Lecture Notes in Artificial Intelligence 3782

Edited by J. G. Carbonell and J. Siekmann

Sublibrary of Lecture Notes in Computer Science

Klaus-Dieter Althoff Andreas Dengel
Ralph Bergmann Markus Nick
Thomas Roth-Berghofer (Eds.)

Professional Knowledge Management

Third Biennial Conference, WM 2005
Kaiserslautern, Germany, April 10-13, 2005
Revised Selected Papers

Series Editors

Jaime G. Carbonell, Carnegie Mellon University, Pittsburgh, PA, USA
Jörg Siekmann, University of Saarland, Saarbrücken, Germany

Volume Editors

Klaus-Dieter Althoff
Universität Hildesheim
Marienburger Platz 22, 31141 Hildesheim, Germany
E-mail: althoff@iis.uni-hildesheim.de

Andreas Dengel
Thomas Roth-Berghofer
Deutsches Forschungszentrum für Künstliche Intelligenz DFKI GmbH
Erwin-Schrödinger-Straße 57, 67663 Kaiserslautern, Germany
E-mail: {andreas.dengel,thomas.roth-berghofer}@dfki.de

Ralph Bergmann
Universität Trier, 54286 Trier, Germany
E-mail: bergmann@uni-trier.de

Markus Nick
Fraunhofer Institut Experimentelles Software Engineering IESE
Fraunhofer-Platz 1, 67663 Kaiserslautern, Germany
E-mail: markus.nick@iese.fraunhofer.de

Library of Congress Control Number: 2005937929

CR Subject Classification (1998): I.2, H.4, H.3, J.1, K.6, K.3-4

ISSN 0302-9743
ISBN-10 3-540-30465-7 Springer Berlin Heidelberg New York
ISBN-13 978-3-540-30465-4 Springer Berlin Heidelberg New York

Springer is a part of Springer Science+Business Media

springer.com

Printed in Germany

Typesetting: Camera-ready by author, data conversion by Scientific Publishing Services, Chennai, India
Printed on acid-free paper SPIN: 11590019 06/3142 5 4 3 2 1 0

Preface

Professional knowledge management is imperative for the success of enterprises. One decisive factor for the success of knowledge management projects is the coordination of elements such as corporate culture, enterprise organization, human resource management, as well as information and communication technology. The proper alignment and balancing of these factors are currently little understood—especially the role of information technology, which is often regarded only as an implementation tool, though it can be a catalyst by making new knowledge management solutions possible.

This conference brought together representatives from practical and research fields for discussing experiences, professional applications, and visions through presentations, workshops, tutorials, and an accompanying industry exhibition. The main focus of the conference was the realization of knowledge management strategies with the aid of innovative information technology solutions, such as intelligent access to organizational memories, or integration of business processes and knowledge management. Also of interest were holistic/integrative approaches to knowledge management that deal with issues raised by the integration of people, organizations, and information technology.

The third conference on "Professional Knowledge Management—Experiences and Visions" (WM 2005) in Kaiserslautern continued the success of the former conferences in Baden-Baden (WM 2001) and Lucerne (WM 2003). It was organized by the German Informatics Society (*Gesellschaft für Informatik GI e.V.*), especially by its Artificial Intelligence and Business Informatics division and its regional subsection (*GI Regionalverband Saar-Pfalz*), together with the German Society for Knowledge Management (*Gesellschaft für Wissensmanagement e.V.*) with support by the German Research Center for Artificial Intelligence DFKI GmbH, the Fraunhofer Institute for Experimental Software Engineering IESE, the University of Hildesheim, the University of Kaiserslautern, the University of Trier, FZI Karlsruhe, and conference consulting Harms. This conference could not have been such a success without the generous support of the sponsoring organizations Klaus Tschirra Stiftung, empolis GmbH, Filenet GmbH, Mindjet GmbH, ontoprise GmbH, Pylon AG, SAP AG, and Siemens AG.

These post-conference proceedings contain a selection of the best papers submitted to and presented at the conference. The papers have been carefully selected by the Workshop Co-chairs/organizers and the participants. The authors revised their original conference submissions according to feedback and results from the discussions.

We would like to thank the authors of the papers included in this book, the Workshop Co-chairs/organizers, and the Program Committee members for their additional work on these post-conference proceedings. We thank the keynote speakers of the conference, the tutorial authors, the organizations explaining their products and services, as well as all the presenters. We also appreciate very much all the effort invested by the local organization team and the various members of our research teams involved in this conference. They all contributed considerably to the success of WM 2005.

Last but not least we would like to thank Rudi Studer, Steffen Staab, Ulrich Reimer, Gerd Stumme, Andreas Abecker, their respective organizing teams of WM 2001 and WM 2003, the management board of the GI Special Interest Group on Knowledge Management (*GI-Fachgruppe Wissensmanagement FGWM*), and the *Gesellschaft für Wissensmanagement* for starting this conference series with much enthusiasm, courage, and foresight.

September 2005

Klaus-Dieter Althoff
Andreas Dengel
Ralph Bergmann
Markus Nick
Thomas Roth-Berghofer

Organization

The conference was organized by the following societies and groups:

Gesellschaft für Informatik e. V.:

- FG Adaptivität und Benutzermodellierung in interaktiven Softwaresystemen
- FG Computer Supported Cooperative Work
- FG Information Retrieval
- FG Management Support Systems
- FG Vorgehensmodelle für die betriebliche Anwendungsentwicklung
- FG Wissensmanagement
- AK Grundlagen der Modellierung und Ausführung von Workflows
- AK Philosophie und Informatik
- AK Wissensmanagement in der Praxis
- GI-Regionalgruppe Saar-Pfalz

Gesellschaft für Wissensmanagement e. V.

Conference Chairs

Klaus-Dieter Althoff (University of Hildesheim)
Andreas Dengel (DFKI GmbH, Kaiserslautern)

Workshop Chair

Ralph Bergmann (University of Trier)

Tutorial Chair

Andreas Abecker (FZI, Karlsruhe)

Conference Management

Christine Harms (conference consulting Harms, Bonn)
Markus Nick (Fraunhofer IESE, Kaiserslautern)
Thomas Roth-Berghofer (DFKI / University of Kaiserslautern)

Keynote Talks

Irma Becerra-Fernandez (Florida International University, USA)
Andreas Günter (HITec e. V., Hamburg, Germany)
Larry Kerschberg (George Mason University, USA)
Klaus Kornwachs (Brandenburg University of Technology, Cottbus, Germany)
Naoyuki Nomura (Ricoh, Japan)

Conference Sponsors

Klaus Tschirra Stiftung	www.kts.villa-bosch.de
empolis GmbH	www.empolis.de
Filenet GmbH	www.filenet.de
Mindjet GmbH	www.mindjet.de
ontoprise GmbH	www.ontoprise.de
Pylon AG	www.pylon.de
SAP AG	www.sap.com
Siemens AG	www.siemens.de

Press and Media Partners

DoQ	www.doq.de
interim 2000	www.interim2000.de
Voice of Information	www.voi.de
Wissensmanagement	www.wissensmanagement.net

Tutorials

Industrielles Wissensmanagement mit Fallbasiertem Schließen
Ralph Bergmann (University of Trier, Germany)
Mehmet Göker (PricewaterhouseCoopers, San Jose, USA)

Systematische Nutzung von Wissen in Geschäftsprozessen - Modellierung und Analyse wissensintensiver Geschäftsprozesse
Norbert Gronau (University of Potsdam, Germany)
Claudia Müller (University of Potsdam, Germany)
Julian Bahrs (University of Potsdam, Germany)

Referenzmodellgestütztes Wissensmanagement - Wissensorientierte Analyse, Gestaltung und Unterstützung von Geschäftsprozessen in kleinen und mittleren Unternehmen
Thomas Mühlbradt (GOM Gesellschaft für Organisationsentwicklung und Mediengestaltung mbH, Aachen, Germany)

Methoden zur engen Integration von Arbeiten und Lernen - Ansätze zur Integration von Wissensmanagement und eLearning
Stefanie Lindstaedt (Know-Center Graz, Austria)
Tobias Ley (Know-Center Graz, Austria)

Ontologien und Semantic Web Technologien für das Wissensmanagement
York Sure (University of Karlsruhe, Germany)
Hans Peter Schnurr (Ontoprise GmbH, Karlsruhe, Germany)

Tutorials (contd.)

Wissensmanagementsysteme
Ronald Maier (Martin Luther University, Halle-Wittenberg, Germany)
Thomas Hädrich (Martin Luther University, Halle-Wittenberg, Germany)

Praktische Erfahrungen bei der Wissensbewertung und Wissensbilanzierung in Unternehmen
Claus Nagel (EBIS GmbH, Hof, Germany)

Human Resource Management und Wissensmanagement
Ernst Biesalski (DaimlerChrysler, Wörth, Germany)
Andreas Abecker (FZI, Karlsruhe, Germany)

Workshop Co-chairs/Organizers

Sven Abels (University of Oldenburg, Germany)
Thomas Allweyer (University of Applied Sciences Kaiserslautern, Zweibrücken, Germany)
Susanne von Baeckmann (Denken & Wissen, Munich, Germany)
Brigitte Bartsch-Spörl (BSR Consulting GmbH, Munich, Germany)
Ansgar Bernardi (DFKI GmbH, Kaiserslautern, Germany)
Andreas Birk (sd&m, Germany)
Gregor Büchel (University of Applied Sciences Cologne, Germany)
Heike Dalinghaus (University of Osnabrück, Germany)
Björn Decker (Fraunhofer IESE, Kaiserslautern, Germany)
Torgeir Dingsøyr (SINTEF ICT, Norway)
Ludger van Elst (DFKI GmbH, Kaiserslautern, Germany)
Hiromichi Fujisawa (Hitachi, Japan)
Markus Gelhoet (University of Osnabrück, Germany)
Norbert Gronau (University of Potsdam, Germany)
Axel Hahn (University of Oldenburg, Germany)
Liane Haak (University of Oldenburg, Germany)
Harald Holz (DFKI GmbH, Kaiserslautern, Germany)
Hisashi Ikeda (Hitachi, Japan)
Larry Kerschberg (George Mason University, USA)
Bertin Klein (DFKI GmbH, Kaiserslautern, Germany)
Jan Kuhlmann (Attorney-at-Law, Hamburg, Germany)
Edith Maier (Danube University Krems, Austria)
Heiko Maus (DFKI GmbH, Kaiserslautern, Germany)
Kerstin Maximini (University of Trier, Germany)
Martin Memmel (DFKI GmbH/ University of Kaiserslautern, Germany)
Marita Muscholl (formerly Sergl) (University of Trier, Germany)
Dirk Muthig (Fraunhofer IESE, Kaiserslautern, Germany)
Naoyuki Nomura (Ricoh Company Ltd., Bunkyo-ku, Tokyo, Japan)

Workshop Co-chairs/Organizers (contd.)

Klaus North (University of Applied Sciences Wiesbaden, Germany)
Peter Pawlowsky (University of Chemnitz, Germany)
Dirk Ramhorst (Siemens Business Services, Germany)
Eric Ras (Fraunhofer IESE, Kaiserslautern, Germany)
Ulrich Reimer (Business Operation Systems, Switzerland)
Bodo Rieger (University of Osnabrück, Germany)
Martin Schaaf (University of Hildesheim, Germany)
Steffen Staab (University of Koblenz-Landau, Koblenz, Germany)
Armin Stahl (DFKI GmbH/ University of Kaiserslautern, Germany)
Ralph Traphöner (empolis GmbH, Kaiserslautern, Germany)
Stephan Weibelzahl (National College of Ireland, Dublin, Ireland)
Oliver W. Wendel (PYLON AG, Frankfurt / Main, Germany)
Marcus Willamowski (Latham & Watkins LLP, Hamburg, Germany)
Michael Wolters (University of Osnabrück, Germany)

Program Committee

Pekka Abrahamsson (VTT Electronics, Finland)
Gerhard Ackermann (Siemens, Austria)
John D'Ambra (UNSW, Australia)
Fulvio D'Antonio (IASI, National Research Council (CNR), Italy)
Dimitris Apostolou (Planet Ernst & Young, Greece)
Aybuke Aurum (University of New South Wales, Australia)
Gabriela Avram (Centre de Recherche Public Henri Tudor, Luxembourg)
Yukika Awazu (The Engaged Enterprise, USA)
Steven Bashford (Business Solutions Group, Mindjet GmbH, Germany)
Stephan Baumann (DFKI GmbH, Kaiserslautern, Germany)
Irma Becerra-Fernandez (Florida International University, Miami, USA)
Wolfgang Behme (Continental AG, Hannover, Germany)
Katy Börner (Indiana University, Bloomington, USA)
Frank Bomarius (University of Applied Sciences Kaiserslautern/Fraunhofer IESE, Germany)
Matteo Bonifacio (University of Trento, Italy)
Paolo Bouquet (University of Trento, Italy)
Peter Brössler (msg systems AG, Munich, Germany)
Peter Chamoni (Universität Duisburg-Essen, Duisburg, Germany)
Jürgen Cleve (University of Wismar, Germany)
Hans Czap (University of Trier, Germany)
Jürgen Dammert (Robert Bosch GmbH, Stuttgart, Germany)
Jörg Denzinger (University of Calgary, Canada)
Kevin C. Desouza (University of Illinois, USA)
Virginia Dignum (University of Utrecht, The Netherlands)
Georg Disterer (University of Applied Sciences and Arts Hannover, Germany)

Program Committee (contd.)

Jörg Eckardt (Maria Hilf GmbH, Dernbach, Germany)
Dieter Ehrenberg (University of Leipzig, Germany)
Jörn Erbguth (Juris GmbH, Germany)
Walter Fabbri (Coop, Italy)
Raimund Feldmann (Fraunhofer USA Center for Experimental Software Engineering, USA)
Luciano Floridi (University of Oxford, United Kingdom)
Ulrich Frank (University of Koblenz, Germany)
Tessen Freund (altavier GmbH, Berlin, Germany)
Beatrice Fuchs (University Lyon III, France)
Peter Funk (Mälardalen University, Sweden)
Roland Gabriel (University of Bochum, Germany)
Peter Gluchowski (University of Düsseldorf, Germany)
Mehmet Göker (PricewaterhouseCoopers, San Jose, USA)
Reiner Gratzfeld (Henkel KGaA, Düsseldorf, Germany)
Alexander Greisle (FhG IAO Competence Center New Work, Stuttgart, Germany)
Pierre Grenon (Centre for Ontology, Geneva, Switzerland)
Gunter Grieser (University of Darmstadt, Germany)
Dieuwke de Haan (Technical University of Eindhoven, The Netherlands)
Ruth Hagengruber (University of Koblenz-Landau, Koblenz, Germany)
Axel Hahn (University of Oldenburg, Germany)
John D. Haynes (University of Central Florida, USA)
Kai U. Heitmann (University of Cologne, Germany)
Scott Henninger (University of Nebraska-Lincoln, USA)
Knut Hinkelmann (University of Applied Sciences Solothurn, Switzerland)
Josef Hofer-Alfeis (Siemens, Munich, Germany)
Wilhelm Hummeltenberg (Universität Hamburg, Germany)
Jozef Hvorecky (College of Management, Bratislava, Slovakia)
Ioannis Iglezakis (DaimlerChrysler, Ulm, Germany)
Josef Ingenerf (University of Lübeck, Germany)
Hayo Iversen (Jurion GmbH, Germany)
Makoto Iwayama (Hitachi, Kokubunji, Japan)
M. Letizia Jaccheri (Norwegian University of Science and Technology)
Norbert Jastroch (MET Communications GmbH, Bad Homburg, Germany)
Manfred Jeusfeld (Tilburg University, The Netherlands)
David Jonassen (University of Missouri-Columbia, USA)
Bernd-Ulrich Kaiser (Bayer AG Leverkusen, Germany)
Noriko Kando (National Institute of Informatics, Chiyoda-ku, Japan)
Dimitris Karagiannis (University of Vienna, Austria)
Hans-Georg Kemper (University of Stuttgart, Germany)
Stefan Kirn (University of Hohenheim, Germany)
Koichi Kise (Osaka Prefecture University, Japan)
Matthias Klusch (DFKI GmbH, Saarbrücken, Germany)

Program Committee (contd.)

Rob Koper (Open University of the Netherlands, The Netherlands)
Klaus Kornwachs (Brandenburg University of Technology, Cottbus, Germany)
Hermann Krallmann (TU Berlin, Germany)
Dirk Krechel (SER Solutions GmbH, Germany)
Stefanie Kreis (Freshfields Bruckhaus Deringer, Germany)
Franz Kurfeß (CalPoly, San Luis Obispo, USA)
Steffen Lange (University of Applied Sciences Darmstadt, Germany)
Manfred Langen (Siemens, Munich, Germany)
Ulrike Lechner (University of the Federal Armed Forces, Munich, Germany)
Peter Lehmann (Stuttgart Media University of Applied Sciences, Germany)
Franz Lehner (University of Passau, Germany)
Stefanie Lindstaedt (Know-Center Graz, Austria)
Jørgen Madsen (Oracle, Denmark)
Edith Maier (Danube University Krems, Austria)
Ronald Maier (Martin Luther University, Halle-Wittenberg, Germany)
Simone Marinai (University of Florence, Italy)
Wolfgang Martin (Wolfgang Martin Team, Annecy, France)
Eitel von Maur (University of St. Gallen, Switzerland)
Frank Maurer (University of Calgary, Canada)
Hermann Maurer (University of Graz, Austria)
Grigori Melnik (University of Calgary, Canada)
Mirjam Minor (Humboldt University Berlin, Germany)
Harry Mucksch (IT-Beratung und Services, Apen, Germany)
Heinz-Jürgen Müller (University of Cooperative Education Mannheim, Germany)
Klaus Müller (Robert Bosch GmbH, Germany)
Wolfgang Nejdl (University of Hannover, Germany)
Anja Neubauer (Cognilexus Knowledge Management Consultants, Germany)
Markus Nick (Fraunhofer IESE, Kaiserslautern, Germany)
Takahiko Nomura (Fuji Xerox Co. Ltd., Japan)
Dietmar Pfahl (Fraunhofer IESE, Kaiserslautern, Germany)
Sofia Pinto (University of Lisbon, Portugal)
Klaus Pommerening (University Hospital of Mainz, Germany)
Steve Probert (Cranfield University, Swindon, United Kingdom)
Thomas Reinartz (DaimlerChrysler, Ulm, Germany)
Michael M. Richter (University of Kaiserslautern, Germany)
Bodo Rieger (University of Osnabrück, Germany)
Knut-Helge Ronæs Rolland (Norwegian University of Science and Technology)
Francis Rousseaux (University of Reims and IRCAM Paris, France)

Program Committee (contd.)

Emil Røyrvik (SINTEF Technology Management, Norway)
Günther Ruhe (University of Calgary, Canada)
Alexander Schieffer (Center of Excellence for Leadership and Learning GmbH, Munich, Germany)
Rainer Schmidt (University of Rostock, Germany)
Sascha Schmitt (SAP AG, Germany)
Georg J. Schneider (University of Applied Sciences Trier, Germany)
Kurt Schneider (University of Hannover, Germany)
Detlev Schoder (University of Cologne, Germany)
Andy Schürr (University of Darmstadt, Germany)
Stefan Schulz (TU Berlin, Germany)
Barry Smith (University at Buffalo, USA)
Rini van Solingen (LogicaCMG, The Netherlands)
Marcus Spies (University of Munich, Germany)
Heiner Stuckenschmidt (Free University Amsterdam, The Netherlands)
Jürgen Taeger (University of Oldenburg, Germany)
Carsten Tautz (Mondia, Dubai, United Arab Emirates)
Rainer Telesko (Robert Bosch GmbH Stuttgart, Germany)
Oliver Thomas (DFKI GmbH, Saarbrücken, Germany)
Huaglory Tianfield (Glasgow Caledonian University (GCU), United Kingdom)
Klaus Tochtermann (Know-Center Graz, Austria)
Bidjan Tschaitschian (empolis GmbH, Germany)
Wolfgang Uhr (TU Dresden, Germany)
Thomas Uthmann (University of Mainz, Germany)
Daniel Veit (University of Karlsruhe, Germany)
Ivo Vollrath (SAP AG, Germany)
Oliver Vopel (Ernst & Young, United Kingdom)
Holger Wache (Free University Amsterdam, The Netherlands)
Aldo von Wangenheim (Federal University of Santa Catarina, Brazil)
Patrick Waterson (Fraunhofer IESE, Kaiserslautern, Germany)
Rosina Weber (Drexel University, USA)
Mathias Weber (BITKOM e. V. Berlin, Germany)
Stefan Wess (empolis GmbH, Germany)
Boris Wyssusek (Queensland University of Technology, Australia)
Hideo Yamazaki (NRI, Japan)
Sandra Zilles (DFKI GmbH/University of Kaiserslautern, Germany)

Table of Contents

Keynote Contributions

Intelligent Office Appliances (IOA)

Learning Software Organizations (LSO)

Learner-Oriented Knowledge Management and KM-Oriented E-Learning (LOKMOL)

Peer-to-Peer and Agent Infrastructures for Knowledge Management (PAIKM)

Knowledge Intensive Business Processes (KiBP)

German Workshop on Experience Management (GWEM)

Knowledge Management in Medicine (KMM)

Knowledge Management in International Professional Services Firms (KMIPSF)

Knowledge Management for Distributed Agile Processes: Models, Techniques, and Infrastructure (KMDAP)

Knowledge Management and Business Intelligence (KMBI)

Intelligent IT Tools for Knowledge Management Systems: (KMTOOLS 2005)

Semantic Model Integration (SMI)

Workshop on Philosophy and Informatics (WSPI)

Workshop on Information Just in Time (WIJIT)

Knowledge Management in Small and Medium Enterprises (WMKMU)

Just-in-Time Knowledge Management

Larry Kerschberg and Hanjo Jeong

E-Center for E-Business, Department of Information and Software Engineering,
George Mason University, MSN 4A4, Fairfax, Virginia 22030-4444
{kersch, hjeong}@gmu.edu
http://eceb.gmu.edu/

Abstract. This paper presents the requirements for just in time knowledge management (JIT-KM). In order to deliver high-value information to user for decision-making, one must understand the user's preferences, biases and decision context. A JIT-KM architecture is presented consisting of user, middleware and data services to search for information from heterogeneous sources, and to rank and deliver this to decision-makers. The search process is described using concepts from Knowledge Sifter, an agent-based system that accesses heterogeneous sources using Semantic Web Services.

1 Introduction

The concept of just-in-time knowledge management (JIT-KM) is appealing in that the goal is to provide the *right information*, to the *right people*, at the *right time* – just in time – so they can take action based on that information. While the just-in-time concept originated with Toyota in its drive to improve its manufacturing processes, the concept can also be applied to the timely delivery of information. There are a number of inter-related current trends that impact our study of JIT-KM. They are: On Demand Computing, On Demand Business, On Demand Retail, and On Demand Organizations.

On Demand Computing allows users to treat the computing infrastructure as an *information utility*, which can marshal the required resources (computers, storage, etc.) and charge based on usage. Users do not have to be aware of where the computers and storage facilities reside – they are virtual. On Demand Organizations, or Virtual Organizations, can be configured on the fly from existing Web services offered by vendors. The goal is dynamically configure a collection of Web services by searching for candidates, negotiating with service providers for quality-of-service agreements, vetting the selected services, composing them, orchestrating their workflow and managing the virtual organization life-cycle [8, 9].

Both On Demand Computing and On Demand Organizations are based on the *virtualization* of resources and services that are then managed on behalf of users to deliver the desired functions. They are both related to the notions of GRID computing [6] and Semantic Web Services [20, 26]. The amount of meta-data [13, 27] required to manage these virtual environments is considerable.

K.-D. Althoff et al. (Eds.): WM 2005, LNAI 3782, pp. 1 – 18, 2005.

On Demand Business integrates the enterprise with its suppliers by optimizing business processes and the supply chain to reduce inventories. On Demand Retail treats stores shelves as space to be managed by suppliers who are paid when customers actually purchase the merchandise. The main concept is the *integration and interoperation of information* among business partners and suppliers to achieve a high degree of transparency and efficiency among their business processes. In a recent *New York Times* article [7], Wal-Mart, the world's largest retailer, was using its 460-terrabyte data warehouse to monitor worldwide operations in near real-time. They have created an extranet called Retail Link that allows suppliers to see how well their products are selling. Eventually, Wal-Mart will have the capability the conduct *scan-based trading* in which the supplier will own the product until it is scanned for purchase. This will reduce inventory costs for Wal-Mart. Wal-Mart will be requiring its major suppliers to use RFID tags on its shipments, in order to keep track of inventory as it enters the warehouses.

This example indicates that Wal-Mart is providing virtual shelf space for its suppliers; they are responsible for stocking those shelves and maintaining their inventories in a just-in-time fashion. Wal-Mart collects and uses massive amounts of data to obtain an up-to-the-minute picture of world-wide operations and can make command decisions based on their analysis of the data.

The above trends inform the concept of Just-in-Time Knowledge Management, which might also be called On Demand Knowledge Management. The sheer volume of data and information available to us make it imperative that we be able to sift and winnow through the mountains of data to find those *knowledge nuggets* so crucial to effective decision-making.

This paper is organized as follows. Section 2 deals with issues associated with requirements and technologies for JIT-KM. Section 3 presents Knowledge Sifter, which is an agent-based search tool based on Semantic Web Services. We stress that search is crucial to JIT-KM. The section also presents a meta-model for Knowledge Sifter that can be used to populate a repository with user queries, associated results and user feedback. Section 4 presents a service-oriented architecture for JIT-KM and discusses some of the services needed to support JIT-KM. Section 5 presents our conclusions.

2 Just-in-Time Knowledge Management

The notion of Just-in-Time Knowledge Management (JIT-KM) is that the right information should be available to decision-makers at the right time and in the right place, just in time. This simple concept has very widespread implications for the systems needed to support it. First, how do we determine what is the right information? How do we know who should receive that information? What is the right format of the information based on the decision-maker's location, context, and type of presentation device? How can we capture and represent the user's preferences, bias, context, and most importantly, his or her information requirements?

We explore these issues within the context of a research project called Knowledge Sifter, which is being conducted at George Mason University's E-Center for E-Business. We show how the Knowledge Sifter architecture can be used for JIT-KM.

2.1 Requirements for JIT-Knowledge Management

In order to deliver JIT-information, we must ensure that the information is timely, authentic, trusted and tailored to the decision-maker's needs. These *knowledge nuggets* are pieces of information that make a quantifiable difference in the decision-making process. Timeliness is important in that out-of-date (stale) information can be irrelevant to the current context and task. Authenticity and trust are related in that the decision-maker should have confidence in the information and the sources that provided it. Finally, there are the issues of *data lineage* and *data provenance*, that is, how was the data processed to derive the information? What is the quality of the original and derived data, and how reliable is the source of the data?

These issues are all crucial for the decision-makers to have confidence in the information products, how they were derived, and the assessment of the quality and reliability of the data provider.

2.2 Technologies for JIT-Knowledge Management

The JIT-information requirements suggest that active technologies are needed to support the timely delivery of JIT services. These include *pull scenarios* in which standing queries are posed to heterogeneous sources, both internal to the enterprise and external such as the Internet and World Wide Web. These queries represent items of interest to the decision-maker and evidence substantiating an existing decision scenario would help him to take action. Alternatively, *push scenarios* deliver content to users via syndication such as RSS feeds or by means of specialized subscriptions services. These messages can be searched for content related to the decision-maker's profile and alerts generated and delivered to a preferred device.

An important component of JIT-KM is the use of *meta-data* — data about data — to model and manage the JIT services. Metadata is important in capturing data lineage as information objects are processed throughout the various phases of the activity life cycle. This may include the evolution of user preferences; historical information regarding the results of standing- and ad-hoc queries; the ranking of search results; the authoritativeness of data sources; and the user's perceptions regarding the quality and timeliness of information provided. We now address these issues in the context of the Knowledge Sifter research.

3 The Knowledge Sifter Architecture

The Knowledge Sifter project, underway at George Mason University, has as its primary goals: 1) to allow users to perform ontology-guided semantic searches for relevant information, both in-house and open-source, 2) to refine searches based on user feedback, and 3) to access heterogeneous data sources via agent-based knowledge services. Increasingly, users seek information outside of their own communities to open sources such as the Web, XML-databases, and the emerging Semantic Web.

The Knowledge Sifter project also wishes to use open standards for both ontology construction and for searching heterogeneous data sources. For this reason we have chosen to implement our specifications and data interchange using the Web Ontology

Language (OWL) [4, 30], and Web Services [2] for communication among agents and information sources.

3.1 Knowledge Sifter Agent-Based Web Services Framework

The rationale for using agents to implement intelligent search and retrieval systems is that agents can be viewed as autonomous and proactive. Each agent is endowed with certain responsibilities and communicates using an Agent Communication Language [5]. Recently, Huhns [10] has noted that agents can be thought of a Web services, and this is the approach we have taken to implement the agent community comprising Knowledge Sifter. The family of agents presented here is a subset of those incorporated into the large vision for Knowledge Sifter. This work is motivated by earlier research into Knowledge Rovers [11, 12] performed at GMU. This research is also informed by our previous work on WebSifter, [15, 16, 18] a meta-search engine that gathers information from traditional search engines, and ranked the results based on user-specified preferences and a multi-faceted ranking criterion involving static, semantic, categorical and popularity measures.

The Knowledge Sifter architecture [13, 14] may be considered a service-oriented architecture consisting of a collection of cooperating agents. The application domain we are considering is that of Image Analysis. The Knowledge Sifter conceptual architecture is depicted in Figure 1. The architecture has three layers: User Layer, Knowledge Management Layer and Data Layer. Specialized agents reside at the various layers and perform well-defined functions. This collection of cooperating agents supports interactive query specification and refinement, query decomposition, query processing, ranking, as well as result ranking and presentation. The Knowledge Sifter architecture is general and modular so that new ontologies and new information resources can be easily incorporated [22]. The various agents and services are described below.

User and Preferences Agents

The User Agent interacts with the user to elicit user preferences that are managed by the Preferences Agent. These preferences include the relative importance attributed to terms used to pose queries, the perceived authoritativeness of Web search engine results, and other preferences to be used by the Ranking Agent. The Preferences Agent can also learn the user's preference based on experience and feedback related to previous queries.

Ontology Agent

The Ontology Agent accesses an imagery domain model, which is specified in the Web Ontology Language (OWL). In addition, there are two authoritative name services: Princeton University's WordNet and the US Geological Survey's GNIS. They allow the Ontology Agent to use terms provided by the name services to suggest query enhancements such as generalization or specialization.

For example, WordNet can provide a collection of synonyms for a term, while GNIS translates a physical place in the US into latitude and longitude coordinates that are required by a data source such as TerraServer. Other appropriate name and translation services can be added in a modular fashion, and the domain model would be updated to accommodate new concepts and relationships. We now discuss the various sources used by the Ontology Agent.

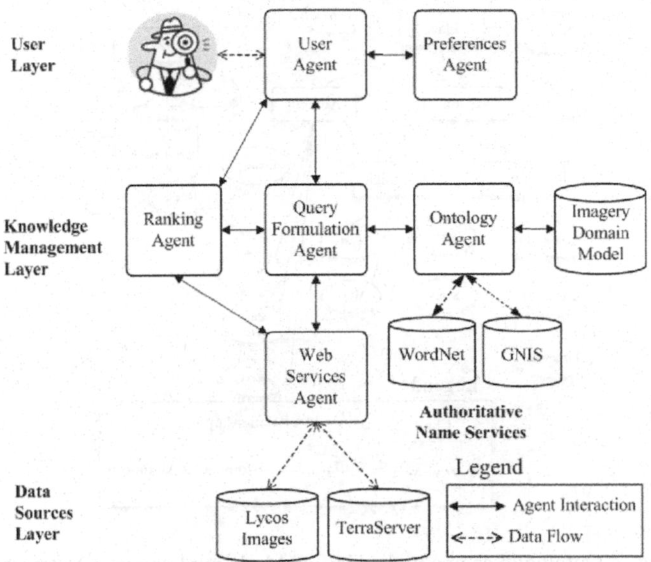

Fig. 1. The Knowledge Sifter Agent-Based Web Services Architecture

Imagery Domain Model and Schema

The principal ontology used by Knowledge Sifter is the Imagery Domain Model, specified using the Web Ontology Language, OWL. A UML diagram of the ontology is provided in Figure 2.

The class Image is defined as having *source*, *content*, and file descriptive *features*. Subcategories of content are *person*, *thing*, and *place*. Since we are primarily interested in satellite and geographic images, the class *place* has two general attributes, *name* and *theme*, together with the subclasses *region* and *address*. The Region is meant to uniquely identify the portion of the Earth's surface where the place is located, either by a *rectangle* or a *circle*. In the case of a rectangle we need two latitude values (*north* and *south*) and two longitude values (*east* and *west*), while to specify a circle we need the *latitude* and *longitude* of its center point, and a *radius*. The *address* of our location is identified by *country*, *state*, *city*, *zip code* and *street*. Each image belongs to a specific online source, the *server*, and has *URI-1* as a unique identifier, together with a secondary *URI-2* for a thumbnail (if any). Some qualitative and quantitative attributes are also modeled as subclasses of the general class *features*, namely *resolution* (in square meters per pixel), *projection* and *datum* (for future GIS utilizations), a *date* range, and image *size* (with *height* and *width* expressed in pixels).

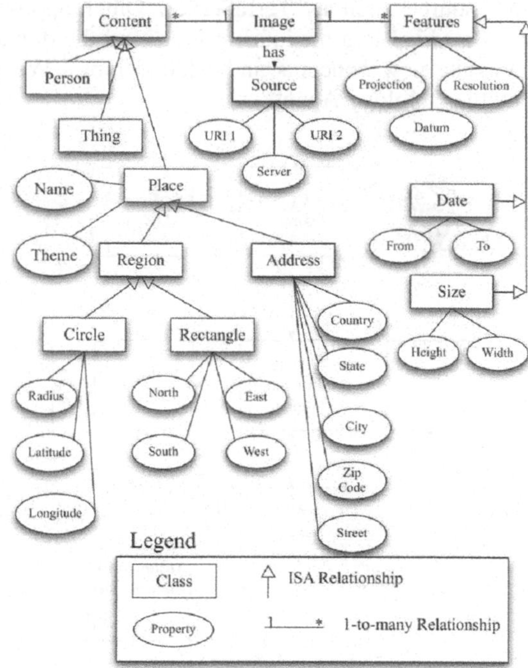

Fig. 2. Ontology Schema in the Unified Modeling Language Notation

Authoritative Name Services

The two name services are WordNet, developed at Princeton University, which is a lexical database for the English language. When the initial query instance, specifying whether a person, place, or thing, is sent to the Ontology Agent, it then consults WordNet to retrieve synonyms. The synonyms are provided to the Query Formulation Agent to request that the user select one or more synonyms. The decision is communicated to the Ontology Agent which updates the appropriate attribute in the instantiated version of the OWL schema. If the attribute value is the name of a class of type *place* then the Ontology Agent passes the instance to the USGS GNIS.

The second name service is the USGS Geographic Names Information System (GNIS) which is a database of geographic names within the United States and its territories [29]. GNIS was developed by the USGS and the U.S. Board on Geographic Names to meet major national needs regarding geographic names and their standardization and dissemination. It is an integration of three separate databases, the National Geographic Names Data Base, the USGS Topographic Map Names Data Base, and the Reference Data Base. Records within the database contain feature name, state, county, geographic coordinates, USGS Geographic Map name, and others. Other specialized name and translation services can be integrated into Knowledge Sifter and linked to the Domain Model.

Query Formulation Agent
The user indicates an initial query to the Query Formulation Agent. This agent, in turn, consults the Ontology Agent to refine or generalize the query based on the semantic mediation provided by the available ontology services. Once a query has been specified by means of interactions among the User Agent and the Ontology Agent, the Query Formulation Agent decomposes the query into subqueries targeted for the appropriate data sources. This involves semantic mediation of terminology used in the domain model ontology and name services with those used by the local sources. Also, query translation is needed to retrieve data from the intended heterogeneous sources.

For example, if the user specifies the domain of his search as *place*, Lycos and TerraServer will be chosen. In cases of *person* and *thing*, only Lycos will be chosen. In the case of person and thing, the user is asked to choose a specific meaning from the list retrieved from WordNet, and then the synonym set and hypernym set regarding that particular meaning are retrieved. Synonyms can be chosen as alternate names. Hypernyms can be used to generalize the user's concept. The terms chosen by the user are used to query Lycos. For example, if the user specifies the concept 'Rushmore' the following synonym set is returned by WordNet:

> Rushmore, Mount Rushmore, Mt. Rushmore – (a mountain in the Black Hills of South Dakota; the likenesses of Washington and Jefferson and Lincoln and Roosevelt are carved on it)

In this case, the synonym set {Rushmore, Mount Rushmore, Mt. Rushmore} and the hypernym set {Mountain Peak} are retrieved from WordNet. If user chooses "Mount Rushmore" and "Mountain Peak", two different queries, "Mount AND Rushmore" and "Mountain AND Peak" are posed to Lycos, because the Lycos image search doesn't support the logical connector "OR" in search terms.

In the case of place, the user-selected synonym set and hypernym set are requested from GNIS server using a similar approach, that is, the queries ("Mount AND Rushmore" and "Mountain AND Peak") are posed to the GNIS server in order to collect a list of locations from which the user can choose. The user can specify a state to restrict the GNIS results. After the user chooses one specific location, the name of the location is also used to submit queries to the Lycos server. Concurrently, a query is sent to TerraServer Web service with the appropriate latitude and longitude for the selected place.

In our future research, we will endow the Query Formulation Agent with more rules and policies to help it to make more intelligent decisions about query specification and query optimization. For example, in the case of image databases, a strategy might be to query the image metadata, retrieve and view thumbnails, and then request the collection of selected images. In addition, Knowledge Sifter will have a repository of processed queries, instantiated and annotated according to the OWL schema. This information will be used by the Query Formulation Agent as a Case Base that can be searched and the results reused. For example, a user query might be specified in stages, and the Case Base could be used to retrieve a relevant query processing strategy, send a request to the Web Services Agent and the results returned for user consideration. If needed, the Ontology Agent could assist in query enhancement as described above.

Web Services Agent

The main role of the Web Services Agent is to accept a user query that has been refined by consulting the Ontology Agent, and decomposed by the Query Formulation Agent. The Web Service Agent is responsible for the choreography and dispatch of subqueries to appropriate data sources, taking into consideration such facets as: user preference of sites; site authoritativeness and reputation; service-level agreements; size estimates of subquery responses; and quality-of-service measures of network traffic and dynamic site workload [21].

The Web Services Agent transforms the subqueries to XML Protocol (SOAP) requests to the respective local databases and open Web sources (TerraServer or Lycos) that have Web Service published interfaces; this is the case for the TerraServer, while Lycos provides an HTTP interface.

Ranking Agent

The Ranking Agent is responsible for compiling the sub-query results from the various sources, ranking them according to user preferences, as supplied by the Preferences Agent, for such attributes as: 1) the authoritativeness of a source which is indicated by a weight – a number between 0 and 10 – assigned to that source, or 2) the weight associated with a term comprising a query.

Data Sources and Web Services

At present, Knowledge Sifter consults two data sources: Lycos Images and the TerraServer. The Lycos server supports keyword-based image search via the web page http://multimedia.lycos.com. It makes use of both an image server and external data sources such as web pages for the image search. For a Lycos image search, no advanced search is supported and only conjunctions of terms are used. Therefore, the user cannot specify the image metadata such as *size* or *resolution*, so the results of search are limited. To address these problems the Query Formulation Agent generates a collection of conjunctive and disjunctive queries, while the evaluation and ranking process is left to the Ranking Agent.

The TerraServer is a technology demonstration for Microsoft. There is a Web Service API for TerraServer. TerraServer is an online database of digital aerial photographs (DOQs – Digital Orthophoto Quadrangles) and topographic maps (DRGs– Digital Raster Graphics). Both data products are supplied by the U.S. Geological Survey (USGS). The images are supplied as small tiles and these can be made into a larger image by creating a mosaic of tiles. The demonstrator at terraserver-usa.com uses a mosaic of 2x3 tiles.

Our purpose is to take the ontology-enhanced query and generate specific sub-queries for the TerraServer metadata. The resulting image identifiers and their metadata are wrapped into an instance of our image ontology. And an array of these is returned to the Web Service Agent to compile with other results.

3.2 Knowledge Sifter End-to-End Scenario

Consider the following scenario in which a user wishes to search for the term 'Rushmore'. This scenario shows how the various agents, name services, and data sources interact in handling a user query.

1. The user provides the User Agent with a keyword query: 'Rushmore'.
2. The user identifies the term as being a person, place or thing via radio buttons in the query form. The user has chosen 'Place'.
3. The User Agent passes the query to Query Formulation Agent.
4. The Query Formulation Agent invokes the Ontology Agent to instantiate an OWL schema for the 'Place' with Name = 'Rushmore'.
5. The Ontology Agent chooses a service agent based on the initial query. In this case, it requests from WordNet a list of concepts for 'Rushmore'. WordNet then passes the results back to the Ontology Agent which then passes the results to the User Agent via the Query Formulation Agent for the user decision.
6. The user chooses the 'Mount Rushmore' concept, which has three synonyms ('Rushmore', 'Mt. Rushmore', and 'Mount Rushmore').
7. The Ontology Agent then submits the synonym set to the USGS Geographic Name Information Server and receives a list of candidate geographic coordinates.
8. The list of candidate coordinates is sent to the Query Formulation Agent and the user chooses the desired location.
9. The Ontology Agent then updates the OWL schema instance with the chosen latitude and longitude.
10. The Query Formulation Agent then passes the fully-specified query to the Web Service Agent.
11. The Web Services Agent forwards appropriate sub-queries to both Lycos and TerraServer. The TerraServer and Lycos data sources are queried, and the results are sent back to the Web Services Agent. The results are compiled into new OWL instances that describe image metadata.
12. All results are combined and sent to the Query Formulation Agent.
13. The Query Formulation Agent sends the result sets and the original query to the Ranking Agent for ranking.
14. Within the Ranking Agent the image metadata for each returned item is ranked using the weights and preferences provided by the Preferences Agent. The Preferences Agent maintains the user preferences.
15. The Ranking Agent generates a score for each image result, and returns the scored list to the User Agent.
16. The User Agent then sorts the results by ranking and presents them to the user.
17. The user can then select an item from the list to download and view the image.

3.3 Knowledge Sifter Meta-model

The previous sections have described how the cooperative agents and web services support the search for relevant knowledge from both local and open-source data sources. The end-to-end scenario shows how the various agents and sources interact. The OWL schema is instantiated with information regarding query and its various transformations into the final ranked results. In this section we elaborate on this concept by presenting a meta-model of the Knowledge Sifter framework so that relevant information can be captured regarding the *lineage* and *provenance* of all aspects of the search process, from query specification, to query reformulation, web service decomposition, results ranking and recommendation presentation. This includes information on the various Knowledge Sifter activities (managed by agents),

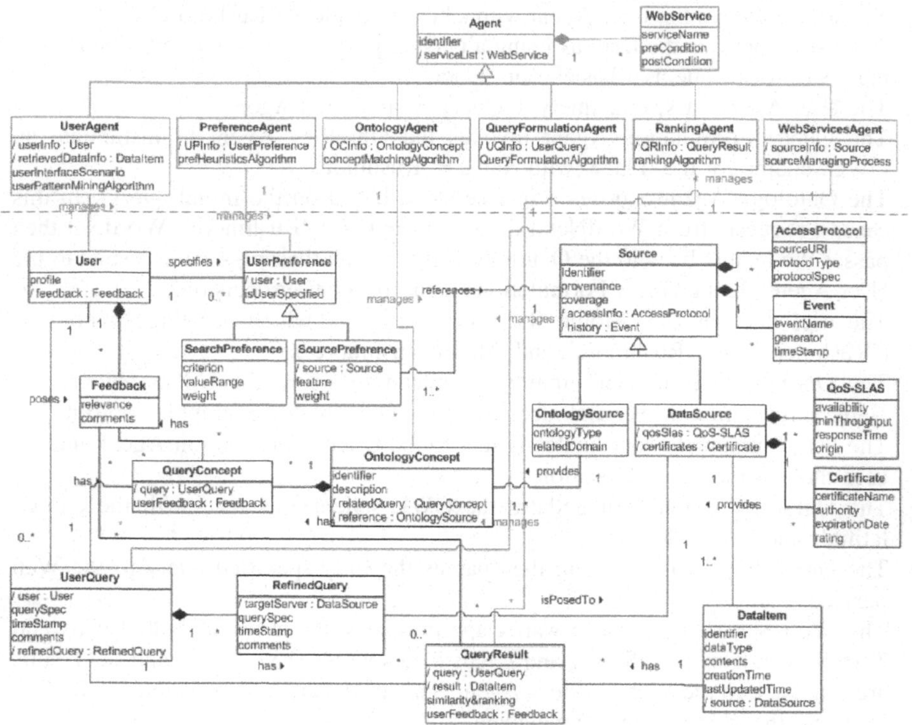

Fig. 3. The Knowledge Sifter Meta-Schema

the outcomes of those activities, the quality of the ranked results, measures of Web service performance, and the authoritativeness and reliability of data sources.

This meta-model is then used to capture and store metadata for future analysis, filtering and mining for JIT-KM. By stepping back and abstracting the agents, classes, their relationships and properties, we can construct the Knowledge Sifter Meta-Model (KSMM) [25]. Figure 3 depicts the UML Static Model for the KSMM. At the top is the Class Agent, which is specialized to those agents in the KS framework, specifically the UserAgent, PreferencesAgent, OntologyAgent, QueryFormulationAgent, RankingAgent and WebServicesAgent. These agents manage their respective object classes, process specifications, and WebServices. For example, the UserAgent manages the User Class, the UserInterfaceScenario, the User PatternMiningAlgorithm, and the WebServices. The User specifies User Preferences that can be specialized to Search Preferences and Source Preferences. The User poses UserQuery that has several QueryConcept, which in turn relates to an OntologyConcept. The Ontology Agent manages both the UserQuery and the OntologyConcept that is provided by an OntologySource. Both OntologySource and DataSource are specializations of Source. Source is managed by the WebServicesAgent and has attributes such as provenance, coverage, access protocol and history. DataSource has attributes such as Quality-of-Service Service-Level-Agreements (QoS-SLAS) and Certificate.

A UserQuery consists of several RefinedQuery, each of which is posed to several DataSource. DataSource provides one-or-more DataItem in response to a RefinedQuery as the QueryResult. Based on the returned QueryResult, the User may provide Feedback as to the result relevance and other comments. These may impact the evolution of metadata associated with UserPreference, query formulation, data source usage and result ranking. A KSMM has been specified by a Protégé ontology [24] and a screen shot of the main panel is shown in Figure 4.

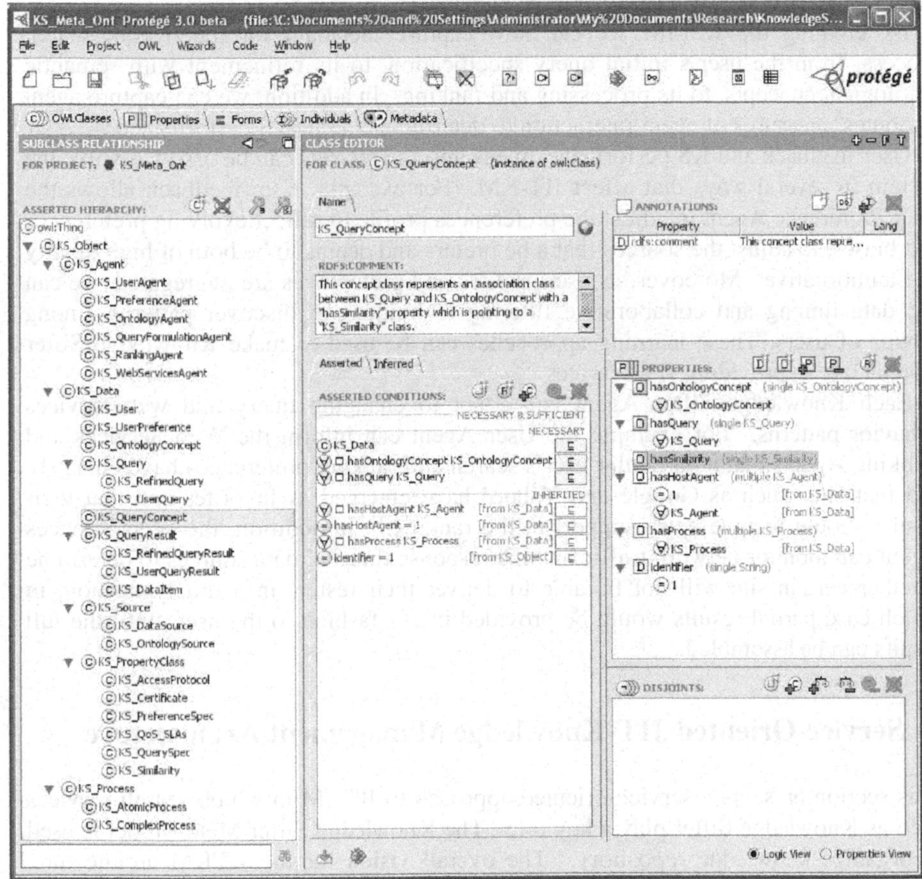

Fig. 4. The Knowledge Sifter Meta-Model in Protégé

The KS meta-classes correspond to those of the UML diagram in Figure 3. The Protégé KSMM can also be exported to a Web Ontology Language (OWL) specification. This specification can be consulted via a namespace hyper-link, thus making the agents, which are implemented as Web Services, portable and able to reside on different computers.

3.4 Data/Knowledge Lineage for JIT Customization

The notion of data/knowledge lineage is crucial to the JIT-KM approach. The Knowledge Sifter Meta-Model provides a specification of the object classes, their properties, relationships and constraints. It can also specify workflow processes among the agents that handle user requests and the processing of those requests. This concept can be extended to dynamically configure semantic web services for virtual organizations [8, 9]. In this discussion we focus on how the KSMM can address the just-in-time aspects of Knowledge Management.

By creating the KSMM we can now capture metadata for the overall search process, from the user's initial query specification, to its refinement with semantic ontological concepts, to its processing and ranking. In addition, we can capture agent attributes, measures of agent interaction to determine overall KS performance.

User feedback and KS performance measures and metrics can be used to evolve the system in several ways that affect JIT-KM. For example, User feedback allows the User Preference Agent to adjust the preferences profile to reflect evolving preferences and biases, to adjust the sources that a he prefers and deems to be both of high quality and authoritative. Moreover, as user profiles and preferences are aggregated, we can use data mining and collaborative filtering techniques to discover patterns among groups of users. These learning approaches can be used to make Knowledge Sifter more active in providing JIT-services.

Each Knowledge Sifter Agent can adapt to changing query and web services behavior patterns. For example the User Agent can inform the Web Services and Ranking Agents that a particular user's search and ranking preferences have changed, and that sites such as Google and Yahoo! have emerged as favorites and that their results should receive extra support in the rankings. In addition, the Web Services Agent can monitor network traffic and the response times of data sources to determine whether certain site will not be able to deliver their results in a timely fashion, in which case partial results would be provided in JIT-fashion to the user, until the full results can be assembled.

4 Service-Oriented JIT-Knowledge Management Architecture

This section presents a service-oriented approach to JITKM in which search services such as Knowledge Sifter play a key role. The Knowledge Sifter Meta-Model is used to organize knowledge repository. The overall vision for the JITKM architecture, shown in Figure 5, has three layers: Knowledge Presentation and Creation, Knowledge Management, and Data Sources. At the top layer, knowledge workers may perform searches, communicate, collaborate as well as create and share knowledge. They are provided information by means of the Knowledge Portal, which can be tailored to the profile of each knowledge worker.

The Knowledge Management Layer depicts the Knowledge Repository and the services that are used to acquire, refine, store, retrieve, distribute and present knowledge. These processes are used to create knowledge for the repository. In this paper we are focusing on search services and the just-in-time aspects of KM. One

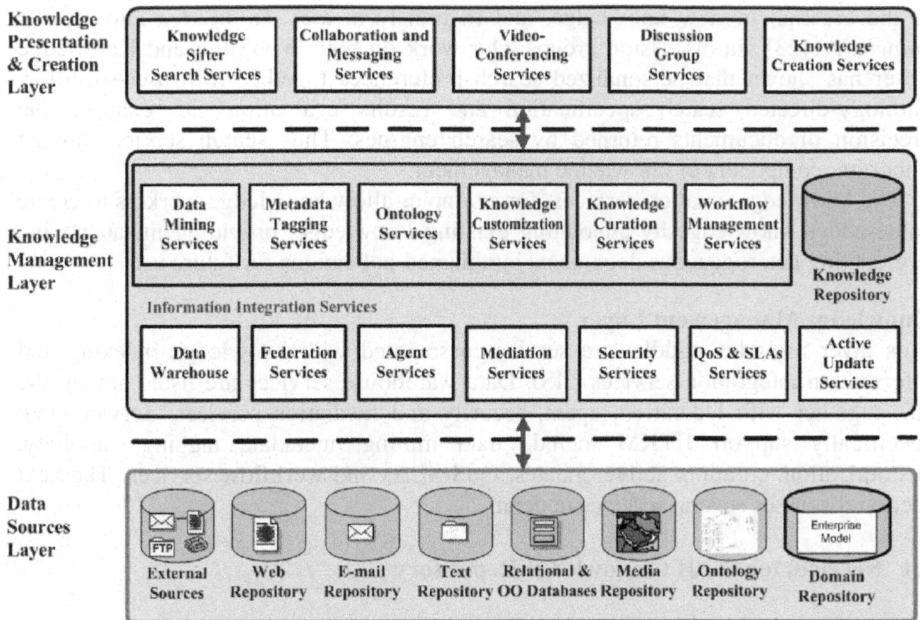

Fig. 5. The Just-in-Time Knowledge Management Architecture

important component of the Knowledge Repository is the Knowledge Sifter Meta-Model, which is instantiated with data from user queries, query processing, the ranked results, and user feedback. In addition, new knowledge can be added to the repository as it becomes available. The services at the Knowledge Management Layer assist in the creation of this knowledge, and its storage in the Knowledge Repository.

The Data Sources Layer consists of the organization's internal data sources including documents, electronic messages, web site repository, media repository of video, audio and imagery, ontology repository and the domain repository, which contains the organization's enterprise model. Also depicted are the heterogeneous external sources of data, including web services that can be used to augment the internal holdings.

Particularly noteworthy are the Ontology Repository and Domain Repository. Organizations may define multiple ontologies used by various divisions in the enterprise, and these organizational ontologies can guide the search process. The Domain Repository contains the Enterprise Model, which is a conceptual model for the organization. It can be used to define the concepts, relationships and constraints that govern the enterprise. For example, in Knowledge Sifter, the ontology sources are WordNet, GNIS, the Imagery Ontology, while the Knowledge Sifter Meta-Model depicts how Knowledge Sifter operates and indicates what data should be captured regarding it processes.

The Knowledge Presentation and Creation Layer

The services provided at this layer enable knowledge workers to obtain personalized information via portals, to perform specialized search for information, to collaborate in the creation of new knowledge, and to transform *tacit knowledge* into *explicit knowledge* [23] via discussion groups. Our work on both WebSifter and Knowledge Sifter has shown that personalized search preferences together with user-specified, ontology-directed search specification and results evaluation can enhance the precision of documents returned by search engines. Thus search services are an important component of knowledge management.

The knowledge creation services, for example, allow knowledge workers to create value-added knowledge by annotating existing knowledge, providing metatags, and aggregating heterogeneous documents into named collections for future use.

Knowledge Management Layer

This layer provides middleware services associated with knowledge indexing and information integration services (IIS). Data warehouse services are listed among the IIS, together with federation, agent, security and mediation services. Services that specifically support JITKM include data mining, metadata tagging, ontology, customization, curation, active updates, QoS-SLAs and workflow services. The next section discusses several services in detail.

4.1 Services for the JIT Knowledge Repository

Data Mining Services. These services include vendor tools for deducing rules from numeric data, as well as concept mining from text. This knowledge can be used to enhance the Knowledge Repository and to provide refined knowledge to decision-makers. Experience with Knowledge Sifter indicates that understanding the user is crucial to being able to provide relevant search results, based on user intent and context. Mining such information from multiple user queries, and across several users, can improve the user preference model. The research in collaborative filtering can be helpful in suggesting to users other sources of information and related users having similar interests.

Meta-tagging Services. Appropriate indexing of knowledge assets is crucial as collections grow. XML and Resource Description Framework (RDF) are emerging as open standards for tagging and metadata descriptions [19]. The Digital Library community has proposed the Dublin Core Metadata Initiative [3] for tagging books. The tagging of data from heterogeneous sources from the data sources layer is important to allow information to be associated with the concepts defined in the Enterprise Model. Manual tagging is simply too slow for JIT-KM requirements and automated tool and techniques are needed. This is an active research area and a more detailed discussion can be found in [1].

Ontology Services. The construction of domain-specific ontologies is of utmost importance to providing consistent and reliable terminology across the enterprise. Hierarchical taxonomies are an important classification tool, and the trend to use automated tools to specify them [24]. Our research in this area includes the Intelligent Thesaurus [17] and we have used user-specified taxonomies to guide the WebSifter meta-search engine. The intelligent thesaurus is an active data/knowledge dictionary capable of supporting multiple ontologies to allow users to formulate and reformulate requests for information. The intelligent thesaurus is similar to the thesaurus found in a library; it assists analysts in identifying similar, broader or narrower terms related to a particular term, thereby increasing the likelihood of obtaining the desired information from the information sources. In addition, active rules and heuristics may be associated with object types as well as their attributes and functions. This has been used very effectively in our work on WebSifter and Knowledge Sifter. Some of services needed for JIT-KM include ontology mapping, curation, inter-operation, reasoning and merging. Our recent work on the MAKO framework [22] indicates that XML Topic Maps can be used define multiple complementary ontologies that can be merged and used to search a knowledge repository.

Agent Services. The Knowledge Sifter prototype is implemented using agents for each major component. Each agent is implemented as a Web Service and they use standard protocols for communication. Agents exhibit autonomy and are proactive, capabilities that are crucial to JIT-KM. Agents should monitor user behavior to assess not only intent, but also the context for a user query. Agents can cooperate to solve-problems, to access relevant information from data sources, to package information for decision-makers. Other agents, call staff agents, can monitor the performance of the overall system and provide feedback to line agents to have them adapt to changing behavior and usage patterns.

Mediation Services. Mediation refers to a broad class of services associated with the Intelligent Integration of Information (I*3). Mediation services [28, 31] facilitate the extraction, matching, and integration of data from heterogeneous multi-media data sources such as maps, books, presentations, discussion threads, news reports, e-mail, etc.

Knowledge Customization Services. These JIT services access, customize, package and deliver value-added and focused "knowledge nuggets" to decision-makers. The services consult the User Agent to obtain user preferences, biases and context, including how the user prefers to have information delivered and presented. For example, the curator of the knowledge repository might want to obtain a report regarding the number of users who requested information on 'Rushmore' as well as the associated ontological concepts used in query reformulation. This report would be prepared for the curator who might then update the ontology. Another user might want to obtain meta-data associated with the data lineage of his query, including the workflow scheduling, the sources queried, their responses and the results presented. The user might also wish to peruse those results that ranked lower, but might still be relevant to the task at hand.

QoS and SLAs Services. Quality of Service is an important feature that needs to be considered to retrieve the data from heterogeneous distributed environments. For instance, availability, response time, and throughput of data providers should be measured to optimize resources and provide users data in a timely fashion. These services could monitor the QoS of the data providers and adapt the Web services workflow to compensate for QoS problems. In addition, these services would manage the longer-term relationship using Service Level Agreements (SLAs) [21]. For example, QoS measures could be used by the Knowledge Sifter Web Service Agent to schedule queries, find alternative sources if a data source disconnects from the network, and devise ways to deliver partial information to decision-makers, rather than waiting for all subqueries to finish processing.

Active Update Services. These services ensure that the JIT-KM knowledge repository is up-to-date with respect to JIT requirements. For example, users could create subscriptions to have alerts via e-mail regarding a new paper published by a respected colleague, or the fact that an important event has taken place. User could also pose 'standing queries' that would be run periodically to look for new and interesting results. These queries could be mediated [28] using approximate consistency criteria based on temporal and spatial constraints.

Another agent could examine RSS News Feeds and filter them based on topic and keywords. These could be presented to the user in a newsreader. The agent could also monitor newly tagged messages from the Metadata Tagging Services and present those pertinent to users' context and scenarios. Our research on MAKO [22] indicates how user scenarios, specified as XML Topic Maps, can be shared among users who are collaborating on a problem.

Discovery agents could be tasked to seek out new data sources with information relevant to enterprise needs. They could obtain the Web Service WSDL specification, probe the data source with prototype queries, and assess the overall data quality and the reliability of the source. If accepted, the new source would provide its ontology and the Ontology Services would incorporate the ontology into the Enterprise Model.

5 Conclusions

This paper has presented the concept of Just-in-Time Knowledge Management (JIT-KM) and has discussed a service-oriented Knowledge Management Architecture, together with a collection of services needed to support and realize JIT-KM.

One very important aspect of JIT-KM is to understand the user's information needs, his preferences, biases, and decision-making context. These help to package information into actionable knowledge.

One example of this framework is Knowledge Sifter, the search service of the JIT-KM Architecture. The agents that constitute Knowledge Sifter accept a user's initial query, consult the User Preferences Agent, reformulate the query based on user preferences and ontological concepts, decompose it into subqueries handled by the Web Services Agent, and rank the query results according to user preferences, biases and context.

The Knowledge Sifter Meta-Model (KSMM) is a specification of the agents, activities, and communications of the system's operation. This has been specified in Protégé, which automatically generates an OWL specification that can be shared with other services via a namespace. The KSMM is one of many holdings of the JIT-KM Knowledge Repository. The KSMM schema can be instantiated with actual user queries, their reformulations, the query processing strategies, the Web Services invocations, the result sets, the rankings, and user feedback regarding the relevance of the results to the task at hand.

In future research we intend to implement the Knowledge Sifter Knowledge Repository based on the KSMM. We hope to use Protégé as a system component to assist the Ontology Agent. Protégé plug-ins such as JessTab and owlTab can be used to provide reasoning and semantic web support, respectively.

Acknowledgements. This work was sponsored by a NURI from the National Geospatial-Intelligence Agency (NGA). The authors with to acknowledge the work on the Knowledge Sifter prototype by M. Chowdhury, A. Damiano, S. Mitchell, J. Si, and S. Smith.

References

1. Cheng, J., Emami, R., Kerschberg, L., Santos, E., Jr., Zhao, Q., Nguyen, H., Wang, H., Huhns, M., Valtorta, M., Dang, J., Goradia, H., Huang, J. and Xi, S., OmniSeer: A Cognitive Framework for User Modeling, Reuse of Prior and Tacit Knowledge, and Collaborative Knowledge Services. in *Hawaii International Conference on Systems Science (HICSS-38)*, (Island of Hawaii, 2005).
2. Chinnici, R., Gudgin, M., Moreau, J.-J. and Weerawarana, S. Web Services Description Language (WSDL) Version 1.2 (http://www.w3.org/TR/wsdl12/), W3C, 2002.
3. DublinCore. Dublin Core Metadata Element Set, Version 1.1: Reference Description, 2003.
4. Fensel, D. Ontology-Based Knowledge Management *IEEE Computer*, 2002, 56-59.
5. Finin, T., Fritzson, R., McKay, D. and McEntire, R., KQML as an Agent Communication Language. in *International Conference on Information and Knowledge Management (CIKM-94)*, (1994), ACM Press.
6. Foster, I., Kesselman, C. and Tuecke, S. The Anatomy of the Grid: Enabling Scalable Virtual Organizations.
7. Hayes, C.L. What Wal-Mart Knows About Customer' Habits, The New York Times, New York, November 14, 2004.
8. Howard, R. and Kerschberg, L. A Framework for Dynamic Semantic Web Services Management. *International Journal of Cooperative Information Systems, Special Issue on Service Oriented Modeling, 13* (4).
9. Howard, R. and Kerschberg, L., A Knowledge-based Framework for Dynamic Semantic Web Services Brokering and Management. in *International Workshop on Web Semantics - WebS 2004*, (Zaragoza, Spain, 2004).
10. Huhns, M. Agents as Web Services *IEEE Internet Computing*, July/August 2002.
11. Kerschberg, L. (ed.), *Knowledge Management in Heterogeneous Data Warehouse Environments*. Springer, Munich, Germany, 2001.
12. Kerschberg, L. The Role of Intelligent Agents in Advanced Information Systems. in Small, C., Douglas, P., Johnson, R., King, P. and Martin, N. eds. *Advanced in Databases*, Springer-Verlag, London, 1997, 1-22.
13. Kerschberg, L., Chowdhury, M., Damiano, A., Jeong, H., Mitchell, S., Si, J. and Smith, S. Knowledge Sifter: Agent-Based Ontology-Driven Search over Heterogeneous Databases using Semantic Web Services. in Bouzeghoub, M., Goble, C., Kashyap, V. and Spaccapietra, S. eds. *Semantics for a Networked World, Semantics for the Grid Databases, LNCS 3226*, Springer, Paris, France, 2004, 278-295.
14. Kerschberg, L., Chowdhury, M., Damiano, A., Jeong, H., Mitchell, S., Si, J. and Smith, S., Knowledge Sifter: Ontology-Driven Search over Heterogeneous Databases. in *SSDBM 2004, International Conference on Scientific and Statistical Database Management*, (Santorini Island, Greece, 2004), IEEE.
15. Kerschberg, L., Kim, W. and Scime, A., Intelligent Web Search via Personalizable Meta-Search Agents. in *International Conference on Ontologies, Databases and Applications of Semantics (ODBASE 2002)*, (Irvine, CA, 2002).

16. Kerschberg, L., Kim, W. and Scime, A. A Semantic Taxonomy-Based Personalizable Meta-Search Agent. in Truszkowski, W. ed. *Innovative Concepts for Agent-Based Systems*, Springer-Verlag, Heidelberg, 2003, 3-31.
17. Kerschberg, L. and Weishar, D. Conceptual Models and Architectures for Advanced Information Systems. *Applied Intelligence*, *13* (2). 149-164.
18. Kim, W., Kerschberg, L. and Scime, A. Learning for Automatic Personalization in a Semantic Taxonomy-Based Meta-Search Agent. *Electronic Commerce Research and Applications (ECRA)*, *1* (2).
19. Klien, M. XML, RDF, and relatives *IEEE Intelligent Systems*, 2001, 26-28.
20. McIlraith, S.A., Son, T.C. and Zeng, H. Semantic Web Services *IEEE Intelligent Systems*, 2001, 46-53.
21. Menascé, D.A. QoS Issues in Web Services *IEEE Internet Computing*, 2002.
22. Morikawa, R. and Kerschberg, L., MAKO: Multi-Ontology Analytical Knowledge Organization based on Topic Maps. in *Fifth International Workshop on Theory and Applications of Knowledge Management*, (Zaragoza, Spain, 2004).
23. Nonaka, I.O. and Takeuchi, H. *The knowledge-creating company : how Japanese companies create the dynamics of innovstion*. Oxford University Press, New York, 1995.
24. Noy, N.F., Sintek, M., Decker, S., Crubezy, M., Fergerson, R.W. and Musen, M.A. Creating Semantic Web contents with Protege-2000 *IEEE Intelligent Systems*, 2001, 60-71.
25. ObjectManagementGroup. Meta Object Facility (MOF) Specification Version 1.3, 2000.
26. Paolucci, M. and Sycara, K. Autonomous Semantic Web Services *IEEE Internet Computing*, Sept - Oct 2003, 34-41.
27. Pouchard, L., Cinquini, L., Drach, B., Middleton, D., Bernholdt, D.E., Chanchio, K., Foster, I.T., Nefedova, V., Brown, D., Fox, P., Garcia, J., Strand, G., Williams, D., Chervanek, A.L., Kesselman, C., Shoshani, A. and Sim, A., An Ontology for Scientific Information in a Grid Environment: the Earth System Grid. in *CCGRID 2003*, (2003), 626-632.
28. Seligman, L. and Kerschberg, L. A Mediator for Approximate Consistency: Supporting 'Good Enough' Materialized Views. *Journal of Intelligent Information Systems*, *8* (3). 203 - 225.
29. USGS. USGS Geographic Names Information System (GNIS), http://geonames.usgs.gov/.
30. W3C. OWL Web Ontology Language Overview, http://www.w3.org/TR/owl-features/. McGuinness, D.L. and van Harmelen, F. eds., W3C, 2003.
31. Wiederhold, G. Intelligent integration of information. *Journal of Intelligent Information Systems*, *6* (2/3). 203 p.

Actor Model and Knowledge Management Systems: Social Interaction as a Framework for Knowledge Integration

Irma Becerra-Fernandez[1], TeWei Wang[1], Gul Agha[2], and Thant Sin[1]

[1] Florida International University, College of Business Administration, Decision Sciences and Information Systems, University Park Campus, RB250, Miami, FL 33199
{becferi, wangte, thant.sin}@fiu.edu

[2] University of Illinois at Urbana-Champaign, Siebel Center for Computer Science, 201 N. Goodwin Avenue, Urbana, Illinois, USA 61801
agha@cs.uiuc.edu

Abstract. Expertise locator systems (ELS) are a special type of knowledge management systems that are used to help locate intellectual capital. The searchable answer-generating environment (SAGE) is an expertise locator system that was developed to identify experts in the state of Florida. This presentation describes an application of the actor model of computation to the development of expertise locator systems (ELS). The actor model describes an approach to modeling intelligence in terms of *a society of communicating knowledge-based problem experts* where each expert may in turn be viewed as a society of primitive actors. A conceptual implementation for SAGE, and ELS in general, based on the actor model as a design paradigm is described. Practical applications for an actor-model based ELS are also discussed.

1 Introduction to Expertise Locator Systems

Expertise-locator systems (ELS) are a special type of knowledge management systems that are used to help locate intellectual capital [1, p. 317]. Typically ELS aim to catalog knowledge competencies across an organization in such a way, that it can later be queried to identify "who knows what" in the organization. ELS are knowledge sharing systems that point to those that have knowledge of the domain, rather than to the knowledge content itself, which is the subject of knowledge repositories.

Although ELS across organizations serve a similar purpose, they may differ across a number of characteristics [1] including:

- The purpose of the system, for example to help identify experts to solve technical problems or to identify potential applicants to fill vacant positions in the organization.
- The ELS access method, for example via the company's Intranet or via the Internet.
- The method that the ELS uses to capture the expertise domain of it's experts, for example does the system require featured experts to complete a self-assessment of their areas of expertise, or does the system infer domains of expertise based on information resources in the organization, such as Web pages and other structured and unstructured databases.

K.-D. Althoff et al. (Eds.): WM 2005, LNAI 3782, pp. 19 – 31, 2005.

- Member participation , that is, does the system require all the organizational members to be represented or only a subset of volunteers.
- The approach used to organize the knowledge in the ELS. A knowledge taxonomy refers to the specific classifications used to index knowledge competencies within the organization. In this respect, an ELS may require that organizational knowledge taxonomy be defined a-priori in order to index knowledge competencies in the organization. ELS developers would then face the decision of using a standard published taxonomy (like for example O*Net by the US Department of Labor) or their own specified taxonomy.
- Levels of competencies, for example does the system define experts across various levels.

Translating the above characteristics into ELS design issues, the three essential design concerns are described as:

- The design structure of an ELS database, that is, how knowledge about experts is represented in an ELS.
- The infrastructure upon which an ELS is built, for example, is the system built on a centralized environment or a distributed environment.
- The method required to discover and capture new knowledge represented in the ELS.

Various computing technologies have played a significant role in the development of ELS. To address the first and second design concern, research on ontologies and semantic networks have been the focus of contemporary ELS design [1, 2]. For example, semantic networks serve to structure concepts and terms in networks, which could be useful to represent knowledge taxonomies (Becerra-Fernandez et al. 2004). Ontology study is also relevant to ELS in that they may be used to represent complex relationships between knowledge competencies in a taxonomy. On the other hand, the third design concern has been addressed through the application of artificial intelligence and decision support techniques, for example text data mining. Web text data mining could be instrumental in mitigating the need for ELS to depend on expert's self-assessment and taxonomy development, by inferring from the employee's Web pages their corresponding areas of expertise. An example of one of those systems is the National Aeronautics and Space Administration's Expert Seeker or SAGE [1, 3, 4], which uses Web text mining to infer areas of expertise from their employee-published Web pages. Both structure-design concerns and knowledge-discovery and capture concerns are context dependent. From a system designer's perspective, the infrastructure or context of an ELS can determine both the choices of ELS structure and knowledge acquisition mechanism. The following section describes briefly the context of one ELS: the SAGE Expert Finder system.

2 A Description of the Searchable Answer Generating Environment ELS

The Searchable Answer Generated Environment (SAGE) Expert Finder is an ELS developed for the purpose of creating a searchable repository of experts in Florida universities. Currently, each university in Florida keeps a database of funded research, but these databases are disparate, dissimilar, and can't be queried on the Web. The SAGE Expert-Finder creates a searchable repository of funded research information, by incorporating a distributed database scheme, which can be searched by a variety of fields, including research topic, investigator name, funding agency, university, or combination of fields.

The SAGE system is essentially a global-schema multi-database system [5]. It combines the unified database by masking multiple databases as if they were one. The main interfaces developed on the query engine use text fields to search the processed data. Figure 1 represents the SAGE architecture.

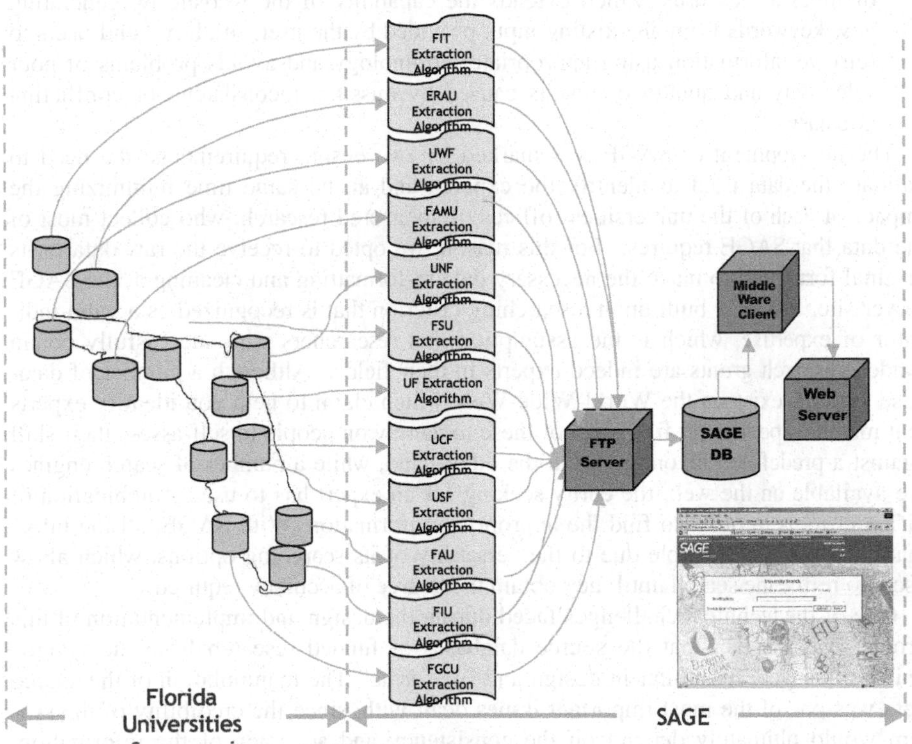

Fig. 1. SAGE Architecture

SAGE provides the following benefits to the participating institutions:

- Helps locate Florida researchers for collaboration with industry and federal agencies, thereby increasing potential research funding to the universities.
- Combines and unifies existing data from multiple sources into one Web-accessible interface.
- Gives university researchers more visibility, and simultaneously allows interested parties to identify available expertise within Florida universities. This application helps to identify a researcher's proficiency within a discipline, and to facilitate a point of contact.

- Is a flexible tool since there is no reconfiguration required to fit data into one template. Furthermore, the system is not dependent of the type of program used to collect the information at the source.
- Incorporates a File Transfer Protocol (FTP) client, an application that resides at each of the participating universities to automate data transfer to the SAGE server.
- Includes a newsletter with more than 200 subscribers from a variety of commercial, education, government, and military institutions. This newsletter allows subscribers to announce their own news, and to be up-to-date with the most recent information concerning to SAGE.
- Includes a thesaurus, which extends the capability of the website by generating new keywords from an existing input provided by the user. It allows end-users to retrieve information using appropriate terminology and avoids problems of poor selectivity and quality of results caused by missing, inconsistent, or conflicting vocalary.

The development of SAGE was marked by two design requirements: the need to validate the data used to identify the experts, and at the same time minimizing the impact of each of the universities' offices of sponsored research, who collect most of the data that SAGE requires. For this reason, we opted to receive the raw data in its original form, and to make the necessary data re-formatting and cleaning at the SAGE server site. SAGE is built upon a searching criterion that is recognized as a valid indicator of expertise, which is the assumption that researchers who successfully obtain funded-research grants are indeed experts in their fields. Although a number of database systems exist on the World-Wide-Web, which claim to help you identify experts that match a specific profile, most of these tools rely on people to self-assess their skill against a predefined taxonomy. On the other hand, while a number of search engines are available on the web, the entity seeking for an expert has to use a combination of different tools in order to find the appropriate information. With SAGE, all the information is easily accessible due to the versatility of its searching options, which allow users to refine the search until they obtain the degree of accuracy required.

One of the technical challenges faced during the design and implementation of this project was the fact that the source databases of funded research from the various universities were dissimilar in design and file format. The manipulation of the source data was one of the most important issues dealt with, since the credibility of the system would ultimately depend on the consistency and accuracy of the information. Manipulating the data included the process of cleansing the data, followed by the data transformation into the relational model, and ultimately the databases migration to a consistent format.

The SAGE system design depends on participating institutions to forward the most recent funded research data to a human agent. Then, this human agent uploads the new data to keep the data repository current. Recently a file transfer protocol (FTP) utility was developed to facilitate the maintenance of SAGE in a more automated fashion, which makes the data maintenance process as human independent as possible. This utility is implemented as a daemon running on each of the universities' servers, working according to a pre-scheduled transfer rule. This daemon obtains the data from the universities databases and transfers the information to the SAGE server, making the data transfer process to the SAGE server human independent. However, the use of such daemon limits the SAGE system's ability to identify expertise using only a limited criterion: funded research projects. To overcome this limitation, we propose integrating SAGE with other Web-based systems, which is the main topic of this paper.

3 Actor Model and Its Applicability to Distributed Systems

In this section we discuss some of the aspects of the actor model of computation. The actor model describes an approach to modeling intelligence in terms of a "society of communicating knowledge-based problem experts" [6], where each expert may in turn be viewed as a society of primitive actors. The actor model of computation provides a framework for effective problem solving, by investigating the nature of the communication mechanisms by a society of experts.

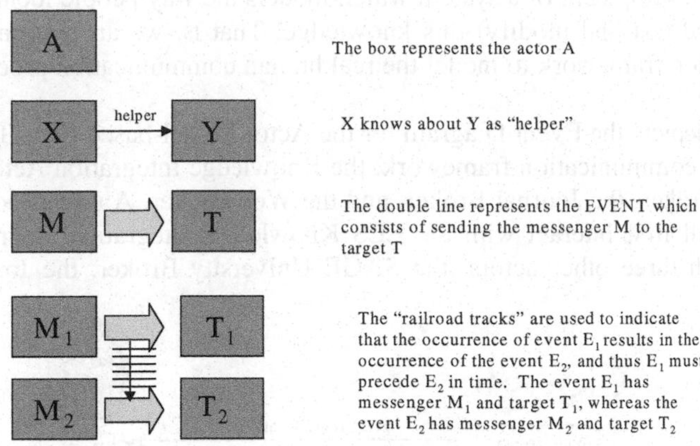
A
The box represents the actor A
X
helper
Y
X knows about Y as "helper"
M
T
The double line represents the EVENT which consists of sending the messenger M to the target T
M_1
T_1
M_2
T_2
The "railroad tracks" are used to indicate that the occurrence of event E_1 results in the occurrence of the event E_2, and thus E_1 must precede E_2 in time. The event E_1 has messenger M_1 and target T_1, whereas the event E_2 has messenger M_2 and target T_2

Fig. 2. Hewitt's Legend for Event Diagrams (Hewitt, 1977)

Actor model is a computation model designed to facilitate distributed computing. Its basic principles are very similar to many other models and formalisms, such as object-oriented design and agent models [7]. In the actor model, actors represent a local model of computation, and they interact by sending messages to each other. Regardless of its application, the actor model has two distinct characteristics: asynchronous communication among actors and fairness of message passing [8]. Due to these two features, actors in any actor model based design typically execute within an actor framework [7]. Various actor frameworks have been designed to resolve different distributed computation problem. Many recent actor frameworks are trying to resolve real-time computation problems [9]. Here we propose to utilize actor model to improve knowledge management systems, such as ELS. Nonetheless, the asynchronous communication feature makes actor model suitable for integrating heterogeneous database systems.

Actor frameworks are usually documented by providing actor descriptions, communication frameworks, and a design architecture. We present our communication framework using an event diagram as suggested by Hewitt [6]. Various actors are introduced in the events diagram. Then, a service-oriented architecture is introduced to realize the conceptual communication framework.

According to Hewitt [6] "the *behavior* of each actor, is *defined* by the relationships among the events which are caused by the actor", and each actor is characterized by both 1) the action it should take when it's sent a message, and 2) it's acquaintances, which is the finite collection of actors that it directly knows about. Figure 2 provides the legend for event diagrams for the actor model of computation. Event diagrams allow displaying the relationships among the events of an actor computation

4 A New Vision for SAGE Based on Actor Model

In this paper, we propose a concept for the communication model of an ELS, whose behavior approximates the behavior of a group of expertise brokers (actors), each one with the knowledge of those who are experts in a particular domain. Our goal is to propose the development of a system which models the way people identify and communicate (and test and modify) this knowledge. That is, we are presenting an actor communication framework to model the real human communication process of identifying experts.

Figure 3 depicts the Event Diagram for the Actor Model-based ELS. There are four actors in our communication framework: the Knowledge Integration Actor, the SAGE University Broker, the Journal Broker, and the Web Broker. A user needing to locate an expert will first interact with the ELS Knowledge Integration actor. This actor interacts with three other actors: the SAGE University Broker, the Journal Broker,

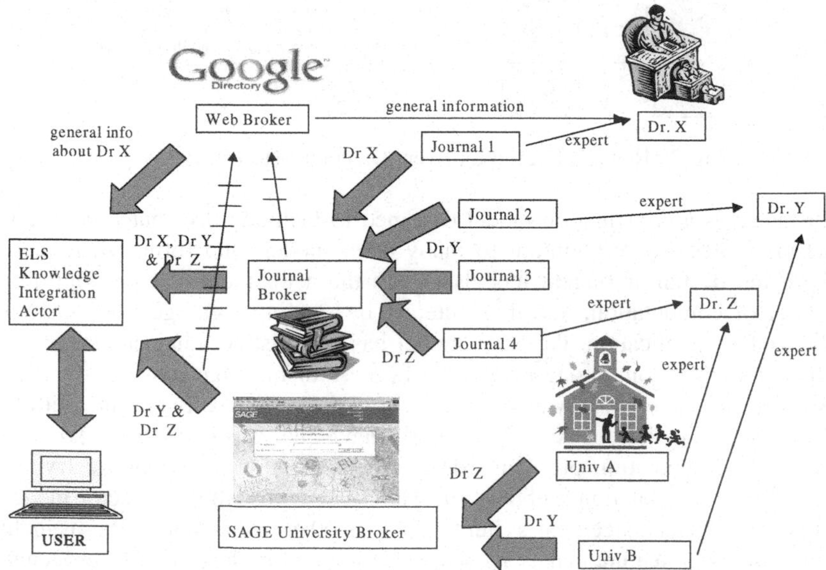

Fig. 3. Event Diagram for an Actor Model-based ELS

and the Web Broker. The SAGE University Broker interacts with each of the University Actors, which knows of a specific set of experts through its access to the corresponding university sponsored research database. For example, in the event diagram example shown in Figure 3, the University A actor knows that Dr. Z is a domain expert at that university, and the University B knows that Dr. Y is a domain expert at the corresponding university. Simultaneously, the Journal Broker interacts with each of the Journal Actors for Journal 1, Journal 2, Journal 3, and Journal 4. Journal 1 knows that Dr. X is a domain expert who publishes in that journal; Journal 2 knows that Dr. Y is a domain expert for the corresponding journal, and Journal 4 knows that Dr. Z is a domain expert for that journal as well. Once the domain experts have been identified by the University Broker actor (Dr. Y and Dr. Z) and the Journal Broker actor (Dr. X, Dr. Y, and Dr. Z), the railroad tracks show a timed event where the Web Broker (for example Google) will generate additional information about each of the domain experts previously identified (in this case Drs. X, Y, and Z). All of this information is integrated by the Knowledge Integration Actor and presented to the user.

The popular service oriented architecture (SOA) of information system design is essentially an extension of the actor computation model. A true SOA encapsulates application logic within services that interact via a common communication protocol. Therefore, it is natural to explore the applicability of SOA-related technologies as a strategy to improve the accuracy and breadth of the SAGE system.

Services are intended as independent (autonomous) building blocks that collectively represent an application environment. Due to the autonomous nature of service components, systems based on SOA do not need to comply to any one platform or technology set [10, p. 49]. The most wildly used SOA is the extended-markup language (XML)-based Web service [11]. The first-generation XML-base Web service is based on three specifications: Web Service Description Language (WSDL), Simple Object Access Protocol (SOAP), and Universal Description Discovery and Integration (UDDI). In the conceptual design model presented in Figure 3, each actor is required to provide a description or service definition about itself, so that it can receive requests from other trusted actors. A necessary pre-condition to establish communication between actors is to have a trust-based relationship among the same actors. Each actor's own WSDL documents are used to establish trust-based relationships between the actors in the model.

SOAP is an XML-based standard message format. Actors can dynamically join the actor framework as long as they use the same message standard. By Implementing SOAP messages in a SOA, the existing SAGE ELS system could be improved in terms of flexibility and scalability. For example a user would access the Knowledge Integration actor, which uses the UDDI directory to gain knowledge about other actors providing services in the model. The UDDI registry is an essential directory service, which describes the service actors in the SOA environment. In Figure 4, we present a vision of the next generation SAGE ELS based on SOA. The concept presented in Figure 4 extends the event diagram previously described in Figure 3. The fundamental idea here is that the SAGE UDDI registry coordinates all communication between our actors. Therefore, the ELS Integrator Actor is able to know about all other actors who have information about a particular expert.

In the current SAGE system, the University Broker actor is currently presents many limitations. For example, to maintain the SAGE current, an FTP process is initiated to transfer the data from each of the university databases to the SAGE server. Furthermore, this data most then be manually cleansed and integrated to the existing data in the SAGE server. For the new vision Actor-based SAGE system, we propose to develop a new University Broker actor, which interacts with each of the University Broker actors. Each individual University actor has access to their corresponding university database and therefore has knowledge of the experts at that particular university. Every University actor interfaces with the University Broker actor, and submits the required information. The University Broker will then be responsible to provide the required information to the information sent to the Knowledge Integration actor.

The Journal Broker is responsible to acquire expert information through external journal databases or citation indexes. Many of these databases now have their own UDDI registry. Therefore, Journal Broker can automatically acquire the required information about experts known to that specific journal (or collection of journals by a publishing house), by querying the journal's UDDI registry. Web Search Broker, on the other hand, is essentially a content analyzer. It utilizes the power of popular search engines and augments the information available about the domain experts of interest. Through proper content analysis, this information can be used to supplement the information about the expert known by each of the actors.

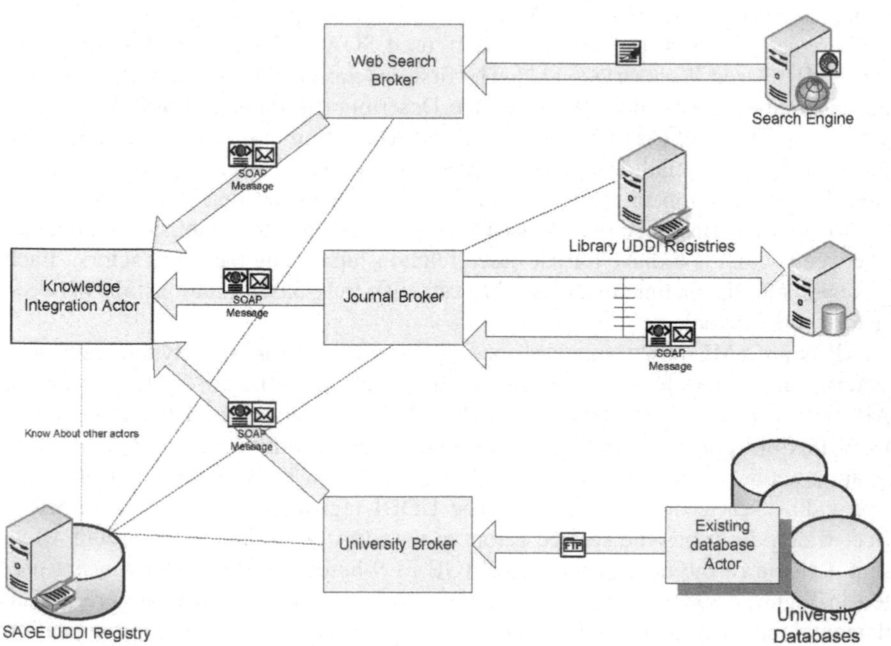

Fig. 4. New Vision for the SAGE ELS architecture

5 Validation of the Actor Model Architecture for SAGE

We tested the proposed actor model-based SAGE ELS by using a computer simulation model. The model was written and run in NetLogo[1] multi-agent programming language and modeling environment. We selected NetLogo as our test-bed language and development environment because of the following characteristics:

- Relatively user-friendly development environment
- Easy-to-understand language structure
- Low threshold required to build the initial models
- Includes a tool to support learning, based on a portable Java runtime environment

In order to characterize the interaction between the actors, we defined a trust-based collaboration relationship among the actors [12]. The basic premise in this model of collaboration, is that trust between each of the actors increases with the completion of every successful collaboration cycle. For example, in the relationship between the University Broker and each of the University Actors, every time a University Actor is able to accurately identify an expert according to the expertise category defined by the University Broker, the trust level between the University Broker and the University Actor increases.

In order to effectively implement the trust-based relationship between the actors, we designed a heuristic that defined the meaning of *accuracy* in expert location. Our heuristic is based on the use of the Google Search engine, defined here as the Google Broker. The Google Broker serves to validate the accuracy of results returned by the University Actor by performing an *and* search (or *search with all*) of the *expert* and his/her area of *expertise*. If the number of 'hits' returned by Google Broker is large (hundreds or thousands of hits) then the expert is validated within his/her area of expertise. If the number of hits from the search is small (tens of hits or less) then the result is not valid, and the identified name could not be validated as that of an expert in that expertise domain. To the extent that Google Broker is able to validate the results of the University Actor, the trust level between the University Broker and the University Actor increases. Otherwise, the trust level betweem the two will decrease.

Figure 5 presents a graphical illustration of the SAGE Actor-based simulation model. The construction of the SAGE Actor Model enabled us to better investigate the effects of a number of important factors such as the impact of increasing the number of universities represented and increasing the number of journals that are accessible to the ELS via the Journal Broker. The respective variables representing the number of universities and the number of journals can be assigned values by modifying the sliders at the top left corner of the screen.

The relationships between the Actor Broker (such as Journal Broker, SAGE…) and each of the individual actors are shown using straight lines with numbers depicting the applicable level of trust between each entity. For example, in Figure 5, the trust level of the relationship between the Journal Broker and the Journal number 2 is 5 (based on the scale of 100), indicating a relatively low level of trust. Plots are drawn

[1] http://ccl.northwestern.edu/netlogo/

to aid in visually studying the changes in the trust level of relationships. As an example, Figure 6a is a snapshot of how the trust level of each of the Journal Actors changes over time. As each Journal Actor successfully identifies an expert in a specific domain, and given that Google Broker (terminology) is able to validate the accuracy of the Actor's response, the trust of the Actor increases.

Figure 6a represents the how the level of trust of each actor progresses over time. Figure 6b shows the number of experts affiliated with each journal. Figure 6c plots the total number of requests for experts (bars in black) as compared to the total number of successfully identified experts (represented by the red bars).

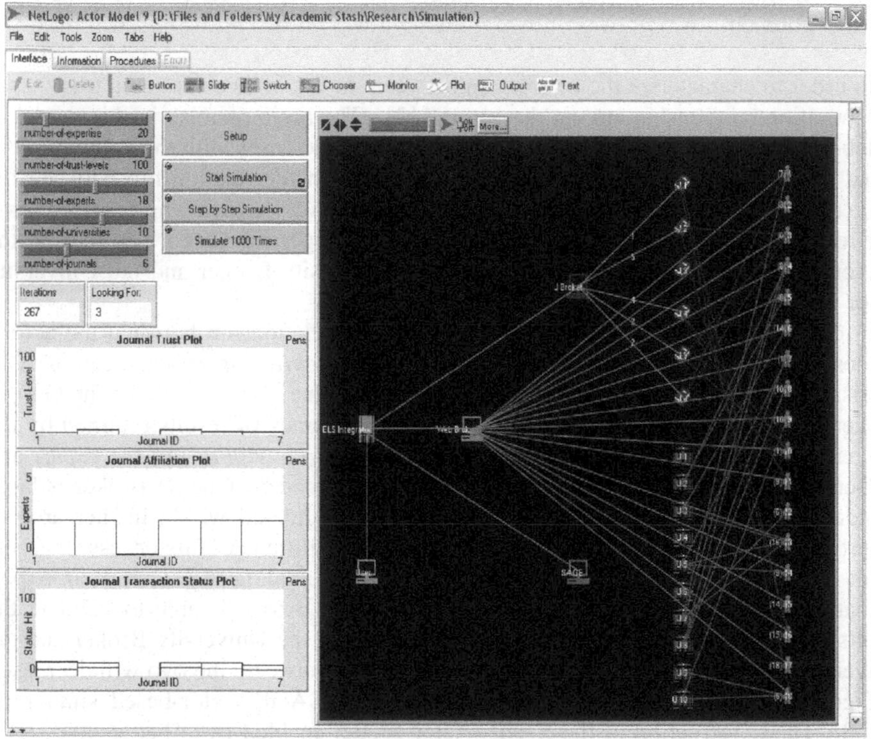

Fig. 5. Simulation model for the Actor-based SAGE ELS

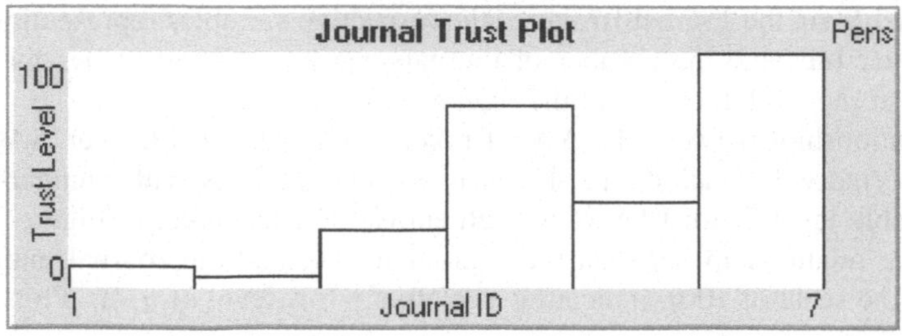

Fig. 6a. Progression of 'trust' of each Journal Actor over time

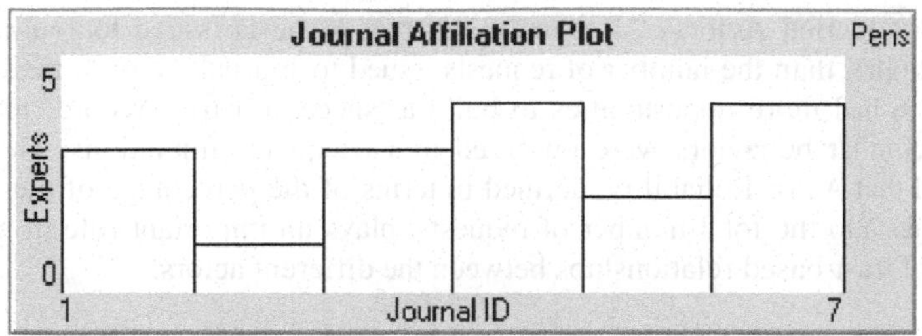

Fig. 6b. Number of experts affiliated with each Journal Actor

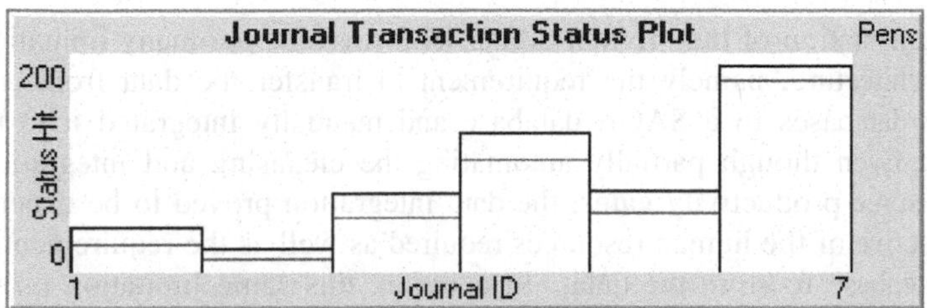

Fig. 6c. Total successful expert requests (red) over total number of expert requests (black)

The simulation model was setup to run successively until either stopped by the command button, or the number of runs reached a pre-determined arbitrary number. We set the number of runs to an arbitrary number (1000 times) in order to be able to observe the changes in the trust relationships over time. The number of runs was chosen arbitrarily based on computing power limitations.

From the simulations, we observed the development of some interesting patterns. First, the number of individual experts affiliated with one or more journals or institutions was found to be a major determinant in building a trust-based relationship between an Actor Broker (SAGE or Journal Broker) and the related Actor (Individual Journal or Institution). Actors with more connections to experts have in general a higher probability of accurately identifying an expert, and therefore increasing their relationship trust level with their respective Actor Broker, faster than actors with less connections within the given time period. (See Figures 6a and 6b).

Also, we observed that reliability or 'trustworthiness' is the next major factor that determines the wellbeing of the trust relationships between brokers and actors. The higher the percentage of the number of requests that are completed successfully over the total number of requests received, the higher the probability of increasing the relationship trust level between brokers and actors. For example, Figures 6a and 6c can be used to explain the difference between the trust levels of Journals Actors 4 and 6. Figure 6a effectively depicts at a particular point in time, that the trust level of Journal 6 was higher than that of Journal Actor 4. Although both journals had the same number of affiliations with experts (as seen from Figure 6b), the trust level of Journal Actor 6 at the end of the simulation was higher than that of Journal Actor 4. A glance at Figure 6c explains the reason for the discrepancy in trust levels between the two Journal Actors. The reliability of Journal Actor 6, shown by the percentage of the number of successfully completed requests to the total number of requests honored (i.e. the location of the red line compared to the size of the bar), is found to be higher than that of Journal Actor 4. But the number of requests issued to Journal Actor 6 was also higher than the number of requests issued to Journal Actor 4; therefore Journal Actor 6 had more opportunities to build a 'successful trust record' than Journal Actor 4. Similar behaviors were observed in subsequent simulations. Therefore we concluded that Actor Reliability, defined in terms of the percentage of the number of valid requests to the total number of requests, plays an important role in moderating the level of trust-based relationships between the different actors.

6 Conclusion

The implementation of the original SAGE ELS revealed the many limitations of that system architecture, namely the requirement to transfer the data from each of the university databases to a SAGE database and manually integrated it to the SAGE database. Even though partially automating the cleansing and integration process produced some productivity gains, the data integration proved to be expensive from the perspective of the human resources required as well as the requirement for a centralized database to store the data. In addition, this same limitation prevented the system to be easily scalable to include other experts at other universities. Finally, the system offered a limited representation of expertise, only those with funded research.

The actor model-based ELS proposed here is an important concept in that it provides a scalable and more comprehensive expert profile. In addition, the proposed paradigm eliminates the need for data owners to relinquish the ownership of their data resource, which is often a barrier to information integration. Finally, in modeling the relationship between the actors, we incorporate the concept of trust between actors, and the need for validating the actor's responses. Trust between the actors and the actor broker increases as each actor successfully identifies a domain expert. We also introduced a heuristic for expertise location, which serves to validate the domain expert located by the actor. We expect to continue to refine this heuristic, as well as to continue with the implementation of the actor-model based ELS.

References

1 Becerra-Fernandez, I., Gonzalez, A., Sabherwal, R. *Knowledge Management: Challenges, Solutions, and Technologies*, 1st ed. Upper Saddle River, NJ: Prentice Hall, (2004).

2 Becerra-Fernandez, I.: "The Role of Artificial Intelligence Technologies in the Implementation of People-finder Knowledge management Systems," *Knowledge Based Systems*, Vol. 13, (2000), 315-320.

3 Becerra-Fernandez, I.: "Searching for Experts on the Web: A Review of Contemporary Expertise Locator Systems," *ACM Transactions on Internet Technology*. Forthcoming in Vol. 6 (4), (2006)

4 Becerra-Fernandez, I.: "Locating Expertise at NASA - Developing a Tool to Leverage Human Capital," Knowledge Management Review, Vol. 4, (2001), 34-37.

5 Wang, T.-W, Murphy, K. E.: "Semantic Heterogeneity in Multidatabase Systems: A Review and a Proposed Meta-Data Structure," Journal of Database Management, Vol. 15, (2004), 71-87.

6 Hewitt, C.: "Viewing Control Structures as Patterns of Passing Message," Journal of Artificial Intelligence, Vol. 8, (1977), 323-364.

7 Allen, A.: "Actor-Based Computing: Vision Forestalled, Vision Fulfilled," presented at Agent'98 2nd International Conference on Autonomous Agents, Minneapolis/St. Paul, Minnesota, 1998.
8 Agha, G. A., Mason, I. A., Smith, S. F., Talcott, C. L.: "A Foundation for Actor Computation," Journal of Functional Programming, Vol. 7, (1997), 1-72.
9 Liu, J., Eker, J., Jamneck, J. W.: "Actor-Oriented Control System Design: A Responsible Framework Perspective," IEEE Transactions on Control Systems Technology, Vol. 12, (2004), 250-262.
10 Erl, T.: Service-Oriented Architecture; A Field Guide to Integrating XML and Web Services. Upper Saddle River, NJ: Prentice Hall, (2004).
11 Gottschalk, K., Graham, S., Kreger, H., Snell, J.: "Introduction to Web Service Architecture," IBM Systems Journal, Vol. 41, (2002), 170-177.
12 Kumar, K. and Becerra-Fernandez, I. Interaction Technology: Speech-Act Based Information Technology Support for Building Collaborative Relationships and Trust. Decision Support Systems, Forthcoming (2006).

Knowledge + Skills + "x"

Klaus Kornwachs

Lehrstuhl Technikphilosophie,
Brandenburgische Technische Universität Cottbus, D-03044 Cottbus
kornwachs@tu-cottbus.de
http://www.tu-cottbus.de/techphil

Abstract. A conceptual analysis of the knowledge concept shows that the distinction between tacit and explicit knowledge is not sufficient. The concept of good informant and good doer is introduced in order to show that effective knowledge is closely connected with the concept of "body". The neglecting of this connection seems to be one of the reason that we have too much information and too less knowledge.

"*Mephisto:* ... Das stolze Licht, das nun der Mutter Nacht
Den alten Rang, den Raum ihr streitig macht,
Und doch gelingt' s ihm nicht, da es, so viel es strebt,
Verhaftet an den Körpern klebt.
Von Körpern strömt' s, die Körper macht es schön,
Ein Körper hemmt' s auf seinem Gange,
So hoff' ich, dauert es nicht lange,
Und mit den Körpern wird's zugrunde gehn. "[1]

1 Introduction

The problem how to acquire and to handle information, how to generate worthy knowledge and how to hand knowledge on to other users and even to future generations has been widely discussed during the centuries;[2] and it is still an actual and – predominantly – an organizational problem.

This task occupied abbeys, monasteries, universities, academies, authorities and enterprises as well. A better generation of knowledge, its conservation, transfer and handing on to future generations or to the neighboured research department within the same company were and are not only a technical problem for libraries and computers, when copying, distributing or storing. If one looks on specific network architecture, it is also an organizational problem.

The technologies of writing, already subject of critique by Plato,[3] the invention of printing technology and the historically complete new possibility to distribute and store information electronically in a large scale never experienced before have

[1] J. W. Goethe: Faust. Eine Tragödie, 1. Teil, Studierzimmer. In. Goethe, J. W.: Werke. Band 3, Insel, Frankfurt a.M. 1966, S. 43.
[2] Cf. [8] Doren (1992).
[3] Cf. Platos dialogue Phaidon and the 7th letter. In: [32] Plato (1990).

K.-D. Althoff et al. (Eds.): WM 2005, LNAI 3782, pp. 32 – 47, 2005.

brought up new technologies themselves and new forms of organizations and means in order to handle knowledge in an interlinked wired world. With the new possibilities new problems with these knowledge technologies arose.

But knowledge is not enough as we know, and information is not sufficient if we have to solve a problem, e.g. to design a better product or to shape a better production technology or service. Even the teaching of skills and abilities is a problem that has not yet been solved satisfactorily by the distinction between explicit and implicit knowledge. Nevertheless knowledge and skills are not sufficient for making a good decision and a well-shaped problem solving.

The term of knowledge has always been an important concept in the History of Philosophy and later in Cognitive Psychology. To know something was regarded to be better than to know nothing, it was brought together with power,[4] despite the dictum of Socrates that he knew to know nothing.[5] Knowledge has become a societal normative concept when Nico Stehr coined the term of knowledge society as a follower of information society.[6]

Generally speaking, a society could be named an *xy*-society, if a considerable – if not essential – portion of good exchange, economical creation of values and transfers is based even such on *xy*.[7] Thus a knowledge society is handling and dealing with knowledge as an economic good. This can be considered as a basis of its transfers and exchanges that may stabilize the societal structure.[8]

In the meanwhile the descriptions of Nico Stehr and its popular and political adaptations[9] do not seem to be pure descriptive ones – a normative component may be figured out due to the fact that the concept of knowledge has been used to put forward political aims, social welfare and economic advantages as well. The usual speaking about information and / or knowledge as "raw material" is leading in this direction.

Consequently, enterprises with dedicated aims in hard technology have started to develop a kind of knowledge management, i.e. the trial to control the generation, handling and transfer of knowledge under the regime of effectiveness and efficiency as a ratio between costs and utility.

Here a lot of misunderstandings arose since some proponents of technologically aimed solutions stated openly their belief that for every problem there would exist always a technical solution.[10] Along to this argument it seemed to be clear that such solutions should encompass a formal, i.e. computer supported knowledge processing. But the rise and fall of expert systems has shown drastically that there is a difference between information, available on a quite semi-intelligent database machine and the

4 F. Bacons dictum is slightly different. He did not say: "Knowledge is power", but: "*ipso scientia potestas est*". Here he pointed out rather Science as a method and as an institution than knowledge as such. Cf. [1] Bacon (1597) in (1864), p. 79.

5 Cf. Apology. In: [32] Plato (1990).

6 Cf. [42] Stehr (1994).

7 Cf. [22] Kornwachs (2000)(b).

8 Cf. [42] Stehr (1994).

9 As given earlier already by [3] Beck (1986), in [37] Radermacher (2001) and other contributions in [15] Hubig (2001).

10 For example the former Secretary of State for the Science Department of German Federal Republic, Dr. Heinz Riesenhuber, at the Annual Conference of the Fraunhofer-Society for Applied Sciences in Aachen 1984.

generation of knowledge by receiving, understanding, modifying and integrating the information into the realm of an already existing knowledge.[11]

Therefore any operative theory of an approach how to handle knowledge must take into account the fundamental difference between knowledge and information.[12] Hence this difference seems to be crucial for each trial to shape a good technology that is driven by knowledge on the one side and advances information processing on the other side.

The aim of my lecture is to show some characteristics of the interaction between technology, organization and conceptual framework with respect to information and knowledge. The main problems can be summarized by some questions:

- How to estimate the quality, reliability and actuality of information gained by a network or data warehouse or other information service, that is part of a knowledge management system? This is not only a question of IC Technologies, but also a matter of trust.
- How to ensure a well qualified understanding process that makes information to knowledge? This is not only a question of our mental abilities, but also a matter of contextual preparation of information design. In former times this was described as cognitive ergonomics.
- How to bridge the gap between time pressure in decision process and knowledge acquiring time? This is the actual reason for the information dilemma. I will discuss this a little bit later.

In Philosophy we will not be able to answer these questions such that a concrete result may be applicable in an operative way for executives or Chief Information Officers. But we can give some hints why these questions have not yet been solved satisfactorily. Our guess is that there may be some conceptual pitfalls and obstacles.

Thus, let us begin with the trivial circumstance that we need knowledge to make good decisions. Generally speaking a decision seems to be determined if the goals have been defined, if the options to act have been ruled out and if the evaluation of the options has been done exhaustively. This is not only the standard for any philosophical theories of actions but also for the still tentative design of automated decisions, i.e. to design self-deciding machines. But such a standard decision situation is not trivial: To find an appropriate goal is sometimes not easy and the options to act depend sensitively upon the knowledge and the skills and abilities. This is the set of possible executable operations and relations between them. Moreover the evaluation of options needs a lot of additional knowledge.

The hypothesis of my talk will be that knowledge and abilities must be completed which has something to do with the situation.

- In computer science a situation is formally modelled by ontology. Such ontology provides a formal and material framework in which one can make definitions, conclusions and arguments. It gives rise to the structure of the relevant universe of discourse.

---

[11] As an early study in this field, cf. [6] Bullinger, Kornwachs (1990).

[12] The difference has been discussed widely in [20] Kornwachs (1999), [23] (2000 (c)), [25] (2005 (a)) and [26] (2005 (b)).

- In natural sciences our general knowledge is expressed by natural laws, frequently given in form of differential equations. The situational knowledge is given by the start and boundary conditions in an experiment. They define the possibility to make forecast as well as they describe the preparation of the experiment.
- In technology, the situation is given by the actual availability of materials, controllable processes and the existence of necessary co-systems in which every technological system is embedded.
- In social and linguistic sciences, the situation is known as the context.

All these types of representations of situations have something to do with how the interaction between the object in question and its situation is organized. This can be clearly shown in the case of technology. Therefore we have firstly to look on what is known as organizational closure.

2 The Organizational Closure

The concept of technology has been changed during the time. The original notion was about the restricted technical knowledge that was necessary to design, to build, to use and to deal with technical instruments, i.e. man made artefacts in order to solve problems and to act purposefully. An apparatus or a technical device was the focus of technological efforts and knowledge. Techniques have been considered as procedures, methods and skills. This both concepts indeed reflect the twofold meaning of τέχνη: the production of something that is useful, a mean with respect to a class of goals (material concept) and the trickery, the art, the method how to do things successfully (formal concept).

But if one looks for instance on a contemporary car, it is easy to realize that such a car cannot unfold its technological functions, if numerous co-systems are not working. There must be a simultaneous co-functioning. Thus, without any roads and traffic control, road prizing (by taxes or in some other way), highways, vocational training for drivers license, electronic and public communication, laws and regulation systems up to the proliferation of fuel and of parts, a car as a part of a mean goal relation is technologically meaningless, it remains a nice peace of metal, rubber and electronics on a green meadow.

The term "organizational closure" is introduced to describe the circumventing circle of interacting co-systems that are not only technical but also mostly organizational systems.[13]

One important part of this organizational closure for each technical device is the knowledge handling. Knowledge is needed to enable a subject to use any technology, e.g. for getting drivers licence, to run and to repair, but it is also necessary to install

[13] Due to an extensive system theoretical analysis, [40] Ropohl (1979, 1999) has widened the general concept of technology that includes not only the instruments and methods, but also the production, the way of use as well as its waste management. Also the relevant forms of communication, organisation and societal co-systems are included. In a new approach, [10] Erlach (2001) introduced three dimensions of technology; i.e. the prosthesis, the game and the risk form the so-called technotop.

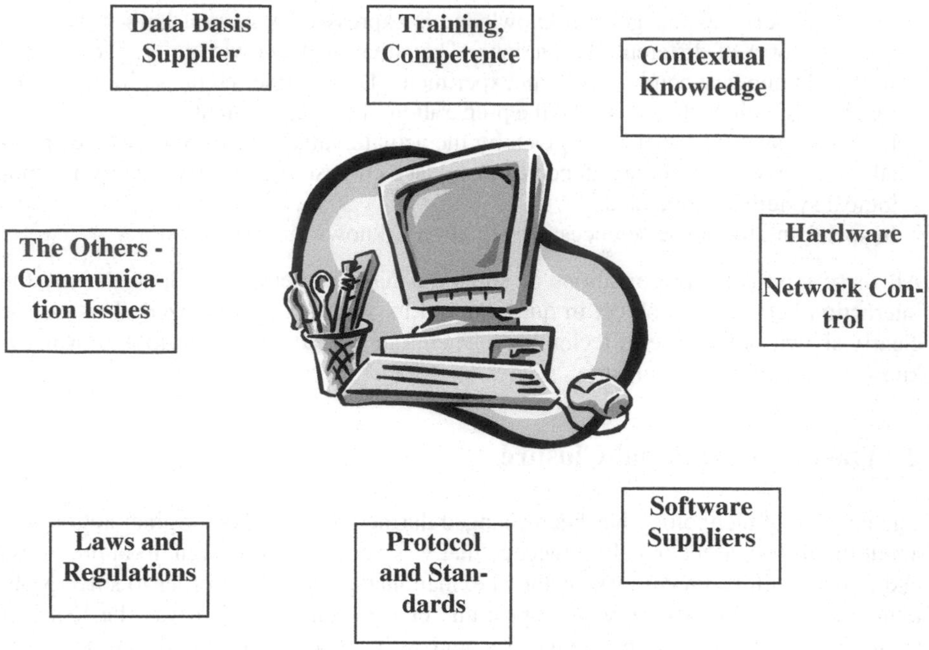

Fig. 1. Organizational closure of an ICT-system

and optimise the relevant organizational closure. Thus, knowledge acquisition must be organized by knowledge itself. And exactly these self-referential characteristics produce the difficulties that have been expressed in the questions above.

Fig. 1 shows an organizational closure of an everyday Information and Communication Technology (ICT-system). The basic variables in order to answer the above questions about the use of information are then related a priori on the organizational closure of an ICT system, not only on the hardware: the problems of trust in the deliverer of information, the question of quality, reliability and actuality, and the problem of security are all closely connected with the surrounding institutions. The problems of process understanding, the problem how to come from information to knowledge, the time pressure in decision process and the knowledge acquiring time, that cannot be compressed by technical means – all this problems are situated primarily on the side of the user.

3 Information and Knowledge

In this chapter a short excurse should be allowed in order to sketch roughly the conceptual distinction between information and knowledge.

Knowledge is information that has been understood. Every process of understanding requires a kind of "zero-knowledge" that allows to interpret the incoming information and to integrate it. Any information has physical carriers. Data are information arrangements under the regime of a certain purpose. The location of knowledge is considered to be the human conscious mind.[14] A necessary but not sufficient condition to understand information is that it contains an adequate portion of novelty (firstness or surprise) and confirmation (redundancy). We will call this pragmatic information, i.e. information that can be understood actually.[15] The acquisition of information is comparably easy because it encompasses an access with the mean of an adequate labelled carrier. The real problem starts with the selection of information with respect to the knowledge wanted.

Philosophically speaking[16] we could recognize knowledge as something what information has produced as understanding within a human cognitive system within this realm. Here we have a difference that influences the societal definition of an information society respective knowledge society: Information is what has been communicated; knowledge is what has been generated by communicated information. In communication we transform knowledge into information that can be handed on, which becomes knowledge again by the receiver. This knowledge owned by the receiver as a result of interpretation may be different from knowledge intended by the sender, seen as the original meaning the sender has. The individuality of the sender, the individuality of the receiver, and the situation conditions determine this difference considerably.

As a consequence we have already a remarkable result. At least only information can be a subject of good exchange, but it is impossible to do so with knowledge.

From a formal point of view the reception of a foolish or misplaced TV show may represent the same information processing procedures as the understanding of a mathematical textbook or a philosophical lecture. The difference was not quite clear when Plato put forward the emphatic meaning of knowledge: he defined knowledge as a true justified opinion. But the generation procedure of this knowledge was struggled on a high level in Plato's dialogue Theaitetos and this problem was not solved there.[17] Heidegger has made a decisive step toward a pragmatic interpretation. Knowledge, as a result from a cognitive act, is knowledge about a thing or a situation and how to handle it adequately. The meaning of this interpretation may be paraphrased in terms like "(s)he knows how to behave oneself" or "s(h)e knows how to handle it", as equivalent with "(s)he knows something".[18] This interpretation could bridge the gap between knowledge and abilities or skills.

The interpretation of [5] G. Böhme (1999) seems to adapt smoothly this meaning. According to him knowledge is participation, i.e. to share something like facts, things or processes, that is represented by knowledge. It is not the participation with the original images in terms of Plato's ideas, but taking part as a process in the community of knowing individuals who are able to inform, to perform adequate acts, and to develop knowledge further. Peer groups, or professional groups, or individuals who define acceptable and justified knowledge can represent such knowledge. It is said that the early Greek sophists have offered knowledge as a useful good. More precisely

[14] Here the term "knowledge" is used in a restricted meaning. In this view, knowledge is neither present nor stored in nonhuman natural or artificial systems. Cf. my arguments in [25] Kornwachs (2005 (b)) against a position in [37] Radermacher (2001).

[15] For a theory of pragmatic information that relates to the effect when being received, cf. [18] Kornwachs (1987), [25] (2005 (a)); earlier [44] E. U. von Weizsäcker et al. (1974).

[16] Cf. [26] Kornwachs (2005(b)).

[17] Cf. Theaitetos, 200d-201c. In: [32] Platon (1990, Bd. 6, S. 1-217).

[18] Cf. [14] Heidegger (1988), p. 149 ff.

they have offered information and skills, how to train rules that may allow to have some success in rhetoric and struggles at courts. With this good they earned money in the same manner as Ghost Writers and consulting firms are doing today. Any moralization of this activity must explain the values that may be in conflict with that.

The usefulness of knowledge can be defined by its power for problem solving. Therefore the value of information can be estimated as the difference between the effectiveness of a problem solving with and without having available the relevant information in order to produce the necessary knowledge. This presupposes a very restrictive and precise definition what the problem is for which given information is needed.[19]

Knowledge must be communicable. As a scientific knowledge, the relevant given information must be explicit and comprehensible in order to check the statement. The claim to be valid normally is given by the methodology used to generate the knowledge that has lead to the information communicated. This claim is stronger than for everyday knowledge and it must prove oneself to be of good quality against critics and trials of refutations. Knowledge can be explicated in statements that can be maintained and defended with good reasons ([5] Böhme 1999). These statements are information that can be understood. Therefore, scientific knowledge as well as everyday knowledge presupposes successful communication processes.

A decisive critique that leads us further has been given by the analysis of [11] Gettier (1963). He showed that the definition in Plato's Theaitetos, according to which knowledge is a true, justified opinion, couldn't be sufficient formally. It is always possible to construct counterexamples, in which a mental content (opinion) can be true and justified and despite of this there is no knowledge about the fact that is represented.[20] We cannot report this analysis here; it remains to say that this critique has provoked an operative definition of knowledge by [8] Craig (1993) that can be usefully introduced here.

4 The Information Dilemma

It may be helpful to distinguish between information, available on a carrier like data, and pragmatic information, i.e. information, that is available and able to be understood. Then we have the process of understanding information as a cognitive act, producing knowledge for the individual. The knowledge itself can be characterized by a state in which an individual may be. The useful knowledge can be described that it may be applied successfully. This can be done by transformation of a more law-oriented knowledge (like in natural sciences) into a technical knowledge that is oriented to rules of action. Last, but not least the communication about this knowledge by producing pragmatic information (like a users manual or explanation) is the end of this chain and its very new beginning.

Thus the information dilemma can be reformulated, regarding these distinctions:

- The information you have is not the knowledge you want.
- The knowledge you want is not the knowledge you need.

---

[19] We cannot discuss details here. For a definition of problem logics and solving expressions cf. [18] Bunge (1967, Chap. 11) and applications in [18] Kornwachs (1987), [19] (1989).

[20] Cf. [11] Gettier (1963), Counterexamples are discussed by [8] Craig (1993, p. 53-64).

- The knowledge needed is not obtainable by the information that is currently available.
- The information available is more expensive than you are ready to pay.[21]

These questions represent also the basic problems of an effective knowledge management.

- How to shape a better information and knowledge technology by regarding organisation issues more in detail?
- How to manage concurrent (simultaneous) processes of knowledge handling?
- How can be established a well-shaped organizational closure for a so-called Good Informant?

5 The Good Informant and the Good Doer

5.1 Epistemological Knowledge

The concept of a "Good Informant" has been coined by [8] Craig (1993), when he was excited by a critique of Plato's concept of knowledge by [11] Gettier (1963). In order to precise more the notion of "having knowledge" that has been discussed in Plato's dialogue Theaitetos, Craig tried to make the term knowledge operational according to a certain ability.

The very starting point of Graig[22] is the platonic formula: knowledge is a true, justified opinion. Knowledge is considered to be a set of justified, coherent convictions an individual or a group of individuals has and which is believed to be true by sufficient reasons. The formal analysis of the statement: "Individual S knows that fact p" by Gettier leads to the following conditions:

- "S knows that p" if and only if
  - p is the case (is factual),
  - S believe that p ,
  - S is justified to believe that p.[23]

Craig moved to the definition that knowledge might be a system build up by conviction that an individual has won during a certain time of experience, receiving information and impressions. This knowledge must be able to be expressed (it refers to the explicit knowledge) by the "bearer". Therefore a reconstruction of this knowledge by an expert inquiry should be possible. The idea behind is that knowledge, an individual has, can be reconstructed by asking this individual for existing facts and the well-founded relations between them. Who is able to do so is called a good informant.

A human beeing with a knowledge able to be reconstructed is called a good informant, if

---

[21] This is an adaptation of a joke, made by a former Yugoslavia journal. The source could not be found again.

[22] Cf. [8]Craig (1993). The hints for the concept of the good informant that Stefan Berndes gave me during his dissertation project are gratefully acknowledged. Cf. also [4] Berndes (2001). We skip here the discussion about scepticism Craig is pursuing as a main goal in his book.

[23] Cf. Craig (1963), p. 53.

- (s)he provides an access to me now and here (operationally speaking);
- (s)he is recognizable as an individual being probably right concerning the question whether p or not;
- the probability for him (her) being right is sufficient for my actual purpose;
- the communication channels are open and available.

According to [8] Craig (1993) knowledge is a state that enables the subject to be a good informant with respect to a defined question. Thus knowledge became only a useful knowledge with respect to a certain context. This good informant can be a subject, a group of individuals and even an institution. The criteria to adjust the sufficient subjective probabilities of expectation represent institutional facts. This presupposes a certain trust and a history of the relation between the good informant and the questioner. Shortly: there is no certain knowledge but it can be communicated.

We will call this type of knowledge "pragmatic knowledge" since it can be closely related to the term of pragmatic information as mentioned in Section 3 of this contribution: only pragmatic information can produce pragmatic knowledge.

5.2 Explicit and Implicit Knowledge

For technological knowledge, that has been characterized by a lot of differences with respect to other kinds of knowledge,[24] there is an important consequence. As far as abilities and skills are not communicable within the realm of language[25] they are not able to be represented as explicit knowledge. This non-explicit knowledge cannot be made fluent in form of information. This knowledge is called implicit. It is generated by direct acts of experience without language, not by an understanding of information expressed in communicative acts.[26]

At a first glimpse Craigs operational concept of a good informant ([8] Craig 1993) seems to be related only to explicit knowledge. This may encompass also all paralinguistic possibilities, i.e. the good informant is allowed to answer a question sufficiently by any understandable gesture or other signs, if the meaning and content of this sign(s) fulfil the condition for a solution of the problem in question.

The success of the communicative act is given when the utterance of the good informant is a speech act with clear defined illocution of maintaining without any differing or further embedding intention.[27]

One could now introduce a good informant, which is responsible for implicit knowledge like skills, abilities, competence, habits and so on. Since implicit knowl-

---

[24] For conceptual reflections cf. [34] Poser (2001), [35] (2003(a)), [36] (2005), [26] Kornwachs (2003(b)), [24] (2004) and [27] (2005(c)); another approach [28] Krämer (2003). Cf. also the reader edited by [2] Banse, Ropohl (2004). A popular distinction between orientation and dispositive knowledge has been recently criticized by [13] Hanekamp (2003).

[25] Here, every kind of „showing" using sign systems and non- or paralinguistic entities like gestures should be included.

[26] The difference between implicit (tacit) and explicit knowledge has been introduced by [33] Polanyi (1985). For further discussions see [29] Layton (1974), later [39] Ropohl (1997), [43] de Vries (2003). See also [38] Rammert (2001).

[27] Speech acts are the basic pragmatic unit "how to do things with words", as Austin stated. For the theory of speech acts, which are characterized by the reference, predicate, illocution and intention of an utterance in a concrete situation, cf. [41] Searle (1969), further applications cf. [17] Kornwachs (1975) and [19] (1989).

edge is acquired mainly not by linguistic means, the respective good informant may be a "good doer".[28] In analogy we could then define:

- A good doer is able to put into practice a technical function that is a solution with respect to a given problem.

The basic idea is then to reconstruct implicit knowledge by asking a subject (or group of subjects) to put into practice technological functions (including the relevant concatenations between them) respective to build an artefact that can perform this function. The good doer is available here and now. He is recognisable to be competent enough, to put into practice a function that is a solution for my problem with a certain probability. For my actual purposes this probability may be sufficient *hic et nunc*. The communication channels (whatsoever) and the (physical and organisational) possibilities to build, to demonstrate and to apply the function or the artefact must exist and must be open. Exactly this last condition gives us a hint to what the "x" in the title of this lecture "Knowledge + Skills + x" could be related.

According to this the analogy to Craigs good informant can be expressed as follows: implicit technological knowledge is a state that enables a subject (group, institution) to be a good doer in a given problem situation. The form of linguistic or formal expressions like in a database cannot handle this. These abilities are mediated by a "body". The term "body" can also be used metaphorically as a set for all necessary physical, biological and technical co-systems, i.e. the organisational closure as mentioned in the forgoing section 2.

The criteria to define the necessary probability are represented again as an institutional fact. Therefore there is no certain implicit knowledge, but if one is able to be successful with it, this knowledge becomes a kind of true knowledge.

6 Knowledge Acquisition

How to acquire knowledge? This processes run differently for explicit and implicit knowledge. Technical knowledge is very often implicit, even when using computer for non-computer purposes. This implicit technological knowledge is determining the action of an individual subject, but the subject cannot tell explicitly what (s)he is doing or thinking. Therefore the implicit knowledge must be deduced from the actions and procedures of the subject when successfully putting into practice a useful technological function. Of course, this deduction is actually an induction.

For explicit knowledge a principal ability to be formalized even in terms of hard (i.e. apparatus) technology is given.[29] This is not the case for implicit knowledge that is often deposited within operative "theories" like the development of organizations or the shape of the organizational closure of a given technology.[30]

---

[28] Here the term "doer" (germ. *Macher*) may comprehend making, generating, producing, putting into practise, performing etc.

[29] Cf. also the Table 1 in [24] Kornwachs (2004).

[30] As examples of formalizing technological knowledge, including default logics; see textbooks in Artificial Intelligence, e.g. [12] Görz (1995). For principles of design and construction, very early cf. [45] Wögerbauer (1943)and [16] Kesselring (1954) as examples.

The task of formalization is made difficult by exceptions that characterize the limitation of the well-known rules. The exceptions are tried to be handled with so-called default logics.[31] These difficulties are well known in knowledge engineering when trying to "transfer" knowledge from elder and very experienced experts to a knowledge base of an expert system. The same difficulty is to "learn" from expert systems with huge data or knowledge bases. But beside this, the existence of exceptions is characteristic for all frames of rules in the area of organisation. The trials to formalize the exceptions lead to the effect that the contents became poorer. The impossibility for laymen to shape their knowledge into a formal framework has its place here. The same holds for the problem to use a complex user interface with a too high requirement of abstraction.[32]

On the other hand we have the incapability of expert, to explain and make explicit their long experienced and accumulated implicit knowledge to laymen who had not the opportunity to experience such a long time.

Here we have the limits of formal representation as a usual problem. But the conceptual damage is not given by the alleged inability of the implicit everyday knowledge to cope with a certain kind of problems, but the source is given by the paradigm of a machine information processing. This states that any knowledge leading to a successful action is not only an explicit knowledge but also a knowledge that can be formalized.[33] This conjecture is wrong. This leads to the paradox of the Non-Formal, indicated in Table 1:

Table 1. The relation between the formal and the explicit is not trivial

	Formal	Non-formal
Explicit	All explicit knowledge can be expressed in a language: Therefore it can be formalized.	To express in a language: This is not yet the same like to formalize
Implicit	Only possible on a Meta-Level: Explicit description of a behaviour of which the generating programme is not known.	On the level of objects implicit knowledge. It can be neither linguistically expressed nor formalized.

According to this short analysis that may be generalized cautiously, the transformation from information to knowledge (understanding) and the transformation from knowledge to information (communicating) are slightly modified in the field of technology. The fulfilment of the problem solving expression is simpler in case of technology, if one reduces it to an artefact in a narrow sense. Using a wider concept of

[31] Cf. textbooks of Artificial Intelligence.

[32] There are many bad examples, for instance the ticket automaton of German Rail Road Company.

[33] As a consequence this knowledge can be mapped on a model of a Turing machine, i.e. a finite discrete automaton. There are a lot of other machines that does not fit to this very universal machine concept and that cannot be emulated by a Turing machine. Paraphrasing a joke of Bochenski, we could say: "The world is full of non-Turing machines".

technology, including the organizational closure, things become more complex since the rules can no more explicitly be represented and the real situation comes into the game.[34]

Since the times of G. W. Leibniz the formal representation has opened the possibility to delegate any formal process to a rule based repetitive procedure that is executed by a machine. Today, this is still a Turing Machine. This has two consequences for the good informant and the good doer as well:

All what may be recalcitrant against formalization is cut away when defining the problem and answering the questions by the good informant. Otherwise it cannot be delegated to a machine. Consequently one has always tried to substitute the good informant by a machine or an expert system. This is only possible for a restricted concept of technology that does not contain organizational issues. Therefore restricted technological knowledge is easier to formalize and to communicate by standardized information.

Technological functions are – at least – only understandable with respect to artefacts, embedded in an organizational closure. Since the organizational closure is too complex, it is omitted when we perform a modelling of technical functions. Thus any automation of knowledge processing reduces considerably any understanding of technology in a wider sense.

It is not necessary to say that the trial to substitute the cognition process by machines may lead to new risks that are counterproductive to shape good technologies.

7 Too Much Information, too Little Knowledge

The instantaneous availability of information at any time, at any place for every user, due to the permanent accelerating life cycles, has not compressed or shortened the time that is necessary to understand an information and to convert it into a personal knowledge, that is useful, communicable and making the bearer a good informant or at least a good doer.

Due to the surplus of information we have to find new criteria for selecting useful information, since our time is limited. Thus our third hypothesis comes into scope: a management of forgetting is necessary in order to handle knowledge in a wired, i.e. extremely interconnected unfolded world with highly nested contexts.[35]

This contextualisation can be explained again by the organizational closure of every technology. If it is true that the forms of institutions and organizations of our contemporary society are primarily mediated by technologies and their organizational closure, then every technological mediated act must take into account the mutual interaction between technical device and relevant organizational issues. This give rise to a world in which no strong separation can be made, i.e. no local solution of a problem can be certain for a longer time. The contextualisation of technology means the technological dependence upon knowledge about organizational issues. The contextualisation of knowledge means its dependence upon technology and upon the physically defined ability and skills. This leads to the assumption, that knowledge is

---

[34] This seems to be a reason that technology might be more complex than science.

[35] Cf. [21] Kornwachs (1996). There the problem of forgetting knowledge and the waste management for knowledge are discussed.

already a technological concept and, vice versa, that technology is an epistemic concept also.

If this assumption could be established by better reflections and investigations, one consequence for shaping better technologies could be given very easily: "to know" is not yet equal with "to be able to build", but "to be able to build" is not equivalent with the real fact of building. Thus having built something shows a certain, not yet necessarily explicit knowledge.

In terms of knowledge and skills: Both, knowledge and skills have a carrier (or a bearer). In Information Theory as well as in Computer Science usually one can neglect this fact – a program and its execution do not depend upon the material basis on which the performance take place. The concept of algorithm is invariant from any material substrate.

Whereas in Cognitive Science, theoreticians like Roger Penrose and others have argued that the material substrate of information processing may have indeed an influence on the mode of processing,[36] one still believes in decision theory, artificial intelligence, in knowledge management, even in economy and politics, that the situation of the bearer of knowledge would not be a factor that should be taken into account.

The "x" for which we are looking for in the title of this talk, is not only a context that may clarify linguistic ambiguities, but also something what has to do with the fact, that a bearer of knowledge (as well as a carrier of information) is a physical entity. Together with skills we call this entity a body. A body needs place and exists for a certain time interval. Therefore the concrete topology of this space-time extension is a serious candidate to be a factor for decision processes that can be reduced neither on knowledge nor on skills. The ability to operate in a certain manner extremely depends upon the restrictions within the space and time of operations. This space and time distances are determined by the situation.

Meaningful decisions in automated systems as well as wise decisions in economy, science and politics are therefore bounded not only to knowledge and available skills, but also to a genuine situated condition that has to do with physics, body and form (i.e. topology).

The reason, why we have too much information and too less knowledge, can be found here. Information can be transferred and stored in a given technology by data manipulation and a rather restricted highly prepared organizational closure. Thus the body dependence of these processes is comparatively small.

Knowledge exists in cognitive processes, it can be generated and forgotten and it "lives" in an organisational closure, that is much more complex than in case of information. This organisational closure is the "body" for knowledge and it's processing. Implicit knowledge requires an explicit body that can express the relevant information, able to be observed and understood.

To have a body, and to have a form cannot be reduced to knowledge already known before the decision has been made, i.e. by a formal ontology. Therefore for any decision this "x" should be concerned seriously.

---

[36] Cf. [30] (Penrose 1989), Chapter 10; and [31] Penrose (1994).

References

1. Bacon, F.: Meditationes Sacrae (1597). In: Spedding, J.v. (ed.): The Works of Francis Bacon. Vol. 14. New York 1864
2. Banse. G., Ropohl, G.: Wissenskonzepte für die Ingenieurspraxis. VDI Report Nr. 35, Düsseldorf 2004
3. Beck, U.: Risikogesellschaft - Auf dem Weg in eine andere Moderne. Edition Suhrkamp, Frankfurt a. M. 1986
4. Berndes, S.: Zukunft des Wissens. Vergessen, Löschen und Weitergeben. Ethische Normen der Wissensauswahl und -weitergabe. Reihe Technikphilosophie, Bd. 7. Lit, Münster, London 2001
5. Böhme, G.: Bildung als Widerstand. In: DIE ZEIT Nr. 38 vom 16. September 1999, S. 51
6. Bullinger, H.-J. K. Kornwachs, K.: Expertensysteme im Produktionsbetrieb - Anwendungen und Auswirkungen. C.H. Beck, München, 1990
7. Bunge, M.: Scientific Research II - The Search for Truth. Springer, Berlin, New York 1967, Chap. 11
8. Craig, E.: Was wir wissen können. Suhrkamp, Frankfurt a.M. 1993
9. Doren, van Ch.: A History of Knowledge. Ballantine, New York 1992; in German: Geschichte des Wissens. Birkhäuser, Basel, Boston, Berlin 1996
10. Erlach, K.: Das Technotop. Die technologische Konstruktion der Wirklichkeit. Reihe Technikphilosophie, Bd. 2. Lit Verlag Münster, London 2001
11. Gettier, E.: Is Justified True Belief Knowledge? In: Analysis 23 (1963), pp. 121-123
12. Görz. G. (Hrsg.): Einführung in die Künstliche Intelligenz. Addison, Wesley, Bonn, Paris 1995
13. Hahnekamp, G.: All Knowledge is Oriental Knowledge. In: Newsletter of European Academy of Bad Neuenahr, Nr. 43, December 2003, pp. 1-2
14. Heidegger, M.: Vom Wesen der Wahrheit - Zu Platons Höhlengleichnis und Theätet. Gesamtausgabe Klostermann Bd. 34, Frankfurt a.M. 1988, S. 149 ff.
15. Hubig, Ch. (Hrsg.): Unterwegs zur Wissensgesellschaft – Zukunftsdialoge im VDI. Edition Sigma, Berlin 2001
16. Kesselring, F.: Technische Kompositionslehre. Springer, Berlin, Göttingen, Heidelberg 1954
17. Kornwachs, K.: Kontext und Sprechakttheorie. Masch. Diss., Universität Freiburg 1976
18. Kornwachs, K.: Offene Systeme und die Frage nach der Information. Masch. Habilitationsschrift, Institut für Philosophie der Universität Stuttgart, Fakultät 11, Stuttgart 1987
19. Kornwachs, K.: Contextual Knowledge and Knowledge Acquisition. In: Elzas, M., Ören, T., Zeigler, B. P. (eds.): Modelling and Simulation Methodology: Knowledge Systems Paradigms. North Holland, Amsterdam 1989, pp. 267 -281
20. Kornwachs, K.: Von der Information zum Wissen? In: Ganten, D. et al. (Hrsg.): Informationswelt - Welten der Information/Forschung-Technik-Mensch. Verhandlungen der Gesellschaft Deutscher Naturforscher und Ärzte, 120. Versammlung, Berlin, 19.-22. September 1998. Wissenschaftliche Verlagsgesellschaft Stuttgart 1999
21. Kornwachs, K: Entsorgung von Wissen. In: Das Denkmal als Altlast - auf dem Weg in die Reparaturgesellschaft. ICOMOS Hefte des Deutschen Nationalkommittees XXI (1996), S. 26-33
22. Kornwachs, K.: Vom Wissen zur Arbeit. In: Mittelstraß, J., (Hrsg.): Die Zukunft des Wissens. XVIII. Deutscher Kongreß für Philosophie. Konstanz, 4.-8. Oktober 1999. Vorträge und Kolloquien. Akademie Verlag, Berlin 2000, S. 237-266 (2000 (b))

23. Kornwachs, K.: Data - Information - Knowledge - a Trial for Technological Enlightenment. In: Banse, G., Langenbach, C. J., Machleidt, P. (eds.): Toward the Information Society – The Case of Central and Eastern European Countries. Wissenschaftsethik und Technikfolgenbeurteilung, Bd. 9. Springer, Berlin, Heidelberg u.a. 2001, S. 109-123 (b). Also in: Science, Technology, Society (Veda, Technika, Spoleènost) IX (XXII)/1 (2000), pp. 5-27 (2000 (c))
24. Kornwachs, K.: Technik wissen. Präliminarien zu einer Theorie technischen Wissens. In: N. C. Karafyllis, T. Haar (Hrsg.): Technikphilosophie im Aufbruch. Festschrift für Günter Ropohl. Edition Sigma, Berlin 2004, S. 197-210
25. Kornwachs, K.: Pragmatic Information and the Generation of Knowledge. In: V. Braitenberg, G. Longo, F. J. Radermacher, (eds.): Interdisciplinary Approaches to a New Understanding of Cognition and Consciousness. Universitätsverlag Ulm, Ulm 2005 (a), pp. 35-75
26. Kornwachs, K.: Technikwissen – Wissenstechnik. In: Kornwachs, K.: Die Struktur technologischen Wissens. Lit, Münster, Hamburg, London 2005, Chap. E (forthcoming) 2005 (b)
27. Kornwachs, K.: Handling Knowledge in a Wired World. In: Kornwachs, K., Hronszky, I. (eds.): Shaping better Technologies. Lit, Münster – Berlin – London 2005 (c) (forthcoming), pp. 123-136
28. Krämer, S.: Verkörpertes Wissen. Eine performative Perspektive oder: Über das Wissen jenseits von Theorien und Kompetenzen. – Skizze von Forschungsfeldern für die Clusterbildung „Wissenschaftsforschung" der Berlin-Brandenburgischen Akademie der Wissenschaften", Berlin, April 2003
29. Layton, E.T.: Technology as knowledge. In: Technology & Culture, Vol. 15. (1974), pp. 31-41
30. Penrose, R.: The Emperor's new Mind. Concerning Computers, Minds and Laws of Physics. Oxford University Press. Oxford, New York 1989
31. Penrose, R.: Shadows of the Mind. Oxford University Press, Oxford New York 1994
32. Platon: Werke. Hrsg. von G. Eigler. Wiss. Buchgesellschaft, Darmstadt 1990
33. Polanyi, M.: Implizites Wissen. Frankfurt a.M., Suhrkamp 1985
34. Poser, H.: On structural differences between sciences and engineering. In: Hans Lenk, Evandro Agazzi and Paul Durbin (eds.): Advances in the Philosophy of Technology: Proceedings of the International Academy of the Philosophy of Science, Karlsruhe, Germany, May 1997. In: Philosophy and Technology: Quarterly Electronic Journal 4.2 (Winter 1998), 81-93. – Reprinted in: Hans Lenk, Matthias Maring (eds.), Advances and Problems in the Philosophy of Technology (= Technikphilosophie 5), Münster / Hamburg / London: LIT 2001, pp. 193-204
35. Poser, H.: „Technisches Wissen". Vortrag in der Arbeitsgruppe „Cluster Wissenschaftsforschung" der Brandenburgischen Akademie der Wissenschaften, Berlin am 23. Mai 2003 (a)
36. Poser, H.: Entwerfen als Lebensform – Elemente technischer Modalität. In: Kornwachs, K. (Hrsg.): Technik – System – Verantwortung. Reihe Technikphilosophie, Bd. 10. Lit, Münster, London, New York 2003, S. 561-575, (2003)(b)
37. Radermacher, F. J.: Wissensmanagement in Superorganisationen. In: Hubig, Ch (Hrsg.): Unterwegs zur Wissensgesellschaft – Zukunftsdialoge im VDI. Edition Sigma, Berlin 2001
38. Rammert, W.: Nicht explizites Wissen in Soziologie und Sozionik – ein kursorischer Überblick. In: Forschungsinstitut für angewandte Wissensverarbeitung (FAW Ulm) (Hrsg.): Management von nicht explizitem Wissen. Noch mehr von der Natur lernen? Abschlußbericht, Teil 3. Im Auftrag des BMBF, Bonn Berlin 2001, pp. 113-136.
39. Ropohl, G.: Knowledge Types in Technology, in: Vries, M.J. de and Tamir, A. (eds.), Shaping Concepts of Technology: From Philosophical Perspectives to Mental Images. Kluwer Academic Publishers, Dordrecht 1997, pp. 65-72

40. Ropohl, G.: Eine Systemtheorie der Technik. Hanser, München 1979. 2. Auflage: Allgemeine Technikwissenschaft. Hanser, München 1999
41. Searle, J. R.: Speech Acts. Cambridge 1969. German in: Searle, J. R.: Sprechakte, Suhrkamp, Frankfurt am Main 1971.
42. Stehr, N.: Arbeit, Eigentum und Wissen. Zur Theorie von Wissensgesellschaften. Suhrkamp, Frankfurt a.M. 1994
43. Vries, M. J. de: The Nature of Technological Knowledge: Extending Empirically Informed Studies into What Engineers Know. In: Techné: Journal of the Society for Philosophy and Technology Vol 6 (2003), Nr. 3, http://scholar.lib.vt.edu/ejournals
44. Weizsäcker, E. U.: Pragmatische Information. In: Weizsäcker, E. U. (Hrsg.): Offene Systeme I. Klett, Stuttgart 1974, pp. 83-112
45. Wögerbauer, H.: Die Technik des Konstruierens. Oldenbourg, München, Berlin 1943

1st Intelligent Office Appliances (IOA 2005): Knowledge Appliances in the Office of the Future

Ansgar Bernardi[1], Björn Decker[2], Harald Holz[1], Dirk Muthig[2], and Naoyuki Nomura[3]

[1] DFKI GmbH, Erwin-Schrödinger-Str. 57, 67663 Kaiserslautern, Germany
bernardi@dfki.uni-kl.de, harald.holz@dfki.de
[2] Fraunhofer IESE, Sauerwiesen 6, 67661 Kaiserslautern, Germany
Bjoern.Decker@iese.fraunhofer.de, Dirk.Muthig@iese.fraunhofer.de
[3] Ricoh Company Ltd., 1-1-17 Koishikawa, Bunkyo-ku, Tokyo 112-0002, Japan
naoyuki.nomura@nts.ricoh.co.jp

About the Workshop

IT technology for ubiquitous work has reached a degree of maturity and usability that can turn every environment into a place for office work. However, this technology needs to be tightly integrated into the knowledge infrastructure and with other appliances to support knowledge work effectively, efficiently and nonintrusively. Experiences with focused aspects of future office work are already available, e.g., from applied and emerging technologies (Tablet PC, PDA, Electronic Paper, etc.). However, an integrative approach to future office work is still missing. The goal of the first workshop on Intelligent Office Appliances (IOA) was to present aspects of this integrative approach by discussing how knowledge work in the office of the future can be effectively supported by intelligent appliances. For this issue we selected two papers that address the usage and engineering aspects of intelligent office appliances:

- How to make use of knowledge captured in a paper-based form is covered in Maus et al.[1]: Scanned and OCR-processed documents are integrated in a user's personal knowledge space.
- The technology for efficient implementation of intelligent office appliances is presented in Keuler et al. [2] by combining workflow specifications and software product lines.

Further submissions to IOA can be found in [3].

Program Committee

- Klaus-Dieter Althoff: University of Hildesheim, Germany
- Steven Bashford: Business Solutions Group, Mindjet GmbH, Germany
- Frank Bomarius: University of Applied Science Kaiserslautern, Fraunhofer IESE, Kaiserslautern, Germany
- Joerg Denzinger: University of Calgary, Canada

K.-D. Althoff et al. (Eds.): WM 2005, LNAI 3782, pp. 48 – 49, 2005.

- Alexander Greisle: FhG IAO Competence Center New Work, Stuttgart, Germany
- Manfred Langen: Siemens AG, Knowledge Management and Business Transformation, CT IC 1, Munich, Germany
- Hermann Maurer: University of Graz, Austria
- Markus Nick: Fraunhofer IESE, Kaiserslautern, Germany
- Takahiko Nomura: Fuji Xerox Co. Ltd., Japan
- Alexander Schieffer: Center of Excellence for Leadership and Learning GmbH, Munich, Germany
- Georg J. Schneider: University of Applied Science Trier, Dept. of Computer Science, Chair Multimedia /Media-Informatics, Germany
- Stefan Wess: empolis AG, Kaiserslautern, Germany

References

1. Maus, H., Holz, H., Bernardi, A., Rostanin, O.: Leveraging Passive Paper Piles to Active Objects in Personal Knowledge Spaces (2004)
2. Keuler, T., Lehner, T., Decker, B., Muthig, D.: Efficient Implementation of Intelligent Office Appliances with Software Product Lines (2004)
3. Althoff, K.-D., Dengel A., Germann, R., Nick, M., Roth-Berghofer, T.: WM 2005 Professional Knowledge Management – Experience and Visions, Deutsches Forschungszentrum für künstliche Intelligenz, ISBN 3-00-016020-5 (2005)

Leveraging Passive Paper Piles to Active Objects in Personal Knowledge Spaces

Heiko Maus, Harald Holz, Ansgar Bernardi, and Oleg Rostanin

DFKI GmbH – German Research Center for AI, Kaiserslautern, Germany
<firstname>.<lastname>@dfki.de

Abstract. Office workers tend to produce paper piles of documents to read or to process sometime later. The information contained in these piles is often lost if it is not transferred to electronic format and connected to knowledge structures. Information that is not part of the knowledge worker's electronic information space is frequently overlooked because it is not proactively provided during actual processes or tasks he is involved in. This paper presents a novel prototype for an intelligent office appliance, which results from an integration of three state-of-the-art office applications/appliances: a workflow system, a document classification system, and a multi-functional peripheral. The resulting system allows for leveraging an office worker's papers to her personal knowledge space in order to realize a pro-active and context-sensitive information support within knowledge-intensive tasks and processes.

1 Motivation

Office work, from an abstract point of view, comprises a wide variety of activities which are concerned with paper handling, information processing, thinking, and decision-making. Although sometimes despised as bureaucratic overhead, office work is nevertheless at the heart of knowledge and value creation and the indispensable basis for innovation and progress. The ever-increasing percentage of office work in today's economic activities, ranging from standard administrative processes to complex and unique decisions, clearly illustrates this significance.

Modern office appliances offer valuable support for routine activities in office work. In spite of such support, it is claimed that knowledge-intensive office work has not reached satisfying increases in productivity in recent years (cf. [7]). The reason for this perceived lack of productivity increase in such office work is seen in the insufficient understanding of the nature of knowledge-intensive work and the lack of adequate integration of information support and work activities.

Typical examples of such inadequate integration are media gaps, in particular between paper and electronic documents. Due to its various advantages, paper documents still prevail today, and the often-proclaimed paperless office seems to be as far as ever. Whereas a few companies exist whose post office scans in all incoming paper mail for further processing, and immediately destroys the original mail as soon as possible, the majority of office workers involved in knowledge-intensive tasks is still surrounded by paper piles. In addition to

K.-D. Althoff et al. (Eds.): WM 2005, LNAI 3782, pp. 50–59, 2005.

the standard "in" and "out" piles, we can typically observe piles with various different semantics (e.g. "must read", topic-related, or project-specific piles) on a knowledge worker's desk(s). Often, these piles arise out an "hunter-gatherer" mentality, or they serve as visual reminders of tasks with varying degrees of importance and urgency.

The problem with paper piles is that, firstly, knowledge workers often spend an unduly amount of time searching for a piece of information hidden in documents that are hidden in piles; secondly, awareness of existing, relevant paper documents is not ensured, i.e. even though the situation finally arises when reading the printout of an article would be useful, its piled existence escapes the knowledge worker's attention during the task at hand.

In the following, we present a novel prototype for effective, light-weight information support within knowledge-intensive processes and work environments by realizing just-in-time knowledge delivery in agile knowledge workflows (cf. [3]). The prototype results from an integration of three state-of-the-art office applications/appliances: (i) a workflow system, (ii) a document classification system, and (iii) a multi-functional product.

2 Office Worker's Dilemma

An office worker faces a dilemma: on the one hand she depends on well organized knowledge structures for effective work but on the other hand maintaining such structures as well as connect information items accordingly is an immense amount of work and therefore often neglected.

Moreover, considering office environments, further problems can be identified: Whereas for a company's inbox processing solutions are on the market and research has shown how to bridge the gap between paper-based business letters and workflows with knowledge-based document analysis systems [10], we still can find a media gap in the knowledge worker's office between paper documents and her electronic information archives. As long as this material is in electronic format, there is an increasing number of search and indexing tools which provide access to this material. But, due to the working style in offices, ideas and material are widespread in the office. For instance, notes taken on paper during meetings or an interesting newspaper article found during a coffee break are in danger to get lost in the everyday rush of office work.

Office workers tend to produce paper piles of things to do or to read. Whereas e-mail allows to be searched, the notes are lost if not transferred to electronic format and connected to knowledge structures. Lost means, that they are no active part of the knowledge worker's electronic information space and therefore also not accessible for the processes a knowledge worker is involved in.

Many ways to structure information have already been introduced in office environments. Support ranges from file directories where documents are stored in a specific directory structure to document management systems with metadata of documents such as title, authors, topic, abstract, and project. And not to forget different filing means within the paper-based world such as in- and outboxes (or simply stacked on the desktop), folders, drawers, and shelves, or archives in designated rooms. For both worlds the statement holds that the more structure is provided and used, the better are the chances to find the information later on.

Thus, a considerable amount of knowledge-intensive office work is also information structuring which involves relating information items to structures, models, or ontologies given by the company.

But office workers in knowledge-intensive areas also tend to create their own structures such as categories for grouping documents or e-mail folders. These structures depend on their personal view and therefore differ among office workers (which in turn makes them hard to share). But it can even be worse if an office worker is using no structures at all or neglects the annotation with metadata, especially if it is not obligatory within the company. Another problem in office environments is the amount of effort an office worker has to put in the administration of such structures (like file directories or folders in drawers) or the annotation of documents with metadata. All this results in ineffective searches, missed information, or even outdated or wrong information.

Hence, effective support in the office environment has to cope with the office worker's behavior and working style. Many systems fail because they simply rely on the user's will (and competence) to classify and store information in the right way. Just to introduce a document management system into a company does not guarantee an effective information sharing. Moreover, there is the danger of a death spiral of such systems [6]: stored information is not appropriately annotated in the system, search and retrieval of relevant information gets difficult, therefore, users start to think negative about the system and tend to neglect the annotation of information (or, even worse, neglect to add new information at all), which in turn contributes to the ineffectiveness of the system. Because of this, the system is doomed to become a wasteland. Consequently, successful approaches have to be aware of the death spiral and consider this accordingly in their way to design the system and to foster an information sharing culture.

Effective support of the create, classify, and store activities in the office environment therefore needs to consider structures and models for classification and furthermore provide unobtrusive and pro-active support as much as possible which is integrated in the office environment. As a consequence, current research focuses on means to take away the burden of annotating information and to provide pro-active and just-in-time information delivery. Therefore, our research department investigates the use of process enactment by workflows to retrieve the workflow context for and to realize proactive and context-sensitive support. Such a system has been accomplished in the KnowMore-project [2] where documents were annotated with their creation context from the workflow instance. The FRODO project introduced a comprehensive workflow context model [5] into the weakly-structured workflow system FRODO TaskMan which provides full access to the workflow's context for services such as planning and coordinating processes resp. tasks, pro-active information support, unobtrusive creation of metadata for documents used in the workflow, as well as context visualization for the user.

The research conducted at the competence center "Virtual Office of the Future"[1] established at DFKI transfers these approaches into a real office environment with smart devices and establish synergy effects to realize intelligent office appliances. The remainder of the paper addresses one of these research efforts in more detail along two steps: First, from passive piles of paper to active objects in the personal knowledge space and second, the context-aware service of task-specific information delivery based on workflow context.

3 Building a Personal Knowledge Space

Modern office work relies also on personal computers. Thus, as with the knowledge worker's real wooden desktop, a large amount of knowledge is contained in his computer desktop, whether formulated in documents or within the structures of the file directory where projects or topics are organized. But as with the passive paper piles, these structures and the associated documents are also passive, which leads to not finding needed information, searching too long for the correct places where to put things resp. that there is no organization at all, etc. Thus, nothing would have been won if the paper piles solely are electronically transferred and put somewhere on the computer desktop, which would lead to electronic document piles.

This observation motivated the EPOS-project (*Evolving Personal to Organizational Knowledge Spaces*[2]) to have a closer look at structures and documents on the computer desktop because they represent the user's subjective view on the world and especially on his knowledge work. Therefore, EPOS investigates how a personal information model (PIM) can be constructed starting from the native structures of a knowledge worker. Such structures can be found in file directories, bookmarks, or e-mail folders dealing with topics, projects, contacts, tasks, etc. The structures, their respective content, and the user's interaction with these structures and contained information gives valuable hints on the user's subjective view as well as on how to evolve the PIM. Thus, as depicted in Fig. 1, EPOS investigates the knowledge worker's electronic footprints on his desktop to build a personal information model representing the user's subjective view. Such a model can be utilized for supporting knowledge workers by user adaptive services. The services are now able to consider the knowledge worker's subjective view. The PIM, the associated information objects, and the user adapted services together realize the user's personal knowledge space. Furthermore, but out of scope of this paper, EPOS investigates methods on how the combination of personal information models within an organization can be evolved to come up with a shared understanding for building organizational models and ontologies which is detailed in [9].

Now, for importing structures and documents and to build up an initial PIM which can be used by other services, EPOS uses the *BrainFiler*™ (see Fig. 2) – a system that we developed as a first implementation of these ideas together with

[1] `http://www.ricoh.rlp-labs.de/`

[2] `http://www.dfki.de/epos`

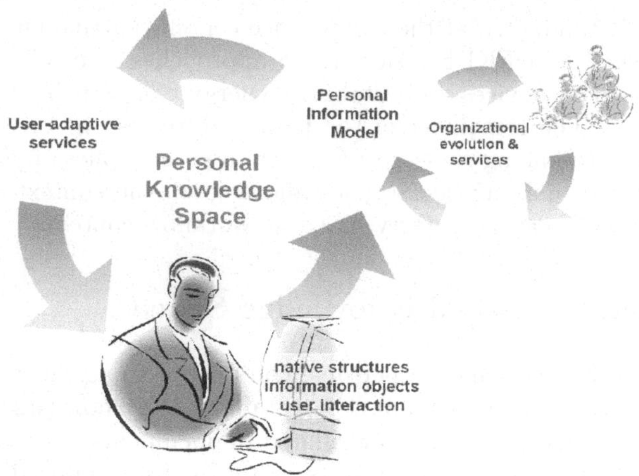

Fig. 1. EPOS Personal Knowledge Space cycles

brainbot technologies[3] – which realizes a personal document management environment allowing multicriterial classification of documents, search functionality such as Boolean search and document similarity evaluation, and incorporation of remote BrainFiler instances to build up peer groups. BrainFiler enables a user to build a personal information model by allowing to import native structures such as e-mail folders, bookmarks, and file directories together with contained documents. The imported structures are shown as trees (usually interpreted as an *is-a* hierarchy). The nodes (interpreted as concepts) get their meaning by a document term-similarity vector generated by the assigned documents. A user is now able to evolve his PIM by creating new structures, making relations between concepts (a concept can have multiple parents), and assigning documents to concepts. These structures then can be used for a conceptual search (all documents having the concepts `X` and `Y`) as well as a combination with the keyword-based search.

Moreover, the BrainFiler also allows to introduce remote classifications from colleagues (in a Peer-to-Peer-manner) or from the organization (as an organizational peer) as complete views or as single concepts which are added to personal views. This enhances the personal knowledge space with views and information items from other sources and reflects the organizational aspect of the knowledge worker.

With the BrainFiler, the knowledge worker has a personal desktop search spanning nearly all information sources, allowing multicriterial classification and views and this also in workgroups, thus, it can be seen as one user-adapted service on top of a PIM for a knowledge worker in the EPOS scenario. Now, EPOS uses the created structures as an initial personal information model which will be further evolved by introducing concepts such as projects, persons, events, tasks, topics, etc. and mapping of structures (cf. [9]). Together with the connected doc-

[3] `http://www.brainbot.com`

uments a personal knowledge space is realized and value added services can be provided. For instance, the EPOS AssistantBar realizes context-specific proactive support by offering relevant documents, concepts, persons, and tasks to the user by observing the user's desktop activities (see [8]).

A further service is the introduction of scanned documents into the knowledge worker's personal knowledge space which will be addressed in the next section. This is achieved by combining the research done in EPOS with the work in the 'Virtual Office of the Future'.

4 Leveraging Paper Piles to Personal Knowledge Spaces

Considering the development of office appliances, a clear trend towards integration can be observed. This is exemplified in the success of multi-functional products (MFP, e.g. as developed by Ricoh) that combine a copier, (color) printer, scanner, and fax machine, featuring a built-in hard drive, network access, as well as a minimal web server for administrative tasks and document management. Moreover, these office devices get smarter, e.g., Ricoh's ScanRouter Delivery Server™ allows for delivering and storing scanned document in various formats (TIFF, JPG, RTF, PDF, etc; also with reproduction of the original layout – so called *TruePage*) in the user's inbox at the delivery server, Ricoh's own document management system, any network drive, or sending it as an attachment to a user-defined e-mail-account.

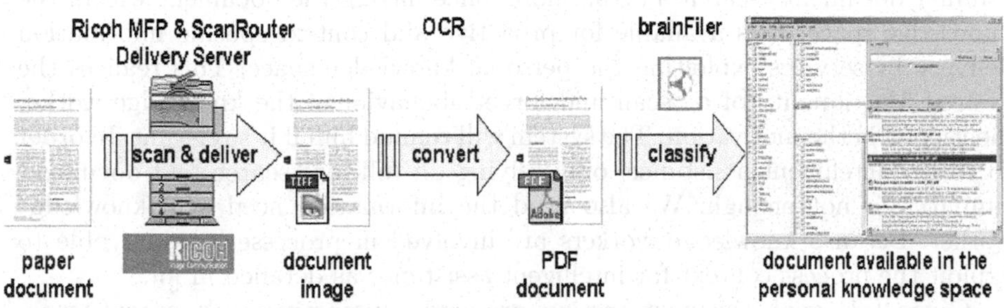

Fig. 2. From passive paper piles to active documents in the personal knowledge space

Such an MFP is the starting point to transfer the aforementioned piles of paper into an electronic format in which it can be handed over to a document classification system, in our case the BrainFiler, as depicted in Fig. 2. Technically, the introduction of paper documents in the personal knowledge space is done by handing over the scanned, transformed (as PDF), and delivered document to the BrainFiler. BrainFiler in turn analyzes the document and suggests those of the user's concepts which fit the best, based on the learned information structures of the user. The user can accept one or more proposed concepts as classification for the document, freely choose others, or simply ignore the assignment task.

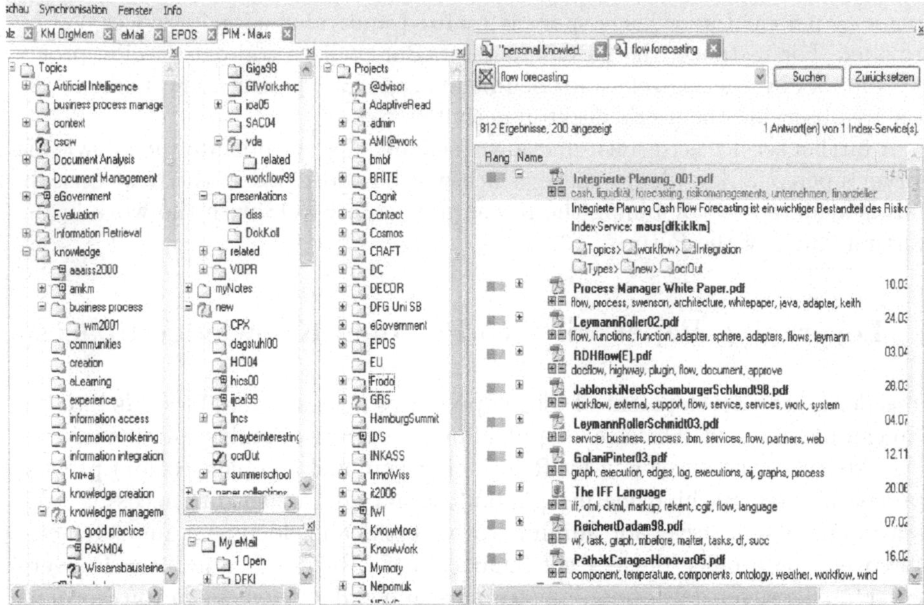

Fig. 3. BrainFiler™: Proposal of several categories to a scanned & delivered document

Although ignoring such assignments does not evolve the knowledge space further, it still allows to find the document via keyword search as well as via a "similar document" search. Furthermore, once having the document within the knowledge space, it is available for proactive and context-specific information delivery by services exploiting the personal knowledge space. This realizes the desired functionality of a "scan and forget"-behavior of the knowledge worker mentioned in the motivation. The system will remind him if it's relevant. In order to realize intelligent assistance, only relying on full-text search and document similarity is not enough. We also need the information need of a knowledge worker. Because knowledge workers are involved in processes, we are able to exploit the process context for intelligent assistance as detailed in [5].

Given this goal, the next section presents a proactive and context-aware information delivery for a knowledge worker based on the personal knowledge space and introducing a process-oriented view.

5 Task-Specific Document Delivery

In order to be able to proactively provide users with access to relevant documents stored within their personal knowledge space, we make use of an explicit representation of a knowledge worker's current tasks. The basis of this approach is the use of an application which provides a to-do list (or: task list) for knowledge workers that allows to manage their current tasks, e.g. such as in MS Outlook or workflow systems. Typically, the representation of a task covers a short task name and a due date, together with an (optional) longer task description that describes the task's goal and objective in more detail, or – depending on the system – is used as scratchpad to jot down things to remember with regard to the task. Fig. 4 shows a screenshot from the FRODO TaskMan[4] [3] workflow system that we used to realize the prototype: the left-hand pane shows the user's to-do list, with the task "Write BrainFiler project-proposal" currently being selected.

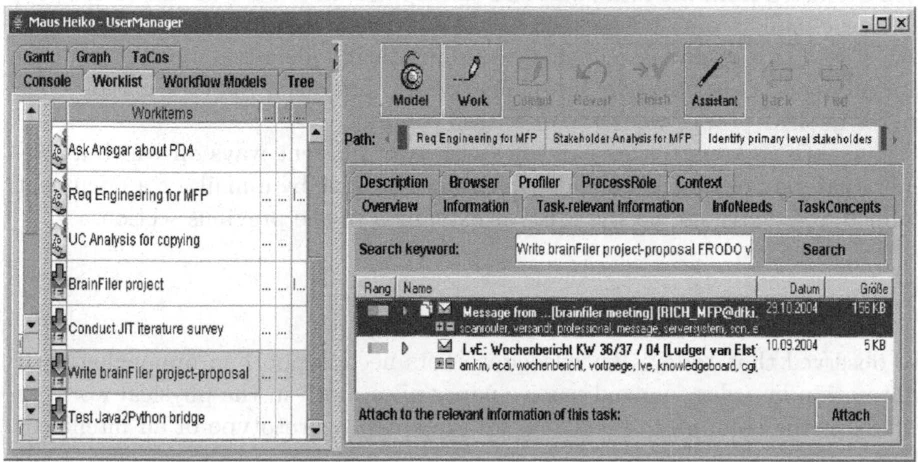

Fig. 4. Task-specific, proactive document provision from the personal knowledge space within FRODO TaskMan

As the list of a knowledge worker's current tasks reflects the work contexts he is currently involved in, it can be assumed that the majority of business e-mails received and sent, as well as all other documents handled by the worker are related to one or more of the tasks on his to-do list. However, current technology does not adequately support the organizing and filing of documents around tasks. Instead, knowledge workers are forced to manually browse to (or search for) the documents relevant to the task at hand, resulting in a considerable waste of time (and hence: money) [1].

In order to address this problem, we extended this to-do list by a component that displays the results of BrainFiler's classifications of documents with regard to the current task. Technically, a corresponding concept is automatically created for each task, containing a file with the task name and description, as well as documents (including e-mails) that the knowledge worker manually associated with the task (e.g. by simple drag-and-drop). This extends the knowledge worker's personal knowledge space with a process-oriented view and yields the benefit of providing the knowledge worker with immediate access to the heterogeneous set of all documents related to a given task. However, what is most important, any newly "incoming" documents are automatically analyzed by the component and tentatively associated with all of the worker's current tasks that

[4] `http://www.dfki.de/frodo/taskman`

the new document seems to be related to, by making use of the BrainFiler's classification suggestions. For example, Fig. 4 shows two emails being provided to the user by the component in the context of the currently selected task; a double-click on one of these emails will open the email with the user's default email application. The two emails have been automatically retrieved by using the relevant terms displayed in the text field labeled "Search keywords", that have been extracted from the task name and already associated documents. That way, relevant e-mails are no longer easily overlooked, e.g. because important e-mails with regard to a given task can now be automatically identified among the unorganized flood of continuously incoming e-mails, and displayed to the knowledge worker in their proper workflow resp. task context.

Currently, our prototype can cope with two different ways on which a document can be "incoming": the document can be sent by e-mail, or a document scanned and delivered via the MFP as explained in the previous section.

6 Conclusion

We observed that today's knowledge workers need support in organizing their information in order to avoid passive paper piles, both in the physical world as well as in the computer. Therefore, we presented a prototype of an intelligent office appliance which brings together research and state-of-the-art office tools and devices in order to realize a light-weight approach to task-specific, proactive document delivery. The term vector similarity-based approach used here is intended to complement our earlier work on more heavy-weight approaches based on process models and ontologies [3][4], which require considerably more modeling effort on behalf of the user.

The concept of the Personal Information Model which is constructed from the knowledge worker's native structures, allows to reduce this modeling effort as well as enabling intelligent services to consider the user's subjective view by using this model. Although this part is ongoing research in the EPOS-project, we could provide a first implementation of these ideas in the BrainFiler tool which we used for the prototype presented in this paper.

This prototype is currently being developed within the competence center "Virtual Office of the Future" established at DFKI and will be evaluated as part of a distributed software development case study in 2005. Based on the positive evaluation results for our process-embedded information support [3], we believe that an efficiency gain can also be achieved in an everyday office setting with the approach presented here, by making documents more easily available during the office worker's tasks, and helping to prevent that relevant documents might be overlooked.

Acknowledgements

Work funded in part by "Stiftung Rheinland-Pfalz für Innovation" (InnoWiss) and BMBF (EPOS, contract number ITW 01 IWC 01).

References

1. Taxonomy & content classification. Market milestone report, Delphi Group, 2002.
2. Andreas Abecker, Ansgar Bernardi, Knut Hinkelmann, Otto Kühn, and Michael Sintek. Context-aware, proactive delivery of task-specific knowledge: The KnowMore-project. *Int. Journal on Information Systems Frontiers (ISF), Special Issue on Knowledge Management and Organizational Memory*, 2000.
3. Ludger van Elst, Felix-Robinson Aschoff, Ansgar Bernardi, Heiko Maus, and Sven Schwarz. Weakly-structured workflows for knowledge-intensive tasks: An experimental evaluation. In *IEEE WETICE Workshop on Knowledge Management for Distributed Agile Processes (KMDAP03)*. IEEE Computer Press, 2003.
4. Harald Holz. *Process-Based Knowledge Management Support for Software Engineering*. dissertation.de Verlag, 2003.
5. Heiko Maus. Workflow context as a means for intelligent information support. In Akman et al., editors, *Modeling and Using Context. 3rd International and Interdisciplinary Conference, CONTEXT'01*, volume 2116 of *LNAI*. Springer, 2001.
6. Gilbert Probst, Steffen Raub, and Kai Romhardt. *Wissen managen: Wie Unternehmen ihre wertvollste Ressource optimal nutzen*. Gabler, Wiesbaden, 1997.
7. Peter Schütt. The post-Nonaka Knowledge Management. *Journal of Universal Computer Science*, 9(6):451–462, 2003.
8. Sven Schwarz. A context model for personal knowledge management. In *Proceedings of the IJCAII'05 Workshop on Modeling and Retrieval of Context*, Edinburgh, 2005.
9. Ludger van Elst and Malte Kiesel. Generating and integrating evidence for ontology mappings. In *Engineering Knowledge in the Age of the Semantic Web: Proceedings of the 14th International Conference, EKAW 2004*, volume 3257 of *LNAI*, pages 15–29, Heidelberg, 2004. Springer.
10. Claudia Wenzel and Heiko Maus. Leveraging corporate context within knowledge-based document analysis and understanding. *Int. Journal on Document Analysis and Recognition, Special Issue on Document Analysis for Office Systems*, 3(4), 2001.

Efficient Implementation of Intelligent Office Appliances with Software Product Lines

Thorsten Keuler, Theresa Lehner, Björn Decker, and Dirk Muthig

Fraunhofer Institute for Experimental Software Engineering,
67661 Kaiserslautern, Germany
{bjoern.decker, thorsten.keuler, theresa.lehner, dirk.muthig}@iese.fraunhofer.de

Abstract. To support the handling of documents in organizations, office appliances have to adapt to the work processes of that organization. To efficiently handle changes in the software imposed by these adaptations, we present an approach to use business process models to compose the basic features of an office appliance into customer-oriented, process-specific services offered by office devices. Software product lines shape the key concepts that enable cost-effective and therefore realistic implementations of the ideas presented[1].

1 Introduction

In the office domain, an intelligent work environment means that office applications and devices actively adapt their services with respect to the role of their user or to the states of workflows a user is actually involved in. This includes that users have secure access to all their documents anywhere and any time. In addition to document access, a virtual office of the future should provide all kinds of other services, for example, services that continuously locate printers or copier machines that are accessible to mobile users.

The implementation of this intelligent work environment is the goal of the project 'Virtual Office of the Future'. The basic approach for this implementation is depicted in Figure 1. Starting point is to specify office processes as adaptive workflows. The interface (e.g., handheld devices, PC) provides task-specific access to knowledge resources (e.g., document databases) and office services (e.g., print, scan). The specification of the workflow is also used to define requirements for the services and the underlying support by devices. Based on these requirements, the software of the underlying devices can be implemented via software product lines [4, 11], accelerating the development process with ensured quality.

In this paper, we present a first step in the endeavour described above. In more detail, we present an approach to generate applications of a product line based on service -oriented architectures (SOA). These applications are considered as instances of a product line, providing services and composed services needed to enact the adaptive workflow. The reasons for selecting these methods are as follows:

[1] This work has been funded by the project "Virtual Office of the Future", "Stiftung Innovation Rheinland-Pfalz".

K.-D. Althoff et al. (Eds.): WM 2005, LNAI 3782, pp. 60 – 69, 2005.

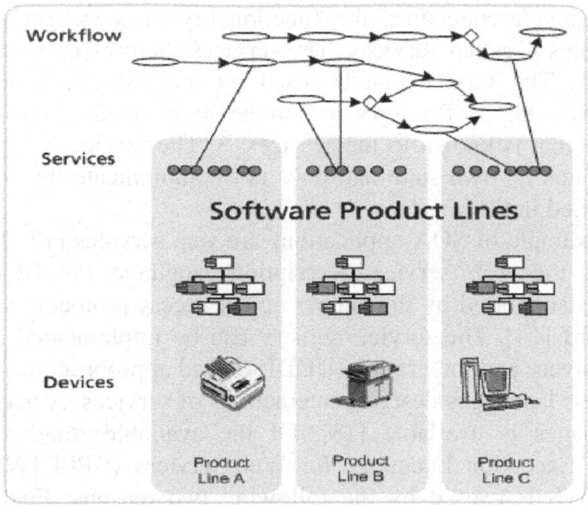

Fig. 1. Approach of the project Virtual Office of the Future

The capturing of application requirements by process and workflow descriptions is meaningful for non-technical customers as well as for system developers: The notation is understandable by the customer, but includes enough details to support transitioning activities towards the executable application. In this paper, all processes and workflows are described by Business Process Modeling Notation (BPMN).

In general, SOA offers flexibility in composing services: Services can be combined statically during compile-time or dynamically during the runtime of an application. Furthermore, SOA enables feature-oriented modeling of applications in a reusable way by encapsulating its functionalities into services. This is an essential advantage if the approach is applied to software product lines [4, 11].With respect to software product lines, defining a concrete workflow can be regarded as instantiating a concrete application. Hence, high-level modeling of concrete processes and workflows leads to an implicit resolution of all variability within a product line.

The overall development process applying BPMN and SOA is strongly model-driven. Following model-driven development paradigms, the workflow description can be considered as a service-independent modeling artifact and the service composition as a service-specific modeling artifact. Due to implementation independence, the transfer of business processes to other domains is facilitated. SOA and business process models coalesce into a method bridging the gap for complete application generation by integrating functionality provided by self-contained services.

2 Concepts and Related Standards

In this section we present the main concepts used in this paper: service-oriented architecture, business process languages, and model-driven software development. In addition, we give an overview of established and emerging standards in these areas.

In service-oriented architecture, the functionality of a system is composed of reusable components – called services. The services themselves share the following principles [13]: 1. The service can be used by its interface independent of the implementation aspects. 2. The service can be dynamically located and invoked through a registry that is known to the services. 3. The service is self-contained, i.e. the service maintains its own state and does not communicate this state beyond the information specified in the interface.

A prominent example of SOA applications are web services [12, 2]. The interface is defined using the web service description language (WSDL) standard [5]. Communication is supported by the simple object access protocol (SOAP), an open, http-based standard [14]. The service registry can be implemented using Universal Description, Discovery and Integration (UDDI) to find appropriate web services [19].

Business process languages describe interactions of services. A magnitude of those description languages is available [18]. Of the available standards, we use the Business Process Execution Language for Web-Services (BPEL4WS) [8, 21]. The focus on BPEL4WS is caused by the following two reasons: First, it is the only standardized language that offers support for essential business process modeling concepts [MM03]. Furthermore, BPEL4WS has gained a prominent market share due to its support through vendors [18, 23]. To express the process in a way understandable to the developer as well as to the user, we use the Business Process Modeling Notation (BPMN) [7]. This language allows expressing processes in a graphical notation that can be transferred into BPEL4WS.

Model-driven software development (MDSD) includes implementation support for business process models that are mapped to SOA [20, 3]. As implied by the name, model-driven software development is about transforming a model representing an application (e.g., by UML models) into more concrete representations (e.g., Code). By restricting these transformations to certain application domains, an optimal generation of code frameworks is leveraged. The models themselves are expressed in a domain-specific language, which defines the semantics of the models. Besides the models and a domain-specific language, MDSD implies the existence of a (domain-specific) platform. According to [16], the platform is defined as a set of subsystems and technologies that provide a coherent set of functionality through interfaces and specified usage patterns. Any application supported by that platform can use the functionality provided by the platform without concerns for implementation details. A standard in the area of MDSD is the model driven architecture (MDA) of the Object Management Group [16, 17]. The interrelation between MDSD and MDA is covered in [20].

We combine the presented approaches to build a software product line [4, 11]. Since the variability mechanisms and the commonalities are prominent aspects of a product line, they are here described in more detail. For an overview of the general interrelation of software product lines, SOA and MDSD please refer to [20, 3].

3 Approach

The approach allows set-up of an individual office infrastructure in a way that is efficient for the organization requiring the infrastructure as well as for the organization selling the office devices supporting the infrastructure. Before explaining the approach in more detail, we describe the set-up scenario. The organization selling office devices and setting up the infrastructure together with the customer identifies the features, especially workflows that need to be supported by the infrastructure. Based on that, the office devices and their services are automatically selected and instantiated for the individual infrastructure.

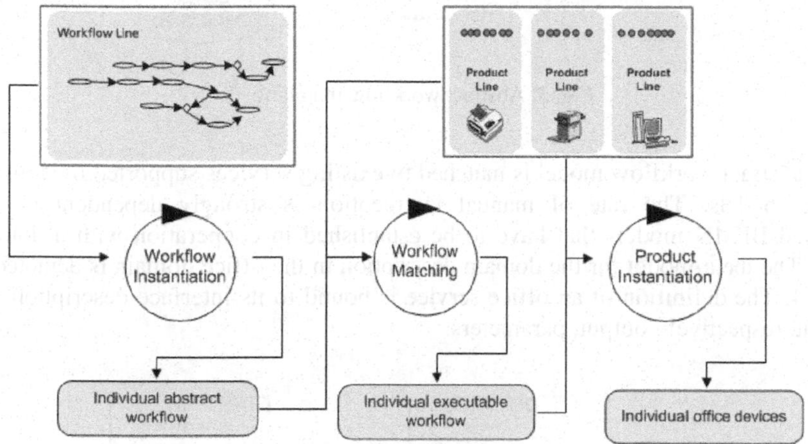

Fig. 2. Process Overview

The set-up scenario is realized as described in Figure 2. The main drivers of the set-up process are the workflow-based product line and the product lines for the office devices. The idea of product lines is to realize features of all products identified in the line as generic infrastructure, which is concurrently instantiated for each product development. The instantiation first selects features needed for the specific product, and then resolves the generic infrastructure regarding the selected features. The generic infrastructure of the workflow line is a generic workflow model comprising all variants of workflows executable by the office infrastructure. In contrast, the product lines for the office devices contain generic services offered by the devices. For more details about product lines and their life cycle, see [4, 6, 11].

The first step in the set-up process is to model the workflow that needs to be supported by the infrastructure together with the requiring organization. This process step is an instantiation of the workflow line, which first identifies the needed workflow features and, based on that, resolves the generic workflow model. The generic workflow model as well as the resulting model is described in BPMN. For more details about workflow lines and the workflow model in BPMN, see [1, 7].

The second step in the set-up process is an automatic match of the abstract workflow model to an executable workflow. It maps workflow activities and sub workflows to executable services offered by the office devices. The resulting workflow is described in BPEL4WS as illustrated in Figure 3.

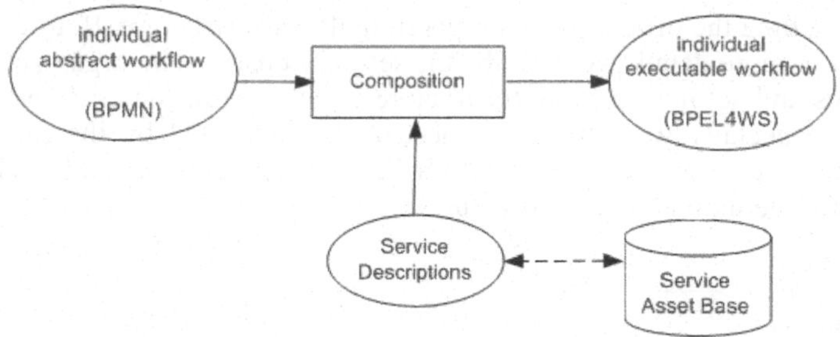

Fig. 3. Abstract workflow matching

The abstract workflow model is matched to existing services supported by domain-specific models. The rate of manual interception is strongly dependent on the annotated BPMN models that have to be established in cooperation with a domain expert. The meta-model for the domain description in the office domain is depicted in Figure 4. The definition of an office service is bound to its interface description and its input, respectively output, parameters.

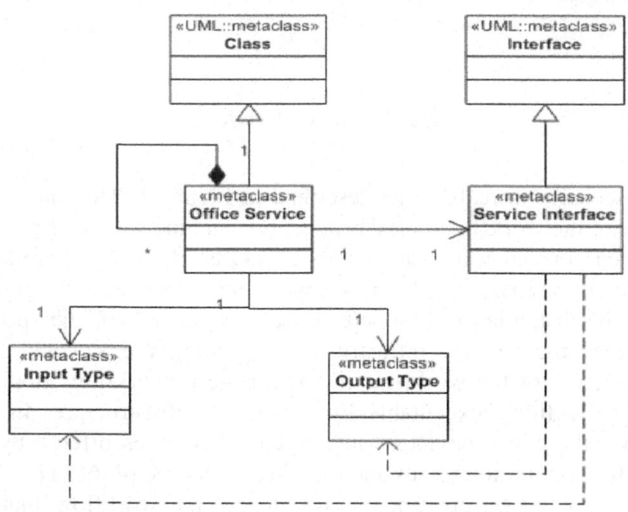

Fig. 4. Meta-model of the office service definition

Based on this meta-model, concrete service descriptions can be deducted. A concrete service model is shown in Figure 5. It is remarkable that due to the explicit service definition with precisely defined input and output types, the mapping is defined for all services that are based on this meta-model. Thus, a mapping of the BPMN model to the BPEL4WS can be performed. How the mapping works is shown in more detail in the example below.

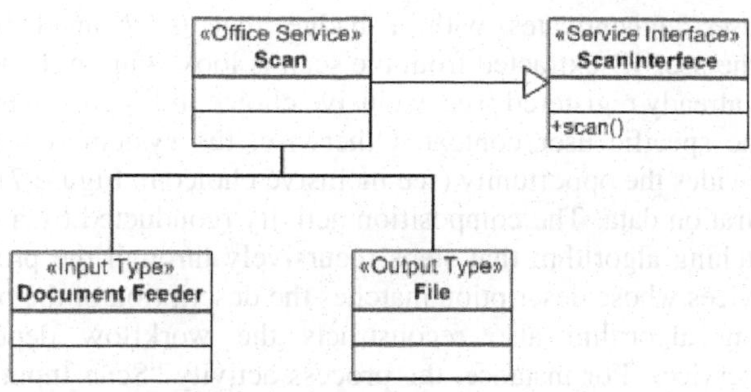

Fig. 5. Concrete service definition

The last step in the set-up process is the automatic instantiation of the device product lines regarding the services needed by the workflow. The resulting office devices are able to execute the activities and sub-workflows of the workflow needed to be supported by the required infrastructure. Figure 6 describes the automated instantiation in more detail.

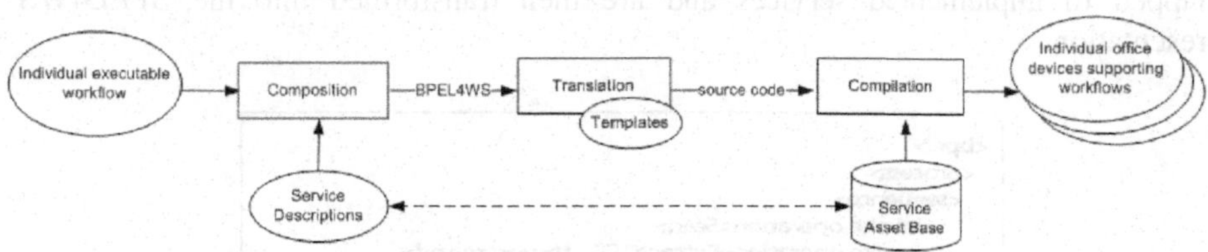

Fig. 6. Instantiation process and artifacts

The composition designs the application by mapping existing services to the individual executable workflow. The service descriptions as well as the workflow description are input for the composition. Figure 7 gives an example of a workflow modeled with BPMN.

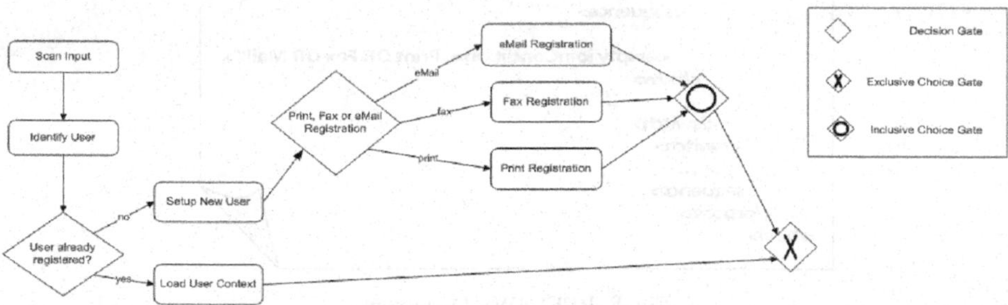

Fig. 7. Workflow Example

The process describes the accreditation mechanism for a document management system. The user authenticates with a badge that is scanned by the system. Subsequently, the user-ID extracted from the scan is looked up in the user registry. In case the user is already registered (see exclusive choice in Figure 7), the system loads and displays the specific user context. Otherwise, the system sets up a new user account and provides the opportunity (see inclusive choice in Figure 7) to print, fax or email the registration data. The composition activity (conducted by a domain expert) performs a matching algorithm that steps recursively through the process and looks for existing services whose description matches the description of the process activity.

The matching algorithm also reconstructs the workflow depending on the availability of services. For instance, the process activity "Scan Input" is (manually) matched to the service definition in the DSL shown in Figure 5. Thus, the input and output types are instantiated to "Document feeder" and "File", respectively.

As output of the matching algorithm the composition of services is translated in to BPEL4WS. BPEL4WS allows the creation of complex processes by wiring together different activities that can, for example, perform service invocations, manipulate data, throw faults, or terminate a process [8]. These activities may be nested within structured activities such as in sequence, or in parallel, or depending on certain conditions. Applied to the complete workflow example, the resulting BPEL4WS document is shown below. Basically all activities of the workflow were previously mapped to implemented services and are then transformed into the BPEL4WS presentation.

```
<bpel>
 <process>
  <sequence>
    <invoke operation=Scan>
    <invoke operation=ExtractOCR att=unresolved>
    <invoke operation=ValidateID att=unresolved>

   <switch>
     <case condition=„ID_registered==true">
        <invoke operation=LoadUserCtxt>
     </case>

    <case condition=„ID_registered!=true">

        <switch condition=„ID_valid==true">
          <invoke operation=SetupNewUser>
            <flow>
              <sequence>
                ...
                <empty joinCondition=„Print OR Fax OR Mail">
            </flow>
                ...
          </switch>
        </switch>
            ...
      </sequence>
     </process>
</bpel>
```

Fig. 8. BPEL4WS Document

The XSLT-templates [9] drive the translation activity by means of selecting the appropriate target language constructs, correlating to the defined workflow tags (see Figure 6). For instance, the *template match="case"* in Figure 9 would result in an *if*-construct, evaluating the variable specified by *@condition*. Due to referencing already implemented services based on a service-oriented architecture, the resulting source code is complete and includes all functionalities according to the specified workflow. Concluding the instantiation process described in Figure 6, the compilation accesses the service asset base to link the services supporting the functionality of the process to the source code. After compilation, the application can be deployed.

```
<xsl:template match="switch">
 if
   <xsl:apply-templates/>
</xsl:template>

<xsl:template match="case">
      if(<xsl:value-of select="@condition"/>){
  <xsl:apply-templates/><br/>
}
</xsl:template>

<xsl:template match="invoke">
  <xsl:if test="@outputVariable!=' '">
     <xsl:value-of select="@outputVariable"/>=
  </xsl:if>
  <xsl:value-of select="@operation"/>
      (<xsl:value-of select="@inputVariable"/>);

  <xsl:apply-templates/>
</xsl:template>
```

Fig. 9. Part of XSLT Template

4 Summary and Future Work

We presented a first step in the endeavor of developing intelligent office appliances efficiently. Concerning the overall vision, our approach supports service-providing organizations by applying a method that efficiently instantiates applications of software product lines based on service-oriented architectures (SOA). Therefore, we fused the strengths of paradigms like high-level modeling by BPMN, service-oriented architectures, model-driven development, and code generation. The high-level workflow modeling advantages are that it is understandable by the customer as well as by the system developer; moreover, it supports the transfer of business processes to other domains. In conclusion, the service-orientation leverages two major aspects: The first aspect is the automated derivation of an executable application based on an abstract process description by integrating already implemented services. The second aspect is the easy instantiation of products defined by a product line. That is, all generated products are per se tailored in regard to a supported workflow by a service selection mechanism. In terms of model-driven development, we solved the lack of behavior in regard to generated components by referencing existing services.

Our approach does not only provide a means for reducing the complexity of software development. Especially with respect to customized office workflows, the complexity of user interfaces in office devices can be reduced: First, the workflow itself may imply several settings of the device. Second, only the settings and functions to perform a certain workflow need to be shown to the user.

Nevertheless, we encountered problems that have to be solved in the future. In service-oriented architectures, the kind of service description influences the interaction, discovery and composition of services. Furthermore, discovery and composition of services are based on a comparison of service request and service descriptions. For service composition in our approach, we assumed that the description of the service request (workflow activity) is based on the same ontology as the description of the service. For future work, the introduction of semantic descriptions of Web Services like the Web Service Modeling Language [22] is inevitable. (For a comparison of those semantic description languages, refer to [10].

Besides, for efficient application of the approach a tool is needed that provides the transformation of a graphical modeling notation into XML format. There exist solutions for partial aspects of that transformation, but a holistic tool support for model import, export and consistency checking is not available yet.

Workflow enactment commonly includes explicit user interactions. Thus, we have to create concepts for automatic user interface integration with regard to the underlying process description. The creation of user interfaces is strongly domain-driven due to the fact that processes abstract from concrete implementation technologies. In SOA, platform-specific concerns like user interfaces can potentially be delegated to domain-specific service implementations. Based on this premise, each service definition has to provide information about its interfaces and how they are accessed. That yields an automatic user interface generation, based on the service composition tree during the translation phase. Respecting our implemented translation approach, XSLT templates offer fast pattern integration, but are sensitive in regard to the complexity of the matching rules, especially if user interfaces have to be generated.

References

1. Bayer, Buhl, Giese, Lehner, Ocampo, Puhlmann, Richter, Schnieders, Weiland: "Process Family Engineering Modeling variant rich processes", PESOA Report, June 2005.
2. Berners-Lee, T.: Web Services (2003) http://www.w3.org/DesignIssues/WebServices.html
3. Bettin, J.: Model Driven Software Development (2004) http://www.softmetaware.com/mdsd-and-isad.pdf
4. Bayer, Joachim; Flege, Oliver; Knauber, Peter; Laqua, Roland; Muthig, Dirk; Schmid, Klaus; Widen, Tanya: PuLSE. Product Line Software Engineering. Kaiserslautern, 1999
5. Booth, D., Liu, C.K.: Web Services Description Language (WSDL) Version 2.0 Part 0: (2005) http://www.w3.org/TR/wsdl20-primer/
6. Bayer, J., Lehner, T., Muthig, D.,: Asset Scoping: dentification of Reusable Software Components - Defining Service Components. Kaiserslautern, (2004)
7. Business Process Modeling Notation, BPMI.org (2004) http://www.bpmi.org/bpmn-spec.htm (Alternative: http://xml.coverpages.org/ni2003-08-29-a.html)

8. Business Process Execution Language for Web Services (2003) http://msdn.microsoft.com/library/default.asp?url=/library/en-us/dnbizspec/html/bpel1-1.asp
9. Burke, E. .: Java und XSLT, O'Reilly, (2002)
10. Cabral L., Domingue J., Motta E. , Payne T. Hakimpour F: Approaches to Semantic Web Services:An Overview and Comparisons, In proceedings of the First European Semantic Web Symposium (ESWS2004); 10-12 May 2004, Heraklion, Crete, Greece (2004) http://kmi.open.ac.uk/projects/irs/cabralESWS04.pdf.
11. Clements, P., Northrop, L. M.: Software Product Lines: Practices and Patterns. Addison-Wesley (2001)
12. Gardner, T.: An Introduction to Web Services, (2001) http://www.ariadne.ac.uk/issue29/gardner/
13. Hashimi, S.: Service-Oriented Architecture Explained, (2003) http://www.ondotnet.com/lpt/a/4108
14. Mitra, N.: SOAP Version 1.2 Part 0: Primer (2003) http://www.w3.org/TR/soap12-part0/
15. Mendling, J., Müller M.. A Comparison of BPML and BPEL4WS (2003) http://wi.wu-wien.ac.at/~mendling/publications/03-BXML.pdf.
16. Miller, J., Mukerji, J.: , MDA Guide Version 1.01, Object Management Group OMG (2003) http://www.omg.org/docs/omg/03-06-01.pdf
17. OMG: Model Driven Architecture (2005) www.omg.org/mda/,
18. Peltz C.: Web Service Orchestration. A review of emerging technologies, tools and standards, Hewlett Packard, Co. (2003) http://devresource.hp.com/drc/technical_white_papers/WSOrch/WSOrchestration.pdf
19. UDDI: Universal Description, Discovery and Integration (2002) Specification http://www.uddi.org/specification.html
20. Völter, M: Modellgetriebene Softwareentwicklung (2005) http://www.voelter.de/data/articles/MDSD.pdf
21. White, S.A.: BPMN overview (2004) http://www.bpmn.org/Documents/Introduction%20to%20BPMN.pdf
22. www.wsmo.org, Web Service Modeling Ontology (2005) http://www.wsmo.org/TR/d2/v1.1/
23. Yushi, C., Wah, L.E., Limbu D.. Wah, L.E.: Web Services Composition - An Overview of Standards (2004) http://www.itsc.org.sg/synthesis/2004/4_WS.pdf.

Trends in Learning Software Organizations: Current Needs and Future Solutions

Andreas Birk[1] and Torgeir Dingsøyr[2]

[1] sd&m AG, software design & management,
Löffelstraße 46, D-70597 Stuttgart, Germany
andreas.birk@sdm.de
[2] SINTEF Information and Communication Technology,
NO-7465 Trondheim, Norway
torgeir.dingsoyr@sintef.no

Abstract. The 7th learning software organizations workshop focused on interdisciplinary research on several aspects of learning: From personal competence development to cultural and technological frameworks for organization-wide knowledge-sharing ("knowledge management in software engineering"). We put special emphasis on experience reports and empirical work.

We define what a learning software organization is, present lessons learned from workshop sessions and suggest some ideas for the future development of the field.

1 Introduction

Software development is essentially an intellectual task. The success of software organizations is partly shaped by their abilities to make learning happen on individual, team, and organizational levels. Therefore they must foster and balance people issues, organization, method, and appropriate tool support.

The Learning Software Organizations (LSO) workshop series is a forum for software professionals and researchers interested in organizational learning within software development environments. The workshop fosters interdisciplinary experience sharing on topics such as software process improvement, personal competence development, technology transfer and innovation management, socio-psychological aspects of learning, as well as enabling technology. LSO places special emphasis on experience reports and empirical research.

In addition to the LSO workshop series, there has been much interest in this topic within the software engineering community, for example through a special issue on knowledge management in IEEE Software [12] and the textbook *Managing Software Engineering Knowledge* [3].

LSO 2005 was held in conjunction with the WM2005 conference. It emphasized the relation between organizational learning and software process improvement. Conference and workshop complemented each other and provided practical insights into current approaches used to establish and further develop learning software organizations.

K.-D. Althoff et al. (Eds.): WM 2005, LNAI 3782, pp. 70 – 75, 2005.

The workshop consisted of discussions, paper presentations and special sessions focused on sharing experience on characteristics of learning software organizations. It provided a forum for professionals from software engineering and knowledge management as well as the applied research community.

In the next chapters of this book you find selected papers from the LSO workshop 2005 [1]. In the next section we discuss the term "learning software organizations" and give an overview of broad present lines in the field, continue by presenting the main topics discussed at the workshop, and finally present our view of how the field should develop in the future.

2 What Is a Learning Software Organization?

A learning software organization is an organization that develops or maintains software and intentionally acts as a "learning organization". There are many definitions on what is required to achieve a "learning organization" or "organizational learning". In a review article, Dodgson [10] describes learning organizations as organizations that "build, supplement and organize knowledge and routines around their activities and within their cultures, and adapt and develop organizational efficiency by improving the use of the broad skills of their workforces". He further writes that this definition incorporates the following assumptions:

- Learning generally has positive consequences even though learning can be caused by failure.
- Corporate and group culture is influenced by individual learning and can assist the direction of the learning.
- Learning occurs throughout all activities of an organization. Encouraging and coordinating the variety of interactions in learning is a key organizational task.

"Learning organizations" are then organizations that "purposefully construct structures and strategies as to enhance and maximize organizational learning".

Studies on organizational learning in general build on theories from different disciplines, from Argyris and Schön's theory of learning [2], Nonaka and Takeuchi's theories of knowledge creation [13] to Wenger's theories on Communities of Practice [14].

When we discuss organizational learning in software organizations, this intersects to a high degree with the subfield of software engineering called *software process improvement;* where for example the total quality management (TQM) "philosophy" [7] and it's version related to software, the quality improvement paradigm (QIP) focuses on learning [4]. The concept of "Experience factory" [5] is the first well known systematic approach to organizational learning in the software engineering field. However, the main focus of the literature in software engineering has been on technological issues [9].

3 Lessons Learned from Learning Software Organizations

The LSO 2005 workshop discussions revealed several lessons learned that show what learning software organizations have achieved during the past years. These lessons learned also indicate needs for future investigations, industrial experience gathering, and research. In the following, we outline the lessons learned along with brief explanations. The explanations refer to concrete examples from the presented workshop contributions, which can also be found in the subsequent chapters of this book.

Organizational learning in the software domain must be integrated well with project processes, engineering work practices, and software architecture.
Fægri et al. describe an approach to increase the knowledge transfer in product family engineering through more effective coordination of people and organizational units by seeing software architects as a community of practice. The expected benefit is that communities offer a more adaptive approach for supporting the transition towards product family engineering as compared to formal organizational restructuring.

The German software company sd&m has experience from seven years of comprehensive, organization-wide knowledge management. Buch and Humm describe the company's experience from integrating organizational learning with substance (i.e., information contents, software architecture, good practice etc.), people, and tool issues.

Project retrospectives and feedback meetings should be the backbone of every learning software organization.
Many software organizations are applying various kinds of project retrospectives and feedback meetings (cf. [6, 8, 11]). Fajtak presents how kick-offs and project retrospectives are organized at the Program and System Engineering division of Siemens in Austria. Kick-offs and retrospectives are supported with a company wide network of facilitators, which enables several learning loops at different organizational levels. Salo of VTT in Finland describes how agile software development teams have improved and adapted their software development processes using iterative project retrospectives.

Knowledge and experience exist on several levels of sophistication. Learning software organizations must address each knowledge level by appropriate methods and techniques.
Buch and Humm have structured knowledge assets into a pyramid of increased sophistication and reuse-benefit. On the foundation level, there is basic factual information needed to derive problem solutions. The middle level is mature knowledge, which offers guidance for finding and developing solutions. The top level is solution knowledge, which is problem-specific and detailed, and can be reused "as is". Nick et al. indicate how a knowledge-based for code inspections can provide support for two distinct levels of knowledge and learning: (1) The inspection process itself and (2) the whole software lifecycle. Dingsøyr and Bjørnsson show how process

guides, that in the first place offer factual process definitions, can be enriched by solution-oriented guidelines and good practice knowledge.

Communities of practice and experience repositories can complement and leverage each other very well.
In a panel discussion, we discussed three major topics: what techniques are most important in spreading software engineering knowledge throughout an organization? What is the major fault when implementing a learning software organization? How should one combine experience packaging and communities of practice to establish a highly effective learning software organization? The conclusion of the discussion was that software engineering knowledge is of a kind which requires both packaging and leveraging through communities. As for leveraging, post-iteration workshops and "open" tools like wikis were viewed appropriate. Experience packaging can either be very focused on a topic (like inspections knowledge) or have a broad thematic horizon.

Motivational factors and drivers of learning software organizations must be managed actively.
Several of the LSO workshop discussions touched the question of motivational factors that enable and foster organizational learning. The following ingredients of motivational ecosystems for organizational learning were identified: (1) Openness for intrinsic learning motivations of individuals and teams. Often, the possibilities to satisfy such intrinsic learning motivations add much to an individual's perceived work satisfaction. (2) Meritocracy, which is a common motivational factor in open source communities. (3) Organizational support that enables and facilitates learning. (4) Technical infrastructure and budget needed to perform learning-related activities.
The workshop contribution of Salo describes an infrastructure that enables bottom-up learning of software teams, which eventually provides organization-level knowledge assets. Also Fajtak as well as Buch and Humm describe elements of organizational infrastructure for learning. Zuser and Grechenig discuss proper ways of giving feedback in typical situations occurring in software development projects.

Communities of practice across company borders can be a powerful means for strengthening smaller organizations and for accelerating adoption of new software engineering technology.
The papers by Santos et al. and the work of Smolander show how organizational learning principles can be applied to networks of smaller organizations. These networks are similar to company-internal networks within larger enterprises. For instance, a community of practice can span across many units within a large company, or across several smaller organizations within a network. Santos et al. describe a Brazilian initiative that supports process introduction in small and medium-sized enterprises. Smolander reports on a Finnish network of IT-suppliers to the timber industry that wants to improve its competitive position against large consulting companies.

Learning software organizations can benefit from a variety of promising enabling technologies. However, technology must be balanced well with content, people, and organization issues.
The LSO workshop presented several examples of new tools and technologies that can improve organizational learning or ease the introduction of organizational learning principles into the various software engineering processes:

- Schneider's modeling of information flows (in Smolander et al).
- The modeling of causal networks in the paper by Al-Shebab et al.
- A new approach to building infrastructures for E-Learning systems for Learning Software Organizations in the paper by Dedene et al.
- Combining electronic process guides and experience repositories as described in a case study by Bjørnsson and Stålhane.
- Experience-based support for code inspections by Nick et al.
- The TABA workstation, which configures and instantiates software development environments in the paper by Villela et al.

We also found approaches to transferring tacit knowledge through Open Space Technology by Dingsøyr and Bjørnsson (in Smolander et al.). The importance of achieving the right balance between technology and other non-technological issues has been addressed by Buch and Humm.

4 Future Needs

What are the main needs of the software industry where researchers and industry should cooperate on in future learning software organizations workshops? And what are the main needs of learning software organizations as a research field?

As for the industry, we think many companies still need to focus more on establishing what we can call learning practices. For example, an easy and obvious learning mechanism such as project retrospectives (or postmortem reviews) is still not used to a large extent in software companies.

As for learning software organizations as a research field, we think learning in agile software development will become an interesting area, increasing the focus on tacit knowledge. Also, we think that learning software organizations should – as the whole software engineering field – be focusing more on empirical work, and for studying learning organizations, this means primarily case studies and action research. There is also a lack of connecting work in this area to theory – we could make much more use of knowledge management work in general, and fields like organization development in particular.

Acknowledgement

We are very grateful to the workshop participants, the program committee, and additional reviewers. See [1] for a complete list of program committee members and additional reviewers for the 7th International Workshop on Learning Software Organizations.

References

1. Klaus-Dieter Althoff, Andreas Dengel, Ralph Bergmann, Markus Nick, and Thomas Roth-Berghofer, Professional Knowledge Management: Experiences and Visions. Proceedings from WM2005. Kaiserslautern, Germany: DFKI, Kaiserslautern, Germany, 2005,
2. Chris Argyris and Donald A. Schön, Organizational Learning II: Theory, Method and Practise: Addison Wesley, 1996,
3. A. Aurum, R. Jeffery, C. Wohlin, and M. Handzic, Managing Software Engineering Knowledge. Berlin: Springer Verlag, 2003,
4. Victor R. Basili, "Quantitative Evaluation of Software Engineering Methodology," Proceedings of the First Pan Pacific Computer Conference, Melbourne, Australia, 1985.
5. Victor R. Basili, Gianluigi Caldiera, and H. Dieter Rombach, "The Experience Factory," in Encyclopedia of Software Engineering, vol. 1, J. J. Marciniak, Ed.: John Wiley, 1994, pp. 469-476.
6. Andreas Birk, Torgeir Dingsøyr, and Tor Stålhane, "Postmortem: Never leave a project without it," IEEE Software, special issue on knowledge management in software engineering, no. 3, vol. 19, pp. 43 - 45, 2002.
7. Edwards W. Deming, Out of the Crisis. Cambridge, Massachusetts: The MIT Press (first published in 1982 by MIT Center for Advanced Educational Services), 2000, ISBN 0-262-54115-7.
8. Torgeir Dingsøyr, "Postmortem reviews: Purpose and Approaches in Software Engineering," Information and Software Technology, no. 5, vol. 47, pp. 293-303, 2005.
9. Torgeir Dingsøyr and Reidar Conradi, "A Survey of Case Studies of the Use of Knowledge Management in Software Engineering," International Journal of Software Engineering and Knowledge Engineering, no. 4, vol. 12, pp. 391 - 414, 2002.
10. Mark Dodgson, "Organizational Learning: A Review of Some Literatures," Organizational Studies, no. 3, vol. 14, pp. 375 - 394, 1993.
11. Norman L. Kerth, Project retrospectives : a handbook for team reviews. New York: Dorset House Publishing, 2001, ISBN 0-932633-44-7.
12. Mikael Lindvall and Ioana Rus, "Knowledge Management in Software Engineering," IEEE Software, no. 3, vol. 19, pp. 26 - 38, 2002.
13. Ikujiro Nonaka and Hirotaka Takeuchi, The Knowledge-Creating Company: Oxford University Press, 1995, ISBN 0-18.509269-4.
14. Etienne Wenger, Communities of practise : learning, meaning and identity. Cambridge, UK: Cambridge University Press, 1998, ISBN 0-521-43017-8.

Kick-Off Workshops and Project Retrospectives

A Good Learning Software Organization Practice

Fred Frowin Fajtak

Siemens AG Österreich, Program and System Engineering PSE,
Werner von Siemens-Platz 1, A-5021 Salzburg
fred-frowin.fajtak@siemens.com

Abstract. Program and System Engineering, in short PSE, is a division of Siemens AG Austria and one of Europe's largest software houses. Kick-off workshops and project retrospectives are an important instrument of PSE as a learning software organization. PSE supports this with a company wide network of facilitators, organized in the Support Center Project Experience. Kick-offs and retrospectives combined with a network of facilitators enable several learning loops in different organizational levels.

1 Introduction

In the high tech world of computer technologies, we sometimes forget the fact that software is built by groups of people. We concentrate on development paradigms and new approaches to software architecture. We focus on performance and reliability and we invest in advanced configuration management tools and automated testing. But we often ignore that none of these technical aspects influence a project's success as much as the experience of our developers and their ability to work as part of a team.

At PSE, the software development division of Siemens AG Austria, we have realized significant benefits by providing carefully designed facilitated rituals at the beginning and at the end of projects, called kick-off workshops and project retrospectives respectively. The high return-on-investment for the time spent is unchallenged and confirmed by the regular feedback of developers, project leaders and managers. They attest a positive influence of these rituals on many subjects such as team cooperation, process effectiveness, quality assurance, know-how sharing, reliability of estimations, and so on. This helps to improve the development cycle and increases the financial success of our projects.

These facilitated sessions have specific goals and structure which will be discussed below, but to understand how kick-off workshops and retrospectives have become a key part of our culture, we first need to look at PSE and the Support Center Project Experience that nurtures and administers these rituals.

2 PSE and the Idea of Support Centers

Program and System Engineering, in short PSE, is a division of Siemens AG Austria and one of Europe's largest software houses. PSE has more than 5000 highly educated

K.-D. Althoff et al. (Eds.): WM 2005, LNAI 3782, pp. 76 – 81, 2005.

software experts, located in seven European countries, as well as in Turkey and China. PSE offers services in the field of product and system development, system integration and consulting for most of the various Siemens divisions worldwide.

To ensure a company-wide technology management PSE developed the Technology Tree Concept [1] that allows all employees to initiate networks for promising technologies or topics. Ten of these networks with particular high impact on the PSE business have been organized into Support Centers. Each Support Center is an internal consulting center with a part of its resources sponsored centrally by PSE. Any project within PSE can use their services at a reasonable internal consulting rate. One of these internal consulting centers is the Support Center Project Experience, in short SC-PE.

3 The Support Center Project Experience

There are two main goals of SC-PE: On the one hand SC-PE supports groups and individuals in learning from their own experiences for lasting improvements in their projects. On the other hand SC-PE spreads experiences and solutions anonymously throughout the whole company. Project retrospectives and kick-off workshops are two of the main tools to reach these goals. Since 1996 the team of SC-PE has facilitated retrospectives and kick-offs for several hundred projects.

Only two members of SC-PE do this job full-time. More than twenty work for different business units at a variety of locations, most of them as project leaders, consultants, unit managers or quality managers. This makes SC-PE a highly distributed PSE network.

SC-PE members spend between ten to thirty percent of their time for SC-PE, mainly as workshop facilitators. Each facilitator has attended a basic course on workshop moderation and additional trainings for topics like group dynamics or conflict management.

New members are coached by more experienced ones during their first workshop facilitations. But also the experienced members of the network always work in twos. It is not always possible to do the facilitation as such as a pair of co-facilitators, but at least the preparation of the workshop and the reflection afterwards is done together with another member of the SC-PE network. As the pairs are always changing, there is a continuous knowledge exchange of facilitation skills and project experiences between the network members. In addition there are network meetings taking place twice a year, where important insights and highlights are discussed.

4 Kick-Off Workshops

At PSE the term kick-off designates an internal workshop at the beginning of a project or at the start of a project phase. A kick-off at PSE usually lasts for 1-2 days.

Kick-offs usually have the following goals:

- Explain goals, requirements and tasks of the project to the whole team
- Inform the team about planned dates and milestones

- Clarify the allocation of responsibilities and the interfaces within the team
- Lay down the mechanisms for risk management and claim management
- These goals can be supplemented, e.g. with management statements, team-building actions, or anything else that helps the team to have a successful project start

To organize a kick-off as a sequence of frontal slide presentations is a common mistake in our branch. To avoid this, the agenda has to be designed as an interactive workshop that encourages the whole team to contribute.

Of course essential presentations are necessary, but there are many ways to lend variety to the agenda. For example the talks should be held by different persons, not only by the project leader. The mission statement should be presented by the management. The quality responsible can inform about obligatory tools and quality goals. Depending on the team size and the project's focal points, other speakers could be the architect, the configuration management expert or the leader of the test team. This also introduces the main contact persons of the project to the team.

To have several speakers requires that the presentations are well coordinated during the preparation phase of the workshop to avoid redundancies and to reduce the given information to what is really essential.

Each presentation has to be followed by a phase of clarification to ensure the commitment of the whole team. In this phase the independent facilitator guarantees the effectiveness of the workshop process and makes sure that each participant can focus entirely on the content.

Apart from presentations, a kick-off agenda should always include some interactive workshop parts. A good example is the search for project specific risks as a basic input for the project's risk management. The involvement of everybody in the team makes it possible to detect risks from different points of view and different areas of responsibility. And it also results in a higher awareness of and attention for the project risks in the whole team.

A further approach to bring more life into a kick-off is to carry out team building activities. A lot of workshop games can be used for this purpose, however a game should always have a clear relation to the project goals or the present content.

Furthermore some kind of social event should always be part of the kick-off agenda.

5 Project Retrospectives

The idea of project retrospectives originally came from Norm Kerth [2] and was introduced at PSE in 1996. Since then the method has been continuously adapted for PSE needs by the SC-PE team. Retrospectives are internal workshops at the end of a project or at the end of a project phase. At PSE the typical duration of a retrospective is 1-3 days.

The specific timeout from daily business allows a thorough discussion of success factors and problems, technical as well as social ones. A professionally facilitated retrospective guarantees that the important hard facts and soft facts become transparent throughout the team.

A typical project retrospective agenda at PSE includes at least the following steps:

- Welcome and warm-up phase
- Collect everyone's memories of the whole project period
- Identify and prioritize core topics: problems, puzzles and success factors
- Selected topics are analyzed in greater depth in parallel working groups
- Plenary presentation of the group work results and derivation of mandatory measures or insights
- Welcome the management to add their point of view and for a final discussion of the results
- Agree on the next steps to ensure that the workshop results will be integrated into daily life

6 Success Factors for Kick-Off Workshops and Project Retrospectives

Kick-offs as well as retrospectives require skilful preparation and objective guidance during the workshop and should therefore be led by a neutral and professional facilitator.

The most important preparation step is the contracting between the facilitator and the project leader. This is the time the facilitator gets the first information on the project and the project leader has to define his objectives for the workshop. The facilitator must find out who else has to be involved in the workshop preparation. Usually this will be at least the management, but in addition it can be any other involved in the project.

During contracting the facilitator develops his first idea of the workshop agenda and he will advise his customers in setting the frame conditions for the workshop. This includes for example the question of who will participate, the duration of the workshop and the location. Kick-offs and retrospectives should always involve as many members of the project team as possible, ideally the whole team. The workshop location should be a place away from the usual place of work and have all the characteristics of a good training environment. The duration depends on many factors such as the number of participants and the relationship between them, the viewed period, the complexity of the project and the goals that have to be reached in the workshop. Another important question in this connection is whether participants will use their native tongue or a foreign language. To make a correct estimate of the expenditure for the workshop at such an early time of planning requires a lot of experience in this field.

In the further preparation there is a big difference between kick-off workshops and project retrospectives. A retrospective is led by the facilitator with the objective to give each participant the same space to bring in their topics and experiences. In a kick-off workshop the project leader has to be in the limelight and the facilitator supports him with the moderation in transition phases and interactive working parts. To enable the project leader to be in the focus of attention, the facilitator has to develop the kick-off agenda in close cooperation with the project leader. This fact gives the facilitator the opportunity to transfer his knowledge and experiences gained during other projects to the project leader. And he can adapt his input exactly to the needs of this project.

In any case the facilitator has to be aware of his different roles in kick-offs and retrospectives and consider them very carefully.

In the workshop an atmosphere of trust has to be created that allows every participant to be absolutely honest. This can be supported by special safety exercises or methods that guarantee anonymity. In addition it has to be acknowledged that it is not only the hard facts that are important, but also everyone's feelings. Therefore the agenda has to allow focusing on technical as well as social topics.

The real success of a workshop is not visible until the results of the workshop are integrated into daily project life. To increase the probability of this success the results have to be mandatory measures and recorded insights. High-quality workshop minutes will support this aim very effectively.

To establish kick-offs and retrospectives as a regular ritual in development teams encourages continuous improvement and makes workshops more effective. Therefore workshops should be held not only at the beginning and at the end of a project, but also at any timely moment such as at the beginning or the end of each project phase, each version or iteration.

There are lots of other parameters influencing the success of kick-off workshops and project retrospectives, but the ones above have turned out to be the basis of daily practice in SC-PE.

7 Learning on Several Organizational Levels

Retrospectives at the end of a project are the most effective way to ensure that the empirically gained knowledge of a project team gets identified and becomes reusable. Whether or not the team splits up after the project, learning will happen. If the team continues it is easier to put concrete measures into practice. On the other hand the insights are spread to several different projects if the team splits up.

Another level of learning is implemented through the SC-PE network. With each workshop the facilitator learns a lot about PSE projects and daily practices in other business units. And as the SC-PE members share their experiences, this knowledge is multiplied. Therefore the network guarantees a permanent knowledge exchange between the business units.

The facilitators transfer this knowledge to other projects in different ways. For example they offer consulting to project leaders while kick-offs are prepared. Another way is to tell stories and pass recommendations during retrospectives and kick-offs. Furthermore you have to consider that most of the SC-PE members work in functions that allow them to spread knowledge in their own business units and projects.

And finally, there is also a company-wide use. SC-PE identifies patterns of common problems and best practices at PSE. The result is authentic input for PSE wide best practice reports and patterns, quality goals and improvement campaigns.

8 Current Developments and Future Prospects

At the beginning of the SC-PE activities most of the retrospectives were held on projects in acute crisis situations or on projects that failed. Today SC-PE services are well-known and many projects use them regularly, regardless of whether or not these projects are running smoothly. Therefore best practice analysis and the identification of success factors are becoming explicit workshop objectives more frequently.

Depending on their project structures and team sizes some of the PSE business units hold kick-offs and retrospectives for each project. Others use them only in specific circumstances, e.g. for larger or exceptional projects.

In the past years the number of projects with distributed teams has increased rapidly at PSE. To have team members at three or four locations, often with different cultures and mother tongues, offers new challenges. Daily practice shows that especially kick-off workshops are a crucial success factor for such projects. Project retrospectives turn out to be an important element for further team development during such projects.

One obvious fact is that the personal contact between all team members helps to reduce the cultural barriers and results in distinct improvements in daily work. Especially a kick-off or an early retrospective helps the individuals in the project to feel and perform as one team. Another important effect of early workshops is that they counteract negative rivalry between different locations.

Apart from the known effects of project retrospectives, some additional benefits can be gained from them for distributed projects. First and foremost they help to counteract the lack of informal contact, which in local teams is a matter of course, such as the daily contact during coffee breaks or project celebrations, but also the chance for spontaneous knowledge exchange and readily available mutual aid within the team. Retrospectives are very well suited for satisfying the social needs in distributed teams, and especially for the management of latent or open conflicts.

PSE also benefits from retrospectives in distributed projects as they increase the knowledge exchange and experience sharing between the different PSE locations.

Another trend comes with the new paradigm of agile software development methods. These methods require shorter iterations of retrospective-like meetings and for this reason new ways of organizing and facilitating such meetings.

More and more development teams recognize that they need basic facilitation skills to moderate such meetings on their own. Some SC-PE facilitators offer support to them and advise interested persons on how to make such meetings more effective. But as agile development methods demand a high culture of reflection, it is not surprising that during these projects almost always real project retrospectives are held in addition to iteration meetings.

For years now, PSE has benefited from the well-tried and reliable learning loops through kick-off workshops and project retrospectives. It should come as no surprise that SC-PE will continue to utilize, refine and extend these techniques as their value is vast and their cost is slight.

References

1. M. Heiss, J. Jankowsky: The Technology Tree Concept – An Evolutionary Approach to Technology Management in a Rapidly Changing Market. Proceedings of the IEEE int. Eng. Manage. Conference 2001, Albany, N.Y., 2001.
2. N. Kerth: Project Retrospectives. A Handbook for Team Reviews. Dorset House Publishing, 2001, ISBN: 0932633447

Substance, People, and Tools – Knowledge Management at sd&m

Arnim Buch and Bernhard Humm

sd&m Research,
sd&m – software design & management,
Carl-Wery-Str. 42, 81739 München, Germany
{Arnim.Buch, Bernhard.Humm}@sdm.de

Abstract. This paper distils the experience from seven years of knowledge management at sd&m, a German software company with more than 900 employees. For sd&m, knowledge management is a strategic investment with the goal to acquire the right knowledge, to make it accessible to all employees, and to increase their proficiency. Effective knowledge management depends on the right combination of the key elements: substance, people, and tools.

1 Introduction

Some people state that *knowledge management* is one of the key success factors of business. Others warn against the term knowledge management since knowledge as such cannot be managed [Mal04]. For sd&m, knowledge management is a *strategic investment* with the goal to acquire the right *knowledge*, to make it accessible to all employees, and to increase their *proficiency*.

More than 900 sd&m employees develop custom software solutions and provide IT consulting services. They work in about 200 projects at a time for several dozen different customers in nine sd&m offices and on numerous customers' premises. In order to get the best benefit for the customers from the experience of the whole company, sd&m has established a dedicated knowledge management group in 1997. Today, *sd&m Research* comprises seven years of experience with knowledge management.

Of course, there is no "silver bullet" for implementing knowledge management effectively in an organisation. It depends on the business, on the company size, and on the culture. Nevertheless, some of sd&m's experience can be applied to other companies, too. In this paper, we present some of our key learnings.

2 Seven Years of Experience in Knowledge Management

What is the knowledge that will bring you ahead of your competitors? In IT business, there is a constant headline-making for so-called break-through technologies. To differentiate technologies with the potential to change the whole industry (like, e.g., web technology) from mere hypes (like, e.g., 4GLs) is a key success factor for a software company. For this reason, sd&m has established an *innovation management*

K.-D. Althoff et al. (Eds.): WM 2005, LNAI 3782, pp. 82 – 85, 2005.

process: a small group of experts regularly screens and assesses current IT trends. Those trends considered important will then be elaborated in *communities*. Community members study literature, gain first experience with the new technology in pilot projects, and produce point-of-view papers. Those papers state the principles, maturity, and potentials of the technology under investigation. At every point in time, a topic can be dropped.

Communities are central for knowledge management at sd&m. A community is a team of topic experts from all over sd&m, either as members of sd&m Research or as project team members. They do research on their subject, and propagate their insights to the projects by trainings, temporary collaboration, and support. Communities have been evolved out of the knowledge broker model described in [Brö99]. Compared to the knowledge brokers, a team offers a broader scope, better availability, and a deeper understanding of the subject. sd&m Research provides communities with a budget and community work is encouraged via personal goals. However, most importantly, the community members are enthusiastic about sharing their expertise with other experts. We have made the experience: it is better to leave a topic for a while rather than establish a community with members who yield little expertise or enthusiasm.

This is because *substance* is most important. This can be made clear with the example of *Quasar* (quality software architecture, [Sied04]). There are two core topics in the business of sd&m. One is project management, and the other is software design – both focussing on successful software projects on time and in budget. For this reason, sd&m has developed Quasar over the last seven years as a reference architecture for custom software solutions. Quasar distils thousands of person years of project experience and is the result of the enthusiasm of very few visionaries, the contribution of tens of people and numerous discussions within the whole company. Quasar has substance and it is vivid. In one-week schools, young sd&m colleagues learn the Quasar concepts and their application. Today, we can state that the principles and notions of Quasar have been widely accepted within the company and are being applied throughout all projects. And this closes the circle: Quasar holds a lot of past project experience, and the trainings bring it into future projects.

One central concept of Quasar is *reuse*. In the 1990s, sd&m started the first attempt to organise software reuse with the intranet-based repository *SINUS* (software in use). Projects dropped pieces of software they considered reusable into the repository. SINUS was a flop. This was because the environment for its use was not set up properly: no common understanding of reusable components, no reliable statement on the quality, nobody responsible for the software in the repository, and, finally, no support in the case of problems with the code.

From the SINUS experience we learned and took the consequences for the second attempt: *QuasarComponents*. A dedicated team develops and supports technical basic components on the basis of the Quasar architecture. The result is software components with guaranteed levels of quality and support. People about to apply the components in the projects are offered three-day schools in using the components.

Over the years, sd&m has established a knowledge organisation. It is run by a full-time *knowledge manager* who reports via the head of research to the board of managing directors. They in turn provide a budget for research and knowledge management annually, e.g., 15 person years for 2004. The knowledge manager has a team of 20 part-time *knowledge consultants* who help projects find relevant knowledge and, in turn, extract knowledge from the project for future use.

3 Conclusion: Substance, People, and Tools

Knowledge management at sd&m distils to the three essentials: *substance, people, and tools* – see Fig. 1 for a categorization of the for sd&m relevant topics (substance), processes (people) and tools.

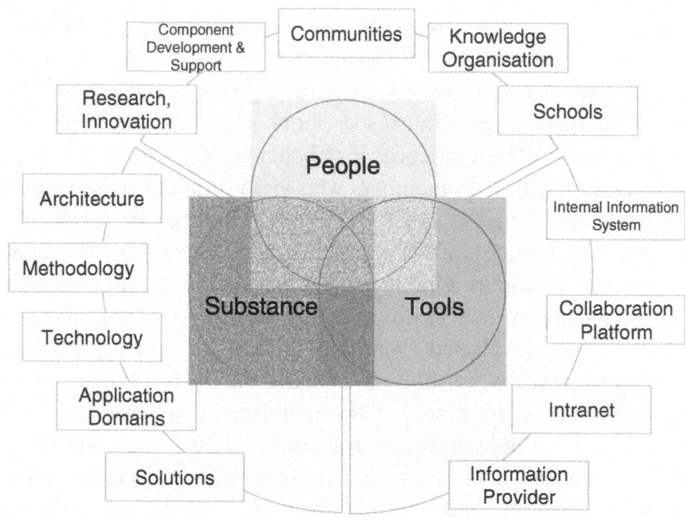

Fig. 1. Substance, People, and Tools

- The first is *substance*: if there is no substantial knowledge to be shared all knowledge management efforts are in vain. Substantial knowledge includes the selection of the relevant topics (at sd&m: via innovation management) and the high quality of results (Quasar is a positive example at sd&m).
- *People* are in the centre of knowledge management: they gather experience (at sd&m: via projects). They share expertise and do research (at sd&m: in communities). And people are being taught (at sd&m: in schools and trainings). More important than the knowledge as such is proficiency, i.e., the ability to apply it. The right organisation is essential (at sd&m: with a knowledge manager, knowledge consultants, communities, annual budgets, etc.).
- The last element comprises knowledge management *tools*: They ease the handling of knowledge for producers and consumers and can increase the acceptance and motivation of sharing knowledge. In a distributed

organization like sd&m they play an important role. But contrary to the statements of some tool vendors, knowledge management tools are the least important of the three elements.

In seven years we have learned: stamina is essential for effective knowledge management. But it is worth it.

References

[Brö99] Peter Brössler: Knowledge Management at a software House. A Progress Report. In: Frank Bomarius (ed.): Proceedings of the Workshop on Learning Software Organisations (1999) 77-86.

[Mal04] Malik on Management 1/2004; managermagazin.de 27.11.2001

[Sied04] Johannes Siedersleben: Moderne Softwarearchitektur – umsichtig planen, robust bauen mit Quasar. dpunkt.verlag. Heidelberg, 2004

Harvesting Knowledge Through a Method Framework in an Electronic Process Guide

Finn Olav Bjørnson and Tor Stålhane

Department of Computer and Information Science,
Norwegian University of Science and Technology,
NO-7491 Trondheim, Norway
{bjornson, stalhane}@idi.ntnu.no

Abstract. A key leverage for small software consultancy companies is the collective knowledge possessed by their consultants. There have been some studies in the literature on how to harvest and transfer this knowledge, but most studies are aimed at large multinational corporations. In this paper we describe an ongoing research project, aimed at improving knowledge sharing in a small software consultancy company through the use of a method framework in an electronic process guide coupled with an experience repository.

1 Introduction

Small software consultancy companies have to leverage their position in the market to stay ahead of their competitors. One way to achieve this is by providing their customers with tailored solutions to their problems. They can do this by drawing upon the collective knowledge of their consultants. When the company is small and the consultants are spread over the sites of many customers, it becomes difficult to gain access to and draw upon the collective experience of all the co-workers. Consequently the solutions provided by the consultants might not be of sufficient quality to make their customers return to the company when they need consultants for a new project.

One solution to the problem with a dispersed workforce is experience repositories. A lot of research has gone into this field, however most of this research has been focused on large companies and little data exists on the application of this in small companies [1, 2].

In [3] the authors examine challenges facing small businesses when implementing knowledge management efforts. Small businesses are particularly vulnerable to knowledge erosion, yet they seldom have the time and resources needed to implement the knowledge management programs described for larger companies. However, the authors suggest that small businesses can benefit just as much from well thought out knowledge management efforts.

According to [1], which describes the successful use of an experience repository in a small software company, detailed data on its use and structure can be used to better understand how experience supports activities in the company. This can in turn lead to improvements in experience management concepts, techniques and tools.

In this research report we describe our work in a small software consultancy company that wish to manage their knowledge through a method framework

K.-D. Althoff et al. (Eds.): WM 2005, LNAI 3782, pp. 86 – 90, 2005.

implemented in an Electronic Process Guide (EPG) coupled with an Experience Repository (ER).

2 Context

The company we investigated currently has 17 employees. Their main activities are hiring out consultants as developers, developing complete solutions for customers and hiring out consultants as advisors for selecting technology, strategy or process. Typically, no more than four to five consultants are at any time working for the same customer.

The managers of the company wish to leverage the company in the market by providing solutions to the problems of their customers. The solutions should make them stand out and increase the probability that the customers later returns with new projects. In order to do this, they wish to foster an environment were all ideas and knowledge are shared freely among the employees, and where the employees can draw upon the experience of each other to provide good services to their customers. This work is difficult since a lot of the employees at any given time are out at the site of customers where they don't have direct access to their colleagues.

To remedy this situation they wish to collect the experience of their employees in an Experience Repository (ER). This will allow their employees to have easy access to the experience of their coworkers.

3 Method

Due to the cooperative nature of this research project, we decided to adopt action research as our approach. The most prevalent description of action research is found in [4]. The approach requires the establishment of a client-system infrastructure or research environment. In our case this was already taken care of through the researchers' and company's involvement in a mutual research program. The approach further specifies five identifiable phases, which are iterated: diagnosing, action planning, action taking, evaluating and specifying learning. This paper sums up our work and findings from the initial phases and what effect this has had on the development of the new tool. The plans for the next phases are outlined up in section 6: Future work.

For the initial diagnosing phase, we decided to use semistructured interviews. We scheduled interviews with 12 of the employees. The interviews were carried out using an interview guide. Basically we wanted answers to three questions: What was the current approach to knowledge sharing, what should the new tool contain, and what kind of functionality should it provide? All of the interviews were taped using a dictaphone and were subsequently transcribed. The material was then coded and analyzed using the constant comparison method and the NVivo tool [5].

The problem with the adopted approach is that our results will be difficult to generalize due to our single case. Rather they will contribute to the understanding of the concepts of Experience Repositories. If the results from our study should coincide with the research literature some generalization might be possible.

4 Interview Results

The company seemed to have a good environment for informal sharing of experience in that people knew one another and knew whom to contact if they were stuck. There did not seem to be much formal gathering of experience. If experience from a project was collected, it was mostly done in an ad hoc manner, and it was not easily available. The gathering of experiences today was mostly done through private initiative and saved for personal use.

Lately a few employees had begun using post mortem analysis [6] at the end of their projects, but they did not have a place to structure and access this information. The fact that a lot of work was done at the site of customers was also seen as a hindrance to collecting project experience. It seemed to be easier to get help with technical problems than problems related to process. More structure and information related to process was seen as desirable.

When asked about what information they wanted the new tool to contain, the employees provided us with a myriad of elements. A few, however, was mentioned more often than the others: document templates, patterns, a good process, help with customer relations and practical experience.

Document templates were seen as potential help to increase productivity. Both inexperienced and experienced project managers saw a benefit from having a set of standardized templates in order to save time on documentation.

Patterns were also mentioned as something that should be readily available. Good ideas and smart solutions that other people had thought of were worth repeating. However, the employees stressed the need for trust. It was important for them to know that a pattern could actually deliver what it promised.

A good development process and the need for help with questions related to process was often mentioned during the interviews. This need was considered especially important for the start-up of new projects. Inexperienced project managers expressed a need for a process that would help and guide them through the initial phases. Experienced managers expressed the need for a process that would help them keep on track throughout the project. A well-defined process was also seen as something they could market to their customers to gain an edge over their competitors.

The employees often mentioned the need for guidelines and advice on how to improve customer relations. There was a broad agreement that more customer involvement would enhance the quality of the end product. The employees agreed that there had not been a lot of focus on this in the past and that guidelines for this would be most welcome in the new method framework.

When it came to choosing a process, a template or a pattern, the employees would like to know what kind of experience others had made when using these items. They saw a great potential in linking the experience of the company's developers to templates, patterns and processes, in order to be able to assess them for their own projects based on their colleagues' experience.

5 Initial Work and Challenges Ahead

After the initial interviews we moved on to the action-planning phase of our research. This phase consisted of meetings with the company where we presented the result of our interviews. The interviews indicated that there was a demand for a tool that would help the employees to share and structure their experience, especially experience surrounding the development process. It also indicated that the culture of the company supported free sharing of information and experience, and that the employees saw the benefits of using such a tool as the management was suggesting.

With the support from the employees established, we arranged a discussion on the functionality and the content of the new tool. It was decided that the company should develop an empty method framework tailored to the development process of the company. This framework would be implemented in a dynamic EPG, which would then be coupled to an ER. The employees would use this tool to enter their experience related to roles, artifacts and activities. The goal is to create a process guide based on the collective experience of all the employees in the company, which can then be used to increase the quality and consistency of their work. Both the decision to couple the ER to the process of an EPG and making the tool highly interactive to enable fast feedback is supported by [7] which describes good practices regarding ER and [2] which describes a successful implementation of an EPG/ER

After the meeting where this was discussed, we moved on to the action-taking part of our research. The company put one consultant on the project of working out a method framework. The framework was based on the Rational Unified Process (RUP), and was tailored to the company's process. During this process the input of both employees and scientists was sought in order to make the framework as similar to the current practice as possible.

One of our main challenges in the time ahead will be to keep the ER alive. An ER that is not used by the developers is of no value to the company. Experience from other ER initiatives [8, 9] has shown that there are three factors that influence the use of an ER:

- The ER must contain a minimum amount of experiences that can be searched. The amount of experience available is critical. If there is little experience available in the ER, the developers will neither use it nor contribute their own experiences to it.
- The experience that is found must be considered to be relevant for the developers in their day-to-day work. It must help them to do a better job and it must be up to date. One of the most de-motivating things that can occur when using an ER is to find an experience with and interesting title but with outdated contents.
- It must be possible to establish a community of practice [10] based on the ER contents. This means that not only must the experience be relevant – it must be possible to discuss, and augment existing experiences, that is; the ER must work as a forum where people can exchange ideas.

All of these mechanisms are used to keep up the interest for the ER among the developers. On the other hand, the interest can only be kept if the content is good. In order to meet these challenges we will use several strategies. The most important mechanisms to achieve our goals are to:

- Keep the ER open. As a consequence of this, everybody can add his or her own experiences. There will only be one restriction – all input must be traceable to the person that contributed it.
- Build discussion treads. These are important both to keep the experiences up-to-date and to keep the community of practice alive.

6 Future Work

When the framework is finished and implemented in the EPG/ER tool it will be presented to the employees. After this, the employees will enter into a period of filling up the framework with relevant experience. The next challenge for the scientists will be to come up with good methods for extracting most of the experience of the employees in a way that is not too intrusive to the regular work of the company, yet still captures the most crucial knowledge.

After an initial trial period the tool will be approved for use in projects. The role of the scientists then switches to an observational role. We plan on following the use of the EPG/ER for two years (the remaining period of our research project). By collecting information along the way and comparing it with the research literature, we hope to be able to ascertain how successful the knowledge initiative have been for the company and how it might apply to companies in similar contexts.

References

[1] Louise Scott, Ross Jeffery: *The Anatomy of an Experience Repository*, Proc. International Symposium on Empirical Software Engineering, 2003

[2] Felicia Kurniawati, Ross Jeffery: *The Long-term Effects of an EPG/ER in a Small Software Organisation*, Proc. Australian Software Engineering Conference, 2004

[3] Wickert Anja, Richard Herschel: *Knowledge management issues for smaller businesses*, Journal of Knowledge Management, vol 5, no. 4, pp. 329-337, 2001

[4] Susman G., Evered R.: *An assessment of the scientific merits of action research*, Administrative Science Quarterly, 23(4), pp. 582 – 603, 1978

[5] Web: http://www.qsrinternational.com, last visited 06.09.04

[6] Birk Andreas, Dingsøyr Torgeir, Stålhane Tor: *Postmortem: Never Leave a Project Without It*, IEEE Software, vol 19, no 3, pp. 43-45, 2002

[7] Kurt Schneider, Jan-Peter von Hunnius: *Effective Experience Repositories for Software Engineering*, Proc. 25th International Conference on Software Engineering, 2003

[8] Louise Scott, Tor Stålhane: *Experience Repositories and the Post Mortem*, Proc. Learning Software Organisations, 2003

[9] Hauge Tor-Erik, *Reuse in IT-companies, evolution and trends*, Master Thesis University of Stavanger, 2003, (in norwegian)

[10] Wenger Etienne: *Communities of Practice*, Cambridge University Press, 1998

Using Feedback for Supporting Software Team Improvement

Wolfgang Zuser and Thomas Grechenig

Research Group Industrial Software, Vienna University of Technology
firstname.lastname@inso.tuwien.ac.at

Abstract. Software process improvement and software team improvement are tightly bound to high quality feedback, which provides valuable information about the status quo and gives hints where improvement activities should take place. Anyhow in many software engineering teams personal feedback is not applied frequently enough. This paper discusses proper ways of giving feedback in typical situations occurring in software development projects.

1 Introduction

Giving the right feedback in the right situation is one of the main assets doing "peopleware" ([2], [3]). However many managers like to avoid giving feedback to their workers because of three main reasons ([5]):

1. They do not like to discuss weaknesses of workers directly. They are afraid of confrontations when discussing which skills or personality attributes could/should be improved.
2. Workers do not like to hear about their weaknesses. In many cases they react quite aggressive being confronted with such matters.
3. Many people overrate their skills enormously.

Feedback as one dimension of a job description besides skill variety, task identity, task significance and autonomy has direct correlations to job satisfaction, performance and motivation [4]. Therefore the rate of feedback for workers has to be as high as possible (with respect to economical issues).

This paper discusses different ways of feedback, which can be applied to software engineering teams (Section 2) and introduces typical patterns, which describe team situations requiring feedback (Section 3). Applying proper ways of feedback in such team patterns helps to improve the team dynamics and team performance more rapidly than without proper feedback.

2 Reasonable Ways of Feedback

For giving valuable feedback different kinds of feedback have to be used in different situations. The selected feedback method strongly depends on the information which should be provided and on the people to whom the feedback should be given.

K.-D. Althoff et al. (Eds.): WM 2005, LNAI 3782, pp. 91 – 95, 2005.

1. Self assessment: Self assessment is a common approach in psychology to investigate personality profiles or personal attitudes and skills. Self assessment technically spoken is a survey with reflective questions that ask the test person to give answers according to personal feelings or to rate certain items. The answers are compiled into profiles according to a theoretical model which underlies the questions (e.g. personality model, performance model).
2. Surveys: The most common way of gathering feedback is a simple survey, which collects data about a certain topic of interest (project experience, work habits ...).
3. Internal team feedback (team member peer evaluation): Teams should stay together as long as possible in order to become a high performing team. A team increases its performance due to improvements in the team dynamics. For reflecting team dynamics feedback from the team members themselves is the most important source (compared to other feedback methods and sources). Only team members have enough insight in the team processes. Peer evaluation in software project teams at college is the best method for getting valid information about team dynamics and individual participation of single team members [8, 1].
4. External feedback for a team: Besides internal feedback in a team, a second (probably more objective, but with less detailed knowledge) feedback source is quite meaningful. The feedback is provided by the project manager(s) or the customer.
5. Tests: Tests are valuable in situations when teams are improving their technical knowledge in workshops, e.g. to get used to a new technology in an innovative project. The importance of the usage of tests for giving feedback to managers as well as team members is stressed in [7].
6. Checklists: Checklists are very helpful assuring that tasks have been finished completely. Therefore they give feedback about the project status or status of a task continuously.
7. Project data collection: Project data (project metrics) is not related to peopleware at all but is an important kind of feedback anyhow. Project data enables the (project) management to evaluate the project status. Therefore assessing the project based on "objective" project data is quite desirable. There are two main problems with this method: project members tend to make wrong statements about the project. There is almost no strategy to avoid this except to raise to level of confidence between project members and management. The second problem is that most software engineers (and not only them) dislike the creation of paper based reports.

3 Team Phase Patterns Requiring Feedback

Feedback should be provided as often as possible throughout all phases of the software development process. Some situations in software development teams (team patterns like team establishment phase pattern, project and process status assessment phase pattern, project team crisis phase pattern, project cut phase pattern) require specialized feedback for such a kind of a situation. Some team patterns exist throughout the whole software development process (e.g. role distribution and (re)definition) and have to be handled (e.g. by giving feedback) regularly (a monthly or every two month basis is appropriate).

3.1 Team Establishment Phase Pattern

The proper composition of software engineering teams is a widely discussed topic. Normally teams have four phases starting with their composition [6]: (1) Forming: The roles and responsibilities are not clear within the team. Strengths and weaknesses of team members are not clarified yet. (2) Storming: Roles become clearer. Power struggle can occur. A first impression of strengths and weaknesses of team members has been gained. (3) Norming: Roles and power distribution is clear and not further discussed. Norms are developed for improving performance. Conflicts can be resolved quickly. (4) Performing: Norms have been developed and proven to be good. Performance is at its peak. A commitment about goals and trust between team members has been established.

The first and second phases have significantly lower productivity than the others. Besides the problem of not being used to the other team members, much time is used to stabilize one's own formal an informal position. Conflicts may be the result of lack of sufficient and qualified information about team colleagues:

(1) Unawareness of strengths and weaknesses of team members. A good distribution of roles and an assignment of responsibilities to roles can only be done upon a profound knowledge of strengths and weaknesses of each team member.
(2) Missing feedback about team colleagues' perceptions. People like to be confirmed about their own perception of their own personality attributes and skills. This strengthens the self-esteem of team members within the team. Missing affirmations of these self-perceptions can spawn overcasted actions, which should provoke the desired affirmations. Instead of producing the desired acknowledgement these actions can continuously influence the perceptions of the team colleagues in a negative way.
(3) Conflicting attraction to roles. In case there are more people attracted to certain positions or roles within the team, conflicts about who occupies the role may arise. Such conflicts may be resolved quickly by investigating the real goals and abilities (skills and traits) of team members. Discussions about the best fit of goals and abilities will lead to a good role assignment.

Internal team feedback and self assessments should be applied to open the possibility for the team to improve within the current and coming projects [9].

3.2 Project and Process Status Phase Pattern

The management needs feedback about what is going on in a project regularly. The frequency (weekly, monthly, milestones) mainly depends on the level of the management (project leader, middle or upper management). Most managers concentrate on the hard facts like existing or non-existing products and reached or not reached milestones. For predicting the future performance "soft" facts (like the current estimations of the programmers about the project status; current motivation and satisfaction levels) are very important and valuable as well.

Checklists and project data collection are good instruments for getting the desired hard facts in this pattern. Surveys can be used for assessing hard facts as well as soft facts.

3.3 Project Team Crisis Phase Pattern

People working together face conflicts regularly. Many conflicts arise because of misunderstandings or misleading expectations. Conflict solving strategies therefore are major skills for project teams and their leaders. There a different possible ways in such a situation. Mediation by an outside professional is a very popular one but is very expensive and time consuming because the mediator needs some time to learn about how the team works. Mediation by the management (if there are managers with such skills) has the advantage that this learning phase can be shortened. Anyhow if the manager is too close to the team or single team members, an objective view and therefore meaningful mediation may not be possible any more.

Self assessments and internal team feedback may help to clarify different points of view and enable a discussion about problems caused of misunderstandings.

3.4 Project Cut Phase Pattern

When a project reaches a major cut (project end, major milestone in long running projects connected with project team changes, integration of so far independent subprojects), precious feedback to the team about the team performance as a whole and to single team members may result from following sources: from the customer, from the management, from team members. Surveys, self assessments and project data collections can help to collect all information from the different sources in a suitable and convenient way.

4 Summary

Feedback is vital for any improvement in software development teams. This paper summarizes different ways of feedback, which can and should be applied in software engineering teams. Furthermore the paper discusses typical situations, in which feedback should take place in order to be most effective.

References

[1] C. Chrisman and B. Beccue. Evaluating students in system development group projects. *SIGCSE-Bulletin*, 19(1):366–73, 1987.

[2] Constantine Larry L., *Constantine on Peopleware*; Yourdon Press, Prentice Hall, 1995.

[3] DeMarco T., Lister Th., *Peopleware: Productive Projects and Teams*, 2nd ed., Dorset House, 1999.

[4] J.R. Hackman and G. R. Oldham. Motivation Through the Design of Work: Test of a Theory. *Organizational Behaviour and Human Performance*, pp. 250-79, 1976.

[5] St. P. Robbins: *Organizational Behaviour: Concepts, Controversies, Application*. Prentice Hall, 9th ed., 2001.

[6] B. Tuckman. Developmental sequence in small groups. *Psychological Bulletin*, 63:384–399, 1965.

[7] K. White. Mis project teams: An investigation of cognitive style implications. *MIS Quaterly*, 8(2):95–101, 1984.

[8] D. E. Wilkins and P. B. Lawhead. Evaluating individuals in team projects. *SIGCSE-Bulletin*, 32(1):172–5, 2000.

[9] W. Zuser, Th. Grechenig. Reflecting Skills and Personality Internally as Means for Team Performance Improvement. In *Proceedings IEEE Conferenc. on SE Education and Training 2003*, pp. 234-41, 2003.

Exploring Communities of Practice for Product Family Engineering

Tor Erlend Fægri[1], Björn Decker[2], Torgeir Dingsøyr[1], Letizia Jaccheri[3], Patricia Lago[4], Dirk Muthig[2], and Hans van Vliet[4]

[1] Sintef Information and Communication Technology, Trondheim, Norway
[2] Fraunhofer Institute for Experimental Software Engineering, Kaiserslautern, Germany
[3] Dept. of Computer and Information Science, Norwegian University of Science and Technology, Trondheim, Norway
[4] Vrije Universiteit, Amsterdam, The Netherlands

Abstract. Product Family Engineering (PFE) is an approach to software engineering that seeks to reduce the global effort in producing multiple software products by actively promoting and governing the reuse of assets between the family members. However, PFE is highly demanding, putting stringent demands on careful planning and management in the organization. To leverage the full opportunities offered by PFE, its introduction and use requires effective coordination of people and organizational units. This paper presents a solution to support this coordination by exploring concepts from the area of communities of practices for PFE. The expected benefit is that communities offer a more adaptive approach supporting the transition towards PFE compared to formal organizational restructuring. In this paper, we will describe our considerations about the building principles for organizations using a shared platform for the family members and a study proposal that will examine the effects of knowledge brokering among Communities of Practice as a means to assist PFE.[1]

1 Introduction

Software engineering is a knowledge intensive activity. The demand for increasingly complex and sophisticated products that must be delivered faster and at lower cost, fuels the search for more efficient techniques, processes and methods in the field. Modularization and component-based software engineering techniques are practices that have been widely adopted by many organizations producing software products. They allow for a certain amount of flexibility in the development process that helps to address these challenges. Modules can be developed in parallel or may be supplied by external organizations. Simultaneously, as a consequence of component-orientation

[1] Parts of the reported work has been funded by the project “Virtual Office of the future”, "Stiftung Innovation Rheinland-Pfalz". Other parts of the reported work have been funded by the project Software Process Improvement through Knowledge Engineering (SPIKE) project, a research/industry collaboration partly funded by the Norwegian research Council.

K.-D. Althoff et al. (Eds.): WM 2005, LNAI 3782, pp. 96 – 105, 2005.

and increased complexity, developers loose their holistic view on systems and become specialists of certain subsystems only.

This often causes problems when organizations want to exploit the potential in component-based software engineering of producing multiple products based on common assets. We call this Product Family Engineering (PFE)[2]. PFE seeks to optimize the resource usage in this production process through management of business, architecture, process and organization [1]. Therefore, PFE adds another level of complexity to software engineering processes: individuals are faced with challenges of managing profound and deep knowledge related to performing their own tasks. Specialization increases the boundaries between the individuals, hindering creative collaboration among the groups and may ultimately lead to reduction in job satisfaction.

Communities of Practice (CoP) [2] promise to solve parts of this problem. On the one hand, they enable concurrent and somewhat independent development of products. On the other, they effectively stimulate knowledge sharing among groups of people. As little research is done in the field of knowledge management in PFE organizations so far, we will use a rather open approach in our investigations. We want to examine four different questions to explore CoP in a PFE context: 1) Are there particular aspects of PFE that can benefit from applying communities as organizing principle? 2) Can brokering activities from CoP support PFE organizations in ensuring good knowledge distribution among the workers? 3) How should responsibilities be assigned within the communities? 4) How should we deal with the evolution of assets?

The remainder of the paper is structured as follows: First we introduce PFE and some key problems related to knowledge management. Then we describe Communities of Practice and explain why we see it as an interesting approach to address the problems. In Sections 4 and 5 we explain our proposed techniques; firstly the set of responsibilities (roles) that will benefit the organization of the communities and subsequently a proposed scheme for supporting change management of evolving assets. In Section 6 we describe our research framework in which our investigations will be conducted. Finally we give an overview of related work and an outlook to future research.

2 Product Family Engineering

As the complexity and size of software systems increases people need methods, processes and principles to cope with the scale. One commonly used principle is *divide and conquer*. This may manifest itself as recursive modularization and component-based development. That is, at a certain level of complexity, the software system is partitioned into multiple levels of modules or components (i.e. modules consisting of sub modules, components consisting of sub components). As the complexity reaches a certain level, these components are likely to be developed by different people, different parts of the organization or even different organizations.

---

[2] We use the term Product Family Engineering throughout in this paper. We regard the term Product Line Engineering, used by others, fully equivalent.

After some time, many organizations will establish a repository of such assets, including significant experience related to their use and limitations.

Now, the company might see a potential to exploit this repository to support a product family – for example with the objective to target different markets with somewhat similar products, using distinct combinations of these assets. This reduces the amount of product specific code that goes into each product, thus promising to reduce cost of development and time to market. Similarly, valuable experience related to the use of the assets is maintained. We believe it is important to understand aspects related to how the organization can use this experience to support continuous learning. The figure below illustrates the problem context.

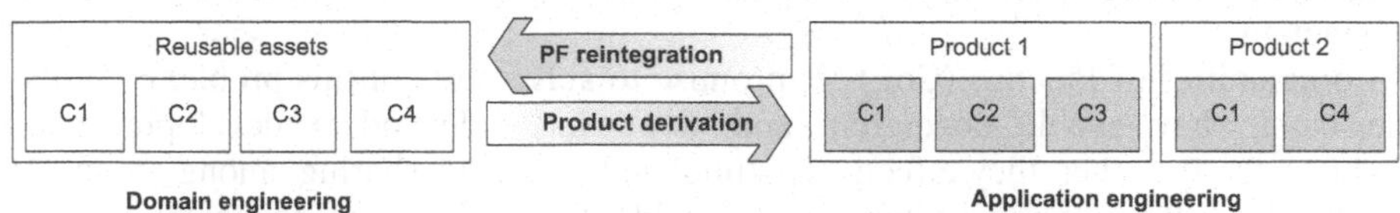

Fig. 1. Product derivation and asset reintegration

According to [3], a software product family is a set of software-intensive systems that share a common, managed set of features satisfying the specific needs of a particular market segment or mission and that are developed from a common set of core assets in a prescribed way. Therefore, PFE is the key approach for managed, intra-organizational, large scale reuse, thus leveraging the opportunities that are offered by the application domain of a software organization. On a high level, the activities to achieve this reuse are subdivided into domain engineering and application engineering (see figure 1). Domain engineering encompasses the activities to create and maintain a complete and consistent set of artifacts to be reused by developments of software systems in a certain domain (i.e., a product family platform). Application engineering subsumes all activities reusing artifacts in such a platform while developing single systems (i.e. family members) [4]. For assets within the product family platform, the variability is explicitly captured. This explicit management of variability differentiates PFE from other reuse approaches like framework or library engineering, which mostly focus on the identification of commonalities.

However, facilitating large-scale reuse – and thus justifying the investments in the software product family - implies a two-way evolution. First, the PFE approach itself has to be adapted to the changing needs of the organization. Second, PFE implies a controlled evolution of these assets to keep the integrity of the product family platform. On the one hand, PFE has to coordinate more people across more organizational sub-structures like project, business units or departments compared to single systems engineering. On the other hand, the freedom of those sub-structures should be kept to the largest extent.

Achieving these ambitions requires elaborate planning, operative support and careful attention to organizational capabilities [5]. An often touted benefit of PFE is the potential for streamlining the product production process by organizing the workforce into two groups, one building reusable assets (i.e. domain engineering), and one building products from these assets (i.e. application engineering). In this way, the organization can foster specialist knowledge among the people developing reusable assets while allowing people with solution building strengths to exploit the asset repository in assembling complex products. However, the effects of this segmentation have not yet been thoroughly investigated [1]. Furthermore, another problem from practice with this style of development is that specialists only receive indirect and sometimes insufficient feedback from field applications.

Capturing, representing and sharing domain knowledge in a PFE organization can be assisted by artifacts such as patterns, frameworks and reference architectures [6]. Also, proper knowledge representation eases communication of architectural principles through the development organization [7]. Additionally, relevant domain knowledge not only concerns the structure and contents of the domain, but also organizational and managerial aspects. For example, if a company has a divisionalized structure such as a set of business units, this may impact its software assets. Capturing and explicitly documenting such attributes enriches our knowledge of these assets. Furthermore, experience with PFE evolution shows that it is often hampered by tacit assumptions. These may be technical (such as standards concerning the underlying platform on which products rely), but equally often they are managerial or organizational in nature [8]. Thus, we believe it is worthwhile to further investigate knowledge management practices within PFE organizations.

This leads to the following three challenges concerning PFE: introduction, asset usage and asset evolution: During *introduction* of PFE, the members of an organization need to learn how to work together in a product family context. The most promising approach is to incrementally add assets to a product family platform, which implies a scaleable organization of this learning effort. The *asset usage* needs to be supported by platform developers that help appliers in integrating assets into the systems derived from the product family (i.e. during application engineering). Concerning *asset evolution*, feedback gained from asset usage gives the asset developers directions on how to evolve asset to met the needs of the appliers (i.e. during domain engineering). The summarized, underlying challenge is to optimize communication among product family stakeholders, thus reducing the overhead to coordinate their activities.

3 Communities of Practice and Brokering

To address this coordination we investigate an online community of practice as a flexible organization form addressing these challenges. In the course of this paper we adapt the definition of [2, 9, 10]: Communities of practice are understood as a group of people sharing the same (professional) interest and who interact regularly to learn how to do their jobs better. Such communities differ from normal business units in that their purpose is knowledge-creation, and they are usually loosely connected, self-managed and informal. Communities of Practice enable the capturing and transferring of tacit knowledge by letting people from different departments in an organization discuss common topics of interest.

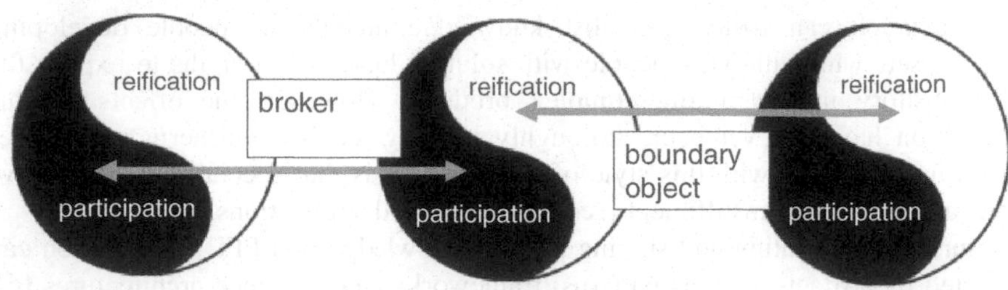

Fig. 2. Communities of Practice

Communities of Practice are said to consist of two main parts: *participation* in the community – interacting and "active involvement in social enterprises" [2] and *reification*, the process of creating artifacts from the community, like documents (see figure above).

Knowledge sharing between Communities of Practice is referred to as *boundary relations,* where connecting communities through participation is called *brokering,* and through reification *boundary objects.* Many practices can classify as brokering – like job rotation, physical design of work-environment to stimulate cross-sectional discussions etc. Typical boundary objects are documents that are shared between communities. In the case of PFE communities, brokers are prominent stakeholders in product family. The boundary objects are the assets within the product platform. Organizations report that such communities help improve communication and save time by "working smarter" [10]. Communities depend on communication, but not on a specific way of communication. The community can be organized around regular meetings, face to face or on-line, but also on interacting through mailing list or news group discussions between meetings. Communities often also include a role as a contact point to get relevant knowledge in a topic area for people not participating in the community. Because most people who are involved in a Community of Practice have their main responsibility in one of the business units, it is important to organize it in a flexible manner. Work should not depend on particular individuals being active at all times. Usually, one person in the core group is appointed as coordinator with the responsibility of arranging meetings.

We therefore define a product family community within an organization as the group of people using and contributing to the product family platform. The purpose (or mission) of this community is: To support the exchange of experience about product family related issues among members, to facilitate the adaptation and evolution of product family practices and to introduce new members to PFE. In this paper, we will present our considerations on how such communities can be established in a PFE context. In particular, we will describe a more detailed role model that focuses on the brokering aspect of communities, while the evolution of assets is emphasizing how boundary object are used within PFE communities.

4 Distributing Responsibilities for Product Family Assets

One major influence on optimizing coordination is a clear definition of responsibilities. Furthermore, this distribution of responsibilities needs to be clear and simple to avoid creating overhead while assigning and determining responsibilities. Our suggestion for this distribution is a simple general assignment based on the impact of assets, combined with a role model to clarify the responsibilities of the individual member of the community.

The classification in [11] provides a distinction of the assets within the platform: On the top level, it distinguishes domain assets and application assets. Application assets are work-products of application engineering, while domain assets capture the domain experience in a reusable form. A special sub-category of domain assets are meta-assets that contain information to reuse other assets. Since these meta-assets can be documentation of methodologies of PFE, they can also be used to introduce such methodologies.

To maintain the integrity of the platform, responsibilities have to be assigned to knowledgeable persons, preferably people with a good overview of the platform (i.e. platform developers). This is of particular importance for meta-assets, where each asset describes a certain view of the whole platform. This structure also helps to evaluate appropriate mechanisms for evolution management: Assets with a high impact are more likely to receive more feedback, since more users are involved compared to assets with lower impact. In addition, faults in these assets will affect more users. Therefore, the evolution mechanisms should be simple and impose low overhead. The quality control of the evolved asset should be more rigid. For less impacting assets like application assets, the feedback can be more complex, whereas inconsistencies can be (temporarily) tolerated.

Based on these considerations, we adopt the generic role model for communities presented by [12]: Visitor, newbie, member, leader, senior. Furthermore, we will also investigate the motivation of being in the product family community: The *visitor* could be any software developer inside the organization that is not already a member of the product family community. To allow the visitor to decide whether to become a member, meta-assets and description of generic assets should be readable with no registration. However, to get an overview of the product where a certain asset is used, the access to solution assets might be restricted. A visitor becomes a *newbie* when s/he actively wants to use the results of the product family, i.e., when the visitor registers to download a component. Therefore, the membership of the newbie can be recognized, and further educational activities can be triggered. The newbie becomes a regular *member* when s/he provides feedback about asset application, which implies that the applied solution asset is used inside a development project. The main motivation for *newbies* as well as members is to use the assets within the product family platform. Since the product family platform provides more support to a member as long as changes do not affect the integrity, there is also motivation to invest extra effort in maintaining this integrity. The next role level is the *leader*, when the regular member coordinates community activities. For each asset, at least one leader is assigned that is responsible for coordinating further implementing members during the evolution of the asset and for handling feedback and questions. Since this role needs additional effort that might not be covered, the organization should provide additional effort for performing this role. Some of the active leaders might become *seniors*, which take care of evolving the product family as a whole. These seniors also act as leaders for meta-assets supporting product family application.

The application of communities in PFE allows measuring the impact on the business of an organization in a concrete way: First, the impact of an asset is explicitly described by its variability. Second, the quality and benefit of assets are validated by application in systems derived from the product family. This allows an organization to justify investments into the community like the assignment of effort for experts mentioned above.

5 Issue Management for Evolving Assets

Controlling the evolution, i.e. managing the changes to an asset in the product family platform, is key to avoid architecture degradation. The explicit variability of product family assets allows identifying affected users not only on an asset level, but based on the variability actually used by certain members. These subgroups created by variability usage allow handling the following communication procedures even if a large number of members are using a certain asset. We propose three communication procedures for managing asset related issues: Relate and comment, consensus based, and transfer and re-integrate.

Relate and comment is used when the users of an asset might detect problems during reusing an asset, but do not have the competence or experience to decide whether this change affects the integrity of the product family or not. In this case, users are allowed to comment the asset, but are not allowed to change its content. An example would be a change in a meta-asset like a process description about product family methodologies.

Consensus-based is used when an asset is used by several users which also have the knowledge to change it in a way such that the product family integrity is not affected. Then, consensus about how the changes are implemented is reached through discussion. An example is a code component, where the implementation of missing variability is distributed among the users of this component.

Transfer and re-integrate is used when project pressure avoid changing an asset in a controlled way or when the effort to gain a consensus exceeds the effort to re-integrate the changed asset in the product family later. In this case, the asset is transferred into the baseline of the project an integrated later on.

6 Suggested Study

As depicted in Fig. 3 (below), PFE represents knowledge about the product families mainly from two perspectives: the representation of the common and variable features in the product family (feature models - depicted in the left part of the figure) and the representation of technical assets like code components (structural models - depicted in the right part of the figure). Feature and structural models can be used by the Communities of Practice as the core mechanisms for brokering: feature models are domain-level representations that can be easily understood by people that want to decide on the functionality of products; structural models are representations (of generic/reusable and concrete/product-specific solutions) that can be used by people producing or using reusable assets.

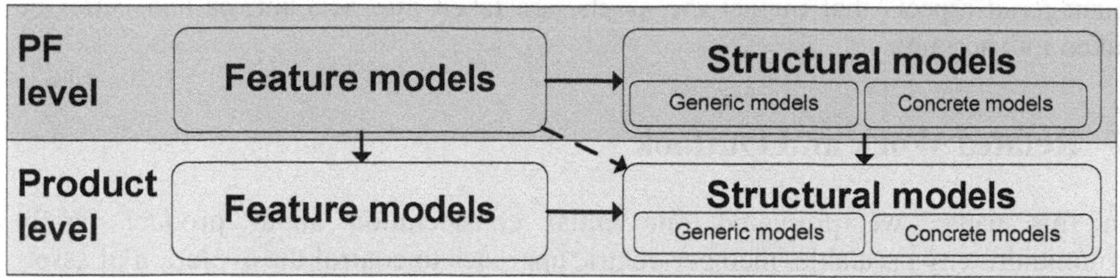

Fig. 3. Product Family modeling framework

Further, PFE knowledge can be represented at the family level (in the top half of the figure above) and at the product level (in the lower half of the figure). The Product Family level describes the aspects shared by all products in the family, whereas the Product level focuses on aspects that are specific to individual products.

The arrows represent traceability links that model the derivation dependencies between models. They can be navigated to share knowledge about artifacts. For example, the horizontal arrows (between feature model and structural model) can be used to learn how a feature has been implemented by a selected component. The vertical arrows (crossing the two levels) can be used to learn if/how elements at the product family level are supported by corresponding elements in different products (e.g. which features shared by the product family are supported in which products, or how a product family component is refined within a selected product).

For a product family to be successful, it is important to understand the factors related to adoption and refinement of reusable assets in the products. It is also important to understand how these aspects relate to the scoping of the PF level feature models, i.e. the ability of the asset repository to reflect the real needs in the product development groups. This is paramount in order to maintain a vital repository that is able to support the required variability in the product family. It is an enabler for organizational learning.

We intend to investigate how knowledge sharing through brokering between people working with reusable assets and products affects the dynamics of the product family, in particular the level of alignment of the repository of reusable assets at the system family level compared to the assets actually used in the delivered products. We will also study the effects of knowledge brokering with regards to reintegration of capabilities developed in the product organizations back into the system family. We will classify these effects for the different roles defined above (visitor, newbie, member, leader and senior) and across the three proposed communication schemes (relate and comment, consensus based, and transfer and re-integrate). The development repositories and issue management systems might act as a source of data for this.

Due to lack of validated metrics [13, 14], we have chosen a qualitative study. Through semi-structured interviews, we suggest studying two different organizations working with product families, and choose a) a company that has few or no brokering between reusable asset and product departments, and b) a company that has many brokering practices in place. We will study brokering on functional and non-functional aspects of assets, as well as the extent to which organizational and managerial aspects that impact the assets, are taken into account, or had better be taken into account.

7 Related Work and Outlook

In this paper, we presented our initial consideration about product family communities as a scalable, member-centric approach to control the evolution of assets in product families. Other approaches address this issue from an organizational point of view:

Bosch [15] gives an overview of four different explicit organizational structures suitable for product families (Development Department, Business Units, Domain Engineering Units, Hierarchical Domain Engineering Units) and also gives criteria when to apply which organizational structure. In [16] he organizes these structures according to the three dimensions concerning scope of product family platform, responsibilities level and lifetime of product family activities. Schmid [17] explains why an organizational structure based on features rather than on development phases offers a more promising approach. He also lists a range of communication patterns and organizational success factors of product family approaches. In between the organizational and individual point of view is the experience report of the Owen software cooperative at HP by [18].

Our approach to establish product families with communities does not contradict these approaches. Product family communities can be organized according to these approaches, in particular when product families have been established within an organization.

Beyond the survey presented in this paper we see two major directions for future research in software product families: 1) Analyzing and adapting organizational principles in Open Source development. Product family communities are based on voluntary participation like open source communities. Successful organizational patterns (e.g. meritocracy) from open source development might support the instantiation of product family communities. However, these patterns might need adaptation due to the commercial and intra-organizational setting. 2) Quantifying the business benefits generated by communities. This is a problem for communities in general [19]. However, product family communities create a magnitude of analyzable artifacts (code, documentation), which builds a promising basis for such analysis.

References

1. Linden, F.v.d., *Software product families in Europe: The ESAPS and CAFÉ projects.* IEEE Software, 2002. **19**(4): p. 41-49.
2. Wenger, E.C., *Communities of Practice: Learning, meaning and identity.* 1998: Cambridge University Press.
3. Clements, P. and L. Northrop, *Software product lines: Practices and Patterns.* The SEI series in software engineering. 2002: Addison Wesley. 563.
4. Muthig, D., *A Light-weight Approach Facilitating an Evolutionary Transition Towards Software Product Lines.* 2002, Stuttgart: Fraunhofer IRB Verlag.

5. Bühle, S., et al. *Exploring the context of product line adoption*. in *5th International workshop on Product Family Engineering*. F.V.d. Linden, Editor. 2003. Siena, Italy: Springer Verlag.
6. Hallsteinsen, S., T.E. Fægri, and M. Syrstad. *Patterns in Product Family Architecture Design*. in *5th International workshop on Product Family Engineering*. F.V.d. Linden, Editor. 2003. Siena, Italy: Springer Verlag.
7. Mustapic, G. *Real World Influences on Software Architecture - Interviews with Industrial System Experts*. in *WICSA-4*. 2004. Oslo, Norway.
8. Lago, P. and H.v. Vliet. *Observations from the Recovery of a Software Product Family*. in *Third software product line conference*. 2004: Springer.
9. Wenger, E.C., *Communities of practice: A brief introduction*.
10. Wenger, E.C., R. McDermott, and W.M. Snyder, *Cultivating Communities of Practice*. 2002, Boston: Hardvard Business School Press.
11. Becker, M., *Anpassungsunterstützung in Software-Produktfamilien*, in *Technical Universität of Kaiserslautern, Department of Computer Science*. 2004.
12. Kim, A.J., *Community Building. Strategien für den Aufbau erfolgreicher Web-Communities*. 2001, Bonn: Galileo Press.
13. Fenton, N. and M. Neil, *Software metrics: A roadmap*, in *The future of software engineering*, A. Finkenstein, Editor. 2000, ACM Press: New York.
14. Seaman, C.B., *Qualitative Methods in Empirical Studies of Software Engineering*. IEEE Transactions on Software Engineering, 1999. **25**(4): p. 557-572.
15. Bosch, J. *Organizing for Software Product Lines*. in *In Third International Workshop on Software Architectures for Product Families*. 2000.
16. Bosch, J. *Software Product Lines: Organizational Alternatives*. in *In Proceedings of the 23rd International Conference on Software Engineering*. 2001: IEEE Computer Society Press.
17. Schmid, K. *People Managemement in Institutionalizing Product Lines*. in *In Proceedings of Net.ObjectDays*. 2003.
18. Toft, P., D. Coleman, and J. Ohta. *A Cooperative Model for Cross-Divisional Product Development for a Software Product Line*. in *Proceedings of the First Software Product Line Conference*. P. Donohoe, Editor. 2000: Kluwer Academic Publishers.
19. Millen, D.R., M.A. Fontaine, and M.M. J., *Understanding the benefits and costs of communities of practice*. Communications of the ACM, 2002. **45**(4): p. 69-73.

Systematical Validation of Learning in Agile Software Development Environment

Outi Salo

VTT Technical Research Centre of Finland,
P.O. Box 1100, FIN-90571 Oulu, Finland
Outi.Salo@vtt.fi

Abstract. This paper illustrates implications from four case studies in which Agile software development teams conducted iterative project retrospectives to improve and adapt their software development processes. It was detected that the existing techniques lack a systematic approach to iteratively validate the implementation and effectiveness of software process improvement actions with both quantitative and qualitative data. Also, the case studies revealed that the organizational level can only benefit from the learning of project teams if the knowledge and reasoning behind the process improvements is converted into such an explicit format that it can be utilized for learning in organizational level also. Thus, this paper illustrates how these deprivations were accomplished in the case projects with the support of a structured template.

1 Introduction

Agile software development offers both need and opportunity for adapting and improving the software development process rapidly and effectively. One of the Agile principles (http://agilemanifesto.org/principles.html) is that the team should regularly reflect on how to become more effective, and tune and adjust its behavior accordingly. The short development cycles provide continuous and rapid loops to iteratively enhance the process during Agile software development projects.

Some techniques suggest how the learning of the project team could be iteratively transferred into concrete software process improvements in Agile software development, namely a reflection workshop technique [1] and postmortem reviews [2]. While both of these techniques most likely accomplish this goal, they both seem to lack the means to systematically validate the effects of the improvements. However, Extreme Programming (XP) [3], for one, requires that the teams can change the rules only if they also agree on how they will assess the effects of the change [4]. Nor do the existing techniques provide guidance on how the tacit or even explicit knowledge and learning of the project teams can be converted into an explicit form that can be utilized in organizational learning as well.

In this paper, an extension for the existing project retrospective techniques is proposed to support the systematic implementation and validation of software process improvements in Agile projects using both quantitative and qualitative data, and to provide organizational level with insights into the projects. The propositions

K.-D. Althoff et al. (Eds.): WM 2005, LNAI 3782, pp. 106 – 110, 2005.

presented in this paper are particularly suitable for Agile software development context where the continuum of short iterations provide the opportunity for such activities.

2 Research Context

The research was conducted at VTT Technical Research Centre of Finland in four Agile case studies (Table 1). The case projects used an XP [3] based software development process that evolved during the case projects to include relevant extensions such as SPI activities.

Table 1. Characteristics of the case projects

Characteristic	eXpert	zOmbie	bAmbie	uniCorn
Team size	4 developers	5.5 developers	4 developers	6 developers
Total team effort	7.5 PM	10 PM	5.5 PM	5.2 PM
End product	Intranet app	Mobile app	Mobile app	Mobile app
Iterations	3 x two weeks 3 x one week	1 x one week 3 x two weeks 2 x one week	1 x one week 3 x two weeks 2 x one week	2 x two weeks 7 x one week

In all case projects, project retrospectives were conducted iteratively to improve and adapt the software development process. The last retrospective in every project was considered a project postmortem, contributing more directly to the organizational level software process improvement. All the previous retrospectives, however, concentrated on the iterative learning and improvement of a single project yet also supported a "bottom-up approach" for organizational learning.

The technique used, i.e. Post-Iteration Workshops, (hereafter referred as PIWs) combines and adapts certain elements from both the workshop technique [1] and the postmortem review technique [2] (as presented in [5]). Furthermore, it includes modifications and extensions evolved and experimented in the series of case studies.

3 Systematic Validation of Process Improvements

Soon after the first case study it was realized that a systematic way to validate the effects of learning (i.e., the process improvement actions agreed by the project team in the retrospectives) was needed for two specific reasons. Firstly, the project itself could control the implementation of the agreed process enhancements and evaluate whether they actually improved the process. Secondly, the organization needed a way to examine how and why individual projects adapted their base process, and how successfully. Without this kind of explicit knowledge supported with qualitative and quantitative data, the process changes in organizational level would be a shot in the dark rather than validated learning to be shared and diffused organizationally.

A structured template (i.e., an Action Point List) was generated to provide guidance for project team on the issues to be considered for every process improvement action and information for both project and organizational levels of how the SPI in individual

Improvement Topic: Test-Driven Development				
Finding	**Action Point**	**Actor**	**Validation plan**	**Validation**
Deficiency and lacking of TDD test cases caused by absent knowledge of TDD.	Support team will coach the team the next planning day Analyse the quality and coverage of test cases (1st and 2nd iteration)	Project Manager Tracker	Team will interpret the data from 1st and 2nd iteration in the next PIW to evaluate the improvement.	Situation not improved based on the experiences of the team and the metrics data. More support needed for the next iteration (=> new ap).
Improvement Topic: Configuration management				
Finding	**Action Point**	**Actor**	**Validation plan**	**Validation**
Corrections made during release day caused irrecoverable situation.	Baseline made at the beginning of release day (instead at the end)	Project Manager	Team will discuss the improvement of the situation in the next PIW.	Working fine according to the team. Ongoing practice.
Improvement Topic: Task estimation				
Finding	**Action Point**	**Actor**	**Validation plan**	**Validation**
Task estimations too inaccurate in release 1. => release delayed.	Analyse task data to evaluate the cause of delays in each task.	Tracker	Team interprets the data in the next PIW to find ways to improve.	Data revealed too big tasks. Splitting needed.
Splitting of tasks needed to improve effort estimation.	Task will be split to max. 4 hours size. Analysis of effort estimations.	Project Manager Tracker	Interpret the metrics data in the next PIW to see if effort estimations improved.	Smaller task size seemed to improve effort estimation. 4 hours is a good size for task when possible.

Fig. 1. Example of filled Action Point List

projects made progress. It was filled in every PIW session with the moderator and the project team. Also, the list from the previous PIW was updated regarding the validation of earlier SPI actions according to the validation plan. Figure 1 illustrates the structure of the template along with a set of examples from the case projects.

In the PIW's, the problematic issues that the software developers had faced during the previous iteration were generated and structured using the KJ method [6], as also suggested in postmortem review technique [2]. These grouped and labeled findings were then the basis for focus group discussion [7] that aimed for discovering and agreeing process enhancements for the subsequent iteration. The "Improvement Topic" field in Action Point List refers to the labels of the grouped findings that the project team generated on the flap board during the PIW. This way the process improvements could be traced all the way back to the groups of findings in certain workshop. The purpose of the "Finding" field is to provide sufficiently detailed explicit knowledge of the specific problems in each topic area based on the discussion of the project team. "Action point" field clarifies what is the mutually agreed concrete action to be taken in the next iteration to improve the situation. "Actor" defines the responsibilities for each action point to ensure its implementation. The "Validation plan" field is used to record the project team's decisions on how the success of the improvement will be assessed effectively and also to reveal the schedule of the action. The validation should be carefully considered for each action point. The qualitative data (i.e. experience) of the software developers is always needed in validating if a certain process enhancement really is an improvement. Often, however, quantitative verification is also needed, especially for the organizational level. In such a case the availability and analysis of the metrics needed should be planned at this point. The "Validation" field is filled in the next PIW as the validation is carried out as planned including the possible interpretations of analyzed data. In practice, the data interpretation and sharing of experiences during a group discussion often generated new improvement opportunities and action points. Also, one goal of validation is to agree if the specific process improvement should be further employed or rejected.

It can be said that the changes made in the project level were usually fairly small, yet effective enough to ease up the daily work of the project team and increase their motivation [5, 8]. The more radical decisions on improving the process were made in the organizational level often based on the ideas generated by the project teams. These improvement opportunities (e.g., changes to organizational data tracking tools) could not be done on the project level alone.

4 Discussion

Agile software development provides an opportunity to iteratively generate and implement enhancements during the software development process. In the case studies, the PIWs were conducted based partly on the two existing Agile techniques, namely a reflection workshop technique [1] and postmortem reviews [2]. They were found to be effective and motivating in improving and adapting the software development process in Agile case projects [5, 7]. However, it was realized that the earlier suggested techniques lacked the mechanisms to support the iterative implementation and evaluation of the process improvement actions, and thus, they were included in the PIW technique. Also, it was realized that the organizational level will benefit from the learning of projects only if the knowledge and reasoning behind the process improvements are converted into such an explicit form that can be utilized for learning on the organizational level as well.

Thus, this paper discusses how the systematic implementation and verification of the software process improvements as well as the flow of process knowledge from projects to organizational level can be supported with a template. It guides the project team to the issues to be considered for every process improvement action, including the quantitative follow-up of the process enhancements. The sequential "Action Point Lists" also provide a means to transfer the knowledge between project and organizational levels and should be supplemented with the analysis and interpreted of quantitative data when needed. As the organizational level can view concrete chains of reasoning behind the software process improvement actions - supported with both quantitative and qualitative data, it can gain new ideas and insights from single projects which is essential if learning is to take place on the organizational level [8].

The focus of this paper is to point out the importance of the systematic follow-up and validation of software process improvements in iterative SPI cycles during Agile software development and to discuss how the benefits of this kind of project level software process improvement should be utilized in organizational level also. This paper is an important part of research of continuous software process improvement in Agile software development context. The thorough analysis of the research data for validating the proposed solution and as well as the presentation of the PIW technique are out of the scope of this paper.

Acknowledgements

This study is done in Agile-ITEA project funded by TEKES (National Technology Agency of Finland). It is part of larger research topic of continuous software process improvement in Agile software development context. Acknowledgements to the software developers of all the case projects for their thorough participation in the process improvement activities. Also, sincere thanks to Dr. Pekka Abrahamsson, Hanna Hulkko and Minna Pikkarainen for their valuable comments.

References

1. Cockburn, A., *Agile Software Development*. The Agile Software Development Series, ed. A. Cockburn and J. Highsmith. 2002, Boston: Addison-Wesley. 278.
2. Dingsøyr, T. and G.K. Hanssen. *Extending Agile Methods: Postmortem Reviews as Extended Feedback*. in *4th International Workshop on Learning Software Organizations (LSO'02))*. 2002. Chicago, Illinois, USA.
3. Beck, K., *Extreme Programming Explained: Embrace Change*. 2000: Addison Wesley Longman, Inc. 190.
4. Beck, K., *Embracing Change with Extreme Programming*. IEEE Computer, 1999. **32**(10): p. 70-77.
5. Salo, O., et al. *Self-Adaptability of Agile Software Processes: A Case Study on Post-Iteration Workhops*. in *5th International Conference on Extreme Programming and Agile Processes in Software Engineering (XP 2004)*. 2004. Garmisch-Partenkirchen, Germany: Springer.
6. Scupin, R., *The KJ Method: A Technique for Analyzing Data Derived from Japanese Ethnology*. Human Organization, 1997. **56**(2): p. 233-237.
7. Kerlinger, F.N. and H.B. Lee, *Foundations of Behavioral Research*. Fourth Edition ed. 2002: Harcourt College Publishers. 890.
8. Salo, O. *Improving Software Process in Agile Software Development Projects: Results from Two XP Case Studies*. in *EUROMICRO 2004*. 2004. Rennes, France: IEEE Computer Society Press.
9. Garvin, D.A., *Learning in Action*. 2000, Boston, Massachusetts: Harvard Business School Press. 256.

Knowledge Management in a Software Development Environment to Support Software Processes Deployment

Gleison Santos[1], Karina Villela[2,*], Mariano Montoni[1], Ana Regina Rocha[1], Guilherme H. Travassos[1], Sávio Figueiredo[1], Sômulo Mafra[1], Adriano Albuquerque[1], Benito Diaz Paret[3], and Márcio Amaral[3]

[1] COPPE/Federal University of Rio de Janeiro,
Caixa Postal 68511, CEP 21945 –970, Rio de Janeiro - RJ, Brazil
{gleison, mmontoni, darocha, ght, sávio, somulo, bessa}@cos.ufrj.br

[2] University of Salvador
Rua Ponciano Oliveira 126, Rio Vermelho, CEP 40170–100, Salvador - Ba, Brazil
kvillela@unifacs.br

[3] Riosoft – Núcleo Softex do Rio de Janeiro,
Rua Buenos Aires 68, 32° andar, Rio de Janeiro - RJ, Brazil
{benito, mpamaral}@riosoft.softex.br

Abstract. Software Engineering is a wide area of knowledge and various other types of knowledge are required during the software development and maintenance. This paper describes a survey carried out to characterize the importance given by software developers to varying types of knowledge mentioned in the technical literature on Software Engineering. The survey results have been used to guide the elaboration and incorporation of content and tools to the TABA workstation, which allows one to configure and instantiate software development environments for different companies. This paper also addresses the use of the TABA workstation to support software processes deployment in small and medium size Brazilian companies. The goal is to increase the capability of software organizations by the adequate use of Software Engineering techniques in their development and maintenance processes.

1 Introduction

Software engineering is a wide knowledge area made up of various sub areas [1]. In addition to this, the activity of software development requires computing knowledge, knowledge of the intended application domain as well as knowledge of the application itself. Another aspect to be taken into account is the experimental, evolutionary and non-repetitive characteristics of the software engineering area [2], which means that there are approaches that work best in certain situations and it is necessary to tailor them in order to deal with new situations. Moreover, unforeseen events may occur despite careful software project planning. This implies making constant choices from among the many feasible options throughout the software life cycle [3]. As a result, many software companies have recognized the importance of

* This is the affiliation of the author after she finished her PHD thesis at the Federal University of Rio de Janeiro, where the work presented here was carried out.

K.-D. Althoff et al. (Eds.): WM 2005, LNAI 3782, pp. 111 – 120, 2005.

administrating knowledge effectively, productively and creatively at both the individual and organizational levels [4].

Software Development Environments (SDE) has been playing an important role to support software engineers in the execution of software processes through the application of specific procedures that combine integrated tools and techniques in accordance to particular software paradigms. Process-Centred Environments are the most recent generation of SDE, whose goal is to guide and assist developers in the application of software development methods, by exploiting an explicit representation of the process [11]. Moreover, SDE are evolving to integrate knowledge management activities within software processes aiming to foster the institutionalization of a learning software organization [9]. Nevertheless, a fundamental step towards the successful introduction of Knowledge Management in software development environments is the identification and the prioritization of the required knowledge in such environments so as to guide the elaboration and/or incorporation of content and the development of services and tools gradually.

This paper describes a survey carried out to characterize the importance given by software developers to varying types of knowledge mentioned in the technical literature on Software Engineering. The survey results have been used to guide the elaboration and incorporation of content and tools for the TABA workstation. This paper also addresses the use of the TABA Workstation to support the deployment of software processes in small and medium size Brazilian companies.

2 Survey on the Importance Attributed to Different Knowledge in Software Development Environments

A survey was planned and carried out using an experimentation process adapted from Wohlin *et al.* [5]. The goal was to identify the types of knowledge programmers, analysts, project managers and company directors based in Salvador[1] considered the most important in the organizational environments for software development.

2.1 Survey Description

Table 1 presents the survey definition according to the GQM (Goal Question Metric) template [5].

Table 1. Survey definition

Analyse	the organizational environments for software development and maintenance
For the purpose of	characterizing the knowledge mentioned in the technical literature on Software Engineering
With respect to	perceived importance in terms of the need to have the knowledge available throughout the development and maintenance of software
From the point of view of	programmers, analysts, project managers and company directors
In the context of	software projects carried out in the year 2002 by companies located in Salvador

[1] Salvador is a city of 2.5 million inhabitants located in the Northeast of Brazil.

The professional population involved in the development and maintenance of software in the city of Salvador was estimated at 472 according to figures from the Brazilian Ministry of Labour. A sample of this population was selected from two national survey reports and a census carried out by the Brazilian Ministry of Science and Technology. Of the 27 companies mentioned in the reports, 18 were located and agreed to take part in the survey which made an initial sample of 99 programmers, 203 analysts, 61 managers and 30 directors, 393 people in total.

The survey planning also included the formulation of hypotheses, survey design, preparation for its instrumentation, identification of threats to its validity [5] and the adoption of procedures to deal with these threats.

The survey instrument was represented by a set of questionnaires including 19 questions for company, project and professional description as well as 96 questions for collecting software professionals' opinions on the importance of the many types of knowledge. The survey participant could answer that each type of knowledge was *not important*, *of little importance*, *important*, *very important*, *indispensable* or *not evaluated*. Despite the number of questions, all 96 questions could be answered using this same scale, which made the questionnaire easy and fast to answer. The terms which were thought might cause misunderstanding or be unknown were explained by using footnotes and the participants had the opportunity to ask the meaning of any terms at anytime. However, only the participants who were personally interviewed did so.

The rate of non-response was 55.56% for programmers, 62.56% for analysts, 44.26% for project managers and 66.67% for directors. 153 valid questionnaires were received, 41 from programmers, 70 from analysts, 32 from managers and 10 from directors.

Groups of companies, projects and participants were established to test the hypotheses. This was done to investigate the independence of the importance attributed to the type of knowledge in terms of size of company, size of project and the qualifications and experience of the professionals. To test the hypotheses Pearson's chi-squared test was applied.

The results obtained, while being statistically significant, are in themselves insufficient to establish a strategy for the construction and/or introduction of Knowledge Management Systems in Software Organizations. Therefore ordered lists of the types of knowledge mentioned in the questionnaires were drawn up according to the importance attached by each group of participants (for example: programmers of small companies). Following this, a list of the types of knowledge was drawn up according to the occurrence of each type of knowledge among the 25 most important and the 25 least important of each previous list. The rationale used was that the more important the type of knowledge, the greater the number of its occurrences among the most important 25 and the lower the number of occurrences among the least important. In the table below the 45 types of knowledge considered the most important are listed.

2.2 Interpretation of Results

From Table 2 it is possible to notice the descending order of importance among the following groups of knowledge: best practices identified by the organization and other types of organizational knowledge related to software development and maintenance;

Table 2. General classification of the types of knowledge as regards their attributed importance

	Type of Knowledge
1º	Organization best practices for coding
2º	Organization best practices for tests
3º	Organization best practices for software documentation
4º	Organization best practices for quality assurance
5º	Knowledge about the organization software processes
5º	Organization best practices for the problem solving process
7º	Organization best practices for specification and analysis of software requirements
8º	Organization best practices for software design
9º	Knowledge about the application domain
10º	Organization best practices for project management
11º	Organization best practices for system engineering
12º	Templates of documents, including real examples of their use
13º	Organization best practices for the evaluation and improvement of software processes
14º	Software items such as specifications, system architecture, source code and test cases
15º	Organization best practices for process modelling
16º	Organization best practices for software maintenance
17º	Knowledge about the evaluation of the organization software processes
18º	Knowledge about the distribution of competences among the organization professionals
19º	Reports on the best practices in the software industry
20º	Knowledge about organizational objectives and goals
20º	Organization best practices for training
22º	Organization historical data related to project management
23º	Organization best practices for system operation (hardware, software etc.) and support to users
23º	Knowledge about the types of software developed in the organization
25º	Organization best practices for reuse of software items
26º	References to technological developments in Software Engineering
26º	Reports on the lessons learned by the software industry
28º	Knowledge about the critical organizational areas to the achievement of organizational objectives
29º	Organization historical data related to product metrics
30º	References to theoretical knowledge about Software Engineering
31º	Knowledge about the organization's restrictions and about its weaknesses and strengths
32º	Organization historical data related to quality assurance
33º	Organization historical data related to process metrics
34º	Knowledge about the organizational processes
35º	Knowledge about the mission of the organization
36º	Organization best practices for configuration management
37º	Organization best practices for risk management
38º	Knowledge about organizational guidelines and standards
39º	Answers for the most frequent questions made by organization software developers
40º	Representation of the organizational structure
41º	Knowledge about the organizational processes of client companies
42º	Organization best practices for the process of supplying software products
43º	Representation of the organizational structure of client companies
44º	Knowledge about the allocation of client companies' staff to their respective organizational units
45º	Knowledge about the technical partners' restrictions and about their weaknesses and strengths

knowledge about the applicatioon domain; knowledge about the organization which develops and maintains software, knowledge from technical literature and historical data related to software development and maintenance; knowledge about the clients and finally knowledge about technical partners.

Further comments can be made with regard to the results:

- the most important types of knowledge identified were related to software product engineering rather than project management,
- we believe organization best practices were so well evaluated because they represent knowledge already consolidated and tailored and thus ready for use,
- the knowledge about the organizational processes was not considered so important. It was expected that the importance of this type of knowledge would be higher in companies that develop and maintain software for their own use, as would the knowledge about the organizational processes of client companies in companies that develop and maintain software for third parties. However, the rating above can be partially explained due to the fact that these types of knowledge are usually obtained as a result of the project activities regardless of the type of company. We believe that the availability of this type of knowledge can benefit both maintenance projects and new development projects which involve organizational processes already understood by someone else,
- many participants answered the questionnaires taking into consideration software reengineering projects. However, the types of knowledge related to reverse engineering and reengineering do not appear in Table 2. Though both terms were explained in footnotes, we believe the terms were not familiar to many survey participants due to the difficulty in characterizing projects as software reengineering ones and the high rate of non-response for the respective question among systems analysts and programmers,
- from the previous lists with the importance attached by each group of participants, we found that groups of systems analysts and project managers considered the knowledge about risk management as very important, while many groups of directors did not. This is reflected in the results presented in Table 2;
- the knowledge considered important concerning technical partners and suppliers of products and/or services is quite specific. As regards technical partners, it is important to know about their restrictions, weaknesses and strengths and occasionally about the products and services offered by them and the organizational guidelines and standards adopted. As regards suppliers, only knowledge about their restrictions, weaknesses and strengths seems to be of importance.

3 TABA Environments

The results of the survey described in the previous section were used to guide elaboration and incorporation of content and the development of tools for the Taba Workstation which allows one to configure Enterprise Oriented Software Development Environments (EOSDE) [6] for different companies. The content is incorporated into the TABA workstation or a specific EOSDE using a tool called Acknowledge [7].

Until 2003, the TABA workstation was exclusively used in the academic area and involved more than 50 master and doctoral theses in the Federal University of Rio de Janeiro. It was created from the perception that different domain applications have distinct characteristics and such characteristics influence the environment the software engineers use to develop software [8].

During the last years, the TABA Workstation also evolved to comply with the different levels of capability maturity models of software organizations. The CASE tools integrated in the environments offer automated support to: (i) adaptation of the organization standard processes for a specific project; (ii) definition of the organizational structure [9]; (iii) acquisition, filtering, packaging and dissemination of organizational knowledge [7]; (iv) planning the organization of specific projects; (v) time, costs, risks, human resources planning, monitoring and control [9, 10]; (vi) planning and execution of Configuration Management activities; (vii) identification of software product quality requirements; (viii) documentation planning; (ix) planning and monitoring of corrective actions; (x) measurement and analysis activities based on the GQM method; (xi) project monitoring through the generation of periodic reports and measures; (xii) controlling of the activities executed during a specific project; (xiii) requirements management; and (xiv) *post mortem* analysis.

Other approach [12, 13] aims at providing an infrastructure that integrates process-centred software development environments and Knowledge Management by implementing the Experience Factory proposed by Basili et.al. [16].

3.1 QualiSoft Project

The objective of the QualiSoft project is to increase the capability of organizations through the adequate use of Software Engineering techniques in their software processes. By achieving this objective, not only the organizational competitive advantages increases, but also the quality of software products enhances.

Although the academic results of the TABA Workstation were excellent, the system was not intended to be used as a commercial product. The QualiSoft project made significant changes in the project goals. At the beginning of the QualiSoft project, a representative of RioSoft affirmed that some automated support should be provided to the organizations in order to facilitate the application of software processes. Therefore, we decided to make available the TABA Workstation to all organizations at no costs.

Since the focus is on small and medium organizations, we executed the project with a pool of organizations with similar characteristics aiming to decrease the overall cost and increase the project feasibility. This project is a result of a contract between RioSoft (a non-governmental organization that integrates the Softex Program - Society for Supporting Brazilian Software Production and Exportation) and the Federal University of Rio de Janeiro. The first phase of the project started on August 2003 and aimed to address a pool of 10 organizations. The second phase started on January 2004 and addressed a second pool of 9 organizations.

The following activities were conducted:

(i) definition of software development and maintenance processes adjusted for small and medium companies;
(ii) training on Software Engineering methods and techniques and in the software processes defined;

(iii) use of CASE tools integrated in a software development environment configured using the TABA Workstation [8] and strongly supported by Knowledge Management during the deployment and use of the software processes defined; and
(iv) follow-up of the companies in the deployment of the software processes throughout the execution of pilot projects.

Therefore a configured environment was delivered to each organization considering its specific characteristics and the development and maintenance standard processes. A hands-on in the environment tools was carried out. From this environment, specific environments for each pilot project were created by the adaptation of the standard processes according to the project specific characteristics.

3.2 Software Process Definition and Training

The first step in the execution of the project was to be acquainted of the individual characteristics of the organizations. In order to do so, each organization filled out a detailed form and the process specialists had to schedule regular visits on the organizations. The form contained questions related to the organizational culture, software process stages and quality management systems, adopted software development practices, main problems in the current software development and maintenance processes, and organizational objectives related to software process improvement.

The following step was to define software development and maintenance standard processes adequate to small and medium organizations. The processes defined on the first project phase were based exclusively on the international standard ISO/IEC 12207 [14]. In the second phase, these processes were refined and adjusted to be completely adherent to the practices defined in the CMMI [15] Level 2 process areas.

In parallel to the processes definition activity, the members of the organizations were trained in the Software Engineering methods and techniques. During the first phase, approximately 32 hours were spent on training. This training was performed under the form of lectures on the following topics: Software Engineering, Software Process, Requirements Engineering, Configuration Management, Project Management and Software Products Quality. Approximately, 80 professionals were trained during this phase. After the theoretical training, project managers and software developers participated on a specific training on the standard software processes defined. The training during the second phase considered other important topics, such as Peer-review, Tests, Measurement and Analysis, Supplier Agreement and Knowledge Management, constituting more 44 hours to the overall training time. In the second phase, more than 70 organizational members were trained.

The following steps focused on the deployment of the processes and the configured environment in the organizations. These steps had been carried out individually considering the particularities of each organization. Initially, the standard processes had been adapted to each company considering the characteristics identified in the beginning of the project, such as types of software developed, documents produced and software development paradigms adopted. After the approval of the adaptations by the organization, a software development environment was configured based on these adaptations.

3.3 Lessons Learned

During the first phase of the QualiSoft project, we learned the following lessons:

(i) the deployment of software processes in a group of organizations in a common project and at low cost is feasible (the amount of money spent by each company was about 40% of which would be spent in a similar project to be conducted by only one organization);

(ii) the configured environments facilitates training, deployment and institutionalization of software processes by providing case tools to assist and automate the carrying out of repetitive tasks like process instantiation, project planning, controlling and monitoring;

(iii) the knowledge management approach adopted in the environments is determinant for the success of the approach, because it helps the developer in executing its activities by providing useful knowledge when the developer needs it the most;

(iv) the knowledge acquisition approach integrated into the CASE tools [7] enables the gradual evolution of the knowledge repository by allowing the acquisition and dissemination of lessons learned, best practices and ideas to improve the software processes.

The lessons learned were identified during the regular meetings to support the software process deployment in the organizations. They were also confirmed through a formal report one of the organizations sent to the QualiSoft project team after successfully applying to an ISO 9000:2001 Certification.

Another survey was planned and executed with the objective to analyze the processes deployed and the TABA Workstation supporting tools. The questionnaire was applied to 16 key members of the companies that took part of the first phase of the QualiSoft Project. More than 90% of the participants recognized that the TABA Workstation significantly reduced the effort for executing most of the process activities. The participants of the experiment also identified that both the processes and the TABA Workstation facilitated the dissemination of best practices from the project planning until the post–mortem analyses. Moreover, the centralization of information and knowledge related to processes execution also supported decision-making situations, because project managers could easily find information about similar projects.

4 Conclusion

The results presented in the table 2 (the most general) and those that report the importance attributed by each group of participants (more specific) are of practical importance to any company in Salvador that wishes to introduce Knowledge Management in their software engineering context. The results obtained should not been thought as prescriptive but rather as descriptive and be analyzed when deciding on what to prioritize. Some observations made during the carrying out of the survey can explain the importance given to certain types of knowledge, and therefore provide additional support to the decision. The experimental study package can be used for future surveys, which can widen the scope and validity of the results or explain any findings. These results have been used to guide the elaboration and incorporation of content and the development of tools for the TABA workstation which allows one to configure and instantiate software development environments for different companies.

This paper also presented a successful approach for deployment of software processes in small and medium organizations supported by the TABA workstation. The results of the QualiSoft Project are excellent under different aspects. First, it showed the feasibility of carrying out a project involving various organizations with very particular characteristics since the costs were significantly diminished. Second, it showed that it is possible to promote technology transfer between universities and other kinds of organization producing good results to all the involved parts.

Currently, more than 30 Brazilian companies use the TABA environments to support the execution of their software processes, some of which participated in the survey on the importance attributed to different knowledge in Software Development Environments.

Further information about Enterprise-Oriented Software Development Environment and its case tools can be found at http://www.cos.ufrj.br/~taba.

Acknowledgement

The authors wish to thank CNPq and CAPES for the financial support granted to the project Enterprise Oriented Software Development Environments. We also acknowledge SEBRAE for the financial support granted to the QualiSoft project.

References

1. Desouza, K. C.: Barriers to Effective Use of Knowledge Management Systems in Software Engineering. Communications of ACM, Vol. 46(1) (2003) 99-101
2. Lindvall, M., Frey, M., Costa, P., *et al.*: Lessons Learned about Structuring and Describing Experience for Three Experience Bases. Lecture Notes in Computer Science, Vol. 2176. Springer-Verlag (2001) 106-119
3. Oh, E., Hoek, A.: Adapting Game Technology to Support Individual and Organizational Learning. Proceedings of SEKE'2001, Buenos Aires, Jun (2001) 347-362
4. Kucza, T., Nattinen, M., Parviainen, P.: Improving Knowledge Management in Software Reuse Process. Lecture Notes in Computer Science, Vol. 2188. Springer-Verlag (2001) 141-152
5. Wohlin, C., Runeson, P., Höst, M., *et al.*: Experimentation in Software Engineering: An Introduction. The Kluwer International Series in Software Engineering. Kluwer Academic Publishers, Norwell (2000)
6. Villela, K., Oliveira, K., Santos, G., *et al.*: Cordis-FBC: an Enterprise-Oriented Software Development Environment. Lecture Notes in Informatics, Vol. 28. Verlag (2003) 91-96
7. Montoni, M., Miranda, R., Rocha, A. R., *et al.*: Knowledge Acquisition and Communities of Practice: an Approach to Convert Individual Knowledge into Multi-Organizational Knowledge. Lecture Notes in Computer Science, Vol. 3096. Springer (2004) 110-121
8. Oliveira, K, Zlot, F., Rocha, A. R., Travassos, G., Galotta, C., Menezes, C. Domain Oriented Software Development Environment, Journal of Systems and Software, vol 72/2 (2004) pp 145-161
9. Santos, G., Villela, K., Schnaider, L., Rocha, A. R.. Travassos, G. H., Building ontology based tools for a software development environment, In: Workshop Learning Software Organization, Banff, Canada, 2004 (Lecture Notes in Computer Science, vol 3096, pp 19-30)

10. Farias, L., Travassos, G. H., Rocha, A. R. C., Knowledge Management of Software Risks In:. Journal of Universal Computer Science, vol 9 n 7 (2003), 670- 681
11. Arbaoui, S. Derniame, J., Oquendo, F., *et al.*, A Comparative Review of Process-Centered Software Engineering Environments", Annals of Software Engineering, v. 14, n. 1-4, pp. 311-340, Dec. 2002.
12. Maurer, F., Holz, H., Integrating Process Support and Knowledge Management for Virtual Software Development Teams, Annals of Software Engineering, v. 14, n. 1-4, pp. 145-168, Dec. 2002.
13. Holz, H., Könnecker, A., Mauerer, F., "Task-Specific Knowledge Management in a Process-Centred SEE". In: Advances in Learning Software Organizations, v. 2176, Lecture Notes in Computer Science, Springer, pp. 163-177, 2001.
14. ISO/IEC 12207, 1995, Information Technology – Software Life-Cycle Processes.
15. CMU/SEI, Capability Maturity Model Integration (CMMI) Version 1.1 - Staged Representation, Carnegie Mellon University, Software Engineering Institute, Pittsburgh, 2002.
16. Basili, V. R., Caldiera, G., and Rombach, H. D. (1994). Experience Factory. In Encyclopedia of Software Engineering (J. J. Marciniak, ed.), vol. 1, John Wiley Sons.

Experience-Based Support for Code Inspections

Markus Nick, Christian Denger, and Torsten Willrich

Fraunhofer Institute for Experimental Software Engineering (IESE),
Sauerwiesen 6, 67661 Kaiserslautern, Germany
lastname@iese.fraunhofer.de

Abstract. According to recent surveys, software developers still perceive current inspection tools as insufficient. One reason might be that most of the existing tools focus their support on organizational aspects of the inspection. We present a knowledge-based tool that provides intelligent support in the defect detection step. This tool is embedded in two learning loops: one for the inspection process itself and one loop that goes across the whole software lifecycle.

1 Introduction

Software inspections are a well established quality assurance technique. After their invention by Fagan [4], a considerable effort was put into optimizing the inspection process. The focus of the optimization approaches was the improvement of the effectiveness and efficiency of software inspections, that is, more defects should be detected with less effort. With our research, we address the following issues:

1. Support inspections with experience management in order to enable systematic sharing of experiences and learning across inspections, across software development process phases, and across projects. This is motivated by experience being one of the major factors that impact the success of inspections [1, 8].
2. Advanced support for the defect detection by adapting checklists to document and development context at hand as well as telling the inspectors more precisely where it is worthwhile to check for what. This is motivated by a lack of tool support for the defect defection step, which has been identified as the most essential step in soft-ware inspections [7, 5, 6, 2].

For supporting code inspections with experience management, we embed a learning loop into the inspection process itself (Section 2) as well as an inspection experience-related learning loop into the surrounding software development and maintenance processes (Section 3). The system is step-wisely developed and evaluated (Section 4).

2 Inspection Process and Experience-Based Support

To provide experience management support and intelligent tool support for inspections, it is important to understand the underlying inspection process that should be supported.

K.-D. Althoff et al. (Eds.): WM 2005, LNAI 3782, pp. 121 – 126, 2005.

In Figure 1 (left side), a commonly accepted inspection process is presented [3, 5, 4], which consists of four main steps: *planning*, *defect detection*, *collection*, and *correction*. In the following, we shortly describe each step. For the experience-based support, we focus on the support for defect detection and the respective issues to be addressed during planning. Figure 1 shows both, the inspection process and its experience-based support.

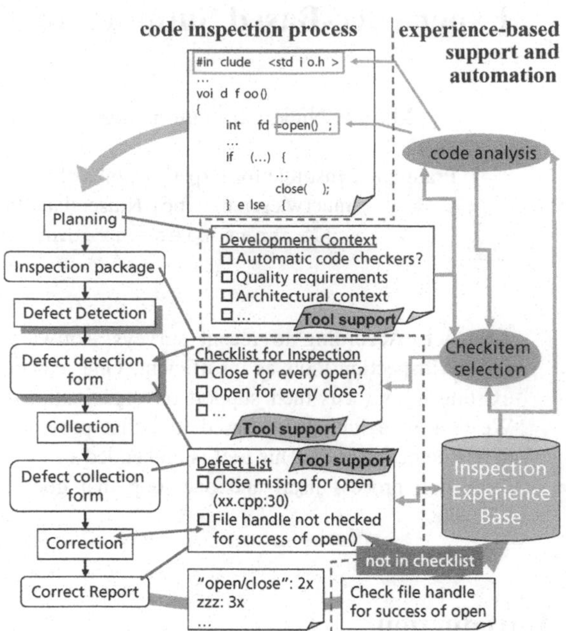

Fig. 1. Enhancing the code inspection process with experience-based tool support

Planning Phase: The organizer of an inspection is, beside other things, responsible to prepare the materials for the inspection (e.g. checklists), to select and invite the inspectors for the inspections, and to distribute the inspection material. This step comprises mainly organizational issues of the inspection process.

Regarding the Experience-Based Support: The development context is characterized. The relevant issues are the architectural context of the code, the quality characteristics that should be checked (e.g., performance, security, compliance with coding standards, type of reading approach), and information about the usage of automatic code checkers. While the quality characteristics select the checkitems that are potentially relevant for the code at hand, the information about the usage of automatic code checkers identifies checkitems that do not have to be checked in the inspection because a tool has already done that job (e.g., conformance checks by Quido's tool (www.quido.at)).

Using the development context characteristics and results of a code analysis for the relevance of checkitems for the code at hand, a checklist is automatically composed that contains only checkitems that are relevant for the code at hand. Furthermore, the code analysis also delivers the *checkpoints*, i.e., locations/lines in the code to which the checkitems are relevant. This enables advanced support during defect detection because a supporting tool now has the knowledge about the relevance of checkitems for each line of the code.

Defect Detection Phase: The inspectors search individually for defects in the document under inspection. During this step, the inspectors document all their findings (defects, questions, comments) in a *defect detection form*. The inspectors are supported by checklists or other reading techniques in detecting the defects.

Regarding Experience-Based Support: Using the knowledge about checkpoints and checkitems from the planning phase, the defect detection support tool (a) points an inspector to code parts that have to be inspected for a specific checkitem as well as (b) shows the inspector the checkitems that are relevant for his current focus in the code (e.g., the current line, code block, or method). Thus, during the inspection, the tool can (1) dynamically adapt the checklist to the part of the code currently being analyzed by the inspector and (2) let the inspector give feedback on which checkitems were checked for which part of the code and if the code is "ok" or not. The latter gives a better picture about the progress and completeness of an inspection at a very detailed level. The feedback "ok"/"not ok" and respective comments comprises the defect collection form, which is the result of the defect detection step. If a checkitem is irrelevant, the inspector can give respective feedback, which helps to identify shortcomings or errors in the inspection experience base itself, which triggers respective maintenance activities.

During the *collection or meeting step*, the results of the individual inspectors are merged into one *defect list*. The main goal of the collection step is to agree on defects; that is, to resolve whether a finding of an inspector is really a defect or not. The outcome is a consolidated defect list that should be corrected by the author of the document. This defect list supports the correction by showing, where a defect was detected and by describing in detail what the defect is.

The code author has to *correct* the document under inspection, based on the defect collection form. In addition to the collected defects, it is possible to collect data regarding the inspection process to allow further evaluations. For example, the effort spent for the defect detection and the collection step, found defect classes, etc.

3 Using Experiences from Other Sources in the Software Lifecycle

Besides the closed experience feedback loop for the inspection process itself, there are relations to other subprocesses and phases of the software development and maintenance processes (Figure 2).

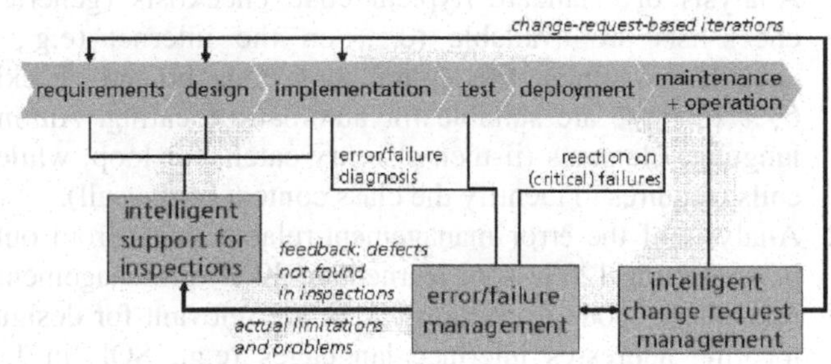

Fig. 2. The software lifecycle has further sources for inspectionrelevant experiences

The error/failure management allows deriving checkitems from experiences about actual problems encountered during testing and operation of developed software. Of particular interest are problems that are difficult to detect during tests or take long to detect during operation (e.g., memory management mistakes). This becomes more and more an issue with today's increasing use of "off-the-shelf" components, where modifications of such components are too expensive or simply not possible because the source code is not available. Also standard interfaces like JDBC or ODBC with SQL leave room for variation regarding interface language and provided functionality and its limitations. Finding such limitations and problems takes long, which justifies collecting them and transforming them into experience-based checkitems (e.g., checkitem in Figure 3). Besides the checkitem itself, the respective problem-solution experience from the error/failure management experience base (1) illustrates the problem to be check for and its consequences (e.g., as online help to an inspector during defect detection) and (2) provides a solution to the problem in the correction phase. From the measurement perspective, the later phases also provide measurable feedback about the effect-tiveness of the inspections viewed from the perspective of the complete software lifecycle.

- *Experience-based checkitem:*
  Is an attribute value of a SQL query's ResultSet accessed more than once?
- *Development context & problem's situation:*
  MS Access is used as database and accessed from Java via the JDBC-ODBC bridge
- *Related problem:*
  The ResultSet of SQL queries is emptied by reading – in contrast to other JDBC drivers.
- *Solution:* [...]

Fig. 3. Example for an experience-based checkitem, its development context, and the related problem from which the checkitem has been derived

4 Evaluation of the Approach

The first step of the evaluation was to analyze if the knowledge (i.e., checkitems) are available and if these are suitable for automatically locating respective checkpoints in the code. For this purpose, we made three different studies:

1 Analysis of "standard"/typical code checklists (generic, Java, C, C++): Such check-lists are available (e.g., on the internet (e.g., www.reviewtechnik.de/checklis-ten.html)). We compiled a consolidated checklist of 117 checkitems. 69% of these are suitable for automatic locating. Automatic location addresses language elements (if-then-else, try-catch, for loop, while loop, etc.) and method calls (requires to identify the class context of the call).

2 Analysis of the error management-related items from our department experience base: Among 120 lessons learned are 39 error management items. 36% of these are relevant for code inspections, 31% are relevant for design inspections. Automatic locating addresses interface languages (e.g., SQL in Java, XML in Java) and architectural dependencies on "standard" components ("standard" means typical for the organization where the inspection tool is used) - e.g. see Figure 3.

3 Analysis of security checklists and related material: We compiled 127 checkitems from available material, which was provided by IESE's secure software engineering team. Automatic locating addresses mainly specific library function calls (100 function families) and also array definition.

In the second step, the feasibility of automatic code analysis has been demonstrated. Using a lexical scanner with some additional logic, we have implemented the code analysis module.

Table 1. Study results and current contents of Experience Base

Checklist sources	*#Checkitems available*	*% suitable for automatic locating*	*Locating of*
Standard checklists	117	69%	• Language elements • Method calls
Error management database	36% -> code 31% -> design	100%	• Interface languages • Architectural dependencies
Security checklists and related material	127	100%	• Library functions • Array definition

An overview on these study results is given in Table 1:. The experience based has been filled with the checkitems and code patterns from studies 1 and 3 from the first step.

In the third step, the applicability of defect detection support tool will be evaluated with empirical studies (prestudy inhouse, controlled experiments with students, case studies with industrial customers). This is related to question about how software engineers use the tool and what is the right/good granularity of the checkitems (e.g., relate correctness of arithmetic expressions to each expression, to the surrounding code block, or to the surrounding method?). Based on the answers to these questions, we expect to be able to provide a better, more focused tool support.

5 Future Work

Further future work is concerned with the following issues: Advanced maintenance support for checkitem and code pattern knowledge editing will make it easier to add and maintain new knowledge items. A tighter integration into existing software development environments (e.g., Eclipse) allows having other code and documentation available and conveniently accessible. For supporting iterative development and changes, the changes to the code are analyzed in order to limit a follow-up inspection to the parts of code and checkitems where the change might have an impact.

References

1. Biffl, S., and Halling, M. Investigating the influence of inspector capability factors with four inspection techniques on inspection performance. In *Proceedings of the Eighth International Software Metrics Symposium*, Ottawa, 2002. IEEE Computer Society Press.
2. Ciolkowski, M., Laitenberger, O., and Biffl, S. Software reviews: The state of the practice. *IEEE Software*, pages 46–51, Dec. 2003.

3. Dreyer, H., and Laitenberger, O. Evaluating the usefulness and the ease of use of a web-based inspection data collection tool. International Software Engineering Re-search Network (ISERN) Technical Report ISERN-98-13, Fraunhofer Institute for Experimental Software Engineering, May 1998.
4. Fagan, M. E. Design and code inspections to reduce errors in program development. *IBM Systems Journal*, 15(3):182–211, 1976.
5. Gilb, T., and Graham, D. *Software Inspection*. Addison-Wesley Publishing Compa-ny, 1993.
6. Laitenberger, O., Vegas, S., and Ciolkowski, M. The state of the practice of review and inspection technologies in germany. ViSEK ViSEK/010/E, 2002.
7. MacDonald, F., and Miller, J. A Comparison of Computer Support Systems for Soft-ware Inspection. *Automated Software Engineering*, 6(3):291–313, Sept. 1999.
8. Wong, Y.-K., and Wilson, D. An investigation of industry software review experi-ence and performance. In *Proceedings of the 16th International Conference on Soft-ware and Systems Engineering (ICSSEA 2003)*, Paris, France, 2003. Centre pour la Maitrise des Systemes et du Logiciel.

New Generation E-Learning Technology by Web Services

Guido Dedene[1,2], Monique Snoeck[1], Manu De Backer[1], and Wilfried Lemahieu[1]

[1] Katholieke Universiteit Leuven, Department of Applied Economic Sciences, Naamsestraat 69, B-3000 Leuven, Belgium
{Guido.Dedene, Monique.Snoeck, Manu.DeBacker, Wilfried.Lemahieu}@econ.kuleuven.ac.be

[2] Universiteit Van Amsterdam, Faculty of Economics and Econometrics, Roetersstraat 11, 1018 WB Amsterdam, The Netherlands

Abstract. This paper discusses a new approach to build infrastructures for E-Learning systems for Learning Software Organizations on the basis of Web Services. A requirements context is developed to determine which type of E-Learning applications that can be Web Service Enabled. This is illustrated with a case study on an Encapsulated Software Teaching Environment. Additional facilities, such as didactical agents and deep personalization to facilitate Learning Software Organizations are discussed at the end.

1 Introduction

The Web Services technology has introduced a revolution in the way how software component interfaces can be invoked over the Internet by means of the XML-message-based SOAP protocol [1]. The commercial deployment of Application Service Provider (ASP) type of Web Services [2] seems to take off slower. Nevertheless, the concept to provide access to complex applications through (extreme) Thin Clients is very appealing in terms of lowering the Total Cost of Ownership. In particular, for Learning Software Organizations, support costs of the learning infrastructure can dramatically be reduced..

This paper will explore the possibilities of Web Services for building E-Learning applications that may provide a better infrastructure for Learning Software Organizations. In Section 2 a requirements context is presented to select E-Learning applications that can be based on Web Services. Not every learning application can be Web Service enabled. In Section 3 a major learning environment case study is reported, where first year economics students are exposed to basic software concepts based on a strict object-oriented approach. Finally Section 4 explores some further developments, discussing the added value of *didactical agent* technology and deep *personalization*. These features are particularly relevant for Learning Software Organizations, because they allow the environment to learn from the learners behavior, and make the learning process more effective.

K.-D. Althoff et al. (Eds.): WM 2005, LNAI 3782, pp. 127 – 133, 2005.

2 Web Services and Education Environments

Whenever education institutes decide to add computer-based training elements to their courses, and introductory first-year courses in particular, they may face some significant organizational problems. In particular, in a typical non-computer science department, such as economics students, the computer background of the average student is limited to Web surfing and using Text editors and Spreadsheets. Installing and running a (learning) software environment is not an easy process for this type of students. Moreover, first-year students are typically huge groups. In general, the following set of requirements holds for this type of education environments:

a. The education environment should have a simple *installation* and *configuration* procedure.
b. The education environment should provide maximal *usability* for the students, based on intuitive as well as defensive style of User Interfaces.
c. The education environment should provide *clearly structured*, *step-by-step* simple *exercises.*
d. The education environment should allow the student to construct solutions for the exercises, whereby the education environment should contain *hints* and/or *guidance* in the construction of the solutions.
e. The education environment should support *maximal automation* in the process of *creating, changing, maintaining and distributing exercises.*
f. The education environment should require *minimal maintenance* from a *technical infrastructure* point of view.
g. The education environment should *integrate* in a frictionless fashion with other Internet or Intranet based education tools.

Traditional education environments make use of a physical distribution of the training programs (e.g. distributing CDROM's) or a distribution through Website-based downloading of the educational software. This solution may result in significant Total Cost of Ownership (TCO) disadvantages. Every student needs a workstation that is powerful enough to support the software. Moreover, the (educational) support staff may suffer from a serious load in terms of installation or technical support questions on behalf of the students. Also, the CDROM as well as the Web-download distribution may result in situations where multiple, potentially conflicting versions of the education environment must be supported. It is also cumbersome to distribute corrections, modifications and additional exercises.

The idea of using Web technologies and server-based education environments is not new as such. One successful development is Ceilidh, which meanwhile evolved in Coursemarker [5]. However, the specific capabilities of Web Services as a new innovative technology, create the opportunity to reduce significantly the Total Cost of Ownership and the organizational effectiveness of education environments. Perhaps the most interesting aspect of Web Services is the fact that they enable a single point of control in an easy way. The center is a Web-based server infrastructure, which eliminates the need to distribute (any) software to the client computers.

Not every education tool can be transformed into a Web Services based implementation. These are some context requirements that make it easier for a learning environment to transform it into a Web Service:

a. when the education environment has clearly *isolated "user sessions"* and has the capability of distinguishing and maintaining the usage data of *multiple users* within the same environment.
b. in case a simple user interaction, preferably on the basis of *forms* is used.
c. when *XML documents* can be processed by the education environment, or XML formats can be used to *import* and *export information* with the education environment.
d. when there is *no need to store* and maintain *local data* about the user on the user workstation.

Many E-Learning software programs may satisfy the above context requirements. The use of Web Services results in the following Total Cost of Ownership changes for both the students (the learners, or "consumers") as well as the educational staff (the "suppliers" or providers):

Potential TCO reductions	Party	
	Learner	Educational Staff
Lower Equipment Costs	X	
Lower Software Costs	X	X
No Installation Costs	X	
No Installation Support Costs		X
Flexible Access to the E-Learning application (any thin client Web Browser)	X	X
Better reliability of the E-Learning application	X	
Lower Software Distribution Costs		X
Flexible maintenance of the E-learning software and exercises		X
E-Learning environment can reach more students		X

Also, Web Services provide some unique opportunities that were largely impossible with the traditional distribution mechanisms. In particular:

- a complete transparency of subsequent versions of the learning environment. Due to the "interface"-nature of Web Services, students should not know the actual version of the learning environment that they are using.
- a possibility to monitor from a central viewpoint (i.e. without using local data, such as "cookies") how the students are using the education environment.

Finally, in case the learning organization or education institute is using workstation-based training rooms, such as PC-classrooms, it can run the E-Learning tool also as an Intranet application, resulting in further reductions in the Total Cost of Ownership for the training rooms.

3 An Encapsulated Software Education Environment Case Study

The Department of Applied Economic Sciences at K.U.Leuven (the Catholic University of Leuven) has a long tradition of offering an intensive Information Systems class to all its first year students. Today, the software part of this course is based on Object-oriented Software Development, based on the Eiffel Language [3]. The Eiffel Environment that is used is ISE Eiffel, and its implementation in the Microsoft .NET framework. The EiffelBench, and its successor, EiffelStudio (which is integrated with the Windows Visual Studio Development Tool) have been used as educational tools. Even with some customization of these tools, it turned out that many options in the tool were overwhelming for a first-year student (although it is clear that these features are needed for a professional use of the tool). Moreover, it was not straightforward for this type of students to set up the Assembly configuration files and libraries that are typically needed to develop an object-oriented application.

Until 2 years ago, students were required to install the Eiffel Environment on their own computers, using distribution CDs and/or download from a central (Blackboard-based) Web Server. The K.U.Leuven has a University Partner Program with ISE Eiffel [6]. One of the complications of the previous environment was the secure distribution of the license keys for the software environment.

From a pedagogical point of view, the exercises are incomplete program fragments which must be completed by the students. This requires a basic knowledge of the software capabilities, but also the skills to gain understanding of existing software components. The basic learning idea is to learning software from sharing experience that is already imbedded in software fragments. The traditional environment could only facilitate the downloading of documents, which the students could fill in, without any straightforward automatic checking. *The learning environment that was needed fulfills most of the context requirements of the previous section.* Consequently a Web Services based E-Learning tool E^3 , the Eiffel Education Environment [4], was developed and put into production for the students two years ago.

This education environment is largely simplifying the procedure for making, compiling and running exercise solutions. In fact, the user is driven by a number of ASP.NET based Web forms for the exercises. One advantage is that students can "drop" their session at one Web station ("in class") and continue - "resume" – next on another Web interface ("at home"). When a student wants to compile a solution, the completed form is submitted as an XML/SOAP document and is presented to the (encapsulated) Eiffel compiler, which runs now as a .NET-based Web Service. Error messages, as well as a successful compilation of the program are reported back as standard SOAP answers. In case a student wants to enjoy the results of the compilation on his own workstation, an option is provided to download the compiled program, including the run-time environment for the programs. *The students are not required to install anything to run the exercises. Any access to the Internet is sufficient to access and use the education environment.*

The following diagram shows the collaboration of the ASP.NET pages (*.aspx) and the encapsulated Eiffel Compiler (Compile.asmx).

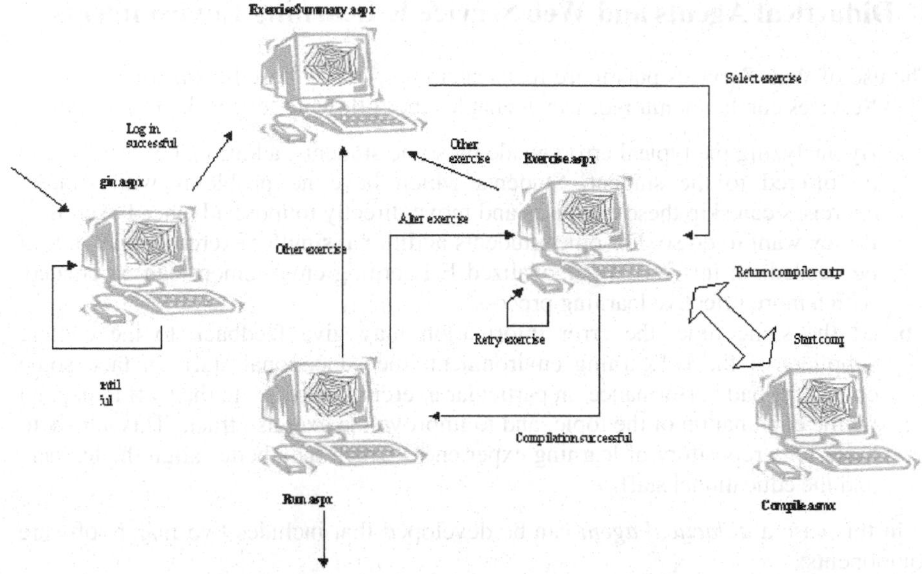

Significant improvements have been observed in the student results after the introduction of the Web Services based E-Learning environment. The following table summarizes the improvements for the same type of exams, indicating the average exam results before and after introducing E^3, for two groups of students, Applied Economics students (who are less ICT-skilled) and Business Engineering student (who have more affinity with ICT):

Average Exam Results	Before E^3	After E^3	Improvement
Applied Economics	8,1 / 20	9,3 / 20	15%
Business Engineers	9,3 / 20	11, 1 / 20	19%

The TCO reduction was spectacular. The main TCO reduction factors are:

- no installation support costs (previously taking up to 50% of the time of the teaching assistants).
- no software distribution costs (elimination of CDs and download spaces).
- no more installation costs in student PC-rooms (no more local installations).

Compared to the previous education environment (without Web Services) the total TCO reduction is 70%. This does not include the TCO reductions on the side of the users.

Finally, it is interesting to note the absolute transparency of the versioning of the Eiffel environment to the students. In fact, switches happened in the Web Service to newer versions of the Eiffelstudio without any noticing of it on the side of the students.

4 Didactical Agents and Web Service E-Learning Environments

The use of Web Services puts more focus again on Service-based Infrastructures. The Web Services can be monitored, which enables the following feedback possibilities:

a. By analyzing the typical errors made by some students, additional exercises may be offered to the student. Students which have no problems with simpler exercises can skip these exercises and move directly to more advanced exercises, if they want to do so. For other students additional simpler exercises may indeed be needed. In this way a personalized E-Learning environment can be created, with a more effective learning process.
b. At the same time, the error information may give feedback to the content suppliers of the E-Learning environment, the educational staff. In fact, some consistent bad performance on particular exercises may invite the staff to expand on the explanation of the topic, and to improve the exercise track. This allows to build up a repository of learning experience, which may better align the learners and the educational staff.

In this case a *didactical agent* can be developed that includes two major software components:

- The *Web Service Analyzer and Advisor*. This tool will categorize the students and their solutions to the exercises into consistent, coherent groups, who need a customized track through this technology. Various scheduling options should be available, such as a weekly checkup of the student results. The advisor may formulate recommendations to the teachers and assistants, for example, to indicate parts of the courses that need to be explained better, or for which more exercises or other types of exercises are needed.
- The *Web Service Customizer* implements in a real-time mode the rules that have been proposed by the Web Service Advisor. . It takes the form of a rule-based part of the User-Interaction, which guides the students through the E-Learning track that has the best fit with their individual needs.

Didactical agents which are conceived in this way can also enable another contemporary didactical issue: guided self-study. Instead of reducing this self-study to some boring uniform document loading application, didactical agents create the possibilities for attractive, personalized self-study environments. *In some ways didactical agents reverse the pedagogical process: instead of just having guided users (learners), a fully guided interoperation of the learners and the information providers (the educational staff) is facilitated in this way.*

One word of caution is appropriate here, as monitoring the individual behaviour against some server-based software application requires legally the permission of the end-user. This is of course related to privacy legislation, as it emerges in many states today.

Observe how it is precisely the (central) Server-based nature of Web Services that makes this type of didactical agent technology feasible. With traditional education environments, difficult and dispersed evaluation systems are needed to try to obtain analogous results. Moreover there is a significant delay in the data analysis: Web Services can be monitored as frequently as needed from a Quality Improvement perspective.

5 E-Learning Web Services Outlook

Web Services based learning environments are very suitable technology for Learning Software Organizations. In the case that was presented here, the students as well as the staff learns from the central server-based learning environment and build a common repository of expertise in the Web Service environment. The environment can dynamically be adapted and evolves as the technology and the didactical insights progress.

Really interesting new types of education environments can emerge when Choreographies of Web Services are applied to the didactical process. In such an environment, several Web Services are combined in the joint didactical process, and can share common repositories of expertise (for example, based on student profiles).

Several Web Service-based learning environments are under construction at K.U.Leuven at this moment:

- A didactical learning environment for SQL-training. The fact that the latest versions of the Microsoft Office technology have build-in Web Service technology components is the basis for the construction of this learning environment.
- A design tool for decision tables and rule-based Business Validations. In this case an existing Delphi-based application is Web-enabled through the standard Web Service facilities of the Delphi environment.
- Another project is focusing on the expansion of the learning environment that was described in this paper into a complete software visualization environment. In particular, this includes the visualization of software applications that are composed by means of Web Services.
- An intelligent Business Modeling environment, which support the process of building organizational models, Business Models in particular, by using formal event-based object-oriented modeling techniques [7]. Not only internal organizational models, but also E-Business cooperative collaborations can be represented in this environment. Hence, such an environment may significantly contribute to organizational learning processes.

The experiences from this paper suggest indeed to further explore and develop the possibilities of applying Web Services in Learning Software Organizations.

References

1 Seely, S.,Sharkey, K. : SOAP: Cross Platform Web Services Development Using XML, Prentice Hall PTR Upper Saddle River, NJ(2001)

2 Walsh, Kenneth R. : Analyzing the Application ASP Concept: Technologies, Economies and Strategies, Communications of the ACM, Vol. 46, No. 8 (2003) 103-107

3 Meyer, B. : Eiffel the language, Prentice-Hall, Inc. New York, 1992.

4 De Backer, M., Dedene, G., Snoeck, M. : An encapsulated Eiffel education environment, based on Web Services, Journal of Object Technology, Vol. 1,No. 3, Special issue: TOOLS USA 2002 proceedings (http://www.jot.fm/issues/issue_2002_08/article6), 97 – 106.

5 http://www.cs.nott.ac.uk/~ceilidh/

6 http://www.eiffel.com

7 Michiels, C., Snoeck, M., Lemahieu, W., Goethals, F. Dedene, G. : A Layered Architecture Sustaining Model Driven and Event Driven Software Development, Andrei Ershov International Conference "Perspectives of Systems Informatics", Novosibirsk, Russia, Lecture Notes in Computer Science, vol. 2890, (2003), 58 – 65

Future Studies of Learning Software Organizations

Kari Smolander[1], Kurt Schneider[2], Torgeir Dingsøyr[3], Finn Olav Bjørnsson[4], Pasi Juvonen[1], and Päivi Ovaska[1]

[1] South Carelia Polytechnic, Koulukatu 5 B, 55120 Imatra, Finland
[2] Software Engineering Group, Universität Hannover, Welfengarten 1, 30167 Hannnover, Germany
[3] SINTEF Information and Communication Technology, NO-7465 Trondheim, Norway
[4] Dept. of Information and Communication Systems, Norwegian University of Science and Technology, NO-7491 Trondheim, Norway

Abstract. We suggest to study learning software organizations in three projects; one to analyse the current situation for local software and system houses, one to study improvement and learning through examining knowledge flows, and a third to study the impact of a large-scale interaction process: Open Space Technology to share domain knowledge.

1 Introduction

This paper presents three suggested future studies on learning software organizations, discussed at the learning software organizations workshop in 2005.

The first suggested research project [21] examines with the practices of local software and systems houses who wish to operate with global industrial customers. The objectives of the project include analysis of the current situation and enabling organizational learning initiatives.

The second project [17] builds on the fact that successful software projects depend project specific information, as well as basic knowledge and experience gained in other projects. The FLOW research project investigates flows and containers of various kinds of information.

The third project [9] identifies domain knowledge as a crucial ingredient for companies developing software, and propose a study on a large-group intervention technique – Open Space Technology – to increase the domain knowledge of developers in a software project.

The three projects are described in the following.

2 Local Software Organizations with Global Customers: A Survival Quest

The Southeast Finland has one of the world's densest concentrations of forest industry, consisting of pulp, paper and paperboard mills, wood saws, surfacing and impregnation mills, and plywood factories. During its history, this concentration has

K.-D. Althoff et al. (Eds.): WM 2005, LNAI 3782, pp. 134 – 144, 2005.

also created a cluster of service companies, including IT service providers, automation experts, and specialized software and systems houses. These service companies of various sizes must cooperate with multinational and globally operating forest industry enterprises.

We introduce our research project Katapultti-SCP, its objectives, research methods, and expected outcomes. With our research partners[1], we are making a study of the present status of the software industry in Southeast Finland. In Katapultti-SCP, our part of the study includes fostering of organizational learning and development of the software and systems development organizations supplying forest industry.

2.1 Objectives of the Study

Our study seeks ways to improve the practices of local software and systems development organizations who wish to operate with global industrial customers. The relationship between the local companies and their global customers can be characterized as asymmetrical [2, 8], i.e. their resources and sizes are not equal and their dependencies are more or less one-way. In this kind of a situation a global customer could easily replace its local software supplier in a way or another. We assume that this kind of a situation has a profound effect on the software development process between the two parties.

In particular, we are interested in how a local software organization operates in such an asymmetrical situation. This requires attention to be paid on

- those software development methods and processes that are usable in asymmetrical relationships,
- the skills that are required from the local software professionals to cope with asymmetry, including also the skills of how to keep up already gained customer relationships with global enterprises,
- what kind of learning and development can be practically and economically introduced into local software organizations, and
- the needed technical skills and learning – what kind of technologies and tools are used at the moment within the industry sector and what kind of visions and development are related to them in the foreseeable future.

Our ultimate objective is to enable organizational learning concerning software development practices that are applicable to an asymmetrical business environment. Our plan includes also the introduction of organizational learning initiatives to selected companies and thereby a demonstration of the effects and benefits of such initiatives.

2.2 Research Methods

The research project is organized into two phases:

Current state analysis: We analyze the current practices of the local software and systems houses that operate with the global forest industry. The phase includes the identification and explanation of key issues in software and systems development in an asymmetrical industrial context.

---

[1] Lappeenranta University of Technology and Kymenlaakso Polytechnic, Finland.

Interviews will be made both in the local software and systems houses and in their customer organizations. In addition, our partners have already collected basic information (including key figures, customers, competitors, partners, etc.) of all software and systems development organizations in the geographical research area. The collected data will be analyzed qualitatively using grounded theory [11, 22]. Our aim is to establish a coherent explanation of the situation and issues of software and systems development that the local companies are facing when dealing with their global customers. The analysis will include an explanation of observed common problems and good practises concerning software and system development in target organizations.

Introduction of learning and development initiatives: The second phase aims at enabling learning and development of methods and processes in the local companies. The main instrument in this will be the increased awareness of the identified issues and problems caused by the asymmetry. A learning and development initiative will be planned and experimented with selected pilot companies. Experiences will be collected and reported to the companies.

2.3 Expected Outcomes

The analysis of the data is about to begin. At the moment, we are not yet able to make any accurate forecasts of the final results of the analysis. However, we can describe and list in no specific order some of the observations of the organizations and their operating environment that we regard as the most essential ones:

- *There are no occurrences of middle-sized organizations.* Almost all local software organizations delivering software for the forest industry are small – except one organization that operates globally and have the largest share of the world markets in specific areas. It seems that even large industrial corporations need small, flexible and service-oriented software organizations that can deliver and tailor for specialized local needs. However, there seems to be no room for middle-sized organizations, having for example from 30 to 100 employees.
- *Tailored software or "software as a service" prevails.* Almost all of the local small software organizations make tailored software. With global customers, product-orientation eventually leads to global markets. Small organizations have problems with their credibility and resources related to global operation. Global forest industry customers see the asymmetry as a problem and consider that small organizations are not able to act as their global software partner.
- *Local "niche" is hard to transform to growth.* Although there are many examples of small organizations that have been successful locally with forest industry, we have not identified any that have grown from local to international level during the last ten years. Local knowledge is not enough for international markets.
- *Industrial domain knowledge is essential for success.* Most of the local software organizations have specific knowledge on certain industrial processes or practices.
- *Flexibility and local, personal presence is the strength of small organizations.* From the global customer point of view small software companies could view agility to react as their strength. It is easier for a big customer to cope with a small company, which will rapidly react to any change in customer needs. Flexibility also means that re-scheduling of projects is easier with small software companies.

- *Personal relationships are important for small organizations.* We heard many comments on how it is important for small software organizations to know personally the customers. This importance might be related to the limited resources. Small organizations do not have dedicated sales nor marketing personnel and they cannot spend much time for searching sales leads.
- *Large customer organizations are difficult to grasp for small software organizations.* It was mentioned in many interviews of small organizations that as long as they are dealing with local paper mills, customer relationships are relatively easy to manage e.g. in requirements analysis. The problem starts when the enterprise level of a global corporation enters to the development process. In this situation small organizations have difficulties to understand who the responsible persons are and where the decisions are made.
- *Small ones are willing to network with others, but they do not know how.* One of the most famous buzzwords of our time is the networked economy [23] which emphasizes the role of information technology in forming business structures and networking between organizations. However, most of the small organizations do not have means and experience to form networks with others, and in practice, only rare occasions of networking between small organizations exist in this area.

After the current state analysis phase, our project will produce a plan about the types of organizational learning initiatives that can be introduced to local companies that must cope with global competition. We will particularly focus on software and systems development processes and the issues and problems identified in the current state analysis. The initiatives will be piloted in selected software organizations and the experiences on the learning and development initiatives will be collected.

2.4 Summary and Discussion

In this position paper, we have introduced Katapultti-SCP project, its objectives, methods and some of its preliminary findings.

We believe that qualitative research methods are particularly suitable in this kind of research settings, where hypotheses are not ready to be tested and even the research problem evolves through empirical observations. We have already found strong evidence about the difficulties of small software organizations to cope with globalization of industries. Current research in software engineering is not particularly useful for resolving problems of small organizations because it is mostly focused on large-scale software production and its problems. It is already noted that the field of software engineering is largely influenced by and based on the needs of large organizations like US Department of Defence [cf. 10, 15] and military applications, whose problems are in many ways different from the problems of small organizations.

Local and small software organizations would benefit much from increased awareness of the problems and risks brought by the globalization of industries. They would also benefit much from knowledge and experiences on how small organizations could network and complement each other in the pressures of globalization and heavy international competition. Our project in this field has just begun and there is certainly much to do.

3 Software Process Improvement from a FLOW Perspective

Software development can be seen from a knowledge and learning perspective: A software process routes project information through a sequence of activities. Project information (from requirements over project plans to quality priorities) needs to be available to the software knowledge workers where and when they need it.

Various different flows need to be combined in order to optimize the outcome of a given project activity. An explicit focus on *experience as a catalyst* flow is integrated with more conventional project information flows. This research paper reports on concepts considered relevant for a FLOW-perspective of software projects. Flows provide a viewpoint that reveals a number of interesting research questions and practical implications for software development and for software process improvement.

3.1 Information Flow in Software Processes

Software process models tend to emphasize activities and documents [6]. These elements are related by reading/writing relationships. In figure 1, a simple example process is depicted which highlights the flow of project information through activities.

Requirements are one of the sources of project information. A systematic software project has to channel this information to all places in which it will be needed for subsequent process steps. For example, requirements will directly flow to design activities.

Fig. 1. Project information flow through activities

Figure 1 implies information flowing from one **activity** (or phase) to the next. In many process models, flow of information is drawn from an activity to a **document** and to the subsequent activity [6]. The difference may seem subtle. In the latter, information is passed *through documents*, whereas Figure 1 does not say which information carriers will be used.

Differences become more obvious when looking *into* one of the activities. Figure 2 (left) depicts the fine-grained flow of information from a person to a document and further on to another person. On the right, there is a direct flow from one person to the other.

Traditional process models and software projects tended to rely on a strict document interface [6]. Agile approaches (among others) tend to rely more on people interfaces, on their ability to communicate fast and efficient. In extreme programming[4], code and direct communication is explicitly preferred as value and

Fig. 2. Left: Document-based information flow. Right: Person-to-person flow

as guiding principle. Direct information flow has drawbacks: misunderstandings, danger of oblivion, and less documentation for maintenance. However, from a flow perspective, direct people-to-people flow of information is highly efficient – in particular when additional practices (like in XP [4]) support it. Gained efficiency stems from a lower threshold and richer communication between people. Weaving in additional flows may further enhance communication efficiency.

3.2 Related Work

Several authors have looked at the flow of information in software projects: Abdel-Hamid and co-authors presented System Dynamics models to study software project dynamics [1]. Their main interest was looking at so-called "policies" within software projects and their outcomes, as investigated by System Dynamics simulation runs. Rodriguez et al. [16] used similar models for a slightly different purpose.

Lately, the core of SESAM models, software quantums, was distilled out and re-focused to support mental models and direct explanations of project dynamics - rather than highly complex simulation models [18]. There are a few techniques that explicitly produce or exploit different kinds of flows in software projects. Some are directly intended to improve project activities: LIDs [19] is an experience elicitation technique. FOCUS is a documentation support approach for software prototypes and legacy systems [20]. There are probably many more examples.

3.3 Experiences Taken Seriously

Project information needs to flow through project activities: One cannot design a product when requirements are missing. However, project information is not sufficient. Projects participants will need access to basic software engineering knowledge, and they will perform much better when they operate on a higher level of experience.

Many large companies started to take experience seriously as an asset [7, 12]. Risk management is just one area in which experience reuse has been studied and published [14]. In this domain, experience is the best guide to estimate probability and relevance of a (theoretical) risk category to one´s own project.

Figure 3 shows a typical cyclic process of experience elicitation (activation) and reuse (re-infusion). Software projects and techniques that want to capitalize on experience exploitation need to accommodate iterations (e.g. LIDs [19] and FOCUS [20]).

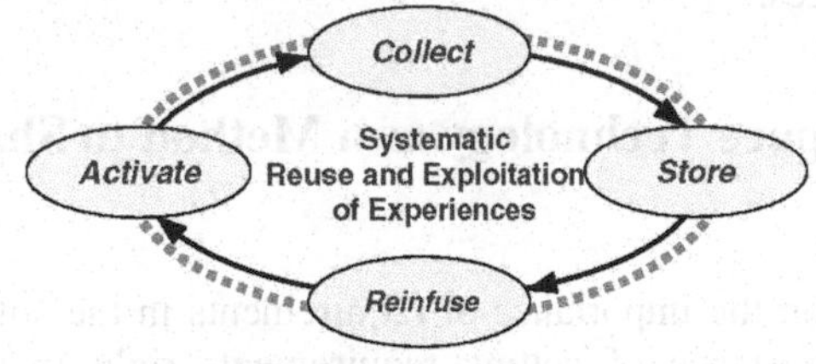

Fig. 3. Iterative experience exploitation and flow (arrows)

3.4 The FLOW Project: Vision and Implications

The FLOW project focuses on flows of information and flows of experience, and intends to reveal opportunities for *focused* software process improvement.

When applying the approach to fine-grained process improvement, an organization will first draw a flow graph of relevant projects. Experience flows cut across projects. When they intersect with other flows (e.g., with prior experiences during risk management), activities can be denoted in a notation similar to IDEF0. Figure 4 (left) shows a situation in which project information is processed by a design activity. It comes in as an input *from the left* and passes on to subsequent activities *to the right*. Carrying out this activity is supported (*bottom*) by basic design capabilities (a flow that may originate in course learning), and it is *guided (from top)* by a flow of experiences on what works in design and what does not.

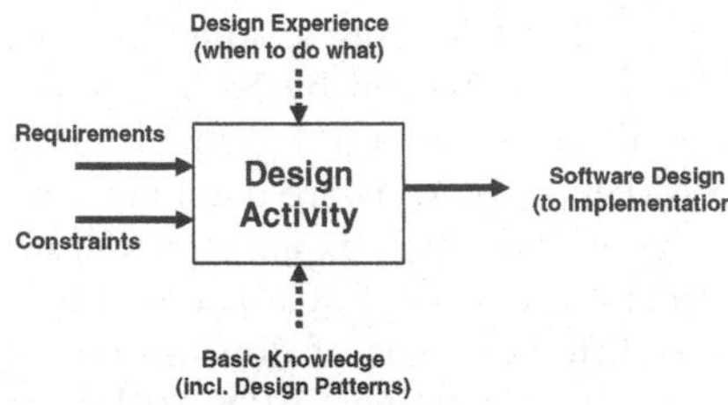

Fig. 4. Activity and associated flows

Process improvement from a FLOW perspective envisions all requested input flows to be provided *at a reasonable intensity and volume*. Software quantums will be used to model quantitative issues [18]. Techniques like LIDs and FOCUS are optimized for both information and experience flows.

Although FLOW is only at its beginning, we have already seen several effects in practical environments that can be explained and improved by a FLOW perspective. One example involved a company that suffered from a legacy system. Project information flows were *disrupted*, which is typical for legacy situations. Although they had the resources, the team was not able to get basic capabilities (good people) and experience flows (about the system) *in place*. A FLOW perspective could have pointed them to missing links or dangling flows. We are currently investigating further FLOW analysis steps in order to constructively guide tailoring: Software quality activities are made to best fit an organization's needs in between traditional and agile work practices.

4 Using Open Space Technology as a Method to Share Domain Knowledge

Many studies report on the importance of requirements in the software development process, and the importance of getting requirements right in the early stages of development [13]. The requirement specification is a negotiation process between user needs, technical possibilities and cost, where stakeholders learn about other stakeholder's expectations for the new system to be developed.

There have been many studies in software engineering on the process of defining requirements, or requirement engineering. However, studies also indicate that in order to deliver software products with high quality for a low cost, it is important that developers have an understanding of the domain where the application is to work [24].

This suggests that there might be other needs than agreeing on requirements that are important in first encounters with a software customer. We will refer to this as increasing the domain knowledge of the people who are to participate in the software development project.

From organization science, a range of methods known as large-group interventions or interactions exist. The aim of these methods are to [5]: 1) enhance the amount of information brought to bear on a problem, 2) build commitment to problem definitions and solutions, 3) fuse planning and implementation and 4) shorten the time needed to conceive and execute major projects.

We suggest a study of one particular large-group intervention technique, which might help increase the domain knowledge, namely Open Space Technology.

4.1 Open Space Technology: What Is It?

Open Space Technology [3] is a group process where all stakeholders are invited to discuss a topic of common concern. It differs from other group processes in that the topic is defined on an overall-level. When arriving, participants are presented to the overall-topic, and asked to identify sub-topics they themselves are interested in. From suggestions a large schedule with topic, time and place is made for the whole event, and people are told to participate in discussing the topics where they think they can contribute. People who have suggested topics act as moderators in their sessions, and are responsible for writing a short minute about the discussion. Such an event can be organized for a large number of people, and usually lasts from one to three days.
The Open Space Technology makes people from many environments find each other to discuss topics of common interest. It also makes the participants themselves responsible for the outcome of the event.

According to [5] there are four assumptions underlying the Open Space Technology method:

1. "Events must focus on an issue of concern, and when the purpose becomes clear, the appropriate event and project structures will follow as a natural expression or embodiment of the purpose."
2. "People can and will self-organize based on their interests. Everyone has the right and responsibility to put items on the agenda. Everyone has creative potential, and his or her energy can be tapped. Groups will generate their own leadership."
3. "Experts and analysts are needed among the participants. There should be no expert help from outside the group."
4. "You can work with the chaos of these events. It represents an opportunity for growth, organizational learning, and improved effectiveness."

The method has a very optimistic view of people. There is a basic belief that good things will happen if people get together to discuss topics of mutual interest.

4.2 Open Space Technology: Why Use It?

The formulation of good requirements in a development project depends on good understanding of the project domain [24]. Not having a good understanding of the

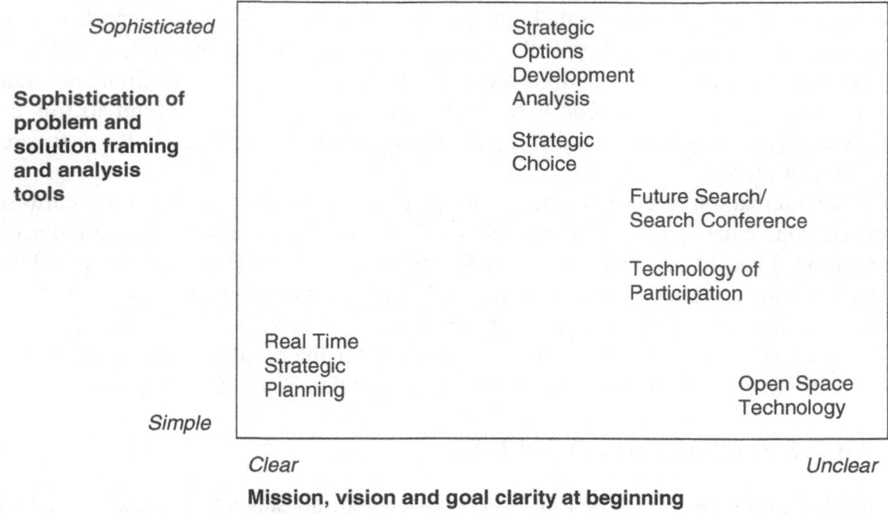

Fig. 5. Suitability of Large Scale Group Interventions, taken from [5]

domain can lead to incomplete requirements and a lot of extra work during implementation when this becomes apparent.

A lot of information is usually captured through structured requirement engineering, yet there is still a risk that some problems might be overlooked due to poor domain knowledge. Our suggestion of using Open Space Technology in the beginning of a development project aims at rectifying this by allowing developers and domain experts to mingle freely and discuss topics in a far more unstructured way than is usually done in requirement engineering. Hopefully this will result in creative dialogue, which surfaces topics and problem areas that would otherwise be overlooked.

Bryson and Anderson [5] compare seven large-scale interaction methods. These knowledge management methods are compared along the scales in figure 5 of (1) their usefulness in dealing with different clarity of mission, vision and goal and (2) the sophistication level of the tools needed to use the method. Open Space Technology is categorized as being good for unclear mission, vision and goal, and only needing a simple sophistication level of the tools to use. This fits well with our need for a simple technique for use early in the requirement phase when the goals of the project are still somewhat unclear.

We think this process can be an interesting one to try out to make developers know the domain better. Instead of only letting developers get into the domain through project managers or internal domain experts who often participate in the requirement process, this process lets them communicate directly with users on what the system should do. It also lets them get contact points in various parts of the receiving organization, and let them take part in different discussions – which should lead to new discussions when working internally.

4.3 Open Space Technology: Strengths and Weaknesses

The underlying positivistic assumptions and philosophy of Open Space Technology is its major strength and at the same time its major weakness.

The method makes for flexible agendas. This is at the expense of control by positional leaders of the group or organization. This is a critical point because project managers might not want to employ a method over which they have little or no control. However we argue that it is exactly this kind of flexible method that will allow points of interest to emerge that might not otherwise have emerged in a more structured process.

The method facilitates dialogue and organizational learning and in so doing enhances the human performance. It also gives the participants a sense of responsibility and ownership for their ideas. On the other hand this can only be achieved if the participants take responsibility for their own actions and involvement. It is also crucial that the participants are open and that they do not have advance expectations about the outcome. Therefore it is vital that the participation is voluntary and not forced upon them in any way as this might put a damper on the process.

4.4 Suggested Research Project

We are interested in investigating how the technique Open Space Technology functions in a small software company in order to give developers insight in domain knowledge, and if the technique makes them better able to find domain knowledge after the requirement process is over.

We intend to investigate this question by organizing an Open Space Technology workshop for a development project – involving both user representatives and developers for a half-day or one-day event. We will ask the project leader of the development project to briefly introduce the project, and describe some of the main challenges. We will then ask participants to suggest topics they are interested in discussing, which relate either development or use of the software system in question. The participants will then discuss the topics according to the Open Space Technology principles.

We will observe the discussions that arise in the workshop, and later interview the participants from the software company about their thoughts about the process. We will ask them to compare the process with work done in other projects. When the project completes, we will study the amount of re-work due to domain misunderstandings and compare this to another similar project in the company. We will focus on one of the four main outcomes of large-group interventions mentioned earlier, namely to what degree such a process is able to enhance the amount of relevant domain knowledge for a project.

References

1. Abdel-Hamid, T. and S.E. Madnick, Software Project Dynamics. 1991, Englewood Cliffs, NJ: Prentice Hall.
2. Blomqvist, K.: Asymmetry in Partnership Formation between Small and Large Technology Firms. In: Proc. Proceedings of 15th Annual Conference on Industrial Marketing and Purchasing, "Interactions, Relationships and Networks: Towards the New Millenium" (1999)
3. Bunker, B.B. and Alban, B.T. Large Group Interventions. San Francisco, California: Jossey-Bass Publishers, 1997.
4. Beck, K., Extreme Programming Explained. 2000: Addison-Wesley.

5. Bryson, J.M., Anderson, S.R., Applying Large-group Interaction Methods in the Planning and Implementation of Major Change Effort", Public Administration Review, vol 60, no 2, pp. 143 – 162, 2000.
6. Bröhl, A.-P. and W. Dröschel, The V-Model. 1995: Oldenbourg-Verlag.
7. Daskalantonakis, M., A practical view of software measurement and implementation experience within Motorola, in IEEE Trans. SW. Eng. 1992.
8. Doz, Y. L.: Technology Partnerships between Large and Smaller Firms: Some Critical Issues. In: F. J. Contractor and P. Lorange, (eds.): Cooperative Strategies in International Business. Lexington Books (1988)
9. Dingsøyr, T. and Bjørnsson, F. O., *Using Open Space Technology as a Method to Harvest Domain Knowledge*, Proceedings from WM2005: Professional Knowledge Management Experiences and Visions, Kaiserslautern, Germany, DFKI, Kaiserslautern, Germany, 2005, pp. 102 – 106.
10. Fayad, M. E., Laitinen, M., Ward, R. P.: Software Engineering in the Small. Communications of the ACM 43 (2000) 115-118
11. Glaser, B., Strauss, A. L.: The Discovery of Grounded Theory: Strategies for Qualitative Research. Aldine, Chigago (1967)
12. Houdek, F. and K. Schneider, Software Experience Center. The Evolution of the Experience Factory Concept., in International NASA-SEL Workshop. 1999.
13. Kauppinen, M., Vartiainen, M., Kontio, J., Kujala, S. and Sulonen, R., Implementing requirements engineering processes through organizations: success factors and challenges, Information and Software Technology, vol. 46, pp. 937 - 953, 2004.
14. Kontio, J., G. Getto, and D. Landes. Experiences in improving risk management processes using the concepts of the Riskit method. in Sixth International Symposium on the Foundations of Software Engineering (FSE-6). 1998. Orlando, USA.
15. Naur, P., Randell, B.: Software Engineering: Report on a Conference Sponsored by the NATO Science Committee, Garmisch, Germany, 7-11 Oct. 1968. Scientific Affairs Division (1969)
16. Rodriguez, D., M. Satpathy, and D. Pfahl. Effective software project management education through simulation models. An externally replicated experiment. in PROFES. 2004. Kansai Science City, Japan: Bomarius, F.
17. Schneider, K., Software Process Improvement in a FLOW Perspective, Proceedings from WM2005: Professional Knowledge Management Experiences and Visions, Kaiserslautern, Germany, DFKI, Kaiserslautern, Germany, 2005, pp. 82 - 86.
18. Schneider, K. A Descriptive Model of Software Development to Guide Process Improvement. in Conquest. 2004. Nürnberg, Germany: ASQF.
19. Schneider, K. LIDs: A Light-Weight Approach to Experience Elicitation and Reuse. in PROFES 2000. 2000. Oulo, Finland: Springer.
20. Schneider, K. Prototypes as Assets, not Toys. Why and How to Extract Knowledge from Prototypes. in ICSE-18. 1996. Berlin, Germany.
21. Smolander, K., Ovaska, P. and Juvonen, P., Local Software Organizations with Global Customers: a Survival Quest, Proceedings from WM2005: Professional Knowledge Management Experiences and Visions, Kaiserslautern, Germany, DFKI, Kaiserslautern, Germany, 2005, pp. 57 - 61.
22. Strauss, A. L., Corbin, J.: Basics of Qualitative Research: Grounded Theory Procedures and Applications. Sage Publications, Newbury Park, CA (1990)
23. Tapscott, D., Caston, A.: Paradigm Shift: The New Promise of Information Technology. McGraw-Hill (1993)
24. Tiwana, A., An empirical study of the effect of knowledge integration on software development projects, Information and Software Technology, vol. 46, pp. 899 - 906, 2004.

Facilitating Organisational Learning Through Causal Mapping Techniques in IS/IT Project Risk Management

Abdullah J. Al-Shehab, Robert T. Hughes, and Graham Winstanley

School of Computing, Mathematical and Information Sciences,
University of Brighton,
Watts Building, Moulsecoomb, Brighton, BN2 4GJ, UK
{A.A.Shehab, R.T.Hughes, G.Winstanley}@brighton.ac.uk

Abstract. Information System and Information Technology (IS/IT) development and implementation have become more difficult with the rapid introduction of new technology and the increasing complexity of the marketplace. IS/IT projects often encounter a range of problems that can be described as failure. Thus, learning from an analysis of past projects and from the issues contributing to failure is becoming a major stage in the risk management process. In IS/IT projects, it is common for groups of stakeholders to participate in planning and management. One important element in these activities is risk assessment, that is, the identification of potential risks and their interrelationships throughout the project lifecycle. The ability to visualise cause and effect risk networks and the capability for interactive network building and modification have the potential for individual and group risk identification, justification and prediction. In this paper we introduce Causal Mapping as a method of accomplishing this, and describe two experiments: one carried out with a group of masters-level students and a second with practitioners from a government organization who had experienced an IS/IT project failure. These two exploratory experiments have demonstrated the potential (and also some of the problems) of the approach in identifying problem areas in past projects, through the collaborative construction of cause and effect maps that allow project participants to visualise their perceptions.

1 Introduction

One survey of over 13,000 IT Projects [1] estimated that US corporations spent more than $255 billion per year on software development projects of which $55 billion was wasted on failed projects. The project success rate was just 34%, while the project failure rate was 15%, with 51% of projects suffering from cost overruns, time overruns, or a reduction in the features and functions delivered.

For some time IT projects have been notorious for their proneness to fail (see, for example, [9]). In the United Kingdom, recently reported problems include delays to an online hospital booking application in September 2004 [10], to the national firearms database in October 2004 [12] and to the implementation of a secure national radio system for ambulance and fire services in November 2004 [11]. A very well known

K.-D. Althoff et al. (Eds.): WM 2005, LNAI 3782, pp. 145 – 154, 2005.

supermarket chain reported a write-off of £260 millions associated with IT and supply chain systems [13]. The United Kingdom is not alone in suffering from these setbacks.

One reason that has been put forward for the prevalence of these failures is that information systems/information technology (IS/IT) applications are not constrained by physical laws [3]. "Software is largely free of constraints and its potential is therefore unlimited", according to [2]. Thus it is easy to embark on over-ambitious and ill-advised projects. This is perhaps exemplified by the supermarket project mentioned earlier: in that report [13] an analyst is quoted as suggesting that the organization "was too ambitious on the business side, trying to over-segment its customer base which meant that it, in turn, created an overly complex IT system that wouldn't scale."

This paper discusses issues of differing perceptions among project stakeholders during the post-evaluation process, and techniques of identifying and rationalising them into a combined and agreed model. Within this process, a method is introduced which is capable of presenting, in a visual diagrammatic fashion, the factors that have a bearing on project failure and their interrelationships. This allows the different stakeholders in a project to use the diagram to collaborate in the creation of risk models that can simulate the propagation and evolution of risks throughout the project life cycle.

2 Learning in the Risk Management Process

An effective organizational learning cycle can increase the capability and maturity levels of the team, project and organisation. However, although risk management is focussed on identifying future problems, it is usually difficult for people to foresee future events and problems [14]. The study of past projects, however, can help to 'sensitise' project participants to the potential obstacles to a new project's success. Pitagorsky [15] sums this up neatly: "The most important step to improve the quality of decision making is the Post-Implementation Review."

The processes by which an organisation can learn from past experiences are core elements of the concept of the 'learning organization' [16]. As Argyris [16] shows in his survey of the literature on learning organizations, some writers have identified obstacles that prevent organizations using past lessons as a basis for improving future performance. Leavitt and March [17] for example point out that organizations often adopt strategies that have worked in the past but which do not work in new situations. The lessons may be based on a small number of cases that might not in fact be typical. The links between cause and effect in past projects may not in fact be obvious or can be subject to controversy. What exactly happened in a past project may not be clear, and judgements about the relative success or failure of a project may depend on the viewpoint of individual stakeholders.

These obstacles to effective organizational learning do not in themselves invalidate the argument that organizations need to learn from past experience. In fact it is argued that they underline the need to make explicit the nature of the lessons learnt from past experience.

The research described below attempts to address some of these issues through the collaborative creation of causal mapping. This has been influenced by the constructivist paradigm that focuses on the way in which human actors use their experiences to construct mental models of the likely outcomes of future actions. Where actions are collaborative in nature, as in IS/IT projects, shared common cognitive models need to be constructed as the basis for future effective action. Causal mapping is examined as one possible tool to assist in the construction of such models. One issue to be considered is the degree to which individuals have common or differing perceptions of the same situation.

3 Causal Mapping

Our research is focussed on the use of the diagrammatic technique of Causal Mapping (CM) as a method of documenting past experience using IS/IT case studies. It involves assessing the ability of stakeholders to identify the relationships among problem areas in a case study by creating a visible map.

According to [5] "A causal map is a word-and-arrow diagram in which ideas and actions are causally linked with one another through the use of arrows. The arrows indicate how one idea or action leads to another." This approach is well established - one early use [6] was to analyse how diplomats and government officials decided and applied policies, particularly in the field of foreign policy. In the field of project management and operational research, they have been used extensively [5],[6]. It should be noted that causal maps are often referred to as "cognitive maps", which generally represent people's perceptions of the relationships between cause and effect in a situation. Huff [4] suggests that an advantage of causal maps is that they can portray information about a system more succinctly than a corresponding textual description. An example of a causal map is shown in Figure. 1.

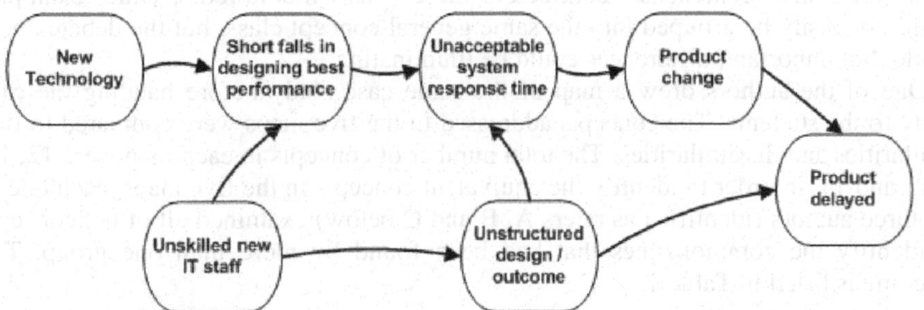

Fig. 1. Example of a causal map drawn in the student experiment

Each oval shape represents a problem area as a concept (variable) and the whole map represents a situation. The example above represents problem areas which have led to a delayed product.

4 Exploratory Experiment Using Causal Mapping with Students

There is a question about the degree of similarity in the perceptions that different observers have of the same situation. To explore this question, causal mapping was used to support the learning of students enrolled in the Master of Science (MSc) Information Systems programme within the School of Computing, Mathematical and Information Science at the University of Brighton. Fifteen MSc students were asked to use causal mapping to examine a case study of project failure, identifying different problems which led to the failure of an IT system. They were also required to identify the interrelations between the different variables they had identified. One of the objectives of the experiment was to familiarise students with post-mortem or post-evaluation processes.

The students were given a one-hour session to introduce Causal Mapping and explain how it could be used in such cases. They were divided into four groups to encourage discussion and were asked to draw a cognitive map of the case study. the one-hour tutorial group session explored the following:

- The case study being investigated
- How to identify problem areas in terms of cause and effects
- Methods of drawing CM and applying it to the data extracted from case study
- Analysis of resulting CM via group session.

The result was four different Causal Map diagrams representing four perceptions of the case study.

All four of the original groups could be said to have similar backgrounds as they were all masters students on the same programme. They were all detached from the case study in the sense that they had not been involved in the original project and should not therefore have any personal bias. All groups were provided with the same textual description of the case study and so were working from the same evidence.

Differences in how concepts were described by each group were observed. For example, while "contractors are – are not monitored" could be deemed to have the same declarative content as "contractors more – less monitored.". Other examples could not easily be grouped into the same general concept class, but the debate about subtle, but important, differences could be illuminating.

One of the authors drew a map of the same case study before handing the case study to the students. The concepts addressed in the five maps were compared to find similarities and dissimilarities. The total number of concepts in each map were 12, 11, 9, 11 and 14. In order to identify the equivalent concepts in the five maps, each one of the three authors (identified as raters A, B and C below) examined all of the concepts to identify the common ones that had been found by more than one group. The outcome is listed in Table 1.

Table 1. illustrates the equivalent concepts common to more than one map

	Identified concepts common to more that one map				
Rater	one group	two groups	three groups	four groups	five groups
A	25	3	2	5	-
B	18	5	3	5	-
C	26	7	-	3	1

All raters counted a large number of factors that were only identified by a single group. It is noticeable that in addition to the lack of agreement between the original groups, the raters themselves also often disagreed about which of the identified factors could be regarded as the same. The differences between the three raters often arose from disagreements about what an identified concept really meant. For example 'Need for Web presence' concept was considered by one of the authors equivalent to 'New Technology' but was not by the other two authors.

Even where groups agreed on the important concepts or factors, there could be disagreement over the relationships between the concepts. A particular problem was where two concepts were agreed to be related in terms of cause and effect, but some identified intermediate factors between the two while others did not – see Figure. 2 where the lower fragment has additional intermediate factors.

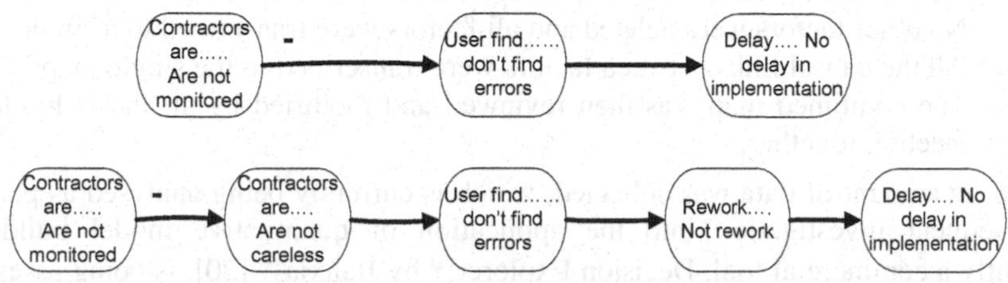

Fig. 2. Two examples of relationships from different maps

Note that in Figure 2 a slightly different notation is used to that in Figure 1. Two extremes, positive and negative, have been identified for each factor. A positive value at one node would normally lead to a positive value in any dependent nodes, while a negative value would lead to negative values in the dependent nodes. A minus sign by the arc indicates that this is reversed: that a positive value will lead to a negative value in the dependent nodes etc.

Despite these differences, students found the mapping exercise useful. They were asked to complete an evaluation form on how useful the causal mapping method was and how easy it was to grasp. The majority of the students supported the use of causal mapping and also found that the method was easy to grasp and could be used on such cases in the IS/IT world. Furthermore, the use of CM as a focus for debate appeared to stimulate the learning process.

5 An Exploratory Experiment Using IS/IT Practitioners

It might be expected that different results might be found when dealing with real IS/IT practitioners and a real project. One of the authors has documented a longitudinal case study in Kuwait. This was accomplished during several field trips from 2003 to 2005. The problematic project started in 1998-1999 and raised many failure issues at the beginning of 2000, and suffered from various setbacks during the following two years. At one point the project was stopped for a period of time, and many stakeholders thought that it had failed and been abandoned. However it was reinitiated and went through much revision of the project design and management approaches, but problems and issues remain with the project up to the current time.

For experimental purposes, the project team members were divided into two groups, managers (5 participants) and technical staff (8 participants). One of the objectives at this stage was to produce a combined diagram reflecting the perceptions of each group. It was considered that having both groups in one group session was undesirable because of the effect that managers might have on staff opinion in an open session.

The possible causes of the problems with the project were explored with project participants in each group using causal mapping. Casual maps were drawn individually by project team members facilitated by one of the authors. Individual maps were then combined to produce a single map for each of the two groups using the following protocol:

- Similar factors identified by different participants were combined
- No other factors were deleted and all factors were transcribed to a single map
- All the causal links between factors were transcribed to the single map
- The combined map was then reviewed and modified by all the individuals meeting together.

A large amount of data was collected, which is currently being analysed as part of a subsequent investigation into the application of quantitative model building. Currently a commercial tool, Decision Explorer™ by Banxia™ [20], is being assessed for use in this case study.

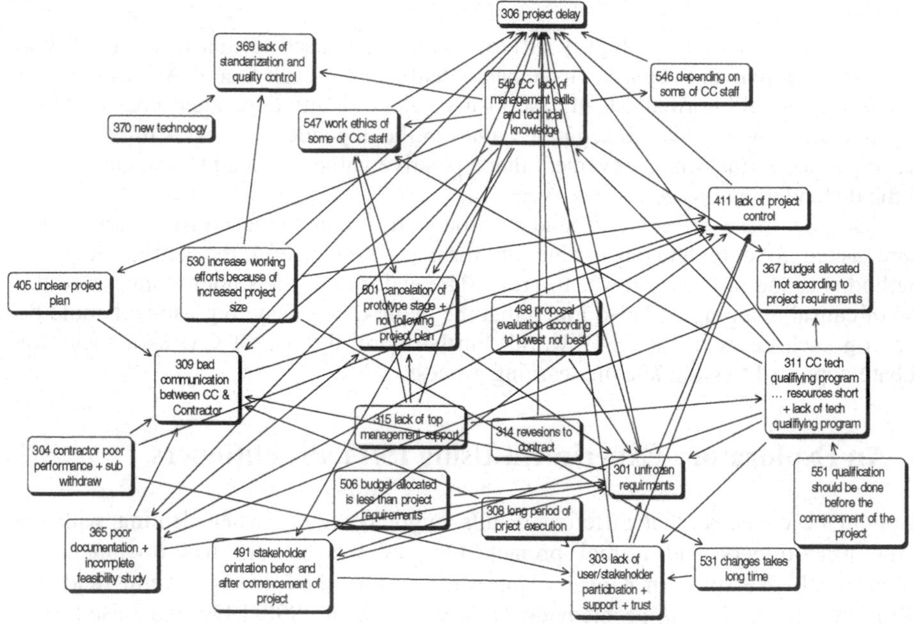

Fig. 3. Managers combined map

The managers' combined map consolidated 92 concepts from five individual maps, and was then discussed by the mangers in a group session. This led to a final version of the combined map with a total of 25 concepts. Figure 3 shows the combined managers' map and illustrates how complex the combined map can be.

This process was repeated for the employees' (analysts and programmers) group. The first version of the map produced a total number of 123 concepts and the final combined map had 24 concepts.

6 Similarity of Concepts in Management and Staff Maps

The combining of individual maps clearly leads to complicated models, even after group review. Two issues arise from these complex models:

- Are the maps a good reflection of the situation being examined? It could be that the underlying pattern of causality really is complex.
- Are the maps effective guides to future action? Even if a model is a good representation of what has happened in a particular project, it may not be easy to apply to future projects.

These questions are the basis for ongoing research. An immediate task has been to measure the differences in perception between the two groups and also differences between members in each group.

At group level, each of the authors acted as a rater and identified those factors that were shared by the two groups. There were some interesting differences – see Table 2 below.

Table 2. Illustrating the equivalent concepts common to two maps

	Identified concepts common to more that one map	
Rater	one group	two groups
A	35	7
B	39	5
C	33	8

The small number of factors common to both groups is striking. There is also, once again, much variation between the raters' evaluations.

Taking the managers' group alone, the three raters attempted to highlight factors that had been identified by all five group members on an individual level, four of the members, three members and so on. This was followed in the usual way by a group session for the raters in which apparent differences in interpretation were identified and debated. The combined results are shown in Table 3.

Table 3. Concepts identified in group-session by more than one group Members

	Identified concepts common to more that one map				
Rater	one group	two groups	three groups	four groups	five groups
A	28	9	6	2	4
B	28	6	3	2	4
C	32	5	5	2	5

A major reason for the differences between raters was that it was only rarely that exactly the same wording was used by different participants. This led to problems of interpretation. In some cases it was simply that the wording used was ambiguous. In other cases, different raters might use different criteria for associating concepts – for example one rater might group together 'little project management experience' and 'little development experience' as both relate to inexperience, but other raters might take a different view.

The exercise above did not look at cause and effect relationships, but was limited to the factors (that is, the nodes rather than the arcs). When a broader view was taken of both factors and the relationships between them, then many of the ambiguities were resolved. For example, in the case of 'little project experience' and 'little development experience', these clearly had different effects on the outcomes and should therefore have been distinguished.

Another cause of contention was where similar but arguably distinct factors could be grouped under some collective title. An example of this was 'changing requirements' and 'new requirements'. While both would have some outcomes in common, 'changing requirements' could have additional ones, such as the need to examine and modify existing code. Differences in outcomes was agreed to be a reason for not merging factors.

7 Discussion and Conclusion

Despite the differences in perceptions and the consequent complexity of the negotiated common maps, the participants still reported that the exercise was useful in terms of organisational learning. The series of experiments had the dual advantage of improving the participants' knowledge base in risk management, and also served to illustrate how the method could be used to facilitate a collective continual learning process in project risk management. It may be that the value was in the process rather than the final product.

As far as organisational learning is concerned, the participants reported the following advantages of causal mapping (CM):

- Group discussions guided by CM encourages participation.
- CM-facilitated group discussions tends to enhance communication between the project members.
- Using CM provides a clear picture of the project situation through its diagrammatic representation.
- The diagram enables identification of the interrelations between risks.

Ontological issues remain, as is the apparent problem of the disparity of perceptions between participants. However, the processes involved in producing causal maps describing risks within a project are useful as an elicitation method, and the differences that emerge are in themselves important in brainstorming (group) sessions. The ability to visualise cause and effect networks, plus facilities to dynamically modify them, has the potential, not only to create agreed and justified risk models, but also to facilitate documentation, model re-use and knowledge management and to reach a level of consensus.

It should be recognised that the ontological issues that emerged were accentuated by having disparate groups of people, with different roles and with potentially different ways of expressing concepts. As Gruber [7] points out, "One problem is how to accommodate the stylistic and organizational differences among representations while preserving declarative content."

We are involved in exploring the usefulness of CMs in identifying what has gone wrong in past projects. The concept of subsequently applying this to new projects is the motivation for our investigation, but this is not the focus of this paper. We have found that individuals tend to have different views of what has happened in a project, and this is the case whether all individuals are looking at the same textual description or considering a real project that they have been involved in. We have found in the experiments forming the basis of this paper, that managers and staff may have different views of what has gone wrong within a project. While there are apparent differences of opinion, the problem that we need to address for new projects is how to build a consensus that can form the basis for future co-ordinated action. Some of the problems are caused by ambiguity in terminology and some through differences in the granularity of defining concepts. This paper has reported some of our research which is concerned with seeking ways of building consensus, by making explicit through CM techniques the assumptions that people base their opinions on.

Another line of research is the investigation of tools and methods that would allow participants to test out assumptions by allowing them to exercise the models they have created. This could be based on capturing the strength of beliefs and the likelihood of occurrence of concepts from the experiments' participants, and translating these perceptions into values, which may then be used to simulate the map as a working model. One approach being considered is 'Fuzzy Cognitive Maps' [18], and what Montibeller, et al [20] refers to as 'Reasoning Maps'.

Acknowledgment

We would like to thank those of our colleagues who have contributed to this work, especially Tim Brady and Nick Marshal of CENTRIM at University of Brighton.

References

1. Standish Group International, Inc. "CHAOS Chronicles report", Yarmouth, Massachusetts,USA,[online]< http://www.standishgroup.com/press/article.php?id=2>(2003)
2. The Royal Academy of Engineering : The Challenges of Complex IT Projects. (April 2004) ISBN 1-903496-15-2
3. Brooks, F.P: No silver bullet, essence and accidents of software engineering. IEEE Computer (1987) April 10-19
4. Huff, A.: Mapping Strategic Thought., Wiley and Sons, USA(1990)
5. Bryson, J., M., Ackermann, F., Eden, C., Finn, C., B.: Visible Thinking: Unlocking causal mapping for practical business results. John Wiley & Sons, Ltd. England (2004)
6. Axelrod, R. (ed.) Structure of decision: The cognitive maps of political elites. Princeton University Press, Princeton, NJ, USA (1976)

7. Gruber, T., R.: A Translational Approach to Portable Ontology Specifications. Knowledge Systems Laboratory technical Report KSL 92-71, Stanford University, CA. (1993)
8. Al-Shehab, A., Hughes, B., Winstanley, G.: Using Causal Mapping Methods to Identify and Analyse Risk in Information System Projects as a Post-Evaluation Process: ECITE 2004: The 11th European Conference on Information Technology Evaluation. Amsterdam (2004)
9. Flowers, S. Software Failure: Management Failure, John Wiley & Sons (1996)
10. Arnott, S. "Delays hit NHS bookings trial" Computing 2 September (2004a) p1
11. Arnott, S. "Emergency services face network delays" Computing 18 November (2004b) p1
12. Nash, E :"Firearms database delayed once again" Computing 28th October(2004) p1
13. Knights, M :"Sainsbury's dumps inefficient systems" Computing 21st October(2004) p1
14. Wiegers, K. :Know Your Enemy: Software Risk Management. Software Development magazine, October 1998.[16] Pitagorsky, G. (2000) PM Network, Project Management Institute, March, (1998) pp 35-39
15. Pitagorsky, G :PM Network, Project Management Institute, March, (2000) pp 35-39
16. Argyris, C. :On organizational learning. (2nd Edition) Blackwell, London(1999)
17. Leavitt, B., and March, J.G. :"Organizational learning", Annual Review of Sociology 14 (1988)
18. Kosko, B. :Fuzzy cognitive maps. International Journal of Man-Machine Studies. (1986) 24, 65-75
19. Decision Explorer is manufactured by Banxia Software,www.banxia.com
20. Montibeller G., Ackermann, F., Belton, V., Ensslin, L. "Reasoning maps for decision aiding: An integrated approach for problem structuring and multi-criteria evaluation", the 46th Conference of the British Operational Research Society, 7-9 Sep, York, UK (2004)

Integration of E-Learning and Knowledge Management – Barriers, Solutions and Future Issues

Eric Ras[1], Martin Memmel[2], and Stephan Weibelzahl[3]

[1] Fraunhofer Institute for Experimental Software Engineering,
Fraunhofer-Platz 1, 67663 Kaiserslautern, Germany
Eric.Ras@iese.fraunhofer.de
[2] German Research Center for Artificial Intelligence DFKI GmbH,
Erwin-Schrödinger-Straße 57, 67663 Kaiserslautern, Germany
Martin.Memmel@dfki.uni-kl.de
[3] National College of Ireland, Mayor Street, Dublin 1, Ireland
sweibelzahl@ncirl.ie

Abstract. The findings of the Workshop on Learner-oriented Knowledge Management and KM-oriented e-Learning (LOKMOL 2005) are summarized in this paper. The results are derived from the presented papers as well as from the moderated discussion during the workshop. First, the main barriers that have to be passed in order to integrate KM and e-Learning are discussed. Secondly, the approaches and technologies of the LOKMOL contributions are summarized and thirdly we provide issues that should be addressed in the future in order to successfully integrate KM and e-Learning.

1 Introduction

The high potential for synergies between Knowledge Management (KM) and e-Learning seems obvious given the many interrelations and dependencies of these two fields. However, the relationship has not yet been fully understood and harnessed. The Learner-oriented Knowledge Management and KM-oriented e-Learning Workshop (LOKMOL 2005) held at the Third Conference on Professional Knowledge Management (WM2005) therefore aimed at bringing together researchers and practitioners who are interested in combining findings from both fields. On the one hand, learning is considered to be a fundamental part of Knowledge Management because employees must internalize, or learn, shared knowledge before they can use it to perform specific tasks. So far, research within KM has addressed learning mostly as part of knowledge sharing processes and focuses on specific forms of informal learning (e.g., learning in a community of practice) or on providing access to learning resources or experts. On the other hand, learning might also benefit from KM technologies. Especially those technologies that focus on the support of technical and organizational components can play an important role in relation to the development of professional e-Learning systems.

The LOKMOL workshop placed a great deal of emphasis on the view that KM needs to take into account findings from the social sciences such as pedagogics or psychology, to be effective in terms of learning and that learning can profit from available KM concepts and technologies.

K.-D. Althoff et al. (Eds.): WM 2005, LNAI 3782, pp. 155 – 164, 2005.

2 The Workshop

A total of 32 participants from research as well as from industry from all over the world attended the one and a half day workshop. The participants' background was manifold: computer science, mathematics, as well as instructional design and pedagogics. Some of them are working in the KM domain, others are engaged mainly in the learning or e-Learning domain. Amongst all participants, about a dozen mentioned that they are working in between the two domains, i.e., not explicitly in the KM or e-Learning domain. The mix up of different interests, meanings, and expertise brought up interesting discussions. Many important findings have been gathered.

The workshop was structured in four sessions. Each session started with three short presentations and concluded in a moderated discussion. The presentations served as a good basis for the sub-sequent discussion. In addition, each discussion was motivated by prepared questions posed by the moderators. During the discussion mind maps and wall papers were used to capture the main findings. These findings are presented in the next section by starting first with the identified barriers, then with solutions presented by the authors. We conclude with future issues to be solved.

3 The Workshop Findings

As Schmidt motivated in his paper, KM and e-Learning serve both the same purpose: facilitating learning and competence development in organizations. However, they follow two different perspectives. KM is related to an organizational perspective, because it addresses the lack of sharing knowledge among members of the organizations by encouraging the individuals making their knowledge explicit by creating knowledge chunks which can be stored in repositories for later re-use or participating in communities of practice; opposed to that, e-Learning emphasizes an individual perspective, as it focuses on the individual acquisition of new knowledge and the technical means to support this construction process [12].

In organizations where KM and e-Learning systems are used, most working processes are very knowledge intensive and involve many people working at different locations and on different tasks. The context in which people are working is changing constantly through changing work processes, different tasks or problems to be solved. These facts require continuous competence development. Ley, Lindstaedt & Albert refer in their paper to recent work stating that one can differentiate between short-term performance support that would involve learning simple procedures or problem solving strategies, and long-term people development [8]. Regarding the short-term performance support, learning is often based on getting involved in communities of practice, accessing knowledge repositories in order to find suitable knowledge, or on receiving the right information for a specific situation pro-actively by the system. Learning is happening just-in-time and in context. *Just-in-time learning* can be defined as the acquisition of knowledge and skills as needed. As Bonar stated in the late 80s, learning becomes fragmented and bite-sized because of the small portions of information and learning content delivered to the learner [2]. It is obvious that a lot of information chunks are stored within the KM repositories. Hence, there are many opportunities for just-in-time learning using relatively small information chunks in the context of use. Opposed to that from a long-term learning perspective, "people develop competencies that enable them to perform competently in a broad area range of situations" and not just for the current situation the learner is currently in [8].

Another important issue is that individuals should be able to recognize trends and to identify correlations within their daily work or the subjects they are working on [6]. Thus, different and innovative ways of learning are required, and hence a new type of learning systems.

Ley et al. mention interesting studies that show "that only 20-30% of what is being learned in formal training is actually transferred to the workplace in a way that enhances performance and that 80-90% of what employees know of their job, they know from informal learning" [8]. Does this mean hat we should focus on informal learning and reduce formal education in organizations? The following section shows that we should not reject formal education, it rather explains why learning in organizations has to follow some guidelines to make it more successful. We capitalize on the integration of KM and e-Learning as a solution for better job performance through learning.

3.1 Identified Barriers for Integration

An interview-based study demonstrated that perceived connections between KM and e-Learning are not operationalized, i.e., integration ideas are rarely implemented in practice [5]. The reasons for the so far weak integration of KM and e-Learning on a conceptual and technical level are related to several barriers that are elaborated next. They are mainly based on the written contributions to the workshop, the discussions done during the workshop and other problems identified in the literature that have not been explicitly addressed during the workshop:

1. Problems on a Conceptual Level

Ley et al. propose a division of a typical workplace into a work space, a learning space, and a knowledge space. In order to enable effective learning, these spaces have to be linked. One of the arising problems is *cognitive disconnection* between the three spaces, because "each of the spaces has an inherent structure which mirrors to some extent the mental model of the people who are using it" [8]. Benmahamed, Ermine & Tchounikine state in their work that one of the problems is to connect already available conceptual KM models to learning activities and existing learning standards such as IMS Learning Design [1].

2. Problems on a Technical Level

Each of the spaces listed above (i.e., work, learning, and knowledge space) is implemented on different technical systems [8]. Examples of these spaces include specific desktop applications, e-Learning platforms, and KM System such as the Intranet or a Wiki system. Each of these systems potentially has its own content structure, which makes the integration of the systems more difficult.

3. Problem of Neglecting Learning Processes

KM addresses learning mostly as a part of knowledge sharing processes and focuses on specific forms of informal learning (e.g., learning in a community of practice) or on providing access to information resources or experts. KM systems focus on knowledge acquisition, storage, retrieval, and deployment of knowledge. However they do not explicitly address learning processes themselves, which is essential for effective learning and competence development [10]. In addition, Schmidt states that "KM does not fully realize that it is mainly about facilitating purpose-oriented learning in organizations" [12].

4. Problem of the Amount of Guidance Provided
As described above competency development takes mostly place during informal learning at the workplace. The learning process is characterized by self-organized activities such as selecting the environment for learning (e.g., Internet), defining learning goals (e.g., related to a work problem), finding and selecting content for learning (e.g., websites or colleagues), and following a preferred learning path. As motivated above, the competence development process largely relies on the learner's own initiative. Performing these activities requires certain skills and expertise in the domain. This is considered to be one of the main barriers for an integration of KM and e-Learning: While many KM systems provide little or no guidance to inexperienced individuals, many e-Learning courses provide too much guidance and prevent the learner from self-directed learning. They are not flexible in terms of their navigation, or content selection/hiding.

According to constructivist learning perspectives, knowledge cannot be transmitted to learners, but must be individually constructed and socially co-constructed by learners [7]. Learning systems should provide learners with a wide range of services to assist and facilitate knowledge construction, because learners may construct their own meaningful understanding of a learning theme from different paths rather than imposing them on a particular learning method. This means that the amount of guidance provided to the learner should be adapted to his/her needs and context.

5. Problem of Context Neglect
Situated learning approaches developed mainly at the end of the 1980s emphasize that a human's tasks always depend on the situation they are performed in, i.e., they are influenced by the characteristics and relationships of the *context* [3]. Because of the relation between cognition and context, knowledge and the cognitive activities meant to create, adapt, and restructure the knowledge can't be seen as isolated psychological products – they all depend on the situation in which they take place.

Schmidt highlights the problem that both KM and e-Learning have a limited and isolated consideration of context. First, e-Learning solutions often do not consider that corporate learning takes place in an organizational context and that learning goals are based on real-world needs. In addition, the author states that also the authoring process takes place (and is encouraged to take place) in the same context as the learning itself, which relates obviously to the peer-to-peer knowledge sharing philosophy where the "knowledge re-users" (i.e., the learners) also become knowledge creators. Secondly, many KM approaches neglect the fact that the delivery of information chunks does not necessarily mean that the user acquires new knowledge. In particular, if the individual's context and characteristics are ignored (i.e., his/her knowledge structures, preferred needs, and learning styles) learning might not take place at all [12].

6. Problem of Structuring and Annotating Content
Ideally, integrating KM and e-Learning also means to use all available knowledge resources in an organization (e.g., documents, humans, experiences, how-tos, process

descriptions) as learning material. This entails some difficult problems, because e-Learning in contrast to KM puts much more emphasis on delivering personalized content and exploiting relations, links and cross references existing within the learning material. This of course requires to structure the material into relatively small fragments which can then be combined into bigger objects in the preferred way. In addition to that, all fragments and combined objects have to be annotated with adequate metadata to provide information about relations to other objects, technical prerequisites, presentation style and so on. Only a small part of this work can be done automatically, most of it has to be done by hand and takes a lot of time. In a typical e-Learning scenario, most of the content is produced in advance, and the repository is usually not very dynamic. In contrast to that, content is produced all the time and often by the employees themselves in a KM scenario. This makes the process of structuring and annotating very difficult, because in most cases there is simply no time available for these tasks. A middle course, meeting the demands of both easy authoring on the one hand as well as enabling interconnectedness and personalization of content on the other hand is required.

7. Problem of Lack of Interactivity
Another barrier in the use of KM for e-Learning is the fact that information chunks in KM systems often lack interactivity [13]. Learning tasks and activities are an important characteristic of good instructional design. Engaging learners and actively involving them in the learning process often increases motivation and learning gain. However, the information chunks in KM systems are usually not designed for instruction. To be successfully re-used for learning these information chunks need to be embedded in interactive learning activities.

Another strategy to make instruction effective is tailoring of content and teaching strategy to the learner's individual needs and preferences. "The effectiveness of human tutors generally does not stem from an overabundance of training and preparation but from the tutor's ability to work one-to-one with a student, and to provide constant feedback that enables constructivist learning" [13]. However, the concept of interactivity is suffering from lack of operational definitions.

8. Problem of Dynamic Adaptation
Adaptive systems strive to monitor students and select next learning steps. In fact, Brusilovsky and Vassileva [4] distinguish between two types of adaptive course sequencing: adaptive and dynamic courseware generation. While adaptive courseware generation creates a course suited to the needs of the students based on a static student model before they encounter it, systems with dynamic courseware generation observe and dynamically regenerate the course according to the student's progress. Especially the latter type of adaptation might encounter more and more attention in the future, because it is able to adapt learning to the current context during the learning process. Thus, adaptivity might help to re-use existing information in KM systems for instruction. However, conventional e-Learning systems are usually not prepared for dynamic selection and sequencing of learning material yet.

9. Presentation of Content not Cognitively Adequate
Another important issue is that individuals should be able to recognize trends and to identify correlations within their daily work or the subjects they are working on. So far, most e-Learning systems do not support recognizing trends or correlations

between subjects. Jantke, Lunzer & Fujima emphasize that e-Learning could be much more successful by making it more cognitively adequate, entertaining, and illustrating to the learner [6].

3.2 Solutions

Several methods and approaches have been proposed at the workshop to address the gap between KM and e-Learning. While some of these approaches aim to facilitate or improve learning with KM systems, others extend learning management systems by exploiting KM technologies.

Ley et al. [8] identified competence management as a possible approach to facilitate learning with KM systems. The authors describe a framework that establishes a connection between competencies and tasks or performance outcomes. Competency development can be seen as an individually controlled learning process rather than a centrally-managed development initiative. It acknowledges the fact that organizations need to support individual, work task related learning paths, so called informal learning. The authors suggest that an environment that supports working and learning needs to take into account two aspects: First, it must provide content for learning purposes and support learners in finding appropriate content. Secondly, it has to support learning interactions, e.g., a lessons-learned meeting at the end of a project, or asking supervisors and experts for advice.

Moreover, competence management can be used for developing training paths by means of weighting training methodologies according to their potential application in order to meet defined pedagogical as well as psychological objectives [9].

Yacci [13] illustrates an approach that creates interactive instruction out of static knowledge components as often found in KM systems. Based on this approach, existing material might be augmented and reused for learning purposes. A so called *Conversational Diagnostic Agent* (CDA) provides a diagnosis, in terms of skills, that can be used by students or faculty members to access instructional resources. The CDA uses a student model that is based on a learning hierarchy, where skills are decomposed into requisite sub-skills and where relationships amongst the skills are specified.

Other approaches aim at extending learning management systems by exploiting existing KM technologies. In particular, approaches that support social and collaborative learning have been proposed. For instance, Richter, Allert & Nejdl [11] show that *Minimal Activity Plans* (MAPs) can foster self-organized learning in an organization. Those plans are described by a more heuristic description framework and have to be interpreted by each recipient. MAPs do not describe work procedures in isolation but aim to encode the meaning of the activity within the organization and enable learning by involving individuals in purposive activities.

Schmidt [12] suggests to integrate working and learning on a process level, as well as through learning management, knowledge management, human capital management, and collaboration solutions on a technical level. By the incorporation of context-awareness of employees into the design of learning solutions, learning in organizations could be improved. In particular, a learning environment should capture the learner's context and characteristics (e.g., position, role, task, prior knowledge, goals). The environment's delivery method should take the context into account, e.g., by tailoring content for learning on demand or long term strategic learning. Finally, most resources stored in KM systems are created in context which must be considered when reusing the material for information or learning purposes.

Jantke, Lunzer & Fujima [6] proposed to integrate KM and exploratory e-Learning with so called *Subjunctive Interfaces*. Exploratory learning aims at learning experiences that offer opportunities to recognize patterns of knowledge. Subjunctive interfaces support users in this process by offering multiple enquiries in parallel. The authors demonstrated the feasibility of their approach in two kinds of domains relevant to e-Learning: dynamic simulation, where a learner may need to explore how a simulation's outcome is affected by various conditions; and information retrieval, including exploratory studies in which a student may systematically gather information from Internet sources.

Standards play an important role both in e-Learning systems as well as in KM systems, and KM technologies can support the learners' needs and individual learning processes. Benmahamed et al. [1] show that the IMS Learning Design modeling language supports an integration of learning and KM; they use the Knowledge Management Mask methodology for knowledge capitalization to design e-Learning activities. This is done by matching Mask models and the concepts of the IMS Learning Design modeling language.

3.3 Future Issues

The variety of approaches presented in this workshop demonstrates that there is a recognizable trend towards a stronger cooperation between the fields of e-Learning and KM, and that there are ways to narrow the gap between these two related fields. Such integration has the potential to dramatically change today's understanding of education towards lifelong learning, particularly when linked to contributions from dynamically changing public and organizational knowledge repositories. The contributions to this workshop showed that the integration of e-Learning and KM is more than just topic-oriented delivery of information chunks by following non-adaptive processes that are prescribed by a centrally managed learning initiative. In particular, the contributions from the workshop point to the following considerations, which in turn have implications for future research in the area:

- Pedagogical and psychological aspects as well as the adherence of the current context are considered when learning methodologies and learning content is chosen to meet certain learning objectives; an issue for the future will be dealing with imperfect and dynamic user context information.
- Learning objectives are more related to the development of competencies, which are connected to task outcomes, instead of learning specific topics; learning hierarchies (e.g., skill decomposition methods) are applied to support the connection between e-Learning and KM.
- Solutions that are developed focus more and more on facilitating self-directed and self-organized learning instead of prescribed instructions provided by the

system; competency development should be an individually controlled learning process rather than a centrally managed development initiative.

- Automatic competency profiling could be automated by using competence performance structures. Due to the fact, that these structures integrate competencies with the tasks performed, profiling can be done within the usual work processes.
- Some of the presented approaches are more flexible because they are based on heuristics instead of descriptive frameworks. Adaptation of instruction during run-time seems to be a promising approach; the concept of *Automated interactivity* is an idea that would create interactive instruction out of static knowledge components. The problem of structuring and annotating content available in a KM system to suit the needs of e-Learning could be solved by matching existing standards for KM and e-Learning.
- The requirement for more interactivity, more personalization through adaptation of delivered learning content, and more reuse of content will lead to a higher relevancy of sound Software Engineering (SE) principles, methods, and techniques: e-Learning content has to be considered more and more as *Software* due to its increasing complexity in terms of interactivity with the learner and the system, different media used, increased set of metadata, and the demand for adaptability. Since component-based SE, Product Lines Architectures, and agent-oriented SE have systemized the reuse process and have made software reuse more comprehensive, these approaches could also play a crucial role for the development of future e-Learning content.
- Other problems that remain to be solved are: How long should a system remember the context of the conversation? How long should the computer believe the evidence that a student possesses any given skill when a learning process stops and starts over time?
- New approaches should emphasize more on mapping existing well-developed KM models to e-Learning specifications and standards. This will facilitate the transformation of knowledge structures and knowledge chunks to learning activity structures and learning content.
- Finally, learning is not just enabled by providing content and using the right methods but also by enabling learning through the involvement of individuals in purposive activities and real working tasks.

The discussions and results show that the integration of KM and e-Learning will only be mastered when researchers and developers of many different disciplines work together. It is clear that we will not be able to find a final solution during the next years since the development of both KM and e-Learning systems are evolving fast and hence, a lot of new research issues will arise.

As is perhaps always the case in research of this kind, more empirical research is necessary to validate the latest developments in the field of integrated e-Learning and KM. Further workshops like LOKMOL are essential to keep the community informed about recent developments in this research field and to keep the integration process ongoing.

Acknowledgements

We would like to thank all individuals and institutions who contributed to the success of the workshop: the committee of the WM2005 conference for providing a perfect basis for organizing and conducting this workshop, the authors for submitting their papers and lending us their insight into recent developments in their research areas and the program committee members (see below) for their hard work reviewing the submitted papers.

- Gabriela Avram, Centre de Recherche Public Henri Tudor, Luxembourg
- John D'Ambra, University of New South Wales, Sydney, Australia
- Jürgen Cleve, Wismar University, Wismar, Germany
- Gunter Grieser, Technical University Darmstadt, Darmstadt, Germany
- Dieuwke de Haan, Technische Universiteit Eindhoven, Eindhoven, The Netherlands
- Jozef Hvorecky, College of Management, Bratislava, Slovakia
- David Jonassen, University of Missouri-Columbia, Columbia, USA
- Rob Koper, Open University of the Netherlands, Heerlen, The Netherlands
- Steffen Lange, Darmstadt University of Applied Science, Darmstadt, Germany
- Stefanie Lindstaedt, Know-Center Graz, Graz, Austria
- Frank Maurer, University of Calgary, Calgary, Canada
- Patrick Waterson, Fraunhofer IESE, Kaiserslautern, Germany
- Sandra Zilles, DFKI GmbH, Kaiserslautern, Germany

References

1. Benmahamed, D., Ermine, J.-L., Tchounikine, P.: From MASK Knowledge Management Methodology to Learning Activities Described with IMS-LD. Lecture Notes in Artificial Intelligence, this volume. Springer-Verlag, Berlin Heidelberg New York (2005)
2. Bonar, J.G.: The Bite-Sized Architecture. Technical Report, Learning Research and Development Center, University of Pittsburgh, Pittsburgh, Pennsylvania (1988)
3. Brown, J.S., Collins, A., Duguid, P.: Situated Cognition and the Culture of Learning. Educational Researcher, 18 (1) (1989) 32-42
4. Brusilovsky, P., Vassileva, J.: Course sequencing techniques for large-scale web-based education. Int. J. Continuing Engineering Education and Lifelong Learning, 13 (2003) 75-94
5. Efimova, L., Swaak, J.: KM and (e)-learning: towards an integral approach? Proc. of KMSS02, EKMF (2002) 63-69
6. Jantke, K., Lunzer, A., Fujima, J.: Subjunctive Interfaces in Exploratory e-Learning. Lecture Notes in Artificial Intelligence, this volume. Springer-Verlag, Berlin Heidelberg New York (2005)
7. Jonassen, D.: Designing constructivist learning environments. In C. M. Reigeluth (Ed), Instructional Design Theories and Models: A New Paradigm of Instructional Theory. Marwah: Lawrence Erlbaum Associates, Publishers, Vol. II (1999) 215-240
8. Ley, T., Lindstaedt, S. N., Albert, D.: Supporting Competency Development in Informal Workplace Learning. Lecture Notes in Artificial Intelligence, this volume. Springer-Verlag, Berlin Heidelberg New York (2005)

9. Pannese L., Lenardon S., Nitti V., Santalmasi M., Festorazzi V.: Competence Tracking and Automatic Training Design Simulation, In: K.-D. Althoff, A. Dengel, R. Bergmann, M. Nick, T. Roth-Berghofer (Eds.). WM 2005: Contributions to the 3rd Conference Professional Knowledge Management - Experiences and Visions, April 10-13, 2005, Kaiserslautern, Germany. DFKI, Kaiserslautern (2005) 156-159
10. Ras, E., Avram, G., Weibelzahl, S., Waterson, P.: Using Weblogs for Knowledge Sharing and Learning in Information Spaces. Journal of Universal Computer Science, 11 (3) (2005) 394-409
11. Richter C., Allert H., Nejdl W.: Minimal Activity Plans: Artifacts for Self-Organized Learning within Organizations. In: K.-D. Althoff, A. Dengel, R. Bergmann, M. Nick, T. Roth-Berghofer (Eds.). WM 2005: Contributions to the 3rd Conference Professional Knowledge Management - Experiences and Visions, April 10-13, 2005, Kaiserslautern, Germany. DFKI, Kaiserslautern (2005) 166-169
12. Schmidt, A.: Bridging the Gap between Knowledge Management and E-Learning with Context-Aware Corporate Learning. Lecture Notes in Artificial Intelligence, this volume. Springer-Verlag, Berlin Heidelberg New York (2005)
13. Yacci, M.: The Promise of Automated Interactivity. Lecture Notes in Artificial Intelligence, this volume. Springer-Verlag, Berlin Heidelberg New York (2005)

From MASK Knowledge Management Methodology to Learning Activities Described with IMS – LD

Djilali Benmahamed[1], Jean-Louis Ermine[1], and Pierre Tchounikine[2]

[1] Institut National des Télécommunications, Département Systèmes d'Information,
9, rue Charles Fourier, 91011 Evry Cedex – France
{djilali.benmahamed, jean-louis.ermine}@int-evry.fr
[2] Laboratoire d'Informatique de l'Université du Maine – CNRS FRE 2730,
Avenue Laennec, 72085 Le Mans cedex 9 – France
pierre.tchounikine@lium.univ-lemans.fr

Abstract. In this paper we present how the way knowledge capitalized using the Knowledge Management Mask methodology can be used to design E-learning activities by matching Mask models and the concepts proposed by the IMS-Learning Design modelling language. Our study consists in highlighting the e-learning aspects encapsulated in these MASK models carried out around a domain of activity, via a writing these elements in the description language IMS - Learning Design; in a preoccupation of reusability and reengineering.

1 Introduction

The general context of the work is the integration of Knowledge Management principles and methodologies and E-Learning requirements. More precisely, we are interested in the construction of learning activities from Knowledge Management systems. Learning activities are activities designed to make learners/employees achieve a given set of actions that will help them internalize knowledge. This follows the pedagogic constructivist approach that promotes "learning by doing" rather than just reading documents. Let us consider an organization that uses a given project management methodology and has to train its employees to this method. Presenting documents that describe the method (i.e., inert e-learning material) is necessary, but not sufficient. It can be powerfully completed by a learning activity that consists in proposing to a group of n employees to achieve a project following the methodology that they are supposed to learn, using E-Communication (Mail, Forum, Collaborative tools, etc.) to achieve this collaborative e-learning activity.

Building such a learning activity requires first identifying the scenarios that will be proposed to the trainees, the different tasks to perform, the different roles to be distributed, etc. and then modelling these different aspects. When the knowledge that is to be acquired is part of the company Knowledge Management system, it appears natural to build the learning activities scenarios from the data stored in the Knowledge Management system.

In this paper, we present the way proposed suggested to achieve such a process and, more precisely, the way proposed to construct learning scenarios from the Mask

K.-D. Althoff et al. (Eds.): WM 2005, LNAI 3782, pp. 165 – 175, 2005.

Knowledge Management methodology and to represent them using the IMS-Learning Design language. The paper shows the way that the educational scripts and training units can prove to be applicable to the objective of sharing and appropriation of knowledge capitalized within the MASK models. Also, it justifies the necessity of a rewriting step of the MASK toward educational engineering modeling norms, in particular the IMS - Learning Design language.

The second section of this paper briefly explains the Mask Knowledge Management methodology and the IMS-LD standard. We then explain the matching between the different Mask models and the different components of an IMS-LD scenario. In order to illustrate the process we take examples from the construction of a project management scenario. This example was used as a full-scale theoretical example (the KM model description is approximately of 30 A4 pages, however this was not processed in a company as we are only at the first steps of the methodology development).

2 Mask, a Method for Knowledge Capitalization

Mask is an evolution of the MKSM method [1], [3] and [4]. It is now a robust, validated and operational method. It takes its origins in cognitive-based knowledge engineering approaches in which problem solving methods are represented under several aspects: classification of concepts, relations between concepts, prescriptive actions and behaviour laws [4]. Mask proposes seven models to help experts and knowledge engineers structure knowledge under systemic, ergo-cognitive, psycho-cognitive, historical and evolution analyses (see references for details): knowledge patrimony model, domain model, activity model, historical model, concept model, task model and temporal line model.

Mask method allows, through various models describing various points of view, to study in-depth the experts' knowledge and their systems of values at different levels of granularity. This facilitates its use for dividing, decentralizing, learning and adapting this knowledge and describing the company's activities. One of the benefits is the ease in updating the model, according to the evolution of knowledge [7]. This allows a better description and practice thus reducing differences between documentation and reality.

3 IMS – Learning Design

Learning Design aims at an evolution of e-learning by capturing the "process" of education rather than simply content. By describing sequences of collaborative learning activities, Learning Design offers a new approach to re-use in e-learning [2]. Learning Design has emerged as one of the most significant recent developments in e-learning. From a standards/specifications perspective, IMS Global Learning Consortium has recently released the IMS Learning Design specification [5], based on the work of the Open University of the Netherlands (OUNL) on "Educational

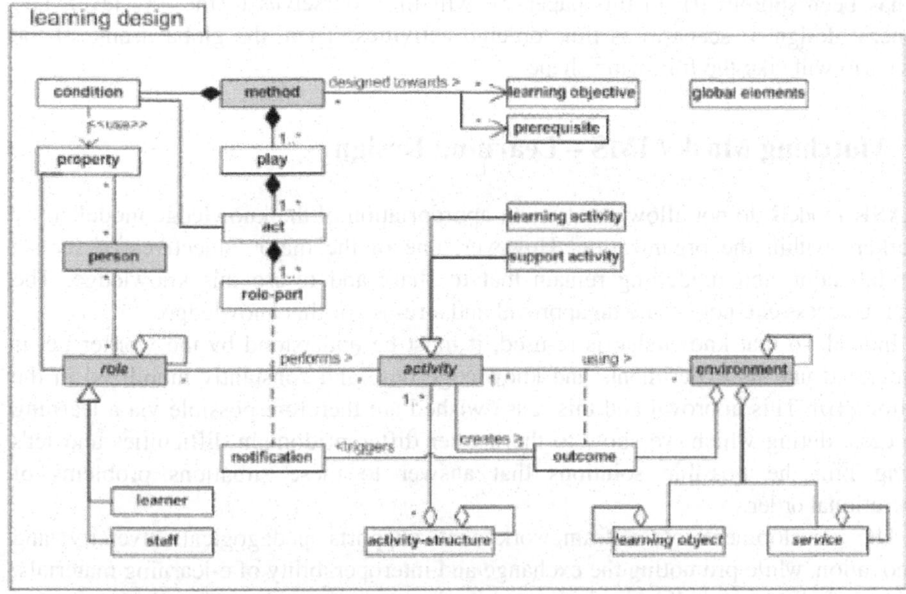

Fig. 1. Conceptual model of the overall Learning Design structure [5]

Modelling Language" [6], a notational language to describe a "meta-model" of instructional design. The OUNL coordinates an international EML/IMS Learning Design implementation group known as the Valkenburg group (2003), and OUNL has recently stated its intention to no longer continue developing EML, but instead focuses its energies on the new IMS Learning Design specification [8].

Three levels of representation suggested by IMS - Learning Design allow the specification and implementation of a great variety of e-learning teaching contents [5]. Level A specifies a time ordered series of *activities* to be performed by learners and teachers (*role*), within the context of an *environment* consisting of *learning objects* or *services*. Analysis of existing design approaches revealed that this was the common model behind all the different behaviorist, cognitive and (social) constructivist approaches to learning and instruction. For more advanced learning purposes, *properties*, *conditions* and *notifications* are required. This corresponds to Levels B and C. *Properties*, specified at Level B, are needed to store information about a *person* or a group of persons (*role*) e.g., for a student, its progress. *Conditions*, also part of Level B, constrain the evolution of the didactic scenario. They are set in response to specific circumstances, preferences or characteristics of specific learners (e.g., prior knowledge). *Notifications*, specified at Level C in addition to the *properties* and *conditions* of Level B are mechanisms to trigger new *activities*, based on an event during the learning process (e.g., the teacher is triggered to answer a question when a question of a student occurs or the teacher should grade a report once it has been submitted). In this paper we will limit ourselves to the "A" level, i.e., general design of scenario as time ordered activities. Then, the global frame of the scenario will take the following shape:

4 Matching Mask / IMS – Learning Design

MASK models do not allow an efficient appropriation of the knowledge modelled by workers within the organization. However, one of the major objectives of such a capitalization and modelling remain that to share and re-use this knowledge. The simple access can not ensure an approval and a re-use of this knowledge.

Indeed, so that knowledge is re-used, it must be understood by the worker i.e. is integrated into its experiments and knowledge base and constantly mobilized in the action [10]. This approval and this reuse wished are therefore possible via a learning process, during which we show to the learner different domain difficulties and let's bring him the possible solutions that answer to these situations problems of operational order.

The development of a framework that supports pedagogical diversity and innovation, while promoting the exchange and interoperability of e-learning materials, is one of the key challenges in the e-learning industry today. The IMS Learning Design allows the elements and structure description of any unit of learning, including resources, instructions for learning activities, templates for structured interactions, conceptual models (e.g., problem-based learning), learning goals, objectives and outcomes and finally assessment tools and strategies [5].

The idea is to exploit the different concepts and aspects that contain the MASK models to extract and to structure the content of this learning. It justifies a step of MASK models rewriting toward modelling norms derived of the learning engineering, in particular the IMS-Learning Design language.

In the beginning, we tried to achieve this matching using the patrimony model. For us, it was a starting point that permits a global vision described by the general phenomena, basis of the professional knowledge to distribute. The advantage is the faithful transcription of this global vision. The continuation was the deepening of every element representing a flux (of data, of information or cognitive). Once the definite global frame, deepening gives an indication on the granularity level of the learning scenario. We noted that such a gait denotes a very general starting due to the generic level of the patrimony model that can generate several main activity models.

Seen this first report, we experimented a matching from the main activity model as a starting point. The idea is to continue to describe the different steps of the scenario from the different correspondent's activities models and to continue while going until tasks models. Such a passage leads to a granularity level more and more refined. This gait proves to be interesting for the very detailed learning scenarios or that aim a training rather of initiation, thanks to the very detailed description level.

Seen this second report, we opted for a third way: to consider, since the departure, the granularity level of the learning scenario as defined by activities models. Patrimony, tasks and concepts models will remain elements to complete the different descriptions that ensue. The advantage of such a gait is that we launch the matching with a maximum of precision and clarity. It's the choice that we kept and that we will retail in the following paragraphs, while starting with the general scenarios identification from the domain Model.

MASK domain model proposes a vision sufficiently global of modeled knowledge that justifies its exploitation to identify the general scenario(s) of the learning activities. The continuation will be the deepening of each sub-element of this general model denoting a flow. This process emphasizes the principle based on the perception of a field like a recursive decomposition of phases and sub-phases. The idea is thus to describe the various headings of the teaching scenario by going through these phases. The general framework will be defined starting from the domain model and the succession of the decompositions will give an indication about the granularity level of the teaching scenarisation. So, a domain model can provide several scenarios corresponding to its different activities (Fig. 2). As an example, in the project management field, different scenarios can be identified corresponding to different general activities such as "definition of project", "team management", "dealing with the project resources" or in a more general manner "managing a project".

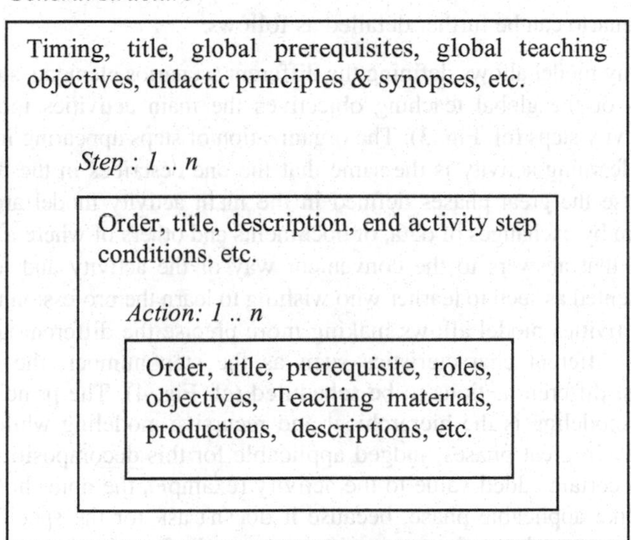

Fig. 2. The scenario global frame

4.1 Identifying General Scenarios from the Domain Model

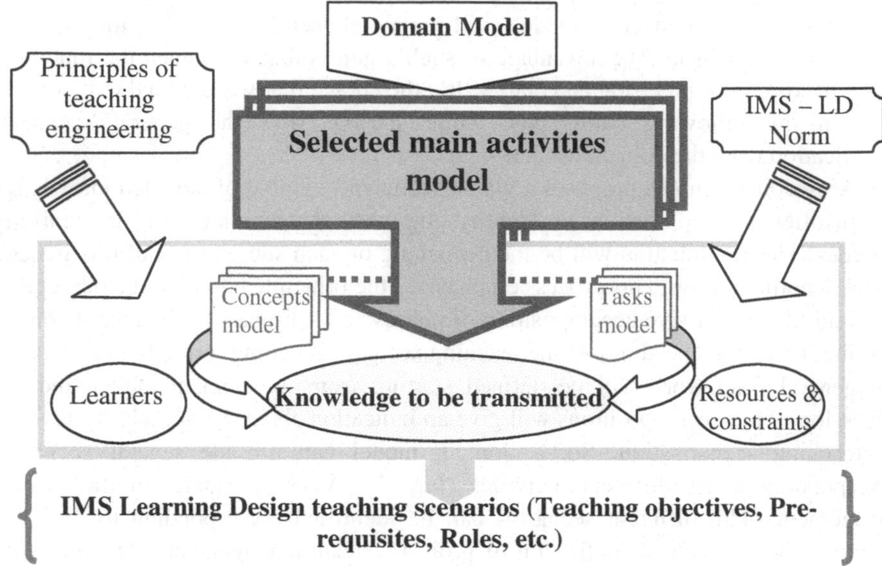

Fig. 3. Domain model generates various possibilities of scenarisation

4.2 Defining the Scenarios from the Main Activities Model

The general scenario can be further detailed as follows:

- The patrimony model allows defining the different scenarios elements such as global prerequisites or the global teaching objectives the main activities model and the different activity steps (cf. Fig. 3). The organization of steps appearing in the general structure of learning activity is the same that the one describes in the main activity model because the great phases defined in the main activity model are articulated between them by exchanges of data, of documents and others of where a "functional" organization that answers to the convenient way of the activity and, exactly, that must be presented as such to learner who wishing to learn the profession techniques.
- The main activities model allows making more precise the different activity steps by defining different characteristics such as the step number, the title and in particular the different actions to be scheduled (cf. Fig. 4). The principle adopted for activity modeling is the hierarchical and recursive modeling while cutting up every activity in great phases, judged applicable for this decomposition since this last brings a certain added value to the activity (example, the notes hold cannot be considered like applicable phase, because it doesn't ask for the specific cognitive resources, except to know how to write or to read). To introduce every activity actors, at the modeling time, is made by their experienced functions within the enterprise or by their roles implied in the activity, according to waited results of this activity, the manipulated objects and the action level (takes decisions,

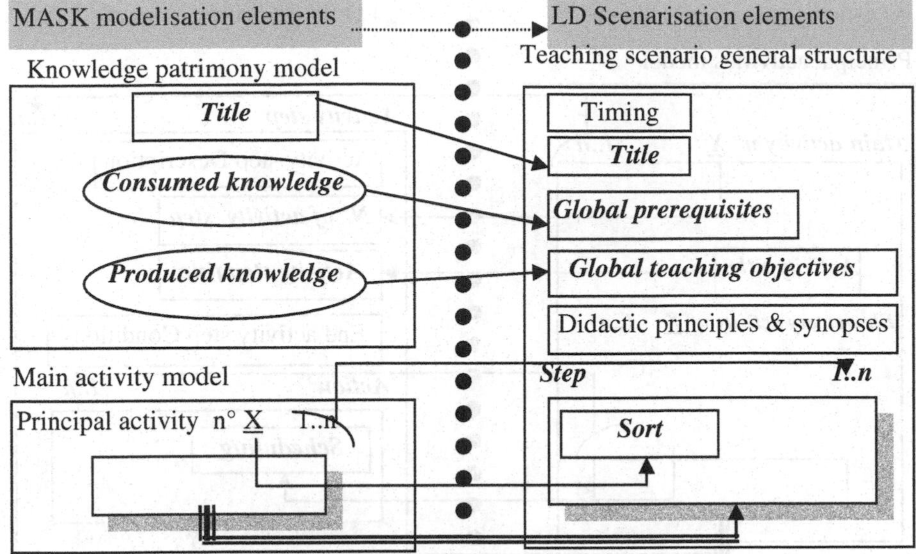

Fig. 4. Defining the scenario general structure

definition of strategies, execution of instructions, etc.) and in this last case, a role can be assigned therefore, to several actors. The set of resources definition carried on activity models denote the material resources remarkable by their roles in the realization of the concerned activity (necessary software, documents, etc.).

- Taking account of the nature of this modeling and the description of every step of the learning scenario that declines it in a succession of actions, the correspondence is direct: the content of the table of actions (corresponding to a step frame) is inspired from the model (or from models, according to the decomposition) of activity retailing the main activity model that corresponds to the step. Thus, every action in a step corresponds to a non decomposed activity in an activity model affiliated to the main activity model correspondent to this step.
- The different activity sub-models and their corresponding tasks models and concept models allow making more precise the different features of the learning activities such as the different roles, the teaching objectives or the intended production (cf. Fig. 5).
- Objectives can be formulated according to fluxes that will be provided in the activity results, while putting in evidence transformations waited from fluxes used by the activity in entry. These output fluxes will be in input for other activities representing among the MASK models and in the same way they will be able to constitute the prerequisite for learning activities that will follow. Most often, these productions are expressed as documents achieved by learner.

If necessary, when the objective of the learning is to work out accurately a given procedure, the learning activity can be further detailed using the tasks model of the considered activity (the task model describes, in particular, the "expert" problem resolving strategy). Finally, Table 1 presents an example of general learning scenario obtained following this process in the case of project management.

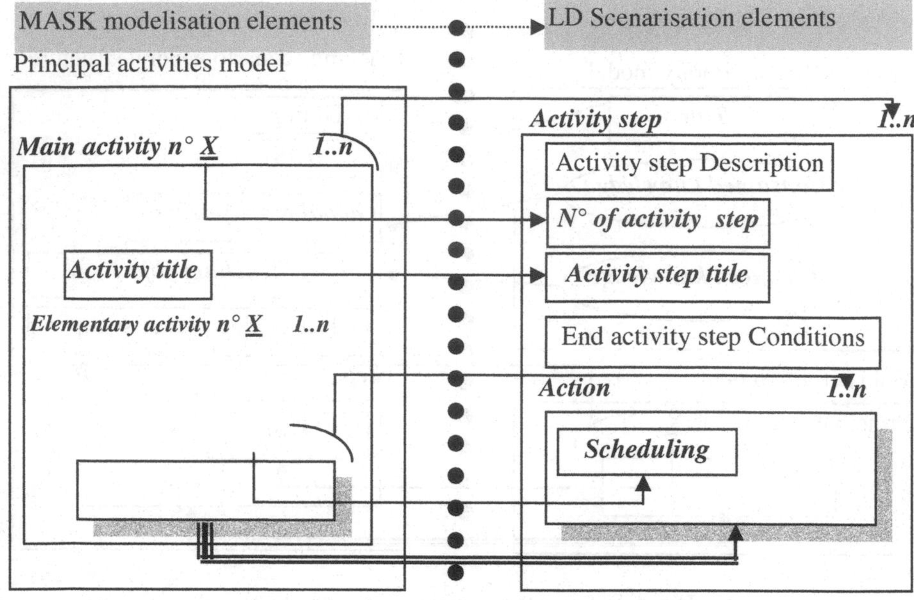

Fig. 5. Defining the different activity steps

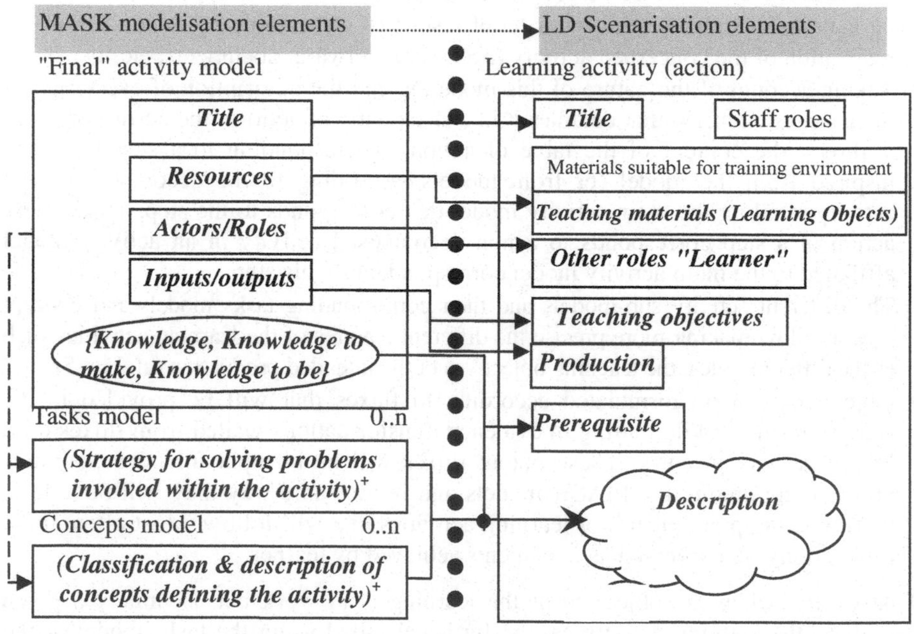

Fig. 6. Defining the details of the different activities

Table 1. A learning scenario

Learning activity general structure for "project management"				
Course title: Learning how to manage a project. Timing: xxx Global teaching objectives: • Developing high level competences in the project scenario definition, dashboard construction, men management, etc. Global prerequisites: fundamental knowledge on the project devices & knowledge of the project ecology, etc. Didactic principles & synopses: How does the course achieve its objectives? - alternate individual and collective learning steps, - alternate synchronous and asynchronous learning steps, etc.				
Learning steps (Learning steps references and execution conditions)				
Ref.	Starting with?	Waiting the end of learning step	Learning step title	Next Learning step
1	Yes	/	Preparation of the upstream project	2
2	No	1	Project beginning	3, 4, 6
Learning steps scheduling : developer choice ☒ actors choice ☒ cf. previous table ☑				

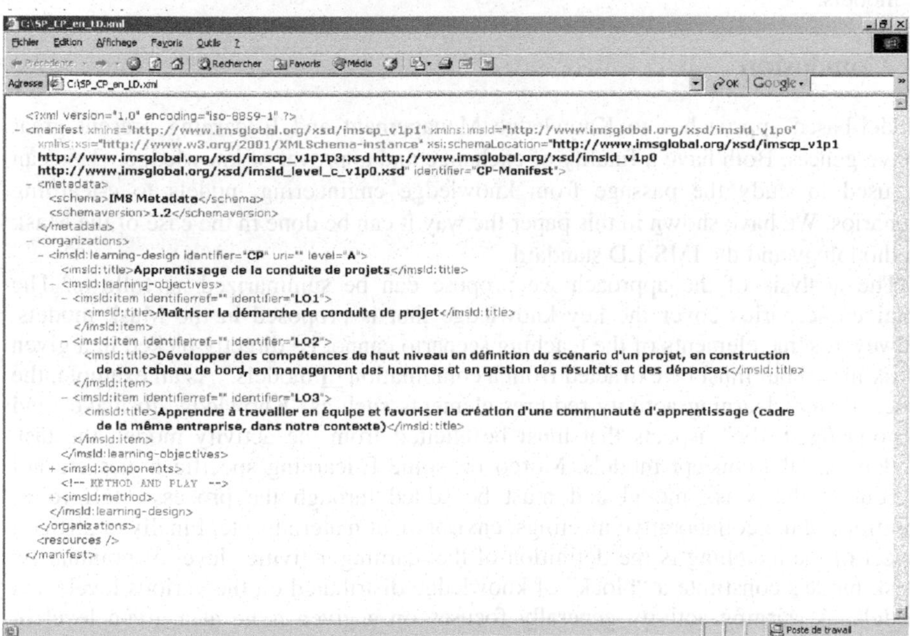


```
<?xml version="1.0" encoding="iso-8859-1" ?>
- <manifest xmlns="http://www.imsglobal.org/xsd/imscp_v1p1" xmlns:imsld="http://www.imsglobal.org/xsd/imsld_v1p0"
   xmlns:xsi="http://www.w3.org/2001/XMLSchema-instance" xsi:schemaLocation="http://www.imsglobal.org/xsd/imscp_v1p1
   http://www.imsglobal.org/xsd/imscp_v1p1p3.xsd http://www.imsglobal.org/xsd/imsld_v1p0
   http://www.imsglobal.org/xsd/imsld_level_c_v1p0.xsd" identifier="CP-Manifest">
 - <metadata>
     <schema>IMS Metadata</schema>
     <schemaversion>1.2</schemaversion>
   </metadata>
 - <organizations>
   - <imsld:learning-design identifier="CP" uri="" level="A">
       <imsld:title>Apprentissage de la conduite de projets</imsld:title>
     - <imsld:learning-objectives>
       - <imsld:item identifierref="" identifier="LO1">
           <imsld:title>Maîtriser la démarche de conduite de projet</imsld:title>
         </imsld:item>
       - <imsld:item identifierref="" identifier="LO2">
           <imsld:title>Développer des compétences de haut niveau en définition du scénario d'un projet, en construction
             de son tableau de bord, en management des hommes et en gestion des résultats et des dépenses</imsld:title>
         </imsld:item>
       - <imsld:item identifierref="" identifier="LO3">
           <imsld:title>Apprendre à travailler en équipe et favoriser la création d'une communauté d'apprentissage (cadre
             de la même entreprise, dans notre contexte)</imsld:title>
         </imsld:item>
       </imsld:learning-objectives>
     + <imsld:components>
       <!-- METHOD AND PLAY -->
     + <imsld:method>
     </imsld:learning-design>
   </organizations>
   <resources />
</manifest>
```

Fig. 7. IMS-LD general structure of the scenario for "project management" training

This general scenario, describe as a structured document, is based on 6 activity steps, each step being then refined into 24 activities. An IMS – Learning Design description as an XML file can be very easily generated from the standard description of this material.

The result obtained was a teaching scenario which is characterized by:

- The existence of the main part of the e-learning aspects such as defined, distributed in various models MASK.
- Some missing elements: they acts primarily of the elements which are specific to the training process (staff roles, durations of the meetings, environment materials, etc.) and thus of the elements which were not taken into account at the time of modeling, nor thought by the expert during the interview of clarification.
- Difficulties noted for the definition of the level of granularity: MASK Models such as they are designed constitute "a block" of knowledge distributed on the various levels and models. In order to keep intact the direction of the knowledge-making, we had the constraint to adopt the same levels of granularity and decomposition.
- Other constraints: elements in the teaching scenario cannot be directly inspired by the models MASK but which can be extracted well while choosing a combination from models. As an example, the description of the Learning activity requires elements of Knowledge, "Knowledge-to make" and "Knowledge-to be" corresponding activity model, descriptions of the task models and those of concept models.

5 Conclusion

Model-based approaches to Knowledge Management and E-learning present great convergences. Both have a finality of exchange and approval of knowledge. This can be used to study the passage from knowledge engineering models to e-learning scenarios. We have shown in this paper the way it can be done in the case of the Mask methodology and the IMS-LD standard.

The analysis of the approach we propose can be summarized as follows. The obtained scenarios cover the key knowledge that is proposed in the Mask models. However, some elements of the teaching scenario cannot be directly picked in a given Mask model but must be extracted from a combination of models. As an example, the description of learning activity requires elements such as "Knowledge-to make" and "Knowledge-to be" aspects that must be elicited from the activity model, the task models and the concept models. Moreover, some E-learning specific issues are not present in the Mask model and must be added through the process: staff roles, durations of the collaborative meetings, environment materials, etc. Finally, a difficult aspect of the matching is the definition of the learning activities level of granularity. Mask models constitute a "block" of knowledge distributed on the various levels and models. A learning activity generally focuses on a given issue at a given level of detail. Keeping coherent the levels of granularity of the two systems requires an accurate work that must be driven by pedagogic considerations.

Our definition of contents, design and scenarisation is intended to the actors of the field through an E-Learning platform and described in IMS - LD. That thus requires reflections to reinforce the assets of such a passage and to answer the difficulties and/or lacks recorded at the time of the passage. For that, we propose for future developments:

- The expert can be called, during the interviews, to indicate some elements which it consider essential so that one learning can comparable its mode of reasoning and/or its way of resolution of problems
- To exploit the book of knowledge rather than the simple MASK models. The book of knowledge is, in fact, the "real" production of the method MASK and which includes the models. The book of knowledge has the advantage, compared to the models, to be content of complementary descriptions which answer the lacks that one noted theoretically and confirmed by our passage experimentation.

Then, we believe that the development of methods that focus on constructing E-learning activities from KM systems is absolutely necessary to manage the complexity of E-learning issues in industrial companies. As an example, the Mask model of the "project management method" produced more than thirty models (plus their documentations). This cannot be managed “by hand”. Although the process of building E-learning activities and curricula cannot be straightforward, approaches such as the one we propose guides and facilitates the process. Moreover, such an approach maintains the knowledge life cycle within the organization and allows reusability and reengineering thanks to IMS - Learning Design descriptions. We believe that knowledge engineering and teaching engineering issues models and systems can then progress towards interoperability.

References

1. Barthelmé F., Ermine J.L., Rosenthal-Sabroux C. *An architecture for knowledge evolution in organisations*, European Journal of Operational Research 109, 414-427 (1998)
2. Dalziel J., *Implementing learning design: Then Learning Activity Management System (LAMS)*, Macquarie E-learning Centre of Excellence (MELCOE) - Macquarie University, Australia 2003
3. Ermine J-L., Chaillot M., Bigeon P., Charreton B., Malavieille D. : *MKSM, a method for knowledge management,* Knowledge Management, Organization, Competence and Methodology, Advances in Knowledge Management Volume 1, Jos. F. Shreinemakers Ed., pp 288 - 302, Ergon, 1996
4. Ermine J-L: Les systèmes de connaissances, Edition Hermès, Paris, 2000
5. IMS Learning Design specification: http://www.imsglobal.org/learningdesign/index.cfm
6. Koper, R., r*From change to renewal: Educational technology foundations of electronic environments*. EML website http://eml.ou.nl/eml-ou-nl.htm
7. Matta N., Ermine J.L., Aubertin G., Trivin J.Y., *Knowledge Capitalization with a knowledge engineering approach: the Mask method*, proceedings of IJCAI'2001 Workshop on Knowledge Management and Organizational Memory, August 2001.
8. Tattersall, C., *EML and IMS Learning Design. Presentation for the Valkenburg Group*, Vancouver, February 2003
9. Tixier B., Rapport de recherche n° 01.9, Institut de recherche en informatique de Nantes, Septembre 2001
10. Tounkara T., Ermine J-L., Matta N., *L'approbation des connaissances avec MASK*, In proceedings of Extraction et Gestion des Connaissances EGC'2002 (industrial session), Montpellier 2002

Subjunctive Interfaces in Exploratory e-Learning

Klaus P. Jantke[1,2], Aran Lunzer[2], and Jun Fujima[2]

[1] FIT Leipzig at HTWK Leipzig,
P.O.Box 30 11 66, 04251 Leipzig, Germany
jantke@fit-leipzig.de

[2] Meme Media Laboratory, Hokkaido University,
Kita-13, Nishi-8, Kita-ku Sapporo 060–8628, Japan
{jantke, lunzer, fujima}@meme.hokudai.ac.jp

Abstract. E-learning deals with knowledge management, for sure, and knowledge management very frequently results in learning. So far, there is an obviously close relationship between the two disciplines. However, deeper insights do not arise easily. Here we investigate how one approach to enhancing information-access interfaces may inspire an improvement in knowledge management for e-learning. Subjunctive interfaces support users in investigating and visualizing information obtained in parallel through multiple enquiries. A wide spectrum of exploratory e-learning approaches may benefit from adopting and adapting the subjunctive interface concept.

1 Introduction and Motivation

It seems that *Knowledge Management* and *e-Learning* have quite contrasting perspectives on knowledge. Knowledge management depends very much on the assumption that knowledge is carried by data, as knowledge management systems are typically complex information processing systems designed to serve the human user by a variety of interactive data manipulations. In contrast, the e-learning community believes that the knowledge they are interested in is not sitting in the data. Learning is understood as some process of knowledge (re-)construction, with the implication that different learners may learn quite different things when dealing with the same data.

Under these roughly sketched assumptions we are trying to bridge the gap by means of an original approach [14,15,16] that aims to go beyond the limits of current support for exploratory use of computer applications.

Knowing about deficiencies of many current e-learning systems and services, our point of departure is the urgent need to promote didactics in technology enhanced learning. Exploratory learning is just one of the prominent didactic concepts that should help to prove e-learning more successful by making it more cognitively adequate, entertaining and illustrating to the learner.

K.-D. Althoff et al. (Eds.): WM 2005, LNAI 3782, pp. 176–188, 2005.

2 Perspectives on e-Learning

Complex e-learning systems in practical use (see [11] for an example) employ a wide spectrum of didactic concepts [2,5]. It is a folklore saying that there are as many didactic concepts in the literature as authors writing about didactics.

Thus, the authors have chosen a pragmatic approach and decided to focus on a single didactic concept on which there is little debate: exploratory learning. In exploratory learning, learners who already have some motivation and are, perhaps, already driven by some learning goal are being presented with material that has to be explored carefully. Insights or even vague ideas gained through such explorations may be used systematically in subsequent learning phases[1]. This concept nicely fits the potentials of technology enhanced learning where computer systems and, in particular, the World-Wide Web may serve as a rich source of information to be explored. Exploratory learning goes clearly beyond the limits of traditional instruction practice where a teacher is very limited in the material he can present to his audience. Furthermore, e-learning allows for individually tailored explorations at any time and with any frequency and intensity preferred by an individual learner.

From this perspective, exploratory learning looks like a great idea that should be employed in e-learning wherever possible. A closer look reveals severe difficulties. When learners are sent out to search for information, to collect information, to compare information, to evaluate their results of comparison, and to draw conclusions from what they have explored with respect to their learning tasks or goals, they usually face serious problems of knowledge management.

When you get many pieces of information about some subject one after the other, how to do comparison? How to recognise trends? How to identify correlations? These are questions of knowledge management that are clearly fundamental to e-learning.

Depending on the goal/task of learning, on the knowledge source, and on the structure of the information to be explored, a large variety of knowledge management technologies may apply.

The present paper does not intend to provide a universal answer to these questions. The proposed solution of subjunctive interfaces has been demonstrated in two kinds of domain relevant to e-learning: dynamic simulation, where a learner may need to explore how a simulation's outcome is affected by various conditions, and exploratory access to information over the Web.

It is worth mentioning that applications of the latter kind are particularly attractive to many learners, because they prove – at least implicitly – that the studies undertaken are based on the most recent information and deal with truly practical data. It is important to pay attention to such opportunities to motivate students [1,2,3,4].

[1] We do not go into further details of arranging deeply structured technology-enhanced learning experiences. Storyboarding is currently seen as the way in which learning processes are anticipated and learning experience is organised [9].

3 Technology Enhanced Didactics

In addition to dynamic simulation and information access (details in Section 4), a third case study has been undertaken within the framework of the e-learning system DaMiT [10,11,12], a data mining tutor available over the Internet for higher education as well as for workplace training. In the DaMiT system, collections of Java applets are offered for exploratory learning purposes.

To get an impression of those applets, here is a first illustration. The learner must challenge a system that has been set up to learn decision trees over regular patterns – a task that has attractive applications in, for example, bioinformatics. Strings entered in the left-hand side of the form are treated as positive examples,and strings in the right-hand side as counter-examples. When the learner switches to the decision tree display 'Entscheidungsbaum', the input form is replaced by a view of the currently learned decision tree, as shown in the lower two screen shots.

For the purpose of illustration in the present paper, the authors have chosen an extremely simple case study to allow a wide audience to follow in every detail.

Decision trees contain patterns p in every internal node. A pattern p is just a string of constants and variables. For readability, symbols in input strings are separated by blanks. Patterns are seen as generators of formal languages, as variables may be substituted by non-empty strings. Every pattern p defines some language $L(p)$. A pattern p in an internal node represents the test "$s \in L(p)$?" for a given input string s. In such a way, decision trees classify strings.

It is a typical machine-learning task to learn decision trees from provided examples and counter-examples, but decision-tree induction over regular patterns is an ambitious task.

What makes a particular task difficult? When does it happen that small changes in the data result in dramatic changes of the generated tree? How much does the task complexity depend on the size of the database given? Are there intrinsic difficulties that show already on very small data sets? Knowledge in the area can hardly be transmitted in a declarative way. Learners need to experience decision-tree induction. They need to get a feeling. This is a case for exploratory learning. The applets of the DaMiT system, one of them depicted in Figure 1 above, provide an excellent basis for a variety of exploratory learning approaches including learners' competition in exploration.

The core motivation for employing exploratory learning derives from the characteristics of machine learning in general, and data mining in particular, which is both an art and a science at the same time. Key knowledge is implicit. Learning is interactive knowledge construction, to a large extent.

Another motivation derives from cognitive psychology [3,4,1] and from neurophysiology [18]. Learning may succeed optimally if environmental conditions are set up appropriately and the human learner is well prepared. To prepare the learner also involves alerting and orienting. Getting human learners engaged in exploratory problem solving means to focus their attention. Through the novelty of discoveries in exploratory learning, the brain's hippocampus gets activated – a crucial step in knowledge acquisition [19,20].

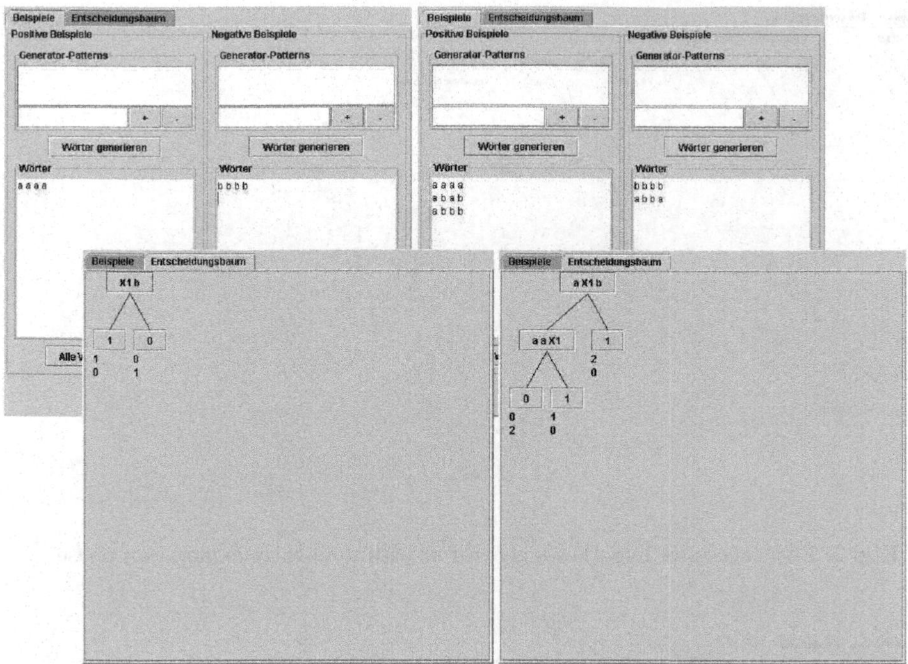

Fig. 1. Two trials of decision-tree induction requiring four windows for inspection

In the decision-tree case study, human learners are asked to explore the difficulties of tree induction. They have to pose learning problems to the computer, making it hard for the computer to generate small decision-tree hypotheses. One may launch a competition among learners, to find small samples that cause big problems for the learning computer. Exploration becomes a game.

When challenging the computer, learners have to try varying inputs and can check the related outputs as illustrated in Figure 1.

But when dealing with complex problems, it is easy to get lost in the exploration. Instead of success, learners may feel boredom or, even worse, frustration.

Let us study the present case in more detail. The exploration task given to the learner is to challenge the decision-tree induction applet with a sequence of strings presented either as positive examples or as counter-examples. The goal is to force the computer to build comparatively large decision trees for only small sample sets, where the decision tree's size is characterised by its number of (internal) nodes and by the length and structural complexity of the patterns in those nodes.

Note that there are some limitations. For every set of n examples and counter-examples, there is trivially a decision tree of at most $n-1$ internal nodes that performs correct classification. The length of patterns in internal nodes is bounded by the length of the longest example presented.

The sequence of output trees presented in Figures 2 and 3 reflect the DaMiT system's response to the input of the following string examples (where the

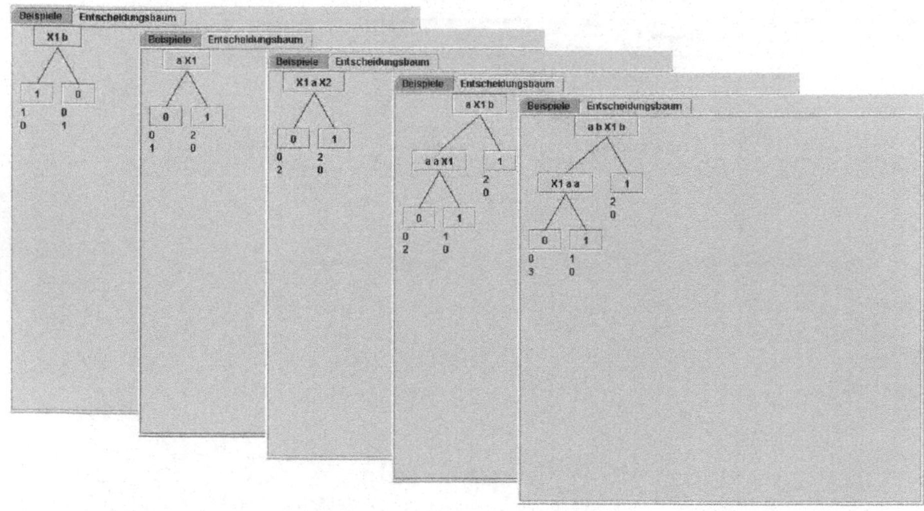

Fig. 2. Five successive hypotheses generated within an early exploration phase

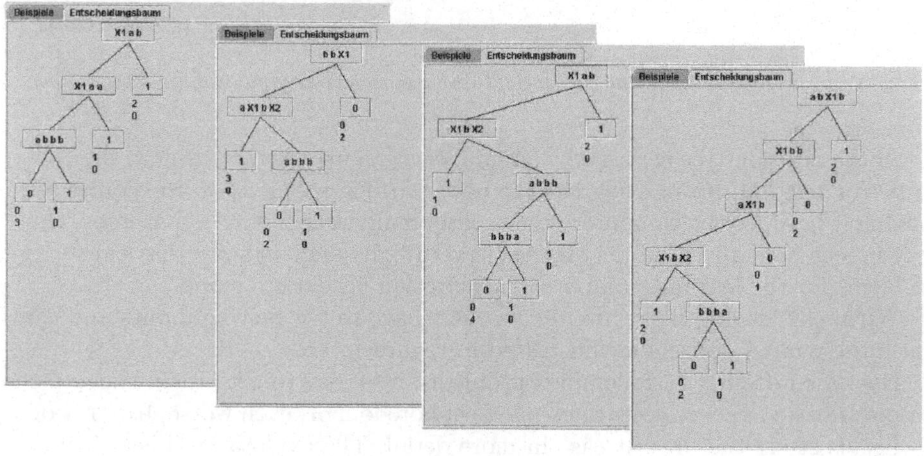

Fig. 3. Successfully challenging decision-tree induction with a sample of 10 strings

suffix 1 indicates a positive example and 0 a counter-example): (aaaa,1) (bbbb,0) / (abab,1) / (abba,0) / (abbb,1) / (aabb,0) / (baab,1) / (bbaa,0) / (bbba,1) / (aaab,0). At the end of such an exploration '*at that moment of triumph when we learn something or master a task*' [13], the release of endorphins results in feeling good and properly contributes to learning.

But it is not easy to perform such a session. The learner must switch back and forth between windows, taking notes or screenshots to relate the contents of one window to the now-hidden contents of another, and to earlier cases.

If a teacher has the bad attitude of forcing students to read enormous amounts of papers, then file systems, the Internet, and transfer protocols like http and ftp may represent the right technology to enable this type of didactics.

But where is the technology to enable exploratory learning? It comes next!

4 Subjunctive Interfaces Introduced and Illustrated

The need to explore alternative results arises not just in e-learning, but in common activities including the navigation of Web sites, querying from databases, experimentation with simulations or spreadsheets, and design of artifacts. Typically, the applications available for such activities provide results only in response to explicit, pinpoint specifications by the user. A user who wishes to explore alternatives is therefore faced with the following kinds of burden:

1. A high number of interface actions
   Making the different specifications needed to obtain the results may require many actions, such as mouse clicks or key presses – especially if the user wants to revisit earlier results.
2. A need to remember results
   When only one result is visible at a time, comparing results requires the user to remember the relevant details of those that are currently out of sight.
3. Mental effort in organizing the exploration
   In cases where the results of interest depend on varying two or more aspects of the specification, the user must expend effort in working through the desired combinations of settings for those aspects.

The concept of subjunctive interfaces was inspired by Hofstadter's [7] playful notion of a subjunc-TV – a magical television whose tuning knobs would provide access to alternative versions of a given broadcast. An application equipped with a subjunctive interface lets the user establish and control multiple scenarios, based on alternative specifications, at the same time. The key features of a subjunctive interface are therefore as follows:

- The user should be able to set up multiple scenarios that differ in arbitrary ways. In general, when offered some choice in the application's interface, the user should be able to say 'maybe I want value X, but maybe Y or Z – so let me try all three and see how things turn out in each case'.
- The scenarios should be viewable side by side, in a way that helps the user to compare them and also to understand each scenario individually – i.e., the correspondence between a given input specification and its results.
- The user should be able to control scenarios in parallel, for example by adjusting an input parameter that is shared by many scenarios and seeing instantaneously the effect of this adjustment on each scenario.

By making use of such facilities, a user can reduce the need to re-specify a scenario to revisit its results, can make side-by-side comparisons that would not

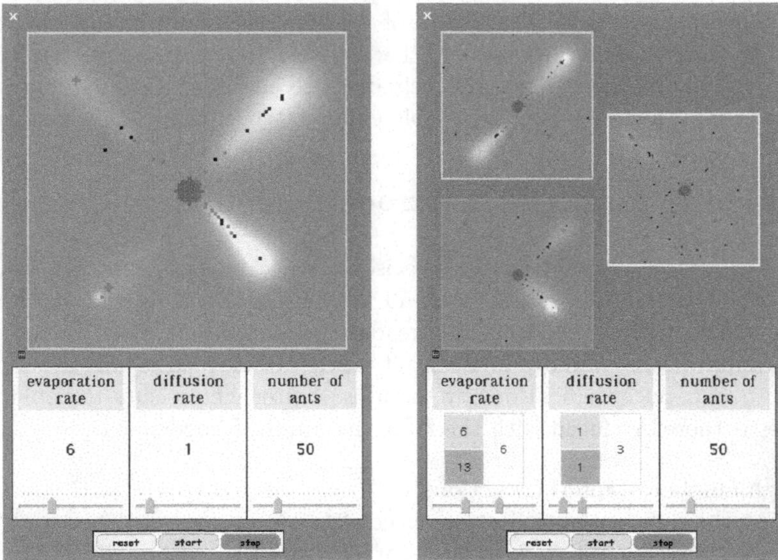

Fig. 4. A simulation of ants foraging for food, influenced by various environmental conditions. A single scenario is shown on the left; three scenarios on the right.

be possible in a single-scenario interface, and can efficiently work through large numbers of alternative specifications.

Figure 4 shows how a subjunctive interface can be used in studying a simulation. This simulation, of the food-foraging behaviour of ants, takes into account three parameters that the student can vary. In the normal, single-scenario presentation, it may be difficult for a student to grasp the impact of some parameter variation; with the addition of a subjunctive interface it becomes possible to create and observe many scenarios side by side (the current interface supports up to twelve scenarios), which can help in observing even subtle differences.

We are also investigating how the subjunctive-interface approach can reduce the burden in pursuing and comparing alternative retrievals from the Web. C3W (Clip, Connect and Clone for the Web; for details see [6]) is a prototype that lets a user capture input/output relationships from form-based Web applications, creating custom applications that explicitly support the execution of multiple retrievals in parallel.

As a simple illustration of these capabilities, Figure 5 represents the operations carried out by a user in capturing part of the behaviour of Google. Viewing the Google site using our enhanced Web browser, the user is able to highlight individual HTML elements within the viewed pages and to 'clip' them, pasting them onto a substrate (called a C3Sheet) that records where each element was found and the navigation relationships between them. Interactive elements on the C3Sheet retain the roles that they had on their original Web pages, so in this example entering new keywords runs a new Google search and delivers its

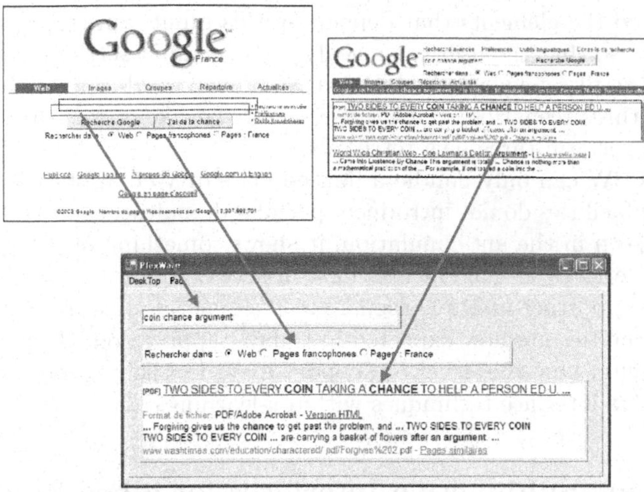

Fig. 5. Creating a simplified interface to google.fr, by clipping the keyword input field, search-scope switch, and top result

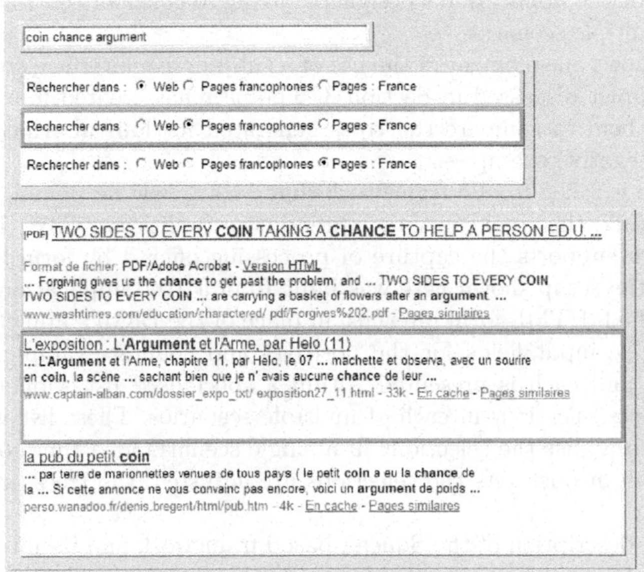

Fig. 6. After cloning the scope switch, three different scopes of search can be requested and viewed in parallel

top result, while clicking on the scope switch would run a new search with the chosen scope.

In Figure 6 the user has set up a number of parallel Web retrievals, just by 'cloning' the scope switch in the captured application. The C3Sheet has automatically cloned the elements that depend on this input – in this case, just the result display – so that the user can specify distinct input settings and see their corresponding results side by side. In this case the keyword-input element is still shared by the three scenarios, so if the user enters new keywords the system will automatically perform three new retrievals.

Although C3W can only handle a limited class of Web applications, and its simple cloning facilities do not introduce specialised, multi-scenario widgets such as the sliders seen in the ant simulation, it shows something of the potential of subjunctive interfaces in general information-access activities. As such, it is a step towards supporting multiple scenarios as a generic software feature, much as clipboard facilities are now expected in today's applications. In the following section we discuss how this level of support may be a key to deriving benefit from subjunctive-interface techniques within e-learning.

5 Delivering Subjunctive Interfaces for e-Learning

In this section we show an example of a subjunctive interface supporting exploration in e-learning, and we describe how this kind of interface might be created without the application's designers having to consider the complexity of supporting multiple scenarios.

Figure 7 shows one moment in the use of a subjunctive interface created from the DaMiT applet discussed in Section 3. The user has created four scenarios, and is using them to compare the trees generated for four alternative sets of positive and negative examples.

This figure is taken from a framework that we are now developing, based on Squeak Smalltalk, that replicates and extends the facilities of C3W. Like C3W, this framework supports the capture of processing offered by form-based Web applications; the setup shown here was built from a Web application that provides a simplified, HTML-form interface in place of the DaMiT applet's original Java forms. The input fields for the positive- and counter-example lists have been clipped, and each is presented within a specialised list widget that can support multiple selections in each of multiple scenarios. These list widgets allow the user to adjust the selections in a single scenario at a time, or in many scenarios simultaneously. As the selections are adjusted, the trees are updated immediately.

A detailed description of the Squeak-based framework and its interface widgets would be beyond the scope of this paper. However, it is relevant to discuss the techniques and steps involved in delivering to learners the kind of multi-scenario exploration support shown here.

Of particular interest to us is the provision of multi-scenario support for applications that were not originally designed with this in mind. We believe that transforming some elements of application behaviour from single- to multi-scenario support can be partially abstracted, so that application developers can rely on a common framework to provide this transformation for free. Naturally, just as when developing an application to benefit from framework services such

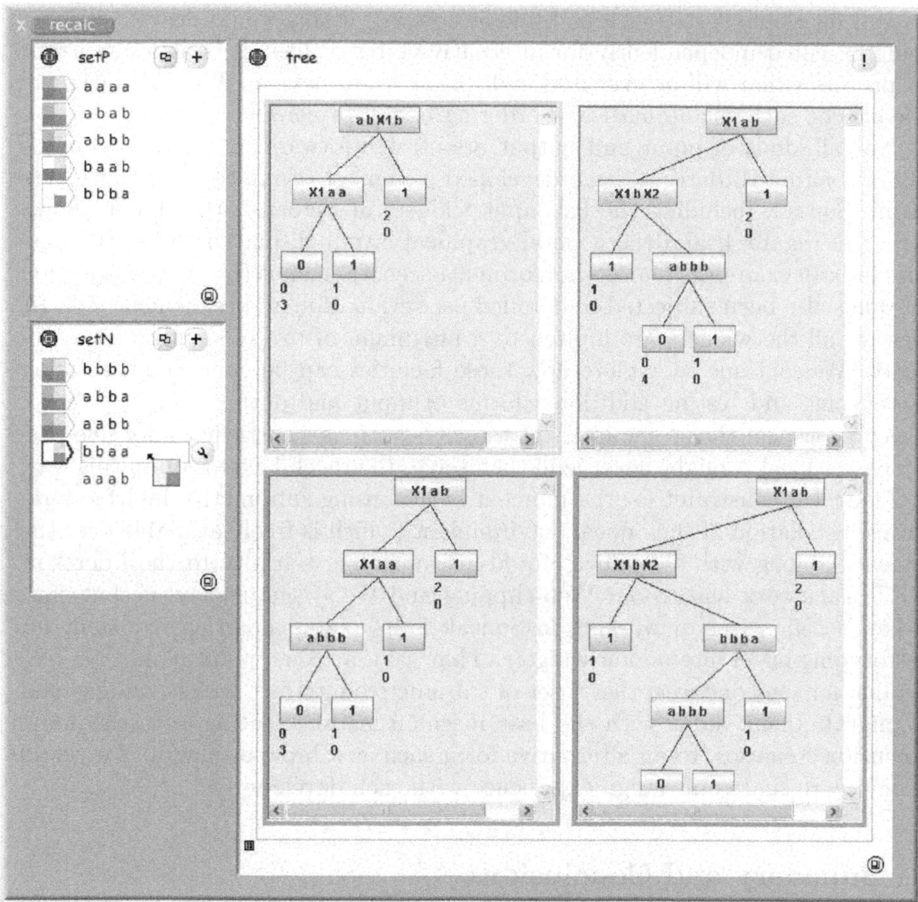

Fig. 7. Four scenarios being explored in a wrapped version of the DaMiT decision-tree induction applet. The markers to the left of the strings in lists setP and setN (positive and negative examples, respectively) show that all scenarios contain the top three strings from each list; the bottom-left (blue) scenario adds one positive example (b a a b); the top-right (yellow) scenario adds a further negative (b b a a); and the bottom-right (red) scenario then adds a fifth positive (b b b a).

as a clipboard or undo, automatic extension to multiple scenarios will place various design constraints on the original application. We now describe some of the constraints that apply to our current framework.

The behaviour of interest must be suitable for capture as a black-box process that accepts values for a fixed number of inputs, can be executed on demand, and produces outputs that can always be extracted in the same way. For example, a Web application that sometimes requires an additional interaction step depending on the input values – to disambiguate certain place names, say – cannot be handled by our existing system. Additionally, the processing must not depend on global state (such as browser cookies) if this would prevent it from being executed independently for alternative input values. It is also important for processes that will be executed multiple times to have no dramatic or costly side-effects, such as automatically ordering books, or aeroplane tickets.

Not all kinds of input and output are straightforward to present in multi-scenario form. To date we have developed a number of multi-scenario widgets within Squeak, including the list-input widgets in Figure 7, the sliders shown earlier in Figure 4, and the general graphical layout display used for the outputs in both examples. Our design for multi-scenario menus (i.e., single-selection lists) has also been subjected to detailed user evaluation and refinement [16]. At present, all the widgets are limited to a maximum of twelve simultaneous scenarios. We continue to explore how these facilities can be enhanced, including prototyping and testing additional forms of input and output widget. We do, however, suspect that some kinds of widget – such as inputs that offer live predictive feedback – might never lend themselves to graceful extension in this way.

One clear constraint for the moment is that using subjunctive interfaces requires installation of the Squeak environment (which is freely available over the Internet), along with a number of add-ins, including a bridge to the Microsoft .NET framework and to our Web-clipping and Web-page display mechanisms. A key benefit to us of working in Squeak is its power as an environment for prototyping novel interaction widgets. That said, at some point it may be reasonable for someone to gather a set of subjunctive-interface widget designs and to migrate them, along with the base mechanisms for creating and scheduling execution scenarios, to an alternative form such as a browser plugin. We would be happy to share our design experience with such developers.

6 Summary and Conclusions

Human brains are, by their very nature, pattern-recognition machines. Humans feel good when they recognise patterns, and brains release endorphins as a reward for successful pattern recognition. Humans learn more successfully when they feel better. The art of didactics lies in organising learning experiences in a satisfying and, thus, sustainable way.

Exploratory learning is a key didactic principle, which aims at learning experiences that offer opportunities to recognise patterns of knowledge. Such pattern recognition is particularly satisfying if the human learner has the impression that it is her personal success to arrive at a certain insight, and if the insight has a touch of novelty. This novelty on the one hand excites the hippocampus, and on the other hand stimulates the release of dopamine. Both events usually contribute to longer-lasting neurophysiological changes.

Though exploratory learning is well respected in the e-learning community, a larger number of settings suffer from the kinds of deficiency that we have pointed out in applets drawn from the DaMiT system. Although exploration is supported, the crucial support for comparison and evaluation of individual exploration results is missing. Patterns of insights can hardly emerge.

As a way out, we wish to draw attention to the idea, principles and techniques of subjunctive interfaces. Subjunctive interfaces may be seen as a general approach to knowledge management, with particular relevance to technology enhanced learning.

Our developments and experiments reveal that supporting exploration by adding subjunctive interfaces to existing applications is feasible in principle, given a framework with similar properties to those that we have prototyped, and applications built in a way that the framework can handle.

Among the questions left open – and in every future-oriented research and development endeavour there should be open questions – there is the problem that the real end-user activities involved in using such a framework have yet to be figured out. Would students be presented with applications already embedded within it, or would they be expected to build their own exploration interfaces by tinkering with the base applications? Would they catch on?

Acknowledgements

We gratefully acknowledge the efforts of the Squeak development community, and especially the developers of its recently added bridge to .NET.

References

1. J. D. Bransford, A. L. Brown, and R. R. Cocking, editors. *How People Learn: Brain, Mind, Experience, and School.* Nat. Acad. Press, 2000.
2. R. M. Briggs, Gagne L. J., and W. W. Wager. *Principles of Instructional Design.* Thomson Learning, 1992.
3. A. Damasio. *The Feeling of What Happens: body and emotion in the making of consciousness.* Hartcourt, 1999.
4. B. Davis, D. Sumara, and R. Luce-Kapler. *Engaging Minds. Learning and Teaching in a Complex World.* Lawrence Erlbaum Associates, 2000.
5. K.-H. Flechsig. *Kleines Handbuch didaktischer Modelle.* Neuland, 1996.
6. J. Fujima, A. Lunzer, K. Hornbæk, and Y. Tanaka. Clip, connect, clone: Combining application elements to build custom interfaces for information access. In *ACM Symp. on User Interface Software and Technology, UIST 2004, Santa Fe, NM, USA*, pages 175–184, 2004.
7. D. R. Hofstadter. *Gödel, Escher, Bach: an Eternal Golden Braid.* Basic Books, 1979.
8. W. Jank and H. Meyer. *Didaktische Modelle.* Cornelsen, 2002.
9. K. P. Jantke and R. Knauf. Didactic design through storyboarding: Standard concepts for standard tools. In Beate R. Baltes, Lilian Edwards, Fernando Galindo, Jozef Hvorecky, Klaus P. Jantke, Leon Jololian, Philip Leith, Alta van der Merwe, John Morison, Wolfgang Nejdl, C. V. Ramamoorthy, Ramzi Seker, Burkhard Shaffer, Iouliia Skliarova, Valery Sklyarov, and John Waldron, editors, *First International Workshop on Dissemination of E-Learning Technologies and Applications, DELTA 2005, in: Proceedings of the 4th International Symposium on Information and Communication Technologies, Cape Town, South Africa, January 3–6, 2005*, pages 20–25. Computer Science Press, Trinity College Dublin, Ireland, 2005.

10. K. P. Jantke, S. Lange, G. Grieser, P. Grigoriev, B. Thalheim, and B. Tschiedel. Learning by doing and learning when doing. In Isabel Seruca, Joaquim Filipe, Slimane Hammoudi, and Jóse Cordeiro, editors, *International Conference on Enterprise Information Systems, Porto, Portugal, April 14–17, 2004, Proc., Vol. 5*, pages 238–241. INSTICC, 2004.
11. K. P. Jantke, S. Lange, G. Grieser, P. Grigoriev, B. Thalheim, and B. Tschiedel. Work-integrated e-learning – the DaMiT approach. In Oliver Sawodny and Peter Scharff, editors, *49. Internationales Wissenschaftliches Kolloquium, TU Ilmenau, 27.-30. September 2004, Conference Proceedings, Volume 2*, pages 333–339. Shaker Verlag, 2004.
12. K. P. Jantke, M. Memmel, O. Rostanin, and B. Rudolf. Media and service integration for professional e-learning. In *E-Learn 2004, World Conference on E-Learning in Corporate, Government, Healthcare & Higher Education, November 1–5, 2004, Washington D.C., USA*, 2004.
13. R. Koster. *A Theory of Fun for Game Design.* Paraglyph Press, 2005.
14. A. Lunzer. Choice and comparison where the user wants them: Subjunctive interfaces for computer-supported exploration. In *IFIP TC. 13 Intern. Conf. on Human-Computer Interaction, INTERACT 99*, pages 474–482. IOS Press, 1999.
15. A. Lunzer. Benefits of subjunctive interface support for eploratory access to online resources. In Gunter Grieser and Yuzuru Tanaka, editors, *International Workshop on Intuitive Human Interface for Organizing and Accessing Intellectual Assets, International Workshop, Dagstuhl Castle, Germany, March 1-5, 2004, Proceedings*, volume 3359 of *Lecture Notes in Artifical Intelligence*, pages 14–32, Berlin, Heidelberg, New York, 2005. Springer-Verlag.
16. A Lunzer and K. Hornbæk. Usability studies on a visualisation for parallel display and control of alternative scenarios. In *7th Intern. Working Conf. on Advanced Visual Interfaces, AVI 2004, Gallipoli, Italy*, pages 125–132, 2004.
17. W. J. Rothwell and H. C. Kazanas. *Mastering the Instructional Design Process: A Systematic Approach (Third Edition).* Pfeiffer, 2004.
18. M. Spitzer. *Lernen. Gehirnforschung und die Schule des Lebens.* Spektrum Akademischer Verlag, 2002.
19. M. A. Wilson and B. L. McNaughton. Dynamics of the hippocampal ensemble code for space. *Science*, 261:1055–1058, 1993.
20. M. A. Wilson and B. L. McNaughton. Reactivation of hippocampal ensemble memories during sleep. *Science*, 265:676–679, 1994.

Supporting Competency Development in Informal Workplace Learning

Tobias Ley[1], Stefanie N. Lindstaedt[1], and Dietrich Albert[2]

[1] Know-Center, Inffeldgasse 21a,
A-8010 Graz, Austria
{tley, slind}@know-center.at
http://www.know-center.at

[2] University of Graz, Cognitive Science Section,
A-8010 Graz, Austria
dietrich.albert@uni-graz.at
http://wundt.uni-graz.at

Abstract. This paper seeks to suggest ways to support informal, self-directed, work-integrated learning within organizations. We focus on a special type of learning in organizations, namely on competency development, that is a purposeful development of employee capabilities to perform well in a large array of situations. As competency development is inherently a self-directed development activity, we seek to support these activities primarily in an informal learning context. AD-HOC environments which allow employees context specific access to documents in a knowledge repository have been suggested to support learning in the workplace. In this paper, we suggest to use the competence performance framework as a means to enhance the capabilities of AD HOC environments to support competency development. The framework formalizes the tasks employees are working in and the competencies needed to perform the tasks. Relating tasks and competencies results in a competence performance structure, which structures both tasks and competencies in terms of learning prerequisites. We conclude with two scenarios that make use of methods established in informal learning research. The scenarios show how competence performance structures enhance feedback mechanisms in a coaching process between supervisor and employee and provide assistance for self directed learning from a knowledge repository.

1 The Importance of Work-Integrated Learning

In order to operate economically in business education the ratio between outcome and investment needs to be maximized. Investment in business education consists of financial contributions for courseware, learning management systems, training hours, and costs for employees being away from their workplaces. Outcome in business education should be learning results that can directly be transferred to employees' workplaces and which have a high reinforcing impact on job performance. However, studies reveal that only a small amount of knowledge that is actually applied to job activities comes from formal training:

K.-D. Althoff et al. (Eds.): WM 2005, LNAI 3782, pp. 189–202, 2005.

1. Formal training is the source of only 10 – 20% of what we learn at work, although it accounts for about 80% of spending in business education [1].
2. Only 20% to 30% of what is being learned in formal training is actually transferred to the workplace in a way that enhances performance [2].
3. 80 – 90% of what employees know of their job, they know from informal learning [3].

At the same time companies invest large amounts of money in formal training initiatives. Haskell in [4] informs us that in 1998 $70 billion were spent on formal training. He argues that half of this has been misspent due to the fact that what people are taught in formal training is not sufficiently transferred to and applied to the job.

In spite of these findings, in current business practice and eLearning research projects most spending is applied to enhancing knowledge transfer of formal training interventions. These initiatives try to answer the question: "How much does the learner *know* after engaging in the formal training?" Instead, as suggested by the above numbers, the question which should be asked is: "To which extend can the learner *apply* the newly acquired competencies to improve her work performance?" This is why in our work we focus on *learning transfer*. This is the effective and continuing application of knowledge and competencies to new (and often unexpected) contexts.

Let's now take a look at organizations in which both the content being created within the usual work processes and the changing requirements of the tasks employees are working in create a dynamic environment. Such organizations have been referred to as knowledge intensive; examples are R&D companies, consultancies, etc. In knowledge intensive organizations weakly structured work processes are predominant, leaving enough space for flexibility and creativity. In such environments, it is neither possible nor feasible to predetermine all possible "learning paths" employees may be pursuing. In order to ensure a high degree of learning transfer in such knowledge intensive organizations the focus of business education has to be shifted. The trend goes away from enforcing predetermined, general learning paths (as attempted by formal training) towards supporting individual, work task related learning paths (the goal of informal learning). We refer to this type of informal, work-integrated learning as *AD-HOC learning* [5], since it happens ad hoc during work.

In addition, the separation of working, learning, and teaching becomes blurred in knowledge intensive organizations. Increasingly interdisciplinary teams work together to perform a task. They all have to learn from each other (and thus also teach each other) to be able to solve the given problems. Most of the time, mutual learning and teaching happen unconsciously during work. Often "simple" work documents (such as reports, project plans, etc.) serve as learning/teaching content. This content already exists in knowledge intensive organizations (e.g. in the organizational memory) and is generated continuously during work. But unfortunately it is mostly not linked to the work processes where it is needed by other people to learn and within the content generation activities didactical aspects are not taken into account. In order to support informal learning related to individual work tasks a large amount, and especially a large variety of learning content is needed. Obviously this content can not be created solely for learning purposes. Instead, an environment supporting learning and working can tap into an organizational memory and *reuse available content* for learning. Metadata associated with the content plays a central role in this pursuit.

Based on the argumentation given above we argue that what is needed is an environment which supports AD-HOC learning: the acquisition of new competencies in the context of the current work task, thus enabling the user to perform the task better, faster, or more reliably. Such an environment will support working as well as learning and will take into account the following aspects:

1. Provide available content for learning purposes: The environment should support a "learner" or a "teacher" in finding any existing content from an organizational memory which could be used for learning or teaching purposes.
2. Support learning interactions: The environment should provide support for interactions that take place for learning purposes. Examples are: a coaching interaction between employee and supervisor, a lessons learned meeting at the end of a project, or an interaction between an expert and novices in a certain topic.

In Chapter 2 we introduce the *AD-HOC concepts* which are the basis for creating environments to support specific work tasks according to the requirements given above. Chapter 3 serves to make the relation between effective competency development and workplace learning explicit. Chapter 4 illustrates the notion of *competencies as a conceptual layer*. This conceptual layer formalizes the tasks employees perform and the competencies needed to do so. Relating tasks and competencies results in a competence performance structure, which structures both tasks and competencies in terms of learning prerequisites. Chapter 5 then illustrates – using two scenarios – how competency performance structures can be applied within AD-HOC environments to support the competency development of the users.

2 AD-HOC Concepts and Environments

In order to create environments which support AD-HOC learning we have developed the AD-HOC methodology [6]. In this paper we will shortly introduce the main AD-HOC concepts and then (as one example) present an AD-HOC environment for project management.

2.1 AD-HOC Unifying Structure: Enabling Content Reuse for Learning

A typical workplace of a knowledge worker and its structure consisting of three separate spaces: a work space, a knowledge space, and a learning space.

Work space represents the user's desktop PC and shared document storage devices such as a common file structure or document management systems. It contains the work documents which are needed by an employee on a day-to-day basis, such as project related documents. In many knowledge intensive organizations this space is structured according to projects and their work packages.

Learning space stands for conscious learning situations, e.g. attending seminars and taking eLearning courses. The learning space is either completely outside any technical system or combined with an eLearning platform. Sometimes information about current seminars is available through the Intranet. The structures of learning spaces mirror the structures of the learning topics as it is seen by course providers. It follows the didactical abstraction of the topic and provides generally no information about the relationship of work tasks to courses. In addition, the available course material is fairly general and has to be adapted to employees' work contexts.

Knowledge space represents unconscious learning, application of past experiences (own and from others) to new situations, spontaneous search for information and use of examples in order to understand how to apply newly found information. The knowledge space of an organization is often distributed over different systems such as the Intranet, a common file server, etc. Here the structure again is different: Organizational knowledge often does not have one clear structure, but mirrors the internal cognitive map of each person providing the knowledge. Often a mix of the organizations' processes, topics and department structures are found here.

Based on the description of these three spaces, two main problems can be identified when linking the spaces together and integrating teaching and learning support and everyday work:

- *Cognitive disconnection* between the three spaces: Each of the spaces has an inherent structure which mirrors to some extent the mental model of the people who are using it.
- *Structural separation* of the three spaces: Each of the spaces is implemented on different technical systems. And here the contents' structure is predetermined by the system's design.

The cognitive disconnection between the three spaces cannot be overcome as long as users are confronted with the structural separation all the time during their daily work. Thus, it is the structural separation that has to be changed first. In working towards that goal attention has to be paid not only to the properties of the content in

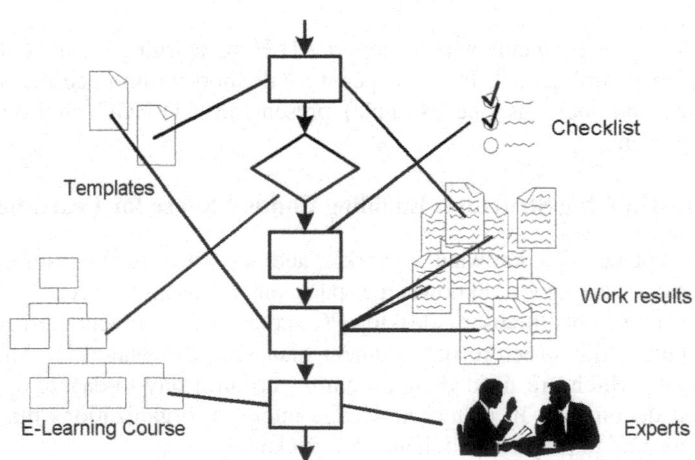

Fig. 1. Using the work process as unifying structuring element to link elements of the three spaces together

question, but also to the mental models of the users. This will ensure that the three spaces will not be connected in some arbitrary way, but in a way that is actually useful and intuitive for the target group.

In order to bridge the cognitive disconnection the AD-HOC method identifies one unifying structuring element for each AD-HOC environment. This unifying element is then used to reference the content from the different spaces. In Figure 1 the work process is used as unifying structural element. This has the advantage that (learning) content can be linked to the work task in which it was created an in which it will likely be used again. Choosing the work processes as unifying structure does not imply automatically that the processes will be used as navigational element. The structural element can be used for navigation (as is described in the case study) however it can also be maintained in the background simply providing implicit structure and using another navigation metaphor (interested readers can refer to the AD-HOC RESCUE environment [7].

2.2 AD-HOC Spectrum: Supporting Self-directed Learning

As motivated above the competence development process largely relies on the learners' own initiative. Within this work we refer to this process as *self-directed learning* [1], [8]. Autonomously defining learning goals and learning paths are important activities within self-directed learning. In order to perform these activities learners need to have a certain level of expertise of the knowledge domain learned. According to [9] there are five different levels of expertise:

- Novice: Learns from facts and context-free rules
- Beginner: Application of facts and context-free rules to other contexts, making first experiences
- Competent: Application of facts, context-free rules and own experiences to other contexts
- Versatile: Holistic perception of 'gestalt' and similarities
- Expert: Holistic perception of 'gestalt' and similarities, intuition

Novices and Beginners need to be supported and led during learning. Only up from the level Competency, learners are able to direct their own learning. Additionally, levels of expertise are dynamic in that one person can have differing levels of expertise in differing knowledge domains. In one domain, she might be an expert, thus behaving as a master (informally) teaching others, in another domain she may be a novice, thus incorporating the role of an apprentice. With informal self-directed learning, learners are able to change between levels of expertise and participate in groups of experts and other learners in order to gain the greatest advantage for themselves and for the community [10].

This illustrates that the needs of a learner are influenced to a large extend by the level of expertise she has reached within one domain. Also, as shown in the section above, the current work context sets certain prerequisites of which learning resources are perceived useful in a situation. In addition, the current personal situation influences immensely which learning content is needed: a person under time pressure is much less likely to read a long report or take an eLearning course than a person who has more time or a more in-depth interest in the subject.

Thus, an environment which aims to support AD-HOC learning must offer a variety of learning content to the user. The more this content is already tailored to the user's situation, the better. We believe however, that it is always useful to get an overview of the different learning resources available within the organization. That is, Novices and Beginners – who still need guidance in their learning activities – will be made aware of formal training offerings (such as seminars and eLearning courses). But at the same time other learning resources will be made available via self-directed learning. The individual learner thus has the choice of which offering fits best his personal preferences and work related needs. We refer to this variety of possible learning resources as the AD-HOC Spectrum (see Figure 2). It bridges the gap between continuously searching the company's intranet and formal courses.

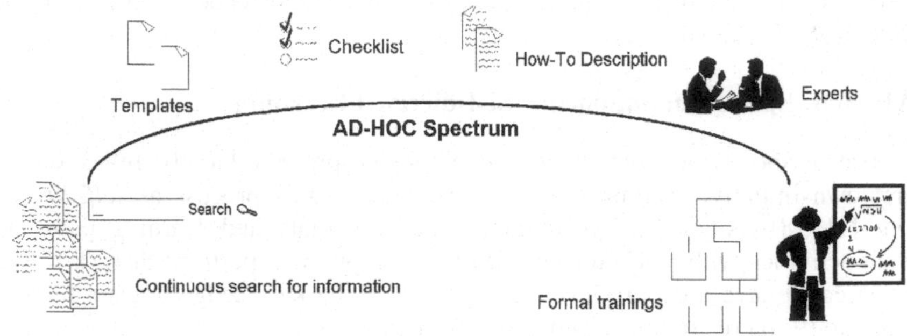

Fig. 2. The AD-HOC Spectrum

Many short task-oriented unconscious learning experiences and few long general conscious learning episodes represent the two extremes of the AD-HOC Spectrum. Between those extremes, AD-HOC offers the learners (workers) a variety of different resources relevant for their specific work tasks. These resources range from example documents and templates, checklists, how-to descriptions, guidelines, contacts to dedicated experts, etc.

3 Competency Development and Workplace Learning

It is generally agreed that learning at the workplace can take different forms. As we have discussed in the previous section, one can differentiate between short-term performance support that would involve learning simple procedures or problem solving strategies, and long-term people development (e.g. [11], [12]). In this paper we look at the latter kind of these learning activities, namely at how employees develop competencies that enable them to perform competently in a broad range of situations.

Up to this point, the use of information technology at the workplace has been primarily concerned with providing performance support, and many knowledge management applications give account of this focus. Learning, however, does also involve permanent changes in the underlying cognitive structures[12]. If we intent to consider a more holistic idea of learning at the workplace, it would therefore be essential to look at human competencies, how they are developed in the workplace and how they are used to produce performance.

We define competencies as personal characteristics (knowledge, skills, abilities) of employees which are relatively stable across different situations (see also [13]). Competencies can be described in terms of distinguishable elements of underlying capacities or potentials which allow job incumbents to act competently in certain situations [14]. Employees dynamically combine these elements according to the requirements of the situation in a self-organising process [15].

Traditionally, competency-based training was targeted at specific behaviors that constitute superior performance. Recently it has been argued that instead of a set of behaviors, competencies should be understood as a set of attributes that allow for superior performance, and that development should be targeted at the underlying competencies rather than at the behavioral level [11]. In accordance with this view, competency development aims to extend the capacity of a person to act competently in a number of situations by helping this person acquire additional competencies applicable for performance in several tasks.

Our view of competency development is such that people acquire new competencies predominantly in interaction with real job situations and tasks (see [14]). New competencies are being developed when a person enters a new situation or task in which action is not predetermined. Reflecting on the outcomes or receiving feedback from a more experienced person helps in this development. This view is in accordance with a large body of research showing the importance of informal learning as opposed to formal training when it comes to learning at the workplace [16].

Baitsch [12] and Conlon [17] have discussed a whole variety of methods that can be used for informal learning, including mentoring, coaching, networking, modeling, effective leadership and interactions in a team environment. Employees consider alternative ways to think and behave, and reflect on processes to assess learning experience outcomes.

How such development can be integrated into workplace learning scenarios is the central concern. In recent times, methods derived from competency-based human resource management (also termed "competency or skills management") have been suggested to improve both knowledge management (KM) and eLearning. Within these methods, competencies of individual employees are being described and rated in order to improve accessibility of these assets or to develop them further.

In KM, competencies have been used to create yellow pages or expert searches (see [18], [19]) in order to leverage "tacit knowledge". Others have suggested that competencies be defined as a means to derive goals for strategic knowledge development [20]. In eLearning, comparing profiles of required competencies for different jobs to profiles of available competencies of individual employees has been utilized in an attempt to assign eLearning courses to employees who need them [21]. Some authors see competencies as a way to closer relate KM and eLearning activities in companies (e.g. [22]).

In this paper we argue that KM and eLearning initiatives aimed at developing competencies of the workforce by employing competency management methods may be improved in two ways: (1) By providing a closer connection between competencies on the one hand and tasks or performance outcomes on the other, and

(2) by seeing competency development as an individually controlled learning process rather than a centrally managed development initiative.

Issue (1) will be addressed by a framework which establishes a competency-performance connection (see section 4). We present results of a case study in a research institute of 30 members, in the following referred to as *Research Ltd.*, where the framework was applied. Issue (2) will be addressed by two scenarios that show how our framework can be applied within an informal workplace learning approach (see section 5). The scenarios emphasize self directed learning from a knowledge repository (rather than the utilization of static courseware) and feedback mechanisms in a coaching process (rather than off the job training).

4 A Competence Performance Approach

Any model for describing competencies should therefore aim to offer a tight integration between competencies and task performance. Using Korossy's competence-performance conception (see [23]), we have developed a framework that achieves this integration. By relating competency descriptions to descriptions of task in which the competencies are being used (*task competency matrix*), we derive a structure on the set of competencies and on the set of tasks (*competence performance structure*).

Table 1 gives an extract from a *task competency matrix* for *Research Ltd.* In this case, the competencies (A-G in the rows) denote typical competencies that deal with different issues of communication. The tasks (the numbers in the columns) denote several documents actually produced by employees working in projects, for example a project requirements document or a management summary. Each document represents a specific task in the project management process that encompasses all actions necessary for producing it.

The document competency matrix was derived by asking project managers, which competencies (knowledge and skills) they had used when producing the documents. Competencies were both general (e.g. communicating in a team setting or with partner companies) and domain specific (e.g. knowledge of streaming technologies). While the first are used for coaching purposes, the latter ones may be used in the context of self-directed learning from a knowledge repository (see next section).

Table 1. Extract from a task-competency matrix for *Research Ltd*

		Project Documents									
Competencies		10	11	12	13	14	17	24	26	33	41
A	Communication about client requirements		x	x	x		x	x	x		x
B	Discussing ideas on an informal level		x				x	x	x		x
C	Understanding goals of others	x	x				x				x
D	Discussing a common practice in a team		x	x	x	x	x		x		x
E	Employing effective interview techniques						x				
F	Presenting and selling own ideas		x				x	x		x	x
G	Defining goals and persuading others		x	x		x	x			x	x

Figure 3 shows the *competence performance structure* that can be derived from the matrix. The boxes in the figure represent *competence states*, which are characterized by a specific combination of competencies (A-G). States are connected by lines denoting a subset relation. Below the competencies, numbers of documents are given that can be created in the state (documents are only listed in the minimal state). For example, in the state {A, D, G} the documents 12, 13 and 14 can be created. The method for deriving a competence performance structures is described in [13].

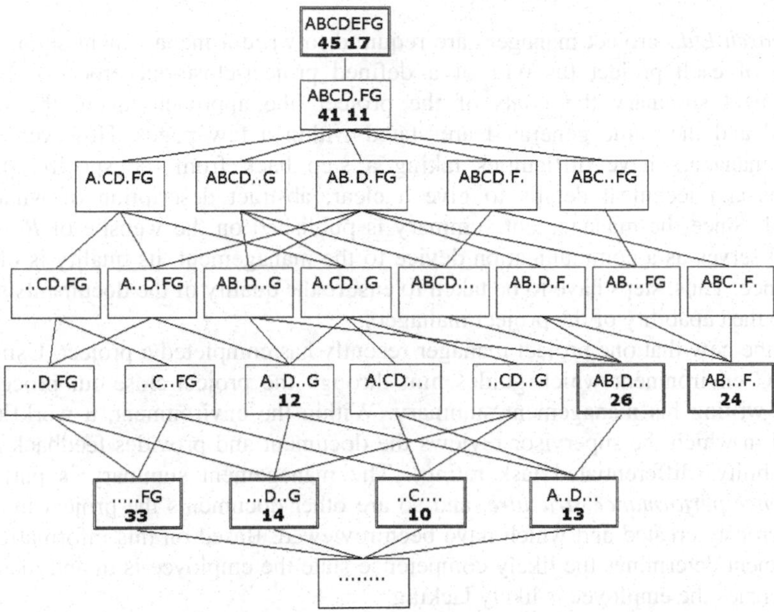

Fig. 3. Structure for competencies A-G and documents corresponding to the states (see [13])

Competence performance structures are based on dependencies that exist both within the set of documents and the set of competencies. Within the competence performance framework, these dependencies can be interpreted as learning prerequisites which can be used for diagnosing learning needs. For example, Figure 3 suggests that there exists a dependency between documents 12 and 13 in that document 12 requires the same competencies as document 13 (A and D) plus one additional one (G). The diagnosis of learning needs happens through an assessment of the performance outcomes (documents in this case). So from good and poor performance in any of these performances, missing competencies can be derived. As competencies are directly connected to performance outcomes, this diagnosis may happen within the usual work processes.

5 Supporting Informal Workplace Learning

Competence performance structures as described in the previous chapter can be the basis for a more effective support of technology enhanced learning interventions at the workplace. They provide the basis for dynamically modeling learning goals and prerequisites, and in conjunction with an AD HOC environment can be used for supporting workplace learning. As competency development is inherently an individual learning activity, we focus on two scenarios that illustrate their use in informal workplace learning.

5.1 Scenario A: Enhancing Supervisor-Employee Learning Interaction

At *Research Ltd.,* project managers are required to write a management summary at the end of each project (as part of a defined project-close-out process). In this management summary the goals of the project, the approach taken, the results achieved and the value generated are stated within a few pages. However, many project managers have difficulties taking a step back from the specific project problems and technical details to give a clear, abstract description of what was achieved. Since the management summary is published on the website of *Research Ltd.* and serves as a communication device to the management, its quality is of high importance. Thus, steps have to be taken to ensure the quality of the documents and to improve the capability of the project managers.

Imagine now that one project manager recently has completed a project. Using the AD-HOC environment which guides him through the project-close-out process he finishes writing his management summary. Within the environment, a workflow is initiated in which the supervisor reviews the document and provides feedback about its suitability (differentiated task rating). The management summary is part of a *competence performance structure,* and so are other documents the project manager has previously created and which have been reviewed. Based on this information the environment determines the likely competence state the employee is in and identifies competencies the employee is likely lacking.

In this case the environment finds out that the project manager in the past had low ratings in the competencies "problem abstraction" and "structured writing" which are essential for writing a management summary. The environment displays these findings to the supervisor thereby supporting the supervisor in his role as a learning coach by helping him assess strengths and weaknesses of the project manager. In this case, the project manager has made considerable improvements in "problem abstraction" but still has some deficiencies in "structured writing". Since the development of this competency is best done by providing feedback and discussing the paper together the supervisor meets with the project manager and coaches him.

This scenario illustrates the connection between the competencies "problem abstraction" and "structured writing" and the task of management summary writing. With a competence performance structure that models the relation of competencies and tasks, it becomes possible to integrate learning in the working process. From the quality of the management summary, the system suggests that the project manager should focus on the development of these specific competencies. Since these competencies are also crucial for other tasks (e.g. writing of user requirement definition) improving them will help to improve overall performance. The scenario also underlines the trend to perform competency development within the business unit as opposed to relying on centrally controlled human resource activities.

5.2 Scenario B: Using a Document Repository for Self-organized Learning

Searching the company's document repository for documents that have been produced in previous projects and finding pointers to the people that have produced them is a different form of informal learning that takes place at knowledge intensive workplaces. The problem is that the document repository is usually not structured according to learning requirements. Again, we suggest that competence performance structures may offer such structuring that is based on learning prerequisites among the documents that have been created.

Fig. 4 shows part of the structure that was created from the data provided by the employees. The part that is shown in the figure focuses on a subset of knowledge used in e-Learning projects (domain specific competencies). The structure was visualized using Formal Concept Analysis [24], which creates concepts (the nodes in the graph) that consist of subsets of objects (documents) and subsets of attributes (competencies). Two documents (5 and 7) can be seen in the structure. The other descriptions denote competencies. All competencies used for producing a specific document can be found by following all paths upwards in the graph.

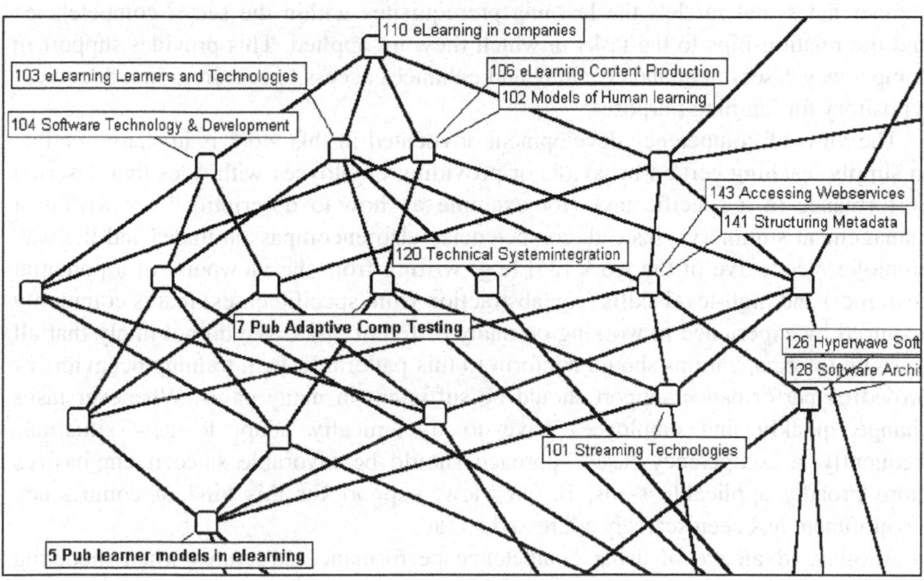

Fig. 4. Formal Context of the documents (5 and 7) and domain specific competencies (101-143) needed for producing them

From the graph, relationships between competencies are readily apparent. For example, we find technological knowledge ("Accessing Webservices", "Structuring Metadata" and "Streaming Technologies") closely related as these were evidently applied in similar contexts. Also, the two documents are related, as document 7 (a publication on adaptive competence testing) used a subset of competencies that was used for document 5 (a publication on learner models). When supporting a self-directed search in the document repository, these relationships can be exploited: For the author of document 7 who is searching for information on technologies used in e-Learning, document 5 might be a valuable learning resource.

This scenario shows that knowing which competencies are available improves self-organized learning by offering documents and information applicable to the user in question. In this case, the environment can take on the role of the "coach" in the sense that for the initial building of the competency "technologies in eLearning" available documents are provided. Initially, no human coach is needed but can later be accessed through the environment as well.

6 Conclusion

We have shown how competence performance structures that establish a connection between tasks and competencies can support informal workplace learning. Two scenarios illustrate possible areas of application. Both utilize a structure of competencies that models the learning prerequisites within the set of competencies and the relationships to the tasks in which they are applied. This provides support in competency assessment and coaching and enhances access to resources in a document repository for learning purposes.

The view of competency development advocated in this work is in sharp contrast to simply teaching certain behaviors or providing employees with rules that describe performance in a specific task (for example a "how-to description" for writing a management summary). Instead, competencies also encompass attitudes and the way employees conceive of the work [25] (e.g. writing from the viewpoint of a potential customer) and high-level skills (e.g. abstraction from specific cases) that is commonly acquired by experience in working on many different tasks. We do not imply that all learning in organizations should conform to this pattern. In fact, training behaviors or providing performance support should be sufficient in many cases. Whenever tasks change quickly and employees have to dynamically adapt to new situations frequently, a competency-based approach should be favorable since it emphasizes more broadly applicable skills. In our view, support for this kind of competency development has been scarcely addressed so far.

Another advantage of using competence performance structures when modeling competencies is that they offer substantial potential for automating the process of competency profiling. Because the structures integrate competencies with the tasks performed in an organization, profiling can be done within the usual work processes. Additionally, the prerequisites in the structures reduce the amount of information that has to be provided manually. If the AD-HOC environment utilizes a document management system, a workflow may be introduced in which only little information (i.e. document-competency ratings) have to be provided in order to place a certain document into the structure, and to make it accessible for technologically enhanced learning purposes.

References

1. Cross, J.: Informal Learning - The other 80%. http://www.internettime.com/Learning/The%20Other%2080%25.htm (2003)
2. Adkins, S.: We are the problem: We are selling Snake Oil. http://www.internettime.com/lcmt/archives/001014.html (2003)
3. Dickover, N. T.: The Job is the Learning Environment: Performance-Centered Learning to Support Knowledge Worker Performance. In: Journal of Interactive Instruction Development, 14, 3 (2000)
4. Haskell, R. E.: Reengineering Corporate Training. Intellectual Capital and Transfer of Learning. Quorum Books, (1998)
5. Lindstaedt, S.: AD HOC - Integration von Arbeits- und Lernprozessen. (2002)
6. Lindstaedt, S. N., Farmer, J., Ley, T.: Betriebliche Weiterbildung. In: Haake, J., Schwabe, G., Wessner, M. (eds.): CSCL-Kompendium - Lehr- und Handbuch zum computerunterstützten kooperativen Lernen. Oldenbourg, München (2004) 423-434
7. Farmer, J., Lindstaedt, S. N., Droschl, G., Luttenberger, P.: AD-HOC - Work-integrated Technology-supported Teaching and Learning. (2004)
8. Tobin, D. R.: All Learning Is Self-Directed: How Organisations Can Support and Encourage Independent Learning. American Society for Training & Development, (2000)
9. Baumgartner, P., Payr, S.: Lernen mit Software. Österreichischer Studienverlag, Innsbruck (1994)
10. Lave, J., Wenger, E.: Situated Learning: Legitimate Peripheral Participation. Cambridge University Press, Cambridge (1991)
11. Hackett, S.: Educating for competency and reflective practice: fostering a conjoint approach in education and training. In: Journal of Workplace Learning, 13, 3 (2001) 103-112
12. Baitsch, C.: Lernen im Prozess der Arbeit - Zum Stand der internationalen Forschung. In: Arbeitsgemeinschaft Qualifikations-Entwicklungs-Management (eds.): Kompetenzentwicklung '98: Forschungsstand und Forschungsperspektiven. Waxmann, Münster (1998) 269-337
13. Ley, T., Albert, D.: Identifying Employee Competencies in Dynamic Work Domains: Methodological Considerations and a Case Study. In: Journal of Universal Computer Science, 9, 12 (2003) 1500-1518
14. Bergmann, B.: Arbeitsimmanente Kompetenzentwicklung. In: Bergmann, B., Fritsch, A., Göpfert, P., Richter, F., Wardanjan, B., Wilczek, S. (eds.): Kompetenzentwicklung und Berufsarbeit. Waxmann, Münster (2000) 11-39
15. Erpenbeck, J., Rosenstiel, L. v.: Einführung. In: Erpenbeck, J., Rosenstiel, L. v. (eds.): Handbuch Kompetenzmessung. Schäffer-Poeschl, Stuttgart (2003) IX-XL
16. Staudt, E., Kriegesmann, B.: Weiterbildung: Ein Mythos zerbricht (nicht so leicht!). In: Staudt, E., Kailer, N., Kottmann, M., Kriegesmann, B., Meier, A. J., Muschik, C., Stephan, H., Ziegler, A. (eds.): Kompetenzentwicklung und Innovation. Waxmann, Münster (2002)
17. Conlon, T. J.: A review of informal learning literature, theory and implications for practice in developing global professional competence. In: Journal of European Industrial Training, 28, 2/3/4 (2004) 283-295
18. Reich, J. R., Brockhausen, P., Lau, T., Reimer, U.: Ontology-Based Skills Management: Goals, Opportunities and Challenges. In: Journal of Universal Computer Science, 8, 5 (2002) 505-515
19. Ehrlich, K.: Locating Expertise: Design Issues for an Expertise Locator System. In: Ackerman, M., Pipek, V., Wulf, V. (eds.): Sharing Expertise - Beyond Knowledge Management. MIT Press, Cambrigdge (2003) 137-158
20. Probst, G. J. B., Deussen, A., Eppler, M. J., Raub, S. P.: Kompetenz-Management: Wie Individuen und Organisationen Kompetenz entwickeln. Gabler, Wiesbaden (2000)

21 Ley, T., Ulbrich, A.: Achieving benefits through integrating eLearning and Strategic Knowledge Management. In: European Journal of Open and Distance Learning (2002) o.S.
22 Efimova, L., Swaak, J.: Converging Knowledge Management, Training and e-learning: Scenarios to Make it Work. In: Journal of Universal Computer Science, 9, 6 (2003) 571-578
23 Korossy, K.: Extending the theory of knowledge spaces: A competence-performance approach. In: Zeitschrift für Psychologie, 205 (1997) 53-82
24 Ganter, B., Wille, R.: Formal Concept Analysis: Mathematical Foundations. Springer, Heidelberg (1999)
25 Sandberg, J.: Understanding Human Competence at Work: An Interpretative Approach. In: Academy of Management Journal, 43, 1 (2000) 9-25

Bridging the Gap Between Knowledge Management and E-Learning with Context-Aware Corporate Learning

Andreas Schmidt

FZI Research Center for Information Technologies, Karlsruhe, Germany
Andreas.Schmidt@fzi.de

Abstract. Knowledge management and e-learning both address the same fundamental problem: facilitating learning in organizations. But they approach the problem with two different paradigms, resulting in two different types of system. This paper proposes context awareness with respect to the learner's or employee's context as a solution to bridge the gap. The project *Learning in Process* is illustrating a step into that direction.

1 Introduction

Learning in Organizations. That's what both (corporate) e-learning and knowledge management are about. It may appear as simple as that, but in practice there are two different paradigms resulting in two different types of systems. But with the shift to constructivist learning environments and the support of collaborative knowledge building in knowledge management systems, it becomes apparent that this separation does not make much sense and is an obstacle to more effective applications. Still, there are two rather different perspectives. In this paper, these differences and the respective shortcomings are briefly discussed (section 2). These shortcomings can be traced back to the unawareness of certain aspects of the context of the respective user. Therefore, a more thorough consideration of context is proposed as a solution (section 3). As an illustration, the work conducted in the project "Learning in Process" (LIP) is presented in section 4.

2 E-Learning and Knowledge Management — Two Paradigms

2.1 Knowledge Management

Knowledge management is a discipline originating from management studies, but always going hand in hand with information technologies both as a reason for its necessity and as a technical solution for the implementation. Knowledge management takes an organizational perspective on learning, and the main problem it tries to address is the lack of sharing knowledge among members of the organization. Its solutions try to enable and encourage the individuals' making explicit their knowledge by creating knowledge assets or engaging in discussion forums.

K.-D. Althoff et al. (Eds.): WM 2005, LNAI 3782, pp. 203 – 213, 2005.

The language of knowledge management is to some degree naïve because it assumes that knowledge is an (almost tangible) good that can be "produced", "captured" or "transferred" and that can be summed up to a corporate memory. Starting from metadata-driven document management, knowledge management has now adopted communication and collaboration solutions in order to address the problem of tacit knowledge. Still, knowledge management does not fully realize that it is mainly about facilitating purpose-oriented *learning* in organizations and that thus understanding how *learning* takes place is extremely important to consider. And learning – in the view of modern constructivist learning theories – is not just transferring knowledge; it is a highly individualized task of construction.

2.2 E-Learning

E-Learning, or better computer supported learning, focuses on the individual's acquisition (or rather construction) of new knowledge and the technological means to support this construction process. One of the main assumptions in e-learning coming from pedagogy is that learning needs can be improved through *guidance*. The typical form of guidance is the teacher or tutor organizing the learning process. But e-learning has also transferred the concept of lessons to computer-based courses, consisting of several learning resources that are connected with one another in a meaningful way. This comes from the pedagogical insight that it matters for the efficiency of learning in which order learning resources are offered, which can encompass both more traditional courses, modular learning objects, but also more elusive interaction possibilities. This concept of guidance also leads to an asymmetry and a separation of the roles author/tutor and learner. Authors and tutors are pedagogically and didactically trained persons while learners typically are not.

State of the art e-learning approaches provide very sophisticated ideas for improving the learning process. However, its focus on didactically well-founded learning material with rich media content and complex interaction profiles makes it impractical, especially in cost-sensitive corporate settings. While it is true that a clear didactical approach and rich learning programs facilitate the learning of the individual significantly, e-learning approaches have so far not been able to solve the problem of producing these kind of materials. Simulations close to the real world are the perfect answer to constructivist learning theories, demanding situated learning [8] with a high degree of engagement of the learner. But the "real world" in companies looks different. There are some more advanced courses, mostly bought from external training providers. But the majority of learning occurs from less perfect things, authored in a more peer-to-peer manner that still provide significant opportunities to learn. This is especially true for innovative topics, constituted by "less mature" knowledge for which there is no consolidated view, or highly specialized, company-specific subjects.

3 Towards an Integrated View with Context-Awareness

What separates the world of e-learning and the world of knowledge management is their respective limited and isolated consideration of context. If context is perceived on a broader scope, e-learning solutions can "learn" that corporate learning takes place in an organizational context, that learning processes are most often triggered by immediate real-world needs. e-learning can also "learn" that the authoring takes place (and is encouraged to take place) in the same context as the learning itself, thus integrating the peer-to-peer knowledge sharing philosophy.

On the other hand, knowledge management can "learn" that the context of the individual matters, that delivery of information pieces does not help if the individual is ignored, her current state of knowledge into which the new knowledge pieces should be integrated, her most efficient form of learning, which probably includes more than just a document.

On a technical level, what do we have to do?

- We need to **capture the context** of the learner and the situation in which learning occurs. This encompasses both the work context (the individual's position and role in the organization, current process or task) and the personal characteristics with respect to learning (previous knowledge, personal goals, cognitive style etc.). This context should be managed in a way so that several applications can view and update this context in a mutually enriching way.
- We need to **provide context-aware delivery methods** to account for the fact that a learner in a company is not primarily learning, but usually working and interrupting their work for learning. Current methods are only suitable for long-term strategic learning, but not for immediate learning on demand (although there is some research in that direction, e.g.[9]).
- We need to perceive that **resources themselves are created in context and interrelated** with other resources and this context makes a difference in making sense of the individual resources.

In knowledge management research, there have been some approaches to exploit context for improving the solution (e.g. process context in [1] or [2]). An approach to the problem from the e-learning point of view was taken by the project "Learning in Process" the results of which are briefly summarized in the following section.

4 The Case of LIP

4.1 Overview

Learning in Process ([3], [4]) has been a project with a consortium with learning technology experts, knowledge management companies and researchers of context-aware information systems. Its primary goals have been the integration of working and learning on a process level and learning management, knowledge management, human capital management and collaboration solutions on a technical level. The focus of the project has been on the incorporation of context-awareness into the design of learning solutions[5].

As a first step, the different types of learning processes in a corporate setting were identified according to the primary initiating or controlling instance. Then it was analyzed how the consideration of context can improve those learning processes. LIP considered the following types of learning processes:

- **Course-steered learning.** This type of learning process currently is in the focus of corporate learning strategies. Learning activity is controlled by the pre-defined course structure, where courses typically are relatively large learning units, which can be subscribed to or assigned to. It is important to note that this encompasses both e-learning courses and presence seminars (and, of course, "blended learning" arrangements). Context-awareness in course-steered learning primarily is the adaptivity of course structures based on contextual variables, allowing for alternative (but still pre-defined) learning paths.
- **Self-steered learning.** In this type of learning process, the learner initiates and controls the learning process herself. Typically, she actively searches for learning resources which help to satisfy the current knowledge need. This includes purposefully contacting colleagues for help on a particular problem. Context-awareness can make the selection process more efficient by adding implicit assumptions of the learner (e.g. her current task). This can be used both for exploratory and for descriptive search strategies.
- **Context-steered learning.** The main drawback of course-steered learning is that it only allows for a limited integration of working and learning activities due to the coarse-grained nature. Self-steered learning on the other side allows for interweaving these processes, but it requires non-trivial cognitive abilities (e.g. becoming aware of knowledge gaps and formulating a corresponding query in whatever form). In order to overcome these problems, LIP has elaborated a third type of learning process: context-steered learning. Here the system observes the (potential) learner's work activities, while she interacts with her everyday applications. The system deduces from its domain knowledge and the knowledge of the learner potential knowledge gaps. For these gaps, the system can compile small learning programs from available learning resources and recommend them to the learner, who can decide whether to learn now, to postpone it, or discard the recommendation completely. Here information about the context is used for several purposes: when and how to recommend, what to recommend and how to compile individual learning resources into personalized learning programs.

4.2 Context Model

Essential for any context-aware system is the formalization of what "can used to characterize the situation of an entity" [10], i.e. the definition of a context model or schema for context information. Past research approaches have shown that there is no canonical set of context feature for a certain problem domain. So the system was designed in a generic way so that appropriate features (together with their acquisition and exploitation strategies) can be added to the schema without affecting the core functionality or the interfaces of the involved services. The core of this generic infrastructure is a data model for context information based on RDFS that is capable of representing imperfection and dynamic phenomena like aging as well as the context history [6] for all context features.

For defining the LIP context schema, a pragmatic approach was chosen that is based on three pillars: (1) the analysis of existing approaches (including both research and standardization activities like IMS Learner Information Profile and PAPI), (2) a scenario-based end users requirements elicitation phase and (3) the identification of potential context sources and usage strategies (e.g. by considering the IEEE Learning Object Metadata (LOM) standard). This ensures that the context schema incorporates both *relevant* and *realistic* context features for the two pilot installations. The result was a context schema that can be divided into three groups, which correspond to the research communities of adaptive e-learning systems [11], business process oriented knowledge management [2] and context-awareness:

- Personal
  - previously acquired knowledge or competencies
  - goals (divided into short-term and long-term)
  - preferred interactivity level (from LOM)
  - preferred semantic density (from LOM)
- Organizational
  - organizational unit
  - role(s)
  - business process (or process step)
  - task (as an activity that cannot be easily mapped to a business process)
- Technical
  - user agent (operating system, browser, plugins etc.)
  - bandwidth
  - available audio

Additional context information, e.g. like the learner typology used in [12], is certainly desirable, but was discarded for the prototypes because there was no appropriate learning material available.

This holistic view of the context in which learning takes place brings together the aspects that are typically the domain of knowledge management (the organizational aspect) and learning management (the personal perspective). Semantic linkage of these two aspects is achieved through a competency catalog, which forms also the semantic basis for current approaches to holistic human resources development (e.g. [13]). Apart from a hierarchical structure, this competency catalog also allows for (currently) five different competency levels. Competencies are linked directly to the individual context as existing competencies and future goals and indirectly by associating the organizational context entities with competency requirements (see Fig.1). On the other side, learning objects are described by their objectives (expressed as competencies that are acquired after successful completion) and their prerequisites (expressed as competencies that are required to understand the presented resources). This enables the context-aware matching procedure, which is described in the following section.

4.3 Matching Procedure for Context-Steered Learning

The overall aim of LIP was the context-aware *delivery* (encompassing both the time of delivery and the delivered items) of available e-learning resources, which can be

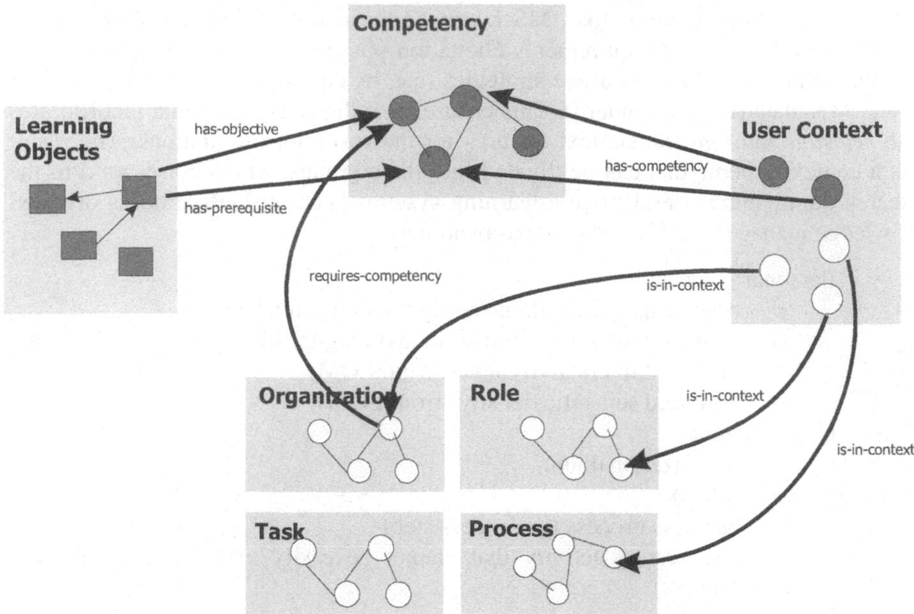

Fig. 1. Competencies as the semantic glue between the context and learning resources

traditional courses, learning objects, but also other resources like colleagues/experts or discussion forums. Learning objects themselves are expected to be modular and self-contained; they are described by their objectives and prerequisites in terms of competencies. It was realized that it is of crucial importance that they can have dependencies on other learning objects, which have to be taken into account by the system. This is an important distinction to pure (just-in-time) information retrieval applications and typical document-oriented knowledge management applications. This consideration of semantic dependencies represent a form of pedagogical guidance, which avoids overstraining the individual with the unknown and thus helps to reduce (or at least not increase) the feeling of uncertainty typically associated with an information or knowledge need [14].

The technical nucleus of LIP is a matching procedure (see Fig. 2) that allows for compiling on demand personalized learning programs based on the current competency gap. This matching procedure can be divided into the following three parts:

- In the **knowledge gap analysis**, the system checks the user's current context or situation. The current knowledge gap is the set of current competency requirements minus the set of current competencies of the user. For this knowledge gap, the system can retrieve appropriate learning objects. In order to fill the knowledge gap, we retrieve all learning objects that deliver one of the competencies in the knowledge gap.
- **Learning Program Compilation.** Usually a single learning object will not be enough to bridge the gap, because the gap is too big, and because learning objects themselves can have prerequisites that the user does not meet yet. Therefore we

need to provide the user with a complete learning program. This is accomplished by recursively adding learning objects for unsatisfied prerequisites and pruning based on features in the user's context (for details see [3]).

- **Preference-based Ranking.** After compiling several possible Learning Programs, the system ranks the alternatives according to the user or organizational preferences. This includes the following properties, which correspond directly to IEEE LOM metadata elements: interactivity level, semantic density, but also overall estimated learning time. As a result of this process, the user can be presented with the ranked list, from which he can select the desired learning program.

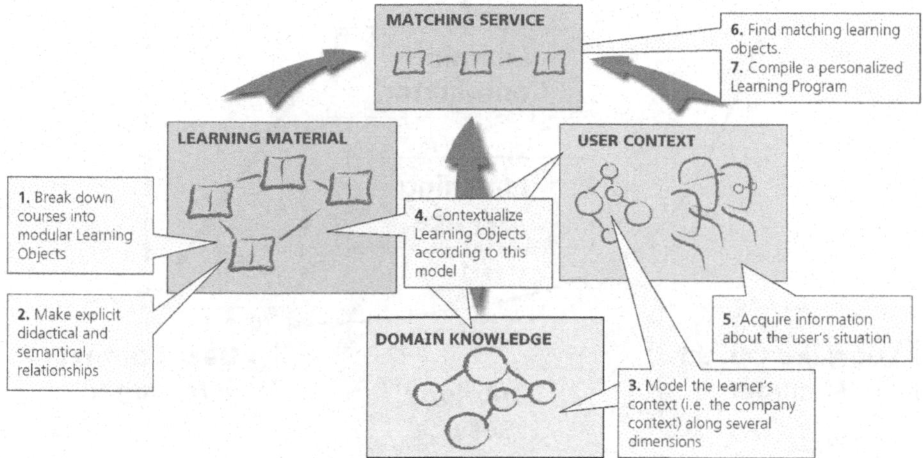

Fig. 2. LIP Matching Procedure for learning material

Although LIP has concentrated on the delivery, it has also enabled context-aware execution of learning objects. Current learning objects are typically unaware of the context in which they are actually executed, apart from some limited awareness of learner preferences. Especially, these learning objects do not take into account the organizational or business context. Apart from pedagogical difficulties, this can be traced back to the technical problem of not being able to access any context-related information from within a standardized execution environment like SCORM. Therefore, LIP has extended the standardized SCORM API available to learning objects at execution time with direct access to context information. This is achieved through mapping the context features to the CMI data model of SCORM. This technically enables the creation of truly adaptive learning objects.

4.4 System Architecture

The integration of context-aware functionality into a learning system architecture was guided by the principle of loose technical coupling while retaining a high level of semantic coherences between the different parts of the system. Complex corporate environments typically do not allow for a complete new, all-in-one system. Rather, there are specialized systems already in place. To account for that, LIP was taking a a service-oriented approach that defines a set of services with well-defined interface and interaction patterns so that existing systems can continue to exist autonomously while being able to take a role in the LIP architecture. The following services (which are further decomposed into subservices on the level of implementation):

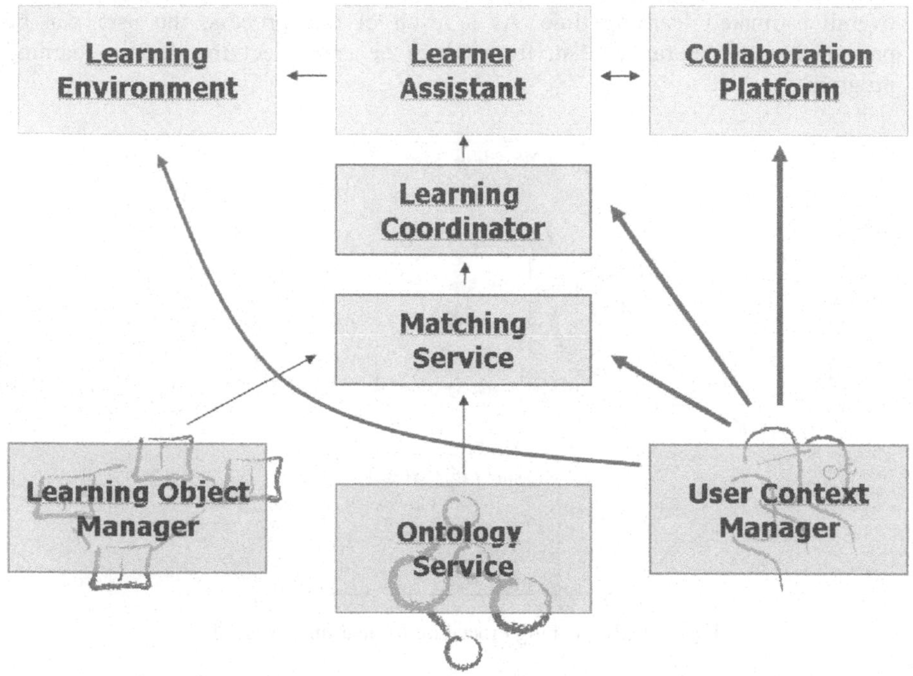

Fig. 3. Loosely coupled architecture of LIP

- The **Learning Object Manager** represents the functionality that is typically offered by a Learning Content Management System (LCMS). It stores learning resources and their metadata and allows for metadata-based retrieval.
- The **Ontology Service** allows for persistence storage and querying of the ontologies involved, i.e. the organizational structure, the competency catalog and the context schema.
- For managing the context, a generic **User Context Manager** [6] was developed that can collect this information from various sources and support different services with a specific views.
- As sketched above, a **Matching Service** can compile personalized learning programs from the available learning material (*Learning Object Manager*), the user's current context (User Context Manager) and the context's knowledge requirements (provided by the *Ontology Service*).

- A **Learning Coordinator** decides based on context changes when to display suggestions about available personalized learning programs and communication or collaboration spaces. There can be several strategies to implement this behavior.
- The **Learning Assistant** represents the component that displays recommendations to the user and captures context changes from the user's interactions with her applications. This component typically resided on the user's machine, although some server-side processing is involved.
- Learning can be organized by the learner in the **Learning Environment**, which allows for finding, scheduling and executing learning programs. Additionally, it makes available through the SCORM API the user's current context in order to enable adaptive learning content.
- A **Collaboration Platform** was "contextualized" with the help of this service by providing contextualized expert finder functionality, group formation and interaction spaces, where learners can themselves create "knowledge assets" which can be made available (e.g. by recommendation or in self-steered learning processes) to other learners based on the context in which they were created.

With the matching service in the center of the architecture, this architecture can be characterized as applying the "Context Matcher" pattern as described in [15].

5 Related Work

There is a long tradition of research in the area of *adaptive systems* (especially in domain of learning) where context information about a user is typically called "user model" [11]. The major limitation of those approaches was (1) that they were always geared towards a single application, whereas corporate environment typically require a wide range of applications that can exploit information about the user's context, and (2) that they are usually biased towards the personal characteristics part of the user context. As shown in the previous section, the consideration of both context aspects can help to overcome the separation of the disciplines of knowledge management and e-learning and provide more holistic context-aware functionality.

On the *knowledge management* side, there has also been some research on linking KM systems to their organizational context, in particular to their business process context [2]. These approaches were a major step into the direction of facilitating workplace learning with a broader scope, but they have not acknowledged the importance of pedagogical guidance. Context-aware delivery of e-learning material is not just the same problem as just-in-time information retrieval.

The idea of supporting *learning on demand* and the interweaving of learning and working processes has also been the foundation for the "Knowledge on Demand" (KOD) project[17], which has concentrated on resource metadata rather than "user metadata", and the AD-HOC platform [9], which demonstrates the potential of knowledge management systems for learning. However, these approach do not fully realize neither the full potential of a thorough consideration of context, nor the non-trivial problem of dealing with imperfect and dynamic user context information. This becomes most apparent with their lack of a generic user context management functionality.

6 Conclusions and Outlook

The LIP approach has shown how e-learning systems can be made more aware of the context in which learning takes place. This allows for a natural integration with knowledge management functionality which has a more peer-to-peer philosophy *and* for the creation of higher quality e-learning objects which are adaptable to the context in which they are executed. Evaluation studies have shown that the user acceptance of such systems is fairly high and suggest that this blending of e-learning and knowledge management functionality can help to improve workplace learning.

It has been recognized as essential that semantically deep integration of different corporate systems via their common (or at least related) usage context needs generic user context management functionality which also acknowledges the complexity of this acquisition and management task. Especially change (including the phenomenon of aging) and the imperfection of acquisition and reasoning techniques pose severe challenges to deep contextualization of systems.

Apart from researching the fundamental problem of user context management, we plan to explore the possibilities of automatically contextualizing resources to provide contextually enhanced navigation support [7] as a next step. This will allows for an exploratory learning environment in which both didactically prepared learning resources and knowledge assets created by users can be presented in a uniform way. These navigational support elements will not only be based on the user's context, but also on the context of the resource. This will include research on how the resource context relates to the user's context and how the context of creators and users of resources can be exploited for improving content creation and learning processes [16].

Acknowledgments. This work was conducted within the project "Learning in Process" (http://www.learninginprocess.com), which was co-funded by the European Commission within the Fifth Framework Programme of IST.

References

1. Maus, H.: Workflow context as a means for intelligent information support. In: 3rd International Conference on Modeling and Using Context (CONTEXT '01), Dundee, Scotland (2001)
2. Abecker, A., Bernardi, A., Hinkelmann, K., Kuehn, O., Sintek, M.: Context-aware, proactive delivery of task-specific information: The Know-More Project. DFKI GmbH International Journal on Information Systems Frontiers (ISF) 2 (2000) 139–162
3. Schmidt, A.: Context-steered learning: The learning in process approach. In: IEEE International Conference on Advanced Learning Technologies (ICALT '04), Joensuu, Finland (2004)
4. Schmidt, A., Winterhalter, C.: User context aware delivery of e-learning material: Approach and architecture. Journal of Universal Computer Science (JUCS) 10 (2004) 28–36
5. Nabeth, T., Anghern, A., Balakrishnan, R.: Integrating context in e-learning systems design. In: IEEE International Conference on Advanced Learning Technologies (ICALT 04). (2004)
6. Schmidt, A.: Management of dynamic and imperfect user context information. In: 2004 International On The Move Federated Conferences (OTM). (2004)

7. Suranyi, Gabor; Nagypal, Gabor; Schmidt, Andreas: Intelligent retrieval of digital resources by exploiting their semantic context. In: 2004 International On The Move Federated Conferences (OTM), Proceedings of International Conference on Ontologies, Databases and Applications of Semantics (ODBASE 2004). Lecture Notes in Computer Science (LNCS), Larnaca/Cyprus, Springer (2004)
8. Lave, J.; Wenger, E.: Situated Learning: Legitimate Peripheral Participation. Cambridge: Cambridge University Press (1991)
9. Farmer, Johannes; Lindstaedt, Stefanie N.: AD HOC: Work-integrated Technology Supported Teaching and Learning, Proceedings of Organisational Knowledge, Learning and Capabilities, Innsbruck, Austria (2004)
10. Dey, Anind K.: Understanding and Using Context, Personal and Ubiquitous Computing Journal, Volume 5 (1), (2001) 4-7
11. Brusilovsky, P.: Adaptive hypermedia, User Modeling and User Adapted Interaction, 11 (1/2), (2001) 87-110
12. Abrahamian, E.; Weinberg, J.; Grady, M.; Stanton, C.M.: Is Learning Enhanced by Personality-Aware Computer-Human Interfaces?, Proceedings of I-KNOW Graz, Austria (2003)
13. Biesalski, E.: Abecker, A.: Ansätze zum ontologiebasierten Human Resource Management, Proceedings Professional Knowledge Management – Experiences and Visions (WM2005), Workshop on IT Tools for Knowledge Management Systems: Applicability, Usability, and Benefits (KMTOOLS), Kaiserslautern (2005)
14. Kuhlthau, C.: Seeking Meaning: A Process Approach to Library and Information Services Ablex Publishing (1993)
15. Flora, C.d.; Riva, O.; Russo, S.; Raatikainen, K.: A Pattern-Oriented Approach to Enhance Context Infrastructures, The 2005 Symposium on Applications and the Internet Workshops (SAINT-W'05), Trento, Italy (2005)
16. Schmidt, A.: Knowledge Maturing and the Continuity of Context as a Unifying Concept for Knowledge Management and E-Learning, Proceedings of I-KNOW '05, Special Track on Integrating Working and Learning (IWL), Graz, Austria (2005)
17. Sampson, D.; Schenone, A.: Knowledge-on-Demand in e-Learning and e-Working Settings, Educational Technology & Society 5 (2) 2002

The Promise of Automated Interactivity

Michael Yacci

Rochester Institute of Technology,
Rochester, NY 14623, USA
may@it.rit.edu

Abstract. This paper discusses issues and potential methods that can be applied to create instruction and interactive instructional material automatically from knowledge components. Knowledge management systems generally promote a static recombination of text and images, with little concern as to how these objects and components will actually work as useful, well-designed instruction. Interactivity itself has historically been poorly defined; the structural model of interactivity created an operational definition of instructional interactivity that will be used as the basis for the discussion of automated interactivity. A prototype system that uses automated interactivity in diagnosis is illustrated.

1 Introduction

In 1999 an idea called the *knowledge warehouse* [1] was introduced. The article discussed reusable *knowledge components*, and suggested various ways in which these knowledge components could be re-assembled for multiple purposes. At the time, this concept was relatively new and under-explored. The idea of warehousing knowledge (as opposed to information or data) and recombining it into reusable pieces for the purposes of instruction or performance support was rarely mentioned in the literature of the day. In the time since the publication of that article, many initiatives and technologies have developed to support this idea, including the emergence of XML as a technology and SCORM as a technical standard for sharing and reuse.

However, critical design issues still have not been addressed, in particular the means by which these knowledge components will be recombined into useful instructional resources. The article pointed out that a major design issue was "the development of proper client-side control systems so that (in the case of training) instructional presentation rules are applied to knowledge content to produce instruction rather than reference materials." More succinctly, the goal is to create *instruction* rather than instructional *materials*. The term "materials" implies the static assembly of text and images, like an engine without a driver. Instruction itself is an activity in which many interactive and adaptive processes occur, such as diagnosis of a student's current state, selection of next topics, and assessment of current knowledge state of the student.

The emerging literature on "learning objects" reflects a lack of agreement on terms, purposes, and structures for learning objects. For example, Mohan and Daniel [2] note that learning objects are sometimes thought of as content resources which might be

K.-D. Althoff et al. (Eds.): WM 2005, LNAI 3782, pp. 214 – 221, 2005.

re-used. However, this is clearly the "instructional materials" approach to the design of these objects.

A line of research that deals with automating the instructional process comes from the development of intelligent tutoring systems (ITS) that are generally attempting to model the interactive nature of instruction, rather than the static creation of instructional materials. Most ITSs are dialogue-based, and the instructional process is created by the interactions between student and ITS system. In some cases [3], these interactions are modeled after actual transcripts from human tutors. However, it is paradoxical that the effectiveness of human tutors generally does not stem from an overabundance of training and preparation; most tutors in higher education, for example, receive little to no training in tutoring techniques. Instead, it appears that the effectiveness of tutoring comes from the tutor's ability to work one-to-one with a student, and to provide constant feedback that enables constructivist learning.

The semi-spontaneous nature of tutoring contrasts with a more general, structured approach used by many instructional designers: specify the outcome, determine a strategy that has a likelihood to succeed, provide opportunities to practice and provide the student with feedback and remediation if necessary.

In 1999, we suggested that knowledge components might consist of tagged instructional components. If tagged correctly, they can be recombined into various lessons and modules according to a set of instructional design rules. A major enhancement to this process would be an attempt to automate the pedagogical interactivity that surrounds the modules; this would include diagnosis, feedback, branching, and remediation.

2 Adaptation

An adaptive system is central to this distinction between instruction and instructional materials. The system's ability to adapt – whether teacher controlled or computer controlled – creates the linkages between instructional materials and creates "life" in an otherwise static environment. Adaptation in instruction has been promoted in varying degrees since the inception of computer based instruction more than 30 years ago. Initially, adaptation consisted of branching programs, in which the student was provided with rather broad-stroke alternative paths and presentations within a module, based upon correct answers to embedded questions. This model continues today, in a variety of forms of increased complexity. However, the basic premise of providing alternative materials based upon student responses is the basis of most adaptive systems.

3 Interactivity

Adaptive systems, by their nature, require interactivity between student and system as the primary basis for monitoring students and selecting alternatives. However, interactivity has been an elusive concept, suffering from the lack of a clear definition.

The *structural model of interactivity* was developed to address the lack of operational definitions for the construct of *interactivity* [4]. While numerous researchers claimed to be investigating the phenomena of interactivity, there was no consensual definition of the term [5]; researchers were often exploring very different phenomena. The need for a clear, operational definition of interactivity prompted the structural model to provide this definition, along with numerous conjectures concerning the likely variables of interest within the model. Within the structural model, interactivity is seen as a multivariate *process* with critical process factors. In essence, a system doesn't have *more* or *less* interactivity, but rather it has different *factors* of interactivity.

Instructional interactivity is a particular subset of interactivity in which one or both entities has the goal of *learning*. The structural model made four basic claims about interactivity, particularly in instruction:

- interactivity is a loop of messages passed between entities (called a message loop);
- instructional interactivity occurs from the learner's point of view and does not occur until a message loop *from* and *back to* the student has been completed;
- instructional interactivity has two distinct classes of outputs: content learning and affective benefits;
- messages in an interaction must be mutually coherent to qualify as interactivity.

There are additional process factors that might influence the interactive process; several of these factors are suggested as areas of research, that could begin to "add flesh" to the bare bones of the structural model (see figure 1).

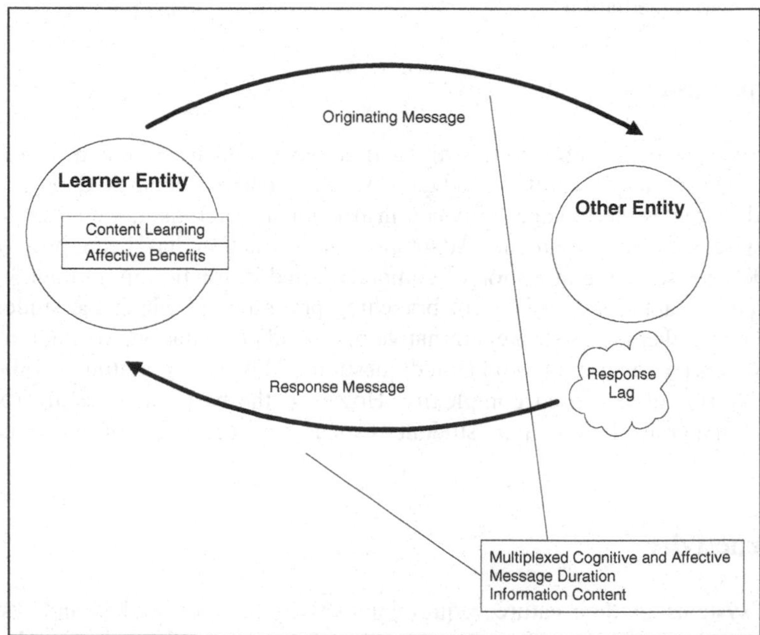

Fig. 1. Additional variables that relate to the structural model

These additional process factors are inherent within almost any interactive system, although they are most commonly found in interactive instructional systems.

4 Student Modeling

Intelligent Tutoring Systems (ITS) additionally introduced the idea of a *student model*. Generally speaking, a student model is a map of a student's current cognitive state. According to Ragnemalm [6] a student model is "a collection of data about the student that is used by the other components in the system in a number of different tasks… and include such as planning the sequence of instruction, remediating misconceptions, generating feedback and explaining the reason for an error made by the student." It can be thought of as an abstract concept map of a student's structural knowledge [7].

In most ITS, the student model is (in some way) compared to an expert model (a map of an expert's knowledge) or a content model (a generalized map of the desired knowledge). Gaps or discrepancies between student model and content model are referred to as a "diagnosis" and are treated as possible topics for investigation or instruction.

At the moment, student modeling is generally ad hoc; there is no standard approach nor is there consensus as to what constitutes an appropriate student model [6]. Depending upon the task circumstances, and the desired characteristics of the complete system, different aspects of a student may be modeled and monitored, such as learning style preferences, presentation modality strengths and weaknesses, or time and speed preferences. For this article, we limit our discussion to a *cognitive* model, limited to monitoring a student's structural knowledge, rather than learning style or other potentially adaptive characteristics.

5 Automated Interactivity

We now introduce the idea of automated interactivity as an aspect of a learning object. If we assume that a learning object is a collection of tagged knowledge components (or content pieces) that are arranged and presented according to an instructional design theory, then a basic instructional module can be automatically created from "standard" pieces. However, the rules for interactivity (or adaptation) are often not clearly stated in an instructional design model. For example, remediation is suggested in many Computer-Based Training (CBT) design approaches, but detailed specifications for remediation (how much, what type, etc.) in mediated environments are rarely researched. In contrast, most ITS systems use plan-based approaches which attempt to determine a "next tutoring step" as they go. These approaches often combine remediation techniques with instructional practices and the developers of these systems note the difficulty in removing the pedagogical activities from content and communication [8].

However, we believe that interactivity in the forms of diagnosis, feedback, and remediation might be handled separately, in a modular manner, so that *existing materials could be made into interactive instruction.* Such an approach holds great promise for knowledge management systems that hope to reuse existing materials, rather than re-write them. Systems and technologies that would allow existing materials to be sequenced and made interactive would be a promising direction.

We chose to work initially with the process of *diagnosis*. Diagnosis (comparison between student model and content model) is frequently done informally in a classroom by teachers and instructors. Diagnosis is done by computer in Intelligent Tutoring Systems; in essence, the ITS engine does a type of similarity comparison, then selects a next topic for discussion. We believe that a similar form of automated interactive process could be used with knowledge components that exist in a knowledge base or knowledge management system.

One attempt to create such a system is the Conversational Diagnostic Agent [9]. The Conversational Diagnostic Agent (CDA) is a software agent that communicates in a variety of ways with students. Specifically, its purpose is to work with a student one-on-one, using a semi-natural language within a series of questions and skill-based tasks to diagnose a student's inability to complete a course-related task.

The Conversational Diagnostic Agent has several significant features that are useful in the creation of automated interactivity and diagnosis. First, the CDA is integrated with Instant Messenger (IM), the most popular real-time conversation tool on the Internet. This provides easy access via any networked computer and enables real-time, text-based "chat" from any machine on the Internet to our agent. This networked linkage is central to most visions of knowledge management systems.

Second, the student model (and exert/content model) is based on a learning hierarchy as popularized by Robert Gagne and his colleagues [10, 11]. Gagne's approach claims that skills can be decomposed into requisite subskills. If any of those subskills are lacking, a higher level of skill cannot be achieved. This much-researched theory is axiomatic in the field of instructional design, and creates a relatively well-structured student model. The diagnostic algorithm is much more systematic because it is based on a learning hierarchy that fully explores gaps in subskills through a depth-first search, guaranteeing that no missing subskill will be overlooked or missed.

A learning hierarchy differs from many existing help systems that are organized as "content outlines." A learning hierarchy has structural rules that specify the relationships of the skills in the hierarchy; a content outline, on the other hand, generally deals with topics rather than skills, and the organization of the outline is somewhat idiosyncratic. That is, there are no established relationships between topics within the outline, and there is no requirement that the content outline be exhaustive and complete. This is the major advantage of the learning hierarchy.

The CDA uses *content nodes* (written in XML) as a central structure. Each content node encapsulates several types of information:

- A behaviorally stated objective
- A prompt question
- A pointer to assessment items (in a related file)
- A list of pointers to prerequisite sub-skills (other content nodes)

The CDA's content nodes each have a minimum of required information. For example, each content node must "know" its subskills. These are, essentially, pointers to other content nodes. Each content node must also have a mechanism for determining if a student has achieved the skill described in the content node – the assessment items. The content nodes for the prototype CDA were created specifically for the project, but we believe that these nodes could have been arranged from existing resources with a reasonable amount of design effort.

The CDA user interface uses a *conversational agent*, a conceptual software approach that communicates about a limited range of topics using natural and semi-natural language [12]. The current CDA uses a question-response format, which allows for both semi-natural language [14] and menu-driven responses. This approach can be modified to create more realistic dialogues, without necessarily requiring true natural language processing. (see [13] for examples). The conversational pieces will be linked to keywords from the content nodes, and will use templates of functionally-centered questions, such as "Do you believe that you have the ability to do X?" These can be randomized to provide variety and interest. Student responses are generally constrained to multiple choice responses. Open-ended input is parsed for keywords, from which the CDA attempts to paraphrase what it believes the student has said.

In the following example transcript from the CDA prototype, *UMachine* is a student who has contacted the CDA using Instant Messenger. The student seeks help in learning about JAVA programming.

```
CDA: Do you feel that you understand loops in
Java?
UMachine: No not really

CDA: OK, Let's explore some more. Do you think you
understand 'while' loops in Java?
1) Yes, I understand while loops.
2) No, I need help with while loops.
UMachine: 1

CDA: Just to be sure, let's check how well you
understand 'while' loops. Click on this link to
view some charts:

http://www.it.rit.edu/~phl/ritlearn/whileloops/q1.
gif

After you look at the three charts, which of these
diagrams best represents a 'while' loop?

UMachine: 3

CDA: Hmmm. Not quite. Let me ask you another: How
many times does a 'while' loop execute?
```

The CDA, at present time, separates the diagnostic process from the overall tutoring or instructional process. It provides a diagnosis, in terms of skills, that can be used by students or faculty members to access instructional resources. This project in its prototype stage connects with a server-side flat file database, which contains its content model and which maintains the student model. However, the CDA's conclusion could be linked to a an associated database.

6 Issues of Automated Interactivity: Time

Although the CDA is only in a prototype stage, there are two issues in its design that we have not seen addressed in other work; both involve the factor *time*.

First, when a conversation stops and starts over time, a major unresolved issue is: how long should the computer remember the context of the conversation? For example, if two people are involved in a discussion, and they are momentarily interrupted, they can often resume the conversation in the exact point in which they left off. However, this ability to resume generally only lasts for a few minutes. If they do not pick up the thread of the discussion again in a few minutes, they will likely both forget. Of course, the computer will never "forget" and will pick up the dialogue weeks later at the same spot, much to the confusion of the student. Thus the computer must be explicitly told when to "forget where we left off." However, a mechanism for this forgetting must be created and tested.

A second time-based issue concerns how long the computer will believe the evidence that a student possesses any given skill. Again, when a conversation happens over a short period of time, we wouldn't expect a student to forget during the course of the conversation. But, again, a student could use instant messenger to contact the CDA weeks or months later; much forgetting could occur during that time. The CDA must have a model for "skill decay" on the part of the users of the system. Otherwise it will assume that a skill that was once demonstrated is permanently learned by the student. We know that this is rarely true of student skills, which often decay over time due to non-use or new learning.

7 Conclusion

Automated interactivity is an idea that would create interactive instruction out of static knowledge components. The benefits of active, adaptive diagnosis of a student's current state would be the first steps in turning knowledge management systems into instructional systems. The Conversational Diagnostic Agent is a prototype of this process. Issues relating to time and conversational memory are still unresolved, and future research will look at these concerns.

References

1. Yacci, M.: The Knowledge Warehouse: Reusable knowledge components. Performance Improvement Quarterly, Vol 12, No. 3, (1999)
2. Mohan, P.& Daniel, B.K. The Learning Objects' Approach: Challenges and Opportunities. The proceedings of E-Learn 2004 World Conference on E-Learning in Corporate, Government, Healthcare, & Higher Education. November 1-5, Washington, DC. (2004)
3. Freedman, R., Cho, B., Glass, M., Zhou, Y., Kim, J.H., Mills, B., Yang, F., & Evens, M.W. Workshop on Adaptation in Dialogue Systems, NAACL, Pittsburgh. (2001)
4. Yacci, M.: Interactivity Demystified: A Structural Definition for Online Learning and Intelligent CBT. Educational Technology, July/August (2000)
5. Moore, M.G.: Editorial: Three types of interaction. The American Journal of Distance Education. Vol. 3 No. 2. (1989) 1-6

6. Ragnemalm, E.L.: Student Diagnosis in Practice: bridging a gap. IDA Technical Report 1995. Department of Computer and Information Science. Linkoping University, Linkoping Sweden (1995)
7. Jonassen, D.H., Beissner, K., & Yacci, M.: Structural Knowledge: Techniques for Representing, Conveying, and Acquiring Structural Knowledge. Lawrence Erlbaum & Associates, Hillsdale, NJ (1993)
8. Freedman, R. An Approach to Increasing Programming Efficiency in Plan-Based Dialogue Systems. Artificial Intelligence in Education, J.D. Moore (Ed.) IOS Press (2001)
9. Yacci, M. & Lutz, P.: Conversational Diagnostic Agent. Proceedings of AACE World Conference on Educational Multimedia, Hypermedia, and Telecommunications, Lugano, Switzerland (2004)
10. Gagne, R. M., & Briggs, L. J.: Principles of Instructional Design. Holt, Rinehart, Winston, Inc., New York (1974)
11. Gagne, R..M. & Medsker, K.L.: The Conditions of Learning: Training Applications. Harcourt Brace College Publishers, Ft. Worth (1996)
12. Cassell, J., Sullivan, J., Prevost, S. & Churchill, E.: Embodied Conversational Agents. MIT Press, Massachusetts (2000)
13. Plantec, P.: Virtual Humans: A Build-it-yourself Kit. American Management Association (2003)
14. Shata, O.: An Interactive System for Electronic Course Delivery on the WEB. (1997) http://naweb.unb.ca/proceedings/1997/shata/shata.html

PAIKM-2005 — Peer-to-Peer and Agent Infrastructures for Knowledge Management

Andreas Abecker[1], Ludger van Elst[2], and Steffen Staab[3]

[1] Forschungszentrum Informatik (FZI), Karlsruhe, Germany
abecker@fzi.de

[2] German Research Center for AI, Kaiserslautern, Germany
elst@dfki.de

[3] Institute for Computer Science, Univ. Koblenz-Landau, Koblenz, Germany
staab@uni-koblenz.de

Today's IT infrastructures for knowledge management often build on centralized information systems architectures, e.g., Web servers. Such systems have shown their benefits in many situations where knowledge processes are comparatively rigid and where the value of knowledge to be contributed to such a centralized repository can be easily assessed. Unfortunately, knowledge-intensive work frequently exhibits some different characteristics:

- It happens sporadically;
- It is not tightly embedded in standardized processes or knowledge structures;
- It includes previously unseen domains of interest to the knowledge worker;
- It requires a lot of ad-hoc interaction with other knowledge workers;
- Its value is hard to be assessed and it will end up in a set of best-practices only after a long time.

Hence, a lot of results of such knowledge-intensive work do not make it into centralized repositories. They remain closed away on PCs or laptops and are unaccessible to the organisation. Thus, a lot of redundant work may be performed and people do not fully benefit from the work of their colleagues.

Peer-to-Peer (P2P) and agent infrastructures serve the needs of knowledge workers for a more flexible knowledge sharing environment adapted to their personal needs and up-to-date with regard to ad-hoc knowledge provided by others.

In the workshop, we saw a set of techniques that contribute to this overall goal spanning the full breadth from reusing existing servers to finding the right peer to talk to. In particular, the latter topic is germane to knowledge management. While we interact with computers as one of the main parts of our knowledge work these days, it appears very promising to let our computers communicate with each other in order to find the right peers to talk to—for human communication as well as for retrieval of facts and documents at the technical level.

Thus, P2P and agent infrastructures in KM do enhance our individual capabilities for collaboration and our individual capabilities for socializing for the purpose of knowledge management.

The two papers that are included in this conference post-proceedings emphasize on linking peers in P2P networks, thus showing the potential of P2P

K.-D. Althoff et al. (Eds.): WM 2005, LNAI 3782, pp. 222–223, 2005.

technology to reflect the need on social constructs in IT for knowledge management. Courtenage & Williams present a publish/subscribe mechanism for automatic hyperlink creation where authors can *express an interest* about the kind of content a page should link to. In contrast to this content-oriented view on linking peers, Schenk's approach explicitly includes a social concept, namely a *reputation measure*, into his strategy for connecting peers.

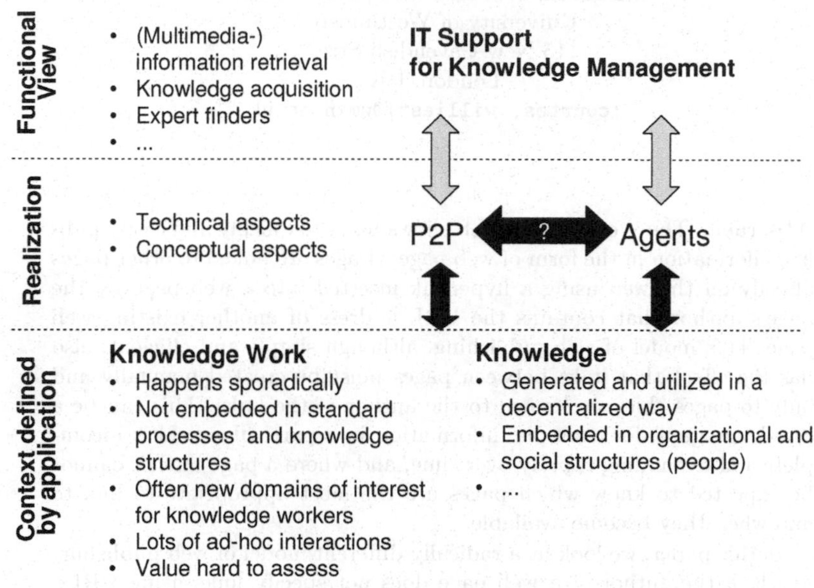

Fig. 1. Discussion space of the PAIKM workshop

The workshop's lively closing discussion—Figure 1 sketches the topic space—showed the agreed-upon demand of knowledge management for distributed IT support. Nevertheless, there are still many technical and conceptual challenges with respect to the question how agent and P2P architectures have to be structured for the special demands of knowledge management environments.

Enjoy reading!

Andreas Abecker, Ludger van Elst, Steffen Staab

Automatic Hyperlink Creation Using P2P and Publish/Subscribe

Simon Courtenage and Steven Williams

Cavendish School of Computer Science,
University of Westminster,
115 New Cavendish Street,
London, UK
{courtes, williast}@wmin.ac.uk

Abstract. The World-Wide Web allows users to quickly and easily publish information in the form of web pages. Pages are linked to other pages already on the web using a hyperlink inserted into a web page by the page's author that contains the URL address of another existing web page. This model of web publishing, although simple and efficient, also has the effect that links between pages must be created manually and only to pages that are known to the author of the links. This can be a disadvantage if, for example, information in a particular field is incomplete and expanding rapidly over time, and where a page author cannot be expected to know which pages are the most appropriate to link to and when they become available.

In this paper, we look at a radically different model of web publishing in which the author of a web page does not specify links using URLs. Instead, the page author *expresses an interest* about the kind of content the page should link to and as new content comes online that matches that interest, links are inserted automatically into the original page to point to the new content. This leads to the possibility that a hyperlink from a particular location in a web page can lead to multiple destinations, something we call a *multi-valued hyperlink*.

We also describe a prototype implementation of our web architecture, based on the CHORD-based peer-to-peer overlay network, which uses publish/subscribe to communicate page author interests to other peers in order to create links between pages.

1 Introduction

The web has been a source of enormous benefit to a great many people. The great advantages of the web are, of course, the ease with which information can be published and made available to a wide audience, and the ability to organize and connect different documents in a graph-based structure using hyperlinks. However, the way in which the web is constructed, through the addition of new documents, can be at odds with the different ways in which knowledge expands. New pages link to pages that already exist in the web graph (as described in,

K.-D. Althoff et al. (Eds.): WM 2005, LNAI 3782, pp. 224–233, 2005.

for example, [1]), but are not linked to by other pages as yet, because they are new.

The web graph, therefore, does not grow *forwards.* We do not write a web page with links from locations in the page to pages that do not as yet exist, nor is a new page immediately linked-in to existing pages, even though it may expand on information contained in those existing pages. But this is one possible model for how human knowledge grows, both in terms of a particular individuals understanding of a subject and in terms of research in general. Research sometimes makes use of undefined terms in particular models, expanding or completing the definition of these terms at some later date. There is a disparity, in some circumstances therefore, between how the web is constructed and how human knowledge is constructed. The web is a great tool for organizing and connecting existing knowledge, but not always for knowledge that is incomplete and expanding.

In this paper, we describe a new architecture for the web that models how human knowledge expands when that knowledge is incomplete, but which is fully compatible with the existing web and existing web pages. The key feature of this web architecture is that authors of web pages do not insert links to other pages as they create or edit the page. Instead they indicate which parts of the content of the page from which links should be established as soon as pages with matching content become available. The basis for this feature is a distributed content-based publish-subscribe system [2] [3] [4]. We show how this publish-subscribe system can implement our *forward web* (which we refer to in this paper as *FWEB*) over a peer-to-peer network of web servers. We also describe a prototype implementation of FWEB, based on CHORD [5] [6], an efficient P2P architecture that provides an single operation, node lookup, efficiently using distributed hash tables.

2 A Forward Web with Multi-valued Hyperlinks

Consider the following scenario: A geneticist may publish, as a web document, results of research into a particular gene and its effect on a genetically-inherited disease. This research may involve factoring in the presence of a second gene in the DNA of a patient, which is not the primary subject of the geneticist's research. Research results into the second gene may not be available at the time the web document is published. At some later time, a web document into the effect of the second gene on patient susceptibility to disease may be published. The geneticist ought now to edit the original document to point to the new document describing research into the second gene. In other words, the web must be *revised backwards* as new knowledge *expands forwards.*

To help the geneticist in this example, we propose a new web infrastructure that allows the web to grow *forwards,* in the same direction as knowledge. However, the current web grows backwards as a consequence of the fact that pages must exist in order to be targeted by an anchor in another tag. To grow forwards, therefore, we must allow anchors to pages that do not yet exist but which may exist at some point in the future. Clearly, we cannot target specific pages that do not yet exist, since their URL is unknown. Instead, therefore, we indicate, through the anchor text *what kind of pages* we want to link to.

2.1 FHTML – A Forward HTML

Web authors need to be able to state where links should be inserted into their documents, as and when new and relevant content is made available. To provide authors with this capability, we first add a new SUMMARY tag, to be included in the header of a page and which acts as an aid to matching page content to link requirements. The SUMMARY tag is similar to the use of the META tag in existing HTML. We have defined a separate tag, rather than reuse `<META`, in order to avoid confusion and also to allow future extension of use.

The syntax of the SUMMARY tag is: `<SUMMARY>` *keyword-list* `</SUMMARY>` and is placed between the `<HEAD>` and `</HEAD>` tags in an HTML document. For example,

```
<HTML> <HEAD> <TITLE>CGI Programming Notes</TITLE>
<SUMMARY> CGI, Web Server, Protocol, HTTP </SUMMARY>
</HEAD>
<BODY> <!-- body of web page --> </BODY> </HTML>
```

A web document author can indicate where new links should be inserted into a document as and when new and relevant content is found by using a `<LINKTO KEY="..."> ... </LINKTO` tag, rather than an HTML anchor tag. The `<LINKTO>` tag is used around text which the author would like to act as a hyperlink to other documents (that may or may not exist in the web graph when the document is created). The `KEY` attribute of the tag contains those keywords to be used in finding matching content on other pages. For example

```
<HTML> <HEAD> <TITLE>Web Servers</TITLE>
<SUMMARY> Web servers </SUMMARY>
</HEAD> <BODY>
<H1> The role of web servers </H1>
The role of an
<LINKTO KEY="web servers"> HTTP-enabled web server </LINKTO>
is to respond to
<LINKTO KEY="HTTP">HTTP(Hypertext Transfer Protocol)</LINKTO>
requests. <!-- rest of page --> </BODY></HTML>
```

At present, the matching between the content of the `KEY` attribute in a `<LINKTO>` tag and the `<SUMMARY>` content in other web documents is done using simple keyword matching.

The author of an FHTML document does not have complete control over which documents will be linked to, since this depends on the matching carried out between the keywords in a `<LINKTO>` tag and the summary in a `<SUMMARY>` tag. In fact, using the `<LINKTO>` tag in a web document creates the distinct possibility that the anchor text in a `<LINKTO>` tag can refer to more than one web document, leading to what we term a *multi-valued hyperlink*. In our current implementation, this means the browser displays a drop-down list of URLs when the user clicks on an multi-valued hyperlink, from which the user can select one as the page to actually visit.

3 An Architecture for the Forward Web

The Forward Web demands more from the components of its infrastructure than the current web. Links between pages must be found and created automatically when a match is found between the content of a <LINKTO> tag in one document and the content of a <SUMMARY> tag in another document. The infrastructure must be aware of the contents of both tags in all documents, therefore, in order to infer which documents should link to which other documents. Our solution to this problem is to use the publish/subscribe communications paradigm for connecting the components of the web infrastructure. Specifically, we use content-based publish/subscribe, over a peer-to-peer (P2P) network. The use of a publish/subscribe network overcomes the problems in matching <LINKTO> keywords with web page <SUMMARY> content posed by the asynchronous nature of web publishing, while the use of a P2P network enables document repositories to provide services to each other to allow new hyperlinks to be formed.

3.1 Publish-Subscribe and Content-Based Routing

Publish/Subscribe systems [7] form an important communications paradigm in distributed systems, one in which servers (or producers of messages) are decoupled from clients (or consumers) by the network. Instead of clients contacting servers directly to request services or information, clients register a subscription with the network to receive messages satisfying certain criteria. Servers publish information onto the network, without knowing who will receive it, and the network undertakes to route messages to the appropriate clients based on the set of subscriptions currently in effect.

Traditional publish/subscribe systems create channels, groups or topics, sometimes hierarchial, under which messages may be classified, where a subscription is simply the identity of the channel, group, or topic that a user wants to receive messages from. Once subscribed, the user or subscribe receives all messages that are published under that channel, group or topic. Recently, another approach to publish/subscribe has been developed that allows subscriber to specify their interests in terms of the kind of *message content* they want to receive: this is known as content-based routing.

The advantage of combining content-based routing and publish/subscribe, to create *content-based publish/subscribe* [3] [2] [4], over more conventional systems is the far greater flexibility that is permitted in creating subscriptions. Subscribers are in effect allowed to create their own message groupings rather than simply sign up to predefined ones, by defining predicates over the structure of a particular message type. When the subscription has been registered with the network (typically a network of servers overlaying a TCP/IP-based network), the network undertakes to route to the subscriber all messages of that type whose content satisfies the subscriber's criteria, typically using an overlay network of *brokers*, servers whose role is to match up subscriptions with publications.

3.2 Implementing the Forward Web

The infrastructure for FWEB is a P2P network of *brokers* based on CHORD [5] [6]. CHORD is a popular distributed P2P service with a single operation: node lookup based on Distributed Hash Tables (DHTs). Given a particular hash key, the CHORD architecture allows fast and efficient lookup of the P2P node associated with that particular key. Each FWEB server participates in the P2P system, acting not only as a web server, therefore, but also as a broker node in a content-based publish/subscribe system in order to link pages together.

Placing a new web page in the document root of an FWEB server triggers the server to parse the document and extract the content of any `<SUMMARY>` or `<LINKTO>` tags (currently, the parsing of new or updated pages is implemented in our prototype FWEB server using directory polling). If a `<LINKTO>` tag is found, then its keywords are used to create subscriptions. Each keyword is hashed using a hash function to locate the FWEB server in the CHORD-based P2P network which will act as broker for the subscription. The located server is then contacted with the details of the subscription (unhashed keyword and URL of the document containing the `<LINKTO>` tag). Similarly, the keywords in the page summary are used to create publications, by hashing the keywords to locate the nodes in the FWEB P2P network that the publications should be sent to.

For example, given a new web page containing the following `<LINKTO>` tag

```
<LINKTO KEY="cerebrovascular disorders"></LINKTO>
```

the keyword phrase is hashed to find locate the node that should receive the subscription for content that match this description. If a page is published with the `<SUMMARY>` tag

```
<SUMMARY>cerebrovascular disorders, Hypoxia </SUMMARY>
```

then publications are created for the keyword content.

When an FWEB server receives a subscription, it attempts to match the subscription against the web pages that it knows have already published summaries[1].

Since both the page and the subscription are sent to a node on the basis of hashing a keyword, then if they contain the same keyword, they will be sent to the same node. If the match is successful, then details of the publication are sent back to the FWEB server that made the subscription.

Using the example `<LINKTO>` and `<SUMMARY>` tags above, we show how subscriptions and publications are matched to create hyperlinks. In Figure 1, the placement of a new page under the FWEB server that is node 3 in the P2P network creates a subscription for "cerebrovascular disorders". Hashing the keyword

[1] Because of this, FWEB is related to work on continuous querying in P2P systems, for example, [8].

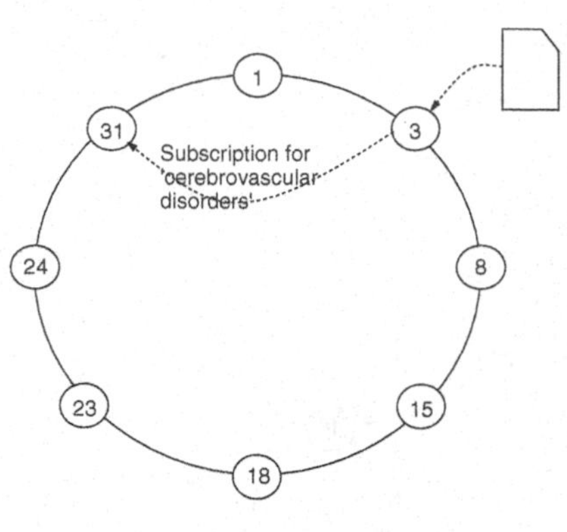

Fig. 1. Distributing subscriptions

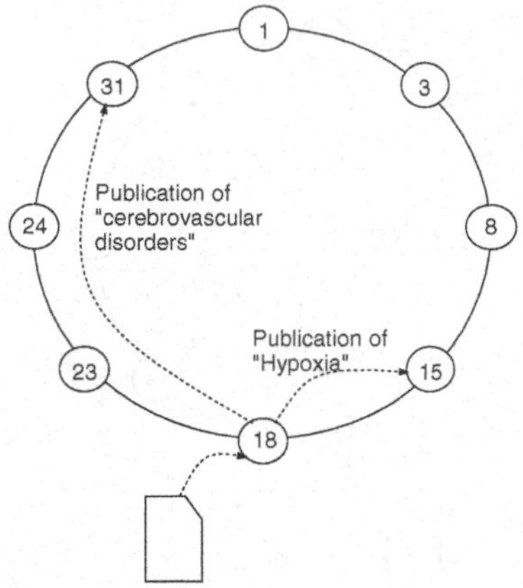

Fig. 2. Distributing publications

phrase produces 31 as the id of the node acting as broker for the subscription. Figure 2 shows a similar process on the FWEB server at node 18, where a new page creates a publication based on the content of the `<SUMMARY>` tag in the page. The FWEB server at node 31, when ir receives the publication, matches against the subscription received earlier. Hence the publication is forwarded to node 8, as in Figure 3. Finally, Figure 4 shows the establishment of a hyperlink between the page with the `<LINKTO>` tag and the page with the `SUMMARY` tag, once the publication is received by the node that originated the subscription.

In FWEB, a hyperlink is only accepted if its summary contains all the keyword phrases in a `<LINKTO>` tag (by collecting and collating the publications received). Effectively, therefore, the keywords in a `<LINKTO>` tag form a conjunction which must be satisfied for a link to be created. This mimics the basic structure of a query in a conventional search engine, and is intended to help restrict the number of returned search results.

In our current version of FWEB, the hyperlink is established by creating a file (with a .url file extension) associated with the original HTML file that stores the hyperlinks received for `<LINKTO>` tags. When the file is requested by a browser, the web server parses the HTML document and the file of received hyperlinks, replacing the `<LINKTO>` tags with hyperlink anchors. To do this, the current web server implementation redirects on every request to a Java Servlet that performs the parsing and replacement process, using a DHTML drop-down menu to display the multi-valued hyperlinks. This ensures compatibility with current web browsers. Figure 5 show a screenshot of a web page sent by an FWEB server with multi-valued hyperlinks displayed using a drop-down menu.

4 Related Work

There has been a great deal of work in designing and developing content-based publish/subscribe systems, for example, [3] [9] [10] [4] [11] [12], which have suc-

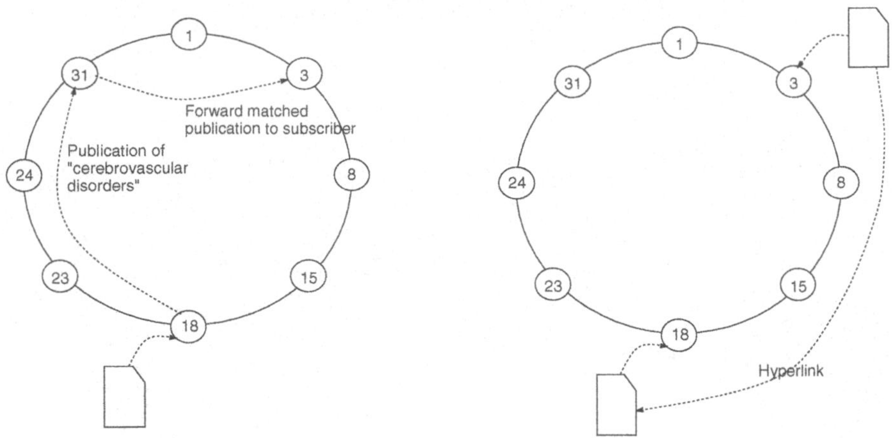

Fig. 3. Forwarding matched publication

Fig. 4. Establishing hyperlink

The HTTP (Hypertext Transfer Protocol) web server .

HTTP - Wikipedia, the free encyclopedia
HTTP - Hypertext Transfer Protocol Overview
Network Working Group Request for Comments: 2616

Fig. 5. Displaying a page with multi-valued hyperlinks

cessfully tackled many of the problems involved in routing a message from its source to a client based solely on its content. Our work makes use of this research in its use of a broker-style network to mediate between subscriptions and publications, in a manner similar to Hermes [4]. However, unlike Hermes (and most other content-based publish/subscribe systems), FWEB servers keep track of past publications in order to create hyperlinks to documents that already exist. Moreover, we do not use subscriptions that have filters more complex than simple equality.

Lewis *et al* [13] describe the use of a content-based publish/subscribe system as part of a complete semantic-based information dissemination system, allowing client browsers to make subscriptions to create information spaces, and then receive notifications when new information becomes available. Our system, however, uses publish/subscribe only to create ordinary hyperlinks between HTML-compliant web pages based on matching content, which is a much simpler proposition. Moreover, the documents received by web browsers are fully HTML-compliant, whereas the system described in [13] depends heavily on Semantic Web markup and associated technologies.

P2P systems have been used before to implement publish/subscribe systems: for example, content-based publish/subscribe systems using Chord is described in Triantafillou *et al* [14] and Terpstra *et al* [15]. The primary goals of [15] are the robustness of the routing strategy for content-based publish/subscribe and the implementation of a filtering strategy on top of a DHT-based P2P system, neither of which are currently handled by FWEB (FWEB's current concept of filters is limited to simple keyword equality which does not pose a problem in DHT-based P2P systems). In [14], the concern is with how range predicates (more complex filters on content, such as *less-than* or *greater-than*) can be implemented in DHT-based P2P systems such as CHORD where the use of hashing to locate nodes makes support of filters other than equality difficult.

5 Conclusions and Future Work

This paper has described the use of a P2P-based content-based publish/subscribe system to augment the current web and allow web authors to specify what kind of pages they want to link to, rather than explicit URLs. The advantage of this approach is that links to matching pages are automatically added, maintained and updated without intervention from the web page author. This may suit domains where information is incomplete and expanding.

The principal disadvantages of our approach are (i) that each server must act as the subscription/publication rendezvous node for a large number of keywords, and (ii) that, at the moment, we allow free-text in the keyword lists of the `<LINKTO>` and `<SUMMARY>` tags, resulting in a very large namespace, as well as problems dealing with synonyms etc.

We have experimented with a prototype FWEB system, using 4-5 FWEB servers. The FWEB servers are written in Java and use JXTA to create the CHORD P2P ring, while documents in the system use free-form keywords to create subscriptions and publications. Standard browsers, such as IE, are used to request documents and display the results. We have found, in this small setting, that FWEB performs as we expected, and that hyperlinks are created for `<LINKTO>` tags as and when documents are added to FWEB servers whose publications of summary content matches their subscriptions.

However, we have not as yet been able to test or simulate the behaviour of FWEB in a large-scale setting. It is likely that the performance of FWEB in our small-scale study is due in part to the limited domain (in terms of documents and users) within which it has been deployed, which in effect enforces an informal ontology that makes it easier to match up links and page descriptions. we envisage, however, that in a real-world internet-scale deployment of FWEB, it should be no more difficult to specify the right keywords for link and page descriptions than it is to specify a query for a search engine, although without the possibility of receiving immediate feedback to improve the query.

Moreover, the impact of the role of FWEB servers as brokers in a P2P publish/subscribe system on their performance as web servers needs to be investigated. If there is any detrimental affect, then the two roles may need to be separated, as in, for example, web servers and servlet engines.

One approach to this problem is to allow keywords only from agreed ontologies, although this limits application to specific communities where such ontologies can be agreed on and predefined. The use of ontologies would, however, eliminate the problem of dealing with synonyms etc. that are created when using free-text in conjunction with DHTs. This would bring our work closer to that of the W3C's Semantic Web Initiative, although currently we are only proposing the use of the term hierarchies of ontologies, rather than any reasoning capability, in order to solve problems of matching terms.

Future work includes exploring the possibilities implied by FWEB, as well as the need for more structured descriptions in <LINKTO> and <SUMMARY tags. For example, since the network automatically inserts hyperlinks into web pages when it detects a matching page for a hyperlink subscription, it could also to the obverse and tell the referred-to page that it has a link from another page. This would allow bi-directional hyperlinks between pages.

Acknowledgements

We gratefully acknowledge the support of the UK Engineering and Physical Sciences Research Council (EPSRC Grant GR/S01573/01).

References

1. Broder, A., Kumar, R., Maghoul, F., Raghavan, P., Stata, R.: Graph structure in the web. In: Proceedings of the 9th International World Wide Web Conference. (2000) 247–256
2. Carzaniga, A., Rosenblum, D., Wolf, A.: Content-based addressing and routing: A general model and its application (2000)
3. Carzaniga, A., Rosenblum, D.S., Wolf, A.L.: Design and evaluation of a wide-area event notification service. ACM Transactions on Computer Systems **19** (2001) 332–383
4. Pietzuch, P.R., Bacon, J.M.: Hermes: A Distributed Event-Based Middleware Architecture. In: Proc. of the 1st Int. Workshop on Distributed Event-Based Systems (DEBS'02), Vienna, Austria (2002) 611–618
5. Dabek, F., Brunskill, E., Kaashoek, M.F., Karger, D., Morris, R., Stoica, I., Balakrishnan, H.: Building peer-to-peer systems with Chord, a distributed lookup service. In IEEE, ed.: Eighth IEEE Workshop on Hot Topics in Operating Systems (HotOS-VIII). May 20–23, 2001, Schloss Elmau, Germany, 1109 Spring Street, Suite 300, Silver Spring, MD 20910, USA, IEEE Computer Society Press (2001) 81–86
6. Stoica, I., Morris, R., Karger, D., Kaashock, M., Balakrishman, H.: Chord: A scalable peer-to-peer lookup protocol for internet applications. In: Proceedings of the ACM SIGCOMM. (2001) 149–160
7. Eugster, P., Felber, P., Guerraoui, R., Kermarrec, A.M.: The many faces of publish/subscribe (2001)
8. Idreos, S., Koubarakis, M., Tryfonopoulos, T.: P2P-DIET: an extensible P2P service that unifies ad-hoc and continuous querying in super-peer networks. In Weikum, G., König, A.C., Dessloch, S., eds.: Proceedings of the 2004 ACM SIGMOD International Conference on Management of Data (SIGMOD-04), New York, ACM Press (2004) 933–934

9. Courtenage, S.A.: Specifying and detecting composite events in content-based publish/subscribe systems. In: 1st International Workshop on Discrete Event-Based Systems. (2002)
10. Fabret, F., Llirbat, F., Pereira, J., Shasha, D.: Efficient matching for content-based publish/subscribe systems. Technical report, INRIA (2000) http://wwwcaravel.inria.fr/pereira/matching.ps.
11. Segall, B., Arnold, D.: Elvin has left the building: A publish/subscribe notification service with quenching. In: Proceedings of AUUUG'97. (1997)
12. Strom, R., Banavar, G., Chandra, T., Kaplan, M., Miller, K., Mukherjee, B., Sturman, D., Ward, M.: Gryphon: An information flow based approach to message brokering (1998)
13. Lewis, D., Feeney, K., K., Tiropanis, T., Courtenage, S.: An active, ontology-driven network service for internet collaboration. In: Workshop on Application of Semantic Web Technologies to Web Communities (SWWC) at ECAI'04. (2004)
14. Triantafillou, P., Aekaterinidis, I.: Content-based publish/subscribe over structured p2p networks. In: 1st International Workshop on Discrete Event-Based Systems. (2004)
15. Terpstra, W.W., Behnel, S., Fiege, L., Zeidler, A., Buchmann, A.P.: A peer-to-peer approach to content-based publish/subscribe. In: Proceedings of the 2nd international workshop on Distributed event-based systems, ACM Press (2003) 1–8

Introducing Social Aspects to Search in Peer-to-Peer Networks

Simon Schenk*

FH NORDAKADMIE, Köllner Chaussee 11, 25337 Elmshorn, Germany
simon.schenk@whitepla.net

Abstract. Searching social networks is determined by two factors: reputation and relevance. Reputation is the memory and summary of behavior from past transactions. Relevance is the probability that useful information can be obtained from a person. Search in social networks is performed by asking persons of high relevance and a good reputation or persons who are supposed to know somebody like that. We describe how these social aspects can be used in peer-to-peer networks in order to increase efficiency and scalability. Based on a social peer-to-peer network a knowledge management application with advantages over centralized approaches can be implemented.

1 Introduction

Knowledge management (KM) has become an important issue over the last ten years. The increasing complexity and quantity of knowledge generated in and necessary for organizations demanded methods and tools supporting search for and access to knowledge. Many of the tools used did not provide the expected results[20]. Reasons were:

(r1) Most tools support either the storage of explicit knowledge or the localization of experts.
(r2) Many tools are complex to use. Prior to use the information stored has to be adapted to the tools' requirements and to be stored in the tool. These operations are time-consuming and therefore are often avoided by users.
(r3) Many tools started with little content, being of no great use initially. As a result these tools were not accepted by their users. [18].
(r4) Tacit knowledge cannot be stored in a database. It must be transferred from person to person. [21]

The common approach to searching knowledge without a tool is asking other persons (actors), e.g. colleagues, kins etc. and using one's social network to locate an expert. Social networks usually follow a small world-characteristic. Thus persons sharing similar interests are grouped together. This fact makes it possible to locate experts relatively fast [23]. Personal communication then enables actors to share tacit knowledge [17]. These facts lead to four theses:

* This work results from a diploma thesis [19] by Simon Schenk, August 2004.

K.-D. Althoff et al. (Eds.): WM 2005, LNAI 3782, pp. 234–242, 2005.

(t1) KM-tools must support networking actors as well as storing explicit knowledge.
(t2) Personal, small world networks support knowledge sharing.
(t3) Tools can assist the forming of a network between actors by providing rich communication channels and search mechanisms for experts.
(t4) A tool's knowledge repository must be able to be filled easily or – if possible – automatically.

2 An Application for Social Peer-to-Peer Networks

Traditionally an actor first has to choose to read or to communicate. Then he searches for either a document or a person. Here, in order to support networking as well as storing information, the typical answer to a user's query can be various objects, for example a document, a user's contact data, a hyperlink to a related website etc. So the decision what to search for (file or person) is no longer necessary a priori. As experts on each topic requested are always displayed, actors are encouraged to communicate resulting in the social network becoming denser.

In order to support networking the tool needs to know the interests of each participant. Traditionally this question has been answered explicitly by the user. Social applications like FOAF [5] use information explicityl provided by users. Applications like KEEx [2] need little additional information, but do not allow expert search. As we want to reduce the necessary amount of time and work needed to make the tool work, implicit sources of information must be used to answer questions, e.g. the pool of documents an actor possesses.

An actor will usually work on topics she has many documents about. Other sources are prior search requests or for websites [10]. Of course an explicit description done by the user is possible as well. Obviously a centralized approach will not be useful here, as the greater part of this information has to be collected locally on the user's computer. More arguments for P2P based distributed knowledge management (DKM) are described in [3].

In the following section we will explain how a clustering of the peers according to the interests of their users can be achieved.

3 Search in Social Peer-to-Peer Networks

The basic idea for shaping the network is to build new connections between peers who worked together successfully. Two peers have worked together successfully if one peer has been able to give a good answer to a search request of the second peer. Both peers then add each other to their repositories of known peers. They also exchange indexes of their interests (i.e. the interests of the users owning the peers as they are perceived by the peers). That way peers with similar interests are grouped together building a small world network. Additionally they can develop an idea of the abilities and interests of others. In order to make this possible unique identifiers for peers are necessary. Indexes are exchanged in the form of compressed bloom filters [1]. Using bloom filters we can determine if a peer's index contains a set of keywords. It is not possible, however, to list all keywords contained in a bloom filter. The solution proposed here is less susceptible against peers temporarily leaving the network than other concepts. Contact information for these peers and the corresponding users can still be found using the exchanged indexes which are more extensive.

As contact information of actors using peers with relevant information is a possible result of a search request, communication between actors with similar interests is encouraged. The grouping of peers on a technical level is expected to be followed by a grouping of actors on a social level. Prior work has shown that information flowing over a media like email represent the structure of the corresponding social network well [25]. We expect that tools supporting the information flow among certain actors can therefore influence the social network.

In social networks messages are forwarded to actors who are supposed to have a smaller social distance to the target [23]. Technically speaking the important question is: How can peers with interesting content be found in order to establish new connections? The following definitions are needed for the description of the search mechanism:

Definition 1. *The relevance rel of a peer related to a given topic or search query is the probability of this peer being able to deliver relevant information on this topic. rel is a value between 0 and 1. rel is always subjective to the perspective of an other peer, which assumes rel to be of a certain value based on information it has.* $rel(a)$ *is a mapping of peers a to* [0..1].

With a view to social network theory relevance can be seen as a measure of social distance [24], where $rel = 1$ of a peer means that the peer is identical to the target. *rel* can be determined from the number of matches of search terms in a peers index. The index must be known from a prior index exchange.

Definition 2. *The reputation rep of a peer is the memory and summary of behavior of that peer from past transactions [16]. rep is a value between 0 and 1, 0 meaning very bad experience and 1 meaning very good experience. rep also is subjective to other peers.* $rep(a)$ *is a mapping of peers a to* [0..1].

rep is initialized with 0.5 as a neutral initial value. Each transaction with an other peer could be assigned a value of 1 if it has been successful and of 0 if the search results provided have not been used by the actor. *rep* can then be determined as the arithmetic mean of these values. See e.g. [4] [8] and [13] for other possible solutions.

It should be noted that reputation in this context is not only related to the quality of service a peer offers (number of broken connections etc.) but also to the quality of the information provided or it's use for the questioner respectively. If the information provided has been useful for the questioner reputation is increased, otherwise it is reduced. Therefore reputation also measures the similarity of the vocabulary of two actors. A peer providing high quality information but having a very different understanding of the terms in the search request will be assigned a bad reputation by the requester.

Definition 3. *The arithmetic mean of the values of rel and rep is called competence c. As a consequence c is a subjective value between 0 and 1.*

Search messages are forwarded in a unstructured way: Incoming search requests are forwarded to a number of known peers, unless the time to live (TTL) of the search request has expired. A disadvantage of this strategy as it is implemented for example in in Gnutella [14] is that only part of the network is searched. The part selected is not chosen based on useful criteria but merely based on distance in network topology. Useful decision criteria will be introduced in the following paragraphs.

In social networks messages are forwarded to actors who are supposed to have a smaller social distance to the target [23]. The analogous measurement used here is *rel*, determined based on the indexes of interests from the peer-repository. Additionally the quality of information provided by others is taken into account, represented by their reputation *rep*. These are aggregated to the competence c of a peer.

Having these measurements the peers to forward to can be chosen as the n peers with the highest competence related to the current search request. Thus it is possible to search a sensible part of the network in more detail (higher TTL) and at the same time to reduce the over-all bandwidth usage by not searching less sensible parts of the net.

In order to avoid overfitting, however, a part of the forwarded messages should be sent to randomly chosen peers. This also allows search for new peers. In the latter case the peers to forward to must be located using lower layers of the network, e.g. JXTA broadcasts.

A parameter "accumulated competence" a in each forwarded message is used to choose when to stop forwarding a search request. It is initialized with 1 and multiplied by the competence of the peer the message is sent to by every forwarding peer: $a_{i+1} = a_i \cdot c_{i+1}$ where c_{i+1} is the competence of the peer the message is forwarded to. If a falls below a certain level the message is dropped. Simulations have shown that 0.2 to 0.3 are useful values for a.

Due to the multiplication the values of a fall rapidly. We assume that different computations will lead to better efficiency of searches.

Figure 1 illustrates the changes in a during the lifetime of a query originating at the peer at the top. The values of c of each peer are printed along the edges. The value of a at each peer is printed underlined below the peer. For fig. 4 a minimum of 0.4 has been chosen for a.

The strategy described above makes it possible as well as necessary for each peer to have a greater number of connections as e.g. in Gnutella. The average number of contacts used for search in social networks is 200 [7]. As the Peer-to-Peer network is less komplex than a real-live social network a smaller repository containing for example $s = 100$ peers does make sense. If the repository is too small, however, we have little advantage compared to simple Gnutella-style flooding. When a peer gets to know more than s peers, the peer which has been contacted least recently is dropped from the repository.

New members should join the network at an appropriate position. Using the social network this can be achieved through invitations by a user, who is already a member of the network. The new peer can use the existing connections of

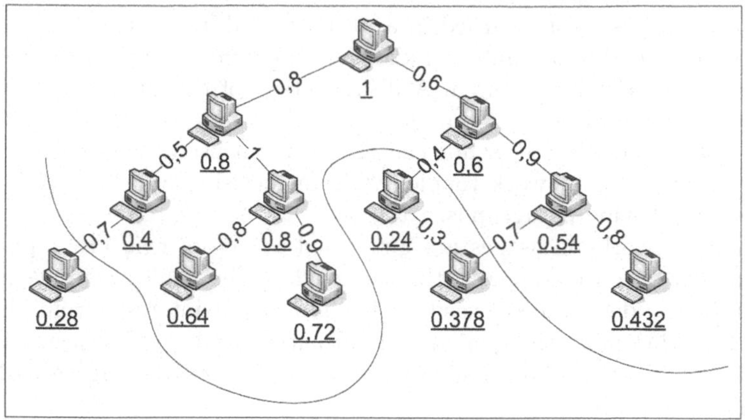

Fig. 1. Changes in a over time

the inviting peer. These lead to other relevant peers, because the new and the inviting user share interests, as they have similar social backgrounds. Providing lists of more or less random peers as entries to the network or broadcasts on lower network layers would also be possible. The new peer would probably be assigned low relevance though, as local neighbors would not necessarily be neighbors with regard to social distance. After some time of operation the peer would have migrated to a more relevant part of the network, so the difference is especially important right after joining the network.

4 An Outline of the Application

Figure 2 shows an overview of the application. The core consists of a desktop search engine for searching resources provided by the peer[1] and a query forwarding engine which searches the local peer repository for peers relevant for a given query. It then forwards the query to the selected peers updating the a attribute of the query. The peer repository and local index are updated after each selection of contact information or a document by the user.

The feedback loop for refinement of peer repository and knowledge about the users' interests is emphasized using dotted lines.

On top of the core layer services are provided to the user and to other peers as well as interfaces to communication channels like email, instant messaging and telephone services.

Search queries can be entered by the user into a graphical user interface (GUI) or be received from other peers via the P2P infrastructure. Search queries are executed locally and forwarded to other relevant peers. Afterwards, documents can

[1] For this application also keywords describing interests of the user of this peer should be contained in the index. A hit for one of these keywords would not result in returning a document but in returning contact information of the user.

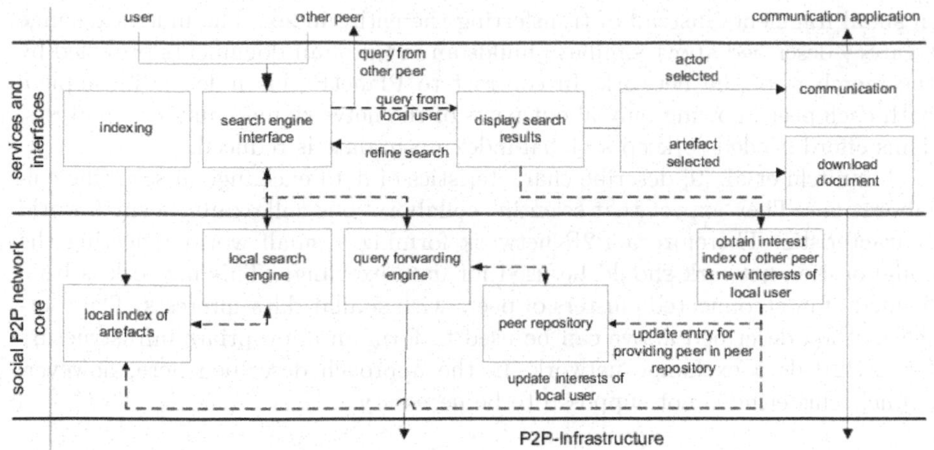

Fig. 2. overview of the application

be downloaded or persons can be contacted. Search results selected by the user are supposed to be of use to her. Therefore the reputation of the providing peer is increased. On the other hand results provided but not selected are supposed to be of no use, thus they reduce reputation. For a more detailed discussion on this point see [10].

5 Related Work

In [3] Bonifacio et al. describe KEEx, a P2P based application for DKM. Each Peer is used to organize the knowledge of a limited group of users. Among the peers a search is performed by matching queries semantically and lexically to the local knowledge repository. Queries can be forwarded based on semantical or local neighborhoods. Semantic matching is not possible with the application described here. On the other hand social discovery and propagation is raised as a research issue in [3]. The mechanism described above can be a starting point for further development of KEEx.

The NeuroGrid project [10] aims at building a distributed meta data search system. While the measure of relevance of peers in relation to a search query is different from the approach described here the method is basically the same. A fundamental difference lies in the data basis on which the decision is performed. In NeuroGrid a list of relevant peers for each word in a search query is built up during a number of queries. In the P2P networks described here an index of all resources offered by other peers is available. Therefore a faster adaption to shared interests between users is possible. Changing interests of a user do not lead to the necessity of rebuilding the entire relevance repository, as prior unasked keywords also are already contained in the repository.

Gossiping is a technology used by the PlanetP project [6] to build a global index over all resources available in a P2P network. This index is replicated to every peer. It is updated by "gossiping" occurring changes to other peers in small fragments instead of transferring the entire index. The index exchange strategy described above similarly builds an index of all documents provided by the members of the network. In contrast to PlanetP this index is incomplete with each peer knowing only about parts of the network matching it's interests. Thus efford needed to keep a global index up-to-date is reduced.

Iamnitchi et al. [9] describe characteristics of data exchange in scientific collaborations. They expect that scientific collaborations will exhibit a small world characteristic. Therefore a P2P network forming a small world reflecting the collaboration network should be used for data exchange. This network is been formed of interconnected clusters of peers with similar data interests. The routing method described above can be used to form an appropriate infrastructure for a P2P data exchange network. In the approach described here, however, explicit clustering is not supposed to be necessary.

6 Future Work

Ways of determining the reputation and relevance of peers must be chosen prior to an implementation. They should integrate well with the communication necessary for search and not use too much bandwidth. It is unclear today how the routing strategy described here can be enhanced to use ontologies instead of simple text-based search. This is perhaps not too critical as studies in the SWAP project have shown that semantic search is not broadly accepted by todays users [15].

Comparisons to semantic routing algorithms like REMINDIN [22] are still missing, as the work this paper is based on has been written before their release.

Simulations in a realistic testing network can be used to investigate the efficiency of searching and the scalability of the described kind of P2P network. An implementation is necessary to prove whether or not social networks can be influenced by search results and communication links produced in a P2P network. If this proves possible "rewiring" social networks will be an important tool for KM in the future.

7 Conclusions

We have introduced the parameters reputation and relevance of peers as a way to improve search in P2P networks. They are used to determine the competence of each queried peer. An accumulation of the competences of all peers a search request has passed is used to determine when to drop a search request. The search method described above leads to a clustering of peers with similar interests. Together with an application designed to encourage communication among users with similar interests this can lead to a rewiring of the social network among the users to better fit the requirements for knowledge exchange. We described an architecture of an application providing document and expert search.

References

1. Burton H. Bloom: Space/time trade-offs in hash coding with allowable errors. Communications of the ACM, 13(7), pp. 422–426, 1970.
2. M. Bonifacio, P. Bouquet, P. Busetta, A., A. Donè, G. Mameli, M.: KEEx: A Peer-to-Peer Solution for Distributed Knowledge Management. P2PKM 2004
3. M. Bonifacio, P. Bouquet, G. Mameli, M. Nori: Peer-Mediated Distributed Knowledge Management. In: L. van Elst, V. Dignum, A. Abecker (Eds.): AMKM 2003, LNAI 2926, pp. 31-47, 2003.
4. F. Cornelli, E. Damiani, S. De Capitani: Choosing Reputable Servents in a P2P Network. In Proc. of the Eleventh International World Wide Web Conference, Honolulu, Hawaii, May 2002.
5. the foaf project: http://www.foaf-project.org/ [2005-04-15]
6. Francisco Matias Cuenca-Acuna, Christopher Peery, Richard P. Martin, and Thu D. Nguyen: PlanetP: Using gossiping to build content addressable peer-to-peer information sharing communities. 12th IEEE International Symposium on High Performance Distributed Computing, 2003.
7. Alain Degenne and Michel Forsé: Introducing Social Networks. SAGE Publications, London, 1994. Translation by Borges, 1999.
8. Holger Eggs, Stefan Sackmann, Torsten Eyman, and Günter Müller: Vertrauen und Reputation in P2P Netzwerken. In Detlef Schoder, Kai Fischbach, and René Teichmann, editors, Peer-to-Peer, pp. 229–251. Springer, Berlin, 2002.
9. Adriana Iamnitchi, Matei Ripeanu, and Ian Foster: Locating Data in (Small-World?) Peer-to-Peer Scientific Collaborations. 1st International Workshop on Peer-to-Peer Systems (IPTPS'02), Cambridge, MA, March 2002.
10. S. Joseph: NeuroGrid: Semantically Routing Queries in Peer-to-Peer Networks. In Proceedings of the International Workshop on Peer-to-Peer Computing (co-located with Networking 2002), Pisa, Italy, May 2002.
11. S. Joseph: P2P MetaData Search Layers. Second International Workshop on Agents and Peer-to-Peer Computing AP2PC 2003.
12. Sun Microsystems Inc.: Project JXTA Vision. http://www.jxta.org/project/www/background.html [2004-09-01].
13. Sepandar D. Kamvar, Mario T. Schlosser and Hector Garcia-Molina: The EigenTrust Algorithm for Reputation Management in P2P Networks. WWW2003, Budapest, Hungary, 20-24 May 2003, pp. 640–651, ACM, 2003
14. Gene Kan: Gnutella. In Andy Oram, editor, Peer-to-Peer: Harnessing the Powers of Disruptive Technologies, pp. 94–122, O'REILLY, 2001
15. E. Lladó, S. Pinto, C. Tempich: SWAP Deliverable 7.5 Evaluation Report, http://km.aifb.uni-karlsruhe.de/projects/swap/public/public/Publications/D7.5_Evaluation_Report.pdf [2005-04-15]
16. Richard Lethin: Reputation. In Andy Oram, editor: Peer-to-Peer: Harnessing the Benefits of a Disruptive Technology, chapter 14, pp. 203–241. O'REILLY, Bejing, 2001.
17. Ikujiro Nonaka, Noboru Konno: The concept of "ba": Building a foundation for knowledge creation. California Management Review, 40(3), pp. 40–55, 1998.
18. Gilbert J. B. Probst.: Wissen managen: wie Organisationen ihre wertvollste Ressource optimal nutzen. Frankfurter Allg. Zeitung für Deutschland, Gabler, Frankfurt am Main, Wiesbaden, 1999.
19. Simon Schenk: Unterstützung von sozialen Netzwerken durch Wissenstauschbörsen auf Basis von Peer-to-Peer Technologie. diploma thesis, FH NORDAKADEMIE, 2004.

20. Peter Schütt: Die dritte Generation des Wissensmanagements. KM-Journal, 2003(1), 2003.
21. Karl E. Sveiby: Tacit knowledge. In James W. Cortada and John A. Woods (Eds): The Knowledge Management Yearbook 1999-2000, pp. 18–27. Butterworth-Heinemann, 1998.
22. C. Tempich, S. Staab, and A. Wranik. REMINDIN': Semantic query routing in peer-to-peer networks based on social metaphors. In Proc. of the 13th Int. World Wide Web Conference, WWW 2004, 2004.
23. J. Travers and S. Milgram: An experimental study of the small world problem. Sociometry, 32, pp. 425–443, 1969.
24. D. J. Watts, P. S. Dodds, M. E. J. Newman: Identity and Search in Social Networks. Science, 296, pp. 1302–1305, 2002.
25. M.H. Zack, J.L. McKenney: Social Context and Interaction in Ongoing Computer-Supported Management Groups. Organization Science, 6(4), pp. 394–422, 1995.

Modelling and Analysis of Knowledge Intensive Business Processes

Julian Bahrs and Claudia Müller

University of Potsdam,
14482 Potsdam , Germany
{julian.bahrs, claudia.mueller}@wi.uni-potsdam.de

Abstract. This contribution gives an overview on the scientific discipline of business process oriented knowledge management. It presents results and recent developments as well as an overview of this year's workshop on Modelling and Analysis of Knowledge Intensive Business Processes (KiBP 2005).

Motivation and Results of the Workshop

Knowledge management is a dynamic evolving discipline. So far, two main directions to tackle the challenges of knowledge management have been identified: human-oriented and technology oriented [11]. Though there are more knowledge management approaches which encompass both directions, no ultimate solution has evolved. Business process oriented knowledge management approaches can be seen as a mediator, since they (in general) do not privilege either direction. Instead they allow for an individual configuration of knowledge management [9]. Through the connection of business processes and knowledge related activities the in depth analysis of knowledge work becomes possible. The context gained from business processes provides purpose for knowledge work. This context is therefore seen as central key to value creation through applying knowledge.

Past experience has shown that many knowledge management projects did not fulfill initial expectations. For example sophisticated infrastructures to store, structure and retrieve information, including the massive collections of information, as well as communication infrastructures were developed but in practice not utilized to a satisfying degree. Even human-oriented approaches, such as communities of practice, may face difficulties in applying gained knowledge in business processes and oppose targeted knowledge creation [13]. Among others, one major reason is that these activities are not aligned to business processes and therefore do not respect the context. The resulting solutions are not part of peoples' day to day work procedures.

In addition these solutions rely on knowledge offerings, which have to be created before any application of the knowledge is predictable. This means an investment through efforts of employees and paid work time for companies which may have no return at all. Process oriented knowledge management offers a chance for a paradigm shift towards orientation on demand since the context provides information where knowledge can be applied. Discussions on WM 2005 have shown this to be one of the hot topics e.g. using the Just-in-Time metaphor.

K.-D. Althoff et al. (Eds.): WM 2005, LNAI 3782, pp. 243 – 247, 2005.

In order to tap the full potential of process oriented knowledge management a thorough understanding of the described context has to be gained. Therefore relevant aspects of the real world are captured in models, which represent these aspects in a formal, mostly visualized, way. This allows further analyzing (and simulating) aiming at optimizing the models towards defined goals, e.g. return on investment. Therefore the selection of aspects which are modeled and analyzed is critical for relevance of measures taken as well as success of derived actions.

In previous years, well-engineered modeling approaches have been developed for business processes including those with intensive information processing. However, such modeling methods are not appropriate for task sequences, which strongly rely on the employment of tacit knowledge. The difficulty is that tacit knowledge cannot be detached from individuals and hence, its transfer cannot easily being captured and represented as objects in a business process model. In recent years, a specific set of methods for modeling knowledge intensive processes have emerged. At WM 2003 the approach PROMOTE [7] has been introduced during the tutorial "Geschäftsprozessorientiertes Wissensmanagement" ("Business Process oriented Knowledge Management"). New aspects were discussed at the workshop "Wissensmanagement im Kontext der Modellierung und Ausführung wissensintensiver und schwach strukturierter Geschäftsprozesse" ("Knowledge Management in the context of Modeling and Execution of knowledge intensive as well as weak structured Business Processes"). More approaches towards business process oriented knowledge management have been published afterwards, e.g. [6].

In order to structure approaches to business process oriented knowledge management Abecker et al. use (among others) the following three categories: on the top layer, strategic business process-oriented knowledge management is a top-down perspective, which derives knowledge objectives from the long-term business objectives. The bottom layer deals with the design of KM interventions based on communication analysis and diagnosis. It primarily deals with communication aspects of knowledge work and development of appropriate methods or tools. It is thus very hard to be separated from the middle layer, where he allocates approaches of business process-oriented design, where methods and tools for business process analysis are extended to meet the new requirements of knowledge management [1]. This middle layer is dealing with modeling methods derived from business process management and the modeling of existing processes to find potentials for improvement.

The approaches Business Process oriented Knowledge Management (BPO-KM) [6], Business Knowledge Management [3], KODA [8], Knowledge Process Redesign [2] and PROMOTE [7] have been analysed during the tutorial „Systematische Nutzung von Wissen in Geschäftsprozessen – Modellierung und Analyse wissensintensiver Geschäftsprozesse" ("Systematic Use of Knowledge in Business Processes – Modelling and Analysing knowledge intensive Business Processes") at WM 2005 by Prof. Dr.-Ing. Norbert Gronau and the authors.

Most of the mentioned approaches have a rather strategic and top-down oriented focus [1]. Also, most approaches are based on tools and methods of classic business process management with only little extensions to deal with knowledge. The given characteristics of knowledge and knowledge intensive business processes (cp. [12]) are not fully modeled or analyzed as indicated [4].

In the workshop "Modeling Knowledge intensive Business Processes" (KiBP) at WM 2005 the authors aimed to evaluate the recent state in this scientific area.

The workshop targeted practically oriented or scientific contributions, focusing on modeling, analysis, and re-engineering in the following topic areas: automatic generation of basic structures for knowledge intensive business processes, integration of Business Process Management and Knowledge Management, continuous monitoring of knowledge intensive business processes, simulation of knowledge intensive business processes, validation of models for knowledge intensive business processes, practical examples in the areas of product development, software engineering, consult-ing, or e-government, patterns and Anti-Patterns in modeling knowledge intensive business processes, and extension of existing modeling methods (e.g. UML, EPC).

Surprisingly, most authors of popular approaches in business process oriented knowledge management have moved on to new challenges (e.g. [10]). Nevertheless, selected results of current research in these areas were presented and discussed at the workshop. In order to provide an overview and guideline all workshop contributions are positioned on a process for modeling Knowledge intensive Business Processes (Fig. 1).

The first contribution introduces and evaluates a methodology and basic fundamentals of modeling. This includes identification of possible points for initial modeling (starting points), detail level of modeling (level of granularity) and the question whether the specific characteristic of knowledge can be addressed in structured workflows (units of description).

The second contribution shows that the process of modeling knowledge intensive processes itself can be significantly enhanced by utilizing an ontology in order to externalize process knowledge. For that purpose design decisions are allocated to single elements of the business process. Benefits include increased transparency as well as a greater flexibility for adapting to changing environmental parameters.

The third contribution introduces a concept to economic evaluation of knowledge intensive processes by identifying and modeling cohesions. The new concept of 'evaluation chains' describes the structure of cause and effect. The resulting model not only provides insightful transparency but can also be analyzed using mathematical methods.

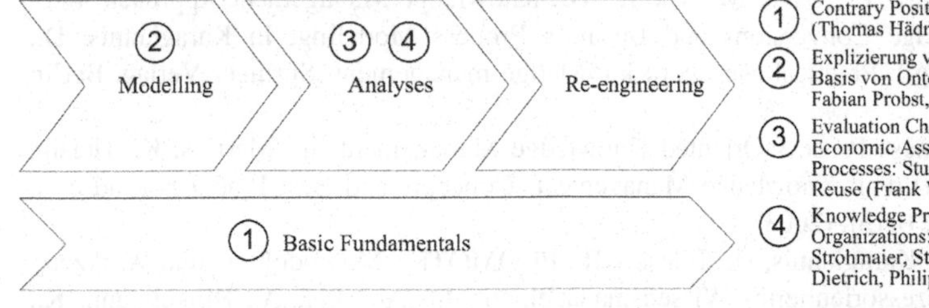

Fig. 1. Generalized Process of Modelling and Analysis of KiBP

In alignment with business strategy, knowledge processes in specific knowledge domains are analyzed using a pattern-based approach. Nine patterns of knowledge process problems have been identified of which one is addressed in the in the fourth contribution. Furthermore, the procedure of the pattern-based identification of knowledge problems is introduced.

All accepted contributions all available either from the conference proceedings or, in an extended version, from our website[1]. The post proceedings feature contributions (1) dealing with aspects to be modelled and (4) analysis of business process models.

At the workshop an additional presentation showing the application of the Knowledge Modeling and Description Language (KMDL) in practice was given. KMDL is the author's subject of research towards modelling, analyzing and improvement of knowledge intensive processes [5].

The results of the workshop KiBP in the year 2005 were ambivalent. New approaches and basic considerations in the area of process-oriented knowledge management were presented. However, many challenges in this scientific area are not addressed. A critical examination through the scientific exchange of successes or failures and improvement of existing approaches in the field leads to the presented solutions. It appears that the field of business process oriented knowledge management turns to a funded scientific work and evaluation, interested in long term success. Still, this field contains many unaddressed potentials.

References

1. Abecker, A., Hinkelmann, K., Maus, H., Müller: H.-J.: Integrationspotenziale für Geschäftsprozesse und Wissensmanagement. In: Abecker, A., Hinkelmann, K., Maus, H., Müller: H.-J. (Eds.): Geschäftsprozessorientiertes Wissensmanagement. Springer-Verlag, Berlin (2002)
2. Allweyer, T.: Wissensmanagement mit ARIS Modellen. In: Scheer, A.-W. (Eds.) ARIS - Vom Geschäftsprozess zum Anwendungssystem (4th ed.).Springer-Verlag, Berlin (2002)
3. Bach, V.: Business Knowledge Management: Wertschöpfung durch Wissensportale. In: Bach, V., Österle, H., Vogler, P.: Business Knowledge Management in der Praxis. Springer-Verlag, Berlin (2000)
4. Gronau, N.: Modellierbarkeit wissensintensiver Geschäftsprozesse mit herkömmlichen Werkzeugen. In: Horster, P. (Eds.): Elektronische Geschäftsprozesse 2004, Sysses (2004) 408 - 421.
5. Gronau, N.; Müller, C.; Uslar, M.: The KMDL Knowledge Management Approach: Integrating Knowledge Conversions and Business Process Modeling. In Karagiannis, D.; Reimer, U. (Hrsg.): Practical aspects of knowledge management. Springer-Verlag, Berlin (2004) 1-10
6. Heisig, P.: Business Process Oriented Knowledge Management. In: Mertins, K., Heisig, P., Vorbeck, J. (Eds.): Knowledge Management. Concepts and Best Practices (2nd ed.), Springer-Verlag, Berlin (2003)
7. Hinkelmann, K., Karagiannis, D., Telesko, R.: PROMOTE - Methodologie und Werkzeug für geschäftsprozessorientiertes Wissensmanagement. In: Abecker, A., Hinkelmann, K., Maus, H., Müller, H.-J. (Eds.): Geschäftsprozessorientiertes Wissensmanagement. Springer-Verlag, Berlin (2002)

[1] http://www.wi.uni-potsdam.de/homepage/potsdam.nsf/kibp05

8. Kühnle, H., Sternemann, K.-H., Harz, K.: Herausforderung Geschäftsprozesse. LOG_X Verlag (1998)
9. Maier, R.: IT-gestütztes Wissensmanagement in Organisationen. BIT Banking and Information Technology, Band 6, Heft 1, March 2005 (2005) 7-20
10. Mertins, K., Alwert, K., Heisig, P. (Eds.): Wissensbilanzen. Springer-Verlag, Berlin (2005)
11. North, K.: Wissensorientierte Unternehmensführung - Wertschöpfung durch Wissen. (3rd ed.), Gabler Verlag (2002)
12. Remus, U.: Prozeßorientiertes Wissensmanagement, Konzepte und Modellierung. Dissertation, Universität Regensburg http://www.bibliothek.uni-regensburg.de/opus/volltexte/2002/80 (2002)
13. Wenger, E., McDermott, R., Snyder, W. M.: Cultivating communities of practice. Harvard Business School Press, Boston (2002)

Contrary Positions About Modeling Knowledge Work

Thomas Hädrich

Martin-Luther-University Halle-Wittenberg,
06099 Halle (Saale), Germany
thomas.haedrich@wiwi.uni-halle.de

Abstract. Modeling for knowledge management (KM) is fundamentally influenced by decisions about which approach, focus, perspectives or modeling language should be used. This paper characterizes three key decisions with regard to what modeling should focus on, which units of description are appropriate and what level of granularity is suited and relates them to a general framework that structures the quality of conceptual modeling. For each decision, contrary positions are highlighted and based on this investigation theses about modeling knowledge work are formulated. It is argued for a more flexible modeling of knowledge work by starting from hot spots of knowledge work with high potential for improvement, using situations as basic units of description and modeling on task level to provide starting points for KM support. The theses developed are related to the concept of knowledge stance that seems to be a promising approach to describe recurring situations of knowledge work.

1 Introduction

Modeling is a key task in order to analyze and understand knowledge work in the context of business processes and to guide the design of supporting information and communication technologies (ICT) and especially knowledge management systems (KMS). Recently, a number of approaches for knowledge-oriented analysis and modeling of knowledge work have been introduced, examples are the extensions of ARIS for KM [2], B-KIDE [39], GPO-WM [16], KMDL [14], Knowledge MEMO [31], PROMOTE [44], and PROMET®I-NET [3]. All of these approaches focus on business processes with the goal to establish a close link between KM measures and value creation and by this way to an organization's success. They differ with respect to several aspects, e.g., the points that are focused during analysis of business processes, the concepts and metaphors considered to be suited for describing knowledge work, the perspectives that are modeled (e.g., person, process, knowledge, resource), and the level of granularity of modeling. Reasons are different views on knowledge work, its characteristics, how it can be described and the type of support the approaches aim at.

Thus, the underlying premises of these approaches should be discussed with respect to their applicability to describe knowledge work - which relates to the quality of the models created. This paper investigates three fundamental decisions that emerged when applying and comparing selected approaches: the starting points of modeling, appropriate units of description and the level of granularity.

Goals are a) to highlight contrary positions concerning these decisions and to discuss which position is suited best, b) to develop theses about how modeling languages

K.-D. Althoff et al. (Eds.): WM 2005, LNAI 3782, pp. 248 – 258, 2005.

should be designed that are appropriate to model knowledge work in the context of business processes, and c) to discuss the concept of knowledge stance presented in an earlier publication [15] against the background of the proposed theses.

Firstly, a framework to understand quality of modeling and to classify issues discussed here is presented (section 2). Afterwards, key decisions for modeling and contrary positions with respect to them are characterized (section 3), theses for modeling knowledge work are formulated (section 4) and related to the concept of knowledge stance (section 5). The paper is concluded with a summary of results and an outlook.

2 Quality of Modeling

Lindland et al. present a general framework to assess the quality of conceptual modeling [24]. Since modeling basically is making statements in a defined language, it is based on linguistic concepts. This is reflected by the four cornerstones of the framework (see Fig. 1): (1) Modeling language consists of all statements that can be made according to the syntax of the language, i.e. the alphabet and grammar. (2) Domain represents the relevant knowledge for solving a problem and consists of all statements that would be correct and relevant for solving this problem. (3) Model is the set of statements that are actually made. (4) Audience includes everyone who needs to understand the model and thus audience interpretation is the set of statements that the audience thinks the model contains.

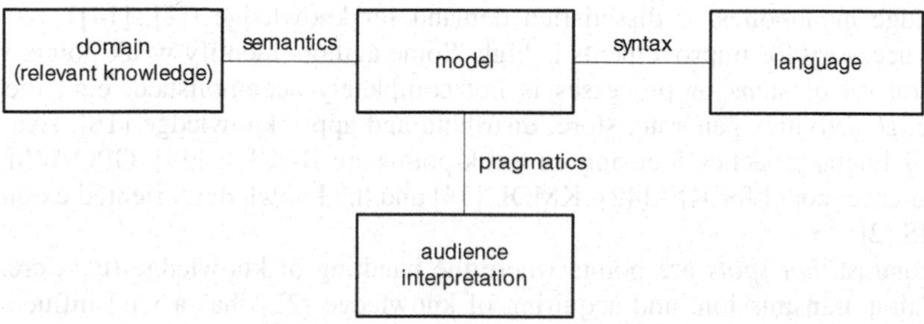

Fig. 1. Cornerstones for quality of modeling and their relationships [24]

Quality of conceptual modeling depends on interrelationships between these elements. Syntactic quality refers to the extent the model adheres to the language rules. Semantic quality describes how well the model corresponds to the domain. Pragmatic quality refers to how good the model supports correct audience interpretation. Other factors such as the extent to which the audience is familiar with the domain may also play an important role. However, they are not directly linked to the model and thus not included within the framework.

The framework broadens the view on quality of modeling to the pragmatic applicability of a modeling notation which later is included in other frameworks or sets of requirements (e.g., in [13]). Moreover, it helps to understand and structure the quality of models and by this way enables the definition of quality goals and measures to reach them. From the view of this framework, a thorough evaluation of modeling approaches should consider all elements of the framework and all aspects of quality.

As a first step, this paper focuses on three key decisions that affect the element *language* of the presented framework: (1) Where and how starting points for analysis and modeling can be identified, (2) which basic units of description are appropriate to structure knowledge work, and (3) what level of granularity is suited best. They emerged during analysis and application of the approaches to concrete examples and are fundamental decisions that are worth to be discussed prior to a detailed evaluation of the approaches that comprises all aspects of quality.

3 Key Decisions

Starting Points: Weak Points vs. Hot Spots. KM can be characterized as being responsible for the selection, implementation and evaluation of strategies and measures to improve knowledge handling of an organization in order to enhance the overall organizational performance [25]. KM instruments are part of an ICT-supported systematic intervention into an organizational knowledge base and to implement KM strategies [26]. Examples are skill management [6], knowledge mapping [9], and best practice sharing [28]. The question is how and where to start with applying them and thus where modeling should focus on. Two alternative views can be identified that can be characterized as weak point and as hot spot approaches.

Weak points are areas in business processes where knowledge processing is inhibited by personal, organizational, technical or cultural barriers. Examples are multiple generation of similar knowledge, media breaks, missing actualization of knowledge, knowledge monopolies or dissatisfied demand for knowledge ([2], [14]). At these points, necessity for improvements is high. Some authors identify weak points where a generic set of steps or processes is not completely accomplished, e.g., the core knowledge activities generate, store, distribute and apply knowledge [16]. Examples for modeling approaches focusing on weak points are B-KIDE [39], GPO-WM [16], the reference model for KM [42], KMDL [14] and the knowledge-oriented extensions of ARIS [2].

In contrast, *hot spots* are points where the handling of knowledge (e.g., creation, application, transmission, and acquiring of knowledge [22]) has a vital influence on the organization's success. This especially is knowledge that is related to the organization's core competencies [23]. These actions depend largely on the capabilities and the experience of individuals as well as an environment that supports knowledge sharing. Hot spots are regularly conceptualized as selected functions or tasks of business processes, e.g., as knowledge-intensive tasks such as "check credit-worthiness" or "determine credit conditions" opposed to more routine tasks such as "collect personal data" or "administer credit" [21]. An example for a modeling approach focusing on hot spots is PROMOTE [44], examples for research projects dealing with workflow support of knowledge-intensive tasks and thus with hot spots of knowledge work are KnowMore [1] and FRODO [41].

Units of Description: Workflows vs. Situations. From an ICT perspective, workflows are an important instrument to automate and to support structured tasks in business processes. It is commonly agreed in the literature that knowledge work does not fit into the category of structured work as it can be characterized by a high degree of variety and exceptions, teamwork and participation in social networks as well as strong communication needs ([25], [27]). Nevertheless, two contrary positions can be distinguished concerning how knowledge work can be modeled. They can be denoted as workflow and as situational perspective.

The *workflow perspective* assumes that workflows are generally appropriate to model and to support knowledge work in business processes, at least fragments or parts of it. Some approaches expand and enrich workflows to support knowledge-intensive business processes, examples are ad-hoc or flexible workflows [35] as well as weakly structured workflows [41]. Other approaches conceptualize knowledge processes ([18], [27]), postulate closed cycles of knowledge-oriented tasks [16] or generic knowledge processes [42].

The *situational perspective* regards the activities of knowledge work as inherently linked to and dependent on the actual context. Deflections, exceptions and breakdown situations are not simply errors, but they are the basis for learning and enhancing plans for future actions [4]. Plans such as structured workflows are resources for reasoning about action rather than controlling structures [40]. The foundation of actions are the actual context and environment as well as goals of joint activities ([8], [27]). Moreover, human expertise can principally not be described with context-free rules or in an algorithmic form since it is based on intuition, creativity and experience [7]. This calls for alternative units of description to structure knowledge work like models of situation handling [43] and new design metaphors like "situations in life" [5].

Level of Granularity: Process vs. Task Level. Modeling can take place at different levels of granularity, depending on the purpose of models. Generally, models can target at description, explanation, support of decisions and design [36]. Models for KM can focus either predominantly on whole processes or on single tasks in the context of business processes.

A well-known example for knowledge-oriented modeling at *process level* is ARIS with extensions for knowledge management [2]. Additional object types (e.g., knowledge object, documented knowledge) and diagrams (e.g., knowledge map, knowledge structure diagram, communication diagram) are suited to give a general overview of knowledge domains and communication between organizational units relevant for business processes.

Modeling at *task level* aims at identifying and designing ways to support knowledge-intensive tasks of individuals. In PROMOTE for example, "knowledge processes" are assigned to knowledge-intensive tasks of business processes. They represent workflows that automate structured sub-tasks of knowledge-intensive tasks (e.g., "find expert", "find similar case") and are supported by topic maps and skill models [17].

Discussion. Weak point approaches have a tendency to focus on optimization of information flows within and across business processes rather than on spots where knowledge that is important for the business process is generated or applied. In contrast, the hot spot approach is a pragmatic, engineering-oriented approach that focuses on design and development of supporting ICT for selected knowledge-oriented actions. It thus seems to be feasible to combine hot spots and weak point approaches, i.e. to focus on those areas in business processes with a high potential for enhancements and where handling of knowledge has a high importance for the organization's success.

Arguments supporting the workflow perspective are that knowledge work in a broad view includes routine fractions that can be automated with workflows [35] and that beyond automating activities, workflows could be used for information support and reflection on steps to solve recurrent problems when they are modeled lazy or late on instance level [41]. Nevertheless, a fundamental advantage of the situational perspective is its closeness to common characterizations of knowledge work, which calls for units of description that enable and operationalize this view and incorporate it into modeling.

Models that should support the design of KMS must provide insights on how individual knowledge-oriented tasks can be supported and how an environment can be created that supports knowledge sharing. Thus, modeling on task level seems to be better suited than models on process level that give a general overview of whole knowledge-intensive business processes.

4 Theses for Modeling Knowledge Work

Based on the investigation of these positions, the following theses are formulated:

Starting Points

- *Hot spots with a high potential for enhancements are good starting points.*
  Hot spots are crucial points of knowledge work in that they are vital for an organization's success. Modeling and KM should focus on knowledge-oriented actions accomplished at hot spots that have a high potential for improvement – which combines hot spot and weak point approaches.
- *Hot spots should be conceptualized broadly to include learning.*
  Business processes depend on exploitation and application of knowledge. Hot spots should be conceptualized in a broad sense that includes exploration and creation of knowledge apart from business processes, e.g., related to other initiatives, projects or to communities.

Units of Description

- *Situations that are linked to business processes should be preferred for modeling knowledge work.*
  KM needs units of description that, like workflows, do not primarily focus on recurring sequences of tasks, though workflows are one pragmatic way to support fractions of knowledge work. Situations as units of description are a promising direction. In a business context, they need to be linked to business processes to ensure the link of knowledge-oriented actions to value-creating activities.
- *Reference knowledge processes are not generally appropriate.*
  The generic cycles or processes of knowledge-related tasks or processes ([16], [19], [42]) such as the fixed sequence generate, store, distribute and apply can be criticized and have not yet been empirically validated. For example, an idea or experience not necessarily has to be stored before it can be handed on to colleagues. However, that created knowledge is not applied (waste of resources) and applied knowledge is not created within the organization (knowledge outage)

[38] each could be an indicator for weak points. Practices of knowledge work are a promising way to analyze and to describe how individuals deal with knowledge, e.g., by expressing, monitoring, translating and networking ([33], [34]).

Level of Granularity

- *Modeling should focus on task level.*
  Models to support knowledge work must provide indications which ICT supported KM instrument is suited best and where. This can only be accomplished with models at task-level.
- *Modeling needs different levels of abstraction.*
  Models on task level tend to become very detailed and complex. Thus, a modeling language must provide different levels of granularity and should allow giving an overview of an organization's knowledge infrastructure.

Table 1 gives an overview of the key decisions and the theses developed above.

Table 1. Overview of contrary positions and theses

starting points		
weak points approach	*hot spots approach*	*thesis*
focuses on barriers and gaps inhibiting knowledge processing	focuses on value-adding knowledge-oriented actions	modeling should focus on hot spots with high potential for improvement in a broad sense that includes learning
units of description		
workflow perspective	*situational perspective*	*thesis*
a substantial portion of knowledge work can be described, structured and supported with workflows	knowledge work depends inherently on the actual context and environment as well as on individual expertise	situations and practices are best suited to describe knowledge work; links to business processes need to be established
level of granularity		
process level	*task level*	*thesis*
models give a general overview of knowledge-intensive processes	modeling is accomplished on task level to design support of knowledge-intensive tasks	task level models are necessary to support knowledge-intensive tasks; multiple levels of granularity need to be combined

5 Concept of Knowledge Stance

Summing up, modeling should focus on hot spots of knowledge work in a situational perspective at task level. A first step into this direction could be the concept of knowledge stance presented in a previous publication [15]. This approach concentrates on reoccuring situations of knowledge work in the context of business processes rather than on knowledge processes or flows within and between business processes.

An example for a knowledge stance is "learning about factors that influence long-term credits" that is connected to the task "check credit-worthiness" in the business process "lending". Knowledge stances are initiated by occasions for generating new knowledge that occur in connection to knowledge-oriented tasks in business processes, for example an unusual long time for repayment of a concrete credit that makes approving or disapproving the credit more complex or risky. The knowledge stance results in knowledge-oriented actions, for example to "contact an expert for long-term credits", to "look-up experiences with previously approved long-term credits" or to "access guidelines regulating approval/disapproval of credits".

A knowledge stance connects two perspectives on knowledge work: a process-oriented perspective and an activity-oriented perspective (see Fig. 2). The process-oriented perspective is based on concepts known from traditional process-modeling approaches such as ADONIS [20], ARIS [32], IEM [37], MEMO [12], PROMET [29], and SOM [11], i.e. processes and workflows that link actors, functions or tasks and resources. They distinguish between three corresponding levels of granularity: (1) Value chains arrange value-adding activities [30], (2) business processes connect functions and (3) workflows orchestrate tasks. The approaches discussed above (see sections 1 and 3) extend this perspective to include some of the specifics of knowledge work. However, they are still limited mainly to routine work solving structured problems that primarily aims at the exploitation or application of knowledge.

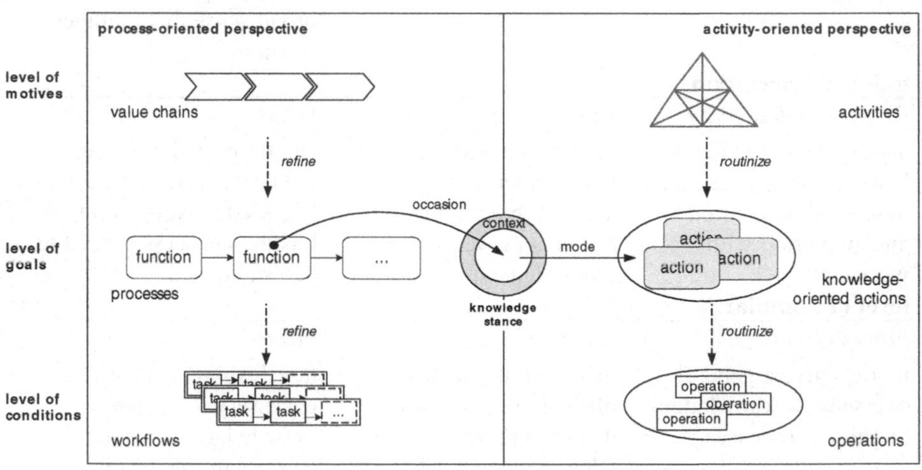

Fig. 2. The concept of knowledge stance [15]

In contrast, the activity-oriented perspective stresses the learning-oriented, creative and unstructured part of knowledge work and is based on the ideas of activity theory (for an integration of process modeling and activity modeling see [15]). An important difference is that in the process-oriented perspective, a change from a higher to a lower level of granularity corresponds to refinement whereas in the activity-oriented perspective, a change from a higher to a lower level is associated with routinization which enables to conceptualize learning.

A *knowledge stance* is a class of recurring situations in knowledge work defined by occasion, context, and mode resulting in knowledge-oriented actions [15]. It describes a situation in which a knowledge worker can, should, or must switch from a business process-oriented function to a knowledge-oriented action. In a process-oriented perspective, an employee accomplishes functions on the level of goals that belong to a value chain on the level of motives by fulfilling a sequence of tasks on the level of conditions. Simultaneously, she can be involved in an activity framing knowledge-oriented actions and corresponding operations.

As mentioned above, a business process may offer several *occasions* to learn and to generate knowledge related to the core competencies of the organization. Occasions trigger knowledge stances and are associated with the functions of the business process by offering the opportunity or the need for knowledge-related actions. A knowledge stance may also include the translation and application of knowledge created outside the knowledge stance. Those functions of business processes that carry occasions should be taken as starting points for modeling. They represent hot spots that should be investigated further with regard to how knowledge-oriented actions could be supported to enhance the effectiveness of knowledge work.

The *context* includes all dimensions suitable to describe the current situation of the worker. It comprises the process context consisting of elements such as involved organizational units, roles, and resources as well as elements of the activity or learning context, e.g., purpose and outcomes of related activities, experts or communities in relevant domains as well as individual or organizational learning goals. Additionally, person-related data and information such as required skill level and communication relationships between roles are part of the context.

The *mode* classifies what actions can be performed and refers to four informing practices [34]: (1) expressing is the practice of self-reflexive conversion of individual knowledge and subjective insights into informational objects that are independent of the person, (2) monitoring describes continuous non-focused scanning of the environment and gathering of useful "just in case"-information, (3) translating involves creation of information by ferrying it across different contexts until a coherent meaning emerges, and (4) networking is the practice of building and maintaining relationships with people inside and outside the organization.

During the process of modeling, context, mode and occasion are means to specify the set of available, allowed or required *knowledge-oriented actions*. Thus, modeling knowledge stances is accomplished on task level with the goal to support single knowledge-oriented actions. Examples for actions are evaluate source, indicate level of certitude, compare sources, link content, relate to prior information, add meta-data, notify and alert, ask questions, and offer interaction [10]. In contrast to the clearly defined sequences of functions in the process-oriented perspective, there is no predetermined flow of actions. They are accomplished by executing operations suited to serve the goals of the action.

6 Conclusion

This paper has highlighted three key decisions for modeling knowledge work concerning starting points, units of description and level of granularity that emerged when analyzing and applying recent approaches for modeling knowledge work. They have been classified with the help of a general framework of quality of conceptual modeling. Contrary positions for each of these decisions have been characterized and as a result theses have been formulated that propose to start from hot spots of knowledge work with high potential for improvement, to use situations as basic units of description and to model on task level. The concept of knowledge stance has been characterized and has been related to these theses.

For a thorough comparison and analysis of the proposed modeling approaches, all aspects of quality of conceptual modeling need to be investigated. To evaluate the concept of knowledge stance, a modeling notation needs to be defined. This is also a foundation to answer emerging questions such as how the context of knowledge stances could be structured and at which level of detail it should be described, which heuristics could be applied to identify occasions and by this way hot spots of knowledge work, how multiple knowledge stances are connected and whether typical knowledge stances in organizations can be identified, which KM instruments are suited to support specific knowledge-related actions and how a modeling language could give hints for the design of KMS and selection of supportive services of an enterprise knowledge infrastructure. Altogether, this paper calls for a flexible modeling of knowledge work by taking its unstructured, communicative and creative features into account. The concept of knowledge stance may be a promising step into this direction.

References

1. Abecker, A., Bernardi, A., Hinkelmann, K., Kühn, O., Sintek, M.: Context-Aware, Proactive Delivery of Task-Specific Knowledge: The KnowMore Project. International Journal on Information Systems Frontiers, 2(3), (2000) 253-276
2. Allweyer, T.: Modellbasiertes Wissensmanagement. Information Management, 13(1), (1998) 37-45
3. Bach, V., Österle, H., Vogler, P.: Business Knowledge Management in der Praxis. Prozessorientierte Lösungen zwischen Knowledge Portal und Kompetenzmanagement. Springer-Verlag, Berlin (2000)
4. Bardram, J. E.: Plans as Situated Action: An Activity Theory Approach to Workflow Systems. In: Proceedings of the 5th European Conference on Computer Supported Cooperative Work, Kluwer Academic Publishers, Lancaster UK (1997)
5. Bleek, W. G.: Situations in Life to Support the Use and Modelling of Municipal Information Systems. In: Bleek, W.-G., Dittrich, Y., Eriksen, S. (Eds.): Multimode Access to Public Service, Technical Report 2002:14, Blekinge Institute of Technology, Sweden (2002)
6. Deiters, W., Lucas, R., Weber, T.: Skill-Management - Ein Baustein für das Management flexibler Teams. Information Management & Consulting, 15(3), (1999) 54-60
7. Dreyfus, H. L., Dreyfus, S. E.: Mind Over Machine. The Power of Human Intuition and Expertise in the Era of the Computer. Free Press, New York (1986)
8. Engeström, Y.: Expansive Visibilization of Work: An Activity-theoretical Perspective. Computer Supported Cooperative Work, 8(1-2), (1999) 63-93
9. Eppler, M. J.: Making Knowledge Visible Through Intranet Knowledge Maps: Concepts, Elements, Cases. Paper presented at the Proceedings of the 34th Hawaii International Conference in System Sciences (2001)
10. Eppler, M. J.: Managing Information Quality: Increasing the Value of Information in Knowledge-intensive Products and Processes. Springer-Verlag, Berlin (2003)

11. Ferstl, O. K., & Sinz, E. J.: From Business Process Modeling to the Specification of Distributed Business Application Systems - An Object-Oriented Approach (Research Paper): Dept. of Business Information Systems, University of Bamberg (1994)
12. Frank, U.: Multi-Perspective Enterprise Modeling (MEMO) - Conceptual Framework and Modeling Languages. In Proceedings of the 35th Hawaii International Conference on System Sciences (HICSS-35). Honolulu (2002)
13. Frank, U., van Laak, B. L.: Anforderungen an Sprachen zur Modellierung von Geschäftsprozessen. Koblenz: Institut für Wirtschaftsinformatik, Fachbereich Informatik, Universität Koblenz-Landau (2003)
14. Gronau, N., Weber, E.: Modeling of Knowledge Intensive Business Processes with the Declaration Language KMDL. In: M. Khosrow-Pour (Ed.): Information Technology and Organizations: Trends, Issues, Challenges and Solutions. Proceedings of the IRMA International Conference, May 18th-23th, 2003, Idea Group (2003) 284-287
15. Hädrich, T., Maier, R.: Modeling Knowledge Work. In: Chamoni, P. , Deiters, W., Gronau, N., Kutsche, R.-D., Loos, P., Müller-Merbach, H., Rieger, B., Sandkuhl, K. (Eds.): Multikonferenz Wirtschaftsinformatik (MKWI 2004), University Duisburg-Essen 9th-11th March 2004 (Vol. 2). Akademische Verlagsgesellschaft GmbH, Berlin (2004)
16. Heisig, P.: Business Process Oriented Knowledge Management. In: Mertins, K., Heisig, P., Vorbeck, J. (Eds.): Knowledge Management. Concepts and Best Practices (2nd ed.), Springer-Verlag, Berlin (2003)
17. Hinkelmann, K., Karagiannis, D., Telesko, R.: PROMOTE - Methodologie und Werkzeug für geschäftsprozessorientiertes Wissensmanagement. In: Abecker, A., Hinkelmann K., Maus H., Müller, H. J. (Eds.): Geschäftsprozessorientiertes Wissensmanagement. Springer-Verlag, Berlin (2002) 65-90
18. Hoffmann, M., Goesmann, T., Kienle, A.: Analyse und Unterstützung von Wissensprozessen als Voraussetzung für erfolgreiches Wissensmanagement. In: Abecker A., Hinkelmann K., Maus H., Müller, H. J. (Eds.): Geschäftsprozessorientiertes Wissensmanagement. Springer-Verlag, Berlin (2002) 159-184
19. Holsapple, C. W., Joshi, K. D.: Knowledge Manipulation Activities: Results of A Delphi Study. Information & Management, 39(6), (2002) 477-490
20. Junginger, S., Kühn, H., Strobl, R., Karagiannis, D.: Ein Geschäftsprozessmanagement-Werkzeug der nächsten Generation - ADONIS: Konzeption und Anwendungen. Wirtschaftsinformatik, 42(5), (2000) 392-401
21. Karagiannis, D., Telesko, R.: The EU-Project PROMOTE: A Process-Oriented Approach for Knowledge Management. In: Reimer, U. (Eds.), PAKM 2000, 3rd International Conference on Practical Aspects of Knowledge Management (2000)
22. Kelloway, E. K., Barling, J.: Knowledge Work as Organizational Behavior. International Journal of Management Reviews, 2(3), (2000) 287-204
23. Leonard-Barton, D.: Core Capabilities and Core Rigidities: A Paradox in Managing New Product Development. Strategic Management Journal, 13, (1992) 111-125
24. Lindland, O. I., Sindre, G., & Sølvberg, A.: Understanding Quality in Conceptual Modeling. IEEE Software, 11(2), (1994) 42-49
25. Maier, R.: Knowledge Management Systems: Information And Communication Technologies for Knowledge Management (2nd ed.). Springer-Verlag, Berlin (2004)
26. Maier, R., Hädrich, T., Peinl, R.: Enterprise Knowledge Infrastructures. Springer-Verlag, Berlin (2005)
27. Nardi, B. A.: Context and Consciousness: Activity Theory and Human-Computer Interaction (2nd ed.). MIT Press, Cambridge, Mass. (1997)

28. Neumann, R., Stingl, A., Grillitsch, W.: Best Practices and Lessons Learned in Knowledge Management Projects. Paper presented at the 3rd European Conference on Knowledge Management, Dublin, Ireland (2002)
29. Österle, H.: Business Engineering. Prozeß- und Systementwicklung. Band 1: Entwurfstechniken. Springer-Verlag, Berlin (1995)
30. Porter, M. E.: Competitive Advantage: Creating and Sustaining Superior Performance. Free Press, New York London (1985)
31. Schauer, H.: Knowledge MEMO: Eine Methode zur Planung, Steuerung und Kontrolle ganzheitlichen betrieblichen Wissensmanagements. Unpublished PhD thesis, University of Koblenz, Koblenz (2005)
32. Scheer, A.-W. ARIS - Modellierungsmethoden, Metamodelle, Anwendungen. Springer-Verlag, Berlin (2001)
33. Schultze, U.: A Confessional Account of an Ethnography About Knowledge Work. MIS Quarterly, 24(1), (2000) 3-41
34. Schultze, U.: On Knowledge Work. In: Holsapple, C. W. (Ed.), Handbook on Knowledge Management - Volume 1: Knowledge Matters, Springer-Verlag, Berlin (2003) 43-58
35. Schwarz, S., Abecker, A., Maus, H., & Sintek, M.: Anforderungen an die Workflow-Unterstützung für wissensintensive Geschäftsprozesse. In: Müller, H. J., Abecker, A., Hinkelmann K., Maus H. (Eds.): WM'2001-Workshop "Geschäftsprozeßorientiertes Wissensmanagement", Baden-Baden, Germany, March 14th-16th, (2001)
36. Sinz, E. J.: Modellierung. In: Back, A., Becker J., König, W., Krallmann, W., Rieger B., Scheer, A.-W., Seibt, D., Stahlknecht, P., Strunz, H., Thome, R., Wedekind, H. (Eds.): Lexikon der Wirtschaftsinformatik. Springer-Verlag, Berlin (2001) 312-313
37. Spur, G., Mertins, K., Jochem, R.: Integrated Enterprise Modelling. Beuth, Berlin (1996)
38. Strohmaier, M., Lindstaedt, S. N., Dietrich, W., Koronakis, P.: Knowledge Problems in Process-Oriented Organizations: A Pattern Approach. Paper presented at the 3rd Conference Professional Knowledge Management, 10th-13th April 2005, Kaiserslautern, Germany (2005)
39. Strohmaier, M. B.: B-KIDE: A Framework and a Tool for Business Process Oriented Knowledge Infrastructure Development. Institute for Knowledge Management and Knowledge Visualization, Graz University of Technology, Graz, Austria (2005)
40. Suchman, L.: Plans and Situated Actions, The Problem of Human-Machine Communication. Cambridge University Press, Cambridge (1987)
41. van Elst, L., Aschoff, F.-R., Bernardi, A., Maus, H., Schwarz, S.: Weakly-Structured Workflows for Knowledge-Intensive Tasks: An Experimental Evaluation. Paper presented at the 11th International Workshop on Enabling Technologies: Infrastructure for Collaborative Enterprises, June 9th - 11th, 2003, Linz, Austria (2003)
42. Warnecke, G., & Stammwitz, G.: Referenzmodell Wissensmanagement - Ein Ansatz zur modellbasierten Gestaltung wissensorientierter Prozesse. Wirtschaftsinformatik, 13(1), 24-29 (1998)
43. Wiig, K. M.: A Knowledge Model for Situation-Handling. Journal of Knowledge Management, 7(5), (2003) 6-24
44. Woitsch, R., & Karagiannis, D.: Process-Oriented Knowledge Management Systems Based on KM-Services: The PROMOTE Approach. International Journal of Intelligent Systems in Accounting, Finance & Management, 11, (2003) 253-267

Application of Knowledge Problem Patterns in Process Oriented Organizations

Markus Strohmaier and Stefanie N. Lindstaedt

Know-Center Graz, Austria
{mstrohm, slind}@know-center.at
http://www.know-center.at

Abstract. This contribution introduces a method for the identification of knowledge problems in process-oriented organizations. On an operative level, knowledge problems occur when the generation, storage, transfer or application of knowledge is not in accordance with an organization's business goals. The introduced method represents an instrument for pointing organizations to such shortcomings and thereby opens up solution spaces for overcoming them. This contribution introduces a set of knowledge problem patterns and an accompanying process of applying them in organizations - both supported by empirical data generated in three conducted case studies. In doing that, this contribution provides new stimuli and insights for current research in the domain of business process oriented knowledge modeling and -audits.

1 Motivation

Modern knowledge-based organizations increasingly face an urgent need to consciously deal with and effectively manage their most critical resource knowledge. On an operational level, many efforts focus on the management of knowledge activities in organizations such as the generation, storage, transfer or application of knowledge [1]. To ensure that KM initiatives focus on *relevant* areas of organizational knowledge work, often a process-oriented approach is pursued [2,3]. By analyzing business processes from a knowledge perspective, *relevant* knowledge activities in organizations can be identified through e.g. the concept of knowledge processes [4]. With knowledge processes, organizational knowledge work within and across distributed business processes can be visualized [5]. Based on such knowledge processes, problems and barriers in organizational knowledge work can be detected. Many factors are known that represent problems for the effective execution of knowledge processes such as a lack of technological resources, transparency or trust [6]. Yet, these factors implicitly assume the suitability of existing knowledge processes and do not question the design or execution of them. Therefore, the contribution at hand introduces a set of hypothetical knowledge problem patterns on a generic level together with empirical experiences that aim to 1) point organizations to wrongly defined or sub-optimally executed knowledge processes and 2) sketch up solution spaces in order to enable organizations "to do the right things" (vs. "to do things right") when it comes to

K.-D. Althoff et al. (Eds.): WM 2005, LNAI 3782, pp. 259–268, 2005.

managing their most critical resource. Successfully addressing these challenges would enable organizations to increase their level of maturity concerning the management of knowledge processes [7,8].

2 Approach

Knowledge problem patterns build on the existing concepts of knowledge processes [4,5] and patterns [9]. *Knowledge processes* represent an approach of visualizing organizational knowledge work based on business processes and thereby are considered to *represent the generation, storage, transfer and application of certain knowledge domains across or within business processes* [4] while *patterns* represent a *relation between a certain context, a problem, and a solution* [9].

2.1 Knowledge Processes

Figure 1 depicts the main elements of knowledge processes. The concept of knowledge processes intends to depict knowledge activities that themselves are considered to run within and/or orthogonally to business processes [10,11,7]. In addition to the elements depicted in figure 1, extensions to these elements illustrate how knowledge is e.g. stored and transferred within certain knowledge domains. Today, organizational knowledge processes can be identified, modeled and visualized with available frameworks and software tools (such as [5]).

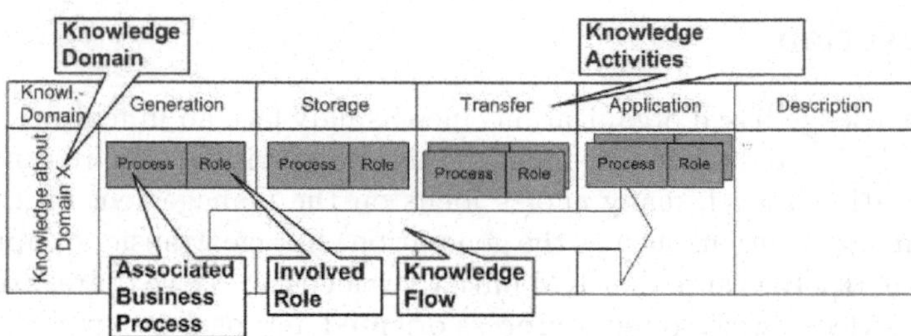

Fig. 1. Knowledge Processes Visualize Distributed Organizational Knowledge Work

Observations of reoccurring knowledge work patterns (e.g. [12]) and the supposition that patterns of certain knowledge process constellations are able to indicate relevant knowledge problems give reason for the following definition of the term *knowledge problem pattern*:

> *Knowledge problem patterns are generic constellations of knowledge processes that indicate potential knowledge problems and -deficits in organizations.*

By having such knowledge problem patterns available, organizations would be able to algorithmically investigate their knowledge process models and identify potential knowledge problems and -deficits. In this contribution, we present a set of hypothetical knowledge problem patterns and report on practical experiences made from applying them in 3 case studies. Therefore, we introduce a set of 10 *knowledge problem patterns* in section 2.2 and an accompanying *process of applying them* in section 2.4 for the identification of potential knowledge problems in process-oriented organizations.

2.2 Knowledge Problem Patterns

Based on an inductive (empirically driven[1]) and deductive (hypothesis driven) approach, a set of 10 knowledge problem patterns emerged. The set consists of the following patterns:

1. Implicit Knowledge
2. Undefined Responsibility
3. Mythos
4. Knowledge Detour
5. Knowledge Outage
6. Long Term Indirect Communication
7. Chaos
8. Broadcasting
9. Culmination
10. External Dependency

Each of them will briefly be explained in the following: 1) Implicit Knowledge points to situations where knowledge of a certain knowledge domain is only available in implicit form. 2) Undefined Responsibility indicates situations where knowledge work is implicitly carried out, with no official responsibilities defined by the organization. 3) Mythos points to knowledge management instruments including storage- or transfer mechanisms (such as databases, intranets, e-mail lists) that were established within organizations, but are not actively used or do not contribute to key value-generating activities. 4) Knowledge Detour identifies situations where knowledge is transferred between two actors through a series of mediators, potentially causing misunderstandings or loss of information. 5) Knowledge Outage refers to situations where knowledge needs of knowledge workers respectively business processes are not fulfilled. 6) Long Term Indirect Communication takes place whenever the generation of knowledge occurs in business process activities only *after* the knowledge is applied. While this seems to be contradictory at first, it makes sense when taking multiple process instantiations into account. An example for such a case would be a process activity 'project requirements definition' that needs to consider experiences gained from past project activities 'project realization'. While on a business process level the activity 'project realization' takes place after the 'requirements definition'

[1] Empirical data from 3 conducted case studies represented the basis for the empirically-driven identification of patterns. The case studies were performed with partners from automotive, software and consulting industry. Each case study focussed on the identification of and support for knowledge processes based on [4].

activity, across multiple instances it might as well be the other way around. 7) Chaos points to situations where a broad range of transfer mechanisms is applied within a single knowledge process. While this might identify creative activities in organizations, it might as well be desirable to reduce variety of these instruments for the sake of traceability or standardization. 8) Broadcasting identifies situations where a single actor transfers knowledge to a series of other actors. Various knowledge management instruments, such as push technologies, exist to support such activities. 9) Culmination points to situations where a single actor needs to acquire knowledge from several other actors. Knowledge management instruments such as portals could integrate different sources and thereby support such situations. 10) External Dependency identifies situations where knowledge that is needed to perform well in business processes is generated outside of the organization. This may indicate critical dependencies from external knowledge suppliers.

It is important to note that all of these patterns are supposed to be applied on a generic level and do not take specifics of certain process instantiations into account. The benefit that can be reaped from such a restriction is that the patterns are potentially applicable across business process instances and organizations as well. Also, although patterns in the sense of [9] include the elements 1. problem 2. context and 3. solution, the knowledge problem patterns at hand predominately focus on the elements *problems* and *context* and only sketch out *solution spaces.* Experiences gained in the three case studies indicated that the development of concrete solutions strongly depends on organizational environments and conditions and therefore is strongly context dependent (in contrast to the *generic* knowledge problem descriptions).

2.3 Details on Two Selected Knowledge Problem Patterns

In order to enhance understanding about these patterns, two of them are introduced in greater detail:

Knowl.-Domain	Generation	Storage	Transfer	Application	Description
Knowledge about Domain X	Process Role	?	Process Role	Process Role	

Fig. 2. Knowledge Problem Pattern 1: Implicit Knowledge

Pattern 1 "Implicit Knowledge", schematically depicted in figure 2, refers to constellations of knowledge processes that do not include any kind of knowledge storage respectively explication, inferring that the only knowledge available in such situations is considered to be implicit. Organizations suffering from high employee turnover rates might increase the degree of explication concerning the affected knowledge domains in order to overcome this knowledge problem.

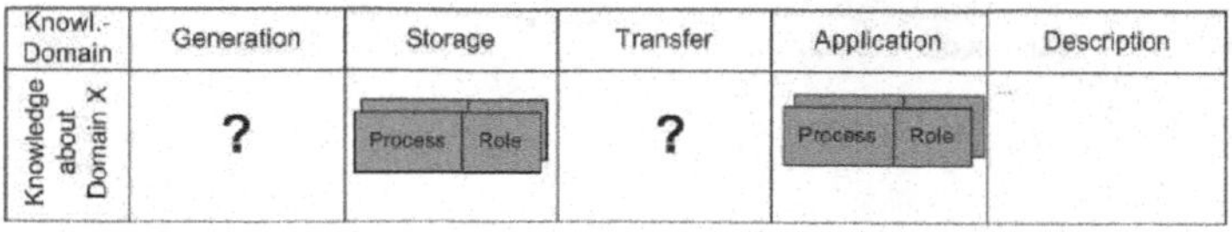

Knowl.-Domain	Generation	Storage	Transfer	Application	Description
Knowledge about Domain X	?	Process Role	?	Process Role	...

Fig. 3. Knowledge Problem Pattern 5: Knowledge Outage

Pattern 5 "Knowledge Outage", depicted in figure 3, refers to situations in which either the generation or the transfer of knowledge is not appropriately anchored within a business process. A critical business processes BP depending on knowledge domains where the generation and/or transfer of knowledge is not sufficiently managed may suffer from this unreliable "knowledge supply chain". Organizations aiming to tackle this problem might emphasize on the stronger integration of these knowledge activities in their respective business processes and thereby increase organizational knowledge support for business process BP.

Since all introduced knowledge problem patterns build on *formal* descriptions of knowledge processes (as introduced in greater detail in [5]), they easily can be applied by performing automated analysis on top of identified knowledge processes.

2.4 Pattern-Based Identification of Knowledge Problems

Knowledge problems *do not exist per se.* They represent current conditions that prevent organizations from effectively achieving their business goals. Therefore, in order to identify knowledge problems in organizations, first a set of business goals need to be recognized and/or defined (Step 1 - depicted in figure 4). Based on business goals, organizational knowledge domains and according identified knowledge processes can be selected (Step 2) that are considered to be of utmost importance for achieving these goals. Subsequently, knowledge problem patterns are applied to the selected knowledge processes in order to identify *potential* knowledge problems (Step 3).

In this step, the identified *potential* knowledge problems need to be evaluated, discussed and reduced to a set of *relevant* knowledge problems, as depicted in figure 5. This is done by e.g. involving experts and investigating if the poten-

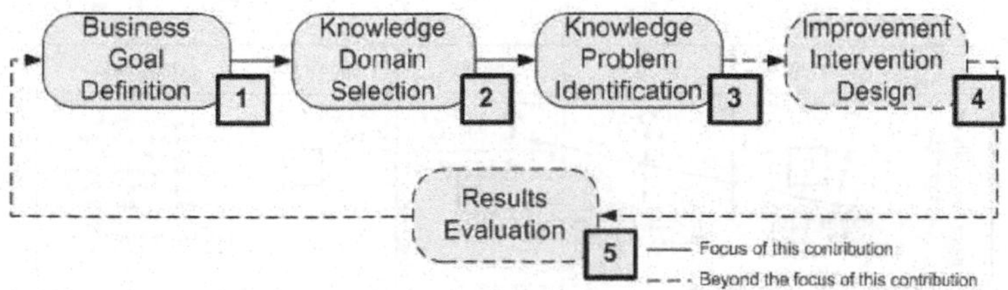

Fig. 4. The Process of Knowledge Problem Identification

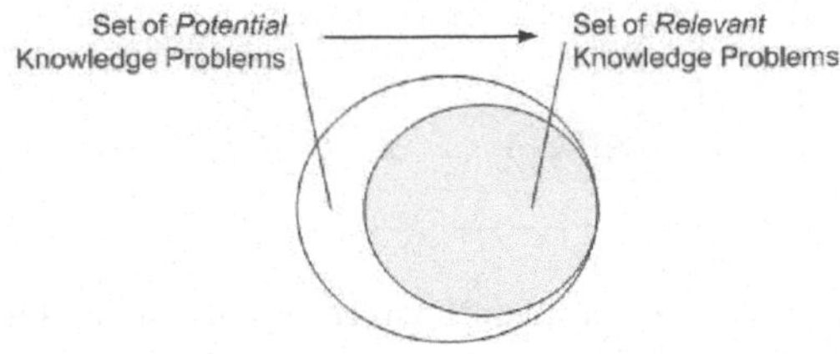

Fig. 5. Potential and Relevant Knowledge Problems

tial knowledge problems represent real problems for organizations. A detailed investigation of *relevant* knowledge problems yields the design of improvement interventions (Step 4) that themselves need to be evaluated (Step 5) regarding their contribution to the addressed business goals (Step 1).

The next section introduces two cases in which the method of this contribution is applied to identify relevant knowledge problems in organizations.

3 Application of Knowledge Problem Patterns

3.1 Knowledge About Customers

Improvement of customer satisfaction is among the top prioritized business goals of organization O. Acknowledging that knowledge about customers plays a key role in achieving higher customer satisfaction, the organization follows a knowledge-oriented approach to address this challenge. Figure 1 depicts the knowledge process "Knowledge about Customers" that was identified and considered to be important by organization O. In this knowledge process, researchers (Resear.) of organization O need to apply knowledge about customers in their respective product development (Product Dev.) business process (see situation 'A' in figure 1). They receive that kind of knowledge through informal meetings (see situation 'B') with sales agents (see situation 'C') that generate that knowledge through customer interaction.

After applying knowledge problem patterns to the knowledge process constellation of figure 6, the following can be concluded for organization O: 1. No knowledge is being explicated in that knowledge process (Pattern 1 "Implicit

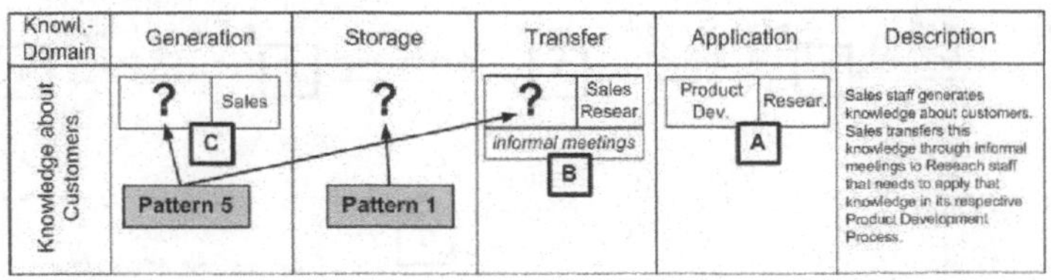

Fig. 6. Pattern-based Knowledge Problem Identification

Knowledge" in figure 6) and 2. The generation as well as the transfer of knowledge about customers is not covered respectively organizationally supported in any business process (Pattern 5 "Knowledge Outage" in figure 6). Findings like these might pose severe problems for organization O's goal to improve satisfaction among its customers. Based on these insights, the organization might focus on increased explication of knowledge (e.g. introduction of meeting minutes) or on the detailed modeling and implementation of sales processes that take knowledge aspects into account to overcome the identified knowledge problems and thereby meet their respective business goals. In doing that, organizations are enabled to implement *necessary* knowledge management interventions that *visibly contribute* to organizational business processes.

3.2 Knowledge About Part Lists

In the second case, the effective design and ongoing improvement of its supply chain is a critical business goal for organization P. When manufacturing automobiles, knowledge about automotive components (part lists) is important to both organizations and their suppliers. Figure 7 depicts the knowledge process related to knowledge about part lists within organization P. In this knowledge process, engineers (Engin.) generate this knowledge within planning processes and store it in engineering data systems. Logisticians (Logist.) and controllers (Contr.) need to apply that knowledge in their respective administrative business processes while suppliers need it in their product delivery processes.

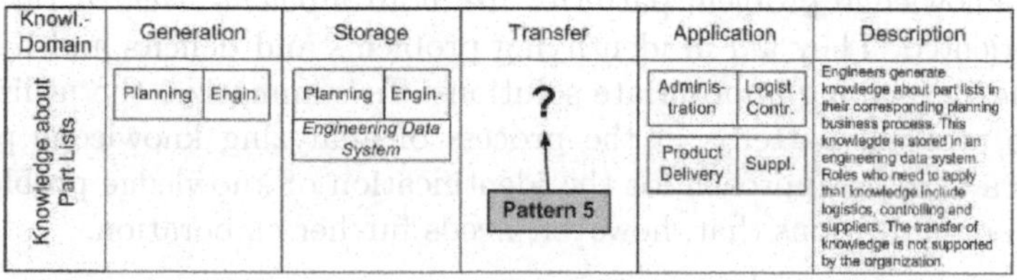

Knowl.-Domain	Generation	Storage	Transfer	Application	Description
Knowledge about Part Lists	Planning / Engin.	Planning / Engin. *Engineering Data System*	? Pattern 5	Adminis-tration / Logist. Contr. Product Delivery / Suppl.	Engineers generate knowledge about part lists in their corresponding planning business process. This knowlegde is stored in an engineering data system. Roles who need to apply that knowledge include logistics, controlling and suppliers. The transfer of knowledge is not supported by the organization.

Fig. 7. Pattern-based Knowledge Problem Identification

After applying knowledge problem patterns to this knowledge process, pattern 5 indicates a potential knowledge problem by highlighting a lack of knowledge transfer. After investigating this potential knowledge problem in greater detail with representatives of organization P, a relevant knowledge problem could be identified: The reason for the lack of transfer in this knowledge process was the technical separation between the engineering data system, used by engineers to store knowledge about part lists, and the logistics software, used by logisticians, controllers and suppliers. This issue led to duplication of data and subsequently to inefficient process cycles. Therefore, the improvement suggestion developed in this case was the technical integration of the two currently separated technological software systems. By doing that, organization P leverages explicit knowledge already available within its software systems for further reuse, to increase efficiency of their supply chain.

4 Experiences

Interesting experiences could be gained from applying the knowledge problem patterns in real world situations. First of all, *relevant* knowledge problems could be identified by following the outlined approach. In discussions with representatives of the case study partners, we received positive feedback concerning the severeness of the identified problems. Second, some patterns were found to be *more stable* than others. Among others, especially the patterns 1 and 5 that were introduced in greater detail led to the identification of *relevant* knowledge problem problems. Furthermore, we experienced that the availability of knowledge problem patterns aids in focus setting. Since we have identified between 20 and 50 knowledge processes in each of our case studies so far, instruments that aid in focus setting are crucial. Knowledge problem patterns help in focussing on relevant areas for improvement.

On the downside, pattern application at the moment is labor intensive and needs interpretation. While the patterns can be applied algorithmically by a computer program, during the time of conducting this research we had to apply them manually because of our explorative research approach. Furthermore, each potential knowledge problem needed to be investigated, verified and discussed with representatives of the organization in detail. This again turned out to be a labor-intensive, yet effective, approach. As indicated in their name, the suggested knowledge problem patterns are more *problem-oriented* rather than solution oriented. They aid in identifying problems and deficits and hardly aid in selecting/developing appropriate solutions. To summarize, the utilization of knowledge problem patterns in the process of analyzing knowledge processes represents a feasible approach for the identification of knowledge problems and -deficits in organizations that, however, needs further elaboration.

5 Future Work

Based on our experiences made with knowledge problem patterns, we suggest two main directions for future work: 1) A software tool that applies knowledge problem patterns to the identified knowledge processes in an automated way would allow for easily testing further empirical data and would significantly speed up the process of experimenting. 2) Quality metrics for the assessment of different knowledge problem patterns need to be introduced. In analogy to retrieval metrics, we suggest to use the notion of precision/recall as indicators for the quality of knowledge problem patterns. While high precision would increase the ratio between identified *relevant* and *potential* knowledge problems, a high recall would increase the set of *relevant* knowledge problems that can be identified with a knowledge problem pattern approach at all.

6 Conclusions

Knowledge problem patterns point organizations to conditions that potentially prevent them from effectively achieving their business goals. In this contribution, a set of knowledge problem patterns and an according process of applying them was introduced. Thereby it is important to keep in mind that the introduced knowledge problem patterns represent indicators for *potential knowledge problems* and no bullet-proof triggers for improvement actions. They thereby represent "objects-to-think-with" for analysts who aim to improve knowledge work in organizations. By identifying knowledge problems in organizations, knowledge problem patterns bear the potential to significantly accelerate analysis efforts and aid in the design of improvement interventions in *critical* business areas. Thereby, organizations are enabled to exploit previously unknown improvement potentials from a knowledge management perspective for successfully addressing their business challenges.

Acknowledgments

The Know-Center is a Competence Center funded within the Austrian Competence Center program K plus under the auspices of the Austrian Ministry of Transport, Innovation and Technology (www.kplus.at).

References

1. Heisig, P.: Business Process oriented Knowledge Management - Methode zur Verknüpfung von Wissensmanagement und Geschäftsprozessgestaltung. In: Proceedings of WM2001, 1. Konferenz Professionelles Wissensmanagement, Baden - Baden. (2001)
2. Abecker, A., Hinkelmann, K., Maus, H., Müller, H.: Geschäftsprozess-orientiertes Wissensmanagement. Springer, Berlin (2002)
3. Remus, U.: Prozeßorientiertes Wissensmanagement - Konzepte und Modellierung. PhD thesis, Wirtschaftswissenschaftliche Fakultät der Universität Regensburg, Regensburg, Deutschland (2002)
4. Strohmaier, M.: A business process oriented approach for the identification and support of organizational knowledge processes. In: 4. Oldenburger Fachtagung Wissensmanagement, Potenziale - Konzepte - Werkzeuge. (2003)
5. Strohmaier, M.: B-KIDE: A Framework and a Tool for Business Process Oriented Knowledge Infrastructure Development. PhD thesis, Institute for Knowledge Management and Knowledge Visualization at the University of Technology, Graz, Austria (December 2004)
6. Kundermann, S.: Ansätze zur Qualitätsverbesserung von Wissensprozessen. Master's thesis, Johann Wolfgang Goethe-Universität, Lehrstuhl für Entwicklung betrieblicher Informationssysteme, Frankfurt am Main (2002)
7. Paulzen, O., Perc, P.: A maturity model for quality improvement in knowledge management. In Wenn, A., McGrath, M., Burstein, F., eds.: Enabling Organisations and Society through Information Systems, Proceedings of the 13th Australasian Conference on Information Systems (ACIS 2002), Melbourne (2002) 243–253

8. Oberweis, A., Paulzen, O.: Kontinuierliche qualitätsverbesserung im wissensmanagement - ein prozessbasiertes reifegradmodell. In: Proceedings der KnowTech 2003 - 5. Konferenz zum Einsatz von Knowledgemanagement in Wirtschaft und Verwaltung. (2003)
9. Alexander, C.: The timeless way of building. Oxford Press (1979)
10. Diefenbruch, M., Hoffmann, M., Misch, A., Schneider, H.: Situated knowledge management - KM on the borderline between chaos and rigidity. In: Proceedings of PAKM 2000 - Conference on Practical Aspects of Knowledge Management. (2000) 8–1–8–7
11. Oxendine, E., Nissen, M.E.: Knowledge process and system design for the carrier battle group. Knowledge and Innovation: Journal of the Knowledge Management Consortium International **1** (2001)
12. Swaak, J., Efimova, L., Kempen, M., Graner, M.: Finding in-house knowledge: Patterns and implications. In: Proceedings of I-Know'04 - 4th International Conference on Knowledge Management, Graz, Austria (2004)

Third German Workshop on Experience Management (GWEM 2005)

Armin Stahl[1], Martin Schaaf[2], and Ralph Traphöner[1]

[1] German Research Center for Artificial Intelligence (DFKI) GmbH,
Research Group Image Understanding and Pattern Recognition (IUPR),
67663 Kaiserslautern, Germany
stahl@informatik.uni-kl.de

[2] University of Hildesheim, Institute for Mathematics and Applied Computer Science,
Data and Knowledge Management Group,
31113 Hildesheim, Germany
schaaf@dwm.uni-hildesheim.de

[3]empolis GmbH,
67657 Kaiserslautern, Germany
ralph.traphoener@empolis.com

1 Workshop Description

Experience Management (EM) as a sub-discipline of Knowledge Management (KM) deals with collecting, modeling, storing, reusing, evaluating, and maintaining experience knowledge, i.e., specific knowledge situated in a particular problem solving context.

The Third German Workshop on Experience Management, initially held in the year 2001 as a event of the Special Interest Group on Knowledge Management, a fusion of the former Knowledge Management Group and the Special Interest Group on Case-Based-Reasoning, was focused on the development and integration of intelligent systems and methodologies for managing experience. Its aim was to provide an interdisciplinary forum where practitioners and researchers can exchange ideas concerning the development of EM systems, present practical experiences about the application of such systems, and discuss future research directions.

The workshop started with an invited talk of Michael M. Richter about the differences between wicked and traditional planning problems. He showed that wicked planning problems require much more interaction with the users and that they cannot be specified exactly without, at least partially, executing them. In the rest of his talk he discussed how experience management may help to solve complex wicked planning problems and illustrated the ideas for some real world application scenarios.

For the following sessions of the workshop we accepted seven submissions for oral presentation and subsequent discussions; four of them addressed the utilization of EM techniques like Case-Based Reasoning (CBR) to various application areas. Virginia Dignum considered Communities of Practice (CoP) as a basis for experience management and presented an approach facilitating their creation and maintenance. Rosina Weber, Ilya Waldstein, Amit Deshpande, and Jason M. Proctor addressed the problem of detecting inconspicuous content in text documents by combining notions from information extraction, case-based reasoning, and computational linguistics. Alexander Tartakovski, Martin Schaaf, and Rainer Maximini provided an approach

K.-D. Althoff et al. (Eds.): WM 2005, LNAI 3782, pp. 269 – 271, 2005.

for the retrieval and configuration of temporary life insurance policies that is based on generalized cases, an extension of traditional CBR technology. From the area of experience management applications in medicine, Olga Vorobieva and Rainer Schmidt reported on a system for therapy recommendations that incorporates, beside former cases, additional knowledge like medical histories of patients.

Two submissions focused on foundational aspects of Case-Based-Reasoning (CBR) technology: Thomas Gabel described in his work the utilization of vocabulary knowledge for learning similarity measures. Thomas R. Roth-Berghofer, Jörg Cassens, and Frode Sørmo addressed the ongoing research for explanations in CBR. They proposed a classification scheme motivated by different perspectives on explanations.

Finally, Mirjam Minor reported on lessons learned from the application of the *Experience Book II*, a repository intended for students that contains textual problem descriptions and solutions to computer related issues.

The four papers published here were selected based on the program committee's evaluation as well as the audience's feedback after the workshop.

The organizers would like to thank all participants for the lively and fruitful discussions.

2 Program Committee

The following people participated in the program committee; we gratefully acknowledge their time and energy:

- Andreas Abecker, FZI Karlsruhe, Germany
- Klaus-Dieter Althoff, Universität Hildesheim, Germany
- Irma Becerra-Fernandez, Florida International University, Miami, US
- Ralph Bergmann, Universität Trier, Germany
- Virginia Dignum, Utrecht University, The Netherlands
- Beatrice Fuchs, Universite Lyon, F
- Peter Funk, Mälardalen University, Sweden
- Mehmet Göker, PricewaterhouseCoopers, San Jose, USA
- Norbert Gronau, Universität Potsdam, Germany
- Ioannis Iglezakis, DaimlerChrysler, Ulm, Germany
- Franz Kurfeß, CalPoly, San Luis Obispo, US
- Mirjam Minor, Humboldt Universität Berlin, Germany
- Markus Nick, Fraunhofer IESE, Kaiserslautern, Germany
- Frank Maurer, University of Calgary, Canada
- Uli Reimer, Swiss Life, Zürich, CH
- Thomas Reinartz, DaimlerChrysler, Ulm, Germany
- Michael M. Richter, Technische Universität Kaiserslautern, Germany
- Thomas Roth-Berghofer, DFKI, Kaiserslautern, Germany
- Rainer Schmidt, Universität Rostock, Germany
- Sascha Schmitt, SAP AG, Germany
- Steffen Staab, Universität Karlsruhe, Germany

- Ivo Vollrath, SAP AG, Germany
- Rosina Weber, Drexel University, US

Finally, we'd like to thank Jane Bogen, Universität Potsdam, for providing us with additional reviews.

On the Use of Vocabulary Knowledge for Learning Similarity Measures

Thomas Gabel

University of Osnabrück, Neuroinformatics Group,
49069 Osnabrück, Germany
thomas.gabel@uos.de

Abstract. A very recent topic in CBR research deals with the automated optimisation of similarity measures—a core component of each CBR application—by using machine learning techniques. In our previous work, a number of approaches to bias and guide the learning process have been proposed aiming at more stable learning results and less susceptibility to overfitting. Those methods support the learner by incorporating background knowledge into the optimisation process. In this paper, we focus on one specific form of knowledge, namely vocabulary knowledge implicitly contained in the model of the respective application domain, as a source to enhance the learning of similarity measures.

1 Introduction

Similarity is a central concept in Case-Based Reasoning. Each case-based application is in need of adequate similarity measures in order to retrieve those cases that are most useful for a given query. The history of CBR has seen various approaches towards modelling similarity measures. On the one hand, simple distance metrics, that base their similarity assessment on a syntactic match between case and query, have been used frequently. Though being definable in a rather straightforward manner, they lead to poor retrieval results in many cases. The alternative is represented by the manual definition of similarity measures, that are highly sophisticated and complex in structure, by knowledge engineers who take the specifics of the respective application domain into consideration. Both alternatives feature certain inherent advantages and drawbacks [9].

Though there have been a number of approaches to learn some elements of a similarity measure (e.g., feature weights [12]), the completely automated construction of an entire similarity measure depicts a rather new idea. Stahl [10] presented a comprehensive framework that is capable of acquiring knowledge-intensive similarity measures from utility feedback and applicable not only to conventional tasks, such as classification, but also in typical CBR domains (e.g. in e-commerce).

In our recent work we have introduced a way to utilise evolutionary algorithms for the learning of similarity measures in the context of the framework mentioned before [11]. Although the application of these machine learning algorithms featured convincing results, under certain circumstances some weaknesses were revealed. For example, when learning on the basis of a small amount

K.-D. Althoff et al. (Eds.): WM 2005, LNAI 3782, pp. 272–283, 2005.

of training data, the algorithms tended to overfit. Tackling this and other problems, we developed a methodology to enhance the optimisation process by incorporating background knowledge [5]. The paper at hand directly builds upon that work and presents further possibilities to stabilise the learning of similarity measures.

The remainder of this article is structured as follows: Section 2 reviews in short the mentioned strategies on exploiting background knowledge to improve the learning process. For more details on that topic the reader is referred to [5,4]. In Section 3 we introduce new concepts on the utilisation of vocabulary knowledge, which may be implicitly contained in the domain model of the CBR system's respective application, as a promising source to support the learning process. Section 4 presents some experimental results gained when applying the concepts explained in the preceding section, and Section 5 concludes.

2 Exploiting Background Knowledge When Learning Similarity Measures

When learning similarity measures, there is a high risk of overfitting the learning results to the training data given. This is due to the enormous search space being taken into consideration during learning. In particular, our representation of local similarity measures (similarity tables for symbolic data types with a small amount of of values and difference-based similarity functions for numeric types, see [11]) allows for learning very complex and specific measures. However, the learnt measures may eventually show poor performance when used for some independent test data set.

Consequently, a self-evident idea is to exploit easily available background knowledge in order to restrict the hypothesis space considered by the evolutionary learning algorithm and thus to bias the optimisation process.

Another crucial issue regarding similarity measures in CBR concerns the modelling effort. Completely manual definition and fully automated learning of knowledge-intensive similarity measures represent two extremes of modelling techniques which both feature certain advantages and drawbacks [9]. When considering a knowledge engineer's (partial) definition of a similarity measure as background knowledge and feeding that into the learning algorithm, a hybrid modelling approach is possible and allows for gaining benefits from both extremes.

2.1 Motivation

The knowledge exploited to enhance the learning can be divided into two groups. Here, we give only a short overview on those knowledge sources, a more detailed description can be found in [5].

Similarity Meta Knowledge. determines general demands on the appearance of learnt similarity measures.

On the one hand, it is possible to define heuristic constraints on the "typical" syntactical shape of local similarity measures. These heuristics refer to several basic properties of similarity measures and can be implemented as weak or strong constraints restricting the search space. A descriptive example concerns the reflexivity of similarity measures: In most application domains a non-reflexive similarity measure would be unpropitious.

On the other hand, the case knowledge container holds a certain amount of unexploited knowledge potential, too. Assumed that the case base contains a sufficient number of cases, the distribution of those cases throughout the entire space of possible cases and especially the distribution of their attribute values, reveals interesting opportunities to improve the learning process. Here, it is possible to employ a statistical case base analysis ("mining" knowledge from the case base) to find out which regions of the space of similarity measures are really worth to be searched thoroughly.

Expert Knowledge. The aid of a knowledge engineer and the incorporation of his/her expert knowledge into the learning process may be very valuable.

Defining similarity measure bottom-up is a complex, time-consuming and probably error-prone task that is reliant to a human domain expert. Searching the whole space of possible similarity measures with the help of a learning algorithm can be time-consuming and is often susceptible to overfitting, if the amount of available training examples is rather small. As already indicated above, here the idea is to meet in the middle, i.e. to incorporate the expert's partial knowledge into the learning process.

Furthermore, when building a CBR system, the expert settles the domain vocabulary, which in turn may include some implicit similarity knowledge to be exploited as well. This kind of expert knowledge is represented as vocabulary knowledge—which corresponds to one of the knowledge containers as introduced [8]. More precisely, the vocabulary provides possibilities to constrain the search space by utilising the information that is contained within *structured data types*, such as symbolic types with an ordered or taxonomic value range. This paper in particular focuses on that vocabulary knowledge source.

2.2 Knowledge-Based Optimisation Filters

To realise the actual restriction of the search space we have introduced the concept of knowledge-based optimisation filters (kbOF) [4]. With that name we denote objects that, on the one hand, store some gathered knowledge concerning the learning of similarity measures. On the other hand, they actively interfere with the learning process, in order to bias and direct the search for optimal similarity measures. For the implementation of the evolutionary algorithm this means that a kbOF exerts its influence during offspring generation: Newly generated individuals contradicting too much to the filter's knowledge are discarded. Furthermore, the kbOF is allowed to explicitly give advice to genetic operators adapting their behaviour in such a way that more realistic similarity measures are created.

During kbOF-based learning the evolutionary population for each local similarity measure to be learnt is equipped with a knowledge filter. Together with an additional filter for the feature weights, $n + 1$ filters are employed for a case representation consisting of n attributes.

3 Utilisation of Vocabulary Knowledge

Before having the first thought about the definition of similarity measures, a knowledge engineer has usually already invested a lot of modelling effort: Prior to settling similarity measures, the respective application domain—in terms of attributes and corresponding data types[1]—must be modelled. This involves tasks such as determining which case attributes are to be used, which are indiscriminant and which are possibly dependent on each other. Moreover, each attribute must be associated with an appropriate data type and domain, respectively. In other words, the expert is fully responsible for the definition of the CBR system's vocabulary knowledge. In this section we want to show how a little of this knowledge implicitly encoded into the domain vocabulary can be exploited to support the learning of similarity measures. We focus on two specific forms of symbolic data types whose domains can be organised in a structured way: taxonomic symbolic and ordered symbolic data types.

So far, we represented any local similarity measure for a symbolic data type as a similarity table and conducted the optimisation on corresponding matrices (consisting of ϕ^2 entries for an attribute A using a data type with $|D_A| = \phi$ elements in its domain). However, local similarity measures for attributes based on taxonomic and ordered symbolic data types are of course definable with respect to the characteristics of those types: This property will be exploited by the concepts we introduce in the following.

3.1 Taxonomic Symbolic Attributes

The elements of a symbolic data type for a specific attribute may be structurable in a taxonomy. Of course, that taxonomic ordering effects the belonging local similarity measure and the way the similarity between a query and a case is computed. In Figure 1 we show the example of a taxonomic data type used for a *MaritalStatus* attribute.

Definition 1. (Taxonomic Symbolic Attribute)
*Let A be a symbolic attribute with value range $D_A = \{d_1, \ldots, d_n\}$. A is called a **taxonomic attribute**, if there exists an accentuated root element $r \in D_A$ for the taxonomy. Furthermore, the remaining elements $d \in D_A \setminus r$ must be arranged in a tree structure $\mathcal{T}_A$ with r as root of the tree. The predicate $isChild(d_i, d_j)$ is true, if d_i is a (possibly indirect) successor of d_j within $\mathcal{T}_A$.*

In [1] the author describes very detailed how taxonomies can be used for representing case features and also addresses the resulting implications for appropriate local similarity measures. There, the focus is laid upon possible semantics

[1] We assume the commonly used attribute-value based representation.

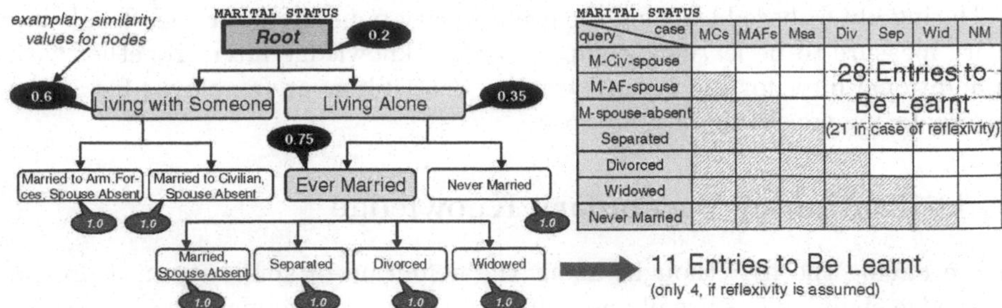

Fig. 1. Representation of Taxonomic Symbolic Similarity Measures as Individuals (left) and Comparison to a Representation as Similarity Table Individual (right)

for leaves and inner nodes as well as on the respective similarity assessments. Here, we employ a simplified approach to calculate the similarity for taxonomic attributes.

Definition 2. (Taxonomic Similarity Measure)
Let A be a taxonomic attribute with its taxonomic value range $D_A = \{d_1, \dots, d_n\}$ arranged in $\mathcal{T}_A$. Moreover, let each node d of $\mathcal{T}_A$ be annotated with a similarity value $s_d \in [0;1]$ so that it holds:

$$s_i \leq s_j \quad \textit{iff} \quad dist(i,r) \leq dist(j,r) \tag{1}$$

where dist measures the distance (number of edges) between two tree nodes and r denotes $\mathcal{T}_A$'s root element.

Then, the ***taxonomic local similarity measure*** *for A is defined as*

$$\begin{aligned} sim_A : D_A \times D_A &\rightarrow [0;1] \\ (q,c) \quad &\mapsto s_{NCP(q,c)} \end{aligned}$$

where $NCP(q,c)$ determines the nearest common parent node for q and c.

Sometimes, it can be advantageous to allow the leaves of $\mathcal{T}_A$ to be elements of D_A only, i.e. it holds $D_A \subsetneq nodes(\mathcal{T}_A)$. Then, the notation introduced above is still appropriate, if we consider D_A to be extended by $\mathcal{T}_A$'s inner nodes.

Representing Taxonomic Individuals

When intending to learn similarity measures for taxonomic attributes, we need to determine an appropriate representation of such measures as individuals. In [11] we made use of vectors of sampling points to represent difference-based similarity functions and of similarity matrices to represent symbolic attributes' similarity tables. Here, we propose to employ trees as individuals that correspond to the taxonomically ordered value range of the respective attribute.

Definition 3. (Similarity Tree Individual)
An individual I representing a taxonomic local similarity measure sim_A for the taxonomic symbolic attribute A is coded as a tree T_A^I whose structure is identical to $\mathcal{T}_A$. The nodes of that ***similarity tree*** *T_A^I are real numbers whose values*

are determined by the node annotations s_i $(i \in \{1, \ldots, n\})$ *that are made to the nodes in* $\mathcal{T}_A$.

When realising similarity tree individuals according to Definition 3, essentially the condition given by Equation 1 must be fulfilled. This means, when creating a new similarity tree individual care must be taken that the similarity values in a similarity tree are increasing from the root towards the leaves of the tree.

Genetic Operators

The application of mutation operators (for their accurate definition see [11]) is straightforward, when using the similarity values of a tree node's predecessor node (i.e., s_p) and the maximum of its m child nodes ($max\{s_{c_1}, \cdots, s_{c_m}\}$) as lower and upper bound, respectively, for the determination of the adapted (mutated) value. Arithmetic crossover's [7] application is trouble-free as well, since an averaged similarity tree individual created from two parent individuals, that fulfill all relations, is consistent with those relations, too.

Crossover variants that make use of splitting the parental genome and composing the offspring by genome parts from its parents (e.g. simple crossover) are also applicable to similarity tree individuals. On the one hand, the similarity tree may be mapped to a flat vector of similarity values, so that the operators introduced for similarity function and similarity table individuals [11] can be used without change. However, in addition to the existing crossover operators we also suggest and make use of another specialised genetic operator that is designed for taxonomic individuals specifically:

- *Sub-tree crossover:* Given a taxonomic attribute A whose value range is arranged in a tree $\mathcal{T}_A$ and two parent similarity tree individuals $\mathcal{T}_A^{I_1}$ and $\mathcal{T}_A^{I_2}$, sub-tree crossover randomly picks a node d from $\mathcal{T}_A$. Then, it creates the offspring $\mathcal{T}_A^{I_{new}}$ according to
$$t_i^{I_{new}} = \begin{cases} t_i^{I_1} & \text{if } d \rhd i \\ t_i^{I_2} & \text{else} \end{cases} \quad \text{for all } i \in \mathcal{T}_A$$
where the operator $\rhd$ denotes that i is a node within the sub-tree of $\mathcal{T}_A$ having root d.

Search Space Restriction

Analysing the restriction of the search space that can be achieved, when utilising information about an attribute's taxonomic value range, we ought to consider the worst case scenario in which the minimal restriction is reached.

First of all, we need to stress that our current realisation does not yet allow to use inner tree nodes as values for queries or cases, i.e. the values from D_A are to be found in the leaves exclusively. This entails the following implications:

- Differentiated semantics for inner nodes, as depicted by [1] cannot be employed. As asymmetries in the respective similarity measure result from different interpretations of inner nodes when used as query or case, only symmetric taxonomic similarity measures can be learnt up to now.

- Since we allow values from D_A ($|D_A| = \phi$) in the leaves of a similarity tree individual only, additional nodes (including a root element) are necessary to form the tree. Thus, in the worst case (binary tree) $\phi - 1$ additional nodes are needed, i.e. a similarity tree individual maximally consists of a total of $2\phi - 1$ similarity values.

Accordingly, for a similarity tree individual I for attribute A with $D_A = \{d_1, \ldots, d_\phi\}$ maximally $2\phi-1$ independent similarity values have to be optimised. If we had treated A as a (non-taxonomic) symbolic attribute and used similarity matrices instead (assuming symmetric measures only), there would have been $\frac{\phi^2+\phi}{2}$ free parameters to be tuned[2]. Hence, the utilisation of vocabulary, here taxonomic, knowledge in fact results in a search space restriction as it holds $2\phi - 1 \leq \frac{\phi^2+\phi}{2}$ for all $\phi \in \mathbb{N}$. Note, that the actual gain is in fact higher than maybe presumed from that inequality: Due to the taxonomic structuring of D_A and due to the relations associated with all nodes (cf. Equation 1) within the tree, most of the $2\phi - 1$ similarity values cannot be chosen from $[0; 1]$ but from a smaller subinterval of $[0; 1]$ only.

3.2 Ordered Symbolic Attributes

A simpler ordering of a symbolic attribute's allowed values $d_1, \ldots, d_n$ (simpler in comparison to a taxonomic ordering) is given, when the elements d_i are ordered totally.

Definition 4. (Ordered Symbolic Attribute)
Let A be a symbolic attribute with value range $D_A = \{d_1, \ldots, d_n\}$. A is called an ***ordered symbolic attribute****, if each d_i is associated with a numeric scaling value $o_i \in \mathbb{R}$, so that it holds $o_i < o_j$ for all $i < j$.*

The mentioned associations o_i may then be employed as representative for the actual elements d_i in order to realise an ordered symbolic similarity measure on the basis of a difference-based similarity function.

Definition 5. (Ordered Symbolic Similarity Measure)
Let A be an ordered symbolic attribute with its ordered value range $D_A = \{d_1, \ldots, d_n\}$ and belonging numeric associations $o_1, \ldots, o_n$. Then, the ***ordered symbolic local similarity measure*** *is defined as*

$$\begin{aligned} sim_A : D_A \times D_A &\to [0; 1] \\ (q, c) &\mapsto sim_{A_O(q,c)} \end{aligned}$$

where sim_{A_O} is a difference-based similarity function that is defined on $I_d = [o_1 - o_n, o_n - o_1]$ and that assigns $sim_{A_O}(o_i, o_j)$ on the basis of the difference $o_i - o_j$.

[2] The denominator is 2 as we only consider symmetric similarity measures, here.

Representing Ordered Symbolic Individuals
An ordered symbolic similarity measure sim_A shall be represented by an individual that consists of two real-valued vectors. The first one is to define the association o_i mentioned above and in so doing affects the scaling of A's value range. Thus, it basically determines the x-axis on which the second vector with its similarity values operates: Figure 2 illustrates how we represent individuals for local similarity measures with an ordered value range, giving an example for an ordered symbolic attribute *RainbowColour.*

Definition 6. (Ordered Symbolic Individuals)
*Let A be an ordered symbolic attribute with value range $D_A = \{d_1, \ldots, d_n\}$ and belonging associations $o_1, \ldots, o_n$. An **ordered symbolic individual** representing an ordered symbolic similarity measure sim_A is coded as a tuple of two vectors: $I = (O_A^I, V_A^I)$. Here, $O_A^I = (o_1^I, \ldots, o_n^I)$, called **scaling vector**, represents a normalisation of the associations $o_1, \ldots, o_n$ according to*

$$o_i^I = \frac{o_i - o_1}{o_n - o_1} \qquad \text{for all } i \in \{1, \ldots, n\}$$

so that it holds $o_i^I \leq o_j^I$ for all $i < j$ as well as $o_1^I = 0$ and $o_n^I = 1$.

*$V_A^I = (v_1^I, \ldots, v_s^I)$, called **similarity vector**[3], represents a collection of a difference-based similarity function's similarity values at sampling points distributed equally over $[o_1^I - o_n^I, o_n^I - o_1^I] = [-1; 1]$, where s denotes the number of sampling points used.*

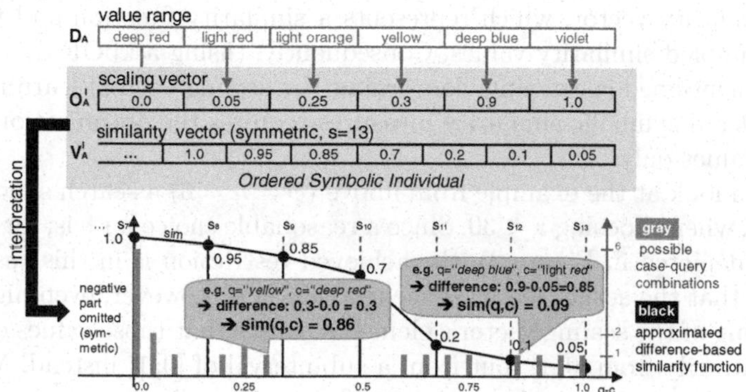

Fig. 2. Representation of Ordered Symbolic Similarity Measures as Individuals

During optimisation, when ordered symbolic individuals are used in the scope of an evolutionary algorithm, both vectors are learnt simultaneously. For the constraints related to the scaling vector O_A^I, the functionality provided by kbOFs can be utilised. Here, we mainly need to meet relational constraints ($o_i^I < o_j^I$ for all $i < j$) as well as predefined values ($o_1^I = 0$ and $o_n^I = 1$).

---

[3] Note, that a similarity vector V_A^I corresponds to a similarity function individual, as defined in [11].

Genetic Operators
Regarding genetic operators the situation for ordered symbolic individuals (in particular for its first component, the scaling vector) is not much different from the situation for taxonomic ones (see Section 3.1). In addition to the previous operators, we introduce a further specialised, heuristic crossover operator that is responsive to the constraints that must be fulfilled by the respective individual's scaling vector:

– *Information exchange crossover:* Given two parent scaling vectors $O_A^{I_1}, O_A^{I_2} \in [0;1]^n$, this operator mingles both vectors' elements and sets
$$z = (z_1, \dots, z_{2n}) \text{ with } z_i \leq z_j \text{ for all } i < j$$
$$\text{and } \forall i \exists j \text{ so that } z_i = o_j^{I_1} \text{ or } z_i = o_j^{I_2}$$
The offspring is formed according to
$$O_A^{I_{new}} = (z_1, z_3, \dots, z_{2n-1}) \text{ or } O_A^{I_{new}} = (z_2, z_4, \dots, z_{2n}).$$

Search Space Restriction
Let us again assume an ordered symbolic attribute A with an ordered value range $D_A = \{d_1, \dots, d_\phi\}$ (note, that $\phi = n$). Treating that attribute as a "normal" symbolic one and modelling its similarity measure with a similarity table—using, so to say, an empty knowledge filter—, there would be ϕ^2 independent entries to be adjusted. Making use of the total ordering of D_A's value range, however, the search space becomes restricted: Doing so, the modelling of ordered symbolic local similarity measures requires the scaling vector, which consists of ϕ elements, and the similarity vector, which represents a similarity function and thus consists of s sampled similarity values. Consequently, (using a kbOF that contains the above-mentioned constraints concerning the scaling vector) learning on the basis of ordered symbolic similarity measures requires the optimisation of $\phi + s$ similarity values only.

Having a look at the example from above ($\phi = n = 6$) a search space restriction occurs, when choosing $s < 30$. Since a reasonable choice for s is, for instance, $s = 13$ (as depicted in Figure 2), the achieved restriction is in this case almost 50%. Note, that the actual search space restriction is, however, even higher. The total ordering of the scaling vector's elements causes that those values cannot be chosen arbitrarily from $[0;1]$, but from a subinterval of $[0;1]$ instead. Moreover, for $o_1^I = 0$ and $o_n^I = 1$ the values are even fixed.

4 Experiments

In the following we present some experimental results gained from an evaluation of the concepts presented in the previous section. We here focus on the exploitation of taxonomic symbolic attributes only, leaving an analysis of using ordered symbolic individuals for future work.

For this purpose we have chosen a classification domain from the UCI Machine Learning Repository [3]—the *Adult* domain where the task is to predict whether a person earns more than 50k dollar a year—in which the employment of taxonomically structured data types seemed advisable. The case representation in this domain consists of 14 attributes, six of which are real-numbered, the remaining eight ones being symbolic attributes. We processed these attributes as follows:

1. First, we removed all the numeric attributes, since in the scope of this evaluation we want to analyse the influence of taxonomically structured data types only. Of course, we are aware that this removal of case attributes will significantly impair the system's overall performance in producing correct classifications. However, we need to stress that it is not our aim here to create the best CBR-based classifier possible, but to examine the usability of vocabulary background knowledge for the process of learning similarity measures.
2. The data records contained in the *Adult* domain originate from the the "CPS Current Population Study"[4]. With the help of a description of the data [6] and using our common-sense knowledge we derived taxonomies for the domains of six out of the eight symbolic attributes (the domains of two symbolic attributes turned out to be not structurable in a taxonomy, so these attributes were removed as well). An example for such a taxonomy is depicted in Figure 1 for the attribute *MaritalStatus*.
3. In a third step, we constructed a kbOF for each of the taxonomies created in the previous step. These so-called t-Filters primarily included the relations resulting from Definition 2. Apart from these constraints, those filters were not enriched with any further knowledge—this is in contrast to the experiments described in [5] where filter classes were introduced and each single filter incorporated a number of different knowledge pieces. As a consequence, we here can investigate the effects of taxonomic vocabulary knowledge solely.

The actual experiments we conducted were based, on the one hand, on filterless learning (i.e. not using any background knowledge at all and thus learning conventional similarity matrices, cf. the right part of Figure 1) and, on the other hand, on the t-Filters we created in step 3.

In Figure 3 (left) we summarise the achieved error reductions in the *Adult* domain for increasing training data sizes (x-axis). The baseline similarity measure represents, on the one hand, a knowledge-poor (default) similarity measure, into whose construction no further knowledge engineering effort has been put, i.e. the similarity assessment here is based on an uninformed syntactic match. On the other hand, we illustrate the accuracies that resulted from a similarity measure that was obtained from filterless learning. The charts' third data row sketches the increased accuracies that could be gained due to the incorporation of explicit vocabulary background knowledge through the use of a t-Filter.

Obviously, the classification accuracy on some independent test data set can be increased by up to 2%, depending on the amount of training data used (left chart). It is worth remembering that this improvement can be reached with almost no effort, simply by "switching a flag", i.e. by prompting the learning

[4] `http://www.bls.census.gov/cps`

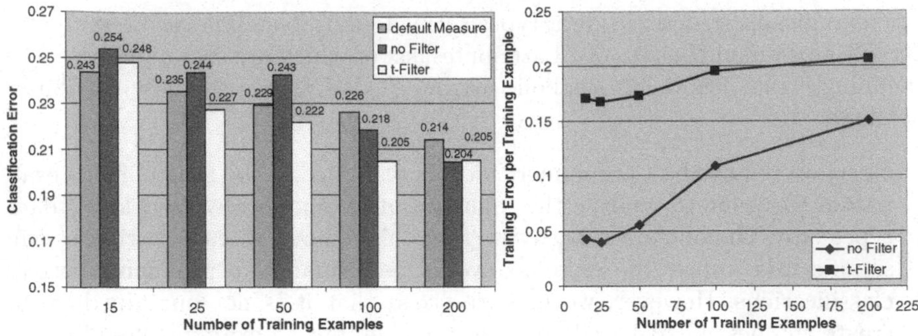

Fig. 3. Experimental Results: Gains Due to the Incorporation of Vocabulary Knowledge (left) and Hindering from Overfitting (right)

algorithm to make use of the taxonomic structures found in the case representation's attributes.

In the right chart we illustrate how the learning algorithm yields those improvements: There the values of the error on the training data (a specialised measure corresponding to the fitness of individuals within the scope of the evolutionary algorithm, see [4] for details) is shown. Apparently, the additional knowledge included in the t-Filter impedes the learner from specialising too much to the training data—especially for small amounts of training data used—, which means that its tendency to overfitting is reduced and its ability in generalising is increased.

5 Conclusions

Different forms of knowledge may be exploited when intending to bias and support the learning of knowledge-intensive similarity measures in CBR. Similarity meta knowledge comes with almost no acquisition effort [4]. Expert knowledge, on the other hand, is more expensive in terms of acquiring it, but is likely to yield higher learning improvements [5]. This paper dealt with a specific sub-form of expert knowledge: vocabulary expert knowledge. Modelling a CBR application's domain vocabulary represents a time-consuming and demanding process which, however, a knowledge engineer indispensably must perform as one of the first steps when creating a CBR system. Accordingly, after that modelling phase, the vocabulary is fixed and the knowledge it inherently contains can be exploited for supporting the settling of similarity measures without any further cost.

We developed concepts to utilise the knowledge implicitly contained in structured (taxonomic and ordered symbolic) data types during the learning process. Our evaluation proved empirically that the knowledge encoded in taxonomic data types indeed helps to bring about better learning results. Possible directions for future research involve more comprehensive evaluation studies, in particular an investigation on how the gains due to the incorporation of vocabulary knowledge described in this article can be combined with other knowledge sources and to which extent synergies can be achieved. Moreover, an extension of our framework to incorporate background knowledge into the optimisation process, so that it can handle even more complex forms of vocabulary knowledge, e.g. by utilising object-oriented case representations [2], is aspired.

Acknowledgements

The author would like to thank Gilbert Esser for his support during data collection and preparation.

References

1. R. Bergmann. On the Use of Taxonomies for Representing Case Features and Local Similarity Measures. In *Proceedings of the 6th German Workshop on CBR*, 1998.
2. R. Bergmann and A. Stahl. Similarity Measures for Object-Oriented Case Representations. In *Proceedings of the 4th European Workshop on CBR*, 1998.
3. C.L. Blake and C.J. Merz. UCI repository of machine learning databases, 1998.
4. T. Gabel. Learning Similarity Measures: Strategies to Enhance the Optimisation Process. Master thesis, Kaiserslautern University of Technology, 2003. http://www.inf.uos.de/tgabel/publications/GabelDA.ps.
5. T. Gabel and A. Stahl. Exploiting Background Knowledge When Learning Similarity Measures. In *Proceedings of the 7th European Conference on CBR*, 2004.
6. J.M. Jungblut. LES — Methods and Variables of CPS 97, 2000.
7. Z. Michalewicz. *Genetic Algorithms + Data Structures = Evolution Programs.* Springer Verlag, 1996.
8. M.M. Richter. The Knowledge Contained in Similarity Measures. Invited Talk, The First International Conference on Case-Based Reasoning, Portugal, 1995.
9. A. Stahl. Defining Similarity Measures: Top-Down vs. Bottom-Up. In *Proceedings of the 6th European Conference on Case-Based Reasoning.* Springer, 2002.
10. A. Stahl. *Learning of Knowledge-Intensive Similarity Measures in Case-Based Reasoning.* Ph.D. thesis, Technical University of Kaiserslautern, 2003.
11. A. Stahl and T. Gabel. Using Evolution Programs to Learn Local Similarity Measures. In *Proceedings of the 5th International Conference on CBR.* Springer, 2003.
12. D. Wettschereck and David W. Aha. Weighting Features. In *Proceeding of the 1st International Conference on Case-Based Reasoning.* Springer, 1995.

Introduction Strategy and Feedback from an Experience Management Project

Mirjam Minor

Institut für Informatik, Humboldt-Universität, Berlin
minor@informatik.hu-berlin.de

Abstract. The ExperienceBook is case-based system to support Experience Management activities in organizations. In this article, we will describe lessons learned from an employment of the ExperienceBook II within a discussion forum for students. This application has a been in use at our university's institute for informatics from October 2003 until January 2004 and in a second turn since October 2004. The article focusses rather on organisational aspects than on the technical details of the used concepts. Success factors and drawbacks are discussed. The article gives the basic functions of the system, presents the system introduction and motivation strategy, explains the feedback results, and discusses some conclusions and related work.

1 Introduction

Experience Management (EM) deals with the experiential knowledge of an organisation, i.e. the experiences of the people that are mainly stored in their heads and are used for solving current problems. EM is a special form of knowledge management that is restricted to task-based knowledge (see [Bergmann, 2002]). The main processes of an EM system handle the following four issues (compare also with [Minor, 2001]): making knowledge explicit, storing the knowledge, making it available in a task-based context, and keeping the knowledge up-to-date. It is crucial for the success of an EM system to let the users participate in all developing phases of the system: before the system is started, during the first weeks of usage, and after the system has been established or failed.

The ExperienceBook II is an EM application that provides a discussion forum and a shared repository for experiential knowledge. The repository is a case base consisting of textual cases with descriptions of the students' daily problems and their solutions. This includes computer science related problems like hints how to use a certain software but also very general issues like a list of the best pubs on the campus. The ExperienceBook has an intelligent search mechanism for the case data that computes the best matching cases concerning a query. An advertising strategy aims to motivate the students to query the system, write new cases, and comment existing cases. So, experiential knowledge that is hidden in the heads shall be transformed into explicit knowledge.

K.-D. Althoff et al. (Eds.): WM 2005, LNAI 3782, pp. 284 – 292, 2005.

2 Basic Design of the System

Before we will discuss the organisational aspects of the ExperienceBook, we will give a quick introduction to the basic design of the system. It has a client-server architecture with a central server holding the case data in a Case Retrieval Net [Lenz and Burkhard, 1996]. The server waits for requests from CGI clients. The Web interface allows easy access from different operating systems via html browsers; the server queue handles multi-user access.

Queries consist of a text in natural language that can be enriched with an attribute value for *SUBDOMAIN* representing the application area of the requested cases. The real application deals with German texts, but we have translated the examples into English. A sample query in the subdomain UNIX is 'How can I list the content of a directory?'. For the users, the cases are semi-structured texts that are enriched with attribute-value pairs. The left hand side of Table 1 contains a sample case in XML, Figure 3 shows the same case as it is displayed on the graphical user interphase.

Table 1. Sample case in both representation forms: in XML and as set of information entities

<CASE> **<CASE_NUMBER>** 12 **</CASE_NUMBER>**	**CASE_IDENTIFIER** = 12
<RETRIEVAL_ATTRIBUTES> SUBDOMAIN=UNIX **</RETRIEVAL_ATTRIBUTES>**	**IE_LIST_RATTR** = [(SUBDOMAIN, UNIX)]
<INFO_ATTRIBUTES> author = M. Minor email = minor@informatik.hu-berlin.de time_stamp = 1064844043 last_edited_at = 09-29-2003 revision = 1 **</INFO_ATTRIBUTES>**	
<DESCRIPTION> How to send an email from the UNIX pool? **</DESCRIPTION>**	**IE_LIST_DESCRIPTION** = [SEND, EMAIL, UNIX POOL]
<SOLUTION> mail <mail_address> from command line sends the following text to <mail_address>, end of input with Ctrl-D **</SOLUTION>**	**IE_LIST_SOLUTION** = [MAIL, COMMAND LINE, SEND, TEXT, END, INPUT, CTRL-D]
<COMMENTS> send the content of a file as email, e.g. myLetter: mail hdb@informatik.hu-berlin.de < myLetter.txt use a mail tool like elm or pine **</COMMENTS>** **</CASE>**	**IE_LIST_COMMENTS** = [SEND, CONTENT, FILE, EMAIL, MAIL, MAIL TOOL, ELM, PINE]

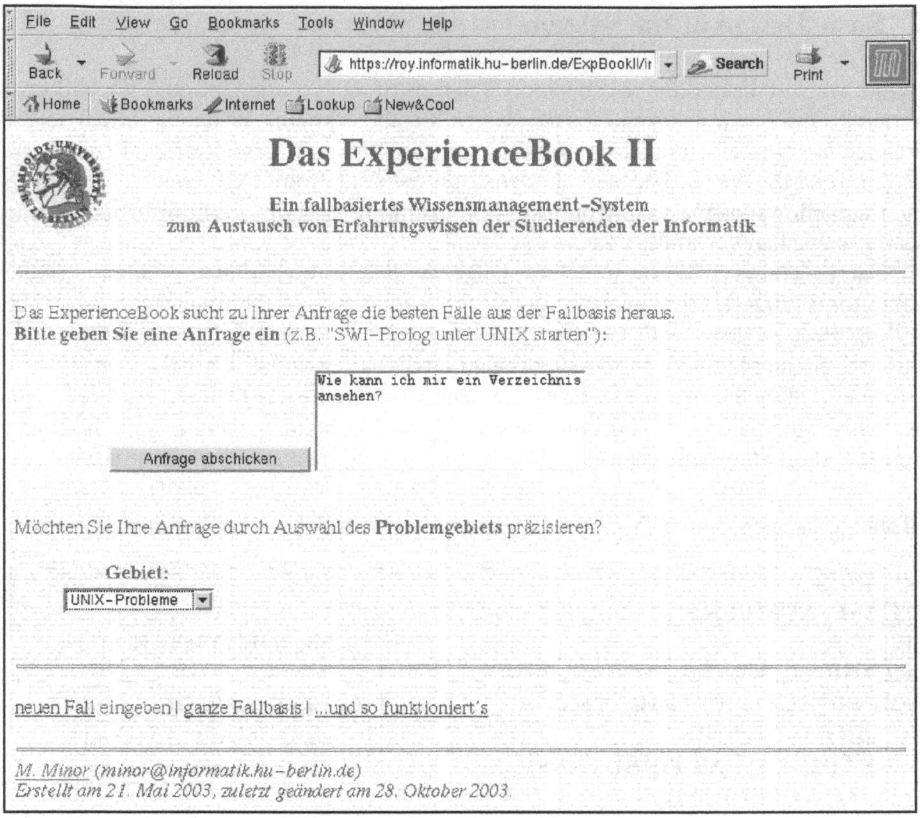

Fig. 1. Query page of the ExperienceBook II

The meaningful concepts are extracted automatically from the textual sections following the method of [Lenz *et al.*, 1998]: A text parser uses dictionaries with important technical terms of the domain and general language terms. The dictionaries contain also different spellings, grammatical forms, and abbreviations of a concept. After the parsing process, a case has a set of information entities for each section (see right hand side of Table 1). The queries are parsed in the same way.

The similarity of a query and the particular cases of the case base is computed by means of a composite similarity function *SIM*. It compares the query with the *DESCRIPTION* and the *RETRIEVAL_ATTRIBUTES* section of the case by means of the extracted sets of information entities of both. *SIM* uses as well a dictionary of local similarity values between information entities, e.g. sim(__LINUX__, __UNIX__) = 0.5 or sim(__ASCII PRINTER__, __POSTSCRIPT PRINTER__) = 0.3. The similarity of a query and a case is a weighted sum of local similarity values:

$$SIM(Query, Case) = \sum_{e_i \in Query} \sum_{e_j \in Case} sim(e_i, e_j).$$

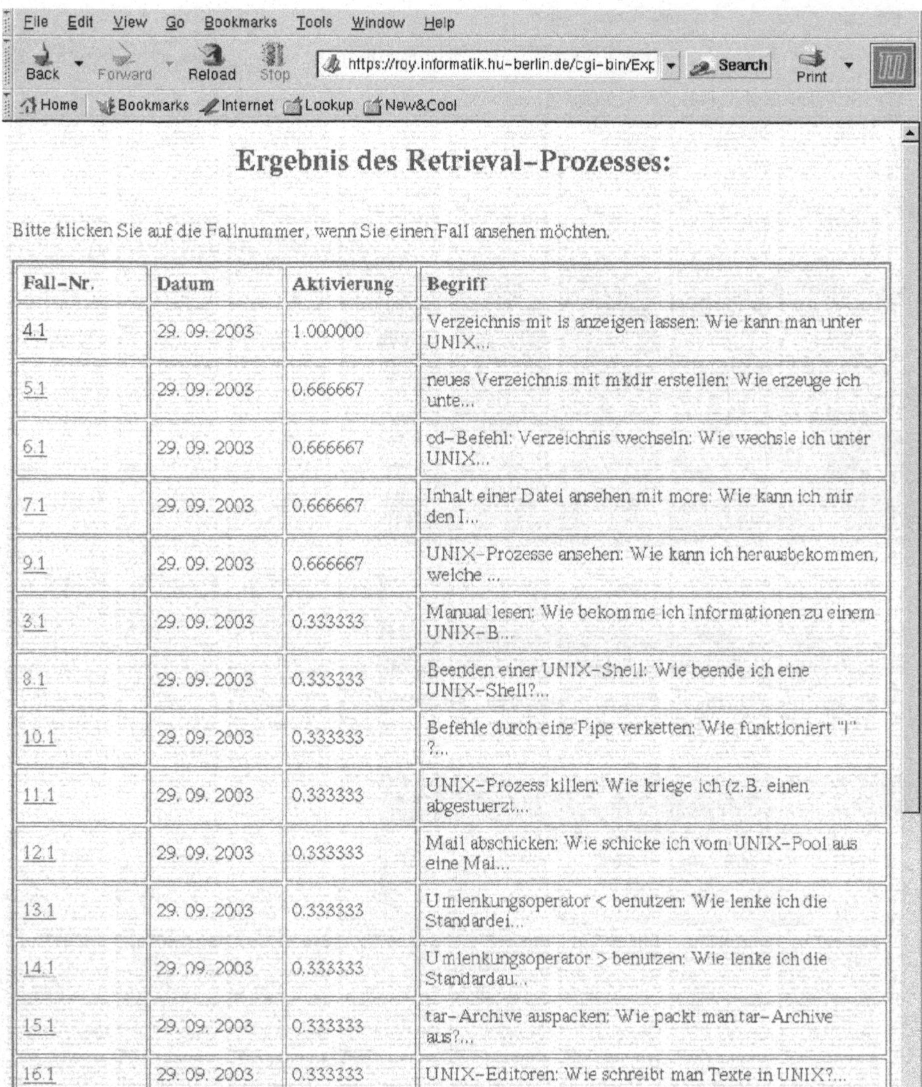

Ergebnis des Retrieval-Prozesses:

Bitte klicken Sie auf die Fallnummer, wenn Sie einen Fall ansehen möchten.

Fall-Nr.	Datum	Aktivierung	Begriff
4.1	29. 09. 2003	1.000000	Verzeichnis mit ls anzeigen lassen: Wie kann man unter UNIX...
5.1	29. 09. 2003	0.666667	neues Verzeichnis mit mkdir erstellen: Wie erzeuge ich unte...
6.1	29. 09. 2003	0.666667	cd-Befehl: Verzeichnis wechseln: Wie wechsle ich unter UNIX...
7.1	29. 09. 2003	0.666667	Inhalt einer Datei ansehen mit more: Wie kann ich mir den I...
9.1	29. 09. 2003	0.666667	UNIX-Prozesse ansehen: Wie kann ich herausbekommen, welche ...
3.1	29. 09. 2003	0.333333	Manual lesen: Wie bekomme ich Informationen zu einem UNIX-B...
8.1	29. 09. 2003	0.333333	Beenden einer UNIX-Shell: Wie beende ich eine UNIX-Shell?...
10.1	29. 09. 2003	0.333333	Befehle durch eine Pipe verketten: Wie funktioniert "|" ?...
11.1	29. 09. 2003	0.333333	UNIX-Prozess killen: Wie kriege ich (z.B. einen abgestuerzt...
12.1	29. 09. 2003	0.333333	Mail abschicken: Wie schicke ich vom UNIX-Pool aus eine Mai...
13.1	29. 09. 2003	0.333333	Umlenkungsoperator < benutzen: Wie lenke ich die Standardei...
14.1	29. 09. 2003	0.333333	Umlenkungsoperator > benutzen: Wie lenke ich die Standardau...
15.1	29. 09. 2003	0.333333	tar-Archive auspacken: Wie packt man tar-Archive aus?...
16.1	29. 09. 2003	0.333333	UNIX-Editoren: Wie schreibt man Texte in UNIX?...

Fig. 2. Retrieval result for the query in Figure 1

The query result is an ordered list of best matching cases. An example of a query and the result of the retrieval is shown in the snapshots in Figure 1 and Figure 2. This case-based retrieval mechanism is more precise than a simple string matching, for instance. To ensure the quality of the retrieval results over time, the dictionaries with information entities and local similarity values have to be maintained when some new cases have been written. Our experiences have shown that 'non-CBR experts' quickly understand the dictionaries and that the time effort for filling them is between 30 seconds and 10 minutes per new case. So, this text comparison method lies in a good

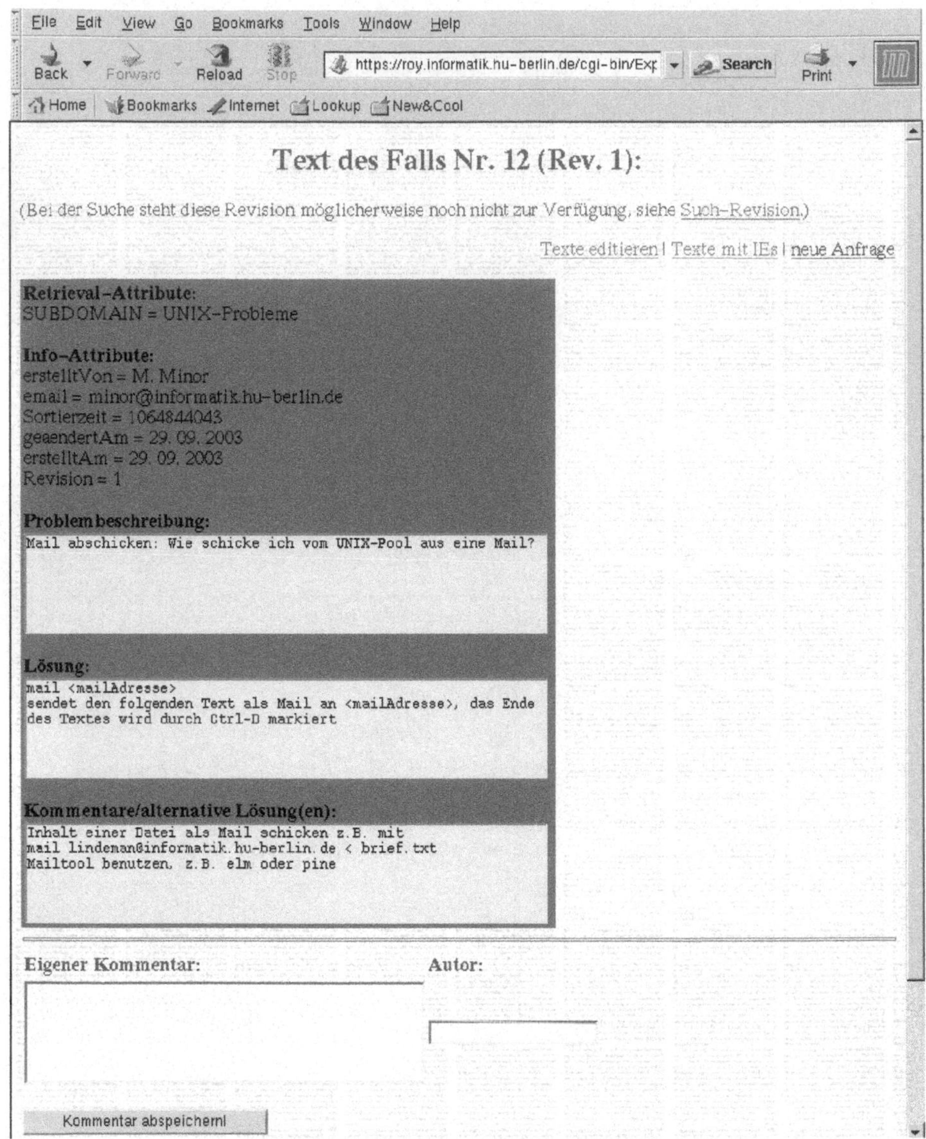

Fig. 3. Sample case of Table 1 as it is presented to the user

balance between a low-effort modelling process and a satisfying solution of the text comparison problem that is independent on the actually used terms (the so-called 'paraphrase problem'). Before the system waits for queries, the texts are mapped on sets of information entities and linked in the net of local similarity relationships. With this pre-compiling, the retrieval is very quick and has a performance of less than a millisecond.

3 System Introduction and Motivation Strategy

We followed the principle of user participation in all developing phases of the system: before the system has been started, during the first weeks of usage, and after the system has failed in the first turn and has been established in a second turn with a new generation of users. This principle led us to four different kind of activities:

- Some of the users helped us to prepare an initial case base.
- All potential users were informed by advertising activities.
- The system works with intrinsic motivation and in a privacy-keeping manner only.
- The system is embedded in an environment that aims to stimulate communication.

The system has been filled with some dozens of initial cases to motivate the users to ask queries from the beginning. These cases have been created from three different sources:

1. From teaching material to a lecture on practical informatics from the year before
2. From the Web pages of the system administration group of our institute
3. From the results of a writing session of second-year students after a presentation of the project

Secondly, the potential users of the system have been informed on several channels: per email, per link from the Web page of the lecture on practical informatics, and via face-to-face communication in a meeting of the students' self-administration and in the lecture. The access statistics showed that the face-to-face advertisment has been the most successful. The results of a feedback questionnaire (see Section 4) has confirmed this observation.

The retrieval is anonymous to avoid an atmosphere of being controlled by lecturers. We decided to abstain from extrinsic motivation like giving extra scores for writing a case, for instance. The usage of the system and the authoring of new cases is voluntary, the motivation is intrinsic and has to be done by convincement only.
We aim to stimulate the communication between the users:

- All users can read and write cases. The access is restricted to institute members.
- Cases can be commented, e.g. extended with an alternative solution.
- Cases can be edited, i.e. false information can be deleted by each person detecting it. A copy of all revisions of the case base is dumped to be able to restore cases that have been damaged by uncautious or malicious users.
- The case format includes email addresses for contacting the authors.
- The case-based system is integrated with a discussion forum (see below).

The discussion forum is situated on the Web page of the lecture on practical informatics that has to be visited by many first-year students. The ExperienceBook can be queried directly from the forum's user interface via a simple text field as search mask. A CGI script transforms the search text into a query by extending it with the attribute-value pair 'SUBDOMAIN=PI1 problems' and sends it to the ExperienceBook. The retrieval result is presented on the ExperienceBook's usual result page.

4 Feedback Results, First Extensions, and Second Turn

We took two means to measure the success of the initiative and to improve the quality of the system: The access statistics from the Web log files (see Table 2) and the feedback of the users. Some weeks after the introduction of the ExperienceBook II at the end of October 2003, we could see that the system works in principal and was queried frequently. However, the plan to let the community members contribute new case knowledge failed. Very few new cases had been typed in. Only two authors wrote cases without being explicitely asked to do this. This was surprising as we made good experiences with a similar system, the ExperienceBook I, which is in use at the AI lab successfully. The ExperienceBook I gets regularly new cases by the members of our lab. After some more weeks, the usage rates were decreasing, too. In opposite to this, the discussion forum 'survived' until July 2004. 60 different authors produced 33 entries with one to 14 contributions each.

Table 2. Access statistics of the first turn of the ExperienceBook II

	# accesses	# queries	# new cases
October 2003	291	9	19
November 2003	1925	369	10
December 2003	289	43	3
January 2004	299	44	0
Oct. 2003 – Jan. 2004	2804	465	32

Additionally to the access statistics, we got oral feedback from discussions with two initiatives of the students some weeks after introduction of the ExperienceBook II. Furthermore, we sent a questionnaire to 298 students in January 2004. The return rate was low (15 of 298 students, i.e. about 5%), but rather informative. The target community had installed an own discussion forum meanwhile that was stored outside the university. We analysed what had happened and draw our conclusions for the second turn.

Still during the first turn of the system, we extended the case base by new cases generated from the entrie of the discussion forum and, secondly, installed an additional Web page for open questions derived from the Web log files of the query page. But this did not help much and we assume that the main problem were psycho-social barriers. We took care on two potential psycho-social barriers for the second turn:

1. *The power relationships*: We told the new generation of students several times that the lecturers don't read the students' cases and comments.
2. *The access from the normal working context*: We placed a link to our system on the 'GOYA' course management Web page that is used by all students nearly daily to download exercises, look up credits and so on.

The success of the second turn confirms this assumption, but can not proof it in general. Since October 2004, the system is accessed constantly about 1,500 times per month. Nearly 500 accesses come from the GOYA Web page. The number of new cases written by students is still low (about one or two per month), but lecturers are contributing new cases so that we have over 50 cases meanwhile. This number is, of course, still improvable.

5 Discussion and Related Work

In this paper, we presented a holistic approach of a case-based EM project that integrates technical, organisational and psycho-social aspects. We extracted the following success factors and drawbacks:

- It worked well to integrate a case-based system with a discussion forum. 227 of 421 analysed queries from the first turn came directly from the lecture's forum page. A few forum contributions could be transformed into new cases for the case base. [Morgan *et al.*, 2003] makes similar observations.
- Advertising is necessary, face-to-face motivation was the most successful: The access rate was significantly increasing for some days after each oral presentation.
- Participating the users was useful to improve the system. Discussions with two initiatives of the students led to the creation of an additional Web page for open questions gained from the Web log files.
- Both, advertising and user participation helped to overcome psycho-social barriers and to create:
  - A well-informed and positive attitude of many users towards the system,
  - A basic trust in the use of the system concerning power relationships and misuse,
  - A direct access from the usual working context, as we learned where to reach the users.
- The intrinsic motivation of the community worked partly. The students asked many queries but wrote few cases in both turns. [Wikipedia, 2004] is a prominent example for the success of the voluntariness principle. In the questionnaires, the ExperienceBook students asked for more cases from the lecturers. This or extrinsic motivation might be countermeasures for the low authoring rate.
- The possibility to evaluate single cases in the questionnaire has not been used at all. [Nick *et al.*, 2003] come to similar results. For the purpose of acquiring case-related feedback, we think about an automatic observation of the navigation behaviour (see [Berendt *et al.*, 2003]).

Acknowledgements to all department members supporting the project, especially Olga Schiemangk, Benjamin Altmeyer, Kay Schröter, Holger Schlingloff, Klaus Bothe, Gabriela Lindemann and Hans-Dieter Burkhard.

References

[Bergmann, 2002] Ralph Bergmann. *Experience Management Foundations, Development Methodology, and Internet-Based Applications*. LNAI 2432, Springer Verlag, 2002.

[Berendt *et al.*, 2003] Berendt, B., Hotho, A., Mladenic, D., van Someren, M., Spiliopoulou, M., Stumme, G. (Hrsg.): *Proceedings of the First European Web Mining Forum*, Ruder Boskovic Institute, Zagreb, Croatia, 2003, Workshop at the 14th European Conference on Machine Learning / 7th European Conference on Principles and Practice of Knowledge Discovery in Databases (ECML/PKDD-2003), Cavtat, Croatia, September 22nd, 2003 http://km.aifb.uni-karlsruhe.de/ws/ewmf03

[Lenz and Burkhard, 1996] Mario Lenz, Hans-Dieter Burkhard. *Case Retrieval Nets: Basic Ideas and Extensions*, In: Görz, Hölldobler (eds.), Proceedings of the KI'96, LNAI 1137, pages 227 -- 239, Springer, 1996.

[Lenz *et al.*, 1998] Mario Lenz, André Hübner, Mirjam Kunze. *Textual CBR*, In: Lenz, Bartsch-Spörl, Burkhard, Wess (eds.), Case-Based Reasoning Technology –From Foundations to Applications, LNAI 1400, Springer Verlag, 1998.

[Minor, 2001] Mirjam Minor. *Experience Management – Case-Based Reasoning for Knowledge Management*, In: Czaja (ed.), Proceedings of the CS&P'01, pages 150 -- 159, Warsaw, 2001. online version http://www.informatik.hu-berlin.de/~minor/Publications/CsuP01.ps.gz.

[Morgan *et al.*, 2003] Alexander P. Morgan, John A. Cafeo, Diane I. Gibbons, *et al.* *The General Motors Variation-Reduction Adviser: Evolution of a CBR System,* In: Proceedings of the ICCBR'03, LNAI 2689, pages 306 -- 318, Springer Verlag, 2003.

[Nick *et al.*, 2003] Markus Nick, Klaus-Dieter Althoff, Andreas Jedlitschka. *Acquiring Knowledge for Linking Software Engineering Experience Maintenance with Evaluation*, Proceedings of the Net.ObjectDays, pages 93 – 107, Ilmenau, 2003.

[Wikipedia, 2004] http://www.wikipedia.org (last visited November 2004)

Applying Generalized Cases to Retrieval and Configuration of Life Insurance Policies

Alexander Tartakovski[1], Martin Schaaf[2], and Rainer Maximini[1]

[1] University of Trier,
Department of Business Information Systems II,
54286 Trier, Germany
{Alexander.Tartakovski, Rainer.Maximini}@wi2.uni-trier.de
[2] University of Hildesheim,
Institute for Mathematics and Applied Computer Science,
Data and Knowledge Management Group,
31113 Hildesheim, Germany
schaaf@dwm.uni-hildesheim.de

Abstract. When searching for the right life insurance product, one can either confide in her/his insurance broker or use internet portal sites providing interactive assistance for finding suitable insurance products based on questionnaires. While the first alternative is risky, the second one is cumbersome because of many successive query formulations required. Since a single product is normally a tradeoff between customer requirements, the possibility of providing its priorities could speed up the search significantly. In this paper, we present an approach, which takes priorities in account, while searching for and configuring of insurance products. It makes use of Structural Case-Based-Reasoning (SCBR) extended by the concept of generalized cases. Here, each insurance product is represented as a generalized case what consequently allows the application of similarity assessment and retrieval techniques to the insurance domain.

1 Introduction

In this paper, we present an approach for selecting life insurance policies that makes use of the *Structural Case-Based-Reasoning* (SCBR) extended by the concept of *generalized cases* [3]. It is developed to overcome several drawbacks by searching for a suitable policy by a prospective customer.

Nowadays, trading life insurance products is usually done in cooperation with an insurance broker who can offer several products from a limited amount of insurance companies. Life insurances are configurable and the decision about their suitability requires the broker to perceive the personal and financial situation of the client, to consider the desired degree of protection and, of course, to keep in mind his own acquisition commission. However, even the best insurance broker can offer only a small fraction of insurance products available on the market. As a consequence, clients are required to obtain additional information like independent comparisons of insurance products. Meanwhile, some dedicated portal sites on the internet provide

K.-D. Althoff et al. (Eds.): WM 2005, LNAI 3782, pp. 293 – 303, 2005.

interactive assistance for finding suitable insurance products based on questionnaires. However, such questionnaires either cover only a small amount of important facts or are cumbersome to fill out. In addition, they do not allow the client to emphasize personal preferences, ignoring the fact, that every police is a tradeoff between customer requirements.

The approach, presented in this paper, overcomes above mentioned disadvantages. Following the approach, the products can be retrieved and configured according to customer requirements. The potential customer is free to provide as much information about his desired degree of protection, financial, and personal situation as she/he wants. Furthermore, it is possible for her/him to emphasize specific requirements to the insurance by providing weights, leading to a reduced number of query formulations and therefore to more comfort for a customer.

According to this approach each insurance product is represented as a generalized case. Similarity assessment and retrieval methods already developed for generalized cases are applied here, solving the task of finding and configuring of insurance products.

Section 2 introduces the concept and details to temporary life insurance products. Section 3 provides an approach for similarity assessment between a customer query and a life insurance product and furthermore, an approach for indexing of product databases. The methodology presented in this section is generic and can be used for other domains where items to be retrieved can be represented as generalized cases.

2 Temporary Life Insurance

There are several different types of insurance products on the market. Among them the well-known cash value life insurance, temporary life insurance, property-linked life insurance and so on. Furthermore, products of the same type offered by diverse insurance companies often differ in their price structure and benefits.

We demonstrate our approach on an example of the classical temporary life insurance described in [1, 6]. Of course, it can be applied to temporary life insurance products of different companies and also to the other types of life insurance products.

We start this section with a brief introduction to the general temporary life insurance. Then we continue with a classical example and go hereby especially into the corresponding insurance formula and its parameters.

2.1 Concept of Temporary Life Insurance and Search for Right Policy

A temporary life insurance is a special form of life insurance. It is a contract where the insurer pays the insurance sum if the death of the assured person occurs within a specific period [1]. During this period the assured person pays the insurance premium e.g. on an annual base. The aim of a temporary life insurance is first of all the financial security of the assured person's affiliates.

To pick the right policy, the customer should provide some personal data and requirements to the insurer or insurance broker. Important personal data is e.g. the age, the sex, the health status, and some lifestyle information e.g. smoker/ no smoker, sports and so on. The requirements can contain the favored insurance duration, insurance sum, and insurance premium. They have not to be completely specified, e.g. providing insurance duration and insurance sum could be sufficient for insurance broker to choose some offers. Furthermore, the broker is usually not strictly bound to fulfill all requirements exactly. For instance he may propose to slightly reduce the insurance sum or duration if this results in a favorable premium.

2.2 Parameters and Formula of Temporary Life Insurance

A single insurance product is, to a certain degree, parameterized and therefore configurable. The personal data reflects data that cannot be changed within a short period of time. Therefore, from the customer perspective, they are constant values. Contrary, the requirements to the contract are parameters that can be affected directly by the customer.

For simplicity but without loss of generality, the insurance formula (1) [1, 6] regarded in this work is limited to healthy males with a normal lifestyle. The parameters used in the formula are:

- age - x,
- period of insurance – n,
- insurance sum – C,
- insurance premium p.a. - Π.

The formula defines the dependencies between the parameters and therefore all their valid assignments:

$$\Pi = C\frac{f(x,n) + \alpha(1 - g(x,n)) + \gamma h(x,n)}{(1-\beta)h(x,n)} \tag{1}$$

It is based on the principle of equivalence between expected benefit of the insured person and expected benefit of an insurance company. Both expected values are calculated using mortality tables. Furthermore, this formula includes different fees reflecting the costs of the insurance company: α-, β- and γ-costs:

- α-costs are acquisition costs. A customer pays them only once when signing the contract. This kind of costs covers expenditure for advertisement, for medical examination, broker's acquisition commission, and so on.
- β-costs are collection costs. This kind of costs covers all activities concerning the collection of fees.
- γ-costs are administration costs. This kind of costs covers all internal costs except acquisition costs.

The functions *f(x,n), g(x,n), and h(x,n)*[1] are the standard functions for the insurance mathematics and therefore, they can be found in product-formulas of different insurance companies. Their values depend on customer age *x*, period of insurance *n*, but

---

[1] Insurance mathematicians often use other names for the functions *f(x,n), g(x,n), and h(x,n),* namely: $A^1_{x\overline{n}|}, A_{x\overline{n}|}{}^{1}, \ddot{a}_{x\overline{n}|}$.

also on the mortality table and the assumed interest. The exact explanation of these terms goes beyond the scope of this paper. The interested reader may refer to the books [1, 6].

3 Configuration and Retrieval of Temporary Life Insurance Policies

This section provides a new method for solving the task of configuring and selecting life insurance policies. It will be demonstrated using an example of the classical temporary life insurance described in [1, 6].

The approach is applicable for systems supporting customers as well as insurance brokers and is based on structural CBR extended by the concept of *generalized cases.* The section begins with an introduction of its general idea and carries on with a detailed description of its realization.

3.1 General Idea of Configuration and Retrieval

Before the beginning of configuration and retrieval process the customer provides her/his personal data and requirements to a wanted contract. The requirements shouldn't be complete and exact, e.g. the customer provides a wanted period of insurance and an insurance sum, but doesn't provide an exact insurance premium, since the wanted contract price is unknown to her/him. In this case the customer might communicate if she/he is interested on chip policies with a possibility of not satisfying other requirements or if the other requirements have greater priority than the price. Since every contract could be a trade-off between requirements the customer might provide their priorities e.g. through weights. This approach offers more flexibility than questionnaires known from internet portal sites, since on the one hand, it allows the customer to provide incomplete information and on the other hand, it allows a providing of priorities (cp. figure 1).

Please enter your Birthdate:	01.01.1975		
Sex:	M		
Do You Smoke or use tobacco?:	N		
Initial Level Term Period:	20 Year	Weight:	exact
Select the Amount of Insurance:	225.000 $	Weight:	slightly variation
Insurance Premium:	?	Weight:	prefer low costs

Fig. 1. Extended Questionnaire

When received information from a customer most suitable products are presented according to their best configuration (cp. figure 2). Hereby, every retrieved product is configured according to the customer requirements and their priorities. To get the most suitable products a retriever component ranks the products according to a satisfaction grade of requirements. If the products or these configurations do not meet the

product	premium $	amount $	period
Product A	165	225.000	20
Product B	170	215.000	20
Product C	184	200.000	20

Fig. 2. Result Set

customer demands, then she/he has a possibility to adjust the weights or requirements in order to improve the result set.

Since this idea can be realized using the concepts of generalized cases and structural CBR, the next section begins with a brief introduction of the both concepts.

3.2 Extension of Structural CBR Approach through Generalized Cases

The structural CBR (SCBR) approach has been proven useful when modeling and searching for products within e-commerce scenarios. Its extension by the new concept of generalized cases allows the representation of complex and configurable products, for instance, parameterized insurance products. SCBR with generalized cases has been successfully applied and tested for management of reusable electronic design components [2, 4, 10]. Following the structural CBR approach, each case is described by a finite set of attribute-value pairs that characterize the problem and the solution. In contrast to a traditional case, a generalized case doesn't cover only a point of the case space *CS* but a whole subspace of it [3] (cp. figure 3).

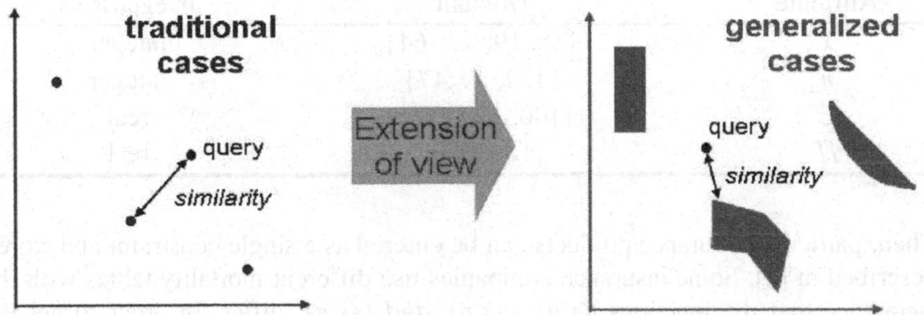

Fig. 3. Extension to Generalized Cases

Therefore, the simple formalization for a generalized case *GC* is:

$$GC \subseteq CS \tag{2}$$

The usual way for representing generalized cases defined over numerical domains is applying constraints for the definition of a subspace like (real domain, here):

$$\begin{aligned} GC = \{x \in IR^n \mid c_1(x) \geq 0 \wedge \ldots \wedge c_k(x) \geq 0 \\ \wedge\, c_{k+1}(x) = 0 \wedge \ldots \wedge c_l(x) = 0\} \end{aligned} \tag{3}$$

The concept of generalized cases implies the extension of similarity measures. In [3, 10] the similarity between a query and a generalized case has been defined as the similarity between the query and the most similar point-case contained in the generalized case:

$$sim^*(q,GC) := \max\{sim(q,c) \mid c \in GC\} \tag{4}$$

According to this definition, the value of the extended similarity function *sim*(q,GC)* is equal to the similarity *sim(q,c)* between a query *q* and the most similar point case *c* contained in the generalized case.

The similarity assessment problem can be viewed as a specific optimization problem [7], which is maximizing or minimizing an objective function under restrictions given through constraints. By defining the objective function as $f(x):=sim(q,x)$ and the feasible set $F:=GC$ the similarity assessment problem is transformed to a specific optimization problem.

3.3 Modeling of Temporary Life Insurance Products

A single temporary life insurance product can be viewed as a generalized case with parameterized attributes: age - *x,* period of insurance – *n,* insurance sum – *C,* and insurance premium - Π. The first step is the definition of the description space that is a Cartesian product spanned by attribute domains. The domains regarded in this work are summarized in the following table:

Table 1. Domains of the description space

Attribute	Domain	Integer/Real
x	{18, 19, … , 64}	integer
n	{1, 2, … ,47}	integer
C	[100, 1000000]	real
Π	[10, 5000]	real

Then, particular insurance products can be entered as a single constraint and stored as described in [2]. Some insurance companies use different mortality tables with the consequence that the functions $f(x,n)$, $g(x,n)$, and $h(x,n)$ differ. In order to get the right values, none standard tables should be saved together with product constrains.

3.4 Modeling Similarity Measures

Since the definition of a similarity measure for generalized cases is based on traditional similarity measures, the first step is to define the local similarities for each attribute. The local similarities for *n, C,* and Π shouldn't be symmetric. For example, the customer is satisfied when getting a cheaper product or a product with a greater period of insurance as required.

The aggregation function is usually the weighted sum, with weights provided by a user in the query. By specifying the weights the customer emphasizes attributes that are important for him. For example the insurance sum is a very important criterion for some customer and he chooses a great weight for this attribute.

The similarity measure for generalized cases defined in [3] is adequate for insurance products retrieval. This measure defines the similarity between a query and a product as a similarity between the query and the most similar configuration of the product. It means that each product is qualified according to its best configuration.

3.5 Similarity Assessment and Configuration

In this work we use the methods of mathematical optimization for solving the similarity assessment and configuration problem for generalized cases [2]. As mentioned before, the similarity assessment can be viewed as a specific optimization problem. When making use of optimization software, it should be transferred to the adequate standard class of optimization problems. Since, the formula types regarded in this work have numerical parameters – real and integer, the adequate class is *Mixed Integer Nonlinear Problem (MINLP)* [5,8]. The standard problem of this class has the following formulation:

$$\begin{aligned}
&\min_{x,y} f(x,y) \\
&s.t.\ \ c_1(x,y) \geq 0, \\
&\qquad \ldots \\
&\qquad c_k(x,y) \geq 0, \\
&\qquad c_{k+1}(x,y) = 0, \\
&\qquad \ldots \\
&\qquad c_l(x,y) = 0, \\
&\qquad x \in IR^m,\ y \in Z^n
\end{aligned} \tag{5}$$

The transformation should map the insurance formula to a single or several constraints and the similarity function to the objective function *f*. Such a mapping introduces a difficulty with the functions *f(x,n), g(x,n), and h(x,n)*, which values are depending on integer age and period of insurance. The following table provides values of insurance terms for a 40 years old male using mortality table: 1960/62 males, Germany [6].

Table 2. Values of *f(x,n), g(x,n), and h(x,n)*

n	f(x,n)	g(x,n)	h(x,n)
24	0.17	0.36	16.24
25	0.18	0.34	16.6
26	0.19	0.32	16.94

The generalized case and hereby the configuration space according to these values is represented in figure 4.

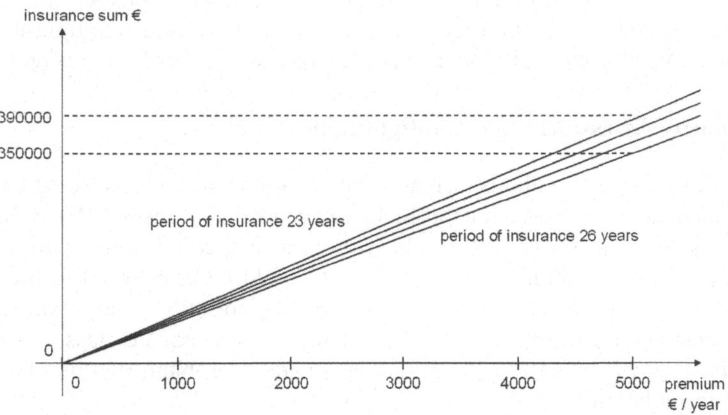

Fig. 4. Temporary life insurance as a generalized case

In [2] a first approach is presented, which transforms the similarity assessment problem for generalized cases defined over mixed, continuous and discrete, domains into a MINLP problem. Using this approach, the insurance formula can be transformed into constraints used by MINLP taking the discrete character of insurance values into account. The transformation will be explained on the concrete temporary life insurance product, which is derived from formula (1) by using the values of $f(x,n)$, $g(x,n)$, and $h(x,n)$ according to the table 2 and by assuming the interval $n\in\{24,\dots,26\}$, and costs $\alpha=0.025$, $\beta=0.01$, $\gamma=0.002$.

By applying *if-then* conditions the instantiated formula can be understood as the following one:

$$\begin{aligned}
&\textit{if } n = 24 \textit{ then } \Pi = C\frac{0.17+0.025(1-0.36)+0.002\cdot 16.24}{(1-0.01)\cdot 16.24},\\
&\textit{if } n = 25 \textit{ then } \Pi = C\frac{0.18+0.025(1-0.34)+0.002\cdot 16.6}{(1-0.01)\cdot 16.6},\\
&\textit{if } n = 26 \textit{ then } \Pi = C\frac{0.19+0.025(1-0.32)+0.002\cdot 16.94}{(1-0.01)\cdot 16.94}.
\end{aligned} \tag{6}$$

In order to get MINLP compatible constraints, the following steps are necessary: Instead of the variable n, three new binary variables must be introduced: n_{24}, n_{25}, $n_{26}\in\{0,1\}$. These correspond to the variable n as follows: $n=i$ iff $n_i=1$. To avoid that several variables get the value 1 a new constraint must be introduced: $n_{24} + n_{25} + n_{26} = 1$. Consequently, the formulas (3) can be transferred to standard MINLP constraints as follows:

$$\begin{aligned}
&n_{24}\left(C\frac{0.17+0.025(1-0.36)+0.002\cdot 16.24}{(1-0.01)\cdot 16.24}-\Pi\right)=0,\\
&n_{25}\left(C\frac{0.18+0.025(1-0.34)+0.002\cdot 16.6}{(1-0.01)\cdot 16.6}-\Pi\right)=0,\\
&n_{26}\left(C\frac{0.19+0.025(1-0.32)+0.002\cdot 16.94}{(1-0.01)\cdot 16.94}-\Pi\right)=0,\\
&n_{24}+n_{25}+n_{26}=1,\\
&C,\Pi\in IR,\quad n_{24},n_{25},n_{26}\in IB
\end{aligned}\qquad (7)$$

Because of the substitution the corresponding local similarity must be changed to:

$$\begin{aligned}
&sim_{period}(q_{period},n)\Rightarrow sim'_{period}(q_{period},n_{24},n_{25},n_{26})=\\
&n_{24}\cdot sim_{period}(q_{period},24)+n_{25}\cdot sim_{period}(q_{period},25)+n_{26}\cdot sim_{period}(q_{period},26)
\end{aligned}\qquad (8)$$

The objective function of the MINLP is then the following one:

$$\max_{n_{24},n_{25},n_{26},C,\Pi}\ w_1 sim'_{period}(q_{period},n_{24},n_{25},n_{26})+w_2 sim(q_{sum},C)+w_3 sim(q_{premium},\Pi)\qquad (9)$$

The objective function (9) together with the constraints (7) is the wanted MINLP.

The majority of available optimization software tools calculate not only an optimal value of an objective function, but additionally a feasible variable assignment corresponding to the optimal value. This assignment is the desired configuration of temporary life insurance products for the scenario regarded in this work.

Furthermore, it is possible to control the accuracy of the optimization software. Increasing the accuracy leads to a better configuration, but a poorer performance. Respectively, decreasing the accuracy decrease the configuration quality, but improves the performance.

3.6 Index Based Retrieval Methods

This section includes an overview of indexing methods presented in [2] and an approach to apply them to case bases consisting of insurance.

Similarity Based Index Method

This method presented for the first time in [2] consists of two parts: an index-builder and a retriever.

Because of the high complexity of the similarity assessment problem for generalized cases the index-builder uses a fix similarity measure for generating an index structure. It partitions the case space into hyperrectangles with faces parallel to the coordinate planes. Every subspace is a potential place holder for a query. Regarding some subspace and some generalized case one can estimate the upper and the lower similarity bounds between the query belonging to an arbitrary point in the subspace, and the case. Doing this not for one case, but for a whole case base, the partial order in terms of similarity can be estimated. The cases having many predecessors, e.g. 10, can be directly excluded, since the customer usually doesn't like to get a large result set. The index-builder stores the remaining cases in conjunction with the partition.

When a customer provides the query, the retriever determines the subspace the query belongs to. Furthermore the retriever load the cases stored together with the subspace and performs the sequential retrieval.

Kd-Tree Based Retrieval Method

The second method presented in [2] adopts the idea of kd-trees [9]. In contrast to the first method it doesn't use the similarity measure, but only the case base for building an index-structure. It consists also of two parts: an indexer, building the adopted kd-tree, and a retriever searching in the tree using a backtracking strategy.

The adopted kd-tree differs from the standard one in the way of storing cases. The original structure is, among other things, the partition of a description space with cases allocated to subspaces including them. Every common point case is allocated to exactly one subspace. Since the generalized cases are sets of possibly infinitely number point cases it is allowed in the adopted variant to allocate cases to subspaces having a not empty intersection with them. Therefore, one generalized case can be allocated to several subspaces.

Indexing Insurance Products

As noticed in section 2, a single insurance product is configurable with respect to personal data of a customer and his requirements to the contract. Since a customer is usually not interested in products that don't match his personal data, e.g. his age, it makes sense to take this fact in account by building of index structures.

The main idea to achieve the improvement of a retrieval performance is to construct, as far as possible, a separate index structure for each individual configuration of personal data.

The personal data in case of the regarded formula for temporary life insurance products is reflected through the age parameter. Therefore index structure can be constructed for every age-value using insurance products restricted to the selected age. After a customer provides his age and his requirements the corresponding index structure is chosen and the products are configured with respect to the customer's requirements.

4 Conclusion and Future Work

In this paper we showed an approach for the retrieval and selection of temporal life insurance policies based on Structural CBR that makes use of generalized cases, a concept that allows the representation of configurable products as cases. In contrast to the widespread questionnaires, which currently provide some kind of assistance for assessing insurance products, this facilitates to emphasize personal preferences and works even in the case when the user provides only incomplete information about his personal and financial situation. For the next months it is planned, to launch an experiment with three different student groups. Each group has to select insurance products for a set of imaginary clients respective their personal and financial situation. One group has to use only the Internet; another will work in cooperation with professional insurance brokers; the third group uses the approach developed so far.

References

1. Gerber, H.U.: Life Insurance Mathematics. Springer-Verlag, Berlin Heidelberg (2001)
2. Tartakovski, A., Schaaf, M., Maximini, R., and Bergmann, R.: MINLP Based Retrieval of Generalized Cases, Proceedings of 7th European Conference, ECCBR 2004. In Peter Funk, and Pedro A. González Calero, editors, Advances in Case-Based Reasoning, LNAI3155, pages 404-418, Madrid, Spain, Springer Verlag, Berlin Heidelberg New York (2004)
3. Bergmann, R.: Experience management. Springer-Verlag Berlin Heidelberg New York (2002)
4. Maximini, R. and Tartakovski, A.: Approximative Retrieval of Attribute Dependent Generalized Cases. In Workshop on Knowledge and Experience Management (FGWM 2003), Karlsruhe Germany (2003)
5. Leyffer, S.: Deterministic methods for mixed integer nonlinear programming. PhD Thesis, Department of Mathematics and Computer Science, University of Dundee (1993)
6. Isenbart, F., and Münzner H.: Lebensversicherungsmathematik für Praxis und Studium. Dr. Th. Gabler Verlag (1994)
7. Mougouie, B., and Bergmann, R.: Similarity Assessment for Generalized Cases by Optimization Methods. In S. Craw, and A. Preece, editors, European Conference on Case-Based Reasoning (ECCBR'02), volume 2416 of LNAI, Springer (2002)
8. Tawarmalani, M., Sahinidis, N.: Convexification and global optimization in continuous and mixed-integer nonlinear programming: Theory, algorithms, software, and applications. Kluwer Academic Publishers, Boston MA (2002)
9. Wess, S., Althoff, K.D., Derwand, G.: Using k-d trees to improve the retrieval step in case-based reasoning. University of Kaiserslautern (1993)
10. Bergmann, R., Vollrath, I., and Wahlmann, T.: Generalized cases and their application to electronic designs. In E. Melis, editor, *7th* German Workshop on Case-Based Reasoning, 1999.

Integrated Approach to Detect Inconspicuous Contents

Rosina Weber, Ilya Waldstein, Amit Deshpande, and Jason M. Proctor

College of Information Science and Technology, Drexel University,
3141 Chestnut Street, Philadelphia, PA 19104, USA
{rw37, imw22, asd28, jp338}@drexel.edu

Abstract. This paper describes an integrated approach for detecting inconspicuous contents in text. Inconspicuous contents can be an opinion or goal that may be disguised in some way to mislead automated methods but keeps a clear message for humans (e.g., terrorist sites). Our methodology hypothesizes that patterns that convey inconspicuous contents can be extracted, represented, generalized, and matched in unknown text. The proposed approach is meant to complement data-intensive methods (e.g. clustering). Data-intensive methods are fast but are susceptible to variations in frequency, do not discern meaning, and require a large corpus for training. Our approach relies on manual engineering for natural language interpretation and pattern extraction using no more than ten examples, but is sufficiently fast to complement a real-time application.

1 Introduction

The approach we introduce in this paper integrates intelligent methods and manual engineering to collect, store, and reuse knowledge for the timely identification of inconspicuous contents. We refer to content as inconspicuous if its message is easily recognized by humans but not as easily recognized by automated methods.

Terror-related [1] web pages are an example of inconspicuous contents. Their authors have a focused audience they need to reach, but they do not wish to be recognized by others outside that targeted audience. Email spam [2] is another example of inconspicuous contents. It is not uncommon to see keyword lists inserted in email spam messages. These are attempts to disguise their contents, preventing these email messages from being automatically detected by methods that can delete them. Sentiment can also be classified as inconspicuous contents. The task of sentiment analysis [3] aims at automatically recognizing opposing views, e.g. when a customer reviews a product showing satisfaction or dissatisfaction.

The detection of terror-related web pages with a data mining approach was proposed in [1]. Their method can be viewed as data-intensive because it relies on clustering training data to learn a model of a *typical terrorist behavior*. Their studies demonstrated the proposed method reaches almost 90% accuracy when detecting terror-related pages. Similar to clustering, the detection of email spam also relies on training large amounts of training instances, such as the method in [2]. Sentiments are detected by Yi et al. [3] using natural language processing (NLP) techniques. NLP is

K.-D. Althoff et al. (Eds.): WM 2005, LNAI 3782, pp. 304–315, 2005.

expensive in terms of complexity and time and its accuracy, although high, is no match for humans.

Our goal is to create a method that can improve the current accuracy of detection of inconspicuous contents. Given the high accuracy obtained by data-intensive methods (i.e. around 90% [1]), we want to complement such methods and contribute with an increase in their accuracy. For this purpose, we assume that lack of meaning is one of the reasons limiting accuracy of data-intensive methods. Another reason we consider is that they rely on generalizations that are usually detrimental to their specificity. In addition, in the context of inconspicuous contents, authors may try to disguise the contents by inserting keywords or excerpts from extraneous text. Therefore, we also take into account that data-intensive methods are susceptible to artificial variations of word frequencies.

The input of our approach is the output of a data-intensive method such as [1]. Their clustering method succeeds in classifying around 90% of the documents. Thus, the remaining 10% of the documents that are undetected become the input to our approach. These undetected documents are likely to contain some surface features that are relevant to the targeted topic, but these words or features are not enough to assign these documents a clear classification so the documents fall below that method's threshold. Therefore, we envision our detection task as one that requires a more specific test. Our assumption is that there are different purposes or perspectives a document may underlie if it is an instance of a given topic. Our purpose is then to detect whether these documents are instances of one of a set of potential perspectives within a topic. If a document carries a perspective of a topic, then it is highly likely it is an instance of that topic. For example, if we assume that terrorist web pages may have one of many perspectives such as organizing a meeting, a document that is around the classification threshold of terrorist pages that also has elements of organizing a meeting is more likely to be an instance of terrorism than not.

The problem we face has a number of characteristics we must take into account. First, we may not have a training corpus available for training. We may have a few examples but we may also need to rely on humans to assume how different angles of a given domain may be expressed. Second, if we want to incorporate our approach into a data-intensive method for real-time detection, the execution time has to be very fast. Detection speed is crucial in domains such as terrorism: detecting terrorist contents on the web is only useful if done in real time so that authorities can be notified to take necessary measures.

Given the definition of the problem and its characteristics, we propose an approach to detect inconspicuous contents that relies on a highly simplified representation formalism for patterns. The proposed approach consists of two steps. A manual engineering step that targets a very small set of training instances, where humans perform the complex understanding offline, extract semantic patterns, and represent them in a simplified representation formalism. In the second step, the patterns are used in real-time detection.

As a complementary method, it takes advantage of the preliminary screening produced by the data-intensive method and only processes the text that ranks below the threshold. Therefore, our classification task aims at detecting when a given text presents a specific perspective or *view* of a topic, and not the topic. Having previous knowledge about the domain of the text to be classified allows us to make some assumptions about semantics in the incoming texts. The essence of the approach is that humans can identify when a combination of words in a given topic indicates one or another view.

The next section highlights related work. Section 3 presents our proposed approach. Section 4 describes our preliminary studies. Conclusions and future work are discussed in Section 5.

2 Related Work

The particular data-intensive application for web detection that motivated our research is Elovici et al. [1]. Their method relies on modeling terrorist behavior based on the particular characteristics of this problem. The distribution of terrorists on the web is neither stable nor balanced. The cost of missing one terrorist is higher than suspecting many legal users [ibid.]. Authors [ibid.] showed their results in a ROC chart [4] where the rate for true positives reached 93% when false positives were at 11.7%, with classification accuracy at 88.9%. These results are hard to improve. Nevertheless, we wanted to develop a method to account for the texts that may fail to classify in their method.

The problem we address is more specific than a topical classification. We already know the domain of the text, what is left to determine is which specific view a text conveys. A view is usually defined by the author's intention. Intent classification for email messages as done in [2] focuses on the goals of the authors of the text. As in [2], our goal is to identify the illocutionary speech act that may trigger some effect on the reader [5]. We are not considering the actual impact as in the modeling of perlocutionary [ibid.] speech acts.

Computational linguistics methods take into account the rhetorical and illocutionary structure of documents. Marcu [6] uses cue phrases to locate and classify rhetorical relations. Branting and Lester [7] represented the rhetorical and illocutionary structure to reuse documents with similar intentional structure. These structures can reveal the intensions of the document's author, which are not necessarily visible in the document's surface text. Consequently, the identification of these structures facilitates interpretation of documents. Cohen et al. [2] also rely on the notion of this analysis to identify illocutionary points of speech acts for classifying email according to intent. The rhetorical structure of a document has also been used for Information Extraction. Template mining [8] is a form of information extraction that makes use of the illocutionary structure of textual documents to extract information from text without using natural language processing.

The patterns we propose here are related to the *factors* concept [9][10]. Factors are portions of text that support one or another argument, which relate to our patterns that are meant to support a view. However, it is much easier to represent an opinion than a factor supporting a legal argument. Different formalisms to represent text excerpts that are evidences of factors were studied in [11]. They have found that using bag-of-words is an adequate representation for factor assignment [ibid.]. However, when they incorporated reasoning, they found their representation formalism called Propositional Patterns (ProPs) is more effective [ibid.]. Bag-of-words are easy to build but they include all words without keeping any reference to ordering or meaning. ProPs are sophisticated representation formalisms that keep ordering, semantics and syntax; but require use of NLP for their construction. In our problem, we wanted to combine sophistication of preserving meaning with simplicity of detection.

Sentiment analysis is performed in [3] with a feature extraction method that relies on NLP. Their resulting accuracy is over 90%. They also use human analysis for validating their patterns. Because their purpose is increasing automation and accuracy, they will explore the use of NLP even further. They are not concerned with real time detection.

Yi et al. [3] used Wordnet to generalize words in a pattern through synonyms. Cohen et al. [2] used ontologies to identify speech acts. Brüninghaus and Ashley [10] used a legal thesaurus for generalizing rules. For generalizing our approach, we rely on humans to define *similars* – alternating words that can be exchanged without altering the validity of a pattern. Although it is theoretically possible to represent similars in highly specialized ontologies of intentional entities [12], given the small number of training instances, it is faster, easier, and maybe less prone to error having humans finding similars.

3 Approach

Fig. 1 shows the problem we address with our proposed approach. We are assuming to complement a data-intensive method that may reach accuracy levels around 90% in text classification. Therefore, the input to our module is roughly about 10% of the documents for which the previous method cannot provide a correct classification. In practice, the documents input in our module are the ones whose classifications fall below a predefined threshold of classification.

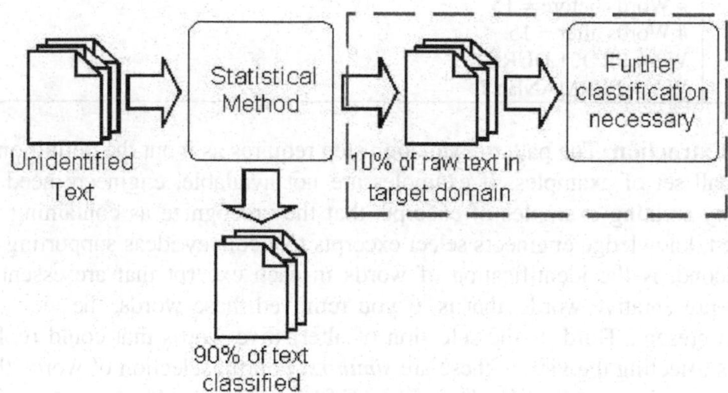

Fig. 1. Context of integrated approach

Figures 2 and 3 show the major steps in our approach, which are described in this section. The approach is based on the hypothesis that there is a combination of words that should appear in a text excerpt to characterize it as a view to be understood by

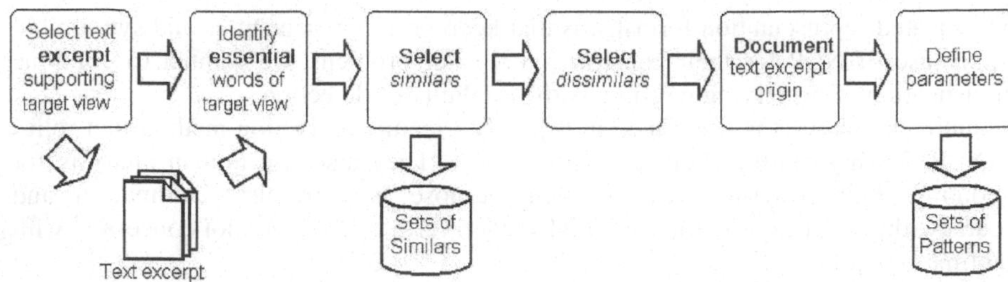

Fig. 2. Steps of the Manual Engineering step

human readers. In the manual engineering step, humans extract view structures that represent the target view with patterns and similars, which are used in the detection step.

3.1 Manual Engineering

The manual engineering step consists of humans interpreting samples of text and extracting and representing patterns that characterize views. A view is described as a set of patterns. A new text is classified as an instance of a view when it contains a minimum number of patterns that characterize such a view.

Table 1. Text and corresponding pattern

Original text	Text excerpt pattern is based on: "And like many other ads for the diet industry (and yes Weight Loss **Surgery** is another diet only it forces the individual to diet by **permanently damaging** their digestive system), the long term results of this **surgery** are seldom if ever, even mentioned.[1]"

Pattern	Star word, W1 = DEFORMATION
	# Words before = 15
	# Words after = 15
	W2 = PROCEDURE
	W3 = PERMANENT

Pattern Extraction. The pattern extraction step requires as input the definition of views and a small set of examples. If examples are not available, engineers need to define patterns by creating examples of excerpts that they recognize as containing the target view. First, knowledge engineers select excerpts that convey ideas supporting the target view. Second, is the identification of words in each excerpt that are essential to the view – representative words, that is, if you removed these words, the view would no longer be present. Third, is the selection of alternative words that could replace these words not affecting the view – these are *similars*. Fourth, selection of words that would invalidate the view – these are *dissimilars*. Fifth, numbering the excerpt and the set of similars to store the location and title of original text where the excerpt came from for future verification of detection efficacy. At the end of this step, all the steps are revised for confirmation of results. The final task is to define the parameters, of the pattern representation (to be detailed next). The label is the word with which all the occurrences

[1] From http://gastricbypass.netfirms.com/wlssell.htm

in the set of similars will be replaced to create a *canonical* version of the text. Next, the patterns and sets of similars are revised by replacing words in patterns with words in the sets of dissimilars. This step is for verification of the patterns. Table 1 shows an example of an excerpt and the pattern extracted from it.

It is important to note that although it is desirable to reduce human judgment from the methodology, the selection of similars is not done exclusively from the training examples. Common sense reasoning and background knowledge is used to select similars and can be used to create additional patterns if it is believed that they can represent a view.

Pattern Representation. Patterns are represented through a list of words and a range where all these words should occur. The representation for the patterns consists of the star word (w_1) and the remaining words (w_2, w_3, ..., w_n). The number of words defined in a pattern (n) is the sum of the star word plus the number of remaining words. The star word is the reference for the pattern's range. Each pattern has a range that is defined with respect to the star word. The range has two directions, before (r_1) and after (r_2) the star word. The representation can be presented as: Pattern #, n, w_1, w_2, w_3,..., w_n, r_1, r_2. For example, Pattern 19 discussed above will be represented as follows, *" 19 3 deformation procedure permanent 15 15."*

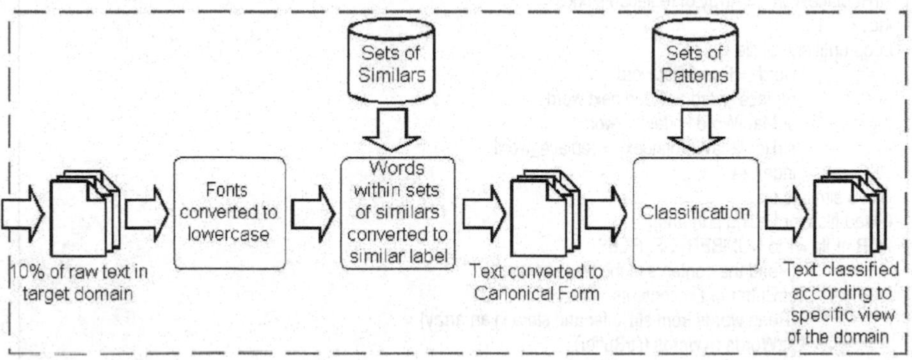

Fig. 3. The Detection step

3.2 Detection

Detection consists of pre-processing and pattern matching. In the preprocessing, all fonts are converted into lower case. Then, all words within the sets of similars are converted into the label of the similar, i.e. creating a canonical text. To match a pattern, all words in the pattern must be found within the pattern's range. First, the star word is found, and then the pattern's range is delimited. When the program reaches the end of the text without finding a star word, there is no need to evaluate other patterns that contain this word. The detection returns which patterns are matched in each text. Table 2 shows pseudocode for pattern detection. The study we discuss next will shed some light on the number of patterns required to match in a text for classification.

When implementing the proposed approach, it is important to note that the role of the patterns is to generalize from specific instances found in the small training set.

It is a generalization that does not follow induction, since it generalizes based on human perception and not based on a large sample of training examples. The guidelines for the conception of sets of similars is very unrestrictive. Therefore, it is not only prone to error but also possible that the freedom given to human engineers result in patterns that are not able to detect their own excerpt that originated the pattern. Therefore, it is necessary that, after patterns and similar sets are finished, one verification round of tests confirm that patterns are actually able to detect the texts that originated them. This is the reason why we recommend the recording of every source excerpt during pattern extraction.

Table 2. Pseudocode for pattern detection

```
{Read identified patterns from the file patterns.txt and store in an array}
strPatterns := Array of pattern strings
index := 1
Loop until end of file
        pattern := Read one word
        strPatterns[index] := word
        index ++
Close pattern.txt
{Read identified similars from the file similars.txt and store in two arrays}
strMainWord := Array of strings to be replaced
strReplaceWord := Array of replaced strings
index := 1
Loop until end of file
        word := Read first word
        replace_word := Read next word
        strMainWord [index] := word
        strReplaceWord[index] := replace_word
        index ++
Close similars.txt
{Read files for finding patterns}
FOR nFile =1 to NUMBER_OF_FILES
        {Read the contents of the file in an array}
        strBuffer := file contents
        {Read words from strBuffer and store in an array}
        strWords := words (strBuffer)
        {Find and replace the similars}
        IF strWords = strMainWord THEN
                strWords := strReplaceWord
        END IF
        FOR nPattern =1 to NUMBER_PATTERNS
                bFound := Find_Patterns
                IF bFound = 1 THEN
                        DISPLAY "Pattern Found"
                END IF
Function: Find_Patterns
        Input: text as array of String
                patterns as array of String
                before as Int
                after as Int
        Output: Bool
        WHILE end of text DO
                IF text = pattern THEN
                        bFound := 1
                END IF
        END WHILE
```

4 Evaluating Detection of Views About Cosmetic Procedures

In this section, we describe an implementation and an evaluation of the introduced approach in the domain of cosmetic procedures. This domain is suitable to evaluate the approach because among several texts on the topic, we found texts conveying opinions against cosmetic procedures – one view – and others in favor – the opposing view. The existence of opposing views is useful for testing the approach.

In order to guarantee consistency among knowledge engineers, we started with the definition of the view. Our purpose was to detect one view only, the view against cosmetic procedures. The overall goal of the approach is to detect text on the target view that could have an impact on a reader. In the context of negative propaganda against cosmetic procedures, we considered whether the text conveyed an idea that could potentially cause a person to change her or his mind about undergoing a cosmetic procedure. For example, the statements "*The death of Olivia Goldsmith, a well known writer aged 54 yrs, from a heart attack while undergoing a neck lift operation, illustrates its potential dangers*[2]." has the potential to change a readers mind because it implies extremely high risk. The statement "*only vain and insecure people get a face lift*" has the potential to change a readers mind because it attacks the candidate. On the other hand, statements such as "*the media is providing too much favorable coverage for plastic surgery*" do not imply anything about the candidate (reader) or the procedure and thereby are not considered as supportive of a negative view.

Table 3. Three patterns extracted from texts with views against cosmetic procedures

Pattern #	n	w_1	w_2	w_3	r_1	r_2
3	3	complications	deformation	procedure	10	10
16	2	death	procedure	-	10	10
19	3	deformation	procedure	permanent	15	15

4.1 Methodology

We selected eight positive training texts from the web to extract patterns. We used the manual engineering step described in Subsection 3.1 to extract thirty-one patterns. Table 3 shows three patterns we extracted from different texts. Table 4 shows sets of similars selected for pattern 19 in Table 3. One can notice that synonyms are sometimes used, but there is no relation to sentence structure, and the relation to meaning is loose. The only rule is that the word, when combined with other words in the pattern, conveys an idea supporting the target view. These similars were selected from the texts and based on human judgment.

Dataset. The entire test dataset has fifteen positive and fifteen negative instances, a total of thirty texts. We randomly selected three subsets with ten texts each to submit ten texts at a time and observe the average time for classifying ten texts.

Hypothesis. The hypothesis we want to evaluate is whether it is possible to classify unknown texts as offering a particular view of a previously known domain by using

[2] http://menshealth.about.com/cs/surgery/a/cosmetic.htm

patterns extracted manually from eight examples. For this purpose, we use three metrics (also used in [1]) namely, *true positives* (TP), *false positives* (FP), and *accuracy* (Ac). True positives measure the proportion of correctly classified texts that are positive instances of the target view. False positives indicate the proportion of texts that are falsely classified as instances of the target view. Accuracy measures the proportion of correct classifications out of the total number of texts classified.

Table 4. Sets of similars

Set label	Elements
permanent	eternal lifelong life-long eternally permanently
procedure	surgery lasik procedures surgeries implant operation augmentation liposuction breast botox implants lipoplasty bariatric facelift
deformation	deformity pain disfigurement limitation handicap disaster damage injured suffering damaged damaging injury injuries wounded wounds deformations deformation aberrated abnormality defects aberration vision-robbing debilitating harmful traumatic excruciating intensely painful agonizing extreme torture torturing dangerous hazardous alarming robbing serious life threatening lifethreatening life-threatening extreme radical unnecessary radical drastic seriously unwanted unneeded

Results. The results obtained from sets A, B and C, and their averages are presented in Table 5. The numbers of patterns are the minimum required to match in a text so it will receive a positive classification. The best results were obtained with one pattern, with average rates TP = 0.7, FP = 0.2, and Ac = 0.6 (shaded in Table 5). Overall for true positives, there is a significant difference between the number of patterns: $F(3, 56) = 6.222$, $p = 0.001$. Specifically, the number of true positives detected with one pattern is different from three patterns at significance level $p = 0.008$, and different from four patterns at significance level $p = 0.002$ (no other pairs of numbers of patterns were statistically different). For false positives and accuracy, there was no significant difference between number of patterns ($p = 0.056$ and $p = 0.764$, respectively).

Table 5. Results for different number of patterns

	True Positives				False Positives				Accuracy			
No. of patt.	A	B	C	Ave.	A	B	C	Ave.	A	B	C	Ave.
1	0.8	0.8	0.6	0.7	0.3	0.1	0.3	0.2	0.6	0.8	0.5	0.6
2	0.8	0.4	0.4	0.5	0.2	0.1	0.3	0.2	0.7	0.6	0.4	0.6
3	0.2	0.2	0.2	0.2	0.2	0.0	0.1	0.1	0.4	0.6	0.5	0.5
4	0.0	0.2	0.2	0.1	0.1	0.0	0.0	0.0	0.4	0.6	0.6	0.5

These values support the conclusion that it is possible to classify unknown texts as instances of a particular view of a previously known domain by using patterns extracted manually from eight examples. They also suggest focusing on a small number of matching semantic patterns as we work towards improving the method's accuracy. We did not evaluate the elapsed time in these runs, though most runs took around one second to run, which is our target speed.

Discussion. As we increase the number of required patterns for detection, it becomes harder to get TP. Analogously, FP also reduce, which is usually good. However, depending on the domain, the impact of reducing FP may be too costly on TP or vice-versa.

Receiver Operating Characteristic (ROC) analysis is meant to provide a visual evaluation of the tradeoffs between TP and FP [4]. The ROC space is represented with TP in the Y axis and FP in the X axis [ibid.]. The ROC analysis of our method is depicted in Fig. 44. The growth in TP is accompanied by increasing values for FP.

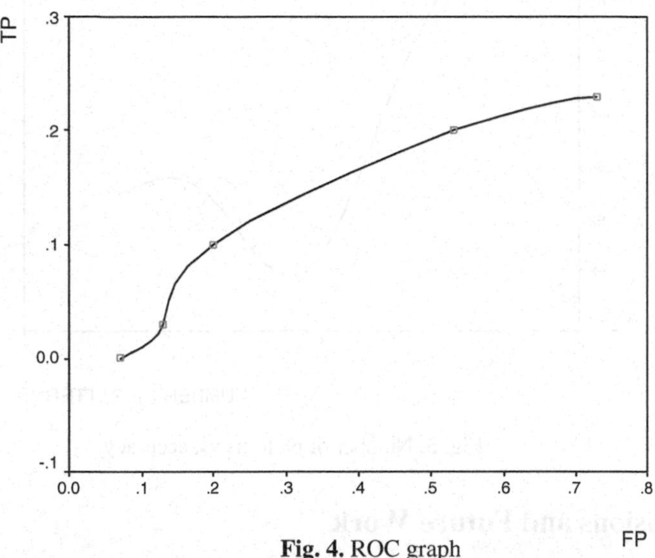

Fig. 4. ROC graph

For a more detailed evaluation of the tradeoffs between TP and FP, Table 6 shows the sensitivity of the average (ave.) of absolute numbers of documents that changed classifications. When the number of patterns varies from one to two, there is a reduction of .3 in FP, but its cost is one less TP. This trade-off suggests the minimum of one pattern for the classification. In a domain such as terrorist detection, it is considered preferable to suspect of one more innocent person than to let one guilty terrorist go undetected [1].

Table 6. Sensitivity of TP vs. FP

# patterns	TP average	Difference	FP average	Difference
1	3.7		2.3	
2	2.7	-1.0	2.0	0.3
3	1.0	-1.7	1.0	1.0
4	0.7	-0.3	0.3	0.7

Another result in our study is how accuracy behaves with changes in the number of patterns required for classification. This information is important because it gives a measure of the power of detection of the patterns. Fig. 5 shows this relation in the data we studied. Additional studies are necessary for verifying these results because we did not observe consistent behavior in the relation between accuracy and the number of patterns.

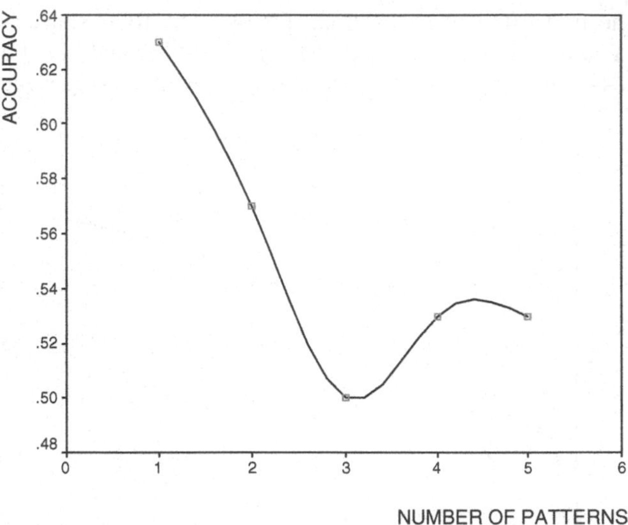

Fig. 5. Number of patterns vs. accuracy

5 Conclusions and Future Work

Our goal was to conceive a method that would complement and improve the accuracy of detection of inconspicuous contents obtained by data-intensive methods. Our proposed method relies on a highly simplified pattern representation extracted in a manual engineering step that uses a very small set of training instances. Additionally, we attempted to process and classify ten input texts under one second to support collaboration with real-time data-intensive applications.

The main contribution of this work refers to the development of a classification approach that does not require a training corpus and uses a simplified representation of semantic meaning while potentially bringing data-intensive methods such as [1] from 90% accuracy to 96% accuracy.

The preliminary evaluation of the ability of the manually extracted patterns to classify text shows promise. We found that it is possible to classify unknown texts as instances of a particular view of a previously known domain, with the results suggestive of focusing on a small number of matching semantic patterns while working towards improving accuracy.

The processing time varied between one and two seconds. The entire design of the method has focused on speed but we have not empirically validated the execution time yet.

The main limitations of this work relate to the use of humans in the process. Humans can be expensive and are not usually consistent. Consequently, human judgment may interfere in the quality of the results. Nevertheless, we believe this is a cost worth paying if the final results improve the overall accuracy and may help detect one more web page retaining inconspicuous contents.

The representation of patterns may be used in different textual methods such as textual case-based reasoning. Any classification task where a large training corpus is not available may also benefit from this approach. The real-time detection offered by the aggregated methods that combines data-intensive plus our patterns can be used to detect a variety of inconspicuous contents.

Acknowledgements

We would like to thank Dr. Mark Last for his suggestions on this work. Dr. Rosina Weber, Amit Deshpande, and Jason M. Proctor are supported in part by the National Institute for Systems Test and Productivity at USF under the USA Space and Naval Warfare Systems Command grant no. N00039-02-C-3244, for 2130 032 L0, 2002.

References

[1] Elovici, Y., Kandel, A., Last, M., Shapira, B., Zaafrany, O.: Using Data Mining Techniques for Detecting Terror-Related Activities on the Web. Journal of Information Warfare 3, 1 (2004) 17 – 29

[2] Cohen, W. M., Carvalho, V. R., Mitchell, T. M.: Learning to Classify Email into Speech Acts. In: Lin, D., Wu, D. (ed.): Proc. of the 2004 Conference on Empirical Methods in Natural Language Processing (2004) 309-316

[3] Yi, J., Nasukawa, T., Bunescu, R., Niblack, W.: Sentiment Analyzer: Extracting Sentiments about a Given Topic using Natural Language Processing Techniques. Proc. of the Third IEEE International Conference on Data Mining. IEEE Computer Society (2003)

[4] Provost, F., Fawcett, T.: Robust Classification for Imprecise Environments. Machine Learning 42, 3 (2001) 203-231

[5] Haller, S.: An Introduction to Interactive Discourse Processing from the Perspective of Plan Recognition and Text Planning. Artificial Intelligence Review 13 (1999) 259–311

[6] Marcu, D.: The Theory and Practice of Discourse Parsing and Summarization. MIT Press, Cambridge, Massachussetts (2000)

[7] Branting, L. K. and Lester, J. C.: Justification Structures for Document Reuse. In: Smith, I., Faltings, B. (eds.): Advances in Case-Based Reasoning. LNCS, Vol. 1168 Springer, Berlin (1996) 76-90

[8] Weber, R.: Intelligent jurisprudence research. In: Proc. of the Seventh International Conference on Artificial Intelligence and Law. ACM, New York (1999) 164-172

[9] Ashley, K. D.: Modeling Legal Argument: Reasoning with Cases and Hypotheticals. A Bradford book. The MIT Press, Cambridge, Massachussetts (1990)

[10] Brüninghaus, S., Ashley, K. D.: Bootstrapping Case Base Development with Annotated Case Summaries. In: Althoff, K-D, Bergmann, R., Branting, LK. (eds.): Case-Based Reasoning Research and Applications. LNAI, Vol. 1650. Springer, Berlin (1999) 59-73

[11] Brüninghaus, S., Ashley, K. D.: Reasoning with Textual Cases. In: Munoz, H. and Ricci, F. (eds.): Case-Based Reasoning Research and Applications. LNAI Springer, Berlin (2005)

[12] Chandrasekaran, B., Josephson, J.R., Benjamins, V. R.: What Are Ontologies, and Why Do We Need Them? IEEE Intelligent Systems 14, 1 (1999) 20-26

Workshop on Current Aspects of Knowledge Management in Medicine (KMM05)

Marita Muscholl[1] and Kerstin Maximini[2]

[1] International Healthcare Management Institute, University of Trier, 54286 Trier, Germany
muscholl@uni-trier.de
[2] Department of Business Information Systems II, University of Trier, 54286 Trier, Germany
Kerstin.Maximini@wi2.uni-trier.de

1 Current Challenges for Medical Knowledge Management

Traditional Knowledge Management systems in the medical field mainly focus on medical knowledge and problem solving like diagnosis, prognosis, therapy planning and critiquing, image processing with image classification, and teaching or practising medical knowledge. Today, also economical, organizational, and quality aspects move into the centre of medical knowledge management, such as efficiency, analysis, and optimisation of hospital processes, workflow management and collaborative treatments by physicians of remote health care facilities. Using the changing accounting system based on flat rates, health care organizations have to change their operating philosophies to become profitable, enterprise-like organizations.

The Workshop KMM05 presented concepts and solutions that show how knowledge management can be applied profitably to solve today's problems and challenges in the medical domain. The Program Committee accepted the six most interesting papers out of a total of 15 submissions for inclusion in these post-conference proceedings.

Medical documentation and the availability and usability of document knowledge play an important role during the daily routine in healthcare environments. Knowledge Management Systems can support medical documentation as well as knowledge processing and retrieval. Three contributions deal with the management of clinical document knowledge: Puppe et al. present an evaluation study of SonoConsult, a knowledge based solution for sonography. They show amongst others that physicians are more interested in the support of the documentation task and see this support as more helpful than diagnosis support. They analyzed also the documentation behaviour of physicians with data mining methods. These methods could help to analyze and control the quality of clinical documentation and DRG coding.

The paper of Katirai and Sax deals with the challenge of availability and usability of clinical document knowledge between different hospital departments. They present an approach that uses "compilable templates" for translating CDA conforming clinical documents into relevant key data and vice versa. As a result many common tasks like creating and installing web services belonging to it can be automated and the compilable templates become a single point of maintenance.

K.-D. Althoff et al. (Eds.): WM 2005, LNAI 3782, pp. 316 – 318, 2005.

Bobrowski and Kreymann report their experiences with realizing a solution that provides medical knowledge in a big university hospital mainly by means of standard software. They established a knowledge management system infrastructure based on Lotus Notes/Lotus Domino and used it to distribute several kinds of clinical knowledge. As a result of their a posteriori system analysis according to the knowledge management paradigm of Probst they found that knowledge identification and knowledge acquisition could be well realized by their approach. But knowledge development, knowledge maintenance, and knowledge evaluation were too difficult to be supported in a satisfactory way.

Another incentive for introducing Knowledge Management systems in healthcare is the need to control cost and quality of treatment. The support of workflow processes and clinical pathways respectively is one approach to meet this requirement.

Muscholl introduces a model-based architecture to support clinical pathways in hospitals and networks of shared care. The main characteristics of the architecture are its open design that allows the integration of existing systems and the ability to support pathway execution in distributed environments.

Cost control in health systems also means avoidance of unnecessary costs. Pechenizkiy et al. propose a data mining method for prognosis and early detection of nosocomial infections in microbiology data.

Curé introduces a system that supports patients to act more independent with a knowledge based system for self-medication in case of mild clinical signs. The system is realized with ontology mapping methods in order to easily enrich and maintain the ontology from a database.

2 The Workshop KMM05

The workshop KMM05 was held at April 11/12, 2005 and attracted scientists and practitioners in computer science, medical informatics and medicine. The topics ranged from new theoretical concepts to prototypes and field reports. Besides presentations and interesting discussions about the six contributions mentioned above, four additional contributions were presented and discussed. The complete workshop program and all presentation slides are accessible at http://www.wi2.uni-trier.de/conferences/kmm05/.

Short versions of all papers are published within a joint conference proceedings as well as in the online proceedings of this workshop at http://ceur-ws.org/Vol-131.

Acknowledgements

Each submission was reviewed by at least two members of the KMM05 Program Committee and we would like to thank each member for participating and for assuring the workshop's success. All members in alphabetical order:

Prof. Dr. Hans Czap	University of Trier, Germany
Dr. med. Jörg Eckardt	Maria Hilf GmbH, Dernbach, Germany
Dr. med. Kai U. Heitmann	University of Köln, Germany

Dr. med. Josef Ingenerf	University of Lübeck, Germany
Prof. Dr. Stefan Kirn	University of Hohenheim, Germany
Dr. rer. nat. Dirk Krechel	SER Solutions GmbH, Germany
Dipl.-Inform. Kerstin Maximini	University of Trier, Germany
Juniorprof. Dr. Marita Muscholl	University of Trier, Germany
Prof. Dr. Klaus Pommerening	University Hospital of Mainz, Germany
Prof. Dr. Huaglory Tianfield	Glasgow Caledonian University, Great Britain
Prof. Dr. Thomas Uthmann	University of Mainz, Germany
Prof. Dr. Aldo von Wangenheim	Federal University of Santa Catarina, Brasil

In addition, we would like to thank Mariana Bortoluzzi and Herculano de Biasi (University of Trier, Germany) for contributing additional reviews.

Of course, we thank all participants of the KMM05 Workshop for their attendance and for the challenging and exciting discussions.

June 2005, *Marita Muscholl and Kerstin Maximini*

Clinical Experiences with a Knowledge-Based System in Sonography (SonoConsult)

Frank Puppe[1], Georg Buscher[1], Martin Atzmueller[1], Matthias Hüttig[2], and Hans-Peter Buscher[2]

[1] Universität Würzburg, Lehrstuhl Informatik VI, Am Hubland, 97074 Würzburg
[2] DRK-Kliniken Berlin Köpenick, Medizinische Klinik 2, Salvador-Allende-Str. 2-8, 12559 Berlin

Abstract. We evaluated the clinical effects of the knowledge-based documentation and diagnosis system SonoConsult for sonography, which has been used in clinical routine for more than 2 years. The evaluation focuses on the following aspects from the clinical point of view: quality of documentation, quality of diagnostic conclusions, training effects, and research effects. In contrast to wide-spread expectations in the knowledge-based community, the diagnostic conclusions were less important than the other aspects, being much more welcomed by clinicians.

1 Introduction

Knowledge-based systems in medicine may serve many functions. Traditionally the main focus was on diagnostic and therapeutic recommendations [Darmoni et al. 92, Berner et al. 99]. However, this may not be perceived as the primary need by most physicians. Instead, other functions such as support for high quality documentation might be more important in clinical routine. We implemented a multifunctional knowledge-based system for sonography and evaluated both its acceptance and its clinical impact.

2 Structure and Function of SonoConsult

SonoConsult (SC) [Hüttig et al. 04] was developed with the diagnostic shell kit d3web [www.d3web.de], which allows the input of expert knowledge via a graphical user interface [Puppe 98]. It covers the entire field of abdominal ultrasound. The implementation makes use of medical heuristics as a knowledge source [McDonald 96] and was performed according to the principles of construction of HepatoConsult [Buscher et al. 02]. The web interface is adaptable for communication with clinical information systems. The terminology of symptoms is descriptive and follows that of textbooks and publications.

SC uses five main object types: symptoms, symptom classes, symptom abstractions, diagnoses, and rules. Symptoms are the input and diagnoses the output of the system. Symptoms consist of a pair (attribute, value), where attribute is the symptom

K.-D. Althoff et al. (Eds.): WM 2005, LNAI 3782, pp. 319 – 329, 2005.

name (e.g. liver size) and value is the symptom value (e.g. increased). In interactive settings, attributes are questions and values are the answers by the user. There are two main types of attributes: choice and numerical. Choice attributes have a predefined range (e.g. for liver size: decreased, normal, increased) and are differentiated according to their cardinality as one-choice (1, i.e. exactly one value is allowed, like liver size) or multiple choice (0 .. n). Symptoms are grouped to symptom classes if they are usually asked together. It is possible to define rules in a symptom class that specify, which questions have to be asked in which order depending on the values of previously answered questions. Symptom abstractions are very similar to symptoms except that their values are inferred by rules. They allow a stepwise abstraction of the input data. Diagnoses are also inferred by rules from symptoms, symptom abstractions or other diagnoses ("criteria"). They usually aggregate uncertain evidence. D3 allows case-based, heuristic and probabilistic mechanisms for representing and accumulating evidence. In SC a score-based scheme is used, i.e. the rules are assumed to be independent and add or subtract points to the score of a diagnoses, which is rated by thresholds in one of the linguistic categories "probable", "possible" and "unclear or excluded". Rules consist of a condition, an action and exceptions. The condition may be a nested logical combination of criteria. Besides the operators "and", "or" and "not", an additional convenience operator, which states that a minimum and maximum of a list of criteria must be fulfilled, is offered by D3 and is widely used in SC. Rules are typed according to their actions. These include to rate diagnoses, to compute values for symptom abstractions, to indicate symptom classes, to trigger

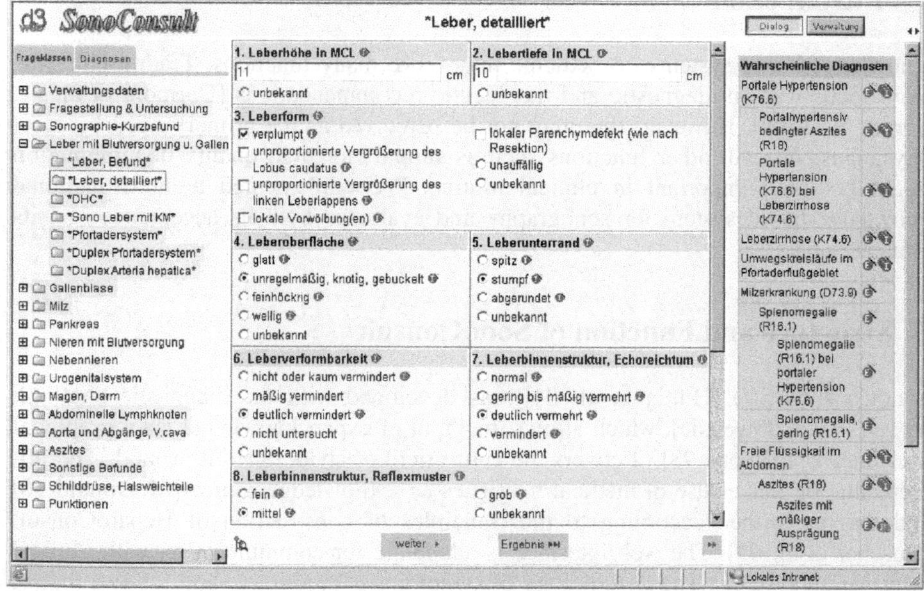

Fig. 1. Screenshot of a section of an SC-questionnaire with part of the hierarchy of questionnaires (partially opened) exemplarily showing the degree of specification (left panel) and the currently generated probable system diagnoses (right panel)

questions and other actions. Exceptions allow to differentiate between two types of negations, whether a fact is yet unknown or definitely wrong, e.g. if C is unknown, a rule "A → B ||- C" [with exception C] may fire, but the similar rule "A ∧ ¬C → B" is blocked. Exceptions are also widely used in SC.

The diagnostic procedure of SC follows the hypothesis-and-test- and the establish-refine-strategy. The selection of a specific questionnaire, (symptom class) depends on the overall clinical question and on the inferred diagnoses. Data gathering stops when all suspected diagnoses (category "possible") are either "probable" or "unclear or excluded" by means of the program's expertise. Subsequently, the case record is stored in a data base. On the basis of the case record a structured text document (medical report) is generated using a predefined rule-based template. It consists of four parts: basic patient data, differentiated report of symptoms, system diagnoses (automatically inferred) and examiner comment (free text). This document is added to the patient record. The screenshot in Fig. 1 exemplifies the data input in SC und Fig. 2 shows the corresponding generated report.

Sonographie

Name, Vorname: **Mustermann, Manuel, 01.10.40**
Fragestellung: Oberbauch-Screening; Leberzirrhose

Befund vom 17.11.04; gute Untersuchungsbedingungen

Leber: Höhe in MCL 11 cm; Tiefe in MCL 10 cm; verplumpt; Oberfläche unregelmäßig, knotig, gebuckelt; Unterrand stumpf; Verformbarkeit deutlich vermindert; Binnenstruktur deutlich echovermehrt; mittleres Reflexmuster; Kalibersprung der Pfortaderäste intrahepatisch; Rarefizierung der Pfortaderäste intrahepatisch
D. hepatocholedochus: Durchmesser 5 mm; unauffällig
Gallenblase: unauffällig
Milz: längs 14 cm, tief 6 cm; Parenchym unauffällig
Pfortadersystem: Pfortaderdurchmesser 14 mm; keine wesentliche Zunahme des Durchmessers bei Inspiration; Milzvenendurchmesser 12 mm; Hinweis auf wiedereröffnete Nabelvene
Duplexsonographie: Pfortader Fluß orthograd mit gleichmäßigem Flußprofil, Flußgeschwindigkeit 12 cm/s; Milzvene Flußgeschwindigkeit 12 cm/s; wiedereröffnete Nabelvene
Flüssigkeit im Abdomen: freie Flüssigkeit im Sinne von Aszites, mäßig ausgeprägt
Abdominelle Gefäße: *Arteria hepatica (duplexsonographisch):* nicht durchgeführt
Vena cava: unauffällig
Lymphknoten: in beurteilbaren Regionen nicht erkennbar bzw. nicht vergrößert
Pleuraerguss: beidseits nicht nachweisbar
Perikarderguss: nicht nachweisbar

Beurteilung:
Schlussfolgerungen von SonoConsult:
Portale Hypertension (K76.6) bei Leberzirrhose (K74.6); portalhypertensiv bedingter Aszites (R18); Splenomegalie (R16.1) bei portaler Hypertension (K76.6)

Die diagnostischen Schlussfolgerungen müssen durch den Untersucher/Befunder geprüft werden.

Bemerkung des Befunders:
Leberzirrhose mit portalhypertensiv bedingtem Aszites und mäßiger Splenomegalie. Kontrolle nach Ausschwemmung des Aszites empfohlen.

Fig. 2. Generated exemplary SC-report corresponding to the ultrasound examination in Fig. 1

The program includes an explanation tool enabling the user to retrace a diagnostic pathway of inferences from symptoms to diagnoses. Additionally, most symptoms and diagnoses are linked to a text-book-like information system for rapid information lookup.

SC was developed continuously on the basis of user feedback. It contains about 430 questions, 140 symptom abstractions and 230 diagnoses. The analysis of the data base of 770 consecutive cases exhibited a mean of 61 answered questions per case with an average of 20 symptom abstractions and 6 diagnoses inferred by the program.

3 Clinical Experience and Evaluations

3.1 Acceptance

For more than three years SC is in routine use as the only documentation system for ultrasound examinations in the DRK-hospital of Berlin-Köpenick. According to the users' opinion, the most important preconditions for the program's introduction into clinical routine were (a) an acceptable account of symptom representation, (b) a time-efficient input procedure, and (c) the ability to convert the case data into structured text documents for the medical record of the procedure.

These preconditions were met before the program was put into routine use. While a self written report took about 3-5 minutes for senior examiners, the input time for a complete case in SC was about 5-8 minutes when starting to work with the program and 2-4 minutes after being familiar with it after about 2-3 weeks of continuous use.

The expectations of the prospective users of SC were asked prior to its first presentation. We provided a questionnaire that was answered by 19 sonographic examiners:

A1 Influence on examination procedure: 3.1 (1 = not probable; 5 = highly probable)
A2 More time for documentation: 3.6 (1 = no willingness; 5 = high willingness)
A3 Standardized data input: 4.3 (1 = unimportant; 5 = very desirable)
A4 Indication of incomplete examination: 3.7 (1 = unimportant; 5 = very desirable)
A5 Presentation of system diagnoses: 3.0 (1 = unimportant; 5 = very desirable)
A6 Simple usability: 4.9 (1 = unimportant; 5 = very desirable)
A7 Rapid access to previous results: 4.6 (1 = unimportant; 5 = very desirable)
A8 Training effects: 3.9 (1 = unimportant; 5 = very desirable)
A9 Statistical analysis: 3.8 (1 = unimportant; 5 = very desirable)
A10 Explanation function: 3.8 (1 = unimportant; 5 = very desirable)

After gaining experience with the use of SC, the physicians were asked again about their opinions using a questionnaire that was answered by 14 examiners:

B1 Structured questionnaires: 3.8 (1 = inconvenient; 5 = very helpful)
B2 Input of findings: 3.7 (1 = insufficient; 5 = too differentiated)
B3 Reminder function: 3.8 (1 = unnecessary; 5 = very helpful)
B4 Use of help: 2.5 (1 = never; 5 = very often)
B5 Relevance of system diagnoses: 2.9 (1 = unimportant; 5 = important)
B6 Influence of system on own diagnoses: 2.2 (1 = unimportant; 5 = important)
B7 Standardization of nomenclature: 4.4 (1 = unimportant; 5 = important)
B8 Comparability of sonographic records: 4.5 (1 = unchanged; 5 = improved)

The answers to these questions show that expectations and experiences agree in many aspects: the standardization of nomenclature is most acknowledged by the examiners (A3 | B7, B8), the input procedure is well accepted (A2, A6 | B1, B2) and the reminder function of the program is perceived as helpful (A4 | B3). This is also true for the effect of the system diagnoses, which is perceived as not so important (A5 | B5, B6). A difference between expectations and experiences exists with respect to the explanation function, which was declared as rather desirable, but rarely used (A10 | B4). The expected training effect (A8) was compared with the experiences of 5 beginners and clearly confirmed the expectations. They all emphasised that the program's most positive effect was to conduct an examination in a complete and structured way as well as in a standardized and reasonable examination sequence. The diagnostic properties of the program had been of only medium or transitory interest during the learning phase.

Since the sonographic report is sent to the referring physicians in the clinic, we also asked for their opinion about the significance of the new record types with a questionnaire that was answered by 35 clinicians:

C1 Differentiated report on organ findings:	3.8 (1 = never read; 5 = always read)
C2 System diagnoses:	3.0 (1 = never read; 5 = always read)
C3 Examiner comment:	4.9 (1 = unnecessary; 5 = necessary)
C4 Standardization of nomenclature:	3.5 (1 = unnecessary; 5 = necessary)
C5 New records:	3.6 (1 = neutral; 5 = positively acknowledged)
C6 Significance of sonographic records:	2.3 (1 = unchanged; 5 = enhanced)

The results indicate that the clinicians most strongly rely on the examiner comment, but often read the differentiated report with all observed findings and the automatically inferred system diagnoses. They welcome the new record and the standardization of nomenclature, but judge them only as a small enhancement.

3.2 Clinical Impact

We also tried to measure whether the use of SC improved the quality of the sonographic records: Potential improvements are a more complete documentation of symptoms and a higher quality of the reported diagnoses. To answer the first question, we entered the data of 103 hand written reports which had been documented before the program's introduction into SC and noted whether all questions asked by SC could be answered with the available data. If not, two senior examiners judged the information gaps in the free text reports as relevant or dispensable. From the 287 information gaps found, the domain experts judged nearly half of them (132) as relevant. For the second question concerning the diagnoses, the senior examiners compared the diagnoses in the free text reports with those generated by the program and used their own diagnoses based on the same patient data as gold standard. They found 179 problematic diagnoses form a total of about 600 diagnoses (103 cases with 6 diagnoses on average) in the free text reports and 86 problematic diagnoses generated by SC.

Since this evaluation is difficult to interpret, because there is some scope to answer standardized questions from free text reports, we conducted a second evaluation, where we used 112 prospective, consecutive records and compared the documented conclusions of the examiners with those of SC. There were almost no relevant information gaps. This is due to the guided data acquisition strategy of SC, which had a significant clinical impact. The diagnostic conclusions were judged by three domain experts as "correct" or "problematic", when they all agreed on the same assessment. From the 412 diagnoses in these records (i.e. in this sample an average of 3.7 per case), the examiners missed 107 (26%) true diagnoses and stated an additional 32 diagnoses, which were not supported by the documented findings. In contrast, all diagnostic conclusions of SC were judged as adequate. When the 412 diagnoses are differentiated into simple and complex conclusions (the latter are based on the combination of more than one symptom), there were 145 complex diagnoses, from which the examiners missed 57 (39%) and stated an additional 15 unsupported diagnoses. Again the figures are difficult to interpret with respect to the clinical correctness of the diagnoses, since the evaluation was based on text documents, not on sonographic pictures, because these were not included in the records. Therefore, in general it is not possible to differentiate between incorrect symptom descriptions and incorrect conclusions, although the high degree of problematic simple diagnoses (50 from 267, i.e. 19%) indicates documentation errors. Nevertheless the inconsistence between documented findings and diagnostic conclusions is rather high. This is quite astonishing, since the SC-diagnoses were visible to the examiners before writing their final comment. This fact is consistent with the low influence of the system's diagnoses on the own diagnoses of the examiners in the questionnaire (B6). To investigate this phenomenon further, we plan several steps: Follow-up evaluations to investigate the hypothesis that the acceptance of the system diagnoses by the examiners takes a longer period of time, an additional interface enabling the examiners to copy the system's diagnoses quite easily in their free text report and a critic component to compare the free text diagnoses and the system's diagnoses. The critic component generates warnings in case of serious discrepancies and offers generated forms for correction of the discrepancies. The latter requires an information extraction component for identifying coded diagnoses in a free text format.

3.3 Statistical Analysis

The physicians considered statistical analysis as one of the desirable features (A9) before SC was introduced. About 300 detailed patient records are documented per month. Typical questions concern correlations among pathological states of different organs, since the intra organ relations are usually well known.

The data mining technique of subgroup mining [Klösgen 02, Atzmueller et al. 05] is quite suitable for common medical questions, e.g. whether a certain pathological state is significantly more frequent if combinations of other pathological states exist. Since the efficient use of a subgroup data mining tool requires some experience and statistical knowledge, we implemented a process consisting of two steps for the clinical introduction. In the first step, a simple tool with standard reports similar to the OLAP [Han & Kamber 00] interface for data warehouses is used: the data can be manually refined along predefined hierarchies, e.g. time hierarchies like day, week, month; general patient attributes like age, gender and body weight with categories and diagnostic hierarchies like organs and special diseases concerning an organ. This simple interface is directly integrated into the user-interface of SonoConsult.

In the second step, the powerful (subgroup) mining tool VIKAMINE (Visual, Interactive and Knowledge-Intensive Analysis and Mining Environment) is utilized, which is applied for interactive and automatic subgroup mining. This tool is adapted to particularities of the medical domain like many missing values in the records, due to intelligent data gathering strategies minimizing the number of asked questions, Furthermore, often background knowledge can be utilized, since known knowledge should not be rediscovered, but the available knowledge should be used to find new, often subtle correlations, to increase the interestingness of the discovered results. Additionally, often (known) confounding factors (like age, gender, body weight etc.) need to be controlled.

VIKAMINE offers different search options for automatic subgroup discovery and various interactive visualizations for active user involvement. Both tools operate on the same data base. When the user discovers something unexpected/interesting in the data using the simple tool, then, after switching to VIKAMINE, these unexpected features can be inspected and analyzed in detail, e.g. to discover subgroups corresponding to the unexpected features which might serve as an explanation.

First experiments with VIKAMINE were quite promising. We describe our current experiences and present results in the following two case studies. The first case study concerns subgroup mining for knowledge discovery, i.e. discovering criteria describing a subgroup in which the presence of a disease is significantly more probable than in the whole population. The second case study aimed to identify certain examiner profiles: these profiles – concerning documentation habits of individual examiners – can be used to detect significant deviations in personal documentation patterns which can then be utilized for discussion and training of the examiners.

3.3.1 Subgroup Mining for Knowledge Discovery

Table 1 exemplary shows discovered interesting subgroups concerning the target variable *gallstones*. While their general probability in the documented cases was about 17%, the factor "age >= 70" increases their probability to ca. 25% (#7). "Age >=70" together with "sex = female" and "liver size = slightly, moderately or highly enlarged" increase the probability of gallstones already to ca. 35% (#5). The probability is further increased to ca. 39%, if "aorta sclerosis" is observed in addition (#2), and if the "aorta sclerosis is calcified" even to ca. 42% (#1). The rows 1-6 in table 1 show the effect of different combinations of age, sex, liver size and aorta sclerosis on gallstones, which are all significant at least at the 10^{-6} level, while the rows 7-13 show the effects of single factors for comparison.

The interestingness of subgroups depends primarily on the increase in probability ("relative gain" = RG) and the subgroup size. In addition, the simplicity of the subgroup description is an important clinical factor. Therefore the expert can interactively vary the precise subgroup description by including or excluding an attribute value by a simple cross in the respective cell.

Table 1. Examples of interesting discovered subgroups in lines 1-6 and reference probabilities in lines 7-13. Subgroup oparameters given in the columns are: (Subgroup) Size, TP (true positives), FP (false positives), Pop. (defined population size), p0 (default target share), p (target share in the subgroup), RG (relative gain of the subgroup) and the binomial quality function BQF (Bin. QF), which combines subgroup size and the target share. The following relations hold: TP+FP = size; p = TP/(TP+FP)), RG = (p– p0) / p0(1-p0)) and $BQF = \frac{(p - p0)}{\sqrt{p0(1 - p0)}} \sqrt{Size} \sqrt{(Pop. - Size) / Pop.}$

Target Variable: Gallstones																					
#	Age			Sex		Liver size						Aorta sclerosis									
	1	2	3	m	f	1	2	3	4	5	6	n	c	Size	TP	FP	Pop.	p0	p	RG	Bin. QF
1			X		X				X	X	X		X	89	37	52	3171	0.172	0.416	1.71	6.17
2			X		X				X	X	X	X	X	119	46	73	3171	0.172	0.387	1.5	6.31
3		X	X		X				X	X	X		X	132	51	81	3171	0.172	0.386	1.5	6.66
4					X			X	X	X	X		X	190	68	122	3177	0.172	0.358	1.3	6.99
5			X		X				X	X	X			207	72	135	3171	0.172	0.348	1.23	6.92
6		X	X		X					X	X	X	X	64	22	42	3171	0.172	0.344	1.2	3.67
7			X											1651	414	1237	3743	0.177	0.251	0.51	10.57
8		X	X											3019	620	2399	3743	0.177	0.205	0.2	9.43
9												X	X	1334	310	1024	3749	0.177	0.232	0.38	6.66
10					X									1776	408	1368	3749	0.177	0.23	0.37	8.1
11									X	X	X			894	178	716	3177	0.172	0.199	0.19	2.52
12										X	X			316	65	251	3177	0.172	0.206	0.24	1.66
13											X			95	16	79	3177	0.172	0.168	-0.02	-0.09

Age:	**Sex:**	**Liver size:**		**Aorta sclerosis:**
1 = <50	m = male	1 = smaller than normal	4 = slightly increased	n = not calcified
2 = 50-69	f = female	2 = normal	5 = moderately increased	c = calcified
3 = >=70		3 = marginally increased	6 = highly increased	

The individual subgroups are shown in the rows of the table, e.g. the first line depicts the subgroup (89 cases) described by *Age >= 70 AND Sex=female AND Liver size={slightly or moderately or highly increased} AND Aorta sclerosis=calcified* with a target share (gallstones) of 41.6% (p) compared to 17.2% (p_0) in the general population, with a relative gain of 171% (RG).

3.3.2 Subgroup Mining for Profiling Examiners

The goal of the second case study was to discover interesting, i.e. unexpected or unusual, documentation patterns of sonographic examiners. Individual examiners rotate according to a defined schedule (e.g., every 6 months). Before performing the examinations, they get special training and can always consult experienced colleagues. However, while performing the examination they are on their own. Then, it is easy to see that the quality of the examinations is dependent on the individual experience and skills of the examiners. Therefore, documentation and interpretation habits of examiners may differ significantly, which is problematic considering the consistency and quality of the documented examinations. For example, some examiners may be more competent in identifying specific symptoms concerning certain diagnoses/organ systems than others.

To identify deviations regarding the documentation habits of examiners, subgroup mining is used for analytical questions concerning individual examiners. Then, if cer tain symptom combinations are observed significantly more (in-)frequently in

Table 2. Interesting subgroups and individual factors concerning liver diseases. We refer to Table 1 for a description of the subgroup parameters. The first line depicts the subgroup (target variable *Examiner=E1*) described by *Liver surface = uneven, knotty* with a target share of 19.9% (p) in the subgroup compared to 16.4% (p_0) in the total population, with a relative gain of 24% (RG).

#	E	LP		LS		LE		LV		LC		Subgroup Parameters						
		mr	sr	uk	kn	mi	si	rp	tp	po	pr	Size	TP	FP	Pop.	p0	p	RG
1	E1			X								221	44	177	2295	0.164	0.199	0.24
2	E1						X					435	41	394	2295	0.164	0.094	-0.51
3	E1	X	X									420	28	392	2295	0.164	0.066	-0.71
4	E1				X							13	0	13	2295	0.164	0	-1.19
5	E2		X									248	19	229	2295	0.123	0.076	-0.43
6	E2							X				689	25	664	2294	0.123	0.036	-0.8
7	E3	X	X					X		X		129	91	38	2294	0.129	0.705	5.12
8	E3	X										248	116	132	2295	0.128	0.467	3.01
9	E3							X		X	X	385	131	254	2294	0.129	0.34	1.87
10	E3	X	X									420	132	288	2295	0.128	0.314	1.64
11	E3				X							13	4	9	2295	0.128	0.307	1.59
12	E3								X		X	102	0	102	2294	0.13	0	-1.14
13	E5				X							13	9	4	2295	0.057	0.692	11.8
14	E5	X				X	X					227	85	142	2295	0.057	0.374	5.89
15	E5	X										248	87	161	2295	0.057	0.35	5.45
16	E5	X	X									420	96	324	2295	0.057	0.228	3.18
17	E5									X	X	440	56	384	3918	0.053	0.127	1.46
18	E5	X	X			X	X	X		X	X	271	39	232	2294	0.057	0.143	1.61
19	E5			X								221	6	215	2295	0.057	0.027	-0.55
20	E5			X		X		X		X	X	109	0	109	2294	0.058	0	-1.06
21	E5					X	X					1493	110	1383	2295	0.057	0.073	0.3
22	E5							X				689	44	645	2294	0.057	0.063	0.12

LP = Liver Plasticity
mr = moderately reduced
sr = strongly reduced

LS = Liver surface
uk = uneven, knotty
kn = knaggy

LC = Cirrhosis of the liver
po = possible
pr = probable

LE = Liver Echogenicity
mi = moderately increased
si = strongly increased

LV = Liver Vessels
rp = rarefication of portal branches
tp = tapering of portal branches

conjunction with certain examiners, then appropriate measures such as special training courses or discussion with colleagues can be suggested.

We show examples of the results in Table 2, considering liver diseases, especially focussing on *cirrhosis of the liver*. The cases used in the case study were acquired by 8 different examiners (E1 - E8). Concerning liver examinations, each examiner contributed 200-600 cases, resulting in a total population of 3931 cases where an examination of the liver was performed. Then, we analyzed the factors concerning the individual examiners as the target concept (dependent variable).

The results in Table 2 show significant differences in the documentation habits of the individual examiners. Negative relative gain (RG) values indicate that the examiner documented/interpreted certain findings less frequently than his colleagues, while a positive relative gain indicates the opposite.

For a comprehensive overview, we also show some single factors in addition to significant combinations, which were interesting in their own. Especially significant deviations are shown in lines 7, 14 and 15, which are very descriptive for the respective examiners. Line 7 also shows a significant correlation with the diagnosis cirrhosis of the liver combined with the relevant findings.

Lines 4, 11, and 13 show a surprising result: the examiners E3 and E5 are the only examiners that document a specific finding, i.e., Liver surface = knaggy in comparison to their colleagues. Further investigation showed that the specific attribute value was added to SC in a later step. Since therefore only some examiners had the opportunity to use this finding, this result may be viewed as an artifact.

More relevant is a closer look on examiner E5 (lines 14-20), since the shown documentation habits differed most significantly compared to the peer examiners. Especially interesting were the subgroups depicted in line 17, 18 and 20: it is easy to see that examiner E5 documents a *cirrhosis of the liver = probable or possible* more frequently than his peers. An even more significant subgroup is shown in line 18 that shows a specialization of the subgroup in line 17. For the very indicative finding combination in line 20 (regarding the diagnosis cirrhosis of the liver) even no case of E5 could be identified. It is striking that E5 uses very special patterns for inferring the diagnosis *cirrhosis of the liver* compared to his colleagues: e.g., symptoms of plasticity are much more frequent (lines 14-16) whereas *liver surface = uneven, knotty* is significantly infrequent (lines 19, 20).

In summary, these results show a high variability of documentation and interpretation habits of the different examiners. These results can be used to initiate a discussion on training or standardization actions to increase the inter-examiner homogenity of the sonographic reports.

4 Summary and Further Work

The evaluations of SonoConsult showed (1) its benefits as an intelligent documentation system producing more complete records in a standardized nomenclature in about the same amount of time as hand-written reports, (2) its training value for beginners, (3) its high diagnostic accuracy, and (4) its potential for knowledge discovery and quality control by data mining techniques. Although the system was well accepted in general, its diagnostic conclusions were largely ignored. This evaluation result requires further investigations. Our plan to investigate the discrepancies between the diagnoses contained in final free text reports of the examiners and the diagnoses automatically inferred by SonoConsult is to rate the discrepancies with a tailored information extraction tool. First results are quite promising with a precision of 94% and a recall of 92% based on a prospective evaluation with 220 reports containing 1804 diagnosis [Dressler 05]. This tool will be the basis for a critiquing component, which informs the users, if major discrepancies are detected.

References

Atzmueller, M.; Puppe, F.; Buscher, H.-P.: Exploiting Background Knowledge for Knowledge-Intensive Sub-group Discovery. Proc. 19th International Joint Conference on Artificial Intelligence (IJCAI-05), 2005.

Berner, E., Maisiak, R., Cobbs, G., Taunton, O.: Effects of a Decision Support System on Physicians´ Diagnostic Performance. J Am Med Inform Assoc 6, 420-427, 1999.

Buscher, H. P., Engler, C., Fuhrer, A., Kirschke, S., Puppe, F.: HepatoConsult: a Knowledge-Based Second Opinion and Documentation System. Artif. Intell. Med. 24, 205-216, 2002.

Darmoni S., Poynard T.: Computer-Aided Decision Support in Hepatology. Scand J Gastroenterol 27, 889-896, 1992.

Dressler, A.: Diagnosecodierung medizinischer Freitexte – am Beispiel sonographischer Befundberichte, [Coding of diagnosis from free texts – with a case study of sonographic reports], Diploma Thesis, Würzburg University, Institute for Informatics, 2005.

Han, J., and Kamber, M.: Data Mining, Concepts and Techniques, Chap. 2, 2000.

Huettig, M., Buscher, G., Menzel, T., Scheppach, W., Puppe, F., Buscher, H.-P.: A Diagnostic Expert System for Structured Reports, Quality Assessment, and Training of Residents in Sonography, Med Klin 99: 117-122, 2004.

Klösgen, W.: Handbook of Data Mining and Knowledge Discovery, Chapter 16.3 Subgroup Discovery, Oxford University Press, 2002.

McDonald C.: Medical Heuristics: The Silent Adjudicators of Clinical Practice. Ann. Intern. Med. 124, 56-62, 1996.

Puppe, F.: Knowledge Reuse among Diagnostic Problem-Solving Methods in the Shell-KIT D3. Int Journal of Human-Computer Studies 49, 627-649, 1998.

Unlocking the Value of Clinical Information: What You Need to Do Now to Enjoy the Benefits in the Future

Hooman Katirai[1,2] and Ulrich Sax[2]

[1] Clinical Decision Making Group,
MIT Computer Science and Artificial Intelligence Laboratory,
32 Vassar Street, Area 250, Cambridge, MA 02139, USA
hooman@MIT.edu

[2] Children's Hospital Informatics Program (CHIP),
Harvard-MIT Division of Health Sciences & Technology,
320 Longwood Ave, Boston, MA 02125, USA
Current address: Department of Medical Informatics,
Robert-Koch-Str. 40, 37075 Goettingen, Germany
usax@med.uni-goettingen.de

Abstract. Electronic communication and connectivity are among the core functionalities of an Electronic Health Record (EHR) infrastructure with comprehensive life-long records. But clinical data is still mostly locked up in disjoint data silos, and often stored in non-standard formats. This paper elucidates the opportunities and drawbacks of using the HL7 Clinical Document Architecture (CDA) as a standard for storing clinical information for computer decision support and knowledge management. As EHR document standards are continually being improved, we argue that the ease in upgrading to new standards should be a significant factor in the design of an EHR infrastructure. To achieve this upgradeability, we need to decouple a document's data from the standards used to represent the data. We argue that this separation between data and form can be achieved using a technique called *compilable templates,* which was recently developed by the authors in a Personal Health Record (PHR) project. Web services offer a compelling means of implementing such templates owing to their language and platform neutrality. Finally we show that some software that one would typically expect to find in a knowledge management context can be automatically generated from a compilable template, saving time and money while reducing the possibility of error.

1 Introduction

Communication and interoperability are the main goals in creating a useful electronic infrastructure in the healthcare system[1]. Patient data should be available both to the patient and all subsequent institutions dealing with the patient. This is not the case today. In the current situation, a patient's data will typically be scattered across numerous databases housed in different points of care. These data silos will each utilize a proprietary data format – often incompatible with the data standards of other organizations. In fact many institutions in healthcare are not interested in sharing their data

K.-D. Althoff et al. (Eds.): WM 2005, LNAI 3782, pp. 330 – 338, 2005.

except financial transactions and in terms of clinical studies. As a result clinical data can rarely be exchanged between different organizations[2].

The person being the most interested in compiling her healthcare related data is the patient. So a patient demanding her hospital data electronically could for instance be a strong motivation for the hospital to share patient data. The longitudinal, maybe life long collection of healthcare related data of one patient across many institutions is called Personal Health Record (PHR). PHRs offer the possibility of medical records that can be easily accessed and annotated both within and between organizations[3, 4]. Post-genomic clinical studies and the application of data mining methods imply standardized patient data and standardized terminology being accessible to knowledge discovery tools[5]. Early attempts on standardizing medical vocabulary show the complexity of this task[6-8]. The lion's share of clinical phenotype data is not encoded for automated processing.

The main goals of enabling clinical data for decision support systems (DSS) and knowledge management (KM) are (a) minimizing the number of fields that express similar concepts in the federated databases and where it makes sense (b) codifying the data to obtain the best tradeoff between specificity and practicality.

An examination of the data models of a number of standards shows that the HL7 Reference Information Model (RIM) and the HL7 CDA architecture are well positioned to fulfill the goal of communication and interoperability of health information systems in general and EHRs in particular[9, 10].

The compilable template technologies introduced in this document were developed while integrating data from hospitals into the Personal Internetworked Notary and Guardian (PING) – a multi-institutional Personal Health Record designed to integrate health information from multiple sources[4, 11].

PING is an open source system representing a fully distributed electronic medical record in which patients have control over who can read, write or modify components of their records. It is designed to be a comprehensive compilation of all medical data longitudinally across the patient's history[4].

2 The HL7 CDA

The HL7 Clinical Document Architecture (CDA) is a document markup standard, which specifies the structure and the semantics of clinical documents in extensible Markup Language (XML). Persistence, stewardship, potential for authentication, wholeness and human readability are the main characteristics of the CDA[10, 12].

CDA documents consist of a header and a body. The header includes the context in which the document was created, and the body contains the actual content of the document. The purpose of the header is to support the communication across and within institutions; facilitate clinical document management; and facilitate the compilation of an individual patient's clinical documents into a lifetime electronic health record[12].

The body of a CDA document can be either an unstructured blob, or can be represented by structured markup. Figure 1 shows a structured body, which is wrapped by the <StructuredBody> element, and which is divided up into recursively nestable document sections[10].

```
<ClinicalDocument>
  ... CDA Header ...
  <StructuredBody>
    <section>
      <text>...</text>
      <Observation>...</Observation>
      <Observation>
        <reference>
          <ExternalObservation>...</ExternalObservation>
        </reference>
      </Observation>
    </section>
    <section>
        <section>...</section>
    </section>
  </StructuredBody>
</ClinicalDocument>
```

Fig. 1. XML structure of a HL7 CDA document containing a header and a structured body[10]

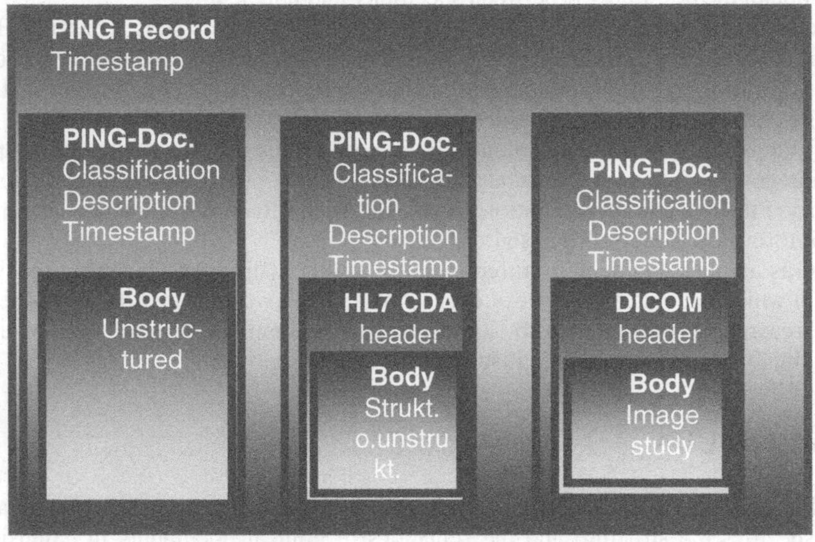

Fig. 2. Simplified PING example Record containing (a) an unstructured Blob, (b) a HL7 CDA document and (c) a DICOM object

CDA defines three levels; in level one only the document header is fixed with a certain set of document and object identifiers. Level two additionally defines a structured document body, which has to be fully RIM-derived in level three[10]. The document type in the header as well as the universal observation identifiers have to be defined according to Logical Observation Identifier Names and Codes (LOINC)[13] document codes. European projects like PICNIC[14] and SCIPHOX[15] have successfully made use of CDA level one documents.

Though the intention of CDA is to facilitate the creation of PHRs, it is very unlikely that all medical information will be encoded in one standard format like

CDA. On the other hand side a PHR like PING has to include all types of documents it get from different healthcare providers. Therefore PING does not rely on one standard format, but wraps any document of any type in a PING document. This document contains a PING header with items like a PING classification, a description and a timestamp. Figure 2 shows an example record containing (a) an unstructured Blob, (b) a HL7 CDA document and (c) a DICOM object.

3 Compilable Templates[1]

To date, only a few CDA document types have been defined[9, 17] . Because changes to the HL7 CDA standard are likely, the effort required to upgrade to new standards should be a consideration in the design of a PHR infrastructure. One way to achieve upgradeability is to decouple the code that generates CDA documents from the code that queries a database via a functional abstraction layer. The code that generates CDA documents can be treated as a black box function that writes CDA documents given a tuple whose elements represent the values of individual fields. We term this

(a) A SNIPPET FROM A COMPILABLE TEMPLATE:

```
<!--#INCLUDE: "header.inc" -->
<person_name>
<nm>
  <v3dt:GIV V="___firstName___"/>
  <v3dt:MID V="___midInitial___"/>
  <v3dt:FAM V="___lastName___ "/>
</nm>
</person_name>
<!-- #INCLUDE: "footer.inc" -->
```

(b) PRODUCES THE FOLLOWING FORWARD FUNCTION:

```
String Toy_example(String first_name, String middle_initial,
      String last_name)
```

(c) CALLING THIS FUNCTION WITH A SET OF VALUES GIVES:

```
<levelone xmlns="urn:hl7-org:v3/cda"
 xmlns:v3dt="urn:hl7-org:v3/v3dt"
 xmlns:xsi=http://www.w3.org/2001/XMLSchema-instance
 xsi:schemaLocation=
 "urn:hl7-org:v3/cda levelone_1.0.attachments.xsd">
<clinical_document_header>
<person_name>
<nm>
   <v3dt:GIV V="George"/>
   <v3dt:MID V="F"/>
   <v3dt:FAM V="Carson"/>
</nm>
</person_name>
</clinical_document_header>
</levelone>
```

Fig. 3. This snippet from a compilable template shows (a) a simplified compilable template, (b) the automatically generated forward function and (c) the CDA document produced after calling the forward function with a set of values. Full examples of templates are available online20.

---

1 Our use of the word 'template' should not be conflated with the HL7 usage of the term 'template' in the sense of Archetypes[16].

function the *forward function*; it produces a CDA document given a tuple of values. Fig. 3 shows a simplified example of a compilable template.

Data mining algorithms generally do not accept XML documents as input; rather, they require their training sets to be in the form a table (where each row in the table represents a tuple). The act of transforming a CDA document into a tuple implies the existence of what we call an "*inverse function*". An inverse function is the opposite operation as the forward function; that is, given a CDA document, it returns a tuple of values. Figure 4 shows a simple example of an inverse function.

(a) SNIPPET FROM A CDA Document:

```
<levelone xmlns="urn:hl7-org:v3/cda"
    xmlns:v3dt="urn:hl7-org:v3/v3dt"
    xmlns:xsi=http://www.w3.org/2001/XMLSchema-instance
    xsi:schemaLocation=
    "urn:hl7-org:v3/cda levelone_1.0.attachments.xsd">
  <clinical_document_header>
    <person_name>
      <nm>
        <v3dt:GIV V="George"/>
        <v3dt:MID V="F"/>
        <v3dt:FAM V="Carson"/>
      </nm>
    </person_name>
  </clinical_document_header>
</levelone>
```

(b) USING THE FOLLOWING INVERSE FUNCTION:

```
Toy_example( String Toy_Example_CDA_Document)
```

(c) CALLING THIS FUNCTION WITH A CDA DOCUMENT GIVES (assumed a table person does not exist yet):

```
CREATE TABLE Persons (firstName,  midInitial, lastName);
INSERT INTO Persons values ('George', 'F', 'Carson');
```

Fig. 4. This snippet shows (a) a CDA document, (b) the automatically generated inverse function and (c) the resulting SQL-query to write the content in a database table

Compilable Template

```
<!--#INSERT:
for (int i=0; i<first_name.length;i++){ -->
 <person_name>
  <nm>
   <v3dt:GIV V="___firstName [i]___"/>
   <!-- #INSERT: if (mid_Initial[i]!=null) -->
   <v3dt:MID V="___midInitial[i]___"/>
   <v3dt:FAM V="___lastName[i]___ "/>
  </nm>
 </person_name>
<!--#INSERT: } // closing brace for staatement -->
```

Resultant Function

```
String Toy_example
(
 String firstName[],
 String midInitial[],
 String lastName[]
)
```

Fig. 5. The 'for' statement above shows how variable length arguments can be incorporated into compilable templates (resulting in arrayed inputs in the resultant function) while the 'if' statement shows how optional arguments can be encoded (i.e the line following the "if-statement" will not be output for patients that have no middle initial)

Inverse functions have to deal with the fundamental difference between XML documents and relational databases. An XML document is a hierarchical data structure, whereas a database table represents a flat data structure. When one converts an XML file into a database table, all implicit hierarchic information in the CDA document is lost. This emphasizes the need for a hybrid approach: "convert the content into database tables for data mining, but store the original CDA document as well".

Both the forward function and the inverse function can be automatically generated from a file we term a "*compilable template*". The file is a *template* insofar as it is similar to a CDA document but it contains variables in place of data values. The file is also termed *compilable* because it contains commands that be processed by a compiler[21] to generate outputs such as the forward and inverse functions.

Web services are functions that execute on a remote server. Given an XML file called a Web Service Description Language (WSDL)[18] file, one can automatically generate the code required to access a web service in just about any programming language of significance. Owing to the language and platform neutrality of web services, we believe that web services represent an ideal means of implementing the forward function – particularly in the context of a PHR where one can expect the cooperating institutions to utilize a variety of platforms and programming languages. Web services are elegant. In our demonstration system the invocation of the function to produce a CDA document takes only two lines of source code in the C# programming language and three lines in Java.

The use of compilable templates can automate many common tasks. To give the reader an idea of the scope of automation possible, consider the automation already achieved in the PING project. In addition to automating the production of the code for the forward and inverse functions, our template compiler also (1) creates web services for the forward and inverse functions (2) installs the web services on a web server (3) generates WSDL files for each web service (4) uses the WSDL file to generate the functions needed to access these web services corresponding to the forward functions

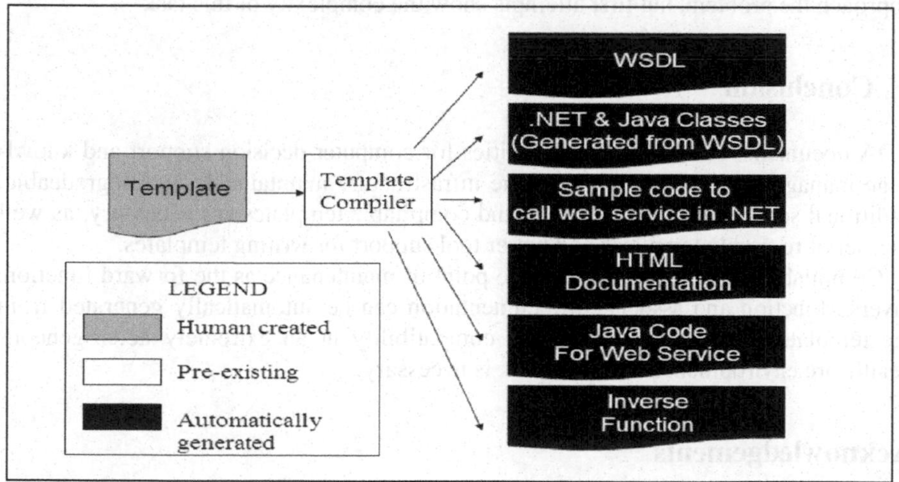

Fig. 6. A compilable template represents a single point of maintenance from which one can generate software and elements whose production would normally require human effort

in two languages (C#.Net and Java), and (5) installs on a web server appropriate documentation to allow authorized programmers to access the web services.

It is in this vein that we refer to compilable templates as a *single point of maintenance,* because all of the above functionality is automatically generated from a single compilable template file. When compared to the alternative approach of writing the CDA document manually (in which each step would represent a point of maintenance) the time and cost savings become compelling.

4 Opportunities and Challenges

The opportunity of our approach is it reduces the cost of moving existing documents to new standards, while immediately reducing the work required to produce software commonly needed for KM applications.

Electronically signed documents present special challenges since the alteration of a single bit is sufficient to void the signature. As a result, signed documents cannot be upgraded to a new standard per se without abandoning the validity of their signature. Therefore we recommend the following hybrid approach. A copy of a signed document should be stored for archival purposes, while an unsigned version of the document can be upgraded to the newer standard, with a URL pointing to the old document.

The effort to create sustainable CDA templates is quite high, as there are no suitable tools available to support the process of writing CDA templates. So the templates we regarding this paper are more or less "hand carved". Better tools and a set of consistant template would facilitate this process and would possibly broaden the usage of CDA documents.

An even bigger obstacle yet is the lack of ontological compatibility on the clinical domain. Using terminologies like LOINC or SNOMED CT etc. and the appropriate mapping to the Unified Medical Language System (UMLS)[19] could be a first step to approach the problem, but first attempts show the complexity of this task[6-8].

5 Conclusion

CDA documents offer many opportunities for computer decision support and knowledge management. In order to keep the infrastructure maintainable and upgradeable, additional services like web services and compilable templates are necessary, as well as a set of re-usable templates and better tool support for writing templates.

Compilable template enable a single point of maintenance as the forward function, inverse function and associated documentation can be automatically generated from the template. To achieve ontological compatibility in an extremely heterogeneous healthcare environment still more work is necessary.

Acknowledgements

The authors are grateful to (1) Peter Szolovits at MIT for reviewing this manuscript and for his sage advice and criticism and to (2) Isaac Kohane at Children's Hospital, for helpful discussions and insights and for suggesting that web services be used in this project.

This work was supported by Deutsche Forschungsgemeinschaft (DFG, SA1009/1-1) and by the National Institutes of Health through contract N01-LM-3-3515 from the National Library of Medicine.

References

1. (IOM) IoM. Key Capabilities of an Electronic Health Record System - Letter Report. July 31, 2003. Available at: http://books.nap.edu/html/ehr/NI000427.pdf. August 16, 2004.
2. Waegemann CP. Status Report 2002: Electronic Health Records. *MRI.* Available at: http://www.medrecinst.com/resources/ehr2002/index.shtml. August 16, 2004.
3. Simons WW, Mandl KD, Kohane IS. The PING Personally Controlled Electronic Medical Record System: Technical Architecture. *J Am Med Inform Assoc.* 10 18 2004.
4. Riva A, Mandl KD, Oh DH, et al. The personal internetworked notary and guardian. *Int J Med Inf.* Jun 2001;62(1):27-40.
5. Kohane I, Glaser J. Informatics for Integrating Biology and the Bedside (I2B2). Available at: http://www.i2b2.org/index2.html. October 18, 2004.
6. Holloway E. Meeting Review: From Genotype to Phenotype: Linking Bioinformatics and Medical Informatics Ontologies. *Comp Funct Genom.* 2002;2002(3):447-450.
7. Verschelde J-L, Dos Santos MC, Deray T, Smith B, Ceusters W. Ontology-assisted database integration to support natural language processing and biomedical data-mining. *Journal of Integrative Bioinformatics.* 15.01.2004 2004(0001, 2004).
8. HL7 Clinical Genomics SIG. HL7 Clinical Genomics SIG San Diego Meeting Minutes Jan 21-22, 2004. *HL7.* Available at: http://www.hl7.org/library/committees/clingenomics/minutes/HL7%20CG%20SIG%20Meeting%20Minutes%202004%2001%2021% 20v2.doc. October 18, 2004.
9. Lovis C, Lamb A, Baud R, Rassinoux AM, Fabry P, Geissbuhler A. Clinical Documents: Attribute-values Entity Representation,Context, Page Layout And Communication. *Proc AMIA Symp.* 2003:396-400.
10. Dolin RH, Altschuler L, Boyer S, Beebe C, Behlen FM, Biron PV. HL7 Clinical Document Architecture (Release 2.0). *Health Level Seven, Inc.* Available at: http://www.hl7.org/library/committees/structure/CDA.REleaseTwo.CommitteeBallot02.Dec.2003.zip. October 18, 2004.
11. PING - Personal Internetworked Notary and Guardian. *Children's Hospital Informatics Program (CHIP).* Available at: http://www.ping.chip.org/IntroductionToPing.html. September 1, 2004.
12. Dolin RH, Alschuler L, Beebe C, et al. The HL7 Clinical Document Architecture. *J Am Med Inform Assoc.* Nov-Dec 2001;8(6):552-569.
13. McDonald CJ, Huff SM, Suico JG, et al. LOINC, a universal standard for identifying laboratory observations: a 5-year update. *Clin Chem.* Apr 2003;49(4):624-633.
14. Bray B. The PICNIC approach to regional care networks. *Stud Health Technol Inform.* 2003;96:80-87.
15. Heitmann KU, Schweiger R, Dudeck J. Discharge and referral data exchange using global standards--the SCIPHOX project in Germany. *Int J Med Inf.* Jul 2003;70(2-3):195-203.
16. Kernberg M, Elkin PL. HL7 Template and Archetype Architecture. *HL7.* Available at: http://www.hl7.org/Library/Committees/template/HL7_San_Diego_v2.3.zip. August 27, 2004.

17. Health_Level_Seven. HL7 Additional Information Specification Implementation Guide (Release 2.0 Ballot, August 2003). *Health Level Seven, Inc.* Available at: http://www.hl7.org/Special/committees/claims/HL7ClmAttIG.PDF. 09.02.2004.
18. W3C WWWC. Web Services Description Language (WSDL) 1.1. *W3C*. Available at: http://www.w3.org/TR/wsdl. September 3, 2004.
19. Bodenreider O. The Unified Medical Language System (UMLS): integrating biomedical terminology. *Nucleic Acids Res.* Jan 1 2004;32 Database issue:D267-270.
20. More complete examples of compilable templates and our template compiler. Available at: http://members.rogers.com/hoomank/templates.
21. Apache Foundation. Apache Web Services Project - an open source Java web services framework. Available at: http://ws.apache.org/axis. November 22, 2004.

Knowledge Management in Internal Medicine Using Lotus Notus – A Knowledge Management Perspective

Christoph Bobrowski and Georg Kreymann

Medizinische Klinik und Poliklinik I, Zentrum für Innere Medizin,
Universitätsklinikum Hamburg-Eppendorf,
D-20246 Hamburg
bobrowski@uke.uni-hamburg.de

Abstract. There is growing demand for the presentation and retrieval of clinical guidelines which are relevant for the everyday usage of clinicians. An intranet-based solution compares favorably to paperwork, but a standard web based on plain HTML does not support very well features such as document structuring and text retrieval. At the start of this project (year 2000), content management systems were rudimentary and expensive. We have therefore implemented an Intranet which is entirely based on Lotus Notes/Lotus Domino. The essential advantages of this solution are the integration of full-text retrieval, structured documents and document hierarchies into a departmental intranet. The outcome of the project is evaluated from the perspective of knowledge management.

1 Introduction

Within the department of Internal Medicine, there was demand for the presentation of guidelines and local procedural standards. An intranet solution based on a web server alone was rejected because this solution lacked document structuring, authoring, and workflow support. Content management systems (CMS), on the other hand, were less developed then (year 2000) than they were now, and they were expensive.

Our essential requirements were: System development and integration costs should be marginal, and authorization and production of documents should be supported by the software. We decided to base the intranet entirely based on Lotus Notes/Domino. Principles governing the design and the structure of websites containing guidelines have been described before. e.g. by the American Medical Association [1] and the National Guideline Clearinghouse project [2]. These principles have focused on quality and efficiency. In the project described here, our modest objective was to start a pilot project based on groupware as a tool for document management in an intranet. The project has resulted only in a partial success. Reasons for this are reviewed from the viewpoint of knowledge management [3].

2 Material, Methods, and Clinical Setting

The Medizinische Klinik and Poliklinik I is a department of the University hospital's Center for Internal Medicine of the Universitätsklinikum Hamburg-Eppendorf (UKE).

K.-D. Althoff et al. (Eds.): WM 2005, LNAI 3782, pp. 339 – 348, 2005.

The department serves the specialties Pneumology, Endocrinology/Metabolism, Gastroenterology/Hepatology, Infectiology, Intensive Care and Emergency Admissions. There are 106 hospital beds and 13 ICU beds in the department. Server and clients run under Windows NT4, newer clients under Windows 2000. Hardware was installed in the years 2000 and 2001. Lotus Notes/Domino Release 5 was used. Network infrastructure consisted of the two disjoint networks of the hospital. The "scientific net" is connected to the internet using UKE's web server, and the "medical net" is used for patient care.

The knowledge management paradigm

The knowledge management paradigm developed by Probst and the Geneva knowledge group [3] has been used to evaluate this project *a posteriori*. In this framework, knowledge management entails

1. Knowledge objectives
2. Knowledge identification
3. Knowledge acquisition
4. Knowledge development
5. Knowledge dissemination
6. Knowledge usage
7. Knowledge maintenance
8. Knowledge evaluation

These eight entities are sometimes referred to as building blocks of knowledge management (KM). Building blocks 2 to 7 form the core of KM. A continuous improvement cycle (à la plan-do-check-act [4]) can result when knowledge management follows predefined objectives, when it is evaluated after implementation and when a feedback loop is closed between knowledge evaluation and knowledge objectives. Iteratively, a new set of knowledge objectives is conceivable. Figure 1 illustrates the feedback loop.

Knowledge management is a discipline of general management. It aims at providung management tools for managing "knowledge" as a production factor, in addition to the classical production factors labour, capital and real estate. In all KM approaches, concepts of data, information, and knowledge are defined. This means that these concepts are clearly discriminated in knowledge management. Data, interpreted in a given context, yields information. Correlating information with other pieces of information, particularly under the aspect of decisions between alternatives, delineates the transformation of information to knowledge. In a hospital setting, data (and also information) needs to be distinguished with respect to its reference to patient cases. Patient-related data (or information) comprises all the information generally relevant for treatment. Non-patient-related information (or data) describes the information needed in the diagnostic and therapeutic process as a whole. Administrative information such as on-call schedules and phone books are part of this, as is all the specific medical information provided in textbooks, in journals, or in therapy manuals.

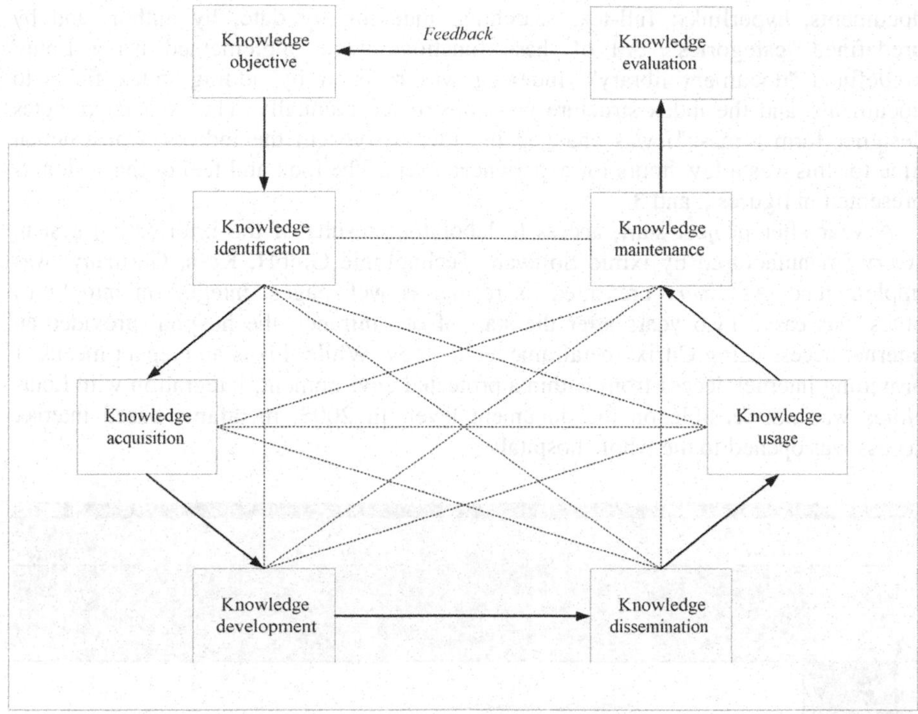

Fig. 1. Building blocks of knowledge management

3 Results

Classes of relevant information were identified by us as follows:

1. Procedural orders issued by the Department
2. Quality guidelines issued by the whole hospital
3. Medical information about laboratory procedures
4. Guidelines issued by the professional societies
5. Medical information from within the hospital but beyond the intranet
6. Medical information from the internet

The intranet based on Lotus Notes provides the user with documents from the above classes 1 to 4. Guidelines from the professional societies were downloaded regularly from the AWMF (Arbeitsgemeinschaft der Wissenschaftlichen Medizinischen Fachgesellschaften). Information from classes 5 and 6 was not presented in the intranet initially. Additionally, the intranet provides ancillary information: Local "yellow pages" (who is in charge of particular medical functions in the department), a rotation schedule, and the night shift schedule. It should be noted that these classes of information are very similar to the *four S model* for evidence based medicine proposed by Guyatt et al. [5].

Lotus Notes provides a rich set of tools and functions. Of these, we have used the following: Hierarchical organization within a document; hierarchical organization of documents, hyperlinks; full-text searching, indexing by date, by author, and by predefined "categories". All of these functions were implemented using Lotus' predefined "document library". Indexing was realized by adding index fields to documents, and the index structure was constructed manually. The associated Notes designer form ("mask") was changed in order to present the indices. Construction time for this was a few hours for experienced users. The look and feel of the system is presented in figures 2 and 3.

A year after project start, access to laboratory results of the information system *ixserv* (manufactured by ixmid Software Technologie GmbH, Köln, Germany) was implemented. As *ixserv* presented its results as web pages, integration into Lotus notes was easy. Two years after the start of our intranet, the hospital provided an internet access using Citrix' metaframe technology. While this is an elegant means of providing internet access from within a protected environment, integration with Lotus Notes was not feasible on the document level. In 2003, metafame based internet access was opened to the whole hospital.

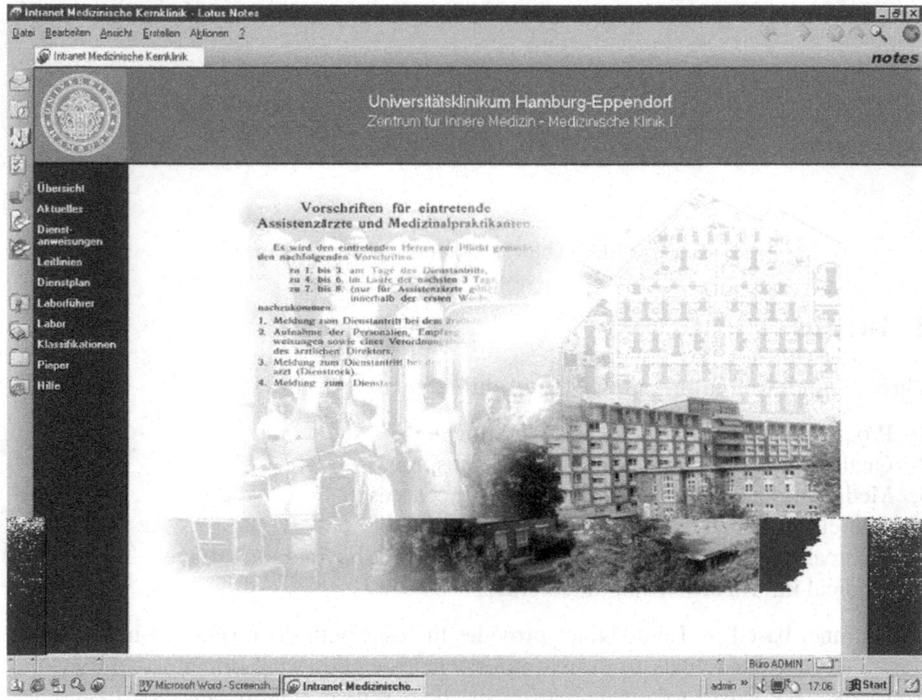

Fig. 2. Initial screen of the departmental intranet, resembling the look and feel of the hospital's internet site

Access to the medical information system UpToDate [6] was initially local to the intranet. When metaframe technology was installed, the decision was made to provide UpToDate's services to the whole hospital. The end result was an internet access to UpToDate instead of the local intranet access. The same migration path was

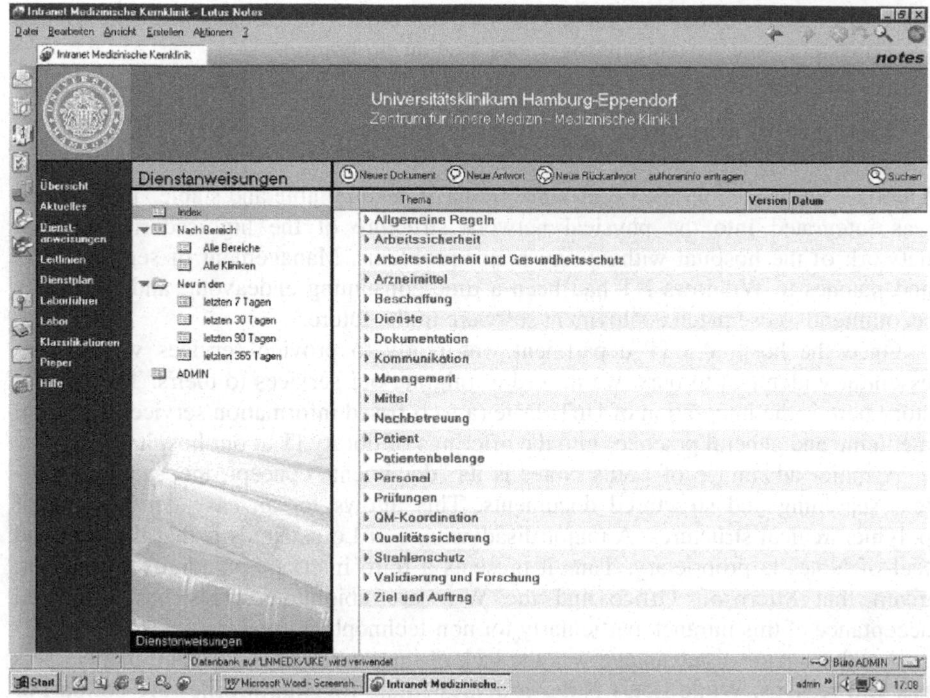

Fig. 3. Access to the document database

employed for the German coding software DIACOS [7]: Once it became avaliable on a dedicated server, the intranet provided access to that central service via metaframe technology.

Once the planning phase was finished, implementation of the network, implementation of the software and customizing/programming the document database required no less than 9 person-months (PM):

Roll-out of hardware and build-up of network	0.5 PM
Acquiring proficiency with Lotus Notes	2.5 PM
Identification of source documents	1.0 PM
Identification of ancillary information	0.5 PM
Designing a web-like portal	0.5 PM
Programming the document database	2.0 PM
Programming the PERL interface to HMTL source	1.0 PM
Roll-out of software and education of users	0.5 PM
Integration of loosely coupled components	0.5 PM

After the system was up and running, it required at least 2.0 PM per year for Windows NT maintenance and document maintenance. By the end of the introduction phase, two staff members of the department were thoroughly familiar with the programming of the document database (one physician, one student-programmer). By the end of 2004, three staff members were thoroughly acquainted with the system (one physician, one systems manager, one student-programmer).

4 Discussion and Directions for the Future

The base hardware and the Lotus software have been reliable and stable. The intranet was integrated into the physical network structure of the high-security medical network of the hospital without any major problems. Management of service packs and patches to Windows NT had been a time-consuming endeavour, and we highly recommend to use patch deployment software in the future.

Once the hospital's IT department was ready to provide services which were essentially identical to ours, we moved to migrate our services to theirs. The success story here is the integration of UpToDate (a web-based information service in internal medicine and general practice) into the offerings of library IT at our hospital.

A major advantage of Lotus Notes is its "document" concept, incorporating full-text searching and structured documents. This allows for an easy construction of polyhierarchical structures. A major disadvantage of Lotus Notes is that the look and feel of Notes is proprietary. Thus it presents a third interface paradigm to the user, given that Microsoft Office and the Web are ubiquitous. This has hampered acceptance of this intranet, particularly for non-technophile users.

Another major disadvantage was the lack of integration of mail functionality. This has two reasons: While Lotus Notes provides email, roaming profiles are not part of Lotus Notes version 5. This means that user specific mail profiles reside on a client which is fixed for the user profile. Clearly, this restriction stems from the typical office usage, but lack of roaming profiles has been a major obstacle for integration into the clinicians' workflow. Secondly, central IT had maintained two disjoint mail systems and mail domains for the hospital, namely internet mail for physicians and scientists and Novell intranet mail for the hospital administration and the IT department. Implementation of a gateway for a third mail domain was stopped for tactical reasons put forward by central IT.

On a more fundamental level, success (and lack thereof) of this system have been evaluated *a posteriori* from a knowledge management viewpoint. We discuss this briefly. Tacit knowledge was never addressed in this system, that is, we have focused on written, well-defined and accepted knowledge; see classes of information above.

It might be argued that only part of the information that we have provided in the intranet constitutes knowledge in the above defined sense. This means that only part of the information could be viewed as knowledge, and that the other part might have lacked the aspect of alternatives of action. This is intrinsic to knowledge management in medicine, however. There may be information provided by a technical or sociological system which can be transferred into knowledge using only implicit information. In clinical jargon, the term "experience" is used for such situations in which experience helps make the transition from information to knowledge.

Knowledge objective: The objective of knowledge management based on non-patient-related information is provide state-of-the-art-knowledge for at least the common clinical decisions. In our context, this means availability and dissemination of the relevant knowledge for every physician and every ward in the department. The concept of "state-of-the-art-knowledge" is clearly naive. We have not addressed the issues of conflicting information or of clinical inferences. An example for the former is contradictory information from similar sources, e.g. similar clinical trials. As an example for the latter, one might consider the question whether a side of effect of a drug might be an idiosyncrasy or a "class effect", thus being generalizable to similar drugs.

Knowledge identification: Identification of the pertinent knowledge for a KM system in internal medicine is hard. Clearly, there is conflicting evidence in the primary literature. Contradictions may even be found when guidelines are compared with each other. In the system reported here, knowledge identification was performed by clinical judgement of the authors. Systems like this one suffer from an "encyclopedic" approach, however. From a knowledge management viewpoint, transparency in knowledge identification is mandatory, and this was achieved only partially. Junior physicians, in particular, need to identify the knowledge that they must absolutely know or access in clinical practice.

Knowledge acquisition: Relevant information was defined in structural terms (procedural orders by the department, national guidelines). This has been well-defined and successful. A major source of knowledge acquisition in academic medicine not addressed by us is the knowledge provided from review articles and national conferences. The limitation to procedural orders and national guidelines has spared us from considering borderline cases (i.e. which sources should have been included in the knowledge acquisition process). We point out in passing that knowledge management in internal medicine ought to address the question how the process of knowledge identification, acquisition, and evaluation should be designed and reviewed.

Knowledge development: The goal of knowledge development is to produce innovation. In clinical medicine, innovation is developed predominantly through clinical trials. Thus, the roles of "knowledge producers" and "knowledge users" are distinct in clinical medicine, and knowledge development is not an issue for KM in our context. (Note that while roles are disjoint, the actors need not be.)

The second aspect of knowledge development in clinical internal medicine concerns bringing the knowledge to the bedside, to the hands of the clinician as it were. Writing and publishing a specific procedural order may be one thing. For example, any of the problem conditions in emergency medicine may be reflected in a respective procedural order.

The other required part is to get all physicians to follow these orders and to understand the description as applied to their clinical situation. Our point here is that discussion and dialogue may help to clarify procedural orders. When discussion without regard to the all-important clinical seniority status is not fostered in a clinical department, groupware providing discussion services may be useless. For the current project, we have already described that the lack of a discussion mechanism was a major shortcoming of this project.

Knowledge dissemination: As we have not evaluated usage patterns, nothing can be reported about this building block of knowledge management. Conventionally, dissemination of new knowledge in medicine utilizes a case-based discussion. It is known that presentation and discussion of relevant cases is a major incentive for the acquisition of knowledge in medicine [8]. We have not provided mechanims to support this, however. In retrospect, mail functionality should have been integrated in a very early phase in order to facilitate a discussion mechanism.

Knowledge maintenance: We believe that knowledge maintenance in internal medicine should be performed by experienced physicians. It must be noted that they are carriers of tacit knowledge which enables them to review information by its clinical relevance [9]. In our scenario, there have been no organizational provisions for this.

Knowledge usage: A typical problem of knowledge usage in internal medicine is the implementation of new information into the daily workflow routine (e.g. usage of a new laboratory parameter in intensive care). We had identified an instance of this problem as we had provided an annotated laboratory guide. There has been no systematic approach to knowledge usage, however.

Knowledge evaluation: Simply, the feedback loop toward a systematic evaluation was never closed in our scenario.

Table 1 summarizes this evaluation according to the knowledge management principles of the Geneva model.

Table 1. Evaluation of project according to knowledge management requirements.

Knowledge objective	+
Knowledge identification	+
Knowledge acquisition	+
Knowledge development	–
Knowledge dissemination	?
Knowledge maintenance	–
Knowledge usage	?
Knowledge evaluation	–

Legend: "+" task has been accomplished satisfactorily
"–" task has not been accomplished satisfactorily
"?" unclear whether this was satisfactory

Lotus Notes has been tried as base software for clinical information solutions before. Little is published in MEDLINE though, but there are interesting reports on Notes based solutions in the web [10, 11, 12]. Most of these applications have centered on form management and document management. In fact, Notes is very strong in these applications, and it has the potential for inexpensive, successful solutions once the Lotus Notes infrastructure is installed. Database access and access to archive tools using Lotus Notes is, in our opinion, initially expensive because it requires the management of a complex interface. Lotus Notes seems to be weak in the integration of biosignal and picture information into documents [13]. Recently, efforts to foster collaborative computing in a clinical setting have been supported by IBM's new Center for Healthcare Management [14].

Lotus Notes provides the user with a powerful set of tools for network-based collaboration ("collaborative computing"). The system's interface is proprietary, however. In our experience, the anticipated learning curve for Lotus Notes is intimidating for some users. This can only be alleviated by a strong user support and by a firm commitment to this groupware solution which is perceived as "exotic" in a hospital setting. This observation also holds for the technical aspects: Administering and customizing a Lotus Notes infrastructure requires access to specialist knowledge. In our case, we secured support from a Lotus Notes third party partner for the initial phase.

For a Lotus Notes based solution, there seem to be only two viable strategies: Pervasive introduction of this groupware system, requiring also strong technical knowledge of the system, or the usage of Lotus Notes "in a box" for limited projects. In the area of content management systems, Notes now competes with a number of commercially available or open source products for content management. In 2004, we believe that a Notes interface to a CMS is not enough, both for the readers and the authors.

We are convinced that departmental intranets need content management systems (CMS) in the short term because only CMSs provide easy management of authoring, versioning, access control, and security defined by "users" and "roles". A CMS might be termed middleware, representing an additional layer on top of base software such as Lotus Notes. Giving a web interface to users is an additional strong asset. A strict adherence to the principles described by the Geneva knowledge management paradigm is hard to achieve for the application domain of internal medicine. We are convinced, however, that a successful realization of a departmental information system depends on following these principles; this requires only a pragmatic definition of the building blocks of knowledge management applied to internal medicine. It seems crucial to close the feedback loop and to utilize and apply all the building blocks of KM.

Acknowledgement

Christopher Peters has been of tremendous help in programming and maintaining the system. We thank the reviewers for suggesting to discuss practice examples of Lotus Notes applications.

References

1. Winker MA, Flanagin A, Chi-Lum B, White J, Andrews K, Kennett RL, DeAngelis CD, Musacchio RA. Guidelines for medical and health information sites on the internet: principles governing AMA web sites. JAMA 2000; 283 (12): 1600-6.
2. Bernstam E, Ash N, Peleg M, Boxwala A, Mork P, Greenes RA, Shortliffe EH, Tu S. Guideline classification to assist modeling, authoring, implementation and retrieval. Proc AMIA Symp 2000; (20 Suppl): 66-70
3. Probst G, Raub S, Romhardt K. Wissen managen. 4th ed., Wiesbaden 2003: Gabler
4. See http://www.isixsigma.com/me/pdca (Accessed May 15,2005)

5. Guyatt GH, Haynes RB, Jaeschke RZ, Cook DJ, Green L, Naylor CD, Wilson MC, Richardson WS. Users' guide to the medical literature XXV. Evidence-based medicine: principles for applying the Users' Guides to patient care. JAMA 2000; 284: 1290-1296
6. See the homepage of UpToDate, Inc.: http://www.uptodate.com (Accessed May 15, 2005)
7. See the homepage of the makers of DIACOS, ID GmbH, at http://www.id-berlin.de (Accessed May 15, 2005)
8. Wyatt JC. Practice guidelines and other support for clinical innovation. J R Soc Med. 2000; 93: 299-304.
9. Wyatt JC. Management of explicit and tacit knowledge. J R Soc Med. 2001; 94: 6-9.
10. Report on a Lotus Notes solution at LaGrange Oncology, LaGrange, Illinois: http://www.eletra.com/rainmakers/e_article000057538.cfm (Accessed May 15, 2005)
11. Report on a Lotus Notes solution at Cincinnatti Childrens' Health Medical Center: http://radio.weblogs.com/0105504/categories/Random (Accessed May 15, 2005)
12. Transcription and forms management system at Carson City Hospital, Michigan: http://itpapers.zdnet.com/abstract.aspx?scid=&kw=domino&dtid=3&docid=81566 (Accessed May 15, 2005)
13. We thank a reviewer for pointing this out.
14. Compilation of healthcare applications compiled by IBM 's Center for Healthcare Management: http://www-1.ibm.com/services/us/bcs/html/chm_overview.html (Accessed May 15, 2005)

Integrated Clinical Pathways in Health Information Systems – An Architectural Concept

Marita Muscholl

International Healthcare Management Institute,
Am Wissenschaftspark 29, 54286 Universität Trier, Germany
muscholl@uni-trier.de

Abstract. Nowadays Clinical Pathways are used in a number of hospitals in order to control quality and cost of treatment. Clinical Pathways can help to collect knowledge about treatments and to automate some organizational tasks, but only if they are highly integrated into clinical knowledge processing systems. On one hand process management tools are used for modelling and simulation and on the other hand providers of health information systems have begun to integrate pathway support into their systems. But there is still no interchange between these applications and no possibility for different hospitals to share pathway definitions. This paper introduces a concept for sharing Clinical Pathway knowledge among different systems and hospitals. It is intended to be one step towards a common reference architecture.

1 Introduction

Increasing costs for health care and the resulting changes of the accounting systems forced health care organizations to think about knowledge management not only concerning medical aspects like diagnose and therapy but also economic aspects like specialization and process optimization. One major problem of knowledge management in health care organizations is the separation of medical knowledge, organizational knowledge and management information in different information systems without any connection to each other.

The integration of clinical pathways into healthcare information systems (HIS) is one approach to interconnect knowledge about medical and economic goals, tasks and processes. Clinical pathways are multidisciplinary plans of best clinical practice for a homogeneous group of medical cases. Each clinical pathway model defines the range of actions in the areas of diagnose, therapy, care and administration that could and should be performed as part of the treatment [1, 2]. Clinical pathways include medical as well as economic aspects and are part of a continuous quality improvement process. The range of pathway validity can either be one individual healthcare provider or – more general – a group of institutions. The execution of Clinical pathways take place in single healthcare environments as well as in networks of shared care.

Today's most important objective for healthcare providers is to be competitive. The use of clinical pathways can help with it by

- Improving quality,
- Reducing costs of treatment,

K.-D. Althoff et al. (Eds.): WM 2005, LNAI 3782, pp. 349 – 359, 2005.

- Relating conflicting aspects of treatment like medical requirements, economy of treatment and patients satisfaction
- Building integrated treatment processes within distributed environments and
- Deriving knowledge about profitability of treatments, efficiency of organizational structures and further optimizations for strategic decisions.

A workflow process that is generated from the clinical pathway can help to control medical and administrative tasks as well as cost and quality of care, if it is used by a workflow engine and critiquing functions contained in the HIS. Systems that integrate clinical pathways can assist the clinical staff in planning the schedule and the resources or at best automatically do the schedule and resource planning by interoperating with other systems. The documentation of applied clinical pathways gives the basic knowledge for analysis and improvement of the pathway model and – in case of universally applicable pathways – for comparing the results of different healthcare providers.

On the one hand clinical pathways can help healthcare providers to work more efficiently, but on the other hand the implementation and use of Clinical pathways cause additional effort, e. g. during the design and optimization phase, during application, monitoring and documentation or during the analysis of results. Knowledge management methods can successfully be applied to limit this effort mainly by sharing of knowledge among different applications, decision support, alerting functions, automatic time and resource control, but also by automatically deriving additional knowledge about costs, profitability and possibilities of improvement.

Today a few software providers of HISs offer basic knowledge based functions for the support of clinical pathways [3, 4]. And also a number of powerful process management tools with comprehensive functionality for modelling and simulation of workflows are already used in the clinical pathway field [5, 2].

2 Requirements for "Integrated Clinical Pathways"

As part of our work within the working group "Medical Controlling" of the German "Society for Medical Informatics, Biometrics and Epidemiology (GMDS)" we identified requirements for an all-embracing implementation of clinical pathways in daily routine and the computer-based knowledge processing needed for this. The most important requirements are listed below:

Functional Requirements: Pathway Management includes the whole pathway lifecycle as shown in Fig. 1. Knowledge based functions have to be implemented to support *modelling* of the clinical workflow processes, *workflow execution*, *monitoring* and *documentation* as well as *simulations* based on the pathway models and *analysis* of models and of applied pathways.

Architectural Requirements: The architecture of pathway supporting systems should be modular and distributable. A huge number of clinical pathways are already modelled with today's process modelling tools. They could – at least partially – be reused by different hospitals treating similar cases and shared by different departments and institutions that are concurrently or sequentially involved in the treatment process. Information about already executed pathway steps and treatment results

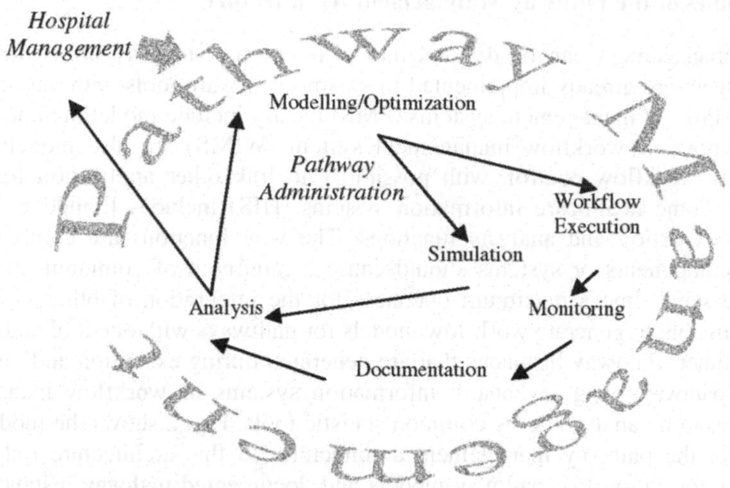

Fig. 1. Steps of clinical pathway management

should also be sharable among different applications for analysis and for sequentially workflow control in networks of shared care.

Requirements to the Information Infrastructure: In order to profit from the use of clinical pathways in the most efficient way data entry devices should be available at each place where data result from pathway execution. At best, the medical staff need only to acknowledge the execution of workflow tasks at execution time at the touch of a button. Delays due to late orders, missing to get an appointment in good time or resource conflicts could be avoided, if the information and communication infrastructure supports automatic order entry, scheduling and dynamic resource control.

Models and Standards for Communication and Interoperability: Pathway models and instances of applied pathways must be exchanged between different systems. This requires a reference information model and interchange formats for a standardized definition of semantics and syntax of pathways.

3 IT-Concept for Integrated Clinical Pathways

With the object of satisfying the requirements mentioned above we developed an IT-concept for clinical pathway support including the following parts:

1. A **modular architecture** of functional components supporting the pathway management that allows to integrate existing software tools,
2. an **architectural framework** for the execution of clinical pathways in networks of shared care,
3. a **reference information model** for pathway models as well as for instances of applied pathways and
4. the corresponding **communication interface definitions** needed for distributed pathway support.

3.1 Modules of the Pathway Management Architecture

Pathway management can be divided into different functions as shown in Fig. 1. Some of them are already implemented in existing software tools with varying combinations. Process management systems (PMS) mostly include modelling and simulation. Functions of workflow management system (WfMS) are also modelling and additionally workflow control, with possibility to link other application for action execution. Some healthcare information systems (HIS) includes limited modelling, workflow execution and analysis functions. The way functions are combined into software components or systems should cause a minimum of communication need and at the same time a maximum openness for the integration of other systems. It must be possible to generate workflow models for pathways with one tool and execute it with another. Pathway instances that are generated during execution and documentation of pathways e. g. by health information systems or workflow management systems has to be analyzable by common statistic tools. Fig. 2 shows the modules we propose for the pathway management architecture. In this architecture only rarely changing information like pathway models and documented pathway instances have to be exchanged.

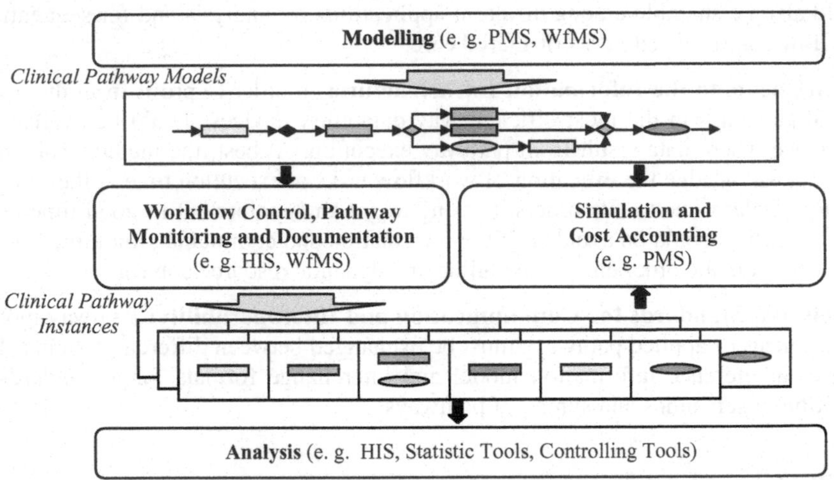

Fig. 2. Functional components involved in the pathway management lifecycle

Workflow control, pathway monitoring and documentation of actions and deviations should not be distributed among different applications because these function are closely linked together and would need a complex and high frequent information exchange. At best these functions are implemented in the HIS where knowledge about treatments is available, where actions can be connected with HIS functions like referral, electronic order entry and time scheduling and so multiple data entry can be avoided.

3.2 Architectural Framework for Pathway Execution in Networks of Shared Care

In networks of shared care partial pathways have to be executed concurrently or sequentially in different information systems. One master system – running at the hospital, which is the primary contractor of the health insurance – must monitor the whole pathway execution and beside execution of partial pathways deliver control data and information about the pathway state to the subordinate systems (Fig. 3). The whole pathway management including modelling, simulations, cost control and further analysis of pathway instances is also done at the primary contractor hospital. The subordinate systems return the partial pathway instances including the documentation of executed actions, deviations, decisions and results.

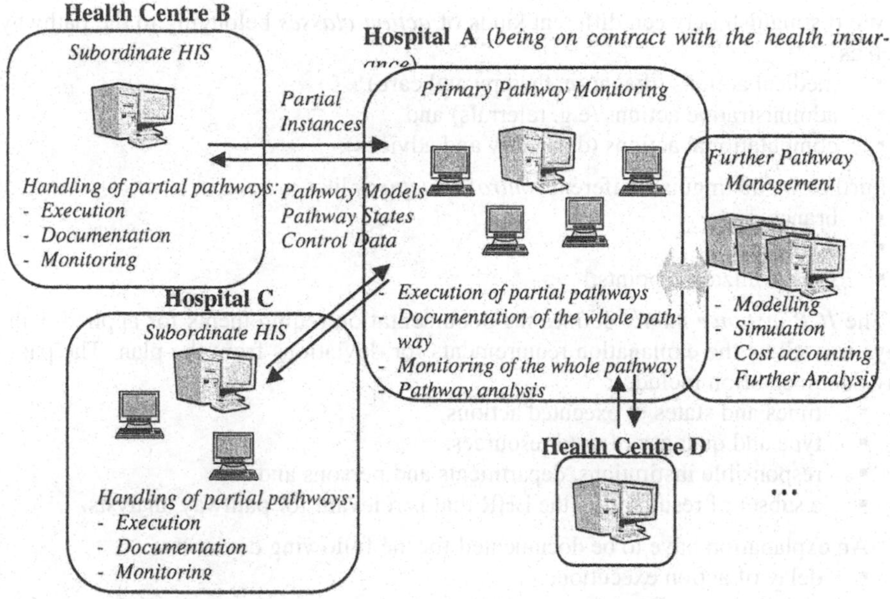

Fig. 3. Architectural framework for pathway execution in networks of shared care

At simplest the pathway can be split into single actions, all decisions are made by the master system and the subordinate systems only have to execute simple actions. But the consequence of this approach is a high frequent communication that needs a very reliable communication infrastructure.

3.3 The Reference Information Model

Every communication between different systems needs besides common formats an agreement about the communicated contents and their meaning. We developed an reference information model for integrated clinical pathways (ICP RIM) consisting of a meta model that describes the ontology of pathway plans (ICP schemes) and a pathway instance model that describes the ontology of applied pathways (ICP instances). The following gives a general idea of the main characteristics of the ICP RIM.

The *ICP schema model* has to combine different views of medical treatment, like diagnose, therapy and care tasks, administrative tasks or resources and costs with target and real consumptions. Also it needs concepts to carry all necessary knowledge e.g. for simulations, workflow control, monitoring of quality and costs, resource control, scheduling and user guidance. The *pathway object* encloses global knowledge like

- the pathway goals,
- inclusion and exclusion criteria,
- stop, cancel and pathway alternation criteria and
- attributes for administration of pathways.

We distinguish between different kinds of *action classes* belonging to the pathway such as

- medical actions (diagnose, therapy and care),
- administrative actions (e.g. referrals) and
- computational actions (data entry and advices).

Further we distinguish different *control structures* like

- branching,
- decision and
- synchronization points.

The *ICP instance model* defines the documentation requirements for applied pathways as well as the explanation requirements for deviations from the plan. The pathway documentation includes:

- times and states of executed actions,
- type and quantity of used resources,
- responsible institutions, departments and persons and
- a subset of results from the EHR that is relevant for pathway analysis.

An explanation have to be documented for the following deviations:

- delay of action execution,
- skipping or adding of actions,
- changing decisions derived by pathway decision rules,
- increased use of resources and
- stopping, cancelling or changing the pathway execution.

Compared to existing clinical guidelines or workflow models our approach mainly focus on characteristics of clinical pathways that are considered in the ICP schema model in an explicit way:

Dealing with Time: Clinical pathways should support the organization of medical treatment in an appropriate way. Therefore ICP schemes allow arranging actions within a coarse timetable based on treatment days or time windows of several hours. Actions can be executed in any order within a time window, and action states must be checked at the end. They can also be triggered by conditions e.g. warnings in case of runaway costs.

Dealing with Deviation: Clinical pathway models have to determine allowed deviations such as usual delays of execution time with additional delay tolerance information and the skipping of an optional action e.g. with an optional flag. Major deviations need to be documented as mentioned above.

Specific Clinical Concepts: The ICP RIM considers all needed actions for medical treatment and clinical organization, like procedures, referral or order entry.

Covering Characteristics of Clinical Guidelines and Workflow Models: The pathway meta model covers guideline specific concepts such as rule based structures for decision support (e.g. for evaluation of actions, pre/post conditions and pathway goals) and concepts that are specific for workflows like costs and resources (e.g. staff, rooms and devices with number and duration or the patients presence, if needed).

3.4 Communication Interfaces

As shown above (Fig. 2 and Fig. 3), the support of clinical pathway management in nowadays healthcare environments requires communication interfaces between several systems. Communication interfaces include besides message transport

Table. 1. Table of interfaces between ICP modules. The last two rows of this table show the interfaces that are only needed for distributed pathway execution.

Source Module	Target Module	Subject of Communication
- modelling	- pathway execution, (*workflow control, documentation and monitoring*)	- pathway schemes
- modelling	- simulation	- pathway schemes
- pathway execution (*workflow control, documentation and monitoring*)	- analysis	- pathway instances
- pathway execution (*workflow control, documentation and monitoring*)	- pathway-oriented cost accounting	- pathway instances
- pathway execution (*workflow control, documentation and monitoring*)	- simulation	- pathway instances
- partial pathway execution (*workflow control, documentation and monitoring*)	- primary pathway monitoring	- partial pathway instances
- primary pathway monitoring	- partial pathway execution	- partial pathway instances - control data (*e. g. the next action*)

mechanisms interchange formats and a semantic mapping between different systems. For an unambiguous semantic mapping a common information model like the ICP RIM introduced above should be referenced. Tab. 1 shows, which interfaces are needed for clinical pathway management.

For reasons of usability and a better acceptance appropriate standards like GLIF or the WfMC standards should be used for communication. We examined both, in order to determine, if they could well communicate the clinical pathway knowledge defined by the ICP RIM [5].

A controlled vocabulary is needed to make all structures and values of the ICP RIM available at modelling time. The vocabulary contains variable identifiers that are linked to knowledge from the EHR (*like the existence of particular symptoms*) or workflow relevant data (*like action states*) as well as action prototypes of system actions that can be configured in order to automatically start their execution at runtime (*like updates of working lists*). It should also contain lists of valid data entries for some variables (*like diagnosis related groups or laboratory test identifiers*). The vocabulary can be individually generated by one master system or developed more generally based on common standards like the HL7 v3 Reference Information Model and terminologies like SNOMED CT and LOINC.

4 Related Work

Besides a few papers in the field of integration of workflow models [6] or clinical guidelines [7, 8], there are two important works that deals with reference models and interchange standards for clinical guidelines and workflow process models respectively. The Guideline Interchange Format (GLIF) was developed by the InterMed Collaboratory [9, 10] with the objective to share clinical guideline definitions among different applications. The Workflow Management Coalition (WfMC) developed a workflow reference model and a few interfaces, e. g. the workflow process definition interface (WfPDI) [11, 12]. They intended to represent workflow models in a standardized way in order to get interoperability between different workflow applications and to link them to other IT services.

4.1 The Guideline Interchange Format

The object model of the current version, GLIF 3.5, includes a guideline object with global information among others about the guideline algorithm, maintenance information, eligibility and aborting criteria. The guideline algorithm is composed by guideline steps that can be actions, decisions, branches, synchronizations, patient state steps and macros. The concepts used in GLIF 3.5 allow to model clinical workflows that define concurrent and alternative sequences of medically oriented actions (therapy and administration) and programming oriented actions (e.g. data and event handling). A RIM determines semantics of data objects. Decisions and eligibility criteria are specified by the object-oriented expression language GELLO.

4.2 The WfMC Workflow Process Definition Interface

The WfPDI allows defining workflow processes as a net of activities supported by various routing strategies that depends on the routing activity type and on each transition information. Execution time of actions is determined by transition conditions. Activities can relate to resources and can be coupled with computer applications or functions by a set of function parameters and by sharing system data. That's why the interface supports resource management and integration into any applications very well. Structures that are not included but needed for a particular domain can be modelled additionally with "Extended Attributes".

Some aspects of the integration of clinical guidelines or workflow management respectively can be transferred to clinical pathways like basic actions and control structures of the models as well as technical or semantic mapping methods, but in the approaches of both fields some characteristics are also missing like the combination of medical and economic aspects and the close integration into the HIS.

5 Results and Future Work

The conceptual work for the open ICP architecture and the architectural framework for distributed pathway execution is finished and will be published in a practice guide for integrated clinical pathway management in autumn 2005 [13]. We also finished the first version of the ICP RIM and examined, if it can be represented by nowadays process management software tools. For this we analyzed the information model and functions of two very common process management systems, ADONIS and ARIS Healthcare Solution [14]. The analysis showed that ADONIS is a powerful tool, which allows to build your own meta process model with all elements and attributes needed. It also offers adaptable XML-based knowledge export. ARIS Healthcare Solution offers several predefined medical elements and environments, but without extensions by the producer some elements important for workflow control are missing.

We also analyzed the possibility of using one of the related standards for the communication of pathway schemes. For this we examined GLIF 3.5 and the WfMC WfPDI. Both meet the characteristics and requirements for clinical pathway models mentioned above only partially. GLIF lacks of concepts for resource management, cost accounting and the possibility of defining and controlling global goals. Full integration into a HIS with a high degree of automation seems also to be not intended. Within the WfPDI specific clinical concepts are missing. Also an explicit timetable how it is usually applied with clinical pathways is not intended. Instructions for deviation documentation are missing in both approaches. The WfPDI approach is more open and powerful than GLIF; all necessary concepts could be added by using the "Extended Attributes".

6 Discussion

If we want clinical pathways to be a part of the clinical knowledge management that helps to optimize quality, efficiency and organization without causing additional effort for the clinical staff, the clinical pathway concept must be fully integrated into daily routine. Clinical pathway models have to correspond with clinical organization and working methods. Healthcare information systems need to be able to adopt clinical pathways modelled with process management tools and to share them among different departments (e. g. hospital management and medical departments) or healthcare institutions.

The proposed architecture meets all requirements to integrate heterogeneous systems for pathway management and to distribute the pathway execution if necessary. The ICP RIM includes all necessary concepts from medical, organizational and economical point of view for all steps of pathway management and also for the integration in the HIS environment. We showed also that some of today's process management systems meet the requirements for the modelling task of clinical pathway management.

There is no specific communication standard or reference model for clinical pathways until now, but there are related models. We plan to define a specific clinical pathway interface based on the WfMC WfPDI for communication of ICP schemes.

The advantages of our concept are:

- the open architecture that allows to integrate every system with the ability to export and/or import pathway schemes and instances,
- the scalability that allows you e. g. to begin with the use of modelling and simulation tools before you integrate the pathway execution in your HIS) and
- that the architecture and the models are well suited for the requirements to clinical pathways in today's health systems.

Disadvantageous is the difficulty to prove it's validity in practice at the moment, because it deals with the integration of existing tools. The implementation and extension of systems and interfaces has to be done in cooperation with today's software providers.

The introduced IT concept for integrated clinical pathways, which was developed together with experts from medicine, economics and informatics and also representatives of HIS providers, is intended to be one step towards a common reference model and architecture.

References

1. Roeder, N., Hindle, D., Loskamp, N., Juhra, C., Hensen, P., Bunzemeier, H., Rochell, B.: Frischer Wind mit klinischen Behandlungspfaden I. Das Krankenhaus 1 (2003), 20-27
2. Greiling, M., Mormann, J., Westerfeld, R.: Klinische Pfade steuern. Baumann Fachverlag (2003).
3. Laprell, S., Begemann, S.: Entwicklung, Integration und Visualisierung von Klinischen Pfaden mit DV-Unterstützung. In: Hellmann (Hrsg.): Klinische Pfade: Konzepte, Umsetzung, Erfahrungen. ecomed-Verlagsgesellschaft, Landsberg/Lech (2002), 194-205.
4. Wetekam, V., Betz, F.: Soarian™ - Workflow Management im Gesundheitswesen. Siemens Healthcare Services. Online: http://www.uniklinikum-giessen.de/ kis-ris-pacs/archiv/2002/mi0940.pdf
5. Bollig, J.: Möglichkeiten und Grenzen von Prozessmanagement-Werkzeugen bei der Umsetzung und Integration klinischer Pfade. Diplomarbeit im Fach Wirtschaftsinformatik, Universität Trier 2005.
6. Junginger, S., Kühn, H., Strobel, R., Karagiannis, D.: Ein Geschäftsprozessmanagement-Werkzeug der nächsten Generation – ADONIS: Konzeption und Anwendungen. WIRTSCHAFTSINFORMATIK 42 (2002) 5, 392-401
7. Gordon, C., Johnson, P., Waite, C., Veleso, M.: Algorithm and Care Pathway: Clinical Guidelines and Healthcare Processes. Proceeding of AIME97, Grenoble (1997), 66-69.
8. Anyanwu, K., Sheth, A., Cardoso, J., Miller, J., Kochut, K.: Healthcare Enterprise Process Development and Integration. Journal of Research and Practice in Information Technology, Vol. 35 (2003) 2, 83-98

9. Ohno-Machado, L., Gennari, J. H., Murphy, S.N., Jain, N. L., Tu, S. W., Oliver, D. E., Pattison-Gordon, E., Greenes, R. A., Shortliffe, E. H., Barnett, G. O.: The GuideLine Interchange Format: A Model for Representing Guidelines. Journal of American Medical Informatics Association Vol. 5 (1998) No. 4, 357-371
10. InterMed Collaboratory: Guideline Interchange Format 3.5 Technical Specification (2004). Online: http://smi-web.stanford.edu/projects/intermed-web/guidelines/GLIF_TECH_ SPEC_May_4_2004.pdf
11. The Workflow Management Coalition: Workflow Process Definition Interface – XML Process Definition Language 1.0 Final Draft (2002). Online: http://www.wfmc.org/standards/docs/TC-1025_10_xpdl_102502.pdf
12. The Workflow Management Coalition: The Workflow Reference Model 1.1 (1995). Online: http://www.wfmc.org/standards/docs/tc003v11.pdf
13. Eckardt, J., Sens, B. (Ed.) : Praxishandbuch Integrierte Behandlungspfade, Economica-Verlag, Heidelberg (2005). (in press)
14. IDS Scheer AG: ARIS Healthcare Solution. White Paper, Saarbrücken 2004. Online: http://www.idsscheer.com/sixcms/media.php/1049/ARIS_Healthcare_Solution_WP_de_2004-04.pdf.

Knowledge Discovery from Microbiology Data: Many-Sided Analysis of Antibiotic Resistance in Nosocomial Infections

Mykola Pechenizkiy[1], Alexey Tsymbal[2], Seppo Puuronen[1], Michael Shifrin[3], and Irina Alexandrova[3]

[1] Dept. of CS and Inf. Systems, Univ. of Jyväskylä, Finland
{mpechen, sepi}@cs.jyu.fi
[2] Dept. of Computer Science, Trinity College Dublin, Dublin, Ireland
tsymbalo@tcd.ie
[3] N.N.Burdenko Institute of Neurosurgery, Russian Academy of Medical Sciences, Moscow, Russia
{Shifrin, IAlexandrova}@nsi.ru

Abstract. Nosocomial infections and antimicrobial resistance (AR) are highly important problems that impact the morbidity and mortality of hospitalized patients as well as their cost of care. The goal of this paper is to demonstrate our analysis of AR by applying a number of various data mining (DM) techniques to real hospital data. The data for the analysis includes instances of sensitivity of nosocomial infections to antibiotics collected in a hospital over three years 2002-2004. The results of our study show that DM makes it easy for experts to inspect patterns that might otherwise be missed by usual (manual) infection control. However, the clinical relevance and utility of these findings await the results of prospective studies. We see our main contribution in this paper in introducing and applying a many-sided analysis approach to real-world data. The application of diversified DM techniques, which are not necessarily accurate and do not best suit to the present problem in the usual sense, still offers a possibility to analyze and understand the problem from different perspectives.

1 Introduction

Nosocomial infections and antimicrobial resistance (AR) are highly important problems that impact the morbidity and mortality of hospitalized patients as well as their cost of care. It is known that 3 to 40 percent of patients admitted to hospital acquire an infection during their stay, and that the risk for hospital-acquired infection, or *nosocomial infection,* has risen steadily in recent decades. The frequency depends mostly on the type of conducted operation being greater for "dirty" operations (10-40%), and smaller for "pure" operations (3-7%). For example, such a serious infectious disease as meningitis is often the result of nosocomial infection.

Antibiotics are drugs that are commonly used to fight against infections caused by bacteria. However, according to the Center for Disease Control and Prevention (CDC) statistics, more than 70 percent of bacteria that cause hospital-acquired infections are resistant to at least one of antibiotics most commonly used to treat infections.

K.-D. Althoff et al. (Eds.): WM 2005, LNAI 3782, pp. 360 – 372, 2005.

Analysis of microbiological data included in antibiograms collected in different institutions over different periods of time is considered as one of the most important activities to restrain the spreading of AR and to avoid the negative consequences of this phenomenon. Traditional hospital infection control surveillance and localization of hospital infection relies on the manual review of suspected cases of nosocomial infections and the tabulation of basic summary statistics; and AR surveillance consists of the construction of annual or semi-annual, hospital-wide antibiogram summaries. Since such manual activities require considerable time and resources, produced measures and patterns are often not up-to-date and certainly many of potentially useful patterns remain undiscovered. Such relatively inefficient analysis results in coping with the increasing complexity of AR, and proves the importance of introducing computer-based surveillance. Recent reports have described effective computer applications for infection control [9].

It has been widely recognized recently that sophisticated, active, and timely intra-hospital surveillance is needed. Computer-assisted infection control surveillance research has focused on identifying high-risk patients, the use of expert systems to identify possible cases of nosocomial infection, and the detection of deviations in the occurrence of predefined events [1].

Numerous DM algorithms have recently been developed to extract knowledge (previously unknown and potentially interesting patterns and relations) from large databases. In this paper we apply a number of different commonly used DM techniques to real clinical data trying to evaluate possibilities to reveal some interesting patterns of AR and to construct data models that would help in the prediction of AR and in understanding its development.

Many real-world DM studies are focused on a few techniques, which have the best performance in a certain sense (generalization accuracy, explanation power, simplicity, speed etc.), even if the accomplishment of a many-sided analysis might be available from the time and computational resources points of view. Furthermore, in the cases when a number of DM techniques are applied the goal is usually to find a single technique (e.g., a classifier) that has the best performance and to disregard the others. However, in this paper we emphasize the data and problem understanding perspective. We see the main contribution of this paper in demonstrating how the many-sided analysis of a real-world problem has been performed and how the application of diversified DM techniques has helped us to enhance our understanding of the nature of the data that represents the problem.

In our experimental study we apply Naïve Bayesian classification (NB), C4.5 decision trees, *k*- nearest neighbor classification (*k*NN), and a rule-based classifier (JRip) to build antibiotic sensitivity prediction models. Besides, we apply the principle of natural clustering, i.e. grouping data into partitions related to certain pathogen and/or antibiotic types. Different filter-based and wrapper-based feature selection techniques are applied in this study to analyze the importance of the features for predicting the sensitivity of pathogens to antibiotics. As the AR concept is rather unstable and changes over time, we try to track possible changes of the concept, applying three different strategies for this purpose, in order to better understand the patterns of AR process development.

The paper is organized as follows: in Section 2 we consider the phenomenon of nosocomial infection and the problem of AR, in Section 3 data collection and organization are described, in Section 4 we present the results of our many-sided data analysis, and in Section 5 we conclude with a brief summary and further research directions.

2 Nosocomial Infections and the Problem of Antibiotic Resistance

Infections acquired during a hospital stay are called nosocomial infections. Formally, they are defined as infections arising after 48 hours of hospital admission. Infections arising earlier are assumed having arose prior to admission, though this is not always true [4].

Nosocomial infections are the inevitable consequence of long treatment, especially in Intensive Care Units (ICUs). The first step of arising nosocomial infection is the colonization of skin and mucous tunic by hospital microorganism cultures. The peculiarity of these cultures is the acquisition of unpredictable AR according to the policy of the use of antimicrobial medications in the present department or institution.

Multiple investigations, conducted in different institutions, have shown the possibility of reduction of the number of nosocomial infections by one third only, even when optimal organization of the treatment process is used. The use of antibiotics with the objective of prophylaxis of nosocomial infections has proven to be ineffective, as pathogens become resistant to antibiotics used.

To treat nosocomial infections, at first a microbiological investigation is normally conducted. In this investigation pathogens are isolated and for each isolated bacterium, an antibiogram is built (represents bacterium's resistance to a series of antibiotics). The user of the test system can define the set of antibiotics used to test bacterial resistance. The result of the test is presented as an antibiogram that is a vector of couples (antibiotic/resistance). The information included in this antibiogram is used to prescribe an antibiotic with a desired level of resistance for the isolated pathogen.

The antibiogram is not uniquely identified given the bacterium species, but it can vary significantly for bacteria of the same species. This is due to the fact that the same bacteria of the same species may have evolved differently and have developed different resistances to antibiotics. However, very often groups of antibiotics have similar resistance when tested on a given bacterium species, despite its strains [6].

Antibiotics, also known as antimicrobial drugs, are drugs that are used to fight against infections caused by bacteria. After their discovery in 1940's they transformed medical care and dramatically reduced illness and death from infectious diseases. However, over the decades bacteria that should be controlled by antibiotics have developed resistance to these drugs. Today, virtually all important bacterial infections throughout the world are becoming resistant. Infectious microorganisms are developing resistance faster than scientists can create new drugs. This problem is known as *antibiotic resistance* (AR), also known as antimicrobial resistance or drug resistance [11].

AR is an especially difficult problem for nosocomial infections in hospitals because they attack critically ill patients who are more vulnerable to infections than the general population and therefore require more antibiotics. Heavy use of antibiotics in these patients hastens the mutations in bacteria that bring about drug resistance[11].

Persons infected with drug-resistant organisms are more likely to have longer hospital stays and require treatment with second or third choice drugs that may be less effective, more toxic, and more expensive [11]. In short, antimicrobial resistance is driving up health care costs, increasing the severity of disease, and increasing the death rates of some infections.

3 Data Collection and Organization

Data for our analysis were collected in the Hospital of N.N. Burdenko Institute of Neurosurgery, Moscow, Russia, using the analyzer *Vitek-60* (developed by *bioMérieux*, www.biomerieux.com) over the years 1997-2003 and the information systems *Microbiologist* (developed by the Medical Informatics Lab of the institute) and *Microbe* (developed by the Russian company *MedProject-3*).

Each instance of the data used in analysis represents one sensitivity test and contains the following features: *pathogen* that is isolated during the bacterium identification analysis, *antibiotic* that is used in the sensitivity test and the *result of the sensitivity test* itself (sensitive S, resistant R or intermediate I), obtained from *Vitek* according to the guidelines of the National Committee for Clinical Laboratory Standards (NCCLS) [3]. Information about sensitivity analysis is connected with *patient,* his or her demographical data (*sex*, *age*) and hospitalization in the Institute (*main department*, *days spent in ICU*, *days spent in the hospital before test*, etc.). These features are summarized in Table 1.

Table 1. Dataset characteristics

Name	Type
Patient and hospitalization related	
sex	{Male, Female}
age	[0;72], mean 29.8
recurring stay	{True,False}
days of stay in NSI before test	[0;317], mean 87.5
days of stay in ICU	[0;237], mean 34
days of stay in NSI before specimen was received	[0;169] mean 31.6
bacterium is isolated when patient is in ICU	{True,False}
main department	{0,…,9}
department of stay	{0,…,11}
Pathogen and pathogen groups	
pathogen name	{Pat_name1, …, Pat_name17}
group1	{True,False}
…	…
group15	{True,False}
Antibiotic and antibiotic groups	
antibiotic name	{Ant_name1, …, Ant_name39}
group1	{True,False}
…	…
group15	{True,False}
sensitivity	{Sensitive, Intermediate, Resistant}

Each bacterium in a sensitivity test in the database is isolated from a single specimen that may be blood, liquor, urine, etc. In this pilot study we focus on the analysis of meningitis cases only, and the specimen is liquor. For the purposes of this exploratory analysis we picked up 4430 instances of sensitivity tests related to the meningitis cases of the period January 2002 – August 2004.

We introduced 5 grouping binary features for pathogens and 15 binary features for antibiotics. These binary features represent hierarchical grouping of pathogens and antibiotics into 5 and 15 categories respectively. Thus, each instance in the dataset had 34 features that included information corresponding to a single sensitivity test augmented with the data concerning the used antibiotic, the isolated pathogen, the sensitivity test result and clinical features of the patient and his/her demographics.

4 Data Analysis

In this section we report both the results achieved by different classification models and our experimental many-sided analysis approach including diversified DM techniques. In our experimental studies we have used various data-mining techniques available in the machine learning library with Java implementation WEKA 3.4.2 [14].

4.1 Basic Classifiers

As one stage of our preliminary analysis we formulated a classification problem aimed to predict the sensitivity of a pathogen to an antibiotic based on the data about the antibiotic, the isolated pathogen, and the demographic and clinical features of the patient (Table 1 above). The classification problem was tried to be solved using six classifiers (columns in Table 2): Naïve Bayes (NB), Bayesian Network (BN), three nearest neighbor-based classifiers (1NN, 3NN, and 15NN with weights), and a decision tree classifier (C4.5). As the seventh classifier the rule-based Jrip (Figure 1) was used.

The main accuracy results are presented as rows in Table 2. From the first row of Table 2 (*34 attributes*) it can be seen that the performance of classifiers in terms of accuracies differs much one to another. The Bayesian approaches performed poorly in

Table 2. Classification accuracy results for different feature subsets and different natural clusters

		NB	BN	1NN	3NN	15NN	C45
34attributes		.660	.665	.820	.782	**.841**	.809
32attrWOant&pat		.642	.660	.727	.723	**.757**	.771
10attrWOanyAnt&pat		.593	.630	.561	.658	**.670**	**.670**
11attrFSbyC45		.674	.686	.824	.802	**.845**	.818
5 attrFSby1NN		.735	.728	.814	.773	**.841**	.794
gram -	2 134	.670	.685	.831	.774	**.840**	.809
gram +	2 296	.756	.768	.803	.785	.830	**.844**
b_lactam	435	.682	.684	.822	.736	**.831**	.819
c_penem	116	.875	.880	.877	.883	**.907**	.858
ceph	183	.626	.615	.775	.665	**.788**	.759
pen	136	.726	.752	.882	.875	**.894**	.865

the case when all the features were used. A possible reason for that is that the features are redundant and highly correlated, with complex inter-feature dependencies.

Interestingly, 1NN was significantly better than the 3NN classifier. Maybe the 34 dimensions result in a situation where the space is not dense enough and the second and the third neighbours are actually quite distant instances. This is partly supported by our finding that when weighing was used with weights equal to *1/distance*, 15NN produced much better results.

The C4.5 decision tree classifier, and also the rule-based JRip classifier performed much better than the Bayesian approaches, yet their accuracy was less than the accuracy achieved by the best NN approaches (1NN and 15NN with weights). When we analyzed the rules selected by rule or tree based classification, we noticed that quite often the Intermediate sensitivity class was completely ignored by those rules. This can be explained by looking at the class distribution of the instances. In our data, classes with instances related to the sensitive and resistant cases of pathogens are dominating and nearly balanced (44.4% and 50.7% correspondingly), and easier to predict. On the contrary, there were very few instances of sensitivity tests where the pathogen sensitivity was intermediate (4.9%). Therefore the behavior of rule-based classifiers becomes clearer – instances of the Intermediate sensitivity class are treated as noise without a loss in generalization accuracy. It would be interesting to see in the future research whether this Intermediate class can be recognized with a reasonable accuracy separately at all, or otherwise it might be reasonable to leave this class out of consideration. At least with the considered in this paper approaches the confusion matrix shows that this class has generalization accuracy no better than random.

4.2 Feature Selection

In order to analyze the importance of features for predicting sensitivity we applied commonly used automatic feature selection techniques. One group of these techniques is related to the so-called filter approach that assumes evaluation of individual features or feature subsets independently from the learning algorithm. We applied ranking procedures based on the *Relief* and *Chi-square* measures. Both of the methods select *antibiotic_short_name, years_old, total_days_in_icu, patogen_short_name, days before_test, dept_of_stay,* and *main_dept* among the top seven features. The feature ranking techniques show that most information is concentrated in the features related to antibiotics, much less information in the features that describe pathogen and even less information is in the features that describe demographics of the patients and the hospitalization context.

The other group of feature selection techniques corresponds to the wrapper approach that assumes evaluation of feature subsets according to the accuracy of predictive model built on these feature subsets. In our experiments we used the same classifiers for the wrapper-based feature selection. Although feature subsets selected with the wrapper approach were different, *days_before_test, patogen_short_name,* and *antibiotic_short_name* have always been selected. The fourth row of Table 2 (*11attrFSbyC45*) includes accuracy results for basic classifiers when the C4.5 decision tree was used with the wrapper approach to select 11 features from the 32 features (patient name and antibiotic name were excluded). The resulting accuracies are slightly higher for all the basic classifiers than using all the features. Because this difference is highest with 3NN it supports our suspect that the multidimensionality of the original space has a negative effect.

It is interesting that the best feature subsets for the 1NN, 3NN, 15NN with weights and C4.5 decision tree classifiers were selected when C4.5 was used as the wrapper learning algorithm. We also tried to use the 1NN classifier in the wrapper approach to select 5 features from the 32 features (patient name and antibiotic name were excluded) and the corresponding results are presented in the fifth row of Table 2 (*5attrFSby1NN*). So, surprisingly, e.g., 1NN classifier performed better (.824 vs. .814) when the C4.5 decision tree (not 1NN itself) was used with the wrapper approach. It is interesting to note that the Bayesian basic classifiers give their highest accuracies with this very limited feature set, which is perhaps due to smaller interdependency of features.

Besides the commonly used automatic feature selection techniques, we applied expert (manual) feature selection. Semantically, the sensitivity concept is related first of all to the pathogen and antibiotic features. Therefore it was interesting for us to see how good accuracy can be achieved if the information about the pathogen and antibiotic is excluded from the models. First we excluded the *pathogen name* and *antibiotic name* attributes but left all the grouping features. The corresponding results for the basic classifiers are presented in the second row of Table 2 (*32attrWOant&pat)*. The accuracies are smaller than using all the 34 features but the accuracies are still much higher than 50% and we can assume that groupings of antibiotics and pathogens into categories were appropriate and the grouping features contained relevant information.

Next, we excluded all the attributes related to the pathogen and antibiotic using only the 10 patient and hospitalization related features. The corresponding results for the basic classifiers are presented in the third row of Table 2 (*10attrWOanyAnt&pat*). The accuracies are smaller than those above but they are still much higher than 50% (the accuracy of naïve prediction of the majority class). This fact indicates that in our data exist some interesting patterns independent from antibiotics and pathogens and they are related to the demographics and hospital stay information only. We applied the rule-based classifier JRip on this feature subset in order to find an explanation.

4.3 Classification Rules

JRip is Weka's implementation of the RIPPER rule learner [2] that efficiently produces easy interpretable *if-then* rules. Association and classification rules are considered to be quite useful in healthcare as they offer the possibility to extract invaluable information and build important knowledge bases quickly and automatically. In general, association and classification rules mining is a common approach in microbiological data that helps to discover new knowledge about the phenomenon or to find support for already known relations between concepts and their features [1].

In collaboration with medical experts we tried to mine interesting patterns by means of classification rules construction. Beside many interesting rules, several expected relationships between pathogens and antibiotics were found during the expert evaluation of discovered rules. There were some interesting rules discovered that determined associations between sex and AR, age and AR, location of a patient in the hospital and AR. However, their clinical relevance and utility await the results of prospective clinical studies currently under investigation. Five of the found rules in our study are presented as an example in Figure 1. The first rule e.g. shows that young patients who have not stayed long in ICU are contracted with bacteria that are quite often sensitive to antibiotics in general irrespective of the pathogen and antibiotic types, and thus the problem of AR concerns young patients to a smaller degree.

```
1: (total_days_in_icu <= 6) & (years_old >= 2) & (years_old <= 14) => pat_ab_sens=S (420/92)
2: (7 < years_old <= 14) & (main_dept = 1)  => pat_ab_sens = S (81/24)
3: (days_fefore_test < 16) & (main_dept = 2)  => pat_ab_sens = S (47/7)
4: (pathogen_short_name = p_aeruginosa) & (recurring = FALSE) and (sex = M) &
   (days_in_ICU < 21) pat_ab_sens = S (82/14)
5: (antibiotic_short_name = vancomycin) => pat_ab_sens = S (44/1)
```

Fig. 1. Classification rule examples produced by JRip on a feature subset that includes information about the patients and their hospitalization only. The numbers in the brackets denote the number of instances satisfying to the left part of the rule (support, 420) and the number of exceptions found for this rule (92).

Based on the discussion with infection control practitioners, we have found that although not all classification and association rules were interesting, some suggested potential nosocomial outbreaks and changes of patterns in microbial resistance. It would be interesting to investigate whether the found classification rules correspond to some of the ones known by medical experts as general dependencies (as it might be the case with the example rules) or are these rules just reflecting the peculiarities of the distribution of our data over the selected attributes (which is often referred to as overfitting).

4.4 Natural Clustering

We continued our experimental study, applying so-called natural clustering of our data. The main reason to do that is to try to find out the possibly different semantics for each group of pathogens and antibiotics. Therefore we were interested in how the accuracy of classification models varies from one cluster to another and whether it is possible to achieve better accuracy applying a classifier locally in each cluster instead of the use of global classification. The basic accuracy results are presented in the lower parts of Table 2. Rows 6 and 7 (*gram–* and *gram+*) include the accuracies of base classifiers for the pathogen clusters 'gram positive' and 'gram negative'. The base classifiers are developed using all the other features than the feature *gram+* which is used to build the clusters. The number of instances in each cluster is presented after the name of the cluster. The clusters *gram–* and *gram+* are approximately of the same size. In Figure 2 the achieved accuracies for each base classifier are presented for both clusters separately, the average of accuracies within those two clusters, and the global accuracy achieved using all the features. For the Bayesian base classifiers the differences of accuracies between the clusters seem to be quite big and at the same time the accuracies for the clusters are always higher than the global accuracies. The NN-classifiers do not manage to achieve higher accuracies in average with clustering compared to the global accuracies. C4.5 base classifiers for clusters result in at least as high accuracies for clusters as globally and inside the cluster *gram+* even higher than 15NN.

Row 8 (*b_lactam*) of Table 2 includes the accuracies of the base classifiers for the antibiotic group, whose subgroups are included in the three following rows (*c_penem*, *ceph*, and *pen*). The base classifiers are produced leaving the excluded antibiotic group features away. The results are presented in Figure 2 (right), subgroups *c_penem*, *ceph*, and *pen* are labeled *ant1*, *ant2* and *ant3* respectively. Inside the clustering related to *b_lactam* the global base classifiers are no worse than the *ceph*-cluster classifiers for every type of base classifiers. On the contrary for the two other clusters (*c_penem* and *pen*) the cluster classifiers outperform the global classifiers for every type of base classifiers. It can also be seen from the figure that the average accuracy of classifiers (except C4.5) is higher when they are applied locally within each cluster comparing to the global classifiers' accuracy.

In [8] different dimensionality reduction techniques have been applied locally in produced pathogen clusters. The results of our experiments show that the proper selection of a local DR technique can lead to a significant increase of predictive accuracy comparing to the global classification with or without DR. The amount of features extracted or selected locally is always smaller than that in the global space that also shows the usefulness of natural clustering in coping with data heterogeneity.

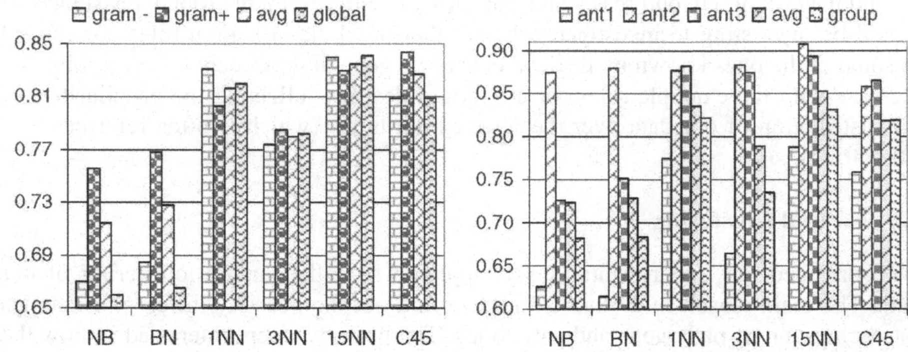

Fig. 2. Classification accuracies for two main pathogen clusters (left) and for b_lactam antibiotics clusters (right)

4.5 Tracking Concept Drift

Most DM algorithms assume that data is a random sample from some stationary distribution, while real data in clinical institutions are gathered over long time periods (months or years) and therefore naturally violate this assumption. Kukar [5] states that even in most strictly controlled environments some unexpected changes may happen due to fail and/or replacement of some medical equipment, or due to changes in personnel. Clearly, the sooner some change is discovered the better, since corresponding actions can be applied to prevent the undesirable effects.

Often the cause of change is hidden, not known a priori, making the learning task more complicated. Changes in the hidden context can induce more or less radical changes in the target concept, which is generally known as the problem of concept drift [12, 13]. An effective learner should be able to track such changes and quickly adapt to them.

It is commonly acknowledged that the sensitivity to antibiotics of many bacteria may change over time significantly due to the antibiotic resistance phenomenon described above causing a significant level of concept drift in the AR domain. Antibiotic resistance is a typical example of concept drift in the medical context. New pathogen strains develop their resistance to antibiotics which were previously effective through mutation and natural selection.

Beside that, a significant level of virtual concept drift is pertinent to the AR domain. Hidden changes in context may not only be a cause of a change of target concept, but may also cause a change of the underlying data distribution. Even if the target concept remains the same, and it is only the data distribution that changes, this may often lead to the necessity of revising the current model, as the model's error may no longer be acceptable with the new data distribution.

In this paper we suggest a window-based approach to analyze the underlying concept drift. We divide the data into blocks of equal size (or equal time intervals) and use these blocks as train and test sets sequentially in order to understand the underlying concept and data distribution changes. We suggest three strategies for that which use different blocks as train and test sets: (I) build a model for each of the blocks sequentially, besides the last one, and test it on the last block; (II) build a model for each of the blocks sequentially, besides the last one, and test it on the next block; and (III) build a model on the first block and test it on each of the next blocks.

These strategies, applied together, and with their results depicted in a single graph, help to better understand underlying changes in the concept and in data distribution. We have constructed such graphs for different time intervals and different learners, and discussed them with medical experts. Discussion of the experimental results with medical experts revealed a few interesting, expected and unexpected, dependencies.

Expectedly enough, the most interesting graphs are built with 15NN, which is the strongest learner in this domain. Most of the graphs constructed confirm our expectations that a significant level of concept and data distribution drift is pertinent to the AR domain. In Figure 3, two graphs are shown for the three strategies with the 15NN learner and 3-month time intervals, corresponding to the seasons of year in Russia (and many European countries), starting with March 2002 (Spring), and December 2002 (Winter).

A few interesting dependencies can be seen in this figure. First, clear periodicity in behaviour is seen (Strategy III). The model for Spring 2002 (left) has its highest accuracy in Springs 2003 and 2004. The same is with the Winter 2002 model (right), which works well again in Winter 2003, and worse in all the other seasons. This is not true, however, with the Summer and Autumn models (not shown here). There is no periodicity with them. After discussion of this phenomenon with medical experts, a hypothesis has been raised that this happens due to the typical bacteria outbreaks which always happen in Winter and in Spring. In terms of these outbreaks, Winter and Spring are more similar seasons to each other, in contrast to Autumn and Summer, which can be drastically different year to year, depending much on the weather. This hypothesis needs to be checked with other data, in other contexts (different hospitals, countries, bacteria, diseases, etc), but it was accepted after

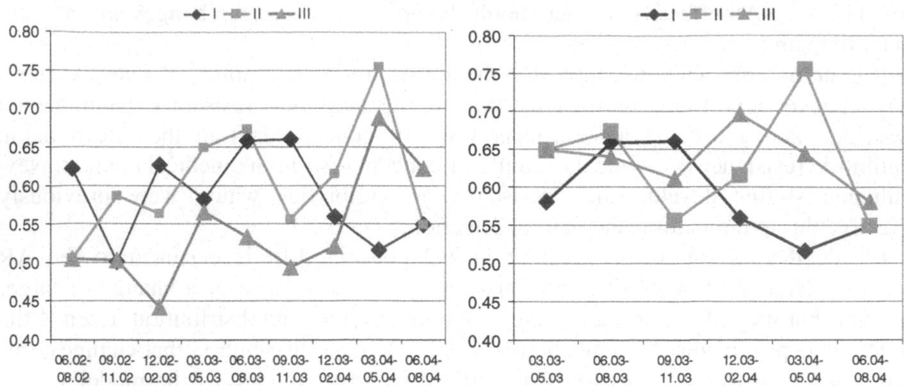

Fig. 3. Tracking CD with the 3 strategies. Accuracy results for Spring 2002 (left) and Winter 2002 (right)

analysis of the tracking concept drift graphs by the experts as very interesting and promising hypothesis.

Among the seasonal models, the Winter models are always much more stable and accurate, with accuracy not dropping much on the other seasons (see Figure 3, right, Strategy III). This behaviour was identified by experts as interesting and a possible explanation for it is that the winter period is characterized by a much bigger variability of bacteria than all the other seasons. In Winter, it is often so that the same bacteria strains appear, common for the other seasons, besides those common for Winter only. This hypothesis needs further research as well and experimental check in other contexts.

5 Conclusions and Directions of Further Research

Surveillance of AR and nosocomial infections is one of the most important functions of a hospital infection control program.

In this paper we have presented the results of our experimental study in AR prediction for nosocomial infections. We have achieved rather high generalization accuracy (84.5%) that is quite promising in terms of better understanding the problem and patterns of AR. The results were achieved using data with patients having meningitis over the last three years only, and we plan to continue our analysis of the whole NSI database of nosocomial infections including older data collected since 1997. Beside good accuracy results achieved, we emphasized the data and problem understanding perspective.

Besides, in this paper we demonstrated how complex many-sided analysis of a real-world problem could have been performed, how application of different DM techniques has helped us to understand better the nature of the data that represents the problem.

DM makes it easy for experts to inspect patterns that might otherwise be missed by usual (manual) infection control surveillance methods. However, the clinical relevance and utility of these findings await the results of prospective studies.

Besides the modeling approaches applied so far, there are also other interesting promising directions to continue. One of these might be to enhance the models to a more fine-grained level considering different sub contexts of interest of the whole domain area separately. These sub contexts can be formed for example from the interestingness or periodicity points of view. For example, specific antibiotic-pathogen pairs could be isolated, certain time intervals chosen, and the peculiarity of behaviour of AR for these clusters analyzed.

Promising area not included in the present study is feature extraction. Our preliminary experiments show that this domain includes many correlated and redundant features, and the inherent dimensionality of the data is relatively low (10 features extracted with PCA is enough to obtain the accuracy of 80% with *k*NN). Feature extraction might be yet another perspective helping to understand better the problem with our many-sided analysis.

Another important direction of further research is to analyze further antibiotic sensitivity as a concept drift problem. Likewise, infection control systems require or will require tools that recognize trends in nosocomial infection and AR in an efficient and timely manner. Tracking and handling concept drift, when applied at the levels of one hospital or many hospitals in one or several countries, helps to start necessary counter actions in time. We are currently developing a technique based on an ensemble of classifiers with dynamic integration to handle concept drift in the AR data.

Besides the issues of data collecting and cleaning (in a timely fashion) for AR analysis, the information on how results of the analysis will be used to make proactive decisions (that possibly would change current practice in a hospital) is of high importance.

Acknowledgments. This research is partly supported by the Academy of Finland, the Graduate School COMAS of the University of Jyväskylä, Finland, and the Science Foundation Ireland under Grant No. S.F.I.-02IN.1I111.

References

1. Brossette SE, Sprague AP, Jones WT, Moser SA A data mining system for infection control surveillance, Methods of Information in Medicine 39(4-5), 2000, pp. 303-310
2. Cohen W. 1995. Fast effective rule induction. In: Proc. of 12th International Conference on Machine Learning (ICML-95), pp. 115-123, Morgan Kaufman.
3. Ferraro M.J., et al. Methods for Dilution Antimicrobial Susceptibility Tests for Bacteria that Grow Aerobically: Approved Standard: Sixth Edition & Performance Standards for Antimicrobial Susceptibility Testing. Wayne, PA: National Committee for Clinical Laboratory Standarts, NCCLS, 2004. (Documents M7-A6 and M100-S14, www.nccls.org).
4. Gaynes R.P. Surveillance of nosocomial infections: a fundamental ingredient for quality. Infect Control Hosp Epidemiol 1997, 18(7): 475–478.
5. Kukar M. Drifting concepts as hidden factors in clinical studies. In: Proc. 9th Conf. on Artifi-cial Intelligence in Medicine in Europe, AIME 2003, Springer, LNCS, 2003, 355-364.

6. Lamma E., Manservigi M., Mello P., Nanetti A., Riguzzi F., Storari S., The automatic discovery of alarm rules for the validation of microbiological data, 6th Int. Workshop on Intelligent Data Analysis in Medicine and Pharmacology, IDAMAP 2001, UK, 2001.
7. Ma L, Tsui FC, Hogan WR, Wagner MM, Ma H. A Framework for Infection Control Surveillance Using Association Rules. In Proc American Medical Informatics Association Annual Fall Symposium, Omni Press CD, pp. 410-414, 2003
8. Pechenizkiy M., Tsymbal A., Puuronen S. 2005. Local Dimensionality Reduction within Natural Clusters for Medical Data Analysis, (to appear) In Proc. 18th IEEE Int. Symp. on Computer-Based Medical Systems CBMS'2005, IEEE CS Press.
9. Samore M, Lichtenberg D, Saubermann L, et al. A clinical data repository enhances hospital infection control. In Proc American Medical Informatics Association Annual Fall Symposium, 1997; 56–60.
10. Streed SA, Sheretz RJ, Reagan DR: Computers in hospital epidemiology. In: Mayhall CG (ed), Hospital Epidemiology and Infection Control, Baltimore:Williams & Wilkins, Chapter8, pp. 115-122.
11. The Problem of Antibiotic Resistance, NIAID Fact Sheet. National Institute of Allergy and Infectious Diseases (NIAID), National Institutes of Health, U.S. Department of Health and Human Services, USA (available at www.niaid.nih.gov/factsheets/antimicro.htm)
12. Tsymbal A. The problem of concept drift: definitions and related work, Technical Report TCD-CS-2004-15, Department of Computer Science, Trinity College Dublin, Ireland, 2004.
13. Widmer G., Kubat M., Effective learning in dynamic environments by explicit context tracking, Proc. 6th European Conf. on Machine Learning ECML-1993, Springer-Verlag, Lecture Notes in Computer Science 667, 1993, 227-243.
14. Witten I., Frank E. 2000. Data Mining: Practical machine learning tools with Java implementations", Morgan Kaufmann, San Francisco.

Semi-automatic Data Migration in a Self-medication Knowledge-Based System

Olivier Curé

ISIS Laboratory, Cité Descartes – 5, bld Descartes,
Champs-sur-Marne – 77454 Marne-la-Vallée Cedex 2 – France
ocure@univ-mlv.fr

Abstract. Self-medication, defined as the act to treat oneself with or without drugs, is a common practice in industrial countries. A study of available computerized solutions in this field highlights that this issue has not been considered with enough attention, although they provide valuable services to both patients and health care organizations. This paper presents XIMSA, a self-medication knowledge-based system, which is supported by a database/ ontology collaboration. This collaboration is guaranteed by DBOM, an application-independent system which enables the end-user to design, enrich and maintain an ontology from an existing database. DBOM's functionalities are presented within XIMSA's application domain.

1 Introduction

In order to become profitable and enterprise-like structures, health care organizations (henceforth HCO) need to provide services to all involved actors. Usually HCOs provide a large attention to health care professionals (physicians, pharmacists, etc.) but rarely concentrate their efforts on patients. Most of the time, this leads the patient to a semantic isolation whenever he is confronted with the idiosyncratic nature medical information, data and knowledge.

Our collaboration with the clinical pharmacology department at the Cochin hospital in Paris (France) has resulted in the implementation of IMSA (Interactive Multimedia for Auto-medication)[6]. This Knowledge-Based System (henceforth KBS) aims at providing information and services to the general-public on mild clinical signs, related treatments and medications. The latest version of this system, XIMSA (eXtended IMSA) bundles together a drug and symptom database, a self-medication ontology, a simplified patient electronic health record and an inference engine. The results provided by the inference engine depend on the ontology/database collaboration efficiency, which is undertaken by DBOM (DataBase Ontology Mapping), a domain independent application providing data integration and maintenance services in a Semantic Web environment [5].

This paper is organized as follows : section 2 presents the main characteristics of self-medication, section 3 focuses on XIMSA's architecture and functionalities, section 4 proposes on overview of DBOM, section 5 emphasizes a database/ontology collaboration, section 6 concludes with a discussion on future extensions of the XIMSA and DBOM systems.

K.-D. Althoff et al. (Eds.): WM 2005, LNAI 3782, pp. 373 – 383, 2005.

2 Self-medication

Self-medication can be defined as the health activities to treat oneself with or without drugs. People self-medicate using information obtained from past health experiences, books, advices, software, web sites, health advertising, radio or TV programs. On the medication side, people usually self prescribe drugs they already have at home, usually left-over of previous general practitioner prescriptions and/or self-medicaiton treatments, and buy Over The Counter (OTC) products. These products are unevenly distributed over therapeutic classes (respiratory and digestive systems drugs are the most self-prescribed) and represent more than half of the drugs available on the french market.

Self-medication is popular in most industrial countries, e.g. a recent study estimated that 91% of French citizens self-prescribe drugs when confronted to a known symptom [1]. The act to self-medicate is also an interesting financial market which represented 9.7% (2 billion euros) of the global pharmaceutical market for 1999 in France [1]. The French government, in its struggle with the French social security system deficit (14 billion euros for 2003), is indirectly encouraging self-medication through series of actions : drug switch, lower the reimbursement rate for some drugs, favoring the emergence of the generics market, etc..

HCOs are as much aware of the semantic isolation of most patients as they are aware of the increasing success of self-medication. A logical correlation between these facts partially explain some alarming French figures for 2004: 128,000 hospitalizations due to drug interactions and 10,000 deaths due to drug over and mis-consumption.

The current policy of the French government is to encourage patients to become responsible and (pro)active health actors, but at the same time, non-commercial and ethical support, in terms of guidelines, books and computer tools, is available to the general public. Officially, the French healthcare system relies on its physician and pharmacist network to provide information on safe practice of self-medication. But with a national average of 6 minutes per consultation, it is hard to believe that general practitioners have the time to analyze a health situation, prescribe some treatements and educate the patient through explainations about the symptom(s) and the drug(s) prescribed. This patient-oriented education approach would be relevant in the french health care system because it is estimated that up to 60 percent of the consultations in general practices can be treated via self-medication.

We believe that KBS is an alternative that has not been sufficiently exploited with the proper attention. These systems are exploited in so-called "intelligent" applications which have the ability to find implicit consequences from their explicitly represented knowledge. Such web-based systems may benefit from rapidly emerging markets, such as high speed Internet access and Internet compliant mobile phones, to reach an important portion of the population.

3 XIMSA

The XIMSA web application proposes self-medication services to the general public and aims to make this health care act a safer one and to free the patient from the semantic isolation related to medical information. The XIMSA system is the result of a long time collaboration with the clinical pharmacology department at the Cochin hospital in Paris and especially Professor J.P. Giroud, its chief and co-author, with Dr. C. Hagège, of several self-medication dedicated french best-seller editions of the "Guide Giroud-Hagège de tous les médicaments", see [10] for the last edition. The success of this book can be attributed to:

- its organization based on two main parts : a section dedicated to symptoms of the self-medication domain which proposes explanations , advices, therapeutic classes and adapted drugs. The second and largest section focuses on drugs (OTC and non-OTC) with Summary of Product Characteristics (SPC) and the authors drug rating.
- the semantic adequacy and readability of its content which is adapted to the understanding of the patient.

XIMSA' architecture is based on 4 distinctive modules (module interactions are presented in figure 1):

- the XIMSA database stores symptom and drug data related to self-medication,
- the XIMSA ontology uses the OWL [8] syntax to represent terminological (usually called the Tbox) and assertional (called the Abox) knowledge in a self-medication context.,
- the Simplified Electronic Health Record (SEHR) stores information (in an XML syntax) concerning data such as clinical antecedents and the history of drug consumption for a particular patient,
- the inference engine makes deduction with respect to the XIMSA ontology, the patient's SEHR and the data acquired during the navigation within XIMSA [6].

The advantages provided by XIMSA's functionalities can be assessed in two categories. The first category is concerned with the quality of treatment which is ensured by:

- the confidence that the system provides advices and drug propositions only for mild clinical signs that can be treated via self-medication,
- the adequacy between the symptom described by the patient and the therapeutic classes proposed,
- the adaptability and accuracy of the drugs provided for a treatment, with respect to the clinical and pharmacological information stored in the patient's SEHR,
- the value of the drugs presented based on their evaluations (a rating between 0 and 20) which is based on an efficiency/tolerance ratio.
- the usage of such systems will increase the overall knowledge of end-users and will improve the communication between patients and healthcare professionals.

The second category is related to the controlling of costs:

- on the patient side, the system provides a direct access to OTC drug prices. Although not reimbursed by the Social Security system, these drugs may cost less to the patients due to their lower prices compared to prescription (partially reimbursed) drugs. This aspect is particularly important in a market driven by drug switches where the number of non-listed drugs (which can be purchased without a prescription) is increasing over the listed ones.

- on the Social Security system side, avoidance of reimbursement are guaranteed on the physician consultation and the drugs proposed.
- Finally, for both patients and the Social Security system, a global visibility of drug prices over all therapeutic classes may encourage the usage of the less expensive generics drugs.

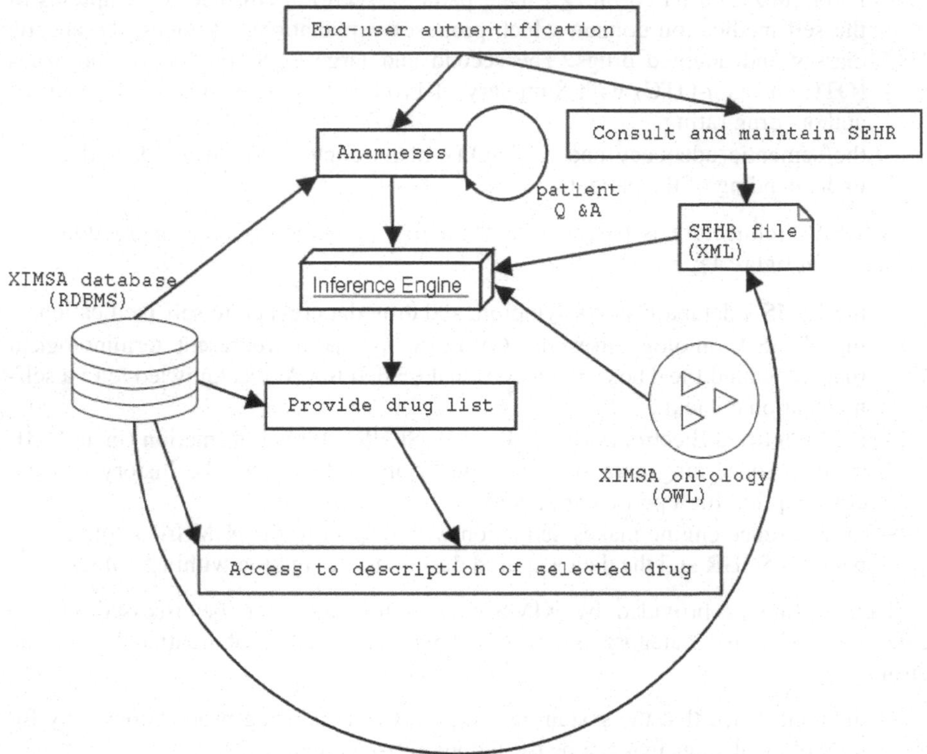

Fig. 1. Interaction-based architecture of XIMSA

4 DBOM

XIMSA's effectiveness is based on the quality and accuracy of the self-medication ontology and the SEHR. Although the patient/end-user is solely responsible for the value of the SEHR, through maintenance's accuracy, the ontology's quality is undertaken by DBOM. An important part of this ontology focuses on drug related data, a field with a high update rate which requires storage in a database. Starting from the fact that "databases are similar to knowledge base because they are usually used to maintain models of some domain of discourse"[3], the idea of DBOM is to tackle the problem of database-to-ontology mapping.

This problem has been addressed by several research groups but DBOM's approach is more concerned with the following issues : data storage redundancy and inference efficiency. The consideration of these issues is done at the price of a non-automatic ontology design. For example, in [9] and [4], the goal is to (fully) automate data migration by transforming the relational database model into corresponding ontological structures, while [2]'s architecture is based on an existing ontology structure (non-automatic).

The approach adopted by DBOM is semi-automatic and involves the end-user to select amongst database components (relations, attributes, keys) which are going to map to the ontology structures. This solution ensures that the ontology will not contain concepts, properties and instances unnecessary to the inference engine. The vision of the DBOM system is to develop applications that use the ontology for inference purposes and is able to bind the inference results to the database thus providing to the end-user, information that may not be contained in the ontology. In order to reach this goal, the designer of the mapping must be aware of the database schema and needs a clear vision of the characteristics of the implemented application, including inferences.

A high potential of the DBOM framework is to design domain and application ontologies [7] from existing databases. An important fact about databases are that update operations may also update the domain of discourse. The XIMSA system makes an intensive use of DBOM via the exploitation of the *automed* database. Below is a sample of its relational schema:

```
drug(drugId, drugName, list, rating, generalInterdiction,
   drugAssociationInterdiction, generalCaution,
   drugAssociationCaution, composition, whenToUseTheDrug,
   whenToStopUsingTheDrug, Incidents, AuthorsComment,
   pharmaceuticalId, drugSystem, posology)
product(drugId, productId, price, cipCode,
   productPresentation, reimbursementRate, generic,
   drugIdRef, productIdRef)
pharmaceutical( pharmaceuticalId, pharmaceutilName)
therapeuticClass2med (classId, drugId)
therapeuticClass (classId, className)
system(systemId, systemName)
rinn(atcCode , rinnName)
rinn2Drug(drugId, atcCode)
```

The data contained in the *drug* and *product* relations provide all thc information proposed in a drug's SPC and additional information such as drug rating, whether the drug is a brand name drug or a link to its reference if it is a generic drug. The *system* relations regroups the different systems of medical practice to treat a disease such as allopathy, homepathy, phytotherapy, etc.. The *rinn* relation store the Recommended International Non-proprietary Name (RINN, the active molecule) available on the market. Each RINN is identified using the Anatomical Therapeutical Chemical (ATC) Classification which is developped and maintained by the WHO Collaborating Centre for Drug Statistics Methodology [11].The data stored in the remaining relations is relatively straightforward.

The comprehension of this relational schema enables the ontology designer to create concepts which can be related via subsumption relations. In the following code sample, two concepts are created. The *Drug* concept is abstract, meaning that no direct individuals of this class will be created in the Abox, while the *AlloDrug* concept is concrete, the Abox will be populated with individuals obtained from the *automed* database via running of the SQL query. The *drugName* (datatye) property used in the following code sample is not presented in this article due to space limitations but is defined in the complete mapping file.

```
<dbom:class dbom:namespace="automed"
   dbom:className="Drug"/>
<dbom:class dbom:namespace="automed"
   dbom:className="Drug"/>
  <dbom:class dbom:namespace="automed"
   dbom:className="AllotherapyDrug"
   dbom:subClassOf="Drug">
      <dbom:instance dbom:query="SELECT
        drugId,drugName FROM drug d WHERE
        systemId=1;">
        <dbom:id>
                    <dbom:field dbom:value="1"/>
        </dbom:id>
        <dbom:data>
              <dbom:field dbom:value="2"
                    dbom:datatypeProperty="drugName"/>
        </dbom:data>
      </dbom:instance>
</dbom:class>
```

Object properties are also being created from the relational schema. The following code example defines a relation whose domain is the *AlloDrug* concept and range is the *RINN* concept (not defined in the code sample but mapped from the *rinn* relation and defined as an artificial substance). This property is concrete and individuals will be created running the SQL query.

```
<dbom:objectProperty dbom:namespace="automed"
   dbom:propertyName="containsRINN"
   dbom:domain="AlloDrug" dbom:range="RINN">
   <dbom:instance dbom:query="SELECT d.drugId,
   atccode FROM drug d, rinn2Drug rd
   WHERE system=1 AND d.drugId=rd.drugId;"/>
 </dbom:objectProperty>
```

The processing of the mapping file in the DBOM system will yield a knowledge base Tbox and Abox. The following OWL code sample presents the concepts and the relation designed previously:

```
<owl:Class rdf:about="http://www.univ-
   mlv.fr/~ocure/automed.owl#AlloDrug">
   <rdfs:subClassOf>
      <owl:Class rdf:about="http://www.univ-
        mlv.fr/~ocure/automed.owl#Drug"/>
   </rdfs:subClassOf>
</owl:Class>
<owl:ObjectProperty rdf:about="http://www.univ-
   mlv.fr/~ocure/automed.owl#containsRINN">
   <rdfs:range rdf:resource="http://www.univ-
   mlv.fr/~ocure/automed.owl#RINN"/>
   <rdfs:domain rdf:resource="http://www.univ-
   mlv.fr/~ocure/automed.owl#AlloDrug"/>
</owl:ObjectProperty>
```

In order to present a complete example, we present the Abox, also in the OWL format :

```
<RINN rdf:ID="DCI_R05DA09">
 <rinnName
   rdf:datatype="http://www.w3.org/2001/XMLSchema#string">
   Dextromethropane Bromhydrate
 </rinnName>
</RINN>
<Drug rdf:ID="AllDrug_647">
 <drugName
   rdf:datatype="http://www.w3.org/2001/XMLSchema#string">
   Capsyl 15mg
 </drugName>
 <containsRINN rdf:resource="#DCI_R05DA09"/>
</Drug>
```

Considering that operations (insert, update, delete queries) on a database can update the knowledge base, it is necessary to synchronize these two components. The proposed system offers such features and extends them to permit symmetrical maintenance solutions, meaning that controls are done both ways : from database to the ontology (ontology updating, e.g. adding new instances) and from the ontology to the database (e.g. consistency checking).

The main motivation behind the maintenance features remains in the database / ontology systems separation. This separation requires that the database schema is not modified during mapping processing and enables users of the DBOM framework to benefit from database features which are not available in ontology engineering (concurrency control, transaction, crash recovery, advanced storage techniques and query languages) as well as features of OWL ontologies, and underlying Description Logics properties and functionalities [3].

The description of the DBOM framework is divided into four distinct components: design, enrichment, ontology and database maintenances (see figure 2).

The design component supports the creation of the TBox (a set of terminological axioms) in an OWL syntax. This phase is partially done by the end-user who uses his knowledge of the database schema to describe a mapping file (an XML document) to the ontology. This description consists in describing the database relations, attributes and possible conditions implied in the design of the ontology. The approach adopted enables DBOM to generate hierarchies of complex classes and properties in the Tbox.

The enrichment component deals with instantiating the Abox (a set of assertional axioms) with individuals obtained from the database. The performances of this phase are increased due to the storage of SQL queries in the mapping file. A simple parsing of a mapping file enables queries to be executed in the database and thus creates new assertions in the ontology.

The maintenance components are dealing with ABox updates and database consistency checking. The ontology maintenance phase is concerned with (non-schema) updates of the databases, e.g. insertion of a new tuple in the database fires a trigger that may creates a corresponding instance in the ontology. The enrichment phase is usually performed once for an ontology schema while maintenance may be

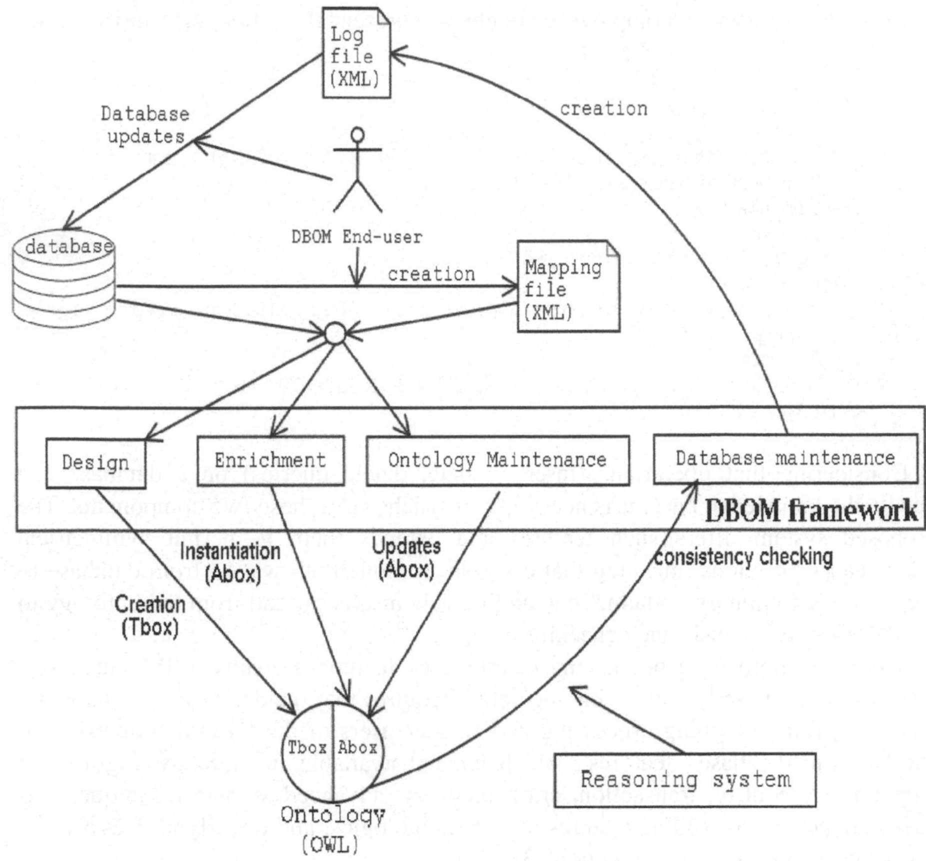

Fig. 2. Global vision of interactions with the DBOM framework

processed several times during the life cycle of a terminology. The last component of DBOM is related to the database maintenance which is ensured by consistency checking of an ABox w.r.t. a TBox. This database maintenance is executed after an effective, at least one trigger has been fired, ontology maintenance. The objective of this maintenance is to ensure that characteristics of new instances are consistent with the semantics of the ontology, something the DBMS can not process due to its lack of detailed semantics. The current philosophy of the database maintenance is not to act directly on the database Thus the approach adopted is to propose a log file, in an XML format, to the end-user.

5 Ontology/Database Collaboration

The main features (design, enrichment and maintenances) of the DBOM application are used on the XIMSA system. An important part of XIMSA's self-medication ontology has been designed using DBOM based on a drug database which contains all drugs available in France. For each drug, the database regroups all the data of the SPC plus extra information such as opinions of the authors and a drug rating.

The integration of the ontology in XIMSA enables the patient to control drug prescription regarding data contained in his SEHR which is created and maintained within the web-based XIMSA interface. The overall goal of the SEHR is to store health related information concerning a particular patient. The formalism adopted for the SEHR is the semistructured XML language. The validation of SEHR documents is supported by an XML Schema document which has been designed to store three categories of patient information:

- general information concerning a patient such as name, gender, date of birth, etc..
- medical information mainly concerning known diseases, allergies, etc..
- drug consumption information which distinguishes consumption start date, dosage and duration of treatment. The system supports the description of discrete and continuous (e.g. Life long treatments) prescriptions. Information concerning the source of prescription, either a health care professional or self-medication, are also provided to emphasize trustworthiness of the data stored.

The following XML extract of an SEHR highlights the consumption of the Marsilid© drug between feburary 1st and february 27th with a dosage of one pill per day. This drug has been prescribed by Dr XXX (kept anonymous in this paper) and is identified in the database by the number 2073.

```
<discretePrescription>
    <prescription>
          <drugId>2073</drugId>
          <drugName>Marsilid</drugName>
          <posology>1 comprime</posology>
          <prescriptionSource>Dr XXX</prescriptionSource>
          <startDate>7/2/2005</startDate>
          <endDate>27/2/2005</endDate>
    </prescription>
    ...
</discretePrescription>
```

A ruled-based mechanism handles the ontology, the SEHR, and a particular request of the end-user (for example requiring an antitussive drug) to propose hyper links of safe to prescribe drugs. The result of the inference mechanisms provides identifiers of eligible ontology instances. Due to the correspondence between the ontology instances and the database tuples, the end-user can click on a hyper link and obtain all the information stored in the database about this drug, including information not contained in the ontology (e.g. drug price).

Finally, updates of the ontology produce a consistency checking. Lets consider the addition of a new drug in the database where the therapeutic class is not consistent with the RINN of the drug. Although the statement recorded in the database is valid, its semantic is wrong. The consistency checking of the ontology will report, in a log file, that an inconsistent statement has been added in the database. A study of the log file will enable the database administrator to change the therapeutic class of this drug.

6 Discussion

The efficiency of XIMSA relies on the quality and quantity of information stored in the SEHR. If the end-user/patient inputs sufficient data concerning clinical (e.g. whether he is suffering from certain diseases) and pharmacological (current consumptions, allergies, etc..) aspects then valuable inferences are provided.

In order to ensure an accurate and up-to-date SEHR, health care professionals may become sources of information. Both patients and physicians would benefit from this collaboration : the physician would be aware of all drugs taken by the patient and the patient would be ensured to have a valid, accurate SEHR concerning non self-medication descriptions and treatments. On the HCO side, such a distributed collaboration may increase the overall quality of self-medication with the possibility to study, understand and control this medical activity.

The DBOM application enables the design and maintenance of high quality ontologies by providing correctness and minimally redundant data. The correctness quality is provided by the capture of the intuitions of domain experts which is facilitated by a conceptual-concerned collaboration with the designer. This collaboration also benefits from a knowledge representation language abstraction and fast access to a realistic, richly instantiated ABox. The minimal redundancy quality is provided by the database/ontology separation considering that the ontology only contains relations and attributes concerned with inference mechanisms.

A study of DBOM also emphasizes economical aspects with the following facts : the database and the ontology can concurrently be accessed and maintained, the knowledge acquisition and updates are done at no extra costs, the guarantee that the system will be adopted by the experts because they were involved in the design of the ontology.

Although the XIMSA auto-medication ontology contains more than 6000 drug products, 1500 RINN and 500 therapeutic classes, we believe that studies with larger ontologies, meaning larger TBoxes and ABoxes, need to be conducted. Performance surveys should also be conducted with such ontologies. The DBOM framework also requires the implementation of a graphical QBE-like solution for the design of database to ontology mapping file.

References

1. AFIPA : "Premier geste". Décembre 1999. On-line at http://www.afipa.org/index/informations/etudes_et_enquetes.html.
2. Astrova, I. : Reverse Engineering of Relational Databases to Ontologies. ESWS 2004: 327-341
3. Baader, F. ; Calvanase , D. ; McGuinness, D. ; Nardi, D. ; Patel-Schneider, P. (editors) : The description logic handbook. Cambridge University Press.
4. Barrasa, J. ; Corcho, O. ; Gómez-Pérez, A. : Fund finder : A case study of database-to-ontology mapping. Proceedings of the Semantic Integration Workshop (ISWC 2003). On-line at http://sunsite.informatik.rwth-aachen.de/Publications/CEUR-WS/Vol-82/.
5. Berners-Lee, T. ; Hendler, J. ; Lassile, O. : The Semantic Web. Scientic American, Vol. 5/01, 2001. (http://www.scientificamerican.com/2001/0501issue/0501berners-lee.html).

6. Curé, O. : Overview of the IMSA project, a patient-oriented medical information system. Codata Journal, Vol 1/ 02, 2002, pp 66-75.
7. Guarino, N. : "Formal Ontology and Information Systems". In the Proceedings of FOIS 1998. Also in Frontiers in Artificial Intelligence and Applications, IOS-Press, Washington, DC, 1998.
8. OWL, Web Ontology Language Guide on-line at http://www.w3.org/TR/owl-guide/.
9. Stojanovic, L. ; Stojanovic, N. ; Volz, R. : Migrating data-intensive web sites into the Semantic Web. SAC 2002: 1100-1107.
10. J.P. Giroud, C. Hagège. Le guide de tous les médicaments. Paris, France. Editions du Rocher. 2001.
11. The WHO Collaborating Centre for Drug Statistics Methodology, on-line at http://www.whocc.no/

Workshop Knowledge Management in International Professional Services Firms (KMIPSF 2005)

Marcus Willamowski[1], Oliver W. Wendel[2], and Jan Kuhlmann[3] (Eds.)

[1] Latham & Watkins LLP, Warburgstrasse 50, 20354 Hamburg, Germany
marcus.willamowski@lw.com
[2] PYLON Aktiengesellschaft, Berliner Str. 44, 60311 Frankfurt am Main, Germany
oliver.wendel@pylon.de
[3] Attorney-at-Law, Dillstrasse 8, 20146 Hamburg, Germany
jan.kuhlmann@novider.com

Abstract. Knowledge Management (KM) has received considerable attention in the past few years. Whereas there are numerous theoretical studies on this topic, practical success stories are still scarce. This is especially the case with professional services firms, usually considered fertile ground for the ideas behind KM. International law firms, most of all, pose exceptional challenges to the ambitions of KM since common cultural, technological and economic obstacles identified by KM theory cumulate in this market.

1 Objectives and Content

The workshop was designed to address the obstacles KM faces in professional services firms and to discuss and develop visions and solutions to these problems beyond standard KM procedures.

In general, scientists and practitioners from Informatics (Computer Science), knowledge managers in international professional services firms, professional support lawyers or from related subjects with interest in a trans-disciplinary discourse were invited to participate.

1.1 Topics

Submissions were encouraged from a variety of perspectives, including, but not limited] to:

- cultural studies
- history
- sociology
- psychology
- communications
- technology
- computer science
- business studies
- process modeling
- performance measurement

K.-D. Althoff et al. (Eds.): WM 2005, LNAI 3782, pp. 384–385, 2005.

Following the conference's subtitle, papers with a clear focus on practical experiences, insights and solutions and/or theoretical visions beyond established KM procedures were preferred.

1.2 Submissions and Review Process

Although authors were encouraged to submit their paper in English language, papers in German language were accepted equally. This workshop solicited full research papers that discuss innovative problems from one of the areas sketched above. All submissions were subject to review by the workshop program committee. Review criteria included originality of ideas, technical soundness, significance of results, and quality of presentation. Each paper was reviewed by three reviewers.

2 Workshop Organizers

- Dr. Marcus Willamowski, LL.M., Knowledge Manager, Latham & Watkins LLP, Warburgstrasse 50, 20354 Hamburg, Fon: +49 (40) 41403-0, Fax: +49 (40) 41403-130, E-Mail: marcus.willamowski@lw.com
- Dr. Oliver W. Wendel, Senior Consultant, PYLON Aktiengesellschaft, Berliner Str. 44, 60311 Frankfurt / Main, Fon: +49 (69) 297287-0, Fax: +49 (69) 297287-70, E-Mail: oliver.wendel@pylon.de
- Jan Kuhlmann, Attorney-at-Law, Dillstrasse 8, 20146 Hamburg, Fon: +49 (40) 45039666, Fax: +49 (40) 45039667, E-Mail: jan.kuhlmann@novider.com

3 Program Committee

- Dr. Peter Brössler, SDS GmbH, Austria
- Prof. Dr. Georg Disterer, Fachhochschule Hannover / ZFWM, Germany
- Jörn Erbguth, Juris GmbH, Germany
- Hayo Iversen, Jurion GmbH, Germany
- Stefanie Kreis, Freshfields Bruckhaus Deringer, Germany
- Anja Neubauer, Cognilexus Knowledge Management Consultants, Germany
- Prof. Dr. Jürgen Taeger, Universität Oldenburg, Germany
- Dr. Oliver Vopel, Ernst & Young, UK
- Dr. Marcus Willamowski, Latham & Watkins, Germany

Creating a Culture of Knowledge Sharing in Law Firms

– Some Obstacles and Solutions –

Martin Schulz[1] and Marcel Klugmann[2]

[1] Attorney-at-Law, Knowledge Management Lawyer, Freshfields Bruckhaus Deringer, Taunusanlage 11, 60329 Frankfurt/M., Germany
martin.schulz@freshfields.com
[2] Attorney-at-Law, Manager Know-How and Information Services, Luther Rechtsanwaltsgesellschaft mbH, Graf-Adolf-Platz 15, 40213 Düsseldorf, Germany
marcel.klugmann@luther-lawfirm.com

Abstract. Creating and fostering a culture of knowledge sharing is, in practice, one of the most difficult tasks when introducing a Knowledge Management system into a law firm. Many obstacles stand in the way of a successful Knowledge Management. Most of the problems described below can only be overcome by strong support and role-modelling of senior management as well as by repeatedly stressing and demonstrating the long-term benefits of Knowledge Management.

1 Introduction

Lawyers are "knowledge workers". In fact, the only product that lawyers sell to their clients is specific Know-how in the form of legal advice. As a knowledge-based business, however, the legal profession faces great challenges and lawyers are permanently being flooded with new information such as frequent changes in legislation, new court decisions etc. The speed of changes in law and the dynamics of new legal developments have steadily increased and so have client expectations on legal services. Clients constantly demand quick results, high efficiency, a sense for cost consciousness and a proactive approach from their legal advisors, without, of course, wishing to compromise on quality. Solutions to these demands can be provided by a professional Knowledge Management. With the aid of an efficient Knowledge Management system lawyers can achieve a significant increase in efficiency, gain advantage over their competitors and thus retain clients and secure motivated staff on a long-term basis. That is why, following the tradition of other professional service sector companies, more and more law firms have discovered Knowledge Management as a tool to cope with the challenges of the above-described "information overload".

We define Knowledge Management as a continuous process of systematically collecting, analysing, organising and distributing Know-how relevant to legal practice. Such a process requires the recruitment of dedicated Knowledge Management staff as well as the design and development of an appropriate IT infrastructure. However, speaking from our own experience of implementing Knowledge Management in a major international law firm, the most important requirement for an effective

K.-D. Althoff et al. (Eds.): WM 2005, LNAI 3782, pp. 386 – 391, 2005.

Knowledge Management system is the creation and fostering of a culture of knowledge sharing amongst lawyers and throughout the firm. We would like to highlight some typical difficulties and problems likely to be encountered when creating such a culture in a law firm and then suggest some steps which have proved to be successful in overcoming such obstacles.

2 Emphasising the Significance of Knowledge Management

When introducing Knowledge Management into law firms for the first time, problems often arise due to a general lack of acceptance. The significance of an effective Knowledge Management system for the day-to-day running of law firms is often either not recognised or not taken seriously enough. Lawyers are constantly being swamped by new developments and accelerated changes in their day-to-day work routine with the result that some tend to regard an innovation like Knowledge Management as a personal attack on well-loved rituals, without actually recognising the need for change from a well-established, yet often ineffective, routine. As many lawyers often already possess their own collection of documents (such as standard forms or precedents) there is a tendency for some to consider a professional Knowledge Management system unnecessary. Others, often more senior practitioners, reject Knowledge Management immediately, considering it to be too "newfangled". After all, they often say, "haven't we managed and, indeed, been successful without "Knowledge Management" for years?". This attitude is, of course, a paradox since lawyers, as knowledge-orientated professionals, are especially in need of professional Knowledge Management. As indicated, Knowledge Management brings significant advantages to law firms, such as increased efficiency in day-to-day practice, an increased quality assurance, a competitive edge as well as protection from loss of Know-how.

The numerous mergers between law firms in recent years do not make the task of implementing Knowledge Management any easier. Different offices, each with their own unique history, have, even within individual jurisdictions, developed their own drafting house styles and other habits over decades. Knowledge Management, as a necessarily central and firm-wide platform, might thus be regarded as a hostile invader into the autonomy of certain offices and their wish to maintain a decentralised culture in the law firm.

To overcome such initial scepticism towards Knowledge Management, it is the role of the senior partner(s) to convince colleagues of the importance of a professional Knowledge Management system and of the long-term benefits of the mutual sharing of knowledge. It is particularly important in the early stages of introducing Knowledge Management that senior managers in the law firm strongly support the system and the Knowledge Management staff; if they can manage to make the importance of Knowledge Management clear, then lawyers will more readily agree to its introduction and will more actively contribute to the Knowledge Management system. Our advice is not to try to gain your colleagues' and staff's support for the system sporadically, but to repeatedly involve all lawyers and employees in identifying relevant Know-how and deciding how best to organize this information. Such repeated emphasis on the significance of Knowledge Management by senior management will lay the foundations for the development of a sustainable Knowledge Management system.

3 Creating Incentives to Contribute to Knowledge Management

A lack of motivation on the part of many lawyers to actively contribute to Knowledge Management is another typical problem faced when introducing Knowledge Management. This problem also often recurs at later stages when expanding and maintaining the Knowledge Management system; lawyers are often too busy with client work and the acquisition of new clients to have the time and continuous interest to support Knowledge Management. Furthermore, lawyers often feel that they already have enough administrative work to deal with in addition to normal client work. The prospect of some additional, not immediately client-related, work is thus, in many cases, not greeted with much enthusiasm. This may, however, be different in a larger law firm where management tasks, including developing and fostering a Knowledge Management system, are often divided up amongst the partners.

Unlike client-related work, Knowledge Management work – particularly in the early stages of building and developing a Knowledge Management system – often does not show any immediate and visible signs of success, i.e. no quantifiable "return on investment". On the contrary, a lot of time and effort must first be invested in human resources and infrastructure before the system starts to bear fruit; the benefits to be reaped by an intelligent standardisation of recurrent legal issues, including the saving of time and money, will not be noticeable until much later. For this reason, many people are discouraged from investing their time in a fledgling Knowledge Management system when, in actual fact, it is precisely at this point that the support of all lawyers is most urgently needed, not only to identify the growing demand for Knowledge Management, but also to systematically collect, analyse and organise the Know-how already available.

Such lack of motivation as described above may also be attributed to a common misconception that can be quite regularly observed upon the introduction of a Knowledge Management system: understandably, the Knowledge Management team focuses in the beginning on creating a suitable IT infrastructure and hiring appropriate Knowledge Management staff. Both such initiatives lead fee earners to believe that Knowledge Management is now being taken care of by Knowledge Management and IT professionals who will run the Knowledge Management system henceforth. So why get involved in Knowledge Management? This is absolutely the wrong conclusion to come to because Knowledge Management is everyone's task – Knowledge Management staff and IT infrastructure are, frankly, only auxiliary tools.

3.1 Praise for Knowledge Contributors

One way to overcome this obstacle is to develop a system of incentives to help improve motivation. Lawyers and other staff actively supporting Knowledge Management should be praised, for example, and if senior management has successfully communicated the importance of effective Knowledge Management, such praise will be recognised as a sign of distinction. Furthermore, in law firms where lawyers are expected to achieve a certain amount of chargeable hours, an incentive for contributions to Knowledge Management could be to put Knowledge Management work on an equal footing with client work, thus encouraging lawyers to spend some of their free capacity on Knowledge Management work without being afraid of losing out on billable hours. Moreover, once contribution to Knowledge Management becomes a regular feature in personnel reviews and ongoing assessments (including the appraisals leading to the decision on the promotion to partnership), lawyers will undoubtedly take Knowledge Management far more seriously.

Other incentive systems may include bonus systems, monetary rewards or other awards/gratifications. However, the effect of such incentives should not be overestimated, particularly since such benefits are more difficult to enforce in law firms than, for example, in larger companies outside the professional service sector.

3.2 Role Model of Senior Staff

One form of incentive which should not be underestimated is the role of (senior) management itself; if a senior partner is willing to share his personal "stores of knowledge" with his colleagues and to put his own collections of precedents, memos etc. at the disposal of other members of the law firm, then this example often encourages other colleagues to follow suit.

3.3 Frequent Presentations of Knowledge Management's Benefits

Frequent demonstrations of the benefits of active contributions to Knowledge Management can also be very effective. By using this technique, the benefits of Knowledge Management will become more visible to all, thus highlighting convincingly its advantages for day-to-day practice and making clear that Knowledge Management is not just "nice to have" but in fact a business driver. Regular meetings or luncheons in the law firm, e.g. where new legal and business developments are discussed, are a good forum for such demonstration of the benefits of Knowledge Management. Participants in these meetings will often realise that, despite their own specialisation, there are many legal issues which are common to all. This typically stimulates their willingness to contribute their own Know-how resources to the Knowledge Management system. In addition, participants in those presentations may, whilst seeing the document collection of another colleague, also recognise practice areas which they too have covered and in which they may have additional information to add. As a result of such Knowledge Management presentations, many colleagues may be more willing to share their knowledge and contribute to Knowledge Management. Since this has often only a temporary effect, it is important to repeat such presentations at regular intervals and to demonstrate the progress being made in the development of the Knowledge Management system. Furthermore, Knowledge Management success stories – in the sense of "how Knowledge Management helped to solve this problem" – should be collected and presented in due time (because of its "easy-to-memorise" anecdotal character, such "storytelling" actually became one of the most sustaining means of persuading lawyers of the necessity of Knowledge Management).

4 Willingness to Share Knowledge with Others

4.1 Positive Effects in the Long Run

Nothing stands in the way of setting up a successful Knowledge Management system more than the lack of willingness of many lawyers to share their knowledge and experience with their colleagues. Frequently, as a result of the daily pressures of work under which lawyers typically find themselves, too little consideration is given to how much one's own results may be of interest and benefit to other colleagues and, consequently, the law firm as a whole. Although most lawyers endorse the ideal of knowledge sharing, the thought of others profiting from one's own work makes some people fear a loss of their competence or power. They fear becoming less important or even dispensable if they part with their own personal Know-how.

Furthermore, the notion of "Knowledge is Power" still prevails in law firms as in many other organizations. Especially in those law firms whose remuneration systems are run on an "eat what you kill" basis, a high level of competitiveness among lawyers can generate a fear of losing influence by sharing one's "unique" knowledge. But even in law firms adhering to a "lockstep culture" and thereby putting strong emphasis on cooperation between their members, one often finds a strong psychological barrier to sharing knowledge: lawyers with specific Know-how in a particular subject-matter typically hope to enjoy a higher standing and reputation within the firm by keeping their expertise instead of sharing it.

These colleagues, however, tend to ignore the long-term detrimental effects of such an attitude. Given the challenges of the above-described "information overload", "going it alone" and creating "monopolies of Know-how" can obviously not be the answer. Many legal problems cover various fields and so require specialist information from all sides. Involving colleagues in the answer to such questions and using their specialist knowledge can only be successful if they in turn can rely on sharing the knowledge of others when the occasion arises. Thus, a system of give-and-take and sharing of knowledge can only be of advantage to each lawyer. Knowledge Management can highlight this interdependence of mutual sharing of Know-how and provide for an efficient way of transferring that knowledge.

4.2 Be Open to Constructive Criticism

Another reason for not sharing one's own knowledge is the aforementioned fear of criticism from one's peer group. Paradoxically, some lawyers think their work is good enough to be sent to clients, but not suitable for the internal Know-how collection. Here, we would strongly recommend being wary of perfectionism. Everything made available to clients should also be good enough to be made available to colleagues. The problem here often lies in the manner in which feedback and criticism are generally handled in law firms. Even if lawyers are in principle willing to contribute their Know-how to a firm-wide system, they regularly fear some kind of negative and derogatory peer judgement by their fellow lawyers, such as: "The contract clause by partner X in the Knowledge Management system is rubbish!". To a certain extent, peer judgement is unavoidable and even desirable as it may contribute to improvements in quality. Apart from that, a sensible approach to criticism throughout the firm, e.g. institutionalised feedback platforms and a "360° feedback culture" may help to ease the fear of peer judgement. It is therefore extremely important to create and foster an atmosphere of open and constructive criticism amongst your colleagues. Any comments and suggestions on how to improve documents should be recognised as a chance to improve Know-how rather than as a personal attack. If you succeed in convincing your colleagues and staff that their suggestions are appreciated, they will volunteer their ideas and help to keep the Knowledge Management system alive.

Once again, a successful way of overcoming the lack of willingness to share knowledge is to constantly stress the advantages of the collective use of knowledge.

4.3 Encouraging Team Players

As already mentioned, another reason for the lack of active contribution to Knowledge Management is often a fear of a loss of competence or authority when handing over a "monopoly" of knowledge. This stems in part from the past when, as law students, many lawyers were forced to fight for space in the lecture hall and for specific books to complete homework, etc. This attitude has unfortunately been retained by many in their working careers. Here it is important to achieve a change of attitude amongst lawyers and to make them team players.

References

Martin Schulz/Marcel Klugmann, Wissensmanagement für Anwälte, Cologne 2005, pp. 21 et seq.

Georg Disterer, Veränderungen der Rechtsberufe durch neue Technologien – Beispiel: Wissensmanagement bei Anwälten, Arbeitspapier 68/2002, FB Wirtschaft FH Hannover, pp. 15 et seq.

Matthew Parsons, Effective Knowledge Management for Law Firms, New York 2004, pp. 96 et seq.

Gretta Rusanow, Knowledge Management and the Smarter Lawyer, New York 2003, pp. 199 et seq.

Networks, Forms of Exchange and Motivations

Insights from Social Anthropology for the Issue of Knowledge Sharing

Dirk Klimkeit

Domstraße 64, 50668 Köln
Dirk.Klimkeit@de.ey.com

Abstract. Sharing of knowledge takes place mainly in social networks. Anthropological methods can help to identify networks where exchange on certain topics takes place. Once transparency about existing networks has been established, they can be fostered cautiously. Conditions for successful knowledge sharing are examined. Where people are in close contact and relationships are multiplex, knowledge sharing works best. Likewise, an anthropological theory of exchange confirms a focus on networks. An example of successful knowledge sharing in practice demonstrates important factors: Direct, oral exchange of knowledge is intrinsically motivating. People sharing knowledge orally can make their name among their peers and get immediate feedback from them. Therefore, a personalized approach is recommended where the supplier of knowledge provides advice following individual requests. KM systems should mainly establish transparency about relevant carriers of knowledge.

A survey of knowledge management in 600 German companies conducted by medienakademie köln has shown that 92% of the respondents from companies who use KM instruments consider a lack of motivation for KM activities as an urgent call for action [1].

The question of suitable conditions for encouraging knowledge sharing suggests a point of view of the social sciences. In this context, it is worthwhile to draw on findings and methods from social anthropology, which can be understood today as a general science of the culturally embedded life of human beings in social contexts. Methods that have been developed originally in order to understand the culturally "other" can contribute to the understanding of corporations in our own society as well.

1 Where Does Knowledge Reside? The Identification of Existing Networks

In each organization, there are informal social networks where sharing of knowledge takes place. The problem is that often only long-standing members are involved in these networks, whereas new staff don't easily get access to them. Moreover, there can be several unconnected networks where knowledge on a certain topic circulates. Here elements from network analysis, in particular methods for the elicitation of network data, can help to create transparency.

K.-D. Althoff et al. (Eds.): WM 2005, LNAI 3782, pp. 392 – 397, 2005.

Network analysis originated in the 1960s when British anthropologists investigated the social organization of labour migrants in Central Africa and developed new models and methods to examine the pattern of their relationships. Later, it was taken up and developed further by other disciplines and has become today an interdisciplinary field of research.

In practice, the survey of a large organization's total network is often too costly. Therefore, methods have been developed in anthropology that investigate so-called personal networks, starting from some selected participants. In this context, so-called name generators are used. The informants are presented with questions asking them to name individuals they would ask for help or information in typical real-life situations. By a snowball-system, persons named in the first round will then in turn be presented with the same questions [2].

The information gathered by such a survey can be helpful for creating transparency about an existing network. It goes without saying that at this, the necessary respect for the sensitivity of the personal data elicited must be applied. For example, the identified members of a core network can be encouraged to enter the relevant knowledge areas into their profile in the corporate yellow pages, if they haven't done so yet. A core network thus identified can then be fostered cautiously. In this context, experience has shown that the support of existing networks with voluntary participation is more successful than the prescription of collaboration. Likewise, at the World Bank, those thematic groups have proven to be most successful that existed already prior to the KM initiative of the bank [3].

2 Symbols, Weak Ties and the Integration of Communities

The cautious fostering of identified networks can help to develop them into communities, for example through the take on of a coordinating role by a member of the network. Here it is important not to blight existing engagement by too much regulation or ill-considered prescriptive actions. In companies dispersed in several locations, spontaneous contacts, e.g. in the canteen, that should not be under-estimated for the maintenance of contacts and sharing, don't occur between all staff. Here a limited number of organized meetings can be helpful. They can be complemented, but never be substituted, by virtual ones.

Once such a community has become known in the company through various activities, further experts, who may not have been identified at first, will soon join. Therefore, the identification of networks in the context of knowledge management suggested here does not need to be as encompassing and thorough as the elicitation of network data for a fully-fledged academic network analysis. Rather, it may serve as a point of departure.

Social anthropology has stressed the importance of symbols and rituals for the development of group identities. Regular meetings, a newsletter with a logo of the community as well as an own section in the corporate intranet can foster identity. A "welcoming message" to new members can help them to integrate quickly.

Nevertheless, naïve euphoria about knowledge communities is not appropriate. Not every community fulfils necessarily all functions praised by some consultants and trainers who "sell" the "implementation" of "communities of practice" as a panacea for successful knowledge management.

Communities can even develop unwanted side effects, e.g. shut themselves off from the rest of the organisation. Theoretical findings of network analysis point out the importance of whether a relatively closely-knit core network is linked to the wider organization by so-called "weak ties". Therefore, it is neither in the interest of the company, nor of the core network itself, if it shuts itself off. Often, important new information reaches a dense core network exactly via such weak ties. Different information comes into play particularly via single contacts to other parts of the organization [2]. Therefore, a sufficient degree of openness and heterogeneity is beneficial to a network.

To foster communities and to integrate them into the wider organization can prove a difficult double role for knowledge management. The alignment of communities with the goals of the company without stinting their dynamism can be a difficult tightrope walk.

3 Multiplex Relationships and Generalized Reciprocity: Focus on Communities

Social anthropology can provide hints about an important factor for knowledge sharing in a network: Anthropologists have noticed that in many rural societies relationships tend to be multiplex. This means that the same person can be at the same time co-worker, neighbour and someone one spends one's free time with. This imposes higher accessibility and social pressure to share.

For example, an investigation of a corporate law firm has revealed that the intensity of the exchange of information and advice correlates strongly with the amount of co-working as well as private contacts between the people in question [4]. Another survey shows that people who are considered as "close" by a participant get current information much faster from him than others [5].

Therefore, knowledge sharing works best where people are in close contact and perhaps know each other beyond the pure business context, as well. Organized social events, where closer contacts can be made, can be helpful in this respect. However, mechanisms that do not serve networking explicitly, like cross-team project work or temporary secondments between locations, can help to build networks, as well.

The anthropologist Marshall Sahlins has distinguished several forms of exchange based on ethnographic descriptions which he arranges on a continuum:[1] One end of the continuum is described as generalized reciprocity, where everyone shares generously and expects a counter-gift only in a delayed manner and possibly only indirectly from others of the group. A point in the middle of the continuum is described as balanced reciprocity, where a transaction stipulates a return of comparable worth within a finite period. The other end is characterized by haggling or even an attempted outsmarting or appropriation without consideration. Real-life situations are to be found

[1] A later summary of research in anthropology around this topic by Stuart Plattner has generally confirmed the main assumptions of Sahlins' contribution. It has stressed in addition its applicability to situations in modern societies as well (Sahlins' had originally in mind mainly what he called - in the terminology of his time - "primitive societies"). Plattner has pointed out how in modern contexts, too, the establishment of long-term exchange relationships between previous strangers can be rational as it can help to reduce risk. [6]

somewhere in between the two end points of this continuum. Sahlins then correlates these form of exchange with the degree of social closeness. Put in a simplified manner: The higher the degree of social closeness between participants, the family being an extreme case in point, the more likely it is for exchange to tend towards the form of generalized exchange. According to Sahlins, in such groups, there is often a norm of reciprocity that inhibits unbalanced taking without giving. This norm is sanctioned by some sort of social pressure as mentioned above. He admits, though, that sometimes mechanisms can be established that enable a sociable form of exchange between previous strangers, too, e.g. by establishing long-term trading partnerships [7].

Many companies encourage their staff to contribute knowledge objects codified in documents to knowledge bases that are accessible to a large number of people many of which are unknown to them. The expectation of knowledge sharing in such a context would have to be placed somewhere towards the end point characterized by generalized reciprocity on Sahlins' continuum. Therefore, it is quite demanding. Sahlins' theory can help to explain why, as is often reported, knowledge sharing based on such a codification approach works best in groups of a manageable size and with an increased level of interaction. Is this bad news for large companies trying to build firm-wide knowledge sharing?

Not necessarily, but this finding stresses again the importance of a focus on networks and communities because as a rule they are made up of people who know each other, if only indirectly. Likewise, they exhibit an increased level of cohesion and interaction as depicted in the model.

Furthermore, corporate culture comes into play here, too. Anthropological network research has pointed out that the position of a participant in a network does not necessarily imply that he actually draws on his network intensively. For this, his attitudes are the decisive factor. They are influenced by his cultural environment [2]. Therefore, a norm of reciprocity can exist to some extent at the level of executives of large corporations, as well. In some companies, executives who generate good business results but whose staff don't participate in the company's knowledge sharing must face criticism from their peers [8].

4 Direct Exchange, Vanity and Feedback: Successful Knowledge Sharing in Practice

The following example of successful knowledge sharing in practice illustrates important motivating factors which suggest a promising approach that can help to encourage knowledge sharing across borders of established communities, too: The anthropologist Julian Orr has accompanied field service technicians from Xerox, who repair photocopiers, at work [9]. In the team investigated by Orr, lively exchange takes place. New solutions to problems are communicated immediately. This is a small team with a high level of social interaction, but other factors come into play as well: For one thing, it is intrinsically motivating for the technicians to communicate about their world. By exchanging war stories, they celebrate their identity. And the telling of stories is fun: A hint to the importance of a motivating configuration of knowledge management tasks as an important factor of success.

However, what is even more decisive: A technician can make one's name among his peers by telling his success at solving known difficult problems. It therefore increases his reputation. And: By oral communication of their stories, e.g. in a joint lunch break in the canteen, they get direct feedback from their colleagues. This is rewarding. Someone who keeps his knowledge to himself will never become known as a proven expert.

What follows from this for knowledge management? This finding tends to support the personalization strategy of knowledge management, which emphasizes much more the identification of carriers of knowledge and the direct exchange with them than the codification and storing of knowledge in databases [10]. When storing a document in a database, one often doesn't get feedback directly. Likewise, one doesn't learn how many and which colleagues access it and how they might use it. So this can provide little in terms of a sense of achievement. Meanwhile, a personalized approach as in the Xerox example can be intrinsically motivating.

Nevertheless, where databases are used for storing existing re-usable documents, there are possibilities for feedback, too: The communication of the page hits of documents, the offering of a feedback or discussion functionality as well as encouraging people to take up contact with the author of a document they are interested in. Particularly, a linking of the knowledge database to corporate yellow pages can encourage contact by highlighting the author of a document.

5 Conclusion

Generally, a system is to be recommended where the supplier of knowledge has the possibility to provide knowledge following individual requests from colleagues. This holds true particularly for the firm-wide exchange across the borders of established communities. Someone approached by a colleague in search of expertise will in most cases feel appreciated and is likely to react positively. In this way, he can experience himself as a competent and sought-after expert, obtain direct feedback and insight into how his knowledge is being used. Furthermore, this creates a moral obligation of the receiver to provide knowledge in return when asked. In this context, modern IT systems can help to enhance transparency about relevant carriers of knowledge and enable direct contact with them.

In order to realize a gain in efficiency with content that is much sought-after, companies may want to use an approach based on the storage of knowledge objects in databases complementarily. Likewise, this can help partly to attenuate the effect of knowledge walking out of the door when experts leave the company. As I have argued above, though, this approach is based on an underlying expectation of generalized reciprocity and is therefore in most cases promising mainly in established communities of manageable size, where coherence and trust have grown. Here, the suggestions made above for the identifying and fostering of networks and for allowing feedback to documents entered into a database should be taken into account.

Nevertheless, another finding of social anthropology is that humility concerning the controllability of socio-cultural change is appropriate. It is in the nature of networks that they are dynamic and don't always behave in the way we want or expect them to.

References

1. Linsinger, L., Kirsten, L.: Wissenserwerb und Wissensmanagement in deutschen Unternehmen. Eine Bestandsaufnahme. medienakademie köln, Köln (2002) 16
2. Schweizer, T.: Muster sozialer Ordnung. Netzwerkanalyse als Fundament der Sozialethnologie. Dietrich Reimer Verlag, Berlin (1996)
3. Cohen, D., Prusak, L.: In Good Company. How Social Capital Makes Organizations Work. Harvard Business School Press, Boston, Mass. (2001)
4. Lazega, E., Pattison, P.E.: Multiplexity, Generalized Exchange and Cooperation in Organizations. A case study. Social Networks 21 (1999) 67-90
5. Shelley, G.A., Bernard, H.R., Killworth, P.D.: Information Flow in Social Networks. Journal of Quantitative Anthropology 2 (1990) 201-225
6. Plattner, S.: Economic Behaviour in Markets. In: Plattner, S.: Economic Anthropology. Stanford University Press, Stanford (1989) 209-221
7. Sahlins, M.: Stone Age Economics, Aldine, Chicago 1972
8. Hansen, M.T., von Oetinger, B.: Introducing T-Shaped Managers. Knowledge Management's Next Generation. Harvard Business Review (2001)
9. Orr, J.E.: Talking About Machines. An Ethnography of a Modern Job. ILR Press, NY (1996)
10. Hansen, Morten T., Nitin Nohria and Thomas Tierney: What's Your Strategy for Managing Knowledge? In: Harvard Business Review March-April 1999: 105-116

Second Workshop on Knowledge Management for Distributed Agile Processes: Models, Techniques, and Infrastructure (KMDAP 2005)

Harald Holz[1], Heiko Maus[1], Naoyuki Nomura[2], and Martin Schaaf[3]

[1] Knowledge Management Department,
German Research Center for Artificial Intelligence DFKI GmbH, Germany
{Harald.Holz, Heiko.Maus}@dfki.de
[2] Software R&D Group,
Ricoh Company Ltd., Japan
naoyuki.nomura@nts.ricoh.co.jp
[3] Data and Knowledge Management Group,
University of Hildesheim, Germany
schaaf@dwm.uni-hildesheim.de

Traditional process-oriented knowledge management (KM) approaches are inadequate for highly dynamic and volatile processes, whose steps cannot be planned in advance, and during which new, unanticipated "knowledge needs" frequently arise: such processes handle mostly informal documents and rely on face-to-face communication between participants. During the workshop, practitioners and researchers presented novel approaches for decision support within agile processes, agile process modeling, and communities of practice.

Decision Support for Agile Processes. In order to support agility in the realm of project management, Karni and Kaner propose a methodology for decision making within project management processes based on case-based reasoning (CBR).

Weber and Wild demonstrate the integration of workflow systems and conversational CBR to enable workflow participants in exceptional situations to change the current workflow instance according to their needs. The problem solving is then retained as case for supporting other participants in similar situations.

Freßmann et al. present a workflow environment for supporting persons and teams in agile processes also using a CBR approach but here with the focus on mobile teams in pressing situations requiring advice and context-dependent information support.

Agile Process Modeling. Zacarias et al. propose to model relations between actors involved in complex processes with action and interaction contexts. The goal is to provide better modeling means for analyzing and finally support people in knowledge-intensive business processes.

Fenstermacher discusses the notion of agility for process-oriented KM systems and presents some next steps towards supporting knowledge workers in agile

K.-D. Althoff et al. (Eds.): WM 2005, LNAI 3782, pp. 398–399, 2005.

processes. He argues that before studying agile processes, means are required for observing user activities and analyze it for a process-based use.

Communities of Practice. Bellini et al. describe an experiment on the impact of the educational background of developers on the knowledge sharing during the design phase. The study offers evidence that forming pairs with the same educational background emphasizes the expected benefits, in contrast to pairs from different educational backgrounds.

Program Committee

- Klaus-Dieter Althoff, University of Hildesheim, Germany
- Dimitris Apostolou, Planet Ernst & Young, Greece
- Torgeir Dingsøyr, SINTEF ICT, Norway
- Ludger van Elst, DFKI GmbH, Germany
- Knut Hinkelmann, University of Applied Sciences Solothurn, Switzerland
- Frank Maurer, University of Calgary, Canada
- Heinz-Jürgen Müller, Berufsakademie Mannheim, Germany
- Dirk Ramhorst, Siemens Business Services, Germany
- Steffen Staab, Karlsruhe University, Germany
- Heiner Stuckenschmidt, Vrije Universiteit Amsterdam, The Netherlands
- Oliver Thomas, Institute for Information Systems (IWi), Germany
- Klaus Tochtermann, Know-Center Graz, Austria
- Bidjan Tschaitschian, empolis GmbH, Germany
- Rosina Weber, Drexel University, USA
- Oliver Wendel, Pylon, Germany
- Hideo Yamazaki, NRI, Japan

Agile Knowledge-Based Decision Making with Application to Project Management

Reuven Karni[1] and Maya Kaner[1,2]

[1] Industrial Engineering & Management, Technion, Haifa, Israel
rkarni@ie.technion.ac.il
[2] Industrial Engineering & Management, Ort Braude College, Karmiel, Israel
kmaya@tx.technion.ac.il

Abstract. Business processes are made up of actions and decisions. Thus an agile process implies both agility in making decisions as well as in performing the necessary actions. When confronted with a sudden change in project scope or an unexpected development, a project manager must make a series of interrelated decisions in response. Knowledge about the content of and interconnections between decisions made in similar circumstances in the past can help the project manager to keep in mind all decisions that need to be taken. We present an integrated case- and cluster-based architecture for supporting multi-domain decisionmaking within project management. The methodology is also applicable to other decision making frameworks.

1 Introduction

The "business process revolution" has introduced a paradigm shift in management – the process view of the firm [1]. This perspective has also been adopted in project management, as emphasized by Brandt and Nick [2]: "There is general agreement today that increasing individualization of business performance and business processes is the reason for the assimilation of routine-oriented business processes to the classic project model".

The business process concept separates organizational processes into two categories: *technological processes* concerned with specifying and creating a product or service; and *business processes* concerned with administering, directing and managing other enterprise activities. In project management a corresponding distinction is made between *product-oriented processes* which specify and create the project product; and *project management processes* which organize the project work. The latter are the concern of the Guide to the Project Management Body of Knowledge (PMBOK) [3], which details 39 project management processes (Table 1).

Processes are made up of two components: actions and *decisions* ([4], [5], [6]). Accordingly, each of the 39 processes incorporates at least one decision [7], usually "selection" (what to choose), so that decisionmaking is an essential *ongoing* feature of project management. Thus project manager must decide in a multi-dimensional range of situations – even for repetitive projects. Moreover, project management processes in general, and decisionmaking in particular, are executed within two contexts: project planning, when actions and decisions can be anticipated; and project execution, when

K.-D. Althoff et al. (Eds.): WM 2005, LNAI 3782, pp. 400 – 408, 2005.

actions and decisions become "agile" – that is, the project manager requires "the ability to demonstrate flexible, efficient and swift responses [in carrying out the necessary actions and decisions in reaction] to changing circumstances" [8]. He must "use this agility for [managerial] advantage, by being able to rapidly respond to changes [and unexpected events] occurring in the [project] environment and through [his] *ability to use and exploit a fundamental resource – knowledge* [our italics]" [9].

As an example of the agility demanded, and the appropriate response, we suppose that a project team member suddenly resigns. The manager urgently needs to choose a substitute. He must implement the decision as part of "staff acquisition" within "project human resource management" [3]. This, however, is not enough – he also has to consider replacement costs by implementing a further decision (choosing a salary for the new member) as part of "cost estimating" within "project cost management" [3]. Thus our first objective is to provide a mechanism for ensuring that the project manager considers all *interrelated* decisions which could be taken.

Moreover, decisionmaking (in project management or any other area) is dependent on knowledge; and the decision quality is directly related to the accessibility and quality of the knowledge provided ([10], [11]). Our second objective is therefore how to provide a *knowledge base* ensuring that the project manager considers *all factors* relevant to the interrelated decisions. This knowledge has several unique characteristics:

- It is heterogeneous: Decisions interact. For example, when project team members are hired, the consequences of their expertise and salary should be considered. Thus knowledge encompasses issues staff acquisition and cost estimating.
- It is dynamic: Knowledge is both created and used during project execution. For example, in the agile environment, project team members may be replaced at more than one stage during the project, due to complications with the project deliverable or problems with customer relationships. The effect is that knowledge regarding staff acquisition and risk response planning is both created and used along the project timeline.
- It is experiential: Project management knowledge is not standardized. Different managers can be expected to react to an unexpected incident and formulate a solution in dissimilar ways. For example, they are likely to have divergent opinions regarding a trade-off between employee cost and skills (staff acquisition and cost estimating processes); or a trade-off between project due date and cost (activity duration and cost estimating processes).

This paper proposes a methodology for agile knowledge-based decision making, specifically in project management, recognizing that decisions are not isolated, but interrelated, and that the knowledge needed to respond effectively is dynamic. Our approach is based upon an extension of *case-based reasoning* (CBR) – comparing two similar decision cases – to *cluster-based reasoning* (CLBR) – comparing two similar interconnected *clusters* of decision cases. The knowledge base comprises a set of case bases, one for each specific domain; and a cluster base [7], containing a series of clusters.

Our objectives are: (a) to provide a mechanism for ensuring that the project manager considers all appropriate interrelated decisions which should be taken, especially when an agile response is required; and (b) to provide a knowledge base for ensuring that the project manager considers all factors relevant to these interrelated decisions.

Table 1. A taxonomy of project management processes according to PMBOK [3]

Knowledge area	Management process
1. Project integration management	1. Project plan development 2. Project plan execution 3. Integrated change control
2. Project scope management	4. Initiation 5. Scope planning 6. Scope definition 7. Scope verification 8. Scope change control
3. Project time management	9. Activity definition 10. Activity sequencing 11. Activity duration estimating 12. Schedule development 13. Schedule control
4. Project cost management	14. Resource planning 15. Cost estimating 16. Cost budgeting 17. Cost control
5. Project quality management	18. Quality planning 19. Quality assurance 20. Quality control
6. Project human resource management	21. Organizational planning 22. Staff acquisition 23. Team development
7. Project communications management	24. Communications planning 25. Information distribution 26. Performance reporting 27. Administrative closure
8. Project risk management	28. Risk management planning 29. Risk identification 30. Qualitative risk analysis 31. Quantitative risk analysis 32. Risk response planning 33. Risk monitoring and control
9. Project procurement management	34. Procurement planning 35. Solicitation planning 36. Solicitation 37. Source selection 38. Contract administration 39. Contract close-out

2 Illustrative Example

We demonstrate our methodology through interactions between two scenarios triggered during the execution of a project and demanding the immediate attention of the project manager. Both scenarios have been invoked by changes in the project deliverable, and thus describe responses to two similar occurrences.

First Scenario. "The project manager estimates the cost of a project deliverable (decision 1: what cost estimate to provide). For this deliverable he tries to understand (a) how similar deliverables in the past were decomposed into activities (decision 2: what activities to formulate); (b) what risks could be encountered (decision 3: what risks to manage); and (c) what resources and quantities were needed for similar deliverables in the past (decision 4: what resources to choose). For each activity he estimates a duration according to past experience (decision 5: what time estimates to provide). For risks pertaining to possible lack of experience he selects the best candidate (decision 6: what candidate to choose)". The graph of this scenario, showing the project management processes incorporating these decisions, and the interactions (causal links) between them, is given in Fig. 1.

Second Scenario. "The project manager defines the work breakdown structure (WBS) according to a WBS template (decision a: what template to adopt). For several deliverables within the WBS he tries to understand (a) how similar items in the past were decomposed into activities (decision b: what activities to formulate); (b) what resources and quantities (decision c: what resources to choose); and (c) what risks could be triggered when developing deliverables (decision d: what risks to manage). For each activity and its resource type the manager estimates a duration (decision e: what time estimate to provide) and a cost (decision f: what cost estimate to provide). For each resource, and for risks pertaining to lack of experience he defines organizational responsibilities (decision g: what functions to allocate); and, finally, he selects the best candidate (decision h: what candidate to choose)". The graph of this scenario, showing the project management processes incorporating these decisions, and the interactions (causal links) between them, is given in Fig. 2.

3 Decision Knowledge Through Monadic and Dyadic Similarity

The two clusters of decision cases are represented by two directed case graphs (Figs. 1 and 2). We refer to the first as the *reference* cluster or *reference* graph (the decision set to be analyzed) and the second as the *benchmark* cluster or *benchmark* graph (the yardstick for analysis). Our aim is to systematize a comparison of the two graphs with the aim of aiding the decisionmaker in understanding and considering all factors constituting the decisions which must be taken. We extend the concept of *monadic* similarity (a measure of the similarity of two cases in a single domain) to *dyadic* similarity (a measure of the similarity of two linked cases in different domains) [7]. A dyad is defined as a pair of cases in a graph, connected directly by a single arc, or indirectly via a linked set of arcs. In the reference graph we consider direct dyads only – i.e. direct causality between two successive decisions. In the benchmark graph we relate to (a) direct or indirect dyads, which (b) refer to the same two domains as some reference dyad, such that (c) the sequence between them is as for the reference dyad. In addition we define *niladic* similarity in the situation where a direct dyad exists in one graph, but only a monad in the other [7].

Monadic, dyadic and niladic similarities provide us with six channels for acquiring knowledge through cluster comparison – the six "As":

- *Monadic analogous knowledge* (reference and benchmark monads: monadic): we learn from parallel decisions in the two clusters, in the same domain. Analogous knowledge indicates that a similar decision has been replicated, thus reinforcing it as a recommended practice.
- *Monadic additional knowledge* (reference monad: niladic): we learn from the absence of a parallel decision pair in the benchmark, that the reference decisionmaking scenario has added knowledge to the case and cluster bases. Additional knowledge indicates that the reference experience has led to a new decision, thus enriching the knowledge base with a new precedent.
- *Monadic absent knowledge* (benchmark monad: niladic): we learn from the absence of a parallel decision pair in the reference cluster, that existent knowledge in the case and cluster bases may have been overlooked. Absent knowledge indicates that the benchmark has not been replicated, and prompts the decision maker to bear this experience in mind when making decisions.
- *Dyadic analogous knowledge* (reference and benchmark dyads: dyadic): we learn from a parallel decision pair in the two clusters and from the causality between them. Analogous knowledge indicates that the decision pair has been replicated, thus reinforcing taking them together as a recommended practice.
- *Dyadic additional knowledge* (reference dyad: niladic): we learn from the absence of a parallel decision pair in the benchmark cluster that the reference scenario has added knowledge to the cluster base regarding a new causality link between two domains. Additional knowledge indicates that the reference experience has led to a second decision coming after a given decision, thus enriching the knowledge base with a new precedent.
- *Dyadic absent knowledge* (benchmark dyad: niladic): we learn from the absence of a parallel decision pair in the reference cluster that existent knowledge in the cluster base, regarding causality links between domains, may have been overlooked. Absent knowledge indicates that the benchmark has not been replicated, prompts the decision maker to take this experience into account when making decisions.

4 Similarity Analysis of Agile Knowledge-Based Decisions

The project manager compares the two scenarios according to the six categories of similarity-based knowledge. The following summarizes the lessons learned from the comparison (reference ↔ benchmark) (cf. Figs. 1 and 2):

- ***In both events (analogous knowledge – reference and benchmark monads)***
  - Benchmark estimating of costs guides the reference estimating of costs (1 ↔ e)
  - Benchmark definition of activities guides the reference definition of activities (2 ↔ b)
  - Benchmark identification of risks guides the reference identification of risks (3 ↔ f)
  - Benchmark planning of resources guides the reference planning of resources (4 ↔ c)
  - Benchmark estimating of durations guides the reference estimating of durations (5 ↔ d)
  - Benchmark staffing of a team can guides the reference staffing of a team (6 ↔ h)

- ***In the benchmark event (absent knowledge –benchmark monads only)***
  - Scope definition should be considered in the reference setting (∅ ↔ a)
  - Organizational planning should be considered in the reference setting (∅ ↔ g)
- ***In both events (analogous knowledge – reference and benchmark dyads)***
  - Activity definition should be followed by duration estimating (2-5 ↔ b-d)
  - Risk identification should be followed by appropriate team recruitment (3-6 ↔ f-<g>-h)
  - Planning resources should be followed by appropriate team recruitment (4-6 ↔ c-<g>-h)

  These practices have been reinforced as they have occurred in both events.
- ***In the reference event (additional knowledge – reference dyads only)***
  - Cost estimating is followed by defining contributory sources – activities (1-2 ↔ e-∅), resources (1-3 ↔ e-∅) and risks (1-4 ↔ e-∅)

  These are new practices and create precedents to be considered in future circumstances.
- ***In the benchmark event (absent knowledge – benchmark dyads only)***
  - Activity duration estimating should be followed by cost estimating (5-∅ ↔ d-e)
  - Risk identification should be followed by a response concerned with organizational planning (3-∅ ↔ f-g).
  - Resource planning should be followed by organizational planning (4-∅ ↔ c-g)
  - Risk identification should be preceded by project scope definition (∅-3 ↔ a-f)
  - Resource planning should be preceded by project scope definition (∅-4 ↔ a-c)
  - Staff acquisition should be preceded by organizational planning (∅-6 ↔ g-h)

  These are augmented practices and should be considered when making decisions.

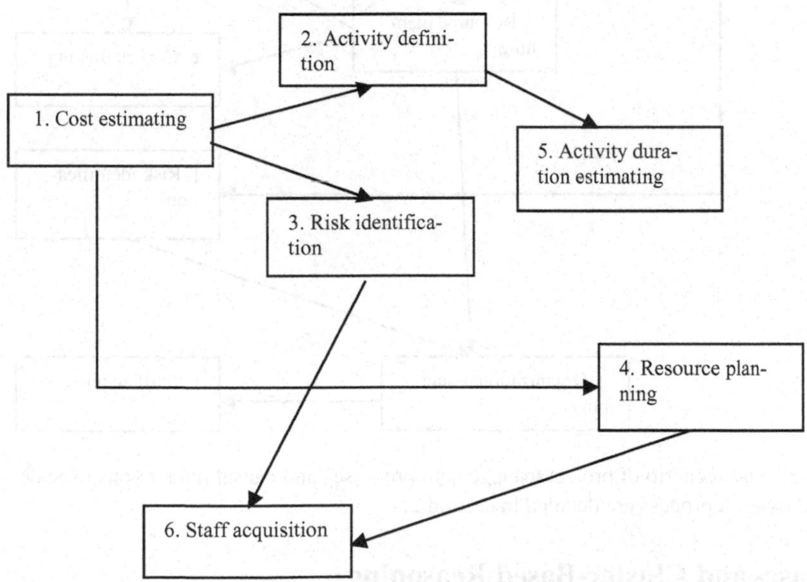

Fig. 1. First scenario of project management processes and causal interactions (The decisions implied by each process are detailed in section 2)

These lessons may be derived cognitively by the project manager, or provided automatically by algorithms ([7]) which compare all monads and dyads in the two graphs, recognize significant relationships (from the six "A"s) between them, and put out the lessons in statements such as:

- benchmark case <X> guides reference case <Y> (monadic similarity)
- benchmark case <X> is not matched by a reference case (niladic similarity - monads)
- reference case <Y> is not matched by a benchmark case (niladic similarity - monads)
- reference case <Y> should be followed by reference case <Z> (dyadic similarity)
- reference case <Y> should be preceded by reference case <Z> (dyadic similarity)
- reference case <Y> should be preceded by a case similar to a benchmark case <X> (niladic similarity - dyads)
- reference case <Y> should be followed by a case similar to a benchmark case <X> (niladic similarity – dyads)
- reference case (Z) following reference case (Y) is not matched by a benchmark case (niladic similarity – dyads)

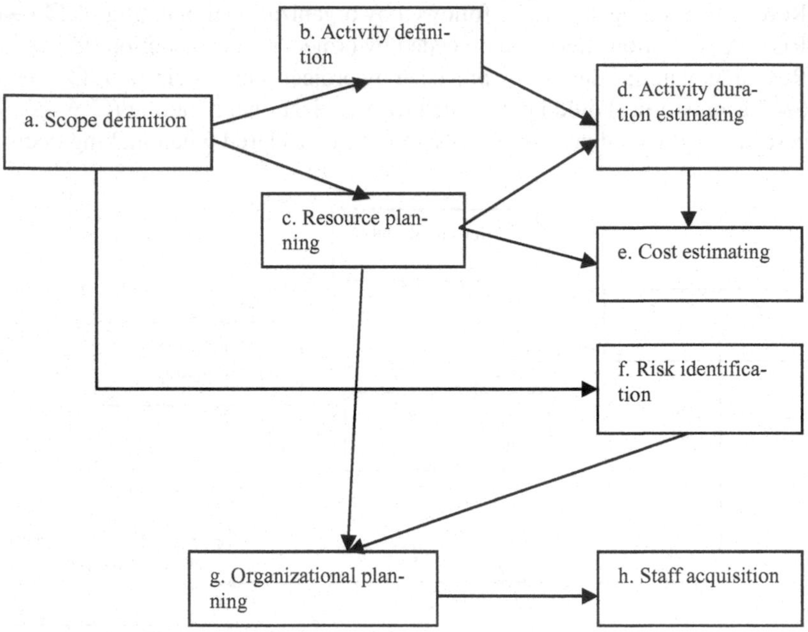

Fig. 2. Second scenario of project management processes and causal interactions (The decisions implied by each process are detailed in section 2)

5 Case- and Cluster-Based Reasoning

We have presented a methodology for analyzing the similarity of two clusters of decisions. This is based on definitions and algorithms ([7] – out of the scope of this paper) for computing quantitative dyadic and cluster similarity measures, by analogy with monadic similarity ([12], [13]). These are applied in CBR and CLBR to retrieve similar cases and clusters from the domain case bases and the cluster base.

We envisage the following procedure: A decision needs to be taken in accordance with an unfolding scenario (e.g. the project manager initially needs to estimate the cost of a deliverable within the WBS). He searches for similar cases in the domain (e.g. project cost) case base using CBR. Using the initial query case, and/or similar cases from the case base, he searches for clusters containing similar cases using CLBR. The retrieved clusters guide him regarding further decisions. As more decisions are taken, the query cluster evolves; and the search for similar cases in the domain case bases, and for similar clusters in the cluster base, is iterated. The process continues until the query cluster (the set of actual decisions taken) is finalized and all required decisions are taken in response to the situation.

6 Experimental Evaluation of Cluster-Based Reasoning

To evaluate the theory and methodology we performed two experiments to answer the following questions: Is the concept of decision cluster understood and can knowledge be obtained from the cluster (i.e. can the decision maker obtain a fast holistic picture)? Can an organized process improve the ability to obtain knowledge from the cluster (i.e. improve agility)? In the first experiment, a decision cluster and a lexicon of case definitions were presented to 30 subjects who were required to interpret the decisions and interactions. Errors that could be incurred were: overlooking the interaction between two successive cases; misinterpreting the interaction between two cases; overlooking a case in the cluster. The average error count (out of 9 possible errors) was 1.87 (variance 1.64). We concluded that the subjects succeeded in interpreting the decision cluster. In the second experiment, a description of a project management decision situation, involving issues of candidate selection, time/cost estimation and risk anticipation, was presented to two groups of 15 subjects, who were required to retrieve and interpret knowledge related to the decisions intimated by the situation. A CLBR system, incorporating three case bases and a decision cluster base, were presented to both groups. The treatment group was further equipped with a detailed process map for carrying out iterative retrieval of cases and clusters. Three important considerations were to be derived: (1) the complexity of the product dictates the employee's ability to handle such complexity; (2) there exists the possibility of an employee leaving because of dissatisfaction with his salary; (3) the task cost and duration are related to the employee selected. Subjects in the control group scored an average of 2.07 correct considerations (variance = 0.50) in an average time of 23.1 minutes (variance = 36.9). Subjects in the treatment group scored an average of 2.47 correct considerations (variance = 0.27) in an average time of 19.4 minutes (variance = 21.3).

Comparing the performance of the two groups, we conclude that the use of the process map led to better interpretation of the knowledge retrieved ($p < 0.001$) and in a shorter time ($p < 0.05$), with more uniform performance.

7 Conclusion

We have demonstrated, using an example of project management (which has been verified experimentally [7]), that a networked architecture of processes and decisions constitutes an effective contribution to agile decisionmaking. The decisionmaker is systematically guided, from a trigger-scenario which demands his attention and intervention, through taking the decisions required. This systematization allows him to gain knowledge incrementally, and thus be able to better control, understand and utilize the knowledge accumulated. Representation of knowledge as cases and clusters in multiple domains accords well with the ongoing and agile nature of project management such as decomposition of a scenario into several issues, the evolution of cases during project execution, and bringing past experiences to bear on the current decisionmaking situation.

Finally, the decision cluster paradigm provides a powerful representation for flexibility in decisionmaking. The composition of the reference cluster evolves in real time in accordance with the requirements of the current situation as seen by the decisionmaker: the decisions to be taken, their content, and their sequencing. This reference cluster is then stored in an historical repository, and, as a benchmark, serves to guide and support – *rather than to dictate* – further decisionmaking through the same three perspectives: suggested decisions, suggested content, and suggested sequences. The paradigm, through the network of decisions and the focusing of knowledge, enables a new set of decisions to be made swiftly and efficiently. And this is the essence of agile decisionmaking.

References

1. Hammer, M., Stanton, S.: How process enterprises really work. Harvard Business Review. November-December (1999) 108-118
2. Brandt, M., Nick, M.: Computer-supported reuse of project management experience with an experience base. In: Althoff, K-D., Feldmann, R.L., Mueller, W. (eds.): LSO 2001. LNCS, Vol. 2176, Springer (2001) 178-189
3. PMI: A Guide to the Project Management Body of Knowledge (PMBOK), Project Management Institute Standards Committee (2001)
4. van Es, R.M., Post, H.A. : Dynamic enterprise modeling: A paradigm shift in software implementation. Kluwer (1996)
5. Vernadat, F.B.: Enterprise modeling and integration: principles and applications. Chapman and Hall (1996)
6. Sparrow, J.: Knowledge in organizations. Sage Publications (1998)
7. Kaner, M.: Project knowledge management using hierarchical case retrieval networks. Unpublished Doctoral Dissertation, Faculty of Industrial Engineering and Management, Technion, Israel (2003)
8. Gartner: The age of agility. Gartner Report prepared for BT (2002)
9. Kidd, P.T.: Agile manufacturing: key issues. Conference on the Human Aspects of Advanced Manufacturing. URL = www.cheshirehenbury.com/agility/ampapers.html.
10. Whalen, T., Samaddar, S.: Problem solving: a knowledge management process. In Holsapple, C.W. (ed.): Handbook on Knowledge Management. Springer, Vol. 1 (2003) 349-365.
11. Holsapple, C.W.: Knowledge and its attributes. In Holsapple, C.W. (ed.): Handbook on Knowledge Management. Springer, Vol. 1 (2003) 165-188
12. Bergmann, R.: Highlight of European INRECA Projects. In Aha D.W., Watson I. (eds.): ICCBR-01. LNCS, Vol. 2080. Springer (2003) 1-15
13. Lenz, M., Bartsch-Sporl, B., Burkhard, H-D., Wess, S. (eds.): Case-based reasoning technology: from foundations to applications. Lecture Notes in Artificial Intelligence, Vol. 1400, Springer (1998)

Towards the Agile Management of Business Processes

Barbara Weber[1] and Werner Wild[2]

[1] Institute of Computer Science – Quality Engineering Research Group, University of Innsbruck, Technikerstraße 13, 6020 Innsbruck, Austria
Barbara.Weber@uibk.ac.at

[2] EVOLUTION Consulting, Jahnstraße 26, 6020 Innsbruck, Austria
werner.wild@evolution.at

Abstract. Today's dynamic and uncertain business environment requires quick reaction to change and frequent deviations from plans, making business agility indispensable. Therefore process-based systems must be able to flexibly adapt to change and provide learning capabilities. This paper proposes an approach to achieve agility in workflow management systems based on the integration of workflow management and conversational case-based reasoning. Keeping semantical knowledge about ad-hoc deviations in cases allows starting with a lightweight initial workflow model and fosters learning from living processes to continuously improve workflow execution.

1 Introduction

Workflow management systems (WFMS) are frequently used to control the execution of business processes and to improve efficiency and productivity. To date, WFMS have been applied to fairly static environments in which the execution of activities follows a highly predictable path. However, today's business is characterized by ever-changing requirements and unpredictable environments (e.g., due to global competition), making business agility indispensable.

The problem of missing flexibility in WFMS has been addressed in the last few years by adaptive workflow management research (e.g., ADEPT [1], METEOR [2], WIDE [3]). In general, these approaches rely on a predefined workflow model and try to avoid user interactions whenever possible. Exception handling mechanisms and (ad-hoc) run-time modifications to the predefined workflow model are suggested in order to provide adaptability and flexibility.

Process-oriented knowledge management systems are suitable for knowledge intensive workflows and are often used to provide additional process information to the users to support them during the execution of activities (e.g., DECOR [4], FRODO TaskMan [5], KnowMore [6]).

However, as described in [7], a firm's business processes are usually not homogenous in the sense that company A has only well-structured processes, while company B's processes are unstructured. To support a company with all its business processes, different types of workflows need to be handled by the WFMS at the same time.

K.-D. Althoff et al. (Eds.): WM 2005, LNAI 3782, pp. 409 – 419, 2005.

The integration of adaptive workflow-management approaches with conversational case-based reasoning (CCBR) allows leaving some parts of the workflow initially undefined. By involving the workflow user in the decision-making process there is no need for a formal and complete a-priori workflow model. Whenever a situation arises that cannot be dealt with in an automatic way by relying on the predefined workflow model the user can take over the initiative. The system then stores the problem-solving knowledge provided by the user for further reuse by this or other workflow users.

In this paper we discuss an approach towards more agility in WFMS by integrating workflow management (WFM) and CCBR. This paper focuses on how this approach contributes towards more agility in WFM and does not cover details of the research prototype CBRFlow, an elaborated description of it can be found in [8].

The structure of the paper is as follows. After giving the backgrounds in Section 2, Section 3 outlines our approach towards agility in workflow management. Section 4 then describes the CBR-cycle as implemented in CBRFlow, followed by a discussion of related work in Section 5 and conclusions and further studies in Section 6.

2 Backgrounds

The background of this paper lies in workflow management and case-based reasoning.

2.1 Workflow Management

WFM involves the modeling, the execution and the monitoring of workflows [9]. During *workflow modeling* an abstract representation of a business process is created, specifying which tasks are executed and in what order. A workflow model thus includes functions (i.e., activities), their dependencies, organizational entities that execute these functions and information objects which provide the functions with data input/output. The *execution* and control of the automated parts of a business process is supported by a WFMS. Each business case is handled by a newly created workflow instance. *Workflow monitoring* provides status information about running instances, supports their evaluation and fosters continuous process improvement.

2.2 Case-Based Reasoning and Learning in Workflow Management

Case-based reasoning (CBR) is a contemporary approach to problem solving and learning where new problems are solved by using past experiences and by adapting their solutions to new problem situations [10]. CBR is also an approach to incremental and sustained learning. Every time a new problem is solved, the information about the problem and its solution is retained and immediately made available for solving future problems [11].

CCBR is an extension to the CBR paradigm, in which a user is actively involved in the inference process [12]. A CCBR system can be characterized as an interactive system that, via a mixed-initiative dialogue, guides users through a question-answering sequence in a case retrieval context.

Unlike in traditional CBR, CCBR does not require the user to provide a complete a priori specification of the problem for retrieval and knowledge about the relevance of each feature for problem solving. The system assists the users to find relevant cases by presenting a set of questions to assess a situation. The users, however, can also supply already known information on their initiative.

3 Towards Agility in Workflow Management

In this section we present our approach towards more agility in workflow management. After a short summary of the approach itself (Section 3.1), we highlight the interaction of WFM and CCBR (Section 3.2) and finally discuss how CCBR contributes to more agility in WFM (Section 3.3).

3.1 Integrating WFM and CCBR

Our approach is characterized by the tight integration of WFM and CCBR as illustrated in Figure 1.

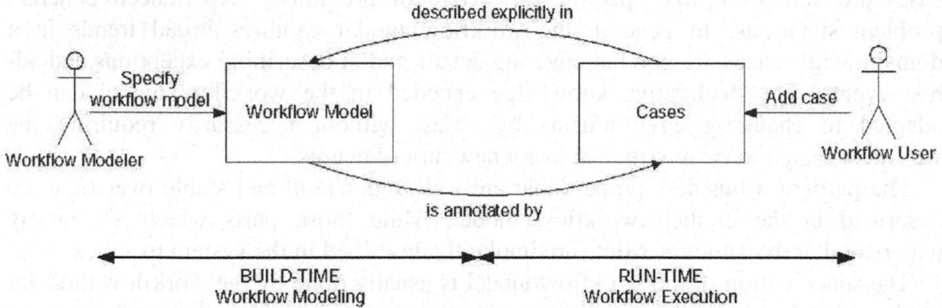

Fig. 1. Integration of WFM and CCBR

During workflow modeling an initial computerized representation of selected business processes is developed. At run-time an instance of the workflow model is created and the process is executed as specified in the workflow model. When run-time changes to the workflow model become necessary due to exceptions or changing requirements, the user annotates the workflow model with context-specific process information in the form of cases. This recently gained knowledge is therefore immediately available for reuse without explicitly changing the process model.

Once the process knowledge captured in cases becomes well-established, the workflow modeler explicitly describes it in the workflow model. CCBR is used to foster the extraction of general knowledge from running workflow instances and therefore supports gaining additional general knowledge. The system and the organization continuously learn how to better handle new situations as more and more experience is gained and the knowledge is always readily available for reuse.

3.2 Using the Synergies Between WFM and CCBR

An integrated system taking advantage of the synergies between traditional WFM and CCBR bridges the gap between highly structured business processes and weakly structured processes such as knowledge-intensive workflows. The complementary strengths and the synergies of both approaches are detailed below and summarized in Table 1.

Table 1. Complementary strengths of WFM and CCBR

	Workflow Model	**CCBR-Case**
Knowledge type	general knowledge	specific knowledge, exceptions, ad-hoc events
Domain	well understood, narrow, stable over time	poorly understood, wide, dynamic over time
Actor	workflow modeler	workflow user
Time of creation	build-time	run-time
Reuse	automated	requires user interaction

The general knowledge of a domain is represented in the workflow model, while cases are able to utilize specific knowledge of previously experienced concrete problem situations. In general, the workflow model captures broad trends in a domain, while cases are good at covering details and at describing exceptions and ad-hoc events. The declarative knowledge encoded in the workflow model can be adapted to changing environments by cases, without necessarily requiring the workflow model to be rewritten at every new turn of events.

The parts of a business process that are well understood and stable over time are described in the explicit workflow model, while those parts which are poorly understood or dynamic over time are implicitly described in the system by cases.

The specification of the workflow model is usually done by the workflow modeler in close collaboration with the domain experts at build-time. Unanticipated situations or situations that are not covered by the workflow model are handled by the workflow user on demand and the problem-solving knowledge is added by using CCBR at run-time.

As the workflow model relies on an explicit and formal definition of a business process it provides support for full automation, whereas the handling of unanticipated situations must be performed in an interactive way. The system only assists the user in the decision-making process, the decision itself is always left to the workflow user.

3.3 CCBR: Key to More Agility

Integrating CCBR into WFM provides the system with learning capabilities and is key to more agility in workflow management. As detailed in [13] CBRFlow's approach follows many of the lean and agile principles advocated in lean [14] and agile software development [15].

Modeling on Demand: In dynamic and uncertain business environments not all eventualities and possible deviations can be considered in advance. Requirements change or evolve over time, exceptions and ad-hoc events may arise. Due to the significant modeling time needed, workflow models are often obsolete right after their specification is "completed". Apart from the limited knowledge available at

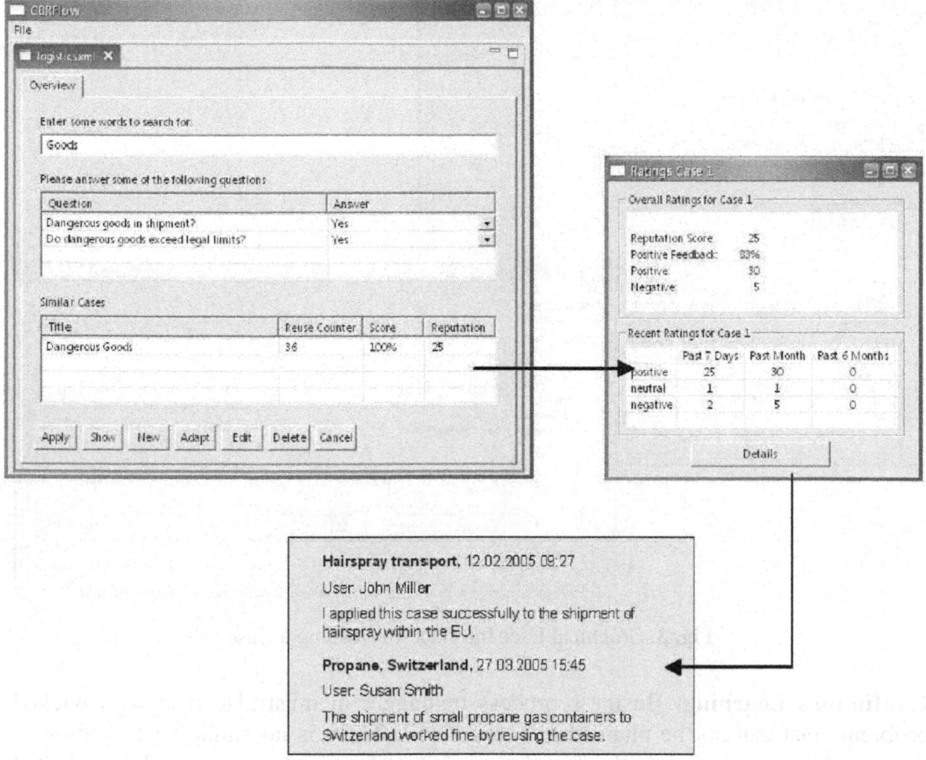

Fig. 2. Graphical User Interface for Retrieving Similar Cases

build-time, modeling every single detail in advance can be time-consuming and involves the risk of including rarely needed parts, not yet needed or even unneeded ones and therefore creates waste.

The integration of WFM and CCBR allows the workflow modeler to start with a preliminary workflow model with a clear focus on the core functionality and supports run-time updates to the workflow model to handle new requirements due to change or unexpected situations.

First an initial workflow model is created, covering a business process only in economically justifiable detail. The decision how to model a business process precisely is delayed until the company's needs are more clearly understood and business value can be achieved. When changes become necessary during run-time, the existing workflow model is extended with additional knowledge stored in cases.

This feedback supports continuous process improvement, resulting in more manageable and more efficient business processes over time. When the knowledge encoded in cases becomes frequently reused, it is refactored and explicitly included in the workflow model.

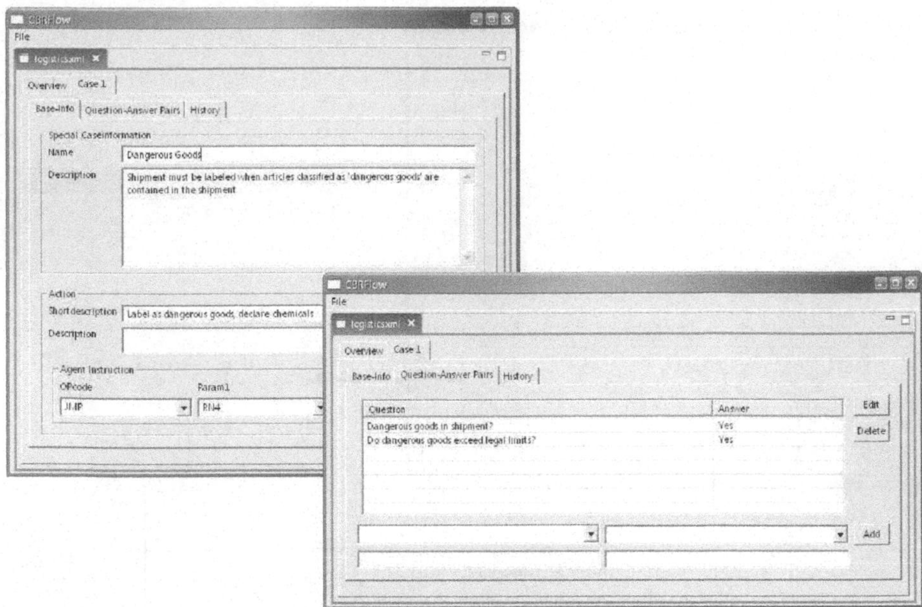

Fig. 3. Graphical User Interface for Adding a Case

Continuous Learning: Business process management must also deal with wicked problems that can not be planned in every detail. There is no single best solution to these problems, so the *right the first time* approach does not work; instead the selected solution has to be continuously improved [16].

In order to efficiently manage business processes, WFMS must provide tight feedback loops, be able to handle modifications when they arise (i.e. short iterations) and memorize them for later reuse. The support of ad-hoc changes to a single workflow instance is not enough, as the results of the learning process must also be fed-back into the system, e.g., by using CCBR, so that the gained knowledge can immediately be reused in subsequent workflow instances.

This short feed-back loop ensures that the workflow model, in combination with the cases in the case-base, closely reflects the real world business processes, which is fundamental for the WFMS in order to achieve perceived integrity.

User Involvement: The involvement of workflow users in the decision-making processes is key to more agility. Workflow users should be regarded as knowledge workers actively contributing to decisions and knowledge elicitation and not as exchangeable resources or uncritical process followers.

During workflow execution exceptions may arise, making deviations from the predefined model necessary. Workflow users are empowered to directly modify the specified flow of activities by creating or adapting cases, thus keeping the knowledge in the system for immediate or later reuse by this or other users. This delegates the decision making authority to the frontline workers and allows them to improve the way they do their work on their own.

User involvement allows dealing with situations that cannot be automated based on the existing workflow model, because the workflow user can take the initiative in such situations and add a new case to the system or retrieve similar previous situations with the help of the system.

4 CBR-Cycle of CBRFlow

The following section describes the CBR-cycle [11] as implemented by our research prototype CBRFlow.

Case Representation: Within CBRFlow a Case *C* represents a concrete ad-hoc modification to one or more workflow instances. It consists of a textual problem description, a set of question-answer pairs $\{QA_1,...,QA_n\}$ and a single action *A*. The problem description briefly describes the problem that made the deviation necessary. The question-answer pairs describe the reasons for the ad-hoc change and the action contains the alternative execution path to be executed. The corresponding XML representation is illustrated in Figure 4.

```
<CASE ID="c15" TITLE="Dangerous Goods" DESCRIPTION "Shipment must be labeled when
articles classified as 'dangerous goods' are contained in the shipment.">
  <QAPAIRS>
    <QAPAIR QUESTION="Dangerous goods in shipment?" ANSWER="Yes"/>
    <QAPAIR QUESTION="Do dangerous goods exceed legal limits?" ANSWER="Yes"/>
  </QAPAIRS>
  <ACTION ID="A1" SHORTDESCRIPTION="Label as dangerous goods, declare chemicals">
        <AGENTINSTRUCTION OPCODE="JMP" PARAM1="RN4 "/>
  </ACTION>
</CASE>
```

Fig. 4. XML-representation of a case

Case Retrieval: For case retrieval CBRFlow uses a CCBR approach as proposed by [11]. When deviations from the predefined workflow model become necessary the workflow user initiates the CCBR sub-system (see Fig. 2). The system then assists the user in finding similar previously stored cases by presenting her a set of questions ranked by their frequency in the case-base. The user can both answer any of the displayed questions in any order she wants and filter the case-base by applying a full-text search. The system then searches for similar cases by calculating the similarity for each case in the case-base; similarity is calculated by dividing the number of correctly answered questions minus the number of incorrectly answered questions by the total number of questions in the case. It then displays the top *n* ranked cases and their reputation score to the user (ordered by decreasing similarity). The reputation score indicates how successfully each case has been applied in the past. As illustrated in Fig. 2, the system also displays the reputation score totals for the past 7 days, the past month and the past 6 months and, if desired, the user can also read the textual comments provided for a case (see below).

Case Reuse: When a similar enough case could be retrieved by the system the user can either directly reuse the case or after adapting it. When a case is reused the solution specified in the action part is executed by the WFMS and a work item is created for evaluating the ad-hoc change later on to maintain the quality of the case-base. The action can either be manual (i.e., a textual description of the required manual steps) or automated (e.g., a workflow action skipping or adding an additional execution step).

Defining deviations from the predefined workflow model requires user experience; however, the reuse of existing ad-hoc changes contributes to hiding as much complexity from users as possible.

Case Evaluation: In addition to the syntactical correctness of an ad-hoc modification, its semantical correctness is crucial for the overall performance of a WFMS and consequently for the trust users have in it. Evaluation mechanisms are needed to learn about semantic failures and to keep the quality of the cases in the case-base sufficiently high. Although we cannot guarantee the semantic correctness of ad-hoc modifications, an evaluation mechanism is at least helpful to avoid the same or similar semantic failures in the future and ensures that semantically incorrect cases are not reused again.

In our approach we use the concept of reputation to indicate how successfully an ad-hoc modification represented by a case has been applied in the past. Whenever a user adds or reuses a case she is encouraged to provide feedback on the performed workflow instance change. For this, a work item representing the feedback task is generated and inserted in the worklist of this particular user. She can later rate the performance of the respective ad-hoc modification either with 1 (positive), 0 (neutral) or -1 (negative), and may optionally specify additional comments. The reputation score of a case is calculated as the number of positive feedbacks minus the number of negative feedbacks regarding the ad-hoc modification specified in this case.

While a high reputation score of a case is an indicator for its semantic correctness, negative feedback probably results from problems after performing a workflow instance change. Negative feedback therefore results in an immediate notification of the process engineer, who can then deactivate the case to prevent its further reuse. The case itself, however, remains in the system to allow for learning from failures and to maintain traceability.

Retain Case: Whenever a user wants to deviate from the predefined workflow model and when no similar enough cases can be found in the CCBR sub-system, the user adds a new case to the case-base in order to make the change possible (see Fig. 3). She creates a new case by briefly describing the problem, entering a set of question-answer pairs describing the reasons for the deviation and the alternative action to take.

Question-answer pairs can be entered by either selecting the question from a list of previously entered questions (i.e., reusing questions from existing cases) or, when no suitable question is already in the system, by defining a new question and giving the appropriate answer.

Finally, the case is retained and thus immediately made available for future reuse. The case is always stored in regard to the location in the workflow where the deviation has happened.

Example: An employee of a parcel delivery service works on a shipment to a drug store, which usually contains pre-defined and agreed-upon articles. However, the new shipment contains hair spray which might be classified as "dangerous goods" if a certain quantity is exceeded. Therefore additional process steps have to be performed (i.e., labelling the shipment as "dangerous goods" and declaring the contained chemicals in detail). As no similar cases are in the system, the user enters a new case describing the situation and applies the case right away (thus labelling the hair spray boxes as "dangerous goods").

5 Related Work

This paper is based on the idea of integrating WFM and CCBR. In related work CBR has been applied to support workflow modeling [17-18], to the configuration of complex core processes [19], to the handling of exceptions [3] and for the composition of Web Services [20]. All of these approaches apply traditional CBR, to our knowledge there are no other approaches relying on CCBR.

Related work also includes adaptive workflow management and process-based knowledge management. Adaptive workflow management research suggests exception handling mechanisms and (ad hoc) run-time modifications to the predefined workflow model in order to provide adaptability and flexibility. Expected exceptions are handled by ECA-rules [2, 3, 21] while unexpected exceptions are either handled by supporting dynamic (ad-hoc) modifications to the workflow model [1, 3, 22] or using knowledge-based approaches [2, 21, 23]. All of these systems rely on a predefined workflow model whenever possible and try to avoid user interactions.

Process-based knowledge management systems are suitable for knowledge intensive workflows and are often used to provide additional process information to the users in order to support them during the execution of activities (e.g., DECOR [4], FRODO TaskMan [5], KnowMore [6]). FRODO TaskMan extends the approach taken in KnowMore by supporting integrated modeling and enactment of weak workflows. Like our approach, FRODO TaskMan allows instance level modifications of the workflow during run-time and additionally supports working with an incomplete workflow model due to its late modeling capabilities.

In WORKWARE [24] interactive process models are used to automate the well-defined parts of the workflow model, and to ask the user to handle ambiguous parts.

6 Conclusions and Further Studies

This paper demonstrates that integrating WFM and CCBR contributes towards more agility in WFM, sharing many of the lean and agile principles and values. The gap between highly structured business processes and weakly structured ones can be bridged by taking advantage of the synergies between traditional WFM and CCBR. Adaptability and flexibility are provided by supporting run-time modifications to the workflow model and by rapidly incorporating the results of the learning processes into subsequent workflow executions.

Ongoing research includes an industrial strength implementation of this approach in the logistics domain and the integration of the research prototype CBRFlow with the well-known adaptive WFMS ADEPT (for details see [25]). By integrating both systems significant synergies can be exploited to foster integrated process life cycle support. On the one hand the combined system provides a powerful process engine, supporting dynamic deviations from the predefined workflow model in a correct and consistent way, including the migration of running workflow instances to the improved workflow model. On the other hand it enables the intelligent reuse of workflow instances and fosters deriving process improvements from the collected semantical information. Currently we implement a prototype that integrates both systems; future work will include process mining tools as well [26], an evaluation of the combined system in a real-life setting is planned (medical domain).

Additionally, clear criteria for the decision when to stop the initial modeling should be defined and a meta-process for the agile management of business processes will be developed.

References

[1] Reichert, M.; Dadam, P.: ADEPTflex – Supporting Dynamic Changes of Workflows Without Loosing Control. In: Journal of Intelligent Information Systems, Special Issue on Workflow Management 10 (1998) 2, pp. 93-129.

[2] Luo, Z.; Shet, A.; Kochut, K.; Miller, J.: Exception Handling in Workflow Systems. In: Applied Intelligence 13 (2000) 2, pp. 125-147.

[3] Casati, F.; Ceri, C.; Pernici, B.; Pozzi, G.: Workflow Evolution. In: Data and Knowledge Engineering 24 (1998) 3, pp. 211-238.

[4] Abecker, A.; et al.: Enabling Workflow-Embedded OM Access With the DECOR Toolkit. In: Rose Dieng-Kuntz and Nada Matta (eds.): Knowledge Management and Organizational Memories. Kluwer Academic Publishers, July 2002.

[5] Elst, L.; Aschoff, F.-R.; Bernardi, Maus, H.; Schwarz, S.: Weakly-structured Workflows for Knowledge-intensive Tasks: An Experimental Evaluation. In: Knowledge Management for Distributed Agile Processes: Models, Techniques, and Infrastructure (KMDAP2003).

[6] Abecker, A.; Bernardi, A.; Hinkelmann, K.; Kühn, O.; Sintek, M.: Context-Aware, Proactive Delivery of Task-Specific Knowledge: The KnowMore Project. In: Int. Journal on Information Systems Frontiers 2 (2000) 3/4, pp. 139-162.

[7] Shet, A.; Georgakopoulos, D.; Joosten, S.; Rusinkiewicz, M.; Scacchi, W.; Wilden, J.; Wolf, A.: Report from the NSF Workshop on Workflow and Process Automation in Information Systems. Technical Report UGA-CS-TR-96-003, Univ. of Georgia, Oct 1996.

[8] Weber, B.; Wild, W.; Breu, R.: CBRFlow: Enabling Adaptive Workflow Management Through Conversational Case-Based Reasoning. In: Proceedings of the 7th European Conference, ECCBR 2004, Madrid, Spain 2004, pp. 434-448.

[9] Gadatsch, A.: Management von Geschäftsprozessen, Methoden und Werkzeuge für die IT-Praxis: Eine Einführung für Studenten und Praktiker, 2. Auflage, Vieweg Verlag, Braunschweig, Wiesbaden 2002.

[10] Kolodner, J. L.: Case-Based Reasoning. Morgan Kaufmann, San Francisco 1993.

[11] Aamodt, A.; Plaza, E.: Case-Based Reasoning: Foundational Issues, Methodological Variations and System Approaches. In: AI Communications 7 (1994) 1, pp. 39-59.

[12] Aha, D. W.; Muñoz-Avila, H.: Introduction: Interactive Case-Based Reasoning. In: Applied Intelligence 14 (2001) 1, pp. 7-8.

[13] Weber B.; Werner, W.: Application of Lean and Agile Principles to Workflow Management. In: Proceedings of the Fifth International Conference on Extreme Programming and Agile Processes in Software Engineering, Springer, Berlin 2004.
[14] Poppendieck, M.; Poppendieck, T.: Lean Software Development: An Agile Toolkit. 1st edition, Addison Wesley 2003.
[15] The Agile Alliance. Agile Manifesto (2001). Available at http://www.agilemanifesto.org, visited on 27/12/2003.
[16] Poppendieck, M.: Wicked Problems (2002). Available at http://www.poppendieck.com/wicked.htm, visited on January 08, 2004.
[17] Kim, J.; Suh, W; Lee, H.: Document-based workflow modeling: a case-based reasoning approach. In: Expert Systems with Applications 23 (2002) 2, pp. 77-93.
[18] Madhusudan, T.; Zhao, J.L.: A Case-based Framework for Workflow Model Management. Netherlands, June, 2003. In: Proc. of Business Process Management 2003, pp. 354-369.
[19] Wargitsch, C.: Ein Beitrag zur Integration von Workflow- und Wissensmanagement unter besonderer Berücksichtigung komplexer Geschäftsprozesse. Diss., Erlangen 1998.
[20] Limthanmaphon, B.; Zhang, Y.: Web Service Composition with Case-based Reasoning, Proceedings of 15th Australasian Database Conferences (ADC2003), Feb. 2002, Australia.
[21] Hwang, S.; Tang, J.: Consulting past exceptions to facilitate workflow exception handling. In: Decision Support Systems 37 (2004) 1, pp. 49-69.
[22] Rinderle, S., Reichert, M., Dadam, P.: Correctness criteria for dynamic changes in workflow systems - a survey. Data and Knowledge Engineering 50 (2004) 1, pp. 9-34
[23] Klein, M.; Dellarocas, C.: A Knowledge-based Approach to Handling Exceptions in Workflow Systems. In: CSCW 9 (2000) 3-4, pp. 399–412.
[24] Jørgensen, H. D: Interactive Process Models. Norwegian University of Science and Technology, Trondheim, Norway, Dissertation 2004. Available at http://publications.uu.se/ntnu/fulltext/nbn_no_ntnu_diva-4.pdf, visited on 23/08/2004.
[25] Weber, B., Rinderle, S., Wild, W., Reichert, M.: CCBR–driven business process evolution. In: Proc. Int. Conf. on Cased based Reasoning (ICCBR'05), Chicago 2005.
[26] Process Mining Research: www.processmining.org (2005).

Towards Collaborative Agent-Based Knowledge Support for Time-Critical and Business-Critical Processes

Andrea Freßmann[1], Rainer Maximini[1], and Thomas Sauer[2]

[1] University of Trier,
Department of Business Information Systems II,
54286 Trier, Germany
{rainer.maximini, andrea.fressmann}@wi2.uni-trier.de
[2] rjm Business Solutions GmbH, 68623 Lampertheim, Germany
t_sauer@rjm.de

Abstract. In this paper, we present the Collaborative Agent-based Knowledge Engine approach for supporting mobile workers performing time-critical and/or business-critical tasks within agile projects. By a combination of sophisticated knowledge management and a light-weight workflow model, this approach provides guidance and knowledge as required to perform the individual activities. Moreover, we discuss aspects for maintaining project history, as well as possibilities for integrating tools regarding computer-supported collaborative work already deployed in organizations.

1 Introduction

In recent years, agile development methodologies have been the subject of intense research [1]. Although agile methods have been put in opposition to more traditional approaches on the planning spectrum [2], agile projects still demand effective planning skills. As explained in [3], planning is required for arranging tasks effectively, i.e. in order to ensure that the agents involved are carrying out the most important tasks. Planning fulfills a documentation purpose as well, e.g. in order to make progress available to the project stakeholders.

However, planning and documentation is not sufficient to support projects including mission-critical or literally life-critical processes. While planning helps to identify *when* to perform these processes, agents working in knowledge-intense domains will require additional support for leveraging the tacit knowledge available in the organization in order to find out *how* to perform these processes effectively.

In addition, the lessons learned are valuable sources of information for future knowledge intense and creative tasks, which clearly includes management activities like designing an initial release plan. As pointed out in [4], this idea of iterative enhancement of the overall methodology is shared among agile approaches and more traditional planning methodologies found in domains like software engineering.

In this paper, we present the Collaborative Agent-based Knowledge Engine (CAKE) approach, which aims at supporting empirical processes [5], i.e. processes that are

K.-D. Althoff et al. (Eds.): WM 2005, LNAI 3782, pp. 420–430, 2005.

mostly unpredictable and unrepeatable. The CAKE concept provides an infrastructure for constant measurement and control through intelligent and light-weight workflow modeling, leading to the idea of planning sketched above. Furthermore, knowledge-intense tasks are supported by sophisticated knowledge management, which allows to present context-dependent information to agents carrying out unknown or unexpectedly difficult tasks.

In the following section, we will discuss background architecture for CAKE, and the CAKE approach is presented in brief. In Section 4, a use case demonstrates how to put this approach into practice. Finally, related and adjacent research will be discussed in Section 5.

2 Business and Time Critical Processes in the AMIRA Context

The presented approach of CAKE is developed domain independently but is motivated by the fire service domain within the AMIRA (Advanced Multi-modal Intelligence for Remote Assistance) project[1]. This domain addresses both business critical and time-critical situations for mobile workers. While wearing operational kits or gloves, accessing information written on paper or stored on laptops is very cumbersome. Hence, the envisaged mobile workers wear head-sets to access diagnoses support by speech. The fire services demand highly flexible processes and collaborative working in the field. Different representative processes are worked out: First, operatives encounter rare problems and want to perform questions to a system or experts. Second, they need pro-active information support for optimizing their collaboratively working procedures. Third, they require support in report activities and review procedures.

2.1 Single Person Request While Collaboratively Working

A fire fighter extinguishes a fire in collaboration with colleagues and encounters a cylinder with unknown abbreviations of chemicals. While collaboratively working he sends a request to the system for getting information about which chemicals are in the cylinders. The response is only sent to the single mobile worker and the headquarters. The others could get this information from the headquarters if necessary.

2.2 Pro-active Context-Based Information Support

In time critical situations it is a demand for headquarters becoming aware of the activities of officers or fire fighters who work under the headquarters' control for making correct diagnoses. Hence, all interactions of the fire fighters with the system are monitored and logged by the system. Based on these logs context-based information is extracted, so that the headquarters are supported in getting corresponding guidelines, important information, and possible instructions for the mobile workers.

---

[1] Funded by the EU. Project partners are Kaidara Software, Fast Datasearch, DaimlerChrysler RIC, the University of Trier, and the Fire Service College.

2.3 Collaborative A-Posteriori Analysis

Collaborative a-posteriori analysis of the operations should be managed. This encompasses pro-actively asking the involved persons, headquarters and/or fire fighters, for information about their last actions concerning possible modifications to guidelines or other information used. Furthermore, it is possible to support methods for capturing information about the incident itself, e.g. in order to alleviate handover procedures. For achieving reliable information sources new or additional information is integrated into the databases.

3 The CAKE Approach

Motivated by the AMIRA context a concept of the collaborative working system CAKE is developed that acts as moderator between several services (e.g. search engines) and user interfaces for providing their communication and context-based information support. For example, information may be retrieved from other search services, and the user interface contains a speech service for converting speech-based requests into machine-processable requests.

For coping with knowledge intensive tasks required for context-based information support CAKE comprises a workflow engine manager. Furthermore, an agent framework enables arbitrary access and communication to different agent-based services mediated by CAKE. At last, for providing highly flexible tasks of mobile workers the collaborative working system integrates a planning component for modifying workflows at runtime.

3.1 Workflow Engine Manager

The CAKE approach describes collaboration using *workflow definitions*. Each workflow definition consists of a set of tasks, as well as a control flow relationship between them. The latter allows arranging the tasks in sequence, in parallel, or by using splits and branches, but does not cover data flow at all. This allows to reuse tasks in different application scenarios easily.

A *task* is either a descriptor for a complex activity (e.g. a real-world activity like "write report") or a machine-executable program, which is denoted as *executor task*. The latter may be implemented as a Java class that can be incorporated into the workflow definition. For instance, an executor task for "send notification" may be defined for use within a workflow definition. Triggering a CAKE workflow definition is also covered by the task definition, so hierarchical decomposition of a complex activity description like "design component" is achieved by following the way a human agent would solve this instead of following a fixed process model.

In order to enact a workflow definition, an *agent* or an *agent role* has to be assigned. Agents may describe either *user agents* (i.e. human actors) or *information agents*, with the latter being connections to arbitrary information providers. Depending on the service provided by agents, information may be accessible read only or with write permissions: While an Internet search engine may be queried as an read-only source, a groupware calendar application deployed in an organization would be available for writing

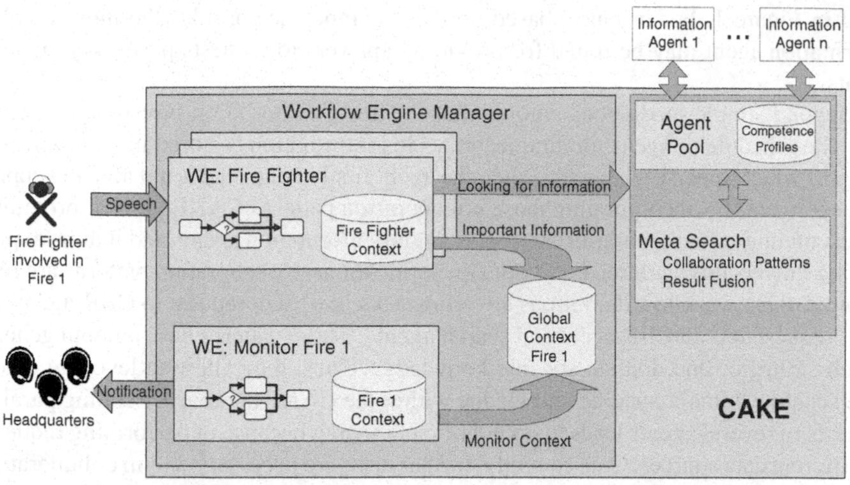

Fig. 1. The CAKE Approach

operations, too. Finally, agent roles describe the competences an agent has to possess in order to follow the workflow definition by providing appropriate agent characterizations.

At runtime, the *Workflow Engine* (WE) initializes an instance of a suitable workflow definition (in the following, *workflow instances* are shortly denoted as workflow). Separating these levels enables modifications on the workflow instances without changing the underlying workflow definitions. Beyond controlling tasks the WE contains the local *context* assigned to a single workflow instance that facilitates capturing, storing, and changing of context-based data. Consequently, the context is an information container for any kinds of objects used by the workflow. The context comprises *administrative data*, *workflow control data*, *workflow relevant data*, and *application data* that have been defined by Maus [6]. Due to the possibility of nested (sub)workflows, local contexts can be nested as well by following the concept of inheritance. Assigned to the higher-level workflow engine manager itself only one global context exists that is accessible by all workflow instances under control.

3.2 Agents Framework

From a more technical point of view, agents are represented as a combination of a *technology component*, a *competence profile*, and a *wrapper*. The technology component enables the service provided by the agent (e.g. speech recognition, search, information delivery), while the competence profile includes characterizations about the agent's competencies which are used for the agent role concept. The wrapper makes sure that communication to CAKE is based on a *unified data model*. Hence, wrappers act as interfaces between agents and CAKE for converting data. For being manageable, agents are able to register in the *agent pool* by publishing their competence profiles. Due to dynamical registrations the agent pool works highly flexible in allocating agents as pictured in Figure 1. For instance, based on these competence profiles the most suitable information agent may be found for providing answers to requests performed by user agents.

Beyond simple mediations among agents, strategies based on best practice structures the schedule of agent communication. This information is stored in *collaboration patterns* which specify what to do when the agent firstly contacted is not able to support the user agent. By incorporating these collaboration patterns CAKE aims at providing representations of collaboration strategies among information agents and it aims at preserving universality with regard to domain applications. Collaboration patterns are represented using workflow definitions covering tasks like "sent request to CBR agent" or "sent request to both CBR agent and search agent". These patterns base on both generic search strategies and domain-specific knowledge. Thus, they allow to leverage otherwise separate domain-specific knowledge within the CAKE approach. Sending parallel requests to several agents leads to a kind of meta search because of performing requests on different data sources. Consequently, further tasks are necessary within collaboration patterns that organize parallel requests to different information agents and the respective result fusions. For finding the most suitable collaboration pattern regarding the current request CAKE provides search facilities on workflow definition representations of the collaboration patterns. Hidden from the end users the search for suitable collaboration patterns is executed.

Furthermore, in order to support a dynamic agent pool the collaboration patterns only contain roles used for agent allocation. Hence, CAKE supports search facilities on agent competence profiles. According to the roles described in the collaboration patterns the most suitable agent is retrieved.

3.3 Pro-active and Context-Based Information Support

By combining the workflow engine manager and the agent framework, CAKE enables pro-active and context-based information support of user agents. The agent technology facilitates the integration of different data sources like external retrieval services or search engines, while the workflow technology enables coordination and collaboration among agents and allows to provide context-based information support.

For realizing the context-based information support, a workflow instance is assigned to one user agent, and the WE monitors all interactions (e.g. requests) of the user agent with this particular instance, whereby more than one user agents can be logged in association to one incident. All collected information is captured by the common parent workflow stored in attribute-value-representations, this information is stored in the global context database of the current incident. Based on the monitored interactions the context-based data already collected is enriched, which ultimately allows the WE to build the application data within the context that can be denoted as repository for all requests, responses, and inputs of the user agents.

The collected application data can be used for analyzing what is going on in the fire ground. CAKE retrieves additional information based on the application data by sending the collected data as request to the search engines, particularly to the search engines that are working on guidelines and working instructions. Consequently, CAKE gets results that match to the application data and contain guideline or working instructions that can be useful for users working in the fire ground. These guidelines can be presented to the headquarters.

The underlying model for building application data is a domain specific ontology. According to this ontology application data can be semantically interpreted and enables retrievals for context-based information, e.g. by using synonyms. A crucial issue is to develop a quality threshold when having achieved enough context-based data for performing the retrieval. Nevertheless, user agents can be pro-actively supported by context-based information. Otherwise, user agents can get notifications about context-based information of other user agents as shown in Figure 1.

3.4 CBR-Driven Planning Support

The CAKE workflow definitions can be used for planning activities which are expected to be performed during project enactment. Each workflow definition describes an individual activity, which may either be refined by introducing tasks (including sub-workflows) and a control flow among them, or which may be defined abstractly in terms of a "black box". This allows coarse-grained planning as required by many application domains in order to represent capricious situations. These situations occur in many application domains incorporating creative or knowledge-intense processes which make it impossible to lay out detailed procedures beforehand (e.g. because selecting a concrete procedure depends on context parameters: a fire fighter has to know about the type of fire before an applicable procedure to extinguish it can be chosen.)

As explained above, by separating workflow definitions from workflow instances, CAKE supports late planning by allowing to apply changes to workflows even during their execution. In addition, abstract tasks allow to specify workflow definitions may at any level of detail, which in combination with late planning leads to support of weakly structured workflows [7]. These concepts overcome limitations of "classic" process models and workflow enactment control known from business process modeling, which are unsuitable in agile environments.

During workflow execution, a user agent may do late planning in order to further refine the situation within the current context when approaching an abstractly defined workflow definition. However, in time and business-critical situations this is insufficient: For instance, while extinguishing a fire, a fire fighter cannot wait until late planning has been completed by the headquarters. In order to overcome this, late planning may be backed by previously recorded planning activities, leading to adaptive workflows supported by Case Based Reasoning (CBR) [8].

CBR technology enables a similarity-based retrieval by incorporating further experience: When proceeding to an abstractly planned task the WE allows the corresponding user agent to retrieve a suitable workflow definition in a special workflow database. In that scope, ad-hoc planning is facilitated during runtime. Procedures how to retrieve suitable workflows are described by collaboration patterns, so when looking for potential replacements for the abstract tasks, domain or organization-specific constraints are respected.

In order to reuse existing knowledge within the organization, the CAKE data model is used to characterize semantics of workflow definitions and agents. For workflows definitions, goals and metrics may be defined with respect to the underlying domain ontology (e.g. "workflow goal is to produce a report"). Goals and metrics are represented using attribute-value pairs based on the unified CAKE data model, which is also used to specify agent characterizations or context data as explained above.

Further modifications on the subworkflow instance can be done by the user agent for adapting. The CBR-driven retrieval mechanism bases on similarity measures derived from the context-based data that annotates the workflow models. In particular, the domain ontology is fundamental for the similarity measure. Though it will be a challenge to develop the similarity measures in detail.

By logging changes to workflow definitions and contexts, the CAKE workflow engine manager allows user agents to conduct further analysis on deviations from a previously laid out workflow definition or additions which have been necessary during workflow enactment. This leads to a Plan-Do-Check-Act cycle, and allows to transform tacit knowledge of the project participants (e.g. experience of a senior fire fighter) into an explicit workflow definition. Notably, domain-specific knowledge is kept aside from the workflow definitions and accessed through the information agents, hence the workflow definitions may be shared across the organization (e.g. between different fire departments). This enables to capture knowledge in the sense of an organizational memory [9].

For business and time critical situations as discussed above, a demand for documentation afterwards is obvious. For example, project stakeholders may request additional reports after having inspected artifacts that have resulted from workflow enactment, or they may request further information on the workflows themselves that led to the results. Thus, the data logged by the workflow engine manager may also be used to automatically generate documentation to handle a-posteriori requests from user agents.

4 Example: A CAKE Use Case

In this section, an example is given how to put the CAKE approach presented above into practice. Especially to fire service domains, the presented approach has to be tailored to the specific domain requirements. For example, the UK fire brigades are strictly organized in a hierarchical order. By following this organizational structure only the incident commander (IC) is equipped by the hands-free information support based on CAKE because he or she is in charge of the incident and of several fire fighters whose number depends on the incident's size. The responsibilities of the IC comprise information gathering, decision making, and keeping contact to the headquarters, the control center to which the IC has a connection via radio. The fire fighters report to the IC and carry out his or her commands.

A use case is sketched to support the IC and the headquarters in performing a routine operation of extinguishing a fire and keeping safe the incident environments. The incident has happened on an industrial production plant. A global workflow is assigned to the incident in CAKE containing a simple workflow definitions "Fire 1". For the IC a standard procedure has been prepared beforehand that is now carried out by the incident commander. This procedure is also represented by a simple workflow definition "extinguishing a fire". Before the incident begins the IC logs into the CAKE system that starts his or her new workflow instance assigned.

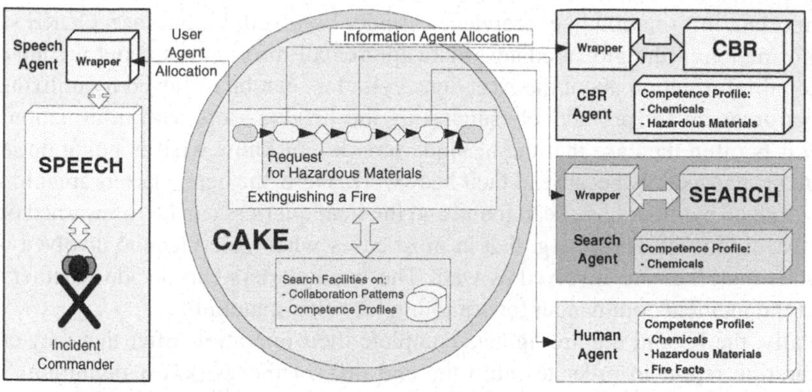

Fig. 2. Illustrations of the Agent Framework tailored to the described Example

In practice, the IC delegates the fire fighters to park all appliances safety, to restrict the zone around the incident, and to begin with extinguishing the fire. Fire fighters collect all available information about the incident and report it to the IC. While working the IC is connected with CAKE using a hands-free voice recognition device that allows the IC to utilize the CAKE information support. When a fire fighter finds a cylinder labeled with an unknown production code, he tells it to the IC who is able to perform a request for detailed information utilizing CAKE: Does this cylinder contain a hazardous material and does it need a special and careful handling?

In order to process the request as illustrated in Figure 2, CAKE enhances the initial workflow instance with the task "request for hazardous materials" and makes use of the respective collaboration patterns. The collaboration pattern says first to ask the CBR-based information agent for seeking on structured chemical data as the agent is an expert for both chemicals and hazardous materials. When no suitable data is retrieved the information agent is asked that works on unstructured chemical data. When no suitable results are retrieved the IC is informed how to connect to a human expert for chemical information. Here, because the CBR-based agent is an expert for chemicals and hazardous materials it delivers the requested information and provides three options in form of short descriptions. The options are sent to the user agent in order to be transformed into natural language, then it is read to the IC. The IC can choose among these results for getting the whole text that contains the information that the found chemical material is Acetylene that has to be dealt in a special manner. Furthermore, the IC can ask for instructions how to deal with the Acetylene cylinder, e.g. first to apply cooling spray from lashed Akron branches on it, to continue cooling for 24 hours, to check if water does not evaporate from cylinder surface when the spray is stopped and to check with a thermal imaging camera does not reveal the presence of any heat. If this is the case, then the cylinders have to be removed into safe area.

Further on the technical level, CAKE has monitored the interactions between IC and CAKE, therefore, the initial workflow is enhanced with this request for chemical materials. Both the request and the response are captured in the context application data of the IC's workflow instance. CAKE monitors this context for extracting critical and important information like Acetylene cylinder involved. In this case, CAKE stores this information in the global context that captures all information about the incident. Additional information about the Acetylene cylinders can be retrieved by utilizing the information agent for pro-actively supporting the headquarters with information. Although it is often the case that the headquarters do not know what is going on in the incident ground exactly because of their busy work. Here, the headquarters are informed that Acetylene cylinder have been found and the headquarters can be forewarned of potential hazardous situations, e.g. that in most cases when Acetylene is involved other hazardous materials are involved as well. The headquarters can decide whether they instruct the incident commander for searching for other materials.

Finally, the IC and the fire fighters complete their operation, after that they create the operation report in order to fulfill the end task of the workflow definition. They decide that for future inspections, querying the company profile should be mandatory in order to prepare for giving safety instructions more carefully.

In the next section, we will discuss related work to the CAKE approach. Finally, we will summarize the core ideas presented above, and discuss possible future work.

5 Related Work

Providing workflow management support for agile methodologies has been discussed before [10]. This approach follows the idea of "heavy agile" [11] methods by suggesting to augment the specific methodology of Extreme Programming with additional documentation, formality, and tools, in order to support larger undertakings like distributed-team projects. However, because of limitation to a specific methodology, scope of application is limited.

In order to model workflows, various concepts have been proposed in the past decades, however none gained broad acceptance. Most rely on process description languages focusing on task dependencies. For instance, formal languages like MVP-L [12] have been designed specifically for expressing relationships between the various aspects of a software project, and to provide a formal execution model. Other efforts propose state and activity charts as means of workflow specification and execution [13]. While these efforts have their advantages to detect infeasible or suboptimal configurations, they require complex tool support, because of their rather non-intuitive model representation.

Workflow management systems have been discussed before as a valuable source of information for supporting knowledge-intense tasks [6]. A promising approach is the concept of weakly-structured workflows that provides knowledge-intense tasks [7]. Here, benefits of explicit process models, workflow-type control, and information support are investigated for process-oriented Knowledge Management support. Building an organizational memory based on process models and workflow information has been used in various systems, as described in [14]. In [15], the author extends this idea by suggesting a framework for explicitly expressing information needs and sources, and how to support team members by proactively providing them. Modeling knowledge creation and management within a workflow environment focused on weakly-strucuterd workflows has been discussed in [16]. However, distributing knowledge to the user agents remains a challenge, and none of the approaches discussed above has been designed to cover the special demands of time and business critical-situations as described in section 2.

An approach for adaptive workflow enactment using multiple agent systems [17] makes use of Business Process Execution Language for Web Services (BPEL4WS or short BPEL) [18]. Here, the XML-based language for expressing the composition of Web services is applied for coordinating agents. Finally, using information agents for providing project history information is known from the field of software metrics [19], and deriving documentation by tracing workflow execution has been suggested in [20]. The idea is to look for patterns within a project history in order to create agile documentation [21] as required, and without obliging users to enter additional information.

6 Conclusion

Motivated by mission-critical or literally life-critical domains from the AMIRA project, in this paper we presented the CAKE approach, a concept for coping with business and time-critical processes. Based on requirements derived from the fire service domain, CAKE rejoins several approaches for supporting application-driven scenarios. Besides providing workflow knowledge and agent mediation the CAKE approach also integrates planning skills and agile documentations as well.

CAKE is currently getting implemented for the application domains of roadside assistance and fire services. In future work, we will research how CAKE can be utilized for providing support in other domains, where knowledge-intense and creative processes are present. This includes, but is not limited to, software engineering and medical processes.

Further applications, e.g. for supporting geographically dispersed collaboration between experts, are taken into account as a generalization of the ideas behind the CAKE approach.

Acknowledgement. The authors acknowledge the European Commission for funding AMIRA under grant number FP6, project IST-2003-511740.

References

1. Abrahamson, P., Salo, O., Ronkainen, J., Warsta, J.: Agile software development methods: Review and anaylsis. Number 478. VTT Publications (2002)
2. Boehm, B.: Get ready for the agile methods, with care. IEEE Computer **35** (2002) 64–69
3. Beck, K., Fowler, M.: Planning Extreme Programming. Addison-Wesley (2000)
4. Glazer, H.: Dispelling the process myth: Having a process does not mean sacrificing agility or creativity. Crosstalk: The Journal on Defense Software Engineering **14** (2001) 27–30
5. Advanced Development Methods, Inc.: Control chaos: Living on the edge. the origins of scrum, http://www.controlchaos.com (1996)
6. Maus, H.: Workflow context as a means for intelligent information support. Lecture Notes in Computer Science **2116** (2001) 261–274

7. van Elst, L., Aschoff, F.R., Bernardi, A., Maus, H., Schwarz, S.: Weakly-structured workflows for knowledge-intensive tasks: An experimental evaluation. In: Proceedings of the 18th International Workshops on Enabeling Technologies: Infrastructures for collaborative enterprises, Linz, Austria, IEEE Computer Society Press (2003) 340–345
8. Weber, B., Wild, W., Breu, R.: Cbrflow: Enabling adaptive workflow management through conversational case-based reasoning. In Funk, P., Calero, P.A.G., eds.: Advances in Case-Based Reasoning, Proceedings of 7th European Conference, ECCBR 2004. LNAI3155, Madrid, Spain, Springer Verlag, Berlin-Heidelberg (2004) 434–448
9. Wargitsch, C., Wewers, T., Theisinger, F.: An organizational-memory-based approach for an evolutionary workflow management system - concepts and implementation. In: HICSS '98: Proceedings of the Thirty-First Annual Hawaii International Conference on System Sciences-Volume 1, Washington, DC, USA, IEEE Computer Society (1998) 174
10. Maurer, F., Mertel, S.: Process support for distributed extreme programming teams. In: Proceedings of the International Workshop on Global Software Development (ICSE'02 GSD), Orlando, FL (2002)
11. Highsmith, J.: Agile Software Development Ecosystems. Addison-Wesley (2002)
12. Bröckers, A., Lott, C.M., Rombach, H.D., Verlage, M.: MVP-L language report version 2 (1997)
13. Wodtke, D., Weißenfels, J., Weikum, G., Dittrich, A.K., Muth, P.: The mentor workbench for enterprise-wide workflow management. In Peckham, J., ed.: Proceedings of the ACM SIGMOD International Conference on Management of Data, Tucson, AZ, ACM Press (1997) 576–579
14. Abecker, A., Bernardi, A., Ntioudis, S., Mentzas, G., Herterich, R., Houy, C., Muller, S., Legal, M.: The DECOR toolbox for workflow-embedded organizational memory access. In: Proceedings of the 3rd International Conference on Enterprise Information Systems, ICEIS 2001. (2001) 225–232
15. Holz, H.: An incremental approach to task-specific information delivery in se processes. In: Proceedings of the 18th IEEE International Conference on Automated Software Engineering. (2003) 295–298
16. Papavassiliou, G., Mentzas, G.: Knowledge modelling in weakly-structured business processes. Journal of Knowledge Management **7** (2003) 18–33
17. Buhler, P.A., Vidal, J.M.: Towards adaptive workflow enactment using multiagent systems. Volume 6., Springer Science + Business Media, Inc. Manufactured in The Netherlands (2005) 61–87
18. Andrews, T., Curbera, F., Dholakia, H., Goland, Y., Klein, J., Leymann, F., Liu, K., Roller, D., Smith, D., Thatte, S., Trickovic, I., Weerawarana, S.: Business process execution language for web services, version 1.1. specification, BEA Systems, IBM Corp., Microsoft Corp., SAP AG, Siebel Systems (2003)
19. Johnson, P.M., Kou, H., Agustin, J., Chan, C., Moore, C., Miglani, J., Zhen, S., Douane, W.E.: Beyond the personal software process: Metrics collection and analysis for the differently disciplined. In: Proceedings of the 2003 International Conference on Software Engineering, Portland, OR (2003)
20. Sauer, T.: Using design rationales as agile documentation. In: Proceedings of the 18th International Workshops on Enabeling Technologies: Infrastructures for collaborative enterprises, Linz, Austria, IEEE Computer Society Press (2003) 326–331
21. Ambler, S.: Agile documentation. Essay, http://www.agilemodeling.com/essays/ agileDocumentation.htm (2001)

Modeling Contexts for Business Process Oriented Knowledge Support

Marielba Zacarias[1,2], Artur Caetano[1,3], H. Sofia Pinto[3,4], and José Tribolet[1,3]

[1] Center for Organizational Engineering, INESC, Lisboa, Portugal
[2] Universidade do Algarve, ADEEC-FCT, Faro, Portugal
[3] Department of Information Systems and Computer Science, IST/UTL, Lisbon, Portugal
[4] ALGOS, INESC-ID, Lisboa, Portugal
mzacaria@ualg.pt, artur.caetano@inov.pt,
sofia@algos.inesc-id.pt, jose.tribolet@inov.pt

Abstract. In this paper, we propose an organizational model to describe the execution of business activities. The model offers a *dynamic, actor centered, context based* and *business process oriented perspective* of the organization that explicitly addresses the information and collaboration requirements derived from human multi-tasking capabilities. Actors are approached as a network of contexts managed by an *"operating system"*. Three kinds of actors are defined; human, business process and organization actor. Two context types are introduced. An *action context* defines the specific behavior and information needs of a *human actor* performing a *task* under a given *role*, at particular *time intervals*. *Interaction contexts* support and regulate activity-related interactions among action contexts. This modeling approach seeks to facilitate a personalized, proactive and timely knowledge support to human business actors. We illustrate these ideas with working examples.

1 Introduction and Motivation

The highly dynamic nature of current organizations continually presses for faster ways of obtaining the information required for their operation. Despite the number of tools and systems developed to collect, organize and disseminate information throughout the organization, people continue to spend time searching the information needed for their work. This situation is aggravated in knowledge intensive tasks, which have greater information and collaboration requirements. When performing business activities, knowledge consumers should receive information according to their specific needs. Furthermore, knowledge provision activities should minimize the disturbance of workers' core activities. In order to meet these requirements, personalized, proactive and timely knowledge distribution services must be devised.

Current knowledge management systems offer limited solutions to the problem of knowledge provision and are frequently deserted by users [2]. Recent research projects [3] are recognizing the subjective, social, and contextual nature of knowledge, and are promoting a distributed approach to knowledge management. Theoretical frameworks and technical solutions are being developed aiming to provide a more appropriate support of knowledge-related processes. However, these developments are

K.-D. Althoff et al. (Eds.): WM 2005, LNAI 3782, pp. 431 – 442, 2005.

not business process-oriented and do not focus the dynamics of individual behavior changing at work. Human business actors perform several tasks under different roles. Therefore, they exhibit different behaviors with different information needs. These needs depend on factors such as individual features, task at hand and role played. A personalized, proactive and timely information provision entails considering not only actor, role and task-related features. It must also take into account the dynamics that governs task and role changing behavior. Capturing these dynamics requires (1) a different organizational perspective, (2) defining new business concepts and (3) adapt existing concepts to the newly defined ones.

Our work pertains to the organizational modeling area. Business models allow organizations to communicate, document and understand its activity [5]. In order to manage organization's complexity, several perspectives are used. A business process perspective of organizations implies relating sequences of activities that deliver some value to internal or external customers. Modeling business processes involves capturing interactions between business objects, such as activities, resources and human or automated actors. Workflow management systems (WFMS) are a supporting technology for business process modeling, optimization and automation [7]. As WFMS enable information dissemination among users and systems, they facilitate a "process oriented" knowledge management [9]. Nevertheless, a process-oriented knowledge support through WFMS has two limitations. First, conventional WFMS support predefined work, offering little flexibility. Second, they describe actors as resources with a specialized behavior. This forces to represent actors' different behaviors as unrelated units [5]. Role based modeling overcomes this limitation by enabling the representation of different "views" of a single actor. However, this approach does not describe actor behavior changing patterns. In order to give business actors a proactive and timely knowledge support, it is necessary to address actor behavior changing dynamics. This entails capturing actor engagement and disengagement patterns to tasks and roles.

In this paper we propose an organizational model to describe the execution of business activities. This model offers a *dynamic, actor-centered, context-based* and *business process oriented perspective* of the organization. It explicitly addresses information and collaboration needs derived from human multi-tasking capabilities. Through this modeling approach we seek to facilitate the design of systems capable of providing a personalized, proactive and timely and knowledge support to human business actors. The remaining of this paper is structured as follows: section 2 reviews related work on context and role-based modeling, section 3 defines the core concepts of our work, section 4 presents the proposed modeling approach. Section 5 illustrates some of these ideas. In section 6, we give our conclusions and future directions.

2 Related Work

This section presents related work supporting our concepts and modeling approach. Section 2.1 summarizes the notion and uses of context developed by context-related research. Section 2.2 describes role-based business process modeling approach.

2.1 The Notions of Context

Although the notion of context plays an important role in disciplines such as pragmatics, natural language semantics, linguistics, cognitive psychology, and artificial intelligence [10], there is no standard concept or theory. The notion of context varies according its area of application. This section briefly summarizes engineering and sociological approaches to context.

Classical Engineering Approach
From an engineering perspective, context is viewed as a collection of things (sentences, propositions, assumptions, properties, procedures, rules, facts, concepts, constraints, sentences, etc) associated to some specific situation (environment, domain, task, agents, interactions, conversations, etc). This consensus is reflected by the "box metaphor" [11]. The intuition is that context can then be seen as a container where its content depends on some set of situational characteristics or parameters. The specific set of parameters varies according to the areas of application. In pragmatics, indexical expressions are defined as expressions dependent on indexes such as place, time, agent and world, which are a subset of context parameters. In Artificial Intelligence, parameters (called dimensions) such as time, location, culture, topic, granularity and modality among others, have been proposed as defining elements of context space [13]. A proposal for a workflow context space in [14] includes the following parameters: function, behavior, causality, organization, information, operation and history. In the area of context aware applications localization, user identity, activity and time have been identified parameters of context [15].

Sociological Approaches
Seeking to improve system sensitivity to specific settings, research in context-aware computing is focusing on a view of context inspired by sociological investigations of real-world practice [25]. This work contrasts the objective account of engineering and the subjective account of phenomenology and discusses the implications of approaching context from the latter perspective. The phenomenological perspective argues that (1) context is a relational property among objects, (2) the scope of contextual features are defined dynamically, (2) context is relevant to *particular* settings, instances of action and participants and (4) context and activity are not separable i.e. context is embedded in activity and arises from it. Under this perspective, the focus moves from context representation to context support.

The apparent contradiction between the objective and subjective positions is denied by Structuration Theory [12], which seeks a balance between both positions. According to this theory, through interactions actors both produce and reproduce social practices. On one side, social practices are produced from interactions among subjects. On the other side, from these interactions emerges an objective structure (interaction context) which provides rules and resources that simultaneously support the reproduction of social practices and constrain subject interactions.

2.2 Role Based Business Process Modeling

Conventional business process models describe actors as resources with a uniform and specialized behavior [5]. This leads to represent the multiple behaviors of a human actor as independent and unrelated units, posing serious limitations to the provision of an integral support to human actors. Role based Business process modeling overcomes this limitation by combining two independent models; the business object model and the role model. The overall motivation for role-based business process modeling is allowing several views on a single business object such as a human actor. An important feature of these views is that they can change dynamically, i.e. be added or removed from a business object. Each one of these views is modeled as a role. A *role* defines the properties of the business object that are relevant when interacting with other business objects, thus defining a part of its observable behavior. The union of all roles that a business object can play defines its complete observable behavior.

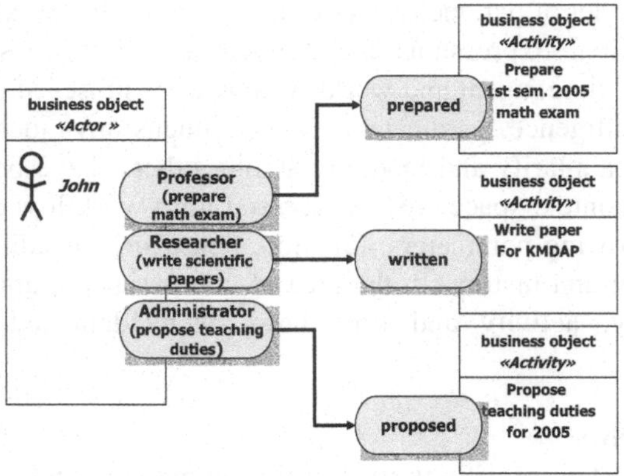

Fig. 1. Role-based modeling example

Figure 1 illustrates how role-based business process modeling enables an integrated view of the human actor John while allowing to represent his different roles when engaged in three different activities. Thus, John *prepares the 1st semester math exam* using the *prepare math exams* capability under the role *professor*. John *writes a paper for conferences* using the *write scientific papers* capability under the researcher role. He *proposes the 2005 teaching duties* using the *propose teaching duties* capability under the administrator role.

3 Action and Interaction Contexts

This section presents the core concepts of our approach. The concepts of action and interaction contexts take into account the multi-tasking nature of human business actors and the inherent complexity of the interactions among them. Analogies with multi-tasking operating systems and distributed systems are established.

3.1 The Action Context

The context of a knowledge worker's information needs is determined by three main factors: (1) the individual person, (2) his/her position in the organizational structure, (3) the task at hand [4]. Taking into account all three dimensions promises better results than focusing on any subset. From our point view, the specific behavior and information needs of an individual is defined by the combination of four factors: an *individual actor* performing a *task* under a given *role* at certain *times* exhibits a specific behavior with specific information needs. Moreover, we regard roles as more restricted, since it refers to specific capabilities rather than broader organizational roles (see fig. 2). Actors are typically modeled according to individual, task or role factors separately. Combining these factors altogether and adding time, enables to further customize human business actors' models.

In terms of the box metaphor, the action context defines the relevant behavior and information needs according to four parameters: *individual, role, task* and *time*. Although we are following an engineering approach in this definition, this is not a discrete notion, since we will consider several degrees of relevance. An action context reflects an actor *state*. This state is to be represented by a sub-set of actor's properties and their values. The main components of action contexts are:

Action Context Parameters:

- *Task:* Part of business activities, which in turn are part of business processes. Tasks are described with a predicate (verb and complements). The task parameter defines formal behavior and information needs.
- *Role:* Capabilities used by an actor in executing a specific task. Although also described with a verb and its complements, tasks and roles are different. The role parameter defines other kind of formal information needs.
- *Individual:* Human actor executing a task. Individual are described with proper nouns. The individual parameter defines preferences and habits such as preferred locations, tools or methods, and informal information needs.
- *Time:* Specific moments or time intervals, defines time-related information needs.

Action Context Contents:

- *Behavior:* Relevant set of actions and interactions relevant for an action context. Action and interactions are the atomic units of behavior of our model. Can be formal (pre-defined by task or roles) or informal (not-predefined).
- *Action:* Described with a verb and its complements. The verb describes a specific act, the direct complement describes an information item used or produced in that act. Circumstantial complements describe action-related preferences or habits.
- *Interactions:* Acts that involve two kinds of actors: senders and receivers. Their description is more complex, we are researching on the appropriate description approach. Verbs are also an important identifier of interactions. Whilst some verbs are related to actions, others are related to interactions.
- *Information needs: Formal* and *informal information items* used, produced and shared in action context actions and interactions.

- *Information items:* Can be *formal* or *informal*. Formal information items are embedded in documents and files of different kinds. Informal items are ideas, facts, meanings, questions, answers, point of views and so on. Embedded in messages.

Action Contexts and the Concept of Knowledge
Despite the consensus around the continuum of data-information-knowledge, the limits among these concepts are still not clear. The context dependence of knowledge has been largely recognized. The borderlines between data, information and knowledge are not sharp because they are relative with respect to the context of use [20]. In our work, action contexts are approached as active entities which dynamically adjust information needs rather than exclusively relying on pre-defined sets of relevant items. In our work, action context relevant information items are considered knowledge items. Thereafter, knowledge is produced and consumed in specific action contexts and its meaning is relative to these action contexts. Consequently, when distributing knowledge the producer and consumer action contexts should be explicit.

3.2 Human Actors' Multi-tasking Nature

Humans typically alternate among several, independent tasks. When engaged in several activities, people "break" these activities and "jump" among them according to criteria such as task priorities, task resource's availability or scheduling-related habits (hour preferences, dispatching shorter tasks first, etc.). Human multi-tasking capabilities and limitations are studied in Experimental Psychology [17]. Several theories claim the existence of mental executive control processes that supervise the selection, initiation, execution, and termination of tasks. An analogy of executive processes with multi-tasking operating systems is established in [18]. Understanding executive mental control, which defines human basic operative behavior, may help to understand and describe the dynamics of human actors' behavior changing. Although business actors exhibit different behaviors and information needs, they are unique entities. Thus, an integral actor support entails capturing not only his specific behaviors and needs, but also his basic operative behavior.

3.3 Modeling Business Actors

Human beings are designed to identify and use context automatically in their daily lives [19]. Due to their multi-tasking behavior, actors are able to handle several action contexts. But scarce resources such as attention and short-term memory [1], forces the activation of only one action context at a time. At some specific time frame, actors' behavior and information requirements depend on the *active* action context. Thus, when modeling actors, not only several action contexts for each actor should be considered but also, the possibility of switching among them. Modeling actors' multi-tasking behavior entails "exploding" the notion of actor. Rather than considering an actor as a single object, we are proposing modeling actors as a network of objects: the action contexts. Action contexts are not autonomous, as they are managed by a different and special object that handles actor's basic capabilities such as action context initiation, termination and switching mechanisms. With this approach we seek to enrich the actors' representation of current business process models.

The "Operating Systems" Metaphor
One goal of our research is to capture and represent both actor specific action contexts and his action context changing patterns. In our work, we use an "operating systems" metaphor as a conceptual framework for several reasons. First, it provides a clear cut separation of actual execution from its management. Second, it enables a dynamic view of actors. Third, it offers a straightforward abstraction of human multi-tasking capabilities. In order to act or interact, upon the reception of messages, multi-tasking actors must first identify and activate the corresponding action context. This metaphor allows and explicit representation of context identification and management operations. Thereafter, the actor management entity is defined in our model as the actor's *"operating system"*.

3.4 The Interaction Context

When modeling actors with an "operating systems" metaphor, their interactions can be approached establishing analogies with distributed systems. All interactions entail a communication process. Distributed system (human or automated) communication can be modeled as the information transfer from a sender to a receiver. This information transfer is supported by a *channel*. According to Communication Theory [21], this channel entails the use of a sign system. Human sign systems (such as natural languages) are described by a layered model with four interdependent layers; *empirics, syntactics, semantics and pragmatics*. Human actors naturally handle all layers. In the case of automated actors, the ISO/OSI model provides the standard communication channel for distributed computational systems, with varying sophistication degrees. The ISO/OSI model addresses empirical and syntactical layers. Advances in Ontology research, are providing higher level syntactics and semantics to communication among automated actors such as agents and web-services [22,23]. The inclusion of role structures and interaction protocols has brought pragmatic-related elements to agent communications [24].

In human environments, interacting individuals always perform some particular tasks under a particular role. This means that human actors always interact from specific *action contexts*: From successive interactions among action contexts emerges a shared space which grows with successive interactions among them. Each business activity in execution originates a *communication space* defined as the **interaction context**. In our work, we focus on certain *pragmatic* elements provided by interaction contexts. Activity-related states of affairs, role structures and interaction rules and protocols belong to the interaction context. Activity-related states of affairs include not only the activity state (activity context) but also, the participants' state i.e., the "observable" part of participating action contexts. Thus, the action and interaction contexts are somewhat overlapped concepts. Nevertheless, both concepts are needed. Whilst action contexts consider the subjective nature of knowledge, interaction contexts consider its social nature.

Figure 2 illustrates the main elements of the interaction context concept. Apart from shared activity and action contexts, interaction context behavior is determined by a number of elements such as specific *interaction rules* and *protocols*. Interaction protocols describe *valid sets of action and interaction sequences* among action contexts that meet specific purposes related to tasks or activities. Interaction rules define the *set of conditions required for successful interactions* among action contexts. The interaction context definition is influenced by sociological approaches to context and it can not be so well described through the box metaphor.

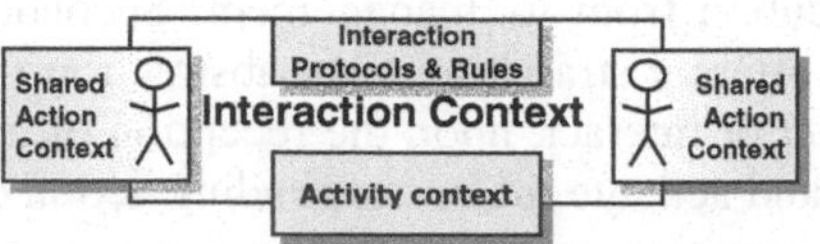

Fig. 2. Interaction Context Elements

The Interaction Context and Knowledge Distribution

Knowledge is distributed in specific interaction contexts and in order to be effective, it must realized according to the interaction context state of affairs and its specific interaction rules and protocols. An explicit interaction context model would greatly enhance the effectiveness of knowledge distribution services. Moreover, knowledge shared among action contexts could be efficiently represented in a single collective element.

4 A Context-Based and Business Process-Oriented Model

Due to their multi-tasking capabilities, human business actors are capable of handling several *action contexts* and participating in several *interaction contexts.* We propose a model to describe the execution of *business activities* that explicitly address human multi-tasking context identification and management operations. Figure 4 illustrates our model. The organization is viewed as a network of individual and collective actors. The model explodes the actor notion and approaches it as a network of contexts managed by actor's own "operating system". Three kinds of actors are defined: *human, business process* actor and *organization* actor. *Human actors* are modeled as a network of *action contexts*. Human "operating system" determines individual habits and action context changing patterns. The *business process actor* is a collective actor modeled as a network of *activity contexts*. Its "operating system" acts as an "engine" managing the execution of pre-defined flows of work. The *organization* actor is another collective actor which represents organized groups of interacting individuals with specific purposes such as teams or departments. It is modeled as a network of *interaction contexts*. The organization "operating system": (1) provides communication services based on shared assumptions, expectations, rules and interaction protocols which support and regulate activity-related actions and interactions and (2) manages ad-hoc behavior and exceptions not handled by business processes.

The inclusion of two kinds of collective actors explicitly acknowledges the organization's capability to act flexibly by combining pre-defined and structured behavior with ad-hoc behavior. The proposed model is a loosely coupled model which separates execution from its management. This approach entails a dynamic composition of business processes, which respond to changing requirements and availability of resources. This offers a more appropriate support to agile processes. However, in our work we do not address business process management issues. Adaptive, agent-based and event-driven WFMS [8,6,16] are working towards this end. Rather, we address the model context-related elements from a *business process perspective*. Explicit context models offer another means to support the execution of agile processes. Since interaction contexts reflect activity-related states of affairs, this enables an empirical control of agile processes.

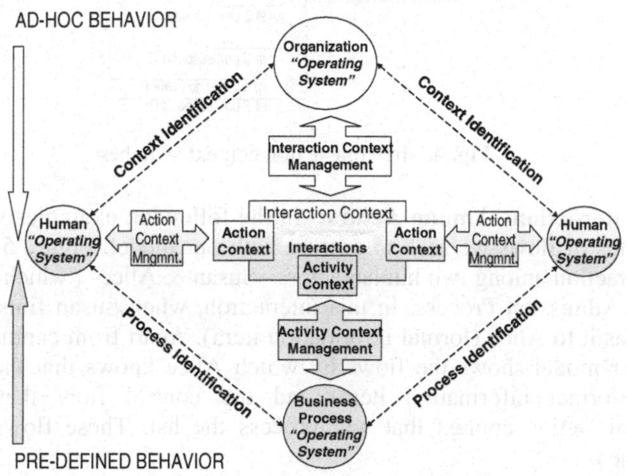

Fig. 3. The proposed model

In our work, we specifically seek to capture *particular* elements of: (1) interaction contexts, i.e. *observable action contexts* (2) human "operating systems", i.e. individual *action context-changing patterns*, and (3) organization "operating system" i.e., supporting and regulating mechanisms of action context interactions, such as interaction *rules* and *protocols.* Capturing and modeling these elements requires different procedures and techniques from those used in business process modeling.

5 Modeling Examples

In order to illustrate some of the previous ideas, we include a modeling example based on observations of a real organizational setting. Alice is the secretary of the CEO of a research institute, At this job, she must handle many action contexts.

Modeling Action Context Switches: Figure 4 illustrates a scenario of Alice's action contexts switching. The figure shows a sequence of action context switches and switching rules. Action context switching rules capture behavior changing patterns. This diagram shows simple scheduling rules and describes one particular scenario. Nevertheless, the goal is to capture lasting patterns of action context switches.

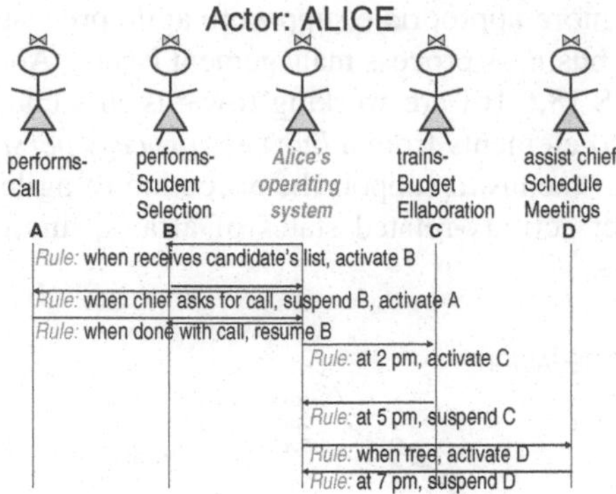

Fig. 4. Modeling action context switches

Modeling Interactions Among Actors: In the following examples we illustrate the different kinds of flows we seek to capture with our model. Figure 5-a shows a pre-defined interaction among two human actors –Susan & Alice- , which is handled by a the Student Admission Process. In this interaction, when Susan finishes the student list, she sends it to Alice (formal information item). Apart from capturing the student list flow, our model shows the flows by which Alice knows that the student list is finished (informal information item) and the control flow that activates the corresponding action context that will process the list. These flows may occur at different times.

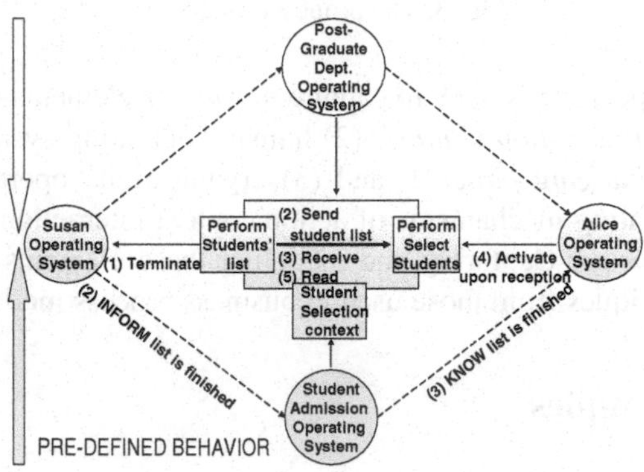

Fig. 5-a. Pre-defined interactions

Fig 5-b shows an ad-hoc flow among two actors, not handled by a business process actor but by the post-graduate department organization. Upon unexpected problems in elaborating student list, Susan asks Alice for help, since she knows from previous interactions, that Alice has the required capabilities and is a collaborative person. The model shows (1) the flows where requests help with student list and Alice's commit to that request (informal information item) (2) Alice control flow activating the corresponding action context when free and (3) the flow where the list is actually sent (formal information item).

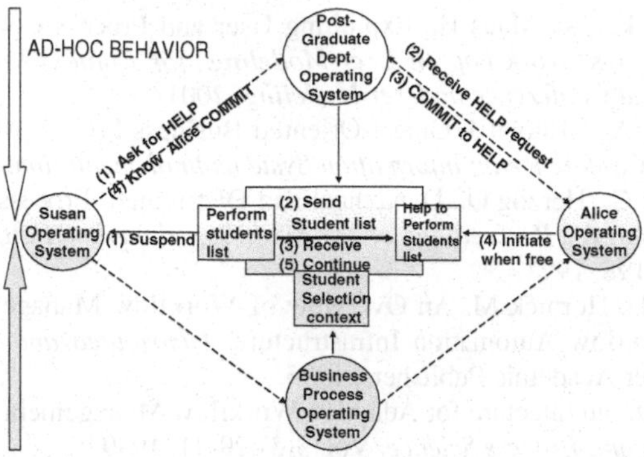

Fig. 5-b. Ad-hoc interactions

6 Conclusions and Future Work

In this paper we define the concepts of **action** and **interaction contexts** as key elements of a *dynamic*, *actor-centered*, *context-based* and *business process oriented* modeling approach to describe the execution of business activities. Action and interaction contexts reflect both the subjective and social nature of knowledge. Three types of actors – human, business process and organization actor- are defined and are approached as a network of activity, action and interaction contexts respectively.

The model offers richer actor representations by addressing human capabilities of handling several action contexts and participating in several interaction contexts. The inclusion of two collective actors acknowledges the organization's capability to act flexibly by combining pre-defined behavior with ad-hoc behavior. Complementing business process models with context models: (1) enables an empirical control of agile processes, providing a means to support its execution and (2) offers an integrated view of actual knowledge flows and business processes, enabling a business process oriented knowledge support to business actors.

The concepts defined and the proposed modeling approach, are preliminary results of our work. The examples illustrate some ideas of our proposal. Additional observation and modeling work is required in order to test, adjust and refine our model. More detailed descriptions of model elements are required. Model is intended to be useful for semi-structured and ad-hoc processes but specific usage and support issues are still to be devised. Model impact on knowledge management projects will be evaluated at a posterior phase.

References

[1] Dix A., Finlay J., Abound G., Beale R., *Human-Computer Interaction*, Prentice Hall, 1998

[2] Bonifacio M., Bouquet P., Distributed Knowledge Management: a Systemic Approach, *Emergence in Complex, Cognitive, Social and Biological Systems*, Kluwer Academic Publishers, 2002

[3] The EDAMOK project, http://www. Edamok.itc.it

[4] Van Elst L., Abecker A., Maus H., Exploiting User and Process Context for Knowledge Management Systems, *Workshop on User-Modeling for Context Aware Applications at the 8th International Conference on User Modeling*, 2001
[5] Caetano A., Silva A., Tribolet J, Object-Oriented Business Process Modeling with Roles, *7th International Conference on Information Systems Implementation Modeling*, 2004
[6] Joeris, G., Klauck C., Herzog O., Dynamical and Distributed Process Management based on Agent Technology, *Proceedings of the Sixth Scandinavian Conference on Artificial Intelligence*, 187-198, 1997
[7] Georgakopoulos D. Hornick M. An Overview of Workflow Management: From Process Modeling to Workflow Automation Infrastructure, *Distributed and Parallel Databases*, 3:119-153 , Kluwer Academic Publishers, 1995.
[8] Siebert R., An open architecture for Adaptive Workflow Management Systems, *Journal of Integrated Design and Process Science*, Vol. 3(3):29-41, 1999
[9] Jablonski S., Horn S., Schlundt M., Process Oriented Knowledge Management, *1. Konferenz Professionelles Wissensmanagement: Erfahrungen und Visionen,* 2001
[10] Bouquet P., Ghidini C., Giunchiglia F., Blanzieri E., Theories and Uses of Context in Knowledge Representation and Reasoning, *Journal of pragmatics - Special issue on context* 35(3): 455-484, 2002
[11] Benerecetti M., Bouquet P., Ghidini C., On the dimensions of context dependence: partiality, approximation, and perspective, *Third International and Interdisciplinary Conference on Modelling and Using Context,* Springer-Verlag, LNAI 2116: 59-72, 2001
[12] Giddens A., The Constitution of Society, University of California Press, 1984
[13] LENAT D., *The Dimensions of Context-Space*, CycCorp, http://casbah.org/resources/cyccontextspace.shtml
[14] Maus H., Workflow Context as a Means for Intelligent Information Support, *Third International and Interdisciplinary Conference on Modeling and Using Context*, Springer-Verlag LNAI 2116: 261–274, 2001.
[15] Dey A., Abowd G., Towards a Better Understanding of Context and Context-Awareness,. *GVU Technical Report*, ftp://ftp.cc.gatech.edu/pu b/gvu/tr/1999/99-22.pdf
[16] http:// itresearch.forbes.com/detail/RES/1062441978_953.html
[17] Rubinstein J., Meyer D., Evans J., Executive Control of Cognitive Processes in Task Switching, *Journal of Experimental Psychology: Human Perception and Performanc,e* 27(4): 763-797, 2001.
[18] Kieras, D. E., Meyer, D. E., Ballas, J. A., & Lauber, E. J., Modern computational perspectives on executive mental processes and cognitive control: Where to from here?, *In Control of Cognitive Processes: Attention and Performance XVIII,* 681-712., MIT Press, 2000
[19] Degler D., Battle L, *Knowledge* Management in Pursuit of Performance: the Challenge of Context, *Performance Improvement* , 39(6):25-31, 2000
[20] Schreiber G., Akkermans H., Anjewierden A., De Hoog R., Shadbolt N., Van de Velde W., Wielinga B., *Knowledge Engineering and Management: The CommonKADS Methodology*, MIT Press, 1999
[21] Beynon-Davies P., *Information Systems: An Introduction to Informatics in Organizations*, Palgrave, 2002
[22] Mc.Guiness D., *Ontologies Come of Age: Spinning the Semantic Web: Bringing the World Wide Web to Its Full Potential.* MIT Press, 2002
[23] McIlraith S., Son T., Zeng H., Semantic Web Services, *IEEE Intelligent Systems*, 16(2):46-53, 2001
[24] H. Parunak, Odell J. Representing Social Structures in UML, *Agent-Oriented Software Engineering II*, Springer-Verlag LNCS 2222:1-16, 2002
[25] Dourish P., What we talk about when we talk about context, Personal and Ubiquitous Computing, 8:19-30,2004

Revealed Processes in Knowledge Management

Kurt D. Fenstermacher

MIS Department, University of Arizona, 1130 E Helen St.,
Tucson, Arizona 85721
KurtF@Eller.Arizona.edu

1 Introduction

The essence of process is repeatability. Organizations, especially for-profit companies, have worked to refine their operations by using well-defined processes that they can manage. In the modern era, many organizations have focused on redesigning their processes by following Hammer's discussion of business process reengineering (BPR). While BPR is not dependent on information technology (IT), reengineering efforts often have complementary IT efforts. In particular, the focus on process has led to the rise of workflow management systems. The importance of process in daily life has also made it a central field within artificial intelligence (AI), where researchers in planning work to automate the construction of processes the achieve user goals [1-3]. The combination of planning, workflow systems and information retrieval has led to work in the burgeoning field of intelligent process-oriented systems for information access. By incorporating a process representation, a process-oriented system can guide users through complex task sequences, while offering relevant information at each step.

Agile techniques [4] for software development have advocated loosening the constraints of so-called heavyweight processes in software development, often represented by the Rational Unified Process, or RUP [5, 6]. In some ways, agile methods are a reaction to the heavyweight methods of software development that incorporate many carefully monitored processes, extensive checklists, and other formal artifacts. Agile methods favor production of code over the production of non-code artifacts. Moreover, agile methods are a sensible approach in dynamic environments. For example, the quickly changing requirements of retail business lead to rapidly changing software specifications and agile methods offer techniques for such environments. While some in the software development community might argue that agile techniques ignore years of strongly process-oriented developments, agile methods bring software development much closer to other kinds of knowledge-intensive work. The tenets of the agile movement, including favoring "customer collaboration over contract negotiation" and "responding to change over following a plan" [4], would seem quaint in the halls of a management consulting firm, while seeming heretical in some IT departments. Agile development can be captured by the sentiment, "Fit the process to the people, rather than the people to the process." For those who rely on processes to develop software applications to support users, whether those applications are for workflow or process-oriented management, fitting the process to the people presents a difficult challenge.

The intersection of process-based approaches and agile approaches offers fertile ground for research and illustrates an internal contradiction within the process-

K.-D. Althoff et al. (Eds.): WM 2005, LNAI 3782, pp. 443 – 454, 2005.

oriented community. Workflow management systems represent the most highly structured of these systems, enacting real-world processes by executing process descriptions written by business process analysts. Rigid processes for software development have been developed to bring repeatability to software development projects, and with repeatability, reliable estimation of future project efforts. The agile development methods described above are in part a reaction to this drive for tightly controlled processes. Creativity in the arts is perhaps the least structured of activities — what is the process for crafting a beautiful sonnet? Knowledge work, whose product is intangible, falls between the extremes of workflow management and poetry. The conflict between strongly and weakly structured processes that today pervades software development is present in all kinds of knowledge-intensive work.

2 Process-Oriented Knowledge Systems

Before considering process-oriented systems further, we should consider the core notion of process. The essence of process is repeatability. By studying alternative strategies for achieving a goal and selecting the best features for achieving a goal, we can capture the strategy in a process. While many business operations can be explicitly described and are highly repeatable (for example, credit card application processing), many other activities are innately highly variable. The repeatability of the process is a function of not only of the underlying activity, but also of the granularity of the process tasks. For example, many projects could be represented as a single process task — `DoProject`. While the single step project process is repeatable, because it can be reused for any project, the process offers very little guidance to those who would apply it to later projects. Process-oriented knowledge management systems must strike a balance among competing factors: reusability of the process and the level of abstraction are two of the most important.

A process description serves as a template, which a process-oriented system must instantiate with contextual information specific to the situation. For example, public companies in the United States are required to prepare annual reports showing a financial summary of their activities over the prior year. A specific company might choose to standardize the process of preparing its report, but each year will establish a different situation. A student writing a research paper is another example of a process (writing a research paper) that must be instantiated with information about the student, topic, and course (the situation). The process and situation together constitute the needed contextual information to support information access for problem solving. By annotating process descriptions with templates for posing queries to information systems, process-oriented systems can instantiate query templates with situational information. Thus, such systems can aid users who not only lack the terms needed to describe a solution, but also are unsure of what to do next.

While implementation details differ among systems, all process-oriented systems must perform at least three tasks: process retrieval, situation determination, and resource suggestion. Process retrieval means matching the user's problem to a process that solves the problem. In some cases, users might initiate retrieval by selecting a problem from a menu of known problems and the solution processes. In other cases, the system may monitor the user's actions to infer which problem the user is working to solve. Once the system determines the relevant process, it must then use situational information. In the previous example, the process is restaurant reservation, and the situation is a business dinner with specific clients in Tucson, Arizona. With the context as specified by the process and situation, a process-oriented system can support a user's access to traditional information systems or simply query such systems on behalf of the user.

What we see as structure in a process is actually a confounding of two distinct characteristics of processes: the degree of structure (i.e., strong or weak) and the level of abstraction. At one extreme, every process is the strongly structured process that consists of the single process step, `AchieveGoal`. At the opposite extreme, we have the loosely structured process where any possible action can succeed any other action. Schwarz and Roth-Berghofer [7] represent multiple levels of abstraction explicitly by considering the workspace, user action, task concept, and process levels separately. While different levels of abstraction are appropriate in different scenarios, my goal is to develop systems that infer which knowledge sources will be helpful to users; this is a less demanding standard than automating access to knowledge sources, but still requires significant detail in the process representation.

2.1 Weakly Structured, Knowledge-Intensive Processes

Others have noted that knowledge-intensive tasks are only weakly structured [7, 8] and have examined strategies for using the structure that is available. Using a top-down approach, [8] gave users the ability to refine processes as they worked, thus giving users control over the process definition. Combining top-down and bottom-up approaches Schwarz and Roth-Berghofer's [7] approach works across abstraction hierarchies by starting at the bottom and inferring user events from workspace actions and then at the top, using a task concept ontology. We are developing a system that combines the approaches of both [7] and [8] by enabling users to define processes for themselves, while also monitoring user interaction and matching it against knowledge-intensive processes using a case-based [9] approach.

2.2 Learning Processes Through Event Monitoring

Thus, the challenge is to identify processes that such knowledge workers follow, and to do so automatically. In collaboration with researchers at Oregon State University, we have been working to develop software that will record semantically significant events (for example, document opens, clipboard copies, and Web browser navigations). By monitoring the actions of knowledge workers through their computers, we hope to add a new perspective to the computer-based portion of their knowledge work. In the early stages, the work will be directed at gathering data on processes that knowledge workers engage in — discovering what we call revealed processes by analogy to the notion of revealed preferences from economics, because people reveal their processes through their actions, rather than an explicit statement of process.

In later stages, our goal is to automate the retrieval of relevant knowledge based on the monitored activities of knowledge workers. By following their actions and the resources they use, we hope to use a case-based approach to supporting just-in-time knowledge delivery. The challenge is that this will require new process representations that enable us to reason at multiple levels of abstraction, much as modern AI planning systems move among differing levels of abstraction.

3 Monitoring User Activity

As argued above, an agile approach to process-oriented knowledge management requires the ability to adapt to the user's style of thinking and working. While agile knowledge management systems can have top-down elements, the final process determination must lie with the user. To provide such adaptation, systems must monitor the user's interaction with her computer, and pay close attention to how she finds and uses data, information, and knowledge. In previous work, I have suggested building tools that "look over the user's shoulder" to monitor her work and use such monitoring as the basis for learning personalized processes. [10, 11]

3.1 Monitoring User Activity with the TaskTracer Suite

The Intelligent Information group at Oregon State has developed a suite of such tools, known as TaskTracer (http://eecs.oregonstate.edu/TaskTracer/). TaskTracer is a set of application listeners to which client programs can subscribe to receive notification of monitored events. [12] By default, the application listeners also echo all events to a MySQL database, providing a permanent record of the user's interaction with tracked applications. Because the TaskTracer system relies on Microsoft's Component Object Model (COM) technology [13], it works only on the Microsoft Windows platform. While a multi-platform tool would be preferable, many knowledge workers use the Windows platform and in some cases, similar data can be gathered on other platforms. In the remainder of this section, I will discuss the monitoring data we will use in learning how knowledge workers find information, and then incorporate it into their own work.

In this section, I present an example based on data collected as part of a test of the TaskTracer system at the University of Arizona. The test participants were all graduate students in the University's masters program in Management Information Systems and all were enrolled in a course in software design. The participants were asked to write a summary (shown in Figure 2) of Radio Frequency Identification (RFID) technology [14] for non-technical, corporate executives and were given 90 minutes to do so. Roughly halfway through the test, the participants were asked to also produce a Microsoft PowerPoint slide show (shown in Figure 3) for a brief presentation to the same executives. While this was simply a test of the technology and its installation, and not a carefully controlled experiment, it demonstrates what kind of data TaskTracer and related systems gather.

Current versions of TaskTracer record monitored events in two related database tables: `events` (a sample is shown in Table 1) and `body` (a sample is shown in Table 2). The portion of the events table shown in Table 1 includes window management (reported by the `Os` listener) and filesystem (reported by the `FileSystem` listener) events. Table 1 also shows an event reported by the Microsoft PowerPoint listener (an `Open` event, reported when the user opened the PowerPoint file with instructions for the test). While the events table also includes a column for recording the user name, it is not shown in Table 1. The events table records information about events — for the event data itself, the system uses the body table, a portion of which is shown in Table 2.

Table 1. The events table of the TaskTracer database, which records event metadata, including the window handle (*Window ID*), the type of event recorded (*Type*), the reporting event listener (*Listener ID*) and the listener version (*Listener version*), the ID of the event detail in the corresponding body table (*Body ID*, shown in Table 2), and a timestamp (*Time*)

id	Window ID	Type	Listener ID	Listener version	Body ID	Time
:	:	:	:	:	:	:
15	4260310	OsWindowCreated	Os	2	15	20050503 17:27:34
16	4260310	OsWindowFocus	Os	2	16	20050503 17:27:34
17	3473820	OsWindowCreated	Os	2	17	20050503 17:27:34
18	4260266	OsWindowCreated	Os	2	18	20050503 17:27:34
19	0	FileChange	FileSystem	2	19	20050503 17:27:35
20	0	FileChange	FileSystem	2	20	20050503 17:27:35
21	0	FileChange	FileSystem	2	21	20050503 17:27:35
22	0	FileChange	FileSystem	2	22	20050503 17:27:35
23	0	FileChange	FileSystem	2	23	20050503 17:27:35
24	4260310	Open	MsPowerPoint	2	24	20050503 17:27:35
25	5374476	OsWindowCreated	Os	2	25	20050503 17:27:35
26	5374476	OsWindowFocus	Os	2	26	20050503 17:27:35
27	4260310	OsWindowFocus	Os	2	27	20050503 17:27:38
28	3015086	OsWindowCreated	Os	2	28	20050503 17:27:45
29	5440012	OsWindowCreated	Os	2	29	20050503 17:27:51
30	3735972	OsWindowCreated	Os	2	30	20050503 17:27:58
31	4260310	Copy	Clipboard	2	31	20050503 17:27:58
:	:	:	:	:	:	:

Detailed event information is stored in snippets of XML that is recorded in the body table of the database, as shown in Table 2. The sample below has three window manager events, all of which include the specific window's handle in the HWND element. The BodyID column of the events table links into the body table as a foreign key.

Table 2. Event data recorded in the body table of the TaskTracer database. Events from the events table (Table 1) are matched with the body table through the BodyID column of the events table.

id	type	guts
1	TaskEvents. WindowEventArgs	<?xml version="1.0" encoding="utf-16"?> <WindowEventArgs xmlns:xsd= http://www.w3.org/2001/XMLSchema xmlns:xsi="http://www.w3.org/2001/XMLSchema-instance"> <HWND>5112150</HWND> <Caption /> </WindowEventArgs>
2	TaskEvents. WindowEventArgs	<?xml version="1.0" encoding="utf-16"?> <WindowEventArgs xmlns:xsd= "http://www.w3.org/2001/XMLSchema" xmlns:xsi= "http://www.w3.org/2001/XMLSchema-instance"> <HWND>5243270</HWND> <Caption>WindowsFormsParkingWindow</Caption> </WindowEventArgs>
3	TaskEvents. WindowEventArgs	<?xml version="1.0" encoding="utf-16"?> <WindowEventArgs xmlns:xsd= "http://www.w3.org/2001/XMLSchema" xmlns:xsi= "http://www.w3.org/2001/XMLSchema-instance"> <HWND>6685050</HWND> <Caption /> </WindowEventArgs>

3.2 Supplementing TaskTracer data

While TaskTracer does monitor Internet Explorer (but not other browser's, which lack IE's extensive COM support), a problem with the test installation prevented the IE events from being recorded. Because the Web browser is central to information-seeking efforts, we looked for data to complement the TaskTracer data with a record of Web activity. As most computer users know, Web browsers keep a list of visited Web sites (known as the browser's *history*) and most cache Web content locally to speed-up subsequent accesses to the same page. Each of the major Web browsers (i.e., Internet Explorer, Mozilla, Firefox, Netscape, Opera, and Safari) stores some history information, but there is no standard format and no consensus on what should be recorded in the history file. Forensic computer investigators have developed tools to process the history files of various browsers [15], which are often stored in non-standard binary formats, however. Because the test participants were asked to use Internet Explorer exclusively, and did so during a short time period, we were able to analyze the single Internet Explorer history file from each participant's computer.

Internet Explorer's history (named `index.dat`) is one of the most informative of browser history files and includes the URL of a browsed page, how the user arrived at the file (e.g., following and link or through a redirect), the Web server's reported modification time for the file, when the user visited the site, a link to the cached copy (if one exists), and the Web server's HTTP response header. A portion of this data is shown in Table 3, was extracted from the user's `index.dat` file by Red Cliff's Web

Historian [16], a forensic analysis tool. For researchers interested in studying information access and usage, Internet Explorer's history is especially helpful because it includes the path to the locally cached version, if a cached copy is available. Thus, researchers can reconstruct large portions of a Web user's experience by replaying the viewed pages. For those researching knowledge processes, the browser history file does hold one pitfall: the history of all open Internet Explorer windows is written into the same file, so the sequence of files shown in the history file is not strictly linear. TaskTracer does record the window handle associated with Internet Explorer events, making a purely sequential analysis feasible.

Table 3. A portion of the subject's Internet Explorer `index.dat` file, which shows each downloaded file's location (*URL Address*, which has had the server's address truncated in the table, for brevity), the Web server's timestamp for the file (*Modified Time*), when the user accessed the file (*Accessed Time*) and the location of the cache copy of the file (*Cached Files*). The `index.dat` file also includes the type of URL, whether the cached file has been deleted, and the HTTP response header sent to the browser, but these are not listed in the table.

URL Address	Modified Time	Accessed Time	Cached Files
/_layouts/1033/owsbrows.js	7/14/2003 23:05	5/6/2005 16:15	S1YFKTMJ\owsbrows[1].js
/_layouts/images/blank.gif	6/3/2002 13:37	5/6/2005 16:15	09A30TEV\blank[1].gif
/images/trans.gif	8/23/2004 16:31	5/6/2005 16:15	RQ061D5U\trans[1].gif
/_layouts/1033/ows.js	7/16/2003 19:06	5/6/2005 16:15	S1YFKTMJ\ows[1].js
/default.aspx		5/6/2005 16:15	KG3F3Z6Y\default[1].htm
/_layouts/images/navgradp.gif	7/31/2003 14:48	5/6/2005 16:15	S1YFKTMJ\navgradp[1].gif
/_layouts/images/vnavicon.gif	7/31/2003 14:48	5/6/2005 16:15	RQ061D5U\vnavicon[1].gif
/ecom.js	1/18/2005 16:13	5/6/2005 16:15	09A30TEV\ecom[1].js

We collected the TaskTracer and browser history data to mine it for knowledge-intensive processes, similarly to the model of Schwarz and Roth-Berghofer [7] but with a focus on learning the instantiated process, rather than the user's goals. Before we began our test, however, we recognized that mining processes without additional constraints would be very difficult. We see the low-level monitoring data as the instantiation of a set of tasks, which taken together, compose the processes of interest. Without higher-level input from users, however, we suspected that effective process mining would be intractable. Thus, we designed a tool that would allow users to associate documents (including their work product) with tasks they defined using a tool called Task Explorer (by analogy to Windows Explorer), shown in Figure 1. To use TaskExplorer, users define tasks by creating folders and then drag-and-drop documents or selected text onto the appropriate folder. TaskExplorer records analogs of user interface actions in a SQLServer database for later analysis. The database record is maintained even for deleted items, enabling researchers to see items that users create and delete.

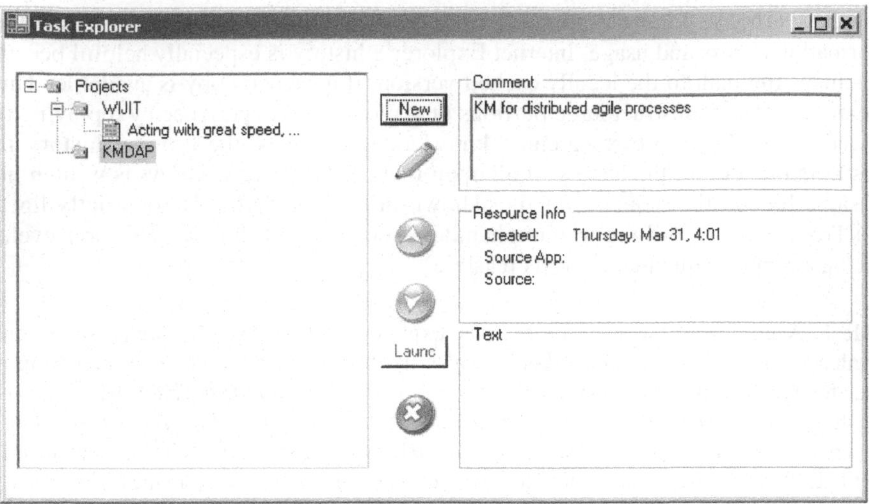

Fig. 1. The TaskExplorer interface, which shows user-defined task folders on the left and metadata, including user-defined comments, on the right. Using the buttons in the middle, the user can create new items, edit them, move them up or down in the order, launch the item's associated viewer, or delete an item.

A key element of the all of the gathered data — TaskTracer database records, Internet Explorer's history data, and the TaskExplorer database — is that every item is time-stamped with the client computer's clock. Thus, we can weave together a complete, ordered sequence of items. Moreover, in addition to the TaskTracer and browser history data, we also have the work produced by the test participants. At the test's outset, the participants were asked to write a report in Microsoft Word (Figure 2) and a PowerPoint slide show (Figure 3). With the data gathered from test and the work product, we have a fairly complete picture of how the participant

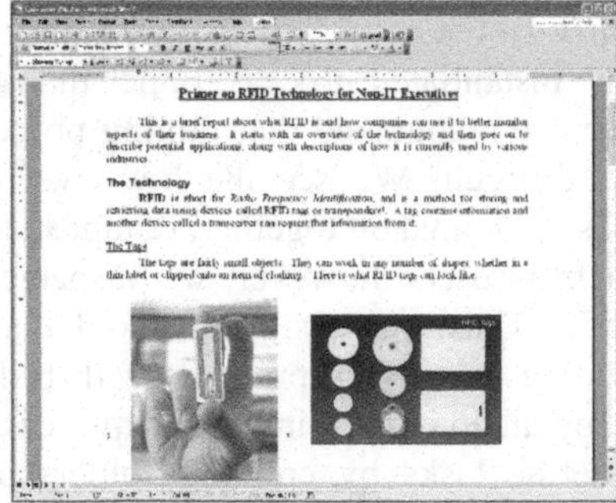

Fig. 2. One of the test participants created the above Microsoft Word document while authoring a report to corporate executives on the potential impact of RFID technology in the supply chain

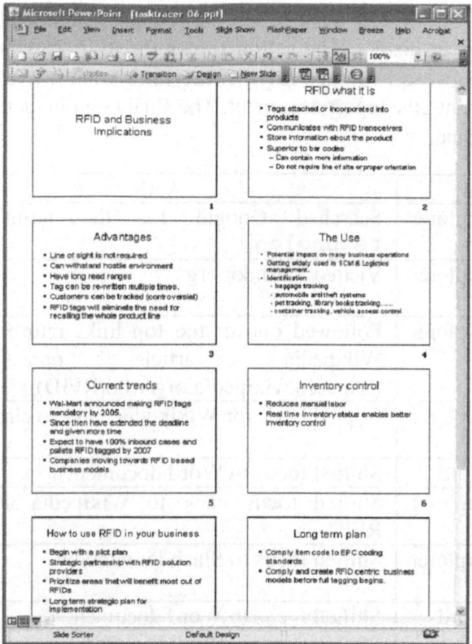

Fig. 3. The Microsoft PowerPoint document created by the test subject in response to a request to produce a short (five-minute) presentation to corporate executives on the impact of RFID technology on supply chain management

defined the task (based on folders created in TaskExplorer), gathered information from the Web (based on the Internet Explorer history), and used that information (based on TaskTracer's data on clipboard and application usage). The next step is to analyze the data to reveal the knowledge-intensive processes of interest.

While we have not yet completed the analysis, we have developed a plan for analyzing the data. First, we will interleave the data into a single ordered sequence, based on the timestamps of each item. A document can act as a *source*, a *sink*, or both. A Web form is a sink that consumes information as the user fills it out; the resulting page is a source. An e-mail that asks the recipient for information is a sink, while a document sent in a reply is a source. A document that was once a sink can become a source if it's later used in modifying a second document. Pipes, which represent user actions, connect sources and sinks. In the simple test we conducted, we asked users to create two closely related artifacts (i.e., the Word and PowerPoint documents) on a single topic, and to do so without interruption for other tasks. Our plan is to mine the collected data for patterns of sources, pipes, and sinks. For example, the participant mentioned earlier entered had the action sequence shown in Table 3 early on in the test.

Table 4 shows the user alternating between parallel sources (the Wikipedia and Slashdot) in the browser before choosing to link the Wikipedia entry on RFID to his

Table 4. A sequence of actions from a single test participant's data, which combines data from TaskTracer and the browser history. The action shows the user searching, following a search result link, alternating between two open Internet Explorer windows, copying a text selection and eventually pasting it into the report document. The final column identifies the action as part of a source, a sink, or a pipe.

Time	Window	Action	S, S, P?
16:18	Internet Explorer (IE #1)	Searched Google for the terms `RFID technology`	Source
16:18	Internet Explorer (IE #2)	Visited Slashdot.org	Source
16:21	Internet Explorer (IE #1)	Followed one of the top links returned to the Wikipedia's article on RFID (http://en.wikipedia.org/wiki/RFID)	Source
16:31	Internet Explorer (IE #1)	Copied URL for Wikipedia entry to clipboard	Pipe
16:31	Microsoft Word	Shifted focus to Word document	Sink
16:32	Internet Explorer (IE #1)	Shifted focus back to Wikipedia article on RFID	Source
16:32	Internet Explorer (IE #2)	Shifted focus to Slashdot window	Source
16:33	Microsoft Word	Shifted focus to Word document	Sink
16:33	Internet Explorer (IE #2)	Shifted focus to Slashdot window	Source
16:33	Internet Explorer (IE #2)	Navigated to Google, searched for terms `RFID tag`	Source
16:33	Internet Explorer (IE #1)	Shifted focus back to Wikipedia article on RFID	Source
16:33	Microsoft Word	Shifted focus to Word document	Sink
16:36	Microsoft Word	Pasted text defining RFID from Wikipedia article	Pipe

report. Despite switching to the Slashdot home page several times, the user never copied any portion of a Slashdot page and abandoned Slashdot in favor of a second Google search. This short action sequence makes several key points. First, we can conclude that Slashdot is not a good source for information on RFID — at least not for an audience of non-technical executives. (In another case, the abandonment of Slashdot might simply signal that it was an inappropriate source for the participant, but here I am confident that this participant was knowledgeable enough to read and follow Slashdot threads.) Second, Slashdot was not useful as a meta-source either, as the participant simply started over by entering Google's address into the address bar, rather than following a link from Slashdot. This coincides with one's intuition that Slashdot would be a poor source of information on the business prospects of RFID. Third, Wikipedia was useful for the definition it provided, but the bulk of the report (including a discussion of Wal-Mart's use of RFID) came from other sources. Wikipedia's entry might have helped enhance the participant's understanding, however, without resulting in a document modification. Until a neural implant version of TaskTracer is developed, we will not be able to observe such changes.

At this stage in our research, we have completed the first in a series of experiments designed to collect data on how people meet knowledge-intensive goals, e.g., writing a report on a new technology. We are currently work to extract simple patterns from sequences of sources, sinks, and connecting pipes to study information flows, which we will report on in follow-on publications.

4 Conclusions

Agile processes are a rational approach to applying processes in dynamic environments. As such, we should expect that traditional AI tools developed to operate in dynamic environments would offer guidance for newly developing process-oriented systems. In business, as in life, however, there are other agents, some with complementary goals, and some with competitive goals. Before we can study agile processes, we must develop the means to track user activity and analyze it for process-based use. By developing common process representation protocols for dynamic process and sharing tools for collecting such representations, we can create a shared base for research that will support not only the study of agile processes in situ, but also enable the development of next-generation process-oriented knowledge management systems. The TaskTracer suite offers a set of tools that, when coupled with other data sources, can gather the data needed for agile process inference — a first step in understanding process-oriented knowledge management "in the wild" of users' environments.

References

[1] J. Hendler, A. Tate, and M. Drummond, "AI planning: systems and techniques," in *AI Magazine*, vol. 11, pp. 61-77, 1990.

[2] E. Sacerdoti, "Planning in a hierarchy of abstraction spaces," in *Artificial Intelligence*, vol. 5, pp. 115-135, 1974.

[3] J. Allen, J. Hendler, and A. Tate, "Readings in Planning," Morgan Kaufmann, 1990.

[4] K. Beck, M. Beedle, A. v. Bennekum, A. Cockburn, W. Cunningham, M. Fowler, J. Grenning, J. Highsmith, A. Hunt, R. Jeffries, J. Kern, B. Marick, R. C. Martin, S. Mellor, K. Schwaber, J. Sutherland, and D. Thomas, "Manifesto for Agile Software Development," [Online document], 2001 [cited 2004 October 6], Available HTTP: http://www.agilemanifesto.org/

[5] IBM, "Rational Unified Process home page," [Online document], 2004 [cited 2004 October 6], Available HTTP: http://www-306.ibm.com/software/awdtools/rup/

[6] P. Kruchten, *The Rational Unified Process: An Introduction*, 3rd ed: Addison-Wesley, 2003.

[7] S. Schwarz and T. R. Roth-Berghofer, "Towards goal elicitation by user observation," presented at Workshop on Knowledge and Experience Management (FGWM 2003), Karlsruhe, Germany, 2003.

[8] L. v. Elst, F.-R. Aschoff, A. Bernardi, H. Maus, and S. Schwarz, "Weakly-structured Workflows for Knowledge-intensive Tasks: An Experimental Evaluation," presented at IEEE WETICE Workshop on Knowledge Management for Distributed Agile Processes: Models, Techniques, and Infrastructure (KMDAP '03), 2003.

[9] A. Aamodt and E. Plaza, "Case-based reasoning: Foundational issues, methodological variations, and system approaches," in *AI Communications*, vol. 7, pp. 39-52, 1994.

[10] K. D. Fenstermacher and M. Ginsburg, "A lightweight framework for client-side monitoring," in *IEEE Computer*, vol. 35, 2002.

[11] K. D. Fenstermacher and M. Ginsburg, "Mining client-side activity for personalization," presented at Fourth Workshop on Advanced Issues in Electronic Commerce and Web Information Systems (WECWIS), Newport Beach, CA, U.S.A., 2002.

[12] S. Stumpf, X. Bao, A. Dragunov, T. G. Dietterich, J. Herlocker, K. Johnsrude, L. Li, and J. Shen, "The TaskTracer system," presented at Twentieth National Conference on Artificial Intelligence (AAAI-05), Pitssburg, PA, U. S. A., 2005.

[13] Microsoft Corporation, "COM: Component Object Model Technologies," [Online document], 2005 [cited 2005 May 15], Available HTTP: http://www.microsoft.com/com/default.mspx

[14] WikiPedia, "RFID," [Online document], 2005 May 16, [cited 2005 May 16], Available HTTP: http://en.wikipedia.org/wiki/RFID

[15] K. J. Jones and R. Belani, "Web browser forensics, Part 1," [Online document], 2005 March 30, [cited 2005 May 16], Available HTTP: http://www.securityfocus.com/infocus/1827

[16] Red Cliff Consulting, "Tools overview," [Online document], 2005 March 29, [cited 2005 May 16], Available HTTP: http://www.red-cliff.com/index.php?fuseaction=tools.overview

The Impact of Educational Background on Design Knowledge Sharing During Pair Programming: An Empirical Study

Emilio Bellini[1], Gerardo Canfora[1], Aniello Cimitile[1], Felix Garcia[2], Mario Piattini[2], and Corrado Aaron Visaggio[1]

[1] RCOST- Research Centre on Software Technology,
University of Sannio, Italy
{bellini, canfora, cimitile, visaggio}@unisannio.it
[2] Alarcos Research Group, University of Castilla-La Mancha, Paseo de la Universidad, 4,
13071 Ciudad Real, Spain
{Felix.Garcia, Mario.Piattini}@uclm.es
http://alarcos.inf-cr.uclm.es/english/

Abstract. The management of knowledge in software processes is becoming a challenging concern for researchers and practitioners. Explicit knowledge can be formalized in many kinds of documents and rules, and consequently transferred in a number of manners. On the contrary, tacit knowledge cannot be formalized, because it is mainly retained in personal cognitive models and consists of individual capabilities of dealing with problems. The design of software systems requires a consistent deployment of tacit knowledge, and pair programming has shown great promises for helping to share knowledge between programmers. It is a common experience that programmers come not only from computer science and engineering curricula, but also from other education degrees, such as mathematics, natural sciences, and social sciences. In this case they attend proper specialist post graduation courses. We have executed an experiment in order to verify the relationship between educational background of pair's components and knowledge sharing throughout working in pairs while designing software systems.

1 Introduction

The management of knowledge when producing and maintaining software, both in the explicit and tacit form [1], is assuming a significant role in software development. Software processes require capabilities which are both technical (e.g., programming languages, network, database, and operating systems), and attitudinal (e.g., problem solving, decision making). Methods for measuring the former exist, generally by listing the skills and the related experience; current literature reports several attempts in this direction [2, 3]. The latter is harder to describe, especially from the perspective of either a project manager or a developer. The two forms of knowledge are commonly classified as explicit and tacit. Explicit knowledge can be formalized and transferred. Tacit knowledge regards the individual capability of solving problem, and it can be built basically *by doing* [5, 6, 7, 8]: applying explicit knowledge, registering personal observations, and making personal models for retaining it (*interiorization* in

K.-D. Althoff et al. (Eds.): WM 2005, LNAI 3782, pp. 455 – 465, 2005.

SEKI Model [4]). This kind of knowledge cannot be easily formalized and transferred, except for the dialogue. Software design asks for a continuous and significant application of tacit knowledge, due to the high abstraction that characterizes software design: as matter of fact, a software programmer becomes a software designer only after some years of practice.

A technique that helps sharing the knowledge is pair programming [10]; it is a practice of extreme programming [9], where two programmers, working side by side, develop and contemporarily review the same piece of code. In the past few years, due to the skill shortage, a scenario has become frequent in Italian software industry: not only computer scientists or computer engineers are called to develop software, but also graduates with different educational profiles (physics, mathematics, engineering, economics) after a period of adequate training. The educational background of the pair's components can affect knowledge transfer within the pair. In order to validate this idea, an experiment has been designed and executed, specially focusing on the design phase rather than on pure coding.

Similarly to pair programming, we name "pair designing" the practice where two designers work side by side at the same design document; one of the two actively edits the document whereas the second performs continuous review.

The research goal of this paper is*: to analyze a pair designing task with the purpose of evaluating how educational background affects the knowledge building within the pair from the viewpoint of the designer, in the context of an actual post graduate student project.*

The paper continues as follows. Section 2 discusses related work. Section 3 describes the experiment, while results are discussed in Section 4; Section 5 discusses the experimental threats. Finally, conclusions are drawn in Section 6.

2 Related Work

When the term 'pair programming' was not yet widespread, Nosek investigated *Collaborative Programming* [13]. Nosek executed an experiment with experienced programmers and it showed that collaborative programmers outperformed the individual programmers. Initially the attention of researchers has focussed mainly on quality and productivity, as in [14, 15, 20]. Recently, the target of pair programming investigation is turning to learning and knowledge transfer [21]. Williams and Kessler [11] found that pair programming fosters knowledge leveraging between the two programmers, particularly tacit knowledge. In [16], authors investigate, throughout an experiment, which are the knowledge needs to be addressed in order to implement effectively pair programming, when pair's components are distributed. Williams and Upchurch [17] examine the ways pair programming may enhance teaching and learning in computer science education. Some authors [18, 19] investigated the effects of pair programming on student performance in an introductory programming class. The main concerns emerging from the state of the art are two: first, the greatest part of the study involves students rather than professionals; second, the analyses accomplished are mainly qualitative instead of quantitative. To our best knowledge, however, no study has been published that addresses pair designing.

The current work is part of a family of experiments, aiming at evaluating the relationship between the practice of working in pairs applied to any phase of software process and knowledge building about the 'big picture' of the system. The results of the first experiment about the relationship between pair designing and knowledge leveraging were discussed in [12]. Two main outcomes were obtained. First, along all the experiment subjects who worked in pair showed a greater knowledge with respect to those who worked as singletons. Second, the knowledge building was more stable for pairs than for singletons: the knowledge growth of pairs can be predictable and repeatable within certain limits.

3 Experiment Description

The experiment was executed with the purpose of testing the following null hypothesis:

H_0: the difference in education between the pair's components does not affect the building of system knowledge realized by the pair's components.

The alternative hypothesis is:

H_1: the difference in education between the pair's components affects the building of system knowledge realized by the pair's components.

Subjects. The experiment was executed with students of the Master of Technologies of Software (MUTS) and Master of Management and Technologies of Software (MUTEGS), high education university courses for post-graduates, at University of Sannio (http://www.ing.unisannio.it/master/). Students of MUTS own a scientific graduation (engineering, mathematics, physics), whereas students of MUTEGS own an economic/humanistic graduation (economics, philology, literature, philosophy). Both the courses provide the same basic education in computer engineering (operating systems, programming languages, network, database, and software engineering), but MUTS students are specialized for developing and maintaining Software Systems, whereas MUTEGS students are trained for dealing with the economic and organizational issues of software lifecycle. The two Master courses are held contemporarily and both last one year, during which students attend theoretical classes and lab sessions, with the same professors and lecturers, develop a large and complex project in connection with an enterprise, participate to seminaries from international experts, perform a three month stage in software companies.

The subjects were organized as follows:

- 4 couples with one MUTS student and one MUTEGS student;
- 5 couples with two MUTS students;
- 5 couples with two MUTEGS students;
- the other 16 subjects, MUTS and MUTEGS, worked as solo designers.

All the groups were formed randomly.

Variables. System's knowledge represented the dependent variable and it was evaluated by grading a questionnaire, answered by subjects after having performed a maintenance task on the system. The questionnaires were evaluated in this way: each correct answer was evaluated 1; each incorrect answer was evaluated 0. The independent variables were the kinds of paired classes of subject's graduation: scientific with scientific, non-scientific with non-scientific, and scientific with non-scientific.

Rationale for the Sampling of the Population. Students of Software Engineering courses are suitable for such an experiment because they study software architecture and software system design. Furthermore they usually are employed as software architects or designers after the graduation. MUTS and MUTEGS students are a fine population's sample, considered that they experienced an actual project work during the overall master. Since the students have comparable curricula, there is not a relevant bias in the sample.

Assignment. In order to evaluate the knowledge built by doing while working on the system, the assignment for the subjects consisted of improving the design of the system. The design of the system was formalized in UML and included: textual specification of the system's requirements, two use cases diagrams, and two class diagrams (for a total of 15 classes). The design was developed by experimenters. Considered the time available, we preferred to avoid bulky documentation. The maintenance tasks were basically two: (i) reduce complexity, by erasing entities or relationships between entities not fundamental for understanding; and (ii) improve readability, by changing existing entities (use cases, actors, classes, methods), or adding new ones.

This kind of assignment was targeted at maximizing the knowledge built by doing; as matter of fact, maintenance needs the programmer to analyze in depth the system. The system design was realized by taking into account the knowledge of subjects, with the aim of making objects representative of the population. An excerpt of the documentation is provided in the appendix.

The Process. The process of the experimental run was the following:

- each subject studied documentation for 30 minutes, individually;
- each subject answered an entry questionnaire, individually, for about 15 minutes. The entry questionnaire was aimed at establishing the baseline, i.e. level of knowledge of the system before working on it;
- the pairs and the solo designers performed the maintenance tasks for 2 hours;
- each subject answered an exit questionnaire individually, in order to understand the knowledge built by practicing the maintenance in the two different ways, pair and solo.

Questionnaires. We prepared two questionnaires, QA and QB, in order to measure the dependent variable. Both the questionnaires were distributed as entry and exit questionnaire, so that each subject had randomly QA (or QB) at entry and, conversely, QB (or QA) at exit. This avoided that the results depended on the questionnaire itself. The questions concerned architectural and functional aspects of the system. One of the two questionnaires is shown in the appendix.

Although we would have liked to use a CASE tool, such as Rational Rose, or ArgoUML, we finally decided to use only pen and paper. The reason was that some subjects could be more familiar with this kind of tools and this could inject bias in the results. As consequence, we would have needed more time for preparation in order to equalize the ability of subjects to work with tools. In Table 1 the experimental design is provided.

Table 1. Experimental Design

<table>
<tr><th>Subjects</th><th>Treatment</th><th>Input</th><th>Output</th></tr>
<tr><td>4 MUTS
4 MUTEGS</td><td>Paired MUTS
MUTEGS</td><td rowspan="6">Requirement Specification;
Use case Diagram;
Class Diagram;
Entry questionnaire QA (or QB);
Exit questionnaire QB (or QA).</td><td rowspan="6">Modifications to Use Case Diagram and Class Diagram;
Answered entry questionnaire QA (or QB);
Answered exit questionnaire QB (or QA).</td></tr>
<tr><td>5 MUTEGS
5 MUTEGS</td><td>Paired MUTEGS
MUTEGS</td></tr>
<tr><td>5 MUTS
5 MUTS</td><td>Paired MUTS
MUTS</td></tr>
<tr><td>8 MUTS</td><td>Solo</td></tr>
<tr><td>8 MUTEGS</td><td>Solo</td></tr>
</table>

4 Preliminary Results

Table 2 shows the descriptive statistics of data. It appears that the pairs MUTS-MUTS obtained results better than all the other subjects. As matter of fact, the average is the greatest one, as well as the maximum and the minimum values. The pairs MUTS-MUTEGS obtained an average value close to that of the pairs MUTEGS-MUTEGS. This suggests that forming pairs with professionals having different background does not give benefits with respect to the pairs formed by people with 'non-scientific' background.

Table 2. Descriptive Statics

Subjects	**Avg**	**Standard Deviation**	**Max**	**min**	**moda**
MUTS MUTS (pairs)	5,8	1,75	9	4	4
MUTS MUTEGS (pairs)	4	0,76	5	3	4
MUTEGS MUTEGS (pairs)	3,9	1,59	7	1	3
MUTS (solo)	4,3	1,04	6	3	4
MUTEGS (solo)	5,1	1,55	7	3	4

The pairs MUTS-MUTS exhibit the greatest variation in results; but also MUTEGS-MUTEGS show high value of standard deviation. This suggests that by coupling individuals with the same background the individual potentialities can be stimulated more than by coupling subjects with different background.

A more surprising result is that solo MUTEGS performed the closest average to the pairs MUTS-MUTS (only 12% less) and anyway higher than the solo MUTS (about 21% more). This can be explained by considering that in the group of solo MUTEGS a few strong individualities were present: this appears evident form the high variance (the std dev = 1,55) and from individual results plotted in Fig.1.

The null hypothesis can be rejected with statistical significance, by fixing the p-level at 0.05. We executed Mann Whitney tests, as the samples' data had no normal distribution. In Table 3 each row denotes one of the tests we made. For example, row 1 shows the results of exit questionnaire of subjects working in pairs MUTS-MUTS compared with those of subjects working in pairs MUTS- MUTEGS; whereas row 6 shows the results of questionnaire QA compared with the results of questionnaire QB.

Table 3. Results of Statistical Tests

Tests	Rank Sum (a)	Rank Sum (b)	p-level	p-level 1 tail
MUTS-MUTS (a) MUTS-MUTEGS (b)	121,00	50,00	**0,020**	**0,020**
MUTS-MUTS (a) MUTEGS-MUTEGS (b)	135,00	75,00	**0,023**	-
MUTS-MUTEGS (a) MUTEGS-MUTEGS (b)	135,00	75,00	**0,020**	**0,023**
MUTS(a) MUTS-MUTS (b)	54,50	116,50	**0,049**	0,054
MUTEGS (a) MUTEGS-MUTEGS (b)	57,50	78,50	0,270	0,278

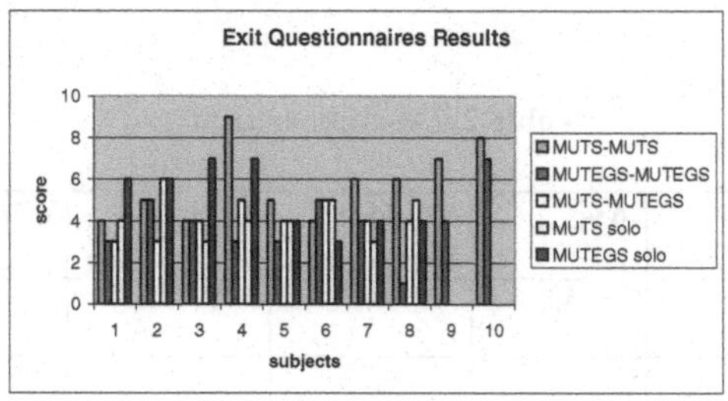

Fig. 1. Exit Questionnaire results

From Table 3 it is evident that: there is empirical evidence that the pairs MUTS MUTS performed better than the other pairs and solo designers, and the difference between the MUTEGS MUTEGS and the solo MUTEGS have not empirical evidence: that can be explained by the fact that the latter group had very strong individualities, as showed in Fig.1.

5 Experimental Threats

This section discusses the validity of the experiment, throughout the analysis of the experimental threats as classified in [26].

Threats to Construct Validity. The dependent variables aims at capturing the knowledge. We proposed questionnaire grading that surely cannot capture the overall aspects of the object to be measured. Tacit knowledge for its intrinsic nature is hard to formally describe and quantify. We consider what we measure an approximation of what we intend to measure.

Threats to Internal Validity. The following issues have been dealt with:

- Differences among subjects. Using a within-subjects design, error variance due to differences among subjects is reduced. In this experiment, students had a good degree in using UML. It is one of the main topics of their curriculum.
- Learning effects. The subjects were required to deal with only one run with only one assignment, so learning threat was cancelled.
- Fatigue effects. On average the experiment lasted a time short enough that fatigue was not very relevant. As a confirmation, the students asked for longer time to accomplish better the assignment.
- Persistence effects. In order to avoid persistence effects, the experiment was run with subjects who had never done a similar experiment.
- Subject motivation. The participants were volunteer, in order to help us in our research. We motivated students to participate in the experiment, explaining to them that they were learning a practice that should be useful in their professional career.
- The experimental package. The results of the run were independent from the experimental package, as showed in Table 4. We made a Mann Whitney test with the p-level fixed at 0.05, and there is no evidence that the differences due to the questionnaires were statistically significant.

Table 4. Testing the independency from the questionnaires

Test Between	Rank Sum 1	Rank Sum 2	p-level
Questionnaire A (1) Questionnaire B (2) in the experiment	540,00	406,00	0,161

Threats to External Validity. Two threats of validity have been identified which limit the possibility of applying generalization:

- Materials and tasks used. In the experiment we have used System design's documentation prepared by experimenters. The system showed a discrete degree of complexity, because it describes an existing system.
- Subjects. Students play a very important role in the experimentation in software engineering, as pointed out in [23]. In situations in which the tasks to perform do not require industrial experience the experimentation with students is viable [24].

Randomization of Sample. In order to accept the outcomes of the experiment as valid, it is necessary to make sure that there are not relevant differences in the samples to compare: the samples of solos and pairs have to be equivalent. If some differences on the entry questionnaires are detected, the randomization was not accomplished correctly. Table 5 shows this analysis for the experiment.

Mann-Whitney's method was used in all the tests because the data of samples were not normally distributed and the p-level threshold value was fixed at 5%.

The tests show that the MUTS subjects working as solos and those working in the pairs did not present significant differences at the entry questionnaire; similarly, the MUTEGS subjects of the solos' set and those of the pairs' set did not present significant differences. It is possible to conclude that the randomization was realized correctly.

Table 5. Testing the randomization of samples

Test Between	Rank Sum 1	Rank Sum 2	p-level
Entry Questionnaires of MUTS Pairs sample (1) MUTS Solos sample (2)	171,000	39,000	0,214768
Entry Questionnaires of MUTEGS Pairs sample(1) MUTEGS Solos sample(2)	112,000	59,000	0,130919

6 Conclusion

A growing interest in the software engineering community is turning toward agile practices, such as pair programming. Moreover, a lack of experimental validation of supposed benefits constitutes a main concern. Pair programming is expected to foster knowledge leveraging between pair's components. We have applied pair programming to the design phase, naming it pair designing. We have performed an experiment in order to validate how different educational backgrounds of the designers forming the pair can affect the knowledge leveraging.

The main conclusions follow:

- Forming pairs with individuals with the same educational background emphasizes the expected benefits of pair designing. Coupling a person with a scientific background and one with a non-scientific background does not seem to improve the latter but to make worst the former. We have evidence of this outcome.
- The individual can apprehend a lot by working alone, but this event is related to the single person; cannot be generalized.
- The tacit knowledge involved in the design is more articulated and complex than the programming knowledge, because concerns different levels of abstraction and includes also the consciousness of the implementation. Thus the scope of pair designing in terms of knowledge diffusion is wider than the one of pair programming.

The experiment owns an (apparent) point of weakness: it is not executed in industrial setting. Students play a very important role in the experimentation in software engineering: in situations in which the tasks to perform do not require industrial experience the experimentation with students is viable [22, 23, 24, 25]. The experiment owns also a point of strength: the number of subjects is approximately 50, and it sounds to us discretely valuable for statistical dependability. Some limitations of the work should deserve a major discussion, but due to matter of space, it is possible only list them: (i) knowledge building is influenced by many other factors of individuals, such as: learning styles, competence, and experience, and (ii) it should be useful to understand deeply the process of knowledge construction in the pair's components, that this study does not address.

Bibliography

[1] IEEE Software Special Issue on Knowledge Management, IEEE Computer Society, 3 (19), 2002.

[2] W. J. Hallinan, *"Improving Software Engineering practice through competency based personnel reviews"*, Master Thesis, College of Graduated Studies, University of Idaho, 2001.

[3] G. Klein, J. J. Jiang, and D. B. Tesch, *"Wanted: Project teams with a blend of IS Professional orientations"*, Communications of the ACM, ACM, 45 (6), 2002.

[4] I. Nonaka, *"A dynamic theory of organizational knowledge creation"*, Organization Science, 5, 1994.

[5] F. Blackler, "Knowledge, Knowledge Work and Organizations: An Overview and Interpretation.", Organization Studies, SAGE Publications, 16 (6),1995.

[6] Y. Engeström, "Developmental Work Research: Reconstructing Expertise through Expansive Learning", in (eds). Nurminen M. and Weir G., Human Jobs and Computer Intefaces, North Holland, Netherlands: Elsevier, 1991.

[7] F. Blackler, *"Knowledge and the Theory of Organizations: Organizations as Activity Systems and the Reframing of Management"*, Journal of Management Studies, Blackwell Publishing, *30* (6), 1993.

[8] C. W. Choo, *The Knowing Organization*, Oxford University Press, 1998.

[9] K. Beck, *Extreme Programming Explained: embrace change*, Reading, Massachusetts, Addison-Wesley, 2000.

[10] http://www.pairprogramming.com/.

[11] L. Williams and B. Kessler, *"The Effects of "Pair-Pressure" and "Pair-Learning""*, proc. of 13th Conference on Software Engineering Education and Training , IEEE Computer Society ,2000 .

[12] G. Canfora, A. Cimitile, and C. A. Visaggio, *"Working in pairs as a means for design knowledge building: an empirical study"*, IEEE International Workshop on Program Comprehension, IEEE computer Society, 2004.

[13] J.T. Nosek, *"The case for collaborative programming"*, Communication of ACM, ACM, 41(3), 1998.

[14] J. Nawrocki and A. Wojciechowski, *"Experimental Evaluation of Pair Programming"*, proc. of European Software Control and Metrics, 2001.

[15] L. Williams, W. Cunningham, R. Jeffries, and R. R. Kessler, *'Straightening the case for pair programming'*, IEEE Software, IEEE Computer Society, 17(4), 2000.

[16] G. Canfora, A.Cimitile, and C.A. Visaggio, *"Lessons learned about Distributed Pair programming: what are the knowledge needs to address?"*, proc. of Knowledge Management of Distributed Agile Process-WETICE, IEEE Computer Society, 2003.

[17] L. Williams and R. L. UpChurch, "*In Support of Student Pair-Programming*", proc. of the thirty-second SIGCSE technical symposium on Computer Science Education, ACM, 2001.

[18] C. McDowell, L. Werner, H. Bullock, and J. Fernald, "*The Effects of Pair Programming on Performance in an introductory Programming Course*", proc. of the 33rd Technical Symposium on Computer Science Education, ACM, 2002.

[19] T. VanDerGrift, "*Coupling Pair Programming and Writing: Learning About Students' Perceptions and Processes*" proc. of SIGCSE, ACM, 2004.

[20] L. A. Williams, *The Collaborative Software Process PhD Dissertation*, in Department of Computer Science. Salt Lake City, UT: University of Utah, 2000.

[21] G. B. Foresythe, J. Hedlund, S. Snook, J. A. Horvath, W.M. Williams, R.C. Bullis, M. Dennis, and R. Sternberg, "*Construct validation of tacit Knowledge for military Leadership*", Annual Meeting of the American Education Research Association, 1998.

[22] J. Carver, L. Jaccheri, S. Morasca, and F. Shull, "*Using Empirical Studies during Software Courses*". Experimental Software Engineering Research Network 2001-2003. LNCS 2765, 2003.

[23] B. Kitchenham, S. Pfleeger, L. Pickard, P. Jones, D. Hoaglin, K. El Emam, J. and Rosenberg, "*Preliminary Guidelines for Empirical Research in Software Engineering*". IEEE Transactions on Software Engineering, IEEE Computer Society, 28 (8), 2002.

[24] M. Höst, B. Regnell, and C. Wholin, "*Using Students as Subjects – A comparative Study of Students & Professionals in Lead-Time Impact Assessment*", proc. of 4th Conference on Empirical Assessment & Evaluation in Software Engineering (EASE), 2000.

[25] V. Basili, F. Shull, and F. Lanubile, "*Building Knowledge Through Families of Experiments*". IEEE Transactions on Software Engineering, IEEE Computer Society, 25 (4), 1999.

[26] Wohlin, C., Runeson, P., Höst, M., Ohlsson, M.C., Regnell, B., Wesslén, A., Experimentation in Software Engineering: An Introduction, Kluwer-Springer, 2000.

Appendix

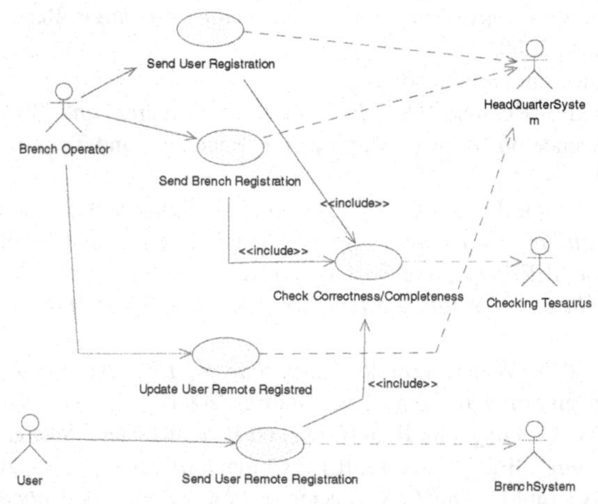

Fig. 2. Exemplar Use Case

Table 6. Excerpt of Use Case Specification

Use Case	Send User Registration
Description	The Branch operator inserts data in the registration form, provided by the user. Validation of the form is launched.
Exceptions	The form is not correct or complete. The sending of data is successfulness.
Actors	BrenchOperator, HeadQuarterSystem.
Use Case Extends	Nn
Use Case Uses	Check Correctness/Completeness
Use Case Inputs	Name, address, offered books list (in case the user is a vendor) with specifications: title, author, publisher, language, publishing year, ISBN.
Use Case Outputs	Recording of data of the new user.
Criterion of Acceptance	Data of the new user are stored in the database of the Local Branch.
Related Expectations	Database management system. Correctness and completeness checks. Data sending to the Headquarter.
Related Reqs/ Use Cases	Check Correctness/Completeness

Table 7. Questionnaire QB

1.Could Remote Registration of User (User Remote Registration Sending) extend local user registration (User registration Sending)?		
a. Yes	b. No and it does not make sense	c. Possible, with proper modifications
2. Does the updating of user data (User Remote Registered Updating) require the correctness and completeness check (Correctness/Completeness Checker)?		
a. Yes	b. No and it does not make sense	c. Possible, with proper modifications
3. Could use cases Notification of Transaction To Buyer and Notification of Transaction To Branch be merged in one use case?		
a. Yes	b. No and it does not make sense	c. Possible, with proper modifications
4. Could the use case Update Database extends the use case Local Book Search?		
a. Yes	b. No and it does not make sense	c. Possible, with proper modifications
5.Given a transaction, can information concerning vendor be obtained through the Book (object)?		
a. Yes	b. No and it does not make sense	c. Possible, with proper modifications
6. A (object) Branch Operator must have executed at least one operation, otherwise it does not exist in the System.		
a. True	b. False	c. This information is not provided by documentation.
7. It is possible to obtain the list of registered users in a local branch through Data contained in a Branch (object).		
a. True	b. False	c. This information is not provided by documentation.
8. DataHandler (object) helps query the Database.		
a. True	b. False	c. This information is not provided by documentation.
9. Checker (object) verifies if all the fields of the form are filled in.		
a. True	b. False	c. This information is not provided by documentation.
10. The user interface is provided only for the remote part of the system.		
a. True	b. False	c. This information is not provided by documentation.

Knowledge Management and Business Intelligence (KMBI 2005)

Bodo Rieger

Institut für Informationsmanagement und Unternehmensführung,
Universität Osnabrück,
Katharinenstr. 3, 49069 Osnabrück, Germany
brieger@uos.de

Workshop Description

Over the past years, the term business intelligence (BI) accompanied a change of focus within management support systems (MSS). Since the early 1980s MSS established as a concept for integrated reporting and analysis tools to support management tasks, but primarily in a passive, retrieval oriented way and based on past data. BI, however, promoted an active, model-based and prospective approach. In BI, intelligence was often defined as the discovery and explanation of hidden, inherent and decision-relevant contexts in large amounts of business and economic data. In an enhanced view, the subsequent phases of business decision processes, e.g. in strategic planning and management, were also included. The successful implementation of BI increasingly required the systematic consideration and professional processing of knowledge types and sources, which so far had only been developed sparse, for example

- to effectively represent and distribute the BI findings, both factual and model-like cognitions,
- to instrumentally apply these cognitions to the modeling of decision support systems (DSS),
- to effectively customize sophisticated methods like data mining or forecasting, and
- to support the valid derivation and interpretation of action-oriented cognitions.

In companies, this prevailing qualitative knowledge of facts and processes is typically distributed on groups of employees, who are organizationally seperated, and concerning business processes, are less integrated. Examples are on the one hand staff divisions of IT and operations research and on the other hand heads of the marketing & sales department. To realize an effective and efficient success of business intelligence in terms of business performance management (BPM), the establishment of any kind of integrative, (inter)active platform of information and communication, capable to manage qualitative knowledge, seems to be essential.

Both preceding workshops on WM'2001 and WM'2003 already had evinced the way how concepts and methods of knowledge management could be applied successfully to support similar problems and tasks of the abovementioned first MSS generation. Thus, the goal of the subsequent workshop on WM 2005 was to extend the spectrum of the "integration of knowledge management and MSS" to the focus of business intelligence.

K.-D. Althoff et al. (Eds.): WM 2005, LNAI 3782, pp. 466 – 468, 2005.

The first contribution [1] structured potential concepts of integration in an application-oriented way. Therefore, three levels of integration were outlined and put into a sequence of migration:

1. A horizontal integration of the BI- and the knowledge management system in a joint user interface.
2. Providing the content of knowledge management systems for BI processes by storing the related metadata into a data warehouse.
3. Distribution and re-utilization of BI analysis and BI analysis models by a knowledge management system

The second contribution [2] presented a knowledge-management-based concept for the integration of enterprise resource planning (ERP)-processes and BI-processes in order to improve MSS-assistance during the initial phase of identifying relevant information sources. Methodologically, this coupling of the ERP- and BI-processes is to be enabled by an ontology-based dynamic mapping of concrete and abstracting process parameters.

The subsequent contribution [3] described an integrated application of Knowledge Discovery in Databases (KDD), related to practical problems. The authors developed a decision table based framework to connect KDD processes with business intelligence system implementations and a knowledge management strategy. The ability of decision tables to offer a highly intuitive visualization of the extracted knowledge was shown by a series of real-life credit scoring cases.

Being an important enabling factor for the mentioned task of integration between knowledge management and business intelligence, the following contribution [4] presented an enabling method for the purposeful distribution of unstructured textual information to decision makers. Therefore, an evaluation environment was developed for the selection of an appropriate classification method as a filter for a user-oriented information supply of unstructured data.

Following the intention of the workshop two presentations were selected for extended contributions in these post-conference proceedings:

Firstly, the KMBI 2005 invited speaker *Oliver Frölich* and his co-authors [5] introduce a basic method enabling the integration of knowledge management and business intelligence. The authors developed a solution for the extraction of semi-structured information from public information sources like the World Wide Web and the integration of these information in web intelligence applications.

Finally, *Christophe Mues et al.* [6] present an extended version of their contribution about the connection of KDD with business intelligence and knowledge management strategies [3]. This contribution focuses on the use of neural network rule extraction and the visualization of extracted rules using decision tables. The authors compare the neural network rule extraction algorithms Neurolinear and Neurorule and discuss implementation strategies based on decision tables.

Workshop Organizers

Prof. Dr.-Ing. Bodo Rieger (Chair)
Institut für Informationsmanagement
und Unternehmensführung (IMU)
Universität Osnabrück
49069 Osnabrück, Germany
brieger@uos.de

Dipl.-Kfm. Markus Gelhoet
Institut für Informationsmanagement
und Unternehmensführung (IMU)
Universität Osnabrück
49069 Osnabrück, Germany
mgelhoet@uos.de

Program Committee

- Dr. Wolfgang Behme, Continental AG, Hannover
- Prof. Dr. Peter Chamoni, University of Duisburg
- Prof. Dr. Dieter Ehrenberg, University of Leipzig
- Prof. Dr. Norbert Gronau, University of Potsdam
- Prof. Dr. Roland Gabriel, University of Bochum
- PD Dr. Peter Gluchowski, University of Düsseldorf
- Reiner Gratzfeld, Henkel KGaA, Düsseldorf
- Prof. Dr. Wilhelm Hummeltenberg, University of Hamburg
- Dr. Bernd-Ulrich Kaiser, Bayer AG Leverkusen
- Prof. Dr. Dimitris Karagiannis, WU Vienna
- Prof. Dr. Hans-Georg Kemper, University of Stuttgart
- Prof. Dr.-Ing. Peter Lehmann, Hochschule der Medien Stuttgart
- PD Dr. Wolfgang Martin, independent analyst, Annecy, France
- Dr. Harry Mucksch, IT-Beratung und Services, Apen
- Prof. Dr. Wolfgang Uhr, TU Dresden
- Dr. Eitel von Maur, University of St. Gallen, Suisse

June 2005 *Bodo Rieger, Markus Gelhoet*

References

1. Baars, H.: Integration von Wissensmanagement- und Business-Intelligence-Systemen – Potenziale. In: Althoff, K., Dengel, A., Bergmann, R., Nick, M., Roth-Berghofer, T. (eds.): WM2005: Professional Knowledge Management – Experiences and Visions. April 10-13, 2005 in Kaiserslautern. Deutsches Forschungszentrum für Künstliche Intelligenz DFKI GmbH (2005) 429-433
2. Felden, C., Kilimann, D.: Aufbau einer Testumgebung zur Evaluation von Verfahren zur Textklassifikation. In: Althoff, K., Dengel, A., Bergmann, R., Nick, M., Roth-Berghofer, T. (eds.): WM2005: Professional Knowledge Management – Experiences and Visions. April 10-13, 2005 in Kaiserslautern. Deutsches Forschungszentrum für Künstliche Intelligenz DFKI GmbH (2005) 444-448
3. Mues, C., Baesens, B., Vanthienen, J.: From Knowledge Discovery to Implementation: Developing Business Intelligence Systems using Decision Tables. In: Althoff, K., Dengel, A., Bergmann, R., Nick, M., Roth-Berghofer, T. (eds.): WM2005: Professional Knowledge Management – Experiences and Visions. April 10-13, 2005 in Kaiserslautern. Deutsches Forschungszentrum für Künstliche Intelligenz DFKI GmbH (2005) 439-443
4. Rieger, B., Wolters, M.: Wissensmanagement-basierte Kopplung von ERP- und BI-Prozessen. In: Althoff, K., Dengel, A., Bergmann, R., Nick, M., Roth-Berghofer, T. (eds.): WM2005: Professional Knowledge Management – Experiences and Visions. April 10-13, 2005 in Kaiserslautern. Deutsches Forschungszentrum für Künstliche Intelligenz DFKI GmbH (2005) 434-438
5. Baumgartner, R., Frölich, O., Gottlob, G., Herzog, M., Lehmann, P.: Integrating Semi-Structured Data into Business Applications: a Web Intelligence Example, this volume (2005)
6. Mues, C., Baesens, B., Setiono, R., Vanthienen, J. : From Knowledge Discovery to Implementation: a Business Intelligence Approach using Neural Network Rule Extraction and Decision Tables, this volume (2005)

Integrating Semi-structured Data into Business Applications: A Web Intelligence Example

Robert Baumgartner[1], Oliver Frölich[1], Georg Gottlob[1], Marcus Herzog[1], and Peter Lehmann[2]

[1] DBAI, Institute for Information Systems,
Vienna Technical University,
Favoritenstr. 9, A-1040 Vienna, Austria
{gottlob, froelich, baumgart, herzog}@dbai.tuwien.ac.at
[2] Department of Information and Communication,
Hochschule der Medien, Fachhochschule Stuttgart,
Wolframstr. 32, D-70191 Stuttgart, Germany
lehmann@hdm-stuttgart.de

Abstract. The World Wide Web, representing a universe of knowledge, provides public domain information about market developments and competitor activities on the market. This information is becoming more and more a critical success factor for enterprises and can be retrieved for example from Web sites or online shops. The extraction from these semi-structured information sources is mostly done manually and is very time consuming. Therefore, powerful and user-friendly tools for extracting and integrating information from various different Web sources, or in general, various heterogeneous semi-structured data sources are needed. In this paper we describe a solution how data from public information sources, in particular from the World Wide Web, can be retrieved and normalized to structured data formats automatically. We also illustrate how this data can be automatically integrated afterwards in – often complex – Web Intelligence applications.

1 Introduction

1.1 Motivation and Distinction of Terms

Today, business management is interested in increasing the internal data retrieval speed because companies from all branches and of all sizes are forced nowadays to make operative decisions within days or even hours – just a few decades ago, similar decisions took weeks or months [1]. At the same time, the external data sources considered should be broadened to improve information quality. This fast, high-quality data is also needed to satisfy increasing investor demands for transparency, and to satisfy today's better informed customers. Fortunately, new technologies like Business Intelligence systems and the internet are available to supply this data. Furthermore, the growing relevance of the internet in developed and developing countries creates new and dynamic sales channels and business opportunities.

K.-D. Althoff et al. (Eds.): WM 2005, LNAI 3782, pp. 469 – 482, 2005.

Based on the described competitive pressure, a systematic observation of competitor activities becomes a critical success factor for business to be able to early identify chances in the market, to anticipate competitor activities, to recognize new and potential competitors, to learn from errors and success stories of competitors, and to validate and enhance own strategic goals, processes and products.

This process of collecting and analyzing information about competitors on the market is called "competitive intelligence" or "competitive analysis" [2],[3]. Nowadays, a lot of basic information about competitors can be retrieved legally from public information sources (public domain information[1]), such as Web sites, annual reports, press releases or public data bases.

Over the last 10 years, the term "Business Intelligence" (BI) has developed from an ambiguously used buzzword to a well-defined, real market. Also, the term BI is often used as a method box for collecting, representing and analyzing enterprise data to support decision makers. Taking a closer look at the word "intelligence", synonyms such as "knowledge, message, reconnaissance, clarification" can be found in a

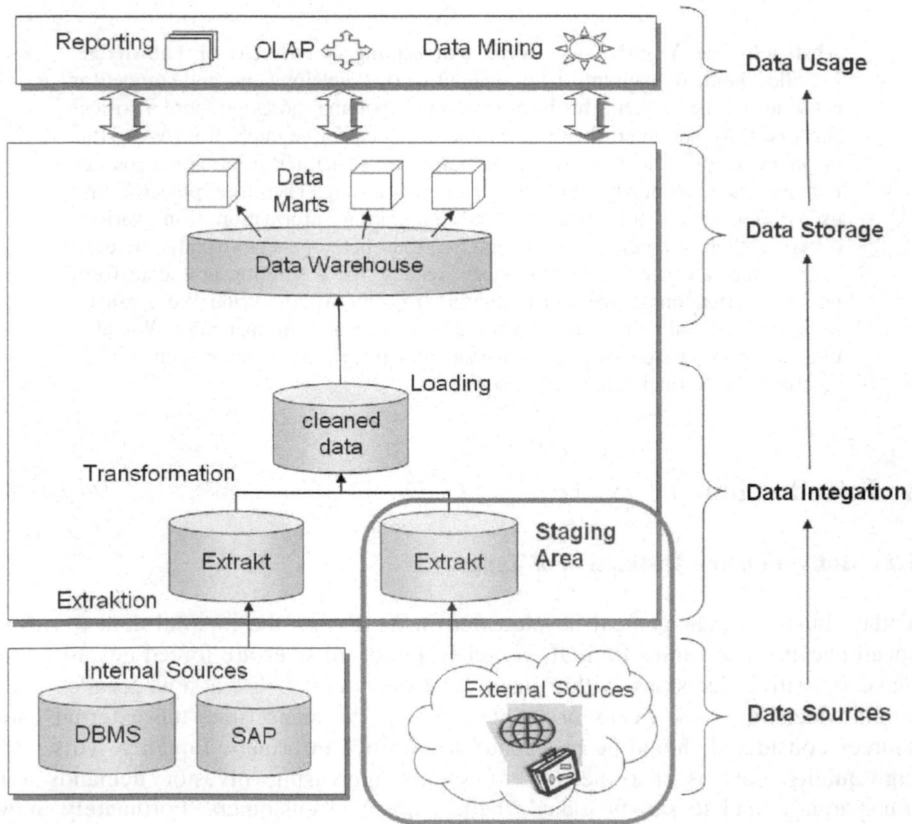

Fig. 1. The Business Intelligence reference process

[1] See [2], p. 59.

dictionary[2]. Thus, in the further course of this paper, "Business Intelligence" will be understood as a process providing better insight in a company and its chains of actions.

The Business Intelligence process covers three main process steps: *data integration*, *data storage* and *data usage* (see fig.1).

Data integration covers methods to extract data from internal or external data sources such as ERP systems[3] or database systems. The data is transferred into a processing area allowing further data transformations like data "cleaning" and data normalization. A load process contains a scheduler which regularly (e.g. daily, weekly, or monthly) uploads the processed data into the final data base storage, the data warehouse.

Data storage in a data warehouse: the basic idea of a data warehouse is to store the relevant data for decision makers in a dedicated, homogeneous database. An important characteristic of the data warehouse is the integration of heterogeneous, distributed, internal and external data. This covers the physical storage of data in a single, centralized data pool, and it also covers the subject-oriented clustering of data organized by business processes, such as sales, production, or finance. The subject oriented organization of data is called a data mart.

Data usage: to support decision making, data in a data warehouse has to be well-organized to fulfill different end-user requirements: predefined reporting for occasional users, ad-hoc data analysis for knowledge workers, or data mining for data analysts.

For the term "Web Intelligence" (WI), a lot of definitions exist, differing in focus and level of specificity. Soon after the World Wide Web started in the early 1990´s, the term WI appeared in the meaning of collecting information about Web page visitor behaviour *(e.g. What items does he/she click on? What Links does he/she follow?)* and the conclusion of a visitor's preferences and interests from this data to create a visitor's profile [4]. Later, the Web Intelligence Consortium[4] (WIC) defined WI as the key technology for the intelligent Web-based business. Combining research results from the fields of Artificial Intelligence (AI) and advanced Information Technology, the WIC defined 9 key topics in the area of WI, including Web mining, Web agents, Knowledge Management and Web information retrieval. In the further course of this paper, we will understand the term "Web Intelligence" in a more specific way: Connecting the terms Business Intelligence and Web Intelligence, WI can be understood as *Business Intelligence based on information from the Web*.

1.2 Problem Definition

Powerful tools for Extracting, Transforming and Loading (ETL-tools) data from source systems into a data warehouse are available today. They support the data extraction from *internal* applications in an efficient way. But there is also a growing need to integrate *external* data, such as market information, into these systems. The World Wide Web, the largest database on earth, holds a huge amount of relevant information. Unfortunately, this data exists in formats intended for human users.

---

[2] See for example http://dict.leo.org.

[3] ERP stands for Enterprise Resource Planning. An example of an ERP system is SAP R/3.

[4] See http://wi-consortium.org. The WIC is an international non-profit organization.

Thus, it cannot be easily processed by computer programs. Advanced data extraction and information integration techniques are required to process Web data automatically. Increasing demand for such data leads to the question of how this information can be extracted, transformed to a semantically useful structure, and integrated with a "Web-ETL" process into a Business Intelligence system using Web Intelligence. A solution proposition to this problem will be illustrated in chapter 2.

2 The Lixto Software Suite

2.1 General Overview

The *Lixto Suite* solution provides tools to access, extract, transform, and deliver information from various semi-structured sources like Web pages to various customer systems. The Lixto software is 100% based on Java technology and standards like XML schema, XSLT, SOAP and J2EE. Internally, the software uses the logic-based data extraction language ELOG [5]. In this chapter, we successively describe the process steps for creating and delivering structured data from semi-structured sources.

At first, so-called *wrappers* are generated. Dynamically and independently, these "intelligent"[5] software agents extract and translate all relevant information from HTML Web pages to a structured XML format that can be queried and processed by other programs. With Lixto, *wrappers* are generated in a graphical user interface with a few mouse clicks. Thus, no special programming knowledge is needed, and *wrappers* can be generated by non-technical personnel. Wrapper agents are typically generated by employees with the relevant business expertise for the project, e.g. from a company's marketing department.

In a second step, XML data generated by wrappers is processed in the *Lixto Transformation Server* [6], the run-time environment for Lixto wrapper agents. A wrapper in the Transformation Server retrieves the Web data automatically, with no developer interaction, based on events. Events are for example a Web page content change, or a defined schedule, such as Web data retrieval *every hour or every 5 minutes.* Additionally, the Lixto Transformation Server can combine, transform and re-format data from *different* wrappers. The Transformation Server also supports the run-time administration and supervision of the whole process. For example, if a wrapper cannot extract data from a specific Web site because the Web server is down, the wrapper generates an error message for the administrator.

Finally, the Transformation Server delivers the extracted, aggregated information into the desired formats to other Business Intelligence systems such as SAP Business Information Warehouse or Microsoft Analysis Server. Also, the Transformation Server interactively communicates with these systems using various interfaces, such as special database formats, XML messaging, and Web services.

2.2 Extracting Data from External, Semi-structured Sources

Creating a wrapper with Lixto starts by highlighting the relevant information with two mouse clicks in a standard internet browser window. Lixto then marks the data in a

[5] See also chapter 2.1.

different colour. Conditions can be defined, allowing the program to identify the desired data even if the structure of the Web page slightly changes. Fig. 2 shows an example: the share prices from the companies listed in the German share index DAX are to be extracted from the Web site *finance.yahoo.de.*

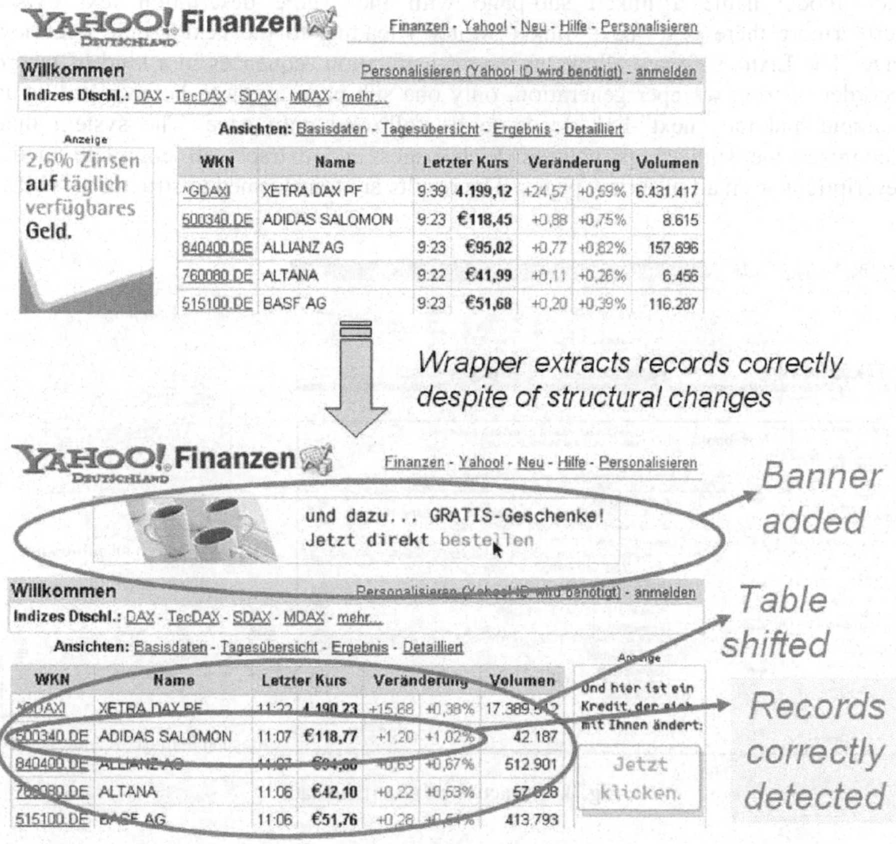

Fig. 2. Wrapper robustness

After a wrapper agent was successfully generated, the layout of the Web site changed after some weeks: the table with the quoted stocks moved from left to right, and additional banners were added. The existing wrapper still extracts all relevant information from the Web site. For a wrapper, an internet page is an HTML tree structure. A wrapper does not extract just the text from a specified HTML tree node, but uses "intelligent" conditions, so-called *logical patterns*. For the wrapper of fig. 2, such conditions could be *„the relevant area should contain the €-symbol in each line"* or *"some specified company's names should occur"* (these names are stored in a system database). For the logical pattern comprised of the conditions, the software searches for the best match within the HTML tree using heuristic methods. So a very high robustness to changes within Web pages can be achieved for the wrapper agents.

Other capabilities of the Lixto software during the wrapper generation process are shown in fig. 3. Here, information about notebooks is to be extracted from the online shop *shop.mediamarkt.de*. Of special interest shall be the information about *manufacturer*, *model name*, *model price* and *model description*. On the overview page shown in fig. 3, only the first two lines of the *model description* are displayed. For each model name a linked sub-page with the whole description text exists. Furthermore there is a "next"-link ("weiter") leading to the next article overview page. The Lixto Software allows to record navigation sequences in a kind of macro recorder. During wrapper generation, only one sub-page needs to be accessed as an example and the "next"-link needs to be followed only once. The system then recognizes the similarly structured Web pages and extracts all complete model descriptions from all overview pages. The results are transformed to structured XML.

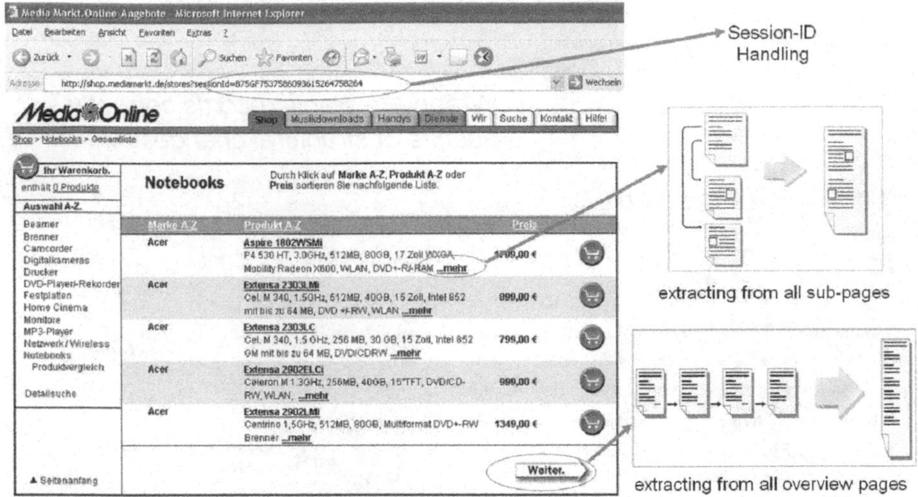

Fig. 3. Extraction of all article data

In addition, the wrapper agents support dynamic handling of session IDs, automatic logon to password-protected pages, filling in form pages and processing the extraction from corresponding result pages (i.e. for Web interfaces of data bases) as well as automatic handling of cookies and SSL. Detailed information on further wrapping capabilities can be found in [7].

As an example, fig. 4 shows how data from the Web page of fig. 3 is extracted using the Lixto software. In the lower section of fig. 4, the Web page has already been loaded in a Web browser window, and the relevant information has been marked with two mouse clicks. The upper windows shows already defined *logical patterns*, such as article and price, arranged in a hierarchical structure. This structure corresponds to the XML output that will later be generated by the wrapper. After loading a Web page with relevant data into the Lixto software, at first a pattern named *article* is defined. This pattern later recognizes lines with article information. Within this line, other patterns are created, identifying information such as *article manufa*cturer and *article* *price*. For this, structures of the HTML document are used, or regular expressions representing logical structures. For example, price can be defined as a number followed by a currency symbol (e.g. the euro symbol "€"). No programming is necessary because all selections are made visually in the browser window. With a "test"-button, all steps during wrapper generation can be evaluated immediately.

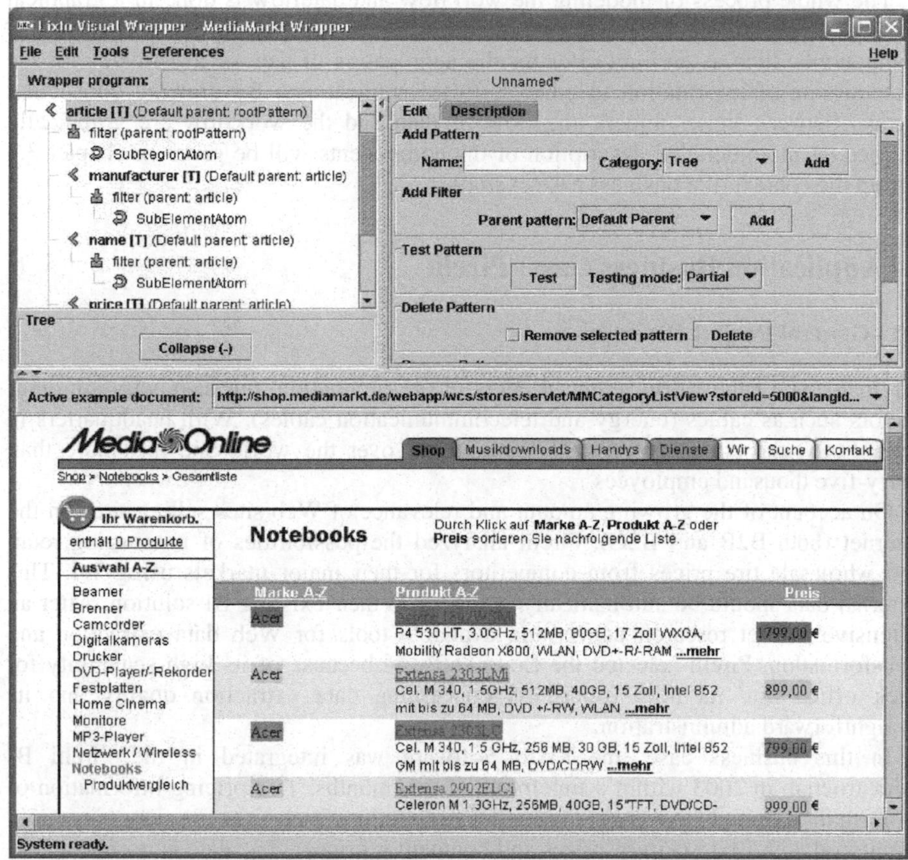

Fig. 4. Visual wrapper generation with Lixto

The resulting XML data created by this wrapper is shown in fig. 5.

```
....
<ARTICLE>
    <MANUFACTURER>Acer</MANUFACTURER>
    <NAME>Aspire 1802WSMi</NAME>
    <PRICE>1799</PRICE>
    <CURRENCY>EUR</CURRENCY>
</ARTICLE>
....
```

Fig. 5. XML data output from the wrapper

2.3 The Transformation Server

Lixto wrapper agents are embedded in the runtime-environment of the Lixto Transformation Server. This server allows post processing the XML data generated by wrapper agents. Here data from different wrappers can be aggregated, reformatted, transformed and delivered.

The whole process of modeling the workflow and dataflow is done in a graphical user interface in the Lixto Transformation Server. Graphical objects symbolize components, such as an *integrator* for the aggregation of data or a *deliverer* for the transmission of information to other software applications. By drawing connecting arrows between these objects, the flow of data and the workflow are graphically defined. A more detailed description of the components will be given in chapter 3.3 within the context of a business case example.

3 Application Business Case: Pirelli

3.1 General Project Description

Pirelli is one of the world market leaders in tire production, but also active in other sectors such as cables (energy and telecommunication cables). With headquarters in Milan/Italy, the company runs 21 factories all over the world and has more than thirty-five thousand employees[6].

On account of the growing amount and relevance of Web sites selling tires on the internet (both B2B and B2C), Pirelli analyzed the possibilities of monitoring retail and wholesale tire prices from competitors for their major markets using WI. This external data should be automatically uploaded to their existing BI solution. After an extensive market research concerning available tools for Web data extraction and transformation, Pirelli selected the Lixto software because of its high scalability for back office use, its high robustness concerning data extraction quality and its straightforward administration.

In this business case, the Lixto Software was integrated in the Pirelli BI infrastructure in 2003 within a timeframe of two months. Tire pricing information of more than 50 brands and many dozens of tires selling Web sites are now constantly monitored with Lixto (Pirelli prices and competitor prices). The data is normalized in the Lixto Transformation Server and then delivered to an Oracle 9 database. From here, the Pirelli BI solution fetches the data and generates i.e. reports in PDF format and HTML format. These reports are automatically distributed to the Pirelli intranet for marketing and sales departments. An overview of the whole system structure is shown in fig. 6.

The success of the project can be measured by the more than 1.000 self-registered Pirelli users receiving the Lixto PDF reports regularly by email. Since its introduction, the Lixto reports are in the top 5 list of all most accessed files from the Pirelli intranet.

[6] See http://uk.biz.yahoo.com/p/p/peci.mi.html and [8].

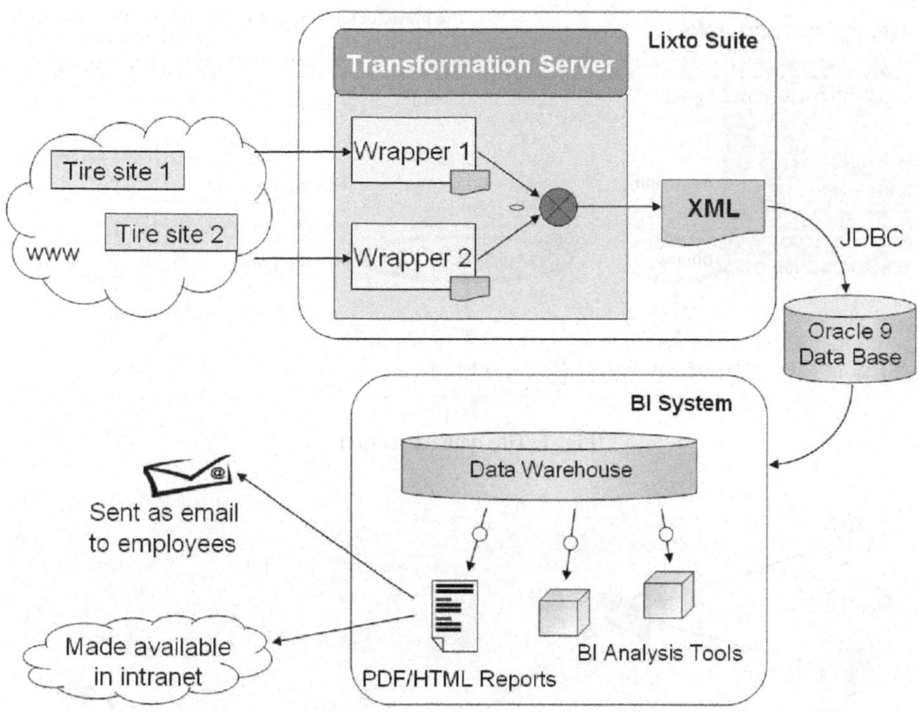

Fig. 6. System structure overview

3.2 Tire Data Extraction with Lixto

The generation of the wrapper agents to extract data in online pricelists from tire selling Web sites is conducted analogous to the procedure described in chapter 2.2. In addition, many of these Web sites require logging in to the site (authentication), and then filling out request forms (what tires are of interested) before the result page with the information needed is displayed and can be extracted. The extracted data can even be inserted iteratively in other forms to extract more detailed data from the corresponding result pages. As depicted in chapter 2.1 and [6] all described processes are completely supported by Lixto. A typical tire Web page containing relevant data is shown in fig. 7.

3.3 Service Generation with the Lixto Transformation Server

In the Lixto Transformation Server, a new service named *PirelliTireMonitor* is created. For this service, components are defined. Every component has a defined input and output behaviour. Configuration data for the components is generated by the system and automatically saved in XSLT stylesheets inside the *PirelliTireMonitor* service.

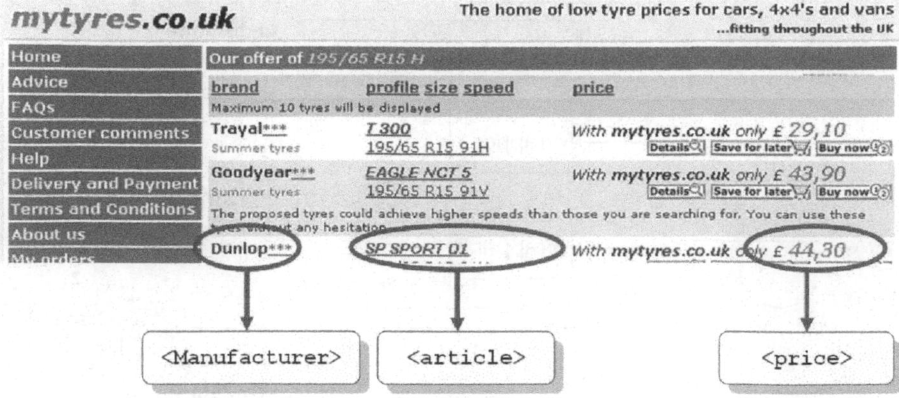

Fig. 7. Tire data extraction

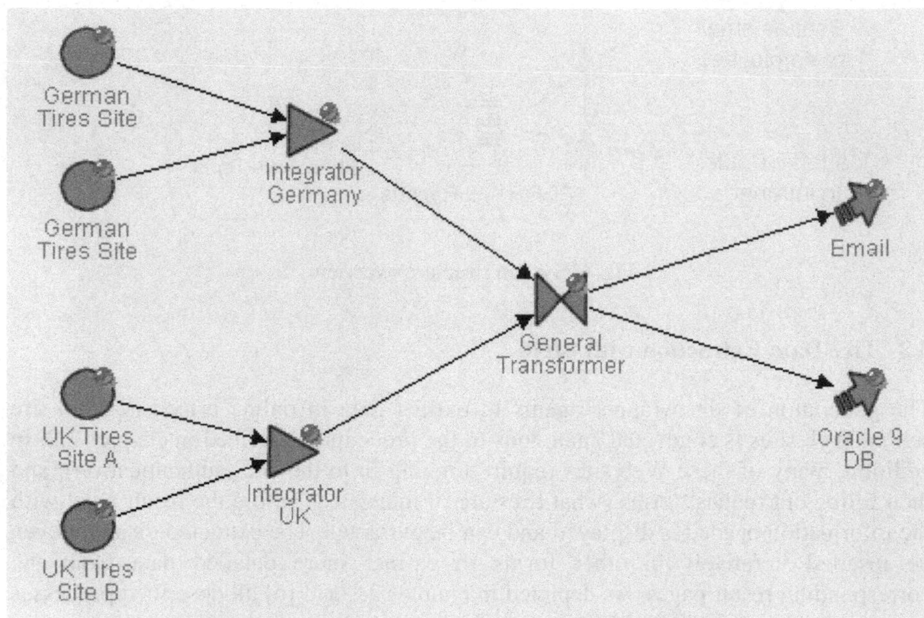

Fig. 8. Modeling the data flow in the Transformation Server

Components are graphically connected by arrows. Every arrow represents a flow of XML data. A simplified data flow as it is created in the Transformation Server is shown in fig. 8.

In the following, the further steps during the process of service configuration are described.

a. Embedding wrappers in the service: At first, the generated wrappers are loaded into the *PirelliTireMonitor* service. They are represented as circular objects (see fig. 10). In the Transformation Server additional wrapper attributes can be set, such as how often a Web site will be queried by a wrapper, for example every 5 minutes or every day.

b. Integrator: In the next step, *Integrator* components are defined ("Integrator Germany" and "Integrator UK" in fig. 8). An integrator allows XML data with different structures from different wrappers to be brought together in a uniform XML format. This is done by drawing arrows from the wrappers to the integrator, and by connecting XML elements by using graphical dialogs. Additionally, content adoptions can be made here, such as converting all *prices* from all currencies to euros, or subtracting local VAT and other taxes to get generally comparable prices.

c. Transformer: The *Integrator* transfers the normalized data to a *Transformer* component ("General Transformer" in fig. 8). It can further restructure the XML data and combine it with other data, e.g. from internal databases. The most important job of a transformer component is to filter incoming data by defining queries, e.g. selecting only the tires from Germany and Spain, or removing double data entries.

d. Deliverer: After filtering the relevant data, it is passed on to a *Deliverer* component ("Email" and "Oracle 9 DB" in fig. 8). This component reformats the information for delivery in the desired output format. Here, data is converted to a valid data stream for transmission via JDBC and SQL store procedures to an Oracle 9 database. If an error occurs during extraction, e.g. if a Web Site is inaccessible, an email notification is sent to the administrator to allow quick response. Furthermore, the error is logged in the internal logs and reports of the Lixto Transformation Server.

After activating the *PirelliTireMonitor* service in the Transformation Server, the Oracle 9 database is incessantly supplied with new data.

3.4 Loading and Processing the Data in Pirelli's BI System

Data in the Oracle 9 data base extracted by the Lixto software is loaded into the BI data warehouse following a predefined schedule. Once integrated in the BI software,

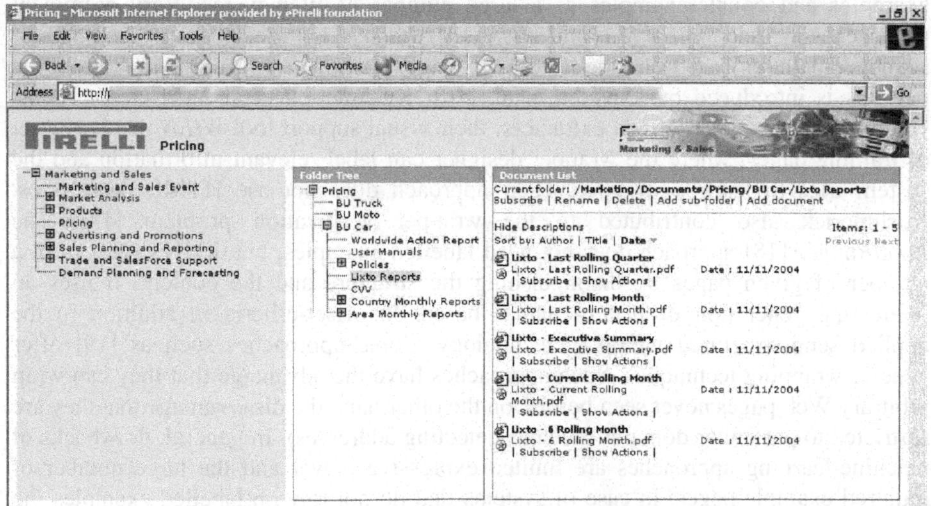

Fig. 9. The Lixto PDF reports on the Pirelli intranet

the data can be analyzed with integrated analysis tools. For example, Pirelli prices are automatically compared with competitor prices, and regional sales and marketing employees can define conditions triggering an alert – if all winter tires from competitors are sold out in Southern Austria due to unexpected heavy snowfall, Pirelli can slightly increase their own prices in this region. Furthermore, the BI system creates different kinds of PDF reports and HTML reports based on the Lixto data, e.g. quarterly reports, monthly reports and executive summaries. These reports are available on the Pirelli intranet. In addition, Pirelli employees can self-subscribe on the intranet to different kinds of Lixto newsletters, and then the corresponding reports will be emailed to them. A screenshot from the Pirelli intranet showing the Lixto reports is illustrated in fig. 9.

4 Related Work

Stand-alone wrapper programming languages are specialized high-level programming languages offering features for web communication, deep web navigation, and web data extraction. Some well-known representatives of wrapper generation languages include *Florid* [9] (using a logic-programming formalism), *Pillow* [10] (an HTML/XML programming library for logic programming systems), *Jedi* [11] (using attributed grammars), *Tsimmis* [12] and *Araneus* [13]. In *Tsimmis*, the extraction process is based on a procedural program which skips to the required information, allows temporary storages, split and case statements, and to follow links. However, the wrapper output has to obey the document structure. In *Araneus*, a wrapper designer can create relational views from web pages by computationally fast and advanced text extracting and restructuring formalisms, in particular using procedural "Cut and Paste" exception handling inside regular grammars. In general, all manual wrapper generation languages are difficult to use by laypersons.

Automated wrapper generation approaches generally rely on learning from examples and counterexamples of a large number of Web pages. Very prominent approaches include *Stalker* [14] and *Wien* [15]. *Stalker* [14] specializes general *SkipTo* sequence patterns based on labelled HTML pages. An approach to maximize specific patterns is introduced by Davulcu et al. [16]. Kushmerick et al. [15] create robust wrappers based on predefined extractors; their visual support tool *WIEN* receives a set of training pages, where the wrapper designer can label relevant information and the system tries to learn a wrapper. Their approach does not use HTML parse trees. Kushmerick also contributed to the wrapper verification problem [17]. The *RoadRunner* [18] approach does not need labelled examples, but derives rules from a number of given pages by distinguishing the structure and the content. It uses an interesting generation of pattern names based on offset-criteria in addition to the applied semi-structured wrapping technology. Some approaches such as [19] offer generic wrapping techniques. Such approaches have the advantage that they can wrap arbitrary Web pages never seen before, on the other hand the disadvantage that they are restricted to particular domains (such as detecting addresses). In general, drawbacks of machine-learning approaches are limited expressive power and the large number of required example pages. In case of systems that do not rely on labelled examples the main drawback is the low percentage of correctness of the extracted data.

Supervised wrapper generation approaches allow for semi-automatic extraction generation and offer convenient visual dialogues to generate a wrapper based on a few examples and user interaction. Supervised interactive wrapper generation tools include *W4F* [20], *XWrap* [21], *Wiccap* [22], *SGWrap* [23], *Wargo* [24] and *DEByE* [25]. *W4F* uses an SQL-like query language called HEL. Parts of the query can be generated using a visual extraction wizard which is limited to returning the full DOM tree path of an element. However, the full query must be programmed by the wrapper designer manually. Hence, *W4F* requires expertise with both HEL and HTML. HEL requires tricky use of index variables and fork constructs to correctly describe a complex pattern structure. *XWrap* uses a procedural rule system and provides limited expressive power for pattern definition. *XWrap* lacks visual facilities for imposing external or internal conditions to a pattern, but instead is rather template-based. The division into two description levels and the automatic hierarchical structure extractor limits the ways to define extraction patterns. In general, many supervised wrapper generation tools require manual postprocessing and do not offer the browser-displayed document for labelling. Additionally, many systems neglect the capabilities of Deep Web navigation such as form filling; however, in practice this is highly required, as most information is hidden somewhere in the Deep Web [26].

5 Summary and Outlook

In this paper we showed how Web Intelligence can be used for extracting data automatically from semi-structured web sites to obtain competitor information for decision support by using the architecture of the Lixto software. The result of the process, a structured XML file, can be used by a Business Intelligence system. We took a closer look at a business scenario for the company Pirelli, where we described the data upload into Pirelli's BI system via an Oracle 9 database.

One major advantage of the integration of external data into BI systems is that Data analysts are able to obtain knowledge about the market situation in nearly real-time. This leads to better pricing decisions, a better positioning of the company and its products on the market, and a faster reaction to competitive activities, such as product innovations, price dumping, or promotions.

Another general advantage is low training costs by using a intuitive graphical user interface. More data sources can be considered in high granularity, and time, cost and personnel efforts for manual information retrieval can be reduced. Moreover, data collection errors caused by manual data input can be reduced, resulting in better data quality and data transparency.

In future we will concentrate on *automating wrapper repairing technologies* and also focus on more *unstructured* formats such as PDF and plain text, using domain ontologies to support rational data validation.

References

1. Tiemeyer, E., Zsifkovitis, H.E.: Information als Führungsmittel: Executive Information Systems. Konzeption, Technologie, Produkte, Einführung; 1st edition; Munich (1995) 95
2. Kahaner, L.: Competitive Intelligence: How to Gather, Analyse Information to Move your Business to the Top. Touchstone, New York (1998)

3. Society of Competitive Intelligence Professionals (SCIP): What is CI? http://www.scip.org/ci/index.asp, accessed on 2004-09-28
4. Raghavan, P.: Social Networks on the Web and in the Enterprise. In N. Zhong, Y. Yao, J. Liu & S.Ohsuga (Eds.), Proceedings of the Web Intelligence: Research and Development, First Asia-Pacific Conference, WI 2001, Springer-Verlag, Berlin (2001) 58–60
5. Gottlob, G., Koch, C.: Monadic datalog and the expressive power of languages for Web Information Extraction, in: Proc. of PODS (2002) 17–28. Full version: Journal of the ACM 51(1) (2004) 74–113
6. Gottlob, G., Herzog, M.: Infopipes: A Flexible Framework for M-Commerce Applications, in: Proc. of TES workshop at VLDB (2001) 175–186
7. Baumgartner, R., Flesca, S., Gottlob, G.: Visual web information extraction with Lixto. In: Proc. of VLDB (2001) 119–128
8. Pirelli& C. SpA: Annual Report 2003. http://www.pirelli.com//investor_relation/ bilanciocompl2003.pdf, accessed on 2004-09-28, p. 7
9. Himmeröder, R., Lausen, G., Ludäscher, B., May, W.: A Unified Framework for Wrapping, Mediating and Restructuring Information from the Web, in: WWWCM. Sprg. LNCS 1727, (1999) 307–320
10. Cabeza, D., Hermenegildo, M.: Distributed WWW programming using Ciao-Prolog and the PiLLoW library. TPLP, 1(3) (2001)
11. Aberer, K., Fankhauser, P., Huck, G., Neuhold, E.: JEDI: Extracting and Synthesizing Information from the Web, in: Proc. of COOPIS (1998) 32–43
12. Atzeni, P., Mecca, G.: Cut and paste. In Proc. of PODS (1997)
13. Aranha, R., Cho, J., Crespo, A., Hammer, J., Garcia-Molina, H.: Extracting semistructured information from the web. In Proc. Workshop on Mang. of Semistructured Data (1997)
14. Knoblock, C., Minton, S., Muslea, I.: A hierarchical approach to wrapper induction. In Proc. of 3rd Intern. Conf. on Autonomous Agents (1999)
15. Doorenbos, R., Kushmerick, N., Weld, D.: Wrapper induction for information extraction. In Proc. of IJCAI (1997)
16. Davulcu, H., Kifer, M., Ramakrishnan, I., Yang, G.: Computat. aspects of resilient data extract. from semistr. sources. In Proc. of PODS (2000)
17. Kushmerick, N.: Wrapper verification. World Wide Web Journal (2000)
18. Crescenzi, V., Mecca, G., Merialdo. P.: Roadrunner: Towards automatic data extraction from large web sites. In Proceedings of 27th International Conference on Very Large Data Bases (2001) 109–118
19. Cafarella, M., Downey, D., Etzioni, O., Kok, S., Popescu, A., Shaked, T., Soderland, S., Weld, D. S., Yates. A.: Web-Scale Information Extraction in KnowItAll (Preliminary Results). In Proceedings of the World Wide Web Conference (2004)
20. Azavant, F., Sahuguet, A.: Building light-weight wrappers for legacy Web data-sources using W4F, in: Proc. of VLDB (1999) 738–741
21. Han, W., Liu, L., Pu, C.: XWrap: An extensible wrapper construction system for internet information. In Proc. of ICDE (2000)
22. Li, F., Liu, Z., Ng, W. K.: Wiccap Data Model: Mapping Physical Websites to Logical Views, in: Proc. of the 21st International Conference on Conceptual Modelling (2002) 120–134
23. Kou, H., Li, C., Meng, X., Wang, H.: A schema-guided toolkit for generating wrappers. In Proc. of WEBSA2003 (2003)
24. Alvarez, M., Hidalgo, J., Pan, A., Raposo, J., Vina, A.: The Wargo System: Semi-Automatic Wrapper Generation in Presence of Complex Data Access Modes. In Proceedings of DEXA 2002, Aix-en-Provence, France (2002)
25. Laender, A. H., Ribeiro-Neto, B. A., da Silva, A. S., Teixeira, J. S: A brief survey of web data extraction tools, in: Sigmod Record 31/2 (2002) 84–93
26. Bergman, M. K.: The deep web: Surfacing hidden value. BrightPlanet White Paper, http://www.brightplanet.com/technology/deepweb.asp, accessed on 2005-01-28

From Knowledge Discovery to Implementation: A Business Intelligence Approach Using Neural Network Rule Extraction and Decision Tables

Christophe Mues[1,2], Bart Baesens[1], Rudy Setiono[3], and Jan Vanthienen[2]

[1] University of Southampton, School of Management,
Southampton, SO17 1BJ, United Kingdom
{c.mues, b.m.m.baesens}@soton.ac.uk

[2] K.U.Leuven, Dept. of Applied Economic Sciences,
Naamsestraat 69, B-3000 Leuven, Belgium
jan.vanthienen@econ.kuleuven.ac.be

[3] National University of Singapore, Dept. of Information Systems,
Kent Ridge, Singapore 119260, Republic of Singapore
rudys@comp.nus.edu.sg

Abstract. The advent of knowledge discovery in data (KDD) technology has created new opportunities to analyze huge amounts of data. However, in order for this knowledge to be deployed, it first needs to be validated by the end-users and then implemented and integrated into the existing business and decision support environment. In this paper, we propose a framework for the development of business intelligence (BI) systems which centers on the use of neural network rule extraction and decision tables. Two different types of neural network rule extraction algorithms, viz. Neurolinear and Neurorule, are compared, and subsequent implementation strategies based on decision tables are discussed.

1 Introduction

Many businesses have eagerly adopted data storing facilities to record information regarding their daily operations. The advent of *knowledge discovery in data* (KDD) technology has created new opportunities to extract powerful knowledge from the stored data using data mining algorithms. Although many of these algorithms yield very accurate models, one regularly sees that the extracted models fail to be successfully integrated into the existing business environment and supporting information systems infrastructure. In this paper, we address two possible explanations for this phenomenon.

Firstly, many of the representations applied by these algorithms cannot be easily interpreted and validated by humans. For example, neural networks are considered a black box technique, since the reasoning behind how they reach their conclusions cannot be readily obtained from their structure. Therefore, we have, in recent work [1], proposed a two-step process to open the neural network black box which involves: (a) extracting rules from the network; (b) visualizing this rule set using an intuitive graphical representation, viz. decision tables. In [1], results

K.D. Althoff et al. (Eds.): WM 2005, LNAI 3782, pp. 483–495, 2005.

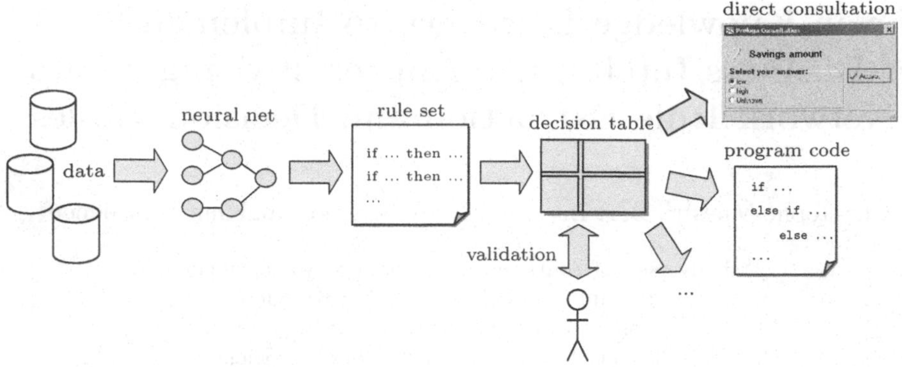

Fig. 1. A framework for business intelligence systems development

were reported on the use of Neurorule, a neural network rule extraction algorithm that requires a pre-processing step in which the data are to be discretized. In this paper, we also investigate the use of an alternative algorithm called Neurolinear, which instead works with continuous (normalized) data and produces oblique (as opposed to propositional) rules. We will empirically assess whether the rules extracted by Neurolinear offer a higher predictive accuracy than those extracted by Neurorule and to what extent they are still easily interpretable.

Secondly, once a satisfactory knowledge model has been obtained, it still has to be implemented and deployed. While, in the KDD literature, much attention has been paid to the preceding stages, relatively few guidelines are supplied with regard to the implementation, integration, as well as the subsequent management and maintenance of *business intelligence* (BI) systems. For example, while neural networks may typically yield a high predictive accuracy, they do so by simultaneously processing all inputs. Hence, direct implementations would need to query the user or a database for all values describing a given input case, regardless of their relative impact on the output. In contrast, decision tables or trees provide more efficient test strategies that avoid querying for inputs that become irrelevant given the case values already supplied. Clearly, this is an important advantage, especially when these operations are quite costly. Another advantage of decision table based systems is that they are easily maintainable: if, at some point, changes are to be made to the underlying decision table, these are either automatically reflected in the operational system, or, depending on the chosen implementation strategy, it requires little effort to modify the system accordingly.

Therefore, in this paper, we advocate that decision tables can play a central role in the KDD process, by bridging the gap that exists between an accurate neural network model and a successful business intelligence system implementation (see Fig. 1) and *knowledge management* strategy. Our approach will be illustrated in the context of developing credit-scoring systems (which are meant to assist employees of financial institutions in deciding whether or not to grant a loan to an applicant), but is also applicable in various other settings involving predictive data mining (e.g., customer churn prediction, fraud detection, etc.).

2 Neural Network Rule Extraction: Neurolinear and Neurorule

As universal approximators, neural networks can achieve significantly better predictive accuracy compared to models that are linear in the input variables. However, a major drawback is their lack of transparency: their internal structure is hard for humans to interpret. It is precisely this black box property that hinders their acceptance by practitioners in several real-life problem settings such as credit-risk evaluation (where besides having accurate models, explanation of the predictions being made is essential). In the literature, the problem of explaining the neural network predictions has been tackled by techniques that extract symbolic rules or trees from the trained networks. These neural network rule extraction techniques attempt to open up the neural network black box and generate symbolic, comprehensible descriptions with approximately the same predictive power as the neural network itself. An advantage of using neural networks as a starting point for rule extraction is that the neural network considers the contribution of the inputs towards classification as a group, while decision tree algorithms like C4.5 measure the individual contribution of the inputs one at a time as the tree is grown [4].

The expressive power of the extracted rules depends on the language used to express the rules. Many types of rules have been suggested in the literature. Propositional rules are simple 'if-then' expressions based on conventional propositional logic. An example of a propositional rule is:

If Purpose = second hand car **and** Savings Account $\leq$ 50 Euro **then** Applicant = bad.

An oblique rule is a rule whereby each condition represents a separating hyperplane given in the form of a linear inequality, e.g.:

If 0.84 Income + 0.32 Savings Account $\leq$ 1000 Euro **then** Applicant = bad.

Oblique rules allow for more powerful decision surfaces than propositional rules since the latter allow only axis-parallel decision boundaries. This is illustrated in Fig. 2. The latter represents a classification problem involving two classes, represented by '+' and 'o' respectively, each described by two inputs x_1 and x_2. The left hand side illustrates an oblique rule separating both classes and the right hand side a set of propositional rules inferred by e.g. C4.5. Clearly, the oblique rule provides a better separation than the set of propositional, axis-parallel, rules. Augmenting the number of training points will probably increase the number of axis parallel decision boundaries. Hence, this example illustrates that oblique rules may provide a more powerful, concise separation than a set of propositional rules. However, this advantage has to be offset against the loss of comprehensibility since oblique rules are harder to interpret for the domain expert.

Neurolinear and Neurorule are algorithms that extract rules from trained three-layered feedforward neural networks. The kinds of rules generated by Neurolinear and Neurorule are oblique rules and propositional rules, respectively. Both techniques share the following common steps [6,7]:

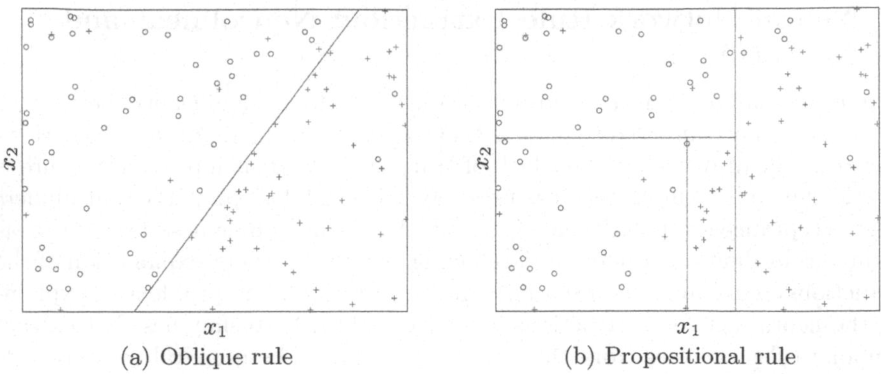

(a) Oblique rule (b) Propositional rule

Fig. 2. Oblique rules versus propositional rules [4]

1. Train a neural network to meet the prespecified accuracy requirement;
2. Remove the redundant connections in the network by pruning while maintaining its accuracy;
3. Discretize the hidden unit activation values of the pruned network by clustering;
4. Extract rules that describe the network outputs in terms of the discretized hidden unit activation values;
5. Generate rules that describe the discretized hidden unit activation values in terms of the network inputs;
6. Merge the two sets of rules generated in steps 4 and 5 to obtain a set of rules that relates the inputs and outputs of the network.

Both techniques differ in their way of preprocessing the data. Neurolinear works with continuous data which is normalized e.g. to the interval $[-1, 1]$. On the other hand, Neurorule assumes the data are discretized and represented as binary inputs using the thermometer encoding for ordinal variables and dummy encoding for nominal variables. Table 1 illustrates the thermometer encoding procedure for the ordinal Income variable (where the discretization into four categories could have been done by either a discretization algorithm, e.g. the algorithm of Fayyad and Irani [2], or according to the recommendation from a domain expert).

Table 1. The thermometer encoding procedure for ordinal variables

Original input	**Categorical input**	**Thermometer inputs**		
		I_1	I_2	I_3
Income $\leq$ 800 Euro	1	0	0	0
800 Euro $<$ Income $\leq$ 2000 Euro	2	0	0	1
2000 Euro $<$ Income $\leq$ 10000 Euro	3	0	1	1
Income $>$ 10000 Euro	4	1	1	1

Both Neurorule and Neurolinear typically start from a one-hidden layer neural network with hyperbolic tangent hidden neurons and sigmoid or linear output neurons. For a classification problem with C classes, C output neurons are used and the class is assigned to the output neuron with the highest activation value (*winner-take-all learning*). The network is then trained to minimize an augmented cross-entropy error function using the BFGS method which is a modified Quasi-Newton algorithm. This algorithm converges much faster than the standard backpropagation algorithm and the total error decreases after each iteration step which is not necessarily the case in the backpropagation algorithm.

Determining the optimal number of hidden neurons is not a trivial task. In the literature, two approaches have been suggested to tackle this problem. A growing strategy starts from an empty network and gradually adds hidden neurons to improve the classification accuracy. On the other hand, a pruning strategy starts from an oversized network and removes the irrelevant connections. When all connections to a hidden neuron have been removed, it can be pruned. The latter strategy is followed by Neurolinear and Neurorule. Note that this pruning step plays an important role in both rule extraction algorithms since it will facilitate the extraction of a compact, parsimonious rule set. After having removed one or more connections, the network is retrained and inspected for further pruning.

Once a trained and pruned network has been obtained, the activation values of all hidden neurons are clustered. In the case of hyperbolic tangent hidden neurons, the activation values lie in the interval $[-1, 1]$. A simple greedy clustering algorithm then starts by sorting all these hidden activation values in increasing order. Adjacent values are then merged into a unique discretized value as long as the class labels of the corresponding observations do not conflict. The merging process hereby first considers the pair of hidden activation values with the shortest distance in between. Another discretization algorithm is the Chi2 algorithm which is an improved and automated version of the ChiMerge algorithm and makes use of the χ^2 test statistic to merge the hidden activation values [3].

In step 4 of Neurolinear and Neurorule, a new data set is composed consisting of the discretized hidden unit activation values and the class labels of the corresponding observations. Duplicate observations are removed and rules are inferred relating the class labels to the clustered hidden unit activation values. This can be done using an automated rule induction algorithm or manually when the pruned network has only a few hidden neurons and inputs. Note that steps 3 and 4 can be done simultaneously by C4.5rules since the latter can work with both discretized and continuous data [4].

In the last two steps of both rule extraction algorithms, the rules of step 4 are translated in terms of the original inputs. First, the rules are generated describing the discretized hidden unit activation values in terms of the original inputs. This rule set is then merged with that of step 4 by replacing the conditions of the latter with those of the former. For Neurolinear, this process is fairly straightforward. In the case of Neurorule, one might again use an automated rule induction algorithm to relate the discretized hidden unit activation values to the inputs.

3 Neural Network Rule Extraction Results

3.1 Experimental Setup

The experiments were conducted on three real-life credit-risk evaluation data sets: German credit, Bene1 and Bene2. The Bene1 and Bene2 data sets were obtained from two major Benelux (Belgium, The Netherlands, Luxembourg) financial institutions. The German credit data set is publicly available at the UCI repository (`http://www.ics.uci.edu/~mlearn/MLRepository.html`).

Each data set is randomly split into two-thirds training set and one-third test set. The neural networks are trained and rules are extracted using the training set. The test set is then used to assess the predictive power of the trained networks and the extracted rule sets or trees. The continuous and discretized data sets are analyzed using Neurolinear and Neurorule, respectively. We also include C4.5 and C4.5rules as a benchmark to compare the results of the rule extraction algorithms. We set the confidence level for the pruning strategy to 25% which is the value that is commonly used in the literature.

All algorithms are evaluated by their classification accuracy as measured by the percentage correctly classified (PCC) observations, and by their complexity. The complexity is quantified by looking at the number of generated rules or the number of leaf nodes and total number of nodes (including leaf nodes) for C4.5.

Since the primary goal of neural network rule extraction is to mimic the decision process of the trained neural network, we also measure how well the extracted rule set models the behavior of the network. For this purpose, we also report the fidelity of the extraction techniques, which is defined as the percentage of observations that the extraction algorithm classifies in the same way as the neural network.

For the Neurolinear and Neurorule analyses, we use two output units with linear or logistic activation functions and the class is assigned to the output neuron with the highest activation value (winner-takes-all). A hyperbolic tangent activation function is used in the hidden layer.

3.2 Results for the Continuous Data Sets

Table 2 presents the results of applying the rule extraction methods to the continuous data sets. Before the neural networks are trained for rule extraction using Neurolinear, all inputs x_i, $i = 1, ..., n$ are scaled to the interval $[-1, 1]$ in the following way: $x_i^{new} = 2[\frac{x_i^{old} - \min(x_i)}{\max(x_i) - \min(x_i)}] - 1$.

As explained, Neurolinear typically starts from a large, oversized network and then prunes the irrelevant connections. This pruned neural network has 1 hidden unit for the German credit and Bene2 data set and 2 hidden units for the Bene1 data set, indicating that there is no need to model more complex nonlinearities by using more hidden neurons. The pruned networks had 16 inputs for the German credit data set, 17 inputs for the Bene1 data set and 23 inputs for the Bene2 data set.

Neurolinear obtained 100% test set fidelity for the German credit and Bene2 data set and 99.9% test set fidelity for the Bene1 data set (cf. Table 3). This clearly indicates that Neurolinear was able to extract rule sets which closely reflect the decision process of the trained neural networks.

It can be observed from Table 2 that the rules extracted by Neurolinear are both powerful and very concise when compared to the rules and trees inferred

Table 2. Neural network rule extraction results for the continuous data sets

Data set	Method	PCC_{train}	PCC_{test}	Complexity
German credit	C4.5	82.58	70.96	37 leaves, 59 nodes
	C4.5rules	81.53	70.66	13 propositional rules
	Pruned NN	80.78	77.25	16 inputs
	Neurolinear	80.93	77.25	2 oblique rules
Bene1	C4.5	89.91	68.68	168 leaves, 335 nodes
	C4.5rules	78.63	70.80	21 propositional rules
	Pruned NN	77.33	72.62	17 inputs
	Neurolinear	77.43	72.72	3 oblique rules
Bene2	C4.5	90.24	70.09	849 leaves, 1161 nodes
	C4.5rules	77.61	73.00	30 propositional rules
	Pruned NN	76.05	73.51	23 inputs
	Neurolinear	76.05	73.51	2 oblique rules

Table 3. Fidelity rates of Neurolinear

Data set	Fid_{train}	Fid_{test}
German credit	100	100
Bene1	99.81	99.90
Bene2	100	100

If [-12.83(Amount on purchase invoice)+13.36(Percentage of financial burden) +31.33(Term)-0.93(Private or professional loan))-35.40(Savings account) -5.86(Other loan expenses)+10.69(Profession)+10.84(Number of years since last house move)+3.03(Code of regular saver)+6.68(Property)-6.02(Existing credit info)-13.78(Number of years client)-2.12(Number of years since last loan) -10.38(Number of mortgages)+68.45(Pawn)-5.23(Employment status) -5.50(Title/salutation)] ≤ 0.31
then Applicant = good

If [19.39(Amount on purchase invoice)+32.57(Percentage of financial burden) -5.19(Term)-16.75(Private or professional loan)-27.96(Savings account) +7.58(Other loan expenses)-13.98(Profession)-8.57(Number of years since last house move)+6.30(Code of regular saver)+3.96(Property) -9.07(Existing credit info)-0.51(Number of years client) -5.76(Number of years since last loan) +0.14(Number of mortgages)+0.15(Pawn)+1.14(Employment status) +15.03(Title/salutation)]≤ -0.25
then Applicant = good

Default Class: Applicant = bad

Fig. 3. Oblique rules extracted by Neurolinear for Bene1

by C4.5rules and C4.5. Neurolinear yields the best absolute test set performance for all three data sets with a maximum of three oblique rules for the Bene1 data set. For the German credit data set, Neurolinear performed significantly better than C4.5rules according to McNemar's test at the 1% level. For the Bene1 and Bene2 data sets, the performance of Neurolinear was not significantly different from C4.5rules at the 5% level.

Fig. 3 depicts the oblique rules that were extracted by Neurolinear for the Bene1 data set. Arguably, although the rules perfectly mimic the decision process of the corresponding neural networks, their interpretability is still rather limited. They are basically mathematical expressions which represent piece-wise linear discriminant functions. Hence, their usefulness for building intelligent, user-friendly and comprehensible credit-scoring systems can be questioned.

3.3 Results for the Discretized Data Sets

After discretization using the method of Fayyad and Irani [2], 15 inputs remained for the German credit data set, 21 inputs for the Bene1 data set and 29 inputs for the Bene2 data set. When representing these inputs using the thermometer and dummy encoding, we ended up with 45 binary inputs for the German credit data set, 45 binary inputs for the Bene1 data set and 105 inputs for the Bene2 data set. We then trained and pruned the neural networks for rule extraction using Neurorule. Only 1 hidden unit was needed with a hyperbolic tangent transfer function. All inputs are binary (e.g. the first input is 1 if Term > 12 Months and 0 otherwise). Note that according to the pruning algorithm, no bias was needed to the hidden neuron for the Bene1 data set. Of the 45 binary inputs, 37 were pruned leaving only 8 binary inputs in the neural network. This corresponds to 7 of the original inputs because the nominal input 'Purpose' has two corresponding binary inputs in the pruned network (Purpose = cash provisioning and Purpose = second hand car).

The network trained and pruned for Bene2 had 1 hidden neuron with again no bias input. Starting from 105 binary inputs, the pruning procedure removed 97 of them and the remaining 8 corresponded to 7 of the original inputs. The network for German credit had also only 1 hidden neuron but with a bias input. The binarized German credit data set consists of 45 inputs of which 13 are retained, corresponding to 6 of the original inputs.

Three things are worth mentioning here. First of all, note how the pruned networks for all three data sets have only 1 hidden neuron. These networks are thus only marginally different from an ordinary logistic regression model. This clearly confirms that, also for the discretized data sets, simple classification models seem to yield good performance for credit scoring. Furthermore, since all networks have only 1 hidden neuron, the rule extraction process by Neurorule can also be simplified. If we would cluster the hidden unit activation values by sorting them, we would find two clusters corresponding to the two output classes. Hence, instead of generating the rules relating the outputs to the clustered hidden unit activation values and merging them with the rules expressing the clustered hidden unit activation values in terms of the inputs, we can

Table 4. Neural network rule extraction results for the discretized data sets

Data set	Method	PCC_{train}	PCC_{test}	Complexity
German credit	C4.5	80.63	71.56	38 leaves, 54 nodes
	C4.5rules	81.38	74.25	17 propositional rules
	Pruned NN	75.53	77.84	6 inputs
	Neurorule	75.83	77.25	4 propositional rules
Bene1	C4.5	77.76	70.03	77 leaves, 114 nodes
	C4.5rules	76.70	70.12	17 propositional rules
	Pruned NN	73.05	71.85	7 inputs
	Neurorule	73.05	71.85	6 propositional rules
Bene2	C4.5	82.80	73.09	438 leaves, 578 nodes
	C4.5rules	77.76	73.51	27 propositional rules
	Pruned NN	74.15	74.09	7 inputs
	Neurorule	74.27	74.13	7 propositional rules

Table 5. Fidelity rates of Neurorule

Data set	Fid_{train}	Fid_{test}
German	99.70	98.80
Bene1	100	100
Bene2	99.71	99.79

generate the rules relating the outputs to the inputs directly by using C4.5rules. Finally, also notice how the binary representation allows to prune more inputs than with the continuous data sets. This will of course facilitate the generation of a compact set of rules. Table 4 presents the performance and complexity of C4.5, C4.5rules, the pruned NN and Neurorule on the discretized credit scoring data sets. It is important to remark here that the discretization process introduces non-linear effects.

When comparing Table 4 with Table 2, it can be seen that the test set performance in many instances actually augments and that the discretization process did not appear to cause any loss of predictive power of the inputs. For the German credit data set, Neurorule did not perform significantly better than C4.5rules at the 5% level according to McNemar's test. However, Neurorule extracted only 4 propositional rules which is very compact when compared to the 17 propositional rules inferred by C4.5rules. The test set fidelity of Neurorule is 98.80% (cf. Table 5). For the Bene1 data set, Neurorule performed significantly better than C4.5rules at the 5% level. Besides the gain in performance, Neurorule also uses only 6 propositional rules whereas C4.5rules uses 17 propositional rules. The rule set inferred by Neurorule obtained 100% test set fidelity with respect to the pruned neural network from which it was derived. The high fidelity rate of Neurorule indicates that it was able to accurately approximate the decision process of the trained and pruned neural network. For the Bene2 data set, the performance difference between Neurorule and C4.5rules is not statistically significant at the 5% level using McNemar's test. However, the rule set

If Term > 12 months **and** Purpose = cash provisioning **and** Savings Account ≤ 12.40 € **and** Years Client ≤ 3 **then** Applicant = bad
If Term > 12 months **and** Purpose = cash provisioning **and** Owns Property = no **and** Savings Account ≤ 12.40 € **then** Applicant = bad
If Purpose = cash provisioning **and** Income > 719 € **and** Owns Property = no **and** Savings Account ≤ 12.40 € **and** Years Client ≤ 3 **then** Applicant = bad
If Purpose = second-hand car **and** Income > 719 € **and** Owns Property = no **and** Savings Account ≤ 12.40 € **and** Years Client ≤ 3 **then** Applicant = bad
If Savings Account ≤ 12.40 € **and** Economical sector = Sector C **then** Applicant = bad
Default class: Applicant = good

Fig. 4. Rules extracted by Neurorule for Bene1

extracted by Neurorule consists of only 7 propositional rules which again is a lot more compact than the 27 propositional rules induced by C4.5rules. Note that the rules extracted by Neurorule actually yielded a better classification accuracy than the original network resulting in a test set fidelity of 99.79%.

Fig. 4 represents the rules extracted by Neurorule for the Bene1 data set. When looking at these rules, it becomes clear that, while the propositional rules extracted by Neurorule are similarly powerful as the oblique rules extracted by Neurolinear, they are far easier to interpret and understand.

However, while propositional rules are an intuitive and well-known formalism to represent knowledge, they are not necessarily the most suitable representation in terms of structure and efficiency of use in every day business practice and decision-making. Research in knowledge representation suggests that graphical representation formalisms can be more readily interpreted and consulted by humans than a set of symbolic propositional if-then rules [5]. Next, we will discuss how the sets of rules extracted by Neurorule may be further transformed into decision tables which facilitate the efficient classification of applicants by the credit-risk manager.

4 Visualizing the Extracted Rule Sets Using Decision Tables

A decision table (DT) consists of four quadrants, separated by double-lines, both horizontally and vertically. The horizontal line divides the table into a condition part (above) and an action part (below). The vertical line separates subjects (left) from entries (right). The condition subjects are the problem criteria that are relevant to the decision-making process. The action subjects describe the possible outcomes of the decision-making process. Each condition entry describes a relevant subset of values (called a state) for a given condition subject (attribute), or contains a dash symbol ('–') if its value is irrelevant within the context of that column ('don't care' entry). Subsequently, every action entry holds a value assigned to the corresponding action subject (class). True, false and unknown action values are typically abbreviated by '×', '–' and '·', respectively.

If each column contains only simple states, the table is called an *expanded* DT (cf. Fig. 5a), whereas otherwise the table is called a *contracted* DT (cf. Fig. 5b). For ease of legibility, we will allow only contractions that maintain a *lexicographical* column ordering, i.e., in which the entries at lower rows alternate before the entries above them. As a result of this ordering restriction, a decision tree structure emerges in the condition entry part of the DT. Importantly, the number of columns in the contracted table can often be further minimized by changing the order of the condition rows (cf. Fig. 5c). It is obvious that a DT with a minimal number of columns is to be preferred since it provides a more efficient representation of the underlying knowledge.

For each of the three rule sets extracted by Neurorule, we used the PROLOGA software (`http://www.econ.kuleuven.ac.be/prologa/`) to construct an equivalent DT. Each expanded DT was converted into a more compact DT, by joining nominal attribute values that do not appear in any rule antecedent into a common 'other' state, and then performing optimal table contraction. As a result of this reduction process, we ended up with three minimum-size contracted DTs,consisting of 11, 14 and 26 columns for the German credit, Bene1 and Bene2

1. Owns property?	yes				no			
2. Years client	≤ 3		>3		≤ 3		>3	
3. Savings amount	low	high	low	high	low	high	low	high
1. Applicant=good	–	×	×	×	–	×	–	×
2. Applicant=bad	×	–	–	–	×	–	×	–

(a) Expanded DT

1. Owns property?	yes			no	
2. Years client	≤ 3		>3	–	
3. Savings amount	low	high	–	low	high
1. Applicant=good	–	×	×	–	×
2. Applicant=bad	×	–	–	×	–

(b) Contracted DT

1. Savings amount	low			high
2. Owns property?	yes		no	–
3. Years client	≤ 3	>3	–	–
1. Applicant=good	–	×	–	×
2. Applicant=bad	×	–	×	–

(c) Minimum-size contracted DT

Fig. 5. Minimizing the number of columns of a lexicographically ordered DT

1. Savings Account	≤ 12.40 €													> 12.40 €
2. Economical sector	Sector C	other												–
3. Purpose	–	cash provisioning							second-hand car				other	–
4. Term	–	≤ 12 months				> 12 months			–					
5. Years Client	–	≤ 3			> 3	≤ 3	> 3		≤ 3			> 3		
6. Owns Property	–	yes	no		–	–	yes	no	yes	no		–	–	–
7. Income	–	–	≤ 719 €	> 719 €	–	–	–	–	–	≤ 719 €	> 719 €	–	–	–
1. Applicant=good	–	×	×	–	×	–	×	–	×	×	–	×	×	×
2. Applicant=bad	×	–	–	×	–	×	–	×	–	–	×	–	–	–
	1	2	3	4	5	6	7	8	9	10	11	12	13	14

Fig. 6. Decision table for the Bene1 rule set

data sets, respectively. In all cases, the contracted tables were satisfactorily concise and did not reveal any anomalies [8]. Fig. 6 depicts the resulting decision table for the Benel data set. Clearly, the top-down readability of such a DT, combined with its conciseness, makes it a very attractive visual representation.

5 Knowledge Implementation: From Decision Tables to Decision-Support Systems

5.1 DT Consultation

DTs can be consulted not only visually, but also in an automated way. In PROLOGA, a generic environment is offered that allows the user to actively apply the decision-making knowledge to a given problem case. During a consultation session, the provided engine will navigate through the DT system structure and inquire the user about the condition states of every relevant condition in the DTs thus visited. Only questions for which relevant condition entries remain are being asked (unlike, e.g., in the rule description shown in Fig. 4, where conditions would typically have to be evaluated on a rule-by-rule basis).

In addition to the built-in engine, a consultation web service has recently been developed (`http://prologaws.econ.kuleuven.ac.be`). Web services may be called by client applications written in various languages and distributed over a network. This allows one to separately manage and update the decision table knowledge (logically as well as physically), while enforcing its consistent use throughout various types of application settings (cf. Fig. 7).

5.2 DT Export

To allow the developer to apply a different tool for the actual implementation, or to integrate the system into a given ICT setting, PROLOGA offers a series of export options. A straightforward transformation of a DT into a decision tree, and from there to Pascal, C, COBOL, Java, Eiffel or Visual Basic program code, is provided. The code takes on the form of a nested if-else selection (or in the case of COBOL, an EVALUATE-statement can be generated as well). It should be noted that the generated code is not intended to be directly executable:variable

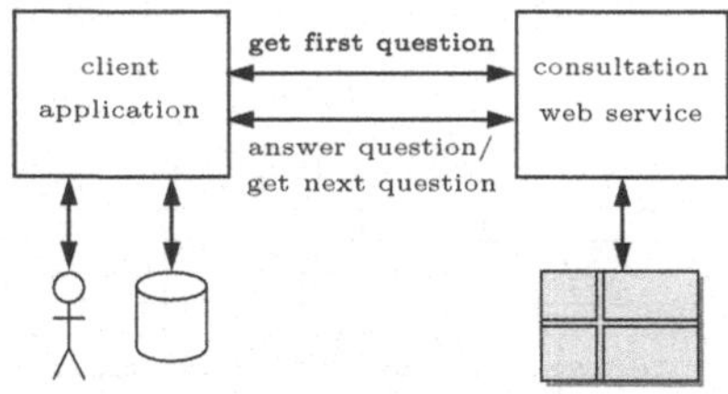

Fig. 7. A simple web service architecture for decision table consultation

declarations must still be added, and the conditions and actions of the DT should constitute valid expressions within the target language. The main idea is to be able to (re-)generate the 'hard' part of the code, quickly and without errors, after which the (updated) piece of code can be plugged (back) into the implementation. In addition to the former standard conversions, one can also generate optimized code for either of the aforementioned languages.

6 Conclusions

In this paper, a framework for the development of business intelligence systems was described, which combines neural network rule extraction and decision table techniques. Using a series of real-life credit scoring cases, it was shown how Neurolinear and Neurorule, two neural network rule extraction algorithms, produce both powerful and concise rule sets, with the rule set extracted by Neurorule being more intuitive. Finally, it was shown how decision tables offer a highly intuitive visualization of the extracted knowledge and can then serve as a basis for an efficient and maintainable system implementation, either by direct or web-based consultation, or through the (partial) generation of program code.

References

1. B. Baesens, R. Setiono, C. Mues, and J. Vanthienen. Using neural network rule extraction and decision tables for credit-risk evaluation. *Management Science*, 49(3):312–329, 2003.
2. U.M. Fayyad and K.B. Irani. Multi-interval discretization of continuous-valued attributes for classification learning. In *Proceedings of the Thirteenth International Joint Conference on Artificial Intelligence (IJCAI)*, pages 1022–1029, Chambéry, France, 1993. Morgan Kaufmann.
3. H. Liu and R. Setiono. Chi2: feature selection and discretization of numeric attributes. In *Proceedings of the Seventh IEEE International Conference on Tools with Artificial Intelligence (ICTAI)*, pages 388–391, 1995.
4. J.R. Quinlan. *C4.5 programs for machine learning.* Morgan Kaufmann, 1993.
5. L. Santos-Gomez and M.J. Darnel. Empirical evaluation of decision tables for constructing and comprehending expert system rules. *Knowledge Acquisition*, 4:427–444, 1992.
6. R. Setiono and H. Liu. Symbolic representation of neural networks. *IEEE Computer*, 29(3):71–77, 1996.
7. R. Setiono and H. Liu. Neurolinear: from neural networks to oblique decision rules. *Neurocomputing*, 17(1):1–24, 1997.
8. J. Vanthienen, C. Mues, and A. Aerts. An illustration of verification and validation in the modelling phase of KBS development. *Data and Knowledge Engineering*, 27(3):337–352, 1998.

Workshop on Intelligent IT Tools for Knowledge Management Systems: Applicability, Usability, and Benefits

Ulrich Reimer[1], York Sure[2], Andreas Eberhart[2], Edith Maier[1], and Hans-Peter Schnurr[3]

[1] University of Applied Sciences St. Gallen, Switzerland
{ulrich.reimer, edith.maier}@fhsg.ch
[2] Institute AIFB, University of Karlsruhe, Germany
{eberhart, sure}@aifb.uni-karlsruhe.de
[3] Ontoprise GmbH, Karlsruhe, Germany
schnurr@ontoprise.de

1 Motivation

Successful knowledge management projects incorporate aspects from the following dimensions: processes, contents, corporate culture, information technologies (IT). IT has the role to facilitate the storage, retrieval and presentation of information and is therefore often called an enabler. An inadequate use of IT can lead to the failure of a knowledge management project, cause considerable delays and detract from the motivation of the people involved.

IT-based knowledge management solutions typically include an organizational memory that contains informal, semi-formal, and formal knowledge needed by a knowledge worker for accomplishing his or her tasks. In order to provide flexible and personalized access to the knowledge, the organizational memory has to model, structure, and interconnect the stored knowledge.

It is therefore important to get a better understanding of

- how best to support knowledge management through intelligent IT tools (including how to structure, store and access knowledge), and
- how to ensure the implementation of efficient knowledge management systems.

To this end, the following issues are of special importance:

- Embedding into the application environment: The functions offered by a knowledge management system must be carefully tailored to the specific requirements of the context of the application and the needs of users.
- Usability: Poorly designed user interfaces cause a loss of efficiency as well as severe quality and acceptance problems due to the high cognitive strain of the users. Since people tend to use knowledge management systems on a voluntary basis and not because they are mandatory for the work to be done, they will refuse to use them if the ergonomic design does not comply with state-of-the-art usability guidelines.

K.-D. Althoff et al. (Eds.): WM 2005, LNAI 3782, pp. 496–498, 2005.

- Process integration: The tasks to be accomplished with the help of a knowledge management system are often part of other processes and should thus be integrated into those processes with respect to information and process flow.
- Information integration: The integration of information from heterogeneous sources is important in order to avoid multiple entering of information, resulting in redundant and possibly inconsistent information. It is to be ensured that information is consistent across all systems and that information can be linked across system boundaries.
- System integration: By integrating a knowledge management system with other systems we avoid the scattering of functions across several systems and relieve the user from having to change between systems when performing a task. This also ensures a uniform look and feel.

2 Selected Workshop Papers

The workshop papers selected for this post-conference proceedings cover the workshop issues outlined above quite nicely. The role ontologies can play in modern knowledge management tools is illustrated by a paper on capturing experience-based knowledge in the context of business processes (Biesalski and Abecker).

The possibility to access knowledge from different sources in a uniform way not only requires ontologies for annotating the contents of the information sources but also a way to align the (in practice typically) different ontologies in a cost-effective manner. The paper by Ehrig et al. deals with this aspect.

A third paper deals with concept recognition to assist browsing and searching information by classifying entities referred to in a document or a web page as being subsumed by certain concepts in a given concept hierarchy (Zhu et al.).

A fourth paper takes a completely different angle on knowledge management by focusing on the exploitation of digital communication structures within an organisation in order to facilitate the access to relevant knowledge (Böhm and Scherf).

The last paper deals with the important topic of how to embed IT-based knowledge management systems into the working context of the intended users so as to increase their usability (Birger et al.).

3 Program Committee

Andreas Abecker, Forschungszentrum Informatik (FZI) Karlsruhe, Germany
Robert Engels, CognIT, Norway
Christian Fillies, Semtation GmbH, Germany
Hermann Kaindl, Siemens AG, Germany
Jürgen Klenk, definiens AG, Germany
Edith Maier, Donau-Universität Krems, Austria
Christian Ohlms, McKinsey, Germany

Axel Polleres, Universität Innsbruck, Austria
Dirk Ramhorst, Siemens Business Services, Germany
Josef Schneeberger, SCHEMA GmbH, Germany
Peter Smolle, Net Dynamics, Austria
Heiner Stuckenschmid, VU Amsterdam, The Netherlands
Ralph Traphöner, empolis GmbH, Germany
Joachim Warschat, Universität Stuttgart, Germany

Human Resource Management with Ontologies

Ernst Biesalski[1,2] and Andreas Abecker[2]

[1] DaimlerChrysler AG, Werk Wörth
ernst.biesalski@daimlerchrysler.com
[2] Forschungszentrum Informatik (FZI), Karlsruhe
{biesalski, abecker}@fzi.de

Abstract. In the first part of our paper we want to depict the dependencies between the two topics „Human Resource Management" (HRM) and „Knowledge Management" (KM). Next we define competency management and describe a concrete scenario at DaimlerChrysler AG, Wörth Plant where we use ontologies in the context of competency management to do strategic training planning.

1 Inter-relations Between HRM and KM

Subject of HRM is the working human being [5]. For the overall function of companies their personnel is the determining factor. The best possible use of human resources has therefore to be a prior strategic aspect for companies. To reach this the HRM hast to be accompanied by holistic strategic considerations. The HRM-department in companies bears the responsibility to keep the company in a „good shape" which means to have adequate skilled employees at the right time in the right place in the right amount you need them. It is one of the major functions to steer a company. Our working definition of HRM is therefore the strategic and target-oriented composition, regulation and development of all areas that affect human resources in a company.

Important areas of HRM (cp. Fig. 1) are:

- Personnel Recruitment, Personnel Placement, Personnel Development, Dismissals
- Personnel Planning, Personnel Controlling, Personnel Administration

As our working definition of HRM shows there is a strong emphasis on the strategic aspect. The so called strategic HRM (SHRM) is defined as: aggregation of all activities that reference the efforts of individuals to reach and formulate strategic goals of a company [6]. This definition is the postulate of the basic concepts of SHRM [4]:

- Consideration of actual and future human resources in companies
- Concatenation of strategic and HRM-goals of the company
- Creation of a strategic competitive advantage by providing an adequate number of employees with the right skills in the right time at the right place.

K.-D. Althoff et al. (Eds.): WM 2005, LNAI 3782, pp. 499 – 507, 2005.

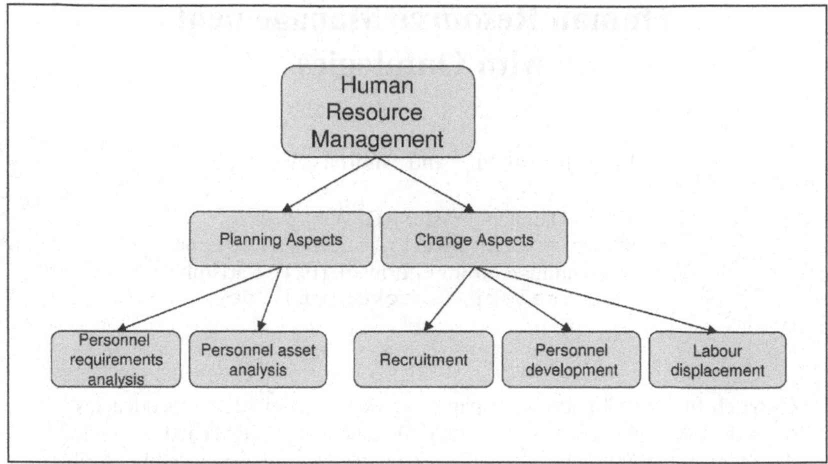

Fig. 1. Fields of HRM

SHRM is closely related to strategic personnel development. Personnel development is hereby an organized learning process that occurs in the social environment of the company [4]. The goal of personnel development is the change of the achievement potential of employees or organizational units. This encloses all planning and controlling instruments, results and processes. Strategic personnel development is the closing of the strategic gap between actual group-based skill requirements and future group-based skill-requirements on a highly aggregated level [7].

Knowledge Management is a structured and holistic approach. Structured means that KM is a management task in a sense, which is the notional execution of measures on a strategic, tactical and operational their implementation and effects, accompanied by continuous monitoring of the activities [1]. This claim is also settled by HRM, because HRM-measures, as depicted in chapter, have as well a strategic and a tactical part as an operational part like for example the recruitment or the dismissal of employees. HRM-measures underlie a continuous monitoring and are re-justified and assessed in yearly planning cycles of the HRM-Controlling.

The holistic approach of KM is characterised by the following four fields of intervention, that have to be processed combined and in a coordinated manner:

- Corporate culture / identity
- Corporate organization
- Process organisation
- Information technology

This means - having a first look at the corporate culture – that there is some kind of basic culture to share knowledge. This postulation is very vague and can seldom be proven in practical experience. It can be that a consciously perception of „knowledge sharing“ is actually recognised because the company accepted it explicitly. It is much easier to proof that corporate organization reflect a culture of knowledge sharing by identifying positions like e.g. Chief Information Officer (CIO) or Chief Knowledge Officer (CKO) or comparable staff positions, that have the special task to organize information or knowledge in companies. There exist some highly specialised roles like *thematic area manager* or *debriefer* which have an operational character but can't be found very often in practical experience. HRM-departments have a well-defined grown structure. Besides staff positions in this area managers always have a human resource oriented task in their leading role. Special processes like *lessons learned* or *communities of practice* depict the process organisation. Each regular communication is an example for process organisation. Basically each human resource-based competency-process is a KM-process. As a last component the information technology with their systems can be found very easily in each company.

The enhancement of the treatment of implicit and explicit knowledge can be found again in the HRM. This can be explicit measures of personnel development like trainings or workshops. On the other hand the transfer of tacit knowledge e.g. by mentoring or rotation on positions is increasing.

The addition „on all levels" can be transferred to HRM again. On the one hand there are all measures concerning the single employee like individual trainings. On the other hand we have all measures concerning the whole organisation.

The last aspect taken from the definition of KM is to reach company-goals better. Again this goal can be substantiated by HRM goals. These can be for example the controlling of the number of employees or the creation of new job profiles.

2 Holistic Competency Management, Competency Catalogues and Ontologies

Felser defined in [13] competence as follows:

"Competence is determined by the knowledge-based and network-driven ability of an actor and his environment to act alone or with partners, to satisfy indirectly or directly existing customer requirements optimally. By this sustainable added values are created in a competitive and superior manner."

During the last years the importance of skill-management approaches has become more and more visible to companies. Companies have recognised that the knowledge of their employees is a decisive competitive factor. Measures like old-age pension and reduction in staff in general imply a constant loss of knowledge. This trend especially on the side of the older employees with a high level of implicit knowledge is dangerous. Companies could get a problem out of the overall demographic change that takes place because they cannot meet their recruitment requirements [2]. Both aspects imply a shorting of human resources and therefore a shortening of knowledge. An accompanying aspect is the speed of technical innovation that takes place. Employees have to be trained to „grow" with the requirements of their positions. A variety of technical systems and the growth of variants e.g. in the automotive sector imply a constant change rate that has effects on the knowledge bases of the workers. Companies therefore feel the pressure to secure their „new blood" on the one side and to train their existing employees on the other side.

Companies that want to cope with these challenges and that want to be versatile have to invest in the target-oriented development of the skill of their employees. Holistic approaches of competency-management solve the fitting of the gap between competency-offers and competency-demands. In an ideal solution this should be done semi-automatically with the support of an intelligent software system. This is the foundation for following measures like the development of competencies (trainings).

2.1 Competency Catalogues

Competency catalogues play a central role in the discussion about competency management. They are the vocabulary to document the actual skills of the employees in their skill-profiles. The catalogue is also used to define the reference skill-profiles for positions. These two types of profiles allow afterwards a matching and an identification of a possible gap-profile. An employee skill-profile depicts the actual skills of an individual employee. Single skills in the profile can be weighted (beginner, advanced, expert, trainer). A reference-position-skill-profile is a list of weighted skills, that are needed to fulfil the working-requirements of this individual position. Both profiles use in an ideal case the same vocabulary from the same competency catalogue [10].

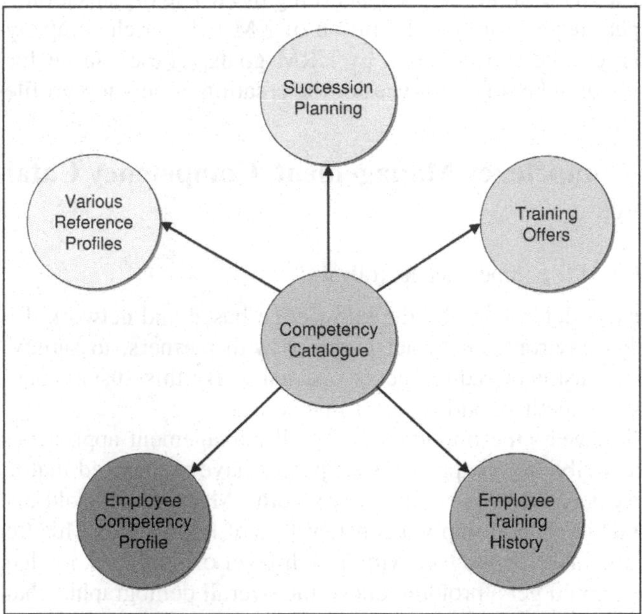

Fig. 2. Use of competency catalogues

The content of a competency catalogue are all skills that are relevant to the company. Normally they are structured in a taxonomy.

3 Scenario at DaimlerChrysler AG, Wörth Plant

Let's now have a look at a real world example from DaimlerChrysler AG, Wörth Plant. It shows an initiative to integrate existing processes in HR with ontologies. Further the example is to show the benefits of ontologies [12] in the context of HR.

First step to get a consistent competency catalogue is to assess all relevant competencies that are needed to fulfil the needs of the company to orderly execute their processes. The modelling of the catalogue was done with the ontology management tool KAON [9]. The catalogue already existed as a simple flat database table and was taken over into KAON as is without any further changes in a first step. The taxonomy has roundabout 700 single competencies. This number results out of the diversification in the automotive sector with its variety of different job profiles throughout all areas of production, management and administration. Without this highly diversificated catalogue it wouldn't be possible to represent all employees with their individual job profiles.

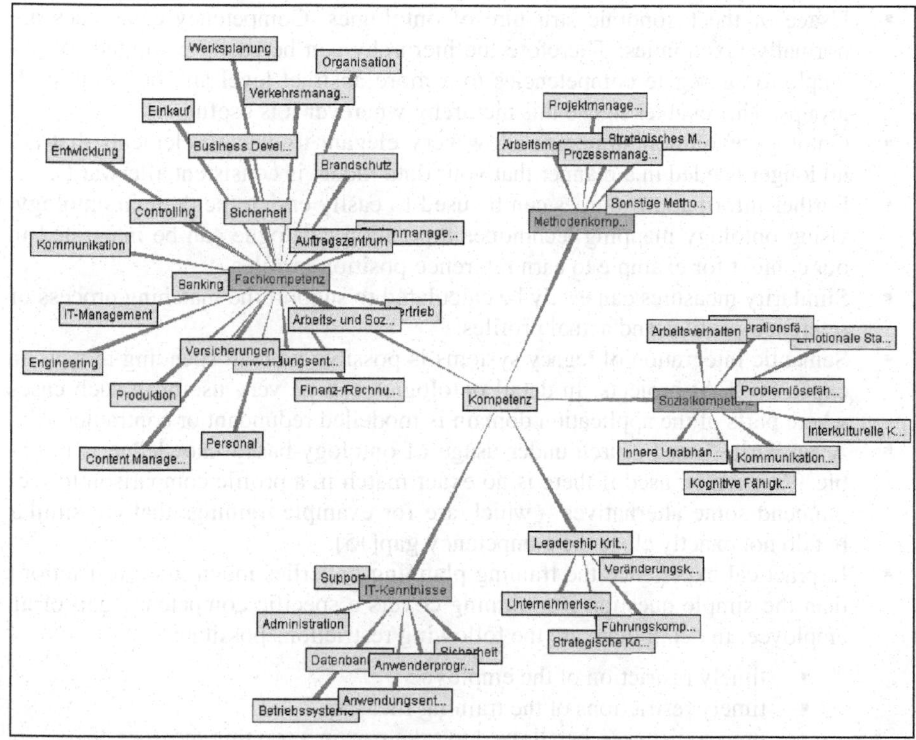

Fig. 3. Extract of the competency catalogue (in german)

To have a concrete look at the benefits of ontologies it is worth to look at the field of training analysis and training planning as to core processes of classic personnel development. To do this we extended our simple skill taxonomy by various relations referencing this application domain (cp. Fig. 2). For example you can do the following basic inference with these modifications:

$$\forall ma \in M, s \in S, k \in K, a \in A:$$

$$(take\_part\_in(ma,s) \wedge imparts\_competency(s,k,a))$$

$$\rightarrow has\_competency(ma,k,a)$$

M = Employee, S = Training, K = Competency, A = Weight of Competency

This means that an employee that has participated in some training, that imparts knowledge – concrete a specific competency with a specific weight (e.g. MS Exel Advanced) – acquires this knowledge by participating in the training measure.

Basically there is always the question where ontologies have benefits over conventional approaches like established ERP-Software with relational data models. Yes – it is true that everything what we can do with ontologies can be done with some other technology as well. But there is always the question how much effort do you have to pay as invest for your solution in contrast to often very elegant ontology-solutions with lots of implicit benefits like:

- Usage of the taxonomic structure of ontologies. Competency catalogues are normally taxonomies. Therefore the hierarchy can be easily exploited for example to aggregate competencies to a more abstract level and build up skill-groups. This enables to use this hierarchy wherever it is useful.
- Ontology-evolution strategies allow very elegant to discard elements that are no longer needed in a manner that your data model is consistent afterwards.
- Further information sources can be used to easily enrich the domain ontology. Using ontology-mapping techniques a position catalogue can be integrated in our context for example to earn reference position profiles.
- Similarity measures can easily be calculated to support the matching process of reference-profiles and actual profiles.
- Semantic integration of legacy systems is possible without spending money on expensive EAI-projects. In detail ontologies can be very useful in such cases where parts of the application domain is modelled redundant or contradictorily.
- A similarity based search under usage of ontology-based knowledge is possible. This can be used if there is no exact match in a profile comparison to recommend some alternatives – which are for example trainings that are similar but do not exactly close the competency gap[15].
- In practical experience the training planning underlies much more restrictions than the simple question if a training covers a specific competency gap of an employee. In detail there are the following restrictions possible:
  - timely restriction of the employee
  - timely restrictions of the training measure
  - pre-requisites to be allowed to take part in a training measure
  - limitation of the number of possible participants per training
  - budget limitations

  Algorithm to handle and optimize these restrictions can be easily declarative formulated with formal rules on the basis of ontologies (cp. Constraint Logic Programming).

At the moment we are working on the above mentioned ideas. Especially the semantic integration of legacy systems is important for real-world applications, specifically if most of the legacy applications have been designed to be isolated applications.

Techniques as the similarity search are partly used in the area of the company intranet and are to some extent used while matching competency-profiles. In the area of planning und optimizing complex situation with lots of restrictions there is still a high level of manual operations. In this case we expect benefits in enhancing underlying processes with our technology.

Besides the sketched module of training analysis we have further modules that are actually in design-phase and partly in prototype-phase. The following figure shows the modules and their interaction with other parts of our concept:

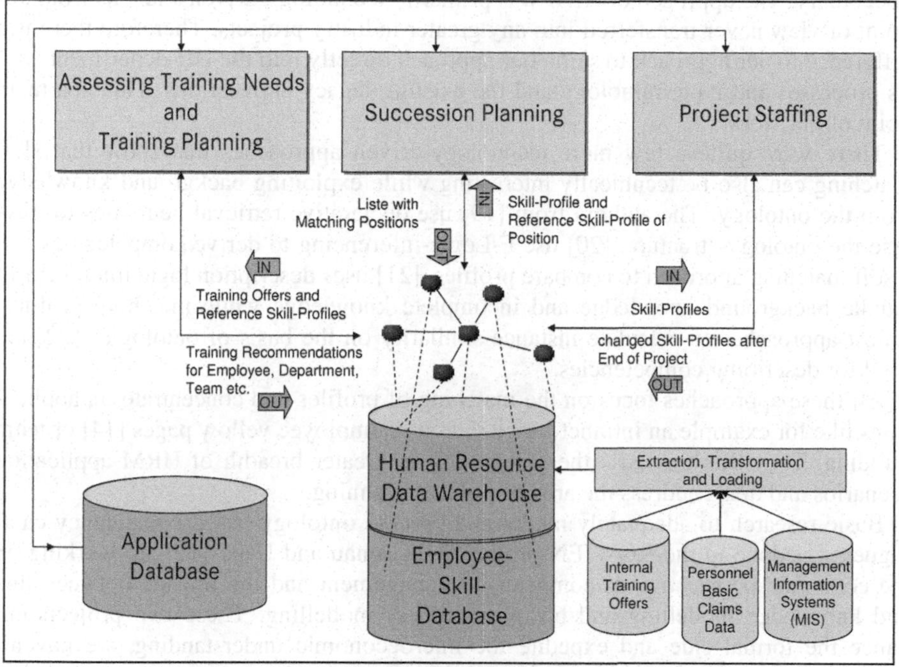

Fig. 4. Overall Architecture

As central database we have a HR-Data Warehouse. In this HR-DW most of the HR-data from legacy-systems is integrated in one place. On top of the HR-DW as a meta-layer between the database and the application modules resides the central domain ontology. It consists mainly of the competency catalogue and some further enriching information sources like organizational structure, reference position catalogue etc. To proof that the concept works, we already implemented the module "Project Staffing", which shows representatively for the other two modules that an ontology-based matching on competency profiles does work.

4 Closing Remarks and Related Work

This paper depicted the inter-relations between Knowledge Management and Human Resource Management and sketched finally how ontologies can be used for training planning. Further we tried to discuss certain benefits of ontologies over conventional methods. The idea to model skills of employees with ontologies is not new in literature. It was propagated already 1999 at AIAI [16; 17]. Especially in [16] possible use cases of ontology-based employee skill profiles are discussed, like: (i) *skill gap analysis* (on the company level and therefore part of the strategic personnel development);

(ii) *project team building*; (iii) *recruitment planning* (strategic personnel planning, too); (iv) *training analysis* (on an individual level of personnel development). The ontologies used there would be classified as "simple ontologies" by McGuiness' Ontology spectrum [18], in essence taxonomies with formal semantics and controlled vocabulary. The approach of AIAI was primarily technology-driven and was from our point of view never transferred into any greater industry projects. Therefore there is a difference to our approach to settle our approach directly into the HR-department with its processes and its terminology and the existing legacy applications. This is a main point of our work.

There were quite a few more technology-driven approaches that show that skill matching can also be technically interesting while exploiting background knowledge from the ontology. The authors from [19] use declarative retrieval heuristics to traverse the ontology-structure. [20] use F-Logic-inferencing to derive competencies and a soft matching approach to compare profiles. [21] uses description logic inferences to handle background knowledge and incomplete knowledge while matching profiles. Latest approaches to calculate instance-similarity on the basis of ontologies [22] are used for describing competencies.

All these approaches focus on the matching of profiles and concentrate on applications like for example an intranet-based search in employee yellow pages [14] or team building. They don't discuss the embedding in greater breadth of HRM-application scenarios and don't address the area of training planning.

Basic research to adequately model and process ontology-based competency catalogues was done in the KOWIEN project [3]. Gronau and Uslar [11] are working on the economic perspective of competency management and the linkage between this and knowledge modelling and business process modelling. These two projects enhance the formal side and expedite the microeconomic understanding, we haven't found a comparable integrating approach like ours that integrates also strategic aspects.

References

[1] Abecker, A. (2004): Tools im Wissensmanagement – Ein Überblick. DTT Symposion 2004 "Terminologie & Wissensmanagement.", Köln.

[2] Buck, H., Kistler, E., Mendius, H. G. (2002): Demographischer Wandel in der Arbeitswelt – Chancen für eine innovative Arbeitsgestaltung, Broschürenreihe: Demographie und Arbeitswelt (BMBF), Stuttgart..

[3] http://www.kowien.uni-essen.de/ (Letzter Zugriff: 31. August 2004.)

[4] Scholz, C., Djarrazadeh, M. (1995): Strategisches Personal-Management – Konzeptionen und Realisationen, in: USW-Schriften für Führungskräfte Band 28, Schäffer Poeschel.

[5] Kolb, M. (1995): Personalmanagement, Berlin: Verlag Arno Spitz GmbH.

[6] Schuler, R. S. (1992): Strategic Human Resource Management: Linking People with the Strategic Needs of the Business, in: Organizational Dynamics.

[7] Scholz, C. (1993): Personalmanagement. Informationsorientierte und verhaltenstheoretische Grundlagen. 3. Auflage, München.

[8] Mädche, A.; Staab, S., Studer, R. (2001): WI - Schlagwort – Ontologien; Wirtschaftsinformatik, Vol.43 . 2001, H.4 , S.393-396

[9] http://kaon.semanticweb.org (Letzter Zugriff: 31. August 2004.)

[10] Faix, W.; Buchwald, C.; Wetzler, R. (1991): Qualifikationsplanung für Unternehmen und Mitarbeiter. Wiesbaden: Gabler.

[11] Gronau, N., Uslar, M. (2004): Requirements and Recommenders for Skill Management. In: R. Dieng-Kuntz & N. Matta (2004): ECAI-04 Workshop on Knowledge Management and Organizational Memory, Valencia, Spanien.

[12] Studer, R.; Oppermann, H.; Schnurr, H.-P. (2001): Die Bedeutung von Ontologien für das Wissensmanagement. Institut AIFB, Universität Karlsruhe.

[13] Felser,W. (2003): Portale für eine kompetente Gesellschaft.URL: http://www.competence-site.de. (Letzter Zugriff: 31. August 2004.)

[14] Lau, T., Sure Y., (2002): Introducing Ontology-based Skills Management at a large Insurance Company , In Modellierung 2002, Modellierung in der Praxis - Modellierung für die Praxis, Tutzing, März 2002, pp. 123-134.

[15] Ehrig, M., Hefke, M., Stojanovic, N. (2004): Similarity for Ontologies – a Comprehensive Framework. Submitted to: 5th Int. Conf. on Practical Aspects of Knowledge Management (PAKM 2004).

[16] Stader, J., Macintosh, A. (1999), Capability Modelling and Knowledge Management. Applications and Innovations in Expert Systems VII, Proc. ES'99 – 19th Int. Conf. of the BCS Specialist Group on Knowledge-Based Systems and Applied Artificial Intelligence, pages 33–50. Springer-Verlag.

[17] Jarvis P, Stader J, Macintosh A, Moore J, Chung P. (1999): What Right Do You Have to Do That? In: ICEIS - 1st Int. Conf. on Enterprise Information Systems; Portugal.

[18] McGuinness, D. L. (2002): Ontologies Come of Age. In: D. Fensel, J. Hendler, H. Lieberman, W. Wahlster (Hrsg.): Spinning the Semantic Web: Bringing the World Wide Web to Its Full Potential. MIT Press.

[19] Liao, M., Hinkelmann, K., Abecker, A., Sintek, M. (1999): A Competence Knowledge Base System for the Organizational Memory. In: F. Puppe (Hrsg.): XPS-99 / 5. Deutsche Tagung Wissensbasierte Systeme, Würzburg, Springer Verlag, LNAI 1570.

[20] Sure, Y., Maedche, A., Staab, S. (2000): Leveraging Corporate Skill Knowledge - From ProPer to OntoProPer. In: D. Mahling & U. Reimer (Hrsg.): 3rd Int. Conf. on Practical Aspects of Knowledge Management (PAKM 2000).

[21] Colucci, S., Di Noia, T., Di Sciascio, E., Donini, F.M., Mongiello, M., Mottola, M. (2003): A Formal Approach to Ontology-Based Semantic Match of Skills Descriptions. Journal of Universal Computer Science (J.UCS) 9(12):1437-1454, 2003. Springer Verlag.

Supervised Learning of an Ontology Alignment Process

Marc Ehrig[1], York Sure[1], and Steffen Staab[2]

[1] Institute AIFB, University of Karlsruhe
[2] ISWeb, University of Koblenz-Landau

Abstract. Ontology alignment is a crucial task to enable interoperability among different agents. However, the complexity of the alignment task especially for large ontologies requires automated support for the creation of alignment methods. When looking at current ontology alignment methods one can see that they are either not optimized for given ontologies or their optimization by machine learning means is mostly restricted to the extensional definition of ontologies. With APFEL (Alignment Process Feature Estimation and Learning) we present a machine learning approach that explores the user validation of initial alignments for optimizing alignment methods. The methods are based on extensional and intensional ontology definitions. Core to APFEL is the idea of a generic alignment process, the steps of which may be represented explicitly. APFEL then generates new hypotheses for what might be useful features and similarity assessments and weights them by machine learning approaches. APFEL compares favorably in our experiments to competing approaches.

1 Introduction

Semantic alignment between ontologies is a necessary precondition to establish interoperability between agents or services using different ontologies. Thus, in recent years different methods for automatic ontology alignment have been proposed to deal with this challenge. Thereby, the proposed methods were constricted to one of two different paradigms: Either, *(i)*, proposals would include a manually predefined automatic method for proposing alignments, which would be used in the actual alignment process (cf. [1,15,5]). They typically consist of a number of substrategies such as finding similar labels. Or, *(ii)*, proposals would learn an automatic alignment method based on instance representations, e.g. bag-of-word models of documents (cf. [2]). Both paradigms suffer from drawbacks. The first paradigm suffers from the problem that it is impossible, even for an expert knowledge engineer, to predict what strategy of aligning entities is most successful for a given pair of ontologies. This is especially the case with increasing complexity of ontology languages or increasing amounts of domain specific conventions. The second paradigm is often hurt by the lack of instances or instance descriptions. Also, knowledge encoded in the intensional descriptions of concepts and relations is only marginally exploited by this way.

Hence, there remains the need to automatically combine multiple diverse and complementary alignment strategies of *all* indicators, i.e. extensional *and* intensional descriptions, in order to produce comprehensive, effective and efficient semi-automatic

K.-D. Althoff et al. (Eds.): WM 2005, LNAI 3782, pp. 508–517, 2005.

alignment methods. Such methods need to be flexible to cope with different strategies for various application scenarios, e.g. by using parameters. We call them "Parameterizable Alignment Methods" (PAM). We have developed a bootstrapping approach for acquiring the parameters that drive such a PAM. We call our approach APFEL for "Alignment Process Feature Estimation and Learning".

2 Foundations

2.1 Ontology

In the understanding of this paper an ontology consists of both schema and instantiating data. An ontology O is therefore defined through the following tuple: $O := (C, H_C, R_C, H_R, I, R_I, A)$. Concepts C of the schema are arranged in a subsumption hierarchy H_C. Relations R_C exist between pairs of concepts. Relations can also be arranged in a hierarchy H_R. (Meta-)Data is constituted by instances I of specific concepts. Theses instances are interconnected by relational instances R_I. Additionally one can define axioms A which can be used to infer knowledge from already existing knowledge. Common languages to represent ontologies are RDF(S)[1] or OWL[2], though one should note that each language offers different modeling primitives.

2.2 Alignment and Similarity

Due to the wide range of expressions used in this area (merging, alignment, integration etc.), we want to describe our understanding of the term "alignment". We define alignment as (cf. [5]): *"Relating similar (according to some metric) concepts or relations from different sources to each other by an equivalence relation. An alignment results in a virtual integration."* We want to stick to this definition, more specific we will demand the *same* semantic meaning of two *entities*. Formally an ontology alignment function can be defined the following way:

- $align : O_{i_1} \rightarrow O_{i_2}$
- $align(e_{i_1 j_1}) = e_{i_2 j_2}$, if $sim(e_{i_1 j_1}, e_{i_2 j_2}) > t$ with t being the threshold entity $e_{i_1 j_1}$ is aligned with $e_{i_2 j_2}$; they are semantically identical, each entity $e_{i_1 j_1}$ is aligned to at most one entity $e_{i_2 j_2}$

So far we only consider one-to-one alignments between singular ontological entities (see above). Neither do we cover alignments of whole ontologies or sub-trees, nor complex alignments such as concatenation of literals (*e.g.* name corresponds to first name plus last name) or functional transformation of attributes (*e.g.* currency conversions).

The alignment function relies on the notion of similarity which we shall describe here (cf. [6]):

- $sim(x, y) \in [0..1]$
- $sim(x, y) = 1 \rightarrow x = y$: two objects are identical.

[1] http://www.w3.org/TR/rdf-schema/

[2] http://www.w3.org/TR/owl-guide/

- $sim(x, y) = 0$: two objects are different and have no common characteristics.
- $sim(x, y) = sim(y, x)$: similarity is symmetric.

Further we define similarity of ontologies through:

- O_i: ontology, with ontology index $i \in \mathbb{N}$
- e_{ij}: entities of O_i, with $e_{ij} \in \{C_i, R_i, I_i\}$, entity index $j \in \mathbb{N}$
- $sim(e_{i_1 j_1}, e_{i_2 j_2})$: similarity function between two entities $e_{i_1 j_1}$ and $e_{i_2 j_2} (i_1 \neq i_2)$; as shown later this function makes use of the ontological structure of the compared ontologies.

3 Alignment Identification

3.1 General Alignment Process

We made the general observation that alignment methods like PROMPT [5] or GLUE [2] may be mapped onto a generic alignment process. Major steps include:

1. Feature Engineering, i.e. select small excerpts of the overall ontology definition to describe a specific entity (e.g., the `label` to describe the concept `o1:Daimler`).
2. Search Step Selection, i.e. choose two entities from the two ontologies to compare (e.g., `o1:Daimler` and `o2:Mercedes`).
3. Similarity Assessment, i.e. indicate a similarity for a given description of two entities (e.g., $\text{simil}_{\text{superConcept}}$(`o1:Daimler` ,`o2:Mercedes`)=1.0).
4. Similarity Aggregation, i.e. aggregate multiple similarity assessment for one pair of entities into a single measure (e.g., simil(`o1:Daimler` ,`o2:Mercedes`)=0.5).
5. Interpretation, i.e. use all aggregated numbers, a threshold and interpretation strategy to propose the alignment (align(`o1:Daimler`)='$\perp$').
6. Iteration, i.e. as the similarity of one entity pair influences the similarity of neighboring entity pairs, the equality is propagated through the ontologies (e.g., it may lead to a new simil(`o1:Daimler` ,`o2:Mercedes`)=0.85, subsequently resulting in align(`o1:Daimler`)=`o2:Mercedes`).

3.2 Feature Engineering and Similarity Assessment

Our implemented approach, which we refer to as QOM (Quick Ontology Mapping, see also [1]), is based on several similarity methods. More specifically we use manually encoded similarity rules which means in a nutshell that we are using rules to identify possible alignments. The manual effort is necessary because coherences in ontologies are

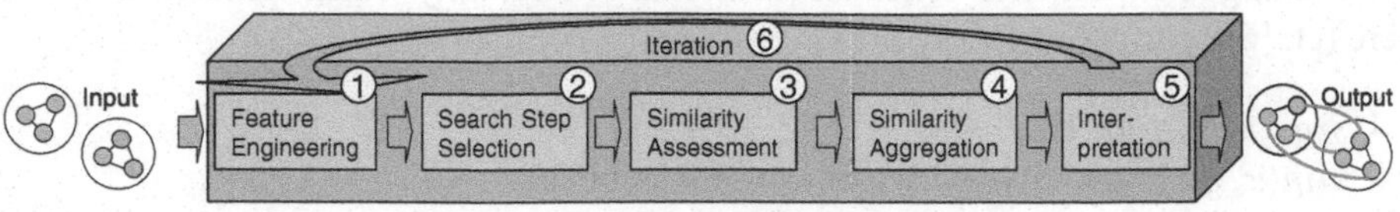

Fig. 1. General Alignment Process in PAM

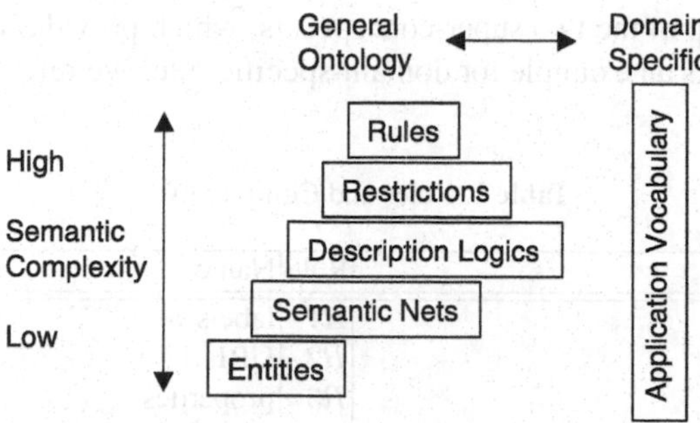

Fig. 2. Similarity stack

too complex to be directly learned by machines. An expert understanding the encoded knowledge in ontologies formulates machine-interpretable rules out of the information. Each rule shall give a hint on whether two entities are identical, but no rule for itself provides enough support to unambiguously identify an alignment. Naturally, evaluation of these manually created rules has to be a core element of the overall process.

The presented general idea will now be explicitly used to determine similarity between ontologies. To get a better understanding, the rules are categorized in a similarity stack as shown in graph 2. Ontologies are based on certain vocabularies which are well-defined, well-understood, and with a generally accepted meaning. The left part shows these aspects arranged along their complexity, which is derived from the "layer cake" of [6], ranging from simple object comparisons over ontology vocabulary up to restrictions and rules. Special shared ontology domains *e.g.* SEKT-common in the mentioned SEKT project, have their own additional vocabulary. The right part therefore covers domain-specific aspects. As this domain-specific knowledge can be situated at any level of ontological complexity, it is presented as a box across all of them.

Labels are human identifiers (names) for entities, normally shared by a community of humans speaking a common language. We can therefore infer that *if labels are the same, the entities are probably also the same* (**R1** as shown in Table 1). Several ideas have already been created to compare labels, *e.g.* the edit distance[8], or the use of dictionaries such as WordNet [9].

```
<owl:Class rdf:ID=''id1''>
    <rdfs:label>telephone number</label>
</owl:Class>
<owl:Class rdf:ID=''id2''>
    <rdfs:label>phone number</label>
</owl:Class>
```

Example 1. Two entities id1 and id2 with similar labels

Further a taxonomy can be created over concepts, in which a concept inherits all the relations of its super-concepts. Another rule is that if concepts are the same, they will probably have the same super-concepts. We turn the rule around: *if super-concepts are the same, the actual concepts are similar to each other* (**R5**). In practice we calculate the degree of overlap of the two super-concept sets, which provides a number between 0% and 100% [9]. As an example for domain-specific rules we refer to **R16** and **R17**.

Table 1. Rules and Complexity

	Rule	Name
Concepts are similar, if ... [rule] ... are similar	$R1$	labels
	$R2$	URIs
	$R3$	properties
	$R5$	super-concepts
	$R6$	concept siblings
	$R7$	sub-concepts
	$R10$	instances
	$R12$	fraction of instances
	$R15$	sameAs relation (links the two)
Relations are similar, if ... [rule] ... are similar	$R1$	labels
	$R2$	URIs
	$R4$	domain and range
	$R8$	super-properties
	$R9$	sub-properties
	$R14$	connected instances
	$R15$	sameAs relation (links the two)
Instances are similar, if ... [rule] ... are similar	$R1$	labels
	$R2$	URIs
	$R11$	mother-concepts
	$R13$	properties and instances
	$R15$	sameAs relation (links the two)
Files are similar, if additionally ... [rule] ... are similar	$R16$	hash-code
	$R17$	mime-type

3.3 Similarity Aggregation

As shown in [11] a combination of the so far presented rules leads to better alignment results compared to using only one at a time. Clearly not all introduced similarity methods have to be used for each aggregation, especially as some methods have a high correlation. A general and straight-forward formula for this integration task can be given by summarizing over the n weighted similarity methods.

$$sim(e_{i_1j_1}, e_{i_2j_2}) = \sum_{k=1}^{n} w_k sim_k(e_{i_1j_1}, e_{i_2j_2})$$

with w_k being the weight for a specific method sim_k and $n \in \mathbb{N}$

Please note our assumption that similarities can be aggregated and are increasing strictly. We add the results of the single methods giving them a weight which indicates their importance. The weights could be assigned manually or learned *e.g.* through maximization of the f-measure (see Section 5) of a training set.

3.4 Interpretation

After performing the just described steps we have a list which consists of the most similar entities of two ontologies plus the corresponding similarity value. Now remains the question which level of similarity is appropriate to indicate equality for the alignment and which strongly indicates inequality? We have chosen here a very simple approach where we predefine the threshold intuitively based on our own experience as modelling experts. Every similarity value above the threshold indicates a match, everything below is dismissed. As future work we will try learn the threshold automatically, *e.g.* by maximizing the f-measure. Further approaches to determine the cut-off criterium are *e.g.* presented in [12].

4 APFEL

In this section the APFEL process is explained in detail following Figure 3. Data structures are illustrated through white boxes and process steps through colored boxes.

4.1 Data Structures

APFEL requires two ontologies O_1 and O_2 as inputs to its processing. Either these are the ontologies for which the further alignment process will be optimized directly. Or, they exemplarily represent a type which requires an optimized alignment method.

Core to APFEL is the representation of the generic alignment process. Relevant data structures for representation include: *(i)* Q_F: features engineered (e.g. label, instances, domain), *(ii)* Q_S: similarity assessments corresponding to the features of Q_F (e.g. equality, subsumption), *(iii)* Q_W: weighting scheme for an aggregation of feature-similarity assessments (e.g. weighted averaging), and *(iv)* Q_T: interpretation strategy (e.g. alignments occur if similarity is above the fixed threshold).

Such a declarative representation can be given to a parameterizable alignment method, PAM, for execution. In fact, we can initialize PAM with a representation of different strategies. Thus, an initial alignment function, $\text{align}_{\text{init}}$, may be defined by $\text{align}_{\text{init}}$:=PAM(PROMPT) or $\text{align}_{\text{init}}$:=PAM(QOM). Then, APFEL uses user validations A_V of the initial proposals of $\text{align}_{\text{init}}$.

In general, the described input does not explicitly require a knowledge engineer. The two ontologies, an arbitrary (predefined) alignment method, and the validation of the initial alignments may be processed by a typical user as well.

The output of APFEL is an improved alignment method, $\text{align}_{\text{optim}}$, defined as $\text{align}_{\text{optim}}$:=PAM(APFEL($O_1, O_2, Q_F, Q_S, Q_W, Q_T, A_V$)). The parameters that characterize APFEL($O_1, O_2, Q_F, Q_S, Q_W, Q_T, A_V$) constitute the tuple ($D_F$, D_S, D_W, D_T) with the indices indicating the same as for Q.

4.2 Generation and Validation of Initial Alignments

Machine learning as used in this paper requires training examples. The assistance in their creation is necessary as in a typical ontology alignment setting there are only a

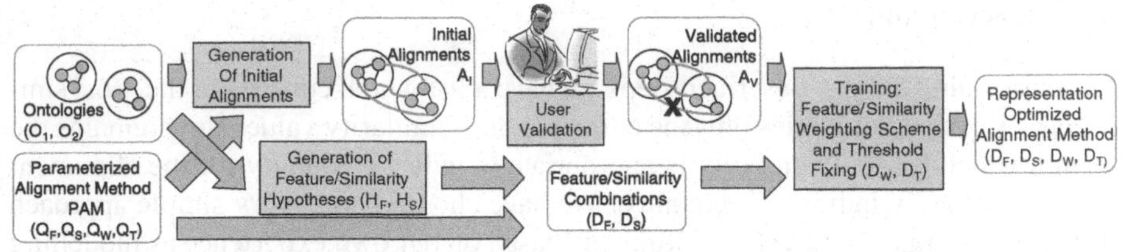

Fig. 3. Detailed Process in APFEL

small number of really plausible alignments available compared to the large number of candidates, which might be possible a priori.

Therefore, we use an existing parametrization as input to the Parameterizable Alignment Method, e.g. $\text{align}_{\text{init}}$=PAM(QOM) to create the initial alignments A_I for the given ontologies O_1 and O_2. As these results are only preliminary, PAM does not have to use very sophisticated processes: simple features and similarities (e.g. label similarity) combined with an averaging and fixed threshold are sufficient in most cases.

This allows the user to easily validate the initial alignments and thus generate correct training data A_V. If the user further knows additional alignments he can add these alignments to the validated list. Entity pairs not marked by the user are by default treated as disjunct entities. Obviously the quality of the later machine learning step depends on the quality and quantity of the validated alignments done at this point.

4.3 Generation of Feature/Similarity Hypotheses

As mentioned in the introduction it becomes difficult for the human user to decide which features and similarity heuristics make sense in indicating an alignment of two entities. Our approach therefore generates these feature/similarity combinations.

The basis of the feature/similarity combinations is given by an arbitrary alignment method such as PAM(QOM) with which we have achieved good results (see [13]).

Further, from the two given ontologies APFEL extracts additional features H_F by examining the ontologies for overlapping features. At this point domain-specific features are integrated into the alignment process. These features are combined in a combinatorial way with a generic set of predefined similarity assessments including similarity measures for, e.g., equality, string similarity, or set inclusion. Thus, APFEL derives similarity assessments H_S for features H_F. Some feature/similarity combinations will not be very useful, e.g. comparing whether one license number is a substring of another one. However, in the subsequent training step machine learning will be used to pick out those which improve alignment results.

From the feature/similarity combinations of (Q_F, Q_S) and of the extracted hypotheses (H_F, H_S) we derive an extended collection of feature/similarity combinations (D_F, D_S) with $D_F := Q_F \cup H_F$ and $D_S := Q_S \cup H_S$.

4.4 Training

After determining the classification of two entities of being aligned or not (A_V), all validated alignment pairs are processed with the previously automatically generated collection of features and similarities. From each feature/similarity combination a numerical value is returned which is saved together with the entity pair.

Based on these example training alignments A_V we can now learn a classifier which distinguishes between those entities which align and those which are disjunct. Different machine learning techniques for classification (e.g. decision tree learner, neural networks, or support vector machines) assign an optimal internal weighting D_W and threshold D_T scheme for each of the different feature/similarity combinations (D_F, D_S). The machine learning methods like C4.5 (J4.8 in Weka) capture relevance values for feature/similarity combinations. If the latter do not have any (or only marginal) relevance for the alignment, they are given a weight of zero.

From this we finally receive the most important feature/similarity combinations (features D_F and similarity D_S) and the weighting D_W and threshold D_T thereof. With this we can set up the final ontology alignment method which we call $\text{align}_{\text{optim}}$:=PAM(APFEL($O_1, O_2, Q_F, Q_S, Q_W, Q_T, A_V$)). Depending on the complexity of the alignment problem it might be necessary to repeat the step of test data generation (based on the improved alignment method) and training.

5 Evaluation

Evaluation Setting. This paper mainly focuses on an approach to improve methods for the alignment of two ontologies. Neither the learning process APFEL itself nor the quality of the alignment method PAM can be evaluated directly. Therefore, we evaluate the results returned by the learned process, i.e. the quality of the alignments. They are compared to an approach using labels only for comparison and the manually defined alignment process QOM.

We use standard information retrieval metrics to assess the different approaches (cf. [14]):

$$\text{Precision } p = \frac{\#correct\_found\_alignments}{\#found\_alignments}$$

$$\text{Recall } r = \frac{\#correct\_found\_alignments}{\#existing\_alignments}$$

$$\text{F-Measure } f_1 = \frac{2pr}{p+r}$$

We consider the f-measure as most relevant for our evaluation since it balances well precision and recall.

Two different scenarios have been used to evaluate the described machine-learning approach. In the first scenario we use two ontologies describing Russia. Students created these ontologies with the objective to represent the content of two independent travel websites about Russia. The ontologies have approximately 400 entities each. The gold standard of 160 possible alignments was derived by the students who assigned the alignments manually. For the second scenario we have only one ontology, but want to identify equal entities (duplicates) within it. In terms of the problem structure this scenario doesn't differ from a scenario where we want to find equal objects in two

Table 2. Results of the Evaluation

Scenario	Strategy (#/name)	No. of FS	Precision	Recall	F-Measure
Russia	1 Only Labels	1	0.990	0.335	0.422
	2 QOM	25	0.679	0.655	0.667
	3 Decision Tree Learner	7	0.887	0.625	0.733
	4 Neural Net	7	0.863	0.539	0.651
	5 Support Vector Machine	8	0.566	0.636	0.593
Bibliographic	1 Only Labels	1	0.909	0.073	0.135
	2 QOM	25	0.279	0.397	0.328
	3 Decision Tree Learner	7	0.630	0.375	0.470
	4 Neural Net	7	0.542	0.359	0.432
	5 Support Vector Machine	6	0.515	0.289	0.370

ontologies, i.e. an alignment. The ontology describes 2100 bibliographical entities, including 275 manually identified equal entities.

Results and Lessons Learned. From several evaluation runs we have obtained the results in Table 2. Although the precision of an approach based on labels only is very high, the very low recall level leads to a low overall f-measure, which is our key evaluation value. Thus, our key competitor in this evaluation, QOM, receives a lot better results with its semantically rich feature/similarity combinations. To investigate the effectiveness of APFEL, we have tested its different strategies against each other (with 150 training examples for the different learning methods). In both scenarios the decision tree learner returns results better than the two other machine learning approaches, i.e. neural nets and support vector machines. The margin on improvement as compared to QOM in the Russia scenario (6.6 percentage points) and in the Bibliography scenario (7.3 percentage points) is both times very good. Alignments for the Russia scenario are identified precisely. In the bibliographic scenario the alignment method can make extensive use of the learned domain-specific features. Finally, the lower number of feature/similarity combinations (maximum of eight for APFEL vs. 25 for QOM) leads even to an increase in efficiency compared to QOM. To sum up, APFEL generates an alignment method which is competitive with the latest existing ontology alignment methods. However, it is important to apply the correct machine learner and a sufficient amount of training data.

6 Concluding Remarks

Many related approaches have already been mentioned throughout the paper. We here cite an approach also using machine learning, GLUE [2]. However, their learning is restricted on concept classifiers for instances based on instance descriptions, i.e. the content of web pages. From the learned classifiers they derive whether concepts in two schemas correspond to each other. Additional relaxation labeling is based solely on manually encoded predefined rules. Nevertheless, from all ontology alignment approaches their work is closest to APFEL. In [14] the same authors introduce the notion of the use of domain specific attributes, thus restricting their work on databases.

The alignment problem arises in many scenarios. We have shown a methodology for identifying alignments between two ontologies based on the intelligent combination of manually encoded rules. Evaluation of QOM proved our initial hypothesis, i.e. the combination of our presented similarity measures leaded to considerably better results than than a simple label based approach. Semantics helps bridging the alignment gap. Further, with the complexity of the alignment task rising it becomes important to use automated solutions to optimize the alignment approaches like PAM without losing the advantages of the general human understanding of ontologies. We contributed to this challenge with our novel approach APFEL, which has shown to be very valuable. The f-measure, the core evaluation measure for all our approaches, is considerably higher than in the manually set QOM approach.

Acknowledgements. Research reported in this paper has been partially financed by the EU in the IST projects SEKT (IST-2003-506826) and SWAP (IST-2001-34103).

References

1. Ehrig, M., Staab, S.: QOM - quick ontology mapping. In van Harmelen, F., McIlraith, S., Plexousakis, D., eds.: Proc. of the Third International Semantic Web Conference (ISWC2004). LNCS, Hiroshima, Japan, Springer (2004) 683–696
2. Doan, A., Domingos, P., Halevy, A.: Learning to match the schemas of data sources: A multistrategy approach. VLDB Journal **50** (2003) 279–301
3. Klein, M.: Combining and relating ontologies: an analysis of problems and solutions. In Gomez-Perez, A., et al., eds.: Workshop on Ontology and Information Sharing, IJCAI'01, Seattle, USA (2001)
4. Bisson, G.: Why and how to define a similarity measure for object based representation systems. Towards Very Large Knowledge Bases (1995) 236–246
5. Noy, N.F., Musen, M.A.: The PROMPT suite: interactive tools for ontology merging and mapping. International Journal of Human-Computer Studies **59** (2003) 983–1024
6. Berners-Lee, T., Hendler, J., Lassila, O.: The Semantic Web. Scientific American **284** (2001) 34–43
7. Levenshtein, I.V.: Binary codes capable of correcting deletions, insertions, and reversals. Cybernetics and Control Theory (1966)
8. Fellbaum, C.: (WordNet: An Electronic Lexical Database)
9. Castano, S.V., Antonellis, M.G.D., Fugini, B., Pernici, C.: Schema analysis: Techniques and applications. ACM Trans. Systems **23** (1998) 286–333
10. Ehrig, M., Sure, Y.: Ontology mapping - an integrated approach. Volume 3053 of LNCS., Heraklion, Crete, Greece, Springer (2004) 76–91
11. Do, H., Rahm, E.: COMA - a system for flexible combination of schema matching approaches. In: Proceedings of the 28th VLDB Conference, Hong Kong, China (2002)
12. Hughes, T.: Information interpretation and integration conference (2004) http://www.atl.external.lmco.com/projects/ontology/i3con.html.
13. Do, H., Melnik, S., Rahm, E.: Comparison of schema matching evaluations. In: Proc. of the Second International Workshop on Web Databases (German Informatics Society). (2002)
14. Dhamankar, R., Lee, Y., Doan, A., Halevy, A., Domingos, P.: iMAP: discovering complex semantic matches between database schemas. In: Proc. of the 2004 ACM SIGMOD International Conference on Management of Data, Paris, France (2004) 383–394
15. Euzenat, J., Valtchev, P.: Similarity-based ontology alignment in owl-lite. In: Proc. of ECAI 2004, Valencia, Spain (2004) 333–337

ESpotter: Adaptive Named Entity Recognition for Web Browsing

Jianhan Zhu, Victoria Uren, and Enrico Motta

Knowledge Media Institute, The Open University, Milton Keynes, MK7 6AA, UK
{j.zhu, v.s.uren, e.motta}@open.ac.uk

Abstract. Browsing constitutes an important part of the user information searching process on the Web. In this paper, we present a browser plug-in called ESpotter, which recognizes entities of various types on Web pages and highlights them according to their types to assist user browsing. ESpotter uses a range of standard named entity recognition techniques. In addition, a key new feature of ESpotter is that it addresses the problem of multiple domains on the Web by adapting lexicon and patterns to these domains.

1 Introduction

Knowledge management faces the classical information overload problem particularly when browsing information from heterogeneous sources on the Web. In the light of this, information extraction has been applied to the Web to extract entities of various types and relations between them [6, 8, 19], where named entity recognition (NER) serves as the basis by identifying entities of various types. However, these tools are either heavily dependent on the domain they are working on [8, 19] or need training data [6, 8, 19].

Browsing Web pages constitutes one important part of the information searching process on the Web. Highlighting key parts of Web pages has been an effective way to help users search information. The Google toolbar [3] highlights keywords to help users navigate among and locate these keywords in the context of Web pages. We extend this approach by integrating NER facilities into a standard browser. We highlight recognized entities to help users get an overview of the content of a Web page without having to read the whole Web page. Users can focus on the content of Web pages in the contexts of these named entities to find desired information. An NER tool can be effective in helping users speed up browsing a lengthy Web page without destroying the context of the text, as a summarization tool might. However, in order to support user browsing, first, an NER tool needs to be able to recognize entities accurately. Mistakenly recognized entities can mislead users. Second, the NER tool needs to be able to recognize entities efficiently. Users are reluctant to wait for an NER tool to finish entity recognition.

NER is a well studied area [9, 12]. NER tackles the problem of finding proper names of various types (such as "John Smith" is a "Person", and "Open University" is an "Organization"). NER relies on lexicon and patterns to find these entities and their types. The lexicon (such as that extracted from dictionaries) is essential to a good NER tool [14]. A lexicon entry typically consists of the content of an entity and its

K.-D. Althoff et al. (Eds.): WM 2005, LNAI 3782, pp. 518 – 529, 2005.

type, e.g., “The Open University” is an entity of the “Organization” type. Patterns are exhibited in the regularities of human language, e.g., in “cities such as London, New York”, “<type> such as <list of instances>” is a pattern describing English usage. “London” and “New York” are entities of “City” type; an entity matching the pattern “University of <Capitalized words>” is of a “University” type. Patterns are also exhibited in Web page layouts, e.g., on a faculty directory web page, people’s names are often followed by their contact information such as email addresses and telephone numbers. Patterns are usually described in regular expressions.

Patterns and lexicon are dependent on domains on the Web. Web pages on the same domain often have similarities in the patterns and lexicon entries, e.g., two researchers’ homepages on the Knowledge Media Institute (KMi) Web site [4] share the same lexicon entry “Knowledge Media Institute” as an “Organization” and same pattern for telephone numbers and fax numbers as “+44[-]{0,1}(\(0\)1|1)908(|-)[0-9-]+” in regular expressions.

Synonymy causes additional problems since the same entity can mean different types of things on different domains, e.g., “Magpie” is a research project on the KMi Web site [4], but a type of bird on the Royal Society for the Protection of Birds (RSPB) Web site [5]. Current NER tools relying on lexicon and patterns specific to a given domain give good NER results on the home domain. Since Web users browse Web pages from various domains during their information searches, these NER tools cannot provide good NER support.

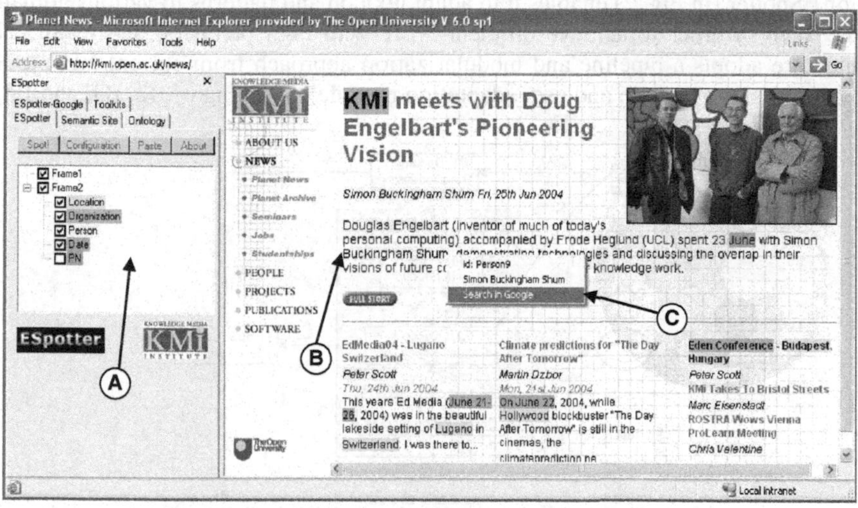

Fig. 1. ESpotter highlighting a page on the KMi Web site [4], showing (A) the ESpotter toolbar (B) entities highlighted according to their types on the Web page (C) services provided for entities (such as search for them in Google)

In this paper, we present a novel NER browser plug-in called ESpotter (in Fig. 1), which adapts patterns and lexicon to domains on the Web and users for efficient NER with high precision and recall. ESpotter allows users to customize lexicon and patterns for NER on various domains. Given a Web page and its domain, ESpotter finds lexicon entries and patterns for NER on the domain, and highlights recognized entities according to their types for helping users search for information on the page.

The remainder of the paper is organized as follows. In Section 2, we present details about ESpotter, an adaptive NER system. In Section 3, we present an evaluation of ESpotter on five different domains. In Section 4, we present related work. Finally we conclude in Section 5.

2 ESpotter

In this section, we first present the architecture of ESpotter. Second, we discuss domain adaptation in ESpotter. Third, we discuss user adaptation in ESpotter. Finally, we present our named entity recognition method based on the ESpotter architecture.

2.1 Architecture

ESpotter builds on the basis of standard NER methods by using a repository of lexicon entries and patterns, which are manually crafted by users, learned from Web pages by machine learning techniques [19], or extracted from domain knowledge such as an ontology [11], to recognize entities of various types. A lexicon entry consists of the content of an entity and its type. A pattern consists of the formal description of the content structure of a type of entity in regular expressions and the type. The architecture of ESpotter (in Fig. 2) enables it to adapt lexicon and patterns to various domains on the Web in order to achieve efficient NER with high precision and recall. The architecture adopts a pipeline and modularization approach from current NER tools, and incorporates a domain and user adaptation module consisting of B2, B4, and B5.

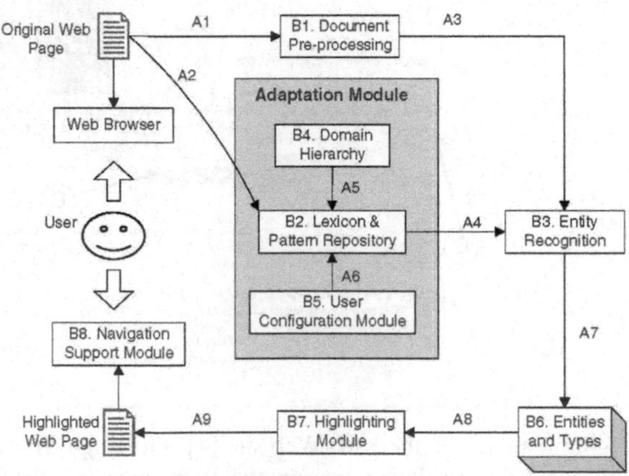

Fig. 2. ESpotter architecture

In Web page pre-processing, the web page content, A1, is pre-processed in B1 by identifying frames in pages (if they exist), extracting text by removing mark-up tags, removing parts of pages which contain irrelevant contents such as advertisements using the Document Object Model (DOM) tree of the page [13], and natural language processing such as removing stop-words and stemming.

Domain adaptation and entity recognition are illustrated in detail in Section 2.2 and Section 2.4 respectively. In summary, lexicon entries and patterns in B2 are given probabilities on domains of B4, a domain hierarchy. The URI of the page, A2, serves as input to B2 for selecting a set of lexicon entries and patterns, A4, which have probabilities above a setting threshold. In B3, lexicon entries and patterns in A4 are sorted in the order of their relevance to the domain and their probabilities, and applied to each text segment in A3 for a list of entities and their types in B3. Recognized entities and their types, A8, serve as input to B7, the highlighting module. B7 uses <span> tags to specify the background colors of recognized entities in the HTML source of the page. Finally, in addition to highlighted web pages, B8, the navigation support module, provides support for users to easily navigate between entities of various types and organize these entities for browsing. Users can switch among highlighted entities and view sorted lists of entities. Users can save highlighted pages and NER results.

User adaptation is illustrated in detail in Section 2.3. In summary, lexicon entries and patterns in B2 are exposed to users for customization operations in B5. Users can select the types of entities they are interested in on Web pages, examine probabilities of patterns and lexicon entries and fine-tune them, and view and update patterns and lexicon entries. Customization results, A6, are used to update B2.

2.2 Domain Adaptation

Domain adaptation in ESpotter tackles two types of behavior of entities on the Web. First, the probability that an entity means a certain type of thing varies on different domains, e.g., the probability that "Magpie" is a bird name is high on the RSPB Web site [5] but low on the KMi Web site [4]. While the probability that "Magpie" is a project name is high on the KMi Web site but low on the RSPB Web site. Second, the probability that a certain type of entity appears on Web pages varies on different domains, e.g., the probability that a UK postal address appears on a Web page on a UK Web site is higher than in another Web page on a non-UK Web site.

Each Web page on the Web is identified by its URI, which contains the URI of the Web site where the page is located. Based on the observation that the URI of a domain often gives clues about the contents of pages on the domain, Kan [16] used URIs of domains to classify Web pages. Based on his work, given the URI of a page, we use a domain hierarchy to determine lexicon entries and patterns for NER on the page.

We define a domain hierarchy (such as in Fig. 3) as a hierarchy which consists of domains on multiple levels and links between two domains on two adjacent levels. Domains are represented by their URIs. The root node is on the zero-level. The top

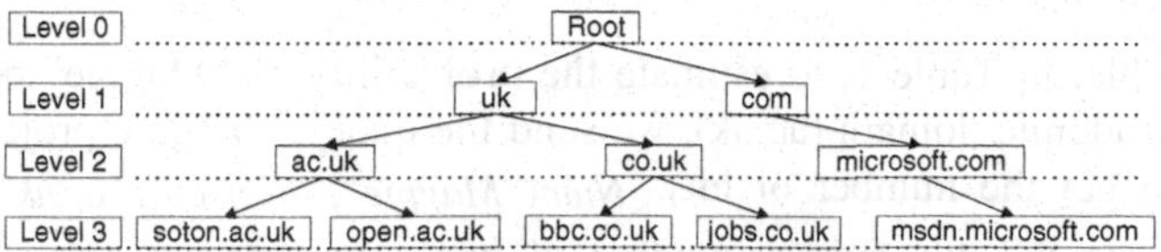

Fig. 3. A domain hierarchy defined on domain URIs

level domains are on the first level, such as "uk". Second level domains are on the second level, such as "ac.uk", and so on. The higher the level of a domain is, the more general the domain is. A link from domain A to domain B means that A is the parent of B. If there is a link from domain A to domain B and a link from domain B to domain C, domain A is the ancestor of domain C.

Each lexicon entry or pattern is given a probability between 0 and 1 on each domain. The higher the probability is, the more accurate it is expected to be for that domain. For example, if a word "Magpie" appears on the KMi Web site [4], the probability that it is a project name is higher than the probability that it is a bird name. A human evaluator may assign 80% to the probability that "Magpie" is a project name, and 10% to the probability that "Magpie" is a bird name on the KMi Web site. However, if it appears on the RSPB Web site [5], the probability that it is a bird name is higher than the probability that it is a project name. Using these probabilities, we can select lexicon entries and patterns with high probabilities for NER on a Web page.

Since manual assignment of a large number of probabilities is not feasible, we propose a search engine based probability assessment method to automatically estimate these probabilities. The method is a variation of the methods that use Google search to associate instances with classes in an ontology [7] and action keywords with activities [18]. Perkowitz et al. [18] proposed Google Conditional Probability (GCP), which is predicted on the assumption that the probability of an entity being associated with a class on a domain is reflected by the probability of the two terms describing the entity and the class co-occurring in Web pages on the domain.

We use a similar approach to estimate probabilities as guidelines for measuring semantic meanings of lexicon entries and patterns on various domains. We use the number of hits returned by a search query to estimate the coverage of the search query on a certain domain. A query constructed from the content of a lexicon entry, L, or the regular expression description of a pattern, P, and a domain, D, is sent to a search engine for the number of hits, $Num(L/P, D)$, which estimates the coverage of the lexicon entry, L, or pattern, P, regardless of the entity type on the domain. The query is joined with the entity type, T, to form a new query. The new query is sent to the search engine for the number of hits, $Num(L/P, T, D)$, which estimates the coverage of the lexicon entry or pattern of the entity type, T, on the domain. In Equation 1, we divide $Num(L/P, T, D)$ by $Num(L/P,D)$ as the probability of the lexicon entry or pattern on the domain, $Pr(L/P, T, D)$, which estimates the probability that an entity matching the lexicon entry, L, or pattern, P, belongs to the entity type, T, on the domain, D.

$$\Pr(L/P, T, D) = \frac{Num(L/P, T, D)}{Num(L/P, D)} \tag{1}$$

For example, in Table 1, to estimate the probability of "Magpie" being a project on the UK academic domain (ac.uk), we send the query, "Magpie project site:ac.uk", to Google to get the number of hits, $Num("Magpie", "project", "ac.uk")$, and query, "Magpie site:ac.uk", to get the number of hits, $Num("Magpie", "ac.uk")$. The estimated probability that "Magpie" is a project name on the UK academic domain is $Num("Magpie", "project", "ac.uk") / Num("Magpie", "ac.uk")$. Google estimated probabilities confirm that "Magpie" is most likely to be a project name on both "kmi.open.ac.uk" and "open.ac.uk" domains. While on the UK academic domain, it has well over 25% chance of being a project name and is twice as likely to be a project name than a bird name. On the UK domain, it is twice as likely to be a bird name than a project name, but the probability is low for both.

Table 1. Google estimated probability for lexicon entry ("Magpie", "Project") and ("Magpie", "Bird") on various domains. The more probable type on a domain is in bold and underlined.

Domain	Type of lexicon entries	Query	Hits	Probability(%)
uk	-	Magpie site:uk	44,900	100
	Project	Magpie project site:uk	3,660	8.2
	<u>Bird</u>	Magpie bird site:uk	7,340	16.3
ac.uk	-	Magpie site:ac.uk	2,440	100
	<u>Project</u>	Magpie project site:ac.uk	628	25.8
	Bird	Magpie bird site:ac.uk	297	12.2
open.ac.uk	-	Magpie site:open.ac.uk	95	100
	<u>Project</u>	Magpie project site:open.ac.uk	55	57.9
	Bird	Magpie bird site:open.ac.uk	6	6.3
kmi.open.ac.uk	-	Magpie site:kmi.open.ac.uk	44	100
	<u>Project</u>	Magpie project site:kmi.open.ac.uk	30	68.2
	Bird	Magpie bird site:kmi.open.ac.uk	0	0

For a pattern that a term consisting of "John" followed by capitalized words in regular expression, "John[ ]+[A-Z][a-zA-Z-]*[.]?([ ]+[A-Z][a-zA-Z'-]*)*", is a person's name on UK academic domain, we transform the pattern into a composite query as Q="("John A*" OR "John B*" OR "John C*"... OR "John Z*")". We join Q with "person" and "person site:ac.uk" respectively to get two queries, which are used to search Google for estimating the probability of the pattern on UK academic domain.

ESpotter contains a probability estimation module, which composes queries from lexicon entries and patterns, uses Google API [2] to search, and computes probabilities. Probabilities of a lexicon entry or pattern are typically computed when it is first added to the lexicon and pattern repository or when the user asks to do so. These probabilities can be computed once and stored for all subsequent NER tasks.

2.3 User Adaptation

Probabilities of patterns and lexicon entries provide users with a fine-grained way to adapt NER to their information searching. NER in ESpotter is adapted to users in three aspects. First, current NER tools are generally targeted for specialists and thus are difficult for ordinary users to customize, e.g., by adding their own knowledge. In ESpotter, they can add lexicon entries and patterns and adjust probabilities of lexicon entries and patterns on different domains. Users can select the types of entities they are interested in for NER. Second, NER tools generally trade off precision against recall. Due to the diversity of domains on the Web, NER tools cannot always achieve both high precision and recall. In ESpotter, users use a probability threshold, which filters out lexicon entries and patterns having low probabilities on a domain, to trade between precision and recall. Third, they can give feedback about recognition results, which is used by ESpotter to adjust the probabilities of lexicon entries and patterns, e.g., reduce the probability of a pattern if the user says that it made a mistake in NER.

In the user configuration module (in Fig. 4), patterns and lexicon entries are grouped according to their purposes and organized in a tree view in Section **A**. The contents of lexicon entries and patterns are shown in Section **B**. The domain hierarchy constructed from domain URIs is visualized as a tree in Section **C**. The probability of a lexicon entry or pattern for a selected URI is shown in Section **D**. Users can view and modify the probability. Users can add, remove, and update patterns and lexicon entries in Section **E**. In Section **F**, users can choose to open lexicon entries and patterns stored in a file. In Section **G**, users can adjust the probability threshold.

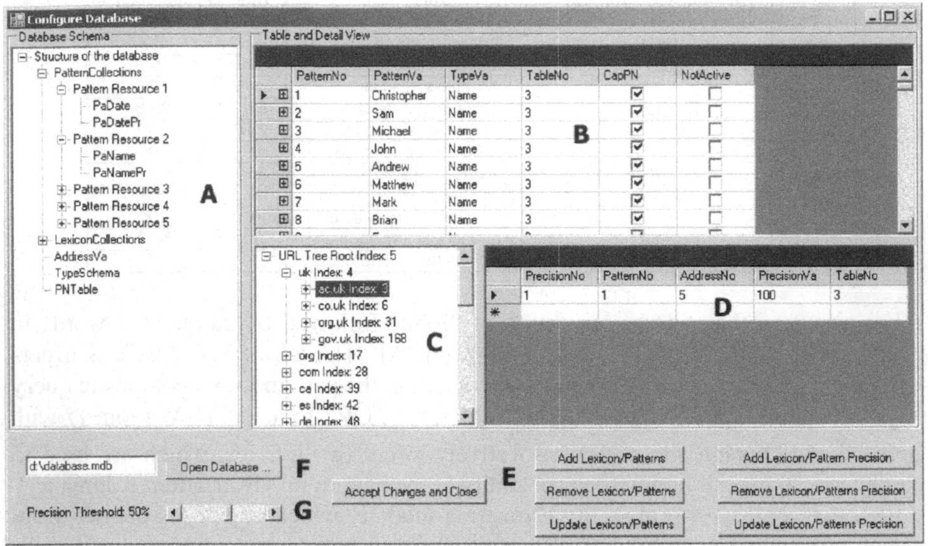

Fig. 4. ESpotter user configuration interface

2.4 Named Entity Recognition

Given the content and URI of a page, NER module finds a list of entities and their types. The page content is pre-processed for text segments separated by HTML tags. Since most entities in English are in the form of proper nouns[1] (PNs) [7], we use a pattern to find PNs and then determine the types of these PNs. Lexicon entries and patterns are divided into PN dependent and PN independent ones, e.g., one PN dependent lexicon entry is that a PN matching "November" is probably a date. A PN dependent pattern is that a PN containing "University" is probably a university's name. A PN independent lexicon entry is that a word "david" with the first letter in lower case is probably a person's name. PN independent patterns include patterns for matching email addresses, telephone numbers, and postal codes.

The domain adaptation module uses the algorithm in Fig. 5 to find lexicon entries and patterns for NER. Given the URI of the page, we can either find it on the domain hierarchy or not. First, if we find its domain on the ith level, $D(i)$. We find the

---

[1] A PN consists of one or more words, which are commonly marked by an initial capital letter, and can contain auxiliary words such as "of", "at". PNs names individuals such as "Open University".

```
Input: D=D(i), K=i, PR(0)
Algorithm:
1. If D(K) found on the Kth level of domain hierarchy
2.     Find patterns & lexicons with probabilities > PR(0) on D(K) and add to set S(K)
   Else
3.     Add D(K) as a new node to domain hierarchy
4.     K=K-1
5.     Goto step 1
   End if
Output: Set S(i), S(i-1), ..., S(j) for NER
```

Fig. 5. Lexicon entry and pattern selection algorithm

lexicon entries and patterns with probabilities on $D(i)$ above the probability threshold, $PR(0)$, and put them in $S(i)$. We find the parent of $D(i)$ on the $i-1$th level, $D(i-1)$, and ancestors, $D(k)$ $(i-1>k\geq 0)$. For each of them, we find the lexicon entries and patterns, which have not been selected already and whose probabilities are above the threshold $PR(0)$ on the domain. Second, if we cannot find $D(i)$ on the domain hierarchy, we add it as a new domain. If we find the parent of $D(i)$, $D(i-1)$, on the hierarchy, we add a link from $D(i-1)$ to $D(i)$, and select lexicon entries and patterns on $D(i-1)$. Otherwise, we add $D(i-1)$ as a new domain and search for the parent of $D(i-1)$, $D(i-2)$, and so on until we find an ancestor of $D(i)$ on the hierarchy. We get sets of lexicon entries and patterns on the domain of the page, its parent, and its ancestors, $S(i)$, $S(i-1)$, …, $S(j)$, for NER.

For example, the domain of Jianhan Zhu's homepage (http://kmi.open.ac.uk/people /jianhan/) is $D(4)$, kmi.open.ac.uk. Suppose we cannot find $D(4)$ on the 4th level of the domain hierarchy, but we find its parent $D(3)$, open.ac.uk, on the 3rd level, we add $D(4)$ to the 4th level and create a link from $D(3)$ to $D(4)$. We find sets of lexicon entries and patterns on $D(4)$, $D(3)$, $D(2)$ (ac.uk), $D(1)$ (uk), and root node with their probabilities above the threshold, respectively.

In entity recognition, for each text segment, we apply the sets of lexicon entries and patterns in order of specificity from the lowest to the highest levels on the hierarchy, i.e., $S(i)$, $S(i-1)$, …, $S(j)$. Lexicon entries and patterns in a set, $S(k)$ $(i\leq k\leq j)$, are divided into PN dependent and PN independent ones, $S(k,Dep)$ and $S(k,Ind)$, respectively. Lexicon entries and patterns in $S(k,Dep)$ and $S(k,Ind)$ are sorted in the descending order of their probabilities on $D(k)$. We apply PN independent lexicon entries and patterns, $S(k,Ind)$, to the text segment to find a list of entities and their types, and tag them if successful. A PN matching pattern is applied to the rest of the text segment to find a list of PNs. The PN matching pattern matches one or more consecutive words consisting of words starting with a capitalized letter, and auxiliary words such as "of", "at". Words and terms which are not real PNs are removed, such as a single word "The", "An". For each PN, we apply PN dependent lexicon entries and patterns, $S(k,Dep)$, to find its type and tag it if successful. We go one level up, if any, to repeat the same process. The output is a list of tagged entities with their types.

Taking Jianhan Zhu's homepage as our example again, for a text segment "I am a research fellow working on the Dot.Kom project in KMi since August 2003", PN independent lexicon entries and patterns are matched to find "research fellow" as "Research-Post". PN matching pattern is used to find three PNs, "Dot.Kom", "KMi", and "August 2003". PN dependent lexicon entries and patterns are matched to find "Dot.Kom" as "Project", "KMi" as "Organization", and "August 2003" as "Date".

Each type is assigned a color by users. ESpotter uses <span> tags to specify the background colors of recognized entities according to their types. ESpotter (in Fig. 1) enables users to switch among highlighted entities and view lists of entities, which are sorted by their types or contents. Users can save highlighted pages and NER results.

3 Experimental Evaluation

We tested ESpotter for NER on five domains: the KMi PlanetNews Web site [6], the KMi Web site [5], the Open University (OU) Web site [8], the University of Ulster (UU) Web site [10], and the BBC News Web site [2]. Twenty Web pages were selected from each domain.[2]

We used ESpotter for recognizing nine types of entities: People, Organizations, Research Areas, Locations, Dates, Projects, Email Addresses, UK Postal Addresses, UK Telephone and Fax Numbers. The results were examined by an evaluator from outside our research group. The evaluator determined the number of entities of each type on a page, $Num(evaluator, page, type)$, before ESpotter performed NER on them. We summed the number of entities of a type on each of the twenty pages on a domain, D, to get the total number of entities of the type on the domain, $Num(evaluator, D, type)$. After ESpotter performed NER on a page, we got the number of annotated entities of the type on the page, $Num(ESpotter, page, type)$. The evaluator decided the number of correctly annotated entities of the type on the page, $Num(ESpotter, page, type, correct)$. We summed the number of ESpotter annotated and correctly annotated entities of the type on each page on a domain, D, to get the total number of annotated and correctly annotated entities of the type on the domain as $Num(ESpotter, D, type)$ and $Num(ESpotter, D, type, correct)$, respectively. For an annotation to be correct, the evaluator compared the automatic annotation and his desired annotation and judged that they are sufficiently similar. For example, for person "Tim Berners-Lee", the automatic annotation, "Tim Berners", is wrong. For organization "the International Web Conference", the automatic annotation, "International Web Conference", is correct. The precision and recall of ESpotter in recognizing entities of a type on a domain, D, are defined as:

$$Precision\ (ESpotter, D, type) = \frac{Num(ESpotter, D, type, correct)}{Num(ESpotter, D, type)}$$

$$Recall\ (ESpotter, D, type) = \frac{Num(ESpotter, D, type, correct)}{Num(evaluator, D, type)}$$

[2] Since the KMi PlanetNews is a sub-domain of the KMi domain, which is a sub-domain of the Open University domain, the same Web page was not selected for two different domains.

In addition, the time taken by ESpotter to mark up a page was recorded. Since ESpotter runs once and generates all the annotations on a page, we averaged the time taken for each page on a domain. The probability threshold for lexicon entries and patterns is set as 50%. The evaluation results are summarized in Table 2.

Table 2. ESpotter NER on five domains in terms of precision, recall and time taken

Type		KMi PlanetNews	KMi	Open University	Univ. of Ulster	UU Customization	BBC News	BBC Customization
People	Precision(%)	99.9	98.8	91.2	83.2	90.2	81.2	94.5
	Recall(%)	85.5	84.4	81.2	75.3	84.7	72.9	89.9
Organizations	Precision(%)	95.0	92.3	87.1	83.3	86.3	81.6	92.3
	Recall(%)	96.1	85.3	80.8	79.4	82.3	77.7	88.9
Research Areas	Precision(%)	92.3	91.3	88.6	87.7	91.3	-	-
	Recall(%)	90.6	88.7	82.3	81.3	87.2	-	-
Locations	Precision(%)	100	100	100	100	100	100	100
	Recall(%)	100	100	100	100	100	100	100
Dates	Precision(%)	97.1	93.2	89.8	82.7	92.4	89.8	93.4
	Recall(%)	83.2	82.7	82.3	77.3	89.4	73.8	89.6
Projects	Precision(%)	92.1	91.4	80.2	76.1	90.3	-	-
	Recall(%)	89.3	83.2	78.3	71.9	86.6	-	-
Emails	Precision(%)	100	100	100	99.1	100	99.2	100
	Recall(%)	100	100	100	95.2	100	100	100
Postal Addresses	Precision(%)	100	100	100	100	100	100	100
	Recall(%)	100	100	100	100	100	100	100
Tele&Fax Numbers	Precision(%)	100	100	100	95.3	100	100	100
	Recall(%)	100	100	83.3	85.3	100	81.1	92.3
TimeTaken	(Secs)	0.7	0.8	0.7	0.7	0.8	0.9	1.0

In Table 2, ESpotter achieved both high precision (>76.1%) and recall (>71.9%) for recognizing nine types of entities on five domains without adding new lexicon entries and patterns. ESpotter provided efficient NER by taking less than 0.9 second on average for each page on a Pentium 4 Desktop, with a 1.80 GHz, and 512 MB RAM. Since there are more lexicon entries and patterns obtained from the domain knowledge of the KMi domain, ESpotter performed better on the KMi domain, its sub-domain, KMi PlanetNews domain, and its parent domain, the Open University domain. The first author customized ESpotter by adding lexicon entries and patterns and tune probabilities of existing lexicon entries and patterns for NER on the University of Ulster (UU) domain and the BBC News domain. 11 lexicon entries and 3 patterns were added for UU domain, and 19 lexicon entries and 2 patterns were added for the BBC News domain. Subsequently both precision and recall for each type of entities were improved as shown in Table 2.

4 Related Work

Perkowitz et al. [18] use the web to mine a large number of human activities. They used Google Conditional Probabilities (GCPs) to measure similarity between concepts and terms. PANKOW [7] uses a pattern-based approach to categorize instances with regard to an ontology consisting of a set of classes. Using a simple capitalized word heuristics, proper nouns (PNs) are extracted from Web pages as candidate instances. A set of patterns, which identify instance-of relationships between an instance and a class, are used to construct search queries to get the number of hits from Google. The number of hits is used to measure the isa-relationship between the instance and the class. An instance is assigned to the class with which it has the strongest isa-relationship measured by the number of hits from Google.

ESpotter uses a method similar to Perkowitz et al. [18] and PANKOW's [7] methods to estimate probabilities of lexicon entries and patterns by querying Google. Search queries are constructed from patterns and lexicon entries. ESpotter uses a method similar to PANKOW's [7] for extracting PNs from Web pages. ESpotter is different from PANKOW in three aspects. First, in PANKOW, the class of a candidate instance is unknown beforehand. Thus the candidate instance is matched against each class in the ontology to get a probability, and assigned to the class with which it has the highest probability. In ESpotter, the class (type) is specified by a lexicon entry or pattern and we only search Google to get a probability to measure the credibility of the lexicon entry or pattern on a domain. Second, probabilities of patterns are assessed in ESpotter while PANKOW only assesses probabilities of lexicon entries. Third, ESpotter assesses probabilities of lexicon entries and patterns on various domains while PANKOW assumes that the domain is the whole Web.

Magpie [11] uses lexicon entries extracted from a domain ontology for NER. Magpie can achieve high precision and recall on Web pages on a certain domain, but precision and recall of its NER degrade dramatically on Web pages outside the domain. ESpotter has been integrated with Magpie to complement ontology based NER by recognizing entities in a much broader range than Magpie. In Magpie [11], entities are highlighted according to their classes, and provided with semantic services based on the ontology. ESpotter highlights entities of various types, enables users to navigate among them, and provides services such as searching Google.

Annotation tools, e.g., SHOE [15] and MnM [20], allow users to manually markup Web pages guided by ontologies. To address the annotation bottleneck problem created by the large amount of information on the Web, systems, such as SemTag [10] which automatically tags a large number of pages with terms from an ontology, are proposed. We use ESpotter to annotate Web pages for KMi semantic Website [17].

5 Conclusions

On the basis of domain specialties on the Web, ESpotter adapts lexicon and patterns to individual domains for efficient NER with high precision and recall. The adaptation can be performed automatically using data from the Web itself to set probabilities for individual lexicon entries or patterns, and these probabilities can be further customized by users. Our experiments on five domains show that ESpotter can be customized for improved precision and recall in NER on these domains. ESpotter's adaptive approach makes NER a viable browsing support for Web users, as well as a scalable information extraction process for the diverse domain environment that is the Web.

Acknowledgements

This research was partially supported by the Designing Adaptive Information Extraction from Text for Knowledge Management (Dot.Kom) project, Framework V, under grant IST-2001-34038 and the Advanced Knowledge Technologies (AKT) project. AKT is an Interdisciplinary Research Collaboration (IRC), which is sponsored by the UK Engineering and Physical Sciences Research Council under grant number

GR/N15764/01. The AKT IRC comprises the Universities of Aberdeen, Edinburgh, Sheffield, Southampton and the Open University.

References

1. Google. http://www.google.com
2. Google API. http://www.google.com/apis/
3. Google toolbar. http://toolbar.google.com/
4. KMi (Knowledge Media Institute). http://kmi.open.ac.uk
5. The Royal Society for the Protection of Birds. http://www.rspb.org.uk
6. Brin, S.: Extracting Patterns and Relations from the World Wide Web. In Proc. of WebDB (1998) 172-183
7. Cimiano, P., Handschuh, S., Staab, S.: Towards the Self-Annotating Web. In Proc. of WWW (2004)
8. Ciravegna, F.: Adaptive Information Extraction from Text by Rule Induction and Generalisation. In Proc. of IJCAI (2001)
9. Cunningham, H.: GATE: a General Architecture for Text Engineering. Computers and the Humanities, Vol. 36 (2002) 223-254.
10. Dill, S., Eiron, N., Gibson, D., Gruhl, D., Guha, R., Jhingran, A., Kanungo, T., McCurley, K. S., Rajagopalan, S., Tomkins, A., Tomlin, J. A., Zien, J. Y.: A Case for Automated Large-Scale Semantic Annotation. Journal of Web Semantics, 1(1) (2003) 115-132
11. Domingue, J. B., Dzbor, M.: Magpie: Browsing and Navigating on the Semantic Web. In Proc. of IUI (2004)
12. Grover, C., Gearailt, D. N., Karkaletsis, V., Farmakiotou, D., Pazienza, M. T., Vindigni, M.: Multilingual XML-Based Named Entity Recognition for E-Retail Domains. In Proc. of the 3rd International Conference on Language Resources and Evaluation (LREC 2002), Las Palmas (2002) 1060-1067
13. Gupta, S., Kaiser, G., Neistadt, D., and Grimm, P.: DOM-based Content Extraction from HTML Documents. In Proc. of WWW (2003)
14. Guthrie, L., Pustejowsky, J., Wilks, Y., Slator, B. M.: The Role of Lexicons in Natural Language Processing. CACM, 39(1) (1996) 63-72
15. Heflin, J., Hendler, J.: Searching the Web with Shoe. In AAAI Workshop on AI for Web Search (2000)
16. Kan, M.-Y.: Web Page Categorization without the Web Pages. In Proc. of WWW (2004)
17. Lei, Y., Lopez, V., Zhu, J.: Engineering Sustainable Semantic Web Sites. Submitted.
18. Perkowitz, M., Philipose, M., Fishkin, K., Patterson, D. J.: Mining Models of Human Activities from the Web. In Proc. of WWW (2004)
19. Soderland, S.: Learning Information Extraction Rules for Semi-Structured and Free Text. Machine Learning, 34(1) (1999) 233–272
20. Vargas-Vera, M., Motta, E., Domingue, J. B., Lanzoni, M., Stutt, A., Ciravegna, F.: MnM: Ontology Driven Semi-automatic and Automatic Support for Semantic Markup. In Proc. of EKAW (2002) 379-391

Using Digital Communication Structures to Support Knowledge Management

Karsten Böhm[1] and Alexander Scherf[2]

[1] University of Leipzig, Institute of Computer Science, Augustusplatz 10-11, 04109 Leipzig, Germany
boehm@informatik.uni-leipzig.de
[2] Detecon International GmbH, Frankfurter Straße 27, 65760 Eschborn, Germany
Alexander.Scherf@detecon.com

Abstract. IT-based knowledge management is often considered under the aspect of information storage and retrieval only. Although the theory of organizational knowledge management reflects on the description of communication structures and communication events between partners, the support of the users by information technology systems does not meet the expectations at all. This contribution describes an approach and a software implementation that uses digital communication structures, which result from the use of new forms of communication infrastructures, to facilitate an easier access to relevant information that can be qualified by identification with the knowledge creator.

1 Introduction

The field of knowledge management is concerned with the support of all processes connected with the generation, distribution, storage and use of knowledge in the widest sense [1, 2, 3]. There is no clear distinction between socio-technical systems, such as businesses or organizations and information-technical applications, such as IT-supported information management systems (see [4] for an overview on the various influences on the area of KM). Nevertheless, there is an emphasis on different aspects and in the field of IT-supported knowledge management the aspect of information management often prevails in the realization of the corresponding solutions.

The approach in the research project *KnowBiT*[1] is based on the central idea that the human urge to communicate as a social being and as an autonomous member of a group is the basic and most used tool for information provision and therefore knowledge acquisition and mediation. This primary characteristic of communication can be used effectively and can be applied in almost every situation. In addition to the preferred means of direct communication, indirect ways of communication have developed in the past, in which a medium has been used as storage and mediator between the parties involved. The factors motivating such indirect communication were especially the missing synchrony regarding time, location, and the number of recipients of a message. While in the past the medium paper has been used most often

[1] KnowBiT is an acronym for "Knowledge Management for the biotechnical industry".

K.-D. Althoff et al. (Eds.): WM 2005, LNAI 3782, pp. 530 – 541, 2005.

(letters, faxes, files, papers, magazines, journals, books, etc. for written language as well as mass media such as radio, TV, etc.), today's communication is increasingly digital. The term digital communication is understood here as the digital creation, storage, transfer and display of messages by the use of computers. This tendency is reflected in the application of digital media for written communication (e-mail, forums, newsgroups, SMS, etc.), which will enable information technology systems in the future to support users beyond the mere storage and management of information (PC, Intranet, Internet, etc.). Digitized communication can be considered a prerequisite for computer systems to take part in the distribution of knowledge actively as the mediator or provider.

In general, it can be observed that humans act according to the principle of the least possible short-term effort in order to obtain the highest possible long-term profit (principle of efficiency). The explicit documentation of ones own knowledge and the acquisition of external knowledge (such as data and documentation as a result of studies) often does not have first priority and remains in the background in favour of inquiring communication with a knowledge medium, since the former requires more time and apparently seems to hold back from the actual tasks. Relevant research in business contexts found that direct communication with colleagues and managers is still the primary and most used source of information in a company [7]. Stored information is often considered as the second-best solution and the effort for finding the needed information plays a key role, as is shown by the growing importance of the internet and of corporation-wide networks (intranets) as reliable sources of information. The figure below contrasts the two main strategies for the acquisition of new knowledge with respect to their advantages and disadvantages.

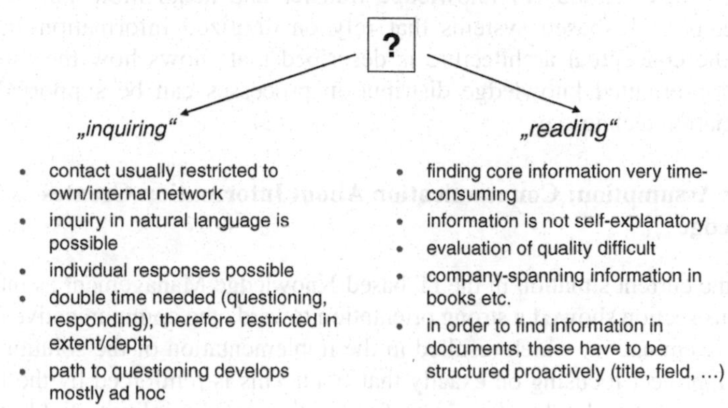

Fig. 1. Two main strategies for knowledge acquisition

The orientation towards efficient knowledge acquisition is probably one of the main reasons why complex knowledge management systems are not yet being used everywhere despite the apparent necessity to use them in order to cope with the growing amount of information.

This is further complicated by the fact that existing modes of operation and business cultures cannot be altered on short notice by introducing a new IT-based knowledge management solution and that the value of knowledge is dependent on situation-specific demand which is therefore subject to constant changes. Thus, only the person that is performing a search can decide which effort for knowledge management is justified at the time of the research.

However, all relevant information in a business is usually documented at least once and is basically available in the form of books, magazines, meeting protocols, presentations, e-mails, etc. Under the assumption that the intended knowledge management solution is targeted at smaller and medium-size enterprises (SME), which normally do not have the additional resources to build up and to operate a knowledge management system, a pragmatic solution has been designed, which facilitates access to information by analyzing digitized communication structures significantly.

The remaining article is structured as follows: The idea of a supported communication will be introduced in the following section and leads to the description of the conceptual architecture. Based on this fundament we outline some technical aspects of the KnowBiT-software solution in section 3, highlight the innovation potential with references to related work in section 4 and some lessons learnt in section 5. The article concludes with a summary and an outlook of future work.

2 The Notion of Supported Communication

This section introduces the approach to support the communicative processes between those persons that have a question and those who actually have a solution in order to support the process of knowledge acquisition and distribution. The intention is not to replace established methods of knowledge transfer and acquisition, but to support them by means of IT-based systems that rely on digitized information structures. Afterwards the conceptual architecture is described that shows how the established communication-oriented knowledge distribution processes can be supported by the use of information technology.

2.1 Project Assumption: Communication About Information Creates Knowledge

Analysis of the current situation in the IT-based Knowledge Management as introduced in the previous section showed a strong orientation towards the communicative aspect in knowledge dissemination, which resulted in the implementation of the solutions within the KnowBiT-project focusing on exactly that field. This is reinforced by the fact that, from the information technological point of view, the interdisciplinary field of knowledge management has always been tailored strongly to the field of information management. The domain of communication management, which sometimes bears relations to information management, does exist separately but only little work can be found that relate *both* fields to knowledge management, which in businesses is often attributed to the field of company organization. Figure 2 shows how these three important fields are related to each other, how they overlap, and which organizational units they are assigned to within typical business departments. The approach attempts to develop a solution, which is in the overlapping area of all three areas.

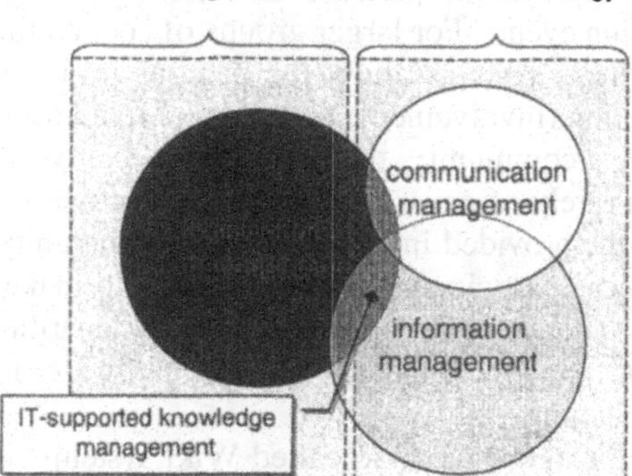

Fig. 2. Overlapping of knowledge management in the fields of communication and information management

The underlying methodology is based on the observation that knowledge distribution and management (in businesses and beyond) is mainly *a communication process about information*, which contains the sought-after knowledge or creates it in the course of the communication (e.g. through collaborative problem solving of the communication partners involved). Thus the working hypothesis for the project is that *communication about information creates knowledge*. The goal of the approach pursued in the KnowBiT project is to support this process by means of information technology.

2.2 Conceptual Architecture

The observations presented in the section suggest a generic approach, which – also in contrast to other approaches for IT-based knowledge management solutions – puts communication into the centre of a knowledge management system and links them to sources of information, in which relevant knowledge is stored in form of information, available in the business. In doing so, the conceptual architecture is based on communication structures existing in a digital form with the objective of (implicitly) recording a knowledge acquisition process once solved in communication so it can be reused for similar problems. Beyond that, providers and inquirers of knowledge can be identified in digitized communication structure to enable the localization of experts which bundle certain knowledge. It is also important that the system does not implement the options for acquisition, storage, and subsequent processing of information and knowledge functionally again but integrates them by using the appropriate systems and refers to the information units contained from the communication process.

Today, systems with digitized communication structures are often available in form of discussion forums, portals etc. Often the geographical distance of many users connected by the same interests was crucial for their formation. Synchronous communication using a software platform was often impossible within internet communities that were spread throughout the world (e.g. because of the different time zones the users live in). Moreover, texts submitted digitally are still the primary medium for the exchange of messages on the internet (e.g. in e-mail messages, news groups or mailing lists). Asynchronous communication architectures also enable a more flexible kind of cooperation because the partners themselves can decide when and how to react to communication events. For larger groups of cooperating persons this is a clear advantage. Finally, these systems allow the persons in a community to control the intensity of participation (involvement) themselves. In addition to active participants, which strongly shape a community, there are also a relatively large number of rather passive users, which rarely or never take part in the active formation of contents, but act as consumers of the provided information. The community is an important source of information for these participants. The possibility to make use of the information without the need of elaborate registration boosts quick distribution just as much as the simple operation and the low standards for the hardware and software to be used (browser-based applications).

In this context, the emergence of so called Wiki systems[2] is an especially interesting trend [5]. Wiki systems are simple web-based applications, which enable the generation and combination of individual websites in a simple way without special editors or expertise of the user being required. By now, many different Wiki installations on almost any topics on the internet have developed, some of which have reached a considerable size (see [6] for an overview on Wiki-based-systems). As an example the free online encyclopedia Wikipedia[3] can be named, which is based on a Wiki system as well. Contents of a Wiki can be seen, altered or supplemented by all users. In doing so, the new contents overwrite the old articles. The members of a community have thus the opportunity to exchange information implicitly with the articles in the Wiki system by searching for interesting contents in the existing collection of articles and then adding their own experiences on a certain topic.

In addition, users of a Wiki system can also discuss the added contents. Similar to news groups and web logging systems[4], discussions for individual Wiki articles can be created and commented on by every user. The contributions are annotated with date and author information and make it possible to reconstruct the reasoning of the users (called a thread) later.

Therefore Wiki systems and their various derivatives are well suited for platforms, which serve not only the purpose of publishing information in form of articles but also for communication. They thus combine the advantages of communication solutions (e-mail, news groups, mailing lists, instant messaging, etc.) and solutions, where the main focus is on the exchange of information (forums, information portals, FAQ lists, etc.). Due to the completely digital environment they also avoid "communicative media breaks" and accessible for automatic information and knowledge structuring technologies for the existing digital communication structures.

On the other hand, the system-functions are knowingly kept simple, which makes them rather unsuitable for storing large and complex information objects. Additionally, such complex information stores are installed and integrated in the value adding

[2] The term *wikiwiki* is Hawaiian and means *fast*. This is meant to stress the simple and quick creation of contents.

[3] The Wikipedia project can be found at http://en.wikipedia.org.

[4] Weblogging systems (also called blogs) document the experiences of an author concerning a certain topic or different sources on the internet chronologically. The option of commenting enables other users to reflect on the content, which can result in discussions focused on contents.

processes in businesses within most companies. For unstructured data, document- and content-management systems (DMS/CMS) are used. In addition to these central and mission critical data stores there are additional digital information sources which do not (need to) comply with such high requirements concerning availability and quality standards but is still important for individual business branches and work groups (e.g. local drives) and which must therefore be considered as well. Finally, the internet is an important source of information, even though quality, topicality and availability of information are difficult to guarantee. Linking to relevant contents, however, can be achieved very easily.

If these kinds of information systems are compared with the information acquisition strategies demonstrated earlier, it becomes apparent, that, due to their digitized communication structures, Wiki-based systems are especially suited for the strategy of inquiring ("coffee-corner" metaphor), while classical information storage systems such as DMS/CMS are more predestined for the strategy of reading (library metaphor). Both investigation strategies can be supported effectively through information technology (e.g. full-text search, information structuring).

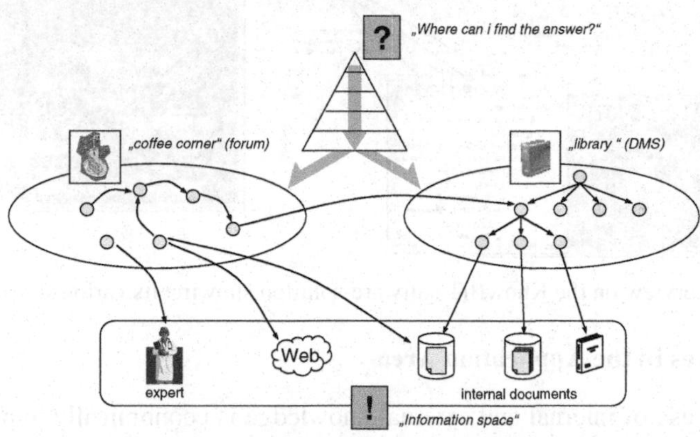

Fig. 3. Conceptual architecture of supported communication

Based on these conceptual preparatory works, a system has been put into working practice within the context of the project, that is based on the information room of the sources of information available in the business (information space) and which, beyond that, provides a communicative way of access on the basis of digital communication structures (inquiry strategy) as well as a classical way of investigation (reading strategy). Both practices are supported by methods of automatic information structuring and are linked to one another, so that the user is provided with a consistent user interface with which he can decide in favour of the adequate investigation strategy depending on the problem. The architecture overview displayed in figure 3 shows how the different systems work on the shared company-internal information room and how they provide different ways of access, which can be used depending on the precise problem and retrieval strategy.

3 Technical Architecture of the KnowBiT Solution

The conceptual model, described above, was transformed into a software solution, shown in figure 4 below and is currently put into practice at a pilot user from the biotechnology business. In this section we describe the practical demands from the chosen application area, sketch the technical architecture of the software and highlight some of their innovative aspects.

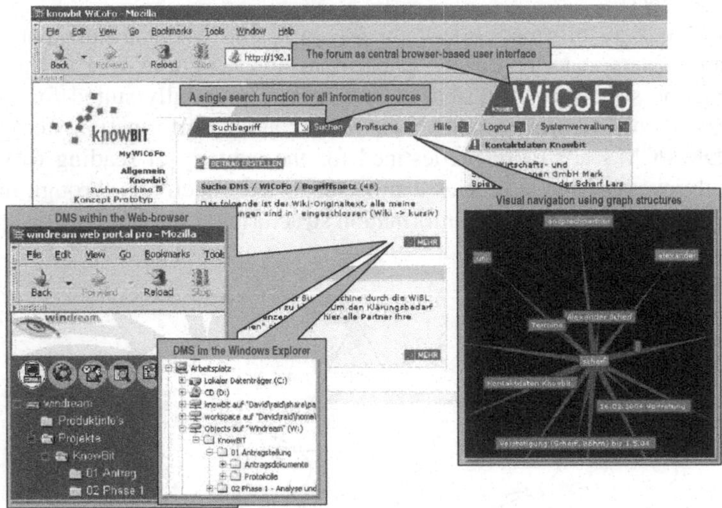

Fig. 4. Overview on the KnowBiT software-solution showing its various components

3.1 Objectives in the Application Area

The effective use of internal and external knowledge is economically important especially for research-oriented businesses with long development cycles and complex processes as in the biotechnological industry. Especially in small businesses knowledge is bound to individuals, who take on a key role in the company.

The more than 30 highly specialized employees of the pilot user ACGT ProGenomics AG are assigned to three business branches. At the moment the processing of the incoming external information flow (studies, patents, etc.) and the internal exchange of information represent a significant challenge for knowledge management. It is the main task of the KnowBiT software to support communication about information actively by linking heterogeneous sources of information such as DMS and Wiki and thus boost the emergence of new knowledge and the distribution of already known facts. A task just as critical is the training and support of measures of quality assurance, whose complete application is a prerequisite for later introduction of new products to the market. Apart from these specific research insights there was a need to share project-accompanying basic knowledge such as:

- contacts and experiences with potential cooperation partners,
- expertise about handling specialized laboratory equipment and
- general observations from the field of protein research.

The management considers the benefits from supporting the employees through active exchange of information as very high but at the same time the willingness of the employees for the manual build-up and the subsequent maintenance of any additional system are seen critically. Therefore it is important for the success of the project to minimize the additional expenses for individual user in using and maintaining the knowledge management system.

The new knowledge management solution was integrated in the existing infrastructure. For this purpose, a database of studies and patents as well as other project databases with specific values from other investigation series were integrated in the module "library" (DMS). The semantic network, which is automatically generated from this information, provides a simple management of information as well as the recognition of relations between heterogeneous topic complexes.

The information base is extended by introducing the Wiki module, which can be thought of as an additional layer on top of the available information sources (the detailed, codified knowledge) that captures the discussions, remarks and annotations (sparsely distributed, light knowledge). Additional information can simply be documented in the form of digital articles. The semantic network is extended and improved qualitatively by linking these articles to each other and to documents stored in the DMS. With this combination, the communication about the individual information objects is supported and initiates the transformation of the information basis into a knowledge basis by easing the access to relevant information using the digitized communication structures to access the information sources.

The concept and the software solution are initially adjusted to the specific needs of the field of biotechnology. It was, nevertheless, intended to develop a platform as flexible as possible, in order to apply it to other knowledge intensive fields with little effort.

3.2 Technical Realisation

The technical architecture as shown in figure 5 consists of several modules which are interconnected, using standardized interfaces that are based on the SOAP-protocol[5] and can be easily extended by new modules. This will make it primarily possible to

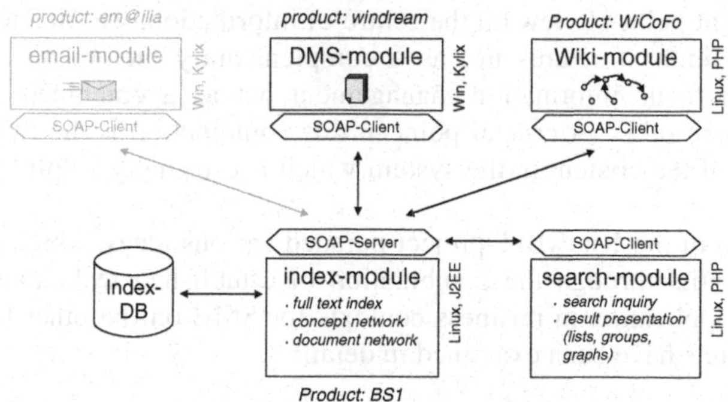

Fig. 5. Technical architecture as basis for a flexible extension

[5] The SOAP protocol is an application layer protocol standardised by the W3C.

connect other sources of information to the system. These include, for example, intranet and internet contents, which are opened up through a content management system and a web crawler, respectively. It is also possible to include part of the e-mail communication as a source of information.

The two current sources of information, the DMS *windream* and the Wiki-similar forum *WiCoFo*, were integrated into the prototype using the same standardized interface of the indexer-module which is responsible for indexing and linking the content using an automatically created semantic network. The DMS solution windream is a high-performance DMS, which is able to extract full-text from numerous file types and which is fully embedded in the Windows environment from the perspective of the user. The proprietary development of the WiCoFo is based on a forum, which was adapted and complemented with Wiki functions in order to facilitate the generation and structuring of small information packages in articles. Special requirements concerning confidentiality and protection of data privacy have to be taken into account to adopt the idea of Wikis in an enterprise setting.

Great emphasis is put on the platform independency of the solution in order to realize the greatest possible flexibility of the application system for future application scenarios. The modules of the existing system are developed in different programming languages and run on Microsoft Windows platforms and on Linux.

4 Related Research

The use of digitized information for the support of knowledge intensive work is a rather new area. Most related work can be found in the area of weblogging systems (Blogs), see for example [8, 9]. Some initial evaluations of applications in company settings [9, 10] suggest, that the use of digitized information can indeed support the search for information and the sharing of knowledge, ideally in environments in which knowledge workers are separated in space (e.g. distributed sites) or time (e.g. retirement problem).

However, most of the work is focussed on networked blogs, which emphasises the individual knowledge worker. Wiki oriented approaches, as we used them in the KnowBiT-project focus on certain topics which are interlinked with each other. Apart from this different point of view on the centre of information, we tried to use the digitized communication structures not as a complementary method to classical KM-solutions which focus information management but as a combined approach that benefits from each other. A crucial point in this combination is the dynamic linking and structuring of the content in the system which is especially helpful for new users of the system.

The approach of the KnowBiT-project pursued various ideas, which promise great innovation potential through the combination of established techniques on the one hand and their application in business contexts for SME on the other hand. The following focal points have been examined in detail:

1. Application and extension of existing Wiki approaches for the use in businesses while maintaining its flexibility and especially the low entry barrier. Basic points of enhancement in this field represent the establishment of security of

information through authentication, authorization, traceability of alterations, and measures of quality assurance (such as evaluation of reliability of information or dynamics of their development).

2. Linking of digitized communication infrastructures (Wikis and forums) with information management systems (e.g. DMS), which hold information and thus represent the primary information and knowledge stores in a business.
3. Provision of automatic methods for structuring the information and communication spaces and of integrated search strategies (using indexing- and mining-techniques), which enable the user to access the sources of information directly and to open up communicative structures and to localize experts within the enterprise.

5 Lessons Learnt

The experiences from the KnowBiT-project, which lasted 12 months, showed that the conception and implementation of an IT-based KM-solution for an SME within the short time frame was possible and that the approach chosen satisfied the immediate needs of the knowledge worker in the company. The project also demonstrated, that the development of the awareness for the need of a Knowledge Management within a company and it support by an IT-system is an evolutionary process. It needs a deficit/problem (e.g. grow of the company) to kick-off this process and a first step solution to create acceptance and directions where to go. Building on the fundament of an initial solution could be extended according to the needs of the users.

Looking back on the on the project we could identify the following major steps which are likely to reoccur in similar projects when introducing the first IT-based KM solution in a SME:

1. The first new tool brings *KM in the consciousness* of the employees. However KM techniques might have been applied before, but mostly without IT-support
2. Some *initial content is entered* in the system to enable a first practical usage scenario. (pilot phase)
3. As a consequence the *demand for new functionalities* increases.
4. The *system will be adapted* according to the needs of the users (gaining direction to drive the development).
5. More content is added, reaching the *critical mass* for the tool to become a productive system that is integrated in the working processes of the users (gaining acceptance).
6. Content *structuring and linking functionalities are demanded* and implemented to keep the information accessible to the users, especially for beginners that are (gaining direction on organizing the content).

There are two loops within this sequence that were important for a successful development and introduction of the system: The initial prototype started with a small set of functions and entered a pilot phase in which users could begin to explore the system and enter some initial information. Out of this user experience developed the request for new functionalities that drove the next development steps and led to another piloting phase (development direction cycle). Another cycle triggered the kind and the amount of structuring of the information when a critical mass was reached (content organization cycle). From our experiences we would suggest to use a cyclic approach as sketched above: start with a lean functionality and put a strong emphasis on content relevant for the daily work of the knowledge worker. New functionalities and more sophisticated methods to structure and organise the contained information are necessary, but should be added when needed.

6 Summary and Outlook

In the KnowBiT project, the concept of supported communication in the context of knowledge management is realized for the first time in connection with information management techniques. By means of automated analysis of the contents and simultaneous documentation of the communication, the information objects are merged from different sources and put in a common retrieval context that can be used by a single interface.

The prototype was installed and tested at the pilot user ACGT ProGenomics AG. For this purpose, the modules have been implemented in a productive status so that all relevant functions can be tried out. The consortium introduced the project to ACGT and communicates with many representatives from the field of biotechnology. The objective of this is the introduction in further businesses and the company-spanning (inter-organisational) use. From a technical point of view, the extension of the current solution to more communication-oriented information source, for example e-mail and the integration of other mining technologies, such as relationship-mining might be useful. More information can be found at http://www.knowbit.de.

Acknowledgements

The KnowBiT-project is a joint research effort of several companies and was supported by the University of Leipzig. The authors would like to thank their colleagues from the eXistand GmbH, Sangerhausen, the SMB GmbH, Leipzig, the WiSL GmbH, Halle/Saale, and bitonic life, Leipzig. The authors appreciate the contribution of the windream GmbH, Bochum, for providing the licenses of their DMS for the project and are grateful for the support for the project from the ACGT ProGenomics AG, Halle/Saale which gave valuable insights into the knowledge intensive work of the biotechnology business. The project was partially founded by the European Fund for Regional Development (EFRE) and from the federal state Saxony-Anhalt under grant number SIG 03 III 07/06.

References

1. J. Hofer-Alfeis, J.: Effective Integration of Knowledge Management into the Business Starts with a Top-down Knowledge Strategy", J.UCS, Vol. 9 (7), 719-728, Springer (2003)
2. Schütt, P.: The post Nonaka Knowledge Management, Proc. of I-KNOW '03, 290-301, Springer Graz (2003)

3. Maier, R.: Knowledge Management Systems. Information and Communication Technologies for Knowledge Management. Springer, Berlin (2004).
4. Maier, R.: State-of-Practice of Knowledge Management Systems: Results of an Empirical Study in: INFORMATIK, Zeitschrift der schweizerischen Informatikorganisationen (SVI), S 14 ff., Nr. 1/2002, Zürich
5. Leuf, B., Cunningham W.: The Wiki Way. Quick Collaboration on the Web. Addison Wesley (2001)
6. Ebersbach, A., Glaser, M., Heigl, R.: WikiTools Kooperationen im Web. Springer, Berlin Heidelberg New York Tokyo (2005)
7. Janine Swaak, J., Efimova, L., Kempen, M., Graner, M.: Finding in-house knowledge: patterns and implications, Proc. of I-KNOW '04, 27-34, Springer Graz (2004)
8. Lehel, V., Matthes, F.: Integration von Weblog-Funktionen in eine betriebliche Standardsoftware zum Wissensmanagement. In Gronau, N., Petkoff, B., Schildhauer, T. (Ed.) Wissensmanagement – Wandel, Wertschöpfung, Wachstum. Proc. of KnowTech 2004, Gito-Verlag, Berlin (2004)
9. Röll, M.: Distributed KM - Improving Knowledge Workers' Productivity and Organisational Knowledge Sharing with Weblog-based Personal Publishing. In T. N. Burg (Ed.), BlogTalks 2.0 The European Conference on Weblogs (2004)
10. Efimova, L., Fiedler, S., Verwijs, C., Boyd, A.: Legitimised Theft: Distributed Apprenticsship in Weblog Networks. Proc. of I-KNOW '04, 494-502, Springer Graz (2004)

Business Process Support as a Basis for Computerized Knowledge Management

Birger Andersson[1], Ilia Bider[2], and Erik Perjons[1]

[1] Royal Institute of Technology, Stockholm, Sweden
[2] IbisSoft AB, Stockholm, Sweden
{ba, perjons}@dsv.su.se.se, ilia@ibissoft.se

Abstract. One of the major factors behind the less successful implementations of computerized knowledge management systems (KMS) is lack of motivation to use such a system on behalf of the end-users. To create such a motivation, i.e., achieve usability, a computerized KMS should be integrated with a business process support (BPS) system and provide three main functionalities: (1) provide a process context, (2) gather automatically experience-based knowledge, and (3) provide an active generalized knowledge base. Such an integrated KMS/BPS can be built using a state-oriented view on business processes. The paper describes a version of a system built according to this view. The system fully implements the first two functionalities, the third one being under development. The system is currently installed at a pilot site. Research work in progress includes creating a formal language for representing an active generalized knowledge base, and investigating the impact of the introduction of an integrated KMS/BPS on the pilot organization.

1 Introduction

This paper concerns so-called practical knowledge, which we consider to be information that can be used by a person to perform an appropriate action in a real-world situation. According to this view, information that has no connection to a context does not constitute practical knowledge. By a context, we understand a description of a real-world situation, or a class of real world situations. Practical knowledge can be divided into the two categories *experience based* and *generalized* knowledge [1]. Experience based knowledge (EBK) can be expressed in the form of records on (memory of) actions undertaken in the past together with description of the contexts in which these actions were completed and the outcomes of these actions. EBK can be used in a current situation by analyzing outcomes of previous actions in similar contexts, when deciding on what to do next. Generalized knowledge (GK) can be expressed in the form of laws and/or rules relevant in a given context. Laws establish limitations on what actions can be valid/successful in a given context; rules prescribe/prohibit/recommend actions for a given context. While EBK is expressed as facts, GK is expressed in an abstract form with explicit or implicit use of variables and/or quantifiers in the descriptions of contexts and actions.

K.-D. Althoff et al. (Eds.): WM 2005, LNAI 3782, pp. 542–553, 2005.

Both type of knowledge are important for adequate behavior. For example, when available GK leaves too many options open, the EBK can be used to choose one of them. Alternatively, past experience in similar contexts may need to be verified against the laws/rules that could have been changed. One more example, if the current situation is completely new, i.e., we can't find similar contexts in our EBK, the selection of actions can be only based on the generalized knowledge. In this paper, we understand as a Knowledge Management System (KMS) a system that facilitate gathering, distribution and utilization of practical knowledge, experience based as well as generalized. Today, KM is considered as a principle success factor and a major force behind business success [2,3]. Effectiveness of practical KM is considered to be achievable through computerization and therefore there is a great interest in computerized KM systems.

Although there exist some successful implementations of KMS, see, for example [2,4,5], several reported implementations of KMS [6,7] are less successful. One of the major factors of failure is lack of motivation to use such a system on behalf of the end-users [8,9]. This leads us to the question of what kind of functionality a computer based KMS should provide in order to motivate people to use it. Based on practical experience and also indicated in the results of [1,3], we understand that the following three features are of particular importance for KMS usability

Context provision: As was pointed out, utilization of practical knowledge requires information on the context in which the knowledge is to be applied. In many situations, getting context information is a far from a trivial task; it may, for example, involve lengthy communication with other people. Therefore, a system that provides full information about the context or helps to find it has more chances to be used than a system that just provide knowledge (be it experience based or generalized).

Automatic gathering of experience-based knowledge: Recording the experience-based knowledge is a tedious and tiresome job that requires not only records the actions undertaken, but also the full context of these actions and their outcomes in the short and long terms. There is no surprise that such records are seldom complete. Notable exceptions are in areas with a strong tradition of keeping records, often enforced by laws or regulations. Examples are the medical (keeping patient records), and the legal profession.

A system that can help in gathering experience-based knowledge without adding extra burden on the workers would have a better chance to be used than a system that just force people to record their actions. To achieve such functionality, the system should not only provide information of the current context (see the previous feature), but also provide, at least some minimum, support for execution of actions. Providing action support ensures that information on actions undertaken will find its way into the system not because people are forced to do it, but because they want to get help from the system to complete the actions.

An active generalized knowledge base: As far as GK is concern, it is not realistic to demand that a system should fully automatically extract it from experience-based knowledge. Manual intellectual intervention will always be required. It is more feasible to concentrate on the utilization part of the generalized knowledge by making it active [10]. For example, if a system could automatically supply the end-user with the part of GKB that fully covers the current situation (context), and nothing else, it would be greatly appreciated by the system users. In addition, if the knowledge is presented in an operational form, e.g., as a list of actions/options appropriate to the current situation, it will make utilization of knowledge easier than the case where it is presented as a list of general laws/rules.

One logical consequence of the above deliberations is that a KMS should be built as an integral part of a system that both support execution of actions and knowledge management. More often than not, the term "integration" is understood as an integration of separately built technical systems. This interpretation is of limited use for our purpose. We consider action support and knowledge management as two special views, or projections, of a unified system. To achieve acceptable results from the technical integration is much more complicated than building one integrated system from the very beginning. In this paper, we describe an approach for building an integrated action support/knowledge management system for one special domain that embraces routine daily operations of a typical organization, be it a private company, non-profit organization or public office.

It is well known that the daily operations are structured in business processes, independently of whether their participants are explicitly aware of it or not. Examples of such processes are processing an order, insurance claim, or correcting a bug in a software system. Any individual action in the domain of interest always takes place in a frame of some business process instance, which constitutes the context of knowledge application. Therefore, the operational knowledge, both experience-based, and generalized should be structured around business processes and their instances. As far as action support is concerned, a system in the chosen domain is always (more or less) aimed at Business Process Support, thus the integrated system we are about to discuss may be referred to as KMS/BPS.

The goal of this paper is to present a conceptual view on business processes that can be used as a basis for building a KMS/BPS and giving an overview of the results achieved so far on our way of exploiting this view. The latter includes system architecture, current installation, and short and long term plans.

The rest of the paper is structured in the following way. In Section 3, we overview the state-oriented view on business processes that served as the basis for building the system. In Section 4, the system architecture is described. In Section 5, a pilot installation is described. Section 6 contains a summarization of the results achieved and research in progress.

Related research: Also in [3,10,11,12,13], integration of KMS with BPS is discussed. The main observation is that business processes are context-giving, structuring elements prevalent in most organizations making the integration of KMS with business process support systems natural. Our basic ideas on the needs of integrating KM and BPS, and providing a combination of experience-based and generalized knowledge are quite similar to those works. Our research differs in two respects. Firstly, we apply these ideas to a specific domain—loosely structured business processes. By loosely structured we mean that it is hard or impossible to pre-determine the necessary activities and their ordering in the processes. Secondly, we are trying to solve integration not through combining systems, but through finding a conceptual view that covers both business process support and knowledge management.

2 State-Oriented View of Business Processes

2.1 General Notions

According to a general definition of a business process, see, for example [14], a business process is a partially ordered set of activities performed to reach a well-defined goal. A process engages a number of participants, which can be divided into two categories *passive* and *active* participants. Passive participants are consumed, produced or changed through the execution of activities. Active participants, or agents, are those participants that perform activities aimed at the passive participants. The roles of passive and active participant can both be filled by human beings as well as artifacts.

When discussing business processes, it is important to differentiate the process type from the process instance. The notion of process type is used to talk about the process in general, like sales process (in general), processing insurance claims, decision-making. The notion of process instance is used to pinpoint a particular process, like processing a sale lead that concern a particular customer, processing insurance claim #1345678, passing an elderly care plan for the year 2002.

2.2 State Orientation

There are many different practical ways of modeling business processes, for example through Petri-nets, IDEF0, Role Activity Diagrams. Most of them are based on the notion of activity and activity ordering. For the sake of creating an integrated view on business process support/knowledge management, the state-oriented view as suggested in [15,16] represents one promising approach. The state-oriented view has its roots in the mathematical systems theory [17] which deals with physical processes. One of the main concepts of the mathematical system theory is the notion of state that, for continuous processes, is defined by a number of state variables accepting real values. A process type in this case is represented as set of trajectories in the state space defined via a set of differential equations of the form

$$\mathbf{P}(\mathbf{x}, \dot{\mathbf{x}}, \mathbf{w}) = \mathbf{0} \tag{1}$$

where $\dot{\mathbf{x}}$ denotes the derivative of the vector of state variables $\mathbf{x}$ with respect to time, and $\mathbf{w}$ is a vector of environment variables. Such equations are binding the direction and speed of movement of the system in the state space to the position of the system in the space and the state of the environment.

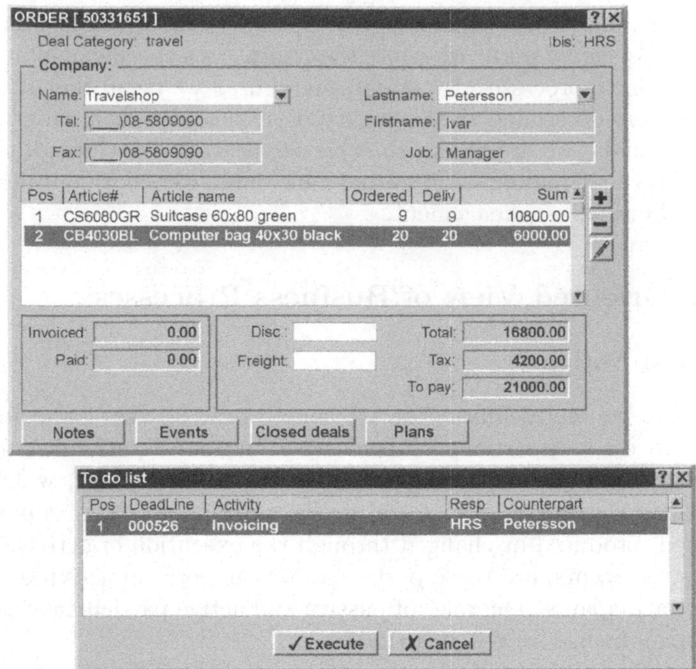

Fig. 1. State of a business process (top). Operative plan that complement the state (bottom)

A state of a business process instance is defined by a construct that reflects the relevant part of the "business world" at a moment in time. The internal structure of the state construct depends on the business process type to which the current instance belongs. An example, of such structure for a business process related to a customer order is represented in fig1 (top). The state structure includes: (a) attributes (variables), like To_pay, Paid, Ordered, etc., and (b) references to various human and non-human participants of the process, like customer, product, etc.

Each business process has an *objective* or *goal*. The goal can be defined as a set of conditions that have to be fulfilled before a process instance can be considered as finished (end of the trajectory). A state that satisfies these conditions is called a *final state* of the process. The set of final states for the process in fig. 1 can be defined as follows: (a) for each ordered item Ordered = Delivered; (b) To_pay = Total + Freight + Tax; (c) Invoiced = To_pay; (d) Paid = Invoiced. These conditions define a "surface" in the state space of this process.

Each instance of a business process is driven forward towards the goal through activities that are executed either automatically or with a human assistance. An *activity* can be viewed as an *action* aimed at changing the process state in a special way. Execution of each activity results in a change in the process state, and thus a jump in the trajectory of the process instance. A change in the process's state can happen not only as a result of completing a planned activity, but also in other, non-anticipated, ways. For example, a customer may change or cancel his/her order in the last moment.

A moment in time when the process's state changes is called an *event* in the process's lifetime. Each completed activity results in an event. The sequence of all events of the given process can be numbered in the ascending order to compose an *internal time* axis of the process. A sequence of the process's states taken after each event up to a certain moment of time forms the *history* of the process. To link the internal time axis to the real or *external time*, event registration can be introduced. A *registered event* is a record that links the change in the state of a process to the reality outside the process. For example, it can record the date-time when the event happened and/or was registered, register the responsible for the event, register comments on the event at the moment of registration (or even later), etc. A list of all events that were registered within the frame of a given process up to a certain moment of time constitutes the *chronicle* of the process, i.e., its written history.

Activities can be planned first and executed later. All activities planned, but not executed for a given process at a particular point of time constitute the process's *operative plan* (to-do list). The plan lists activities the execution of which diminishes the *distance* between the current state of the process instance and the *nearest* final state. The meaning of the term distance depends on the business process in question. Here, the term is used informally. For example, activities to plan for the process in fig.1 can be defined in the following manner: If for some item Ordered > Delivered, shipment should be performed, or If To_pay > Invoiced, an invoice should be sent, etc. The operative plan in fig. 1 (bottom) corresponds to the process instance state shown in fig. 1 (top). Conceptually, the notion of operative plan corresponds to the idea of derivatives of continuous processes. Each activity in the plan shows the direction of movement along some axes in state space and the velocity of the movement (e.g., through a deadline).

A pair ⟨*process_state, operative_plan*⟩ is called a *generalized state*. With regards to the generalized state, the notion of a *valid state* in addition to the notion of *final state* is defined. To be valid, the generalized state should include all planned activities required for moving the process to the next stipulated state. A business process type, i.e. a set of trajectories in the state space, can be defined as a subset of valid generalized states. Each trajectory in the state space that runs through the valid states constitutes a (valid) business process instance. Such a definition corresponds to the differetial equations used to define continuous processes.

A definition of a business process in the form of a set of valid states can be converted into an operational procedure called *rules of planning*. The rules specify what activities could/should be added to an invalid generalized state to make it valid. Using these rules, the process instance is driven forward in the following manner. First, an activity from the operative plan is executed and the state of the process is changed. Then, an operative plan is corrected to make the generalized state valid. Rules of planning can be roughly divided into three categories

- Obligations. Given current state, possibly history or other planned activities, certain activities must be present in the plan.
- Prohibitions. Given current state, and possibly history or other planned activities, certain activities must not be present in the plan.
- Recommendations. Given current state, and possibly history or other planned activities, certain activities should normally be planned for the process instances of the type in question.

While obligation and prohibitions can be enforced automatically by adding or deleting activities, recommendations give to the human participants a choice to follow or not to follow them based on their understanding of the situation. Besides what should be planned, rules of planning should also help to determine when things should be done and by whom, i.e. help in assignment of human resources.

2.3 Analysis from a Knowledge Management Point of View

According to Section 2, the following three representation issues should be clarified, to show that the above model could really be used as a basis for building a KMS: a) how the action context is represented, b) how the experience-based knowledge is represented, and c) how the generalized knowledge is represented.

In the above model, a minimum context that could/should be taken into consideration when executing or planning an action is the state of the business process instance in which frame the action should be undertaken. If this is not enough to make a decision or complete the action, historic information can be consulted, which includes both the process's history and chronicle. The latter could show who produced the previous actions, and why, if it is written in the comments.

The experience-based knowledge is represented by all the histories of all completed process instances. Having such histories, any action undertaken in the past can be connected to the context in which it has been completed, e.g., a state of the process at that point of time. In addition, the action can be connected to its short-term and long-term outcomes. The short-term outcome is the state of the process after completing the action. The long-term outcome is the result of the given process instance, e.g. its final state.

The generalized knowledge can be represented both in the form of laws, i.e., as a set of valid states, and in the form of rules, i.e., rules of planning.

3 The Support System

The heart of the integrated KMS/BPS we built based on the state-oriented view on business processes consists of

- A historical database that automatically stores information on all events and all past states of all processes, documents, and other business objects.
- A principle of dynamic and distributed planning. Dynamic means planning when needed, distributed means users planning to each other. Planning for each other constitute a communication channel between process participants along business process instances. Planning can be partly manual, partly automatic.
- A navigational system that allows the end user to freely navigate through the space of interconnected processes in the present and past.

The system, among other things, provides

- A virtual calendar that allows the users to plan tasks to each other, and gives immediate access to all information required for completing individual tasks. The latter includes information on the currents situation and all relevant events and documents in the past and future.
- Automatic support of history recording that allows not only to see what happened in the past, but also how things looked like at that time.
- Document management that facilitates getting access to any internal or external document without knowing its name or storage placement. The documents are found through association to their usage (e.g., purpose of creation). In addition, via support of history, all internal documents are automatically version controlled.

The current version of the system is called ProBis and the system is built as a client/server solution where clients run under Microsoft Windows, and a server runs an SQL DBMS, Oracle, or MS SQL Server. The historical database is implemented as a set of stored procedures and triggers. The user interface is built with the help of the Prolifics application development tool from Prolifics, Inc.

The end-user operates the system via executing activities in the frame of various process instances he/she is engaged in. This is done in the same manner regardless of the types of the processes and activities.

A process screen of any type has a special tab called 'Tasks', see figure 2. On this tab, both the activities planned for a process instance, and the events already registered in the frame of this process are represented as two adjacent list boxes adjacent. The left box represents planned activities (Tasks in the user-interface terminology), while the right one represents completed ones. In figure 2, one of the planned activities is represented in a "zoomed" form to show more detailed information connected to the planned activity.

To start the execution of a planned activity when observing a particular process instance, the user presses the '>' button placed between the boxes, alternatively drag-and-drop the activity icon from the left box to the right one. The planned activity disappears from the plan box and appears in the event box with a specially designated icon (a Lightning). After that, the user can change various attributes presented on the process screen to reflect changes made during execution of the activity. He/she can also add comments to the registered event by first zooming it, and also add newly planned activities to the left box by pressing the 'New' button placed above this box. After all changes in the process state are done, the user presses the 'Save' button. At this moment, the Lightning icon in the list box is substituted by a Green tick icon used to represent events or completed activities.

If during the execution of an activity, new activities have been added to the process instance, all of them will be shown in virtual calendars of the end-users to whom these activities have been assigned. In addition, if these users are currently logged in, each of them will get a message that somebody has changed his/her plans.

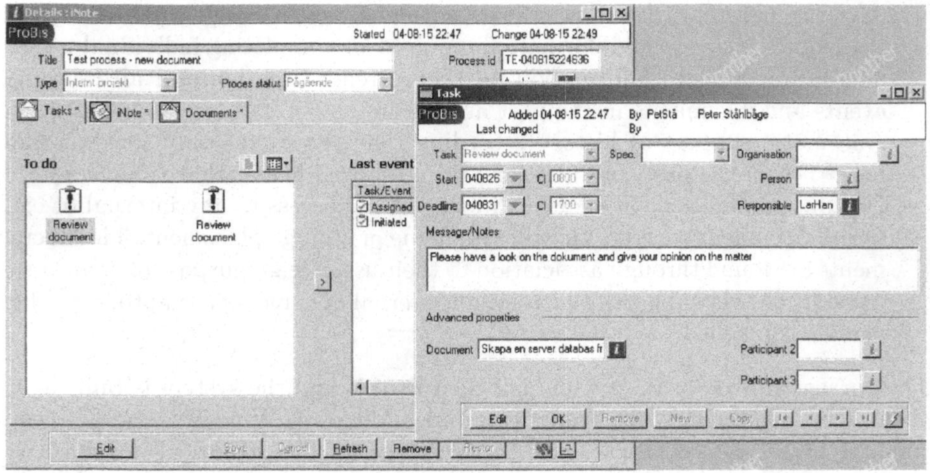

Fig. 2. Activities in the frame of a process instance

ProBis provides/intend to provide features discussed in the Section 2 in the following way

- Context provision. When a user needs to complete an action, planned or not, he/she automatically gets all the knowledge on the current state of the process in which frame the action is about to be executed, see fig. 2. No extended communication with the colleagues previously engaged in the process is required, as they do not have any additional information than what is stored in the system. As was pointed out in Section 2, the state of the process constitutes the immediate context of action. If this is not enough, the user can browse through the chronicle, see right box in figure 2, and see what actions has been completed in the frame of the process, who completed them and when. If need, he can also get a snapshot of the process' state at any time in the past. The system also provides other information that may be needed for execution of actions, like resource availability.
- Automatic gathering of experience-based knowledge. The full history of previously completed processes is automatically stored during the process life-

time, and it is easily available through a number of associations, like time-frame, document used, received or produced, people engaged in the process (own staff as well as external contacts). To stimulate workers using the system and thus avoid historic information bypassing it, the following action support is currently provided by the system: *Planning.* Just add a new task to a process, and it immediately appears in a virtual calendar as a reminder of what should be done, when and in connection to what. *Effective channels for internal communication.* Instead of writing a long message to a colleague explaining things, a user can drop a task, e.g., "review a document" into an appropriate process and assign it to a colleague. The rest of the information needed (including the full process history) is already attached to the process. The task will appear in the colleague's virtual calendar. In addition, he/she will be notified that somebody has changed his/her plans. *Reporting.* To report a completed task, it is moved from the left box in figure 2 to the right one. If needed a comment can be added. There is no need to send any reporting messages since the task list is open for all to read. *Integration with external tools.* In the current version, integration is provided for document processing. For viewing or editing a document, be it text, spread-sheet, voice message, an assigned external program can be called. The results of the editing are "trapped" back and stored in the historic database as the new version of the document.

– An active generalized knowledge base. The current version of ProBis does not provide the means for automated planning but this part is under development. Earlier versions of the system (see [18]) had some automated planning capability, but it was hard coded into the system. Current research is devoted to creating a formal language for expressing rules of planning. Having such a language, hard coding can be substituted by an interpreter.

4 Pilot Installation

The current version of ProBis was developed for the "Association of Tenants, Region West Sweden" (in Swedish: Hyresgästföreningen, Region Västra Sverige), abbreviated to HGF. HGF is a non-profit interest organization that unites more than 60 000 tenants and has as its primary objective to guard the interests of its members. The regional office, where ProBis is deployed and which is used as the main pilot site, has about 50 employees whose task it is to provide service to individual members and to the "grassroots" organizations. The service is provided in a number of areas, such as giving legal and practical advice, conducting rent negotiation with the property owners, lobbying, i.e. influencing decisions made by authorities on the local, national, or international levels.

Most business processes in the pilot organization are of administrative nature, such as negotiations, conflict management, lobbying. We call such processes loosely structured to stress that for these processes it is difficult to pre-determine the order of activities. This term has connotation with the concept of ill-defined problems in AI, see, for example [19], and with such terms as ad-hoc, emergent and dynamic workflows, see for example [20,21].

The first attempt of introducing ProBis at the customer site was worse than expected. Based on the previous experience of setting a support system into one department of this organization, some delays were expected in the introduction process. However, the difficulties of introducing a system aimed at functioning through the whole organization showed to be much greater than in the case of system introduction in a single department. One of the major problems was that the system's user-interface was poorly adapted to the occasional end-users. Based on results of the first try, the user-interface has been totally redesigned to satisfy the less skilled users (fig. 2 is from the redesigned system, whereas fig. 1 is from the old system). The redesigned system was introduced to the staff at the pilot site in 2004 and evaluation of the experiences is currently on-going.

5 Summary and Future Directions

Summarizing the material discussed in the paper, we state that to achieve usability, a computerized system for an operational KM should be integrated with BPS and structured around three main functionalities

- Provision of context in a form which is recognizable for the user.
- Automatically gathered structured experience base.
- Active generalized knowledge base.

We have chosen the state-oriented view on business processes as a basis for creating an integrated KMS/BPS for business processes of administrative nature (loosely structured business processes). We created a system that fully implemented the first two functionalities. The system was tested in our own operational practice, and it is currently installed at a pilot site.

Our research in progress goes in two directions. The first direction is to provide the third functionality. The second direction is to investigate the impact of the introduction of such an integrated system on an organization. More specifically, to find out what are the consequences for productivity, efficiency, transparency, relations between managers and subordinates, gender issues, etc. This investigation is based both on qualitative, mainly interviews with the users of ProBis, and quantitative information, based on information gathered in ProBis' historical database.

Acknowledgement. The project described in this paper is currently supported by the Swedish Agency for Innovation System (Vinnova). The authors would like to thank all people involved in the project.

References

1. Henninger, S.: Case-based knowledge management tools for software development. Journal of Automated Software Engineering **4** (1997)
2. Davenport, T., Prusak, L.: Working knowledge. Harvard Business School Press (1998)

3. Papavassiliou, G., Ntioudis, S., Abecker, A., Mentzas, G.A.: Supporting knowledge-intensive work in public administration processes. Knowledge and Process Management **10** (2003) 164–174
4. Dixon, N.: Common knowledge. Harvard Business School Press (2000)
5. Sharp, D.: Knowledge management today: Challenges and opportunities. Information System Management (2003)
6. Koenig, M.E.D., Srikantaiah, T.K.: Knowledge management lessons learned: What works and what doesn't. American Society for Information Science and Technology Monograph Series (2004)
7. KPMG: Knowledge management research report. Technical report, KPMG Consulting (2000)
8. Henninger, S.: Using software process to support learning software organizations. In: Workshop on Learning Software Organizations, Kaiserslauten, Germany (1999)
9. Malhotra, Y.: Why do knowledge management systems fail? Enablers and constraints of knowledge management in human enterprises. American Society for Information Science and Technology Monograph Series (2004) 87–112
10. Abecker, A., Mentzas, G.: Active knowledge delivery in semi-structured administrative processes. In Wimmer, M., ed.: Knowledge Management in Electronic Government, KMGov-2001, Siena, Italy, Schriftenreihe Informatik (2001) 47–57
11. Reimer, U., Margelisch, A., Staudt, M.: EULE: A knowledge-based system to support business processes. Knowledge-based Systems Journal **13** (2000) 251–260
12. van Kaathoven, R., Staudt, M., Reimer, U.: Organisational memory supported workflow management. In Sheer, A.W., ed.: Electronic Business Engineering. Physica Verlag (1999) 543–563
13. Davenport, T., Jarvenpaa, S., Beers, M.: Improving knowledge work processes. Sloan Management Review **37** (1996) 53–65
14. Hammer, M., Champy, J.: Reengineering the Corporation: A Manifesto for Business Revolution. HarperBusiness (1993) ISBN 0-88730-640-3.
15. Khomyakov, M., Bider, I.: Achieving workflow flexibility through taming the chaos. In: OOIS 2000 - 6th international conference on object oriented information systems, Springer Verlag (2000) 85–92
16. Bider, I.: State-Oriented Business Process Modelling: Principles, Theory and Practice. PhD thesis, Royal Institute of Technology, Stockholm, Sweden (2002)
17. Kalman, R.E., Falb, P.L., Arbib, M.A.: Topics in Mathematical System Theory. McGraw-Hill (1969)
18. Bider, I.: Developing tool support for process oriented management. Data Base Management (1997) Auerbach.
19. Simon, H.: The structure of ill-structured problems. Artificial Intelligence (1973) 181–201
20. Bernstein, A.: How can cooperative work tools support dynamic group processes? bridging the specificity frontier. CSCW 2000 (2000)
21. Jørgensen, H.D., Carlsen, S.: Emergent workflow, integrated planning and performance of process instances. In: Workflow Management'99, Münster, Germany (1999)

Semantic Interoperability Among Models

1st Workshop on Semantic Model Integration (SMI05)

Sven Abels, Liane Haak, and Axel Hahn

University of Oldenburg,
26111 Oldenburg, Germany
{abels, haak, hahn}@wi-ol.de

1 Workshop

The first workshop on Semantic Model Integration (SMI05) took place in Kaiserslautern on the 13th of April 2005. It was held in conjunction with the 3rd Conference Professional Knowledge Management and sponsored by the INTEROP NoE. The workshop was organized by the University of Oldenburg in the Department of Business Information Systems. The following text will give a short summary about the topics of this workshop and about the organization.

2 Topics of the Workshop

System landscapes in today's companies are characterized by a high heterogeneity of systems, which has led to the usage of various data models and formats. Data and models are often stored within varying systems and in different semantics. Due to this variety an integrative use is only possible to a certain extend, although there is an increasing demand of information. Access to information and their integration is essential for an effective companywide knowledge-management.

Today there are several approaches to create a unified access and to merge or to map information such as transformation processes e.g. in EAI, data warehouses implemented by using filters or mediators. Promising solutions to support the merging process are found in the area of meta models, ontologies or other model interoperability technologies.

If capacious data stocks have to be merged or used as a shared knowledge base, concepts of integrating the data are needed to combine these data without loosing meta data. Several knowledge integration approaches can be used to merge and to combine heterogeneous data sources or to integrate them by using concepts of interoperability. It turned out that a formal handling of semantics speeds up this integration process.

3 The Meaning of Semantic Model Integration

Performing a semantic model integration can help to integrate heterogeneous data, based of different models. For example, two models A and B could be mapped by linking their elements. This mapping can afterwards be applied to the data, which is

K.-D. Althoff et al. (Eds.): WM 2005, LNAI 3782, pp. 554 – 556, 2005.

based on model A in order to make it usable for systems that expect data to be based on model B. The following figure shows the mapping and its application.

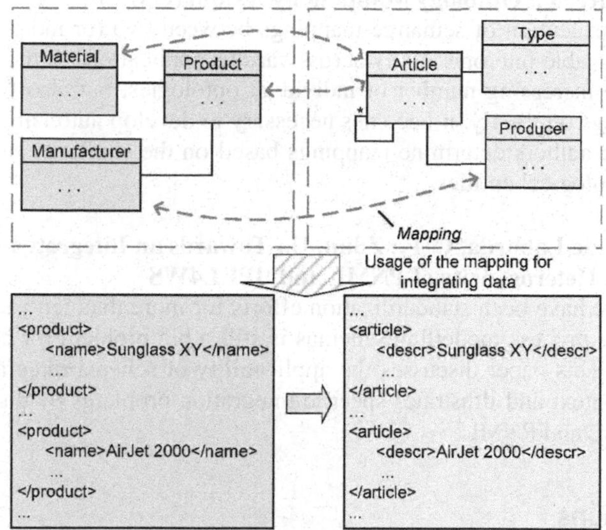

Fig. 1. Mapping between models

In order to realize a semantic model integration, several challenges have to be considered. The following list shows some of the most important challenges and topic that have to be addressed:

- An interoperability of meta models
- A combination of different co-existing "standards" for a domain
- A semantic integration of incompatible concepts
- An automatic meta data extraction and combination
- A combination of heterogeneous formats
- An automatic semantic integration of business processes and their adoption
- An application of knowledge integration concepts to the real-world
- An successful and automatic mapping among different ontologies
- A negotiation of language barriers for interpreting textual data

4 Introduction of the Papers

The following pages contain some of the papers, presented at the workshop. In contrast to the papers of the workshop proceedings, these new version will discuss the topics in more details. They include the feedback and discussions of the workshop as well as new content for completion.

Hasselbring, W.; Pedersen, S.: Metamodelling of Domain-Specific Standards for Semantic Interoperability
To achieve effective communication, not only technical interfaces are required, but also common semantics for exchanged data. This paper focuses on problems of

interoperability on the level of the application architecture, viz. Enterprise Application Integration.

Ehrig, M.; Sure, Y.: Ontology Mapping by Axiom (OMA)
Creation and execution of semantic mappings between two (or more) ontologies is a core issue to enable interoperability across various applications in the Semantic Web. To handle the increasing number of individual ontologies, but also for being able to create mappings on the fly, it becomes necessary to develop automatic approaches. In this paper, the authors determine mappings based on the similarity of the features of individual ontological entities.

Mendling, J.; de Laborda, C. P.; Zdun, U.: Towards an Integrated BPM Schema: Control Flow Heterogeneity of PNML and BPEL4WS
Although there have been standardization efforts for more than ten years, heterogeneity of business process modelling schemas is still a big problem for business process management. This paper discusses the applicability of schema integration methodology in this context and illustrates specific integration problems by discussing the example of BPEL and PNML.

5 Discussions

The workshops main idea was to bring together researchers in order to start discussions and exchange ideas. Actually, the organizers where surprised by the active and yet constructive discussions. We also believe that there will be further contact and cooperation between some of the participants. One of the reasons for the good atmosphere and the active discussions might have been the thematic closeness of all selected papers. Since the topic of the workshop was very special, we believe that we succeeded in bringing together experts of the semantic model integration domain.

Metamodelling of Domain-Specific Standards for Semantic Interoperability

Wilhelm Hasselbring and Susanne Pedersen

OFFIS, University of Oldenburg, Software Engineering Group, Oldenburg, Germany
{hasselbring, susanne.pedersen}@informatik.uni-oldenburg.de
http://www.offis.de/
http://se.informatik.uni-oldenburg.de/

Abstract. The IEEE defines interoperability as the ability of two or more systems or components to exchange information and to *use* the information that has been exchanged. Semantic interoperability problems arise in various business domains [1]. Exemplary, we take a look at the healthcare domain. Connecting heterogeneous information sources in healthcare usually implies problems of semantic interoperability. A typical problem of semantic interoperability in this domain is that the same terms are often used for different concepts (homonyms) and that the same concepts are denoted by different terms (synonyms). Many standardization efforts aim at solving these problems [2]. Standards play an important role for ensuring a common understanding of transferred data among heterogeneous application systems [3]. To achieve effective communication, not only technical interfaces are required, but also common semantics for exchanged data. This paper focuses on problems of interoperability on the level of the application architecture, viz. Enterprise Application Integration [4]. Various health care standards were analyzed, uniformly structured and put into the context of a metamodel that enables interoperability based on domain-specific standards.

1 Metamodelling

Metamodels are models of models, e.g., a UML metamodel describes a model. An example of a metamodel is the UML metamodel, which is an integral part of a layered architecture that also deals with other abstraction levels, such as the meta-meta level. The classes at the meta-meta level are specified by the Meta Object Facility (MOF) and serve as the basic building blocks for classes at the meta UML level. The semantics of UML are defined by instantiating the MOF classes at the meta-meta level. Metamodels may be applied to concisely specify and reason about the semantics of modelling languages. Figure 1 illustrates our metamodel architecture.

2 Domain-Specific Standards in Healthcare

Cooperation of health care providers is required to enable shared care. Well-known problems for interoperability with respect to correct communication among heterogeneous software systems of dissimilar health care providers emerge.

A classification of domain-independent and domain-dependent standards for achieving interoperability may be found in [5]. In the domain of health care there exist

K.-D. Althoff et al. (Eds.): WM 2005, LNAI 3782, pp. 557–559, 2005.

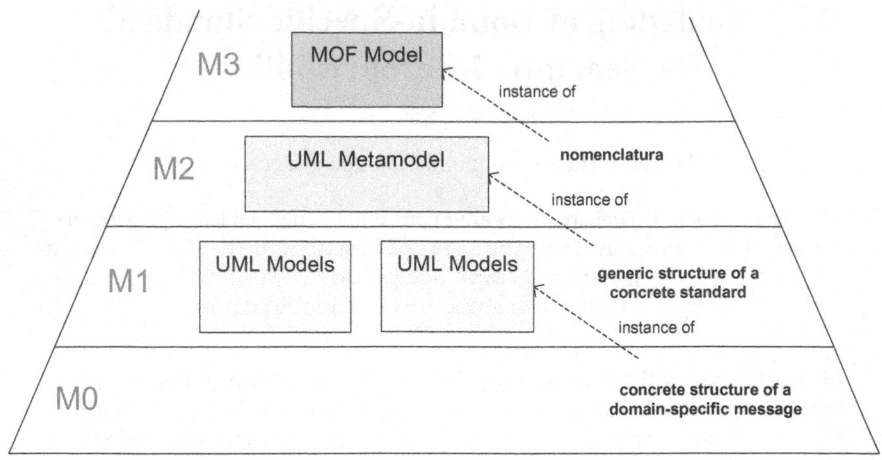

Fig. 1. Metamodel levels

various standards for communication and documentation. We integrate these standards into a common metamodel. HL-7 (Health Level Seven), for instance, is a standard, which is used mainly for communication within hospitals [6]. An accepted standard for exchanging digital images is DICOM (Digital Imaging and Communications in Medicine) [7]. Communication among general practitioners in Germany is supported by the BDT (Behandlungsdatenträger) standard [8]. We modelled the relationships among these standards by means of the standardized modeling language UML (Unified Modeling Language). Figure 2 illustrates in its lower box the resulting structure of communication standards in health care as a UML class diagram. The upper box of Figure 2 contains the corresponding metamodel on the M2 level. We follow the multilevel metamodeling approach of [9].

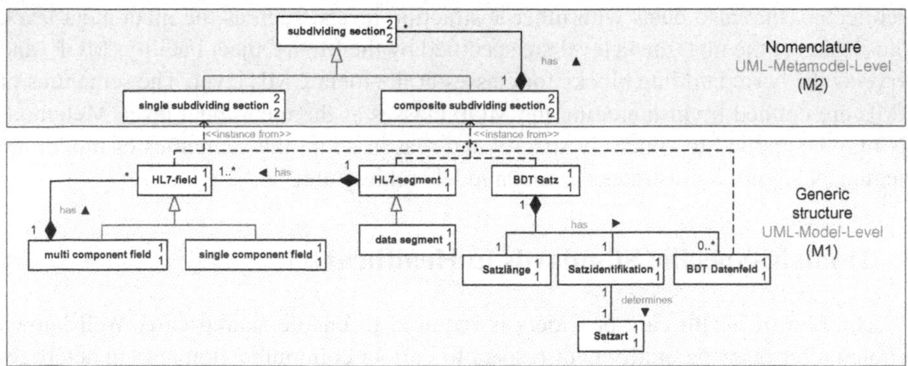

Fig. 2. Top-down structural analysis from the metamodel for communication standards towards the models for HL7 and BDT

3 Summary

Domain-specific standards play an important role for achieving semantic interoperability among federated information systems. In the present paper, we discuss our efforts for uniform structuring of these relevant standards on the metamodel level. The proposed approach is evaluated within the context of an epidemiologic cancer registry system. Our goal is to develop a flexible and scalable software architecture, which enables interoperability among the various institutions in health care. This architecture is based on the presented metamodels for health care standards. Because of our uniform specification of relevant standards for communication and documentation by means of the standardised UML, appropriate metadata for a transformation among heterogeneous models is provided for achieving interoperability among federated information systems of the various institutions in health care.

Top-down integration, based on domain-specific standards, can result in scalable and flexible software architectures for federated information systems [10,11]. In the domain of health care there exist various standards for communication and documentation, which are integrated into a common metamodel. Various health care standards are analysed, uniformly structured on the metamodel level to enable interoperability based on domain-specific standards.

References

1. Hasselbring, W., Weigand, H.: Languages for electronic business communication: State of the art. Industrial Management & Data Systems **101** (2001) 217 bis 227
2. Pedersen, S., Hasselbring, W.: Interoperabilitt für Informationssysteme im Gesundheitswesen. Informatik Forschung und Entwicklung **18** (2004) 174–188
3. Hasselbring, W.: The role of standards for interoperating information systems. In Jakobs, K., ed.: Information Technology Standards and Standardization: A Global Perspective. Idea Group Publishing, Hershey, PA (2000) 116–130
4. Hasselbring, W.: Information system integration. Communications of the ACM **43** (2000) 32–36
5. Chari, K., Seshadri, S.: Desmystifying integration. Communications of the ACM **47** (2004) 58–63
6. Dolin, R.H., et al.: The HL7 clinical document architecture. AMIA The Practice of Informatics (2004)
7. Bidgood, W.D., et al.: Understanding and using DICOM, the data interchange standard for biomedical imaging. AMIA Medical Imaging Informatics (2002)
8. KBV: xDT - Synonym für elektronischen Datenaustausch in der Arztpraxis. http://www.kbv.de/it/xdtinfo.htm (2005)
9. Atkinson, C., Kühne, T.: The essence of multilevel metamodeling. In Gogolla, M., Kobryn, C., eds.: Proc. UML 2001. Volume 2185 of Lecture Notes in Computer Science., Springer-Verlag (2003) 19–33
10. Hasselbring, W.: Web data integration for e-commerce applications. IEEE Multimedia **9** (2002) 16–25
11. Hasselbring, W., van den Heuvel, W.J., Papazoglou, M.: Top-down enterprise application integration with reference models. Australian Journal of Information Systems **8** (2000) 126–136

Ontology Mapping by Axioms (OMA)

Marc Ehrig and York Sure

Institute AIFB, University of Karlsruhe,
76128 Karlsruhe, Germany
{ehrig, sure}@aifb.uni-karlsruhe.de

Abstract. Creation and execution of semantic mappings between two (or more) ontologies is a core issue to enable interoperability across various applications in the Semantic Web. To handle the increasing number of individual ontologies, but also for being able to create mappings on the fly, it becomes necessary to develop automatic approaches. In this paper, we determine mappings based on the similarity of the features of individual ontological entities. We show that mappings can be derived automatically by encoding similarities into logical axioms. Processing these axioms by inference engines allows for detection, creation and processing of mappings on the fly without human intervention. The advantages of this approach are obvious. Firstly, the axioms can easily be reused for mappings of arbitrary ontologies, no additional modelling effort is required. Secondly, the inference engine is the only mandatory technological infrastructure which means that no additional implementation effort is needed. Finally, we evaluate our approach with very promising results.

1 Introduction

Mapping of ontologies generalizes a number of problems occurring in realistic semantic web applications such as the following ones:

(I) *Data integration* is concerned with the use of data from different sources in one application. The data from the different sources needs to be presented to the user in a unified way. Typical scenarios include (a) the integration of relational databases into semantic web applications, where database schemas are first "lifted" to the ontology level and then mapped to the ontologies of the applications, and (b) the usage of different heterogeneous ontologies within semantic web applications (e.g. by reusing different domain ontologies).

(II) *Ontology evolution* deals with the fact that in reality ontologies are typically not static entities but they rather evolve over time. This holds also for ontologies which participate in mappings to other ontologies. Therefore one can further distinguish between (a) evolving ontology mappings, (b) mapping different versions of multiple evolving ontology, and (c) mapping between versions of one ontology.

To handle the increasing number of individual ontologies, but also for being able to create mappings on the fly, it becomes necessary to develop automatic approaches. In this paper, we determine mappings based on the similarity of the features of individual ontological entities. We show that mappings can be derived automatically and on the

K.-D. Althoff et al. (Eds.): WM 2005, LNAI 3782, pp. 560–569, 2005.

fly by encoding similarities into logical axioms and processing them with an inference engine. The advantages of this approach are obvious. Firstly, the axioms can easily be reused for mappings of arbitrary ontologies, no additional modeling effort is required. Secondly, the inference engine is the only mandatory technological infrastructure which means that no additional implementation effort is needed.

In the next section 3 we present our idea of how to identify mappings. Thereafter in Section 4 follows a description how this can be realized through axioms. We briefly evaluate this axiom-based approach in Section 5. Before we conclude in Section 8 we present some related and future work (Sections 6 and 7).

2 Definitions

In this section we define and explain the core notions our work is based on. Firstly, our understanding of ontologies is presented. Secondly, we discuss the general meaning of mapping and similarity. The logics we use will be presented at the end.

2.1 Ontologies

In philosophy an ontology is *a particular theory about the nature of being or the kinds of existence*. The following short definition describes ontologies as used in our scenario. In the understanding of this paper they consist of both schema and instance data. An ontology O is a tuple consisting of the following. The concepts C of the schema are arranged in a subsumption hierarchy H_C. Relations R_C exist between single concepts. Relations (properties)[1] can also be arranged in a hierarchy H_R. Instances I of a specific concept are interconnected by property instances R_I. Additionally one can define axioms A which can be used to infer knowledge from already existing one. An extended definition can be found in [1]. Common languages to represent ontologies are RDF(S) ([2]) or OWL ([3]), though one should note that each language offers different modelling primitives and, thus, a different level of complexity.

2.2 Mapping and Similarity

Due to the wide range of expressions used in this area (merging, alignment, integration etc.), we want to describe our understanding of the term "mapping". We define mapping as (cf. [4]): *"Relating similar (according to some metric) concepts or relations from different sources to each other by an equivalence relation. A mapping results in a virtual integration."* We want to stick to this definition, more specific we will demand the *same* semantic meaning of two *entities*. Formally an ontology mapping function can be defined the following way:

- $map : O_{i_1} \to O_{i_2}$
- $map(e_{i_1 j_1}) = e_{i_2 j_2}$, if $sim(e_{i_1 j_1}, e_{i_2 j_2}) > t$ with t being the threshold entity $e_{i_1 j_1}$ is mapped onto $e_{i_2 j_2}$; they are semantically identical, each entity $e_{i_1 j_1}$ is mapped to at most one entity $e_{i_2 j_2}$

[1] In this paper we treat the words *relation* and *property* as synonyms.

So far we only consider one-to-one mappings between singular ontological entities (see above). Neither do we cover mappings of whole ontologies or sub-trees, nor complex mappings such as concatenation of literals (*e.g.* name corresponds to first name plus last name) or functional transformation of attributes (*e.g.* currency conversions). However, using a logical language such as F-Logic (see later) for deriving mappings and at the same time for representing mappings, creation and execution of such sophisticated mappings is feasible but requires some more scientific efforts.

The mapping function relies on the notion of similarity which we shall describe here (cf. [5]):

- $sim(x, y) \in [0..1]$
- $sim(x, y) = 1 \rightarrow x = y$: two objects are identical.
- $sim(x, y) = 0$: two objects are different and have no common characteristics.
- $sim(x, y) = sim(y, x)$: similarity is symmetric.

Further we define similarity of ontologies through the following. For a more extensive description of similarity for ontologies please refer to [6].

- O_i: ontology, with ontology index $i \in \mathbb{N}$
- e_{ij}: entities of O_i, with $e_{ij} \in \{C_i, R_i, I_i\}$, entity index $j \in \mathbb{N}$
- $sim(e_{i_1j_1}, e_{i_2j_2})$: similarity function between two entities $e_{i_1j_1}$ and $e_{i_2j_2} (i_1 \neq i_2)$; as shown later this function makes use of the ontological structure of the compared ontologies.

2.3 Logics and Inferencing

In our approach we rely on (i) F-Logic as representation language for our mapping model (*cf.* [7], "F" stands for "Frames") and (ii) Ontobroker as the inference engine to process F-Logic (*cf.* [8]). F-Logic combines deductive and object-oriented aspects: *"F-logic ... is a deductive, object-oriented database language which combines the declarative semantics of deductive databases with the rich data modelling capabilities supported by the object oriented data model"* (*cf.* [10]).

F-Logic allows for concise definitions with object oriented-like primitives (classes, attributes, object-oriented-style relations, instances). Furthermore, it also has Predicate Logic (PL-1) like primitives (predicates, function symbols). F-Logic allows for axioms that further constrain the interpretation of a model. Axioms may either be used to describe constraints or they may define coherences, *e.g.* in order to define a relation R by the composition of two other relations S and Q. Throughout this paper we refer to F-Logic every time we use the term 'axiom'.

F-Logic axioms have the expressive power of Horn-Logic with negation and may be transformed into Horn-Logic rules. The semantics for a set of F-Logic statements is defined by the well-founded semantics (*cf.* [11]). This semantics is close to First-Order semantics. In contrast to First-Order semantics not all possible models are considered but one "most obvious" model is selected as the semantics of a set of axioms and facts. It is a three valued logic, *i.e.* the model consists of a set of true facts and a set of unknown facts and a set of facts known to be false.

Unlike Description Logics (DL), F-Logic does not provide means for subsumption [12], but (also unlike DL) it provides for efficient reasoning with instances and for the capability to express arbitrary powerful axioms, *e.g.* ones that quantify over the set of classes. However, it has to be noted that first efforts are being made to put a rule layer on top of the DL-based OWL language [3]. Thus, in future (some kind of) convergence of different representation mechanisms can be expected.

The most widely published operational semantics for F-Logic is the alternating fixed point procedure (*cf.* [13]). This is a forward chaining method which computes the entire model for the set of axioms, *i.e.* the set of true and unknown facts. For answering a query the entire model must be computed (if possible) and the variable substitutions for the query are then derived. In contrast, the inference engine Ontobroker performs a mixture of forward and backward chaining based on the dynamic filtering algorithm (*cf.* [14]) to compute (the smallest possible) subset of the model for answering the query. In most cases this is much more efficient than the simple evaluation strategy. These techniques stem from the deductive data base community and are optimized to deliver all answers instead of one single answer as *e.g.* resolution does.

For detailed introductions to the syntax and the object model of F-Logic, in particular with respect to the implementation of F-Logic in Ontobroker, we refer to [15] and [16].

3 Mapping Identification

Our mapping approach extends the accompanying paper [17] by encoding similarity rules as logical expressions. Our implemented approach is based on several similarity methods which are manually encoded and allow for detection of possible mappings (see also Figure 1). The manual effort is necessary because coherences in ontologies are too complex to be directly learned by machines. An expert understanding the encoded knowledge in ontologies formulates machine-interpretable rules out of the information. This is done in a two step approach.

In a first step, the modeling expert defines similarity rules such as presented in Table 1 in natural language. We here present only some of the identified rules. As a second step, as shown exemplary in Section 4, these rules are encoded into machine processable logical axioms.

In the following we give examples of such encoded similarity rules. Labels are human identifiers (names) for entities, normally shared by a community of humans speaking a common language. We can therefore infer that *if labels are the same, the entities are probably also the same* (**R1**). Several ideas have already been created to compare labels, *e.g.* we rely on the edit distance [19]. Further a taxonomy can be created over concepts, in which a concept inherits all the relations of its super-concepts. *If super-concepts are the same, the actual concepts are similar to each other* (**R4**). In practice we calculate the degree of overlap of the two super-concept sets.

Each rule shall give a hint on whether two entities are identical, but typically no rule for itself provides enough support to unambiguously identify a mapping. A general and straight-forward formula for this integration task can be given by summarizing over the total number of weighted similarity methods. A threshold cuts off relevant

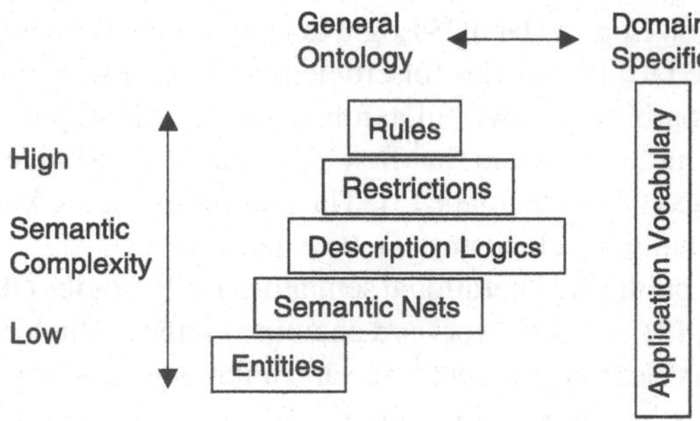

Fig. 1. Similarity stack

Table 1. Similarity Rules

	Rule	Name
Entities are similar, if ... [Name] ... are similar	$R1$	labels
	$R2$	URIs
Concepts are similar, if ... [Name] ... are similar	$R3$	relations
	$R4$	super-concepts
	$R5$	sub-concepts
	$R6$	instances
Relations are similar, if ... [rule] ... are similar	$R6$	domain and range
	$R7$	connected instances
Instances are similar, if ... [rule] ... are similar	$R8$	mother-concepts
	$R9$	properties and instances

from irrelevant mappings. The accompanying paper presents all rules in detail how to combine these rules and how to set the threshold.

4 Formalization of Similarity Rules as Logical Axioms

The similarity rules initially have been defined as natural language. Goal of this subsection is to show how they can be declaratively represented by logical axioms which can be processed by inference engines. In specific we will use F-Logic as ontology language to formalize the similarity rules as axioms and Ontobroker as inference engine to process them. F-Logic combines features from object-oriented programming and frame-logics. ":" is used to represent "instance of" and "::" to denote the "subconcept of" relationship. Arbitrary relationships are specified by the following syntax: $concept[relation =>> concept]$, $->>$ is used for the instantiation of such a relationship. # splits an identifier into namespace and local name. Please refer to [16,20] for further details.

The following F-Logic examples correspond to the above mentioned rule **R5**: *if super-concepts are the same, the actual concepts are similar to each other*. In a similar manner, all other rules have been formalized.

```
a#tele1::c#commuication_device.
a#tele1[#label->>a#telephone].
b#tele2::c#communication_device.
b#tele2[#label->>b#phone].
```

Example 1. Two concepts tele1 and tele2, which are both a subclass of info; encoded in F-Logic

```
FORALL NS1,LN1,NS2,LN2
 similaritySuper(NS1#LN1,NS2#LN2)
 <-
 EXISTS NS3,LN3
 NS1#LN1::NS3#LN3 AND
 NS2#LN2::NS3#LN3.
```

Example 2. Two concepts NS1#LN1 and NS2#LN2 are checked for identical super-concepts (R5)

Example 1 shows a fragment of an ontology: `tele1` and `tele2`, both from different namespaces `a` and `b`, are subclass of `communication_device`. Further they have specific labels (`telephone` and `phone`). Example 2 calculates the similarity based on rule R5. For all namespaces and local names a similarity of super-concepts (`similaritySuper`) is determined if there is one common super-concept from an arbitrary namespace of both individual classes, as it is the case here with `communication_device`. Applying this axiom to the example ontology we receive the predicate `similaritySuper(a#tele1,b#tele2)`.

Ontobroker is able to distinguish different namespaces. The variables `NS1`, `NS2` and `NS3` are bound to namespaces and `LN1`, `LN2` and `LN3` to entity labels (such as concept names or relation names). Please note that to define *e.g.* `NS1` and `NS2` explicitly as disjunct namespaces, one would need to add `AND NOT equals(LN1,LN2)` into the rule body.

For the integration step all similarity predicates are summarized. If a threshold is reached, the two corresponding concepts (or other entities) are declared to be mapped onto each other.

By using the same kind of axioms also mappings themselves can be expressed as F-Logic (as *e.g.* shown in [21]).

4.1 Procedural Strategy

Just for completeness we will briefly explain an alternative way of implementing the similarity rules. Additionally we created a Java program where the rules are explicitly implemented, ontologies are loaded and processed with the KAON-environment[2]. Obviously, a direct procedural implementation can be more focused towards the actual mapping problem. In detail, we emphasized mapping efficiency by e.g. restricting the entity pairs to compare. Also some ontology features are easier to grasp through a procedural approach. A complete evaluation is given in [17,23]. Ordering of rules, which

[2] http://kaon.semanticweb.org

can not be enforced in an inference engine, is currently not used, but might be interesting for the future e.g. only if the labels are similar it is worth looking at the instances of two concepts. In comparison, the procedural approach allows for better efficiency whereas the declarative approach allows for more flexibility and maintenance.

5 Evaluation

To evaluate our implementation we basically take two ontologies and create mappings between the entities based on a given strategy. These mappings are validated against the correct mappings which had been created in beforehand for the evaluation in the accompanying paper where we compared our approach also against other approaches.

In our data set we have two ontologies describing Russia. The ontologies were created by students with the task to represent the content of two independent travel websites about Russia. These ontologies have approximately 400 entities, including concepts, relations, and instances. The total number of theoretical mappings is at 280, which have been assigned manually.

We here compare two strategies. For the *Procedural Strategy (S1)* the presented rules have been implemented in a procedural way with a focus on efficiency. The *Logics Strategy (S2)* represents the approach shown in this paper which has a focus on intuitive modeling, greater flexibility, and easy maintainability.

To allow for comparability not only between our own test series, but also with existent literature we will focus on using standard information retrieval metrics. The definitions of precision and recall is adapted by us to fit the given evaluation scenario [24].

Recall: $r = \frac{\#correct\_found\_mappings}{\#possible\_existing\_mappings}$
Precision: $p = \frac{\#correct\_found\_mappings}{\#all\_found\_mappings}$
F-Measure: combines the two mentioned measures, $f = \frac{2pr}{p+r}$

The following Table 2 shows that our approach works as good as the procedural implementation. More specifically one can see from the results that finding mappings through an inference engine returns results which have a similar quality (precision, recall and f-measure) to the ones provided by a procedural implementation.

Table 2. Comparison of procedural and logics mapping approach

Strategy	Measure	Value
Procedural	Precision	0.772
	Recall	0.652
	F-measure	0.707
Logical Inferencing	Precision	0.784
	Recall	0.652
	F-measure	0.711

6 Related Work

[25] give a general overview of similarity. As the basic ontology mapping problem has been around for some years first tools have already been developed to address this. The tools PROMPT and AnchorPROMPT [26] use labels and to a certain extent the structure of ontologies. Their focus lies on ontology merging i.e. how to create one ontology out of two. [27] already used a general approach of relaxation labelling in their tool GLUE. [28] further present an approach for semantic mappings based on SAT. Most of their work is based on the similarity of instances only. [29] created a tool for mapping called Chimaera. Potential matches are presented to the user in all mentioned tools for confirmation. In their tool ONION [30] the authors take up the idea of using rules and inferencing for mapping, but the inferencing is based on manually assigned mappings or simple heuristics (as e.g. label comparisons). Besides equality first steps are taken in the direction of complex matches. These could also include concatenation of two fields such as "first name" and "last name" to "name"[31]. The other mentioned tools do not raise the issue, they presumably use only naive summarization approaches.

Despite the number of related work, there are very little approaches on how to combine the many methods as we do. Actually, in the work of [32] the notion of using different features and heuristics based upon to determine mappings is first presented.

7 Future Work

Despite the recent work on inference engines, efficiency stays a problem, especially when reasoning on schema and instance level. Our experiment showed that the current implementation of Ontobroker was able to deal with non-toy ontologies. However, more experimental settings with different kinds of ontologies are needed to understand the behavior of our approach in different situations. *E.g.* consider mapping of ontologies which have high number of relationships and only few concepts etc., or consider larger ontologies which include thousands of entities.

Although our simple approach for setting the threshold intuitively for creation of mappings resulted in convincing precision and recall values, we expect an even better result when learning thresholds by *e.g.* maximizing the f-measure value.

To compare our approach on a technical level with other existing approaches, we plan to contribute to the "3rd International Workshop on Evaluation of Ontology-based Tools (EON2004)"[3] at the "3rd International Semantic Web Conference (ISWC2004)". Part of the workshop will be an experiment on ontology mapping and alignment where participants have to proof the abilities of their approaches in a well-defined evaluation setting.

8 Conclusion

To conclude, the mapping problem arises in many scenarios. We are identifying mappings between two ontologies based on the intelligent combination of manually encoded similarity rules. We have shown that this can further be seamlessly integrated

[3] see `http://km.aifb.uni-karlsruhe.de/ws/eon2004/`

into a semantic web infrastructure which contains an inference engine, as the axioms are represented in logic.

The advantages of our approach are mainly twofold. Firstly, the modeled axioms can easily be reused for mapping of arbitrary ontologies, no additional modeling effort is required and the maintenance of the system is performed on the knowledge level. Secondly, the inference engine is the only mandatory technological infrastructure which means that no additional implementation effort is needed.

To sum up, semantic mappings can be effectively retrieved by using inference engines.

Acknowledgements. Research reported in this paper has been partially financed by EU in the IST projects SWAP (EU IST-2001-34103), SEKT (EU IST-2003-506826), and KnowledgeWeb (EU IST-2003-507482). Many thanks to our colleagues for the fruitful discussions.

References

1. Stumme, G., Ehrig, M., Handschuh, S., Hotho, A., Maedche, A., Motik, B., Oberle, D., Schmitz, C., Staab, S., Stojanovic, L., Stojanovic, N., Studer, R., Sure, Y., Volz, R., Zacharias, V.: The Karlsruhe view on ontologies. Technical report, University of Karlsruhe, Institute AIFB (2003)
2. Brickley, D., Guha, R.V.: RDF Vocabulary Description Language 1.0: RDF Schema. W3C Recommendation 10 February 2004 (2004) available at http://www.w3.org/TR/rdf-schema/.
3. Smith, M.K., Welty, C., McGuinness, D.: OWL Web Ontology Language Guide (2004) W3C Recommendation 10 February 2004, available at http://www.w3.org/TR/owl-guide/.
4. Klein, M.: Combining and relating ontologies: an analysis of problems and solutions. In Gomez-Perez, A., et al., eds.: Workshop on Ontology and Information Sharing, IJCAI'01, Seattle, USA (2001)
5. Bisson, G.: Why and how to define a similarity measure for object based representation systems. Towards Very Large Knowledge Bases (1995) 236–246
6. Ehrig, M., Haase, P., Stojanovic, N., Hefke, M.: Similarity for ontologies - a comprehensive framework. In: 13th European Conference on Information Systems. (2005)
7. Kifer, M., Lausen, G., Wu, J.: Logical foundations of object-oriented and frame-based languages. J. of the ACM **42** (1995) 741–843
8. Decker, S., Erdmann, M., Fensel, D., Studer, R. [9] 351–369
9. Meersman, R., Tari, Z., Stevens, S., eds.: Database Semantics: Semantic Issues in Multimedia Systems. Kluwer Academic Publisher (1999)
10. Frohn, J., Himmeröder, R., Kandzia, P., Schlepphorst, C.: How to write F–Logic programs in FLORID. A tutorial for the database language F–Logic. Technical report, Institut für Informatik der Universität Freiburg (1996) Version 1.0.
11. van Gelder, A., Ross, K.A., Schlipf, J.S.: The well-founded semantics for general logic programs. J. of the ACM **38** (1991) 620–650
12. Horrocks, I.: Using an expressive description logic: FaCT or fiction? In: Proc. of the Int. Conf. on Knowledge Representation (KR 1998), Morgan Kaufmann (1998) 636–649
13. van Gelder, A.: The alternating fixpoint of logic programs with negation. J. of Computer and System Sciences **47** (1993) 185–221
14. Kifer, M., Lozinskii, E.: A framework for an efficient implementation of deductive databases. In: Proc. of the 6th Advanced Database Symposium, Tokyo (1986) 109–116

15. Erdmann, M.: Ontologien zur konzeptuellen Modellierung der Semantik von XML. Books on Demand (2001) PhD Thesis.
16. Ontoprise: How to write F–Logic programs – a tutorial for the language F–Logic (2004)
17. Ehrig, M., Sure, Y.: Ontology mapping - an integrated approach. [18] 76–91
18. Bussler, C., Davies, J., Fensel, D., Studer, R., eds.: Proc. of the First Europ. Semantic Web Symp. (ESWS 2004). Volume 3053 of LNCS., Heraklion, Crete, Greece, Springer (2004)
19. Levenshtein, I.V.: Binary codes capable of correcting deletions, insertions, and reversals. Cybernetics and Control Theory (1966)
20. Kifer, M., Lausen, G., Wu, J.: Logical foundations of object-oriented and frame-based languages. Journal of the ACM **42** (1995)
21. Maier, A., Schnurr, H.P., Sure, Y.: Ontology-based information integration in the automotive industry. [22] 897–912
22. Fensel, D., Sycara, K., Mylopoulos, J., eds.: Proc. of the 2nd Int. Semantic Web Conf. (ISWC 2003). Volume 2870 of LNCS., Sanibel Island, FL, USA, Springer (2003)
23. Ehrig, M., Staab, S.: QOM - quick ontology mapping. In: Proceedings of the Third International Semantic Web Conference (ISWC-2004), Hiroshima, Japan (2004)
24. Do, H., Melnik, S., Rahm, E.: Comparison of schema matching evaluations. In: Proceedings of the second int. workshop on Web Databases (German Informatics Society). (2002)
25. Rodríguez, M.A., Egenhofer, M.J.: Determining semantic similarity among entity classes from different ontologies. IEEE Transactions on Knowledge and Data Engineering (2000)
26. Noy, N.F., Musen, M.A.: Anchor-prompt: Using non-local context for semantic matching. In: Workshop on Ontologies and Information Sharing at the Seventeenth International Joint Conference on Artificial Intelligence (IJCAI-2001), Seattle, WA (2001)
27. Doan, A., Madhavan, J., Domingos, P., Halevy, A.: Learning to map between ontologies on the semantic web. In: Proceedings to the Eleventh International World Wide Web Conference, Honolulu, Hawaii, USA (2002)
28. Bouquet, P., Magnini, B., Serafini, L., Zanobini, S.: A SAT-based algorithm for context matching. In: IV International and Interdisciplinary Conference on Modeling and Using Context (CONTEXT'2003), Stanford University (CA, USA) (2003)
29. McGuinness, D.L.: Conceptual modeling for distributed ontology environments. In: International Conference on Conceptual Structures. (2000) 100–112
30. Mitra, P., Wiederhold, G., Kersten, M.: A graph-oriented model for articulation of ontology interdependencies. Lecture Notes in Computer Science **1777** (2000) 86+
31. Do, H., Rahm, E.: COMA - a system for flexible combination of schema matching approaches. In: Proceedings of the 28th VLDB Conference, Hong Kong, China (2002)
32. Euzenat, J., Petko, V.: An integrative proximity measure for ontology alignment. In: Proc. ISWC-2003 workshop on semantic information integration, Sanibel Island (FL US). (2003) 33–38

Towards an Integrated BPM Schema: Control Flow Heterogeneity of PNML and BPEL4WS

Jan Mendling[1], Cristian Pérez de Laborda[2], and Uwe Zdun[1]

[1] Dept. of Information Systems and New Media, WU Vienna, Austria
jan.mendling@wu-wien.ac.at, uwe.zdun@wu-wien.ac.at
[2] Dept. of Computer Science, Databases and Information Systems, University of Düsseldorf, Germany
perezdel@cs.uni-duesseldorf.de

Abstract. Although there have been standardization efforts for more than ten years, heterogeneity of business process modelling schemas is still a big problem for business process management. This paper discusses the applicability of schema integration methodology in this context and illustrates specific integration problems by discussing the example of BPEL and PNML. Different control flow representations are highlighted as a major challenge in this area. Using classical schema integration and the upward inheritance principle can yield an integrated schema that still includes redundant behavioral concepts. We conclude that future research has to identify extensions to the schema integration process in order to capture such specifics of BPM schemas.

1 Introduction

Heterogeneity of Business Process Modelling (BPM) schemas is a notorious problem for business process management. Although standardization has been discussed for more than ten years, the lack of a commonly accepted interchange format is still the main encumbrance to business process management (see e.g. [1]). A commonly accepted interchange format is needed to move business process models between tools and applications of different vendors. Furthermore, such an interchange format implies the availability of a business process modelling schema that defines the interchange format.

The problem of a missing de facto standard for BPM is addressed by various standardization efforts. Currently, there are at least 15 specifications available or in progress of development, for an overview see e.g. [2]. Different BPM schemas are proposed by the Object Management Group (OMG), the Business Process Management Initiative (BPMI), the Workflow Management Coalition (WfMC), the Organisation for the Advancement of Structured Information Standards (OASIS), the United Nations Centre for Trade Facilitation and Electronic Business (UN/CEFACT), the World Wide Web Consortium (W3C), and academic initiatives – some of them addressing only partial aspects of BPM. Recently, various new specifications for Web Service based BPM and Web Service composition including respective XML schemas have been proposed. At least in

K.-D. Althoff et al. (Eds.): WM 2005, LNAI 3782, pp. 570–579, 2005.

the short run, they contribute to a further increase of heterogeneity of schemas for business process modelling.

The variety of these standardization efforts raises several questions. Firstly, the interrelation of these various schemas is too little understood. The mere number of specifications does not allow any conclusion on the heterogeneity of concepts included. Research on the comparison of BPM standards like e.g. [3] gives some evidence, but with a narrow focus. Secondly, there is doubt whether standardization processes are a suitable means to come up with an integrated schema for BPM. Weaknesses of BPM standardization have been mentioned in several publications. [4] discusses the diverging strategies of different stakeholders in standardization highlighting the bargaining character of such processes. This holds also for the upcoming Business Process Definition Metamodel standard of OMG. It is required to be UML2-compliant and it will most probably be inspired by IBM products in its major parts. Furthermore, the case of XPDL suggests that standardization may rather lead to specification of the minimal consensual set of concepts than to a consolidation of concepts [5]. In the case of BPEL4WS (or short BPEL) [6] the control flow concepts of XLANG and WSFL were just put together, but semantic redundancies were not eliminated. Accordingly, there is a choice in BPEL between a block structured and a graph structured specification of control flow [7]. In contrast to that, a schema is needed that reflects the superset of concepts available in various BPM specifications and that is free of redundant concepts.

This paper discusses in how far schema integration offers a suitable methodology for deriving an integrated BPM schema from various input schemas. In Section 2 we present the basic ideas of schema integration. In Section 3 we focus on PNML and BPEL as two examples of heterogeneous BPM schemas. We illustrate how schema integration could be used to integrate the schemas and in how far the result is satisfactory. In Section 4 we give an overview on related research in the context of both schema integration and heterogeneity of BPM schemas. Section 5 concludes the paper and gives an outlook on future research.

2 Schema Integration

Schema integration refers to the construction of a global schema from a set of local schemas. In general, the local schemas are heterogeneous, i.e. semantically related concepts are captured by different local schemas in a different way, e.g. using different names or different structure (cf. e.g. [8]). The global schema is expected to be *complete* in capturing all concepts of the local schemas, *minimal* by including semantically related concepts only once, and still *understandable* [9]. Discovering semantic relationships like equivalence, subsumption, intersection, disjointness, and incompatibility between concepts of local schemas plays a central role for schema integration. On the other hand, design criteria like simplicity, completeness, generality, unambiguity, and extensibility have been identified as important for standardization of schemas (see e.g. [2]). Apart from extensibility these criteria match the schema integration criteria of completeness, minimality, and understandability as reported in [9]. As we discussed in Section 1 these criteria are not always met by BPM standards: e.g. XPDL is not complete and BPEL is not minimal. Therefore, schema integration could be a promising methodology to grant completeness and minimality of an integrated BPM schema that could also serve as a candidate standard.

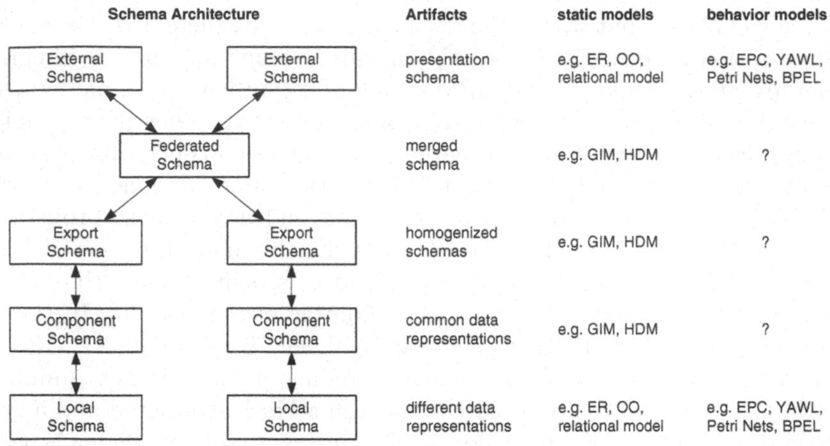

Fig. 1. Schema architecture according to [10] and schema integration

Figure 1 shows a schema architecture as defined in [10]. Typical schema integration problems can be related to this architecture. They are addressed by dedicated transformations from local schemas (bottom) via intermediate steps to external schemas (top). The first step takes the local schemas (that may be represented in heterogeneous data models) as input and transforms them to a common data model representation. This common data model can be low-level or high-level. Low-level models include e.g. the generic integration model (GIM) [11] or the hypergraph data model (HDM) [12]. For a discussion on common data models see e.g. [11]. In the second step, transformations to the export schemas homogenize the component schemas by resolving schema conflicts. The categories of potential conflicts depend on the common data model; a typical example is a concept that is represented by an attribute in schema A and by an object in schema B. In the third step, the export schemas are subject to a merge operation that builds on semantic relationships between concepts of the different schemas. This yields the federated schema which is still expressed in the common data model. In a fourth steps, this federated schema is transformed to external schemas in data models that the user can easily understand. The question is whether schema integration as proposed for static concepts can be applied for deriving an integrated BPM schema. In [11] the straight-forward application of schema integration of static aspects to behavioral aspects is doubted and further research in this area is encouraged. In the following section we discuss problems that may arise when schema integration of static aspects is applied to BPM schemas like e.g. PNML and BPEL.

3 Schema Integration of PNML and BPEL

We will illustrate specific integration problems of BPM schemas by using Petri Net Markup Language (PNML) and the Business Process Execution Language for Web Services (BPEL) as an example. Both define an XML schema. For integration we rely on the definition of intentional relationships like proposed in e.g. [13] and the upward inheritance principle [14].

PNML was designed in order to facilitate the interchange of Petri net models between heterogeneous Petri net analysis tools [15]. PNML includes the standard Petri net elements, i.e. places, transitions, and arcs between them. Furthermore, all these elements can have so-called labels. A label captures the specifics of a certain Petri net type. So-called Petri net type definitions specify the set of allowed labels to define a particular type of Petri net. This extensibility mechanism offers the flexibility to exchange arbitrary Petri net types with PNML. For further details on PNML refer to [15]. *BPEL* is an executable language for the specify Web Service composition. That means BPEL builds on a set of elementary Web Services to define a more complex process that is also accessible as a Web Service. BPEL offers several concepts including *variables* to store workflow data and messages that are exchanged with Web Services. *PartnerLinks* represent a bilateral message exchange between two parties. They are relevant for such *basic activities* that involve Web Service requests. These include the `invoke`, the `receive`, and the `reply` activity. Further basic activities include `wait`, `terminate`, and `assign` to name but a few. Moreover, BPEL offers *structured activities* for the definition of control flow, e.g. to specify sequencing (using `sequence`), concurrency of activities (using `flow`), or alternative branches (e.g. via `switch`). These structured activities can be nested. Finally, there are different handlers in order to respond to the occurrence of a fault, an event, or if a compensation has been triggered. In this paper we concentrate on control flow specification of BPEL, i.e., basic and structured activities. For further details on BPEL see [6].

The example of Figure 2 illustrates a major problem when integrating heterogeneous BPM schemas, i.e. heterogeneous representation of behavioral aspects (also referred to as control flow). There are different formalisms available to represent control flow (see e.g. [16]). Some BPM formalisms are quite different from a syntactical perspective, although they represent similar semantics. Figure 2 gives an example of an AND split with one flow of control branching into two parallel threads of execution. The first grey column provides the XML code for this process in Petri Net Markup Language (PNML), which uses a graph-based representation with places and transitions as special nodes linked via control flow arcs. The second grey column shows the AND split represented in BPEL using a block-structured syntax. The so-called `flow` structured activity is used to specify parallel execution of all its child activities.

Figure 3 illustrates the PNML and BPEL schemas represented as metamodels. Classical schema integration builds on identifying semantic relationships between the intentional domains of schema constructs, i.e. the real world entities identified by the constructs. In [13] equivalence, subsumption, intersection, and

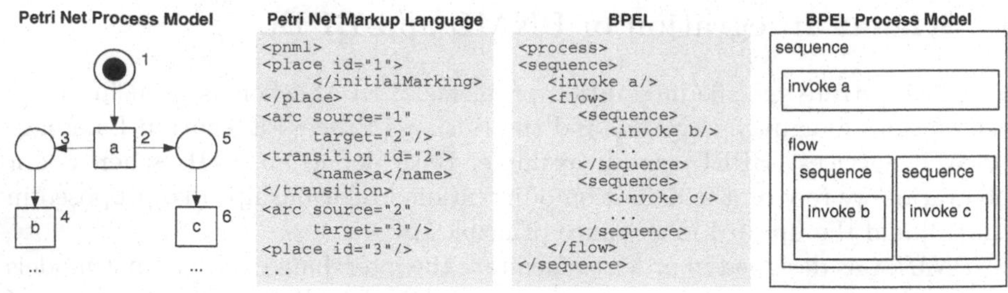


```
<pnml>
<place id="1">
    </initialMarking>
</place>
<arc source="1"
    target="2"/>
<transition id="2">
    <name>a</name>
</transition>
<arc source="2"
    target="3"/>
<place id="3"/>
...
```

```
<process>
<sequence>
   <invoke a/>
   <flow>
      <sequence>
         <invoke b/>
         ...
      </sequence>
      <sequence>
         <invoke c/>
         ...
      </sequence>
   </flow>
</sequence>
```

Fig. 2. A sample process model with its PNML and BPEL representation

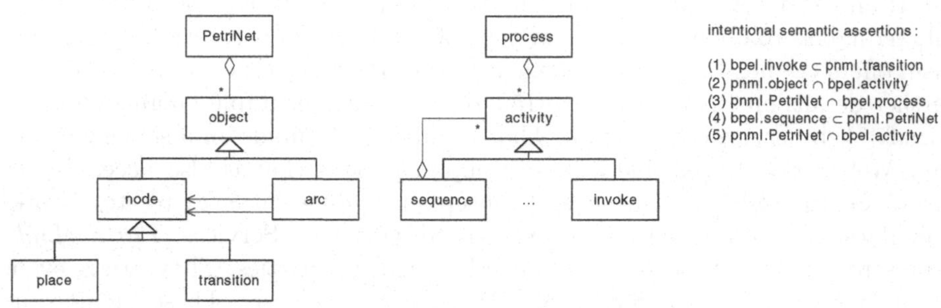

Fig. 3. Metamodel of PNML and BPEL and intentional semantic assertions

disjointness are defined as intentional semantic relationships. Such relationships need to be considered when merging two schemas. On the right hand side of Figure 3 semantic relationships between the schemas are given:

1. The intention of an invoke activity in the BPEL schema can be subsumed to the intention of a transition in the PNML schema.
2. The intention of a PNML object intersects with that of a BPEL activity, because the intention of a structured activity is beyond the intention of a PNML object, and because there is nothing like a PNML place in BPEL.
3. The intention of a PNML PetriNet intersects with that of a BPEL process. In PNML arbitrary cycles of places and transitions are allowed, BPEL offers only structured cycles in terms of a `while` activity. Yet, BPEL offers the OR join that Petri nets cannot express directly.
4. The intention of the BPEL sequence can be subsumed as a special kind of Petri net. There is always a set of places, transitions, and arcs that can capture the behavior of a sequence modelled in BPEL. This holds also for other BPEL structured activities except the `flow`.
5. The intention of a BPEL activity intersects with a Petri net for the same reason as mentioned in 3.

Figure 4 shows a schema that could be constructed according to the intentional semantic relationships given. Relationship 1 would result in an a merged "transition/basic activity" construct that inherits from BPEL activity and

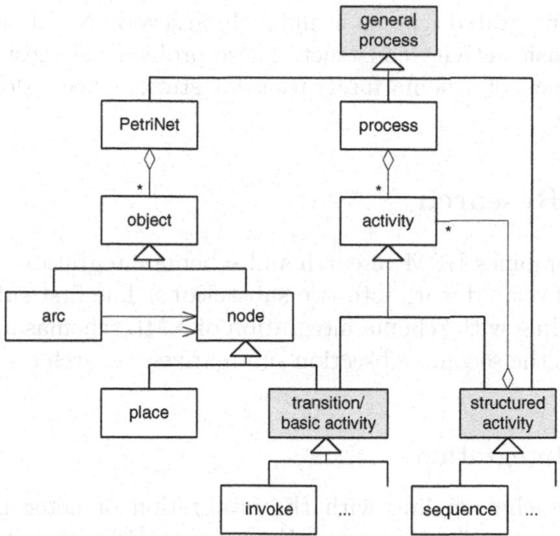

Fig. 4. Integrated schema for PNML and BPEL

PNML node. This relationship implies already relationship 2. The third relationship results in the creation of a "general process" construct following the upward inheritance principle [14]. This construct also generalizes the BPEL structured activity as given in relationship 5. Finally, relationship 4 motivates the introduction of the structured activity construct, too.

The integrated schema in Figure 4 has still some deficiencies. First, further *simplifications* are possible. Some structured activities can be mapped to Petri nets; e.g. a BPEL sequence can always be expressed as a Petri net. Therefore, the sequence is somehow redundant in the integrated schema. The problem is that this kind of redundancy cannot be expressed in terms of a binary intentional relationship, because a BPEL sequence has to be mapped to several nodes and arcs in a Petri net. In order to eliminate this kind of redundancy, both Petri nets and BPEL processes could be mapped to a language with more expressive modelling primitives like e.g. YAWL [17]. Another option could be a mapping to a more basic representation like state charts. Although this representational heterogeneity of behavioral aspects is typical for BPM languages, it seems that it is not inherent to behavior modelling only. Think of two car component schemas: one might use an unordered list of arcs and nodes (analogue to Petri nets) to model subcomponent relationships. The other uses a block-oriented representation by nesting components (analogue to BPEL). The latter allows to model a tree while the first accepts also general graphs. Intentional semantic relationships about mappings between these two different representations could help to eliminate redundant behavioral concepts in the integrated schema. Secondly, as intentional semantic relationships have been used, there is a problem with the *extensional description* of the constructs. A transition in PNML is described by quite different attributes than a basic activity in BPEL. Accordingly, instances stored with the integrated schema would include several NULL attributes, e.g. in the transition/basic activity construct. These problems suggest that a straightforward application of schema integration for static aspects does not yield the desired results.

4 Related Research

As this paper combines BPM research and schema integration, we have divided the discussion of related work into two subsections. The first subsection regards publications dealing with schema integration of XML schemas and of behavioral aspects, whereas the second subsection summarizes research on heterogeneity of BPM languages.

4.1 Schema Integration

Numerous approaches dealing with the integration of heterogenous database schemas have been published so far. We refer to [18] for a detailed overview of different strategies in the context of (semi-)automatic schema matching. A taxonomy of potential conflicts between schema components is given in e.g. [19]. That work builds on an abstract approach regarding real-world objects instead of schema components of relational databases, like it is done in [8]. On the role of identifiers in the integration process refer to e.g. [20,21]. Different data models for schema integration have been proposed, e.g. GIM [11] or HDM [12]. A good overview of research on schema integration in general can be found in [11].

Most BPM schemas are defined as XML schemas. Several approaches deal with the specifics of this schema type. In [22] Behrens addresses the problem of integrating different XML schemas. He proves, that although there is always a new DTD for the intersection of two DTDs, this is not true for their union. Yang et al. introduce in [23] a further XML schema integration concept using a mediator model. Contrary to [22] they transform the XML schema into a semantic rich representation for capturing the implicit semantics stored in an XML schema. Work in the context of the AutoMed project highlights graph restructuring as a promising technique for XML schema integration [24].

The integration of behavioral aspects has received less attention in comparison to integration of static data models. Preuner et al. [25] present an integration strategy for business process models given as a Petri net derivative called object/behavior diagrams (OBD). Yet, heterogeneity of business process modelling schemas is not discussed in this context. Therefore, it is not clear in how far OBD represents a suitable common data model for integration of behavioral aspects. Integration is often related to some notion of inheritance. In [26] four types of inheritance relationships are defined for Petri nets. This work seems to be motivated by model checking as it does not discuss integration aspects.

Yet, there is doubt whether schema integration is suitable as a methodology for standardization of schemas. In [27] schema integration as a bottom-up methodology is contrasted with top-down domain modelling. Schema integration is said to produce schemas that are too much influenced by the local schemas and therefore rather difficult to understand, while domain modelling yields much clearer schemas. The question in this context is how can aspects of domain modelling be included in the integration process to come up with an integrated BPM schema that is clear and straight-forward to understand for a domain expert.

4.2 Heterogeneity of BPM Schemas

In the context of heterogeneous BPM schemas, a lot of research is dedicated to semi-formal comparisons of BPM schemas. Examples include comparisons of BPEL and BPML [3]; DAML-S (predecessor of OWL-S) and BPEL [28]; and XPDL, BPEL, and BPML [29]. Furthermore, a list of 13 high-level concepts of BPM languages has been reported in [2]. This list represents the superset of metamodel concepts extracted from 15 currently available XML-based specifications for business process modelling. Another approach is taken by [30] who identify workflow patterns for control flow semantics. These patterns have been applied as a framework for comparing various BPM languages. Furthermore, that research inspired the specification of a new workflow language called YAWL that is able to capture all pattern (excluding implicit termination). Beyond that, there has been some work on transformations between BPM standards. In [31] a transformation from UML to BPEL4WS is given. Moreover, the BPMN specification includes also a mapping to BPEL4WS. Yet, as both these transformations are one way, it is not clear whether a back transformation is feasible. A general framework for the integration of various BPM schemas is missing.

5 Conclusions and Future Work

In this paper we outlined integration problems in the context of heterogeneous BPM schemas. The example of BPEL and PNML was given to highlight different control flow representations as a major challenge in this area. Using classical schema integration and the upward inheritance principle would yield an integrated schema that could still include redundant behavioral concepts. Basically, further research is needed in at least two areas. Firstly, the specifics of behavioral aspects have to be clearly identified in order to either adapt the schema integration process for static aspects as given e.g. in [11], or to come up with an integration process for behavioral aspects building on a specific common data model. Secondly, the role of such an integration methodology for standardization processes needs to be analyzed. Additional engineering steps might be required in order to further simplify the integrated schemas which represents the output of the integration process.

References

1. Delphi Group: BPM 2003 – Market Milestone Report. White Paper (2003)
2. Mendling, J., Nüttgens, M., Neumann, G.: A Comparison of XML Interchange Formats for Business Process Modelling. In: Proceedings of EMISA 2004 - Information Systems in E-Business and E-Government. LNI (2004)

3. Mendling, J., Müller, M.: A Comparison of BPEL4WS and BPML. In Tolksdorf, R., Eckstein, R., eds.: Proceedings of Berliner XML-Tage. (2003) 305–316
4. zur Muehlen, M., Nickerson, J.V., Swenson, K.D.: Developing Web Services Choreography Standards - The Case of REST vs. SOAP. Decision Support Systems (2005)
5. van der Aalst, W.M.P.: Patterns and XPDL: A Critical Evaluation of the XML Process Definition Language. QUT Technical report FIT-TR-2003-06, Queensland University of Technology, Brisbane (2003)
6. Andrews, T., Curbera, F., Dholakia, H., Goland, Y., Klein, J., Leymann, F., Liu, K., Roller, D., Smith, D., Thatte, S., Trickovic, I., Weerawarana, S.: Business Process Execution Language for Web Services, Version 1.1. Specification, BEA Systems, IBM Corp., Microsoft Corp., SAP AG, Siebel Systems (2003)
7. van der Aalst, W.M.P.: Don't go with the flow: Web services composition standards exposed. IEEE Intelligent Systems **18** (2003) 72–76
8. Kim, W., Seo, J.: Classifying schematic and data heterogeneity in multidatabase systems. IEEE Computer **24** (1991) 12–18
9. Batini, C., Lenzerini, M., Navathe, S.B.: A Comparative Analysis of Methodologies for Database Schema Integration. ACM Computing Surveys **18** (1986) 323–364
10. Sheth, A.P., Larson, J.A.: Federated database systems for managing distributed, heterogeneous, and autonomous databases. ACM Comput. Surv. **22** (1990) 183–236
11. Schmitt, I., Saake, G.: A Comprehensive Schema Integration Method Based on the Theory of Formal Concepts. Acta Informatica (2005) to appear.
12. Boyd, M., McBrien, P., Tong, N.: The automed schema integration repository. In Eaglestone, B., North, S., Poulovassilis, A., eds.: Advances in Databases, 19th British National Conference on Databases, BNCOD 19, Sheffield, UK, July 17-19, 2002, Proceedings. Volume 2405 of Lecture Notes in Computer Science., Springer (2002) 42–45
13. Larson, J.A., Navathe, S.B., Elmasri, R.: A theory of attribute equivalence in databases with application to schema integration. IEEE Trans. Software Eng. **15** (1989) 449–463
14. Schrefl, M., Neuhold, E.J.: Object class definition by generalization using upward inheritance. In: Proceedings of the Fourth International Conference on Data Engineering (ICDE), IEEE Computer Society (1988) 4–13
15. Billington, J., Christensen, S., van Hee, K.E., Kindler, E., Kummer, O., Petrucci, L., Post, R., Stehno, C., Weber, M.: The Petri Net Markup Language: Concepts, Technology, and Tools. In W. M. P. van der Aalst and E. Best, ed.: Applications and Theory of Petri Nets 2003, 24th International Conference, ICATPN 2003, Eindhoven, The Netherlands. Volume 2679 of Lecture Notes in Computer Science. (2003) 483–505
16. Mendling, J., Nüttgens, M.: XML-based Reference Modelling: Foundations of an EPC Markup Language. In J. Becker, ed.: Referenzmodellierung - Proceedings of the 8th GI-Workshop on Reference Modelling, MKWI Essen, Germany. (2004) 51–71
17. van der Aalst, W.M.P., ter Hofstede, A.H.M.: Yawl: yet another workflow language. Information Systems **30** (2005) 245–275
18. Rahm, E., Bernstein, P.A.: A survey of approaches to automatic schema matching. VLDB Journal **10** (2001) 334–350
19. Spaccapietra, S., Parent, C., Dupont, Y.: Model Independent Assertions for Integration of Heterogeneous Schemas. VLDB Journal **1** (1992) 81–126

20. Schmitt, I., Saake, G.: Managing object identity in federated database systems. In Papazoglou, M.P., ed.: OOER'95: Object-Oriented and Entity-Relationship Modelling, 14th International Conference, Gold Coast, Australia, December 12-15, 1995, Proceedings. Volume 1021 of Lecture Notes in Computer Science., Springer (1995) 400–411
21. Pérez de Laborda, C., Conrad, S.: A Semantic Web based Identification Mechanism for Databases. In: 10th International Workshop on Knowledge Representation meets Databases (KRDB 2003), Hamburg, Germany, September 15-16, 2003. Volume 79 of CEUR Workshop Proceedings., Technical University of Aachen (RWTH) (2003) 123–130
22. Behrens, R.: A Grammar Based Model for XML Schema Integration. In: BNCOD 17: Proceedings of the 17th British National Conferenc on Databases, London, UK, Springer-Verlag (2000) 172–190
23. Song, I.Y., Liddle, S.W., Ling, T.W., Scheuermann, P., eds.: Resolving Structural Conflicts in the Integration of XML Schemas: A Semantic Approach. In Song, I.Y., Liddle, S.W., Ling, T.W., Scheuermann, P., eds.: Conceptual Modeling - ER 2003, 22nd International Conference on Conceptual Modeling, Chicago, IL, USA, October 13-16, 2003, Proceedings. Volume 2813 of Lecture Notes in Computer Science., Springer (2003)
24. Zamboulis, L., Poulovassilis, A.: Using AutoMed for XML Data Transformation and Integration. In Bellahsne, Z., McBrien, P., eds.: DIWeb Workshop - CAiSE'04 Workshop Proceedings. (2004) 58–69
25. Preuner, G., Conrad, S., Schrefl, M.: View integration of behavior in object-oriented databases. Data Knowl. Eng. **36** (2001) 153–183
26. van der Aalst, W.M.P.: Inheritance of business processes: A journey visiting four notorious problems. In Ehrig, H., Reisig, W., Rozenberg, G., Weber, H., eds.: Petri Net Technology for Communication-Based Systems - Advances in Petri Nets. Volume 2472 of Lecture Notes in Computer Science., Springer (2003) 383–408
27. Hasselbring, W.: The role of standards for interoperating information systems. In Jakobs, K., ed.: Information Technology Standards and Standardization: A Global Perspective. Idea Group Publishing, Hershey, PA (2000) 116–130
28. McIlraith, S., Mandell, D.: Comparison of DAML-S and BPEL4WS. x, Stanford University, http://www.ksl.stanford.edu/projects/DAML/Webservices/DAMLS-BPEL.html (2002)
29. Shapiro, R.: A Comparison of XPDL, BPML and BPEL4WS. Draft version 1.4, Cape Visions, http://xml.coverpages.org/Shapiro-XPDL.pdf (2002)
30. van der Aalst, W.M.P., ter Hofstede, A.H.M., Kiepuszewski, B., Barros, A.P.: Workflow Patterns. Distributed and Parallel Databases **14** (2003) 5–51
31. Gardner, T.: UML Modelling of Automated Business Processes with a Mapping to BPEL4WS. In: Proceedings of the First European Workshop on Object Orientation and Web Services at ECOOP 2003. (2003)

Working Together in Philosophy and Informatics: An Introduction to the Contributions of the Second International Workshop on Philosophy and Informatics (WSPI 2005)

Thilo Deussen[1], Thomas R. Roth-Berghofer[2,4], Gregor Büchel[3], and Bertin Klein[4]

[1] Department of Artificial Intelligence, University of Ulm, 89069 Ulm, Germany
mail@thilodeussen.de
[2] Knowledge-Based Systems Group, Department of Computer Science, University of Kaiserslautern, P.O. Box 3049, 67653 Kaiserslautern, Germany
[3] Institute of Communications Engineering, University of Applied Sciences Cologne, 50679 Cologne, Germany
gregor.buechel@fh-koeln.de
[4] Knowledge Management Department, German Research Center for Artificial Intelligence DFKI GmbH, Erwin-Schrödinger-Straße 57, 67663 Kaiserslautern, Germany
{trb, klein}@dfki.uni-kl.de

Having people from two sciences come together appears to be a difficult task, especially when one of the sciences has a tradition that can be counted in millennia and where the other one some decades ago simply did not exist. Todays talking about ontologies in informatics (computer science), for instance, can easily be misleading. The term is borrowed from philosophy where there is no such thing as a multitude of ontologies, there is only ontology as the subject of existence.

The Second International Workshop on Philosophy and Informatics WSPI 2005 was organized by the Special Interest Group Philosophy and Informatics (SIG PandI) of the German Informatics Society (*Arbeitskreis "Philosophie und Informatik" der Gesellschaft für Informatik*). This group provides a platform for discussions in form of regular meetings and workshops. Members are scientists from philosophy, informatics, and from related fields. The work of the SIG PandI addresses and encourages especially—but not exclusively—the trans-disciplinary discourse on foundations of artificial intelligence with the help of philosophy. A lot of topics have been discussed already, e.g., the relation between philosophical concepts of ontology and ontologies as a concept of knowledge representation. For further information about the goals and the progress of the SIG and the results of earlier workshops and work meetings, visit the SIG's website[1].

The main goal of this workshop was to identify the influence and potential of philosophy for the theory and practice of knowledge management, along the

[1] http://www.philosophyandinformatics.org

K.-D. Althoff et al. (Eds.): WM 2005, LNAI 3782, pp. 580–585, 2005.

lines of specific questions and scenarios. The papers in these post conference proceedings were selected by the workshop participants as the best workshop submissions being presented.

1 Motivation

It seems clear that scientists of both areas can enter into fruitful discussions. For centuries philosophy has been a seed of ideas used to fertilize other disciplines, such as mathematics or physics.

During the last years, knowledge management is being academically pursued in diverse disciplines and is gaining increasing importance in all business activities. However, the multidisciplinarity of the approaches and the complexity of the notion of knowledge raise many issues, which are often simply ignored or treated offhandedly. Computer scientists are very much involved in system and application modeling while using concepts implicitly or only vaguely grasping them. There are assumptions made or to be made in order to have a coherent view on the subject. Also there is the danger, that the notion of Knowledge Management is misused. It becomes a mere marketing label and one looses track from the ambitious goal.

On the other hand, for millennia, philosophy—as the mother of sciences—addressed the notion of knowledge, the generation of knowledge, and its transfer, with its prospects and limitations. Philosophy is about concepts and clarifying them to the maximum extent, sometimes not bothering about possible applications of the generated knowledge. What, then, seems better than systematically examining the potential of contributions of philosophy to knowledge management and search for mutual promotion and synergy? The philosophical notion of ontology, which gained considerable impact in the information sciences, was an analogous success story.

In this environment the workshop's discussions centered around the topics of knowledge representation as a common field of research in philosophy and informatics, ontologies and ontology, knowledge and context, personalization of knowledge/embodied mind, epistemological framework, and philosophy of information. These topics are addressed in one or more of the presented papers.

2 About the Presented Work

One aim in knowledge management, which is related to the enumerated topics, is formulated by Balke and Mainzer [1]:

> In the current trend of modern informatics, we want to construct effective and appropriate tools and service systems under the conditions of bounded knowledge/rationality which need interdisciplinary cooperation between informatics, cognitive science and philosophy of mind.

The problem of the relation between knowledge and knowledge representation or between knowledge and information concerns some of the workshop's contributions. In an early work, the philosopher Hegel discussed the relation between philosophy as a process and a philosophical system (*Verhältnis des Philosophierens zu einem philosophischen System*) and he outlined this relation as a special type of difference (*Entzweiung*). Hegel characterized the study of those differences as the original need of philosophy ([4] p. 20). The workshop studied differences between informatics and philosophy regarding the foundations of artificial intelligence, and the contributions show a genuine need of philosophy.

As mentioned earlier, assumptions are often made implicitly by researchers and may vary fundamentally. Niehaves et al. [7] come to the same result and offer an approach to how to discuss epistemological assumptions. The so-called "consensus-oriented interpretivist approach to conceptual modeling" is constructed step-by-step where each step requires certain assumptions to be accepted. By making the latter explicit we gain knowledge on possible pitfalls when using a model and can be aware of the forthcoming implications.

Position of "Realism" vs. "Constructivism". This method assumes a view of the world that is partial realistic and partial constructivist. The difference between them is elaborated by Zelic and Stahl [10] interpreting stakeholders' behavior in a case study of Irish voting in 2004 as an assumption of a realist ontology. They argue that a constructivist ontology would have foreseen failure and explain why the development of the electronic voting system failed. Assuming that managers of information systems are sometimes not aware of their ontological commitment, it might be the reason why "technological failures happen on a regular basis".

A realist view gives technology itself a value and claims to be observer independent. Anything can be solved with "the right tool for the task at hand". Realism supposes that a community can be convinced of a certain technology (i.e., information system) if the technology in question is expected to be appropriate for the use case. In contrast to that, constructivists would put technology in function of a society, since it is always observer dependent. Technology is not objective and is created inside a human context. In the case of Irish voting realism demanded the Irish people to accept the—in its point of view—better way of doing and failed, whereas constructivism would have sought to adapt technology to people's demands.

Knowledge Representation—A Common Field of Research in Philosophy and Informatics In a philosophical reflection, the question could arise, whether the manifold of empirically given concepts could be reduced to a finite set of basic concepts (categories). There are constructive answers to this question in the history of philosophy, e.g., the systems of categories by Aristotle and Kant [1]. While Kant's research of this question was oriented to show conditions of cognition, one can find in the mediaeval philosophy or in the philosophy of the early modern times attempts to use basic concepts (like categories) to construct empirically given concepts [3]. The tradition of these experiments of mind (*Gedankenexperimente*) leads to Leibniz's "lingua universalis". Leibniz's concepts of knowledge representation are related to his invention of a mechanical calculator. In designing work for knowledge management systems experiments of mind are done, too, when knowledge is represented by concepts such as ontologies or entity relationship models (ERM).

Ontologies and Ontology. The design of an information system (IS) starts generally with the construction of a semantic model (e.g., an ERM) of the data, which should be stored in the system. From an approach of general model theory semantic models are implementing only one type of ontologies [5]. Kaschek states that proven wrong models can be favored instead of correct ones when a certain task is equally good or even more easily accomplished with the former for the sake of simplicity. Hence the "best" modeled ontology cannot exist.

The universe of discourse in using ontologies for information systems has to be reflected as in the case study by Zelic and Stahl [10].

Hagengruber [3] discusses the problem of "mapping the multitude". In her discussion, the capability of ontologies as representation models are discussed in relation to categories in taxonomies. In her view, the concept of categories are relations with order. Any domain consists of a set of relations and an ordering of its entities, thereby defining the domain's relational structure. Systematic and application-independent design of ontologies is recommended thus achieving precision and redundancy-reduction.

Knowledge and Context. In the discussion of the distinction between practical knowledge and propositional knowledge Riss [8] shows that both concepts of knowledge are based on the same footing, i.e., action. He examines context-restrictions, which determine different types of knowledge. Kornwachs [6] stated in his keynote contribution "Knowledge + Skills + X": "The 'x' for which we are looking for, is not only a context that may clarify a linguistic ambiguity, but also something that has to do with the fact, that a bearer of knowledge (as well as a carrier of information) is a physical entity".

Personalization of Knowledge, Embodied Mind. Modeling user behavior is of vital importance when designing a computer system. Usually, only static user preferences are explicitly modeled and stored in the system to allow adapting to user's favor. This can be done by allowing the user to select certain options or by monitoring user behavior and deducing his preferences for the future. This is very restrictive, as assumptions on the intention of the user, the situation he/she is in or his/her general background are made—if at all—implicitly [1]. The development of advanced personalization in computer systems has to study four main sources of information: long-term preferences, intention, situation, and domain. Balke and Mainzer [1] outline case studies for preference-based personalization. Personalization of knowledge implies that the understanding of basic concepts to grasp knowledge can gravely differ. Rousseaux and Bouaziz [9] give a case study showing what different meanings the basic concept of "collection" can have in the context of arts. Slightly changing its usual meaning, a collection as opposed to mere classifications, sets, or groups, is defined as "a metastable equilibrium between singularity and category". Instead of having a finite set of possible elements and therefore only a limited number of possible combinations, a collection comes to life when its possible components exceed its current components [9]. Each component is part and parcel of the collection and can be treated individually as a unique bit. They can, however, have a feature in common, which can also fall under a certain common category shared with the other components. Due to its openness, potential extensions of a collection cannot be computed exhaustively. This is true, even when the scope of extension is known.

Epistemological Framework. Niehaves et al. [7] claim a lack of epistemological funding in IS research. IS modeling takes place within a multi-disciplinary and multi-cultural context. They describe a consensus-oriented approach to conceptual modeling. A philosophical basis to reflect this consensus-oriented approach could be a theory which is related to aspects of the "critical theory" of the *Frankfurter Schule* (Adorno, Horkheimer, Habermas).

Philosophy of Information. Using computational methods to tackle philosophical problems is very refreshing, since most of the contributions try to apply philosophical background knowledge to current problems of computer science and not vice versa. Greco et al. [2] do the latter in presenting techniques of minimalism, level of abstraction and constructionism.

Applying minimalism when analyzing a system requires the system to be a)—controllable, i.e., when modifications to its structure can be made purposefully, b)—implementable physically or by simulation, making it a white box and c)—predictable, insofar as the maker of the system, who controls and implements it, should be able to predict its behavior [2]. Modeling an environment involves a decision on the level of detail, how many details one wants to implement or—seeing it from the other side—a decision on the level of abstraction, which part one wants to abstract from. Moreover, Levels of abstraction fulfill Poppers requirement of any theory being falsifiable.

Speaking in the maker's knowledge tradition, one is able to know only what one constructs. Constructionism is about implementing and testing a system that models a theory. A good heuristic can be found to evaluate the quality of any theory that can be viewed as a level of abstraction

3 Closing Remarks

With this workshop, another step to build a common vocabulary of philosophers and computer scientists has been taken and is documented with the present proceedings. It shows the many points of contact between the two fields of research and it provided new and interesting questions to ask.

Acknowledgements

Many persons are needed for the success of a workshop. We thank the contributors, the program committee, and the supporters at DFKI, Kaiserslautern.

Program Committee: Stephan Baumann (DFKI GmbH), Luciano Floridi (U. of Oxford, UK), Pierre Grenon, (IFOMIS, Germany), Ruth Hagengruber (U. of Koblenz and Landau, Germany), John D. Haynes (U. of Central Florida, USA),

Norbert Jastroch (MET Communications GmbH, Germany), Klaus Kornwachs (Brandenburg U. of Technology, Germany), Jürgen Müller (U. of Cooperative Education, Mannheim, Germany), Steve Probert (Cranfield U., Swindon, UK), Michael M. Richter (U. of Kaiserslautern, Germany), Christophe Roche (U. of Savoie, France), Francis Rousseaux (IRCAM Paris, France), Stefan Schulz (Carleton U., Canada), Barry Smith (IFOMIS, Germany), Marcus Spies (U. of Munich, Germany), and Boris Wyssusek (Queensland U. of Technology, Australia).

References

1. Wolf-Tilo Balke and Klaus Mainzer. Knowledge representation and the embodied mind: Towards a philosophy and technology of personalized informatics. In *this proceedings*, 2005.
2. Gian Maria Greco, Gianluca Paronitti, Matteo Turilli, and Luciano Floridi. How to do philosophy informationally. In *this proceedings*, 2005.
3. Ruth Hagengruber. Mapping the multitude. categories in a process ontology. In *this proceedings*, 2005.
4. Georg Wilhelm Friedrich Hegel. Werke in zwanzig bänden. In E. Moldenhauer and K. M. Michel, editors, *Jenaer Schriften (1801-1807)*, volume 2, chapter Differenz des Fichteschen und Schellingschen Systems der Philosophie [Difference of Fichte's and Schelling's Systems of Philosophy], pages 1–138. 1801.
5. Roland Kaschek. Modelling ontology use for information systems. In *this proceedings*, 2005.
6. Klaus Kornwachs. Knowledge + skills + x. In *this proceedings*, 2005.
7. Björn Niehaves, Karsten Klose, Ralf Knackstedt, and Jörg Becker. Epistemological perspectives on is-development—a consensus-oriented approach on conceptual modeling. In *this proceedings*, 2005.
8. Uwe Riss. Knowledge, action, and context: Impact on knowledge management. In *this proceedings*, 2005.
9. Francis Rousseaux and Thomas Bouaziz. Collecting or classifying? In *this proceedings*, 2005.
10. Bruno Zelic and Bernd Carsten Stahl. Does ontology influence technological projects? the case of irish electronic voting. In *this proceedings*, 2005.

Knowledge Representation and the Embodied Mind: Towards a Philosophy and Technology of Personalized Informatics

Wolf-Tilo Balke[1] and Klaus Mainzer[2]

[1] L3S Research Center,
Universität Hannover, 30539 Hannover, Germany
balke@l3s.de, http://www.l3s.de/~balke
[2] Chair for Philosophy of Science, Institute of Interdisciplinary Informatics,
Universität Augsburg, 86135 Augsburg, Germany
klaus.mainzer@phil.uni-augsburg.de
http://www.informatik.uni-augsburg.de/I3/

Abstract. Knowledge representation has a long tradition in logic and philosophy. Automated reasoning with ontologies and categories had been discussed in philosophy, before it was formalized in artificial intelligence and e.g. applied in information systems. But, most of our knowledge is implicit and unconscious, situated and personalized. It is not formally represented, but embodied knowledge, which is learnt by doing, applied by self-organization, and understood by bodily interacting with (social) environments. In a complex world, we have to be able to act and decide with incomplete and fuzzy knowledge under the conditions of bounded rationality. The bounded rationality of embodied minds is a challenge of informatics especially in the complex information world of Internet applications and Web-based services offering access to a vast variety of information sources. It overcomes traditional concepts of mind-body dualism in the philosophy of mind, traditional knowledge representation in AI, and rational agents ("homo oeconomicus") in economics. Personalized informatics opens a trans-disciplinary perspective for philosophy and working technology.

1 Knowledge and Representation

Knowledge representation which is today used in database applications, artificial intelligence, software engineering, and many other disciplines of computer science has deep roots in logic and philosophy [15]. In the beginning, there was Aristotle (384-322 B.C.) who developed logic as a precise method for reasoning about knowledge. Syllogisms were introduced as formal patterns for representing special figures of logical deductions. According to Aristotle, the subject of ontology is the study of categories of things that exist or may exist in some domain. Aristotle distinguished ten basic categories for classifying anything that may be said or predicated about anything: Substance, quality, quantity, relation, activity, passivity, having, situatedness, spatiality, and temporality. Many of these categories are today applied in information systems, e.g. spatiality in location-based services. In the middle ages, knowledge representation was illustrated by graphic diagrams and pictures. In the 'summulae logicales' (1239) of Peter of Spain, an ontological hierarchy with

K.-D. Althoff et al. (Eds.): WM 2005, LNAI 3782, pp. 586 – 597, 2005.

aristotelian categories represented knowledge by genus (supertype) and species (subtype). The features that distinguished different species of the same genus were called differentiae. Raimundus Lullus (13th century) illustrated an ontological hierarchy by a tree with branches for categories. Leaves corresponded to questions or to answers which should automatically be found by a system of rotating disks for combining features of things. Actually, Raimundus Lullus applied a kind of British Museum algorithm, the first attempt to develop mechanical aids for problem solving and information retrieval. Today, we use Entity-Relationship (ER)-diagrams in suitable forms to illustrate structures of ontologies in informatics.

In modern times, Descartes considered the human brain as a store of knowledge representation. Recognition was made possible by an isomorphic correspondance between internal geometrical representations (ideae) and external situations and events. Leibniz was deeply influenced by these traditions. In his 'mathesis universalis', he required a universal formal language (lingua universalis) to represent human thinking by calculation procedures and to implement them to mechanical calculating machines. An 'ars iudicandi' should allow every problem to be decided by an algorithm after representation in numeric symbols. An 'ars iveniendi' should enable users to seek and enumerate desired data and solutions of problems. Thus, in the age of mechanics, knowledge representation was reduced to mere mechanical calculation procedures. In Kant's epistemology, recognition is not only a passive mapping of the external world, but an active construction of internal representations by a priori categories of pure reason. In modern terms, categories are considered as tools which must be assumed before ('a priori') any application of knowledge representation. Cognitive constructivism roots back to Kant's epistemology. In the tradition of Brentano's and Husserl's phenomenology, Aristotelian ontologies had been again discussed for knowledge representation. Recognition needs intentional actions, which direct our awareness and consciousness to objects of the world. Thus, according to Husserl, understanding is not possible by symbolic representations of the external world, but by the intentionality of human consciousness [7]. Intentionality also became a prominent criterion to distinguish human consciousness and computer representation of knowledge in recent AI-debates [19].

Computational cognitivism arose on the background of Turing's theory of computability. In his functionalism, the hardware of a computer is related to the wetware of the human brain. The mind is understood as the software of a computer. Turing argues: If human mind is computable, it can be represented by a Turing program (Church's thesis) which can be computed by a universal Turing machine, i.e. technically by a general purpose computer. Even if people do not believe in Turing's strong AI-thesis, they often claim classical computational cognitivism in the following sense: Computational processes operate on symbolic representations referring to situations in the outside world. These formal representations should obey Tarski's correspondence theory of truth: Imagine a real world situation X1 (e.g. some boxes on a table) which is encoded by a symbolic representation A1 = encode(X1) (e.g. a description of the boxes on the table). If the symbolic representation A1 is decoded, then we get the real world situation X1 as its meaning, i.e. decode(A1) = X1. A real-world operation T (e.g. a manipulation of the boxes on the table by hand) should produce the same real-world result A2, whether performed in the real world or on the symbolic representation: decode(encode(T)(encode(X1))) = T(X1) = X2. Thus, there is an isomorphism between the outside situation and its formal representation in Cartesian tradition.

2 Self-organization and the Embodied Mind

Knowledge representations with ontologies, categories, frames, and scripts of expert systems work along the discussion in section 1. However, they are restricted to a specialized knowledge base without the vast, if somewhat unspecific background knowledge of a human expert. Human experts do not only rely on explicit (declarative) rule-based representations, but also on intuition and implicit (procedural) knowledge [6]. Moreover, as already Wittgenstein knew, our understanding depends on situations. The situatedness of representations is a severe problem of informatics. A robot, e.g., needs a complete symbolic representation of a situation, which has to be updated, if the robot's position is changed. Imagine that it surrounds a table with a ball and a cup on it. A formal representation of their respective relative positions in a computer language may be ON(TABLE, BALL), ON(TABLE, CUP), BEHIND(CUP, BALL), etc. Depending on the robot's position relative to the arrangement, the cup is sometimes behind the ball or not. So, unlike the representation ON(TABLE, BALL) the formal representation BEHIND(CUP, BALL) always has to be updated or at least checked in changing positions. How can the robot prevent incomplete knowledge? How can it distinguish between reality and its relative perspective? Situated agents like human beings do not need symbolic representations and constant updating. They look, talk, and interact bodily, e.g., by pointing to things. Even rational acting in sudden situations does not depend on internal representations and logical inferences, but on bodily interactions with a situation (e.g. looking, feeling, and reacting).

Thus, we distinguish formal and embodied acting in games with more or less similarity to real life: Chess for instance is a formal game with complete representations, precisely defined states, board positions, and formal operations. Soccer is a nonformal game with skills depending on bodily interactions, without complete representations of situations and operations, which are never exactly identical. According to Merleau-Ponty, intentional human skills do not need any internal representation, but they are trained, learnt, and embodied in an optimal 'gestalt', which cannot be repeated [16]. An athlete like a pole-vaulter cannot repeat his/her successful jump like a machine generating the same product times and again. Neither can athletes explicitly specify how they exactly achieved the result. Husserl's representational intentionality is replaced by embodied intentionality.

The embodied mind is no mystery. Modern biology, neural, and cognitive science give many insights into its origin during the evolution of life. The key-concept is self-organization of complex dynamical systems [13]. The emergence of order and structures in nature can be explained by the dynamics and attractors of complex systems. They result from collective patterns of interacting elements in the sense of many-bodies problems that cannot be reduced to the features of single elements in a complex system. Nonlinear interactions in multi-component ("complex") systems often have synergetic effects, which can neither be traced back to single causes, nor be forecasted in the long run or controlled in all details. The whole is more than the sum of its parts. This popular slogan for emergence is precisely correct in the sense of nonlinearity.

The mathematical formalism of complex dynamical systems is taken from statistical mechanics. If the external conditions of a system are changed by varying certain control parameters (e.g., temperature), the system may undergo a change in its macroscopic global states at some critical point. For instance, water as a complex system of molecules changes spontaneously from a liquid to a frozen state at a critical temperature of zero Celsius. In physics, those transformations of collective states are called phase transitions. Obviously they describe a change of self-organized behavior between the interacting elements of a complex system. The suitable macrovariables characterizing the change of global order are denoted as "order parameters". They can be determined by a linear-stability analysis. From a methodological point of view, the introduction of order parameters for modeling self-organization and the emergence of new structures is a huge reduction of complexity. The study of, perhaps, billions of equations, characterizing the behavior of the elements on the microlevel, is replaced by some few equations of order parameters, characterizing the macrodynamics of the whole system. Complex dynamical systems and their phase transitions deliver a successful formalism to model self-organization and emergence. The formalism does not depend on special, for example, physical laws, but must be appropriately interpreted for different applications.

Obviously, self-organization leads to the emergence of new phenomena on sequential levels of evolution. Nature has demonstrated that self-organization is necessary, in order to manage the increasing complexity on these evolutionary levels. But nonlinear dynamics can also generate chaotic behavior which cannot be predicted and controlled in the long run. In complex dynamical systems of organisms monitoring and controlling are realized on hierarchical levels. Thus, we must study the nonlinear dynamics of these systems in experimental situations, in order to find appropriate order parameters and to prevent undesired emergent behavior as possible attractors. The challenge of complex dynamical systems is 'controlled emergence'.

A key-application is the nonlinear dynamics of brains. Brains are neural systems which allow quick adaptation to changing situations during the life-time of an organism. In short: they can learn, assess and anticipate. The human brain is a complex system of neurons self-organizing in macroscopic patterns by neurochemical interactions. Perceptions, emotions, thoughts, and consciousness correspond to these neural patterns. Motor knowledge for instance is learnt in an unknown environment and stored implicitly in the distribution of synaptic weights of the neural nets. In the human organism, e.g. walking is a complex bodily self-organization, largely without central control of brain and consciousness: It is driven by the dynamical pattern of a steady periodic motion, the attractor of the motor system. Motor intelligence emerges without internal symbolic representations.

What can we learn from nature? In unknown environments, a better strategy is to define a low-level ontology, introduce redundancy – and there is a lot in the sensory systems, for example – and leave room for self-organization. Low-level ontologies of robots only specify systems like the body, sensory systems, motor systems, and the interactions among their components, which may be mechanical, electrical, electromagnetic, thermal etc. According to the complex systems approach, the components are characterized by certain microstates generating the macrodynamics of the whole system.

Take a legged robot. Its legs have joints that can assume different angles, and various forces can be applied to them. Depending on the angles and the forces, the robot will be in different positions and behave in different ways. Further, the legs have connections to one another and to other elements. If a six-legged robot lifts one of the legs, this changes the forces on all the other legs instantaneously, even though no explicit connection needs to be specified [18]. The connections are implicit: They are enforced through the environment, because of the robot‘s weight, the stiffness of its body, and the surface on which it stands. Although these connections are elementary, they are not explicit and could be easily included if the designer wished. Connections may exist between elementary components that we do not even realize. Electronic components may interact via electromagnetic fields that a designer is not aware of. These connections may generate adaptive patterns of behavior with high fitness degrees (order parameters). But they can also lead to sudden instability and chaotic behavior. In our example, communication between the legs of a robot can be implicit. In general, much more is implicit in a low-level specification than in a high-level ontology. In restricted simulated agents, only what is made explicit exists (cf. the closed world assumption in database applications), whereas in the complex real world, many forces exist and properties obtain, even if the designer does not explicitly represent them. Thus, we must study the nonlinear dynamics of these systems in experimental situations, in order to find appropriate order parameters and to prevent undesired emergent behavior as possible attractors.

But not only ‘low level' motor intelligence, but also ‘high level' cognition (e.g., categorization) can emerge from complex bodily interaction with an environment by sensory-motor coordination without internal symbolic representation. We call it ‘embodied cognition': An infant learns to categorize objects and to build up concepts by touching, grasping, manipulating, feeling, tasting, hearing, and looking at things, and not by explicit representations. The categories are based on fuzzy patchworks of prototypes and may be improved and changed during life. We have an innate disposition to construct and apply conceptual schemes and tools (in the sense of Kant). Moreover, cognitive states of persons depend on emotions. We recognize emotional expressions of human faces (e.g. sadness) with pattern recognition of neural networks and react by generating appropriate facial expressions (e.g. concern) for non-verbal communication. Emotional states are generated in the limbic system of the brain which is connected with all sensory and motoric systems of the organism. All intentional actions start with an unconscious impulse in the limbic system, which can be measured half a second before the actions' actual performance. Thus, embodied intentionality is a measurable feature of the brain [8]. Humans often use feelings to help them navigate the ontological trees of their concepts and preferences, to make decisions in the face of increasing combinatorial complexity: Emotions help to reduce complexity.

The embodied mind is obviously a complex dynamical system acting and reacting in dynamically changing situations. The emergence of cognitive and emotional states is made possible by brain dynamics which can be modeled by neural networks. According to the principle of computational equivalence [13, 14], any dynamical system can be simulated by an appropriate computational system. But, contrary to Turing's AI-thesis, that does not mean computability in any case. In complex dynamical systems, the rules of locally interacting elements (e.g., Hebb's rules of synaptic interaction) may be simple and can be programmed in a computer model. But their nonlinear dynamics can generate complex patterns and system states, which cannot be predicted in the long run without increasing loss of computability and information. Thus, artificial minds could [5] have their own intentionality, cognitive and emotional states that cannot be forecast and computed like in the case of natural minds. Limitations of computability are characteristic features of complex systems.

In a complex dynamical world, decision-making and acting is only possible under conditions of bounded rationality. Bounded rationality results from limitations on our knowledge, cognitive capabilities, and time. Our perceptions are selective, our knowledge of the real world is incomplete, our mental models are simplified, and our powers of deduction and inference are weak and fallible. Emotional and subconscious factors affect our behavior. Deliberation takes time and we must often make decisions before we are ready. Thus, knowledge representation must not be restricted to explicit declarations. Tacit background knowledge, change of emotional states, personal attitudes, and situations with increasing complexity are challenges of modeling information and communication systems. Personalized information systems in dynamic situations should be referred to ubiquitous and invisible computing of world-wide interactive media, in order to improve human-oriented information services and to support a sustainable information world.

3 Towards Advanced Personalization in Computer Systems

Especially for areas in computer science that rely on a user's expression of individual needs like e.g. query processing in databases and information systems, media retrieval in document collections or selection problems in Web services or e-commerce workflows, getting a precise account what the individual user wants or means is mission critical. In practical system implementations such information usually is deduced from a user's profile or some explicitly stated preferences. User modelling is concerned with trying to describe completely what part of the users' interests should influence a computer application. But since research in psychology shows that even in purposeful tasks users are usually not fully conscious of their exact wishes and needs, see e.g. [1], eliciting preferences directly from users is a difficult matter. It often needs a tedious process like the manual selection of services or areas of interest for personalization in publish/subscribe systems. Moreover, given that some knowledge is embodied the elicited information will be naturally incomplete and simply logging and storing and using user-stated keywords/behaviour will sometimes lead to counter-intuitive results. In order to raise a personalized system's performance in terms of relevance, a system thus has not only to focus on explicit user specification, but should also take information into account, that is specified by the user's implicit notions, situation or assumed common knowledge. This information can be gathered mainly from four sources:

- **long-term preferences:** The notion of relevance from previous interactions or generally applicable knowledge about a user is used
- **intention:** The specific user's purpose of the interaction is included in personalizing the system
- **situation:** The present state and environment of a user is used to decide whether specific preferences or rules are applicable
- **domain:** Knowledge on the specific domain (often referred to as expert knowledge) is used within an interaction

Let us consider typical instances of these kinds of personalization information. Among long-term preferences typical re-occurring individual preferences are collected e.g. individual tastes like colours, general areas of interest or preferred layout settings. Generally this kind of preference can always be used to personalize a system for individual users and is the usual kind often stored in user profiles. Systems, however, cannot always rely on these preferences, since they might be either further specified for certain categories or simply not applicable in a certain context. Consider for instance a set of colour preferences in an e-commerce setting. Though a user can be assumed to have a certain favourite colour that will apply to shopping decisions, the preferences might be different for e.g. clothing and cars, since driving an e.g. red car differs from actually wearing red clothing. Moreover, for e.g. book shopping the colour preference becomes entirely inapplicable, since the request to buy a red book is usually not sensible. A first framework for tagging and storing this kind of information can be found in [10].

Of a less general, but more interesting kind for personalization tasks are the preferences for the last three categories. Consider for example intentionality in a real world application like book shopping. Personalized book stores (e.g. Internet portals like www.amazon.com) will usually keep a list of recommendations based on the topics a user was interested in during previous interactions (i.e. a long-term profile of topical categories). Now assume that the same user accesses the book store with the intention of buying a present for some acquaintance. In most cases this present will focus on the preferences of the acquaintance; hence neither is the typical user profile applicable, nor should the interaction and the topics accessed be used to update the user's personal profile. In this example the intention of the user to buy a book for him-/herself or for a different person makes all the difference. Thus, the (assumed) intention of a user will help to decide, which choices a user should be offered in personalization and what characteristics a user generally cares about at a certain point in time during his/her interaction with the system. Typical examples for using these intentions in Web-based systems are also adaptive hypertext applications, where depending on a user's previous interactions and current navigation patterns the environment can be effectively personalized to support users, see e.g. [11].

Also the current situation has an impact on how to personalize a system. Context-aware systems have to use clues from a user's direct environment (like time or location), personal characteristics like emotional states, technical characteristics like client device capabilities, or certain high level situation information like "user in a business meeting" or "user at home" (both are examples for social situations) for personalization tasks. Examples for systems integrating this kind of information are location-based services, situation-based communication routing, or context-aware synthesis of multimedia content like discussed in e.g. [20].

The most renowned realizations of the last kind of preferences for personalization based on domain knowledge are the so-called expert systems that encode domain knowledge elicited from domain expert in a system usually be means of introducing rules for deduction. However, [6] shows that there cannot be a complete set of expert knowledge rules, since most expert knowledge is not represented by rules, but embodied in the experts themselves. Thus, we cannot simply consider domain preferences in the sense of expert systems, but have to rely on domain specific heuristics like which general preferences (and in what combination) might be applicable, or what users generally care about in a certain domain. The notion behind this is often referred to as 'common knowledge' or 'world knowledge', i.e. the knowledge about the environment that is assumed to be common to or implicitly shared by all humans interacting in a certain domain. Ontologies present a good way of representing some of this knowledge for use by non-experts of a domain.

In today's systems the latter three kinds of preferences – if at all – are mostly built directly into the application logic and represent the embodied mind as opposed to collected individual long-term preferences that form a user's individual profile. In the next section we will consider two sample scenarios and focus on how to use these kinds of preferences not in a hard-coded fashion, but flexibly mixed with information from user profiles.

4 Case Studies for Preference-Based Personalization

Let us consider two short application studies where we can see parts of the embodied mind represented by adequate preferences and used for improved system personalization. For effective personalization knowledge from all the four sources discussed above has to be blended with the specific user-provided details/keywords for an individual interaction. Though generally not all embodied knowledge can be captured that way, this method nevertheless provides a useful way of personalizing systems under the notion of bounded rationality.

First consider personalized information search and retrieval tasks in databases and information systems. The classical relational model that is still predominant in today's practical database applications uses relational algebra to specify rigid selection predicates that allow selecting objects with certain characteristics from usually large data sets. Though this model is applicable in a variety of simple cases, e.g. if customer information for a bank account with a certain account number has to be retrieved, modern information-driven environments demand for somewhat fuzzier capabilities in specifying what kind of information a user needs to accomplish his/her task. In most practical applications like e.g. Web search engines, information searches will lead to empty or too many results. If a user does ask a very specific query in necessarily fuzzy tasks like information searches, the query may be overspecified, e.g. by choosing too specific keywords, and lead to an empty result that will not be very helpful to users. On the other hand, asking rather unspecific (i.e. underspecified) queries is bound to lead to the flooding effect, i.e. lots of items that only more or less match a user's needs. However, not knowing the underlying database content or information collection users simply cannot be expected to know the degree of specificness their query needs to show to retrieve a helpful, yet manageable set of results.

Preferences that show the structure of interests for an individual user or ontologies modelling the common understanding of topics in a certain domain can help to tackle this problem. As stated in [2], expanding queries along user-specific preferences goes back to the area of cooperative answering, see e.g. [17] for an overview. The basic notion of cooperative retrieval systems is that they will relax the user-specified terms until a match in a collection of data can be found. Thus even an overspecified query will lead to some 'best efforts' results and avoid empty result sets together with the often necessary tedious manual refinement of queries. This way of dealing with query predicates as 'soft constraints', is also necessary for personalization tasks using individual preferences that have not been explicitly stated for a specific interaction. Since they have been implicitly assumed by the system as representations of common or embodied knowledge either from long-term profiles, intention, situation, or domain, they have to be considered on a lower level than the explicitly provided terms (i.e. as soft constraints that may refine too large result sets, but can be relaxed if empty result sets are retrieved). Recently [12] introduced a system of integrating preferences in the form of strict partial orders with a simple "I like A better than B" semantics into database queries. For example searching for a rental car a user could state that he/she likes a car with automatic transmission better than gear transmissions. If two offers are retrieved meeting all basic requirements, the result set can be ordered by or even limited to those objects fulfilling also the preference on transmissions. Such basic preferences on single aspects like a car's type of transmission can be modelled and combined into more complex queries using operators for deriving Pareto sets (i.e. all preferences are considered as equally important following the Pareto principle from economics), prioritized sets (i.e. a certain order is imposed on the preferences like e.g. lexicographic orders) and ranked result sets (i.e. preferences on numerical domains that are aggregated using suitable utility functions).

As a second example let us consider discovering useful Web services or selecting suitable services to construct complex workflows in a personalized manner like motivated in [3, 4]. Service-oriented application infrastructures are getting more and more common. In times of the ubiquitous Internet the Web service paradigm is expected to substantially alter the world of modern business processes. Essential components of this emerging service paradigm are Internet-based, modular applications that provide standard interfaces and communication protocols for efficient and effective service provisioning between different business units or businesses and customers. Especially the reusability of basic building blocks (or implementations) that are common in certain different workflows and easy customization within complex workflows are particularly appealing. But like in information searches, also here a retrieval model based on exact matches only is not likely to succeed. Users generally are rather interested in accomplishing high-level tasks and do care less about the exact intermediate steps. Thus, making them exactly specify all characteristics of the services needed instead of using a more fuzzy understanding of the workflow in question will be counterproductive. With the number and diversity of Web services expected to grow, enhanced techniques for service discovery and selection will be needed.

When designing a service like e.g. restaurant reservation or flight booking service providers already have quite specific ideas what capabilities the service should provide and what kinds of interaction to expect. Thus providers are domain experts that can provide a set of useful domain preferences and even ontologies for categorizations to foster successful execution/composition of services even for non-expert users. Moreover, providers also may anticipate different possibilities for usage of the service (possibly also in different situation scenarios). Generally in well-defined services only a certain number of typical requests/business processes will exist. These typical interactions for different users/groups also are preference patterns or usage patterns open for our personalization approach. A usage pattern may e.g. depend on the basic intentions of a significant group of users. Different intentions will need different patterns that reflect on both a user's profile stating his or her notion of a service's usefulness or desired characteristics (like execution costs, quality guarantees, etc.) and the service profiles that are employed to carry out the actual business task. Also here the basic method of relaxing demands in the case of empty result sets is necessary to support users in a cooperative fashion.

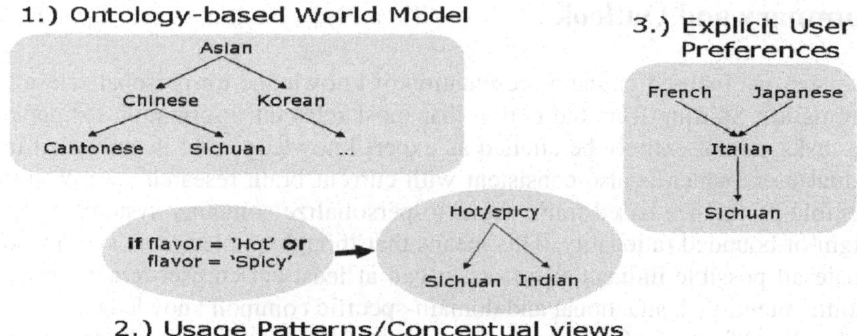

Fig. 1. Preferences derived from different sources

To show some examples for the different types of preferences and how to derive them consider a restaurant booking service. One of the parameters that is important in choosing a restaurant, is the type of cuisine. Every restaurant can be characterized by an adequate parameter, but querying for them is a tedious process, if it is not cooperatively supported. For example, if a user is interested to have lunch in a certain area asking for a restaurant offering Sichuan cuisine might be too specific and often deliver an empty result set. On the other hand just asking for a restaurant offering Asian cuisine might result in a large set of rather unspecific choices offering Chinese, Japanese, Indian, or Thai cuisine. One thing a cooperative system could use is an explicit preference (either explicitly specified with the current service request or derived from previous interactions of the same user). Such a preference could e.g. specify that a user prefers Sichuan cuisine over Italian and over French and Japanese (cf. Fig. 1).

But also in the case that such a preference is not explicitly given the service provider can assume some information. For example the general notion of similarity between cuisines could be made on the notion of geographical closeness reasoning that cuisines in similar geographic regions work with the same kind of ingredients, herbs and spices. A possible assumption would thus be that, since Sichuan is a specific Chinese cuisine, other Chinese cuisines like Cantonese could be acceptable offers for a user asking for Sichuan cuisine. To express this knowledge a domain-specific ontology like shown in Fig. 1 could be provided and in the case of empty results and no explicitly stated preferences be used to relax a user's request. As an example for user intentionality consider the usage pattern (or conceptual view) shown in Fig. 1. If we assume that a user is rather interested in hot and spicy food (i.e. a user has a rather taste-based conception of the similarity in restaurants that the geographical one presented above), some cuisines like Indian or Mexican are rather more similar to Sichuan cuisine (known for its spiciness) than the geographically close ones. Thus, if a user is known to subscribe to a specific conception as induced by his/her conception the more specific pattern has to be used for cooperative request relaxation.

5 Summary and Outlook

In this paper we focused on the representation of knowledge for personalization tasks in Informatics. Starting from the notion that most relevant information for personalization tasks cannot entirely be elicited as expert knowledge, but is embodied in the individual user (which is also consistent with current brain research), we propose to use flexible preference-based frameworks to personalize computer systems under the paradigm of bounded rationality. This means that though an electronic system cannot anticipate all possible influential factors, it can at least enrich user-related processes with some intentional, situational and domain-specific common knowledge.

As discussed for typical user interaction in the areas of personalized retrieval in databases/information systems and proactive Web service discovery/selection personalizing the interaction with preferences from each individual user's long-term profile, intention, situation, and domain will result in an improved effectiveness of the systems. This is because the user-provided information can be expanded with information representing the 'embodied' information necessary for a certain task. Since this information is not conscious, this expansion really adds value to the personalized task. However, since all preferences used for expanding the user information are only used on a lower level of importance than the explicitly provided information (and will be relaxed if necessary), the system's expansion will respect an individual users needs and never violate explicit constraints.

Obviously, personalized computer systems do not aim at complete computational models of the human embodied mind, which was an impractical illusion of traditional AI and the expert systems. In the current trend of modern informatics, we want to construct effective and appropriate tools and service systems under the conditions of bounded knowledge which need interdisciplinary cooperation especially with cognitive science and philosophy of mind.

Acknowledgements

Part of this work was supported by a grant of the German Research Foundation (DFG) within the Emmy Noether Program.

References

1. Ackhoff, R., Emery, F.: On Purposeful Systems. Aldine Atherton, Chicago (1972)
2. Balke, W.-T.: A Roadmap to Personalized Information Systems by Cognitive Expansion of Queries. Int. Workshop on Content-Knowledge Management and Mass Personalization of E-Services (EnCKompass 2002), Paris, France (2002)
3. Balke, W.-T., Wagner, M.: Cooperative Discovery for User-centered Web Service Provisioning. Int. Conf. on Web Services (ICWS'03), Las Vegas, USA (2003)
4. Balke, W.-T., Wagner, M.: Towards Personalized Selection of Web Services. Int. World Wide Web Conference (WWW'03), Budapest, Hungary (2003)
5. Dennett, C.D.: Brainchildren: Essays on Designing Minds, MIT Press1998
6. Dreyfus, H.L.: What Computer's can't do – The Limits of Artificial Intelligence. Harper & Row, New York, USA (1979)

7. Dreyfus, H.L.: Husserl, Intentionality, and Cognitive Science. MIT Press, Cambridge, USA (1982)
8. Freeman, W.J.: How and why brains create meaning from sensory information. Int. J. Bifurcation and Chaos 14 (2004) 515-530
9. Floridi, L. (ed.): Philosophy of Computing and Information. Blackwell, Oxford, UK (2004)
10. Holland, S., Kießling, W.: Situated Preferences and Preference Repositories for Personalized Database Applications. Int. Conf. on Conceptual Modeling (ER'04), Shanghai, China (2004)
11. Kaplan, C., Fenwick, J., Chen, J.: Adaptive Hypertext Navigation Based On User Goals and Context. Int. J. on User Modeling and User-Adapted Interaction. Vol. 3(3) (1993)
12. Kießling, W.: Foundations of Preferences in Database Systems. Int. Conf. on Very Large Data Bases (VLDB'02). Hong Kong, China (2002)
13. Mainzer, K.: Thinking in Complexity. The Computational Dynamics of Matter, Mind, and Mankind. 4th enlarged ed. Springer, New York, USA (2004)
14. Mainzer, K.: KI - Künstliche Intelligenz. Grundlagen intelligenter Systeme. Wissenschaftliche Buchgesellschaft, Darmstadt, Germany (2003)
15. Mainzer, K.: Computerphilosophie – Zur Einführung. Junius Verlag, Hamburg, Germany (2003)
16. Merleau-Ponty, M.: Phenomenology of Perception. Routledge & Kegan Paul (1962)
17. Minker, J.: An Overview of Cooperative Answering in Databases. Int. Conf. on Flexible Query Answering Systems (FQAS'98), Springer LNCS 1495, Roskilde, Denmark (1998)
18. Pfeifer, R., Scheier, C.: Understanding Intelligence. MIT Press, Cambridge, USA (1999)
19. Searle, J.R.: Intentionality. An Essay in the Philosophy of Mind. Cambridge University Press (1983)
20. Wagner, M., Balke, W.-T., Kießling, W.: An XML-based Multimedia Middleware for Mobile Online Auctions. In *Enterprise Information Systems III*, Kluwer, The Netherlands (2002)

Knowledge, Action, and Context: Impact on Knowledge Management

Uwe V. Riss

SAP Research, CEC Karlsruhe,
Vincenz-Priessnitz-Str. 1, D-76131 Karlsruhe, Germany

Abstract. The relation between knowledge and action is discussed. It is argued that knowledge comprises static as well as dynamic aspects that are related to expectation of success of possible action and control over the performance of factual action, respectively. Both views concur in success of action as common point of reference. The main claim of this paper is that regarding this reference to action propositional knowledge does not differ from practical knowledge. In this way action establishes a natural dependency of knowledge on context. The approach is compared to the analytical characterization of propositional knowledge as justified true belief, pointing at existing connections. Consequences for knowledge management are indicated regarding the support of knowledge intensive work and knowledge transfer.

1 Introduction

The opinions about knowledge generally vary between a static object view and a dynamic process view [2]. The respective attitude is not only of theoretical interest but essentially influences the way how we try to manage knowledge. Therefore the question decisively determines our understanding of knowledge management (KM) even if we define the latter in a rather economic way as the "strategies and structures for maximizing the return on intellectual and information resources" [19]. Finally the attitude affects the way how we apply information technology (IT) to support knowledge management. Traditionally IT people tend to a static view of knowledge but many ineffective IT projects that followed this doctrine to leverage knowledge have led to consider alternatives [11]. In this way recent studies have fostered the dynamic approach [27,12,15,24,22], closely relating knowledge and action.[1] This paper will also emphasize the relevance of dynamic aspects of knowledge by means of philosophical arguments and give some hints regarding the consequences for KM.

Referring to Ryle we will distinguish practical knowledge (know-how) and propositional knowledge (know-that) [21]. The relation between both concepts is still discussed quite controversially. While Ryle and Polanyi [16] have argued for a prevalence of practical knowledge, Stanley and Williamson [26] see practical knowledge as some kind of propositional knowledge. Other authors like Hawley

[1] Refer to Wiig [30] for a recent discussion of this relation.

K.-D. Althoff et al. (Eds.): WM 2005, LNAI 3782, pp. 598–608, 2005.

only have pointed at the structural similarity of both concepts [8]. The present study will show that both concepts are based on the same footing, namely intentional action, supporting Ryle's and Polanyi's view.

In section 2 we introduce the notion of action that is used throughout this study and explain the relation of practical knowledge and action. This consideration will reveal a dialectic character of knowledge that comprises a static expectative as well as a dynamic performative aspect. In section 3 these considerations are transferred to propositional knowledge and its relation to action is analyzed in terms of subjective, intersubjective, and objective action. On the basis of this relation propositional knowledge gets a natural reference to context, namely context of action associated to this knowledge. Previous studies in analytical philosophy have mostly concentrated on propositional knowledge characterized as some variant of justified true belief (JTB) [31]. This characterization overemphasizes the static aspect of knowledge. However, a discussion of its constituents shows that the JTB description is essentially compatible to the present approach but leaves the issues discussed here open and abandons them to its constituents. In section 4 we will turn to the impact of the present conception of knowledge by discussing some consequences for KM, placing emphasis on new perspectives to open problems. The final section will give a short discussion of the results, e.g., with respect to unconsidered aspects, and will show relations to other research.

2 Knowledge and Action

Let us first explicate the notion of (intentional) action that is to be used. An action describes the activity of an *agent* that is directed at a specific *goal*. The agent can be an individual person or an organization. The agent's physical or mental activity related to the action is described as *execution* of the action. Before starting the execution the agent needs a *plan* how to approach the goal. In simple cases this plan can only consist in the agent's awareness that a specific body movement must be carried out to reach the goal. The *context* of an action comprises *all* factors that directly or indirectly influence the action. An action can assume the following three states. (1) If the agent realizes that the goal has been achieved, the action is called *successful*. It is to be remarked that a necessary side condition for action success is that this success is attributed to the respective action plan. (2) If the agent consciously gives up the intention to bring the action to a successful end, we call it a *failed* action. (3) If the agent has not yet finished to strive for the goal the action is *unfinished*. These states are also ascribed to actions which the agent does not execute currently since she might resume it later. This notion of action also comprises mental actions if these are directed by goals, e.g., doing mental arithmetic with the goal to determine the sum of two numbers. In the following we will investigate the relation between action and knowledge in more detail since it provides the foundation of the entire conception of knowledge developed the following.

We start the study of the relation between knowledge and action referring to Craig's statement that human beings need knowledge "to guide their actions to a successful outcome" ([6], p. 11). This statement especially holds for practical knowledge that directly refers to successful action [8]. However, practical knowledge cannot be equated with successful action. Actions can be successful by chance, i.e., they are not based on knowledge and succeed owing to favorable circumstances. Moreover, we do not necessarily deny knowledge if a single action fails, e.g., if the failure only owes to unusually unfortunate circumstances. An essential aspect of practical knowledge is the *control* of action. We can equate successful actions with actions that are controlled from start to finish. A failure can be seen as a loss of control. In particular the success of action is not ascribed to knowledge if the agent definitely looses the control during the execution. Furthermore, the existence and observance of an action plan is a necessary precondition for the ascription of knowledge to a successful action. On the other hand, if someone denies that the action success is based on practical knowledge, she has to give reasons for the mismatch. In the long run we always have to adapt our knowledge claims to the action outcome as the final criterion. This can be learned from the sciences in which the reproducible experiment is regarded as final authority.

In particular we have to realize that action plans are not static. Let us consider the example of a surgeon who knows how to perform a certain operation. In an actual operation, however, unexpected events can occur which might necessitate a change of the action plan to adapt the action to the current circumstances. In fact, the success of the action decisively depends on the agent's ability to effectively adapt the execution to the particularities of the context. The adaptability demonstrates the ability to control the action and describes the dynamic aspect of knowledge. The consequence, however, is that knowledge only refers to single actions. Knowing how to q in context c_1 does not imply knowing how to q in context c_2. From this perspective it is not surprising that actions can fail even if we seem to *possess* the respective knowledge.

Indeed, this dynamic view of knowledge contradicts our usual comprehension of knowledge as possession. Let us suppose that a person proves to know how to q at time t_0 and at time $t_1 > t_0$ by successfully performing q. Let us now ask for the agent's knowledge at some time t_2 with $t_0 < t_2 < t_1$. Generally we assume that the person also knows how to q at t_2. This corresponds to the concept of knowledge as a mental state that starts at some time t_i and ends at some later time t_f. On the other hand, we are also aware that we cannot predict with certainty that a person actually executes q successfully at t_2. There can always be factors that temporarily prevent an agent from being successful and we have no guarantee that this failure is only temporary. Only if the agent actually executes q successfully we can say that she knows how to q. If we talk about an agent's knowledge how to q without the agent's successful execution of q we only express an *expectation*. Consequently we will call this aspect of knowledge expectative.

In contrast to the dynamic aspect of knowledge such expectations are mainly context-independent. It is this very property that makes expectative knowledge generally applicable. A mere expectation, however, is not reckoned knowledge.

This means that we have to ask for reasons for the expectation. Here we can refer to experience directly, i.e., having successfully performed similar actions in the past, or indirectly, i.e., tracing it back to a combination of other actions that have been performed successfully. Although expectation fundamentally differs from control of action, both aspects are fundamentally entwined by knowledge:

1. *Expectation* is reckoned knowledge insofar as it is based on experience.
2. *Experience* refers to a sufficient extent of successful actions.
3. *Successful action* is only ascribed to knowledge if it is performed in a controlled way.
4. *Control* refers to a continuously adapted plan that expresses the expectation how the action leads to the intended goal.

This conception of dynamic and expectative knowledge corresponds to John Seely Brown's distinction between *knowing* and *knowledge* (see e.g. [5]). However, he regards the latter as a tool for the former whereas the present approach regards both as aspects of the same concept.

3 From Practical to Propositional Knowledge

Now we regard the relation between propositional and practical knowledge. To this end we consider the prototypical example of the proposition "$5 + 6 = 11$". However, before doing so we first have to answer the question what it actually means to know that "$5 + 6 = 11$". Obviously the mere utterance of "$5 + 6 = 11$" is not sufficient. It is also necessary to understand the proposition but this leads to the question what it means to understand a proposition. According to the present approach this can be best answered in terms of inferential semantics [3]. Doing so we replace the representational view of propositional knowledge by an inferential view, according to which the meaning of a proposition is given in terms of the commitments and entitlements associated with individual performances related to the proposition [23]. With respect to propositional knowledge we even go beyond a practice "in terms of giving and asking for reasons" ([3], p. 141) and generalize it in terms of performing and demanding successful action.

Following this program we have to determine the relation between propositional knowledge and action in more detail. First of all, we have to realize that propositions like "$5 + 6 = 11$" require interpretation to be understood. Referring to Abel ([1], p. 322 n. 21) we can describe the factors which are associated with propositional knowledge in this respect as follows:

1. Articulation and representation in a public language as well as in sensible (linguistic or non-linguistic) signs.
2. Mastering of the practice of interpretation implicitly presupposed in the utilization of such signs.
3. Putting the knowledge claim in a "logical space of reasons" (Sellars [23]).
4. Ability to handle these knowledge representations and symbolizations, i.e., being able to apply the corresponding action rules.

From this description it becomes clear that interpretation of propositions is a central aspect of propositional knowledge. This corresponds to Polanyi's view that the notion of *pure* propositional knowledge is self-contradictory if taken in a strict sense, due to the need for interpretation [17]. In particular the interpretational aspect shows how propositional knowledge is rooted in practical knowledge. This view is also supported by Walsham's model of basic communication [29] that shows that propositions are not carriers for directly transferring knowledge.

In the following the necessity to interpret propositions is discussed on the basis of examples. If we return to the proposition "$5 + 6 = 11$" and regard it as a representation of knowledge, we implicitly assume, for instance, that it refers to the decimal and not to the hexadecimal system of numbers. In the latter case the proposition would be false and would not represent any knowledge. This is only one example how background assumption influence our interpretation of propositions but there are also many other assumption of this kind. The reason why we usually regard the proposition as true is that we have a context in mind or assume a standard context. The decimal system belongs to this standard context. If we realize that another situation can always stipulate another context, we see that the knowledge character of "$5 + 6 = 11$" is not rooted in the expression itself but in its interpretation with respect to the situation in which it is used.

The second example is related to Wittgenstein's problem of rule-following [32]. Let us consider a finite sequence of numbers to be completed. This sequence can be seen as a placeholder for a proposition. Its completion can then be regarded as the adaptation to a concrete action context. In this way we would generally extend the sequence $1, 2, 3, 4$ to $1, 2, 3, 4, 5$ as standard. However, for every number n we can find a rule (or context) that describes the sequence $1, 2, 3, 4, n$ as correct completion. Analogously we can assume that many different interpretations of a proposition can be made true or false if we choose an appropriate context, respectively. Craig has argued for this strategy in his discussion of the attempt to find analytic definitions of knowledge [6]. He has pointed out that we will find counterexamples for all definitions of knowledge that are proposed if we construct suitable counterexamples. Consequently we can state that only the context determines which interpretation (or completion in the case of finite sequences) is correct and not the proposition itself.

The examples show that context plays a decisive role in relating propositions to knowledge. This raises the question which factors actually determine the context. The answer is that the context is fixed by the action that is intended. Thus we have to examine how propositional knowledge is related to action. We can identify three possible types. These are to be explained on the basis of the example "$5 + 6 = 11$". First, a student from primary school performing mental arithmetic might find that $5 + 6$ is actually 11 affirming an idea she already has. This is a mental action and thus completely internal. The action success only depends on the agent's own judgment. The second example describes a teacher asking a student what $5 + 6$ is. The student answers "$5 + 6 = 11$". The success of this action depends on the teacher who accepts or rejects the agent's statement. Finally, a person can refer to "$5 + 6 = 11$" by handling a vending machine that requires 11 cents. The machine displays a remainder of 6 cents. If an agent inserts 5 cents and the machine accepts this she will relate the success to her knowledge of "$5 + 6 = 11$". In this case the success depends on external and non-communicative factors. The examples represent three principles how propositions can be associated with action.

1. In a subjective sense, an action is successful if (after some reasoning) the agent comes to the conclusion that the proposition is *coherent* with her other beliefs.
2. In an intersubjective sense, an action is successful if a proposition is accepted by the communication partners, i.e., if *consensus* is achieved.
3. In an objective sense, the associated action does not depend on communication but on external impersonal factors only. We can call it *correspondence* in a pragmatic sense.

After associating propositional knowledge with action we can treat it in a way that is analogous to practical knowledge.

It is to be remarked that sometimes the relation between propositional knowledge and action is not as obvious as in the considered examples. For instance, which action can be associated with my knowledge that I am *not* able to fly? First of all, I can confirm this in subjective action, checking its coherence with my other beliefs. However, there are also more practical cases. If I am at a place, which I can only leave by flying or swimming, it is important to know that I cannot fly to choose the other alternative. A lack of this knowledge could prompt me to try to fly and thus cause the action to fail.

As discussed in the previous section none of the actions described above is a proof of the respective propositional knowledge. This raises the question if there are additional aspects of propositional knowledge that are not covered in this way. One way to do this is to compare the present approach to the justified true belief (JTB) characterization of propositional knowledge. Here it is to be clarified that the latter conception does not include aspects that go beyond any relation to action.

To this end let us regard the three constituents of the JTB definition. First, we examine the belief condition. To belief that p, expresses the expectation that an action can be successfully based on p so that the belief condition is definitely related to the expectative aspect of knowledge. If we consider the justification condition we realize that justification represents an action. Whether a justification succeeds depends on the context of justification. For instance, in a congress of philosophers we need other justifications for knowledge than in everyday's life. Of course one might ask whether there is not a generally valid justification for a proposition. However, the success of an action is always valued by an observer in a concrete situation and this also holds for justifications. Consequently justification is related to the dynamic aspect of knowledge.

Finally we come to the truth condition which is the most complicated. Our understanding of truth usually assumes the following simple form:

(1) If the proposition p is true,
(2) the action a is based on p, and
(3) the action a failed.

So:

(4) The failure of a is not due to p.

We can also express this as:

(5) If the action a is exclusively based on the propositions $p_1, \ldots, p_n$ and
(6) $p_1 \wedge \ldots \wedge p_n$ is true.

So:

(7) The action a must be successful.

These considerations express an expectation but it obviously goes beyond mere expectation since it refers to factual success. The relation between truth and action had been already discussed in the course of the pragmatist conception of truth as advocated by James [10]. He argued for a conception of truth that takes a proposition for true if it can be verified. This obviously corresponds to a dynamic aspect. Beside verification James also takes verifiability into consideration to characterize truth. Doing so he refers to an expectative aspect. We see that the dialectical character of knowledge is reflected in the dialectical character of truth.[2]

The antithesis can also be shown revealed regarding the example of classical mechanics. This theory has been falsified by relativistic mechanics as well as by quantum mechanics so that we have to regard it as false from a logical point of view. Nevertheless we still base actions on it. Moreover, it is not unusual to say that one *knows* classical mechanics. But how can we know a theory that is admittedly false? Actually it depends on the context of the associated action whether we consider classical mechanics as true or false. In the microscopic realm it is false whereas in the macroscopic realm it is still regarded as valid.[3]

4 Relevance for Knowledge Management

Even today it is the omnipresent conviction in KM that propositional knowledge can be managed by means of documents, models, ontologies etc.. This view completely neglects the dynamic aspects of knowledge, i.e., that users must convert the provided information into successful action. Moreover, it is neglected that only the context determines whether and how this information can be interpreted and applied by the user. The proceeding assumes that the practical

[2] This dialectics of truth has been also observed by Hingst who attributed it to potentiality and actuality of human action ([9], p.140).

[3] Even the argument that we can see it as an approximation is not convincing since it does not change the fact that the theory is false from a logical point of view.

knowledge to do this is always available. This assumption is acceptable as long as the context is largely stable. Then it can be assumed that the users have already learned to manage both difficulties. If the environment is highly dynamic, however, as it is typical for knowledge intensive work, then it breaks down and we face massive difficulties. In the following this will be discussed regarding the example of workflow systems.

Workflow systems have proven themselves as very efficient in situations in which the work process are rather homogeneous. The model on which the system is built represents propositional knowledge in the usual sense. This knowledge allows the support of the corresponding process by a workflow engine that assists users in executing their incoming tasks. Thus the work can be accomplished in very efficient way. Usually the agents are well trained for these situations so that they possess the required practical knowledge to convert the propositional knowledge represented by the model into successful action. The price for this efficiency, however, is the inflexibility of the process. Due to the static model only small deviation from the main proceeding can be tolerated. The adaptability of the process to variable context is limited.

For knowledge intensive work the precondition of static context breaks down. The kind of work requires more variability in defining work steps and the complexity of situations requires better adaptation. In [20] we have presented a paradigm how to deal with this situation directed by the following strategy. Starting a task, the user forms an expectation on the basis of her situation and referring to previous experience. By specification of the respective task goal she can inspect a case repository for similar tasks. Here she finds information how other users have dealt with similar cases. From these cases she can select detailed information that fits to her current context. The case descriptions are transformed into expectational knowledge by the users' interpretational capability. The main difference to traditional workflow systems is that the user determines the proceeding and not the model.

Moreover, case descriptions support sense-giving and sense-reading since they provide information about the respective context of the performed task. In this respect case description resembles storytelling which is intensively discussed nowadays as means of context provision (e.g. [30] , p. 107f.). Case description are much more suitable to make context information available than models. In particular a case description helps users to understand deviations from the standard proceeding and enables them to seize the most suitable patterns and use them to form an action plan.

The next stage consists in the conversion of the action plan into performance. Here it is important to continuously compare the current state of action with the case on which the plan is built. It has to be clarified whether the course of execution is still congruent with the template and if not, in which way the template has to be adapted. In the latter case other cases must be identified or completely new ways be developed. This requires the users' practical knowledge regarding their ability to identify congruence and deviation. In this respect the users' interpretation of the cases and the current situation is essential. After finishing the task its description is added to the case repository for further reuse. In the entire process it is crucial to be aware that the application of propositional artifacts always requires the users' interpretation to transform them into successful action. The approach is completely aligned with the concept of knowledge developed before.

Another example concerns the attempt to transfer knowledge by means of documents. The traditional knowledge conception sees the document as a representation of knowledge that is created by the author and consumed by the reader. However, as Walsham has pointed out there is no transport of knowledge but only of data [29]. What we call knowledge transport requires sense-giving and sense-reading as additional steps. Both are performed in terms of practical knowledge [17]. Therefore knowledge is not transported but newly created on the basis of the existing practical knowledge. The acquired knowledge is never completely identical to the original. This means, however, that the support of sense-giving and sense-reading is crucial for the success of the transfer. The contexts of author and reader must be compared, differences must be identified and closed. How to do this exactly is still a question of ongoing research.

5 Discussion

Established conceptions of KM mostly see its core task in transforming practical and propositional knowledge [13]. Propositional knowledge has been identified with documents, models, ontologies etc. that can be stored in suitable repositories. This proceeding is based on the assumption that it is possible and sufficient to determine appropriate knowledge representations. However, the central aim of knowledge is not transformation but action and a neglect of this aspect, e.g., by lacking adaptation to the action context for which the knowledge is required, often prevents KM initiatives form being successful. The present study points out those aspects of practical as well as propositional knowledge that are related to action. Only against this background it becomes clear how we have to deal with knowledge in concrete situations.

One central advantage of an action theoretic approach is that it clearly emphasizes the relevance of context dependency in the concept of knowledge. Representational conceptions regard context mainly as external to knowledge and therefore overlook that interpretation and adaptation are intrinsic elements of knowledge. Based on this false assumption they largely leave these tasks to the users who are often overstrained, at least if the context significantly deviates from usual situations. Although some attempts have been undertaken to make KM systems more adaptive to individual needs, e.g. by context models [7] or role concepts [28], these approaches have remained incomplete.

The same neglect also appears on the side of philosophy where propositional knowledge is mostly regarded in a static way, too. However, reference to action is not new. For instance, Craig has already strongly emphasized the relevance of action for knowledge [6], even if his good informant solution to the problem differs from the present. One central consequence of the dynamic character of knowledge is the natural context dependency of knowledge. This context dependency of knowledge has been recently taken up by epistemic contextualists [4,25]. Nevertheless this contextualist approach do not consequently reflect on the role of action. Instead they refer to epistemic strength depending on the context of knowledge as seen by the person who ascribes the knowledge. However, this leaves open the question which are the particular aspects of context that establish the standard for epistemic strength. Without a concrete reference the concept of context remains vague so that it remains unclear on which basis a knowledge ascription is to be made.

Finally it is to be remarked that the present study abstain from several aspects that are also quite important for the understanding of knowledge. This concerns normative, social, political and other aspects. Regarding the normative aspects the liaison between *facts* and *values* is in no way unknown if a pragmatist standpoint is taken [18]. With respect to action we find normative aspects in the ascription of success or failure, i.e., there are no *objective* criteria that can be applied to come to an unambiguous assessment. Obviously this is carried forward to knowledge. At the same time the normative aspects point at the social dimension of knowledge. This concerns norms as well as meaning which cannot be established but as a social endeavor. People usually work and live in groups, organizations, and societies. Here they cultivate their values and communication. A deferment of these aspects can help to concentrate on some specifics of knowledge but cannot illuminate the entire body of facets. Various authors like Stacey [27] or Orlikowski [15] have therefore emphasized the social character of knowledge. Consequently, the present focus must not be seen as denial of the social dimension but as a step towards it leaving this task to further studies.

Acknowledgements

The author appreciates discussions with and feedback provided by Oded Nov, Sabine Sczesny, Boris Wyssusek and Bruno Zelic.

References

1. Abel, G.: Sprache, Zeichen, Interpretation. Suhrkamp, Frankfurt a.M. (1999)
2. Alavi, M., Leidner, D.: Knowledge Management and Knowledge Management Systems: Conceptual Foundations and Research Issues. MIS Quart. **25** (2001) 107–136
3. Brandom, R.: Making It Explicit. Havard University Press, Cambridge, MA (1994)
4. Cohen, S.: Contextualist Solutions to Epistemological Problems: Scepticism, Gettier, and the Lottery. Australasian Journal of Philosophy **76** (1998) 289–306
5. Cook, S. D. N., Brown, J. S.: Bridging Epistemologies: The Generative Dance Between Organizational Knowledge and Organizational Knowing. Organ. Sci. **10** (1999) 381–400
6. Craig, E.: Knowledge and the State of Nature. OUP, Oxford (1990)
7. Dey, A.: Understanding and Using Context. Personal and Ubiquitous Computing Journal **5** (2001) 4–7
8. Hawley, K.: Success and Knowledge-How. Am. Phil. Quart. **40** (2003) 19–31

9. Hingst, K.-M.: Zur Sechsten Vorlesung: James' pragmatische Deutung der Korrespondenztheorie der Wahrheit. In: K. Oehler (Ed.): William James: Pragmatismus. Akademie Verlag, Berlin (2000) 131–164
10. James, W.: Pragmatism. Longman Green and Co, New York (1907)
11. McDermott, R.: Why Information Technology Inspired But Cannot Deliver Knowledge Management. California Management Review **41** (1999) 103–117
12. McInerney, C.: Knowledge management and the dynamic nature of knowledge. Journal of the American Society for Information Science **53** (2002) 1009–1018.
13. Nonaka, I., Takeuchi, H.: The Knowledge-Creating Company: How Japanese Companies Create the Dynamics of Innovation. Oxford University Press, London (1995)
14. Noë, A.: Anti-Intellectualism. Analysis **65** (2005) (forthcoming)
15. Orlikowski, W.J.: Knowing in Practice: Enacting a Collective Capability in Distributed Organizing. Organ. Sci. **13** (2002) 249–273
16. Polanyi, M.: The Tacit Dimension. Routledge & Kegan Paul, London (1966)
17. Polanyi, M.: Knowing and Being. Routledge & Kegan Paul, London (1969)
18. Putnam, H.: Pragmatism:An Open Question. Blackwell, Cambridge, MA (1995)
19. Rao, M.: Knowledge Management Tools and Techniques. Butterworth-Heinemann, Burlington, MA (2005)
20. Riss, U. V., Rickayzen, A., Maus, H.: Challenges for Business Process and Task Management. In Proc. of the 5th International Conference on Knowledge Management (I-KNOW '05), Graz, Austria (2005) (forthcoming)
21. Ryle, G.: The Concept of Mind. University of Chicago Press, Chicago (1949)
22. Schütt, P.: The post-Nonaka Knowledge Management. Journal of Universal Computer Science **9** (2003) 451–462
23. Sellars, W.: Empirism and the Philosophy of Mind. Harvard University Press, Cambridge, MA (1997)
24. Snowdon, D.: Complex Acts of Knowing: Paradox and Descriptive Self-awareness. J. of Knowledge Management, Special Edition, July 2002
25. Sosa, E., Kim, J.(eds.): Epistemology. Blackwell, Oxford (2000) pp. 479
26. Stanley, J., Williamson, T.: Knowledge How. J. of Phil. **98** (2001) 411–444
27. Stacey, R.D.: Complex Responsive Processes in Organizations. Routledge, London New York (2001)
28. Vering, M. et al.: The E-Business Workplace: Discovering the Power of Enterprise Portals. John Wiley & Sons, New York (2001)
29. Walsham, G.: Knowledge management systems: Action and representation. In Proc. of the 2nd Intl Conf on Action in Language, Organisations and Information Systems (ALOIS-2004), Linkping University, Sweden (2004)
30. Wiig, K.: People-Focused Knowledge Management, Ch. 3. Butterworth-Heinemann, Burlington, MA (2004)
31. Williams, M.: Problems of Knowledge. OUP, Oxford (2001)
32. Wittgenstein, L.: Philosophical Investigations. Blackwell, Oxford (1958)

Modelling Ontology Use for Information Systems

Roland Kaschek

Department of Information Systems, Massey University, New Zealand

Abstract. This paper is based on a particular concept of model and modeling respectively. A key aspect of modeling is the particular relationship that is presupposed to exist between a model and its original. Ontologies are in this paper distinguished from other kinds of model in terms of that relationship. This paper discusses ontology use and proposes a quality model of that use. In doing so it aims at a better understanding of ontology use. That quality model contains the quality characteristics "role", "justification" and "relevance". It is the position of this paper that an unjustified use of an ontology in a particular role indicate a need for further reasoning. Similarly, if it is not relevant for the role in which a model is used that this model actually is an ontology then further reasoning and a different model might be suited better for that use.

1 Introduction

Among the ontologies used in information systems (IS) are the ones of Bunge (see, e.g.[45]) and Chisholm (see, e.g. [23]). It was already Bunge, [4, p. 3 - 5], who has pointed out that ontologies might differ from each other significantly. With respect to the information systems field a distinction between the ontologies mentioned is important. Bunge's ontology does not cover mental phenomena, as that would lead to the respective ontology in fact being a logic, [4, p. 5]. Bunge in fact says: "Because unreal objects have nonphysical properties, they satisfy nonphysical laws if any. For this reason it is impossible to make any non tautological statements applying to all objects: ontology, ... as a general theory of objects of all kind, and yet different from logic, is impossible." Chisholm's ontology, however, covers mental phenomena. That maybe relevant for its potential applicability in information systems, as one might want to include system quality in particular and requirements in more general into what can be backed up by ontology use. Non-functional requirements are a main reason for considering system quality. They have been excluded from investigation in [33]. The decision to do so appears as conflicting a trend towards more awareness of usability and quality issues in the information systems community as a result of the increased role of the Web, see for example [26, p. 10]. See also [27] and [31, pp. 179]. Chisholm's ontology is not the only one being used in information systems that does not restrict itself to concrete things. The upper level ontology of GOL (general ontological language) for example contains so-called "urelements" and sets as occurring in the world. The latter contrary to the former are collections (in the usual mathematical sense) and thus are not

K.-D. Althoff et al. (Eds.): WM 2005, LNAI 3782, pp. 609–622, 2005.

concrete things, see [11]. The availability of several different ontologies appears to require a sensible choice to be made in case one wants to use an ontology in information systems. This paper aims at aiding in this choice by providing a model of ontology use.

The most wide-spread use of an ontology in information systems appears to be the one that comes with the use of semantic models. Regarding semantic models one, for example, might wish to refer to [12,29,13]. Examples for semantic models are the Entity-Relationship model (ERM), see [5], State Charts, Dataflow Diagrams, [35], Petri Nets, [25], and Function Points, [9]. They have a built-in ontology that aids modelers in: identifying, classifying and relating to each other phenomena in a universe of discourse and by doing so to obtain a specification of a conceptualization that is capable of being shared by a number of individuals. Obviously, that use of ontologies in information systems predates the current respective fashion.

For example, in ER modeling one is guided to (1) define the scope of the universe of discourse D; (2) recognize phenomena within D that appear to be relevant for a task at hand; (3) classify these phenomena as entity, attribute, relationship, or role; and (4) relate classified phenomena to each other following the ERM's syntactic conventions. Defining the scope of D is more formalized in Function Point Analysis (i.e., measuring system size with function points) than it is in ER modeling (i.e., conceptually specifying systems). In Function Point Analysis it is, for example, prescribed to focus on all application systems that are supposed to inter-operate with a system under construction and the size of which has to be assessed. The conceptualizations obtained with a semantic model intentionally often are shared by a number of involved individuals.

A debate has been going on as to what an ontology in IT should be as opposed to what an ontology is supposed to be in philosophy, [50]. This paper contributes to that debate by means of putting forward its own view on what an ontology is. In doing so it reuses an idea in [18] and extends and corrects the approach taken in [17].

The paper is structured as follows. In section 2 we introduce our model concept and in section 3 we discuss the consistency of models, i.e., what models are made of. Finally in section 4 we conceptualize ontologies as particular models and propose a model of ontology use.

2 Models

This paper draws from Stachowiak's general model theory (GMT) (see [41], [40], [39]). A recent discussion of the GMT for software engineering is in [21]. The particular approach to Stachowiak's theory that is chosen here is the author's contribution. Views on models and modeling that are similar to Stachowiak's theory were recently used in [M*03] but were also published earlier, see, e. g., [24,32,34].

Let a cultural unit be something to which one, in a given culture, can intelligibly refer to. This concept according to Eco, see [6, p. 75], was introduced by Schneider. Let A be a group of agents and M, O specifications of cultural units U_M, U_O. Let A refer to O by means of M. Codify this with the predicate

$\mu(O, M, A)$ and call it model relationship. Call the roles of O and M in it original and model respectively. Stachowiak has characterized models by three properties that are expressed in terms of how these roles are related to each other:

1. **a mapping property**, i.e., each model is a model of something, i.e., its original;
2. **a truncation property**, i.e., the model in general lacks some of the specification parts of the original;
3. **a pragmatic property**, i.e., the model is subdue to a purpose and its use for this purpose is only justified with respect to particular users, their objectives, applied techniques and tools, and period of time etc.

In the sequel these properties are intentionally included in the term "model relationship" whenever it is used. According to Stachowiak model and original are classes of predicates. We give a particular class of predicates below that is, in our view, sufficient for capturing all sorts of models. The mentioned reference, according to Stachowiak ([41]) is realized by an icomorphism.[1]. An icomorphism is a bjection between subsets S_M and S_O of M and O respectively. The existence of an icomorphism allows -in principle- to back-propagate findings to the original that were obtained with respect to the model.

This paper deviates from Stachowiak's views on models in that originals do not have to predate their model (violation of what he called principle of methodological order, see [40]). Compatible to Stachowiak's theory is the emphasis on what here is called the **plenty property**, i.e., the observation that models often have important characteristics that the respective originals don't have. Consider, for example, a map M as a model of an intuitive specification W for a world C_W. M can easily be transported and folded, as the map is made of paper. This significantly impacts the map's usability. Using that model does, of course not, suggest the presupposition that the world would also consists of paper and is foldable.

One dimension of the model relationship $\mu(O, M, A)$ is the **reference mode**, i.e., the kind of reference A makes with the thing used in the role of model to the thing used in the role of original. It helps distinguishing from each other particular ways to relate the model to original: Do all agent instances relate the model to the original in the same way, or do they use different ways? In which particular way does the agent relate the model to the original? is it a descriptive, prescriptive, prognostic, idealizing, constitutive, or comprehending way? In the descriptive, prescriptive, prognostic and idealizing reference mode the agent A uses M for specifying what O is like, should be like, expects it to be like under particular stated conditions, and what O will be like under ideal conditions respectively. In the constitutive reference mode replaces agent A original O by M and in this sense constitutes U_O by means of M. In the comprehensive reference the agent includes into M "... all the necessary facts, details or problems ... " regarding O "... that need to be dealt with ... ", [1].

[1] Rather than the German "Ikomorphismus" the English version of it is used in this paper.

A few examples will be discussed to show that in fact all these reference modes occur in information systems.

descriptive mode. Consider a table in a relational database and its primary key. For each primary key there is a table (mapping property). Usually there is a number of table columns that do not belong to the key (truncation property). The primary key only is valid for distinguishing between any two tuples of the table if the table is maintained properly and only for those who are entitled for using it etc. (pragmatic property). Contrary to the table the primary key can be the target of a foreign key reference (plenty property). The model describes the original, i.e., if the latter does not fit well to the model, the model must be updated.

prescriptive mode. Consider the design of an information system. It is a blueprint for that system, i.e., it prescribes the system (mapping property). The design does usually not include the code (truncation property). The design is a blueprint for system construction only for those who can read the language in which it is expressed have the means, capability, and authority to actually implement that system (pragmatic property). The model prescribes the original, i.e., if the latter does not fit to the model, the original must be updated.

prognostic mode. Simulation models of a system often work such that in certain structural aspects they describe the system the evolution of which they are going to forecast. The validity of that structural description is taken as an evidence for the forecast being likely to be true. They are simulation models of a system (mapping property). Simulation models often lack characteristics their originals have, as the latter often happen to be real world systems such as factories etc. (truncation property). Simulation models can only be used to forecast the evolution of the modeled system by those who understand the involved mathematics to some extent. As the forecast is limited to particular aspects of the evolving system the model in total depends on the purpose of the forecast (pragmatic property). The model simulates the original. The difference between them in terms of correctly describing the original could be made go away. However, that would make the model useless.

idealizing mode. Software processes, such as the Rational Unified Process (RUP) are models of how to develop software systems. At least once the RUP was actually used for guiding software developers (mapping property). The RUP lacks all the details of activities of people and the outcomes thereof that are characteristic for real processes happening in space, time, and organization such as the number of individuals in the development team (truncation property). The system development activity can only be conducted by those who have a satisfactory cultural and educational background (pragmatic property). The model idealizes the original, i.e., differences between them are inevitable but not considered as too relevant. The development team is supposed to find a proxy for a prescribed activity that is such that the real conditions do not let it appear as advisable to conduct it though under ideal conditions that would be the case.

comprehensive mode. System quality is often conceptualized on the base of a structured set of so-called quality aspects or characteristics. For each of the latter a scale and a weighting factor is presupposed. The quality of a system is then represented by a vector of weighted score values, i.e., the instances of the scale accredited to the system with respect to each of the quality aspects. In that sense each quality is the quality of a system (mapping property). All concrete system properties have been abstracted away (truncation property). The vector of weighted scores is only a quality model for those who understand the definitions of the quality aspects and accept that quantifying approach to system quality (pragmatic property). Also, the quality model itself depends on the reason for which one is interested in the quality of that system. The weighting factors, the quality aspects, the scales and the definition of the scale values are due to change if that reason changes.

Please note that the descriptive- and the prescriptive reference mode were distinguished from each other in [47] in terms of the so-called direction of fit: While in a descriptive reference mode an unacceptable difference between model and original suggests the model to be changed the contrary suggestion applies in case of the prescriptive mode of reference.

3 The Consistency of Models

So far we have taken a relativistic approach to explaining the term model, i.e., we have related models to original and provided a brief discussion of the properties of that relationship. For going into more depth regarding that we describe what a model is in itself. For that we make use of a naive understanding of the concept "concept". In that understanding a concept enables to refer to phenomena in a universe of discourse. That reference can be a 1:1 reference, as it is the case with the individual concepts "Napoleon Buonaparte", "the United States of America", or "Pope John-Paul 2nd.", "the number π", etc. However, that reference can also be a 1:n reference, as is the case with the universal concepts "the planets in our solar system", "the non-negative integers", "the members of the United Nations". Since there are relations among concepts such as subsumption and composition etc. concepts can be used to gain an overview over a universe of discourse by grouping together those that "fall under" a given concept and relate those groups to each other that fall under related concepts. The perhaps best-known way to gain an oversight is to have a taxonomy, i.e., a tree-like hierarchical concept structure. Regarding what concepts actually are we refer to Kamlah and Lorenzen, [16]. For more detail regarding what kinds of concepts exist we refer to Pfänder, [30].

Our general idea regarding modeling is that it is a process that results in a model relationship $\mu(O, M, A)$ being established. In that relationship models are related to their originals for expressing our opinions, concerns or views etc.

regarding the original. For providing a reasonable approach to the structure of models we therefore need to identify "the atom" of opinion etc. and conceive models as sets of such atoms. In this paper we identify the concept of judgment as that atom. We reuse and extend a bit the theory of judgment in the form published by Alexander Pfänder in 1921, [30]. A judgment according to his theory is a predicate U = (S,P,C,A). Its meaning is that actor A to the instances of the subject notion S relates the predicate notion P in a way specified by the copula notion C. The copula notion C specifies whether the predicate notion is accredited to or denied from the instance set of the subject notion, i.e., the extent of S. The copula notion also specifies whether the predicate notion is related to all instances of the subject notion or only to a subset of it. Pfänder defines the modality of a judgement as the degree of confidence of A in his / her judgment. The judgement (employing the obvious notation) (cat, grey in the dark, ∀+, Peter) says that Peter judges "All cats are grey in the dark."

A signature Σ is a 4-tuple $(\Omega, \mathcal{F}, \mathcal{R}, A)$ such that $\Omega = \{\Omega_1, \ldots, \Omega_m\}$, $\mathcal{F} = \{F_1, \ldots, F_n\}$, $\mathcal{R} = \{R_1, \ldots, R_o\}$, and A is a set of sort symbols, function symbols, relation symbols, and a mapping respectively. The latter associates to each function symbol f and each relation symbol r an arity $A(f) = (i_1, \ldots, i_f, i)$ and $A(r) = (j_1, \ldots, j_r, j)$ respectively such that the i_x and i as well as the j_y, and j are elements of $\{1, \ldots, m\}$. A structure $\mathcal{S}$ over a signature $\Sigma = (\Omega, \mathcal{F}, \mathcal{R}, A)$ is a triple $\mathcal{S} = (S, F_S, R_S)$ such that $S = \{S_1, \ldots, S_m\}$, $F_S = \{f_S^x \mid f \in \mathcal{F},\ x \in \{1, \ldots, a_f\}\}$, $R_S = \{r_S^y \mid r \in \mathcal{R},\ y \in \{1, \ldots, b_r\}\}$ is a set of sets, functions, relations, such that $f_S^x : S_{i_1} \times \ldots \times S_{i_f} \to S_i$, for all $f_S^x \in F_S$, with $A(f) = (i_1, \ldots, i_f, i)$, and $r_S^y \subseteq S_{j_1} \times \ldots \times S_{j_r} \times S_j$, for all $r_S^y \in R_S$, with $A(r) = (j_1, \ldots, j_r, j)$. Given a structure $\mathcal{S} = (S, F_S, R_S)$ the set $\cup S$ is called its support and if no confusion must be expected $\mathcal{S}$ is referred to as S. For each function $f \in F_S$, and each relation $r \in R_S$ the tuples $A(f)$ and $A(r)$ are called the arity of f and r respectively. For each $s \in S$ the elements of s are said to be of sort s

Given a modeler I, and a signature $\Sigma = (\Omega, \mathcal{F}, \mathcal{R}, A)$ the following sets of judgments can be considered $X_1 = \{(\omega, \exists^*, +, I) \mid \omega \in \Omega\}$, $X_2 = \{(f, \exists^*, +, I) \mid f \in \mathcal{F}\}$, $X_3 = \{(r, \exists^*, +, I) \mid r \in \mathcal{R}\}$ where it is assumed that the predicate notion $\exists^*$ means that I with respect to a universe of discourse, UoD, has obtained a definition of the subject notion that allows him or her to classify the phenomena in UoD as either belonging to the extent of the subject notion or not, $\forall \omega \in \Omega, f \in \mathcal{F}, r \in \mathcal{R}$ respectively. As a boundary condition, the subject notions f, and r are subject to the constraint specified by the arities $A(f), A(r)$ respectively. Obviously the signature Σ can be specified as $X_1 \cup X_2 \cup X_3$. If one now permits the use of composite subject notions like $(mammal, dog)$, and $(dog, Lassie)$ then even structures over the signature Σ can be specified as sets of judgements. The judgments $((mammal, dog), ako, +, I)$, and $((dog, Lassie), isa, +, I)$ then mean that the modeler I holds that a dog is a kind of (ako) mammal and that Lassie is a (isa) dog. Similarly one can consider the judgments $(cat, \exists^*, +, I)$, $(mouse, \exists^*, +, I)$, and $(catch, \exists^*, +, I)$, as well as $((cat, mouse), catch, +, I)$, $((cat, Tom), isa, +, I)$, $((mouse, Jerry), isa, +, I)$, and $((catch, (Tom, Jerry)), isa, I)$.

The ER-model, for example, can be specified as the signature $\Sigma = (\Omega, \mathcal{F}, \emptyset, A)$ with $\Omega = \{\Omega_i \mid i \in \{1, \ldots, 6\}\}$, and $\mathcal{F} = \{\alpha, \beta, \gamma\}$ and $A(\alpha) = (2, 4, 1)$, $A(\beta) = (1, 6, 3)$, and $A(\gamma) = (1, 5, 3)$. To make more sense out of it the sort symbols $\Omega_1 \ldots \Omega_6$ are called entity type, relationship type, value type, role, association characteristic, and entity characteristic respectively. According to the arities, as defined above, the function symbol α can be understood as a schema of mappings that each associate an instance of an entity type to a pair of a role instance and a relationship type instance. Similarly, the function symbols β and γ can be understood as mapping schema of a mapping that associates a value type instance to a pair of an entity type instance and an entity characteristic instance and a pair of an entity type instance and an association characteristic instance, respectively. An ER-diagram $\mathcal{D}$ is then a structure $(D, F_D, \emptyset)$ over the signature Σ. For other semantic models similar encodings can be given. Obviously, all semantic models that can be encoded as a structure over a signature can be understood as models.

4 Ontologies and Their Use

Following the frequently used definition of Gruber, see [10, p. 199], an "... ontology is an explicit specification of a conceptualization". And a "... conceptualization is an abstract simplified view of the world that we wish to represent for some purpose." Bunge says the [4, p. 12] "... goals of ... ontology are to analyze and to systematize the ontological categories and hypothesis germane to science." He adds later [4, p. 21]: "True, ontological theories, whatever their degree of scientificity, cannot be tested empirically." Consequently, one cannot justify to be more confident of true ontologies in the sense of Bunge than of other reasonably consistent theories. Ontology use becomes even more problematic due to Bunge's remark. In [42, p. 96] and [38] ontologies more specifically are considered as shared conceptualization. The point of conceptualizations being shared was of course critical for database design, see for example [2] for a good source. In the subarea of schema integration it has led to a lot of work being done. In [42, p. 98] ontologies are viewed as enabling the introduction of normative models.

Gruber's definition of the term ontology is frequently used (see, for example [44,28,7]). For a critical discussion of that definition refer for example to [50]. In that paper additionally to Gruber's definition the definition is discussed of ontology as " a logical theory accounting for the intended meaning of a formal vocabulary". In this paper Gruber's definition is considered as more adequately fitting how ontologies are used in information systems. For an alternative conception of information system ontology as a hermeneutic enterprise see [8]. Given the current time- and resource limitations of not too innovative projects Gruber's definition appears as appropriate for the information systems field. However, it is conceded that for working out the requirements of highly innovative projects the hermeneutic approach is preferable.

4.1 An Ontology Model

A shared conceptualization is a cultural unit. Let an ontology X be used by an agent A to specify a cultural unit U_W. Let a specification W exist that allows for justification of the use of X to specify U_W. Let furthermore U_X be the cultural unit associated with X prior to agreeing that X actually should be used as a specification of U_W. Note that U_X may be void. Conceptualizing the consideration of an ontology X for U_W by an agent A thus leads to the model relation $\mu(W, X, A)$ in which a constitutive mode of reference occurs, i.e., a replacement of W by X.

Let for better understanding of the concept ontology A be an agent, who establishes a model relation $\mu(W, X, A)$. Then X is an ontology that specifies a cultural unit U. The agent A will replace W by X and therefore essentially consider U rather than W after the ontology has become dominant. That can be justified if one presupposes that a proposition is true with respect to U iff it can be implied by X. What therefore is achieved by using an ontology is that a naively reconstructed world can be replaced by a scientifically reconstructed world. Assuming the agent is a human then the specification X can be considered as a media of interaction for the agent and our world as such or, what is supposed to mean the same, the world as such to some extent is reflected in X.

One can exemplify the use of ontology by an example from modern Physics: Quantum Theory is a particular theory that many physicists consider as truly describing a particular part of our world. When theoretical knowledge regarding that part of the world is needed then Quantum Theory is referred to in attempts to provide that knowledge. Quantum theory is used for implying correct statements about the worlds to which it applies. A respective example that directly relates to informatics is not hard to find. For example, at 2. April 2004, the Web edition of the "Neue Zürcher Zeitung" in its science column published the article (in German) "The Quantum Lab in the Matchbox" reporting about an encryption device produced by a Swiss company. The unique selling point of this device is that it uses a Quantum Theory based encryption device that produces encodings that provably cannot be deciphered without access being given to the respective key (if Quantum Theory is correct and applies).

The consequence of characterizing ontologies as models is that they are due to pragmatic concerns. An ontology might thus be suitable for a given purpose, group of users, time of use, or similar, but not so for others. Therefore, from a modelers' point of view the use of ontologies in information systems asks for further investigation. The mentioned pragmatic concerns lead occasionally to puzzling consequences. Sometimes one uses wrong models in favor of correct ones! In primary and secondary education for example the wrong ball-model of molecules (Chemistry) and orbs (Physics) are used rather than (more) correct ones. Behind the scene a tradeoff is arranged for that balances the cognitive load put on the pupils and the benefit they can draw from that load. One can generalize that to a tradeoff taking place between the cost of model usage and the benefit of it.

4.2 Modeling Ontology Use

The usage of ontologies can in a coarse-grained way be conceptualized as a predicate $u(A, M, D, L, T)$, wherein A is an agent that uses ontology M (i.e., the model) with respect to a domain D (i.e., the original) for a task T that is specified in language L. Dimensions of an ontology use can be identified as (1) role, (i.e., the way the ontology is used); (2) justification (addressing as to whether or not A is entitled for using M in role R because M is an ontology); and (3) relevance (addressing as to whether it is relevant for using M in role R that M is an ontology). To each of these dimensions will be associated a scale. For both of the latter dimensions the scale values "+", and "-" will be used in the obvious meaning. The scale for dimension 'role' has the values[2]:

correctness concept provider (ccp), i.e., the ontology is used for providing a concept of correctness of the sentences of L.

communication medium provider (cmp), i.e., the ontology is used for providing a communication media, i.e., the language L.

knowledge provider (kp), i.e., the ontology is used for providing knowledge regarding the domain D.

meaning provider (mp), i.e., the ontology is used for providing a meaning to the sentences of the language L.

quality concept provider (qcp), i.e., the ontology is used for providing a concept of quality regarding items in the domain D.

world view provider (wvp), i.e., the ontology is used for providing a conceptualization of the world D.

Please note that some papers mention more elementary reasons for using an ontology in information systems. In [43, p. 287] these reasons are: the ontology "is directed towards systems", it intends to cover "... a wide range of systems", "... is well formalized", provides a consistent notation, and "... draws upon an extensive body of prior work related to ontology." Evaluations of conceptual modeling practices or theories with respect to that chosen ontology are at least subject to the reservation that these reasons are not rejected.

Let T ve a task. The ontology m in the role ccp, cmp, kp, mp, qcp, and wvp is used for distinguishing the correct from the wrong sentences of L; for providing agents in A the media L for taking about D; for providing knowledge regarding D to members of A; for associating items in D as a meaning to the sentences of L; for establishing the concept of quality regarding items in D; and specifying a conceptualization of D respectively. For an ontology use u the triplet $\alpha_u = (\rho, \iota, \omega)$, with ρ, ι, ω scale values of role, justification and relevance respectively is called use assessment. An ontology use u should be considered as problematic if its assessment α_u scores "-" for 'justification' or 'relevance'.

[2] It is conceded that several of these roles could apply to an ontology in a case at hand. However, that is expected not to cause any difficulties.

Some pragmatic concerns regarding ontology roles are:

1. When a correctness concept is introduced correctness or truth of propositions becomes important. It is only mentioned as an aside that this concept might be rather difficult to use if not a respective criteria is supplied. Truth is not always sufficient as a success criteria. Assume a postman knows a letter's recipient name and street of residence but not the house number. If the street has many houses he is likely not to deliver the letter. What he knows is correct but not precise (enough). Furthermore, as the ontology (in so far as it is true in the sense of Bunge) cannot be checked empirically the justification of being used in that role is not particularly strong.
2. Proving a proposition can let it appear as unrefutable. However, the proven result is at most as correct as the presuppositions of its proof are. With respect to so-called facts it is even worse, as not only truth or correctness of the presupposed theories in their area of applicability play a role. Rather the applicability itself is a source of error. An example for this remark is Bunge's proof of the transitivity of the parthood relationship, [4, pp. 29, 30]. As is known from [48] there are cases of parthood relationship for which it is not transitive. For a more recent discussion of parthood relations see, e.g. [15].
3. The extent and the quality of the knowledge that can be provided by means of an ontology depends on the individual that is targeted at. This is a consequence of both the contextuality of human memory ([22, pp. 121]), and human language understanding and use ([36]). For becoming effective the knowledge needs to be acquired (i.e., incorporated into a mental model) by the respective individual. Obviously that acquisition may impact extent and quality of that what is known.
4. The semantics of a sentence, understood as an object belonging to a separate (i.e., semantic) domain and being associated to that sentence, is a standard model of linguistics regarding how human language works, see for example [49, 115]. Other such models exist, [14, p. 246]. An elementary introduction into Wittgenstein's "meaning-is-use-model" is [19, pp. 58]. Obviously the chosen semantics will significantly impact the human-computer interaction. A list of pros and cons of using natural language for human-computer interaction is reproduced from the literature in [20, pp. 294 - 295]. Obviously, using an ontology in the role of meaning provider requires quite some further elaboration.

Let the predicate $\mu(O, M, A)$ be true and A use M in the constitutive reference mode. Consider an ontology use $u = u(A, M, D, L, T)$.

- Using M as wvp is justified if the overlap of D and C_O is counted as significant. What counts as significant depends on T and A. It is relevant for using M as wvp that M actually is an ontology because that makes M capable of specifying C_O.
- Using M as ccp regarding L turns discriminating true from false propositions in L into drawing implications from M. It is justified to use M in this role. However, it is not relevant for this use that M is an ontology. For a theory to

be used in this role it would be relevant that the important propositions can be implied efficiently. What counts as 'important' or 'efficient' again depends on T and A.

- Using M as kp is justified if the overlap of C_O and D contains key items regarding which knowledge is sought for. It is relevant for this use that M is an ontology.
- Using M as cmp can be justified if C_O. Using M in this role would not be justified if enough or not the right members of A are not fluent in L respectively. What counts as enough or right depends on T and A. It is not relevant for this use of M that M is an ontology.
- It is justified to use M as mp, if L enables A to talk about C_O. It is not relevant for using M in this role that M is an ontology. Note that justification of using M as mp may involve a fluency issue like the one discussed with respect to the role cmp. The characteristics of a model that is suited for use as mp depend on T and A.
- Using M as a qcp can be justified if for T an understanding of quality as ontology compliance is adequate. An ontology does not qualify per-se for the role of qcp. It is less important that a quality concept means ontology compliance than it is that this concept helps A doing T.

The following table contains the results of an investigation of a few papers with respect to the quality model that was proposed in this paper.

role	**justification**	**relevance**	**paper**
wvp	+	+	[5], ...
ccp	+	-	[11,44]
kp	+	+	[37,45]
cmp	-	-	/
mp	-	+	[28]
qcp	-		[46,3]

Fig. 1. Assessment of a few papers with respect to the quality model proposed here

References

1. *Longman Dictionary of Contemporary English.* Langenscheidt-Longman GmbH, München, 1995.
2. Carlo Batini, Stefano Ceri, and Shamkant Navathe. *Conceptual Database Design.* The Benjamin/Cummings Publishing Company; Inc., Redwood City, California, 1992.
3. Francois Bodart, Arvind Patel, Marc Sim, and Ron Weber. Should optional properties be used in conceptual modelling? A theory and three empirical tests. *Information Systems Research*, 12(4):384 – 405, December 2001.
4. Mario Bunge. *Ontology I: The furniture of the world*, volume 3 of *Treatise on basic philosophy.* D. Reidel Publishing Company, Dordrecht, Holland and Boston, USA, 1977.

5. Peter P. Chen. The Entity-Relationship Model: Toward a Unified View of Data. *ACM Transactions on Database Systems*, 1(1):9–37, 1976.
6. Umberto Eco. *Einführung in die Semiotik*. Wilhelm Fink Verlag GmbH & Co. KG, München, 1994.
7. Peter Fettke and Peter Loos. Ontological evaluation of reference models using the Bunge-Wand-Weber model. In *Ninth Americas Conference on Information Systems*, 2003.
8. Frederica T. Fonseca and James E. Martin. Towards an alternative notion of information systems ontologies: information engineering as a hermeneutic enterprise. *Journal of the American Society for Information Science*, 56(1):46 – 57, 2005.
9. David Garmus and David Herron. *Managing the software process: a practical guide to functional measurements*. Yourdon Press Computing Series. Prentice Hall PTR, Upper Saddle River, New Jersey, 1996.
10. Thomas Gruber. A translation approach to portable ontologies. *Knowledge Acquisition*, 5(2):199 – 220, 1993.
11. Giancarlo Guizzardi, Heinrich Herre, and Gerd Wagner. On the general ontological foundations of conceptual modeling. In *Proceedings of 21st. International Conference on Conceptual Modeling (ER 2002)*, Berlin, 2002. Springer Verlag.
12. Richard Hull and Roger King. Semantic Database Modeling: Survey, Applications, and Research Issues. *ACM Computing Surveys*, 19(3):201–260, 1987.
13. Richard Hull and Roger King. A Tutorial on Semantic Database Modeling. In A. F. Cardenas and D. McLeod, editors, *Research Foundations in Object Oriented and Semantic Database Systems*, pages 1–33. Prentice Hall, Englewood Cliffs, New Jersey, 1990.
14. Howard Jackson. *Words and their meaning*. Longman, London and New York, 1988.
15. Ingvar Johansson. On the transitivity of parthood relations. In H. Hochberg and K. Mulligan, editors, *Relations and predicates*, pages 161 – 181, Frankfurt, 2004. Ontos Verlag.
16. Wilhelm Kamlah and Paul Lorenzen. *Logische Propädeutik : Vorschule des vernünftigen Redens*. Verlag J. B. Metzler, Stuttgart, Weimar, 1996.
17. Roland Kaschek. Modelling ontology use for information systems. In Klaus-Dieter Althoff, Andreas Dengel, Ralph Bergmann, Markus Nick, and Thomas Roth-Berghofer, editors, *WM2005: Professional knowledge management, experiences and visions*, pages 559 – 562. Deutsches Forschungszentrum für künstliche Intelligenz, April 2005.
18. Roland Kaschek and Sergiy Zlatkin. Where ontology affects information systems. In HeinrichC. Mayr, Michael. Godlevsky, and Stephen C. Liddle, editors, *ISTA 2003 Proceedings*, Bonn, Germany, 2003. GI.
19. Rudi Keller. *Zeichentheorie*. Francke Verlag, Tübingen, Basel, 1995.
20. Nils Lenke, Hans-Dieter Lutz, and Michael Sprenger. *Grundlagen Sprachlicher Kommunikation*. Wilhelm Fink Verlag GmbH & Co. KG, München, 1995.
21. Jochen Ludewig. Models in software engineering - an introduction. *Software and Systems Modeling*, 2(1):5 – 14, March 2003. Reworked version of Ludewig's presentation at "Modellierung 2002".
22. Margaret W. Matlin. *Cognition*. John Wiley & Sons, New York et al., 5th. edition, 2002.
23. Simon Milton and Ed. Kazmierczak. An ontological study of data modelling languages using Chisholm's ontology. In *European-Japanese conference on information modelling and knowledge bases*, Amsterdam et al., 2001. IOS Press.

24. Marvin Minsky. Matter, mind and models. In Marvin Minsky, editor, *Semantic information processing*, pages 425 – 432. MIT Press, Cambridge, Massachusetts and London, England, 1968.
25. Tadao Murata. Petri Nets: Properties, Analysis and Applications. *Proceedings of the IEEE*, 77(4):541 – 580, April 1989.
26. Jakob Nielsen. *Designing Web usability.* New Riders Publishing, Indianapolis, Indiana, 2000.
27. Donald Norman. *The design of everyday things.* Basic Books, New York, 2. edition, 2002.
28. A. Opdahl, B. Henderson-Sellers, and F. Barbier. Ontological analysis of whole-part relationships in OO-models. *Information and Software Technology*, 43:387 – 399, 2001.
29. Joan Peckham and Fred Marjanski. Semantic Data Models. *ACM Computing Surveys*, 20(3):153–189, 1988.
30. Alexander Pfänder. *Logik.* Verlag von Max Niemeyer, Halle a. d. Saale, 1921.
31. Jennifer Preece, Yvonne Rogers, and Helen Sharp. *Interaction design: beyond human-computer interaction.* John Wiley & Sons, Inc., New York, 2002.
32. Edward S. Quade. Predicting the consequences: Models and modeling. In Hugh Miser and Edward S. Quade, editors, *Handbook of systems analysis: overview of uses, procedures, applications and practice*, pages 191 – 218. Elsevier Science Publishing Co., Inc., New York, 1985.
33. Michael Rosemann, Iris Vessey, Ron Weber, and Boris Wyssuk. On the applicability of the Bunge-Wand-Weber Ontology to Enterprise Systems Requirements. In Steve Elliot, Marie-Anne Williams, Sue Williams, and Carrol Pollard, editors, *Poceedings of the 15th. Australasian Conference on information systems, 2004.* School of information systems of University of Tasmania, 2004.
34. Jeff Rothenberg. The nature of modeling. In Lawrence E. Widman, Kenneth A. Loparo, and Norman R. Nielson, editors, *Artifical intelligence, simulation, and modeling*, pages 75–92. John Wiley & Sons, Inc., New York et al., 1989.
35. James Rumbaugh, Michael Blaha, William Premerlani, Frederick Eddy, and William Lorensen. *Object-Oriented Modeling and Design.* Prentice-Hall, Inc., Englewood Cliffs, New Jersey, 1991.
36. David E. Rumelhart. Some problems with the notion of literal meanings. In Andrew Ortony, editor, *Metaphor and thought*, pages 71 – 82, Camrdidge et al., 1998. Cambridge University Press. 4th. printing of the 2nd. edition of the book from 1993.
37. Klaus-Dieter Schewe, Roland Kaschek, Claire Matthews, and Catherine Wallace. Modeling web-based banking systems: Story boarding and user profiling. In Heinrich C. Mayr and van den Heuvel, Willem-Jan, editors, *Proceedings of eCoMo 2002*, Springer LNCS, Berlin et al., 2002. Springer - Verlag.
38. Peter Spyns, Robert Meersman, and Mustafa Jarrar. Data modelling versus Ontology engineering. *ACM SIGMOD Record*, 31(4):12 – 17, December 2002.
39. Herbert Stachowiak. *Allgemeine Modelltheorie.* Springer Verlag, Wien, New York, 1973.
40. Herbert Stachowiak. Erkenntnisstufen zum Systematischen Neopragmatismus und zur Allgemeinen Modelltheorie. In Herbert Stachowiak, editor, *Modelle-Konstruktionen der Wirklichkeit*, pages 87–146. Wilhelm Fink Verlag, München, 1983.
41. Herbert Stachowiak. Modell. In Helmut Seiffert and Gerard Radnitzky, editors, *Handlexikon Zur Wissenschaftstheorie*, pages 219–222. Deutscher Taschebuch Verlag GmbH & Co. KG, München, 1992.

42. Mike Uschold and Michael Gruninger. Ontologies: principles, methods and applications. *The Knowledge Engineering Review*, 11(2):93 – 136, 1996.
43. Yair Wand, David E. Monarchi, Jeffrey Parsons, and Carson C. Woo. Theoretical foundations for conceptual modeling in information systems development. *Decision Support Systems*, 15:285 – 304, 1995.
44. Yair Wand, Veda C. Storey, and Ron Weber. An Ontological Analysis of the Relationship Construct in Conceptual Modeling. *ACM Transactions on Database Systems*, 24(4):494–528, Dezember 1999.
45. Ron Weber. Conceptual modelling and ontology: possibilities and pitfalls. *Journal of Database Management*, 14(3):1 – 20, July - September 2003.
46. Christopher Welty and Nicola Guarino. Supporting ontological analysis of taxonomic relationships. *Data & Knowledge Engineering*, 39:51 – 74, 2001.
47. Roelf Wieringa. *Algebraic foundations for dynamic conceptual models*. PhD thesis, Free University of Amsterdam, Amsterdam, The Netherlands, Mai 1990.
48. M. Winston, R. Caffin, and D. Herrman. A taxonomy of part-whole relations. *Cognitive Science*, 11:417 – 444, 1987.
49. George Yule. *The study of language*. Cambridge University Press, Cambridge, UK, 1998.
50. Gloria Zuniga. Ontology: its transformation from philosophy to information systems. 2001.

How to Do Philosophy Informationally

Gian Maria Greco, Gianluca Paronitti, Matteo Turilli, and Luciano Floridi

Information Ethics Group, Oxford University Computing Laboratory,
Oxford, United Kingdom

Abstract. In this paper we introduce three methods to approach philosophical problems informationally: Minimalism, the Method of Abstraction and Constructionism. Minimalism considers the specifications of the starting problems and systems that are tractable for a philosophical analysis. The Method of Abstraction describes the process of making explicit the level of abstraction at which a system is observed and investigated. Constructionism provides a series of principles that the investigation of the problem must fulfil once it has been fully characterised by the previous two methods. For each method, we also provide an application: the problem of visual perception, functionalism, and the Turing Test, respectively.

1 Introduction

The Philosophy of Information is a new area of research at the intersection of philosophy, computer science and ICT (information and communication technology) [6] and [8]. It concerns (a) the critical investigation of the conceptual nature and basic principles of information, including its dynamics (especially computation), utilization (especially ethical issues) and sciences; and (b) the elaboration and application of computational and information-theoretic methodologies to philosophical problems. Past work by members of our group has concentrated on (a). In this paper we explore (b). In a nutshell, we ask what computer science can do for philosophy, rather than what the latter can do for the former.

Applications of computational methods to philosophical issues may be approached in three main ways:

1. *Conceptual experiments in silico*, or the externalization of the mental theatre. As Patrick Grim has remarked "since the eighties, philosophers too have begun to apply computational modeling to questions in logic, epistemology, philosophy of science, philosophy of mind, philosophy of language, philosophy of biology, ethics, and social and political philosophy. [...] A number of authors portray computer experimentation in general as a technological extension of an ancient tradition of thought experiment" [12].
2. *Pancomputationalism*, or the fallacy of a powerful metaphor. According to this view, computational and informational concepts are so powerful that, given the right *Level of Abstraction* (see section 3), anything could be presented as a computational system, from a building to a volcano, from a forest to a dinner, from a brain to a company, and any process could be

K.-D. Althoff et al. (Eds.): WM 2005, LNAI 3782, pp. 623–634, 2005.

simulated computationally, heating and flying, eating or knitting. Even non-computable functions would be representable, although by abstracting them to such a high level that they would no longer count as a system (one would have to abstract output and even termination and the existence of output, although a system has to be allowed to terminate or not, even if one does not observe the output). Pancomputationalists (e.g. [3]) have the hard task of providing a credible answers to the following two questions: (1) how can one avoid blurring all differences among systems, thus transforming pancomputationalism into a night in which all cows are black, to paraphrase Hegel? And (2) what would it mean for the system under investigation not to be an informational system (or a computational system, if computation = information processing)? Pancomputationalism does not seem vulnerable to a refutation (to put it in Popperian terms), in the form of a possible counterexample in a world nomically identical to the one to which pancomputationalism is applied.

3. *Regulae ad directionem ingenii*, or the Cartesian-Kantian approach. Are there specific methods in computer science that can help us to approach philosophical problems computationally?

In the following sections we answer this last question by introducing three main methods: *Minimalism*, the *Method of Abstraction* and *Constructionism*. Each one is discussed separately

2 Minimalism

Philosophical questions pose multi-faceted problems. According to Descartes, a problem space can be decomposed by a divide-and-conquer approach [19]. The outcome is a set of more approachable sub-problems, interconnected in a sort of Quinean web of dependencies [18]. When dealing with a philosophical question, the starting problem often presupposes other open problems and the strength of the answer depends on the strength of the corresponding assumptions. A minimalist starting problem relies as little as possible on other open problems, thereby strengthening the final answer to the philosophical question.

Philosophers may improve the tractability of a problem space by choosing discrete systems with which to study it. *Minimalism* outlines three criteria to orientate this choice: *controllability*, *implementability* and *predictability*. Each deserves a brief comment.

A system is *controllable* when its structure can be modified purposefully. Given this flexibility, the system can be used as a case study to test different solutions for the problem space.

The second minimalist criterion recommends that systems be *implementable* physically or by simulation. The system becomes a *white box*, the opposite of a *black box* (see section 4). Metaphorically, the maker of the system is a Platonic "demiurge", fully cognisant of the components of the system and of its state transition rules. The system can therefore be used as a laboratory to test specific constraints on the problem space.

The third criterion follows from the previous two: the chosen system must be such that its behaviour should be predictable, at least in principle. The demiurge can predict the behaviour of the system in that she can infer the correct consequences from her explanations of the system. The system outcomes become then the benchmarks of the tested solutions.

Three properties further characterise Minimalism as we advocate it.

First, Minimalism is relational. Problems and systems are never absolutely minimalist, but always connected with the problem space posed by the philosophical question.

Second, Minimalism provides a way to choose critically the starting problem for the analysis of a problem space, thus guaranteeing the strength of the next step in the forward process of answering the philosophical question. According to a minimalist approach, the tractability of a philosophical problem is a function of the three criteria outlined above. They allow the use of dynamic systems to test possible solutions and to derive properties of the problem space.

Finally, Minimalism is a matter of inferential relations between a problem and its space, but it is not a way to privilege simple or elementary problems. Minimalist problems may be difficult or complex.

Minimalism is an economic method related to, but not to be confused with, Ockham's razor. The two methods are of course compatible. However, whilst Ockham's razor avoids inconsistencies and ambiguities by eliminating redundant explicative or ontological elements in a theory, Minimalism provides a set of criteria for choosing problems and systems relative to a given specific question. Moreover, Ockham's principle of parsimony is absolute and is applied to any theoretical element, while Minimalism's main maxims of strength and tractability are always relative to a given problem space [13].

A practical example of Minimalism applied to the philosophy of perception may be helpful. Suppose our investigation concerns the nature of visual perception. We start from

1. *The identification of the question.* One begins by asking "what is visual perception?". This question poses a wide problem space, hitherto approached with different methods [15].
2. *The Cartesian decomposition of the problem is followed by a Quinean construction of the problem space.* One proceeds by identifying some well-known sub-problems of this problem space, such as the nature of internal representations, the role of mind in perception, and the interpretation of vision as computation.
3. *The identification of the starting problem.* The standard representational interpretation of perception is rich in assumptions about open problems. Perception is based, for example, on the presumed existence of internal representations. The sensorimotor approaches to visual perception are less demanding. Perception is chained to action while information is externalised. James Gibson [10], one of the main advocates of the sensorimotor hypothesis, cannot explain the nature of perceptual errors. This problem does not

rely on other open problems and therefore can be assumed as a minimalist starting problem. It can be referred to as "Gibson problem".

4. *The selection of the system to be used to study the starting problem.* The system selected has to be consistent with the requirements of Gibson's sensorimotor theory and with the criteria for Minimalism. The subsumption architecture, proposed by Rodney Brooks [2], satisfies these requirements. The architecture of Brooks' robots is reactive, parallel and decentralised. Perception and action are directly connected without any explicit internal representation or centralised inferential engines. Moreover, subsumption architectural behaviour is fully specified by the topological structure of its layers, composed of single behavioural units. Its demiurge has full control and predictability power over the system she has built. The Gibson problem can therefore be studied by means of Brooks' mobots.
5. *The solution of the problem.* In the sensorimotor approaches to vision, seeing is something done by agents in their environments. The definition of perceptual errors must be shifted from a representational interpretation, according to which errors are incorrect computations made over internal representations, to an action-based interpretation, according to which errors are unsuccessful actions performed by agents in their environment. If the sensorimotor features of the mobot enable it to move randomly in its environment then perception is successful, otherwise its perception is erroneous. The mobot that collides against a window lacks either the right features or the sensorimotor capabilities relative to a given specific environment and its task of moving around randomly.

We have just seen how Minimalism orientates the choice of problems and systems that are tractable. The answer to the initial question "what is visual perception?" is reached via the solution of localized problems. The minimalist choice of the problem — and possibly of the system — is reiterated to ensure the controllability of the whole inferential process of finding an answer to the initial philosophical question.

The definition of Minimalism is based on two main assumptions. The first concerns the existence of a problem space. Minimalism does not give an account of the decomposition process of the problem space to which it applies. The second assumption is that a dynamic system, whether conceptual or physically implemented, is useful in finding the answer to the investigated question. Minimalism does not explain why and how this approach works. In the next sections, two other methods are presented to ground both these assumptions: the *Method of Abstraction* and *Constructionism.*

The Method of Abstraction is used to describe the observables that compose the problem space and how they are related. Minimalism is always relative to a given Level of Abstraction as the structure of the problem space depends on the LoA assumed by the investigator.

Constructionism is the precise answer to the need to clarify how to choose the system and how to use it in order to investigate the set of minimalist problems that will lead to the required answer.

3 The Method of Abstraction

The process of making explicit the Level of Abstraction (LoA) at which a system is considered is called *Method of Abstraction* [9]. This method pertains to the analysis of discrete systems, by which we mean those systems whose evolution is described by explicit transition rules. It applies both to conceptual and to physical systems. Its pivotal element is the concept of LoA.

The terminology and the study of the method are rooted in a branch of theoretical computer science known as Formal Methods. Intuitively, Formal Methods are a collection of mathematical techniques used to prove that the concrete code implementation fits the abstract specifications of a computer system [23]. More precisely, Formal Methods are a variety of mathematical modelling techniques used to specify and model the behaviour of a computer system and to verify, mathematically, that the system design and implementation satisfy functional requirements.

The metaphor of interface in a computer system is helpful to illustrate what a LoA is[1]. As is well known, most users seldom think about the fact that they employ a variety of interfaces between themselves and the real electromagnetic and Boolean processes that carry out the required operations. An interface may be described as an intra-system, which transforms the outputs of system A into the inputs of system B and vice versa, producing a change in data types. LoAs are comparable to interfaces because:

1. they are a network of observables;
2. the observables are related by behaviours that moderate the LoA and can be expressed in terms of transition rules;
3. they are conceptually positioned between data and the agents' information spaces;
4. they are the place where (diverse) independent systems meet, act on or communicate with each other.

LoAs can be connected together to form broader structures of abstraction, from hierarchy of abstractions to nets of abstraction. One of the possible relations between LoAs is that of simulation.

Traditionally, a simulation is considered a dynamical representation of a system. This means that, if one wishes to produce a simulation, one must extract a model, by selecting some variables from the investigated system; and then construct an update function, which lets the variables in the simulator change as if they were the variables observed in the system [20]. In a nutshell, a simulation is considered the observation of a model that evolves over time. Such definition, though correct, is still imprecise because, in order to understand what a simulation is, one also needs to clarify explicitly and precisely what a model is. This clarification is currently one of the most controversial issues in the philosophy of science, and it is far from clear how one may best deal with it. However,

[1] For a more technical and in-depth introduction the reader should refer to [9].

using the Method of Abstraction it becomes possible to characterize the notion of simulation in a different way and hence bypass this difficulty.

A simulation relation is now the relation between the observables of a simulator system and a simulated one [21]. This relation must occur between pairs of observables in order to guarantee a satisfactory degree of congruence, not only for the current state of the two systems, but also for their evolution. In the simulation relation, the epistemic agent is coupling the state evolution of two systems by observing these two systems at different LoAs. This means that an epistemic agent tries to construct an equivalence relation between the two systems, seeking to understand at what LoA those systems could be considered congruent. By way of explanation, let us consider a simple example. Let us apply the Method of Abstraction and the simulation relation to a new definition of *functionalism*.

Functionalism argues that a physical or abstract entity is identified by its causal or operational role. From this viewpoint, a system is not evaluated by its structures and their interactions, but rather by the functions it shows. If the "stuff" constituting a system is irrelevant for its identification, then the same functional organization can be realized by different systems and substrates, which are usually called realizations [17]. This is the *multi-realizability thesis*.

Some philosophers try to rule out multi-realizability from the functionalist approach [1]. For example, they argue that multi-realizability could lead to a weakening of a neuroscientific approach in the explanation of human behaviour. For why should one be concerned with the actual neural structures if one can execute an algorithm to instantiate the same behaviours shown by these neural structures? It is argued that a computational approach is therefore more suitable for processing those algorithms.

Multirealizability cannot be detached from functionalism since, without it, functionalism becomes inexplicable. This is clear if we consider the mathematical concept of function. A function is usually expressed by an operation on one or more variables, the well-known scheme being $f(x) = y$. However, this simply means that the variables in the equation could be replaced or interpreted by an endless set of numbers or by points over the Cartesian plane or by means of a Turing machine or by set theory. Without all these instantiations, it would be impossible to explain the function $f(x) = y$. We shall therefore conclude that functionalism entails multi-realizability.

Now, in the classic account of functionalism we deal with relata (the *functional organization* and the *realizations*) and relations (the *realization relation* between the functional organization and the realizations, and the *simulation relation* between the various realizations). Our goal is to show that realization and simulation are equivalent. An epistemic agent can observe any functional organization, at a specific LoA, and the realization of that functional organization at another LoA. Then the realization relation between the two LoAs is characterized by: (a) the codification of the inputs of the functional organization LoA into the inputs of the various realizations LoAs, and (b) the de-codification of the outputs of the latter into the outputs of the former. Basically, simulation relation and realization relation are equivalent because they are relations which describe the same processes. The argument is then that:

1. multi-realizability and functionalism are coupled concepts, and
2. a simulation relation is equivalent to a realization relation.

But then it follows that

3. a common functional organization does not exist at a LoA higher than its realizations. The functional organization is the Net of Abstraction constructed by the epistemic agents with the simulation relation between the various realizations conceived at different LoAs.

This means that it is the relational structure produced by various realizations and by the simulation relation that connects them. For example, a carpenter who is making a piece of furniture by following a blueprint is not handling a functional organization (the blueprint) and a realization (the piece of furniture), but two realizations at different LoAs, which are related in a simulation relation specified by his work.

This new interpretation of functionalism leads us to reconsider functionalistic explanations within the philosophy of AI and the philosophy of mind by introducing simulation relation as a new device. The functionalist explanation is configured as a specification of simulations between the LoAs at which the realizations are organised by the epistemic agent.

4 Constructionism

Providing the guidelines for choosing a problem and supplying a method for observing and analysing it are two of the fundamental steps in the informational treatment of philosophical problems. In order to be complete and sound, the general methodology must also give an account of how the problem must be investigated once it has been fully delineated. We refer to this method as *Constructionism.*

Constructionism is at the core of the epistemological theory proposed by PI. As for *Minimalism* and the *Method of Abstraction*, Constructionism finds its roots in both the philosophical tradition and computational theories and practices.

A *black box* is a system whose internal structure, rules and composition remain undisclosed. A *white box* is a system about which one knows everything, because one has constructed it. This perspective, well known in Computer Science and Artificial Intelligence, lays in the wake of the so-called *maker's knowledge tradition*, according to which:

1. one can only know what one makes, and therefore
2. one cannot know the genuine nature of reality in itself.

Like Vico and Hobbes [4], philosophers who emphasise (2) argue that, since any attempt to know the intrinsic nature of the world will inevitably fail, it is better to concentrate on those sciences whose subject is created by us, such as politics and social sciences.

Philosophers who emphasize (1) argue that it is possible to improve our knowledge of reality through the improvement of our knowledge of the techniques by which reality is investigated. This tradition finds its champion in Francis Bacon's philosophy of technology [16] and it is related to Kantism. Following Bacon, technology becomes the main subject of philosophical enquiry, because it is both a human product and the means through which the world is investigated. And when Kant stresses the importance of understanding the conditions of possibility of our knowledge, he is working within the maker's knowledge tradition. One can investigate scientifically the phenomena one experiences only insofar as one is epistemically responsible for them.

Constructionism explicitly refers to the maker's knowledge tradition. Its method consists of the following five principles:

1. The *Principle of Knowledge*: only what is constructible can be known. Anything that can not be constructed could be subject, at most, to working hypotheses.
2. The *Principle of Constructability*: working hypotheses are investigated by (theoretical or practical) simulations based on them.
3. The *Principle of Controllability*: simulations must be controllable.
4. The *Principle of Confirmation*: any confirmation or refutation of the hypothesis concerns the simulation, not the simulated.
5. *The Principle of Economy*: the fewer the conceptual resources used the better. In any case, the resources used must be fewer than the results accomplished.

Constructionism suggests that, given a theory, one implements and tests it in a system. Because one constructs the system, one can also control it. As Newell and Simon remarked "neither machines nor programs are black boxes; they are artefacts that have been designed, both hardware and software, and we can open them up and look inside" [14] (for constructionist approaches in Cybernetics and proto-Cybernetics see [5]).

Consider, for example, behaviour-based robotics. One may observe an ant and offer a hypothesis about its internal structures in order to explain its behaviours. Then one may build a system to test that hypothesis. The resulting system is controllable in that it is *modifiable*, *compositional* and *predictable*. This means that, as far as the constructed system is concerned: (a) one can change its internal structures and rules; (b) the system can be implemented by adding or removing new parts in order to test a variety of hypotheses; and since one knows the rules of the system, (c) one can know its behaviour. Suppose that the mobot one has built behaves like the ant one observed. The Principle of Confirmation prevents her from generalizing the working hypotheses, as if they were the real cause (or internal structure) of the simulated. It is obviously possible to provide an endless number of simulations with different internal structures whilst still obtaining the same behaviour. From this, the *sub-Principle of Context-dependency* is derived:

isomorphism between the simulated and simulation is only local, not global. The mobot accounts for the behaviour of the ant only under the constraints specified by the simulation. If the constraints change, so does the evaluation of the hypotheses.

Constructionism is in plain contrast to any mimetic approach in epistemology. The latter assumes that reality is approached through some reproductive or representational mechanism. Ideas, mental images, corresponding pictures, concepts and so forth are supposed to be mere copies or portraits of some otherwise mysterious reality in itself. From the constructionist point of view, on the contrary, knowledge is a modelling process, which shapes and edits reality to make it intelligible. It therefore rejects more "mimetic" theories such as Plato's, Descartes' or Locke's, in favour of a more Kantian approach. The Principle of Economy refers to the "careful management of resources". On the one hand, in defining knowledge processes, mimetic theories use a large amount of resources. Assuming that there is a reality and that it works in some particular way means making a heavy ontological commitment. On the other hand, Constructionism does not state anything about reality in itself. This more modest commitment makes errors less likely. As in the case of Minimalism, the constructionist Principle of Economy differs from Ockham's razor too. While the latter is a post-production revision tool, for it provides a criterion for choosing among theories already produced, the former is a pre-design planning norm, for it requires to be fully aware of the initial assumptions before one undertakes the investigation process and it binds the construction of any explanatory model to the conceptual resources available.

The Turing Test (TT) is an enlightening example of how the methodology outlined in this paper and, more specifically, the constructionist method, work, since it respects the minimalist criterion, uses the LoAs and is constructionist.

As we saw earlier, Minimalism concerns the choice of the problem, not of the explanation. Turing refuses even to try to provide an answer to the question "can a machine think?". He considers it a problem "too meaningless to deserve discussion", because it involves vague concepts such as 'machine' and 'thinking' [22]. Turing suggests replacing it with the Imitation Game, which is exactly more manageable and less demanding from the minimalist point of view. By so doing, he specifies a LoA and asks a new question, which may be summed up thus: "can one consider that a machine is thinking *at this Level of Abstraction*?". The rules of the game define the conditions of observability [9]. If the machine passes the test at that LoA, one can clearly state that the machine is thinking, at that LoA. By changing the rules of the game, one changes the LoA and consequently the answer. Note how TT respects the constructionist principles:

1. By satisfying Minimalism, that is, by refusing to provide a universal definition of intelligence, Turing also respects the Principle of Knowledge.
2. Turing makes a hypothesis based on the common assumption that conversation skills require intelligence, and then he devises a system to evaluate whether a machine is intelligent comparatively, that means at that LoA (Principle of Constructability).

3. The system is controllable. One knows how it works and how it can be modified, so it can be implemented to test other features such as creativity, learning, and ethical behaviour (Principle of Controllability).
4. If a machine passes the test implies only that the machine can be considered intelligent at that LoA (Principle of Confirmation).
5. Finally, in tackling the problem of artificial intelligence, Turing refuses to avail himself of those approaches that require a large amount of conceptual resources. This is why, for instance, he refuses to deal with any psychological assumption about intelligence (Principle of Economy)[2].

A strongly constructionist approach grounds not only the design of TT but also what Turing conjectured as a potentially successful strategy to obtain a machine that would pass the test. In the final section of his 1950 paper, entitled "Learning Machines", Turing suggests, as a working hypothesis, that a child-machine could learn and gain its own knowledge through educational processes. Then he builds a system, the child-programme, in order to test that hypothesis. This system is controllable, for example through punishment and reward processes. Any hints or results in the process concern only the system and not how a human child learns. The choice itself of a child-machine, instead of a "grown up", respects not only the minimalist criterion but also the Principle of Economy.

5 Conclusion

In this paper, we have introduced three methods and shown how they can be imported, with some adaptations, from computer science into philosophy, in order to model and analyse conceptual problems. We have outlined their main features and advantages. The methods clarify implicit assumptions, facilitate comparisons, enhance rigour and promote the resolution of possible conceptual confusions. Some applications of the methods discussed in this paper have already been successfully provided in computer ethics [9], in epistemology [7], and in the philosophy of information [8]. Of course, the adoption of the methods raises important further questions. We mention only three of them that seem to us particularly pressing: (a) What is the logic of problem spaces? (b) What are the logical relations between LoAs? (c) How can Constructionism avoid solipsism? We have not attempted to answer these questions, which we hope to address in future work[3].

[2] The TT is anti-psychological in the classical Fregean sense.

[3] An earlier version of this paper was presented at NA-CAP@CMU 2004, the annual Computing and Philosophy meeting organised at Carnegie Mellon (4-6 August 2004). We wish to thank the participants in that meeting, especially Seth Casana, Charles Ess, Susan Stuart and John Taylor, as well as the participants in the WSPI 2005, and the two anonymous referees for their feedback. As usual, Jeff Sanders' input was fundamental in shaping our ides. This paper is a revised version of [11]. For Italian legal requirements, Gianluca Paronitti must be considered the author of section 3, Matteo Turilli of section 2, Luciano Floridi of sections 1 and 5, Gian Maria Greco of section 4 and the first author of the whole paper.

References

1. W. Bechtel and J. Mundale. Multiple realizability revisited: Linking cognitive and neural states. *Philosophy of Science*, 66:175–207, 1999.
2. R. A. Brooks. Intelligence without representation. *Artificial Intelligence*, 47(1-3):139–159, 1991.
3. D. J. Chalmers. *The Conscious Mind: in Search of a Fundamental Theory.* Oxford University Press, Oxford, 1996.
4. A. Child. Making and knowing in hobbes, vico, and dewey. *University of California Publications in Philosophy*, 16(13):271–310, 1953.
5. R. Cordeschi. *The Discovery of the Artificial: Behavior, Mind, and Machines Before and Beyond Cybernetics.* Kluwer Academic Publishers, Dordrecht, 2002.
6. L. Floridi. What is the philosophy of information? *Metaphilosophy*, 33(1-2):123–145, 2002.
7. L. Floridi. On the logical unsolvability of the gettier problem. *Synthese*, 142(1):61–79, 2004.
8. L. Floridi. Open problems in the philosophy of information. *Metaphilosophy*, 35(4):554–582, 2004b.
9. L. Floridi and J. W. Sanders. The method of abstraction. In M. Negrotti, editor, *Yearbook of the Artificial. Nature, Culture and Technology. Models in contemporary sciences*, volume 2, pages 177–220. P. Lang, Bern, 2004.
10. J. J. Gibson. *The Ecological Approach to Visual Perception.* Houghton Mifflin, Boston, 1979.
11. G. M. Greco, G. Paronitti, M. Turilli, and L. Floridi. The philosophy of information - a methodological point of view. In K. D. Althoff, A. Dengel, R. Bergmann, M. Nick, and Th. Roth-Berghofer, editors, *WM2005: Professional Knowledge Management. Experiences and Visions*, pages 563–570. DFKI GmbH, Kaiserslautern, 2005.
12. P. Grim. Computational modeling as a philosophical methodology. In L. Floridi, editor, *The Blackwell Guide to the Philosophy of Computing and Information*, pages 337–349. Blackwell, Oxford, New York, 2003.
13. M. McCord Adams. *William Ockham.* University of Notre Dame Press, Notre Dame, 1987.
14. A. Newell and H. A. Simon. Computer science as empirical enquiry: Symbols and search. *Communications of the ACM*, 19(3):113–126, 1976.
15. A. Noé and E. Thompson, editors. *Vision and Mind: Selected Readings in the Philosophy of Perception.* The MIT Press, Cambridge, 2002.
16. A. Pérez-Ramos. *Francis Bacon's Idea of Science and the Maker's Knowledge Tradition.* Oxford University Press, New York, 1988.
17. H. Putnam. Psychological predicates. In W. H. Captain and D. D. Merrill, editors, *Art, Mind and Religion.* Pittsburgh University Press, Pittsburgh, 1967.
18. W. V. O. Quine. Two dogmas of empiricism. *The Philosophical Review*, 60(1):20–43, 1951.
19. A. Raftopoulos. Cartesian analysis and synthesis. *Studies in History and Philosophy of Science, Part A*, 34(2):265–308, 2003.

20. S. Rasmussen and C. L. Barrett. Elements of a theory of simulation. In F. Moràn, J. J. Moreno, P. Merelo, and P. Chacòn, editors, *ECAL 95. Advances in Artificial Life: Proceedings of the Third European Conference on Artificial Life*, pages 515–529. Springer-Verlag, Berlin, 1995.
21. W. P. de Roever and K. Engelhardt. *Data Refinement: Model-oriented Proof Methods and their Comparison.* Cambridge tracts in theoretical computer science. Cambridge University Press, Cambridge, 1998.
22. A. M. Turing. Computing machinery and intelligence. *Mind*, 49(236):433–460, 1950.
23. B. P. Zeigler. *Theory of Modelling and Simulation.* Wiley, New York, 1976.

Epistemological Perspectives on IS-Development – A Consensus-Oriented Approach on Conceptual Modeling

Björn Niehaves, Karsten Klose, Ralf Knackstedt, and Jörg Becker

European Research Center for Information Systems (ERCIS),
University of Muenster, Leonardo Campus 3, 48149 Münster, Germany
{Bjoern.Niehaves, Karsten.Klose, Ralf.Knackstedt, Becker}@ercis.de
http://www.ercis.de

Abstract. Within the information systems (IS) research discipline, conceptual modeling is widely discussed as a fundamental task for IS-development as it leads to shared domain knowledge between IS developers and business personnel. As well as IS-research modeling takes place within a multi-disciplinary and multi-cultural context. Thereby, the (mostly implicit) assumptions made by different researchers may vary fundamentally. As a result, it is important to expose epistemological assumptions which underlie the work of different participants. Thus, we provide a framework which questions help to analyze and systematize the epistemological assumptions underlying IS research. We demonstrate the application of the framework on a special concept (the consensus-orientated approach) of conceptual modeling.

Keywords: IS development, IS research, conceptual modeling, epistemological assumptions, epistemological framework, consensus-oriented approach.

1 Introduction

Information systems (IS) research today already takes places in an international and also multi-disciplinary context. But the (mostly implicit) epistemological assumptions which underlie different research approaches may vary deeply due to the disciplinary and national background of the researchers [34]. E. g., cross-continental comparison between European and North American IS journals shows that the European ones are more receptive to interpretive approaches while North American journals tend to be positivist [11]. Against the background of distinct hidden (epistemological) assumptions, working on the same research topic or studying the same phenomenon of interest [52] does not necessarily mean that mutual understanding prevails. "An important skill we need to develop as researchers is an ability to reflect on, to understand, to evaluate, and to see the interrelationships among the deep assumptions that underlie our work." [53] In this respect, the discussion of epistemological assumptions of IS research is almost mandatory. Nevertheless, the lack of epistemological funding of IS research methods is apparent and discussed extensively

K.-D. Althoff et al. (Eds.): WM 2005, LNAI 3782, pp. 635 – 646, 2005.

within the discipline [33]. The discussion of epistemological assumptions in IS research requires a high degree of systematization.

Within the IS research discipline, conceptual modeling is widely discussed by all epistemological doctrines which are most relevant in the IS field, such as positivism and interpretivism [11]. Conceptual models are regarded as design artifacts which are result of a design science research process [21]. Design artefacts are supposed to deliver value by being applied to a problem situation. Conceptual modeling is a commonly accepted approach to overcome the communicational problem between information system designers and business personnel [51]. Sharing the (modeling) language will lead to shared domain knowledge because interdisciplinary organizational members have the means to communicate. A shared domain knowledge between business personnel and information system designers, positively influences the alignment of business and IT objectives and therefore enhances the quality of IT design artefacts [37]. Hence, in a business situation in practice, conceptual modeling gives a significant value to the quality and usability of information systems.

The aim of this article is to provide a framework which can be used to analyze and systematize the epistemological assumptions underlying IS research (section 2). The framework consists of five epistemological questions and the debate of selected possible answers to each question. We use the framework to explicit the basic epistemological assumptions of a consensus-oriented interpretivist approach to conceptual modeling (also referred to as consensus-oriented approach). The consensus-oriented approach is standing in the tradition of the so-called critical linguistic approach [24], [25], which is also referenced from other related approaches to conception modeling [32], [35], [54]. In section 4, we will draw conclusions and suggest possible future research.

2 Epistemological Framework

The discussion of epistemological questions must, at least presently, be considered as an open issue. For this reason, no theory based on a philosophy of science can be considered as binding for researchers. The individual selection, however, necessitates the extensive publication of the epistemological assumptions made by (individual) researchers. Here, basic epistemological questions can be differentiated from one another. Therefore, in a first step, we discuss what epistemology means, what the main relevant epistemological aspects in the field of MIS (management information systems) development are supposed to be, and how different epistemological schools approach these aspects. In this section we thus will present an epistemological framework that consists of five questions each addressing one core epistemological aspect.

Epistemology can be understood as the science of analyzing the way human beings (researchers in this case) grasp knowledge about what is (perceived to be) existing [8]. It addresses the question of how a person can come to true cognition. Hence, epistemology comprises assorted aspects (cp. Figure 1) which will be addressed ensuingly in detail.

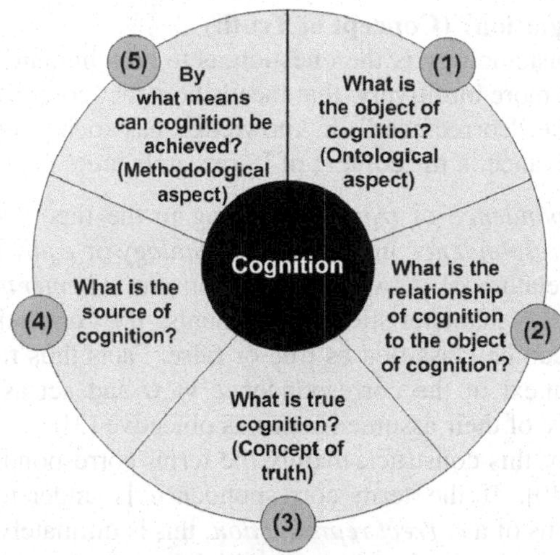

Fig. 1. Epistemological Framework

1) What Is the Object of Cognition? (Ontological Aspect)

Ontology is the science, the theory or the analysis or investigation of 'what is' and 'how it is' [49]. In the context of this epistemological analysis, ontology reveals its relevance in that objects are analyzed, to which the process of cognition refers. The process deals with the question of the way reality exists beyond the realms of pure imagination of the subject [7], [55], [70].

a. If the researcher assumes a real world in his investigation, a world that exists independently of cognition, i. e. independent of thought and speech processes, he thus assumes the position of *(ontological) realism.*
b. If the researcher negates the existence of a real world independent of human thinking and speech, that is, if he perceives reality as a construct dependent on human consciousness, he thus assumes the position of *(ontological) idealism.*

2) What Is the Relationship Between Cognition and the Object of Cognition?

This epistemological question, which is often regarded as central, is about the relationship of cognition obtained by the subject to the object of cognition. The point is whether things beyond human thoughts and speech can at least in principle be recognized as objective. Two possible answers to this question can be differentiated according to their basic notions:

a. In *epistemological realism*, the objective cognition of an independent reality is possible. It claims the possibility of eliminating subject-dependent distortions of the cognition of reality, as soon as suitable measures for the removal of appropriate intervening variables are found [30].
b. The understanding of cognition in *constructivism* is subjective, i. e. „private" [16], [17]. The relationship of cognition and the object of cognition is thus determined clearly by the identifiable subject [31], [56].

3) What is True Cognition? (Concept of Truth)

A central topic of epistemology is the question as to how humans can achieve "true" cognition. Expressed more intuitively, that means how far "correct" knowledge can be obtained and how the "correctness" of knowledge has to be verified. Approaches, which yield high relevance in the context of IS research, are:

a. *Theory of correspondence of truth.* According to the theory of correspondence, truth causes a *correspondence* in terms of an *analogy* or *equivalence* between two relata. The first relatum of a two-digit relation are *statements*. The capacity for truth determines the characteristic of statements. By correlating statements and facts, the former can be classified as true or false. Facts thus represent the second relatum in the context of the correspondence view and act as *truth inducers* for statements, because of their assumed status as objective [3].

   In the context of this construct, mainly the terms correspondence and fact, pose problems [27], [40]. If the term correspondence is understood as *analogy* or *equivalence* in terms of a *correct reproduction*, this is ultimately nothing other than rephrasing of truth, the explanation of which should have been object of the investigation. The solution to this problem can be found in the operationalization of the term correspondence from Wittgenstein, designated as *image theory* (cp. [55]; a reconstruction in [44]; a related theory in [39]). Image theory links the correspondence to two conditions:

   i. The elements of a statement represent appropriate, corresponding, elements of a fact (*semantic condition*).
   ii. The elements of a statement are arranged between each other as the elements of a fact (*condition of structural consistency*).

   This deconstruction of the correspondence term, presents another problem: the likewise unclear term *structural identity*, cannot be perfectly and accurately defined. Thus, image theory creates the dilemma, that it either requires the term *truth* to be clarified or that it is substituted with the less clear term *structural identity* [3].

b. *Consensus theory of truth.* The consensus theory of truth is a social variant of the epistemic truth concept. In its elemental form, truth results from the consensus of everyone [2], [3], [19]:

   i. *A statement is true if, and only if, it is rationally acceptable for everyone under ideal and optimal conditions.*

   A variant of this thought can be, for example, that the range of truth is reduced. No longer is everyone then required for the consensus on the truth or falseness of a statement, only a group of a certain size. With this understanding, statements about truth are thus always to be understood relative to a group. The reference to rationality could also be dropped. To what extent the group now accepts the statements and what the sources of cognition are (from which the acceptance of the statement arises) remains intentionally open. A concept of the consensus theory of truth, altered to this effect, might be:

   ii. *A statement is true (for a group), if and only if, it is acceptable under ideal and optimal conditions for the group.*

This concept of truth implies that nothing exists or proves to be relevant in the context of a test of truth, which would not be apparent to the community/group doing the perceiving. Within the search for consensus and truth, the existence of facts and things which are independent from thought and speech of the subject striving for cognition, are not necessary conditions.

c. *Tarski's concept of truth.* Tarski's so-called *semantic theory of truth* suggests an alternative comprehension of truth and is greatly discussed in the literature. This theory achieves clarity and precision of argumentation by using the compact instrument of modern semantics. Regarding the following remarks on the semantic theory of truth, see [46], [47], [48] as well as [3], [18], [27], [41]. The attempt to enlarge Tarski's concept of truth beyond formalised languages can be found in [13].

Tarski's vision of truth is based to a large degree on linguistics. Thus, truth (T) is determined in terms of Tarski's semantic concept as follows. It applies to: s, L and p:

(T) *„s" is a true sentence of the object language L, if it applies: p*
s: *The statement of the object language, whose validity has to be proven*
L: *object language, which expresses the statement, whose validity has to be proven*
p: *translation of the object language based statement "s" into the meta language M*
M: *meta language, which contains predicates of truth regarding object language based statements*

Thus, the differentiation between object language and meta language is significant. Basically, the object language and meta language must be different from one another. In fact, a language can contain predicates of truth, their application area, though, has to be limited to other languages. Further it becomes clear that truth always refers to a language, the object language, and thus can only be understood as relative linguistic truth.

Tarski does not define the term truth. With his semantic theory of truth he rather expresses a condition for appropriateness, which represents the necessary requirement of a definition of the term truth [3]. He transfers the predicate of truth to the meta language and thus relocates the problem of comprehension of truth into the linguistic area. This limits the scope of application of the theory considerably on the one hand, but on the other hand, the problem of reference to facts or other objects outside the language, does not apply.

4) Where Does Cognition Derive from? (Source of the Cognition Capability)

The question as to the origins of cognition, relates to positions regarding the fundamental capability to perceive. In the context of IS research the relevance of this question becomes clear if formulated as: where does our knowledge derive from?

a. Experience is regarded as one source of knowledge (impressions of senses). Experience-based knowledge is called *a posteriori* or *empirical knowledge* [1]. The assumption of this source of cognition is often oriented towards natural science theory and practical experience and is represented by the school of *empirism* [5], [9], [10], [23], [29], [36].

b. Intellect can also be assumed as a source of cognition. An object can become a matter of cognition through the conceptual efforts of the subject, in turn through the use of a differentiation system. Non-experience-based knowledge is referred to as a priori knowledge. The assumption of intellect as source of cognition is represented by supporters of rationalism, often also known as apriorism [6], [12], [14], [20], [28], [43].
c. Conciliating positions recognise both experience and intellect as sources of cognition. According to Kant, none of these features has to be preferred to another. Without a sensory element, no object would be given, and without intellect, no one perceived. Thoughts are meaningless without content, cognitions are blind without being linked to terms. Thus it is also necessary as well, to make ones terms sensory [26].

5) By What Means Can Cognition Be Achieved? (Methodological Aspect)

The methodological aspect of epistemology deals with the question as to how humans perceive. This question addresses the modes which are considered to be valid for acquiring knowledge within an IS research process.

a. Cognition can be obtained *inductively* on the one hand. Induction is understood as the extension from individual cases to universal phrases [42], the generalisation. An inductive conclusion means the transfer from statements via (observed, empirical) individual cases to a universal law a statement on the basis of an assumption of homogeneity on nature [38]. It is an a posteriori method which is often applied in the natural sciences.
b. On the other hand, cognition can be acquired through a *deductive* method. Deduction is seen as the derivation of a statement (thesis A) from other statements (hypothesis A_1, …, A_n) with the help of logical conclusions [15]. It is the derivation of the individual from the universal and is applied, for example, in mathematical axiom systems.

The presented set of questions forms the basis for an epistemological discussion of research approaches (especially in the field of conceptual modeling and MIS development) and offers the chance to support a comprehensive comparison of particular assumptions made. Where appropriate, this list of questions should be extended to additional issues (e. g., linguistic aspects).[1] Furthermore, we only addressed selected epistemological schools. In certain cases, it surely is useful to address more or different ones (e. g., coherence theory of truth, hermeneutics, or phenomenology). The selection here is based on a comprehensive literature review – especially in the information systems field and in general philosophy.

---

[1] The answers to the questions comprised by the epistemological framework are very much interdependent. E. g., the assumption of the possibility of objective cognition (epistemological realism; question 2, a) is necessarily linked with the assumption of the existence of an objective world that is independent of human consciousness (question 1, a) [11], [22].

3 The Consensus-Oriented Approach to Conceptual Modeling

Here, our concept of conceptual modeling is based on the consensus-oriented approach coined from the work of Kamlah and Lorenzen [25]. Figure 2 provides an overview of its most important elements and their dependencies. At first, the approach aims to create a linguistic community. Against the background of IS-development, this community facilitates information system designers and business personnel to overcome communicational problems [51].

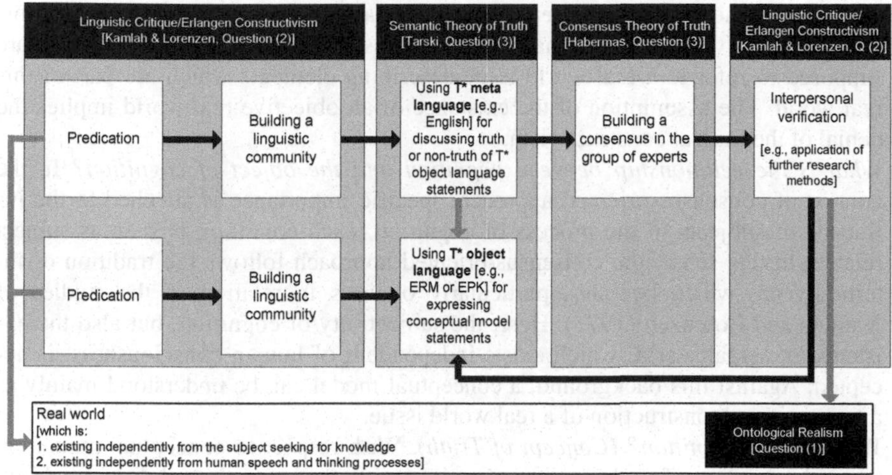

Fig. 2. Elements of the consensus-oriented approach and their dependencies

Linguistic communities can be created through the (re)construction of an ortho-language. First parts of the language can be formed by the alignment of individual (real world) objects to nominators. In the context of IS-development important nominators are terms such as 'customer Meier', 'product 4711' etc. Based on nominators, predicators (in our context e. g. 'customer' and 'product') are introduced in order to expose and communicate similarities of individual objects.

Following Tarski the creation of the linguistic community takes place on two levels. On the first level (here named *T* object language*) conceptual model statements are expressed. E. g. using Entity Relationship Models (ERM) members of the linguistic community have to agree upon the term 'entity type'; in the case of Event Driven Process Chains (EPC) they have to agree upon the term 'event'. Moreover, a distinction between a) the language of model instances and b) the language of the modeling method and technique has to be made. On the second level (here named T* meta language)[2] members of the community have to agree on a language which facilitates them to debate about the truth and nontruth of the statements represented in a model

[2] We use the term T* meta language in order to distinguish them from linguistic-based meta languages that are documented in linguistic-based meta models [45], which describe the language that underlies a modeling technique or method.

(e. g. German or English). In the next step, the meta language T* is used to discuss the modeling system which is formulated on the first level using the T* object language until a consensus of a group of experts is achieved. Afterwards, the results can be evaluated within the scope of the interpersonal verification [25]. Here, research methods such as field experiments, surveys, case studies or action research can be applied. Based on these results a revision of the conceptual model may be required.

From the perspective of the framework presented in Section 2 this approach results in the following epistemological positions:

1. *What is the object of cognition? (Ontological aspect).* The existence of a (real) world is assumed, which is independent of human thoughts and speech and for this reason exists even beyond human consciousness. Conceptual models therefore are supposed to refer to a real world issue describing elements which are part of this real world. The assumption of the existence of an objective real world implies the denial of the radical constructivism.
2. *What is the relationship between cognition and the object of cognition?* In the context of consensus-oriented approach, specific importance is attached to the influence of subjects in the process of cognition: each cognition is seen as subject related. In this sense, the consensus-oriented approach follows the tradition of interpretivism, which becomes particularly obvious in relation to the studies of Kamlah and Lorenzen (1973). Here, the subjectivity of cognition, but also the existence of a real world, which exists independent of human consciousness, is accepted. Against this background, a conceptual model can be understood mainly as a linguistic (re)construction of a real world issue.
3. *What is true cognition? (Concept of Truth).* With respect to conceptual modeling, the understanding of truth is relevant mainly with respect to the validity, reliability and "quality" of conceptual model statements.

   With the *semantic theory of truth*, Tarski develops a concept of truth, which is always relative to a language (object language). Simultaneously, the existence of a meta language is assumed, which contains the predicates of truth about statements of the object language. In this context, both languages ultimately emerge in linguistic communities.

   On the other hand, the consensus theory of truth confirms that a statement is true if and only if it's rationally acceptable to everyone under ideal and optimal conditions. In a modified version, this means that (for a group), a statement is true if and only if it's acceptable to the group. It becomes apparent that, both in the context of the semantic theory of truth and in the context of the consensus theory, that truth is regarded as relative. In the first case, truth is relative to the language in which the statement to be confirmed, is made. The languages which are to be applied for determining the truth, are ultimately the property of a *linguistic community* [25]. In the second case, truth is relative to the community in which consensus was obtained about the truth or non-truth of a statement. The foundation of this truth verification is ultimately the exchange of speech artifacts. Accordingly, finding a consensus within a group requires the existence of a *linguistic community* as well.

   In the context of *consensus-oriented approach* to conceptual modeling it should be assumed that truth emerges through the consensus of a linguistic community. Truth is thus regarded as relative to a language (semantic theory of truth) and relative towards a group (consensus theory of truth), in this case to a linguistic community. According to the consensus theory of truth [2], [3], [19], a statement is true if, and only if, it is acceptable for everyone. Focusing certain business problems and IS solutions suggests, that the reduction of "everyone" to a group of smaller size is permitted. In this context, the concept of the consensus theory of truth, altered to this effect, might be: A statement is true (for a group), if and only if, it is acceptable for the group. This implies that truth is relative to the group in which consensus was obtained about the truth or non-truth of a certain statement. In order to express the statements within conceptual models [50] several modeling languages can be used, e. g. ERM or eEPC. By this means, models can be used as a formalized way of stating the consensus. Here, the formalized modeling language functions as an object-language (L). Natural language, e. g. English, can be used to discuss whether the statements within a conceptual information model are "correct". Hereby, it contains the predicates of truth regarding the object-language based statements and poses as a meta-language (M). Both languages are thus comprised by the linguistic community.

4. *Where does cognition derive from? (Source of the cognition capability).* Both empirical statements [25] and a priori statements can be made, which may form the basis of conceptual models. Conceptual modeling therefore derives its results via theoretical reflection of the model contents, as well as from the implementation of the model in information systems and through observation.
5. *How does cognition emerge? (Methodological aspect).* Conceptual models are one form of artefacts of a formalized language and can contain both empirical and a priori knowledge. Both inductive and deductive conclusions can be accessed firstly in the context of the model creation and secondly in the context of truth verification.

   If in the context of *model creation*, single statements are generalized on the basis of a set of individual tests, for example in the context of reference modeling, the relevant process is that of induction [4]. Creating an information model can, however, can be achieved deductively as well, for example by attaching object-class-specific attributes to model elements on the basis of their linkage to certain object classes.

   Truth verification is based on the procedure of interpersonal verification [24], [25]. The formalized linguistic statements contained in a conceptual model are logically decomposed (deduction) until they are accessible as elemental statements for purposes of truth verification. This takes place by means of a group of experts who obtain a consensus. The main instruments are observation, experiments, interviewing and the interpretation of texts [25]. The validity of statements in the model can be confirmed, for example, in the case of business specific models, with a single case. In case of a pattern or reference model, however, the generalized abstraction of different individual verifications (induction) is necessary. This means that in the context of the procedure of interpersonal verification, additional, mainly empirical research methods are used.

Thus, consensus-oriented approach is characterized by an interpretivist position, which is mainly coloured by the critical linguistic approach of [24]. The information models developed contain formalized linguistic statements to be tested for validity in combination with additional (empirical) research methods. This is done through members of a linguistic community in order to obtain consensus. Therefore, elements of the semantic theory of truth and the consensus theory of truth are considered and used.

With the help of this instance, we demonstrated how the epistemological framework developed in section 3 can be applied for discussion the epistemological assumptions of certain research paradigms and research approaches. Especially regarding the discussion of the concept of truth (question 3), we analyzed the interdependencies in between specific answers to this question, namely the semantic theory of truth and the consensus theory of truth.

4 Conclusions and Future Research

IS research takes place in a multi-disciplinary and international context. As a consequence, the IS field can be described as a rich tapestry of different methodological approaches. Therefore, we developed an epistemological framework for systematically analyzing epistemological assumptions of different research approaches. The framework consists of five questions which are addressing different epistemological aspects appearing most relevant in the context of IS research. By offering a critical perspective on multi-disciplinary and international IS research, the chosen systematization tries to give new impulse to the theoretical discussion distinct research paradigms and approaches.

Furthermore, the epistemological framework was applied to the consensus-oriented interpretivist approach to conceptual modeling. Interdependencies between distinct epistemological theories, namely the semantic theory of truth and the consensus theory of truth, have been discussed intensively. For future research, the discussion of interdependencies between certain epistemological questions and answers has to be carried out in greater extend. Here, a differentiation of distinct types of relations / interdependences – such as '*logically necessary*', '*product of the historical philosophical debate*' or '*can be found in most dominant epistemological paradigms*' – can be very helpful.

Additionally, the analysis of the consequences of epistemological assumptions on research evaluation is of great magnitude. In the current IS literature, several approaches can be found which discuss guidelines for good IS research. But the discussion of epistemological aspects often runs too short. E. g., the assumption of the subject having great influence on the research process reveals great relevance for the validity of research results. In addition to the traditional validity criteria (coined by a positivist paradigm) – such as retrospective, prospective, and structural validity – the idea of an interpersonal validity ought to be debated. The discussion of research rigor is also very much affected by this issue.

References

1. Alavi, M.; Carlson, P.; Brooke, G.: The Ecology of MIS Research: A Twenty Year Status Review. 10th International Conference on Information Systems (ICIS), Boston, MA, (1989) 363-375
2. Apel, K.-O.: Towards a Transformation of Philosophy. Routledge Kegan & Paul, London (1979)
3. Baumann, P.: Erkenntnistheorie. Metzler, Stuttgart/Weimar (2002)

4. Becker, J.; Schütte, R.: Handelsinformationssysteme. Landsberg/Lech (1996)
5. Berkley, G.: Philosophical Works. London (1975)
6. Bonjour, L.: In Defense of Pure Reason: A Rationalists Account of A Priori Justification. Cambridge/MA (1998)
7. Bunge, M. A.: Ontology I: The Furniture of the World. Treatise on Basic Philosophy. Dordrecht, the Netherlands et al. (1977)
8. Burrell, G.; Morgan, G.: Sociological Paradigms and Organizational Analysis. London, UK (1979)
9. Carnap, R.: The Logical Structure of the World and Pseudoproblems in Philosophy. Open Court Publishing Company, Chicago (2003)
10. Carnap, R.; Hahn, H.; Neurath, O.: Wissenschaftliche Weltauffassung: Der Wiener Kreis. Vienna/New York (1929)
11. Chen, W.; Hirschheim, R.: A paradigmatic and methodological examination of information systems research from 1991 to 2001. Information Systems Journal 3 (2004) 197-235
12. Chomsky, N.: Aspects of the Theory of Syntax. Cambridge/MA (1965)
13. Davidson, J.: Inquiries Into Truth and Interpretation. Oxford (1984)
14. Descartes, R.: Meditations on First Philosophy : With Selections from the Objections and Replies. Cambridge University Press, Cambridge (1996)
15. Gethmann, C. F.: Deduktion. In: Mittelstraß, J. (ed.): Enzyklopädie Philosophie und Wissenschaftstheorie. Band 1. Stuttgart, Weimar (1995)
16. Glasersfeld, E.: Steps in the Construction of "Others" and "Reality": A Study in Self-Regulation. In: Trappl, R. (ed.): Power, Autonomy, Utopia. London, New York 1986 107–116
17. Glasersfeld, E.: The Construction of Knowledge. Seaside/CA (1987)
18. Haak, S.: Philosophy of Logics. Cambridge/MA (1978)
19. Habermas, J.: Wahrheitstheorien. In: Fahrenbach, H. (ed.): Wirklichkeit und Reflexion. Walter Schulz zum 60. Geburtstag. Pfullingen (1973) 211-265
20. Hanson, P.; Hunter, B.: Return of the A Priori. University of Calgary Press, Calgary/Alberta (1992)
21. Hevner, A. R. et al.: Design Science in Information Systems Research. MIS Quarterly 1 (2004) 75-105
22. Hirschheim, R.; Klein, H. K.: Four Paradigms of Information Systems Development. Communications of the ACM (1989) 1199-1216
23. Hume, D.: A Treatise of Human Nature. Oxford (1978)
24. Kamlah, W.; Lorenzen, P.: Logical Propaedeutic. Lanham/MD (1973)
25. Kamlah, W.; Lorenzen, P.: Logische Propädeutik. Vorschule des vernünftigen Redens. 3. edn. Stuttgart, Weimar (1996)
26. Kant, I.: Critique of Pure Reason. Cambridge University Press, Cambridge (1999)
27. Kirkham, R. L.: Theories of Truth. A Critical Introduction. Cambridge University Press, Cambridge/MA (1992)
28. Leibniz, G.-W.: Nouveaux Essais sur l'Entendement Humain. In: Leibniz, G.-W. (eds.): Sämtliche Schriften. Berlin (1962) 39-527
29. Locke, J.: An Essay Concerning Human Understanding. Oxford (1982)
30. Loose, J.: A Historical Introduction to the Philosophy of Science. Oxford University Press, New York (1972)
31. Lorenzen, P.: Constructive Philosophy. The University of Massachusetts Press, Amherst, MA, USA (1987)

32. Luft, A. L.: Software-Engineering und konstruktive Wissenschaftstheorie. Ein Beitrag zur Methodologie des Software Engineering. Angewandte Informatik 3 (1981) 93-99
33. Mingers, J.: Combining IS research methods: towards a pluralist methodology. Information Systems Research (2001) 240-259
34. Orlikowski, W. J.; Baroudi, J.: Studying information technology in organizations: research approaches and assumptions. Information Systems Research (1991) 1-28
35. Ortner, E.: Methodenneutraler Fachentwurf. Stuttgart, Leipzig (1997)
36. Quine, W. V. O.: Two Dogmas of Empiricism. In: Quine, W. V. O. (ed.): From a Logical Point of View. Cambridge University Press, Cambridge/MA 1961 20-46
37. Reich, B. H.; Benbasat, I.: Factors That Influence the Social Dimension of Alignment between Business and Information Technology Objectives. MIS Quarterly 1 (2000) 81-113
38. Rott, H.: Schluß, induktiver. In: Mittelstraß, J. (ed.): Enzyklopädie Philosophie und Wissenschaftstheorie. Band 3. Stuttgart, Weimar 1995 710-713
39. Russell, B.: The Philosophy of Logical Atomism. In: Russell, B. (ed.): Logic and Knowledge. Essays 1901-1950. London 1956 177-281
40. Schmitt, F. F.: Socializing Epistemology. The Social Dimension of Knowledge. Lanham/MD (1994)
41. Schmitt, F. F.: Truth. A Primer. Westview Press, Boulder/CO (1995)
42. Seiffert, H.: Einführung in die Wissenschaftstheorie 1. 12. edn. München (1996)
43. Spinoza, B.: The Ethics ; Treatise on the Emendation of the Intellect ; Selected Letters. Hackett Publishing Company, Indianapolis/IN (1992)
44. Stenius, E.: Wittgenstein's Tractatus: A Critical Exposition of its Main Lines of Thought. Oxford (1960)
45. Strahringer, S.: Metamodellierung als Instrument des Methodenvergleichs – Eine Evaluierung am Beispiel objektorientierter Analysemethoden. Aachen (1996)
46. Tarski, A.: The Semantic Concept of Truth and the foundation of semantics. Philosophy and Phenomenological Research (1944) 341-375
47. Tarski, A.: The Concept of Truth in Formalized Languages. In: Tarski, A. (eds.): Logic, Semantics, Mathematics. Papers from 1923 to 1938. Oxford (1956) 152-278
48. Tarski, A.: Truth and Proof. In: Hughes, R. I. G. (eds.): A Philosophical Companion to First-Order-Logic. Indianapolis/IN 1993 101-125
49. von Foerster, H.: Wissen und Gewissen. Versuch einer Brücke. 4. edn. Frankfurt a. M. (1996)
50. Wand, Y.; Weber, R.: Research Commentary: Information Systems and Conceptual Modeling – A Research Agenda. Information Systems Research 4 (2002) 363-376
51. Wand, Y.; Weber, R.: Research Commentary: Information Systems and Conceptual Modeling – A Research Agenda. Journal of Information Systems 2 (2002) 217-237
52. Weber, R.: Editor's Comment: Theoretically Speaking. MIS Quarterly 3 (2003) iii-xii
53. Weber, R.: The Refelexive Researcher. MIS Quarterly 4 (2003) v-xiv
54. Wedekind, H.: Datenbanksysteme I, Eine konstruktive Einführung in die Datenverarbeitung in Wirtschaft und Verwaltung. 2. edn. Mannheim et al. (1981)
55. Wittgenstein, L.: Tractatus Logico Philosophicus. Routledge, London (2001)
56. Wyssusek, B.; Schwartz, M.: Towards a Sociopragmatic-Constructivist Understanding of Information Systems. In: Gordon, S. R. (ed.): Computing Information Technology: The Human Side. Idea Group Publishing, Hershey et al. (2003) 267–297

Collecting or *Classifying*?

Francis Rousseaux[1] and Thomas Bouaziz[2]

[1] IRCAM, Centre Pompidou,
1, place Igor Stravinski, 75004 Paris
francis.rousseaux@ircam.fr
[2] ExperiensS,
36, rue Voltaire, 78500 Sartrouville
thomas.bouaziz@experienss.org

Abstract. Informatics and AI claim, at least implicitly, that the world is made of objects organized into classes (taxonomies, ontologies...). In this paper, we explore another idea: we structure our material relationships by collecting objects within collections, which are never as static as classes. The notion of collection will appear as an efficient way to articulate organic life and conceptual life throughout a metastable equilibrium, more promising than the intensive categorization traditionaly made in informatics, as far as depicting and managing human experience is concerned.

1 Introduction

At the beginning of *La Symphonie Pastorale* by André Gide, the good pastor, having taken in Gertrude, tries to reassure his spouse, whose anxiety is premonitory. He justifies his remarkable interest for the young blind by the particular devotion due to those secluded in infirmity. When later his wife wonders how the pastor comes to neglect even his own children, he claims to be following the Gospel according to Matthieu, which says that "every sheep of the flock, taken separately, is in the eyes of the shepherd more precious than the rest of the flock taken together".

But can a shepherd set aside a sheep that he already keeps away from the herd, to take even better care of her in the following days? Isn't the shepherd already unable to see the rest of the herd otherwise than as a petrified whole? It must be said that Mathieu's metaphor says nothing about selecting the privileged sheep... Thus the love of the pastor for Gertrude grows inexorably, soon conflicting with the legal categories that allowed their meeting: evangelical devotion, conjugal fidelity, filial tenderness, or religious dogma. The promising metaphor of the herd "which sheep are all more precious than the rest of the herd" did not last long. As if Gide wanted to show that no operational fiction, as subtle or as sophisticated as it may be, cannot hold out long against reality, which breaks apart any middle ground under the violent tension of two attractive poles: the forced singularity of an always immediate actual experience (described by Gide as love), and the compulsively re-arranged order of conceptual categories,

K.-D. Althoff et al. (Eds.): WM 2005, LNAI 3782, pp. 647–656, 2005.

which is always local, and which figures in *La Symphonie Pastorale* as moral and spiritual engagement. Is this audacious tentative to articulate organic life to intellectual and spiritual life, by a figure irreducible to the one and to the other, definitely presumptuous and vain?

Today's informatics and AI rely on an implicit epistemology, whose axioms establish that the world is made of objects, that we can categorize those objects into classes, and structure their field of interaction into ontologies, taxonomies, semantic networks... But how far can this knowledge engineering transcribe reality as experienced by human beings? Can an extreme and systematic categorization translate and convey feelings? A computer system could describe a lady in this way: "The woman had brown hair. She had blue eyes. She was 1.73m tall. etc. etc. ". But will a novelist use such a process if he tries to depict beauty, charm, love at first sight? An exhaustive, straight to the point categorization of each and every property of the character would bury any tiny little flame of all the magic the scene is based on. Obviously, doing without the organic reflection of life isn't satisfactory.

But is this audacious tentative to articulate organic life to intellectual and spiritual life, by a figure irreducible to the one and to the other, definitely presumptuous and vain?

From here, I will call collection this specific figure, which the present article means to study. We will show that:

1. This acceptation of the word collection is close to its usual meaning;
2. That a collection differs from the notions of ensemble, class, series, set, group, or clutter but also from that of organic whole or family;
3. That a collection is the institution of a metastable equilibrium between singularity and category, just as other concurrent fictions such as fashion, crises, choreographies, plans, liturgical cycles, scientific projects, or instrumental gestures.

2 Jorge – Reconstitution of an Initiatory Meeting

My meeting with Jorge Helft last spring in Buenos Aires is not foreign to my interest for the collectors' posture. I had met Jorge in Paris, after we had translated together one of Borges' poems. Jorge had talked to me in great length about his meetings with the author of *A History of Eternity* and in the end, he had invited me to see his Borges collection in Argentina.

The profusion of artworks displayed at Jorge's remind me of Gérard Wajcman's analyses (page 89 of the *Catalogue de l'exposition inaugurale de la Maison rouge*) on the status of excess in collections:

> "Excess in collections does not mean disordered accumulation; it is a constitutive principle: for a collection to exist – in the eyes of the collector himself – the number of works has to be greater than the number than can be presented and stored at the collector's home. Therefore someone who lives in a studio can very well have a collection: he only needs to have

> one piece that cannot be hanged in his studio. That is why the reserves are an integral part of a collection. Excess can also be noted at the level of the memorizing capacities: for a collection to exist, the collector just needs to be unable to remember all the artworks he possesses. The collector should not completely be the master of his collection".

As he invited people to dinners, famous or unknown artists, actors of the political or cultural scene and personal friends, Jorge enabled the artists to become known to the people who could help them professionally, therefore making his reputation stronger on the arts scene, as well as making his collection more valuable, and bringing himself closer to the pieces that were being created.

Later, I understood Wajcman better, when he writes that "collecting implies in itself a responsibility towards the artist. Among collectors, it is a common trait that buying a piece of art from someone means accepting responsibility for this artist." Under my eyes, from being a collector-seeker (hunter), Jorge became a collector-finder (fisherman), and to this end was developing his own reticular logistics, throwing nets, constituting a network. "The scene of a collector is not his own apartment, it's the world. The main part of his collection is not at his place – his collection is to be, still scattered across the world, and every gallery and every fair is a way for him to go and find his future collection" ([7], page 29).

With his Borges collection, Jorge had soon become the best collector of the world on this topic; who could have found it worth it to be his competitor? People from around the world told him when an interesting piece became available... and sometimes a famous American university made him an offer for his whole collection.

I was so fascinated by collectors by then that I asked Jorge if I could interview him on the topic. He told me about his hunt for works, the places where he lives haunted by artworks, the intimate ritual that he sometimes establishes with the artworks, the danger that one piece may abolish another, or the whole collection, but also his vision of the collection as an artwork in itself, or the impossibility that he would ever give away his entire collection in exchange for a singular work of art – unlike the pastor in love with Gertrude.

A collection is far from a simple juxtaposition or reunion of individual elements. It is primarily a temporary correlate of an initiatory ritual made sacred by time. Adding works, or revisiting a collection keeps alterating and re-constituting it, leaving it always halfway between the original series of juxtaposed intimate moments and a permanently organized class of objects.

Unlike an organic whole, a collection only exists for each of its parts, and unlike an ensemble, it does not exist as a normative or equalizing unity; it is productive if in tension between singularities and categorical structure.

Collecting is creating an artwork with artworks, hence the ultimate dream of collectors to bequeath their collection as foundations, in the hope that they could be baptized "Collection of Mr. X" ([7], page 38). Indeed, we can very well consider a collection as a work of art (Jorge confesses he dislikes the label:

he finds it too pretentious). Marcel Duchamp said that anything can be looked upon as art, providing it is put into a situation of art. Last year, an exhibition space was inaugurated in Paris, called *la Maison Rouge* ("the Red House"). In each room of that house, collections are exposed the very same way they are usually arranged in their owner's intimate environment. In a way, *la Maison Rouge* makes a collection out of collections; collections are received and shown as works of art.

3 Apostoli – Inaugurating a Collection

My career as an art collector was inaugurated a few weeks ago, by acquiring two paintings from a young Greek artist of Albanian background that I met on the island of Hydra the day of my arrival. I did not spend a day there without going to his home to see a number of paintings that he set in sequence on a large easel, light by the Mediterranean light, and perfumed by jasmine and bay trees.

The liturgy of looking at paintings was greatly facilitated when I accepted the invitation to stay at his place. As Gérard Wajcman writes, thinking probably of Gertrude Stein ([7], page 28), "If nobody ever looks at "a collection", it is because it is not a collection of artworks, but an indefinite series of singular objects, an artwork + another artwork + another artwork..." Apostoli handled the artworks with a musical and ritual precision, careful that each painting was shown only when needed and only when the specific occasion allowed it to be understood. For the artist, the collection of his own works is like Mattthieu's herd: "Every painting on the easel, taken separately, is more precious to the painter than the rest of his collection". But in that case, the election of the next painting to be presented was naturally prescribed par the exhibit/procession, series were never set a priori, and a specific painting never made us forget the rest of the collection.

So Apostoli is in love with his collection, only when he confronts his works one by one, as he is reconstituting his collection, which he does wishing for the next piece of art. When no sheep is set apart, the pastor is more concerned with the future sheep, the one that will join the herd and alter it. The collector, at this point, is interested about what his collection lacks, about its virtual development. Gide's pastor might have overlooked this crucial point: the biblical pastor must live his mission as an apostolic mission, his ultimate goal is to win new disciples by converting them.

When I was about to leave Apostoli, I bought two large paintings from him, and thus started the fantastic epic necessary to bring them back to France. My impressive "hand luggage" was finally flown in the baggage hold, and the paintings were finally safely hanged in my apartment.

Selling these paintings stimulated Apostoli in two ways: It encouraged him to develop an artistic life in France, first by planning an exhibit in Paris. It also stimulated him to paint the painful absence of these two paintings and thus create a new one. As for myself, I felt I was becoming a collector.

4 Jorge and Apostoli – Recollection

Meeting Jorge and Apostoli revealed a key to collections, that is the initiatory ritual built as constitution and differential reconstitutions go along. From this point, the collector matches the artist as a creator himself.

I understood that it is through the repetition of intimate lived moments that a collection is created. By this gesture is instituted not only the same, which unifies the collection through the similarities supposedly going through the collected objects, but also the object nature of the specific things that constitute the collection. Collecting is therefore part of an initiatory journey, between what was lived and what can be communicated, and thus becomes a sacred activity, just as creating.

The process of reconstitution regenerates the coherence of the collection. If the reconstitution is not well done, the collection can soon be abandoned, or dispersed. A collection ceases to exist as something else than a mundane correlate as soon as the collector ceases to be interested in its development. Then he stops repeating the acquiring gesture or the reconstituting gesture for himself or his intimate friends. These two gestures have the same meaning. The reconstitution gives better balance to the heavy tendencies of the collection, makes new relationships appear between artworks, and institutes new similarities which later influence the logic of acquisition. New objects become part of the collection as "different", and they become "same" only later, because they have in common to be different, thus being part of what Jean-Claude Milner calls a *paradoxical class*.

It is rather easy to spot individual cases of collections that were abandoned. The collection can also appear to have been a fake. A question was especially obsessing me: can a collection of immediacies be a real collection?

5 Investigation on a Late Vocation

My friends were very surprised when I told them that I was becoming a collector.

It is true that I throw away books that have not made a great impression on me, just as CDs that I do not listen to very often, fearing the intellectual dispersion that the multiplicity of objects inspires me... I wish I could have expressed what I feel when objects, such as gifts, intrude in my environment, as well as Andy Warhol [8], quoted by Jean-Pierre Criqui: "I live completely in the future, for when I eat a box of candies, I cannot wait to eat the last one. I do not even want to try the others, I want to finish all the candy, throw away the box and be done with it."

The doubts expressed by my friends provoked me to think more about my suspicious calling to become a collector. My investigation revealed the following traits, which are far from the best foundations for my sudden passion:

– Probably to be able to collect love stories, I have been engaged for a long time in a collection of immediacies. To establish a relationship of seduction, one needs to appear as a virgin, and therefore needs to carefully get rid of

all compromising objects, which means of all objects, because they are all compromising;
- The posture is self-aggravating: how can someone collect something else than immediacies when one has started to collect immediacies? First of all, it would probably ruin the collection of immediacies and deny it completely: contrary to a mount, a collection only exists and remains through its development dynamics. And secondly, one would have to face the fear of realizing that it would have been better to start collecting long ago what one starts collecting now. The question of the origin of a collection is, indeed, quite delicate; and a collector can still rationalize his nostalgia by recognizing the very decision of collecting being necessary for the determination process of a collection.
- Collecting mundane objects always seemed inelegant to me, and somewhat despising. I felt like the position of the dandy collecting immediacies was very comfortable in that respect. Indeed, a collector always despises somehow what he does not collect. Collecting immediacies was a way to prevent hierarchizing objects.

This investigation brought to light the impossibility of putting an end to a collection of immediacies on the pretext of inaugurating a fake collection of mundane objects. Now, the *reason* for my artwork collection can be found in the following: either Apostoli's paintings oddly came to me and insisted on my starting a collection, or my collection of immediacies had run out of reconstitution.

6 Colligere Humanum Est

To be able to stay entirely within the immediate, intense and intimate present, I thought I could prevent time from constructing itself, by preventing it to lay its foundations anywhere, by killing in the egg any emergence of an embryo of a collection.

My approach was mnemonic, and consisted in constantly collecting immediacies. A collection of immediacies is not really a collection, because among immediacies, the play of differential similarities is hollow and inconsistent. But letting immediacies play, and let their changing relationships fade, seemed like an excellent heuristic to take time off the beat and tire it out: memory without correlates does not allow for a game of reconstitution. I was thus faithful to immediacy, even if it implied avoiding to collect mundane objects. Because collecting, in the sense of reconstituting a collection, as Mathieu elaborates his herd, is an art of time.

The synthetic nature of an ensemble of objects presented to be seen as a collection is different from the nature of the ensemble that is constituted and shown by the collector. Indeed, the collector does not juxtapose objects, he puts together elements of remembrance, to be prompted by objects. Walter Benjamin [1], quoted by Jean-Pierre Criqui writes:

> "Everything that is present to memory, to thought, to consciousness becomes a base, a frame, a pedestal, a casket for the object possessed.

The art of collecting is a form of practical recollection, and, of all the profane manifestations of proximity, it is the most convincing."

The collector experiences his collection as a summary whose process of composition, by arranging "elements of remembrance", he more or less controls; whereas the receiver experiences it either as a group of objects gathered into a disparate juxtaposition, or as an organic whole whose singular unity seems impenetrable.

Thus, the receiver intends to recreate and give a collection value to the arrangement, in other words to penetrate the secret of the collection; and he tries himself to build a collection by giving objects a certain coherence according to his own personal experience.

Here is another thought from Walter Benjamin:

"What is decisive, in the art of collecting, is to free each object from its primitive functions, in order to establish a relationship as close as possible with similar objects. This relationship is diametrically opposed to usefulness, and belongs to the remarkable category of completeness. What is that completeness? An imposing attempt to go beyond the absolutely irrational nature of the simple presence of the object in the world, by integrating it in a new historical system, especially created, that is the collection. The collector's deepest spell consists in shutting the particular thing up in a magical circle where it freezes while a last thrill runs through it [...]."

The same phenomenon actually does occur with isolated objects. The work of art you chose isn't the work of art I receive (gap of reception). But with a collection, there's not only a repetition of this gap, but also the appearance of another one that distinguishes the collection as a "summary peculiar to the collector" from the collection as "an ensemble whose reason remains a secret", as it is received by its visitor (gap of composition).

Here we can't do without thinking about Schloezer's *paradoxical theorem*, reported by Bernard Sève in his work entitled *L'altération musicale* [6]. It deals with music, but the parallel with collections is amazingly relevant. Let us take the time to visit Schloezer thought as exposed in his *Introduction to Jean-Sébastien Bach* [3], inspired by the *Gestaltheorie*.

The author begins by distinguishing three types of systems: mechanical systems, composed systems and organic systems.

Mechanical systems are additive ensembles: they only have an effective, and not legitimate, unity. Their elements are juxtaposed in a pure contingent manner, like objects in an attic or books thrown in a mess onto the floor.

Composed systems obey an abstract and intelligible rule. As in additive ensembles, each and every element exists apart from its belonging to the system: a book found by chance at the bottom of a trunk (additive system) or carefully arranged by a principle of order in a bookcase (composed system), is in itself an element independent from its place in the system. To turn an additive system into a composed system, you just need to have it bound by a system of intelligible rules.

> On the contrary, in an organic system, elements do not pre-exist the structure. The organic order is not an order that would structure them from the outside – as when we choose to arrange books by themes, by chronological order, by alphabetical order, by sizes, or by a combination of all or part of the latter criterions. An element of an organic system is, rather than an element, a part which exists through and for the whole. As a consequence, "the members of an organic whole are themselves organic systems, and not composed systems nor mechanical ensembles".
>
> To Schloezer, a musical work is an organic whole; and it is interesting just as long as it is something beyond a composition in accordance with rules, and it is the invention of an organicity that cannot be reduced to pre-existing rules. Composition obeys a necessity of understanding, and organisation obeys a necessity of sensitivity, a necessity that can be experienced but cannot be proved. Thus we could conclude that the more organic a work is, the more artistic it is; and that masterpieces of musical art are pure organic wholes that owe nothing to composition.
>
> Well, Schloezer's *paradoxical theorem* (the expression is from Bernard Sève) establishes on the contrary that an exclusively organic whole would be impossible to distinguish from an additive whole. Indeed, for the receiver a mechanical whole is a complete mess, but so is the exclusively organic whole; its rule system forms one body with its material in so peculiar a way that there is no possible analogy with any other rule of organisation already known. Pure organicity is not intelligible as such, since its rule of organisation is absolutely idiosyncratic (think about *Métamorphose* by Richard Strauss, for example).
>
> A pure organic system could not be assimilated as such; we could not distinguish it from a mechanical system. The point is that the listener will not be able to get an organic system as such unless it is not only organic but also composed. There is then a necessary tension in the work, between its organic inventiveness and its composition rules. Thus, the musical organic, whose elements are only worth for the whole, can only be interpreted providing it is projected into a composition order.

So is the case when receiving a collection, as soon as we look upon it as the result of a composition, as opposed to a disparate amount of objects or works. In order to assimilate the arrangement as a collection as such, it is necessary to feel the tension between singularities and the categorical structure – even if it has to be penetrated, interpreted by the receiver.

7 *Collections* in Recent Data Mining Tools

7.1 Musical Data Mining – Interactive Collection Development

Recent data-mining tools prove how working with collections is a powerful alternative to a systematic intensive categorization. Two navigation systems through digital databases of musical pieces are worth mentioning.

The first, called LE MUSICOLOGUE [5], was designed and produced by a small team of computer scientists and musicologists between 1987 and 1990. Among other functionalities, one allows a student, who just practiced musical dictation on a particular piece, to be suggested others by the system. The point is to help the student to evolve in a wide digital space in order to buid a collection of exercices, which constitutes his course, and which must be as coherent as possible with his progress. The methods and criterions to evaluate this progress have been designed so that the collection of exercises that is being made up stimulates the interest of the student, is adapted to his current skills, and still offers him motivated choices for orientations.

There are other systems designed to help the listener to build a path/collection through digital musical pieces, with no other aim than the very desire of listening, and its continuation. The *Music Browser* developed within the framework of European project CUIDADO is one of them: this new generation of digital navigation relies on multiple metadata – including cultural, acoustic, editorial aspects... – through which the user is free to travel, as inspired by his whims. The system keeps proposing adapted and varied opportunities of navigation to the listener/collector within the latter aspects, and he remains free to choose the one over which he will exercise control.

7.2 A System of Generation of Collections of Interactions

The system VIRTUALIS is based on the idea that a live show can be looked upon as a collection of interactions, whose mediatization permits opening the performance (in the sense of Umberto Eco). As applied to a play by Geneviève de Gaulle, *La traversée de la nuit* (1998), VIRTUALIS allowed interactive exchanges between a narrator, a dancer, and a neural network that analyses in real-time the voice of the actress. The collection of these interactions is directly mediatized by the synthesis, the animation, and the projection of images on a wide screen in the background of the stage [2].

8 Conclusion: Towards a New Approach in Software Engineering

When Allen Newell wrote his paper *The Knowledge Level* in 1982 [4], he invented a new meaning for knowledge, that allowed computer scientists to think differently the notions of digital document and browsing among content. But the analysis of recent systems, such as those mentioned above, reveals that the *Knowledge* approach is being built down and replaced by a *Collection* approach.

When asked who was intelligent, between man and machines, Newell answered: "Let's make them intelligent together, as a hybrid couple/group/organisation ". Switching to the interactive constitution of collections sounds like a sensible evolution to remain in this perspective.

References

1. Walter Benjamin. *Paris, capitale du XIXe siècle.* 1989.
2. Alain Bonardi and Francis Rousseaux. A style of theater production directly inspired by interactive data mining. In *Proceedings of the AAAI Workshop Style and Meaning in Language, Art, Music and Design*, pages 71–73, 2004.
3. Boris de Schloezer. *Introduction à Jean-Sébastien Bach.* Gallimard, 1947.
4. Allen Newell. The knowledge level. *Artificial Intelligence*, 18:87–127, 2004.
5. Francis Rousseaux. LE MUSICOLOGUE, a learning apprentice system for music education. *Artificial Intelligence & Music, IJCAI*, août 1989.
6. Bernard Sève. *L'altération musicale.* Seuil poétique, 2002.
7. Gérard Wajcman. *Collection.* Nous Paris, 1999.
8. Andy Warhol. *Ma philosophie de A à B et vice-versa.* Flammarion Paris, 1977.

Does Ontology Influence Technological Projects? The Case of Irish Electronic Voting

Bruno Zelić[1] and Bernd Carsten Stahl[2]

[1] Faculty of Business, Dublin Institute of Technology, Aungier Street, Dublin 2, Ireland
bruno.zelic@dit.ie

[2] Faculty of Computer Science and Engineering, Centre for Computing and Social Responsibility, De Montfort University, The Gateway, Leicester LE1 9BH, UK
bstahl@dmu.ac.uk

Abstract. This paper discusses the relationship between ontology, seen as the doctrine concerned with the nature of reality, and the management of technology. It introduces two ontological positions: realism and constructivism. Realism is the position that holds that reality is objectively given and independent of the observer. Constructivism stands for the belief that reality is constructed by the observer. The implications of this ontological debate are explored using the example of the Irish attempt to introduce e-voting. In order to understand the mistakes made during the Irish e-voting project, it is helpful to consider the ontological position taken by the responsible decision makers. It is argued that only a realist conception of technology can give rise to the sort of mismanagement that was observed in the case study. In conclusion, the paper suggests that following a constructivist ontology would have helped avoid some of the serious mistakes that were made.

1 Introduction

In 2004 the Irish government tried to introduce electronic voting for the local and European elections. This was the first attempt to implement electronic voting holistically within the European Union. E-voting had been implemented over a period of approximately two years. During this time, there were many indicators that e-voting might not be feasible. However the Irish government held on to the idea. Just five weeks before the start of the election, the public opposition became so strong that the government was forced to abandon the idea of electronic voting. In the end, this technological adventure cost Irish taxpayers more than €50 million Euro.

We argue that this so-called Irish e-voting disaster was partly caused by the dominant ontological belief of western society. Based on the case of the Irish e-voting project, this paper will discuss the relationship between ontology and the management of technology. It will be argued that the ontological position used by a researcher or a practitioner, while typically not reflected, is of decisive importance for the success of a technical system. For the purpose of this paper we will analyse two ontological positions, which we will call realism and constructivism.

The prevalent ontology in technology and technological research, particularly in Information Systems (IS) is that of realism, as presented in the research approach of positivism [1, 2]. Realism claims that reality exists independently of the observer's

K.-D. Althoff et al. (Eds.): WM 2005, LNAI 3782, pp. 657 – 667, 2005.

mind, and that this reality can be known by the observer [3]. The realist worldview has been dominating the sciences and the western society from the time of Enlightenment and Descartes until today [4]. The realist ontology is closely linked to an empiricist epistemology and quantitative research methodologies. This is reflected by the fact that the realist pursuit of universal truth is seen as an appropriate way of gaining knowledge and proposing solutions in our societies.

While realism is the dominant ontology, it has also been contradicted frequently and it is not without alternatives. In this paper we will concentrate on that ontological system which we believe is most widely spread and offers most promise to alleviate the problem of realism, namely constructivism. Constructivism holds that reality is not objectively give and subject to impartial observation but rather a (individual or social) construction dependent on the observer [5-7].

The aim of this paper is not only to question the realist ontology in technology and information systems research but also to propose constructivism as a more pragmatic worldview. We will briefly analyse the philosophical underpinnings of realism and constructivism. The case study of the Irish electronic voting failure is used to demonstrate the practical relevance of our theoretical considerations. We put forward the view that the realist ontology tends to overemphasise the use of technology. However, the expected goals are very often not met. The problem lies not in the technology itself but in its poor management, which often takes the technology out of social context. We argue that constructivism might be more applicable and beneficial than realism, leading not only to a better understanding of technology but also to beneficial results in its management.

2 Two Different Ontologies: Realism vs. Constructivism

Ontology is the philosophical discipline that deals with the nature of reality that asks what it means to be [8]. As one of the building blocks of philosophy, it has a history of over 2000 years and we cannot do it justice in a brief paper. We will concentrate on two positions that we believe to be of high relevance in today's discussion of technology in general and information systems in particular: realism and constructivism.

Realism, as we use the word, means that reality is given independent of the observer [1, 9-12]. It is the ontology that used to be prevalent in the natural sciences and it is what Husserl called the "natural attitude" - the ontological assumption that we seem to pick up most easily during our socialisation. A different term sometimes used to denote the same ontological view is "objectivism" [3, 13, 14]. Realism is the ontology of positivism which arguably is the prevalent research paradigm in most natural but also many social sciences [2, 15-20].

There is a close (but not necessary) relationship between the realist ontology and certain epistemological and methodological approaches. Our main focus in this paper is on establishing a link between ontology and the management of information systems. A researcher who believes that reality is objectively given will typically believe that it is possible to gather objective knowledge about this reality by impartial observation. Realism thus leads to empiricism as the epistemological idea that truth is a function of experience. The criterion for truth is the correspondence of the observation with reality. This can best be achieved by using scientific tools, particularly formal and quantitative research methods. The debate we try to recast here is thus closely related (albeit not identical) to the debate between positivism and interpretivism or quantitative and qualitative research.

If realism is so widely spread, then it is worth asking what may be problematic about it. There are many indicators that the realist search for universal 'truth' might be questionable. Albert Einstein argues that: 'Physical concepts are free creation of the human mind, and are not, however it may seem, uniquely determined by the external world. In our endeavour to understand reality we are somewhat like a man trying to understand the mechanism of a closed watch.' [21]

Human beings describe their world according to their paradigmatic lenses. This view is endorsed by many ontologies which have arisen as alternatives to realism in the last decades. This leads to the charge that realist research, instead of describing an objectively given world, actually produces self-fulfilling prophecies or, to put it more simply, that it invents those things that it pretends to be measuring, [22].

If realism is indeed problematic, then we need to ask what alternatives there are. The history of philosophy offers many examples of non-realist ontologies. We will just pick the one we think is most important to current practices in information systems research. The constructivist position is rooted in the notion that there is no observed phenomenon without an observer [23]. The constructivist view of the world 'acknowledges the legitimacy and reality of differing perspectives on social phenomena' [24]. Reality is not given but it is the result of the human action of perception which constitutes the phenomena under investigation. There are different views in the constructivist camp on how exactly this is done and whether it is an individual or social process that leads to reality [5, 6]. The end result, however, is that the reality we are studying is the product of our own minds.

The fundamental ontological ideas developed in this paper have been explored before. They are closely linked to the fields of science and technology studies and, more specifically, to the idea of the social construction of technology [25]. Some of the ideas developed in these fields of study have successfully been transferred to the theory and practice of information systems [26]. The specific contribution of this paper to the discourse is twofold: First, we emphasise the ontological underpinning of the constructivist approach, which is rarely discussed in depth. Second, we provide an empirical example to support our thesis that ontology is a relevant factor in information systems management.

The constructivist view challenges the instinctive drive towards the rational implementation of technology. Constructivist ontology holds a position that technology cannot be seen objectively. It is rather created, invented, and constituted during the process of design, development, and use. Information systems, for instance, should be studied and managed within a specific social context. Furthermore IS would not only be influenced by various technological features but also by human factor.

Under these proposed conditions empirical research of IS and its management takes on a different meaning. One can no longer find out the reality about technology but one can study how it is put to use, what aspects affect its creation and use, which hidden assumptions shape it, etc. Management should not conceptualise technology as a tool [27] that can be used to achieve some purposive-rational aim. Instead, the constructivist's proposal suggests that the managerial use of technology interacts with its use, and forms a part of the environment that shapes its reality.

It should by now have become clear that the ontological assumption influence the decision making in the management of IS. We have so far tried to argue that realism is the prevalent ontology but that it is also defective. Our suggested alternative is constructivism, which should provide more applicable ontology for the research and the management of IS. In order to render this argument plausible, we will now discuss the case study of electronic voting in Ireland.

3 Case Study

The usual way of electing democratic representatives is the collection of ballot papers. On the ballot paper a voter indicates his or her preferences. There are three important factors which have to be assured with ballots issued by the government. Firstly, only eligible voters vote. Secondly, they only vote once. Thirdly, all votes counted are valid votes [28]. These three premises have to be achieved maintaining the voters' privacy, i.e. assurance of anonymous vote [29]. However, the most important aspect during the election process is the protection from manipulation and misuse. One could argue that with the loss of the voter's privacy or potential to manipulate ballots the democratic principles would be in danger.

In 2002 the Irish government started to consider the introduction of electronic voting. During the general elections in 2002, the government piloted electronic voting in three constituencies. Instead of using the traditional way of placing a vote in the ballot box, citizens voted electronically. Despite minor problems government was pleased with the results. The decision was made to introduce electronic voting nationwide for the local and European elections on 11th June 2004, which would give Ireland a pioneering role in Europe. For this purposes a Dutch company was employed to provide Ireland with an electronic voting system [28] and the government started to implement electronic voting system in early 2003.

There were various arguments as to why e-voting should have been implemented. Some of the advantages are: relatively easy usage, accurate results, elimination of the spoiled votes, acceleration of the counting process and the modernisation of the electoral system [28]. The Irish minister for the Environment and Local Government Martin Cullen was convinced that e-voting would make it easier for the public to vote, would improve efficiency and the administration, would provide earlier results, and also would provide a positive image of Ireland as a pioneer in usage of information systems in the democratic elections. In fact, Mr. Cullen was of the opinion that e-voting would modernise the democratic process in all of it facets [30].

Despite the euphoria at the pilot stage, sizeable reasonable amount of Irish citizens, computer experts and also opposition parties cast their doubts from the start that electronic voting would be feasible on the national level. One opposition party, for instance, pointed out that the system did not have a paper trail and therefore was open to manipulation [31]. The lack of a paper trail was also the main reason for the establishment of the lobby group organised by computer experts, called "Irish Citizens for Trustworthy E-voting" (ICTE). A paper trail that allows voters to review a print-out of their expressed preferences, would add confidence to the system.

Without such paper trail an independent random check of the system would not be possible.

The main complaints regarding e-voting were constraints between the verified audit trail and the privacy of the voter. The electronic voting system has to ensure privacy of the vote, i.e. cannot reveal voters' identity. At the same time the system has to ensure a verified audit trail. An example of the verified trail is banking, where in the case of a mistake, the money transfer could be traced backed and corrected. American computer scientists Mercuri [29, 32] had previously identified this stumbling block but seemingly with little response from politicians. Mercuri [29] argues that all electronic voting systems have the same problem, 'unlike automated teller machines at banks, where video cameras are used to deter theft, receipts are issued, such provides a physical audit mechanism, and insurances covers losses'.

A simple solution to avoid the potential jeopardising of voters' privacy would have been the issue of the paper based voter audit trail. This solution, proposed by Mercuri [29], was supported by the Irish Computer Society [33] and the lobby group ICTE. This concept suggests that during the process of election the system would print the ballot containing voter's preferences. This ballot could be examined by the voter and then deposited in a ballot box. Doing so, the chance of possible manipulation would be eliminated. The election would still profit from the accuracy and the counting speed of a computer but the official certification of the election would come later from the paper records.

However, the government's intention, supported by the Dutch contractor, was to eliminate any paper trail. Arguably, by adopting the Mercuri Method, there would not be any economic benefits for the government. On the contrary the cost would increase. According to Minister Cullen, who was the responsible politician for the introduction of e-voting in Ireland, six independent studies verified the security of the system. [31]. Disregarding the warnings from the opposition, many independent citizens, ICTE and Irish Computer Society, the Irish government stood by its decision not to have a paper trail. As Mr. Cullen [31] emphasised: 'Receipts were not issued under the old system and will not be issued under the new system for the same reason to protect voters' privacy'.

The source code of the electronic voting system was another issue in the e-voting debate. The source code was not available for the public. Even the Irish government was not in the possession of the source code provided by the Dutch computer company. This means that a private company, which was based abroad, had the exclusive insights about the source code and nobody else. In the case of an attempt of manipulation of the source code, the Irish government would not have had any power of monitoring and protecting the source code. As Mercuri [29] states: 'any programmer can write code that displays one thing on a screen, records something else, and prints yet another result'.

Despite the growing opposition to the introduction of electronic voting in June, even in February 2004 the Irish government was sticking to the agenda. The Irish Minister for Finance, Charly McCreevy, for instance, advocated electronic voting strongly in front of the Irish parliament. The electronic voting was also strongly supported by the Taoiseach (Irish word for Prime Minister) Bertie Ahern. But in February 2004 some senior members of the ruling party started to doubt the feasibility of electronic voting, which had already cost Irish tax payers more than €40 million.

Finally, due the public resistance against electronic voting the Irish government decided to establish an independent Commission on Electronic Voting. The Commission consisted of five independent members: one judge, two clerks and two computer experts. The Commission also invited the public submissions. The task of the commission was to produce an interim report on secrecy, accuracy and testing of the chosen electronic system. The report [34: 7] published on 1st May stated that the 'Commission finds that it is not in a position to recommend with the requisite degree of confidence the use of the chosen system at elections in Ireland in June 2004'. The majority of the submissions also stated that the electronic voting system was flawed and should be changed radically before being introduced.

The commission's statements on testing, accuracy and secrecy were against electronic voting usage. Regarding the testing of the system, the commission stated that tests, which had been carried out to date, were insufficient to establish its reliability for use at elections. The final software version was not available to the commission, despite the forthcoming deadline of three months. The commission also did not receive the source code of the system. Hence the Commission was not able to give any statement regarding the accuracy issue. In fact, the secrecy of electronic voting was also in danger. During the voting process, the machine would produce certain tones, which meant that an insider would have been able to identify the voter's preferences. The commission underlined also, that a verified paper trail, as argued by many [28, 29, 33], is crucial to assure the integrity of the election.

After the commission's clear recommendation against the introduction of electronic voting the Irish government was forced to rethink its strategy. Mr. Cullen the main politician responsible for the Irish electronic voting disaster was faced with sustained accusation of arrogance, incompetence and neglecting for long time the public voice against electronic voting. The policy has cost the Irish government more than €50 million. Five weeks before the election date government abandoned the proposal to carry out the elections electronically and went back to manual voting [35].

The government's hope to be able to improve the democratic process implementing e-voting proved to be fallacious. It did not only cost the Irish state more than €50 million but it also massively influenced local and European elections. The ruling party experienced the worst election results since the 1920s [36]. Possibly, the Irish government wanted to get an image of being the first European government, which successfully introduced electronic voting for any price. However, one can speculate that the Irish government will find it difficult to rebuild the publics trust to introduce electronic voting for the general election in 2006 [35]. The question which arises is, how was it possible for the Irish government to not be aware of different weaknesses of the system before 1st May 2004.

4 Discussion

This story of the failure of a large scale system will look familiar to many readers who are interested in the development and implementation of information systems. One can see examples of poor management, unclear aims and requirements, lack of communication, non-existing user involvement, and of course many political issues, which are intrinsic to any e-government or e-voting system. There are thus many possible explanations for the failure of the system. In this paper we do not want to discuss any of the choices just indicated but rather look for an underlying cause of the instinctive adoption of a technological invention neglecting social constraints. We believe that there is good reason to argue that the ontological view of an information system is the root cause for many of the problems it encounters and that the Irish e-voting experience is a good example of this.

Researchers and practitioners who subscribe to the position of ontological realism see technology as a tool, which serves humanity by achieving its common objectives. While they would concede that technology is created by humans, it eventually matures from human tutelage and leads an existence of its own. The resulting view is than that a technological tool is tailored towards a certain task, which can successfully be used to address the task and solve the problem. Management of the system thus has to make sure that the right tool for the task at hand is present. Once this has been achieved, the rest is a matter of detail and skilled application.

The story of Irish e-voting fits this description. How else could one explain the fact that the Irish government believed that it could go ahead with the new technology? Ignoring societal resistance and the facts that it has never been used successfully on a nation-wide scale. The opposition that the Irish government faced could only be overcome (or ignored) on the basis of a strong conviction that e-voting, once installed, will eventually be successful and the opposition voices will slowly disappear. Empirical tests, prior the independent Commission, were obediently used to support this conviction.

Under given circumstances, even the realist position should not support the Irish concept of e-voting. There are several reasons for this. Firstly, the voting system has not existed in a ready-made form five weeks before the election. It thus did not have an objective existence by the best of standards. Secondly, the government and also the Commission did not have an access to the source code. The fact that the supplier retained the code meant that it was impossible to verify whether the system actually did what it was supposed to do and how it did so. To return to the metaphor of the tool, if one is shown a hammer but is not allowed to touch it or to hammer with it, then there is probably good reason to doubt it is indeed a hammer. One can thus argue that the main problem of the projcct was bad management and oversight and that does not have anything to do with ontological assumptions. Yet, as we discuss in this paper an inadequate ontology might be the underlying reason for it. If this is true, then one should ask what the alternative would have been.

Had the Irish government (or more specifically Martin Cullen) been of a constructivist persuasion, then the entire project would have presented itself in a different light. Constructivists do not believe in the independent existence of technology but see it in the social context, where technology is being constantly constructed and reconstructed through its use and interaction. The constructivist ontology assumes that technology is not determined by engineers or designers but it is negotiated by all stakeholders. Consequently, apart from responsible politicians and technical consultants the input of the public opinion and independent computer experts would have been crucial in decision-making.

Having the constructivist position in mind, the objections raised by the opposition and by interest groups would not have been interpreted as a politically motivated attempt to hinder the use of a good system but as a legitimate expression about the character of the technology. On the other hand, different stakeholders would have had to come to an understanding of their respective positions and also to be capable of leading a critical discourse regarding this matter. Through the social construction of the electronic voting, the participants of the discourse would have shaped the actual manifestation of the e-voting system as well as the interpretation and understanding thereof.

One example of the constructivist alternative could be the status of the source code. The vendor had a legitimate interest in protecting the source code in order to be able to sell the system to other governments. However, the users and technical specialists among them, had an equally legitimate interest in gaining access to the source code in order to understand it and rule out malfunction and manipulation. The character of the system would then have been constructed through the discourse of these viewpoints. Comparable processes in other countries have led to the installation of systems based on open source code.

Similar processes of negotiation could be used to solve the main stumbling block between Minister Cullen and the public opposition, namely the paper trail, The realist ontology supports the position of using e-voting for rational and economic purposes such as, acceleration of the counting process, accurate results and elimination of the paper trail. Irish experts also welcomed the technical advantages such as accuracy and speed of e-voting. At the same time they argued that elimination of the paper trail could endanger Irish democratic principles. One can argue that the constructivist ontology would put democratic principles into first place, accepting the higher costs, if necessary. A constructivist would advocate, that e-voting should be adjusted to the public requirements, and not vice versa.

5 Conclusion

In this paper we have tried to put forward the idea that the underlying ontology is of great importance for the use and understanding of technology. We used the example of the Irish attempt to institute electronic voting showing that the management of this technology and its eventual failure can be explained by looking at the ontology upon which it is built. We have argued that realism, as the current predominant ontology of the technology, is not tenable. In our view, realists tend to overemphasise the benefits of IS. Furthermore we have proposed constructivism as a more viable alternative, which putts the technology into the social context.

However, most average citizens and voters as well as the people responsible for analysing, designing and building information systems are neither experts nor particularly interested in matters of philosophical ontology. It should nevertheless have become clear that the problem of the choice of ontology is not one to keep the inhabitants of the ivory tower busy but has immediate and manifest consequences for our individual and collective lives. As indicated above, the choice of the constructivist ontology entails approaches to building and using systems that look very different from what we usually see.

Although the IS managers might not be aware of the ontological discourse, they cannot escape the fact that the technological failures happen on a regular basis. The case described above is a typical sample of it. Another good example of the same sort is the unsuccessful attempt of the German government to introduce electronic autobahn toll system. We strongly believe that a shift in ontological thinking would improve the management of technological systems. Instead of seeing technology as 'universal' solution to our societal problems, technology should underlie social rules. When following this line of thought, one would recognise that, despite all technological advantages of e-voting, for instance some societies would still prefer to vote manually. In other words, although the e-voting would speed up the voting procedure, it would not necessarily modernise a country's democracy.

What we are proposing is not a panacea. Constructivism as an ontological theory has to contend with theoretical problems that we did not discuss in this paper. However, it gives us a different perspective and it just may allow us to avoid some of the mistakes that are frequently made. We believe that the story of Irish e-voting supports this contention and is believable to the reader. At the very least, it can be understood as a motivation to reflect upon and question the ontological assumptions one holds and thereby maybe improve the way one deals with technology.

References

1. Chua, W.F.: Radical Developments in Accounting Thought. The Accounting Review. **61**(4) (1986) 601-632
2. Orlikowski, W.J. and Baroudi, J.J.: Studying Information Technology in Organizations: Research Approaches and Assumptions. Information Systems Research. **2**(1) (1991) 1-28
3. Gill, J. and Johnson, P.: Research Methods for Managers. Second ed. Paul Chapman Publishing Ltd, London (1997)
4. Wersig, G.: Knowledge Communication as a Postmodern Phenomenon. in International Conference on Public Communication of Science & Technology "Science without Frontiers - Wissenschaft, Medien, Oeffentlichkeit". (1998). Berlin, Germany.
5. Gergen, K.J.: An Invitation to Social Construction. SAGE Publications, London/Thousand Oaks/New Delhi (1999)
6. von Glasersfeld, E.: Radical Constructivism: A Way of Knowing and Learning. Falmer Press, London (1995)
7. Riegler, A.: Towards a Radical Constructivist Understanding of Science. Foundation of Science. **6**(1-3) (2001) 1-30
8. Heidegger, M.: Sein und Zeit. 17th ed. Max Niemeyer Verlag, Tübingen (1993)
9. Burrell, G. and Morgan, G.: Sociological Paradigms and Organizational Analysis. Heinemann, London (1979)
10. Hirschheim, R. and Klein, H.K.: Four Paradigms of Information Systems Development. Communications of the ACM. **32**(10) (1989) 1199-1216
11. Weber, R.: Theoretically Speaking (Editor's Comment). MIS Quarterly. **27**(3) (2003) iii-xii
12. Hirschheim, R.A.: Information Systems Epistemology: An Historical Perspective. in: Mumford, E., et al., (eds.): Research Methods in Information Systems (IFIP 8.2 Proceedings). North-Holland, Amsterdam (1985) 13-36
13. Guba, E.G. and Lincoln, Y.S.: Competing Paradigms in Qualitative Research. in: Denzin, N.K. and Lincoln, Y.S., (eds.): Handbook of Qualitative Research. SAGE Publications, Thousand Oaks/London (1994)
14. Dougiamas, M.: A Journey into Constructivism, [Online]. Available: http://dougiamas.com/writing/constructivism.html; (1998) 08/09/2003

15. Myers, M., D and Avison, D.: An Introduction to Qualitative Research in Information Systems. in: Myers, M., D and Avison, D., (eds.): Qualitative Research in Information Systems: a Reader. Sage, London (2002) 3-12
16. Varey, R.J., Wood-Harper, T., and Wood, B.: A Theoretical Review of Management and Information Systems Using a Critical Communications Theory. Journal of Information Technology. **17** (2002) 229-239
17. Landry, M. and Banville, C.: A Disciplined Methodological Pluralism for MIS Research. Accounting, Management & Information Technology. **2**(2) (1992) 77-92
18. Darke, P., Shanks, G., and Broadbent, M.: Successfully Completing Case Study Research: Combining Rigour, Relevance and Pragmatism. Information Systems Journal. **8**(273-289) (1998)
19. Visala, S.: Broadening the Empirical Framework of Information Systems Research. in: Nissen, H.-E., Klein, H.K., and Hirschheim, R., (eds.): Information Systems Research: Contemporary Approaches & Emergent Traditions. North Holland, Amsterdam (1991) 347-364
20. Jönsson, S.: Action Research. in: Nissen, H.-E., Klein, H.K., and Hirschheim, R., (eds.): Information Systems Research: Contemporary Approaches & Emergent Traditions. North Holland, Amsterdam (1991) 371-396
21. von Glasersfeld, E.: The Radical Constructivist View of Science. Foundation of Science. **6**(1-3) (2001) 31-43
22. Stahl, B.C.: How We Invent What We Measure: A Constructionist Critique of the Empiricist Bias in IS Research. in Proceedings of the Ninth Americas Conference on Information Systems. (2003). Tampa.
23. Maturana, H.R. and Varela, F.J.: Autopoiesis and Cognition: The Realization of the Living. Vol. 42. D. Reidel Publishing Co., Dordrecht Holand (1980)
24. Hackley, C.: Doing Research Projects in Marketing, Management, and Consumer Research. Routledge, London/New York (2003)
25. MacKenzie, D. and Wajcman, J.: The Social Shaping of Technology. Second ed. Open University Press, Maidenhead (1999)
26. Howcroft, D., Mitev, N., and Wilson, M.: What We May Learn from the Social Shaping of Technology Approach. in: Mingers, J. and Willcocks, L., (eds.): Social Theory and Philosophy for Information Systems. Wiley, Chichester (2004) 329 - 371
27. Orlikowski, W.J. and Iacono, C.S.: Research Commentary: Desperately Seeking the "IT" in IT Research - A Call to Theorizing the IT Artifact. Information Systems Research. **12**(2) (2001) 121-134
28. McGaley, M. and Gibson, P.: Electronic Voting: A Safety Critical System, [Online]. Available: http://www.cs.may.ie/~pgibson/Research/Publications/E-Copies/NUIM-CS-TR2003-02.pdf; (2003) 06/08/04
29. Mercuri, R.: A Better Ballot Box? IEEE Spectrum Online. **October** (2002)
30. Environ: Minister Cullen Announces roll out of electronic voting for 2004 Local Government and European Parliament Elections, The Department of the Environment, Heritage and Local Government, [Online]. Available: http://www.environ.ie/DOEI/DOEIPub.nsf/6fb57b90102ce64c80256d12003a7a0d/97488b6e000fe85380256d2d005e48b1?OpenDocument; (2002) 11/08/2004
31. Environ: Cullen invites All Party Oireachtas Committee for electronic voting demonstration: 6 independent studies verify security of electronic voting, The Department of the Environment, Heritage and Local Government, Available: http://www.environ.ie/DOEI/DOEIPub.nsf/wfInfo/15d88ab7fad648ce80256dd300540874?OpenDocument; (2003) 11/08/2004

32. Mercuri, R.: Florida 2002: Sluggish Systems, Vanishing Votes. Communication of the ACM. **45**(11) (2002) 136
33. O'Duffy, M.: The ICS calls for audit trail in e-voting system, Irish Computer Society, [Online]. Available: http://www.ics.ie/article-027.shtml; (2004) 20/08/2004
34. Commission on Electronic Voting: Secrecy, Accuracy and Testing of the Chosen Electronic Voting System, [Online]. Available: http://www.cev.ie./htm/report/V02.pdf; (2004) 11/08/2004
35. Hennessy, M. and Brennock, M., *E-voting abandoned for elections in June*, in *Irish Times*. 2004.
36. Brennock, M., *An alternative emerges*, in *Irish Times*. 2004: Dublin.

Mapping the Multitude – Categories in a Process Ontology

Ruth Hagengruber

Philosophisches Seminar, Universität Koblenz, Universitätsstrasse 1,
56068 Koblenz, Germany
www.uni-koblenz.de/~hagengru
ruth.hagengruber@uni-koblenz.de

Abstract. One of the main problems with artificial intelligence is the fact that the information which artificial intelligence is typically required to handle is heterogeneously structured. Ontologies are designed to mitigate this effect. From a philosophical perspective, we refer to an ontology when we have a systematic representation whose various relations can adequately describe a domain. Humans use special strategies to reduce the amount of data at their disposal. They apply selection and reorganization techniques to adapt their knowledge to new situations. Categories are understood in this sense as necessary relations that occur due to necessary orders within certain domains. Thus, each domain has its necessary set of relations and a necessary ordering of entities which define the domain-specific relational structure. This kind of representation has far-reaching consequences in applications, for example for Knowledge Management.

1 Introduction

One of the main problems with artificial intelligence is the fact that the information which artificial intelligence is typically required to handle is heterogeneously structured. Data systems developed independently of one another lead to incompatible data structuring, and thus to semantic breaks. This reflects the different approaches and focuses, the different interpretations and backgrounds of various groups of users.

Ontologies are designed to mitigate this effect. The theory is that ontologies can help to provide a common knowledge base. Ontologies are designed to provide a structure or grid that allows us to categorize information no matter where it comes from and to retrieve that information, just like from an ingenious system of drawers. The general applicability of this system of drawers would guarantee general availability and help to achieve the goal of supporting access from anywhere, and with any degree of precision. Ontologies are designed to provide a basis for enabling and supporting multiple perspectives.[1] The most important task regarding ontologies however is to imitate this process of human beings to synthesize and to analyze the given knowledge and to reorganize this in regard to a new situation. The task that computer science firmly places in the hands of philosophical ontology today is only that of mapping the basic principles and structures of reality in an highly generic way, and

[1] The term is taken from [1].

K.-D. Althoff et al. (Eds.): WM 2005, LNAI 3782, pp. 668 – 675, 2005.

thus providing an authoritative basis for categorizing and communicating various concepts or symbolic representations of our world. Today, typical approaches attempt to do this by creating models to represent reality. Within these multiple models, entities can be represented in many different ways. Different perceptions and experiences thus influence the conceptual exemplification of the models involved and lead to completely different orders, which are incompatible in cases, although they refer to the same part of the world. An authoritative structure that allows us to collate varying paths of access to reality can not be designed on this basis. [2]

2 How to Map a Process

In addition to a critical appraisal of the options and consequences related to the use of models, we also need a critical appraisal of the extent to which these models are language models of reality. Representations within information processing systems permit a variety of forms. Generalizations and specifications do not necessarily need to be developed along the lines of language models. On the following pages, I will be outlining an approach that allows the meaning behind a representation to come to the fore through ontological categories (cf. [3]). An ontology based on a "world model", a language model for example, is an ontology *"post quem"*. That is, it assumes things, relations etc. which can *not* be assumed – at least not as fixed points of reference. This ordering method is oriented on an approach that "paradoxically needs a known model prior to the original".[4] It is quite obvious that a model of this kind that maps an existing scenario cannot be applied to any other scenario but its own. Its representation only reflects one view of the world, to be more precise the one it projects of itself. Even if it were possible to map all scenarios and relations, a representation would present only *one* view at *one instant*.

Language entity oriented specification analyses (language models of reality) maintain a world that is assumed by the model builders i.e. by the speaker. But it remains unclear as to what legitimacy these assumptions have, as the extent to which the model truly reflects the world is unknown. This more or less how the ontological issue arises. What justification is there for information models that refer to a world that apparently everyone perceives in a different way, and can map in a different way?

The difference between the models used in information science, and the approach we try here is the assertion that it offers a representation basis capable of mapping a world. Models use categories (i.e. structures or relations) that are meant to refer to a real world scenario, we get to know them usually "post quem" – after being constituted. Our approach introduced here is to map the process that leads to a certain knowledge of the word. Instead of mapping "post quem" we try to map the knowledge of the process.

2.1 Categories as a Basis for Processes

From a philosophical perspective, we refer to categories in an ontology, when we have a systematic representation of principles whose various relations can adequately describe a subset of the world. The interrelation of these principles constitutes the world we know. We refer to these relations as *categories*. An ontology that claims to do this also claims to be authoritative, as the relations that it defines are constitutive for the subset of the world that the ontology defines. The kind of philosophical ontology introduced here does not serve the purpose of presenting a unique set of circumstances or a unique representation of the world, as it exists at the moment. Instead, its focus is to provide a basis for a process. Instead, the aim is to demonstrate that basic relations can be identified within more complex relations. These basic relations can reoccur in a variety of contexts. However, it is also true that basic relations develop in various contexts, thus giving rise to new, differentiated, relational patterns which can be regarded as consolidating the basic relations. Thus, these categories are not defined by a hierarchical representation and ordering of the entities they comprise; instead the ordering of the entities in a given ontology, O_1, depends on the definition of the relations.

3 Mapping the Process

In contrast to machine learning, human achievement in the form of outstanding thought is not typically regarded as the result of a quantifiable process, but as the result of a qualitative process.[2] For human thought, the decisive factor is *how* existing knowledge is associated. "Successful" relations are those in which stored knowledge (=known and readily available representations) are modified to reflect new scenarios to allow us to perceive this knowledge as an adequate representation of reality [5],[6]. Because our world changes constantly, our knowledge of that world must also change. This mainly occurs by restructuring existing knowledge and remapping known coherencies to form new ones. This mapping process is based on reality, whereas a model-based approach prefers the perceptions gained via the model to the original. Cf. [4] We also could refer to this difference in the perspective of a static and a dynamic view of relations. Dynamic knowledge is characterized by its adaptability to specific and changing conditions. They can be determined by environmental as well as social contexts.[11]. In the course of adaptation existing knowledge is rearranged in a context-sensitive way. Consequently, "new" knowledge can be regarded as the result of a recombination of existing entities within new categories.[12]

As machine learning is implemented by mathematical combinatorics, it allows a multifaceted representation which is totally alien. Machine processes can (theoretically] record an infinite number of things, and each term can (theoretically] be characterized by an infinite number of properties. Correspondingly, existing data can be aggregated in an infinite$^{(2)}$ (infinite to the power of two) number of categories. But this variety does not make sense, as it is not real. It only demonstrates the enormous range of possibilities. But reality is not the sum of all options that can be deduced by mathematical operations. On the contrary, experience tells us that certain relations only exist in specific subsets of the world. We only experience these coherencies in specific areas, but not in all areas. We refer to categories as necessary coherencies, whereas relations can include any possible coherencies. And again, not all relations that are theoretically possible have to be real. But we do not have a systematic scheme

[2] Obviously, dynamicism of knowledge was an extremely important topic for Turing too [7]. Turing recommended "educating" computers, as a consequence, an intensive discussion of the question of what learning means ensued [8]. The discussion made it obvious that human intelligence and learning potential are not necessarily equivalent to growth of knowledge, but can even mean reduced performance [9], [10].

of representations that allows us to implement only those relations that are capable of providing the required coherency.[3] This power of association is specific to human thought; the process can be described as follows.

Humans use special strategies to reduce the amount of data at their disposal. They apply selection and reorganization techniques to adapt their knowledge to new situations. We can recognize this as the *analytical* and *synthesizing* part of a process. In one part of the process we *dissect* our knowledge base; in the other we *reassemble* our world. While doing so, we "juggle" with categories. Our aim is to continually modify our knowledge of the world in a way that allows us to generate new knowledge based on existing knowledge, and to modify this new knowledge to reflect new situations. We modify our knowledge of our world by continually creating new relations between entities and by stabilizing these relations in categories to specify domains. Without these categories, that is these stabilized relationships, the world would be confused and chaotic for humans. Our understanding of a system of categories is something that allows us humans to cope with the world around us.[4]

Though these categories may be developed infinitely, they are not arbitrary. Simple relations develop into more complex ones. We can identify new relations by applying basic categories to new situations. A set of simple relations can continually produce increasingly differentiated specifications which allow us to map the world. And the order imposed by these relations is reflected as the current context.

Let's assume that O_1 is an image of the world at a given point in time t_1, and that it comprises 3 entities and 3 relations. If the relation R_1 has two digits, we can form the following associations.

R_{11} (e_1,e_2)
R_{12} (e_1,e_3)
R_{13} (e_2,e_3)
The same principle applies to the relation R_2
R_{21} (e_1,e_2)
R_{22} (e_1,e_3)
R_{23} (e_2,e_3) and so one.

And this also applies to the relation R_3. It is understood that relations$_{11}$ etc. depend on their definitions, that is, whether they are transitive or not, and whether they comprise one, two or three digits.

Let's take this image as a representation of a subset of reality, and as part of the thought process. In the *analytical* part of the process, an image is dissected into its parts: entities and relations. If process 1 has e_1,e_2,e_3 and three relations, r_1- r_3, the synthesizing process gives us the relation r_{11} (e_1,e_2) as a new entity e_4, relation r_{12} (e_1,e_3) is generated as a new entity e_5 by process 2, and so on. Relations lead to new entities. *Knowledge of the world is thus a set of relations produced by synthesis*, and not an image of fixed entities.

---

[3] Research into expert systems was targeted at representing critical relations and synthetic coherencies which were bounded by knowledge and experience, and evidenced by heuristic processes [13],[14].

[4] The formal-ontological method of the Basic Formal Ontology (BFO) suggests an approach in which entities are organized along the lines of basic concepts. Within this formally structured framework it would be possible to identify field-specific relations [17], [18], [19].

But thought is a lot more than just the successful adaptation of entities to a subset of the world by the application of relations. It is also the successful selection of characteristics or terms from a variety of options with respect to a specific goal, and its positioning within a specific relationally defined context. It is important to understand critical relations. Where categories define a certain ordering, we then refer to a pattern of knowledge.

3.1 Patterns of Knowledge – Defining a Domain

Categories are relations that occur due to necessary orders. Let's assume that the original orders, which coincide with the first categories, multiply and continue to differentiate (process 2 and so on). These orders represent meaning. This is quite logical because we say that categorial ordering defines the necessary context[5]. It thus makes sense to generate new meanings via new relational contexts. This also means that semantic content is not defined by the specification of terms, but that the specification of terms is the result of the relational structure.

Let me show this with an example. I will talk of "David" Michelangelo's marble masterpiece. Let's assume that David consists of three decisive entities. E1 consists of r1, r2, r3; e2 consists of r4, r5, r6; e3 consists of r1, r5, r7. Entity 1 is "beauty" and it consists of r1, white marble, r2 is height, r3 is proportion. Entity 2 is "man" and it consists of r4, strong muscles, r5, active attitude, r6, sex. Entity 3 is "work of art" and consists of r3, r5, and r7, made by Michelangelo. In our example, "proportion" is part of Entity 1 and 3 (R_{13}). This doubled relation leads to an intensified path. Although the meaning of "proportion" is something different regarding to the relations that are implicit in e1 or e3, it is a stable category with different "meanings" in different contexts. Our example exemplifies how – within a certain knowledge pattern – some relations are repetitive and thus become more dense than others. These relations are more often used than others to describe a special cutout of reality. The same is true for "beauty" or "work of art" and so on. These categories are gained by a process that helps us to define this field of art.

The most important thing is to understand that each entity reflects a multitude of new ones and a multitude of different relations. Every domain or every pattern of knowledge is thus a specific ordering scheme that reflects a subset of the world in a specific perspective. It is also true, that this diversification starts from a certain point, although it is not important, where it starts. All parts of this process could be traced back to a certain amount of basis relations. As individual representations of specific facts, they differ by their degree of differentiation and their ordering. This is a representation of knowledge. A basic set of entities will turn out during the processes which are differentiated in specific areas and demonstrate specific patterns of relations[6];

Thus, each domain has its necessary context of relations and a necessary ordering of entities which define the domain-specific relational structure, that is a knowledge

[5] Thus the question as to whether the human brain organizes new information along the lines of existing structures becomes irrelevant: they are new, but based on earlier structures, cf. [6, 332].

[6] Since the mid 90s, there have been attempts to design and different taxonomies by applying philosophical categories [15], [16].

pattern, which is not a language dependent pattern. Any pattern can theoretically be dissected into its component parts at any time, and traced back to its origins. Parts of this representation of reality that are far apart, can be associated with each other on the basis of their common ground. Of course, one can imagine that an intelligent machine might be capable of making and recognizing these associations itself. [7]

4 Application

This kind of representation has far-reaching consequences. Let's investigate the practical effect that an ontology like the one we designed here can have. This ontology is not characterized by the fact that it presents an image of "existing" facts. A variety of taxonomic structures can develop from this *process ontology*. The development depends on the circumstances in which the categories and their iterations are valid. Various branches of development can co-exist parallel to one other and are nonetheless interconnected. They are *intensively* interconnected – because they all refer to a common ground of basic relations. And they will always retain their inter-compatibility. As all states of the total structure can be derived from a base structure, theoretically all states can be inter-associated at all levels [20]. They are *extensively* interconnected because the relations include context sensitive information and refer to other relations. But these references are not arbitrary.

Instances occur when the development of an ontology is discontinued. This is always the case when a relational representation is not followed by a further differentiation comprising new relations. The decisive factor, for the purpose of our discussion is whether we can identify strong interconnections within the scope of the web of relations we are investigating. If these strong interconnections exist, we refer to this as a pattern of knowledge. Strong interconnections are relations that continually reoccur, which prove stable in specific contexts, and which thus demonstrate the relations belonging to a context. We refer to them as categories. At the same time, patterns of knowledge, that is domains, are generated and defined by these categories. It is important to realize that these patterns are neither closed nor disambiguated from other kinds of information. When webs of relations are extended, other categories can arise to represent a stable pattern. At the same time, arbitrary extensibility of the web of relations is prevented by categories. Of course, a new relation can be added to the web of relations at any point to extend it. But this does not mean that every relation will be relevant with respect to the pattern of knowledge or its potential changes. The significance of close relations as evidenced within a pattern does not become superfluous due to individual relations. The relational complex which a pattern represents – just like in our example of a "proportion" is supported by multiple stable links. These links are either extended – and thus supported - by new relations, or they are irrelevant to them. New relations which do not support the pattern in question remain ir-

[7] With the rise of the WWW and networked environments, the paradigm of information processing has moved away from monolithic, centralized systems towards heterogeneous, and independent information processing networks capable of interaction. Intelligent agents pursue goals independently, and cooperate with other agents. Cf. [21], [22], [23].

relevant until they themselves have become part of a new pattern. They are stable and can thus be retrieved and referred to from every point of knowledge.[8]

The most important goal that philosophical ontology can hope to achieve is precision, and the reduction of redundancy. To achieve this, we need to represent the elements that form the basis of our knowledge in a way that allows best possible access to them. The critical elements that allow this to happen are relations. Relations are the basic framework of the world. And this is why the world is a process and not just a collection of disconnected entities. We can comprehend categories as a framework of relations, to allow repetition and reintegration.

References

1. Frank, U.: Multiperspektivische Unternehmensmodellierung. Theoretischer Hintergrund und Entwurf einer objektorientierten Entwicklungsumgebung. Oldenbourg München (1994).
2. Hagengruber, R.: Ontologische Strukturen. Gegenwärtige Entwicklungen der philosophischen Ontologieforschung in der Informatik. In: Frank, U. (ed). Wissenschaftstheorie in Ökonomie und Wirtschaftsinformatik. Deutscher Universitätsverlag Wiesbaden (2004) 417-433.
3. Baltzer, U.: Erkenntnis als Relationengeflecht. Kategorien bei Charles S. Peirce. Schöningh Paderborn Wien München Zürich (1994)
4. Müller, W. H. I owe this formulation to him. Cf. his unpublished "Verdikte". See also my comments in: Hagengruber, R.: Philosophie und Wissenschaft / Philosophy and Science. Köngishausen & Neumann, Würzburg 2000, p. 17.
5. Tulving, E., Donaldson, W. (ed.): Organization of memory. Academic Press New York (1972)
6. Strube, G.: Cognition. In: Görz, G. (ed.): Einführung in die künstliche Intelligenz. Addison-Wesley Publishing Company (1993) 303-365.
7. Turing, A.: Computing Machinery and Intelligence in Mind 59 (1950).
8. Simon, H.: Why should machines learn? In: Michalski, R. Carbonell, I., and Mitchell, T. (eds.) Machine Learning: An Artificial Intelligence Approach (1983) 25-38.
9. Michalski, R.: Understanding the nature of learning. In: Michalski, R. Carbonell, I., Mitchell, T. (eds.) Machine Learning: An Artificial Intelligence Approach, Vol. II, Los Altos, CA.: Morgan Kaufmann (1986)
10. Scott, P.: Learning. The Construction of a posteriori knowledge structures. In: AAAI-83, Washington (1983)
11. Riss, U.: Knowledge, Action, and Context: A Process View on Knowledge Management. In: Proceedings of the Second Workshop on Philosophy and Informatics WSPI 2005, Kaiserslautern, Germany. Editor: Buechel, G., Klein, B., Roth-Berghofer. http://CEUR-WS.org/Vol-130. (2005-06-20).
12. Hagengruber, R., Riss, U.: Knowledge in Action. Proceedings of the ECAP 2005. Mälardalen University, Västerås, Sweden. Editor: Dodig-Crnkovic, G.. http://www.idt.mdh.se/ECAP-2005/ (2005-06-20).

[8] This topic is discussed by reference to examples of the relations between three and four dimensional ontologies, that is between ontologies that refer to objects, and ontologies based on processes. Again, this assumes ontological perspectivism. Each area of reality could thus be described by a number of ontological perspectives.

13. Wachsmuth, I. (ed.): Expertensysteme, Planen und Problemlösen. In: Goertz, G. (ed.) Einführung in die künstliche Intelligenz. Addison-Wesley Publishing Company (1993) 713-828.
14. Furbach, U. , Baumgartner, P.: Model based deduction for knowledge representation (position paper). In: S. Frank, M., Noy N.:(eds.) International Workshop on the Semantic Web, Workshop at WWW2002 Hawaii (2002).
15. Guarino, N.: Formal Ontology and Information Systems. In: Formal Ontology in Information Systems, IOS Press (1998)
16. Guarino, N.: The Role of Identity Conditions in Ontology Design In: König, W, Wendt, O. (ed.): Wirtschaftsinformatik und Wissenschaftstheorie, Institut für Wirtschaftsinformatik, Proceedings, Frankfurt a. M. (1999)
17. Smith, B.: The Basic Tools of Formal Ontology. In: Guarino, N. (ed.): Formal Ontology in Information Systems Amsterdam, Oxford, Tokyo, Washington, DC (1998) 19–28.
18. Bittner T., Smith, B.: A Theory of Granular Partitions. In: Duckham, M., Goodchild M., Worboys, M. (eds) Foundations of Geographic Information Science London: Taylor & Francis Books (2003) 117-151.
19. Smith, B., Grenon, P.: The Cornucopia of Formal Relations (2003) Forthcoming in DIALECTICA http://ontology.buffalo.edu/smith/articles/cornucopia.pdf; (September 3, 2004).
20. Hagengruber, R., Schauer, H.: Eco – Economic Ontology. Part 1, Towards a Basal Enterprise Ontology. In: Frank, U., Hagengruber, R., Schauer, H. (eds.): Eco-Reports. Arbeitsberichte des Fachbereichs Wirtschaftsinformatik, Forschungsgruppe Unternehmensmodellierung, Bereich Wissenschaftstheorie, Universität Koblenz, Koblenz (2002) 43-55
21. Mainzer, K.: KI – Künstliche Intelligenz. Grundlagen intelligenter Systeme. Wissenschaftliche Buchgesellschaft Darmstadt (2003).
22. Kohonen, T.: Self-Organizing Maps, Springer-Verlag Berlin Heidelberg New York (1991).
23. Malsburg, C. v. d.: Am I Thinking Assemblies. In: Palm, G., Aertson A. (eds.): Brain Theory. Springer-Verlag Heidelberg New York (1986) 161-176.

Workshop on Information Just-in-Time (WIJIT2005): Seeking a New Knowledge Management Paradigm

Hiromichi Fujisawa[1] and Larry Kerschberg[2]

[1] Central Research Laboratory, Hitachi, Ltd.,
1-280 Higashi-koigakubo, Kokubunji, Tokyo 185-8601, Japan
fujisawa@crl.hitachi.co.jp

[2] E-Center for E-Business, Department of Information and Software Engineering,
George Mason University, MSN 4A4, Fairfax, Virginia 22030-4444, USA
kersch@gmu.edu
http://eceb.gmu.edu/

1 Preface

In seeking a new knowledge management paradigm, the First Workshop on Information Just-in-Time was held as a full day workshop associated with the 3rd Conference on Professional Knowledge Management in Kaiserslautern, Germany.

Ideas and experiences that expand and instantiate the concept of *Information Just-in-Time* (*JIT*) were presented and discussed at the workshop. The goal was to invigorate the long-standing knowledge management paradigm with a new perspective, by injecting the *JIT* concept, which entails the well-known best practices in car manufacturing. The core philosophy of JIT is in the quality, cost, and worker participation. These values can be mapped into the corresponding values in knowledge/information management methodologies and practices, which may include proactiveness, optimal information flow, human-centric information process design, customization based on user context, accuracy in information, and constant improvements through feedback.

Issues addressed in the workshop presentations and discussions included: How can "Information Just-in-Time" be defined and modeled? What are new features of Information JIT that have not been seen in conventional KM? How can the concept be implemented? What kinds of IT functions are more important in light of Information JIT? Have human factors and user context been well considered in conventional KM? How do the cognitive aspects of knowledge-intensive workers affect Information JIT? How well has conventional KM supported human intellectual processes? Has conventional KM succeeded in responding to the new demands that come from globalization of business processes and practices?

The technical papers solicited for this workshop succeeded in providing new insights and new stimuli to incorporate the Information JIT concept into Knowledge Management. We accepted six papers, two abstracts, and one demonstration proposal. They introduced and discussed concepts such as "just-in-time information delivery" and "just-in-time knowledge management" in analogy to "just-in-time manufacturing." As L. Kerschberg defines it in his keynote talk in WM2005, which is also in these proceedings, the concept of just-in-time knowledge management (JIT-KM or JITKM) is to provide the *right information*, to the *right people*, at the *right time* – just in time.

K.-D. Althoff et al. (Eds.): WM 2005, LNAI 3782, pp. 676 – 678, 2005.

The *timeliness* requirement of *information JIT* suggests that researchers study real-time processes rather than static information storage. Three papers proposed a process-oriented approach to knowledge management. Fenstermacher (University of Arizona, USA) first argued convincingly the analogy between JIT knowledge management and JIT manufacturing, and suggested that the analogy was deeper than typically acknowledged. Then, he emphasized the importance of integrating processes and monitoring users and the tasks. Morikawa et al. (George Mason University, USA) proposed a Just-in-Time Process Model for building service-oriented processes that require individualized and timely information. They further proposed Temporal Layer Model based on the temporal ontology. The third paper of this group by Karni et al. (Technion, Israel) introduced an Integrated Enterprise Flow Model that integrates the aspects of business process (workflow) and knowledge management (knowledge flow).

Another group of papers stressed the issue of *timeliness*. The paper by Nguyen et al. (Vienna University of Technology, Austria) presented a model for extracting the latent knowledge within continuous data streams by analyzing the stream on the fly. Another paper by Eikemeier (University of Bremen, Germany) explored the role of implicit knowledge in JIT-KM, and stressed the importance of the source of knowledge. Then, he proposed a Peer-to-Peer (P2P) system that supports the search for the optimal human partners to solve requester's problems in real time. The paper by Siebert (Siemens Business Services, Germany) viewed just-in-time information delivery as a key component for the "knowledge creation process," and described the need for a new approach to solve the context problem in just-in-time information delivery.

An abstract by Hofer-Alfeis (Siemens, Germany) raised the issue of knowledge management itself and discussed it to give better understanding of just-in-time knowledge. Considering JIT Knowledge as the just-in-time capability for effective actions, he discussed knowledge quality in three dimensions, i.e., proficiency, diffusion and codification. He stressed the importance of a comprehensive KM approach. Another abstract by Ikeda (Hitachi, Japan) proposed a timely use of personal handwriting annotations to facilitate information retrieval. He showed a prototype system which uses a digital pen to store annotations and retrieve pertinent portions of digital video. The timing information recorded together with annotations and videos can identify the right portions of the video. A software demonstration by Iwayama (Hitachi, Japan) showed a new user interface for information search that enables the user to browse simultaneously two domains – documents and topics – to conduct search associatively.

The organizing committee members who attended the workshop carefully evaluated these nine papers and presentations, and four papers were selected for publication in these post-proceedings. The four papers are by Fenstermacher, Morikawa, Siebert, and Iwayama.

2 Papers Presented at the Workshop

Papers with an asterisk have been selected for this book.

* A Process for Delivering Information Just in Time
K. D. Fenstermacher

* MAKO-PM: Just-In-Time Process Model
R. Y. Morikawa and L. Kerschberg

JIT Knowledge for Decision Making
R. Karni and G. Molcho

Toward the Stream Analysis Model in Grid-based Zero-Latency Data Stream Warehouse
T. M. Nguyen, A. M. Tjoa, and J. Schiefer

Just-In-Time Access to Implicit Knowledge with Peer-to-Peer Community Systems
C. Eikemeier

* Knowledge Creation Framework - Enabling Just-in-Time Information Delivery
M. Siebert

JIT Knowledge: Expert Proficiency, Organizational Capability and Information to Act Effectively
J. Hofer-Alfeis

Human Memory Expansion by Personal Handwriting for Realizing iJIT
H. Ikeda

* Just-In-Time Interactive Document Search
M. Iwayama

3 Workshop Organizer

Chairs

Larry Kerschberg, George Mason University, USA
Hiromichi Fujisawa, Central Research Laboratory, Hitachi, Ltd., Japan

Executive Chair

Hisashi Ikeda, Central Research Laboratory, Hitachi, Ltd., Japan

Program Committee

Katy Börner, Indiana University, USA
Josef Hofer-Alfeis, Corporate Technology, Siemens AG, Germany
Makoto Iwayama, Central Research Laboratory, Hitachi, Ltd., Japan
Noriko Kando, National Institute of Informatics, Japan
Koichi Kise, Osaka Prefecture University, Japan
Simone Marinai, University Florence, Italy
Heiko Maus, DFKI (German Res. Center for Artificial Intelligence), Germany
Wolfgang Nejdl, L3S Research Center, University of Hannover, Germany

A Process for Delivering Information Just in Time

Kurt D. Fenstermacher

MIS Department, Eller College of Management, University of Arizona, 1130 E Helen St, Tucson, AZ 85719
KurtF@Eller.Arizona.edu

Abstract. Over the last three decades, the idea of just-in-time manufacturing, with its emphasis on quality improvement, streamlining processes, and reducing inventories, has revolutionized manufacturing operations across the industrial world. While there are many interrelated elements in just-in-time manufacturing, the idea's success in producing goods has led others to apply the same ideas in services, and more recently, to knowledge management. In this paper, I explore the analogy implied by the idea of delivering knowledge "just-in-time" and argue that this necessarily requires a process-oriented approach to knowledge management.

1 Introduction

During the 1970's, Toyota's Taiichi Ohno noticed a close relationship between American consumers and their grocery stores. American homes stored relatively little food and households would visit nearby grocery stores several times a week to replenish milk, vegetables and other items. He observed that as customers bought items from grocery store shelves, the stores reordered from their suppliers and the stores were kept stocked without building up large inventories. This insight led him to develop similar ideas in Toyota's manufacturing plants that become known (in the United States) as just-in-time manufacturing.

In traditional manufacturing operations, assembly lines of factory workers combined raw materials with partially assembled products and passed their work down a line. Beginning with Henry Ford's innovations in mass production, assembly line manufacturing continued in this manner for decades. While such operations were far more efficient than the craft style processes they replaced, there have several significant flaws. In attempting to address these flaws, the operations community advanced the notion of *just-in-time manufacturing* (also called *JIT manufacturing* or *lean manufacturing*). In searching for solutions to managing the deluge of information that confronts knowledge workers, many have drawn an analogy just-in-time manufacturing and just-in-time information delivery. In this paper, I argue that while the central notion of just-in-time is helpful in information contexts, but the analogy is more complex than usually discussed.

In the next section, I summarize the principles of just-in-time manufacturing, including the Japanese *kanban* system, and the problems these systems address and create. Following that, I explore whether the analogy to the problems of manufacturing carries over to knowledge management. I will then argue that applying

K.-D. Althoff et al. (Eds.): WM 2005, LNAI 3782, pp. 679 – 687, 2005.

just-in-time notions to knowledge management requires a process-oriented approach to knowledge delivery. Finally, I conclude by offering research directions suggested by the analogy.

2 An Introduction to Just-in-Time, Just-in-Time

In traditional manufacturing operations, products moved along assembly lines where workers combined partly assembled products with raw materials at successive work stations. Often, assembly lines were configured to produce one model of a product at a time and changeovers to other model configurations are very expensive. In addition, most work stations accumulated substantial inventories of partial products ready for work, products ready for the next station, and the station's requisite raw materials. Taiichi Ohno, a Toyota employee, proposed an overhaul of the automaker's production process. Toyota's president, then Eiji Toyoda, had set the company's goal as eliminating waste, i.e. "anything other than the minimum amount of equipment, materials, parts, space, and time which are absolutely essential to add value to the product", quoted in [1]. According to Russell & Taylor's text on operations management [1], just-in-time is a complex set of interacting elements, including flexible resources, cellular layouts, pull production system, kanban production control, small-lot production, quick setups, uniform production levels, quality at the source, total productive maintenance, and supplier networks. While just-in-time production evolved in manufacturing environments, service industries have adopted just-in-time aspects as well [2]. Knowledge-intensive tasks differ from both product manufacturing and more general service provision, but some of the aspects of just-in-time apply to managing knowledge just as well as managing production lines.

While just-in-time is usually thought of as applying strictly to manufacturing, the requirements of just-in-time place significant demands on information systems. Because inventories are low (ideally zero), there is no buffer to absorb supply or demand shocks. Instead, deliveries must be carefully coordinated. Moreover, this coordination must be dynamic as strict schedules are antithetical to just-in-time, where customer demand, not a production schedule, drives the process. Indeed, as notions of just-in-time propagate upstream in a supply chain, entire industries come to depend on the rapid and complex flow of real-time information.

3 Just-in-Time Knowledge Management

In studying the application of just-in-time techniques to service industries, Canel et al. [2] state that just-in-time techniques applies to processes, not products, and so are applicable to services as well as goods. By extending that reasoning, I argue that just-in-time techniques also apply to knowledge work. We can most easily see the analogy to just-in-time production if we consider a knowledge worker's own thoughts and experiences as inventory and their draft work product as work in progress. With this analogy in mind, the elements of just-in-time production most directly applicable to knowledge-intensive tasks are pull production, uniform production levels, quality at the source, total productive maintenance, and supplier networks.

3.1 Pull Production

The notion of push versus pull in production is the same as that in information systems — in a pull system, jobs are completed in response to customer demand. In American grocery stores, as customers "pull" items from the shelves and they are scanned at checkouts, the store inventory system automatically updates replenishment orders. The distinction between push mechanisms (such as the selective dissemination of information [3], or SDI, systems) and pull systems (for example, Web search by users) has been known for decades. The wealth of information now available online has made it almost impossible to target push information narrowly enough to avoid overwhelming the recipient. In effect, the pushed information piles up in inventory — in this case, in the mind of the recipient. Unlike physical inventory, however, the information is often simply lost before it becomes useful. While pull systems have fallen out of favor recently, they do offer a critical advantage in one situation. When users are not aware of relevant information sources, they are obviously unable to request information from those sources. A push system can work to notify users of the existence of previously unknown resources. With a pull perspective, information appears to users as they "ask" for it.

3.2 Uniform Production Levels

Another tenet of just-in-time is the notion of uniform production levels. Because there is no "slack" in a just-in-time system, such systems respond poorly to unanticipated demand. One strategy to cope with this problem is the development of accurate demand forecast. In the knowledge management context, forecasting demand amounts to studying to the knowledge needs of organizations and developing the expertise and identifying the knowledge sources needed to serve those needs.

3.3 Quality at the Source

Because just-in-time supply chains have very little buffer capacity, there is little room for error, including poor quality materials. The importance of quality led Toyota and others to empower assembly line workers with *jidoka* — the power to stop the assembly line when they spot a problem. Moreover, workers exercise this right — production is halted on average twenty minutes per day at Toyota's plant because of jidoka [1]. Beyond the stopping of the line itself, however, each stoppage is recorded on a board and workers spend the end of their shifts not on the production line, but instead analyzing the failure that gave rise to the stoppage. In fact, workers may spend more than 10% of an eight-hour shift in such discussions [1]. While knowledge workers may not need to "stop the line" in the same sense as auto workers, the recognition that all of us need time to reflect on mistakes and consider our performance is an oft-overlooked aspect of implemented programs in knowledge management.

3.4 Total Productive Maintenance

Most of us recognize the importance of preventive maintenance of physical objects, as it is often far easier to prevent machine breakdowns with careful maintenance than to recover from an unexpected failure. In the knowledge management context, this suggests that we must continually maintain the machines (knowledge workers) by training them in new sources of information and new ways of doing their jobs. While many managers see training as a distraction from productive work, just-in-time demonstrates that maintenance is not only important, but must be conducted within the broader context of employee empowerment and overall strategy. This broader focus leads to the term total productive maintenance, rather than the narrower idea of preventive maintenance.

3.5 Supplier Networks

As with other aspects of just-in-time, the lack of buffering demands reliable suppliers who deliver quality products on time. In practice, this means that just-in-time manufacturers must develop close relationships with suppliers and so just-in-time operations often have fewer suppliers than traditional operations. Within knowledge management, adopting this principle would demand careful study of experts and their expertise, as well as evaluating useful external sources of knowledge. The idea of supplier networks in knowledge management is most obvious in the "yellow pages" systems that many organizations develop to identify experts and their specialties.

4 Context and Knowledge Need

In the world of manufacturing, there is little doubt which part to attach next as a physical item moves along an assembly line; factory workers need not ponder which of the tens of thousands of seats would be appropriate for the car model in front of them. In addition, the seats to install remain the same for every shift, every worker who toils on the line. In the world of information, however, there is far more ambiguity and personalization. A key problem is that information sources, whether text documents, multimedia objects, or dynamically generated, which I will collectively call *information items*, information sources often have significant semantic overlap. For example, consider the following items that are relevant to quantum mechanics:

- Kid's Net Australia includes an elementary discussion of quantum mechanics suitable for teenagers. [4]
- Karl Hecht's book, *Quantum Mechanics*. [5]
- The Stanford Encyclopedia of Philosophy's description of quantum mechanics. [6]
- A University of Washington chemist's Web site introduces quantum mechanics to the layperson. [7]

While the above resources overlap in the sense that they are all about quantum mechanics, each is very different in its own way. Moreover, it is unlikely that more than one of these sources would be appropriate for a particular person seeking information, although all of them appear among Google's results for the query "quantum mechanics." How is an information system to differentiate among the types of users and recommend the most appropriate information item from the above?

In the manufacturing world, the need for physical items is highly constrained, whereas in the information world, there are very few constraints. Thus, to identify the appropriate information item, a JIT system must incorporate a model of the user's context, which it must then use to constrain information delivery. While pull systems can mitigate this problem by shifting the burden of context modeling on to the user, users have proven poor modelers of their own contexts — or at least poorly translate their contextual model in specific queries. In analysis of search engine studies, Jansen and Pooch [8] state that "that the vast majority of Web searchers use *approximately two terms in a query*, have *two queries per session*, do not use complex query syntax, and typically view no more than ten documents from the results list" (emphasis added). Moreover, while most users know of several Web search engines, there are many information sources that users may not be aware of, and so cannot pull information from them.

While modeling context is an appealing strategy for any information system and a necessity for JIT systems, the obvious next question is "What constitutes the context?" Context is the Pandora's box of information systems, because once a system purports to consider context, there is no return to a context-free world and context can be fiendishly complex — virtually any element of the world state could be contextually relevant. For example, if I am shortly to embark on a business trip to Frankfurt, the fact that Frankfurt's weather forecast suddenly includes rain is relevant as I decide what to pack for my trip. During the American college basketball championship in March, there is noticeably less traffic on the streets of Tucson, Arizona when the University of Arizona plays and so one might argue that mapping programs should plan shorter travel times during scheduled tournament games. Anticipating all such implications is computationally infeasible, which means that some more parsimonious representation than "the state of the world" is needed. In the next section, I argue that process-oriented approaches strike a good balance between constraining information needs with context and being overwhelmed by the potential scope of user context.

5 Process-Oriented Approaches

As Cole et al. [9] state, "The system's purpose is to provide just-in-time knowledge, thus the system has to be totally integrated to the user's performance. The EPSS interface has to contain a representation of the user's performance, and performance environment.... This performance can be understood and modeled in terms of tasks (or phases), and each task can have resources, constraints and results." Thus, the user's current task and role, and their place within a larger process, determines the moment to know. In manufacturing, the process is well defined and the inputs are completely specified. With knowledge work, however, identifying the relevant knowledge ("the inputs", by analogy) is typically a substantial task in itself. For just-in-time knowledge management, the implication is that the vision of a "pure" pull system, entirely driven by user inquiry is unrealistic. Instead, systems must offer suggestions of relevant knowledge, but must do so at the right moment. As Cole [9] and others (including [10] and [11]) have argued, process is the key to identifying the right moment — what has been called the *process proxy principle* elsewhere [12].

5.1 Well-Defined Processes for Knowledge Work

While there are many aspects of just-in-time production that are applicable to knowledge management practices, the key question is "When is the right time?" In manufacturing operations that adopt pull processes, each work station retrieves goods from the previous station when it is free to work on those goods. With goods removed from the previous station, the previous station's workers know that they can proceed to their previous station to pick up finished products, creating a ripple effect. In knowledge management, how are we to know when to incorporate new knowledge? In cases where there is a strict process to follow, we can likely adopt the manufacturing paradigm directly. When a knowledge worker has no further action in service of a particular task, she can look to the previous worker in the process for finished material. For example, a teacher might grade assignments as students submit them. Once the teacher finishes grading an assignment, he will await the finished product of the previous station, which is the class as a whole in this analogy. The next student to submit an assignment then provides the class's finished output to the next station in line — the teacher. Such "strict" processes are the realm of workflow management systems, which ensure the smooth and correct flow of work among process actors, whether those actors are people or systems.

The problem of process-oriented knowledge management systems is what I call the *knowledge-work process paradox*. The paradox lies in the conflict between the descriptive power of process and the nature of knowledge work, which often requires creativity and intuition, and hence is difficult to capture in a well-defined process. (I call a process *well-defined* if there exists a total order of tasks with known pre-conditions and post-conditions, both of which can be formally stated.) Past experiments with systems such as KnowMore [10] have demonstrated the potential of well-defined processes for aiding in the management of knowledge work, but more recent work in weakly defined processes shows promise with added flexibility.

5.2 Weakly Defined Processes for Knowledge Work

Others have noted that knowledge-intensive tasks are only weakly structured [13, 14] and have examined strategies for using the structure that is available. Using a top-down approach, [13] gave users the ability to refine processes as they worked, thus giving users control over the process definition. Combining top-down and bottom-up approaches Schwarz and Roth-Berghofer's [14] approach works across abstraction hierarchies by starting at the bottom and inferring user events from workspace actions and then at the top, using a task concept ontology. We are developing a system that combines the approaches of both [14] and [13] by enabling users to define processes for themselves, while also monitoring user interaction and matching it against knowledge-intensive processes using a case-based [15] approach.

5.3 A Process-Based Architecture for Just-in-Time Information

While there is extensive variation among process-oriented systems, there have more in common than in contrast. Every process-oriented system must incorporate several key elements, however. First, process-oriented systems must have a process library to store knowledge-intensive process representations. Such processes can be inferred from the analysis of user actions, written by process analysts, or automatically

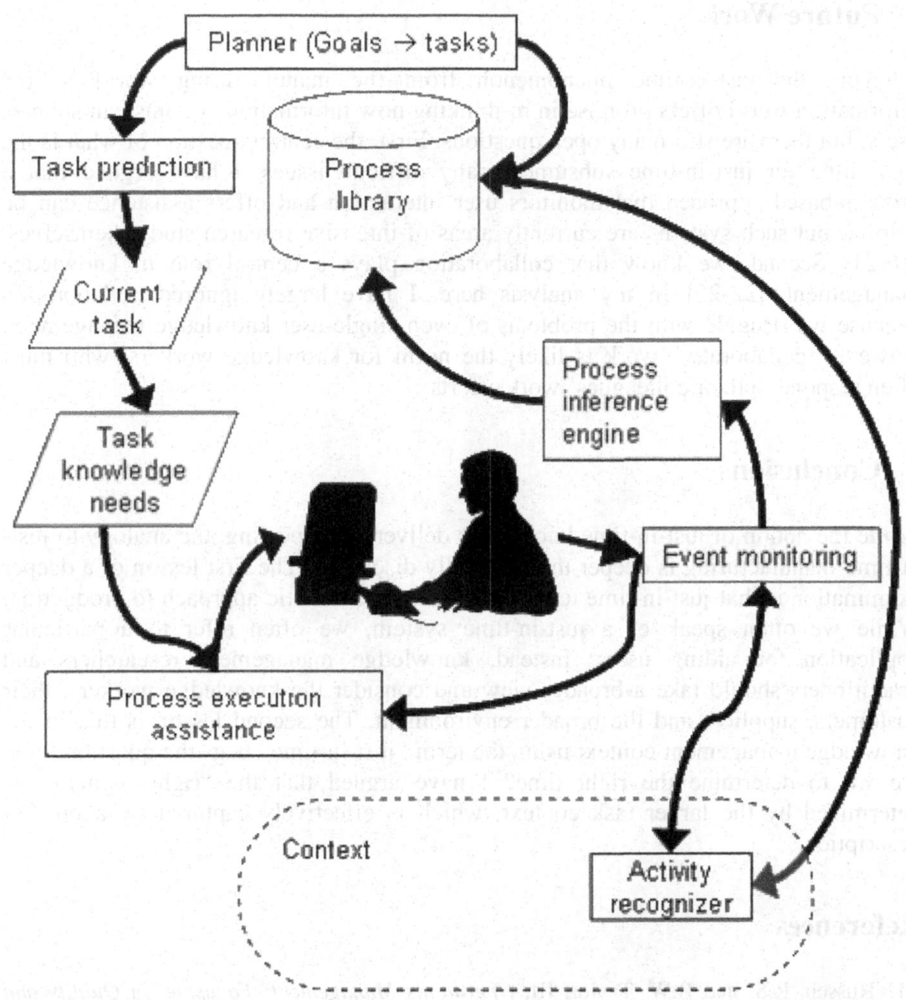

Fig. 1. Process-oriented systems must incorporate elements to monitor user interaction (*event monitoring*), infer semantically rich activities from interaction elements (*activity recognizer*), which form a smaller portion of the much larger context of the user's information needs. With such contextual information, the system can index into a *process library* (which can be either inferred from user observation by a *process inference engine* or produced by a *planner*, possibly a person) and use relevant information to predict the user's *current task*. With task information, the system can aid the user by meeting the *task's knowledge needs.*

generated (was with a planner). Second, process-oriented systems must recognize a user's activity to enable the system to match the user's current activity to known processes (stored in the process library). Third, process-oriented systems must follow through on process recognition by predicting the current and remaining tasks, modeling the user's knowledge needs for those tasks, and aiding the user in performing those tasks — just-in-time. The key elements and their relationships are shown below in Fig. 1.

6 Future Work

Carrying the just-in-time phenomenon from the manufacturing world to the information world offers promise in re-thinking how information systems can support users, but there are still many open questions. First, the central question of what is the right time for just-in-time subsumes many difficult issues. I have argued that a process-based approach that monitors user interaction and offers assistance can be helpful, but such systems are currently areas of intensive research study themselves. [16-21] Second, we know that collaboration plays a central role in knowledge management. [22-25] In my analysis here, I have largely ignored collaboration because we struggle with the problems of even single-user knowledge management. However, collaborative work is likely the norm for knowledge workers, who must often respond to their colleagues' work efforts.

7 Conclusions

While the notion of just-in-time knowledge delivery is appealing, the analogy to just-in-time manufacturing is deeper than typically discussed. The first lesson of a deeper examination is that just-in-time techniques demand a holistic approach to production. While we often speak of a just-in-time system, we often refer to a particular application for aiding users. Instead, knowledge management researchers and practitioners should take a broader view and consider the knowledge workers, their customers, suppliers and the broader environment. The second lesson is that in the knowledge management context using the term "just-in-time" begs the question: how are we to determine the right time? I have argued that the "right moment" is determined by the larger task context, which is effectively captured by a process description.

References

1. Russell, R.S. and B.W. Taylor, III, *Operations Management: Focusing on Quality and Competitiveness*. 3rd ed. 2000, Upper Saddle River, N.J., U.S.A.: Prentice Hall.
2. Canel, C., D. Rosen, and E.A. Anderson, *Just-in-time is not just for manufacturing: a service perspective*. Industrial Management + Data Systems, 2000. **100**(2): p. 51.
3. Luhn, H.P., *A Business Intelligence System*. IBM Journal of Research and Development, 1958. **2**(4): p. 314-319.
4. Kids.Net.Au, *Quantum mechanics (encyclopedia entry)*. 2005, Kid's.Net.Au.
5. Hecht, K.T., *Quantum Mechanics*. 2000, Heidelberg, Germany: Springer. 661.
6. Ismael, J., *Quantum mechanics*, in *The Stanford Encyclopedia of Philosophy*, E.N. Zalta, Editor. 2000, Stanford University: Stanford, CA, U. S. A.
7. Stedl, T., *Intro to Quantum Mechanics*. 2000, University of Washington.
8. Jansen, B.J. and U. Pooch, *A review of Web searching studies and a framework for future research*. Journal of the American Society for Information Science and Technology, 2001. **52**(3): p. 235-246.
9. Cole, K., O. Fischer, and P. Saltzman, *Just-in-time knowledge delivery*. Communications of the ACM, 1997. **40**(7): p. 49-53.

10. Staab, S. and H.-P. Schnurr. *Knowledge and Business Processes: Approaching an Integration.* in *International Workshop on Knowledge Management and Organizational Memory of the International Joint Conference on Artificial Intelligence (IJCAI '99).* 1999. Stockholm, Sweden: AAAI.
11. Abecker, A., et al., *Information supply for business processes: coupling workflow with document analysis and information retrieval.* Knowledge-Based Systems, 2000. **13**(5): p. 271-284.
12. Fenstermacher, K.D. *Process-based knowledge retrieval.* in *35th Hawaii International Conference on System Sciences.* 2002. Waikoloa, Hawaii, U.S.A.
13. Elst, L.v., et al. *Weakly-structured Workflows for Knowledge-intensive Tasks: An Experimental Evaluation.* in *IEEE WETICE Workshop on Knowledge Management for Distributed Agile Processes: Models, Techniques, and Infrastructure (KMDAP '03).* 2003: IEEE Computer Press.
14. Schwarz, S. and T.R. Roth-Berghofer. *Towards goal elicitation by user observation.* in *Workshop on Knowledge and Experience Management (FGWM 2003).* 2003. Karlsruhe, Germany.
15. Aamodt, A. and E. Plaza, *Case-based reasoning: Foundational issues, methodological variations, and system approaches.* AI Communications, 1994. **7**(1): p. 39-52.
16. Palkovits, S., R. Woitsch, and D. Karagiannis, *Process-based knowledge management and modelling in E-government - An inevitable combination.* Knowledge Management in Electronic Government, 2003. **2645**: p. 213-218.
17. Lee, H., *Knowledge Management Enablers, Processes, and Organizational Performance: An Integrative View and Empirical Examination.* Journal of Management Information Systems, 2003. **20**(1): p. 179.
18. Kwan, M.M. and P. Balasubramanian, *Process-oriented knowledge management: a case study.* Journal of the Operational Research Society, 2003. **54**(2): p. 204-211.
19. Dorfler, A., *Business process modelling and help systems as part of KM in e-government.* Knowledge Management in Electronic Government, 2003. **2645**: p. 297-303.
20. Staniszkis, W., *Supporting administrative knowledge processes.* Electronic Government, Proceedings, 2002. **2456**: p. 468-471.
21. Ramesh, B., *Process knowledge management with traceability.* Ieee Software, 2002. **19**(3): p. 50-+.
22. Pease, A. and J. Li, *Agent-mediated knowledge engineering collaboration.* Agent-Mediated Knowledge Management, 2004. **2926**: p. 405-415.
23. Walsh, K.R. and S.D. Pawlowski, *Collaboration and visualization: Integrative-opportunities.* Journal of Computer Information Systems, 2003. **44**(2): p. 58-64.
24. Korner, E.J., M.J. Oinonen, and R.C. Browne, *The power of collaboration: Using Internet-based tools to facilitate networking and benchmarking within a consortium of academic health centers.* Journal of Medical Systems, 2003. **27**(1): p. 47-56.
25. Inkpen, A.C., *Creating knowledge through collaboration.* California Management Review, 1996. **39**(1): p. 123.

MAKO-PM: Just-in-Time Process Model

Riki Y. Morikawa and Larry Kerschberg

E-Center for E-Business, Department of Information and Software Engineering, George Mason University, MSN 4A4, Fairfax, Virginia, 22030-4444
rikimorikawa@yahoo.com, kersch@gmu.edu
http://eceb.gmu.edu/

Abstract. Unlike traditional assembly lines, service-oriented processes require individualized and timely information during the execution of steps or phases. This paper discusses the Multi-layered Analytical Knowledge Organization (MAKO) Just-in-Time Process Model (JITPM), which is a framework and methodology for building service-oriented processes that are interrelated to an organizational knowledge base. Process model instances are connected to a temporal reference, which ensures the timely retrieval of pertinent information, and compliance with procedural constraints

1 Introduction

Today's service-oriented economy requires providers to be flexible in catering to the specific needs of individuals, while still following a predetermined process that guarantees quality and efficiency for both the organization and customer. Unlike traditional assembly line processes, which are typically predictable and unchanging, many service-oriented processes require that a level of customization be made possible through the timely identification of current pertinent information. In the medical field, for example, patients are assigned specific standardized protocols based upon a physical ailment. Depending upon the patient's reaction to the assigned protocol, the attending physician may make modifications, or may decide to terminate treatment in favor of an alternative protocol. In order to enable the making of real-time process decisions, the decision maker must have access to the latest data regarding the specific instance of the process, as well as literature regarding state-of-the-art practices within the field [1, 2].

Previous solutions have addressed knowledge and information requirements using "pull" type scenarios based upon user queries [3, 4]. Other solutions include the introduction of relevant information during specific phases of a process [5], or through the creation of a temporal ontology used to track procedural steps through a protocol [6]. The uniqueness of our approach consists of the adoption of a standards-based knowledge framework, the creation of a simple temporal ontology, and the use of roles to identify process phases or steps.

This paper describes the Multi-layered Analytical Knowledge Organization (MAKO) Just-In-Time Process Model (JITPM) [7], which enables the service worker to follow established processes and to retrieve the latest and most relevant information available in order to make timely knowledgeable decisions. The JITPM provides the worker with the knowledge and information deemed necessary to

K.-D. Althoff et al. (Eds.): WM 2005, LNAI 3782, pp. 688 – 698, 2005.

perform a single phase, or step, of an overall procedure. By doing this, information overload to the worker is minimized. Based upon the XML Topic Map Standard (XTM) [8], the JITPM model ensures interoperability with other systems.

2 Multi-layered Analytical Knowledge Organization (MAKO) Framework

MAKO represents a framework methodology for building, maintaining, modifying, and operating a knowledge base system. The strength of the MAKO concept resides in the fundamental structure of the framework. Any number of customized ontologies can be developed to address the conceptualizations that are most pertinent to an organization.

The MAKO framework, shown in Table 1, is a cross matrix of several major concepts. The Multidimensional Ontology Model (MOM) decomposes the knowledge base into separate conceptualizations based upon common sense groupings. The Temporal Layer Model (TLM) provides a reference by which topics can be segregated according to their time points and intervals. The Interpretive Layer[1] (IL) represents non-validated assessments or opinions that are available for sharing, critiquing, and analysis amongst members of the organization. Although the IL represents information considered to be conjecture or hypothetical, it is vital for the creation of knowledge. Until fully validated by the organization, the new potential knowledge represented in the IL is segregated from the validated part of the MAKO knowledge base.

Table 1. MAKO Framework consists of the MOM, TLM and IL

		Multidimensional Ontology Model		
		Ontology A	**Ontology B**	**Processes**
	INTERPRETIVE LAYER	Interpreted Knowledge		
Temporal Layer Model	**OCCURRENT LAYER**	DYNAMIC Subjects	DYNAMIC Subjects	DYNAMIC Subjects
Temporal Layer Model	**CONTINUANT LAYER**	STABLE Subjects	STABLE Subjects	STABLE Subjects

2.1 Multidimensional Ontology Model (MOM)

An ontology is defined as a "specification for a conceptualization". The conceptualization is comprised of a set of concepts, or classes, that relate to one another in some logical fashion. In essence, an ontology describes concepts that are in a domain of discourse. We use the term Semantic Layer to refer to an ontology that

[1] The IL model is not discussed in this paper. However, its construction is similar to other ontologies within the MOM except for unique scope and class elements that distinguish it from the validated parts contained in the knowledge base.

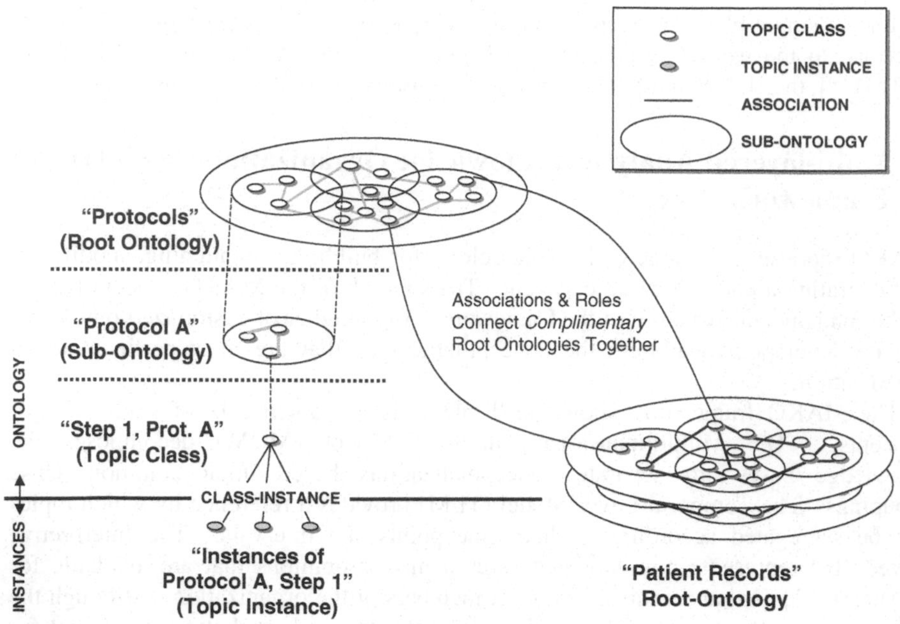

Fig. 1. The Medical Protocol ontology is decomposed into separate sub-ontologies. Multiple instances of each step, or phase, within a specific protocol are created as patients are assigned. The "Protocols" root ontology is connected to the "Patient Records" root ontology via class associations, and they are considered complementary to one another.

has been populated with class instances. The Semantic Layer, combined with rules and constraints, constitute the knowledge base [9, 10].

In terms of the Multidimensional Ontology Model, a set of *root* ontologies are integrated through standard XTM 1.0 association element interfaces. A root ontology represents a specific conceptualization. Within the MOM, several root ontologies co-exist in a complementary manner within the knowledge base. There are several qualities that a root ontology possesses in our model. The first quality is *independence*, which means that the ontology can represent a complete domain of knowledge without depending upon other domains (e.g., temporal, patient records, pharmaceutical domains). The second is *reusability*, where identified reference root ontologies can be reused by other knowledge base applications with minimal, if any, modification. While reusability is required for all reference ontologies (e.g. temporal, almanacs, medical dictionaries, etc.), it is not a necessary condition for other ontologies where highly specialized domains are uniquely specified per organization (e.g., medical treatment protocols may be unique to each medical center). Third, root ontologies must have *standardized interfaces* that enable them to interconnect to other root ontologies. This is accomplished by defining a set of standard association class elements such as "related_to", "begins_on", "ends_on", etc. Finally, root ontologies can be further decomposed into multiple *sub-ontologies* when necessary. As an example, the root ontology containing all medical protocols is decomposed into *sub-ontologies* that represent separate steps within a single protocol. The steps are then decomposed further into separate topics that are pertinent to the execution of the single step. This decomposition process serves to refine conceptualizations into simpler and more manageable representations, and continues until no further simplification is deemed necessary (Figure 1).

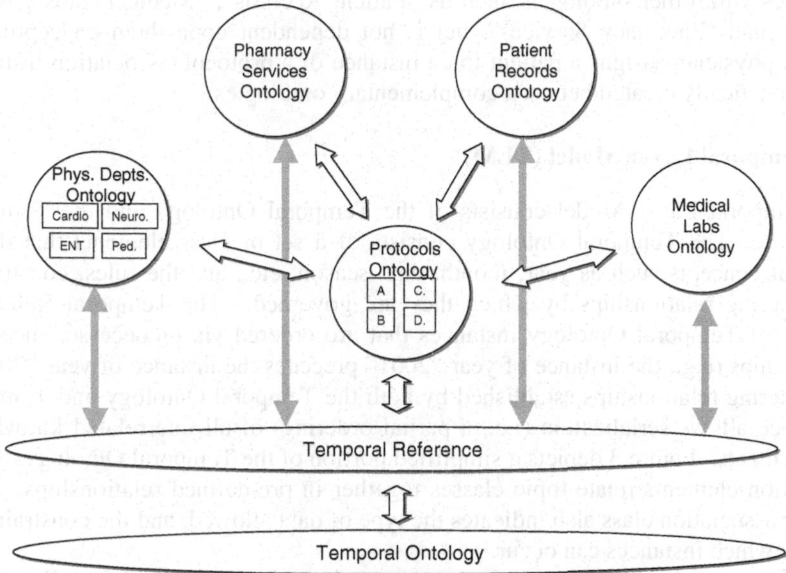

Fig. 2. Multidimensional Ontology Model for medical protocol example. Each ontology is interconnected to other relevant ontologies through the class association elements (depicted as double-headed arrows in figure). Each ontology is also connected to the Temporal Reference. The Temporal Layer Model (TLM) is defined as the combination of the Temporal Reference and Temporal Ontology.

Complementary ontologies are defined as two or more root ontologies that are interrelated to one another, thereby serving to enhance the overall knowledge represented. Complementary ontologies are connected through a subset of ontology defining *association* and *role* class elements. In the case of Figure 1, ontology defining classes within the "Protocols" and "Patient Records" ontologies are interconnected to one another (e.g., patient classes are assigned to particular protocol classes). Through inheritance, any instance of a patient assigned to a protocol, retains this interrelationship. The desired result is to provide relevant patient information to the medical professional when a specific protocol has been assigned (e.g., name, billing information, medical history, etc.). Doing this helps to provide a more complete picture of the patient/protocol instance.

An ontology within the MAKO-MOM is constructed using a set of topic, association and occurrence elements as defined by XTM 1.0. These interconnected sets of elements define the classes, which in turn, define the conceptualization being modeled.

In our example of the medical center, ontologies include "Pharmacy Services", "Patient Records", "Medical Labs", "Physician Departments", and "Protocols" (see Figure 2). Each ontology is considered independent (i.e., each is a complete specification of its conceptualization), and complementary to other ontologies. For example, protocol "A" in Figure 2 represents a complete step-by-step process that interfaces with other ontologies such as "Patient Records", "Medical Labs", "Phys. Depts.", and "Pharmacy Services", but is not dependent upon them conceptually[2]. When a physician assigns a patient to an instance of a protocol, association instances are automatically created between complementary ontologies.

2.2 Temporal Layer Model (TLM)

The Temporal Layer Model consists of the Temporal Ontology and the Temporal Reference. The Temporal Ontology consists of a set of class elements that define temporal concepts such as year, month, day, season, etc., and the rules, constraints, and ordering relationships by which they are governed. The Temporal Reference consists of Temporal Ontology instances that are ordered via predecessor/successor relationships (e.g., the instance of year "2001" precedes the instance of year "2002"). The ordering relationships established by both the Temporal Ontology and Temporal Reference allows serialization (i.e., a partial ordering) of all interrelated knowledge base elements. Figure 3 depicts a simplified portion of the Temporal Ontology. Class association elements relate topic classes together in pre-defined relationships. Each topic or association class also indicates the type of data allowed, and the constraints or rules by which instances can occur.

When an instance of "year" is created, topics for "months", "weeks", "days", "hours", "minutes", etc., which comprise the concept of "year" are also created. When declaring an instance of "year", constraints and ordering relationships are inherited in a straightforward manner. For example, every year has 12 months starting with "JAN" and ending with "DEC", and each month has a predetermined number of days. However, when assigning a day of the week ("SUN" through "SAT") to a particular date, simple algorithms need to be called upon to ensure the correct matching between "date" and "day-of-the-week". This is because assignment is dependent upon the particular year in question. Leap year adjustments are also handled in the same manner. Figure 4 depicts an example of two dates: December 31, 2003 and January 1, 2004. The Temporal Reference provides the following information:

1. The year "2003" precedes the year "2004"
2. The month "DEC" has 31 days, and is the last month of the year.
3. The month "JAN" has 31 days and is the first month in the year.
4. December 31, 2003 occurred on a Wednesday. Therefore, the *variable name* for December 31, 2003 is "Wednesday".
5. January 1, 2004 occurred in a Thursday. Therefore, the *variable name* for January 1, 2004 is "Thursday".

---

[2] Protocol "A" is described as a set of steps. Some of these steps may refer to lab results or patient reactions; however, the existence of the protocol itself is not dependent upon either the medical lab or the patient ontologies.

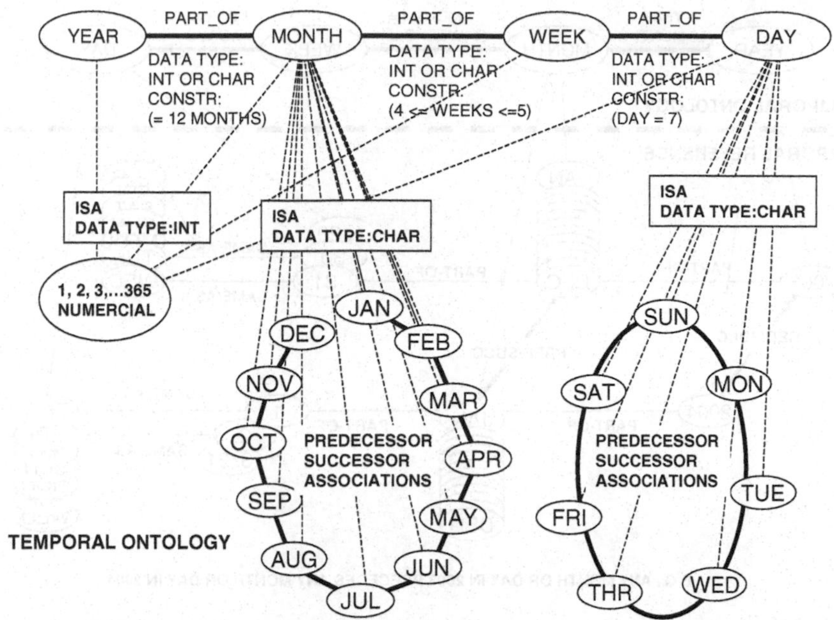

Fig. 3. The Temporal Ontology provides class relationships within the TLM. "ISA", "Part_of", "super-subclass", "aggregate", and "predecessor-successor" relationships are established within this ontology. Figure shows a partial example of the type of relationships and constraints that exist. Instances of ontology elements are constrained by data type and upper/lower bounds. For example, "JAN" must have 31 days, year "2001" must have 12 months (not shown).

6. December 31, 2003 preceded January 1, 2004.
7. Following constraints require "WED" to immediately precede "THR", "DEC 31" to precede "JAN 1", etc.

All ontology-defining class elements and their instances are connected to the temporal reference for the purpose of object serialization and temporal inferencing. Each root or sub-ontology is temporally divided into *occurrent* and *continuant* layers, which serve to maintain order among knowledge base objects. Continuant objects are *stable* topics and associations that do not change over the valid time interval [3] of the knowledge base. Occurrent, or *dynamic*, objects are created, destroyed, or their definitions modified during the valid time interval [11]. Segregating continuant and occurrent objects has benefits when considering knowledge base serialization. The reason is simple, continuant objects, which exist in a stable form regardless of time, are not required to be temporally ordered as long as their core identity (i.e., subject identity, base name, and class) does not change. This reduces computer resource needs during temporal serialization. For knowledge bases that are populated with numerous occurrent elements whose associative "mappings" change frequently, the temporal reference helps to preserve the historical relationships between objects thus making post analysis for any previous time period possible.

[3] The valid time interval of the knowledge base represents the time interval for which the knowledge base was intended.

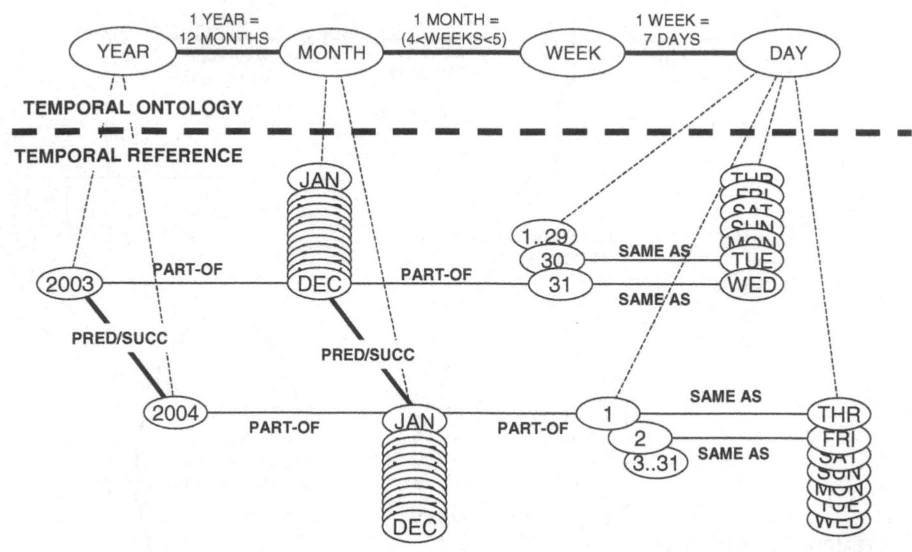

Fig. 4. TLM example for dates December 31, 2003 and January 1, 2004

3 MAKO Just-in-Time Process Model (JITPM)

The JITPM is captured within the MAKO framework as an ontology consisting of a number of separate or integrated processes. Each process is represented by a set of topics, which in turn, represent steps or phases. The relationships between steps (e.g., "predecessor-successor", "overlapping steps", "gap between steps") are represented by XTM 1.0 association class elements and member roles. Processes are connected to complementary ontologies and the temporal reference via association elements. By connecting process steps and complementary ontologies to the temporal reference, time critical information (e.g., patient test results, latest drug information or treatment techniques, etc.), is readily available to the medical professional during specific steps or phases when needed. In addition, since the start of any protocol is relative to the patient (i.e., patients on the same protocol will most likely have differing start-finish times), the temporal reference helps the system automatically keep track of patient progress, and can alert medical professionals when a protocol decision point has been reached.

Each phase within the process is associated with a time interval whose beginning and end time points are represented by t_{open} (i.e., start of the phase) and t_{close} (end of the phase). The relationships between phases (e.g., "gap", "overlap", "pred/succ") are defined by the roles each phase, or topic, plays in the adjacent association. These role types are shown in Figure 5. For example, if two phases are connected to one another in a "pred/succ" relationship, then the predecessor phase takes on the role of SB/EB or "Starts_Before/Ends_Before", and the successor phase takes on the role of SA/EA or "Starts_After/Ends_After". The role assignments in this relationship means that the predecessor phase must start and end before the successor phase begins. From the viewpoint of the successor phase, it cannot start until the predecessor phase has ended. In addition, our model identifies the "pred/succ" relationship as one in which the successor must start immediately after the predecessor has ended. In contrast, the definition of the "gap" relationship with phases that are assigned similar roles, allows a period where neither the predecessor nor the successor are active. Roles dictate "overlap" relationships between phases in a similar manner. In each "overlap" case, the unique relationship between phases is strictly dictated by the roles each plays. Constraints, which are part of the protocol's ontological description, dictate the minimum and maximum times a phase overlap or gap can exist. The concept of applying roles to relationships provides flexibility in representing complex processes that do not adhere to strict sequential order (e.g., several parallel phase paths executed in a concurrent manner).

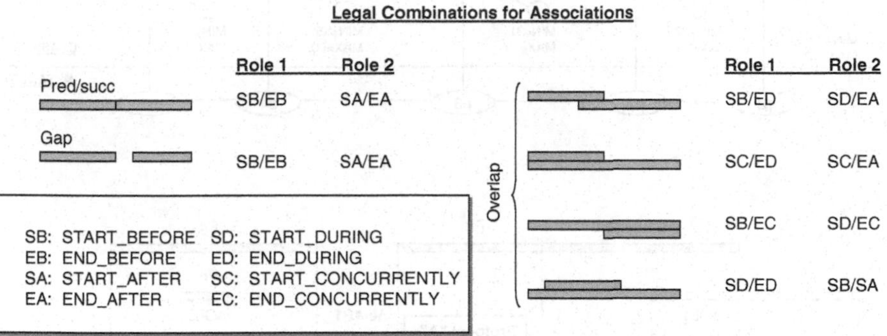

Fig. 5. Protocol process is shown with relative time line for each phase. Each protocol is created as a class of topic and association elements that are linked to relevant ontologies as appropriate. Upon initiation, an instance of the protocol is created with full inheritance, and the first phase is anchored via the temporal reference.

Figure 6 depicts a fictional treatment protocol. Relationships between phases are defined by their roles per Figure 5 and are defined ahead of time in the protocol ontology. The protocol is a set of topics related together via association and role elements. Each protocol within the ontology is carefully created by the organization based upon current medical practices for use in treating a specific ailment. Each step in the protocol is represented by either a single topic or set of topics, which in turn represent an activity such as retrieving patient information or lab results, linking and retrieving relevant medical documentation, executing or terminating a process such as the start of a drug regimen, and identifying decision points within the procedure. Each protocol instance inherits data typing and constraints from parental classes contained within the protocol ontology. Protocol instances, which are essentially copies, i.e., *instantiations*, of the protocol ontology, are uniquely created for individual patients and are attached to the temporal reference. Attaching the individual patient's protocol instance to the temporal reference essentially anchors the start date, enabling the system to automatically track patient progress. Each instance of a protocol also inherits parental associations that are connected to other relevant ontologies such as the "Medical Lab", "RX Services", "Patient Records", and "Phys.

Dept.". In other words, as soon as a patient is assigned to a specific protocol, associations between the protocol and other relevant ontologies are created. For example, upon protocol initiation, the topic "retrieve_patient_history" tells the system to automatically retrieve the patient's medical record from the "Patient Records" database. As the patient progresses through the protocol, timely information, such as lab results, availability of new drugs, or new procedures, are revealed to the physician at the appropriate time when informed decision-making or observation is required.

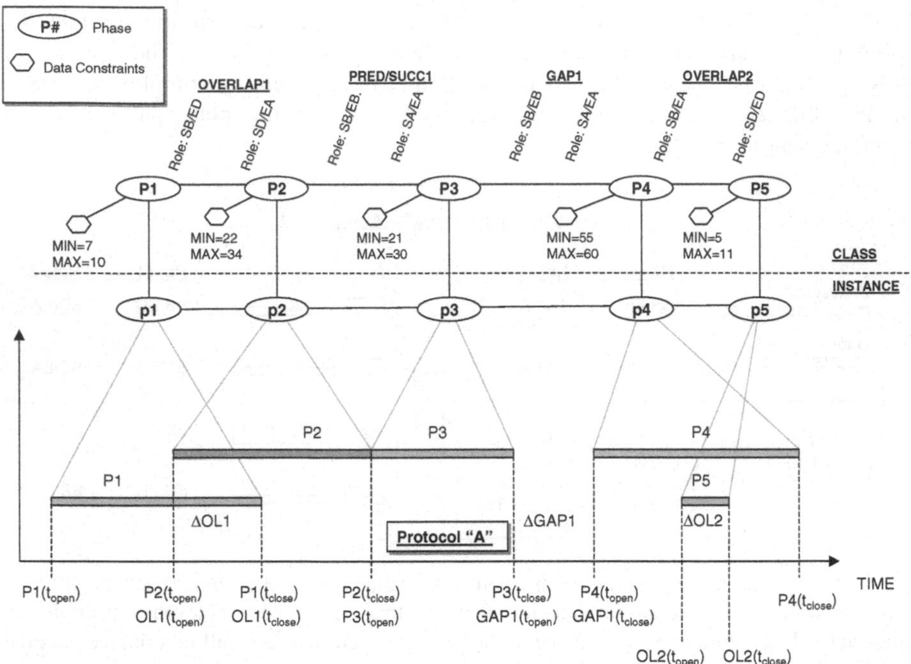

Fig. 6. Protocol "A" is created within the Protocols Ontology as a set of topic and association class elements. Data constraints, such as the minimum and maximum number of days allowed for each phase, are identified as part of the protocol "A" ontology. Upon assignment to a patient, an instance of protocol "A" is created and the start time P1(topen) is anchored to the temporal reference. Bars on the time graph represent the length of each phase, the order in which each phase must occur, phase time limits, and the time in which "gaps" or "overlaps" between phases can occur.

As an example, in Figure 7, patient "X" is assigned to protocol "A" by the physician. Upon assignment, an instance of protocol "A" is created for "X".

At "p1" of the protocol instance "A", information is automatically linked to patient "X's" pertinent drug, medical lab and treatment histories. Only data that is specific to protocol "A" is returned (e.g., patient "X" billing records are not needed, however "X's" medical history is considered relevant and therefore retrieved[4]). By initiating

[4] This applies to drug, medical and physician department information as well. Only patient information deemed necessary for executing the protocol are returned.

an instance of protocol "A", relevant knowledge is automatically pushed to the physician as each phase, "p1" through "p5", is executed. Initiation of "p1" also causes a time stamp, t_{open}, to be created via relationship to the Temporal Reference. This time stamp provides the reference by which the remainder of the protocol is executed.

Finally, the physician is alerted to information (e.g., current studies, research material, medical findings) contained in databases and web sites that are considered relevant to protocol "A", "p1" (Figure 7).

An advantage of modeling protocols using this method is the ability to capture changes within the ontology that can be applied to all future instances of the protocol. This makes the implementation of procedural changes (i.e., between roles or the sequencing of phases, and data constraints) straightforward. Other advantages include the ability to track multiple patients with different start times, mid protocol re-direction per patient, and the system's ability "push" relevant information to the medical professional based upon patient progress and physician decision making.

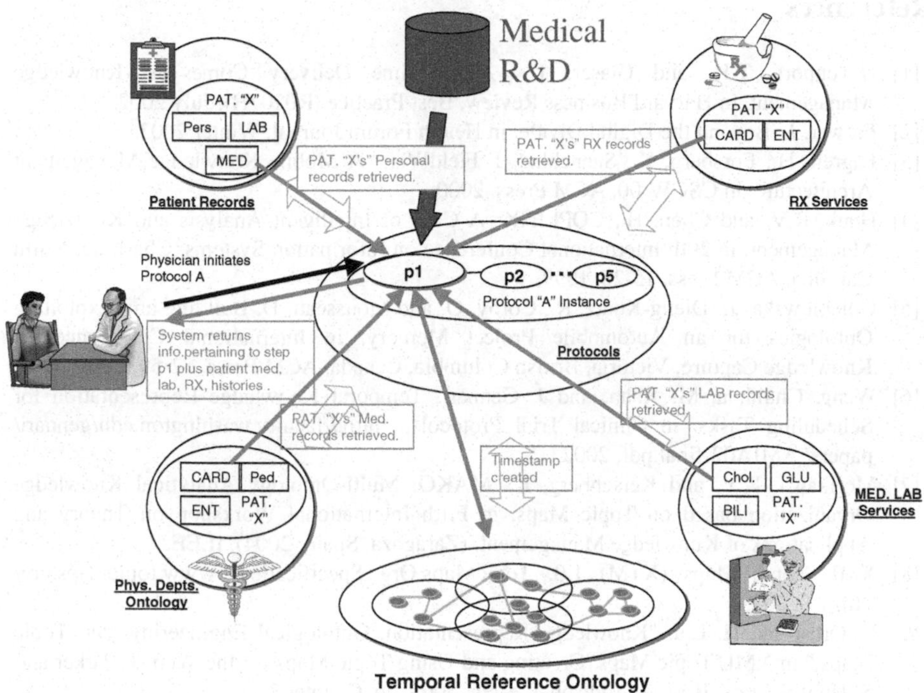

Fig. 7. Protocol is represented by a set of connected topic and association elements. During the execution of each phase, the most recent and pertinent medical treatment data is also pushed to the physician for review.

4 Conclusions

The MAKO-PM model enables timely information to be displayed to a user when specific steps or phases in a process are reached. The information retrieved is derived from separate, and independent, ontologies maintained by subject matter experts for use by an organization. By creating associations between individual steps in a process and related data in complimentary ontologies, the user is supplied with the critical and timely data needed to make informed decisions.

The MAKO-PM uses the XTM standard as a basic building block for maximum interoperability. However, the basic concept should be equally viable using RDF and OWL standards. A deficiency of the current XTM standard is it's lack of a data typing or data constraint mechanism. Future investigation should include ways in which RDFS-like templates can be formally adopted to address such deficiencies.

Acknowledgements. This work was sponsored by a NURI from the National Geospatial-Intelligence Agency (NGA).

References

[1] Davenport, T.H. and Glaser, J. Just-in-Time Delivery Comes to Knowledge Management. in Harvard Business Review, Best Practice (R0207H), July 2002.
[2] Flower, J. Beyond the Digital Divide. in Health Forum Journal, Winter 2003.
[3] Fagrell, H., Forsberg, K., Sanneblad, J. FieldWise: A Mobile Knowledge Management Architecture. in CSCW'00, ACM Press, 2000.
[4] Hauk, R.V. and Chen, H., COPLINK: A Case of Intelligent Analysis and Knowledge Management. in 20th International Conference on Information Systems, Charlotte, North Carolina, ACM Press, 15-28, 1999.
[5] Golebiowska, J., Dieng-Kuntz, R., Corby, O. and Mousseau, D. Building and Exploiting Ontologies for an Automobile Project Memory. in International Conference on Knowledge Capture, Victoria, British Columbia, Canada, ACM Press, 52-59, 2001.
[6] Weng, Chunhua, M. Kahn, and J. Gennari, Temporal Knowledge Representation for Scheduling Tasks. in Clinical Trial Protocols, http://faculty.washington.edu/gennari/ papers/ AMIA02-final.pdf, 2002.
[7] Morikawa, R.Y. and Kerschberg, L., MAKO: Multi-Ontology Analytical Knowledge Organization based on Topic Maps. in Fifth International Workshop on Theory and Applications of Knowledge Management, (Zaragoza, Spain, 2004), IEEE.
[8] XML Topic Maps (XTM) 1.0, TopicMaps.Org Specification, www.topicmaps.org/ xtm/1.0, 2003.
[9] L. Orbst and H. Liu, "Knowledge Representation, Ontological Engineering, and Topic Maps," in XML Topic Maps: Creating and Using Topic Maps for the Web, J. Parker and S. Hunting, Eds. Boston: Addison-Wesley, 2003, pp. Chapter 7.
[10] N. F. Noy and D. L. McGuinness, "Ontology Development 101: A Guide to Creating Your First Ontology," Stanford Knowledge Systems Laboratory Technical Report KSL-01-05 and Stanford Medical Informatics Technical Report SMI-2001-0880 March 2001.
[11] J. F. Sowa, Knowledge Representation: Logical, Philosophical, and Computational Foundations: Brooks/Cole Thomas Learning, 2000.

Knowledge Creation Framework – Enabling Just-in-Time Information Delivery

Mark Siebert

Siemens Business Services GmbH und Co OHG, Munich, Germany
{mark.siebert@siemens.com}

Abstract. Capturing and applying context-information is still a problem for just-in-time information delivery. This paper understands just-in-time information delivery as knowledge creation process and derives a framework. The application to the use case of proposal development within Siemens Business Services shows the potential of the framework enabling intelligent technologies. Future research will focus on elaborating a model of "knowledge intelligence" to support knowledge creation and just-in-time information delivery starting from multi-agent environments.

Keywords: Knowledge creation, Artificial Intelligence, Knowledge Management Systems, Pattern recognition, Context, Perspective taking, (Multi-) Agents.

1 Motivation and Introduction

Quick development of high quality proposals is a main and knowledge intensive process within sales (with knowledge products as output). Sales representatives (sales rep.) spend a *lot of time in producing proposals rather identifying and understanding customer needs.* Technological process optimization could increase productivity, driven by focused usage of the valuable human resources (e.g. to identify the real customer needs).

At Siemens Business Services (SBS) for example, a sales rep. requires various information from different sources to develop the proposal components, like customer facts and contacts from CRM, global service prices from the bidding tool, successful and similar proposals from the knowledge base, templates from project management portal or references and service descriptions from the sales service. For each of them he has to step out of the proposal process into a search process, where he needs to *reformulate his intention into search queries and re-interpret the results.*

He receives his information only passively upon request rather actively according his status in the proposal process. One reason for this might be the complexity of knowledge-intensive processes *are not yet sufficiently understood and described* to develop and provide the right technological support. But modeling methods and frameworks are already described, e.g. [Gro04].

The paper addresses the problem from the user's individual perspective rather than from the technology perspective as knowledge is said to be subjective (see following chapter). Providing just-in-time relevant information (technology point of view)

K.-D. Althoff et al. (Eds.): WM 2005, LNAI 3782, pp. 699 – 709, 2005.

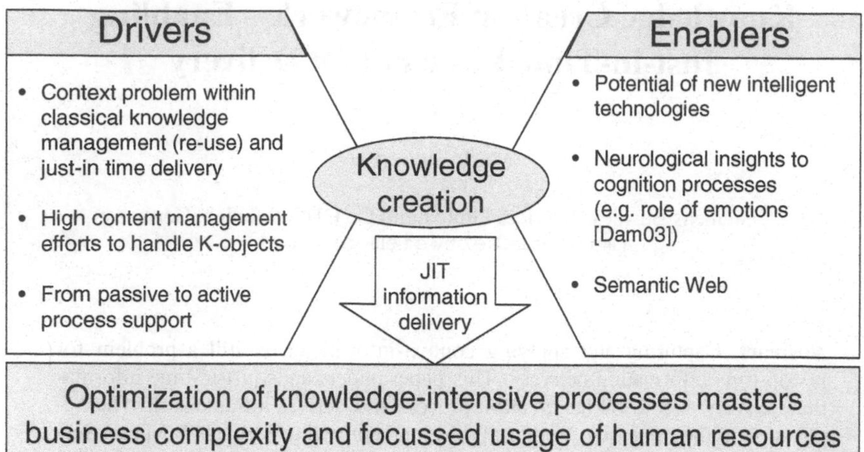

Fig. 1. Motivation for Knowledge creation

means in that sense putting information in relevant context and *creating knowledge* (user's point of view) in the current situation. A better understanding of the creation processes on individual level will support handling of the complexity.

Figure 1 summarizes the key drivers and enablers, which enable enables just-in-time information delivery and optimization of knowledge intensive processes using a knowledge creation framework. Optimized processes allow the organization to focus its resources (e.g. sales representatives) on business critical topics (e.g. relationship management with the customer)

Existing discussions on knowledge management focused on knowledge sharing but struggled with handling of the context and high content management efforts. Neurological insights and developments in intelligent technologies additionally drive the research into knowledge creation, with the following questions for this project:

- What do different disciplines understand in "knowledge creation"?
- How can a better understanding contribute to solve the context problem ?
- How differs individual knowledge creation from organizational ?
- How could the knowledge worker be supported in knowledge creation ?
- Which intelligent technologies and architectures do serve for those requirements and where is the human resource key to success ?

Qualitative research offers with the Grounded Theory a multi-discipline desk research linked to existing use cases at Siemens Business Services for the development of the relevant framework [Gla98, p.8 and 15]. The Grounded theory supports the development of theories and models (e.g. the knowledge creation framework) based on hypothesis and concepts. They derive on an inductive way from a systematic discussion and link to the underlying "data" (here proposals at SBS). The transfer of the theoretical model into technological architectures will proof the concept in practice using the introduced use-case of proposal development at SBS based on action research. Action research aims to combine change in some organization and to increase understanding on part of the researcher. [Dic92]

2 Knowledge and the Knowledge Creation Framework

Most research and applications in business- and artificial intelligence understand knowledge according to the „knowledge stairs" of North [Nor98] as *information in context*. Within Siemens it is understood as potential for action [Dav02] in the dimensions of proficiency, codification and diffusion. Nonaka [Non95, p.59] distinguished the form of knowledge, explicit (KMS focus) and implicit (HR focus).

The (moderate) constructivist theory [Rot94] distinguishes between objective reality and subjective perspective and understands knowledge as *representation* of reality. It offers a wider understanding of knowledge as *subjective perspective* of the individual, understood as a temporary and viable (individual) *state of consciousness*. We experience this state as knowledge in the sense of "justified true belief" [Non95, p.58]. According to v. Glasersfeld [Gla95] knowledge in this sense is *viable*, led by and focused on the application of the knowledge in reality.

Understanding knowledge from a constructivist point of view as a *state of consciousness*, knowledge could only be created inside a *system* or individual [see Luh95]. The system is defined according to its context, understood as *intention* (will) and *situation* (application) [for definition overview: Bré96]. Individual knowledge creation incorporates specific characteristics like reflexivity [Coh95, p.80f.], self-similarity [Pri95, p.26] and circularity [Pri95, p.25]˙ Reflexivity and self-similarity describe the characteristic to apply the framework on different abstraction levels. Each process step could be described by the KCF itself. Circularity describes the characteristic that each step influences the next one based on the individual's memory and experiences.

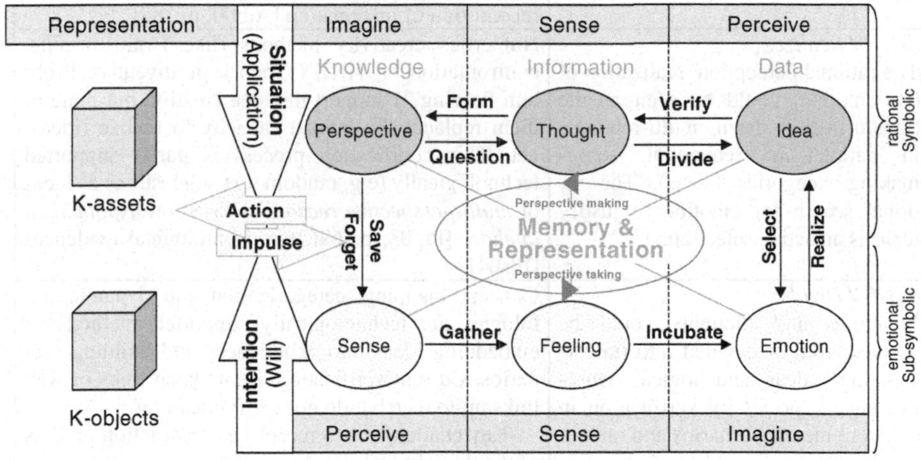

Fig. 2. Knowledge Creation Framework (KCF)

The *framework* starts and ends with the individual perspective (from external interpretated as implicit knowledge) as a state of consciousness. The perspective at the end results from interfering *construction* and *selection* processes based on different forms of memory. The creation process consists in analogy to [Bol95] of two elements: *perspective taking and perspective making.* Perspective taking exists as rational (symbolic) or emotional (sub-symbolic) process. Rationally it is triggered by an impulse or observation and then split into sense-making elements. Re-categorizing and evaluating them emotionally leads to the *perspective making* in order to create a new state of awareness (new knowledge). *Intelligence* is the capability to operate this process by differentiating and deciding. The understanding of each process step should enable technology to better design intelligent solutions supporting the creation process and with this enhancing the just-in-time delivery. First technologies are already in use, each of them with an own user interface (context):

Table 1. Steps within the Knowledge Creation Framework

Process step	Existing technology
Gather: Gathering and bundling of different sensorial impulses evokes a feeling	Agents gather information (e.g. prices), crawl websites and use sensorial data acting as classical search engines. But to create a feeling gathering of sensorial data over time is not sufficient.
Incubate: In an emotional maturity process parallel working scenarios are combined through a selective filter to emerge as an emotion.	Recent avatars show emotions or the robot-dog (Asimo) or a Tamagotchi which both feel offended if they sense and "feel" that a combination of actions and inputs contradicts with their basic set of rules, values or defined scenarios. From a linguistic point of view (language production) the set of rules is represented as internal concepts, which allow quicker recognition of information [Alb00, p. 188]
Select / Realize: The rational perception, realization of the emotion, could be seen as the transformation from multi-relations in parallel to sequential, sense-making categories (ideas). The rational search for emotion to justify ideas is an active selection.	Numerous creativity methods (like Brainstorming, confrontation or TRIZ ("Theory of Inventive Problem Solving")) support the idea creation but none of them replaces the human capacity to realize (ideas) yet. This codification process is partly supported technologically (e.g. random text suggestions as ideas or *multi-perspective reasoning* based on *hypothetical anchors* [Pip03, p.169f.]) and ontological evidences [Els04].
Verify / Divide: Meanings and thoughts could be derived from or devided into (understanding) ideas and logical sense-making categories by verification in different mental scenarios and memorized experiences.	Concept mapping, categorization and dynamic ontologies are technologically supported methods of embedding ideas into experiences and building scenarios. Current verification agents keep links or web links up-to date but do not verify ideas yet. Key challenge is to recap the construction process of the thought (n:1 development).
Form / Question: Based on the individual's ability to abstract and differentiate, thoughts and meanings could be clustered, summarized, categorized to better fit to the application context.	Louçã [Lou93], for instances, describes a model for agent-based decision-making with concept maps (see also "Verify"). Bailini [Bai03] investigates the role of different viewpoints in decision-making (Questioning)

Forget / Save: The current perspective will be interfered by a new one. The intensity of the old one decreases, which we perceive unconsciously as forgetting.	Technology usually follows the aim to save but not to forget. Knowledge Management Systems include dates of expiry within documents or websites. As a question of priority and categorization this process step is directly linked to the form of memory.
Memory: The memory influences each creation step and makes it recursive Science differentiates three forms of memory: sensorial, primary or short-term and secondary or long-term memory	V. Elst [Els01] or Gandon [Gan00] in the CoMMA project provide agent-based middleware for exploitation of distributed organizational memories. Memory has to be seen as a dynamic system of multi-dimensional links rather than a stable and pre-organized information stock or archive.

Nonaka [Non95] already showed ways of knowledge creation (Internalization, Externalization, Socialization and Combination) as *interaction of individuals*. They are *communication* in respect of building a common perspective within a group or organization based on the interaction and space of relations between the individuals described as “ba” [Non98].

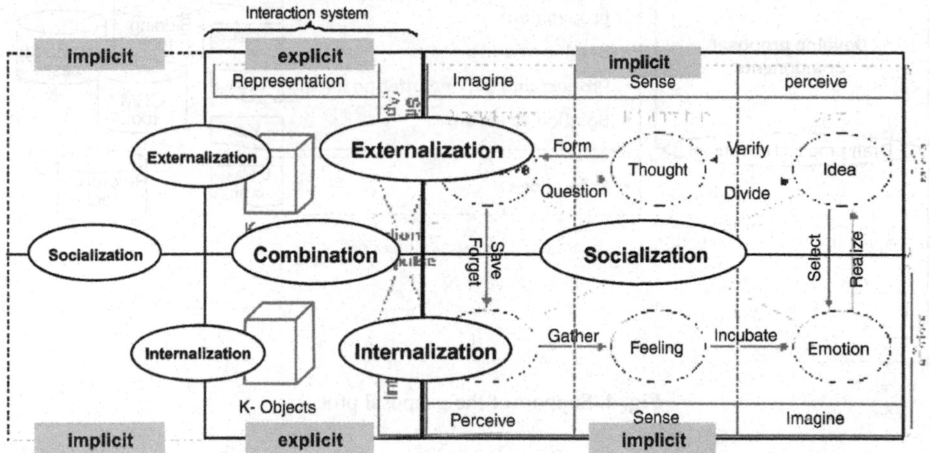

Fig. 3. KCFs are linked through an interaction system

Nonaka does not specify the *individual* knowledge creation and does not distinguish between rational (symbolic) and emotional (sub-symbolic) explanation levels.

As implicit intention, which is derived from the perspective made or taken, is a key element of context, knowledge itself would not be created within the interaction system but *only in the individual*. Externalization and Internalization thus describe more the *transformation* of individual perspectives into explicit knowledge objects rather than creation of individual knowledge. Combining and discussion the perspectives of different individuals leads to Maturana’s [Mat87] understanding of knowledge from an *organizational perspective* as a *co-creation* based on common perspectives and understanding.

3 Application of the Framework in Proposal Development

The application of the framework to the introduced use case illustrates the knowledge creation (a benefit argumentation). The overview in Table 1 showed no significant technologies for the representation of emotional, sub-symbolic processes. In the first step the application of the framework to the use case will focus on the rational, symbolic level.

Proposal Development at Siemens Business Services follows a standard process starting with the customers' request for proposal. Focus for the question of JIT information delivery is the development of proposal components for a draft proposal document.

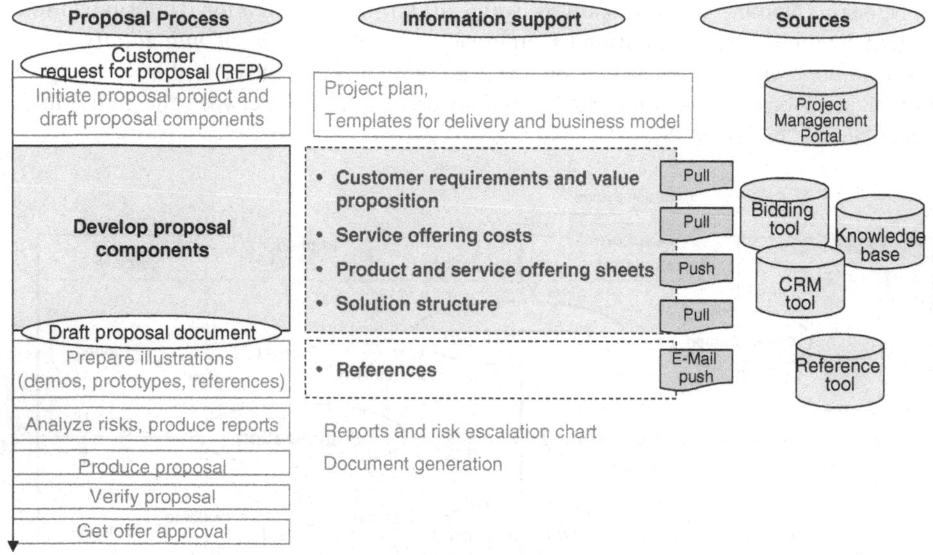

Fig. 4. Support of the proposal process

Part of the draft proposal is an articulated benefit argumentation to discuss with his experts in the proposal team and the organization. With a first (full-text, key word) search on the knowledgebase he identifies various related documents, like: service offering sheets, ROI calculations or project overviews from former projects.

Based on the search results he follows the knowledge creation framework on a symbolic level (upper process in Fig. 3).

The system *perceives* the search results and *identifies key words* (e.g. ROI, CRM, etc.) by full-text and meta-information search.

Questioning the results the system links and clusters the key words into a topic map by the *type of documents*, for instances, they are located in (e.g. calculation or solution description).

Dividing the topics (documents) on content level into their content structures refines the topic map and reveals further relations among the topics. They link content to documents and meta-information (document type) and form new *categories* (e.g. external ROI (content) used in a won project (document-type)).

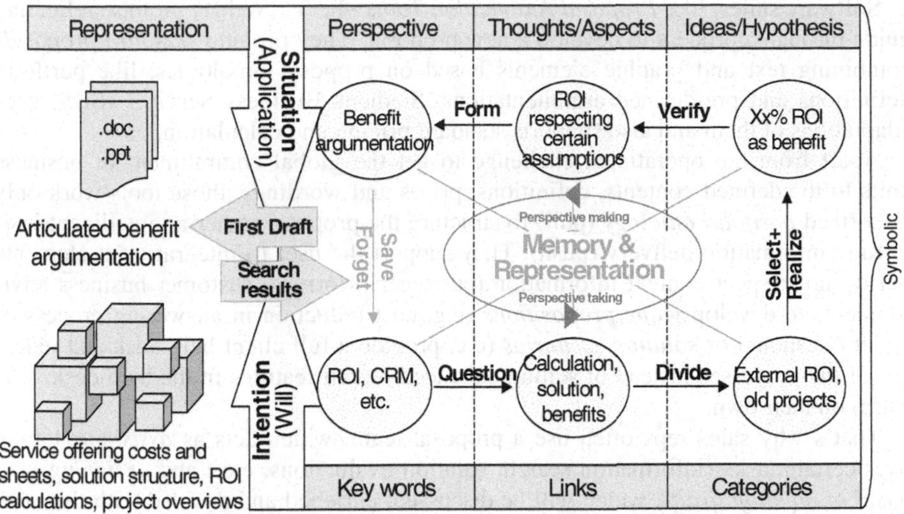

Fig. 5. Development of a benefit argumentation with the KCF

Selecting and realizing the "right" ROI for the benefit argumentation is the shift from perspective taking mode to perspective making mode. Key element is to identify and set *hypothetical anchors* on content level based on *multi-perspective reasoning* over the defined categories. The decision challenges the system to evaluate and choose out of the multiple options in accordance and respect to the requirements and a sense-making argumentation.

The postulated hypothesis ("the proposed solution will bring an ROI of about 20%") now has to be *verified* against the proposed solution concept with its details and expert information. The result will be a modified or restricted thesis with arguments and conditions.

Those arguments have to be formed into a *logical structure,* which could be explicated as a first draft benefit argumentation.

Although a user driven approach illustrated the use case, the technological representation has to combine various technologies and integrate solutions. Agents within a coordinating multi-agent environment promise a possible realization with their flexibility and potential to intelligent behavior.

4 Outlook to an Agent-Enabled Framework

First active information-push functionalities at Siemens Business Services (e.g. provide reference information once he enters a lead into the CRM system) already led to an *information overflow*, as technology was not yet able to capture the whole context, link different information sources autonomously and delivered information specific enough. Addionally this would just provide existing knowledge objects but would not support knowledge creation as no adaptations to the current situation could be made.

Software suites, like *Proposal Automation Tools* –PAT- [Wil01] promise relief and guide through a process to develop a new proposal. They provide *standard proposals* combining text and graphic elements based on proposal ontologies, like portfolio definitions and pre-defined argumentations. Siemens Business Services (SBS) uses adaptations of them and also supports standard pricing and calculation.

Apart from the operational challenge to get the global commitment of business units to the defined contents, definitions, prices and wordings, those tools work only on a fixed *portfolio ontology* (pull) to structure the proposal rather an intelligent just-in-time information delivery (push). They support the user to integrate text elements but do not respect context information (customer priorities, customer business environment) to develop *value propositions* (e.g. cost reduction in answering process of client questions) or *solution scenarios* (e.g. provide a full client help-desk and redesign of the processes instead of selling enhanced search features in the help-desk software) on their own.

That's why sales reps often use a proposal team, which acts as *assistants* taking over certain tasks (information search, solution evaluations, etc.) and *designing proposal or solution drafts*, which will be discussed, enriched and decided with the sales rep. and the customer up to the final version of the proposal. In analogy and based on Tacla [Tac03], active process support could (a) *replace certain tasks* (service agents) and act as (b) *assistant* (personal agents) drafting and proposing solution scenarios.

Personal agents address and describe directly, analytically the *procedural* context and have to cope with issues of *the human-computer interface* (e.g. animated conversation agents) and usability questions. They support externalization and internalization of knowledge and transform knowledge into a usable format within the process.

Service agents in contrast are more likely to support *individual* knowledge development itself and address the context problem indirectly. Each process step described in the KCF could be replaced or supported by an agent. The whole perspective taking and making would though resemble a multi-agent system based on *holistic*, rather than analytical, context capturing or creation (perspective) of the situation and address the context problem though indirectly.

Service agents and agent-based technologies already cover a broad range of use cases within Knowledge Management. [Mac03] and [Mor03] for instances use agents for optimization and enhancement of features in current KM systems, like document classification and mailing list optimization.

Agents dynamically link concept maps, match and merge ontologies to build hypothetical anchors and derive storylines, e.g. a benefit argumentation, as seen in the application example. As addition to existing PAT agent solutions use context information to build a storyline rather just combining content elements according to user-driven steps.

Linking, managing and combining the right agents are the challenge of *multi-agent architectures (MAS)*. They enable agents to work together in social environments, providing a standard language, registration (directory services), identification and security [Cle00].

From an architectural perspective, MAS link the user interface (portal) and the content (Knowledge Management Systems (KMS)) through communication and knowledge-intensive functions.

Literature and research describe different types of agent architectures aiming at technically representing a *rational thinking human being* and model real social systems (by working character – [Mer01], Rao [Rao95], by result orientation [Deb00], by level of abstraction [Els04]). *Merk* [Mer01] distinguishes between logic-based, reactive and belief-desire intention (BDI) architectures. *Debenham* [Deb00] furthermore distinguishes *reactive deliberative and hybrid architectures. Elst et. al.* [Els04, p.23] structure MAS based on their level of abstraction and complexity into *single-agent systems, homogeneous agent systems and heterogeneous systems* on the levels of system development and KM applications. To support learning within MAS Müller proposed and developed the InterRRAP architecture [Mue97] with a *conceptual layer* to describe how agents are specified and a *control layer* to describe how they operate.

Based on the overview further research has to evaluate suitable agent-architectures and agent descriptions to fulfil the requirements of the introduced use case and enable the KCF.

5 Conclusions for JIT Information Delivery and Future Research

The knowledge creation framework (KCF) serves as a new approach to *overcome the context-problem* in just-in-time information delivery understanding knowledge creation as just-in time information delivery from a user's point of view. It therewith expands existing models of knowledge creation (e.g. Nonaka's SECI model) from an organizational point of view to an individual. Knowledge creation is a question of *perspective taking and making*. Illustrating an use case of proposal development within SBS the rational level of KCF serves as process guideline for the development of an example benefit argumentation out of key word based search results.

In general, agents act autonomously based on rules of "artificial intelligence" (AI). AI describes the attempt to artificially simulate human intelligence. *Intelligence* describes a, mostly rational, *capability* to create knowledge. Applying this to the creation of knowledge (in the sense of contextual information), all technologies, processes, models and approaches enabling and supporting knowledge creation could be described as *"Knowledge Intelligence"*. It expresses the technological capability (intelligence) to create knowledge. Special interest lies in the role of perspective-based, intentional context, like [Bla03] (implicit culture based agents) or [Per03] (intentional analysis) started to investigate. To overcome the context-problem findings from *multi perspective reasoning* and *holistic pattern recognition* should be derived and applied.

The KCF of course can be applied on organizational level (e.g. supporting idea and innovation processes), too, but focuses on the individual level. A KCF-based architecture will enable active provision of proposal scenarios to sales representatives within the proposal development use case at Siemens Business Services.

Its further technological representation (most likely MAS and agent technologies) and realization is focus of future research in my dissertation, embedded into SBS co-operations with the SEKT [Sek] and EPOS [Epo] projects.

References

[Alb00] Alber, K.: Kognitive Verarbeitung von Dimensionsadjektiven - ein konstruktivistisch-konnektionistisches Modell zur Produktion von Äußerungen mit dem Dimensionsadjektiv "groß", Diss., University of Bielefeld (2000)

[Bai03] Bailini, S.C., Truszkowski, W., Perspectives: An Analysis of Multiple Viewpoints in Agent-Based Systems, in: van Elst, L., Dignum, V., Abecker, A., (eds.): Agent-mediated Knowledge Management, Proceedings and Lecture Notes of AMKM, AAAI Spring Symposium 2003, Springer, Heidelberg (2003) 369-387

[Bla03] Blanzieri, E., Giorgini, P., Giunchiglia, F., Zanoni, C.: Implicit Culture-Based Personal Agents for Knowledge Management, in: van Elst, L., Dignum, V., Abecker, A., (eds.): Agent-mediated Knowledge Management, Proceedings and Lecture Notes of AMKM, AAAI Spring Symposium 2003, Springer, Heidelberg (2003) 246-261

[Bol95] Boland J., Tenkasi, R.: Perspective making and perspective taking in communities of knowing, in: Organization Science, 6(4), (1995)

[Bré96] Brézillon, P.: Context in human-machine problem solving; technical report 96/29, LAFORIA, Paris (1996)

[Cle00] Clement, M., Runte, M.: Intelligente Software-Agenten im eCommerce, in: der Markt, Nr. 152, 39 Jg., (2000) 18-35

[Coh95] Cohen, J., Steward, I.: Chaos und Anti-Chaos, München (1997), 80f., cited in: Primio, F.: Roboterkognition, GMD Report 16, Sankt Augustin, (1998) 24f.

[Dam03] Damasio, A.R., Der Spinoza-Effekt, München (2003)

[Dav02] Davenport, T., Probst; G.: Knowledge Management Case book – Siemens Best practices; Erlangen (2002)

[Deb00] Debenham, J.K.: Three Intelligent Architectures for Business Process Management, in: Proceedings 12th International Conference on Software Engineering and Knowledge Engineering SEKE2000, Chicago (2000), http://citeseer.ist.psu.edu/debenham00three.html

[Dic92] Dick, B.: Qualitative action research: improving the rigour and economy, in: Bruce, C. S. and Russell, A. L. (eds.): Transforming tomorrow today, 2nd World Congress on Action Learning, Brisbane (1992), http://www.scu.edu.au/schools/gcm/ar/arp/rigour2.html#a_r2_1

[Els01] van Elst, L., Abecker, A.: Domain Ontology Agents in Distributed Organizational Memories, Workshop on Knowledge Management and Organizational Memories (IJCAI), Seattle, Washington (2001)

[Els03] van Elst, L., Dignum, V., Abecker, A., (eds.): Agent-mediated Knowledge Management, Proceedings and Lecture Notes of AMKM, AAAI Spring Symposium 2003, Springer, Heidelberg (2003)

[Els04] van Elst, L., Kiesel, M.: Generating and Integrating Evidence for Ontology Mappings, in: Proceedings of the 14th International Conference, EKAW, Springer, Heidelberg (2004).

[Epo] "Leverage a user's effort for his personal knowledge management for his own benefit as well as to evolve this within the organization" – http://www.dfki.de/epos

[Gan00] Gandon, F: Multi-Agent System to Support Exploiting an XML-based Corporate Memory, in: Proceedings PAKM, Basel (2000)

[Gla95] v. Glasersfeld, E.: Radical Constructivism – A Way of Knowing and Learning, London (1995)

[Gla98] Glaser, B. G., Strauss, A.L.;: Grounded Theory, Bern, Göttingen (1998)

[Gro04] Gronau, N.: Management of Knowledge Intensive Business Processes, in: Proceedings of Second International Conference, Business Process Management, Potsdam, (2004) 163-178

[Lou03] Louçã, J.: Modeling Context-Aware Distributed Knowledge, in: van Elst, L., Dignum, V., Abecker, A., (eds.): Agent-mediated Knowledge Management, Proceedings and Lecture Notes of AMKM, AAAI Spring Symposium 2003, Springer, Heidelberg (2003) 202-212

[Luh95] Luhmann, N.: Die Soziologie und der Mensch, Opladen (1996)

[Mag03] Magalhãe, J.A., de Lucena, C.J.P.: Using an Agent-Based Framework and Separation of Concerns for the Generation of Document Classification Tools", in: van Elst, L., Dignum, V., Abecker, A., (eds.): Agent-mediated Knowledge Management, Proceedings and Lecture Notes of AMKM, AAAI Spring Symposium 2003, Springer, Heidelberg (2003) 193-200

[Mat87] Maturana, H. R. Varela, F. J.:Der Baum der Erkenntnis, Bern, München (1987)

[Mer01] Merk, S.L.: Softwareagenten – mobile Agenten –Aglets, Universität München (2001)

[Mor03] Moreale, E., Watt, S.: An Agent-Based Approach to Mailing List KM, in: van Elst, L., Dignum, V., Abecker, A., (eds.): Agent-mediated Knowledge Management, Proceedings and Lecture Notes of AMKM, AAAI Spring Symposium 2003, Springer, Heidelberg (2003) 118-129

[Mue97] Müller, J.P.: The Design of Intelligent Agents: A Layered Approach, Lecture Notes in Computer Science, 1177, Springer, Heidelberg (1996)

[Non95] Nonaka, I., Takeuchi, H.: The knowledge creating company, New York (1995)

[Non98] Nonaka, I., Konno, N.: The concept of "Ba". Building a foundation for knowledge creation, in: California Management review, 40 (1998) 40-55

[Nor98] North, K.: Wissensorientierte Unternehmensführung, Wiesbaden (1998)

[Per03] Perini, A., Bresciani, P., Yu, E., , Molani, A.: Intentional Analysis for Distributed KM, in: van Elst, L., Dignum, V., Abecker, A., (eds.): Agent-mediated Knowledge Management, Proceedings and Lecture Notes of AMKM, AAAI Spring Symposium 2003, Springer, Heidelberg (2003) 353-367

[Pip03] Pipek, V., Nuderscher, P; Won M.: Periphere Wahrnehmung von Expertise; in: Mambrey, P., Pipek, V., Rohde, M. (eds.): Wissen und Lernen in Virtuellen Organisationen, Heidelberg (2003)

[Pri95] Primio, F.: Roboterkognition, GMD Report 16, Sankt Augustin (1998) 24f.

[Rot94] Roth, G.: Das Gehirn und seine Wirklichkeit, Frankfurt (1994) 314 - 338

[Sek] "Developing the essential semantic knowledge technologies for realizing the European Knowledge Society" - http://www.sekt-project.com/

[Tac03] Tacla, C., Barthè, J-P.: A Multi-agent Architecture for Evolving Memories, in: van Elst, L., Dignum, V., Abecker, A., (eds.): Agent-mediated Knowledge Management, Proceedings and Lecture Notes of AMKM, AAAI Spring Symposium 2003, Springer, Heidelberg (2003) 389-404

[Wil01] Wilson, G. (2001): Proposal Automation Tools, in: Proposal Management Journal, Spring, (2001) 67-73

Just-in-Time Interactive Document Search

Makoto Iwayama and Yoshiki Niwa

Hitachi Ltd., Central Research Laboratory,
1-280, Higashi-Koigakubo, Kokubunji, Tokyo 185-8601, Japan
iwayama@crl.hitachi.co.jp, yniwa@harl.hitachi.co.jp

Abstract. *DualNAVI* is a user interface for "Just-in-Time" document search. Its dual view interface always returns the retrieved results in two views: a list of clustered titles for document space and topic word graphs for word space. They are tightly coupled by their cross-reference relation, and inspire the users with further interactions. *DualNAVI* also supports two kinds of search facilities, conventional keyword search and document associative search, which is searching documents by documents. The dual view interface provides a natural interface to invoke these two search facilities.

1 Introduction

In knowledge management systems, document search is a crucial function for assisting users' knowledge intensive works by providing useful documents to the users. Although there have been proposed many sophisticated algorithms of document searching [1], they still cost much time for users to obtain relevant documents to their information needs. To reduce the total cost of document searching, we have developed a "Just-in-Time" interactive interface called *DualNAVI*, which enables for users to recognize where they are during their searching processes and to find next directions to proceed. In other words, searching with *DualNAVI* can promote interactive and systematic refinement of search results with which users are liberated from blind trails and errors.

DualNAVI provides users with rich interaction both in document space and in word space. Its dual view interface always returns the retrieved results in two views: a list of clustered titles for document space and topic word graphs for word space. They are tightly coupled by their cross-reference relation. Through interactions between two views, users can have the summary of the retrieved results and are inspired with further interactions. *DualNAVI* also supports two kinds of search facilities, conventional keyword search and document associative search (searching documents by documents). Both of them are similarity based search from given items as a query. The dual view provides a natural interface to invoke these two search functions. Document associative search also facilitates the content-based correlation among databases which are maintained independently at distributed places. These functions of *DualNAVI* reduce the total cost of document search process in the "Just-in-Time" meaning.

DualNAVI has been commercially used in an encyclopedia search service over the internet since 1998, a bioinformatics DB search [2] since 2000, and a US/Japan patent search ("PatentRetriever") since 2003. Its effectiveness has been confirmed by many

K.-D. Althoff et al. (Eds.): WM 2005, LNAI 3782, pp. 710 – 718, 2005.

real users. It is also discussed as one of the promising search technologies for scientists in Nature magazine [3].

This paper is organized as follows. In section2 we briefly review the typical process of document searching and discuss the role of document search system in the process. In section 3 we introduce a basic design principle of *DualNAVI*. Two important features, dual view and dual query types, are also discussed. In section 4 we explain algorithms used to realize *DualNAVI* interface, and section 5 concludes the paper.

2 *DualNAVI* in Document Search Process

Figure 1 shows the typical process of document searching. Users first construct a query in the form of a list of keywords. When users are not familiar with their searching domain, the initial query may be vague or ambiguous, and the query should be refined in later steps of searching.

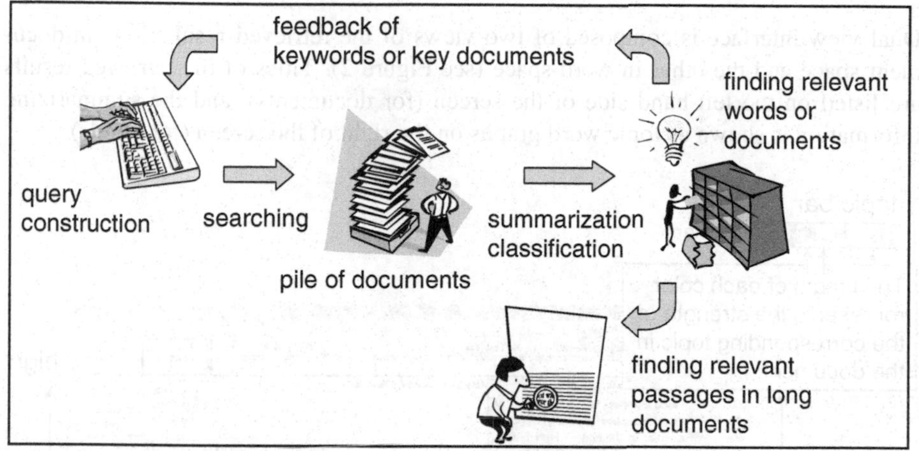

Fig. 1. Document search process

Based on the query, a system retrieves a set of documents and displays them to users. Here users have to understand the overview of the retrieved results to decide weather they stop or continue searching. Since almost all existing systems display search results in the ranked list only, users have to check them one by one. Dual view interface in *DualNAVI* reduces the cost taken in this process of summarization. It offers two kinds of summaries, topic word graph (in word view) and list of clustered documents (in document view), and these two summaries are closely related to each other.

When users are not satisfied with the retrieved results, they have to update the initial query to obtain refined results. One simple method is to add keywords to the query, but finding effective keywords is a hard task for non-expert users without domain knowledge. Topic word graph in *DualNAVI* helps such novice users easily to find relevant keywords, because connected words in a topic word graph suggest new keywords they have not noticed or they have not known. Another method of feedback is to use relevant documents themselves as key items. If users find one or more relevant documents in the search results, document associative search of *DualNAVI* automatically finds more documents similar to the key documents. This association is not limited within the same database, but it is applicable across different databases. For example, users can collect relevant patents to newspaper articles without constructing complicated queries. Using these feedbacks, users can refine search results until they are satisfied with the results.

In the following sections, we explain details of the above mentioned components of *DualNAVI*.

3 *DualNAVI* Interface

DualNAVI is based on two kinds of duality, dual view and dual query types.

3.1 Dual View Interface

Dual view interface is composed of two views of the retrieved results: one in document space and the other in word space (see Figure 2). Titles of the retrieved results are listed on the left-hand side of the screen (for documents), and the summarizing information is shown as topic word graphs on the right of the screen (for words).

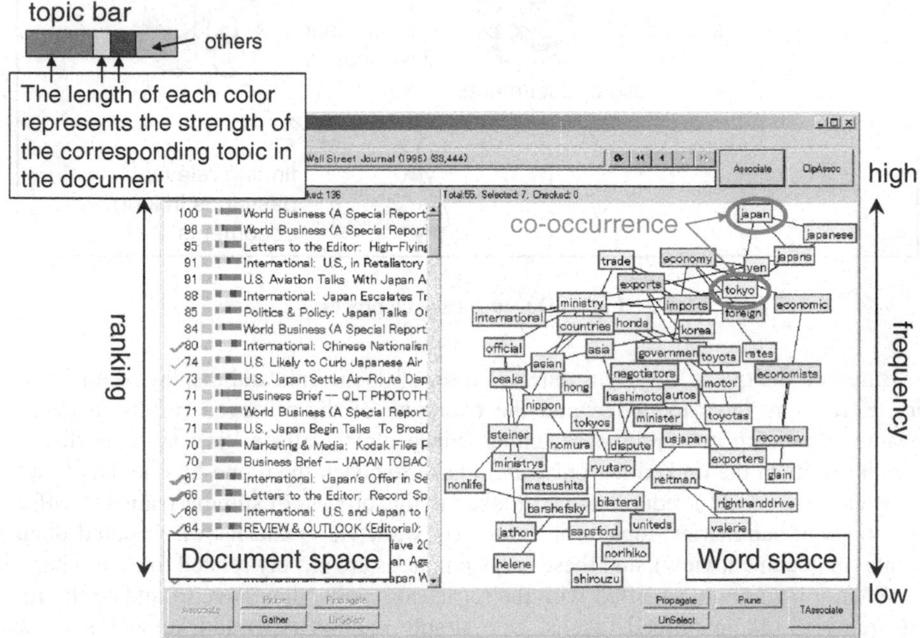

Fig. 2. Dual view interface of *DualNAVI*

Document space is a ranked list of the retrieved documents. Alongside of each document, there is a topic bar (RGB spectrum) which displays the topicalities of the document. We first extract three representative topics (red, green, and blue) from the retrieved documents by using a clustering technique, and the strength of each topic in the documents is calculated and mapped to the length of the corresponding color. This calculation is done dynamically when the set of retrieved document is updated. Users can sort the documents by the length of a specified color and collect the documents having the specified topic. The effectiveness of the topic bar tool has been evaluated in [6, 7].

Topic word graphs are also dynamically generated by analyzing the retrieved set of documents. A set of words characterizing the retrieved results are selected and the statistically meaningful co-occurrence relations among words are shown as links between them. Connected sub-graphs are expected to include effective potential keywords with which to refine searches.

Two views are tightly coupled with their cross-reference relation: Select some topic words, and related documents which include them are highlighted in the list of documents. And vice versa.

3.2 Dual Query Types

Dual query types mean that *DualNAVI* supports two kinds of search facilities, document associative search and keyword search. Document associative search finds related documents to given set of key documents. Keyword search finds related documents to given set of key words. Dual view interface provides a natural way for indicating the key objects for these search methods. Just select the relevant documents or words within the previous search result, and users can start a new associative search. This enables easy and intuitive relevance feedbacks to refine searches effectively. Search by documents is especially helpful when users have some interesting documents and feel difficult in selecting proper keywords.

The effectiveness of these two types of feedback with *DualNAVI* has been evaluated in [7, 9]. The results were significantly positive.

3.3 Dual View Bridges Dual Query Types

The dual view and dual query types are not just two isolated features. Dual query types can work effectively only with dual view framework. Figure 3 illustrates how they relate each other. We can start with either a search by keywords or by documents, and the retrieved results are shown in the dual view. If the title list includes interesting documents, we can proceed to next associative search using these found documents as keys. If some words in the topic word graphs are interesting, we can start new keyword search using these topic words as keys.

Another advantage of dual view interface is that the cross checking function is naturally realized. If users selects some documents of their interest, the users can easily find what topic words appear in the documents. Conversely, it is easy to find related documents by selecting topic words. If multiple topic words are selected, the thickness of checkmarks (See Figure 2) indicated the number of selected words included in each document. Users can sort the title list by this thickness, which approximates the relevance of each document to the topic suggested by the selected words.

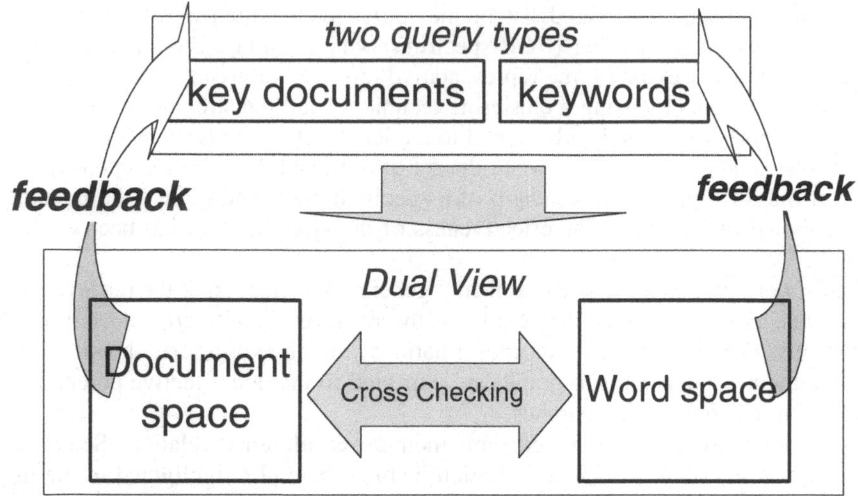

Fig. 3. Dual view bridges dual query types

4 Computation in *DualNAVI*

This section explains how the above mentioned functions of *DualNAVI* work.

4.1 Generation of Topic Word Graph

Topic word graph summarizes the search results and suggests proper words for further refining of searches. The method of generating topic word graph is fully described in [8]. Here we give a brief summary.

The process consists of three steps. The first step is the extraction of topic words based on the word frequency analysis over the retrieved set of documents. Next step is the process of generating links between extracted words based on co-occurrence analysis. The last step is to assign a xy-coordinated position for each word on the display area.

The score for selecting topic word is given by "df(w) in the retrieved documents / df(w) in the whole database" where "df(w)" is the document frequency of word "w", i.e. the number of documents containing "w". In general, it is difficult to keep the balance between high frequency words (common words) and low frequency words (specific words) by using a single score. In order to make a balanced selection, we adopted the frequency-class method, where all candidate words are first roughly classified by their frequencies, and then proper number of words is picked up from each frequency class.

A link between two words means that they are strongly related, that is, they co-appear in many documents in the retrieved results. In the link generation step, each topic word "X" is linked to another topic word "Y" which maximized the co-occurrence strength "df(X&Y) / df(Y)" with "X", among those having higher document frequency than "X". Here "df(X&Y)" means the number of retrieved documents which have both "X" and "Y". The length of a link has no specific meaning.

In the last step to give two-dimensional arrangement of topic word graphs, the y-coordinate (vertical position) is decided according to the document frequency of each word within the retrieved set. Common words are placed in the upper part, and specific words are placed in the lower part. Therefore, the graph can be considered as a hierarchical map of topics appears in the retrieved set of documents. The x-coordinate (horizontal position) has no specific meaning. It is assigned in the way to avoid overlapping of nodes and links.

4.2 Associative Search

Associative search is a type of document retrieval method based on the similarity between documents. It is useful when a user's intention cannot clearly be expressed by one or several keywords, but the user has some documents match with his/her information need. Associative search is also a powerful tool for relevance feedback. If a user find interesting documents in the search results, associative search with these documents as search keys may bring the user more related items which were not previously retrieved.

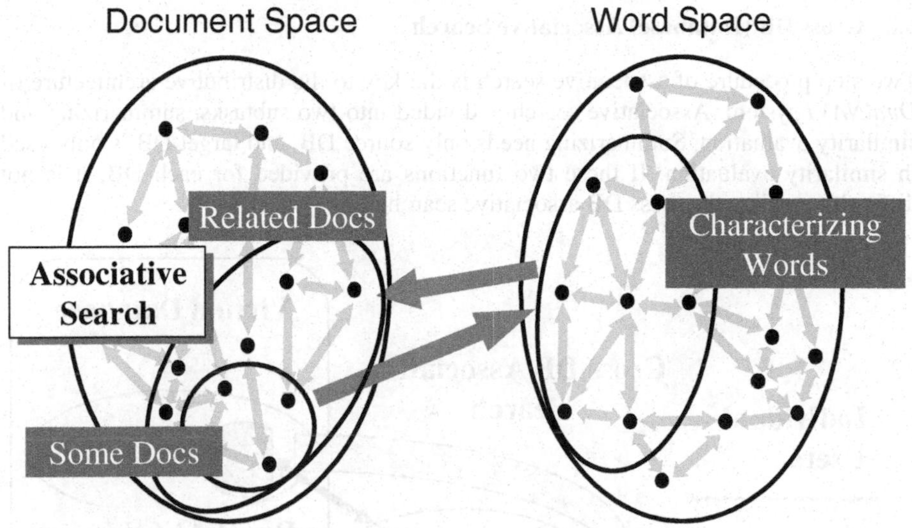

Fig. 4. Associative search

Associative search of *DualNAVI* consists of following steps (also shown in Figure 4):

- Extraction of characterizing words from the selected documents. The default number of characterizing words to be extracted is 200. For each word "w", which appears at least once in the selected documents, its score is calculated by "tf(w) / TF(w)", where "tf(w)" and "TF(w)" are the term frequencies of "w" in the selected documents, and in the whole database respectively. Then the 200 documents of higher score are selected.

- These extracted words are used as a query, and the relevance of each document "d" in the target database with this query "q" is calculated by "sim(d,q)", which is a standard TF.IDF measure described in [10].
- The documents in the target database are sorted by this similarity score and the top ranked documents are returned as the search results

In theory, associative search should not limit the size of the query. The merged documents should be used as the query in associative search from a set of documents. But if we don't reduce the number of the distinctive words in the query, we end up on calculating "sim(d,q)" for almost all the documents in the target database, even when we request for just few documents. In fact this extensive computational cost had prevented associative search from being used in the practical systems.

This is why we reduce the query into manageable size in step one. Most common words which appear in many documents are dropped in this step. We have to do this carefully so as not to drop important words within the query. In above explanation, we simply adopt "tf(w) / TF(w)" for measuring the importance of the words, but it is possible to use any measure for this filtering. Currently we are using a sophisticated probabilistic measure proposed in [4].

4.3 Cross DB (Database) Associative Search

Two step procedure of associative search is the key to the distributive architecture of *DualNAVI* system. Associative search is divided into two subtasks, summarizing and similarity evaluation. Summarizing needs only source DB, and target DB is only used in similarity evaluation. If these two functions are provided for each DB, it is not difficult to realize the cross DB associative search.

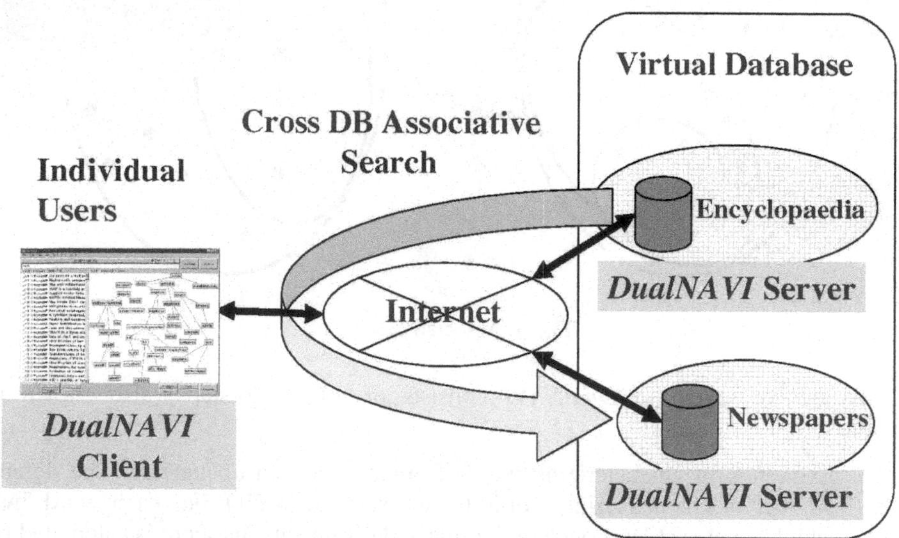

Fig. 5. Cross DB associative search with *DualNAVI*

Figure 5 shows the structure for the cross DB associative search between two physically distributed servers for *DualNAVI*, one for an encyclopedia and the other for newspapers. Users can select some articles in the encyclopedia and search related documents in other DB's associatively and seamlessly. We call these set of DB's a "Virtual Database" because it can be accessed as one big database.

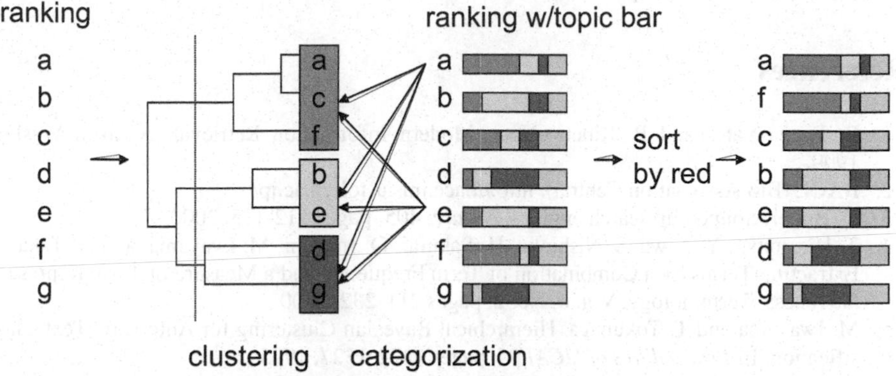

Fig. 6. Generation of topic bar

4.4 Generation of Topic Bar

Topic bar (RGB spectrum bar) beside each document shows the topicality of the document. The length of each color represents the likelihood of the document belonging to the corresponding topic; the three topics are automatically extracted from the retrieved documents.

Figure 6 shows the algorithm used to produce topic bars. We first use a clustering algorithm [5] to divide the retrieved documents into three clusters and regard them as major topics summarizing the retrieved documents. For each document, we calculate the similarities to each of the three topics (clusters), and display the similarity values in the RGB spectrum. Users can see the representative words in each cluster to understand what the corresponding topic means. Users can also focus on a topic by sorting the documents by the length of the corresponding color.

5 Conclusions

We have introduced a highly interactive search interface called *DualNAVI*. Its dual view interface and dual query types enable for users easily to understand the current status of searching, and to find next directions of searching. We believe that *DualNAVI* is a powerful search interface to reduce the total cost of document searching in our knowledge intensive works. *DualNAVI* is used in a number of commercial/public services of document searching and we are reflecting users' feedbacks on the refinement of *DualNAVI*.

Acknowledgements

The work reported in this paper is an outcome of the joint research efforts with Akihiko Takano (National Institute of Informatics, Japan), Shingo Nishioka (National Institute of Informatics, Japan), Toru Hisamitsu (Hitachi, Ltd., Japan), and Osamu Imaichi (Hitachi, Ltd., Japan).

References

1. R. Baeza-Yates and B. Ribeiro-Neto. Modern Information Retrieval. Addison Wesley, 1999.
2. BACE (Bio Association Central). http://bace.ims.u-tokyo.ac.jp/
3. D. Butler. Souped-up search engines. *Nature*, 405, pages 112-115, 2000.
4. T. Hisamitsu, Y. Niwa, S. Nishioka, H. Sakurai, O. Imaichi, M. Iwayama, and A. Takano. Extracting Terms by a Combination of Term Frequency and a Measure of Term Representativeness. Terminology, Vol. 6, No. 2, pages 211-232, 2000.
5. M. Iwayama and T. Tokunaga. Hierarchical Bayesian Clustering for Automatic Text Classification. In *Proceedings of IJCAI'95*, pages 1322-1327, 1995.
6. M. Iwayama. Relevance feedback with a small number of relevance judgements: incremental relevance feedback vs. document clustering. In *Proceedings of ACM SIGIR 2000*, pages 10-16, 2000.
7. M. Iwayama, Y. Niwa, S. Nishioka, A. Takano, T. Hisamitsu, O. Imaichi, H. Sakurai, and M. Fujio. The Effect of Document Clustering in Interactive Relevance Feedback, in *Proceedings of NTCIR Workshop 2*, pages196-203, 2001.
8. Y. Niwa, S. Nishioka, M. Iwayama, and A. Takano. Topic graph generation for query navigation: Use of frequency classes for topic extraction. In *Proceedings of NLPRS'97*, pages 95-100, 1997.
9. Y. Niwa, M. Iwayama, T. Hisamitsu, S. Nishioka, A. Takano, H. Sakurai, and O. Imaichi. Interactive document search with *DualNAVI*. In *Proceedings of NTCIR Workshop 1*, pages 123-130, 1999.
10. A. Singhal, C. Buckley, and M. Mitra. Pivoted Document Length Normalization. In *Proceedings of ACM SIGIR'96*, pages 21-29, 1996.

Knowledge Management in Small and Medium Enterprises (WMKMU 2005): Integration of HR and IT Perspectives

Brigitte Bartsch-Spörl[1], Klaus North[2], and Peter Pawlowsky[3]

[1] BSR Consulting GmbH, Wirtstrasse 38, 81539 Muenchen
brigitte@bsr-consulting.de
[2] FH Wiesbaden, Bleichstrasse 44, 65183 Wiesbaden
k.north@bwl.fh-wiesbaden.de
[3] TU Chemnitz, Reichenhainer Strasse 41, 09107 Chemnitz
p.pawlowsky@wirtschaft.tu-chemnitz.de

1 The Main Topics of the Workshop WMKMU 2005

This workshop was organised in order to create a forum for exchanging, comparing and reflecting lessons learned from knowledge management projects carried out in small and medium enterprises (SME). We wanted show that and how it is possible to establish knowledge management solutions without spending a fortune – but not without creative ideas, a deep understanding of the users requirements, a seamless co-operation between all participating departments, an efficient use of the project members time and contributions and last not least doing the right things at the right time.

We are convinced that this type of lean approaches to knowledge management is interesting for many other small and medium enterprises that feel a need for a better utilisation of their employees' knowledge and experiences but – at least at the moment – can afford only small and pragmatic steps into the right direction. As soon as these small steps pay back their return on investment this opens up more opportunities for bigger steps during the coming years.

2 The Participants

We achieved to have a good mixture of participants coming both from small and medium enterprises currently implementing knowledge management solutions and from scientific institutions active in research and education in this field. This lead to very lively discussions and for every participant to at least some new topics, insights and lessons learned.

3 The Contributions to the Proceedings

The submission of a scientific paper was no mandatory prerequisite for an active participation in this workshop. Therefore we are glad that two teams of authors have succeeded in submitting a paper and that these two papers allow to transfer at least some of the experiences discussed in the workshop to a wider audience.

K.-D. Althoff et al. (Eds.): WM 2005, LNAI 3782, pp. 719–720, 2005.

Alexander Scherf and Karsten Boehm give an overview of the KnowBiT project aiming at the introduction of a particularly easy to use knowledge management system in a small biotech enterprise in the city of Halle, named ACGT ProGenomics AG.

Roman Povalej und Wolffried Stucky share their experiences from the introduction of a skill information and management system called the "Skill Matrix" in a medium size IT enterprise, the ISB AG situated in Karlsruhe.

Both contributions demonstrate that in technology-oriented small and medium enterprises knowledge management is an important challenge and that it is feasible to make substantial progress with small to medium investments that are affordable for this type of SME.

KnowBiT – Knowledge Management in the Biotechnology Industry

Alexander Scherf [1] and Karsten Böhm[2]

[1] Detecon International GmbH, Frankfurter Straße 27,
65760 Eschborn, Germany
Alexander.Scherf@detecon.com
[2] Leipzig University, Department of Computer Science,
Augustusplatz 10-11, 04109 Leipzig, Germany
boehm@informatik.uni-leipzig.de

Abstract. Due to the scarce supply in personnel, the immanent significance of knowledge and the need for company-spanning cooperation, much is demanded from knowledge management solutions in the biotechnology industry. Together with a biotechnology company, an application-oriented solution was developed within the scope of the KnowBiT project to meet these requirements. The main emphasis was put on knowledge inquiry and knowledge transfer without the need to adapt the existing knowledge intensive processes. Thereby, the integrated application of new communication infrastructures was used to facilitate the access to information and to qualify it by identifying it with knowledge carriers or domain experts.

1 Introduction

In many aspects, biotechnology businesses which are dealing primarily with research issues exhibit special features compared to other industries. This results primarily from the high-risk orientation of the company goals for developing new processes or products through long-term research without causing considerable revenues during these research periods. Patenting the results as the first company in the market is essential for the financial safeguarding of the costly development. In order to achieve the necessary development speed (time-to-market) biotechnology companies must pursue an integral knowledge management. Although a number of Knowledge Management systems have been proposed and implemented in numerous applications (see [1] for an overview) only a few have been tailored to the special needs of the biotechnical industry; an example that relies heavily on the manual modelling of knowledge structures is described in [2].

This article describes the KnowBiT project, which was mainly targeted at the biotechnology cluster Halle/Saale. The project consortium pursued the goal of supporting the use of the resource knowledge by building up an IT-based knowledge management platform to collect and transfer the information needed for the research intensive biotechnological research processes.

K.-D. Althoff et al. (Eds.): WM 2005, LNAI 3782, pp. 721 – 728, 2005.

2 Project Goals

In order to determine an appropriate approach to the structure of knowledge management in biotechnology companies, some characteristics of these businesses were established in a preceding analysis phase:

- Biotechnological companies are usually not older than 6 years and possess, with an average of 20 persons, a small but exceptionally well-trained and high skilled workforce.
- They are usually established in universities (spin-offs). This connection usually persists past the starting phase, so that the exchange and the access to resources of the universities (laboratories, material, and personnel) is still available. Therefore, the cooperation with universities is often an intermingled relation with fuzzy boundaries with multidimensional benefits for both sides (win-win situation).
- Furthermore, close contacts or even stable co-operations with companies close to research are maintained in such a way that synergy potentials (as in fundamental research) can be used and the own productivity can be increased. This type of cooperation is made possible through the high specialization of each of the biotechnological company.
- In the field of opposing poles of co-operation and patent protection, the resource knowledge needs to be dealt with extreme sensitivity, as it represents in many cases the *only* valuable asset in the company, besides the human resources. The research results must therefore be protected from unauthorized access by extensive security measures.
- Consequently, the value of biotechnology companies basically corresponds to the value of the existing patents and the knowledge of the employees. Increased knowledge and skills of the employees thus at the same time increase the value of the company, which in turn sets ground for significant efforts in a knowledge management solution.

Despite the limited size of these companies, they have access to various sources of knowledge, which must be included in the integral knowledge management. On the one hand, these are knowledge objects, such as internal protocols and reports, as well as external studies, patent specifications and product specifications. This division is also seen in the owners of the respective knowledge. Beside the own employees, thus also professors, interns, doctorate students, investors, customers and competitors belong to the interconnected knowledge. Through the extension of the knowledge space to the outside of the actual company, the meaning of knowledge management in the small biotechnology companies becomes more apparent but will also add another layer of complexity. Especially the questions concerning quality, availability, comprehensibility and topicality must be dealt with separately for the external knowledge.

In the course of the project, the clarification of these rather organizational topics had to be put in the background due to the short runtime of the project (roughly one year from the first analysis phase to the roll-out of a customized IT-based solution). The emphasis was therefore put on the development and implementation of a conceptional architecture, which supports the established communication-oriented knowledge circulation processes – which is often an implicit activity within companies – by using information technology. The immediate benefits of this approach are the documentation of communication trails, relevant information (questions and related answers) and the possibilities to identify experts within the company for certain topics. Likewise, documented answers for frequently asked questions free the expert from answering the same question again and again. Using an easy to use interface that can be handled with little introduction eases the process of externalizing knowledge significantly, compared to other known approaches (e.g. interviewing techniques).

Therefore, the following premises for the development of such an architecture were defined at the beginning of the project:

- Typically, all relevant information has already been documented at least once within the companies. Due to the legal guidelines and the increasingly digitalized communication (e-mail, newsgroups, mailing lists etc.), one can assume that electronic filing is predominantly used. This, however, does not continually take place in a centralized way as information sources of various types are scattered throughout the company (for example patent- and studies databases, file servers, intranet).
- Communication between the knowledge carriers is currently realized in a way that does not allow others to access the submitted knowledge later (conversations by telephone or personally; the "coffee-corner symptom"). While such a communication is usually very efficient for transferring knowledge it also has the disadvantage that only a few people are involved (mostly only two persons) and that both parties have to be available (synchrony in space and time).
- Within the small companies, there are no additional resources (time/money) available for setting up and operating the knowledge management solution. A pragmatic and modular solution enables the initial step and the further (gradual) development of the knowledge management solution.

The author of an information object is usually unable to determine the sensible additional effort, which is necessary for the processing of the knowledge object, in order to guarantee a later relocation by a third party. Only the searching party (the information recipient) determines the value of the information object and the justified effort for its inquiry. For this reason the support of the searching party with its tasks was brought to prominence and the author was released from any additional effort.

In addition, the communication between the knowledge carriers was identified as another important factor for success and was thus supported by an appropriate module.

The superordinate goal of the project was to build up a holistic knowledge management solution for the field of biotechnology, which – like the example of the pilot user ACGT as a member of the growth area protein research Halle – allows the transfer of knowledge from the individual knowledge carrier into the company and thus leads to the building up of organizational competence[1]. With the successful reference example of the internal use at ACGT, the goal is to construct a platform for the whole growth area, so that the company-spanning knowledge exchange can be supported.

[1] See also the article in Mitteldeutsche Zeitung from 26th of May 2004.

This section was meant to clarify the particularities of biotechnology companies and to derive the conditions for the project from that.

3 Cooperation Partners and Their Roles in the Project

As explained above, the main task of the project was to develop a modular system platform, which supports communication about information actively and which therefore promotes the generation of new knowledge and the circulation of already known facts. The project gained experience, for example in linking heterogeneous information sources such as a DMS and a Wiki-system (see next section). For the evaluation and the early test in practice, the biotechnology company ACGT ProGenomics AG from the biotech cluster Halle/Saale was available as a pilot user. Like many other young biotechnology companies, ACGT was also founded at a university. With approximately 30 highly specialized employees, who are divided into three fields, the company has reached a size, where the management has realized the growing relevance of knowledge management. It is noteworthy to mention that the increasing effort needed to communicate knowledge between the different employees in the company was the main motivation to implement a knowledge management solution; from our experiences we would suggest that the growth factor in a knowledge intensive company is likely to trigger the implementation of a supporting IT-based KM-solution.

Together with the pilot user the concept described before was adapted to the specific needs of the company. A platform was developed, which is as flexible as possible and that can be used for various fields of application with very little effort and without extensive training.

The development of the project idea and the incorporation of the project partners were realized by net4com. This organisation is a partner network, which works in the area of Central Germany and is specialized in knowledge exchange between medium-sized companies and the development of concrete project ideas.

For the implementation of the system, a project consortium was founded, which consists of the three IT service providers: the eXistand GmbH from Sangerhausen, as well as SMB GmbH and WiSL GmbH from Halle/Saale. As a domain expert in the biotechnical domain, the company Bitonic was integrated in the consortium, in order to council the partners. In specific questions concerning knowledge management, existing approaches and scientific background, the group is supported by the department of Business oriented Information Systems, associated with the Institute for Computer Science at the Leipzig University.

4 Realization of the IT-Based KM Solution

During the conception phase the existing prerequisites at ACGT were examined, since the existing elements of the information infrastructure should be integrated as the basis for the future knowledge management. Therefore a studies and patents database, group and project drives (network shares), as well as several project databases with parameters from test series were considered for the integration. The decision as to which information objects should be integrated in the new solution, was made together with the users. It was then decided that the project databases will not yet be integrated due to the sensitivity and structure of the data contained. All other documents (a total of more than 100 GB) were taken over into the document management system windream, so that the work done so far was adapted with group drives. The DMS module now presents a sort of "library" (see Figure 1), in which all project documents were included. The existing studies and patents database were integrated into the DMS as well, so that now internal and external documents are stored centrally in one system.

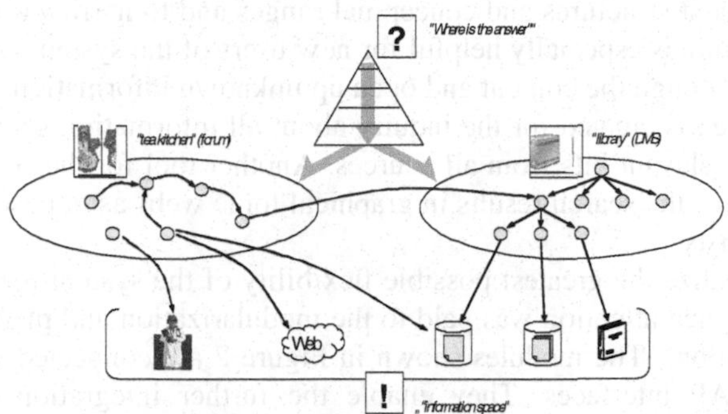

Fig. 1. Conceptional architecture of supported communication

This information base was expanded with the introduction of an adapted Wiki module. So-called Wiki systems[2] are simple web-based applications, which allow the generation and connection of individual websites or articles in a simple way without requiring special editors or special knowledge on the user side. A detailed description of the characteristics of such systems can be found in [3]; an overview on available implementations is given in [4]. The contents of a Wiki can be accessed, changed or supplemented by any user. The new contents thereby overwrite the old articles. A versioning system ensures the transparency of the evolution of the articles. The members of a community are thus able to exchange information implicitly over the articles in the Wiki system by inquiring interesting contents in the existing collection of articles and by adding their own experiences in that field. The project of the free online encyclopaedia[3] Wikipedia is an example of a large Wiki system with a large user group.

It was necessary for the project to limit the free structure and open alterability of a standard Wiki for the company-internal use but without it reaching the administrative complexity of a forum. The solution called WiCoFo, which was developed in this project, is a mixture of a Wiki and a forum, and beside rights management and defined categories for structuring the articles it also contains the simple formatting rules for linking articles and the simple alterability and extendibility for articles. Furthermore, discussion forums and linking with documents from the DMS are possible.

---

[2] The term *wikiwiki* is Hawaiian and means *fast*. This is meant to stress the simple and quick creation of contents.

[3] The Wikipedia project can be found at http://wikipedia.org.

With these links of the articles to one another, but also to documents, a knowledge network is built up, and its quality is improved in an evolutionary way with each new relation. With this combination, the communication about the individual information objects is supported for the first time. This combination of technologies enables the development of the information basis into an actively used knowledge basis for the company.

The manually generated links between articles and documents, which form together the integrated knowledge basis, are supplemented by relations created using text mining methods. This way document relations as well as relations between terms are determined. The searching party is therefore able to refine its searching strategy in unknown document structures and conceptual ranges and to narrow down the number of hits. This feature is especially helpful for new users of the system as they can more easily navigate through the content and open up unknown information sources.

A central index is created for the inquiry about all information sources, so that inquiries produce relevant hits from all sources. Another tool for the searching party is the presentation of the search results in graphical topic webs as opposed to the classic presentation in lists.

In order to realize the greatest possible flexibility of the system for future application scenarios, much attention was paid to the modularization and platform independence of the solution. The modules shown in Figure 2 are connected with each other by defined SOAP interfaces. They enable the further integration of information sources into the system. In the scope of the project at ACGT, at first only a document management systems and the WiCoFo were incorporated. During the initial considerations, the integration of intranet areas via CMS, internet areas via Web Crawler, and the linking with e-mail communication were checked as well.

But since the intranet of ACGT does not play an important role yet, its integration was postponed. The inclusion of internet fields was considered crucial; however dealing with the internal documents had priority, so that the integration of the internet was subordinated. The interface with intranet and internet is scheduled for the next development stage of the KnowBiT solution.

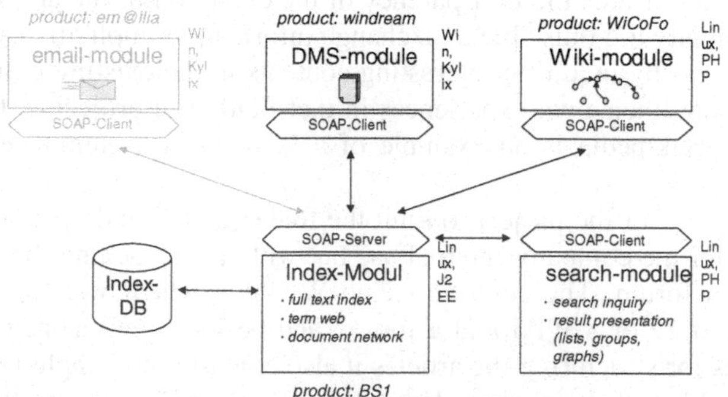

Fig. 2. Technical Architecture as a basis of flexible extension

At the moment the information exchange is mainly realized by e-mail communication. The usefulness of a general integration of e-mail systems into the KnowBiT solution is doubtful, since not every e-mail contains solely information that should be available to the whole company. Therefore, a selective integration seems more advisable to ensure privacy and data protection. An e-mail module was prepared, which provides defined e-mail addresses, to which the employees can forward certain messages. The module then searches the contents and stores the e-mail according to predefined rules. ACGT, however, decided not to use the module in the current version, but to gain experience first with the document management system and with the WiCoFo.

5 Continuity Through Linking Companies

The increasingly necessary linking of value creating chains, which exceed company borders more and more, leads to completely new challenges in the co-operation with companies. This also shows in the international trends to collaborative business as well as cluster linking. The platform developed in the project will take up this topic for the knowledge management in company groups.

After the successful introduction of the platform to the individual companies, it is planned to support the knowledge transfer in the growth area protein research Halle in infrastructure as well. By using the knowledge management platform developed in the project in a company-spanning way, inter-organizational competence in the fields relevant for all biotechnology partners (especially pure research, project management, quality and innovation management, as well as operational experiential knowledge) is achieved.

In order to prepare the establishment of a knowledge management solution for a cluster or growth area, the consortium is currently in touch with various biotechnology companies and bio-centers in Germany. In these conversations the specific needs, but also critical questions concerning the information exchange are discussed. It is becoming apparent that the platform should be used for internal communication within the growth area, but also in other regional clusters for the exchange of process knowledge and the integration of experts. Furthermore an integrated presentation of the services and products of the partner companies is demanded for external interested parties.

The strict separation of company-internal knowledge management and company-spanning information exchange is thereby seen as a prerequisite for the acceptance by the members. The consequence of this is that in this loose co-operation, no competition-critical knowledge is exchanged.

6 Summary and Prospects

In the KnowBiT project, which was introduced in this article, a knowledge management solution for biotechnology companies was developed, in which various information sources, such as DMS and forums/Wiki, were integrated. The open architecture is constructed in a way that further sources, such as e-mail, intranet/internet etc. can be incorporated later. Not only the central access, but also the manual and automated linking of information objects from different sources was realized. In order to meet the specific requirements and conditions for the knowledge management in small research oriented businesses, a pragmatic approach was pursued, so that the solution can be easily integrated in various contexts and it barely costs efforts for adaptation.

The prototype is currently being run and tested at ACGT ProGenomics AG. The modules were implemented in the actual production, so that all relevant functions can be tested. Beside the introduction at ACGT as pilot user, the consortium is planning the construction of a communication and information platform for growth areas or clusters on the basis of the KnowBiT system in a follow-up project.

The emphasis in the next stage is thus put on the clarification of organizational and operational issues. The first answers are expected for the following months from the observation at ACGT, which will influence the next development steps of the solution.

More information can be found at the project website http://www.knowbit.de.

Acknowledgements

The KnowBiT-project is a joint research effort of several companies and was supported by the University of Leipzig. The authors would like to thank their colleagues for their fruitful cooperation and appreciate the contribution of the windream GmbH, Bochum, for providing the licenses of their DMS for the project. The project was partially founded by the European Fund for Regional Development (EFRE) and from the federal state Saxony-Anhalt under grant number SIG 03 III 07/06.

References

1. Maier, R.: Knowledge Management Systems. Information and Communication Technologies for Knowledge Management. Springer, Berlin (2004).
2. Flach, G.: KnowledgeDirect – Einsatz semantikbasierter Wissensmanagement-Technologien im Unternehmensnetzwerk „BioCon Valley“, KnowTech 2003, Online Ressource available: http://www.bitkom.org/files/documents/F2_09_Flach_Vortrag.pdf, last Access 13.05.2005
3. Leuf, B., Cunningham W.: The Wiki Way. Quick Collaboration on the Web. Addison Wesley (2001)
4. Ebersbach, A., Glaser, M., Heigl, R.: WikiTools Kooperationen im Web. Springer, Berlin Heidelberg New York Tokyo (2005)

Introduction of a Knowledge Information System in a SME, "Skill Matrix" as Pilot Scheme

Roman Povalej and Wolffried Stucky

University of Karlsruhe (TH),
Institute of Applied Informatics and Formal Description Methods (AIFB),
D-76128 Karlsruhe
{povalej, stucky}@aifb.uni-karlsruhe.de

Abstract. The procedure model WISKI (S)PUR[1] was developed within the cooperation project EWISU[2] between the institute AIFB[3] (http://www.aifb.uni-karlsruhe.de) and the company ISB AG Karlsruhe (http://www.isb-ag.de). With it you will be able to introduce a knowledge information system (WIS) into a company successfully and also you will be able to use this WIS successfully. The procedure model serves the support of the introduction of a WIS into a company or an organization. WISKI (S)PUR offers a framework for the efficient and actual establishment of a company's specific knowledge information system. Furthermore, a phase model was developed for the introduction of a WIS into a company, as the case may be for the accomplishment of knowledge projects; WISKI (S)PUR is reflected in it. These both models are validated and are verified by knowledge projects in the ISB AG. The introduction of a Skill Matrix was selected as the pilot scheme on the basis of the need in the ISB AG. The generation and utilization of synergies by the implentation and combination of two further completed knowledge projects with the Skill Matrix will be described briefly in this paper.

1 Introduction

An increasingly more competitive market (for example because of market saturation or greater similarity/equality and smaller life cycles of products) forces companies to implement their existing resources as optimally as possible and to activate recumbent resources. Furthermore, a conscious dealing with the production factor knowledge by companies plays an ever-increasing role in gaining or expanding (competitive) advantages over competitors. Only who optimizes the use and implementation of his knowledge based processes and resources, will be able to assert themselves long term against the competition. Keeping the companies' knowledge up to date and readily available will enable these companies to act faster and more cost advantageous than their competition.

---

1 "Knowledge Information System-Circle Layer-ISB Model" with Layers (Strategy Target Layer), Process Layer, Support Layer, Frame Layer.

2 Introduction of Knowledge Information Systems in Companies.

3 Institute of Applied Informatics and Formal Description Methods.

K.-D. Althoff et al. (Eds.): WM 2005, LNAI 3782, pp. 729 – 735, 2005.

The employees belong to the most important resources of a company. Above all the service providers and advisors in the IT industry are dependant on qualified, competent and efficient employees, in order to present high quality results and consequently to satisfy their customers. Therefore, it is absolutely necessary for a company to know the strengths and weaknesses of the existing employees' skills. Based on this knowledge strengths can be used goal orientated and weaknesses can be met by training and advanced training. Further advantages can hereby be won over competitors through quality and efficiency.

2 Motivation

Because of the tense market situation, large-scale companies try to find a foot holds in niches that until now were uninteresting for them and which were occupied successfully by SME. On this occasion market prices are fixed, at a level at which SME can

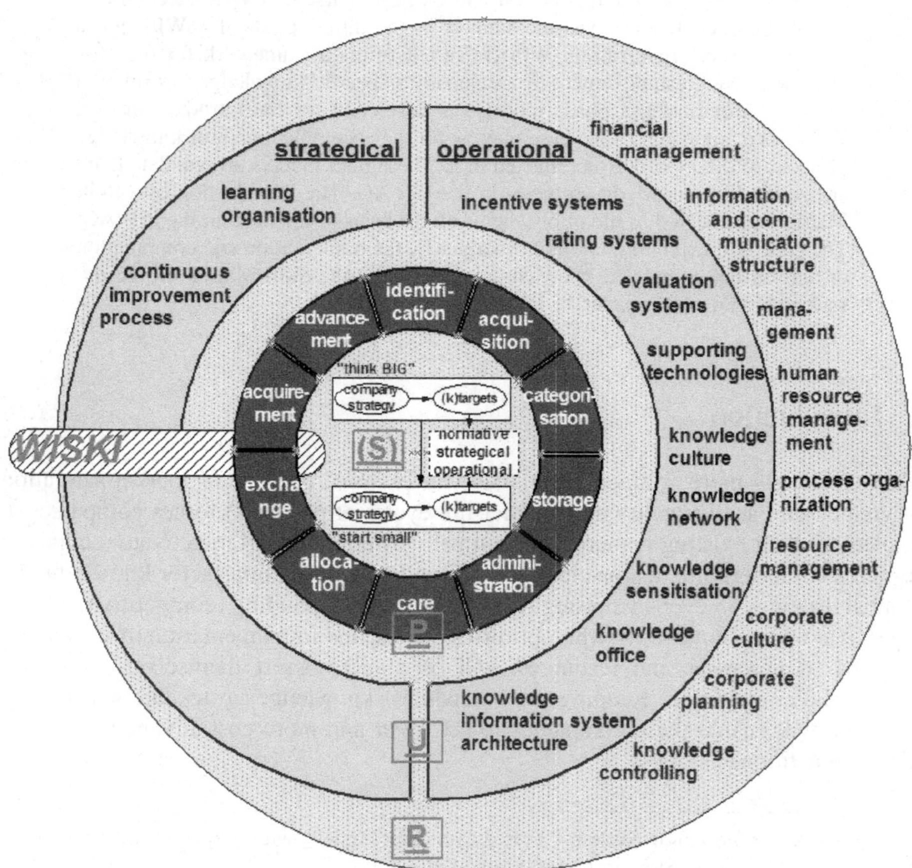

Fig. 1. Procedure Model WISKI (S)PUR

only keep up with some difficulty or not at all. Every SME, that accentuates itself through quality and innovation has nevertheless good chances to become generally accepted against the large-scale companies. Simultaneously the competition between the SME becomes tougher. Therefore, it has become necessary to activate unused resources and to optimize the use of the existing resources, especially the resource knowledge, in order to be able to survive against competitors.

The ISB AG has recognized this and would like to further develop itself to a Knowledge Company. Therefore, amongst others the cooperation project EWISU was founded and in which the procedure WISKI (S)PUR (Fig. 1) and the associated phase model were developed. These are used to support the introduction of a WIS into a company or into an organization. They offer a framework for the efficient and effective set up of a company's specific WIS. A Skill Matrix was chosen as pilot knowledge scheme, because a large demand therefore could be seen. Additionally a quick and successful completion before the end of the EWISU project was foreseeable.

3 Pilot Scheme Skill Matrix

The ISB AG was established in 1981 as a spin-off of the institute AIFB in order to transfer the theoretical research knowledge of relational databases into practice. In 1992/93, the company's concept was completely revised and a change of ownership took place. Because of the low number of employees and the informal atmosphere ("ISB Family"), it was for a long time possible to know each employee's skills and projects and to easily assist if necessary, or call in competent support at short notice. As the ISB AG has grown by 20% per year in the past 10 years, the number of employees has increased and two new offices have been opened, an overview of this type is even for long standing employees barely possible. In order to maintain this qualitatively good overview of the skills of the individual employee, a Skill Matrix was to be developed, that shows the existing skills of the employee and makes a simple access possible for all employees. This should support the change of the ISB AG ("Professional ISB Family") to the Knowledge Company.

3.1 Targets, Benefits, Basic Conditions

By using the Skill Matrix, the scope of the existing know-how and the demand for required know-how should be determined and documented. On this basis, the existing know-how could be used precisely and qualitatively fostered, and the lacking, but required know-how achieved through targeted measures, (for example through internal or external advanced training or courses). In addition, the search for desired know-how should be simplified and optimized, so that for example project plannings are more efficiently executed, or competent contact partners can be quickly found by each employee.

As basic conditions for the pilot scheme, following points were pre-determined to be able to recognize the fastest possible success:

- The company structure serves as the basis for the determination of the skill topics; the demand must always exist.

- Pre-determined basic conditions are to be in accordance with the data privacy protection law.
- Participation in the Skill Matrix takes place on a voluntary basis; no disadvantages should occur for non-participants.
- Synergies are to be used and generated by the use of existing resources during the development.
- The application should be put into operation quickly in order enable the use of the advantages of the Skill Matrix at short notice.
- The evaluation method should be simple.
- The associated controlling should be efficient and simple.

The ISB AG uses their self-developed planning information tool PlanIT. This contains amongst others data, information and knowledge of finances, employees, plans and projects. Through the integration of the Skill Matrix, a fast realization is possible. Additionally double data storage and resulting redundant data maintenance is avoided so that the employees' recognition value and as consequence the probability of their acceptance thereof rises.

3.2 Skill Management in the ISB AG

Before the Skill Matrix was conceived, the principal procedures in the Skill Management of the ISB AG were compiled and recorded (Fig. 2). By this process knowledge aims and benefits which could be achieved in future by the Skill Matrix were validated.

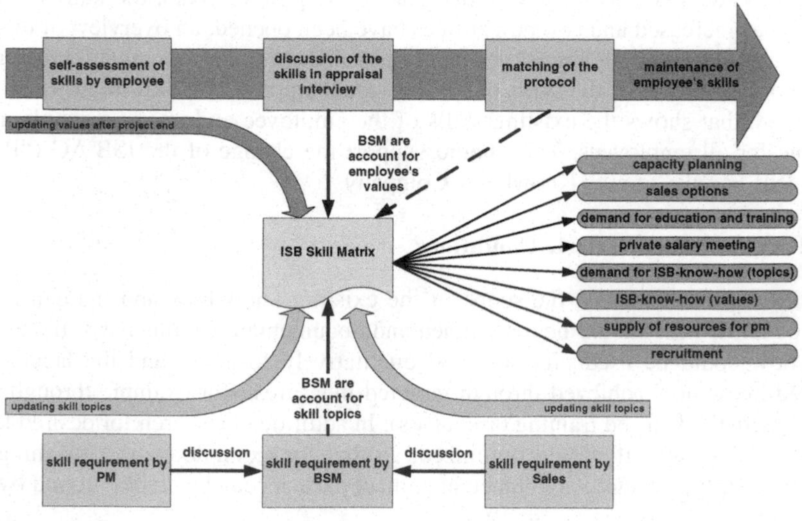

Fig. 2. Skill Management in the ISB AG

At the ISB AG, appraisal interviews take place at the end of the year between an employee and his or her responsible Business Solution Manager (BSM) during which targets and tasks for the coming year are defined. In the middle of the year another appraisal interview takes place that serves as control, in order to be able to react in time to changes or non-achievement of the targets and tasks of an employee. In these appraisal interviews and after project completion, the Skill Matrix maintenance is initiated after agreement with the responsible BSM. The skill topics maintenance is also carried out by the BSM. New requirements are put up for discussion by the project management or sales. Acceptance or refusal thereof is the BSM's responsibility. From the Skill Matrix, following report statements amongst others can be won:

- Which skills or employees require advanced training?
- Required experts should be identified for the project planning. Then the availability of the identified experts has to be checked for the requested period.
- The recruitment of new employees can be well directed to the needed know-how, which is identified by the Skill Matrix.

3.3 Introduction

After establishing that a demand and also the benefit of the implementation of a Skill Matrix exist, planning was begun. In the following two sub-chapters the most important milestones of the pilot scheme, as well as the formulation and evaluation of skill topics are presented briefly.

3.3.1 Milestones

After the targets, basic conditions and the principal procedures of the Skill Management of the ISB AG had been determined, amongst others following milestones were:

- *25.11.2003:* found skill topics are presented to the area management.
- *09.12.2003:* revised skill topics are presented to the company management.
- *19.12.2003:* skill management is presented at the employee meeting.
- *16.01.2004:* Skill Matrix is made available for appraisal interviews.
- *06.03.2004:* first complete Skill Matrix is made available as MS Excel sheet.
- *03.05.2004:* Skill Matrix is designed/implemented for integration into PlanIT.
- *31.12.2004:* boosted controlling during introduction phase.

3.3.2 Skill Topics

The pilot scheme had to fulfill two conditions: (A) Skill topics should be company structure orientated and (B) only implemented if further company demands exist. Therefore, long-standing employees of the ISB AG, with extensive project experience, were appointed to establish the skill topics.

A four-stage classification from zero to three was chosen for the evaluation of the individual skill topics. With a more elaborate scale or a percent scale the differentiation between for example "5 and 6 out of 10" or "50% and 55%" is only possible with difficulties. The classification should not remind anyone of a scoring system in order not to decrease the acceptance from the start:

- "0": know-how is not available, or information is not given.
- "1": basic knowledge (in general: practical experience, or possibly academic knowledge is sufficient).
- "2": advanced knowledge and project experiences are present.
- "3": expertise without restriction of any kind is present.

3.4 Daily Service

Since February/March 2004 the Skill Matrix is available as a MS Excel Sheet. By the use of external tools, skill topic entries, maintenance, its evaluation by PlanIT as well as the data processing possibilities (for example the interpretation of the skill topics indexes and associated evaluations) have been made available since April 2004. The Skill Matrix was successfully used within the ISB AG from the beginning for distribution processes, project planning and the search of experts. After a short time, the employees' participation was at 80% and has continually risen until today. In the following two months, the cyclic appraisal interviews are on the agenda. It is to be expected that an employees' participation of almost 100% will be achieved. This is very strongly related to the ISB AG's company culture. Consequently, a successful launch of the Skill Matrix in the ISB AG can be confirmed.

The Skill Matrix in general, comprises the results of the appraisal interviews. The input of the results and consequently the evaluations of the skill topics take place by the individual employee. On that occasion, no particular control of the completeness or correctness takes place. At first one relies here on self-regulating effects:

- Who values himself too well, will not satisfy project requirements.
- Who values himself too badly, will not be appointed for projects.

It is to be noted that the Skill Matrix is only a supporting tool. It shall be the user's responsibility to produce evaluations with the Skill Matrix, in order to find suitable employees for project tasks, to check whether the possible candidates really have the required skills or whether a mistake has occurred during the data entry.

Above all, new employees receive with the Skill Matrix a tool, with which they can for example, find competent contact partners in a fast and simple way or can execute project planning. So for example, the time required by a new employee for building a team of suitable employees with the required skills for a project, is reduced by almost 50%.

4 Further Knowledge Projects

In the meantime, further knowledge projects were initiated, for which a demand in ISB AG exist. For example applications for the standardized maintenance of employee's profiles and project warrant of apprehension were conceived and already partially integrated in PlanIT. On this occasion, the user is supported with the input and maintenance of the individual data by standardized and centralized entries. Furthermore, through these standardizations, evaluations can be optimally compiled and simultaneously the informational value can be increased. During conception, it was insured amongst others that a triangle relationship between the Skill Matrix application, employee's profile and project warrant of apprehension was upheld so that following statements can be investigated

- *Starting from Skill Matrix:*
  Which employees have certain skills?
  In which projects were certain skills used or required?

- *Starting from employee's profile:*
  Which Skills has the employee?
  In which projects was the employee used?
- *Starting from project warrant of apprehension:*
  Which employees were/are involved in the project?
  Which Skills were/are used in the project or were required?

At the moment, these investigations take place manually; automatisms will be made available for this in the future in order to enhance support and consequently, to partially unburden the employees.

5 Outlook

The procedure model WISKI (S)PUR and the associated phase model, are dynamic models, i.e. new findings from knowledge projects immediately flow into them. The realization of further knowledge projects and the findings won from them will validate and verify these two models. Additionally individual steps of the models taken are looked at in detail. The approach when appraisal and incentive systems are implemented is of great interest. This approach serves as supporting measure when introducing WIS.

The pilot scheme of the introduction of a Skill Matrix into ISB AG was successfully completed. In further projects, improvements and expansions will flow in and be integrated. For example, in future capacity check ups, which are implemented manually at the moment, could be automatically executed. Which evaluations are frequently required will crystallize in the course of further utilization of the Skill Matrix. These could be centrally available as standardized templates. Controls would be carried out in defined cycles in order to investigate which individual skill areas as well as skill topics must be adjusted or expanded regarding new requirements.

Within the ISB AG, further knowledge projects are tackled according to demand, urgency and the availability of resources. A strategic target of the ISB AG is the construction of a successful Knowledge Company under consideration of the current market situation.

Skills play an important role in all companies and organizations. Therefore, it is very interesting to investigate, in what way a model or procedure can be developed, to define matching skill topics for the respective company or organization. The establishment of the skill topics in the ISB AG serves as a basis. Furthermore, it should be examined, which influence skills have on existing job profiles and which connections exist. A further question to be answered is the role of certifications in job profiles and skills, and the way these are interrelated as to achieve added value for a company.

The conclusion of the cooperation project EWISU will be the completion of a dissertation, potentially at the end of 2005. Amongst others the procedure model WISKI (S)PUR and the associated phase model will be introduced into (published in) this dissertation. Finally all results and insights of completed and currently planned projects with the ISB AG will be processed, evaluated and published.

Author Index

Lecture Notes in Artificial Intelligence (LNAI)

Vol. 3835: G. Sutcliffe, A. Voronkov (Eds.), Logic for Programming, Artificial Intelligence, and Reasoning. XIV, 744 pages. 2005.

Vol. 3814: M. Maybury, O. Stock, W. Wahlster (Eds.), Intelligent Technologies for Interactive Entertainment. XV, 342 pages. 2005.

Vol. 3809: S. Zhang, R. Jarvis (Eds.), AI 2005: Advances in Artificial Intelligence. XXVII, 1344 pages. 2005.

Vol. 3808: C. Bento, A. Cardoso, G. Dias (Eds.), Progress in Artificial Intelligence. XVIII, 704 pages. 2005.

Vol. 3802: Y. Hao, J. Liu, Y.-P. Wang, Y.-m. Cheung, H. Yin, L. Jiao, J. Ma, Y.-C. Jiao (Eds.), Computational Intelligence and Security, Part II. XLII, 1166 pages. 2005.

Vol. 3801: Y. Hao, J. Liu, Y.-P. Wang, Y.-m. Cheung, H. Yin, L. Jiao, J. Ma, Y.-C. Jiao (Eds.), Computational Intelligence and Security, Part I. XLI, 1122 pages. 2005.

Vol. 3789: A. Gelbukh, Á. de Albornoz, H. Terashima-Marín (Eds.), MICAI 2005: Advances in Artificial Intelligence. XXVI, 1198 pages. 2005.

Vol. 3782: K.-D. Althoff, A. Dengel, R. Bergmann, M. Nick, T. Roth-Berghofer (Eds.), Professional Knowledge Management. XXIII, 739 pages. 2005.

Vol. 3735: A. Hoffmann, H. Motoda, T. Scheffer (Eds.), Discovery Science. XVI, 400 pages. 2005.

Vol. 3734: S. Jain, H.U. Simon, E. Tomita (Eds.), Algorithmic Learning Theory. XII, 490 pages. 2005.

Vol. 3721: A.M. Jorge, L. Torgo, P.B. Brazdil, R. Camacho, J. Gama (Eds.), Knowledge Discovery in Databases: PKDD 2005. XXIII, 719 pages. 2005.

Vol. 3720: J. Gama, R. Camacho, P.B. Brazdil, A.M. Jorge, L. Torgo (Eds.), Machine Learning: ECML 2005. XXIII, 769 pages. 2005.

Vol. 3717: B. Gramlich (Ed.), Frontiers of Combining Systems. X, 321 pages. 2005.

Vol. 3702: B. Beckert (Ed.), Automated Reasoning with Analytic Tableaux and Related Methods. XIII, 343 pages. 2005.

Vol. 3698: U. Furbach (Ed.), KI 2005: Advances in Artificial Intelligence. XIII, 409 pages. 2005.

Vol. 3690: M. Pěchouček, P. Petta, L.Z. Varga (Eds.), Multi-Agent Systems and Applications IV. XVII, 667 pages. 2005.

Vol. 3684: R. Khosla, R.J. Howlett, L.C. Jain (Eds.), Knowledge-Based Intelligent Information and Engineering Systems, Part IV. LXXIX, 933 pages. 2005.

Vol. 3683: R. Khosla, R.J. Howlett, L.C. Jain (Eds.), Knowledge-Based Intelligent Information and Engineering Systems, Part III. LXXX, 1397 pages. 2005.

Vol. 3682: R. Khosla, R.J. Howlett, L.C. Jain (Eds.), Knowledge-Based Intelligent Information and Engineering Systems, Part II. LXXIX, 1371 pages. 2005.

Vol. 3681: R. Khosla, R.J. Howlett, L.C. Jain (Eds.), Knowledge-Based Intelligent Information and Engineering Systems, Part I. LXXX, 1319 pages. 2005.

Vol. 3673: S. Bandini, S. Manzoni (Eds.), AI*IA 2005: Advances in Artificial Intelligence. XIV, 614 pages. 2005.

Vol. 3662: C. Baral, G. Greco, N. Leone, G. Terracina (Eds.), Logic Programming and Nonmonotonic Reasoning. XIII, 454 pages. 2005.

Vol. 3661: T. Panayiotopoulos, J. Gratch, R.S. Aylett, D. Ballin, P. Olivier, T. Rist (Eds.), Intelligent Virtual Agents. XIII, 506 pages. 2005.

Vol. 3658: V. Matoušek, P. Mautner, T. Pavelka (Eds.), Text, Speech and Dialogue. XV, 460 pages. 2005.

Vol. 3651: R. Dale, K.-F. Wong, J. Su, O.Y. Kwong (Eds.), Natural Language Processing – IJCNLP 2005. XXI, 1031 pages. 2005.

Vol. 3642: D. Ślęzak, J. Yao, J.F. Peters, W. Ziarko, X. Hu (Eds.), Rough Sets, Fuzzy Sets, Data Mining, and Granular Computing, Part II. XXIII, 738 pages. 2005.

Vol. 3641: D. Ślęzak, G. Wang, M. Szczuka, I. Düntsch, Y. Yao (Eds.), Rough Sets, Fuzzy Sets, Data Mining, and Granular Computing, Part I. XXIV, 742 pages. 2005.

Vol. 3635: J.R. Winkler, M. Niranjan, N.D. Lawrence (Eds.), Deterministic and Statistical Methods in Machine Learning. VIII, 341 pages. 2005.

Vol. 3632: R. Nieuwenhuis (Ed.), Automated Deduction – CADE-20. XIII, 459 pages. 2005.

Vol. 3630: M.S. Capcarrère, A.A. Freitas, P.J. Bentley, C.G. Johnson, J. Timmis (Eds.), Advances in Artificial Life. XIX, 949 pages. 2005.

Vol. 3626: B. Ganter, G. Stumme, R. Wille (Eds.), Formal Concept Analysis. X, 349 pages. 2005.

Vol. 3625: S. Kramer, B. Pfahringer (Eds.), Inductive Logic Programming. XIII, 427 pages. 2005.

Vol. 3620: H. Muñoz-Ávila, F. Ricci (Eds.), Case-Based Reasoning Research and Development. XV, 654 pages. 2005.

Vol. 3614: L. Wang, Y. Jin (Eds.), Fuzzy Systems and Knowledge Discovery, Part II. XLI, 1314 pages. 2005.

Vol. 3613: L. Wang, Y. Jin (Eds.), Fuzzy Systems and Knowledge Discovery, Part I. XLI, 1334 pages. 2005.

Vol. 3607: J.-D. Zucker, L. Saitta (Eds.), Abstraction, Reformulation and Approximation. XII, 376 pages. 2005.

Vol. 3601: G. Moro, S. Bergamaschi, K. Aberer (Eds.), Agents and Peer-to-Peer Computing. XII, 245 pages. 2005.

Vol. 3596: F. Dau, M.-L. Mugnier, G. Stumme (Eds.), Conceptual Structures: Common Semantics for Sharing Knowledge. XI, 467 pages. 2005.

Vol. 3593: V. Mařík, R. W. Brennan, M. Pěchouček (Eds.), Holonic and Multi-Agent Systems for Manufacturing. XI, 269 pages. 2005.

Vol. 3587: P. Perner, A. Imiya (Eds.), Machine Learning and Data Mining in Pattern Recognition. XVII, 695 pages. 2005.

Vol. 3584: X. Li, S. Wang, Z.Y. Dong (Eds.), Advanced Data Mining and Applications. XIX, 835 pages. 2005.

Vol. 3581: S. Miksch, J. Hunter, E.T. Keravnou (Eds.), Artificial Intelligence in Medicine. XVII, 547 pages. 2005.

Vol. 3577: R. Falcone, S. Barber, J. Sabater-Mir, M.P. Singh (Eds.), Trusting Agents for Trusting Electronic Societies. VIII, 235 pages. 2005.

Vol. 3575: S. Wermter, G. Palm, M. Elshaw (Eds.), Biomimetic Neural Learning for Intelligent Robots. IX, 383 pages. 2005.

Vol. 3571: L. Godo (Ed.), Symbolic and Quantitative Approaches to Reasoning with Uncertainty. XVI, 1028 pages. 2005.

Vol. 3559: P. Auer, R. Meir (Eds.), Learning Theory. XI, 692 pages. 2005.

Vol. 3558: V. Torra, Y. Narukawa, S. Miyamoto (Eds.), Modeling Decisions for Artificial Intelligence. XII, 470 pages. 2005.

Vol. 3554: A.K. Dey, B. Kokinov, D.B. Leake, R. Turner (Eds.), Modeling and Using Context. XIV, 572 pages. 2005.

Vol. 3550: T. Eymann, F. Klügl, W. Lamersdorf, M. Klusch, M.N. Huhns (Eds.), Multiagent System Technologies. XI, 246 pages. 2005.

Vol. 3539: K. Morik, J.-F. Boulicaut, A. Siebes (Eds.), Local Pattern Detection. XI, 233 pages. 2005.

Vol. 3538: L. Ardissono, P. Brna, A. Mitrović (Eds.), User Modeling 2005. XVI, 533 pages. 2005.

Vol. 3533: M. Ali, F. Esposito (Eds.), Innovations in Applied Artificial Intelligence. XX, 858 pages. 2005.

Vol. 3528: P.S. Szczepaniak, J. Kacprzyk, A. Niewiadomski (Eds.), Advances in Web Intelligence. XVII, 513 pages. 2005.

Vol. 3518: T.-B. Ho, D. Cheung, H. Liu (Eds.), Advances in Knowledge Discovery and Data Mining. XXI, 864 pages. 2005.

Vol. 3508: P. Bresciani, P. Giorgini, B. Henderson-Sellers, G. Low, M. Winikoff (Eds.), Agent-Oriented Information Systems II. X, 227 pages. 2005.

Vol. 3505: V. Gorodetsky, J. Liu, V.A. Skormin (Eds.), Autonomous Intelligent Systems: Agents and Data Mining. XIII, 303 pages. 2005.

Vol. 3501: B. Kégl, G. Lapalme (Eds.), Advances in Artificial Intelligence. XV, 458 pages. 2005.

Vol. 3492: P. Blache, E.P. Stabler, J.V. Busquets, R. Moot (Eds.), Logical Aspects of Computational Linguistics. X, 363 pages. 2005.

Vol. 3490: L. Bolc, Z. Michalewicz, T. Nishida (Eds.), Intelligent Media Technology for Communicative Intelligence. X, 259 pages. 2005.

Vol. 3488: M.-S. Hacid, N.V. Murray, Z.W. Raś, S. Tsumoto (Eds.), Foundations of Intelligent Systems. XIII, 700 pages. 2005.

Vol. 3487: J.A. Leite, P. Torroni (Eds.), Computational Logic in Multi-Agent Systems. XII, 281 pages. 2005.

Vol. 3476: J.A. Leite, A. Omicini, P. Torroni, P. Yolum (Eds.), Declarative Agent Languages and Technologies II. XII, 289 pages. 2005.

Vol. 3464: S.A. Brueckner, G.D.M. Serugendo, A. Karageorgos, R. Nagpal (Eds.), Engineering Self-Organising Systems. XIII, 299 pages. 2005.

Vol. 3452: F. Baader, A. Voronkov (Eds.), Logic for Programming, Artificial Intelligence, and Reasoning. XI, 562 pages. 2005.

Vol. 3451: M.-P. Gleizes, A. Omicini, F. Zambonelli (Eds.), Engineering Societies in the Agents World V. XIII, 349 pages. 2005.

Vol. 3446: T. Ishida, L. Gasser, H. Nakashima (Eds.), Massively Multi-Agent Systems I. XI, 349 pages. 2005.

Vol. 3445: G. Chollet, A. Esposito, M. Faúndez-Zanuy, M. Marinaro (Eds.), Nonlinear Speech Modeling and Applications. XIII, 433 pages. 2005.

Vol. 3438: H. Christiansen, P.R. Skadhauge, J. Villadsen (Eds.), Constraint Solving and Language Processing. VIII, 205 pages. 2005.

Vol. 3430: S. Tsumoto, T. Yamaguchi, M. Numao, H. Motoda (Eds.), Active Mining. XII, 349 pages. 2005.

Vol. 3419: B.V. Faltings, A. Petcu, F. Fages, F. Rossi (Eds.), Recent Advances in Constraints. X, 217 pages. 2005.

Vol. 3416: M.H. Böhlen, J. Gamper, W. Polasek, M.A. Wimmer (Eds.), E-Government: Towards Electronic Democracy. XIII, 311 pages. 2005.

Vol. 3415: P. Davidsson, B. Logan, K. Takadama (Eds.), Multi-Agent and Multi-Agent-Based Simulation. X, 265 pages. 2005.

Vol. 3413: K. Fischer, M. Florian, T. Malsch (Eds.), Socionics. X, 315 pages. 2005.

Vol. 3403: B. Ganter, R. Godin (Eds.), Formal Concept Analysis. XI, 419 pages. 2005.

Vol. 3398: D.-K. Baik (Ed.), Systems Modeling and Simulation: Theory and Applications. XIV, 733 pages. 2005.

Vol. 3397: T.G. Kim (Ed.), Artificial Intelligence and Simulation. XV, 711 pages. 2005.

Vol. 3396: R.M. van Eijk, M.-P. Huget, F.P. M. Dignum (Eds.), Agent Communication. X, 261 pages. 2005.

Vol. 3394: D. Kudenko, D. Kazakov, E. Alonso (Eds.), Adaptive Agents and Multi-Agent Systems II. VIII, 313 pages. 2005.

Vol. 3392: D. Seipel, M. Hanus, U. Geske, O. Bartenstein (Eds.), Applications of Declarative Programming and Knowledge Management. X, 309 pages. 2005.

Vol. 3374: D. Weyns, H. V.D. Parunak, F. Michel (Eds.), Environments for Multi-Agent Systems. X, 279 pages. 2005.

Vol. 3371: M.W. Barley, N. Kasabov (Eds.), Intelligent Agents and Multi-Agent Systems. X, 329 pages. 2005.